Financial Accounting Partner

Financial Accounting Partner is a CD package containing two kinds of powerful software to help students master the most challenging topics in the financial accounting course. It's fully integrated with the text and FREE with every new book.

Topic Tackler

This complete tutorial provides students with help on at least two key topics for every chapter using:

• Video clips
• PowerPoint ® slide-shows that sometimes include animations and/or audio
• Drag-and-drop, fill-in-the-blank exercises
• Self-test quizzes
• Web site hotlinks

Topic Tackler

Concepts appearing in the text that receive additional treatment in Topic Tackler are marked with a unique icon.

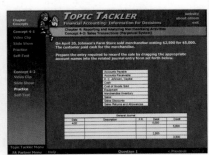

Mastering the Accounting Cycle (M.A.C.)

This software helps students through what is often a very difficult part of the course – the details of the double-entry accounting system. Three components make up the program:

• Approximately 30 additional exercises per chapter, based on those in the text.

• Immediate feedback to the student based on the answers submitted. If students provide a correct answer, M.A.C. tells them so. If they are wrong, M.A.C. guides them through a four-step process to help them discover, review, learn, and apply the appropriate accounting principle.

• After each lesson is completed, M.A.C. provides the student with a Performance Report listing the student's grade, completion time, and a list of the topic areas that the student needs to review. The Performance Report can also be printed and given to the instructor to help identify areas that need more classroom coverage.

M.A.C.

Exercises for which alternates are provided in M.A.C. are marked with a unique icon in the text.

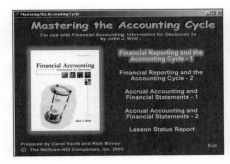

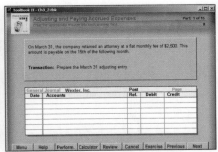

System Requirements: Windows 95, Windows 98 Version 1, SE, 2000, NT, ME, or Equivalent; Pentium Processor (133MHz minimum); 32MB of RAM or greater; PC Compatible sound card (Topic Tackler only); Internet connection (Topic Tackler only); 6x CD-ROM or higher; 16 bit, 640x480 video card (minimum)

2 edition

Financial Accounting:
Information for Decisions

John J. Wild
University of Wisconsin at Madison

McGraw-Hill
Irwin

Boston Burr Ridge, IL Dubuque, IA Madison, WI New York
San Francisco St. Louis Bangkok Bogotá Caracas Kuala Lumpur
Lisbon London Madrid Mexico City Milan Montreal New Delhi
Santiago Seoul Singapore Sydney Taipei Toronto

To my wife **Gail** and children, **Kimberly, Jonathan, Stephanie,** and **Trevor.**

McGraw-Hill Higher Education

A Division of The **McGraw-Hill** *Companies*

FINANCIAL ACCOUNTING: INFORMATION FOR DECISIONS
Published by McGraw-Hill/Irwin, a business unit of The McGraw-Hill Companies, Inc. 1221 Avenue of the Americas, New York, NY, 10020. Copyright © 2003, 2000 by The McGraw-Hill Companies, Inc. All rights reserved. No part of this publication may be reproduced or distributed in any form or by any means, or stored in a database or retrieval system, without the prior written consent of The McGraw-Hill Companies, Inc., including, but not limited to, in any network or other electronic storage or transmission, or broadcast for distance learning.
Some ancillaries, including electronic and print components, may not be available to customers outside the United States.

This book is printed on acid-free paper.

domestic   2 3 4 5 6 7 8 9 0 VNH/VNH 0 9 8 7 6 5 4 3 2
international   2 3 4 5 6 7 8 9 0 VNH/VNH 0 9 8 7 6 5 4 3 2

ISBN   0-07-245691-4

Publisher: *Brent Gordon*
Sponsoring editor: *Melody Marcus*
Senior developmental editors: *Tracey Douglas/Kristin Leahy/Jackie Scruggs*
Senior marketing manager: *Richard Kolasa*
Editorial assistant: *Kelly Odom*
Senior project manager: *Kimberly D. Hooker*
Production supervisor: *Rose Hepburn*
Lead designer: *Matthew Baldwin*
Senior producer, Media technology: *Ed Przyzycki*
Supplement producer: *Matthew Perry*
Senior digital content specialist: *Brian Nacik*
Photo research coordinator: *David A. Tietz*
Photo researcher: *Charlotte Goldman*
Cover and interior design: *Matthew Baldwin*
Typeface: *10.5/12 Times Roman*
Compositor: *TechBooks*
Printer: *Von Hoffman Press, Inc.*

Library of Congress Cataloging-in-Publication Data

Wild, John J.
        Financial accounting: information for decisions / John J. Wild.—2nd ed.
                p. cm.
        A multi-media instructional package is available to supplement the text.
        Includes index.
        ISBN 0-07-245691-4 (alk. paper)
        1. Accounting. I. Title.
    HF5635.W695 2003
        657—dc21   2001051192

INTERNATIONAL EDITION ISBN 0-07-112134-X
Copyright © 2003. Exclusive rights by The McGraw-Hill Companies, Inc. for manufacture and export. This book cannot be re-exported from the country to which it is sold by McGraw-Hill. The International Edition is not available in North America.

www.mhhe.com

ABOUT THE AUTHOR

The author brings a blend of skills uniquely suited to writing an introductory accounting textbook. He combines award-winning teaching and research with a broad view of accounting and business gained through years of practical and teaching experiences to make accounting relevant, understandable, and enjoyable to today's reader.

JOHN J. WILD is a professor of business and the Vilas Research Scholar at the University of Wisconsin at Madison. He has previously held appointments at Michigan State University and the University of Manchester in England. He received his BBA, MS, and PhD from the University of Wisconsin.

Professor Wild teaches courses at both the undergraduate and graduate levels. He has received the Mabel W. Chipman Excellence-in-Teaching Award and the departmental Excellence-in-Teaching Award at the University of Wisconsin. He also received the Beta Alpha Psi and Roland F. Salmonson Excellence-in Teaching Award from Michigan State University. Professor Wild is a past KPMG National Fellow and is a recipient of fellowships from the American Accounting Association and the Ernst and Young Foundation.

Professor Wild is an active member of the American Accounting Association and its sections. He has served as a member or the chair of several committees of these organizations, including the Outstanding Accounting Educator Award, Wildman Award, National Program Advisory, Accounting Publications, and Research Committees. Professor Wild is an author of *Financial Statement Analysis* and *Fundamental Accounting Principles*, both published by McGraw-Hill. His research appears in *The Accounting Review, Journal of Accounting Research, Journal of Accounting and Economics, Contemporary Accounting Research, Journal of Accounting, Auditing and Finance, Journal of Accounting and Public Policy,* and other business periodicals. He is associate editor of *Contemporary Accounting Research,* senior associate editor of the *Journal of International Accounting Research,* and has served on several editorial boards including *The Accounting Review* and the *Journal of Accounting and Public Policy*.

Professor Wild, his wife, and four children enjoy travel, music, sports, and community activities.

TECHNOLOGY SOLUTIONS *(vertical, left margin)*

TECHNOLOGY SOLUTIONS
TO MEET EVERY NEED

TODAY, nearly 200,000 college instructors use the INTERNET in their respective courses. Some are just getting started while others are READY TO EMBRACE the very latest advances in educational CONTENT DELIVERY and COURSE MANAGEMENT.

That's why we at McGraw-Hill/Irwin offer you a complete range of digital solutions. Your students can use **Wild 2e's** complete Online Learning Center (OLC), NetTutor, PowerWeb, GradeSummit, and ALEKS on their own. We can also help you create your own course Web site using McGraw-Hill's PageOut. We can even help you achieve dot-com nirvana with your entire financial accounting course online.

In addition to Web-based assets, **Wild2e** boasts CDs for students and instructors alike. Students will be especially grateful for **Financial Accounting Partner,** the free CD-ROM that offers special assistance for the most demanding financial accounting topics. Instructors will appreciate the convenience of having access to electronic versions of nearly all critical support materials such as the Instructor's Manual and PowerPoint® slides from both the Instructor's CD-ROM and the Internet.

McGraw-Hill is a leader in bringing helpful technology into the classroom. With **Wild,***Financial Accounting 2e,* your class gets all the benefits of the digital age.

Topic Tackler

M.A.C.

FINANCIAL ACCOUNTING PARTNER

Financial Accounting Partner is a CD package containing two kinds of powerful software to help students master the most challenging topics in the financial accounting course. It's fully integrated with the text and FREE with every new book. (See inside front cover for more details.)

Topic Tackler

This complete tutorial provides students with help on two key topics for each chapter.

Topic Tackler

Mastering the Accounting Cycle (M.A.C.)

This software helps students through what is often the most difficult and technical part of the course – the accounting cycle.

M.A.C.

TECHNOLOGY SOLUTIONS

ONLINE LEARNING CENTER (OLC)

www.mhhe.com/wild2e

More and more students are studying online. That's why we offer an **Online Learning Center (OLC)** that follows *Financial Accounting* 2e chapter by chapter. It doesn't require any building or maintenance on your part. It's ready to go the moment you and your students type in the address.

As your students study, they can refer to the OLC Web site for benefits such as:

- Additional alternate exercises to those in the text

- Internet-based activities

- Self-grading quizzes

- General Ledger Applications Software (GLAS) and Excel templates for use with select end-of-chapter problems

- Interactive glossary

- Free links to *Business Week* articles referenced in the assignments

- Links to text Web references

- Links to professional resources on the Web and job opportunity information

- Learning objectives

- Chapter overviews

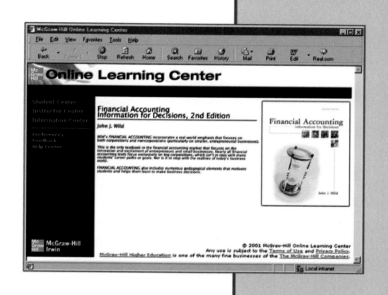

A secured Instructor Resource Center stores your essential course materials to save you preparation time before class. The Instructor's Manual, Solutions, PowerPoint®, and sample syllabi are now just a couple of clicks away. You will also find useful textbook packaging information.

The OLC Web site also serves as a doorway to other technology solutions like PageOut, NetTutor, and PowerWeb, which are free to *Finanical Accounting* 2e adopters.

MORE TECHNOLOGY SOLUTIONS

COURSE MANAGEMENT

PAGEOUT

McGraw-Hill's Course Management System

PageOut is the easiest way to create a Web site for your course.

There's no need for HTML coding, graphic design, or a thick how-to book. Just fill in a series of boxes with plain English and click on one of our professional designs. In no time, your course is online!

Should you need assistance in preparing your Web site, we can help you. In addition to many pre-built course Web sites, we offer a team of product specialists ready to help. Just send them your course materials and after a brief phone consultation, they will build your PageOut Web site from scratch. (For information on how to do this, see "Superior Service" on the next page.)

PageOut is free when you adopt **Wild 2e**! To learn more, please visit **http://www.pageout.net**.

THIRD-PARTY COURSE MANAGEMENT SYSTEMS

For the ambitious instructor, we offer **Wild 2e** content for complete online courses. To make this possible, we have joined forces with the most popular delivery platforms currently available. These platforms are designed for instructors who want complete control over course content and how it is presented to students. You can customize our Online Learning Center content (see page v) and author your own course materials. It's entirely up to you.

Products like WebCT, Blackboard, eCollege, and TopClass (a product of WBT) all expand the reach of your course. Online discussion and message boards will now complement your office hours. Thanks to a sophisticated tracking system, you will know which students need more attention – even if they don't ask for help. That's because online testing scores are recorded and automatically placed in your grade book. If a student is struggling with coursework, a special alert message lets you know.

Remember, the **Wild 2e** content is flexible enough to use with any platform currently available. If your department or school is already using a platform, we can help. For information on McGraw-Hill/Irwin's course management services, including Instructor Advantage and Knowledge Gateway, see "Superior Service" on the next page.

SUPERIOR SERVICE

No matter which online course solution you choose, you can count on the highest level of service. That's what sets McGraw-Hill apart. Once you adopt Wild 2e, our specialists offer free training and answer any question you have throughout the life of your adoption.

KNOWLEDGE GATEWAY

Developed with the help of our partner Eduprise, the **McGraw-Hill Knowledge Gateway** is an all-purpose service and resource center for instructors teaching online.

The First Level of **Knowledge Gateway** is available to all professors browsing the McGraw-Hill Higher Education Web site and consists of an introduction to OLC content, access to the first level of the Resource Library, technical support, and information on Instructional Design Services available through Eduprise.

The Second Level is password-protected and provides access to the expanded Resource Library; technical and pedagogical support for WebCT, Blackboard, and TopClass; the online Instructional Design helpdesk; and an online discussion forum for users. The **Knowledge Gateway** provides a considerable advantage for teaching online—and it's only available through McGraw-Hill.

To see how these platforms can assist your online course, visit **www.mhhe.com/solutions**.

INSTRUCTOR ADVANTAGE and INSTRUCTOR ADVANTAGE PLUS

Instructor Advantage is a special level of service McGraw-Hill offers in conjunction with WebCT and Blackboard. A team of platform specialists is always available, either by toll-free phone or e-mail, to ensure everything runs smoothly throughout the life of your adoption. Instructor Advantage is available free to all McGraw-Hill customers.

Instructor Advantage Plus is available to qualifying McGraw-Hill adopters (see your representative for details). **IA Plus** guarantees you a full day of on-site training by a Blackboard or WebCT specialist for yourself and up to nine colleagues. Thereafter, you will enjoy the benefits of unlimited telephone and e-mail support throughout the life of your adoption. **IA Plus** users also have the opportunity to access the **McGraw-Hill Knowledge Gateway**.

PAGEOUT SERVICE

With McGraw-Hill's PageOut, you can put your course online without knowing a word of HTML, using either our OLC content or your own content. It's free of charge! If you want a custom site but don't have time to build it yourself, we offer a team of product specialists ready to help. Just call 1-800-541-7145 and ask to speak with a **PageOut** specialist. You will be asked to send in your course materials and then participate in a telephone consultation. Our specialist will then help you build your site and maintain it throughout the life of your adoption.

NETTUTOR

NetTutor allows tutors and students to communicate with each other in a variety of ways:

- The **Live Tutor Center** via NetTutor's WWWhiteboard enables a tutor to hold an interactive online tutorial with several students whose questions are placed in a queue and answered sequentially.

- The **Q&A Center** allows students to submit questions at any time and retrieve answers within 24 hours.

- The **Archive Center** allows students to browse for answers to previously asked questions. They can also search for questions pertinent to a particular topic. If they encounter an answer they do not understand, they can ask a follow-up question.

Students are issued 5 hours of free **NetTutor** time when they purchase a new copy of **Wild 2e**. Additional time may be purchased in one hour increments. Live tutor availability will vary throughout the course of the term with a peak availability of around 60 hours a week.

POWERWEB

Keeping your course current can be a job in itself and now McGraw-Hill does that job for you. **PowerWeb** extends the learning experience beyond the core textbook by offering all of the latest news and developments pertinent to your course, brought to you via the Internet without all the clutter and dead links of a typical online search.

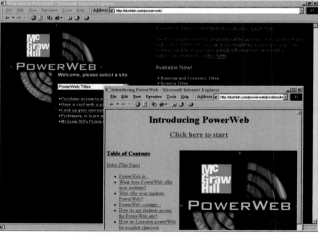

PowerWeb offers current articles related to financial accounting, weekly updates with assessment tools, informative and timely world news culled by a financial accounting expert, refereed Web links, and more.

In addition, **PowerWeb** provides a trove of helpful learning aids, including self-grading quizzes, interactive glossaries, and exercises. Students may also access study tips, conduct online research, and learn about different careers.

Visit the **PowerWeb** site at **http://www.dushkin.com/powerweb** and see firsthand what **PowerWeb** can mean to your course.

GRADESUMMIT

Optimize student study time. Help them elevate their grades!

GradeSummit is an innovative product that helps students make the most efficient use of their study time. This Internet exam preparation service helps students assess exactly where they are in a specific area. By revealing subject strengths and weaknesses and by providing feedback and direction, GradeSummit enables students to focus their study time on those areas where they are most in need of improvement.

GradeSummit is tied directly to Wild 2e with page references. It contains 2,000 unique exam-like questions written by professors and peer reviewed for quality and accuracy. These questions are the vehicle to invaluable information students can only get here. So don't make your students wait to find out what they know by seeing how they do on the exam. Have them use GradeSummit to ensure that they are ready for their next test! GradeSummit can be packaged with Wild 2e or students can buy access directly online.

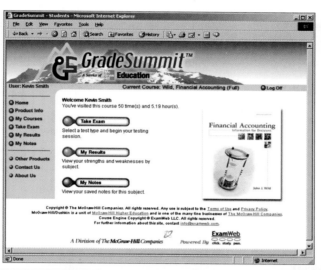

ALEKS

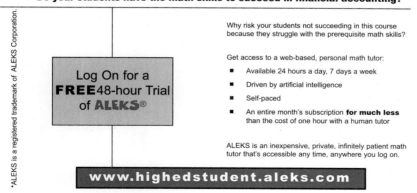

How's Your Student's Math?

Do your students have the math skills to succeed in financial accounting?

Log On for a
FREE 48-hour Trial
of **ALEKS**®

Why risk your students not succeeding in this course because they struggle with the prerequisite math skills?

Get access to a web-based, personal math tutor:

- Available 24 hours a day, 7 days a week
- Driven by artificial intelligence
- Self-paced
- An entire month's subscription **for much less** than the cost of one hour with a human tutor

ALEKS is an inexpensive, private, infinitely patient math tutor that's accessible any time, anywhere you log on.

www.highedstudent.aleks.com

SOLID ACCOUNTING COVERAGE...

THROUGHOUT THE TEXT:

Increased coverage of e-business, the Web, business analysis, and entrepreneurship as related to accounting. Some highlights of changes from the first edition follows:

Chapter 1

Capitalist Pig **NEW opener**

Early introduction to financial statements and analysis

Revised motivation on relevance of accounting in business

Revised section on accounting and related careers

New table on compensation in accounting careers

New section on organizing and interpreting ratio analysis

Chapter 2

Venture Frogs **NEW opener**

Simplified transaction analysis using the accounting equation

Early introduction to statement of cash flows

New, early introduction to corporate accounting

Streamlined section on using T-Accounts as tools

Shortened section on posting of transactions and entries

New discussion of using entries to analyze transactions

Chapter 3

Mellies **NEW opener**

Revised presentation on accounting adjustments

Streamlined discussion of the adjusting process

Revised discussion on relevance of accrual accounting for analysis

Shortened section on closing entries

Streamlined section on account numbering system

Chapter 4

Damani Dada **NEW opener**

Simplified presentation of income statement formats

Streamlined section on merchandising cash flows

Chapter 5

Baby Einstein **NEW opener**

Streamlined presentation of gross profit and retail inventory methods

Removed details of subsidiary inventory records

New analysis of the LIFO reserve

Chapter 6

eBay **Updated opener**

New feature on cyberfraud

Shortened discussion of voucher system of internal control

New analysis of cash and cash flows

Chapter 7

Enginehouse Media **NEW opener**

New, simplified illustrations on adjustments for unrealized gains and losses on securities

New analysis of window-dressing with securities

Streamlined discussion of full disclosure principle

Dell and Apple **Updated**

Chapter 8

House of Bread **NEW opener**

New explanation of intangibles and goodwill per SFAS 141 and 142

Streamlined discussion of partial-year depreciation

Shortened and simplified section on revenue and capital expenditures

Deleted discussion on exchange of dissimilar assets

Coors and Anheuser-Busch **Updated**

Chapter 9

Priority Staffing Solutions **NEW opener**

New section on employee bonus plans

Shortened section on income tax liabilities

Best Buy **Updated**

Revised appendix on employee payroll benefits and records

Chapter 10

David Bowie bonds **Updated opener**

Simplified discussion and analysis of notes payable

Streamlined appendix on present values of bonds and notes

New Appendix 10B on "Leases and Pensions"

Chapter 11

World Wrestling Federation **Updated opener**

Deleted section on issuing stock through subscriptions

Streamlined section on participating and nonparticipating preferred stock dividends

Deleted the Dividends Declared account to streamline journal entries for cash (and stock) dividends

Deleted the section on liquidating cash dividends

Simplified sections on discontinued segments and on changes in accounting principles

Streamlined section on diluted earnings per share

Shortened sections on book value per share and dividend yield

Chapter 12

BlueFly **NEW opener**

Simplified preparation of the statement of cash flows

Shortened section on analyzing cash sources and uses

Chapter 13

The Motley Fool **NEW opener**

Revised discussion on comparative analysis (benchmarking)

Streamlined section on working capital and current ratio

Updated Nike vs. Reebok comparative analysis

Appendix C

Streamlined discussion of long-term investments in securities

Deleted accounting for transactions in a foreign currency

Simplified assignment materials

ENTREPRENEURIAL FLAVOR

An Entrepreneurial Icon calls out all relevant material within the chapters, whether an opening vignette, box, or end-of-chapter assignment.

Today's students live in a world where start-up companies have redefined traditional notions of success in business. To reflect this shift, **Wild 2e** integrates ideas and practices followed by today's entrepreneurs, speaking more directly to students and better preparing them for the workforce they will enter. **This approach is distinctive in the financial accounting market**.

ENTREPRENEURIAL CHAPTER-OPENERS

These opening vignettes focus on young entrepreneurs and the relevance of accounting in their business decisions. We highlight companies like Capitalist Pig, Venture Frogs, Mellies, Damani Dada, Baby Einstein, Enginehouse Media, House of Bread, eBay, Motley Fool, and WWF—names that students will recognize from magazines, newspapers, television, and the Internet. The openers discuss how accounting information and an understanding of it aided these start-ups in successfully launching and running their operations. They serve as excellent motivators—showing the importance of accounting in business.

4 Reporting and Analyzing Merchandising Activities

A Look Back

Chapter 3 focused on the final steps of the accounting process. We explained the importance of proper revenue and expense recognition and described the closing process. We also showed how to prepare financial statements from accounting records.

A Look at This Chapter

This chapter emphasizes merchandising activities. We explain how reporting merchandising activities differs from reporting service activities. We also analyze and record merchandise purchases and sales transactions and explain the adjustments and closing process for merchandisers.

A Look Ahead

Chapter 5 extends our analysis of merchandising activities and focuses on the valuation of inventory. Topics include the items in inventory, costs assigned, costing methods used, and inventory estimation techniques.

"*I felt we should go into something that we had some connection to.*"
Dwayne Lewis

Entrepreneurial Decision

A1 A2 A3 A4 **P3**

BTN 2-9 Liang Lu is a young entrepreneur who operates Lu Music Services, offering singing lessons and instruction on musical instruments. Lu wishes to expand but needs a loan. The bank requests Lu to prepare a balance sheet and key financial ratios. Lu has not kept formal records but is able to provide the following accounts and their amounts as of December 31, 2002:

Cash	$ 1,800	Accounts Receivable	$4,800	Prepaid Insurance	$ 750
Prepaid Rent	4,700	Store Supplies	3,300	Equipment	25,000
Accounts Payable	1,100	Unearned Lesson Fees	7,800	Total Equity*	31,450
Annual net income	20,000				

* The total equity amount reflects all investments, revenues, expenses, and dividends as of Dec. 31, 2002.

Required

1. Prepare a balance sheet as of December 31, 2002, for Lu Music Services.
2. Compute Lu's debt ratio, return on equity, and return on assets (from Chapter 1). Assume average equity and average assets equal their respective ending balances.
3. Do you think the prospects of a $15,000 bank loan are good? Why or why not?

Hitting the Road

BTN 2-10 Obtain a recent copy of the most prominent newspaper distributed in your area. Research the classified section and prepare a report answering the following questions (attach relevant classi-

Learning Objectives

Conceptual

C1 Describe merchandising activities and identify business examples.

C2 Identify and explain the components of income for a merchandising company.

C3 Identify and explain the inventory asset of a merchandising company.

C4 Describe both perpetual and periodic inventory systems.

C5 Analyze and interpret cost flows and operating activities of a merchandising company.

Analytical

A1 Analyze and interpret accruals and cash flows for merchandising activities.

A2 Compute the acid-test ratio and explain its use to assess liquidity.

A3 Compute the gross margin ratio and explain its use to assess profitability.

Procedural

P1 Analyze and record transactions for merchandise purchases

P2

P3

P4

ENTREPRENEURIAL DECISION PROBLEM

A new Entrepreneurial Decision problem is included at the end of each chapter (in the "Beyond The Numbers" assignment section). These problems focus on small businesses and the relevance of accounting in helping solve business problems and guiding business strategy. No other text offers such assignments specifically directed at small businesses.

ENTREPRENEURIAL BOXES

A select number of *Decision Center* boxes focus on entrepreneurial issues and decisions. These boxes are especially effective at engaging students interested in small business and start-up possibilities.

Decision Feature

Dada's Hip

EL SEGUNDO, CA—Dwayne Lewis and Michael Cherry had a dream—a dream to own and run a company. With one lone product (a five-panel polo hat) and $1,000 in pooled paychecks, they launched **Damani Dada (www.DamaniDada.com).** The two dreamed that Damani Dada would bring an ultra-hip style to the urban fashion scene. A mere six years after its launch, Dada projects annual sales of more than $50 million.

The early days, however, were far from easy as Lewis and Cherry struggled alone against long odds. "It was very tricky to try and learn the business without a mentor," recalls Lewis. "We always struggled with the task of maintaining a strong financial backing, and we had to learn a lot by making mistakes." Among those struggles was implementing and learning a merchandising system—one that could capture and communicate the costs and sales information so desperately needed by the young entrepreneurs. A crucial part of their success was tracking merchandising activities. This was necessary for setting prices and making policies for everything from discounts and allowances to returns on both sales and purchases. Also, use of a perpetual inventory system enabled them to stock the right type and amount of merchandise, and to avoid the costs of out-of-stock and excess inventory. This chapter describes how the accounting system captures merchandising information for these and other business decisions. It also introduces analysis tools for assessing the financial condition and performance of merchandisers.

Damani Dada successfully weathered the storm and has expanded to offer a full line of both men's and women's apparel. "Business is war," says Lewis. "You have to be mentally strong, willing to sacrifice, and willing to accept delayed gratification." [Sources: Damani Dada Web site, January 2002; *Entrepreneur,* November 2000.]

Decision Insight

No Place Like Home Home is where the business is—that according to nearly one-half (49%) of entrepreneurs in a recent survey with annual sales between $50,000 to $500,000. More similarities exist between home-based and non-home-based entrepreneurships than commonly assumed—see the table here.

	Home-Based	Non-Home-Based
Similarities		
Years in business	13.9 yrs.	14.5 yrs.
Checking acct. bal.	$ 14,700	$ 15,200
Household income	$108,400	$113,200
Differences		
Importance of growth	11%	21%
Proprietorship	72%	52%

DECISION CENTER

The Decision Center is a pedogogical framework exclusive to this book. See the inside front cover for more details.

A decision icon calls out all relevant material within the chapter, whether a boxed item or end-of-chapter assignment.

THE CAP MODEL

The Conceptual/Analytical/ Procedural (CAP) Model allows courses to be specially designed to meet instructional and learning needs. This model identifies learning objectives, textual material, assignments, and test material by C, A, or P, allowing different instructors to teach from the same materials yet easily customize their courses toward a conceptual, analytical, or procedural approach (or a combination thereof) based on personal preferences.

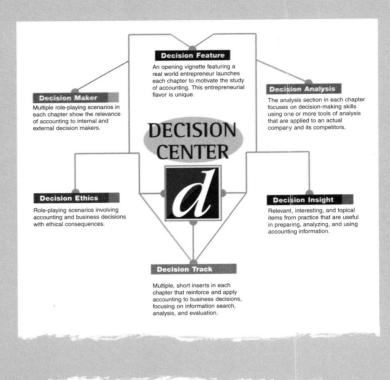

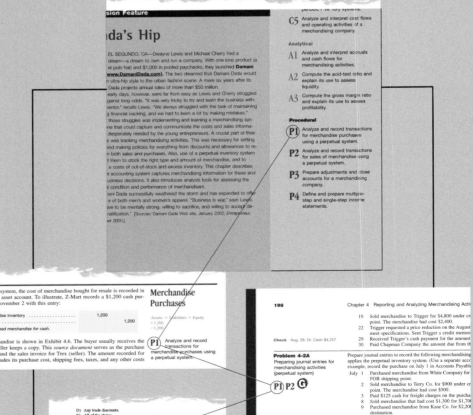

Quick Check

1. Describe one advantage for each of the inventory costing methods: specific identification, FIFO, LIFO, and weighted average.
2. When costs are rising, which method reports higher net income—LIFO or FIFO?
3. When costs are rising, what effect does LIFO have on a balance sheet compared to FIFO?
4. A company takes a physical count of inventory at the end of 2002 and finds that ending inventory is understated by $10,000. Would this error cause cost of goods sold to be overstated or underst

Answers—p. 233

44   Chapter 2   Accountin

Point: Prepaid expenses that apply to current *and* future periods are assets. These assets are adjusted at the end of each period to reflect only those amounts that have not yet expired, and to record as expenses those amounts that have expired.

the income statement on the balance sheet

Office supplies. Comp and pens. These supp are reported as expen asset account.

Store supplies. Many ing sales for customer

---

244   Chapter 5   Reporting and Analyzing Inventories

BEYOND THE NUMBERS

Reporting in Action
C2 A3 ⁊
NIKE

BTN 5-1   Refer to the financial statements of Nike in Appendix A to answer the following:

Required

1. What amount of inventories did Nike hold as a current asset on May 31, 2000? On May 31, 1999?
2. Inventories represent what percent of total assets on May 31, 2000? On May 31, 1999?
3. Comment on the relative size of Nike's inventories compared to its other types of assets.
4. What accounting method did Nike use to compute inventory amounts on its balance sheet?
5. Calculate inventory turnover for fiscal year ended May 31, 2000, and days' sales in inventory as of May 31, 2000. (*Note:* Cost of sales is cost of goods sold.)

Swoosh Ahead

6. Access Nike's financial statements for fiscal years ended after May 31, 2000, from its Web site (www.nike.com) or the SEC's EDGAR database (www.sec.gov). Answer questions 1 through 5 using the current Nike information and compare results to those prior years.

Comparative Analysis
A3 ⁊
NIKE Reebok

BTN 5-2   Key comparative figures ($ millions) for both Nike and Reebok follow:

Key Figures	Nike Current Year	Nike One Year Prior	Nike Two Years Prior	Reebok Current Year	Reebok One Year Prior	Reebok Two Years Prior
Inventory	$1,446.0	$1,170.6	$1,396.6	$ 414.6	$ 535.1	$ 563.7
Cost of sales	5,403.8	5,493.5	6,065.5	1,783.9	2,037.5	2,294.0

Required

1. Calculate inventory turnover for both companies for the most recent two years shown.
2. Calculate days' sales in inventory for both companies for the three years shown.
3. Comment on and interpret your findings from parts 1 and 2.

Ethics Challenge
A1 ⊙ ⁊

BTN 5-3   U-Golf Corp. is a retail sports store carrying golf apparel and equipment. The store is at the end of its second year of operation and is struggling. A major problem is that its cost of inventory has continually increased in the past two years. In the first year of operations, the store assigned inventory costs using LIFO. A loan agreement the store has with its bank, its prime source of financing, requires the store to maintain a certain profit margin and current ratio. The store's owner is currently looking over U-Golf's preliminary financial statements for its second year. The numbers are not favorable. The only way the store can meet the required financial ratios agreed on with the bank is to change from LIFO to FIFO. The store originally decided on LIFO because of its tax advantages. The owner recalculates ending inventory using FIFO and submits the statements to the loan officer at the bank for the required bank review. The owner thankfully reflects on the available latitude in choosing the inventory costing method.

Required

1. How does U-Golf's use of FIFO improve its net profit margin and current ratio?
2. Is the action by U-Golf's owner ethical? Explain.

Communicating in Practice
A1 ⊙ ⁊

BTN 5-4   You are a financial adviser with a client in the wholesale produce business that just completed its first year of operations. Due to weather conditions, the cost of acquiring produce to resell has escalated during the later part of this period. Your client, Juana Peabody, mentions that because the business sells perishable goods, she has striven to maintain a FIFO flow of goods. Although sales

---

QUICK CHECK

These short question/answer features reinforce the material immediately preceding them. They allow the reader to pause and reflect on the topics described, then receive immediate feedback before going on to new topics. Answers are provided at the end of each chapter.

MARGINAL STUDENT ANNOTATIONS

These annotations provide students with additional hints, tips, and examples to help them more fully understand the concepts and retain what they have learned. They also include notes on global implications for accounting.

BEYOND THE NUMBERS, as its name

suggests, is a section designed to encourage your students to look at numerical information as involving more than just mathematical calculations. These end-of-chapter exercises show your students how accounting data apply to a variety of business and analysis situations. It is divided into 10 sections:

- Reporting in Action
- Comparative Analysis
- Ethics Challenge
- Communicating in Practice
- Taking It to the Net
- Teamwork in Action
- *Business Week* Activity
- Entrepreneurial Decision
- Hitting the Road
- Global Decision

Comprehensive and Serial Problems are included in several chapters and focus on multiple learning objectives from multiple chapters. They help integrate and summarize key concepts.

SUPPLEMENTS

INSTRUCTOR SUPPLEMENTS

Instructor's Resource CD-ROM
0072456965

This is an all-in-one resource. It allows instructors to create custom presentations from their own materials or from the following text-specific materials provided in the CD's asset library:

- Instructor's Resource Manual
- Solutions Manual
- Test Bank
- Ready Shows (PowerPoint® Slides)
- General Ledger Applications Software
- Excel Templates
- Tutorial Software
- Link to PageOut
- Video Clips

Ready Shows
(only available on Instructor's Resource CD-ROM and text Web site)
A multimedia lecture slide package using Microsoft® PowerPoint to illustrate chapter concepts and procedures. It includes a viewer so that the screens can be shown with or without the software and it allows revision of lecture slides.

Financial Accounting Video Library
0072376163

These short, action-oriented videos, developed by Dallas County Community College, provide the impetus for lively classroom discussion. The focus is on the preparation, analysis, and use of accounting information for business decision making.

Instructor's Resource Manual
0072456973

This manual contains (for each chapter) a Lecture Outline, a chart linking all assignment materials to Learning Objectives, a list of relevant active learning activities, and additional visuals with transparency masters. A guide to integrating videos and PowerPoints into class sessions is also included. An electronic version is available on the text Web site and on the Instructor's Resource CD-ROM.

Solutions Manual
0072457228

Written by John J. Wild, this manual contains solutions for all assignment materials. An electronic version is available on the text Web site and on the Instructor's Resource CD-ROM.

Solutions Acetates
0072456930

Overhead transparencies present solutions to end-of-chapter activities in large, boldface type.

Test Bank
0072456981

The Test Bank contains a wide variety of questions presented in six categories—true/false, multiple-choice, matching, short essay, quantitative problems, and completion exercises. Test Bank materials are identified by varying levels of difficulty and grouped by learning objectives.

Brownstone Test Bank
Available on Instructor's Resource CD-ROM: 0072456965

Offers a computerized version of the Test Bank questions. It gives instructors the power to write tests that can be administered on paper, over a campus network, or on the Internet. Test results can be merged into Brownstone's gradebook program. Its test-building tools allow question editing and random selection of test questions by question number, learning objective, or level of difficulty.

Peachtree Solutions Manual
0072457244

This booklet presents the solutions for the Peachtree-supported assignments.

STUDENT SUPPLEMENTS

Financial Accounting Partner CD
0072456957

See inside front cover for a complete description.

Student Software CD
0072457287

Not to be confused with **Financial Accounting Partner**, this CD contains four separate software applications:

- General Ledger Applications Software (GLAS)
- Excel Templates
- Peachtree Templates
- Link to Online Quizzes

GLAS, Excel Templates, and Peachtree allow students to use various software programs to help solve selected text assignments. The Online Quizzes gives students a chance to review the material in each chapter of the text using true/false questions and multiple-choice questions.

Study Guide
0072457007

The Study Guide covers each chapter with reviews of the learning objectives, outlines of the chapters, and summaries of chapter materials. It also provides additional problems and solutions.

Working Papers
0072457279

Working Papers (prepared by John J. Wild) are available to help direct students in solving all assignments. Each chapter also contains one set of papers that can be used for either the A or B series of problems.

Building an E-Business: From the Ground Up
0072426365

Steeped in hands-on experience, this book was written by Elizabeth Reding specifically for those entrepreneurs who want to develop Web skills and business plans for use in starting an e-business.

Stock Market Experience
0070397279

This manual provides direction using electronic spreadsheets and the Web to manage a stock portfolio.

Practice Sets

Manual Practice Set
Prepared by William R. Pasewark, Texas Tech University

Instructor	Student
Understanding Corporate Annual Reports	
0072387165	0072387149

Computerized Practice Sets
Prepared by Leland Mansuetti and Keith Weidkamp, Sierra College

Instructor	Student
Granite Bay Jet Ski Inc., Level 1	
0072426896	0072426942
Granite Bay Jet Ski, Inc., Level 2	
0072426209	0072426950
Wheels Exquisite, Inc., Level 1	
0072427531	0072428457
Thunder Mountain Snowmobile	
0072341157	0072341149
Gold Run Snowmobile, Inc.	
0072341092	0072341076

ACKNOWLEDGMENTS

We are thankful for the suggestions, counsel, and encouragement provided by many instructors, professionals, and students in preparing this book. It has truly been a team effort, and we recognize the contributions of many individuals, including the following:

Vernon Allen, Central Florida Community College

Harold Averkamp, Northwestern University

Thomas Badley, Baker College

Edward Banas, Northern Virginia Community College/Woodbridge

Scott Barhight, Northampton Community College

Abdul Baten, Northern Virginia Community College/Manassas

Daniel A. Bayak, Northampton Community College

Peggy A. Boerman, Madison Area Technical College

Shifei Chung, Rowan University

Anthony Cioffi, Lorain County Community College

Bob Coburn, Franklin Pierce College

James L. Cosby, John Tyler Community College

Alan Czyzewski, Indiana State University

Sid Davidson, Foothill College

Victoria Doby, Villa Julie College

Roger Dufresne, Northern Essex Community College

James Forcier, Las Positas College

Albert Frakes, Washington State University

J. Thomas Franco, Wayne County Community College

Paul Franklin, DeVry Institute of Technology – Kansas City, MO

James S. Gale, Northern Virginia Community College/Alexandria

Shirley Glass, Macomb Community College

John J. Godfrey, Springfield Technical Community College

Ellen Goldberg, Northern Virginia Community College/Loudoun

Jennifer Gregorski, Bristol Community College

Gloria Halpern, Montgomery College

Susan Hamlen, SUNY – Buffalo

Jerry C. Y. Han, SUNY – Buffalo

Robert J. Hardin, Henry Ford Community College

Sara Harris, Arapahoe Community College

Frank Heflin, Purdue University

Tom Hoar, Houston Community College

Barbara Houchen, Anne Arundel Community College

Richard Howden, Delta College

Stephen Kerr, Hendrix College

Tom Kimberling, Ventura College

Shirly Kleiner, Johnson County Community College

Jill Kolody, Anne Arundel Community College

Michael Krause, Le Moyne College

Lawrence Kreiser, Cleveland State University

Christopher Kwak, Ohlone College

Phillip Landers, Pennsylvania College of Technology

Betty Lipford, Community College of Baltimore County

Paul Lospennato, North Shore Community College

Eddy McClelland, Roanoke College

William Mundy, Columbus State Community College

Andrea M. Murowski, Brookdale Community College

Christopher Myers, Yuba College

Ramesh Narasimhan, Montclair State University

Leah O'Goley, Holyoke Community College

Rochelle Olive, College of Alameda

Lynn Pape, Northern Virginia Community College/Alexandria

Craig Pence, Highland Community College

Douglas R. Pfister, Lansing Community College

Yvonne Phang-Hatami, Borough of Manhattan Community College

Jim Pofahl, University of Wisconsin/Whitewater

Susan Pope, University of Akron

Allan Rabinowitz, Pace University

George M. Roy, Concordia College

Alphonse Ruggiero, Suffolk County Community College

Jill Russell, Camden County College

Steve Schaefer, Contra Costa College

Linda Schain, Hofstra University

Sara Seyedin, Foothill College

Ed Shoenthal, Brooklyn College

Delta Heath-Simpson, Lewis Clark State College

Daniel Small, J. Sargeant Reynolds Community College

Gerald Smith, University of Northern Iowa

Charles A. Spector, SUNY – Oswego

Philip Stickney, Cocnise Community College

Mary Ston, Oakland Community College

Ron Strittmater, Hennepin Community College

K. R. Subramanyam, University of Southern California

Joseph Tabet, North Shore Community College

Steven Teeter, Utah Valley State College

Thomas Thompson, Madison Area Technical College

Leslie Thysell, Richard Bland College

John C. VanSantvoord, New Hampshire College

Keith Weidkamp, Sierra College

Jan Williams, Morgan State University

Orville Wright, Morgan State University

Theron Ray Wurzburger, New River Community College

ABOUT THE CONTRIBUTORS

Jo Lynne Koehn received her Ph.D. and Master's of Accountancy from the University of Wisconsin at Madison and is an associate professor at Central Missouri State University. Her scholarly articles have been published in a variety of journals including *Issues in Accounting Education, The CPA Journal, The Tax Advisor,* and *Accounting Enquiries.* Professor Koehn is a member of the American Accounting Association and the American Institute of CPAs. She also holds a Certified Financial Planning license and is active in promoting a financial planning curriculum at Central Missouri State University.

Jeannie M. Folk teaches financial and managerial accounting at College of DuPage and mentors accounting students working in cooperative education positions. In addition, she is active in the area of online, distance education. Professor Folk serves on the board of directors and the Scholarship Committee of TACTYC (Teachers of Accounting at Two-Year Colleges) as well as the Illinois CPA Society's Outstanding Educator Award Committee. She is also a member of the American Accounting Association and the American Institute of Certified Public Accountants. She was honored with the Illinois CPA Society's Outstanding Educator Award and was a recipient of the Women in Management, Inc., Charlotte Danstrom Woman of Achievement Award. Before entering academe, Professor Folk was a general practice auditor with Coopers & Lybrand (now PriceWaterhouseCoopers). She received her BBA from Loyola University Chicago and MAS in Accountancy from Northern Illinois University. Professor Folk enjoys travel, camping, hiking, and community activities with her three children.

Carol Yacht is a textbook author and educator with a teaching career spanning more than three decades. Carol has taught at Yavapai College; West Los Angeles Community College; California State University, Los Angeles; and Beverly Hills High School and Adult School. Carol has been teaching accounting for more than 25 years. She has worked for IBM Corporation as an educational instruction specialist and currently serves on the Computer Education Task Force for the National Business Education Association. Carol is a frequent speaker at state, regional, and national conventions; technical school consortium meetings; and Department of Education conferences. Carol earned her AS degree from Temple University, BS degree from the University of New Mexico, and MA degree from California State University, Los Angeles.

In addition to the helpful and generous colleagues listed above, I would like to thank the entire McGraw-Hill/Irwin Financial Accounting team, including Brent Gordon, Melody Marcus, Tracey Douglas, Kristin Leahy, Jackie Scruggs, Kimberly Hooker, Kelly Odom, Matthew Baldwin, Rose Hepburn, David Tietz, Matthew Perry, and Edward Przyzycki. I also owe thanks to a great marketing and sales support staff, including Kurt Strand, Rich Kolasa, Ryan Blankenship, and Melissa Larmon. I would also like to thank my accuracy checker, Barbara Schnathorst, CPA, of The Write Solution Inc. Many talented educators and professionals worked hard to create the supplements for this book, and for their efforts I'm grateful. Finally, many more people I either did not meet or whose efforts I did not personally witness nevertheless helped to make this book everything that it is and I thank them all. *John J. Wild*

ABOUT THE CONTRIBUTORS

Brief Contents

*Appendixes D and E are available as PDF files from the book's Web site and as print copy from a McGraw-Hill representative.

Contents

---

* Appendixes D & E are available as PDF files from the book's Web site and as print copy from a McGraw-Hill representative.

Financial Accounting:
Information
for Decisions

1

Accounting Information for Business Decisions

A Look at This Chapter

Accounting plays a crucial role in the information age. In this chapter, we discuss the importance of accounting to different types of organizations and describe its many users and uses. We see that ethics and social responsibility are crucial to accounting, and that the information age provides many new accounting opportunities.

A Look Ahead

Chapter 2 explains financial statements and the principles underlying them. It also describes and analyzes business transactions. More generally, Chapters 2 through 4 focus on accounting and analysis, and they explain how financial statements reflect transactions and events.

"In the markets, you don't fight with knives, but know-how"—Jonathan Hoenig

Learning Objectives

Conceptual

C1 Explain the aim and influence of accounting in the information age.

C2 Identify forms of organizations and their characteristics.

C3 Identify and describe the three major activities in organizations.

C4 Identify users and uses of accounting.

C5 Explain why ethics and social responsibility are crucial to accounting.

C6 Identify opportunities in accounting and related fields.

Analytical

A1 Describe income and its two major components.

A2 Explain the relation between return and risk.

A3 Explain and interpret the accounting equation.

A4 Compute and interpret return on investment.

Procedural

P1 Identify and prepare basic financial statements.

Decision Feature

When Pigs Fly

e CHICAGO—Jonathan Hoenig is on the fast track. This 25-year-old upstart begins his day about 5 A.M. and doesn't quit until late evening. Jonathan feels that his calling in life is to spread the message of financial opportunity to fellow members of his generation. He has his own radio show, regularly appears on the Fox TV affiliate in Chicago, writes a financial advice column for an ultrahip magazine, runs **CapitalistPig Asset Management (www.CapitalistPig.com),** and took time to write *Greed Is Good: The Capitalist Pig Guide to Investing*.

According to Hoenig, being a capitalist pig isn't about being materialistic. It's about knowing what you want and doing what it takes to get it. From his two-toned hair to his sockless feet in a pair of high-top sneakers, he doesn't look the part of an information guru. Says Hoenig, "In the markets, you don't fight with knives, but know-how." This is where accounting enters. It serves as a reliable, relevant source of business information—to be perused, digested, and acted on. He asserts that too many young businesspeople are ill informed on accounting but that there is hope. Financial statements are free for the taking, but the information they contain is invaluable.

This chapter opens the door to accounting and financial statements. It provides the accounting basics that investors, managers, and others such as Jonathan Hoenig use to make business decisions. This chapter also describes business organizations, activities, and opportunities. Hoenig asserts that all good businesspeople plan to use accounting in their business decisions. In that spirit Hoenig likes to quote the visionary architect Daniel Burnham: "'Make no little plans; they have no magic to stir men's blood.'" [Sources: Capitalist Pig Web site, January 2002; *Business Start-Ups,* March 2000; *Kiplinger.com,* March 2001.]

Chapter Preview

A **Preview** opens each chapter with a summary of topics covered.

Today's world is one of information—its preparation, communication, analysis, and use. Accounting is at the heart of this information age. Knowledge of accounting gives us opportunities. It also gives us the insight to benefit from these opportunities. By studying this book, you will learn about concepts, procedures, and analyses that are useful in everyday activities. This knowledge can help you make better financial decisions throughout your life. In this chapter we describe accounting, the users and uses of accounting information, the forms and activities of organizations, and the importance of ethics and social responsibility. We also explain several important accounting principles. This chapter provides a foundation for those who have little or no understanding of business.

Information Age

Key **terms** are printed in bold and defined again in the end-of-chapter **glossary**.

Topic Tackler icon references additional help on the CD.

Topic Tackler 1-1

We live in an **information age**—a time of communication, data, news, facts, access, and commentary. The information age encourages timeliness, independence, and freedom of expression. Information affects how we live, whom we associate with, and the opportunities we have. We use information to pick and choose among products and services. Examples are product rankings (*Consumer Reports*), investment advice (*The Motley Fool*), and credit ratings (*Standard & Poor's*).

Communication with others and access to data make up much of the *information superhighway*. The information superhighway has redefined communication, especially business communication. Global computer networks and telecommunications equipment allow us quick access to all types of business information. To fully benefit from this information, we need knowledge of the information system. An information system involves the collecting, processing, and reporting of information to decision makers. Knowledge of the information system means personal opportunities and real increases in pay. Studies show that two-year degree graduates with this knowledge can make upward of 40% more than high school graduates, and bachelor degree graduates can make 50% to 75% more than high school graduates. This added pay is for an ability to understand and process information.

Understanding and processing information is the core of accounting. To get the most from our education and opportunities in life, we must know accounting. Your instructor will provide you with many assignments from this book and related materials to help you master accounting. We also encourage you to join us on the information superhighway to explore the opportunities. For your help, we devote an entire Web site solely for your use with this book (**www.mhhe.com/wild2e**).

Influence of Accounting

C1 Explain the aim and influence of accounting in the information age.

One of the most important roles of the information superhighway is the reporting of business activities. Providing information about what businesses own, what they owe, and how they perform is the aim of accounting. **Accounting** is an information and measurement system that identifies, records, and communicates relevant, reliable, and comparable information about an organization's business activities. It helps us make better decisions, including assessing opportunities, products, investments, and social and community responsibilities.

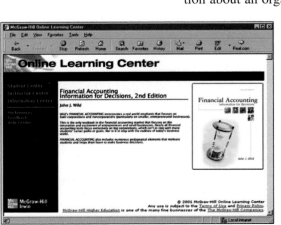

Completing this course will help you apply information in a way you can use in your everyday life. The use of information is not limited to accountants or even to people in business. Often the greatest benefits from understanding accounting come to those outside of accounting and business. You can use accounting to get better terms for a loan, to start a business, and to make better investment decisions. You will use accounting knowledge in whatever career you choose.

Business and Investment

A **business** is one or more individuals selling products or services for profit. Products such as athletic footwear (**Nike, Reebok, Converse**), computers (**Intel, Cisco, Apple**), and clothing (**Levi's, Limited, Gap**) are part of our lives. Services such as information communication (**Yahoo!**, **Microsoft**), fast food (**McDonald's**, **Wendy's**), and car rental (**Hertz**, **Budget**, **Alamo**) make our lives easier. A business can be as small as an at-home Web service provider or as massive as **Wal-Mart**. Nearly 1 million new businesses are started in the United States each year, no different from Jonathan Hoenig's **CapitalistPig** in the opening feature. Most of these are started by people who want freedom from ordinary jobs, a new challenge in life, or the advantage of extra money.

Point: More than 60% of those ages 18–29 want to have their own business.

Business Income

A common feature of all businesses is the desire for income. **Income**—also called **net income, profit,** or **earnings**—is the amount a business earns after subtracting expenses from its sales. **Sales,** also called **revenues,** are the amounts earned from selling products and services. **Expenses** are the costs incurred with producing sales. For CapitalistPig, income is the amount earned from client fees less expenses such as supplies, salaries, advertising, and promotion. Not all businesses make income. A **loss** arises when expenses are more than sales. Many new businesses incur losses in their first several months or years. **Amazon.com** is one example. However, no business can continually have losses and survive.

A1 Describe income and its two major components.

    Nike's income breakdown is in Exhibit 1.1. If we pay $100 for a pair of Nike shoes, $6.44 is income to Nike. The rest goes to cover expenses such as materials and labor ($60.08) and advertising ($10.87). Nike also pays $3.78 in total taxes. One question confronting our society today is, What is the "right" amount of profit? Also, should business give more to charities or community services? Are taxes too high or too low? For us to seriously consider important questions like these, we must understand accounting information.

Return and Risk

Income is often linked to **return.** The word *return* derives from the idea of getting something back from an investment: that "something" is referred to as a return on investment. **Return on investment (ROI)** is commonly stated in ratio form as income divided by amount invested. For example, banks or savings and loans often report our return on investment from a savings account in the form of an interest return such as 4%. We can invest our money in many ways. If we invest it in a savings account or in U.S. Treasury bills, we get a return of around 3% to 7%. We could also invest in a company's stock, or even start our own business. How do we decide among these investment options? The answer depends on our trade-off between return and risk.

    Risk is the uncertainty about the return we will earn. All business investments involve risk, but some investments involve more risk than others. The lower the risk of an investment, the lower is our expected return. The reason that savings accounts pay such a low return is the low risk of our not being repaid with interest (the government guarantees most savings accounts from default). Similarly, U.S. government bonds pay a low return because the U.S. government is not likely to default on its payments. If we buy a share of Nike or any other company, we might obtain a large return. However, we have no guarantee of any return; there is even the risk of loss.

    The bar graph in Exhibit 1.2 shows recent returns for bonds with different risks. **Bonds** are written promises by organizations to repay

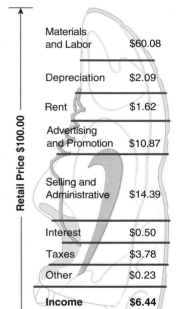

Retail Price $100.00	
Materials and Labor	$60.08
Depreciation	$2.09
Rent	$1.62
Advertising and Promotion	$10.87
Selling and Administrative	$14.39
Interest	$0.50
Taxes	$3.78
Other	$0.23
Income	**$6.44**

Exhibit 1.1

Where Our Money Goes When We Buy a Pair of Nikes

A2 Explain the relation between return and risk.

Decision Insight boxes highlight relevant items from practice.

Decision Insight

Celebrity Investment How do fame and fortune translate into return and risk? A poll asked people which celebrity is the best investment. Similar to business investments, many people named performers with years of earning power ahead—see results to the right.

Oprah Winfrey	27%
Steven Spielberg	19
Tiger Woods	15
Michael Jordan	14
Tom Cruise	8
Rosie O'Donnell	5
Jerry Seinfeld	4
Madonna	2

Exhibit 1.2

Returns for Bonds with
Different Risks

Source: *The Wall Street Journal.*

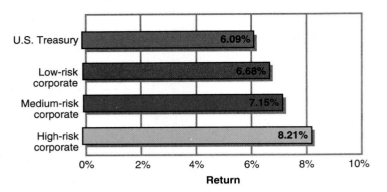

Return

Decision Maker

Programmer   You are considering two job offers. Both require your computer programming skills. One is with a start-up Internet company at an annual salary of $41,000; the other is with an established insurance company for $34,500 a year. Which offer do you accept? [*Answers are at the end of each chapter.*]

Answer—p. 23

amounts loaned with interest. U.S. Treasury bonds provide a low expected return, but they also offer low risk since they are backed by the U.S. government. High-risk corporate bonds offer a much larger potential return but with much higher risk.

The trade-off between return and risk is a normal part of business. Higher risk implies higher, but riskier, expected returns. To help us make better decisions, we use accounting information to measure both return and risk.

Focus of Accounting

We need to guard against a narrow view of accounting. The most common contact with accounting is through credit approvals, checking accounts, tax forms, and payroll. These experiences are limited and tend to focus on the recordkeeping parts of accounting. **Recordkeeping,** or **bookkeeping,** is the recording of financial transactions and events, either manually or electronically. While recordkeeping is essential to data reliability, accounting is this and much more.

The primary objective of accounting is to provide useful information for decision making, as shown in Exhibit 1.3. Accounting activities include identifying, measuring, recording, reporting, and analyzing business transactions and events. *Transactions* are exchanges between businesses. Examples are product sales, money lending, and payment of expenses. *Events* are incidents affecting a business's financial position. Examples are bankruptcies, labor strikes, and casualties. Accounting also involves interpreting information and designing information systems to provide useful reports that monitor and control a company's activities.

Exhibit 1.3

Accounting Activities

Identifying and measuring

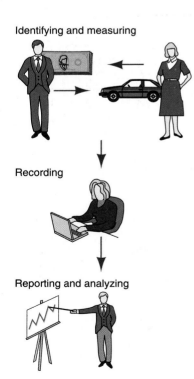

Recording

Reporting and analyzing

Setting Accounting Rules

There are rules for reporting on a business's performance and financial condition. These rules increase the usefulness of reports, including their reliability and comparability. The rules are determined by many individuals and groups and are referred to as **generally accepted accounting principles (GAAP).** Since accounting is a service activity, these rules reflect our society's needs, and not those of accountants or any other single constituency. Congress has charged the **Securities and Exchange Commission (SEC)** with the authority to set accounting rules for companies that issue stock to the public. For the most part, the SEC has passed authority to set accounting rules to the **Financial Accounting Standards Board (FASB),** a private organization consisting of seven full-time members. Many interested groups and individuals lobby the FASB in their self-interest. They include unions, investors, government agencies, lenders, and politicians.

Accounting and Technology

Technology is a key part of modern business and plays a major role in accounting. Computing technology reduces the time, effort, and cost of recordkeeping while improving clerical accuracy. Some small organizations continue to perform various accounting tasks manually, but even these companies are still impacted by information technology.

As technology has changed the way we store, process, and summarize large masses of data, accounting has been freed to expand its field. Consulting, planning, and other financial services are now part of accounting. These services require sorting through data, interpreting their meaning, identifying key factors, and analyzing their implications. Technology is increasingly important in accounting information systems, and is encouraged by advances in computer technology, networks, and enterprise-application software.

Global: Another important group in setting GAAP is the International Organization of Securities Commissions (IOSCO), a group of regulators representing about 90% of global financial markets.

Margin notes further enhance the textual material.

Point: Computing technology is only as good as the accounting data available, and users' decisions are only as good as their understanding of accounting. The best software and recordkeeping cannot make up for lack of accounting knowledge.

Quick Check

1. What is the purpose of accounting?
2. Describe income, sales, and expenses.
3. Explain the trade-off between return and risk.
4. What is the relation between accounting and recordkeeping?
5. Who sets accounting rules?
6. Identify some advantages of technology for accounting.

Quick Check boxes offer a chance to stop and reflect on key points.

Answers—p. 23

Forms of Business Organization

A business is organized and operated to make a profit. It can take one of three legal forms: *sole proprietorship, partnership,* or *corporation.*

Sole Proprietorship

A **sole proprietorship,** or simply **proprietorship,** is a business owned by one person. No special legal requirements must be met to start a proprietorship. It is a separate entity for accounting purposes, but it is *not* a separate legal entity from its owner. This means, for example, that a court can order an owner to sell personal belongings to pay a proprietorship's debt. An owner is even responsible for debts that exceed his or her net investment in the proprietorship. This *unlimited liability* of a proprietorship is sometimes a disadvantage.

Since tax authorities do not separate a proprietorship from its owner, the income of a proprietorship is not subject to a business income tax but is reported and taxed on the owner's personal income tax return. The rate of tax on a proprietorship's income depends on the level of total income from all sources that the owner had for the year. Proprietorship is by far the most common form of business organization in our society. Its characteristics are summarized in Exhibit 1.4.

C2 Identify forms of organization and their characteristics.

Partnership

A **partnership** is a business owned by two or more people, called *partners.* Like a proprietorship, no special legal requirements must be met in starting a partnership. The only requirement is an agreement between partners to run a business together. The agreement can be either oral or written and usually indicates how

Decision Insight

Accounting Web Technology is changing the face of business and accounting. Most organizations maintain Web sites that include substantial accounting information—see Nike's (**www.nike.com**) or Reebok's (**www.reebok.com**) Web sites. The SEC keeps an online database called EDGAR (**www.sec.gov**), which has accounting information for thousands of companies.

Exhibit 1.4

Characteristics of Businesses

Characteristic	Proprietorship	Partnership	Corporation
Business entity	yes	yes	yes
Legal entity	no	no	yes
Limited liability	no*	no*	yes
Unlimited life	no	no	yes
Business taxed	no	no	yes
One owner allowed	yes	no	yes

*Proprietorships and partnerships that are set up as LLCs provide limited liability.

Point: Boston Celtics Limited Partnership (BCLP) directs Celtic basketball. It has about 3 million ownership units. Based on recent transactions, each unit is worth about $11 to $12.

Point: Sole proprietorships and partnerships are usually managed on a regular basis by their owners. In a corporation, the owners (shareholders) elect a board of directors who appoint managers to run the business.

income and losses are to be shared. A written agreement is preferred because it can help partners avoid or resolve disputes. A partnership, like a proprietorship, is *not* legally separate from its owners. This means that each partner's share of profits is reported and taxed on that partner's tax return. It also means *unlimited liability* for its partners.

Two types of partnerships limit liability. A *limited partnership* includes a general partner(s) with unlimited liability and a limited partner(s) with liability restricted to the amount invested. A *limited liability partnership* restricts partners' liabilities to their own acts and the acts of individuals under their control. This protects an innocent partner from the negligence of another partner. Yet all partners remain responsible for partnership debts. **Nike** began as an entrepreneurial partnership and was originally called **Blue Ribbon Sports**. The partners, Philip Knight and Bill Bowerman, each contributed $500 and shipped shoes out of Knight's basement. They represent one of many entrepreneurial success stories.

Most proprietorships and partnerships are now organized as *limited liability companies* (*LLCs*). LLCs offer the limited liability of a corporation and the tax treatment of a partnership (or proprietorship).

Decision Insight

e

Entrepreneurial Age   Entrepreneurship will emerge as the defining trend of business in this century, according to a recent survey of leading Americans. Respondents see the biggest opportunities for entrepreneurship in technology, medicine, food services, hospitality, information services, and management.

Corporation

A **corporation** is a business legally separate from its owners, meaning it is responsible for its own acts and its own debts. It can enter into contracts, and it can buy, own, and sell property. It can also sue and be sued. Separate legal status means that a corporation can conduct business with the rights, duties, and responsibilities of a person. A corporation acts through its managers, who are its legal agents. Separate legal status also means that its owners, who are called **shareholders** (or **stockholders**), are not personally liable for corporate acts and debts. Shareholders are legally distinct from the business, and their loss is limited to their net investment in purchased shares. This limited liability lowers shareholder risk and is a key reason that corporations can raise resources from shareholders. It also encourages riskier investment with higher expected returns.

A corporation is legally chartered (*incorporated*) under state or federal law. Separate legal status results in a corporation having unlimited life. Ownership, or *equity*, of all corporations is divided into units called **shares** or **stock**. A shareholder can sell or transfer shares

Decision Track boxes apply accounting to business decisions—focusing on info acquisition, analysis, and usage.

Decision Track 1.1

d

Decision Point	Information Search	Analyze & Evaluate
How is a company organized and what are its related risks?	Background information or company name: Identifies the company as a proprietorship, partnership, or corporation— the first two are often set up as LLCs.	Proprietorships and partnerships (not set up as LLCs) are subject to unlimited liability, whereas corporations have limited liability. Corporations are subject to double taxation.

to another person without affecting the operations of a corporation. When a corporation issues only one class of stock, we call it **common stock** (or *capital stock*).

A corporation is subject to *double taxation.* This means that (1) the corporation is taxed on its net income and (2) any distribution of corporate income to its owners (through dividends) is taxed as part of the owners' personal income. An exception to this is an *S corporation,* a corporation with certain characteristics that give it special tax status. This special tax status removes its double taxation. Shareholders of S corporations report their share of corporate income or loss as part of their personal income.

Decision Ethics
e

Entrepreneur You and a friend develop a new design for in-line skates that improves speed and performance by 25% to 40%. You plan to form a business to manufacture and market these skates. You and your friend want to minimize taxes, but your prime concern is potential lawsuits from individuals who might be injured on these skates. What form of organization do you set up?

Answer—p. 23

Decision Ethics boxes are role-playing exercises that stress ethics in accounting and business.

Activities in Organizations

Organizations carry out their activities in many different ways. These differences extend to their products, services, goals, organization form, management style, worker compensation, and community giving. Yet the major activities of organizations are similar. There are three major types of business activities: financing, investing, and operating. We discuss each of these, but first we note that all of them require planning. **Planning** involves defining an organization's ideas, goals, and actions. Strategies and tactics must be laid out. Employees must be informed and motivated. Managers must be credible and display leadership and vision. All of these planning tasks are the duties of *executive management.* Executive management sets the organization's strategic goals and policies that are captured in an *organization plan.* An owner leads executive management in most organizations. This responsibility often carries with it the title of president, chief executive officer, or chairman of the board of directors.

External parties benefit from knowledge of an organization's plans. They look for clues on tactics, market demands, competitors, promotion, pricing, innovations, and projections. Much of this information appears in accounting reports. Most public corporations use the *Management Discussion and Analysis* section in their annual reports for this purpose. For example, Nike declares in its annual report that "management believes there is tremendous opportunity for growth in markets outside the United States. The Company continues to invest in infrastructure and local marketing and advertising to capitalize on these opportunities." Planning also involves change and reaction to it. It is not cast in stone. This adds *risk* to both the setting of an organization's plans and analysis of them. Accounting information can reduce this risk.

C3 Identify and describe the three major activities in organizations.

Point: Management must understand accounting data to set financial goals, make financing and investing decisions, and evaluate operating performance.

Financing

An organization requires financing to begin and to operate according to its plans. **Financing activities** are the means organizations use to pay for resources such as land, buildings, and equipment to carry out plans. Organizations are careful in acquiring and managing financing activities because of their potential to determine success or failure.

The two main sources of financing are owner and nonowner. *Owner financing* refers to resources contributed by the owner (common stock) along with any income the owner chooses to leave in the organization (retained earnings). *Nonowner* (or *creditor*) *financing* refers to resources contributed by creditors (lenders). Creditors often include banks, savings and loans, and other financial institutions. *Financial management* is the task of planning how to obtain these resources and to set the right mix between the amounts of owner and creditor financing. Nike's total financing at May 31, 2000, equaled $5,856.9 million. It comprised $3,136.0 million in owner financing and $2,720.9 million in creditor financing.

Point: Retained earnings increase from net income and decrease from net losses and dividends (owner withdrawals).

Investing

Investing activities are the acquiring and disposing of resources (assets) that an organization uses to acquire and sell its products or services. **Assets** are resources that are expected

Real company names are printed in blue when referred to in the text.

to possess current and future benefits and are funded by an organization's financing. Assets include land, buildings, equipment, inventories, supplies, cash, and all investments needed for operating an organization. Nike's assets, at May 31, 2000, totaled $5,856.9 million. Organizations differ on the amount and makeup of their assets. Some organizations require land and factories to operate. Others might need only an office. Determining the amount and type of assets for operations is called *asset management*.

A3 Explain and interpret the accounting equation.

The concept that an organization's investing and financing totals are *always* equal is important. Invested amounts are referred to as *assets,* and financing is made up of creditor and owner financing. Creditors and owners hold claims on assets. Creditors' claims are called **liabilities,** and the owner's claim is called **equity.** This equality can be written as:

$$\text{Assets} = \text{Liabilities} + \text{Equity}$$

This equality is called the **accounting equation.** At May 31, 2000, Nike's assets of $5,856.9 equal its liabilities of $2,720.9 plus its equity of $3,136.0 (all in millions):

$$\text{Assets} = \text{Liabilities} + \text{Equity}$$
$$\$5,856.9 = \$2,720.9 = \$3,136.0$$

The accounting equation works for all organizations at all times. It is an important part of accounting. We will return to and use the accounting equation in our analysis of transactions throughout the book.

Operating

An organization's main purpose is to carry out operating activities. **Operating activities** involve using resources to research, develop, purchase, produce, distribute, and market products and services. They also include management activities such as worker supervision and compliance with laws. Sales are the inflow of assets from selling products and services. Costs and expenses are the outflow of assets to support operating activities. Examples of costs and expenses are salaries, rent, electricity, and taxes. *Strategic management* is the process of determining the right mix of operating activities for the type of organization, its plans, and its market. How well an organization carries out its operating activities determines its success and return.

Exhibit 1.5

Activities in Organizations

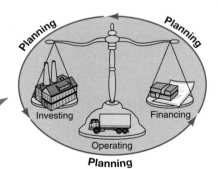

Infographics reinforce key concepts through visual learning.

Exhibit 1.5 summarizes these activities. Planning is part of each activity, and gives the activities meaning and focus. Investing (assets) and financing (liabilities and equity) are set opposite each other to stress their balance. Operating activities are shown below investing and financing activities to emphasize that operating activities are the result of investing and financing.

Quick Check

7. What are the three basic forms of business organization?

8. Identify the owners of corporations and the terminology for ownership units.

9. What are the three major activities in organizations?

Answers—p. 23

Financial Statements

Four basic financial statements report on an organization's activities: income statement, statement of retained earnings, balance sheet, and statement of cash flows. This section introduces these statements using Nike's data. We cover further details of each statement in later chapters.

How these statements are linked in time is illustrated in Exhibit 1.6. A balance sheet reports on an organization's financial position at a *point in time*. The income statement, statement of retained earnings, and statement of cash flows report on financial performance over a *period of time*. The three statements in the middle column of Exhibit 1.6 link balance sheets from the beginning to the end of a reporting period. They explain how the financial position of an organization changes from one point to another.

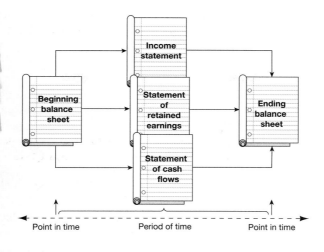

Exhibit 1.6

Links between Financial Statements

Preparers and users (including regulatory agencies) determine the length of the reporting period. A one-year, or annual, reporting period is common, as are semiannual, quarterly, and monthly periods. The one-year reporting period is known as the *accounting,* or *fiscal, year*. Businesses whose accounting year begins on January 1 and ends on December 31 are known as *calendar-year* companies. Many companies choose a fiscal year ending on a date other than December 31. **Nike** is a *noncalendar-year* company as reflected in the headings of its May 31 year-end financial statements in Appendix A near the end of the book. Some companies choose a fiscal year-end when sales and inventory are low. For example, **Gap**'s fiscal year-end is always near February 1, after the busy holiday season.

Topic Tackler 1-2

Point: A statement's heading lists the 3 W's: **W**ho—name of organization, **W**hat—name of statement, **W**hen—statement's point in time or period of time.

Income Statement

An income statement reports on operating activities. It lists amounts for sales and revenues less all costs and expenses over a *period of time*. This yields the "bottom-line" net income amount. Nike's income statement is shown at the top of Exhibit 1.7. Nike's numbers are all in millions, meaning we must multiply its numbers by 1 million to get actual amounts. Net income is $579.1 and is computed as revenues of $8,995.1 less costs and expenses of $8,416.0 (in millions).

P1 Identify and prepare basic financial statements.

Decision Track 1.2		*d*
Decision Point	**Information Search**	**Analyze & Evaluate**
Are company operating activities profitable?	Income statement: Reports revenues and expenses from operations.	Net income (profit) occurs when revenues exceed expenses; net loss occurs when expenses exceed revenues.

Statement of Retained Earnings

A statement of retained earnings reports changes in the retained earnings of the business over a *period of time*. This includes changes due to net income (or loss) and any dividends. Nike's statement of retained earnings is the second report shown in Exhibit 1.7. Two major items affecting Nike's retained earnings are its net income of $579.1 and dividends of $131.5.

Decision Track 1.3		*d*
Decision Point	**Information Search**	**Analyze & Evaluate**
What company activities explain changes in retained earnings?	Statement of retained earnings: Reports changes in retained earnings from mainly net income (loss) and dividends.	Retained earnings increase from net income and decrease from net losses and dividends; a growth company usually pays few, if any, dividends.

Topic Tackler 1-3

Exhibit 1.7

Nike's Financial Statements

NIKE	
Income Statement (in millions)	
For Year Ended May 31, 2000	
Revenues	$8,995.1
Costs and expenses	8,416.0
Net income	$ 579.1

NIKE	
Statement of Retained Earnings (in millions)	
For Year Ended May 31, 2000	
Retained earnings, May 31, 1999	$3,066.5
Add: Net income	579.1
Less: Dividends	(131.5)
Other changes	(627.1)
Retained earnings, May 31, 2000	$2,887.0

NIKE			
Balance Sheet (in millions)			
May 31, 2000			
Cash assets	$ 254.3	Liabilities	$2,720.9
Noncash assets	5,602.6	Equity: Common stock	2.8
		Retained earnings	2,887.0
		Other equity	246.2
Total assets	$5,856.9	Total liabilities and equity	$5,856.9

NIKE	
Statement of Cash Flows (in millions)	
For Year Ended May 31, 2000	
Cash from operating activities	$759.9
Cash used by investing activities	(440.0)
Cash used by financing activities	(263.7)
Net increase in cash	$ 56.2
Cash, May 31, 1999	198.1
Cash, May 31, 2000	$254.3

Balance Sheet

A balance sheet reports on investing and financing. It lists amounts for assets, liabilities, and equity at a *point in time*. The balance sheet for **Nike** is the third report shown in Exhibit 1.7. Its accounting (fiscal) year ends on May 31. Nike's assets total $5,856.9 and is the amount invested. Its liabilities are $2,720.9, and its equity is $3,136.0—their sum equals total financing.

Decision Track 1.4		*d*
Decision Point	**Information Search**	**Analyze & Evaluate**
Are company investing activities mainly financed by owner or nonowner financing?	Balance sheet: Reports company resources and claims on those resources; claims consist of owner (equity) and nonowner (liability) financing.	Compare the equity amount to the liability amount to assess the extent of owner versus nonowner financing.

Statement of Cash Flows

The statement of cash flows reports on cash flows for operating, investing, and financing activities over a *period of time*. **Nike**'s statement of cash flows is the final report shown in Exhibit 1.7. Its cash balance increased by $56.2 million this period. Of this increase in cash, Nike's operating activities provided $759.9 in cash, its investing activities used $440.0, and its financing activities (including exchange rate changes) used $263.7.

Decision Track 1.5		*d*
Decision Point	**Information Search**	**Analyze & Evaluate**
What are a company's sources and uses of cash for its business activities?	Statement of cash flows: Reports cash inflows and cash outflows for operating, investing, and financing activities.	A successful company yields sufficient operating cash inflows in the long run; growth is often accompanied by cash outflows for investing activities and cash inflows from financing and operating activities.

Users of Accounting Information

Organizations set up accounting information systems to help them and others make better decisions. Every organization uses some type of information system to report on its activities. Exhibit 1.8 shows that the accounting information system serves many kinds of users including managers, lenders, suppliers, customers, directors, auditors, employees, and current and potential investors.

External users

- Lenders
- Shareholders
- Governments
- Labor unions
- External auditors
- Customers

Internal users

- Managers
- Officers
- Internal auditors
- Sales staff
- Budget officers
- Controllers

Exhibit 1.8
Users of Accounting Information

External Information Users

External users of accounting information are *not* directly involved in running the organization. They include shareholders (investors), lenders, directors, customers, suppliers, regulators, lawyers, brokers, and the press. External users rely on accounting information to make better decisions. For example, lenders are less likely to make bad loans and shareholders bad investments when they know the current and past income of a business.

Financial accounting is the area of accounting aimed at serving external users. Its main objective is to provide financial statements to help users assess an organization's activities. External users have limited access to an organization's information. Their success depends

C4 Identify users and uses of accounting.

on financial statements that are reliable, relevant, and comparable. Some governmental and regulatory agencies have the power to require statements in specific forms, but most external users must rely on *general-purpose financial statements*. The term *general-purpose* refers to the broad range of purposes for which external users rely on these statements.

Each external user has special information needs depending on the types of decisions to be made. The remainder of this section describes several external users and questions they seek answers for from accounting reports.

Lenders (Creditors)

Lenders loan money or other resources to an organization. Banks, savings and loans, co-ops, and mortgage and finance companies all can act as lenders. Lenders look for information to help them assess whether an organization is likely to repay its loans with interest. Financial statements help them answer questions about an organization such as:

- Has it promptly paid past loans?
- What are its current risks?
- Can it repay current loans?
- What is its income outlook?

The questions can also change for short- and long-term lending decisions. The more long-term a loan, the more a lender's questions look like those of an owner.

Shareholders

Shareholders have legal control over part or all of a corporation. They are its owners and in many cases are not part of management. Shareholders are exposed to the greatest return and risk. Risk is high because there is no promise of either repayment or a return on investment. A shareholder can lose his or her entire investment. On the upside, shareholders have a claim on assets after a business pays its debts. Many businesses do not return income to shareholders but instead invest it in company growth. Financial statements aim to help answer shareholder (owner) questions such as these:

- What is current and past income?
- Are assets adequate to meet plans?
- Do expenses seem reasonable?
- Do customers pay bills promptly?
- Do loan amounts seem too high?

Shareholders typically elect a board of directors to oversee their interests in an organization. Since directors are responsible to shareholders, their questions are similar.

External Auditors

External (independent) auditors examine financial statements and provide an opinion on whether the statements are prepared according to generally accepted accounting principles. Auditors use financial statements of competing organizations to help assess the reasonableness of a client's statements. **Nike**'s auditor is **PricewaterhouseCoopers LLP**.

Employees

Employees have a special interest in an organization. They are interested in judging the fairness of wages and in assessing future job prospects. Financial statements provide information useful in addressing these interests. The statements are also used in bargaining for better wages when an organization is successful.

Regulators

Regulators often have legal authority or significant influence over the activities of organizations. The Internal Revenue Service (IRS) and other tax authorities require organizations to use specific reports in computing taxes. These taxes include income, unemployment, sales, and Social Security. Tax reports usually require special forms and supporting records.

Examples of other regulators include utility boards that use accounting information to set utility rates and securities regulators that require special filings for businesses with publicly traded securities.

Other Important External Users

Accounting serves the needs of many other important external users. Voters, legislators, and government officials use accounting information to monitor and evaluate a government's receipts and expenses. Contributors to nonprofit organizations use accounting information to evaluate the use and impact of their donations. Suppliers use accounting information to judge the soundness of a customer before making sales on credit. Customers use financial reports to assess the staying power of potential suppliers.

Internal Information Users

Internal users of accounting information are individuals directly involved in managing and operating an organization. The internal role of accounting is to provide information to help improve the efficiency and effectiveness of an organization in delivering products and services. **Managerial accounting** is the area of accounting aimed at serving the decision-making needs of internal users. It provides internal reports to help internal users improve an organization's activities. Internal reports are not subject to the same rules as external reports. Internal reports aim to answer questions such as these:

- What are costs per product?
- What service mix is most profitable?
- Are sales sufficient to break even?
- Which activities are most profitable?
- What costs vary with sales?

Information to help answer these questions is important for business success.

Exhibit 1.9 shows seven internal operating functions common to most organizations: research and development, purchasing, human resources, production, distribution, marketing, and servicing. Accounting is essential to the operation of each function. Each unit often has its own internal user (manager) who makes decisions. Depending on the type of business, not all of these functions may be necessary (or some may be combined). For example, publishing companies usually do not require separate research and development units, and banks do not require production units. The following list briefly describes the information needs of each function:

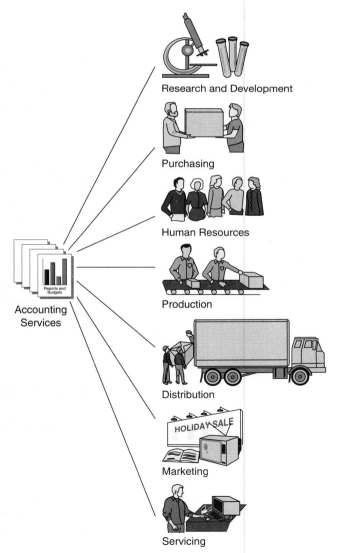

Exhibit 1.9
Internal Operating Functions

Research and Development

Purchasing

Human Resources

Production

Distribution

Marketing

Servicing

Accounting Services

Reports and Budgets

(R10)

- **Research and development**   Research and development seeks to create or improve products and services. Managers need information about current and projected costs and sales.
- **Purchasing**   Purchasing involves acquiring and managing materials for operations. Managers need to know what, when, and how much to purchase.
- **Human resources**   Human resources management locates, screens, hires, trains, compensates, promotes, and counsels employees. Managers need information about current and potential employees' payroll, benefits, performance, and compensation.
- **Production**   Production is the mix of activities to produce products and services. Good production methods depend on information to monitor costs and ensure quality.
- **Distribution**   Distribution involves timely and accurate delivery of products and services. Information is often key to quality, low-cost distribution.
- **Marketing**   Marketing promotes and advertises products and services. Marketing managers use reports about sales and costs to target consumers, set prices, and monitor consumer needs, tastes, and price concerns.
- **Servicing**   Servicing customers after selling products and services is often key to success. Information is needed on both the costs and benefits of servicing.

Point: There are 3 different types of businesses: (1) Services—provide services for profit, (2) Merchandisers—buy products and sell them for profit, and (3) Manufacturers—create products and sell them for profit.

Both internal and external users rely on internal controls to monitor and control these functions. *Internal controls* are procedures set up to protect assets, ensure reliable accounting reports, promote efficiency, and encourage adherence to company policies.

Ethics and Social Responsibility

This section explains ethics and their effect on organizations. The goal of accounting is to provide useful information for decisions. For information to be useful, it must be trusted. This demands ethics in accounting. This section also discusses social responsibility for organizations.

Understanding Ethics

C5   Explain why ethics and social responsibility are crucial to accounting.

Ethics are beliefs that distinguish right from wrong. They are accepted standards of good and bad behavior. Ethics and laws often coincide, with the result that many unethical actions (such as theft and physical violence) are also illegal. Yet other actions are legal but are considered unethical, such as not helping people in need. Since there are differences between laws and ethics, we cannot look to laws to always keep people ethical.

Identifying the ethical path is sometimes difficult. The preferred path is a course of action that avoids casting doubt on our decisions. For example, accounting users are less likely to trust an auditor's report if the auditor's pay depends on the success of the client. To avoid such concerns, ethics rules are often set. For example, auditors are banned from direct investment in their client and cannot accept pay that depends on figures in the client's reports. Exhibit 1.10 gives guidelines for making ethical decisions.

Exhibit 1.10

Guidelines for Ethical Decision Making

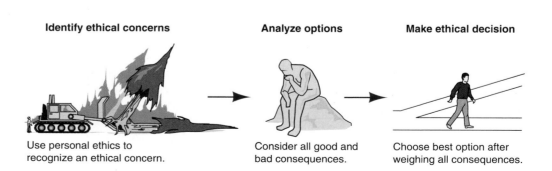

Identify ethical concerns

Use personal ethics to recognize an ethical concern.

Analyze options

Consider all good and bad consequences.

Make ethical decision

Choose best option after weighing all consequences.

Organizational Ethics

Organizational ethics are likely learned through example and leadership. Companies such as **McDonald's**, **Marriott**, and **IBM** work hard to instill ethics in employees, yet we still hear people express concern about what they see as poor ethics in organizations. One survey of executives, educators, and legislators showed that 9 of 10 participants believe organizations are troubled by ethical problems. Yet this same survey revealed that the vast majority of participants believe organizations that are successful over the long run follow high ethical standards. This finding confirms an old saying: *Good ethics are good business.* Ethical practices build trust, which promotes loyalty and long-term relationships with customers, suppliers, and employees. Thus, many organizations have their own code of ethics.

Global: Organizational ethics often differ across countries. This is due to cultural, political, legal, economic, and other important factors.

Accounting Ethics

Ethics are crucial in accounting. Providers of accounting information often face ethical choices as they prepare financial reports. Their choices can affect both the use and receipt of money, including taxes owed and the money dispersed to shareholders. They can affect the price a buyer pays and the wages paid to workers. They can even affect the success of products, services, and divisions. Misleading information can lead to a wrongful closing of a division that harms workers, customers, and suppliers. Accordingly, codes of accounting ethics are set up and enforced. These codes include those of the American Institute of Certified Public Accountants and the Institute of Management Accountants. Ethics codes also can help in dealing with confidential information. For example, auditors have access to an organization's confidential salaries and strategies. Auditors' ethics codes require them to keep this information confidential.

Point: Converse proposed to name a new footwear product Run N' Gun, sparking debate on ethics, social responsibility, and profits. Converse says "run n' gun" is a basketball and football phrase. Critics claim it invites youth violence and links with the gun culture.

Point: The American Institute of Certified Public Accountants' *Code of Professional Conduct* is available at www.AICPA.org.

Social Responsibility

Social responsibility refers to a concern for the impact of actions on society. Organizations are increasingly concerned with their social responsibility. **Reebok** proclaims in its annual report: "We have a deep-felt commitment to operate in a socially responsible way and we stand for human rights throughout the world." Society has increased the pressure on organizations to act responsibly, and they have responded to this challenge. An organization's social responsibility can include donations to hospitals, colleges, community programs, and law enforcement. It also can include programs to reduce pollution, increase product safety, improve worker conditions, support continuing education, and better use our natural resources. Yet most organizations are more likely to invest in their own social programs. For example, **Nike** invests in its *P.L.A.Y.* (*Participate in the Lives of America's Youth*) program, which provides facilities for kids to pursue fitness and fun. We are aware of well over 1,000 businesses that offer social programs to their employees to pursue community service activities. These programs are not limited to large companies. For example, many independently owned theaters and sports businesses offer discounts to students and senior citizens. Still others help sponsor events such as the Special Olympics and summer reading programs.

Point: Does sex sell? Abercrombie & Fitch's *A&F Quarterly* carries an article that touts Costa Rica as a spring break destination because—among other reasons—prostitution is legal. Its "Naked New Wire" tells where to go for nude skiing and volleyball. Reflecting a social backlash, the company's stock plunged from over $50 to under $25.

Point: Paul Newman donates all income from sale of his Newman's Own products to charity.

Graphical displays are often used to illustrate key points.

Decision Insight

Returns on Social Responsibility   Virtue is not always its own reward. Compare the S&P 500, which includes companies selling weapons, alcohol, and tobacco, with the Domini Social Index (DSI), which covers 400 companies that have especially good records of social responsibility. Notice that returns for companies with socially responsible behavior are at least as high if not higher than those of the S&P 500.

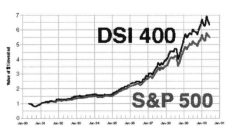

Opportunities in Practice

Accounting information affects many aspects of our lives. When we earn money, pay taxes, invest savings, budget earnings, and plan for the future, we are influenced by accounting. This section discusses four areas of opportunities in accounting: financial, managerial, taxation, and accounting-related. Exhibit 1.11 lists selected opportunities in each area.

Financial Accounting

C6 Identify opportunities in accounting and related fields.

Financial accounting provides information to decision makers who are external to an organization. This information is normally in the form of general-purpose financial statements. The process of preparing financial statements demands the input of many individuals within and outside accounting. There is also a demand for auditing in financial accounting. An **audit** is a check of an organization's accounting systems and records using various tests. It increases the credibility of financial statements. When an audit is complete, an auditor writes an *audit report* expressing a professional *opinion* about whether the financial statements are fairly presented. It is an opinion because an auditor does not verify every transaction and event. Nike's audit report is in Appendix A.

Managerial Accounting

Point: Accounting offers many career opportunities that are both challenging and rewarding and that require strong interpersonal and communication skills.

Managerial accounting provides information to an organization's internal decision makers. Managerial accounting activities generally fall within one of five areas: (1) *General accounting* refers to the recording of transactions, the processing of data, and the preparing of reports for internal use. It is supervised by a chief accounting officer called a *controller*. (2) *Cost accounting* is a process of accumulating the information managers need to identify, measure, and control costs. It involves accounting for the costs of products and services and is useful for evaluating managerial performance. (3) *Budgeting* is the development of

Exhibit 1.11

Opportunities in Practice

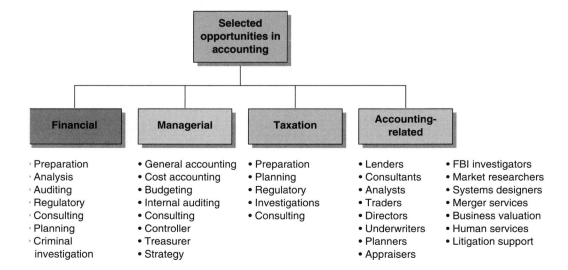

formal plans for an organization's future activities. It provides a basis for evaluating actual performance. (4) *Internal auditing* adds credibility to reports that are produced and used within the organization. Internal auditors assess the effectiveness and efficiency of established operating procedures. (5) *Management consulting* helps organizations design and install new accounting and control systems, develop budgeting procedures, and set up employee benefit plans.

Tax Accounting

Taxes raised by federal, state, and local governments include those based on income reported by taxpayers. *Tax accounting,* a service offered by many organizations including law firms, helps taxpayers comply with the law by preparing tax returns. It also plans future transactions to minimize taxes. The Internal Revenue Service is a major employer of tax services. It is responsible for collecting federal taxes and enforcing tax law.

Point: The Internal Revenue Code is complex. As a result, it is often less costly for small companies to pay accountants to do their tax work than to develop the necessary expertise among their employees.

Accounting-Related Opportunities

Accounting-related opportunities are vast. Accounting is the common language of business communications. It spans professions, continents, and economies. Exhibit 1.11 listed several accounting-related opportunities, including lenders, consultants, analysts, and planners. Less traditional ones include community activist, political consultant, reporter, salesperson, union official, entrepreneur, programmer, and engineer.

Accounting Specialization

The majority of accounting professionals work in **private accounting,** as shown in Exhibit 1.12. A large company can employ 100 or more accounting professionals, but most companies have fewer. Other accounting professionals are employed in **public accounting,** whose services are available to the public. Many in public accounting are self-employed; others work for public accounting firms whose employees number from few to several thousand. Another large number of accounting professionals work in nonbusiness organizations, with many of these in federal, state, or local government. *Government accountants* perform accounting services for government units, including business regulation and investigation of law violations.

Accounting specialists are highly regarded. Their professional standing often is denoted by a certificate. Certified public accountants (CPAs) must meet education and experience requirements, pass the CPA examination, and exhibit ethical character. Most states require a college degree with the equivalent of a major in accounting. The CPA examination covers topics in financial and managerial accounting, taxation, auditing, and business law. Many accounting specialists hold certificates in addition to or instead of the CPA. Two of the most common are the certificate in management accounting (CMA) and the certified internal auditor (CIA). Holders of these certificates must meet examination, education, and experience requirements similar to those of a CPA. The CMA is awarded by the Institute of Management Accountants and the CIA is granted by the Institute of Internal Auditors. Another prestigious certificate is the chartered financial analyst (CFA), awarded by the Association for Investment Management and Research (AIMR). Employers also look for specialists with designations such as certified bookkeeper (CB), certified payroll professional (CPP), and personal financial specialist (PFS).

Point: Many states accept graduate study in accounting as a substitute for experience in meeting CPA requirements.

Outlook and Compensation

Employers are desperately seeking to hire individuals with accounting knowledge. Beyond the usual accounting work, employers want these individuals to help with financial analysis, strategic planning, e-commerce, product

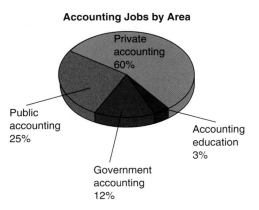

Accounting Jobs by Area

Private accounting 60%

Public accounting 25%

Government accounting 12%

Accounting education 3%

Exhibit 1.12

Accounting Jobs by Area

feasibility analysis, information technology, and financial management. Demand is so great that many employers are offering signing bonuses along with stock options, profit sharing, and performance bonuses. Benefit packages often include flexible work schedules, telecommuting options, career path alternatives, casual work environments, extended vacation time, and child and elder care. Employers are also offering options to full-time work, including temporary employment and project work.

Intense demand for accounting specialists led the American Institute of Certified Public Accountants (AICPA) to send career information to thousands of high schools. Demand for accounting specialists is also boosting salaries. Exhibit 1.13 reports average annual starting salaries for several accounting positions. Note that for each position, salary variation depends on location, company size, professional designation, expertise, experience, and other factors. For example, salaries for chief financial officers range from under $75,000 to more than $500,000 per year. Likewise, salaries for bookkeepers range from under $28,000 to more than $45,000.

Exhibit 1.13
Accounting Salaries

Title (experience)	2000 Salary	2005 Estimate*
Public Accounting		
Partner	$121,000	$155,000
Manager	66,500	82,000
Senior	45,500	59,000
Staff (1–3 years)	39,000	48,000
Entry (0–1 years)	34,000	43,500
Private Accounting		
CFO/Treasurer	149,000	185,500
Controller	111,000	144,000
Asst. treasurer/Controller	70,000	87,500
Manager	64,000	80,000
Senior	46,000	60,000
Staff (1–3 years)	39,000	49,000
Entry (0–1 years)	33,500	42,500
Bookkeeping		
Full-charge bookkeeper	38,000	47,500
Payroll manager	35,000	44,500
Accounts manager	34,500	44,000
Assistant bookkeeper	30,500	38,500
Accounting clerk	26,500	34,500

* Estimates assume a 5% compounded annual increase over current levels; these estimates are likely low since the National Association of Colleges and Employers reported an 8.8% increase in starting pay of accounting graduates for 2000 alone.

 Decision Analysis (a section at the end of each chapter) introduces and explains important ratios and tools helpful in decision making. It illustrates these using real company data.

Decision Analysis d Return on Investment

A *Decision Analysis* section at the end of each chapter is devoted to financial statement analysis. We organize financial statement analysis into four areas, which we identify as the *building blocks* of analysis: (1) liquidity and efficiency, (2) solvency, (3) profitability, and (4) market prospects.

Liquidity refers to the availability of resources to meet short-term cash requirements. *Efficiency* refers to how productive a company is in using its assets. Measures that reflect liquidity and efficiency include

- Current ratio.
- Acid-test ratio.
- Accounts receivable turnover.
- Inventory turnover.

- Days' sales uncollected.
- Days' sales in inventory.
- Credit risk ratio.
- Total asset turnover.
- Working capital.
- Days' cash expense coverage.

Solvency refers to a company's long-run financial viability and its ability to cover long-term obligations. Measures that reflect solvency include

- Debt ratio.
- Equity ratio.
- Free cash flow.
- Pledged assets to secured liabilities.
- Times interest earned.
- Cash coverage of debt.

Profitability refers to a company's ability to generate an adequate return on the amounts invested. Measures that reflect profitability include

- Profit margin ratio.
- Gross margin ratio.
- Return on total assets.
- Return on common stockholders' equity.
- Book value per common share.
- Basic earnings per share.

Market prospects refer to the returns and risks associated with those companies with publicly traded stock. Measures that reflect market prospects include

- Price-earnings ratio.
- Dividends yield.

We introduce many of these ratios in the Decision Analysis section of the most relevant chapters. Definitions for these ratios are also summarized on the back inside cover of the book and again in Chapter 13 for most of these ratios.

When analyzing and interpreting these measures, we need benchmarks to identify good, bad, or average financial performance or condition. These benchmarks can include

- Intracompany—company itself provides benchmarks from prior and current periods.
- Competitor—one or more direct competitors provide the benchmarks.
- Industry—industry statistics serve as benchmarks.
- Guidelines (rules of thumb)—past experiences serve as benchmarks.

Each of these benchmarks can be useful when properly applied, yet comparisons with selected competitors are often best.

In this first chapter we discuss a profitability measure, that of return on investment. Return on investment is useful in evaluating management, analyzing and forecasting profits, and planning activities. **Dell Computer** has its marketing department compute return on investment for *every* mailing. Dell's chief financial officer says it spent over a year teaching its workers how to apply return on investment. *Return on investment (ROI)*, also called *return on assets (ROA)*, is viewed as an indicator of operating efficiency and is defined in Exhibit 1.14.

A4 Compute and interpret return on investment.

$$\textbf{Return on investment} = \frac{\textbf{Net income}}{\textbf{Average total assets}}$$

Exhibit 1.14
Return on Investment

Net income is usually taken from the annual income statement. The average total assets figure is usually computed by adding the beginning and ending amounts of total assets for that same period and dividing by 2. To illustrate, **Nike** reports net income of $579.1 million in 2000. At the beginning of fiscal 2000, its total assets are $5,247.7 million and at the end of fiscal 2000 they total $5,856.9 million. Nike's return on investment for 2000 is:

$$\text{Return on investment} = \frac{\$579.1 \text{ mil.}}{(\$5,247.7 \text{ mil.} + \$5,856.9 \text{ mil.})/2} = 10.4\%$$

Is a 10.4% return on investment good or bad for Nike? To help answer this question and others like it, we can compare (benchmark) Nike's return on investment with its prior per-

Exhibit 1.15

Nike, Reebok, and
Industry Returns

Fiscal Year	Return on Investment		
	Nike	**Reebok**	**Industry**
2000	10.4%	0.7%	1.4%
1999	8.5	1.4	1.8
1998	7.4	7.7	3.7
1997	17.1	8.1	5.9
1996	15.6	10.0	8.6

formance, the returns of similar companies (such as **Reebok, Converse, Skechers,** and **Vans**), and the returns from alternative investments. **Nike**'s return on investment for each of the prior five years is reported in the second column of Exhibit 1.15, which ranges from 7.4% to 17.1%. These returns show a recent decline with Nike's efficiency in using its assets. We can also compare Nike to a similar company such as Reebok, whose return on investment is shown in the third column of Exhibit 1.15. In four of the five years shown, Nike's return exceeds Reebok's, and its average return is higher for this period. We can also compare Nike's return to the normal return for manufacturers of athletic footwear and apparel. Industry averages are available from services such as **Dun & Bradstreet**'s *Industry Norms and Key Ratios* and **Robert Morris Associates**' *Annual Statement Studies.* When compared to its competitors, Nike performs well. The industry ratio, shown in the fourth column of Exhibit 1.15, is the median value computed from 10 competitors, including Fila, Converse, Stride Rite, K-Swiss, Skechers, and Vans, among others. Another useful analysis is to compare Nike's returns to those of companies outside its industry.

Decision Maker concludes each Decision Analysis section with a role-playing scenario to show the usefulness of ratios.

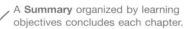

Decision Maker

Entrepreneur   You own a small winter ski resort that earns a 21% return on its investment. An opportunity to purchase a winter ski equipment manufacturer is offered to you. This manufacturer earns a 19% return on its investment. The industry return for this manufacturer is 14%. Do you purchase this manufacturer?

Answer—p. 23

---

*A **Summary** organized by learning objectives concludes each chapter.*

Summary

C1 **Explain the aim and influence of accounting in the information age.** Accounting is an information and measurement system that aims to identify, record, and communicate relevant, reliable, and comparable information about business activities. It helps assess opportunities, products, investments, and social and community responsibilities.

C2 **Identify forms of organization and their characteristics.** Business organizations take one of three basic forms: sole proprietorship, partnership, or corporation. These forms of organization have characteristics that hold important implications for legal liability, taxation, continuity, number of owners, and legal status.

C3 **Identify and describe the three major activities in organizations.** Organizations carry out three major activities: financing, investing, and operating. Financing is the means used to pay for resources such as land, buildings, and machines. Investing refers to the buying and selling of resources used in acquiring and selling products and services. Operating activities are those necessary for carrying out the organization's plans.

C4 **Identify users and uses of accounting.** Users of accounting are both internal and external. Some users and uses of accounting include (a) managers in controlling, monitoring, and planning; (b) lenders for measuring the risk and return of loans; (c) shareholders for assessing the return and risk of stock; (d) directors for overseeing management; and (e) employees for judging employment opportunities.

C5 **Explain why ethics and social responsibility are crucial to accounting.** The goal of accounting is to provide useful information for decision making. For information to be useful, it must be trusted. This demands ethics and socially responsible behavior in accounting.

C6 **Identify opportunities in accounting and related fields.** Opportunities in accounting include financial, managerial, and tax accounting. They also include accounting-related fields such as lending, consulting, managing, and planning. Many other opportunities with accounting knowledge also exist.

A1 **Describe income and its two major components.** Income (also called net income, profit, or earnings) is the amount a business earns after subtracting all expenses necessary for its sales (Sales − Expenses = Income). Sales (also called revenues) are the amounts earned from selling products and services. Expenses are the costs incurred with generating sales. A net loss arises when expenses are more than sales.

A2 **Explain the relation between return and risk.** *Return* refers to income, and *risk* is the uncertainty about the return we hope to make. All investments involve risk. The lower the risk of an investment, the lower is its expected return. Higher risk implies higher, but riskier, expected return.

A3 **Explain and interpret the accounting equation.** Investing activities are funded by financing activities. An organization cannot have more or less assets than its financing and, similarly, it cannot have more or less nonowner (liabilities) and owner (equity) financing than its assets. This relation yields the accounting equation: Assets = Liabilities + Equity.

A4 **Compute and interpret return on investment.** Return on investment is computed as net income divided by the average amount invested. For example, if we have an average balance of $100 in a savings account and it earns $5 interest for the year, the return on investment is $5/$100, or 5%.

P1 **Identify and prepare basic financial statements.** Four basic financial statements report on an organization's activities: balance sheet, income statement, statement of retained earnings, and statement of cash flows.

Guidance Answers to **Decision Maker** and **Decision Ethics**

Programmer As the computer programmer, you confront a trade-off between return (salary) and risk (dependable employment). The start-up company has an uncertain future and is willing to increase your pay to balance the added risk you take in working for it (it could fail). The established company pays less, but you are reasonably assured of employment. If you or others depend on your salary, the risk of the start-up company might be too high. Yet if you depend less on your salary, the increased pay might be worth the risk.

Entrepreneur (p. 9) You should probably form the business as a corporation if potential lawsuits are of prime concern. The corporate form of organization protects your personal property from lawsuits directed at the business and would place only the corporation's resources at risk. A downside of the corporate form is double taxation—the corporation must pay taxes on its income, and you must pay taxes on any money distributed to you from the business (even though the corporation already paid taxes on this money). You should also examine the ethical and socially responsible aspects of starting a business in which you anticipate injuries to others. Formation as an LLC should also be explored.

Entrepreneur (p. 22) The 19% return on investment for the manufacturer exceeds the 14% industry return (and many others). This is a positive factor for a potential purchase. Also, the purchase of this manufacturer is an opportunity to spread your risk over two businesses as opposed to one. Still, you should hesitate to purchase a business whose return of 19% is lower than your current resort's return of 21%. You are probably better off directing efforts to increase investment in your resort, assuming you can continue to earn a 21% return.

Guidance Answers to **Quick Checks**

1. Accounting is an information and measurement system that identifies, records, and communicates relevant information to help people make better decisions. These decisions can involve opportunities, products, investments, and social and community activities.

2. Income is what a business earns after paying for all expenses necessary for its sales. Sales are the amounts earned from providing products and services. Expenses are the costs incurred with generating sales.

3. The lower the risk of an investment, the lower is the expected return. Similarly, higher expected return offsets higher risk (*actual* return usually differs from *expected* return). Higher risk implies higher, but riskier, expected returns.

4. Recordkeeping, also called bookkeeping, is the recording of financial transactions and events, either manually or electronically. Recordkeeping is essential to data reliability; accounting is this and much more. Accounting includes identifying, measuring, recording, reporting, and analyzing business events and transactions.

5. Many individuals and groups determine accounting rules that reflect society's needs, not those of accountants or any other single constituency. Major participants in setting rules include the SEC and the FASB.

6. Technology offers increased accuracy, speed, efficiency, and convenience in accounting.

7. The three basic forms of business organization are sole proprietorships, partnerships, and corporations.

8. Owners of corporations are called shareholders (or stockholders). Corporate ownership is divided into units called shares (or stock). The most basic of corporate shares is common stock (or capital stock).

9. Organizations pursue financing, investing, and operating activities. These three major activities all require planning.

10. External users of accounting include lenders, shareholders, directors, customers, suppliers, regulators, lawyers, brokers, and the press. Internal users of accounting include managers, officers, and other internal decision makers involved with strategic and operating decisions.

11. Internal operating functions include research and development, purchasing, human resources, production, distribution, marketing, and servicing.

12. Internal controls are procedures set up to protect assets, ensure reliable accounting reports, promote efficiency, and encourage adherence to company policies. Internal controls are crucial for relevant and reliable information.

13. Ethical guidelines are threefold: (1) identify ethical concerns using personal ethics, (2) analyze options considering all good and bad consequences, and (3) make ethical decisions after weighing all consequences.

14. Ethics and social responsibility often translate into higher profits and a better working environment.

15. For accounting to provide useful information for decisions, it must be trusted. Trust demands ethics in accounting.

A **Glossary** of key terms concludes each chapter (a complete glossary is on the book's Web site).

Glossary

Accounting An information and measurement system that identifies, records, and communicates relevant information about a company's business activities. (p. 4)

Accounting equation The equality where Assets = Liabilities + Equity. (p. 10)

Assets Resources expected to produce current and future benefits. (p. 9)

Audit An analysis and report of an organization's accounting system and its records using various tests. (p. 18)

Bonds Written promises to repay amounts loaned with interest. (p. 5)

Bookkeeping (See *recordkeeping*). (p. 6)

Business One or more individuals selling products and/or services for profit. (p. 4)

Common stock A corporation's basic ownership share; also called *capital stock*. (p. 9)

Corporation A business that is a separate legal entity under state or federal laws with owners called *shareholders* or *stockholders*. (p. 8)

Earnings (See *net income*). (p. 5)

Equity The owners' (shareholders') claim on an organization's assets. (p. 10)

Ethics Codes of conduct by which actions are judged as right or wrong, fair or unfair, honest or dishonest. (p. 16)

Expenses The costs incurred to earn sales. (p. 5)

External users Persons using accounting information who are not directly involved in running the organization. (p. 13)

Financial accounting Area of accounting aimed at serving external users. (p. 13)

Financial Accounting Standards Board (FASB) Independent group of seven full-time members who are responsible for setting accounting rules. (p. 7)

Financing activities The means (equity and liabilities) organizations use to pay for their resources (assets). (p. 9)

Generally accepted accounting principles (GAAP) Rules that specify acceptable accounting practices. (p. 6)

Income (See *net income*). (p. 5)

Information age A time period that emphasizes communication, news, facts, data access, and commentary. (p. 4)

Internal users Persons using accounting information who are directly involved in managing the organization. (p. 15)

Investing activities The buying and selling of resources (assets) that an organization controls. (p. 9)

Liabilities Creditors' claims on an organization's assets. (p. 10)

Loss Arises when expenses are more than sales; also called *net loss*. (p. 5)

Managerial accounting Area of accounting aimed at serving the decision-making needs of internal users (p. 15)

Net income Amount earned after subtracting all expenses necessary for sales; also called *income, profit* or *earnings*. (p. 5)

Operating activities Use of assets to carry out an organization's plans in the areas of research, development, purchasing, production, distribution, and marketing. (p. 10)

Partnership A business owned by two or more people that is not organized as a corporation. (p. 7)

Planning Term for an organization's ideas, goals, and strategic actions. (p. 9)

Private accounting Accounting services provided for an employer other than the government. (p. 19)

Profit (See *net income*). (p. 5)

Proprietorship (See *sole proprietorship*). (p. 7)

Public accounting Accounting services provided to many different clients. (p. 19)

Recordkeeping Part of accounting that involves recording transactions and events, either manually or electronically; also called *bookkeeping*. (p. 6)

Return The income from an investment; often in percent form. (p. 5)

Return on investment A ratio reflecting operating efficiency; defined as net income divided by average total assets; also called *return on assets*. (p. 5)

Revenues (See *sales*). (p. 5)

Risk The uncertainty about an expected return. (p. 5)

Sales Amounts earned from selling products or services; also called *revenues*. (p. 5)

Securities and Exchange Commission (SEC) Federal agency charged by Congress to set reporting rules for organizations that sell ownership shares to the public. (p. 6)

Shareholders Owners of a corporation; also called *stockholders*. (p. 8)

Shares Equity of a corporation divided into units; also called *stock*. (p. 8)

Social responsibility Being accountable for the impact that one's actions might have on society. (p. 17)

Sole proprietorship Business owned by one person that is not organized as a corporation; also called *proprietorship*. (p. 7)

Stock (See *shares*). (p. 8)

Stockholders (See *shareholders*). (p. 8)

Questions

1. What is the purpose of accounting in society?

2. What is the relation between accounting and the information superhighway?

3. Identify three actual businesses that offer services and three actual businesses that offer products.

4. Explain business income and its computation.

5. *d* Explain return and risk. Discuss the trade-off between them.

6. Why do organizations license and monitor accounting and accounting-related professionals?

7. Technology is increasingly used to process accounting data. Why then do we need to study and understand accounting?

8. Describe the three basic forms of business organization and their characteristics.

9. Identify three types of organizations that can be formed as either profit-oriented businesses, government units, or non-profit establishments.

10. Describe the three major activities in organizations.

11. Explain why investing (assets) and financing (liabilities and equity) totals are always equal.

12. *d* Identify four kinds of external users and their uses of accounting information.

13. *d* What are at least three questions business owners might be able to answer by looking at accounting information?

14. Identify at least four managerial accounting tasks performed by both private and government accountants.

15. Describe the internal role of accounting for organizations.

16. *d* What type of accounting information might be useful to those who carry out the marketing activities of a business?

17. What ethical issues might accounting professionals face in dealing with confidential information?

18. Identify three types of services typically offered by accounting professionals.

19. Why is accounting described as a service activity?

20. Identify at least three tasks performed by government accounting professionals.

21. What work do tax accounting professionals perform in addition to preparing tax returns?

22. *d* Define and explain *return on investment* (return on assets).

23. This chapter introduced **Nike**'s financial statements. Nike was initially organized as a partnership. Identify important characteristics of partnerships and their implications.

24. Access the SEC's EDGAR database (www.sec.gov) and retrieve **Nike**'s 10-K for fiscal year 2000. Identify Nike's chief financial officer. How many directors does Nike have? **NIKE**

25. Identify the dollar amounts of **Reebok**'s 1999 assets, liabilities, and equity shown in its statements in Appendix A near the end of the book. **Reebok**

26. *d* Access the SEC EDGAR database (www.sec.gov) and retrieve **Gap**'s 10-K for year 2000. Identify its auditor. What responsibility does its independent auditor claim regarding Gap's financial statements? **GAP**

The *d* icon highlights assignments stressing business decision-making skills.

Quick Study exercises give readers a brief test of key elements.

QUICK STUDY

There exist several important accounting principles and organizations. Identify the meaning of each of the following accounting and business abbreviations: GAAP, SEC, FASB, and AICPA.	**QS 1-1** Identifying accounting abbreviations C1
Accounting provides information about an organization's business transactions and events. Identify at least two examples of both (*a*) business transactions and (*b*) business events.	**QS 1-2** Identifying transactions and events C3
Executive management is key to an organization's success or failure. Identify at least three responsibilities in the *executive management* (planning) activity of an organization.	**QS 1-3** Identifying management plans C3
An important responsibility of many accounting professionals is to design and implement internal control procedures for organizations. Explain the purpose of internal control procedures.	**QS 1-4** Explaining internal control C4
Identify at least three main areas of opportunities for accounting professionals. For each area, identify at least three accounting-related work opportunities in practice.	**QS 1-5** Accounting opportunities C6

QS 1-6

Identifying ethical **C5**
concerns

Accounting professionals must sometimes choose between two or more acceptable methods of accounting for business transactions and events. Explain why these situations can involve difficult matters of ethical concern.

QS 1-7

Applying the accounting **A3**
equation

a. Total assets of Keller Financial Co. equal $50,000 and its equity is $20,000. What is the amount of its liabilities?

b. Total assets of Echo Valley Co. equal $25,000 and its liabilities and equity amounts are equal. What is the amount of its liabilities? What is the amount of its equity?

QS 1-8

Applying the accounting
equation

A3

Use the accounting equation to compute the missing financial statement amounts a, b, and c.

Company	Assets	=	Liabilities	+	Equity
1	$ 40,000		$ (a)		$10,000
2	$ (b)		$60,000		$20,000
3	$110,000		$20,000		$ (c)

QS 1-9

Identifying and computing
assets, liabilities, and equity

A3   **GAP**

Use **Gap**'s January 2000 financial statements, printed in Appendix A near the end of the book, to answer the following:

a. Identify the dollar amounts of Gap's 2000 (1) assets, (2) liabilities, and (3) equity.

b. Using Gap's amounts from part *a*, verify that: Assets = Liabilities + Equity.

QS 1-10

Identifying items in financial
statements

P1

Indicate in which financial statement each item would most likely appear: income statement (I), balance sheet (B), statement of retained earnings (E), or statement of cash flows (CF).

a. Assets   **d.** Retained earnings   **g.** Total liabilities and equity

b. Revenues   **e.** Dividends   **h.** Cash from operating activities

c. Liabilities   **f.** Costs and expenses   **i.** Net decrease (or increase) in cash

---

EXERCISES

Exercise 1-1

Distinguishing business
organizations

C2

The following describe several different business organizations. Determine whether the description refers to a sole proprietorship, partnership, or corporation.

a. Ownership of Cola Company is divided into 1,000 shares of stock.

b. Trimark is owned by Sarah Gates, who is personally liable for the debts of the business.

c. Jerry Staley and Susan Morris own Financial Services, a financial services provider. Neither Staley nor Morris has personal responsibility for the debts of Financial Services.

d. Nancy Case and Frank Pruitt own Get-It-There, a courier service. Both are personally liable for the debts of the business.

e. WSP Services does not have separate legal existence apart from the one person who owns it.

f. BioLife Enterprises does not pay taxes and has one owner.

g. Tampa Trade pays its own taxes and has two owners.

Exercise 1-2

Identifying business activities

C3

Match each transaction or event to one of the following activities of an organization: financing activities (F), investing activities (I), or operating activities (O).

a. _____ An owner contributes resources to the business.

b. _____ An organization purchases equipment.

c. _____ An organization advertises a new product.

d. _____ The organization borrows money from a bank.

e. _____ An organization sells some of its assets.

Many accounting professionals work in one of the following three areas:

A. Financial accounting   **B.** Managerial accounting   **C.** Tax accounting

Identify the area of accounting that is most involved in each of the following responsibilities:

_____ **1.** Auditing financial statements.

_____ **2.** Cost accounting.

_____ **3.** Budgeting.

_____ **4.** Internal auditing.

_____ **5.** Planning transactions to minimize taxes.

_____ **6.** Preparing external financial statements.

_____ **7.** Reviewing reports for SEC compliance.

_____ **8.** Investigating violations of tax laws.

Exercise 1-3
Describing accounting responsibilities
C6

Much of accounting is directed at servicing the information needs of those users that are external to an organization. Identify at least three external users of accounting information and indicate two questions they might seek to answer through their use of accounting information.

Exercise 1-4
Identifying accounting users and uses   C4

Select the internal operating function from the two choices provided that is most likely to regularly use the information described. *Note:* The information described is likely used in both functions, but it is more relevant to one.

a. Which internal operating function is more likely to use payroll information: marketing or human resources?   *human*

b. Which internal operating function is more likely to use sales report information: marketing or research and development?   *research*   *marketing*

c. Which internal operating function is more likely to use inventory information: purchasing or human resources?   *purchasing*

d. Which internal operating function is more likely to use budget and cost information: production or distribution?   *production*

e. Which internal operating function is more likely to use product quality information: human resources or production?   *production*

Exercise 1-5
Determining accounting use in internal operating functions
C4

Assume the following role and describe a situation in which ethical considerations play an important part in guiding your decisions and actions:

a. You are a student in an introductory accounting course.

b. You are a manager with responsibility for several employees.

c. You are an accounting professional preparing tax returns for clients.

d. You are an accounting professional with audit clients that are competitors in business.

Exercise 1-6
Identifying ethical concerns
C5

Indicate which term best fits each of the following descriptions:

A. Audit   **C.** Cost accounting   **E.** Ethics   **G.** Budgeting

B. Controller   **D.** GAAP   **F.** General accounting   **H.** Tax accounting

_____ **1.** An accounting area that includes planning future transactions to minimize taxes paid.

_____ **2.** A managerial accounting system designed to help managers identify, measure, and control operating costs.

_____ **3.** Principles that determine whether an action is right or wrong.

_____ **4.** An examination of an organization's accounting system and its records that adds credibility to financial statements.

_____ **5.** The task of recording transactions, processing recorded data, and preparing reports and financial statements.

_____ **6.** The chief accounting officer of an organization.

Exercise 1-7
Learning the language of business
C1–C6

Exercise 1-8
Learning the language of business

A1 A2 **C4 C6**

Indicate which term best fits each of the following descriptions:

A. Government accountants   **C.** IRS   **E.** CIA   **G.** Risk   **I.** AICPA
B. Internal auditing   **D.** SEC   **F.** Income   **H.** Public accountants   **J.** CMA

_____ **1.** Process of examining an organization's recordkeeping, assessing whether managers are following established procedures, and appraising the efficiency of operating techniques.

_____ **2.** Amount of uncertainty associated with an expected return.

_____ **3.** Amount a business earns after paying all expenses and costs associated with its sales.

_____ **4.** Federal agency responsible for collecting federal taxes and enforcing tax law.

_____ **5.** Accounting professionals who provide services to many different clients.

_____ **6.** Accounting professionals employed by federal, state, or local branches of government.

Exercise 1-9
Using the accounting equation

A3

Check (c) Beg. equity, $60,000

Answer the following questions. (*Hint:* Use the accounting equation.)

a. Knight's Medical Supplies has assets equal to $119,000 and liabilities equal to $47,000 at year-end. What is the total equity for Knight's business at year-end?

b. At the beginning of the year, Amber Company's assets are $300,000 and its equity is $100,000. During the year, assets increase $80,000 and liabilities increase $50,000. What is the equity at the end of the year?

c. At the beginning of the year, New Navy Company's liabilities equal $70,000. During the year, assets increase by $60,000, and at year-end assets equal $190,000. Liabilities decrease $5,000 during the year. What are the beginning and ending amounts of equity?

Exercise 1-10
Using the accounting equation

A3

Determine the missing amount from each of the separate situations a, b, and c below.

	Assets	=	Liabilities	+	Equity
a.	?	=	$20,000	+	$45,000
b.	$100,000	=	$34,000	+	?
c.	$154,000	=	?	+	$40,000

Exercise 1-11
Return on investment

A4

Fineva Group reports net income of $30,000 for 2002. At the beginning of 2002, Fineva Group had $110,000 in assets. By the end of 2002, assets had grown to $150,000. What is Fineva Group's return on investment?

A **Problem Set B** located at the end of **Problem Set A** is provided for each problem to reinforce the learning process. **Problem Set C** (with solutions) is provided on this book's Web site.

PROBLEM SET A

Problem 1-1A
Computing and interpreting return on investment

A4

Coca-Cola and PepsiCo both produce and market beverages that are direct competitors. Key financial figures (in $ millions) for these businesses over the past year follow:

Key Figures	Coca-Cola	PepsiCo
Sales	$19,805	$20,237
Net income	2,431	2,050
Average invested (assets)	21,623	17,551

Required

Check (1a) 11.24%; (1b) 11.68%

1. Compute return on investment for (*a*) Coca-Cola and (*b*) PepsiCo.

2. Which company is more successful in its total amount of sales to consumers?

3. Which company is more successful in returning net income from its amount invested?

Analysis Component

4. Write a one-paragraph memorandum explaining which company you would invest your money in and why. (Limit your explanation to the information provided.)

All business decisions involve risk and return.

Required

Identify both the risk and the return in each of the following activities:

plum
grape
apricot
peach
cherry

1. Investing $2,000 in a 5% savings account.
2. Placing a $2,500 bet on your favorite sports team.
3. Investing $10,000 in Yahoo! stock.
4. Taking out a $7,500 college loan to earn an accounting degree.

Problem 1-2A
Identifying risk and return

A2

Quadcomm manufactures, markets, and sells cellular telephones. The average amount invested, or average total assets, in Quadcomm is $250,000. In its most recent year, Quadcomm reported net income of $65,000 on sales of $475,000.

$\frac{65,000}{250,000} = .26$

Assets = $250,000
Net Income = $65,000
Sales = $475,000

Required

1. What is Quadcomm's return on investment (also called return on assets)?
2. Does return on investment seem satisfactory for Quadcomm given that its competitors average a 12% return on investment? *yes*
3. What are total expenses for Quadcomm in its most recent year? *410,000*
4. What is the average total amount of financing (liabilities plus equity) for Quadcomm?

Problem 1-3A
Determining expenses, financing, and return on investment

A1 A3 A4

Check (3) $410,000
(4) $250,000

A start-up company often engages in the following transactions in its first year of operations. Classify these transactions in one of the three major categories of an organization's business activities.

A. Financing   **B.** Investing   **C.** Operating

____ **1.** Contributing land to the business.
____ **2.** Purchasing a building.
____ **3.** Purchasing land.
____ **4.** Borrowing cash from a bank.
____ **5.** Purchasing equipment.
____ **6.** Selling and distributing products.
____ **7.** Conducting advertising.
____ **8.** Paying employee wages.

Problem 1-4A
Describing organizational activities

C3

An organization undertakes various activities in pursuit of success. Identify an organization's three major business activities, include descriptions for each of these activities.

Problem 1-5A
Describing organizational activities **C3**

The following is selected financial information for Vasero Energy Company for the year ended December 31, 2002: Revenues, $55,000; costs and expenses, $40,000; net income, $15,000.

Required

Prepare the 2002 calendar-year income statement for Vasero Energy Company.

Problem 1-6A
Preparing an income statement

P1

The following is selected financial information for Sumoco as of December 31, 2002: Liabilities, $44,000; equity, $46,000; assets, $90,000.

Required

Prepare the balance sheet for Sumoco as of December 31, 2002.

Problem 1-7A
Preparing a balance sheet

P1

The following is selected financial information for ComCast for the year ended December 31, 2002:

Cash used by investing activities	$(2,000)
Net increase in cash	1,200
Cash used by financing activities	(2,800)
Cash from operating activities	6,000
Cash, Dec. 31, 2001	2,300

Problem 1-8A
Preparing a statement of cash flows

P1

Required

Prepare the 2002 calendar-year statement of cash flows for ComCast.

Problem 1-9A
Preparing a statement of
retained earnings

P1

The following is selected financial information for Boardwalk for the year ended December 31, 2002:

Retained earnings, Dec. 31, 2002	$14,000	Dividends	$1,000
Net income	8,000	Retained earnings, Dec. 31, 2001	7,000

Required

Prepare the 2002 calendar-year statement of retained earnings for Boardwalk.

PROBLEM SET B

Problem 1-1B 🝜
Computing and interpreting
return on investment

A4

AT&T and GTE produce and market telecommunications products and are competitors. Key financial figures (in $ millions) for these businesses over the past year follow:

Key Figures	AT&T	GTE
Sales	$ 62,391	$25,336
Net income	5,450	4,033
Average invested (assets) . .	130,973	50,832

Required

Check (1a) 4.16%; (1b) 7.93%

1. Compute return on investment for (a) AT&T and (b) GTE.
2. Which company is more successful in the total amount of sales to consumers?
3. Which company is more successful in returning net income from its amount invested?

Analysis Component

4. Write a one-paragraph memorandum explaining which company you would invest your money in and why. (Limit your explanation to the information provided.)

Problem 1-2B 🝜
Identifying risk and return

A2

All business decisions involve risk and return.

Required

Identify both the risk and the return in each of the following activities:
1. Stashing $500 under your mattress.
2. Placing a $250 bet on a horse running in the Kentucky Derby.
3. Investing $20,000 in Nike stock.
4. Investing $25,000 in U.S. Savings Bonds.

Problem 1-3B 🝜
Determining expenses,
financing, and return on
investment

A1 A3 A4

Kasper Company manufactures, markets, and sells snowmobile equipment. The average amount invested, or average total assets, in Kasper Company is $3,000,000. In its most recent year, Kasper reported net income of $200,000 on sales of $1,400,000.

Required

1. What is Kasper Company's return on investment (also called return on assets)?
2. Does return on investment seem satisfactory for Kasper given that its competitors average a 9.5% return on investment?

Check (3) $1,200,000
(4) $3,000,000

3. What are the total expenses for Kasper Company in its most recent year?
4. What is the average total amount of financing (liabilities plus equity) for Kasper Company?

A start-up company often engages in the following activities during its first year of operations. Classify each of the following activities into one of the three major activities of an organization:

A. Financing   **B.** Investing   **C.** Operating

———— **1.** Providing services.   ———— **5.** Supervising workers.

———— **2.** Obtaining a bank loan.   ———— **6.** Contributing money to the business.

———— **3.** Purchasing machinery.   ———— **7.** Renting office space.

———— **4.** Researching products.   ———— **8.** Paying utilities expenses.

Problem 1-4B
Describing organizational activities

C3

Identify in outline format the three major business activities of an organization. For each of these activities, identify at least two specific actions normally undertaken by its owners or managers.

Problem 1-5B
Describing organizational activities C3

Selected financial information for Pricenet Co. for the year ended December 31, 2002, follows:

| Revenues .... $68,000 | Costs and expenses .... $40,000 | Net income .... $28,000 |

Problem 1-6B
Preparing an income statement

P1

Required

Use the information provided to prepare the 2002 calendar-year income statement for Pricenet Co.

The following is selected financial information for MicroUS as of December 31, 2002:

| Liabilities .... $64,000 | Equity .... $50,000 | Assets .... $114,000 |

Problem 1-7B
Preparing a balance sheet

P1

Required

Use the information provided to prepare the balance sheet for MicroUS as of December 31, 2002.

Selected financial information of Intertec for the year ended December 31, 2002, follows:

Cash from investing activities	$1,600
Net increase in cash	400
Cash from financing activities	1,800
Cash used by operating activities	(3,000)
Cash, Dec. 31, 2001	1,300

Problem 1-8B
Preparing a statement of cash flows

P1

Required

Use this information to prepare the 2002 calendar-year statement of cash flows for Intertec.

The following is selected financial information of ComEx for the year ended December 31, 2002:

| Retained earnings, Dec. 31, 2002 . | $47,000 | Dividends .... | $ 7,000 |
| Net income .... | 5,000 | Retained earnings, Dec. 31, 2001 . | 49,000 |

Problem 1-9B
Preparing a statement of retained earnings

P1

Required

Prepare the 2002 calendar-year statement of retained earnings for ComEx.

> **Beyond the Numbers (BTN)** is a special problem section aimed to refine communication, conceptual, analysis, and research skills. It includes many activities helpful in developing an active learning environment.

BEYOND THE NUMBERS

Reporting in Action

A1 A3 A4

NIKE

BTN 1-1   Key financial figures for Nike's fiscal year ended May 31, 2000, follow:

Key Figure	In Millions
Financing (liabilities + equity)	$5,856.9
Net income	579.1
Revenues	8,995.1

Required

1. What is the total amount of assets invested in Nike?
2. What is Nike's return on investment? Nike's assets at May 31, 1999, equal $5,247.7 (in millions).
3. How much are total expenses for Nike?
4. Does Nike's return on investment seem satisfactory if its competitors average a 2% return?

Swoosh Ahead

5. Access Nike's financial statements (Form 10-K) for fiscal years ending after May 31, 2000, from its Web site (www.nike.com) or from the SEC Web site (www.sec.gov). Compute Nike's return on investment using this current information. Compare the May 31, 2000, fiscal year-end return on investment to any subsequent years' returns you are able to compute.

Comparative Analysis

A1 A3 A4

NIKE

Reebok

BTN 1-2   Key comparative figures ($ millions) for both Nike and Reebok follow:

Key Figure	Nike	Reebok
Financing (liabilities + equity)	$5,856.9	$1,564.1
Net income	579.1	11.0
Revenues (sales)	8,995.1	2,899.9

Required

1. What is the total amount of assets invested in (*a*) Nike and (*b*) Reebok?
2. What is the return on investment for (*a*) Nike and (*b*) Reebok? Nike's beginning-year assets equal $5,247.7 (in millions) and Reebok's beginning-year assets equal $1,684.6 (in millions).
3. How much are expenses for (*a*) Nike and (*b*) Reebok?
4. Is return on investment satisfactory for (*a*) Nike and (*b*) Reebok? (Assume competitors average a 2% return.)
5. What can you conclude about Nike and Reebok from these computations?

Ethics Challenge

C5

BTN 1-3   Julian Brown works in a public accounting firm and hopes to eventually be a partner. The management of Vianet Company invites Brown to prepare a bid to audit Vianet's financial statements. In discussing the audit fee, Vianet's management suggests a fee range in which the amount depends on the reported profit of Vianet. The higher its profit, the higher will be the audit fee paid to Brown's firm.

Required

1. Identify the parties potentially affected by this audit and the fee plan proposed.
2. What are the ethical factors in this situation? Explain.
3. Would you recommend that Brown accept this audit fee arrangement? Why or why not?
4. Describe some ethical considerations guiding your recommendation.

BTN 1-4 Refer to this chapter's opening feature about CapitalistPig. Assume that Jonathan Hoenig wishes to launch a CapitalistPig Store to sell paraphernalia related to his radio and TV shows, and that he meets with a loan officer of a Chicago bank to discuss a loan.

Communicating in Practice

A2 C2 ⓓ ⓔ

Required

1. Prepare a half-page report outlining the information you would request from Hoenig if you were the loan officer.

2. Indicate whether the information you request and your loan decision are affected by the form of business organization for the proposed CapitalistPig store.

BTN 1-5 World Wrestling Federation Entertainment, Inc., began selling stock to the public in 1999. A company's first sale of stock to investors outside the company is termed an *initial public offering (IPO)*. Access EDGAR at www.edgar-online.com. Click on the IPO Express link. Next Search IPOs by World Wrestling Federation's ticker symbol WWFE. You should see a link to information regarding WWFE's initial public offering. Search links at this page and determine the initial opening stock offering price for the World Wrestling Federation.

Taking It to the Net

C1 C2 C4

BTN 1-6 Teamwork is important in today's business world. Successful teams schedule convenient meetings, maintain regular communications, and cooperate with and support their members. This assignment aims to establish support/learning teams, initiate discussions, and set meeting times.

Teamwork in Action

C1

Required

1. Form teams and open a team discussion to determine a regular time and place for your team to meet between each scheduled class meeting. Notify your instructor via a memorandum or e-mail message as to when and where your team will hold regularly scheduled meetings.

2. Develop a list of telephone numbers and/or e-mail addresses of your teammates.

BTN 1-7 *Business Week* publishes a ranking of the top 1,000 companies based on several performance measures. This issue is called the *Business Week Global 1000*. Obtain the July 10, 2000, publication of this issue—this book's Web site maintains free access to this article.

Business Week Activity

C1

Book's Web site provides free and easy access to all articles for every *Business Week* Activity.

Required

1. What are the top 10 companies on the basis of market value?

2. Which companies are ranked in the top 10 in both 1999 and 2000 for market value?

3. How many of the top 10 on market capitalization are not U.S. companies?

BTN 1-8 Shanda Lowry is preparing to launch her new business, Your Boards (YB). YB would be a small retail store located on the Pacific coast that buys and sells skateboards, surfboards, snowboards, and related accessories.

Entrepreneurial Decision

C2 A3 ⓔ ⓓ

Required

1. As what organization form should YB be set up? Explain.

2. YB obtains a $25,000 bank loan and Lowry contributes $28,000 of her own assets to the business.

   a. What is YB's total amount of financing?

   b. What is YB's total amount of assets?

Hitting the Road
C2 *d*

BTN 1-9   You are to interview a local business owner. (This can be a friend or relative.) Opening lines of communication with members of the business community can provide personal benefits of business networking. If you do not know the owner, you should call ahead to introduce yourself and explain your position as a student and your assignment requirements. You should request an appointment for a face-to-face or phone interview to discuss the form of organization and operations of the business. Be prepared to make a good impression.

Required

1. Identify and describe the main operating activities and the form of organization for this business.

2. Determine and explain why the owner(s) chose this particular form of organization.

3. Identify any special advantages and/or disadvantages the owner(s) experiences in operating with this form of business organization.

Global Decision
A1 A3 A4 *d*

BTN 1-10   Both Nike and Reebok compete with each other and with Adidas-Salomon (www. adidas.com/investor). Key financial figures for Adidas-Salomon for the 2000 calendar-year follow:

Key Figure*	Euros in Millions
Financing (liabilities + equity)	4,018.5
Net income	181.7
Revenues	5,834.8
Return on investment	4.8%

*Figures prepared in accordance with International Accounting Standards.

Required

1. Identify any concerns you have in comparing Adidas-Salomon's financing, income, and revenues figures to those of Nike and Reebok (in BTN 1-2) for purposes of making business decisions.

2. Identify any concerns you have in comparing Adidas-Salomon's return on investment ratio to those of Nike and Reebok (in BTN 1-2) for purposes of making business decisions.

2 Accounting Information System

"Knowledge of accounting information systems helps start-ups"—Tony Hsieh and Alfred Lin (far left)

A Look Back

Chapter 1 considered the role of accounting in the information age and introduced financial statements. We described accounting for different organizations and identified users and uses of accounting.

A Look at This Chapter

This chapter focuses on the accounting process. We describe transactions and source documents as inputs for analysis. We explain the analysis and recording of transactions. The accounting equation, T-account, ledger, trial balance, and debits and credits are shown as useful tools in the accounting process.

A Look Ahead

Chapter 3 extends our focus on processing information. We explain the importance of adjusting accounts and the procedures in preparing financial statements.

Learning Objectives

Conceptual

C1 Explain the financial reporting environment.

C2 Identify, explain, and apply accounting principles.

C3 Explain the steps in processing transactions.

C4 Describe source documents and their purpose.

C5 Describe an account and its use in recording transactions.

C6 Describe a ledger and a chart of accounts.

C7 Define *debits* and *credits* and explain their role in double-entry accounting.

Analytical

A1 Analyze business transactions using the accounting equation.

A2 Analyze the impact of transactions on accounts and financial statements.

A3 Compute return on equity and use it to analyze company performance.

A4 Compute the debt ratio and describe its use in analyzing company performance.

Procedural

P1 Record transactions in a journal and post entries to a ledger.

P2 Prepare and explain the use of a trial balance.

P3 Prepare unadjusted financial statements from business transactions.

Decision Feature

Leapfrog Competitors

e SAN FRANCISCO—Tony Hsieh, 26, and Alfred Lin, 28, love chicks—the kind that hatch from business incubators. The two run **Venture Frogs (www.vfrogs.com)**, an incubator that funds Internet start-ups—something that few folks, frogs, or humans have recently pursued. Hsieh and Lin see the dot-com downturn as an opportunity. Says Hsieh, "What we see is pretty much opportunity everywhere."

A good incubator, says Hsieh, "creates an environment where companies being incubated can interact and share ideas and stories. We have a break room where people play foosball or talk shop while relaxing." Many incubators charge a fee for space and services as well as take equity stakes in the companies being raised. A crucial part of incubation is setting up a reliable accounting information system. Hsieh and Lin know that business decision makers must have access to timely accounting data. Decision makers must also understand the limitations of those data, including the accounting system underlying its preparation. Says Hsieh, "We started Venture Frogs so that we could invest in and advise [companies, and] . . . help them make fewer mistakes."

The accounting information system is the focus of this chapter. It describes key accounting principles, how the system captures and reports business transactions, and crucial components of the accounting double-entry system. As all managers of incubators know, a grasp of the accounting information system is an advantage in the game to leapfrog your competition. [Sources: Venture Frogs Web site, January 2002, *Entrepreneur,* January 2001, CNN.com, July 6, 2001.]

Chapter Preview

Financial statements report on the financial performance and condition of an organization. Financial statements are the way businesspeople communicate. Knowledge of their preparation, organization, and analysis is important. In this chapter, we describe the information reflected in financial statements. We also discuss the principles and assumptions guiding their preparation. An important goal of this chapter is to illustrate how transactions are recorded and reflected in financial statements and how they impact our analysis. Debits and credits are introduced and identified as a tool in helping us understand and process transactions.

Generally Accepted Accounting Principles

We explained in Chapter 1 how financial accounting practice is governed by rules called *generally accepted accounting principles* (*GAAP*). To use and interpret financial statements effectively, we need to understand these principles. A main purpose of GAAP is to make information in financial statements relevant, reliable, and comparable. *Relevant information* affects the decisions of its users. *Reliable information* is trusted by users. *Comparable information* is helpful in comparing organizations. This section describes the setting of GAAP and identifies several crucial accounting principles.

Financial Reporting Environment

C1 Explain the financial reporting environment.

Point: An audit does *not* attest to the absolute accuracy of financial statements.

Global: Both U.S. and U.K. accounting principles are developed in the private sector. This is likely tied to both countries' legal systems based on English common law, in which professionals tend to make the rules. In contrast, governments set accounting principles in many continental European countries. This is likely tied to their legal systems that tend to be based on codified law.

Accounting principles are developed in response to users' needs. Moreover, accounting principles, auditing standards, and the various users interact in the financial reporting environment. Specifically, accounting principles are applied in accounting for business transactions and events and in preparing financial statements. Audits are performed in accordance with **generally accepted auditing standards (GAAS),** which are the accepted rules for conducting audits of financial statements. Both accounting and auditing help assure users that financial statements include relevant, reliable, and comparable information. An audit report tells whether or not the statements are prepared using accepted accounting principles. **Ernst & Young** states in its audit report of **Harley-Davidson:** "In our opinion, the consolidated financial statements . . . present fairly, in all material respects . . . [and] in conformity with generally accepted accounting principles."

Accounting principles were historically developed through common usage. A principle was acceptable if most professionals permitted it. This history is reflected in the phrase *generally accepted.* As business transactions became more complex, users wanted more concrete guidance. Many users desired more uniformity in practice. Authority for developing accepted principles was eventually assigned to a select group of professionals. The Financial Accounting Standards Board (FASB) is the primary authoritative source of GAAP. [Predecessors to the FASB were the Accounting Principles Board (APB) and the Committee on Accounting Procedure (CAP).] The FASB seeks advice from all users and often holds public hearings. Its goal is to improve financial reporting and balance the interests of all users. The FASB communicates its decisions in various publications. Most notable are its *Statements of Financial Accounting Standards (SFAS).* These statements set generally accepted standards in the United States and often affect international practices.

The FASB draws its authority from two major sources. The first, as noted in Chapter 1, is the Securities and Exchange Commission (SEC), which Congress created to regulate securities markets, including the flow of information from companies to the public. The SEC designates the FASB as its primary authority for setting GAAP. It can overrule the FASB but rarely does so. The second source of authority comes from state boards that license CPAs. State ethics codes require CPAs who audit financial statements to disclose areas where those statements fail to comply with FASB rules. If CPAs fail to report noncompliance, they can lose their licenses to practice. Also, the AICPA's *Code of Professional Conduct* states that a member can be expelled for not objecting to financial statements that fail to comply with FASB rules.[1] In addition, authority for GAAS belongs to the *Auditing Standards Board* (*ASB*), a special committee of the AICPA.

Point: The five largest international accounting firms are Arthur Andersen, Deloitte & Touche, Ernst & Young, PricewaterhouseCoopers, and KPMG.

International Accounting Principles

In today's global economy, companies in different countries increasingly do business with each other. For example, Coca-Cola does business with numerous companies located in nearly 200 countries across the world. Nike says the following in its recent annual report about its global operations: "The Company currently markets its products in approximately 110 countries . . . through independent distributors, licensees, subsidiaries and branch offices . . . Non-U.S. sales accounted for 43 percent of total revenues."

Despite the global economy, most countries continue to maintain a unique set of accounting practices. Consider a Canadian company selling stock to foreign investors. Should it prepare financial statements that comply with Canadian standards or with the standards of another country? Should it prepare different sets of reports to gain access to financial markets in more countries? This is a difficult and pressing problem. One response has been to create an **International Accounting Standards Board (IASB).** The IASB issues *International Accounting Standards* that identify preferred accounting practices. By narrowing the range of alternative practices, the IASB hopes to create more harmony among accounting practices of different countries. If standards are harmonized, one company can use a single set of financial statements in all financial markets. Many countries' standard setters support the IASB, and interest in moving U.S. GAAP toward the IASB's preferred practices is growing; yet the organization does not have the authority to impose its standards on companies.

Global: The IASB has developed its own accounting concepts to help guide the setting of international accounting principles.

Global: IASB standards are frequently adopted by newly industrialized countries such as Malaysia and Singapore, and by developing countries such as Nigeria.

Principles of Accounting

Accounting principles are of two main types. *General principles* are the basic assumptions, concepts, and guidelines for preparing financial statements. *Specific principles* are detailed rules used in reporting business transactions and events. General principles stem from long-used accounting practices. Specific principles arise more often from the rulings of authoritative groups.

C2 Identify, explain, and apply accounting principles.

We need to understand both general and specific principles to effectively use accounting information. Since general principles are especially crucial in using accounting information, we emphasize them in the early chapters of this book. The general principles described in this chapter include business entity, objectivity, cost, going-concern, monetary unit, and revenue recognition. General principles described in later chapters include time period, matching, materiality, full disclosure, consistency, and conservatism. General principles are portrayed as building blocks for the "House of GAAP" in Exhibit 2.1. The specific principles are especially important for understanding individual items in financial statements. They are described as we encounter them.

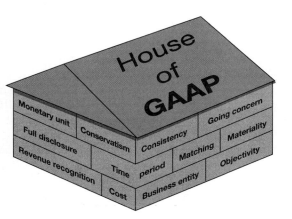

Exhibit 2.1

Building Blocks for the House of GAAP

---

[1] Many other professional organizations support the FASB, including the American Accounting Association (AAA), Financial Executives Institute (FEI), Institute of Management Accountants (IMA), Association for Investment Management and Research (AIMR), and Securities Industry Association (SIA). They increase the board's credibility by participating in its process for setting GAAP. Working alongside the FASB is the Governmental Accounting Standards Board (GASB), which identifies special accounting principles to be applied in preparing financial statements for state and local governments.

Business Entity Principle

The **business entity principle** means that a business is accounted for separately from its owner(s). It also means that we account separately for each business controlled by the same owner. The reason for this principle is that separate information about each business is necessary for good decisions. A company's statements must reflect only the transactions and events of its *own business*. For reports and decision making to be effective, businesses must apply the entity principle.

Decision Insight

Sham-Barter Transactions   Abuse of the objectivity and cost principles brought down executives at Itex Corp who bartered assets of little or no value and then reported them at grossly inflated values—recognizing fictitious gains and assets. The barter deals involved difficult-to-value assets such as artwork and stamp collections.

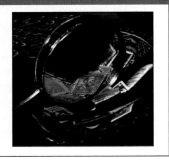

Objectivity Principle

The **objectivity principle** means that financial statement information is supported by independent, unbiased evidence. It demands more than one person's opinion. Information is not reliable if it is based only on what a preparer thinks might be true. A preparer can be too optimistic or pessimistic. An unethical preparer might try to mislead users by misrepresenting the truth. The objectivity principle is intended to make financial statements useful by ensuring they report reliable and verifiable information such as requiring invoices and other documents as evidence.

Cost Principle

The **cost principle** means that financial statements are based on actual costs incurred in business transactions. Cost is measured on a cash or equal-to-cash basis. This means if cash is given for an asset or service, its cost is measured as the amount of cash paid. If something besides cash is exchanged (such as a car traded for a truck), cost is measured as the cash equal to what is given up or received. The cost principle emphasizes reliability and relevance. It is also consistent with *objectivity* in that information based on cost is considered objective. For example, reporting purchases of assets and services at cost is more objective than reporting a manager's estimate of their current value. To illustrate this principle, suppose a company pays $5,000 for equipment. The cost principle requires that this purchase be recorded at a cost of $5,000. It makes no difference if the owner thinks this equipment is really worth $7,000.

Going-Concern Principle

The **going-concern principle** means that a company's financial statements reflect an assumption that the business will continue operating instead of being closed or sold. This means that a balance sheet reports items at cost instead of, say, liquidation values that assume closure. If a company is expected to fail or be liquidated, neither the going-concern principle nor the cost principle is appropriate. Instead, market values are then relevant.

Monetary Unit Principle

The **monetary unit principle** means that we can express transactions and events in monetary, or money, units. Money is the common denominator in business. Expressing transactions and events in monetary units is crucial to the use of financial statements for business communications. Examples of monetary units are the dollar in the United States, Canada, Australia, and Singapore; the pound sterling in the United Kingdom; and the peso in Mexico, the Philippines, and Chile. An *exchange rate* expresses the value of one currency relative to another. Exchange rates change frequently and are tied to many economic and political factors. The monetary unit an organization uses in its financial reports usually depends on the country where it operates, but many companies today are expressing financial statements in more than one monetary unit. Nintendo reports its financial statements in *both* yen and dollars. Accounting generally assumes a *stable* monetary unit. This means that the value of a currency is not expected to change. The more changes in the monetary unit, the more difficult it is to use and interpret financial statements, especially across time.

Accounting provides information to help people make better decisions. The accounting process reflects business transactions and events, analyzes and records their effects, and summarizes and prepares information in reports and financial statements. These reports and statements are used for making investing, lending, and other business decisions. We illustrate the general steps in the accounting process in Exhibit 2.2.

Transactions, Documents, and Accounts

Exhibit 2.2
The Accounting Process

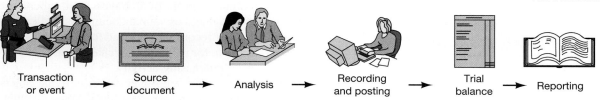

Transaction or event → Source document → Analysis → Recording and posting → Trial balance → Reporting

Transactions and events are the starting points in the accounting process. Relying on source documents, we analyze transactions and events using the accounting equation to understand how they affect company performance and financial position. These effects are recorded in accounting records, informally referred to as the *accounting books,* or simply the *books.* Additional processing steps such as posting and preparing a trial balance help us summarize and classify the effects of transactions and events. A final step in the accounting process is to provide information in useful reports or financial statements to decision makers. We begin our overview of the accounting process with a discussion of transactions and events. Later sections explain the remaining steps.

C3 Explain the steps in processing transactions.

Transactions and Events

Business activities can be described in terms of transactions and events. **External transactions** are exchanges of economic consideration between two separate entities. External transactions yield changes in the accounting equation. **Internal transactions** are exchanges within an entity; they can also affect the accounting equation. One example is a company's use of supplies in its operating activities, which are reported as expenses when used.

Events are happenings that affect an entity's financial position and can be reliably measured. They include financial events such as changes in the market value of certain assets and liabilities, and natural events such as floods and fires that destroy assets and create losses.

Decision Track 2.1   *d*

Decision Point	Information Search	Analyze & Evaluate
Has a transaction or event occurred that impacts financial statements?	Transaction or event details: Assess the financial impact using the accounting equation.	Financial statements are impacted by a transaction or event that is relevant to the accounting equation and can be reliably measured.

Source Documents

C4   Describe source documents and their purpose.

Companies use various documents when doing business. **Source documents,** or *business papers,* identify and describe transactions and events entering the accounting process. They are the sources of accounting information and can be in either hard copy or electronic form. Examples are sales tickets, checks, purchase orders, charges to customers, bills from suppliers, employee earnings records, and bank statements. To illustrate, when we buy an item on credit, the store usually prepares at least two copies of a sales invoice. One copy is given to us. Another copy, often sent electronically, gives rise to an entry in the store's information system to record the sale. Many registers record information for each sale on a tape or electronic file locked inside the register. Total sales for a day, or for any time period, can be obtained immediately from these registers. This record can be used as a source document for recording sales in the accounting records.

Point: To ensure that all sales are rung up on the register, it helps to require customers to have their receipts to exchange or return purchased items.

The accounting information system is designed to ensure that accounting records include all transactions. It also helps prevent mistakes and theft. To encourage employees to follow accounting procedures, stores often give discounts or free goods to any customers who are not provided a receipt. This is part of good internal control. Both buyers and sellers use sales invoices as source documents. Sellers use them for recording sales and for control. Buyers use them for recording purchases and for monitoring purchasing activity.

Decision Ethics   *d*

Cashier   Your manager requires that you, as cashier, immediately enter each sale. Recently, lunch hour traffic has increased and the assistant manager asks you to avoid delays by taking customers' cash and making change without entering sales. The assistant manager says she will add up cash and enter sales after lunch. She says that, in this way, the register will always match the cash amount when the manager arrives at three o'clock. What do you do?

Answer—p. 78

Source documents, especially if obtained from outside the organization, provide objective and reliable evidence about transactions and events and their amounts. Some accounting systems—mostly limited to small businesses—still require manual (pencil-and-paper) recording and processing of transaction data. In today's information age, computers assist us in recording and processing data—yet they are only part of the process, and modern technology still demands human insight and understanding of transactions. In our discussion of the steps making up the accounting process, we often refer to a *manual system* for simplicity in presentation, but the fundamental concepts of the manual system are identical to those of a computerized information system.

Quick Check

6. Describe external and internal transactions.

7. Identify examples of accounting source documents.

8. Explain the importance of source documents.

Answers—p. 79

The Account and its Analysis

C5   Describe an account and its use in recording transactions.

An **account** is a detailed record of increases and decreases in a specific asset, liability, equity, revenue, or expense. Information is taken from an account, then analyzed, summarized, and presented in reports and financial statements. A separate account is kept for each asset, liability, equity, revenue, and expense item important to business decisions. The **ledger** (also called *general ledger*) is a record containing all accounts used by a company. This is often in electronic form and is what we mean when we refer to the *books*. While most companies' ledgers contain similar accounts, a company may use one or more unique accounts because of its type of operations. Accounts are arranged into three general categories (based on the accounting equation), as shown in Exhibit 2.3. The remainder of this section defines and describes accounts common to most organizations.

Exhibit 2.3

Accounts Organized by the Accounting Equation

Asset Accounts

Assets are resources owned or controlled by a company that have expected future benefits. Most accounting systems include separate accounts for the assets described here.

Cash. A *Cash* account reflects the cash balance, and increases and decreases in cash are recorded in it. A Cash account includes money and any medium of exchange that a bank accepts for deposit (coins, currency, checks, money orders, and checking account balances).

Accounts receivable. Products and services are often sold to customers in return for promises to pay in the future. These transactions are often called *credit sales* or *sales on account* (or *on credit*). Promises of payment from buyers are called *accounts receivable* to sellers. Accounts receivable are increased by credit sales and are decreased by customer payments. A company also needs a separate record for each customer's purchases and payments. We describe the system for maintaining these records in Chapters 4 and 7. For now, we use the simpler practice of recording all increases and decreases in receivables in a single account called *Accounts Receivable.* Customers and other individuals and organizations who owe a company are called its **debtors.** The importance of accounts receivable to a company, like many other accounts, depends on its type of business. For example, the **Florida Panthers'** accounts receivable amount to less than 3% of the organization's assets. In comparison, **Nike**'s accounts receivable amount to more than 30% of its assets.

Note receivable. A *note receivable,* or *promissory note,* is a written promise to pay a definite sum of money on a specified future date. A company holding a promissory note signed by another party has an asset that is recorded in a Note (or Notes) Receivable account.

Prepaid expenses. Prepaid expenses are assets because they represent prepayments of future expenses (*not* current expenses). In the future, when the expenses are incurred, the amounts in prepaid expenses are transferred to expense accounts. Common examples of prepaid expenses include prepaid insurance, prepaid rent, and prepaid services (such as club memberships). Prepaid expenses expire with the passage of time (such as with rent) or through use (such as with prepaid meal tickets). When financial statements are prepared, prepaid expenses are adjusted so that (1) all expired and used prepaid expenses are recorded as regular expenses and (2) all unexpired and unused prepaid expenses are recorded as assets (reflecting future use in future periods). An exception exists for prepaid expenses that will expire or be used before the end of the current accounting period when financial statements will be prepared. In this case, the prepayments *can* be recorded immediately as expenses. For example, if a company pays $1,000 for December rent at the beginning of the month, it can record this prepaid rent as rent expense since its benefit will be fully expired when the statements are prepared on December 31.

To illustrate prepaid expenses, consider prepaid insurance, one of the most common prepaid expenses. Insurance contracts provide protection against losses caused by fire, theft, accidents, and other events. An insurance policy usually requires the fee, called a *premium,* to be paid in advance. Protection can be purchased for almost any time period, including a month, year, or several years. When an insurance premium is paid in advance, the cost is typically recorded in an asset account called *Prepaid Insurance.* Over time, the expiring portion of the insurance cost is removed from this asset account and reported in expenses on

Point: College tuition fees are prepaid expenses. At the beginning of the term, they represent an asset that entitles you to attend class, access college libraries, and so forth. This asset decreases in size (benefits expire) as the term progresses. At term-end, prepaid tuition fees (asset) equal zero and their total is now recorded as tuition expenses.

Point: Prepaid expenses that apply to current *and* future periods are assets. These assets are adjusted at the end of each period to reflect only those amounts that have not yet expired, and to record as expenses those amounts that have expired.

the income statement. Any unexpired portion remains in Prepaid Insurance and is reported on the balance sheet as an asset.

Office supplies. Companies use office supplies such as stationery, computer paper and toner, and pens. These supplies are assets until they are used. When they are used up, their costs are reported as expenses. The costs of unused supplies are recorded in an *Office Supplies* asset account.

Store supplies. Many stores keep supplies for circumstances such as wrapping and packaging sales for customers. These include plastic and paper bags, gift boxes, cartons, and ribbons. The costs of these unused supplies are recorded in a *Store Supplies* asset account. When supplies are used, their costs are transferred from the supplies asset account to the supplies expense account.

Point: Some assets are described as *intangible* because they do not have physical existence or their benefits are highly uncertain. A recent balance sheet for Coca-Cola Company shows nearly $2 billion in intangible assets.

Equipment. Most organizations own computers, printers, desks, chairs, and other office equipment. Costs incurred for this type of equipment are recorded in an *Office Equipment* asset account. The costs of assets used in a store such as counters, showcases, forklifts, hoists, and cash registers are recorded in a *Store Equipment* asset account.

Buildings. Buildings owned by an organization can provide space for a store, an office, a warehouse, and a factory. Buildings are assets because they provide expected future benefits. Their costs are recorded in a *Buildings* asset account. When several buildings are owned, separate accounts are sometimes kept for each of them.

Land. A *Land* account records the cost of land owned by a business. The cost of land is separated from the cost of buildings located on the land to provide more useful information in financial statements.

Decision Insight

Wish List   Entrepreneurs were asked whom they would want—if they could have anyone—to help run their businesses for a week. Bill Gates led, with 24%, followed by Donald Trump and Warren Buffet—see selected survey results.

Bill Gates	24%
Donald Trump	6.8
Warren Buffet	5.8
Lee Iacocca	5.2
Ross Perot	3.1
Hillary Clinton	1.4

Liability Accounts

Liabilities are obligations to transfer assets or provide products or services to other entities. Individuals and organizations that own the right to receive payments from a company are called its **creditors.** One entity's payable is another entity's receivable. If a company fails to pay its obligations, the law gives creditors a right to force the sale of this company's assets to obtain the money to meet creditors' claims. When assets are sold under these conditions, creditors are paid first, but only up to the amount of their claims. Any remaining money, the residual, goes to the owners of the company. Creditors often use a balance sheet to help decide whether to loan money to a company. They compare the amounts of liabilities and assets. A loan is less risky if liabilities are small in comparison to assets because there are more resources than claims on resources. An organization often has several different liabilities, each represented by a separate account. The more common liability accounts are described here.

Point: Accounts Payable are also called Trade Payables.

Accounts payable. Purchases of merchandise, supplies, equipment, and services made by an oral or implied promise to pay later create liabilities called *payables*. Accounting systems keep separate records about purchases from and payments to each creditor. We describe these individual records in Chapter 4. For now, we use the simpler practice of recording all increases and decreases in these payables in a single account called *Accounts Payable*.

Note payable. When an organization formally recognizes a promise to pay a future amount by signing a promissory note, the resulting liability is a note payable. It is recorded in either a Short-Term Note Payable account or a Long-Term Note Payable account depending on when it must be repaid. We explain details of short- and long-term classification in Chapter 3.

Unearned revenue. The *revenue recognition principle* requires that revenues be reported on the income statement when earned. This principle means that when customers pay in advance for products or services (before revenue is earned), the seller considers this pay as unearned revenue. **Unearned Revenue** is a liability account that is settled in the future when products or services are delivered. Examples of unearned revenue include magazine subscriptions collected in advance by a publisher, sales of gift certificates by stores, and season ticket sales by sports teams. The seller would record these in liability accounts such as Unearned Subscriptions, Unearned Store Sales, and Unearned Ticket Revenue. When products and services are delivered, the earned portion of the unearned revenues is transferred to revenue accounts such as Subscription Fees, Store Sales, and Ticket Sales.[2]

Decision Insight

MLB Accounting The Cleveland Indians report *Unearned Revenues* of nearly $50 million in advance ticket sales. When the team plays its regular season home games, it settles this liability to its customers (fans) and transfers the amount earned to *Ticket Revenues.*

Accrued liabilities. Accrued liabilities are amounts owed that are not yet paid. Examples are wages payable, taxes payable, and interest payable. These are often recorded in separate liability accounts by the same title. If they are not large in amount, one or more of them may be added and reported as a single amount on the balance sheet. For example, **Harley-Davidson**'s balance sheet reports a single accrued liabilities amount of more than $100 million.

Point: Many companies offer warranties on their products and must report a liability by estimating future warranty costs.

Equity Accounts

The owners' claims on a corporation's assets are called *stockholders' equity, shareholders' equity,* or *owners' equity*. **Equity,** also called **net assets,** is the owners' *residual interest* in the assets of a business after deducting liabilities. There are four subcategories of stockholders' equity: common stock, retained earnings, revenues, and expenses. We show this visually in Exhibit 2.4 by expanding the accounting equation, and we describe each type of equity account below. Information in these separate categories is readily used to prepare financial statements.

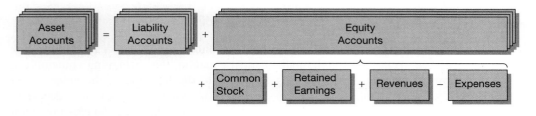

Exhibit 2.4

Expanded Accounting Equation

---

[2] In practice, account titles vary. As one example, Subscription Fees is sometimes called Subscription Fees Revenue, Subscription Fees Earned, or Earned Subscription Fees. As another example, Rent Earned is sometimes called Rent Revenue, Rental Revenue, or Earned Rent Revenue. We must use good judgment when reading financial statements, since titles can differ even within the same industry. For example, product sales are called *revenues* at **Nike** and **K. Swiss,** but *net sales* at **Reebok** and **Converse.** Generally, the term *revenues* or *fees* is more commonly used with service businesses, and *net sales* or *sales* with product businesses.

Global: Global markets present challenges in terminology. For example, U.S. users refer to equity shares as *stock,* while U.K. users refer to inventory as *stock.*

Common stock. When an owner invests in a corporation, the invested amount is recorded in an account titled **Common Stock.** Any further investments also are recorded in this account. Investing in a corporation is done by purchasing common stock. A corporation can issue a stock certificate imprinted with the owner's name as proof of ownership.

Retained earnings. The term **retained earnings** refers to net income that is retained by a company. The *Retained Earnings* account equals cumulative net income earned by the company over its lifetime minus cumulative net losses and dividends. **Dividends** (a corporation's distributions of assets to its owners) are not required, but rather are optional. If a corporation pays a cash dividend to its owners, such payment is recorded by reducing retained earnings.

Revenues and expenses. Decision makers often want information about revenues earned and expenses incurred for a period. Various revenue and expense accounts are used to record this information. Different companies have different kinds of revenue and expense accounts reflecting their own unique activities. Examples of revenue accounts are Sales, Commissions Earned, Professional Fees Earned, Rent Earned, and Interest Revenue. Revenues increase equity. Examples of expense accounts are Advertising Expense, Store Supplies Expense, Office Salaries Expense, Office Supplies Expense, Rent Expense, Utilities Expense, and Insurance Expense. Expenses decrease equity. We can get an idea of the variety of revenues and expenses by looking at the *chart of accounts* that follows the index at the back of this book. It lists accounts needed to solve some of the assignments in the book.[3]

Decision Insight

NBA Accounting The **Boston Celtics** report the following major revenue and expense accounts:

Revenues	Expenses
Basketball ticket sales	Team salaries
TV & radio broadcast fees	Game costs
Advertising revenues	NBA franchise costs

Transaction Analysis and the Accounting Equation

Financial statements reflect a company's business activities. We know that many of these activities, such as purchases and sales, involve transactions. To understand information in financial statements, we need to know how an accounting system captures relevant data about transactions, classifies and records data, and reports data in financial statements. This section starts us on this important path. Recall from Chapter 1 that the basic tool of modern accounting systems is the **accounting equation:**

$$\text{Assets} = \text{Liabilities} + \text{Equity}$$

The accounting equation is also called the **balance sheet equation** because of its link to the balance sheet. Like any simple mathematical equation, the accounting equation can be modified by rearranging terms. Moving liabilities to the left side of the equality, for example, gives us an equation for equity in terms of assets and liabilities: Assets − Liabilities = Equity. The accounting equation can be used to help track changes in a company's assets, liabilities, and equity to provide useful information and to help with analysis, which is the purpose of this section.

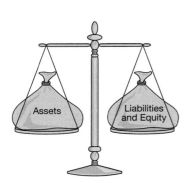

---

[3] Different companies sometimes use different account titles than those in this book's chart of accounts. For example, a company might use Interest Revenue instead of Interest Earned, or Rental Expense instead of Rent Expense. It is important only that an account title describe the item it represents.

Transaction Analysis—Part I

A transaction affects one or more components of the accounting equation. Remember that each transaction leaves the equation in balance. Assets *always* equal the sum of liabilities and equity. We use the accounting equation to analyze the first 11 transactions for FastForward, a start-up consulting business, in its first month of operations.

A1   Analyze business transactions using the accounting equation.

Topic Tackler 2-1

Transaction 1: Investment by Owner

On December 1, Chuck Taylor forms an athletic shoe consulting business. He sets it up as a corporation. Taylor owns and manages the business. The marketing plan for the business is to focus primarily on consulting with sports clubs, amateur athletes, and others who place orders for athletic shoes with manufacturers. Taylor personally invests $30,000 cash in the new company in exchange for common stock, and deposits the cash in a bank account opened under the name of FastForward, Inc. After this transaction, the cash (an asset) and the shareholders' equity (*Common Stock* account) each equal $30,000. The source of increase in equity is identified as an owner investment (stock issuance). The effect of this transaction on FastForward is reflected in the accounting equation as follows:

	Assets	=	Liabilities	+	Equity
	Cash	=			Common Stock
(1)	+$30,000	=			+$30,000 Investment

Transaction 2: Purchase Supplies for Cash

FastForward uses $2,500 of its cash to buy supplies of brand name athletic shoes for testing over the next few months. This transaction is an exchange of cash, an asset, for another kind of asset, supplies. It merely changes the form of assets from cash to supplies. The decrease in cash is exactly equal to the increase in supplies. These supplies of athletic shoes are assets because of the expected future benefits from the test results of their performance. This transaction is reflected in the accounting equation as follows:

	Assets			=	Liabilities	+	Equity
	Cash	+	Supplies	=			Common Stock
Old Bal.	$30,000			=			$30,000
(2)	−2,500	+	$2,500				
New Bal.	$27,500	+	$2,500	=			$30,000
	$30,000						$30,000

Transaction 3: Purchase Equipment for Cash

FastForward spends $26,000 to acquire equipment for testing athletic shoes. Like transaction 2, transaction 3 is an exchange of one asset, cash, for another asset, equipment. The equipment is an asset because of the expected future benefits from using it to test athletic shoes. This purchase changes the makeup of assets but does not change the asset total. The accounting equation remains in balance.

	Assets					=	Liabilities	+	Equity
	Cash	+	Supplies	+	Equipment	=			Common Stock
Old Bal.	$27,500	+	$2,500			=			$30,000
(3)	−26,000				+$26,000				
New Bal.	$1,500	+	$2,500	+	$26,000	=			$30,000
			$30,000				$30,000		

Example: If FastForward pays $500 in cash in transaction 4, how does this cash payment affect the liability to CalTech? What would be FastForward's cash balance? *Answers:* The liability to CalTech would be reduced to $6,600 and the cash balance would be reduced to $1,000.

Transaction 4: Purchase Supplies on Credit

Taylor decides he needs more supplies of athletic shoes. These supplies total $7,100, but as we see from the accounting equation in transaction 3, FastForward has only $1,500 in cash. Taylor arranges to purchase them on credit from CalTech Supply Company. Thus, FastForward acquires supplies in exchange for a promise to pay for them later. This yields a liability for FastForward to CalTech Supply of $7,100. This purchase increases assets by $7,100 in supplies while liabilities (called *accounts payable*) increase by the same amount. The effects of this purchase on the accounting equation are as follows:

	Cash	+	Supplies	+	Equipment	=	Accounts Payable	+	Common Stock
	Assets					**=**	**Liabilities**	**+**	**Equity**
Old Bal.	$1,500	+	$2,500	+	$26,000	=			$30,000
(4)		+	7,100				+$7,100		
New Bal.	$1,500	+	$9,600	+	$26,000	=	$7,100	+	$30,000
			$37,100					$37,100	

Transaction 5: Services Rendered for Cash

A main business objective is to increase the owners' wealth. This goal is met when a business produces *net income*. Net income is reflected in the accounting equation as an increase in equity. FastForward earns revenues by consulting with clients about test results on athletic shoes. FastForward earns net income only if its revenues are greater than its expenses incurred in earning them. In one of its first jobs, FastForward provides consulting services to an athletic club and immediately collects $4,200 cash. The accounting equation reflects this increase in cash of $4,200 and in equity of $4,200. This increase in equity is identified in the far right column under Retained Earnings as a rev-enue because it is earned by providing services. These identifications are useful in later preparing and interpreting both the statement of retained earnings and the income statement.

	Cash	+	Supplies	+	Equipment	=	Accounts Payable	+	Common Stock	+	Retained Earnings	
	Assets					**=**	**Liabilities**	**+**		**Equity**		
Old Bal.	$1,500	+	$9,600	+	$26,000	=	$7,100	+	$30,000			
(5)	+ 4,200									+	$4,200	Consulting Revenue
New Bal.	$5,700	+	$9,600	+	$26,000	=	$7,100	+	$30,000		$4,200	
			$41,300						$41,300			

Transactions 6 and 7: Payment of Expenses in Cash

FastForward pays $1,000 rent to the landlord of the building where its store is located. Paying this amount allows FastForward to occupy the space for the month of December. The rental payment is reflected in the following accounting equation as transaction 6. FastForward also pays the biweekly $700 salary of the company's only employee. This is reflected in the accounting equation as transaction 7. Both transactions 6 and 7 are December expenses for FastForward. The costs of both rent and salary are expenses, as opposed to assets, because their benefits are used in December (they have no future benefits after December). These transactions use up an asset (cash) in FastForward's operations. The accounting equation shows that both transactions reduce cash and equity. The far right column identifies these decreases as expenses.

	Assets					=	Liabilities	+	Equity			
	Cash	+	Supplies	+	Equipment	=	Accounts Payable	+	Common Stock	+	Retained Earnings	
Old Bal.	$5,700	+	$9,600	+	$26,000	=	$7,100	+	$30,000	+	$ 4,200	
(6)	−1,000										− 1,000	Rent Expense
Bal.	$4,700	+	$9,600	+	$26,000	=	$7,100	+	$30,000	+	$ 3,200	
(7)	− 700										− 700	Salary Expense
New Bal.	$4,000	+	$9,600	+	$26,000	=	$7,100	+	$30,000	+	$ 2,500	
			$39,600						$39,600			

Summary of Part I Transactions

FastForward has net income when its revenues exceed its expenses. Net income increases equity. If expenses exceed revenues, a net loss occurs that decreases equity. Net income (or loss) is not affected by transactions between a business and its owners. This means Taylor's initial investment of $30,000 is not income to FastForward, although it increased equity. To stress that revenues and expenses yield changes in equity, we have added revenues directly to equity and subtracted expenses directly from equity in this section. In practice and in later sections and chapters, information about revenues and expenses is compiled separately during the accounting period. These amounts are then added to or subtracted from equity accounts at the *end* of the period. We describe this process in Chapter 3.

Point: To apply these concepts, work Exercises 2-3 and 2-5.

Revenue Recognition Principle

We briefly interrupt the analysis of FastForward's transactions to describe the revenue recognition principle. Companies need guidance in deciding when to recognize revenue. To *recognize* means to record a transaction or event for purposes of reporting its effects in financial statements. If revenue is recognized too early, the income statement reports revenue sooner than it should, and the business looks more profitable than it is. If revenue is recognized too late, the income statement shows lower revenue and net income than it should, and the business looks less profitable than it is. The **revenue recognition principle** provides guidance on when to recognize revenue on the income statement.

1. *Revenue is recognized when earned.* Preparing for services, finding customers, and promoting sales all contribute to revenue. Yet we usually cannot reliably determine revenue earned until services or products are actually delivered. This means revenue is usually not recognized until the earnings process is complete. The earnings process is normally complete when services are rendered or the seller transfers ownership of products to the buyer.

Decision Insight

Revenues for the New York Yankees baseball team include ticket sales, television and cable broadcasts, radio rights, concessions, and advertising. Revenues from ticket sales are recognized when the Yankees play each game. Advance ticket sales are not revenues; instead, they represent a liability for the Yankees to play a game at a later date.

2. *Assets received from selling products and services need not be in cash.* A common noncash asset received by a seller in a revenue transaction is a customer's promise to pay at a future date. The seller views the customer's promise as an account receivable. These transactions are called *credit sales*. If evidence shows the seller has the right to collect from a customer, this seller recognizes an asset (account receivable) and records revenue. When cash is later collected, no additional revenue is recognized. It merely changes the makeup of assets from a receivable to cash.

Example: When a bookstore sells a textbook on credit is its earnings process complete? *Answer:* The bookstore can record sales for these book sales minus an amount expected for returns.

3. *Revenue recognized is measured by the cash received plus the cash equivalent (market) value of any other assets received.* This means, for example, if a revenue transaction

creates an account receivable, the seller recognizes revenue equal to the value of the receivable, which usually is the amount of cash expected to be collected.

Financial statements include an explanation of the revenue recognition method used. **General Motors**, for instance, states in its annual report that "sales are generally recorded by the Corporation when products are shipped to independent dealers."

Transaction Analysis—Part II

To show how revenue recognition works, let's return to FastForward's transactions.

Transaction 8: Services and Facilities Rendered for Credit

FastForward provides consulting services of $1,600 and rents its test facilities for $300 to an amateur sports club. The rental involves allowing club members to try recommended shoes at FastForward's testing grounds. The sports club is billed for the $1,900 total. This transaction results in a new asset, called accounts receivable, from this client. It also yields an increase in equity from the two revenue components identified in the far right column of the accounting equation:

	Assets					=	Liabilities	+		Equity		
	Cash	+	Accounts Receivable	+	Supplies	+	Equipment	=	Accounts Payable	+	Common Stock	+	Retained Earnings	
Old Bal.	$4,000	+		+	$9,600	+	$26,000	=	$7,100	+	$30,000	+	$2,500	
(8)		+	$1,900									+	1,600	Consulting Revenue
												+	300	Rental Revenue
New Bal.	$4,000	+	$1,900	+	$9,600	+	$26,000	=	$7,100	+	$30,000		$4,400	
			$41,500								$41,500			

Transaction 9: Receipt of Cash from Accounts Receivable

The client in transaction 8 (the amateur sports club) pays $1,900 to FastForward 10 days after it is billed for consulting services. This transaction 9 does not change the total amount of assets and does not affect liabilities or equity. It converts the receivable (an asset) to cash (another asset). It does not create new revenue. Revenue was recognized when FastForward rendered the services (transaction 8), not when the cash is now collected. This emphasis on the earnings process instead of cash flows is a goal of the revenue recognition principle and yields useful information to users. The new balances follow:

Point: Note that receipt of cash is not necessarily a revenue.

	Assets					=	Liabilities	+		Equity		
	Cash	+	Accounts Receivable	+	Supplies	+	Equipment	=	Accounts Payable	+	Common Stock	+	Retained Earnings
Old Bal.	$4,000	+	$1,900	+	$9,600	+	$26,000	=	$7,100	+	$30,000	+	$4,400
(9)	+1,900		−1,900										
New Bal.	$5,900	+	$ 0	+	$9,600	+	$26,000	=	$7,100	+	$30,000	+	$4,400
			$41,500								$41,500		

Transaction 10: Payment of Accounts Payable

FastForward pays $900 to CalTech Supply as partial payment for its earlier $7,100 purchase of supplies (transaction 4), leaving $6,200 unpaid. The accounting equation shows that this transaction decreases FastForward's cash by $900 and decreases its liability to CalTech Supply by $900. Equity does not change. This event does not create an expense even though cash flows out of FastForward (the expense is recorded when FastForward derives the benefits from these supplies).

	Assets							=	Liabilities	+	Equity		
	Cash	+	Accounts Receivable	+	Supplies	+	Equipment	=	Accounts Payable	+	Common Stock	+	Retained Earnings
Old Bal.	$5,900	+	$ 0	+	$9,600	+	$26,000	=	$7,100	+	$30,000	+	$4,400
(10)	− 900								− 900				
New Bal.	$5,000	+	$ 0	+	$9,600	+	$26,000	=	$6,200	+	$30,000	+	$4,400
			$40,600								$40,600		

Transaction 11: Payment of Cash Dividend

FastForward declares and pays a $600 cash dividend to its owner. Dividends (decreases in equity) are not reported as expenses because they are not part of the company's earnings process. Since dividends are not expenses, they are not used in computing net income.

	Assets							=	Liabilities	+	Equity			
	Cash	+	Accounts Receivable	+	Supplies	+	Equipment	=	Accounts Payable	+	Common Stock	+	Retained Earnings	
Old Bal.	$5,000	+	$ 0	+	$9,600	+	$26,000	=	$6,200	+	$30,000	+	$4,400	
(11)	− 600												− 600	Dividend
New Bal.	$4,400	+	$ 0	+	$9,600	+	$26,000	=	$6,200	+	$30,000	+	$3,800	
			$40,000								$40,000			

Summary of Transactions

FastForward engaged in transactions with five major entities: the owner (shareholder), its suppliers, an employee, its customers, and the landlord. We identify the transactions by number with the specific entity in Exhibit 2.5. We also summarize in Exhibit 2.6 the effects of these first 11 transactions of FastForward using the accounting equation. Three points should be noted. First, the accounting equation remains in balance after each transaction. Second, transactions can be analyzed by their effects on components of the accounting equation. For example, in transactions 2, 3, and 9, one asset increased while another decreased by equal amounts. Third, the equality of effects in the accounting equation is crucial to the double-entry accounting system. We discuss this system in the next section.

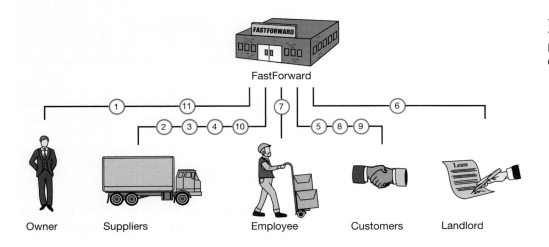

Exhibit 2.5

FastForward's Transactions Grouped by Entities

Exhibit 2.6

Summary of Transactions Using the Accounting Equation

	Assets				=	Liabilities	+	Equity		
	Cash +	Accounts Receivable +	Supplies +	Equipment =		Accounts Payable +		Common Stock +	Retained Earnings	
(1)	$30,000							$30,000		Investment
(2)	−2,500		+$2,500							
Bal.	27,500		2,500					30,000		
(3)	−26,000			+$26,000						
Bal.	1,500		2,500	26,000				30,000		
(4)			+7,100			+$7,100				
Bal.	1,500		9,600	26,000		7,100		30,000		
(5)	+4,200								+$4,200	Consulting Revenue
Bal.	5,700		9,600	26,000		7,100		30,000	4,200	
(6)	−1,000								−1,000	Rent Expense
Bal.	4,700		9,600	26,000		7,100		30,000	3,200	
(7)	− 700								− 700	Salary Expense
Bal.	4,000		9,600	26,000		7,100		30,000	2,500	
(8)		+$1,900							+1,600	Consulting Revenue
									+ 300	Rental Revenue
Bal.	4,000	1,900	9,600	26,000		7,100		30,000	4,400	
(9)	+1,900	−1,900								
Bal.	5,900	0	9,600	26,000		7,100		30,000	4,400	
(10)	− 900					−900				
Bal.	5,000	0	9,600	26,000		6,200		30,000	4,400	
(11)	− 600								− 600	Dividend
Bal.	$4,400 +	$ 0 +	$9,600 +	$26,000 =		$6,200 +		$30,000 +	$3,800	

Answer—p. 79

Quick Check

9. How can a transaction not affect any liability and equity accounts?
10. Describe a transaction increasing equity and one decreasing it.
11. Why is the revenue recognition principle important?
12. Identify a transaction decreasing both assets and liabilities.
13. When is the accounting equation in balance, and what does that mean?

Processing and Analyzing Transactions

This section explains several crucial elements and tools that comprise an accounting system. These include a ledger, T-accounts, debits and credits, double-entry accounting, journalizing, and posting.

Ledger and Chart of Accounts

C6 Describe a ledger and a chart of accounts.

Recall that the collection of all accounts for an information system is called a *ledger* (or *general ledger*). If accounts are in files on a hard drive, the sum of those files is the ledger.

If the accounts are pages in a file, that file is the ledger. A company's size and diversity of operations affect the number of accounts needed. A small company may get by with as few as 20 or 30 accounts; a large company may need several thousand. The **chart of accounts** is a list of all accounts a company uses and includes an identification number assigned to each account. A small business might use the following numbering system for its accounts:

101–199	Asset accounts
201–299	Liability accounts
301–399	Equity accounts
401–499	Revenue accounts
501–699	Expense accounts

These numbers provide a three-digit code that is useful in recordkeeping. In this case, the first digit assigned to asset accounts is a 1, the first digit assigned to liability accounts is a 2, and so on. The second and third digits also relate to the accounts' subcategories. Exhibit 2.7 shows a partial chart of accounts for FastForward.

Account Number	Account Name	Account Number	Account Name
101	Cash	307	Common stock
106	Accounts receivable	318	Retained earnings
126	Supplies	403	Consulting revenue
128	Prepaid insurance	406	Rental revenue
167	Equipment	622	Salaries expense
201	Accounts payable	637	Insurance expense
236	Unearned consulting revenue	640	Rent expense
		652	Supplies expense
		690	Utilities expense

Exhibit 2.7

Partial Chart of Accounts

Debits and Credits

The left side of an account is called the **debit** side, often abbreviated *Dr.* The right side is called the **credit** side, abbreviated *Cr.*[4] To enter amounts on the left side of an account is to *debit* the account. To enter amounts on the right side is to *credit* the account. We must guard against the error of thinking that the terms *debit* and *credit* mean increase or decrease. Whether a debit is an increase or decrease depends on the account. Similarly, whether a credit is an increase or decrease depends on the account. In each account, however, a debit and a credit have opposite effects. In an account where a debit is an increase, the credit is a decrease; in an account where a debit is a decrease, the credit is an increase. Identifying the account is the key to understanding the effects of debits and credits. The difference between total debits and total credits for an account is the **account balance.** When the sum of debits exceeds the sum of credits, the account has a *debit balance.* It has a *credit balance* when the sum of credits exceeds the sum of debits. When the sum of debits equals the sum of credits, the account has a *zero balance.*

C7   Define *debits* and *credits* and explain their role in double-entry accounting.

Point: Think of *debit* and *credit* as accounting directions for left and right.

---

[4] These abbreviations are remnants of 18th-century English recordkeeping practices where the terms *debitor* and *creditor* were used instead of *debit* and *credit.* The abbreviations use the first and last letters of these terms, just as we still do for Saint (St.) and Doctor (Dr.).

Exhibit 2.8

The T-Account

Account Title	
(Left side)	(Right side)
Debit	**Credit**

A **T-account** is a helpful tool in analyzing the effects of transactions and events on individual accounts. Its name comes from its shape like the letter *T*. The T-account is shown in Exhibit 2.8. The layout of a T-account is (1) the account title on top, (2) a left, or debit side, and (3) a right, or credit, side.

To determine the account's balance, we start with the beginning balance and then (1) compute the total increases shown on one side, (2) compute the total decreases shown on the other side, and (3) subtract the sum of the decreases from the sum of the increases. The T-account for FastForward's Cash account, reflecting its first 11 transactions (from Exhibit 2.6), is shown in Exhibit 2.9. The total increases in its Cash account are $36,100, the total decreases are $31,700, and the account balance is $4,400.

Exhibit 2.9

Computing the Balance for a T-Account

Cash			
Issuance of stock (investment)	30,000	Purchase of supplies	2,500
Consulting services revenue earned	4,200	Purchase of equipment	26,000
Collection of account receivable	1,900	Payment of rent	1,000
		Payment of salary	700
		Payment of account payable	900
		Payment of dividend	600
Total increases	**36,100**	Total decreases	**31,700**
Less decreases	**−31,700**		
Balance	**4,400**		

Double-Entry Accounting

Double-entry accounting requires that each transaction affect, and be recorded in, at least two accounts. It also means the *total amount debited must equal the total amount credited* for each transaction. Accordingly, the sum of the debits for all entries must equal the sum of the credits for all entries, and the sum of debit account balances in the ledger must equal the sum of credit account balances.

The system for recording debits and credits follows from the usual accounting equation—see Exhibit 2.10. Assets are on the left side of this equation. Liabilities and equity are on the right side. Two points are important here. First, like any simple mathematical relation, net increases or decreases on one side have equal net effects on the other side. For example, a net increase in assets must be accompanied by an identical net increase on the liabilities and equity side. Also recall that some transactions affect only one side of the equation, meaning that two or more accounts on one side are affected, but their net effect on this one side is zero. Second, we treat the left side as the *normal balance* side for assets, and the right side as the *normal balance* for liabilities and equity. This matches their layout in the accounting equation.

Three important rules for recording transactions in a double-entry accounting system follow from Exhibit 2.10: (1) Increases in assets are debits to asset accounts. Decreases in assets are credits to asset accounts. (2) Increases in liabilities are credits to liability accounts.

Exhibit 2.10

Debits and Credits in the Accounting Equation

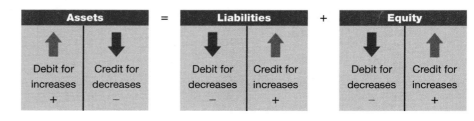

Decreases in liabilities are debits to liability accounts. (3) Increases in equity are credits to equity accounts. Decreases in equity are debits to equity accounts.

We earlier showed how equity increases from owners' investments (via stock issuances) and from revenues and how it decreases from expenses and dividends. These important equity relations are conveyed by expanding the accounting equation to include debits and credits in double-entry form as shown in Exhibit 2.11.

Exhibit 2.11

Debit and Credit Effects for Component Accounts

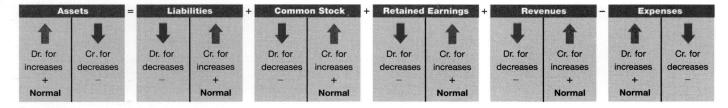

Increases (credits) to common stock, retained earnings, and revenues *increase* equity; increases (debits) to expenses *decrease* equity. The normal balance of each account (asset, liability, equity, revenue, or expense) refers to the left or right (debit or credit) side where *increases* are recorded. Our understanding of these diagrams and rules is especially helpful in analyzing and recording transactions. It also helps us prepare, analyze, and interpret financial statements.

Quick Check

14. Identify each of the following as either an asset, a liability, or equity: (*a*) Prepaid Rent, (*b*) Unearned Fees, (*c*) Building, (*d*) Wages Payable, and (*e*) Office Supplies.

15. What is an account? What is a ledger?

16. What determines the number and types of accounts a company uses?

17. Does *debit* always mean increase and *credit* always mean decrease?

Answers—p. 79

Journalizing and Posting Transactions

Processing transactions is a crucial part of accounting. The four usual steps of this process are depicted in Exhibit 2.12. Steps 1 and 2—involving transaction analysis and double-entry accounting—were introduced in prior sections. This section extends that discussion and focuses on steps 3 and 4 of the accounting process. Step 3 is to record each transaction in a journal. A **journal** gives a complete record of each transaction in one place. It also shows debits and credits for each transaction. The process of recording transactions in a journal is called **journalizing.** Step 4 is to transfer (or *post*) entries from the journal to the ledger. The process of transferring journal entry information to the ledger is called **posting.** This section describes both journalizing and posting transactions.

P1 Record transactions in a journal and post entries to a ledger.

Topic Tackler 2-2

Journalizing Transactions

The process of journalizing transactions requires an understanding of a journal. While companies can use various journals, every company uses a **general journal**. It can be used to record any transaction. A general journal entry includes the following information about each transaction: (1) date of transaction, (2) titles of affected accounts, (3) dollar amount of each debit and credit, and (4) explanation of the transaction. Exhibit 2.13 shows how the first two transactions of FastForward are recorded in a general journal. This process is similar for manual and computerized systems. Computerized journals are often designed to look like a manual journal page. Computerized systems typically include error-checking routines that ensure debits equal credits for each entry. Shortcuts often allow record-

Point: A journal is often referred to as the *book of original entry.*

Point: There are no exact rules for writing journal entry explanations. An explanation should be short yet describe why an entry is made.

Exhibit 2.12

Steps in Processing Transactions

Step 1: Analyze transactions and source documents.

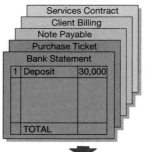

Step 2: Apply double-entry accounting.

Step 3: Record journal entry.

General Journal			
Dec. 1	Cash	30,000	
	Common Stock		30,000
Dec. 2	Supplies	2,500	
	Cash		2,500

Step 4: Post entry to ledger.

keepers to enter account numbers instead of names and to enter account names and numbers with pull-down menus.

To record entries in a general journal, we apply the following standard procedures—refer to the entries in Exhibit 2.13 when reviewing these steps. (1) Date the transaction: Enter the year at the top of the first column and the month on the first line of the journal entry. Enter the day of the transaction in the second column on the first line of each entry. (2) Enter titles of accounts debited. Account titles are taken from the chart of accounts and are aligned with the left margin of the Account Titles and Explanation column. Enter debit amounts in the Debit column on the same line as the accounts debited. (3) Enter titles of accounts credited. Account titles are taken from the chart of accounts and are indented from the left margin of the Account Titles and Explanation column to distinguish them from debited accounts. Enter credit amounts in the Credit column on the same line as the accounts credited. (4) Enter a brief explanation of the transaction on the line below the entry (it often references a source document). This explanation is indented about half as far as the credited account titles to avoid confusing it with accounts, and it is italicized. (5) Skip a line between each journal entry for clarity. When we first record a transaction, we leave the **posting reference (PR) column** blank. Later, when entries are posted to the ledger, we enter individual ledger account numbers in the PR column.

Decision Track 2.2		*d*
Decision Point	**Information Search**	**Analyze & Evaluate**
What accounts are impacted by a transaction or event?	Transaction or event details along with identification of a company's accounts from its financial statements.	Identify the company's accounts and assess the impact of a transaction or event using the accounting equation.

Balance Column Account

T-accounts are simple and direct means to show how the accounting process works. However, actual accounting systems need more structure and therefore use **balance column accounts,** as in Exhibit 2.14.

The balance column account format is similar to a T-account in having columns for debits and credits. It is different in including transaction date and explanation columns. It also has a column with the balance of the account after each entry is recorded. For example, FastForward's Cash account in Exhibit 2.14 is debited on December 1 for the $30,000 owner investment, yielding a $30,000 debit balance. The account is credited on December 2 for $2,500, yielding a $27,500 debit balance. On December 3, it is credited again, this time for $26,000, and its debit balance is reduced to $1,500. The Cash account is debited for $4,200 on December 10, and its debit balance increases to $5,700.

When a balance column account is used, the heading of the Balance column does not show whether it is a debit or credit balance. An account is assumed to have a *normal bal-*

Exhibit 2.13

Partial General Journal for FastForward

General Journal						Page 1
Date			**Account Titles and Explanation**	**PR**	**Debit**	**Credit**
2001 Dec.	1		Cash		30,000	
			Common Stock			30,000
			Investment by owner.			
	2		Supplies		2,500	
			Cash			2,500
			Purchased store supplies for cash.			

Cash					Account No. 101	
Date		Explanation	PR	Debit	Credit	Balance
2001						
Dec	1		G1	30,000		30,000
	2		G1		2,500	27,500
	3		G1		26,000	1,500
	10		G1	4,200		5,700

Exhibit 2.14

Cash Account in Balance Column Format

ance. Unusual events can sometimes temporarily give an account an abnormal balance. An *abnormal balance* refers to a balance on the side where decreases are recorded. For example, a customer might mistakenly overpay a bill. This gives that customer's account receivable an abnormal (credit) balance. An abnormal balance is often identified by circling it or by entering it in red or some other unusual color. Computerized systems often provide a code beside a balance such as *dr.* or *cr.* to identify its balance. A zero balance for an account is usually shown by writing zeros or a dash in the Balance column. This practice avoids confusion between a zero balance and one omitted in error.

Posting Journal Entries

Step 4 of processing transactions is to post journal entries to ledger accounts (see Exhibit 2.12). To ensure that the ledger is up-to-date, entries are posted as soon as possible. This might be daily, weekly, or when time permits. All entries must be posted to the ledger by the end of a reporting period. This is necessary so that account balances are current when financial statements are prepared. When entries are posted to the ledger, the debits in journal entries are transferred into ledger accounts as debits, and credits are transferred into ledger accounts as credits. The usual process is to post debits first and then credits. Exhibit 2.15 shows the four steps to post a journal entry. First, identify the ledger account that is

Point: The ledger is referred to as the *book of final entry* because financial statements are prepared from it.

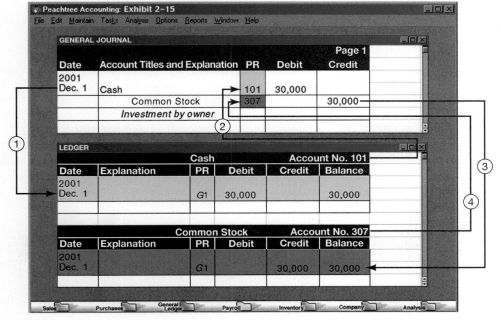

Exhibit 2.15

Posting an Entry to the Ledger

Key:
1. Identify debit account in Ledger: enter date, journal page, amount, and balance.
2. Enter the debit account number from the Ledger in the PR column of the journal.
3. Identify credit account in Ledger: enter date, journal page, amount, and balance.
4. Enter the credit account number from the Ledger in the PR column of the journal.

debited in the entry. In the ledger, enter the date of the entry, the journal and page in the PR column, the debit amount from the journal, and the new balance of the ledger account. (The letter *G* shows it came from the General Journal. Other journals are identified by their own letters. We discuss other journals in Appendix E.) Second, enter the ledger account number in the PR column of the journal next to the entry. Repeat these two steps for credit entries and amounts. The posting process creates a link between the ledger and the journal entry. This link is a useful cross-reference for tracing an amount from one record to another. Computerized systems usually automatically transfer debit and credit entries from the journal to the ledger.

Analyzing Transactions

We return to the activities of FastForward to show how double-entry accounting is useful in analyzing and processing transactions. We analyze each transaction in four stages. First, we review the transaction and any source documents. Second, we analyze the transaction using the accounting equation. Third, we use double-entry accounting to record the transaction, in both the required journal entry form and the optional T-account form (the T-accounts can be viewed as simple ledger accounts). Fourth, we show how each transaction affects (links to) the financial statements. Exhibit 2.17 (on pages 64–65) eventually summarizes these links. We should study each transaction thoroughly before proceeding to the next transaction. The first 11 transactions are familiar to us, and we consider five additional FastForward December transactions (numbered 12 through 16) that were omitted earlier.

Point: Explanations are typically only included in ledger accounts for unusual transactions or events.

A2 Analyze the impact of transactions on accounts and financial statements.

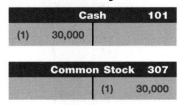

1. Investment by Owner

Cash		101
(1)	30,000	

Common Stock		307
	(1)	30,000

Transaction: Chuck Taylor invests $30,000 cash in exchange for common stock of FastForward on December 1.

Analysis:

	Assets	=	Liabilities	+	Equity
	+30,000	=	0	+	30,000

Double entry: (1) | Cash | 101 | 30,000 | |
| | Common Stock | 307 | | 30,000 |

Statements affected:[5] BS and SCF

2. Purchase Supplies for Cash

Supplies		126
(2)	2,500	

Cash		101
(1)	30,000	(2)	2,500

Transaction: FastForward pays $2,500 cash for supplies.

Analysis:

	Assets	=	Liabilities	+	Equity
	+2,500				
	−2,500	=	0	+	0

Changes the composition of assets but not the total.

Double entry: (2) | Supplies | 126 | 2,500 | |
| | Cash | 101 | | 2,500 |

Statements affected: BS and SCF

3. Purchase Equipment for Cash

Equipment		167
(3)	26,000	

Cash		101
(1)	30,000	(2)	2,500
		(3)	26,000

Transaction: FastForward pays $26,000 cash for equipment.

Analysis:

	Assets	=	Liabilities	+	Equity
	+26,000				
	−26,000	=	0	+	0

Changes the composition of assets but not the total.

Double entry: (3) | Equipment | 167 | 26,000 | |
| | Cash | 101 | | 26,000 |

Statements affected: BS and SCF

---

[5] We use abbreviations for the statements: income statement (IS), balance sheet (BS), statement of cash flows (SCF), and statement of retained earnings (SRE).

4. Purchase Supplies on Credit

Supplies		126
(2)	2,500	
(4)	7,100	

Accounts Payable 201		
	(4)	7,100

Transaction: FastForward purchases $7,100 of supplies on credit.

Analysis:

Assets	=	Liabilities	+	Equity
+7,100	=	+7,100	+	0

Double entry:

(4)	Supplies	126	7,100	
	Accounts Payable	201		7,100

Statements affected: BS

5. Provide Services for Cash

Cash		101		
(1)	30,000	(2)	2,500
(5)	4,200	(3)	26,000

Consulting Revenue		403
	(5)	4,200

Transaction: FastForward provides consulting services and immediately collects $4,200 cash.

Analysis:

Assets	=	Liabilities	+	Equity
+4,200	=	0	+	4,200

Double entry:

(5)	Cash	101	4,200	
	Consulting Revenue	403		4,200

Statements affected: BS, IS, SCF, and SRE

6. Payment of Expense in Cash

Rent Expense		640
(6)	1,000	

Cash		101		
(1)	30,000	(2)	2,500
(5)	4,200	(3)	26,000
		(6)	1,000

Transaction: FastForward pays $1,000 cash for December rent.

Analysis:

Assets	=	Liabilities	+	Equity
−1,000	=	0	+	−1,000

Double entry:

(6)	Rent Expense	640	1,000	
	Cash	101		1,000

Statements affected: BS, IS, SCF, and SRE

7. Payment of Expense in Cash

Salaries Expense		622
(7)	700	

Cash		101		
(1)	30,000	(2)	2,500
(5)	4,200	(3)	26,000
		(6)	1,000
		(7)	700

Transaction: FastForward pays $700 cash in employee salary.

Analysis:

Assets	=	Liabilities	+	Equity
−700	=	0	+	−700

Double entry:

(7)	Salaries Expense	622	700	
	Cash	101		700

Statements affected: BS, IS, SCF, and SRE

Point: *Salary* usually refers to compensation for an employee who receives a fixed amount for a given time period, whereas *wages* usually refers to compensation based on time worked.

8. Provide Consulting and Rental Services on Credit

Accounts Receivable		106
(8)	1,900	

Consulting Revenue		403
	(5)	4,200
	(8)	1,600

Rental Revenue		406
	(8)	300

Transaction: FastForward provides consulting services of $1,600 and rents its test facilities for $300. The customer is billed $1,900 for these services.

Analysis:

Assets	=	Liabilities	+	Equity
+1,900	=	0	+	{+1,600 / + 300}

Double entry:

(8)	Accounts Receivable	106	1,900	
	Consulting Revenue	403		1,600
	Rental Revenue	406		300

Statements affected: BS, IS, and SRE

Point: Transaction 8 is a **compound journal entry.** A compound journal entry affects three or more accounts.

9. Receipt of Cash on Account

Cash			101
(1)	30,000	(2)	2,500
(5)	4,200	(3)	26,000
(9)	1,900	(6)	1,000
		(7)	700

Accounts Receivable			106
(8)	1,900	(9)	1,900

Transaction: FastForward receives $1,900 cash from the client billed in transaction 8.

Analysis:

$$\text{Assets} = \text{Liabilities} - \text{Equity}$$
$$\left.\begin{array}{r} +1,900 \\ -1,900 \end{array}\right\} = \quad 0 \quad + \quad 0$$

Double entry:

(9)	Cash	101	1,900	
	Accounts Receivable	106		1,900

Statements affected: BS and SCF

10. Partial Payment of Accounts Payable

Accounts Payable			201
(10)	900	(4)	7,100

Cash			101
(1)	30,000	(2)	2,500
(5)	4,200	(3)	26,000
(9)	1,900	(6)	1,000
		(7)	700
		(10)	900

Transaction: FastForward pays CalTech Supply $900 cash toward the payable of transaction 4.

Analysis:

$$\text{Assets} = \text{Liabilities} + \text{Equity}$$
$$-900 = -900 + 0$$

Double entry:

(10)	Accounts Payable	201	900	
	Cash	101		900

Statements affected: BS and SCF

11. Payment of Cash Dividend

Retained Earnings			318
(11)	600		

Cash			101
(1)	30,000	(2)	2,500
(5)	4,200	(3)	26,000
(9)	1,900	(6)	1,000
		(7)	700
		(10)	900
		(11)	600

Transaction: FastForward declares and pays a $600 cash dividend to its owner.

Analysis:

$$\text{Assets} = \text{Liabilities} + \text{Equity}$$
$$-600 = 0 + -600$$

Double entry:

(11)	Retained Earnings	318	600	
	Cash	101		600

Statements affected: BS, SCF, and SRE

12. Receipt of Cash for Future Services

Cash			101
(1)	30,000	(2)	2,500
(5)	4,200	(3)	26,000
(9)	1,900	(6)	1,000
(12)	3,000	(7)	700
		(10)	900
		(11)	600

Unearned Consulting Revenue			236
		(12)	3,000

Transaction: FastForward receives $3,000 cash in advance of providing consulting services to a customer.

Analysis:

$$\text{Assets} = \text{Liabilities} + \text{Equity}$$
$$+3,000 = +3,000 + 0$$

Accepting $3,000 cash obligates FastForward to perform future services and is a liability. No revenue is earned until services are provided.

Double entry:

(12)	Cash	101	3,000	
	Unearned Consulting Revenue	236		3,000

Statements affected: BS and SCF

13. Pay Cash for Future Insurance Coverage

Prepaid Insurance 128	
(13) 2,400	

Cash			101
(1)	30,000	(2)	2,500
(5)	4,200	(3)	26,000
(9)	1,900	(6)	1,000
(12)	3,000	(7)	700
		(10)	900
		(11)	600
		(13)	2,400

Transaction: FastForward pays $2,400 cash (premium) for a 2-year insurance policy. Coverage begins on December 1.

Analysis: Assets = Liabilities + Equity

$$\left.\begin{array}{r} +2,400 \\ -2,400 \end{array}\right\} = \quad 0 \quad + \quad 0$$

Changes the composition of assets from cash to prepaid insurance. Expense is incurred as insurance coverage expires.

Double entry:	(13)	Prepaid Insurance	128	2,400	
		Cash	101		2,400

Statements affected: BS and SCF

14. Purchase Supplies for Cash

Supplies		126
(2)	2,500	
(4)	7,100	
(14)	120	

Cash			101
(1)	30,000	(2)	2,500
(5)	4,200	(3)	26,000
(9)	1,900	(6)	1,000
(12)	3,000	(7)	700
		(10)	900
		(11)	600
		(13)	2,400
		(14)	120

Transaction: FastForward pays $120 cash for supplies.

Analysis: Assets = Liabilities + Equity

$$\left.\begin{array}{r} +120 \\ -120 \end{array}\right\} = \quad 0 \quad + \quad 0$$

Double entry:	(14)	Supplies	126	120	
		Cash	101		120

Statements affected: BS and SCF

15. Payment of Expense in Cash

Utilities Expense 690	
(15) 230	

Cash			101
(1)	30,000	(2)	2,500
(5)	4,200	(3)	26,000
(9)	1,900	(6)	1,000
(12)	3,000	(7)	700
		(10)	900
		(11)	600
		(13)	2,400
		(14)	120
		(15)	230

Transaction: FastForward pays $230 cash for December utilities.

Analysis: Assets = Liabilities + Equity

$$-230 \quad = \quad 0 \quad + \quad -230$$

Double entry:	(15)	Utilities Expense	690	230	
		Cash	101		230

Statements affected: BS, IS, SCF, and SRE

16. Payment of Expense in Cash

Point: We could merge transactions 15–16 into one *compound entry.*

Salaries Expense 622	
(7)	700
(16)	700

Cash			101
(1)	30,000	(2)	2,500
(5)	4,200	(3)	26,000
(9)	1,900	(6)	1,000
(12)	3,000	(7)	700
		(10)	900
		(11)	600
		(13)	2,400
		(14)	120
		(15)	230
		(16)	700

Transaction: FastForward pays $700 cash in employee salary.

Analysis:

Assets	=	Liabilities	+	Equity
−700	=	0	+	−700

Double entry:

(16)	Salaries Expense	622	700	
	Cash	101		700

Statements affected: BS, IS, SCF, and SRE

Accounting Equation Analysis

Exhibit 2.16 shows the accounts of FastForward after all 16 transactions have been recorded and the balances computed. The accounts are grouped into three major columns corresponding to the accounting equation: assets, liabilities, and equity. Note several important points. First, as with each transaction, the totals for the three columns must obey the accounting equation. Specifically, assets equal $42,070 ($3,950 + $0 + $9,720 + $2,400 + $26,000); liabilities equal $9,200 ($6,200 + $3,000); and equity equals $32,870 ($30,000 − $600 + $5,800 + $300 − $1,400 − $1,000 − $230). These numbers obey the accounting equation: $42,070 = $9,200 + $32,870. Second, the retained earnings, revenue, and expense accounts reflect the transactions that change retained earnings. Their balances make up the statement of retained earnings. Third, the revenue and expense account balances will be summarized and reported in the income statement. Fourth, components of the cash account make up the elements reported in the statement of cash flows.

Point: Technology does not provide the judgment required to analyze most business transactions. Analysis requires the expertise of skilled and ethical professionals.

Financial Statement Links

Exhibit 2.17 extends the analysis and summarizes how FastForward's transactions impact all financial statements. Some transactions such as purchasing supplies on credit (No. 4) impact only one statement. Others such as receiving cash for services performed (No. 5) impact all of the statements. We should review this exhibit and understand how transactions link to financial statements. We return to explain the details of these links in Chapter 3, including the adjusting and closing processes.

Point: Some small businesses use an outside recordkeeping service to make entries once each month.

Quick Check

18. What types of transactions increase equity? What types decrease equity?

19. Why are accounting systems called *double entry?*

20. For each transaction, double-entry accounting requires which of the following: (a) Debits to asset accounts must create credits to liability or equity accounts, (b) A debit to a liability account must create a credit to an asset account, or (c) Total debits must equal total credits.

21. An owner invests $15,000 cash and equipment having a market value of $23,000 in exchange for stock of the corporation. Prepare the necessary journal entry.

22. Explain what a compound journal entry is.

23. Why are posting reference numbers entered in the journal when entries are posted to ledger accounts?

Exhibit 2.16

Ledger for FastForward (in T-account Form)

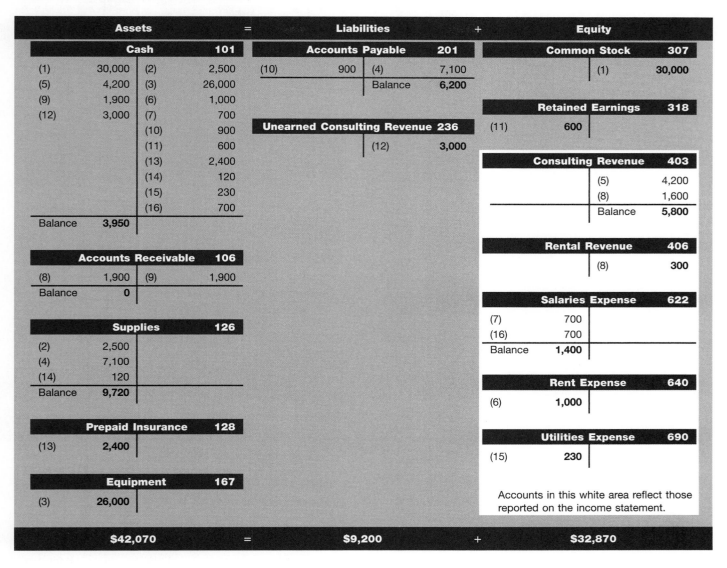

	Assets		=		Liabilities		+		Equity	

Cash   101

(1)	30,000	(2)	2,500
(5)	4,200	(3)	26,000
(9)	1,900	(6)	1,000
(12)	3,000	(7)	700
		(10)	900
		(11)	600
		(13)	2,400
		(14)	120
		(15)	230
		(16)	700
Balance	3,950		

Accounts Receivable   106

| (8) | 1,900 | (9) | 1,900 |
| Balance | 0 | | |

Supplies   126

(2)	2,500
(4)	7,100
(14)	120
Balance	9,720

Prepaid Insurance   128

| (13) | 2,400 |

Equipment   167

| (3) | 26,000 |

Accounts Payable   201

| (10) | 900 | (4) | 7,100 |
| | | Balance | 6,200 |

Unearned Consulting Revenue 236

| | (12) | 3,000 |

Common Stock   307

| | (1) | 30,000 |

Retained Earnings   318

| (11) | 600 | |

Consulting Revenue   403

	(5)	4,200
	(8)	1,600
	Balance	5,800

Rental Revenue   406

| | (8) | 300 |

Salaries Expense   622

(7)	700
(16)	700
Balance	1,400

Rent Expense   640

| (6) | 1,000 |

Utilities Expense   690

| (15) | 230 |

Accounts in this white area reflect those reported on the income statement.

$42,070	=	**$9,200**	+	**$32,870**

Double-entry accounting requires the sum of debit account balances to equal the sum of credit account balances. A trial balance is used to verify this. A **trial balance** is a list of accounts and their balances at a point in time. Account balances are reported in the debit or credit column of a trial balance. Exhibit 2.18 shows the trial balance for FastForward after its 16 entries have been posted to the ledger. (This is an *unadjusted* trial balance—Chapter 3 will explain the necessary adjustments.)

Trial Balance

Preparing a Trial Balance

Preparing a trial balance involves three steps:

1. List each account title and its amount (from the ledger) in the trial balance. If an account has a zero balance, it can be listed with a zero in its normal balance column.
2. Compute the total of debit balances and the total of credit balances.
3. Verify (*prove*) total debit balances equal total credit balances.

P2   Prepare and explain the use of a trial balance.

| Transactions | | Balance Sheet (BS) | | | | | | | | | |
| No. Description | | Assets | | | | | = | Liabilities | | + | Equity | |
No.	Description	Cash	+ Accts. Rec.	+ Prepaid Insur.	+ Supplies	+ Equip.	=	Accts. Pay.	+ Unearned Revenue	+	Common Stock	+ Retained Earnings
1	Shareholder investment	30,000					=			+	30,000	
2	Purch. supp.	(2,500)			2,500		=			+		
3	Purch. equip.	(26,000)				26,000	=			+		
4	Credit purch.				7,100		=	7,100		+		
5	Services for cash	4,200					=			+		4,200
6	Rent exp.	(1,000)					=			+		(1,000)
7	Salary exp.	(700)					=			+		(700)
8	Services for credit		1,900				=			+		1,600 / 300
9	Cash rec'd. on Acct. Rec.	1,900	(1,900)				=			+		
10	Payment of Acct. Pay.	(900)					=	(900)		+		
11	Dividend payment	(600)					=			+		(600)
12	Cash for future service	3,000					=		3,000	+		
13	Payment of future insur.	(2,400)		2,400			=			+		
14	Purch. supp.	(120)			120		=			+		
15	Utilities exp.	(230)					=			+		(230)
16	Salary exp.	(700)					=			+		(700)
	Totals	3,950	0	2,400	9,720	26,000	=	6,200	3,000	+	30,000	2,870

Point: The ordering of accounts in a trial balance typically follows their identification number from the chart of accounts.

The total of debit balances equals the total of credit balances for the trial balance in Exhibit 2.18. If these two totals are not equal, then one or more errors exist. However, equality of these two totals does not guarantee that no errors were made.

Using a Trial Balance

When a trial balance does not balance (when its columns are not equal), usually one or more errors occurred in one of the following steps of the accounting process: (1) preparing journal entries, (2) posting entries to the ledger, (3) computing account balances, (4) entering account balances on the trial balance, or (5) totaling the trial balance columns. When a trial balance does balance, the accounts are likely free of the kinds of errors that create unequal debits and credits, yet errors can still exist. One example is when a debit or credit of a correct amount is made to a wrong account. This can occur when either journalizing or posting. This error would produce incorrect balances in two accounts, but the trial balance would balance. Another error is to record equal debits and credits of an incorrect amount. This error produces incorrect balances in two accounts, but again the debits and credits are equal.

Point: A trial balance is *not* a financial statement but a mechanism for checking equality of debits and credits in the ledger. Financial statements do not have debit and credit columns.

Searching for and Correcting Errors

If the trial balance does not balance, the error (or errors) must be found and corrected before preparing financial statements. Searching for the error is more efficient if we check the journalizing, posting, and trial balance preparation process in *reverse order*. While methods vary, we suggest the following sequence of steps. Step 1 is to verify that the trial balance columns are correctly added. If step 1 fails to find the error, then step 2 is to verify that ac-

Rev.	−	Exp.	=	Net Inc.	Oper. Cash Flow	+	Inv. Cash Flow	+	Fin. Cash Flow	=	Net Cash Flow	No.	Description
	−		=						30,000	=	30,000	1	Shareholder investment
	−		=		(2,500)					=	(2,500)	2	Purch. supp.
	−		=				(26,000)			=	(26,000)	3	Purch. equip.
	−		=							=		4	Credit purch.
4,200	−		=	4,200	4,200					=	4,200	5	Services for cash
	−	1,000	=	(1,000)	(1,000)					=	(1,000)	6	Rent exp.
	−	700	=	(700)	(700)					=	(700)	7	Salary exp.
1,600	−		=	1,600								8	Services for credit
300	−		=	300									
	−		=		1,900					=	1,900	9	Cash rec'd. on Acct. Rec.
	−		=		(900)					=	(900)	10	Payment of Acct. Pay.
	−		=						(600)	=	(600)	11	Dividend payment
	−		=		3,000					=	3,000	12	Cash for future service
	−		=		(2,400)					=	(2,400)	13	Payment of future insur.
	−		=		(120)					=	(120)	14	Purch. supp.
	−	230	=	(230)	(230)					=	(230)	15	Utilities exp.
	−	700	=	(700)	(700)					=	(700)	16	Salary exp.
6,100	−	2,630	=	3,470	550	+	(26,000)	+	29,400	=	3,950		Totals

Income Statement (IS) · **Statement of Cash Flows (SCF)** · **Transactions**

Exhibit 2.17

Financial Statement Links to Transactions

FAST FORWARD
Trial Balance
December 31, 2001

	Debit	Credit
Cash	$ 3,950	
Accounts Receivable	0	
Supplies	9,720	
Prepaid insurance	2,400	
Equipment	26,000	
Accounts payable		$ 6,200
Unearned consulting revenue		3,000
Common stock		30,000
Retained earnings	600	
Consulting revenue		5,800
Rental revenue		300
Salaries expense	1,400	
Rent expense	1,000	
Utilities expense	230	
Totals	$ 45,300	$ 45,300

Exhibit 2.18

Trial Balance (unadjusted)

count balances are accurately entered from the ledger. Step 3 is to see whether a debit (or credit) balance is mistakenly listed in the trial balance as a credit (or debit). A clue to this kind of error is when the difference between total debits and total credits in the trial balance equals twice the amount of the incorrect account balance. If the error is still undiscovered, Step 4 is to recompute each account balance in the ledger. Step 5 is to verify that each journal entry is properly posted to ledger accounts. Step 6 is to verify that the original journal entry has equal debits and credits. At this point, all errors should be uncovered.[6]

If errors are discovered in either the journal or the ledger, they must be corrected. Our approach to correcting errors depends on the type of error and when it is discovered. In one case, if an error in a journal entry is discovered before the error is posted, it can be corrected in a manual system by drawing a line through the incorrect information. The correct information is written above it to create a record of change for the auditor. Many computerized systems allow the operator to replace the incorrect information directly. If a correct amount in the journal is posted incorrectly to the ledger, we can correct it the same way.

Another case occurs when an error in a journal entry is not discovered until after it has been posted. We usually do not strike through both erroneous entries in the journal and ledger. Instead, the usual practice is to correct the error in the original journal entry by creating *another* journal entry. This *correcting entry* removes the amount from the wrong account and records it to the correct account. As an example, suppose we recorded a $1,600 purchase of office supplies in the journal with an incorrect debit to Office Equipment, and we then post this incorrect entry to the ledger. The Office Supplies ledger account balance is understated by $1,600, and the Office Equipment ledger account balance is overstated by $1,600. When we discover the error later, we make the following correcting entry: debit Office Supplies and credit Office Equipment (both for $1,600). The explanation reports exactly what happened.

Presentation Issues

Dollar signs are not used in journals and ledgers. They do appear in financial statements and other reports such as trial balances. The usual practice is to put a dollar sign beside the first amount in each column of numbers, and beside the first amount appearing after a ruled line. The financial statements in Exhibit 2.19 demonstrate this. Another practice is to put dollar signs beside only the first and last numbers in a column. **Nike**'s financial statements in Appendix A show this. When amounts are entered in a journal, ledger, or trial balance, commas are optional to indicate thousands, millions, and so forth. However, commas are always used in financial statements. Companies also commonly round amounts to the nearest dollar, or even to a higher level. Nike is typical of many companies in that it rounds its financial statement amounts to the nearest one-tenth of a million. This decision is based on the perceived impact of rounding for users' business decisions.

Decision Track 2.3

Decision Point	Information Search	Analyze & Evaluate
Where is a listing of accounts and their balances? Do debits equal credits?	Ledger and trial balance: A trial balance lists all accounts in the ledger with their balances.	Prepare a trial balance, total debit and credit columns, and verify equality.

[6] *Transposition* occurs when two digits are switched, or transposed, within a number. If transposition is the only error, it yields a difference between the two trial balance totals that is evenly divisible by 9. For example, assume that a $691 debit in an entry is incorrectly posted to the ledger as $619. Total credits in the trial balance are then larger than total debits by $72 ($691 − $619). The $72 error is *evenly* divisible by 9 (72/9 = 8). The first digit of the quotient (in our example it is 8) equals the difference between the digits of the two transposed numbers (the 9 and the 1). The number of digits in the quotient also tells the location of the transposition, starting from the right. The quotient in our example had only one digit (8), so it tells us the transposition is in the first digit. Consider another example where a transposition error involves posting $961 instead of the correct $691. The difference in these numbers in $270, and its quotient is 30 (270/9). The quotient has two digits, so it tells us to check the second digit from the right for a transposition of two numbers that have a difference of 3.

Exhibit 2.19

Financial Statements and
Their Links

FASTFORWARD
Unadjusted Income Statement
For Month Ended December 31, 2001

Revenues:

Consulting revenue ($4,200 + $1,600)	$5,800	
Rental revenue	300	
Total revenues		$6,100

Expenses:

Rent expense	1,000	
Salaries expense	1,400	
Utilities expense	230	
Total expenses		2,630
Net income		**$3,470** ←

Point: Arrow lines show how the
statements are linked.

FASTFORWARD
Unadjusted Statement of Retained Earnings
For Month Ended December 31, 2001

Retained earnings, December 1, 2001	$ 0
Plus: Net income	3,470 ←
	$3,470
Less: Dividends	(600)
Retained earnings, December 31, 2001	**$2,870** ←

FASTFORWARD
Unadjusted Balance Sheet
December 31, 2001

Assets		Liabilities	
→ Cash	$ 3,950	Accounts payable	$ 6,200
Supplies	9,720	Unearned revenue	$ 3,000
Prepaid insurance .	2,400	Total liabilities	$ 9,200
Equipment	26,000	**Equity**	
		Common stock	$30,000
		Retained earnings	2,870 ←
Total assets	$42,070	Total liabilities and equity .	$42,070

Point: To *foot* a column of numbers
is to add them.

FASTFORWARD
Unadjusted Statement of Cash Flows*
For Month Ended December 31, 2001

Cash flows from operating activities:

Cash received from clients [5 + 9 + 12]	$ 9,100	
Cash paid for supplies [2 + 10 + 14]	(3,520)	
Cash paid for insurance [13]	(2,400)	
Cash paid for rent [6]	(1,000)	
Cash paid to employee [7 + 16]	(1,400)	
Cash paid for utilities [15]	(230)	
Net cash provided by operating activities		$ 550

Cash flows from investing activities:

Purchase of equipment [3]	(26,000)	
Net cash used by investing activities		(26,000)

Cash flows from financing activities:

Investments by shareholders [1]	30,000	
Dividends to shareholders [11]	(600)	
Net cash provided by financing activities		29,400
Net increase in cash		$ 3,950
Cash balance, December 1, 2001		0
→ Cash balance, December 31, 2001		**$ 3,950**

Point: Final totals are double
underlined. Negative amounts are
often in parentheses.

*Numbers in brackets refer to the numbered transactions 1–16.

Unadjusted Financial Statements

This section shows how we prepare *unadjusted financial statements* from business transactions and events. We prepare these financial statements using the December transactions of FastForward. These statements are called unadjusted because we need to make some further accounting adjustments (described in Chapter 3).

Unadjusted Income Statement

An **income statement** reports the revenues earned less the expenses incurred by a business over a period of time. **Net income** occurs when revenues exceed expenses. A **net loss,** or simply *loss,* occurs when expenses exceed revenues. An income statement does not simply report net income or net loss. It lists the types and amounts of important revenues and expenses. **Revenues** are inflows of assets in exchange for products and services provided to customers as part of a company's operations. **Expenses** are outflows or the using up of assets in providing products and services to customers. The income statement heading identifies the company, the type of statement, and the time period covered. Knowledge of the time period is important in judging whether a company's performance is satisfactory.

Point: Knowing how financial statements are prepared improves our analysis of them. We develop the skills for analysis of financial statements throughout the book. Chapter 13 solely focuses on financial statement analysis.

FastForward's unadjusted income statement for December is shown at the top of Exhibit 2.19. Information about revenues and expenses is conveniently taken from the income statement columns of Exhibit 2.17 or from the unadjusted trial balance in Exhibit 2.18. Revenues are reported first on the income statement. They include consulting revenues of $5,800 from transactions 5 and 8, and rental revenue of $300 from transaction 8. Expenses are reported after revenues. We can list revenues and expenses in different ways, such as listing larger amounts first. The expenses are from transactions 6, 7, 15, and 16. Expenses reflect the costs to generate the revenues reported. Net income (or loss) is reported at the bottom of the statement and is the amount earned in December. Shareholders' investments and dividends are *not* part of income.

Point: An income statement is also referred to as an *earnings statement, a statement of operations,* or a *P&L* (profit and loss) *statement*.

Unadjusted Statement of Retained Earnings

The **statement of retained earnings** reports information about how retained earnings changes over the reporting period. This statement shows beginning retained earnings, events that increase it (net income), and events that decrease it (dividends and net loss). Ending retained earnings is computed in this statement and is carried over and reported on the balance sheet. FastForward's statement of retained earnings is the second report in Exhibit 2.19. Its beginning retained earnings is measured as of the start of business on December 1. It is zero because FastForward did not exist before then. An existing business reports the beginning balance as of the end of the prior reporting period (such as from November 30). FastForward's statement shows the $3,470 of net income earned during the month. This links the income statement to the statement of retained earnings. The statement also reports the $600 dividend and FastForward's $2,870 end-of-month retained earnings balance.[7]

Point: While revenues earned increase retained earnings and expenses incurred decrease retained earnings, the amounts are not reported in detail in the statement of retained earnings. Instead, the net effect of revenues and expenses is reflected in net income.

Unadjusted Balance Sheet

The **balance sheet** (also called the *statement of financial position*) reports the financial position of a company at a point in time, usually at the end of a month, quarter, or year. The balance sheet describes financial position by listing the types and dollar amounts of assets, liabilities,

---

[7] The beginning retained earnings balance in the statement of retained earnings is rarely zero. An exception is for the first period of a company's operations. The beginning retained earnings balance in January 2002 for FastForward is $2,870 (this is December's ending balance).

and equity. The balance sheet heading lists the company, the statement, and the date on which assets, liabilities, and equity are identified and measured. The amounts in the balance sheet are measured as of the close of business on that date.

FastForward's unadjusted balance sheet is the third report in Exhibit 2.19. This statement refers to FastForward's financial condition at the close of business on December 31. The left side of the balance sheet lists its assets: cash, supplies, prepaid insurance, and equipment. The upper right side of the balance sheet shows that FastForward owes $6,200 to creditors and $3,000 in services to customers who paid in advance. All other liabilities (such as a bank loan) would be listed here. The equity section shows common stock of $30,000 and retained earnings of $2,870. Note the link between the ending balance of the statement of retained earnings and the retained earnings balance here. (This presentation of the balance sheet is called the *account form*—assets on the left and liabilities and equity on the right. Another presentation is the *report form*—assets on top, followed by liabilities and then equity. Either presentation is acceptable.)

Unadjusted Statement of Cash Flows

The **statement of cash flows** describes the sources (inflows) and uses (outflows) of cash for a reporting period. It also reports the amount of cash at both the beginning and end of a period. This information is important because a company must carefully manage cash if it is to succeed. FastForward's unadjusted statement of cash flows is the final report in Exhibit 2.19.

The statement of cash flows is organized according to a company's major activities: operating, investing, and financing. The first section reports cash flows from *operating activities*. The $9,100 of cash received from clients exceeds total revenue on the income statement because FastForward collected $3,000 of revenues in advance. This section also lists cash paid for supplies, rent, insurance, salaries, and utilities. We put these amounts in parentheses to indicate they are subtracted. The payment for supplies is an operating activity because they are expected to be used up in short-term operations (their benefits are not long term). Net cash provided by operating activities for December is $550. If cash paid exceeded cash received, we would call it "cash used by operating activities." Decision makers are especially interested in the operating section of the statement of cash flows because it helps them assess how much operating income is in the form of cash.

The second section of the statement of cash flows describes *investing activities*. Investing activities involve buying and selling assets such as land and equipment that are held for *long-term use* in the business. Decision makers are interested in this section of the statement because it describes how a company is preparing for its future. If it is spending cash on productive assets, it should be able to grow and increase net income. A user is also concerned that a company does not overly spend on productive assets and face a cash shortage. If a company is selling its productive assets, it is downsizing.

The third section shows cash flows related to *financing activities*. Financing activities include *long-term* borrowing and repaying cash from lenders, and cash investments from and dividends to shareholders. FastForward's statement of cash flows shows it received $30,000 from Taylor's initial investment. If the business had borrowed cash, that amount would appear here as an increase in cash. The financing section also shows the $600 dividend. The total effect of financing activities is a $29,400 net inflow of cash. The financing section shows why FastForward did not run out of cash even though it spent $26,000 on equipment and generated only $550 from operating activities: it used the shareholder's cash investment. Decision makers are interested in the financing section because excessive borrowing can burden a company and reduce its potential for growth.

The final part of the statement of cash flows is the net increase or decrease in cash. It shows FastForward increased its cash balance by $3,950 in December. Since it started with no cash, the ending balance is also $3,950. This ending amount is the link from the statement of cash flows to the balance sheet. We give a more detailed explanation of the statement of cash flows in Chapters 3 and 12.

Example: How would the balance sheet in Exhibit 2.19 change if FastForward pays off $2,000 of its payable on December 31 using its Cash account? What would be the new amount of total assets? Would the balance sheet still balance? *Answers:* Cash would be $1,950, accounts payable would be $4,200, total assets (and liabilities) would be $40,070, and the balance sheet would still balance.

Point: Investing activities refer to long-term asset investments in the company, *not* to owner investments.

Example: How would the cash flow statement in Exhibit 2.19 change if FastForward had paid $27,000 cash for the equipment and had borrowed $5,000 from a bank to help finance future operations? *Answer:* The investing section would show the $27,000 paid for equipment; the financing section would report the $5,000 loan as additional cash provided; and the net increase in cash and ending cash balance would be increased from $3,950 to $7,950.

Quick Check

24. Describe a chart of accounts.

25. Where are dollar signs typically entered in financial statements?

26. If a $4,000 debit to Equipment in a journal entry is incorrectly posted to the ledger as a $4,000 credit, and the ledger account has a resulting debit balance of $20,000, what is the effect of this error on the trial balance column totals?

27. Explain the link between the income statement and the statement of retained earnings.

28. Describe the link between the balance sheet and the statement of retained earnings.

29. Discuss the three major sections of the statement of cash flows.

30. What are the four major financial statements?

31. Define and describe revenues and expenses.

32. Define and describe assets, liabilities, and equity.

Answers—pp. 79–80

Decision Analysis *d*   **Return on Equity and the Debt Ratio**

An important objective for many users is gathering information to help them assess a company's profitability and its risk of failing to pay its debts. This section describes the return on equity ratio and the debt ratio and how they can help in these tasks.

 A3   Compute return on equity and use it to analyze company performance.

Return on Equity

An important reason for recording information about assets, liabilities, equity, and income is to help an owner judge the company's profitability compared to other business or personal opportunities. One measure of success is the **return on equity** ratio, which is computed as net income divided by average equity for the period as shown in Exhibit 2.20.

Exhibit 2.20

Return on Equity

$$\text{Return on equity} = \frac{\text{Net income}}{\text{Average equity}}$$

FastForward's return on equity for the month of December is computed (using data from the unadjusted financial statements) as[8]

$$\frac{\$3,470}{[\$30,000 + \$32,870]/2} = 11.0\%$$

FastForward's December return is high compared to many investments, especially for the first month of operations. An owner would compare this return with other opportunities to determine whether it is adequate. Examples of other opportunities are savings accounts, stocks, and bonds. Taylor likely will continue to operate FastForward because 11% per month exceeds 130% per year. (The annual rate is approximated by taking the 11% monthly rate and

Decision Maker   *d*

Venture Capitalist You are considering launching a corporation to manufacture athletic apparel. You estimate the new business will yield a net income of $2,000 per month and require an average equity balance of $400,000. Do you pursue this opportunity?

Answer—p. 78

---

[8] A simple average is computed as the sum of the beginning and ending balances divided by 2. For a company's *first* period of operations, the owner's initial investment is often used as the beginning balance (as it is here).

multiplying by the 12 months in a year, or 132%.) For further comparison, the table in the margin shows the return on equity for different industries.

Three additional points are important. First, an evaluation of returns should recognize risk. Risk can differ considerably across investment alternatives. Second, income can vary from month to month. Income variation is related to risk. Third, because of company, business, and economic fluctuations, a better measure of return is obtained by computing it over a longer period such as one year.

Point: Return on equity for selected industries follows:
Motion pictures 17.5%
Eating and drinking 17.5%
Book publishing 10.4%
Electronic equipment 15.7%
Food stores 13.0%
Department stores 6.8%
Educational services 9.2%

Debt Ratio

Most companies finance a portion of their assets with liabilities and the remaining portion with equity. A company that finances a relatively large portion of its assets with liabilities is said to have a high degree of *financial leverage*. Higher financial leverage involves greater risk because liabilities must be repaid and often require regular interest payments (equity financing does not). The risk that a company might not be able to meet such required payments is higher if it has more liabilities (is more highly leveraged). One way to assess the risk associated with a company's use of liabilities is to analyze the debt ratio. The **debt ratio** reflects the relation between a company's liabilities and its assets and is defined in Exhibit 2.21.

A4   Compute the debt ratio and describe its use in analyzing company performance.

$$\text{Debt ratio} = \frac{\textbf{Total liabilities}}{\textbf{Total assets}}$$

Exhibit 2.21

Debt Ratio

To see how we apply the debt ratio, let's look at Stride Rite's liabilities and assets. Stride Rite makes Keds, Pro-Keds, and other footwear. Exhibit 2.22 computes and reports the debt ratio for the company at the end of each year from 1996 to 2000.

	2000	1999	1998	1997	1996
Total liabilities (in mil.)	$103	$ 96	$ 91	$102	$103
Total assets (in mil.)	$352	$346	$335	$344	$364
Debt ratio	.293	.277	.272	.297	.283
Industry debt ratio*	.48	.46	.52	.59	.64

Exhibit 2.22

Computation and Analysis of Debt Ratio

* Industry debt ratio is the median value from 10 competitors.

Note that Stride Rite's debt ratio is stable over recent years, ranging from a low of .272 to a high of .297. Stride Rite's ratio is low as compared with the industry ratio. Stride Rite reports that it carries no long-term debt, which is unusual. This analysis implies a low risk from financial leverage for Stride Rite. Still, evaluating a company's debt ratio depends on several factors, such as the nature of its operations, its ability to generate cash flows, its industry, and its economic conditions. Saying that a specific debt ratio is good or bad for a company is not possible. Instead, we need to compare performance over time and across companies both inside and outside the industry. In simplest terms, we need to compare the company's return on the money it has borrowed to the rate it is paying creditors. If the company's return is higher, it is successfully borrowing money to make more money. We also must be aware that company returns change over time due to many factors. Accordingly, a company's success with making money from borrowed money can quickly turn unprofitable if its own return declines.

Decision Maker   *d*

Investor   You consider buying stock in Converse. As part of your analysis, you compute its debt ratio for 1998, 1999, and 2000: 1.35, 1.74, and 2.44, respectively.* Based on the debt ratio, is Converse a low-risk investment? Has the risk of buying Converse stock changed over this period?

*Converse's equity is negative for these years because of cumulative losses.

Answer—p. 78

Demonstration Problem

↑

The **Demonstration Problem** is a review of key chapter materials. The Planning the Solution offers strategies in solving the problem.

After several months of planning, Sylvia Workman started a haircutting business called Expressions. The following events occurred during its first month:

a. On August 1, Workman invested $3,000 cash and $15,000 of equipment in Expressions in exchange for common stock.

b. On August 2, Expressions paid $600 cash for furniture for the shop.

c. On August 3, Expressions paid $500 cash to rent space in a strip mall for August.

d. On August 4, it purchased equipment for the shop on credit for $1,200 (using a long-term note payable).

e. On August 5, Expressions opened for business. Cash received from services provided in the first week and a half of business (ended August 15) is $825.

f. On August 15, it provided haircutting services on account for $100.

g. On August 17, it received a $100 check for services previously rendered on account.

h. On August 17, it paid $125 to an assistant for working during the grand opening.

i. Cash received from services provided during the second half of August is $930.

j. On August 31, it paid a $400 installment toward principal on the note payable entered into on August 4.

k. On August 31, it paid $900 cash dividends to Workman.

Required

1. Arrange the following asset, liability, and equity titles in a table similar to the one in Exhibit 2.6: Cash, Accounts Receivable, Furniture, Store Equipment, Note Payable, Common Stock, and Retained Earnings. Show the effects of each transaction using the accounting equation. Add explanations for each of the changes in equity.

2. Prepare general journal entries for the transactions in part 1.

3. Open the following ledger accounts in balance column format (account numbers are in parentheses): Cash (101); Accounts Receivable (102); Furniture (161); Store Equipment (165); Note Payable (240); Common Stock (307); Retained Earnings (318); Haircutting Services Revenue (403); Wages Expense (623); and Rent Expense (640).

4. Post the journal entries from (2) to the ledger accounts from part (3).

5. Prepare a trial balance as of August 31.

6. Prepare an unadjusted income statement for August.

7. Prepare an unadjusted statement of retained earnings for August.

8. Prepare an unadjusted balance sheet as of August 31.

9. Prepare an unadjusted statement of cash flows for August.

10. Determine the return on equity ratio for August and the debt ratio as of August 31.

Extended Analysis

11. In the coming months, Expressions will experience an even greater variety of business transactions. Identify which accounts are debited and which are credited for the following transactions. (*Hint:* You may have to use some accounts not listed in part 3.)

a. Purchase supplies with cash.

b. Pay cash for future insurance coverage.

c. Receive cash for services to be provided in the future.

d. Purchase supplies on account.

Planning the Solution

• Set up a table with the appropriate columns, including a final column for describing the transactions that affect equity.

• Analyze each transaction and show its effects as increases or decreases in the appropriate columns. Be sure the accounting equation remains in balance after each transaction.

• Use the debit and credit rules to prepare a journal entry for each transaction.

• Post each debit and each credit in journal entries to their ledger accounts and cross-reference each amount in the posting reference (PR) columns of the journal and ledger.

- Calculate each account balance and list the accounts with their balances on a trial balance.
- Verify that total debits in the trial balance equal total credits.
- To prepare the unadjusted income statement, identify revenues and expenses. List those items on the statement, compute the difference, and label the result as *net income* or *net loss*.
- Use information in the ledger to prepare the unadjusted statement of retained earnings.
- Use information in the ledger to prepare the unadjusted balance sheet.
- To prepare the unadjusted statement of cash flows, include all events listed in the Cash column of the account. Classify each cash flow as operating, investing, or financing.
- Calculate return on equity by dividing net income by average equity. Calculate the debt ratio by dividing total liabilities by total assets.
- Analyze the future transactions to identify the accounts affected and apply debit and credit rules.

Solution to Demonstration Problem

1.

	Assets				= Liabilities +		Equity	
	Cash	+ Accounts Receivable	+ Furniture	+ Store Equipment	= Note Payable	+ Common Stock	+ Retained Earnings	Explanation of Change
a.	$3,000			$15,000		$18,000		Investment
b.	− 600		+$600					
Bal.	2,400		600	15,000		18,000		
c.	− 500						−$500	Rent Expense
Bal.	1,900		600	15,000		18,000	−500	
d.				+ 1,200	+$1,200			
Bal.	1,900		600	16,200	1,200	18,000	−500	
e.	+ 825						+825	Haircutting Services Revenue
Bal.	2,725		600	16,200	1,200	18,000	325	
f.		+$100					+100	Haircutting Services Revenue
Bal.	2,725	100	600	16,200	1,200	18,000	425	
g.	+ 100	− 100						
Bal.	2,825	0	600	16,200	1,200	18,000	425	
h.	− 125						−125	Wages Expense
Bal.	2,700		600	16,200	1,200	18,000	300	
i.	+ 930						+930	Haircutting Services Revenue
Bal.	3,630		600	16,200	1,200	18,000	1,230	
j.	− 400				− 400			
Bal.	3,230		600	16,200	800	18,000	1,230	
k.	− 900						−900	Withdrawal
Bal.	$2,330 +		+ $600 +	$16,200 =	$800	+ $18,000 +	$330	

2. General journal entries:

Date	General Journal Account Titles and Explanations	PR	Debit	Page 1 Credit
Aug. 1	Cash	101	3,000	
	Store Equipment	165	15,000	
	Common Stock	307		18,000
	Owner's investment.			
2	Furniture	161	600	
	Cash	101		600
	Purchased furniture for cash.			
3	Rent Expense	640	500	
	Cash	101		500
	Paid rent for August.			
4	Store Equipment	165	1,200	
	Note Payable	240		1,200
	Purchased additional equipment on credit.			
15	Cash	101	825	
	Haircutting Services Revenue	403		825
	Cash receipts from 10 days of operations.			
15	Accounts Receivable	102	100	
	Haircutting Services Revenue	403		100
	To record revenue for services provided on account.			
17	Cash	101	100	
	Accounts Receivable	102		100
	To record cash received as payment on account.			
17	Wages Expense	623	125	
	Cash	101		125
	Paid wages to assistant.			
31	Cash	101	930	
	Haircutting Services Revenue	403		930
	Cash receipts from second half of August.			
31	Note Payable	240	400	
	Cash	101		400
	Paid an installment on the note payable.			
31	Retained Earnings	318	900	
	Cash	101		900
	Paid cash dividend to owner.			

3. & 4. Open ledger accounts and post journal entries from (2):

Date		Cash Explanation	PR	Debit	Account No. 101 Credit	Balance
Aug.	1		G1	3,000		3,000
	2		G1		600	2,400
	3		G1		500	1,900
	15		G1	825		2,725
	17		G1	100		2,825
	17		G1		125	2,700
	31		G1	930		3,630
	31		G1		400	3,230
	31		G1		900	2,330

3. & 4. (continued)

		Accounts Receivable			Account No. 102	
Date		Explanation	PR	Debit	Credit	Balance
Aug.	15		G1	100		100
	17		G1		100	0

		Furniture			Account No. 161	
Date		Explanation	PR	Debit	Credit	Balance
Aug.	2		G1	600		600

		Store Equipment			Account No. 165	
Date		Explanation	PR	Debit	Credit	Balance
Aug.	1		G1	15,000		15,000
	4		G1	1,200		16,200

		. . . . .Note PayableAccount No. 240				
Date		Explanation	PR	Debit	Credit	Balance
Aug.	4		G1		1,200	1,200
	31		G1	400		800

		Common Stock			Account No. 307	
Date		Explanation	PR	Debit	Credit	Balance
Aug.	1		G1		18,000	18,000

		Retained Earnings			Account No. 318	
Date		Explanation	PR	Debit	Credit	Balance
Aug.	31		G1	900		900

		Haircutting Services Revenue			Account No. 403	
Date		Explanation	PR	Debit	Credit	Balance
Aug.	15		G1		825	825
	15		G1		100	925
	31		G1		930	1,855

		Wages Expense			Account No. 623	
Date		Explanation	PR	Debit	Credit	Balance
Aug.	17		G1	125		125

		Rent Expense			Account No. 640	
Date		Explanation	PR	Debit	Credit	Balance
Aug.	3		G1	500		500

5. Prepare a trial balance (unadjusted) from the ledger:

EXPRESSIONS Trial Balance August 31	Debit	Credit
Cash	$ 2,330	
Accounts receivable	0	
Furniture	600	
Store equipment	16,200	
Note payable		$ 800
Common stock		18,000
Retained earnings	900	
Haircutting services revenue		1,855
Wages expense	125	
Rent expense	500	
Totals	$20,655	$20,655

6.

EXPRESSIONS Unadjusted Income Statement For Month Ended August 31		
Revenues:		
Haircutting services revenue		$1,855
Operating expenses:		
Rent expense	$500	
Wages expense	125	
Total operating expenses		625
Net Income		$1,230

7.

EXPRESSIONS Unadjusted Statement of Retained Earnings For Month Ended August 31	
Retained earnings, August 1	$ 0
Plus: Net income	1,230
	$1,230
Less: Cash dividend to owner	(900)
Retained earnings, August 31	$ 330

8.

EXPRESSIONS Unadjusted Balance Sheet August 31			
Assets		**Liabilities**	
Cash	$ 2,330	Note payable	$ 800
Furniture	600	**Equity**	
Store equipment	16,200	Common stock	18,000
Total assets	$19,130	Retained earnings	330
		Total liabilities and equity	$19,130

9.

EXPRESSIONS Unadjusted Statement of Cash Flows For Month Ended August 31		
Cash flows from operating activities:		
Cash received from customers	$1,855	
Cash paid for rent	(500)	
Cash paid for wages	(125)	
Net cash provided by operating activities		$1,230
Cash flows from investing activities:		
Cash paid for furniture		(600)
Cash flows from financing activities:		
Cash from stock issuance	3,000	
Cash paid for dividends	(900)	
Partial repayment of long-term note payable	(400)	
Net cash provided by financing activities		1,700
Net increase in cash		$2,330
Cash balance, August 1		0
Cash balance, August 31		$2,330

10. $\text{Return on equity} = \dfrac{\text{Net income}}{\text{Average equity}} = \dfrac{\$1,230}{(\$18,000^* + \$18,330)/2} = \dfrac{\$1,230}{\$18,165} = \underline{\underline{6.77\%}}$

*Uses the initial $18,000 investment for the start-up period.

$\text{Debt ratio} = \dfrac{\text{Total liabilities}}{\text{Total assets}} = \dfrac{\$800}{\$19,130} = \underline{\underline{4.18\%}}$

11a. Supplies debited
      Cash credited

11b. Prepaid Insurance debited
      Cash credited

11c. Cash debited
      Unearned Services Revenue credited

11d. Supplies debited
      Accounts Payable credited

Summary

C1 Explain the financial reporting environment. Accounting professionals prepare financial statements, independent auditors often examine them and prepare an audit report, and users rely on them to make important decisions. Preparers use GAAP, and auditors are guided by GAAS. Applying both GAAP and GAAS helps ensure that financial statements include relevant, reliable, and comparable information. The FASB is the primary authoritative source of GAAP. It draws authority from two major sources: the SEC and state boards that license CPAs.

C2 Identify, explain, and apply accounting principles. Accounting principles aid in producing relevant, reliable, and comparable information. The business entity principle means that a business is accounted for separately from its owner(s). The objectivity principle means independent, objective evidence supports the information. The cost principle means financial statements are based on actual costs incurred. The monetary unit principle assumes transactions can be captured in money terms. The going-concern principle means financial statements assume the business will continue. The revenue recognition principle means revenue is recognized when earned.

C3 Explain the steps in processing transactions. The accounting process captures business transactions and events, analyzes and records their effects, and summarizes and prepares information useful in making decisions. Transactions and events are the starting points in the accounting process. Source documents help in their analysis. The effects of transactions and events are recorded in journals. Posting along with a trial balance helps summarize and classify these effects.

C4 Describe source documents and their purpose. Source documents identify and describe transactions and events. Examples are sales tickets, checks, purchase orders, bills, and bank statements. Source documents provide objective and reliable evidence, making information more useful.

C5 **Describe an account and its use in recording transactions.** An account is a detailed record of increases and decreases in a specific asset, liability, equity, revenue, or expense. Information from accounts is analyzed, summarized, and presented in reports and financial statements for decision makers.

C6 **Describe a ledger and a chart of accounts.** The ledger (or general ledger) is a record containing all accounts used by a company and their balances. This is referred to as the *books*. The chart of accounts is a list of all accounts and usually includes an identification number assigned to each account.

C7 **Define debits and credits and explain their role in double-entry accounting.** *Debit* refers to left, and *credit* refers to right. Debits increase assets and expenses, while credits decrease them. Credits increase liabilities, common stock, retained earnings, and revenues; debits decrease them. Double-entry accounting means each transaction affects at least two accounts and has at least one debit and one credit. The system for recording debits and credits follows from the accounting equation. The left side of an account is the normal balance for assets and expenses, and the right side is the normal balance for liabilities, equity, and revenues.

A1 **Analyze business transactions using the accounting equation.** A transaction is an exchange of economic consideration between two parties. Examples include exchanges of products, services, money, and rights to collect money. Transactions always have at least two effects on one or more components of the accounting equation which follows: Assets = Liabilities + Equity. This equation is always in balance.

A2 **Analyze the impact of transactions on accounts and financial statements.** We analyze transactions using concepts of double-entry accounting. This analysis is performed by determining a transaction's effects on accounts. These effects are recorded in journals and posted to ledgers.

A3 **Compute return on equity and use it to analyze company performance.** Return on equity is computed as net income divided by average equity. It reflects a company's profitability from the owners' perspectives.

A4 **Compute the debt ratio and describe its use in analyzing company performance.** A company's debt ratio is computed as total liabilities divided by total assets. It reveals how much of the assets are financed by creditor (nonowner) financing. The higher this ratio, the more risk a company faces because liabilities must be repaid at specific dates.

P1 **Record transactions in a journal and post entries to a ledger.** Transactions are recorded in a journal. Each entry in a journal is posted to the accounts in the ledger. This provides information that is used to produce financial statements. Balance column accounts are widely used and include columns for debits, credits, and the account balance.

P2 **Prepare and explain the use of a trial balance.** A trial balance is a list of accounts from the ledger showing their debit or credit balances in separate columns. The trial balance is a summary of the ledger's contents and is useful in preparing financial statements and in revealing recordkeeping errors.

P3 **Prepare unadjusted financial statements from business transactions.** Transactions can be summarized using the accounting equation from which we can prepare financial statements. The balance sheet uses the ending balances in the accounting equation. The statement of retained earnings and the income statement use data from the Equity column for the period. The statement of cash flows uses data from the Cash column.

Guidance Answers to **Decision Maker** and **Decision Ethics**

Cashier   The advantages to the process proposed by the assistant manager include improved customer service, fewer delays, and less work for you. However, you should have serious concerns about internal control and the potential for fraud. In particular, the assistant manager could steal cash and simply enter fewer sales to match the remaining cash. You should reject her suggestion without the manager's approval. Moreover, you should have an ethical concern about the assistant manager's suggestion to ignore store policy.

Entrepreneur   We can use the accounting equation (Assets = Liabilities + Equity) to help us identify risky customers to whom we would likely not want to extend credit. A balance sheet provides amounts for each of these key components. The lower a customer's equity is relative to liabilities, the less likely you would extend credit. A low equity means the business has little value that does not already have creditor claims to it.

Venture Capitalist   The return on equity is relevant for your decision. This return equals 0.5%, computed as $2,000/$400,000. This is about 6% per year, approximated as 0.5% × 12 months. You would not likely take the risk of a new business for an expected return of 6% per year.

Investor   The debt ratio suggests the stock of Converse is of higher risk than normal and that this risk is rising. Industry ratios reported in Exhibit 2.22 further support this conclusion. The debt ratio for Converse is five times the industry norm of 0.48. Also, a debt ratio larger than 1.0 indicates negative equity. Excessive cumulative losses for Converse led to its negative equity.

Guidance Answers to **Quick Checks**

1. The FASB is the primary organization that sets GAAP. Its decisions are reflected in its *Statements of Financial Accounting Standards*. The FASB draws authority from two main sources: the SEC and state boards that license CPAs.

2. *GAAS* stands for "generally accepted auditing standards"; these are the guidelines for performing audits of financial statements. GAAS are set by the Auditing Standards Board.

3. U.S. companies are not directly affected by international accounting standards. International standards are put forth as preferred accounting practices. However, stock exchanges and other parties are increasing the pressure to narrow differences in worldwide accounting practices. International accounting standards are playing an important role in that process.

4. Users desire information about the performance of a specific entity. If information is mixed between two or more entities, its usefulness decreases.

5. The objectivity and cost principles are related in that most users consider information based on cost as objective. Information prepared using both principles is considered highly reliable and often relevant.

6. External transactions are exchanges of economic consideration between an organization and some other entity. Internal transactions are exchanges within an organization, for example, a company using equipment in its operations.

7. Examples of source documents are sales tickets, checks, purchase orders, charges to customers, bills from suppliers, employee earnings records, and bank statements.

8. Source documents serve many purposes, including recordkeeping and internal control. Source documents, especially if obtained from outside the organization, provide objective and reliable evidence about transactions and their amounts.

9. A transaction that changes the makeup of assets would not affect liability and equity accounts. Transactions 2 and 3 of FastForward are examples. Each exchanges one asset for another.

10. Earning revenue by performing services, such as in FastForward's transaction 5, increases equity (and assets). Incurring expenses while servicing clients, such as in transactions 6 and 7, decreases equity (and assets). Other examples include owner investments that increase equity and withdrawals (dividends) that decrease equity.

11. The revenue recognition principle gives preparers guidelines on when to recognize (record) revenue. This is important; for example, if revenue is recognized too early, the income statement reports revenue sooner than it should and the business looks more profitable than it is. The reverse is also true.

12. Paying a liability with an asset reduces both asset and liability totals. One example is transaction 10 of FastForward, where a payable is reduced by paying cash.

13. The accounting equation is: Assets = Liabilities + Equity. This equation is always in balance, both before and after every transaction.

14.

Assets	Liabilities	Equity
a,c,e	b,d	—

15. An account is a record in an accounting system that records and stores the increases and decreases in a specific asset, liability, equity, revenue, or expense. The ledger is a collection of all the accounts of a company.

16. A company's size and diversity affect the number of accounts in its accounting system. The types of accounts depend on information the company needs to both effectively operate and report its activities in financial statements.

17. No. Debit and credit both can mean increase or decrease. The particular meaning in a circumstance depends on the *type of account*. For example, a debit increases the balance of asset and expense accounts, but it decreases the balance of liability, equity, and revenue accounts.

18. Equity is increased by revenues and by owners' investments. Equity is decreased by expenses and dividends.

19. The name *double entry* is used because all transactions affect at least two accounts. There must be at least one debit in one account and at least one credit in another account.

20. Answer is (*c*).

21.

Cash	15,000	
Equipment	23,000	
Common Stock		38,000
Investment by owner of cash and equipment.		

22. A compound journal entry affects three or more accounts.

23. Posting reference numbers are entered in the journal when posting to the ledger as a cross-reference that allows the recordkeeper or auditor to trace debits and credits from one record to another.

24. A chart of accounts is a list of all of a company's accounts and their identification numbers.

25. At a minimum, dollar signs are placed beside the first and last numbers in a column. It is also common to place dollar signs beside any amount that appears after a ruled line to indicate that an addition or subtraction has occurred.

26. The Equipment account balance is incorrectly reported at $20,000—it should be $28,000. The effect of this error understates the trial balance's Debit column total by $8,000. This results in an $8,000 difference between the column totals.

27. An income statement reports a company's revenues and expenses along with the resulting net income or loss. A statement of retained earnings reports changes in retained earnings, including that from net income or loss. Both statements report transactions occurring over a period of time.

28. The balance sheet describes a company's financial position (assets, liabilities, and equity) at a point in time. The retained earnings account in the balance sheet is obtained from the statement of retained earnings.

29. Cash flows from operating activities report cash receipts and payments from the primary business the company is engaged in. Cash flows from investing activities involve cash transactions from buying and selling long-term assets. Cash flows from financing activities include long-term cash borrowings and repayments from lenders and the cash investments and withdrawals (dividends) of the owners.

30. The four major financial statements are income statement, balance sheet, statement of retained earnings, and statement of cash flows.

31. Revenues are inflows of assets in exchange for products or services provided to customers as part of the main operations of a business. Expenses are outflows or the using up of assets that result from providing products or services to customers.

32. Assets are the resources a business owns or controls that carry expected future benefits. Liabilities are the obligations of a business, representing the claims of others against the assets of a business. Equity reflects the owners' claims on the assets of the business after deducting liabilities.

Glossary

Account A record within an accounting system where increases and decreases in a specific asset, liability, equity, revenue, or expense are entered and stored. (p. 42)

Account balance The difference between total debits and total credits (including the beginning balance) for an account. (p. 53)

Accounting equation Relation between a company's assets, liabilities, and equity; Assets = Liabilities + Equity; also called *balance sheet equation*. (p. 46)

Assets Resources a business owns or controls that are expected to provide future benefits to the business. (p. 43)

Balance column account An account with debit and credit columns for recording entries and another column for showing the balance of the account after each entry. (p. 56)

Balance sheet Financial statement that lists the types and amounts of assets, liabilities, and equity at a specific date; also called *statement of financial position*. (p. 68)

Balance sheet equation (See *accounting equation*.) (p. 46)

Business entity principle The principle that requires a business to be accounted for separately from its owner(s). (p. 40)

Chart of accounts A list of accounts used by a company; includes an identification number for each account. (p. 53)

Common stock Category of equity created by shareholders' investments. (p. 46)

Compound journal entry A journal entry that affects at least three accounts. (p. 59)

Cost principle The accounting principle that requires financial statement information to be based on actual costs incurred in business transactions. (p. 40)

Credit Recorded on the right side; an entry that decreases asset and expense accounts, and increases liability, equity, and revenue accounts; abbreviated Cr. (p. 53)

Creditors Individuals or organizations entitled to receive payments. (p. 44)

Debit Recorded on the left side; an entry that increases asset and expense accounts, and decreases liability, equity, and revenue accounts; abbreviated Dr. (p. 53)

Debtors Individuals or organizations that owe money. (p. 43)

Debt ratio Ratio of total liabilities to total assets; used to reflect risk associated with a company's debts. (p. 71)

Dividends A corporation's distributions of assets to its owners. (p. 46)

Double-entry accounting An accounting system in which each transaction affects at least two accounts and has at least one debit and one credit. (p. 54)

Equity The owners' claim on the assets of a business; equals the residual interest in an entity's assets after deducting liabilities; also called *net assets*. (p. 45)

Events Happenings that both affect an organization's financial position and can be reliably measured. (p. 41)

Expenses Outflows or the using up of assets as part of operations of a business to generate sales. (p. 68)

External transactions Exchanges of economic consideration between one entity and another entity. (p. 41)

General journal An all-purpose journal for recording the debits and credits of transactions and events. (p. 55)

Generally accepted auditing standards (GAAS) Rules adopted for conducting audits of financial statements. (p. 38)

Going-concern principle A principle that requires financial statements to reflect the assumption that the business will continue operating. (p. 40)

Income statement Financial statement that subtracts expenses from revenues to yield a net income or loss over a specified period of time. (p. 68)

Internal transactions Activities within an organization that can affect the accounting equation. (p. 41)

International Accounting Standards Board (IASB) A group that identifies preferred accounting practices and encourages global acceptance. (p. 39)

Journal A record where transactions are recorded before they are posted to ledger accounts. (p. 55)

Journalizing Process of recording transactions in a journal. (p. 55)

Ledger Record containing all accounts (with amounts) for a business also called *general ledger*. (p. 42)

Liabilities Claims by others that will reduce the future assets of a business or require services or products. (p. 44)

Monetary unit principle A principle that assumes transactions and events can be expressed in money units. (p. 40)

Net assets (See *equity*.) (p. 45)

Net income The excess of revenues over expenses for a period. (p. 68)

Net loss The excess of expenses over revenues for a period. (p. 68)

Objectivity principle A principle that requires financial statement information to be supported by independent, unbiased evidence. (p. 40)

Posting Process of transferring journal information to the ledger. (p. 55)

Posting reference (PR) column A column in journals where ledger account numbers are entered when entries are posted to those ledger accounts. (p. 56)

Retained earnings A corporation's accumulated net income and losses that have not been distributed (in dividends) to shareholders. (p. 46)

Return on equity Ratio of net income to average equity. (p. 70)

Revenue recognition principle The principle that revenue is recognized when earned. (p. 49)

Revenues Inflows of assets received in exchange for goods or services provided to customers as part of operations. (p. 68)

Source documents The source of information for accounting entries that can be in either paper or electronic form; also called *business papers*. (p. 42)

Statement of cash flows A financial statement that lists cash inflows (receipts) and cash outflows (payments) during a period; arranged by operating, investing, and financing. (p. 69)

Statement of retained earnings A report of changes in retained earnings over a period; adjusted for increases (owner investment and net income) and for decreases (dividends and net loss). (p. 68)

Statements of Financial Accounting Standards (SFAS) FASB publications that establish U.S. GAAP. (p. 38)

T-account A tool used to show the effects of transactions and events on individual accounts. (p. 54)

Trial balance List of accounts and their balances at a point in time; total debit balances equal total credit balances. (p. 63)

Unearned revenue A liability created when customers pay in advance for products or services; earned when the products or services are later delivered. (p. 45)

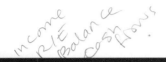

Questions

1. Identify the four main financial statements of a business.
2. What information is reported in an income statement?
3. What do accountants mean by the term *revenue?*
4. Why does the user of an income statement need to know the time period that it covers?
5. Give two examples of expenses a business might incur.
6. Which financial statement is sometimes called the *statement of financial position?*
7. What information is reported in a balance sheet?
8. Define (*a*) assets, (*b*) liabilities, (*c*) equity, and (*d*) net assets.
9. The statement of cash flows reports on what major activities?
10. What FASB pronouncements make up generally accepted accounting principles?
11. Identify two categories of accounting principles.
12. What does the objectivity principle require for information reported in financial statements? Why?
13. A business reports its own office stationery on the balance sheet at its $430 cost, although it cannot be sold for more than $10 as scrap paper. Which accounting principle justifies this treatment?
14. Why is the revenue recognition principle needed? What does it require?
15. What events or transactions change equity?
16. To what should a company's return on equity ratio be compared with to determine whether it is successful?
17. Refer to the financial statements of Nike in Appendix A. To what level of significance are the dollar amounts rounded? What time period does the income statement cover?
18. Review the balance sheet of Reebok in Appendix A. What amount of total assets is re-

ported at December 31, 1999? Prove the accounting equation for Reebok at December 31, 1999.

19. Refer to Gap's income statement in Appendix A. How does the name of this statement differ from FastForward's income statement? How does Gap's 2000 net income compare to its previous year?
20. What is the difference between a note payable and an account payable?
21. Provide the names of two (*a*) asset accounts, (*b*) liability accounts, and (*c*) equity accounts.
22. Discuss the steps in processing business transactions.
23. Are debits or credits typically listed first in general journal entries? Are the debits or the credits indented?
24. What kinds of transactions can be recorded in a general journal?
25. Should a transaction be recorded first in a journal or the ledger? Why?
26. If assets are valuable resources and asset accounts have debit balances, why do expense accounts have debit balances?
27. Why does the recordkeeper prepare a trial balance?
28. Review the Nike balance sheet in Appendix A. Identify three accounts on the balance sheet that carry debit balances and three accounts on the balance sheet that carry credit balances.
29. Review the Reebok balance sheet in Appendix A. Identify three different liability accounts that include the word *payable* in the account title.
30. Locate Gap's income statement in Appendix A. What is the name of its revenue account?
31. If a wrong amount is journalized and posted to the accounts, how should the error be corrected?

QUICK STUDY

QS 2-1

Identifying accounting principles

C2

Identify which general accounting principle best describes each of the following practices:

a. Le Ann Welch owns Sailing Passions and Dockside Supplies, both of which are corporations. In preparing financial statements for Dockside Supplies, Welch makes sure that the expense transactions of Sailing Passions are kept separate from Dockside's statements.

b. In December 2001, Renew-A-Floor received a customer's order to install carpet in a new house that would not be ready for installation until March 2002. Renew-A-Floor should record the revenue from the customer order in March 2002, not in December 2001.

c. If $40,000 cash is paid to buy land, the land is reported on the buyer's balance sheet at $40,000.

QS 2-2

Identifying source documents

C4

Select items from the following list that are likely to serve as source documents:

a. Bank statement   **d.** Trial balance   **g.** Company revenue account

b. Sales ticket   **e.** Telephone bill   **h.** Balance sheet

c. Income statement   **f.** Invoice from supplier

QS 2-3

Identifying financial statement items

C5

Identify the financial statement(s) where each of the following items appears:

a. Service fees earned   **d.** Accounts payable   **g.** Office supplies

b. Cash dividends   **e.** Cash (principal) repaid on loan **h.** Cash from prior period credit sale

c. Office equipment   **f.** Utilities expenses

QS 2-4

Linking debit or credit with normal balance

C7

Indicate whether a debit or credit *decreases* the normal balance of each of the following accounts:

a. Office Supplies   **e.** Salaries Expense   **h.** Buildings

b. Repair Services Revenue   **f.** Common Stock   **i.** Interest Revenue

c. Interest Payable   **g.** Prepaid Insurance   **j.** Retained Earnings

d. Accounts Receivable

QS 2-5

Analyzing debit or credit by account

C7

Identify whether a debit or credit yields the indicated change for each of the following accounts:

a. To increase Store Equipment   **f.** To decrease Unearned Revenue

b. To increase Retained Earnings   **g.** To decrease Prepaid Insurance

c. To decrease Cash   **h.** To increase Notes Payable

d. To increase Utilities Expense   **i.** To decrease Accounts Receivable

e. To increase Fees Earned   **j.** To increase Common Stock

QS 2-6

Preparing journal entries

P1

Prepare journal entries for each of the following selected transactions:

a. On January 13, Bella Woods opens a landscaping business called Showcase Yards by investing $70,000 cash along with equipment having a $30,000 value in exchange for common stock.

b. On January 21, Showcase Yards purchases office supplies on credit for $280.

c. On January 29, Showcase Yards receives $7,800 cash for performing landscaping services.

d. On January 30, Showcase Yards receives $1,000 cash in advance of providing landscaping services to a customer.

QS 2-7

Identifying a posting error

P2

A trial balance has total debits of $20,000 and total credits of $24,500. Which one of the following errors would create this imbalance? Explain.

a. A $2,250 debit to Rent Expense in a journal entry is incorrectly posted to the ledger as a $2,250 credit, leaving the Rent Expense account with a $3,000 debit balance.

b. A $4,500 debit to Salaries Expense in a journal entry is incorrectly posted to the ledger as a $4,500 credit, leaving the Salaries Expense account with a $750 debit balance.

c. A $2,250 credit to Consulting Fees Earned in a journal entry is incorrectly posted to the ledger as a $2,250 debit, leaving the Consulting Fees Earned account with a $6,300 credit balance.

QS 2-8

Applying the accounting equation

A1

Use the accounting equation in the following separate cases to determine the:

a. Equity in a business that has $195,000 of assets and $23,000 of liabilities.

b. Liabilities of a business having $162,400 of assets and $122,900 of equity.

c. Assets of a business having $32,890 of liabilities and $134,655 of equity.

Indicate the financial statement on which each of the following items appears. Use I for income statement, E for statement of retained earnings, and B for balance sheet:

a. Office Supplies   *B*
b. Services Revenue   *I*
c. Interest Payable   *B*
d. Accounts Receivable   *B*

e. Salaries Expense   *I*
f. Equipment   *B*
g. Prepaid Insurance   *B*

h. Buildings   *B*
i. Interest Revenue   *I*
j. Dividends   *R/E*

QS 2-9
Classifying accounts in financial statements

A2

In a recent year's financial statements, Boeing Company, which is the largest aerospace company in the United States, reported the following. Calculate Boeing's return on equity.

Sales	$57,993 million
Net income	2,309 million
Total assets	36,147 million
Total beginning-of-year equity	12,316 million
Total end-of-year equity	11,462 million

QS 2-10
Computing return on equity

A3

$\frac{2,309}{12,316 + 11,462} \cdot 2$

Match each of the following numbered descriptions with the principle it best reflects. Indicate your answer by writing the letter for the appropriate principle in the blank space next to each description.

A. General accounting principle
B. Cost principle
C. Business entity principle
D. Revenue recognition principle

E. Specific accounting principle
F. Objectivity principle
G. Going-concern principle

EXERCISES

Exercise 2-1
Identifying accounting principles

C1 C2

___*E*___ 1. Usually created by a pronouncement from an authoritative body.
___*G*___ 2. Requires financial statements to reflect the assumption that the business continues operating.
___*A*___ 3. Derived from long-used and generally accepted accounting practices.
___*F*___ 4. Requires financial statement information to be supported by evidence other than someone's opinion or belief.
___*C*___ 5. Requires every business to be accounted for separately from its owner or owners.
___*D*___ 6. Requires revenue to be recorded only when the earnings process is complete.
___*B*___ 7. Requires information to be based on costs incurred in transactions.

For each of the following (1) identify the type of account as an asset, liability, equity, revenue, or expense, (2) enter debit (Dr.) or credit (Cr.) to identify the kind of entry that would increase the account balance, and (3) identify the normal balance of the account.

a. Unearned Revenue *liab CR*
b. Accounts Payable *liab CR*
c. Postage Expense *exp DR*
d. Prepaid Insurance *Asset DR*

e. Land *Asset DR*
f. Common Stock *Equ CR*
g. Accounts Receivable *Asset DR*
h. Retained Earnings *Equ CR*

i. Cash *Asset DR*
j. Equipment *liab CR*
k. Fees Earned *rev DR*
l. Wages Expense *exp CR DR*

Exercise 2-2
Identifying type and normal balances of accounts

C5 C7

Sarah Wells began a new consulting firm on January 5. The accounting equation showed the following balances after each of the company's first five transactions. Analyze the accounting equation for each transaction and describe each of the five transactions with their amounts.

Exercise 2-3
Analysis using the accounting equation

A1

invested cash in exchange for common stock

	Assets				= Liabilities +	Equity	
Transaction	Cash	+ Accounts Receivable	+ Office Supplies	+ Office Furniture	= Accounts Payable	+ Common Stock	+ Retained Earnings
a.	$20,000	$ 0	$ 0	$ 0	$ 0	$20,000	$ 0
b.	19,000	0	1,500	0	500	20,000	0
c.	11,000	0	1,500	8,000	500	20,000	0
d.	11,000	3,000	1,500	8,000	500	20,000	3,000
e.	11,500	3,000	1,500	8,000	500	20,000	500

Exercise 2-4
Identifying effects of
transactions on the
accounting equation

A1 A2

Provide an example of a transaction that creates the described effects for the separate cases *a* through *g*.

a. Decreases an asset and decreases equity.
b. Increases an asset and increases a liability.
c. Decreases a liability and increases a liability.
d. Decreases an asset and decreases a liability.

e. Increases an asset and decreases an asset.
f. Increases a liability and decreases equity.
g. Increases an asset and increases equity.

Exercise 2-5
Identifying effects of
transactions on accounting
equation

A1

The following table shows the effects of five transactions (*a* through *e*) on the assets, liabilities, and equity of Benton Boutique. Write short descriptions of the probable nature of each transaction.

	Assets				=	Liabilities +	Equity	
	Cash	+ Accounts Receivable	+ Office Supplies	+ Land	=	Accounts Payable	+ Common Stock	+ Retained Earnings
	$10,500		$1,500	$ 9,500			$21,500	
a.	− 2,000			+ 2,000				
b.			+ 500			+$500		
c.		+$950						+950
d.	− 500					− 500		
e.	+ 950	−950						
	$ 8,950 +	$ 0	+ $2,000	+ $11,500	=	$ 0	+ $21,500	+ $950

Exercise 2-6
Analyzing effects of
transactions on accounts

A2

Fitterling Co. recently notified a client that it would have to pay a $62,000 fee for services. Fitterling agreed to accept the following three items in full payment: (1) $10,000 cash, (2) computer equipment worth $80,000, and (3) assumed responsibility for a $28,000 note payable related to the computer equipment. The entry Fitterling makes to record this transaction includes which one or more of the following items?

a. $28,000 increase in a liability account
b. $10,000 increase in the Cash account
c. $10,000 increase in a revenue account

d. $62,000 increase in an asset account
e. $62,000 increase in a revenue account

Exercise 2-7
Recording effects of
transactions in T-accounts

A2

Record the transactions below for Dejonge Company by recording the debit and credit entries directly in the following T-accounts: Cash; Accounts Receivable; Office Supplies; Office Equipment; Accounts Payable; Common Stock; Retained Earnings; Fees Earned; and Rent Expense. Use the letters beside each transaction to identify entries. Determine the ending balance of each T-account.

a. Robert Dejonge invested $13,325 cash in the business in exchange for common stock.
b. Purchased office supplies for $475 cash.
c. Purchased $6,235 of office equipment on credit.
d. Received $2,000 cash as fees for services provided to a customer.
e. Paid cash to settle the payable for the office equipment purchased in transaction *c*.
f. Billed a customer $3,300 as fees for services provided.
g. Paid the monthly rent with $775 cash.
h. Collected $2,300 cash toward the account receivable created in transaction *f*.
i. Dejonge Company paid $800 cash for dividends.

Exercise 2-8
Preparing a trial balance **P2**

After recording the transactions of Exercise 2-7 in T-accounts and calculating the balance of each account, prepare a trial balance. Use May 31, 2002, as its date.

Exercise 2-9
Analyzing account entries
and balances

A2

Use the information in each of the following separate cases to calculate the unknown amount:

1. During October, Rightlane Company had $102,500 of cash receipts and $103,150 of cash disbursements. The October 31 Cash balance was $18,600. Determine how much cash the company had at the close of business on September 30.

2. On September 30, Rightlane had a $102,500 balance in Accounts Receivable. During October, the company collected $102,890 from its credit customers. The October 31 balance in Accounts Receivable was $89,000. Determine the amount of sales on account that occurred in October.

3. Rightlane had $152,000 of accounts payable on September 30 and $132,500 on October 31. Total purchases on account during October were $281,000. Determine how much cash was paid on accounts payable during October.

Mary Campion began a professional practice on June 1 and plans to prepare financial statements at the end of each month. During June, Campion completed these transactions:

a. Invested $60,000 cash along with equipment that had an $8,000 market value in exchange for common stock.

b. Paid $1,500 cash for rent of office space for the month.

c. Purchased $15,000 of additional equipment on credit.

d. Completed work for a client and immediately collected the $1,000 cash earned.

e. Completed work for a client and sent a bill for $6,000 to be paid within 30 days.

f. Purchased additional equipment for $5,000 cash.

g. Paid an assistant $2,700 cash as wages for the month.

h. Collected $4,000 cash on the amount owed by the client described in transaction *e*.

i. Paid cash for the equipment purchased in transaction *c*.

j. Paid $900 cash in dividends.

Exercise 2-10
Identifying effects of transactions on the accounting equation and computing return on equity

A1 A3

Required

Create a table like the one in Exhibit 2.6, using the following headings for columns: Cash; Accounts Receivable; Equipment; Accounts Payable; Common Stock; and Retained Earnings. Then use additions and subtractions to show the effects of the transactions on individual items of the accounting equation. Show new balances after each transaction. Determine the return on equity for Campion's business assuming a beginning equity balance of $68,000.

Check Net income, $2,800; return on equity, 4.06%

Prepare general journal entries for the following transactions of a new business called Click and Shoot.

Aug. 1   Hannah Hicks, the owner, invested $6,500 cash and $33,500 of photography equipment in the business in exchange for common stock.
  1   Paid $2,100 cash for an insurance policy covering the next two years.
  5   Purchased office supplies for $880 cash.
  20   Received $3,331 cash in photography fees earned.
  31   Paid $675 cash for August utilities.

Exercise 2-11
Preparing general journal entries

A2 P1

Use the information provided in Exercise 2-11 to prepare an August 31 trial balance for Click and Shoot. Open these T-accounts: Cash; Office Supplies; Prepaid Insurance; Photography Equipment; Common Stock; Photography Fees Earned; and Utilities Expense. Post the general journal entries to T-accounts (which will serve as the ledger), and prepare a trial balance.

Exercise 2-12
Preparing T-accounts and a trial balance **P2**

Examine the following transactions and identify those that create revenues for Stout Services, a corporation owned by David Stout. Prepare general journal entries to record those transactions and explain why the other transactions did not create revenues.

a. David Stout invests $39,350 cash in the business in exchange for common stock. N

b. Provided $2,300 of services on credit. R

c. Provided services to a client and received $875 cash. R

d. Received $10,200 cash from a client in payment for services to be provided next year. L (UR)

e. Received $3,500 cash from a client in partial payment of an account receivable. R

f. Borrowed $120,000 cash from the bank by signing a promissory note. N

Exercise 2-13
Analyzing and journalizing revenue transactions

A2 P1

Examine the following transactions and identify those that create expenses for Stout Services. Prepare general journal entries to record those transactions and explain why the other transactions did not create expenses.

a. Paid $12,200 cash for office supplies purchased 13 months previously.

b. Paid $1,233 cash for the two-week salary of the receptionist.

c. Paid $39,200 cash for equipment.

d. Paid utility bill with $870 cash.

e. Paid $4,500 cash dividends to the owner.

Exercise 2-14
Analyzing and journalizing expense transactions

A2 P1

Exercise 2-15
Preparing an income
statement

P3

Check Net income, $2,110

On October 1, Bernice Haddox organized a new consulting firm called Tech Answers. On October 31, the company's records show the following items and amounts. Use this information to prepare an October income statement for the business.

Cash	$11,360	Cash dividends	$ 2,000
Accounts receivable	14,000	Consulting fees earned	14,000
Office supplies	3,250	Rent expense	3,550
Patents	46,000	Salaries expense	7,000
Office equipment	18,000	Telephone expense	760
Accounts payable	8,500	Miscellaneous expenses . . .	580
Stock issued	84,000		

Exercise 2-16
Preparing a statement **P3**
of retained earnings

Use the information in Exercise 2-15 to prepare an October statement of retained earnings for Tech Answers.

Exercise 2-17
Preparing a balance **P3**
sheet

Use the information in Exercise 2-15 (if completed, you can also use your solution to Exercise 2-16) to prepare an October 31 balance sheet for Tech Answers.

Exercise 2-18
Preparing a statement of
cash flows

P3 A2

Check Net increase in cash,
$11,360

Use the information in Exercise 2-15 to prepare an October 31 statement of cash flows for Tech Answers. Also assume the following:

a. The owner's initial investment consists of $38,000 cash and $46,000 in patents for stock.

b. The $18,000 equipment purchase is paid in cash.

c. The accounts payable balance of $8,500 consists of the $3,250 office supplies purchase and $5,250 in employee salaries yet to be paid.

d. The rent, telephone, and miscellaneous expenses are paid in cash.

e. No cash has yet been collected for consulting services provided.

Exercise 2-19
Identifying sections of
statement of cash flows

P3 A2

Indicate the section where each of the following would appear on the statement of cash flows.

A. Cash flows from operating activity

B. Cash flows from investing activity

C. Cash flows from financing activity

_____ **1.** Cash paid for wages	_____ **5.** Cash paid on an account payable
_____ **2.** Cash dividends	_____ **6.** Cash invested by owner for stock
_____ **3.** Cash purchase of equipment	_____ **7.** Cash received from clients
_____ **4.** Cash paid for advertising	_____ **8.** Cash paid for rent

Exercise 2-20 🖉
Computing and interpreting
the debt ratio

A3 A4

1. Calculate the debt ratio and the return on equity using the year-end information for each of the following six separate cases ($ in thousands):

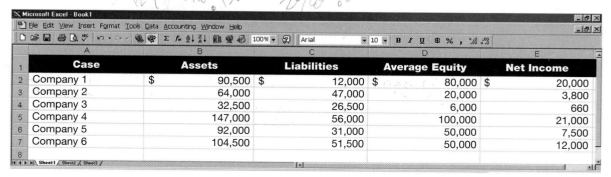

Case	Assets	Liabilities	Average Equity	Net Income
Company 1	$ 90,500	$ 12,000	$ 80,000	$ 20,000
Company 2	64,000	47,000	20,000	3,800
Company 3	32,500	26,500	6,000	660
Company 4	147,000	56,000	100,000	21,000
Company 5	92,000	31,000	50,000	7,500
Company 6	104,500	51,500	50,000	12,000

2. Of the six cases, which business relies most heavily on creditor (nonowner) financing?

3. Of the six cases, which business relies most heavily on equity (owner) financing?

4. Which two companies indicate the greatest risk?

5. Of the six cases, which business yields the greatest return on equity?

6. As an investor, which company would you prefer to invest in based on analysis of the debt ratio and return on equity?

You are told the column totals in a trial balance are not equal. After careful analysis, you discover only one error. Specifically, a correctly journalized credit purchase of a computer for $18,950 is posted from the journal to the ledger with an $18,950 debit to Office Equipment and another $18,950 debit to Accounts Payable. The balance of the Office Equipment account has a debit balance of $37,100 on the trial balance. Answer each of the following questions and compute the dollar amount of any misstatement:

a. Is the debit column total of the trial balance overstated, understated, or correctly stated?

b. Is the credit column total of the trial balance overstated, understated, or correctly stated?

c. Is the balance of the Office Equipment account overstated, understated, or correctly stated in the trial balance?

d. Is the balance of the Accounts Payable account overstated, understated, or correctly stated in the trial balance?

e. If the debit column total of the trial balance is $360,000 before correcting the error, what is the total of the credit column before correction?

Exercise 2-21
Analyzing a trial balance error

A2 P2

The following financial statement information is known about five separate companies:

PROBLEM SET A

Problem 2-1A
Calculating missing information using accounting knowledge

C5 A1 A2

	Company A	Company B	Company C	Company D	Company E
December 31, 2001:					
Assets	$55,000	$34,000	$24,000	$60,000	$119,000
Liabilities	24,500	21,500	9,000	40,000	?
December 31, 2002:					
Assets	58,000	40,000	?	85,000	113,000
Liabilities	?	26,500	29,000	24,000	70,000
During year 2002:					
Stock issuances	6,000	1,400	9,750	?	6,500
Net income	8,500	?	8,000	14,000	20,000
Cash dividends	3,500	2,000	5,875	0	11,000

Required

1. Answer the following questions about Company A:

  a. What is the equity amount on December 31, 2001?

  b. What is the equity amount on December 31, 2002?

  c. What is the amount of liabilities on December 31, 2002?

2. Answer the following questions about Company B:

  a. What is the equity amount on December 31, 2001?

  b. What is the equity amount on December 31, 2002?

  c. What is net income for year 2002?

3. Calculate the amount of assets for Company C on December 31, 2002.

4. Calculate the amount of stock issuances for Company D during year 2002.

5. Calculate the amount of liabilities for Company E on December 31, 2001.

Check   (1*b*) $41,500

Check   (2*c*) $1,600
Check   (3) $55,875

Identify how each of the following separate transactions affects financial statements. For the balance sheet, identify how each transaction affects total assets, total liabilities, and equity. For the income statement, identify how each transaction affects net income. For the statement of cash flows, identify how each transaction affects cash flows from operating activities, cash flows from financing activities, and cash flows from investing activities. For increases, place a "+" in the column or columns. For decreases, place a "−" in the column or columns. If both an increase and a decrease occur, place a "+/−" in the column or columns. The first transaction is completed as an example.

Problem 2-2A
Identifying effects of transactions on financial statements

A1 A2

		Balance Sheet			Income Statement	Statement of Cash Flows		
	Transaction	Total Assets	Total Liab.	Equity	Net Income	Operating Activities	Financing Activities	Investing Activities
1	Owner invests cash for stock	+		+			+	
2	Performs services for cash							
3	Pays wages incurred with cash							
4	Services received on credit							
5	Borrows cash by signing note payable							
6	Pays cash dividend							
7	Buys land by signing note payable							
8	Performs services on credit							
9	Buys office equipment for cash							
10	Collects cash on receivable from (8)							

Problem 2-3A

Analyzing transactions and preparing unadjusted financial statements

C5 A1 P3

J. D. Simpson started a new business called The Simpson Co. that began operations on May 1. Simpson Co. completed the following transactions during that first month:

May 1   Simpson invested $40,000 cash in the business in exchange for common stock.
     1   Rented a furnished office and paid $2,200 cash for May's rent.
     3   Purchased $1,890 of office equipment on credit.
     5   Paid $750 cash for this month's cleaning services.
     8   Provided consulting services for a client and immediately collected $5,400 cash.
   12   Provided $2,500 of consulting services for a client on credit.
   15   Paid $750 cash for an assistant's salary for the first half of this month.
   20   Received $2,500 cash payment for the services provided on May 12.
   22   Provided $3,200 of consulting services on credit.
   28   Received $3,200 cash payment for the services provided on May 22.
   29   Paid $1,890 cash for the office equipment purchased on May 3.
   30   Purchased $80 of advertising in this month's local paper on credit; cash payment is due June 1.
   30   Paid $300 cash for this month's telephone bill.
   30   Paid $280 cash for this month's utilities.
   30   Paid $750 cash for an assistant's salary for the second half of this month.
   30   Paid $1,400 cash for dividends.

Required

1. Arrange the following asset, liability, and equity titles in a table like Exhibit 2.6: Cash; Accounts Receivable; Office Equipment; Accounts Payable; Common Stock; and Retained Earnings. Include an Explanation column for changes in equity.

Check (2) Ending balances: Cash, $42,780; Retained Earnings, $4,590

2. Show effects of the transactions on the accounts of the accounting equation by recording increases and decreases in the appropriate columns. Do not determine new account balances after each transaction. Next to each change in equity, state whether it was caused by an investment, a revenue, an expense, or a dividend. Determine the final total for each account and verify that the equation is in balance.

Check (3) Net income, $5,990; Total assets, $44,670

3. Prepare an unadjusted income statement for May, an unadjusted statement of retained earnings for May, a May 31 unadjusted balance sheet, and an unadjusted statement of cash flows for May.

Problem 2-4A

Analyzing transactions, preparing unadjusted financial statements, and computing return on equity

C5 A1 A2 A3 P3

Curtis Hamilton started a new business and completed these transactions during December:

Dec. 1   Curtis Hamilton transferred $65,000 cash from a personal savings account to a checking account in the name of Hamilton Electric in exchange for common stock.
    2   Rented office space and paid $1,000 cash for the December rent.
    3   Purchased electrical equipment from an electrician who was going out of business for $13,000 by paying $4,800 cash and agreeing to pay the balance in 30 days.

5   Purchased office supplies by paying $800 cash.
6   Completed electrical work and immediately collected $1,200 cash for the work.
8   Purchased $2,530 of office equipment on credit.
15 Completed electrical work on credit in the amount of $5,000.
18 Purchased $350 of office supplies on credit.
20 Paid $2,530 cash for the office equipment purchased on December 8.
24 Billed a client $900 for electrical work completed; the balance is due in 30 days.
28 Received $5,000 cash for the work completed on December 15.
30 Paid the assistant's salary of $1,400 cash for this month.
30 Paid $540 cash for this month's utility bill.
31 Paid $950 cash for dividends.

Required

1. Arrange the following asset, liability, and equity titles in a table like Exhibit 2.6: Cash; Accounts Receivable; Office Supplies; Office Equipment; Electrical Equipment; Accounts Payable; Common Stock; and Retained Earnings. Leave space for an Explanation column to the right of the table.

2. Use additions and subtractions to show the effects of each transaction on the accounts in the accounting equation. Show new balances after each transaction. Next to each change in equity, state whether the change was caused by an investment, a revenue, an expense, or a dividend.

Check   (2) Ending balances: Cash, $59,180; Accounts Payable, $8,550; Retained Earnings, $3,210

3. Use the increases and decreases in the columns of the table from part 2 to prepare an unadjusted income statement, an unadjusted statement of changes in retained earnings, and an unadjusted statement of cash flows for the month. Also prepare an unadjusted balance sheet as of the end of the month.

Check   (3) Net income, $4,160; Total assets, $76,760

4. Calculate the return on equity for the month, using the $65,000 initial investment as the beginning balance of equity.

Analysis Component

5. Assume the investment transaction on December 1 was $49,000 instead of $65,000 and that Hamilton obtained the $16,000 difference by borrowing it from a bank. Explain the effect of this change on total assets, total liabilities, equity, and return on equity.

Roberto Ricci opens a computer consulting business called Financial Consultants and completes the following transactions in its first month of operations:

Problem 2-5A
Preparing and posting general journal entries; preparing a trial balance

A1 P1 P2

April 1   Ricci invests $80,000 cash along with office equipment valued at $26,000 in the business in exchange for common stock.
2   Prepaid $9,000 cash for three months' rent for office space. (*Hint:* Debit Prepaid Rent for $9,000.)
3   Made credit purchases for $8,000 in office equipment and $3,600 in office supplies. Payment is due within 30 days.
6   Completed services for a client and immediately received $4,000 cash.
9   Completed a $6,000 project for a client, who will pay within 30 days.
10 Paid $11,600 cash to settle the account payable created on April 2. 3
19 Paid $2,400 cash for the premium on a 12-month insurance policy. (*Hint:* Debit Prepaid Insurance for $2,400.)
22 Received $4,400 cash as partial payment for the work completed on April 9.
25 Completed work for another client for $2,890 on credit.
28 Paid $5,500 cash for dividends.
29 Purchased $600 of additional office supplies on credit.
30 Paid $435 cash for this month's utility bill.

Required

1. Prepare general journal entries to record these transactions (use account titles listed in part 2).

2. Open the following ledger accounts—their account numbers are in parentheses (use the balance column format): Cash (101); Accounts Receivable (106); Office Supplies (124); Prepaid Insurance (128); Prepaid Rent (131); Office Equipment (163); Accounts Payable (201); Common Stock (307); Retained Earnings (318); Services Revenue (403); and Utilities Expense (690). Post journal entries from part 1 to the ledger accounts and enter the balance after each posting.

Check   (2) Ending balances: Cash, $59,465; Accounts Receivable, $4,490; Accounts Payable, $600

3. Prepare a trial balance (unadjusted) as of the end of this month's operations.

Check   (3) Total debits, $119,490

Problem 2-6A

Recording transactions in T-accounts, preparing a trial balance, and computing a debt ratio

A1 A2 P2

Shelton Engineering completed the following transactions in the month of June.

a. Sandra Shelton, the owner, invested $100,000 cash, office equipment with a value of $5,000, and $60,000 of drafting equipment to launch the business in exchange for common stock.

b. Purchased land worth $49,000 for an office by paying $6,300 cash and signing a long-term note payable for $42,700.

c. Purchased a portable building with $55,000 cash and moved it onto the land acquired in *b*.

d. Paid $3,000 cash for the premium on an 18-month insurance policy.

e. Completed and delivered a set of plans for a client and collected $6,200 cash.

f. Purchased $20,000 of additional drafting equipment by paying $9,500 cash and signing a long-term note payable for $10,500.

g. Completed $14,000 of engineering services for a client. This amount is to be received in 30 days.

h. Purchased $1,150 of additional office equipment on credit.

i. Completed engineering services for $22,000 on credit.

j. Received a bill for rent of equipment that was used on a recently completed job. The $1,333 rent must be paid within 30 days.

k. Collected $7,000 cash in partial payment from the client described in transaction *g*.

l. Paid $1,200 cash for wages to a drafting assistant.

m. Paid $1,150 cash to settle the account payable created in transaction *h*.

n. Paid $925 cash for minor repairs to the drafting equipment.

o. Paid $9,480 cash for dividends.

p. Paid $1,200 cash for wages to a drafting assistant.

q. Paid $2,500 cash for advertisements in the local newspaper during June.

Required

Check (1) Ending balances: Cash, $22,945; Accounts Receivable, $29,000; Accounts Payable, $1,333

1. Open the following T-accounts: Cash; Accounts Receivable; Prepaid Insurance; Office Equipment; Drafting Equipment; Building; Land; Accounts Payable; Long-Term Notes Payable; Common Stock; Retained Earnings; Engineering Fees Earned; Wages Expense; Equipment Rental Expense; Advertising Expense; and Repairs Expense.

Check (2) Trial balance totals, $261,733

2. Record the transactions by entering debits and credits directly in the T-accounts. Use the transaction letters to identify each debit and credit. Prepare a trial balance (unadjusted) as of June 30.

3. Calculate the company's debt ratio. Use $245,095 as the total assets amount. Are the company's assets financed more by debt or equity?

Problem 2-7A

Preparing and posting general journal entries; preparing a trial balance

A1 P1 P2

Eₓ

Stuart Birch opens a Web consulting business called Show-Me-the-Money Consultants and completes the following transactions in March:

March	1	Birch invested $150,000 cash along with $22,000 of office equipment in the business in exchange for common stock.
	2	Prepaid $6,000 cash for three months' rent for an office. (*Hint:* Debit Prepaid Rent for $6,000.)
	3	Made credit purchases of office equipment for $3,000 and office supplies for $1,200.
	6	Completed services for a client and immediately received $4,000 cash.
	9	Completed a $7,500 project for a client, who will pay within 30 days.
	10	Paid $4,200 cash to settle the account payable created on March 3.
	19	Paid $5,000 cash for the premium on a 12-month insurance policy.
	22	Received $3,500 cash as partial payment for the work completed on March 9.
	25	Completed work for another client for $3,820 on credit.
	29	Paid $5,100 cash for dividends.
	30	Purchased $600 of additional office supplies on credit.
	31	Paid $500 cash for this month's utility bill.

Required

Check (2) Ending balances: Cash, $136,700; Accounts Receivable, $7,820; Accounts Payable, $600

1. Prepare general journal entries to record these transactions (use the account titles listed in part 2).

2. Open the following accounts—their account numbers are in parentheses (use the balance column format): Cash (101); Accounts Receivable (106); Office Supplies (124); Prepaid Insurance (128); Prepaid Rent (131); Office Equipment (163); Accounts Payable (201); Common Stock (307); Retained Earnings (318); Services Revenue (403); and Utilities Expense (690). Post the journal entries from part 1 to the accounts and enter the balance after each posting.

Check (3) Total debits, $187,920

3. Prepare a trial balance (unadjusted) as of the end of this month's operations.

The following financial statement information is known about five separate companies:

	Company V	Company W	Company X	Company Y	Company Z
December 31, 2001:					
Assets	$54,000	$80,000	$141,500	$92,500	$144,000
Liabilities	25,000	60,000	68,500	51,500	?
December 31, 2002:					
Assets	59,000	100,000	186,500	?	170,000
Liabilities	36,000	?	65,800	42,000	42,000
During year 2002:					
Stock issuances	5,000	20,000	?	48,100	60,000
Net income	?	40,000	18,500	24,000	32,000
Cash dividends	5,500	2,000	0	20,000	8,000

Problem 2-1B 🎞
Computing missing
information using
accounting knowledge

C5 A1 A2

Required

1. Answer the following questions about Company V:
   a. What is the amount of equity on December 31, 2001?
   b. What is the amount of equity on December 31, 2002?
   c. What is net income for year 2002?
2. Answer the following questions about Company W:
   a. What is the amount of equity on December 31, 2001?
   b. What is the amount of equity on December 31, 2002?
   c. What is the amount of liabilities on December 31, 2002?
3. Calculate the amount of stock issuances for Company X during 2002.
4. Calculate the amount of assets for Company Y on December 31, 2002.
5. Calculate the amount of liabilities for Company Z on December 31, 2001.

Check   (1*b*) $23,000

Check   (2*c*) $22,000

Check   (4) $135,100

Identify how each of the following separate transactions affects financial statements. For the balance sheet, identify how each transaction affects total assets, total liabilities, and equity. For the income statement, identify how each transaction affects net income. For the statement of cash flows, identify how each transaction affects cash flows from operating activities, cash flows from financing activities, and cash flows from investing activities. For increases, place a "+" in the column or columns. For decreases, place a "−" in the column or columns. If both an increase and a decrease occur, place "+/−" in the column or columns. The first transaction is completed as an example.

Problem 2-2B 🎞
Identifying effects of
transactions on financial
statements

A1 A2

		Balance Sheet			Income Statement	Statement of Cash Flows		
	Transaction	**Total Assets**	**Total Liab.**	**Equity**	**Net Income**	**Operating Activities**	**Financing Activities**	**Investing Activities**
1	Owner invests cash for stock	+		+			+	
2	Acquired Web servers by signing note payable							
3	Pays salaries incurred with cash							
4	Performs services for cash							
5	Pays rent incurred with cash							
6	Services received on credit							
7	Buys store equipment for cash							
8	Pays cash dividend							
9	Performs services on credit							
10	Collects cash on receivable from (9)							

Problem 2-3B

Analyzing transactions and preparing unadjusted financial statements

C5 A1 P3

Ken Stone launched a new business called Ken's Maintenance Co. that began operations on June 1. The following transactions were completed by the company during that first month:

June	1	Stone invested $130,000 cash in the business in exchange for common stock.
	2	Rented a furnished office and paid $6,000 cash for June's rent.
	4	Purchased $2,400 of equipment on credit.
	6	Paid $1,150 cash for the next week's advertising of the opening of the business.
	8	Completed maintenance services for a customer and immediately collected $850 cash.
	14	Completed $7,500 of maintenance services for First Union Center on credit.
	16	Paid $800 cash for an assistant's salary for the first half of the month.
	20	Received $7,500 cash payment for services completed for First Union Center on June 14.
	21	Completed $7,900 of maintenance services for Skyway Co. on credit.
	24	Completed $675 of maintenance services for Comfort Motel on credit.
	29	Received $7,900 cash payment from Skyway Co. for the work completed on June 21.
	29	Made a payment of $2,400 cash for the equipment purchased on June 4.
	30	Paid $150 cash for this month's telephone bill.
	30	Paid $890 cash for this month's utilities.
	30	Paid $800 cash for an assistant's salary for the second half of this month.
	30	Paid $4,000 cash for dividends.

Required

1. Arrange the following asset, liability, and equity titles in a table like Exhibit 2.6: Cash; Accounts Receivable; Equipment; Accounts Payable; Common Stock; and Retained Earnings. Include an Explanation column for changes in equity.

Check (2) Ending balances: Cash, $130,060; Retained Earnings, $3,135

2. Show the effects of the transactions on the accounts of the accounting equation by recording increases and decreases in the appropriate columns. Do not determine new account balances after each transaction. Next to each change in equity, state whether it was caused by an investment, a revenue, an expense, or a dividend. Determine the final total for each account and verify that the equation is in balance.

Check (3) Net income, $7,135; Total assets, $133,135

3. Prepare a June unadjusted income statement, a June unadjusted statement of retained earnings, a June 30 unadjusted balance sheet, and a June unadjusted statement of cash flows.

Problem 2-4B 🖊

Analyzing transactions, preparing unadjusted financial statements, and computing return on equity

C5 A1 A2 A3 P3

Swender Excavating Co., owned by Patrick Swender, began operations in July and completed these transactions during that first month:

July	1	Swender invested $80,000 cash in the business in exchange for common stock.
	2	Rented office space and paid $700 cash for the July rent.
	3	Purchased excavating equipment for $5,000 by paying $1,000 cash and agreeing to pay the balance in 30 days.
	6	Purchased office supplies by paying $600 cash.
	8	Completed work for a customer and immediately collected $7,600 cash for the work.
	10	Purchased $2,300 of office equipment on credit.
	15	Completed work for a customer on credit in the amount of $8,200.
	17	Purchased $3,100 of office supplies on credit.
	23	Paid $2,300 cash for the office equipment purchased on July 10.
	25	Billed a customer $5,000 for work completed; the balance is due in 30 days.
	28	Received $8,200 cash for the work completed on July 15.
	31	Paid an assistant's salary of $1,560 cash for this month.
	31	Paid $295 cash for this month's utility bill.
	31	Paid $1,800 cash for dividends.

Required

1. Arrange the following asset, liability, and equity titles in a table like Exhibit 2.6: Cash; Accounts Receivable; Office Supplies; Office Equipment; Excavating Equipment; Accounts Payable; Common Stock; and Retained Earnings. Leave space for an Explanation column to the right of the table.

Check (2) Ending balances: Cash, $87,545; Accounts Payable, $7,100; Retained Earnings, $16,445

2. Use additions and subtractions to show the effects of each transaction on the accounts in the accounting equation. Show new balances after each transaction. Next to each change in equity, state whether the change was caused by an investment, a revenue, an expense, or a dividend.

3. Use the increases and decreases in the columns of the table from part 2 to prepare an unadjusted income statement, an unadjusted statement of retained earnings, and an unadjusted statement of cash flows for the month. Also prepare an unadjusted balance sheet as of the end of the month.

4. Calculate return on equity for the month, using the $80,000 initial investment as the beginning balance of equity.

Analysis Component

5. Assume that Swender's $5,000 purchase of excavating equipment on July 3 was financed from an additional personal investment of another $5,000 cash in exchange for more common stock in the business (instead of the purchase conditions described in the transaction). Explain the effect of this change on total assets, total liabilities, equity, and return on equity.

Check   (3) Net income, $18,245; Total assets, $103,545

Lummus Management Services opens for business and completes these transactions in September:

Sept.	1	Rhonda Lummus, the owner, invests $38,000 cash along with office equipment valued at $15,000 in the business in exchange for common stock.
	2	Prepaid $9,000 cash for three months' rent for office space. (*Hint:* Debit Prepaid Rent for $9,000.)
	4	Made credit purchases for $8,000 in office equipment and $2,400 in office supplies. Payment is due within 14 days.
	8	Completed work for a client and immediately received $3,280 cash.
	12	Completed a $15,400 project for a client, who will pay within 30 days.
	13	Paid $10,400 cash to settle the account payable created on September 4.
	19	Paid $1,900 cash for the premium on an 18-month insurance policy. (*Hint:* Debit Prepaid Insurance for $1,900.)
	22	Received $7,700 cash as partial payment for the work completed on September 12.
	24	Completed work for another client for $2,100 on credit.
	28	Paid $5,300 cash for dividends.
	29	Purchased $550 of additional office supplies on credit.
	30	Paid $860 cash for this month's utility bill.

Problem 2-5B
Preparing and posting general journal entries; preparing a trial balance

A1 P1 P2

Required

1. Prepare general journal entries to record these transactions (use account titles listed in part 2).

2. Open the following ledger accounts—their account numbers are in parentheses (use the balance column format): Cash (101); Accounts Receivable (106); Office Supplies (124); Prepaid Insurance (128); Prepaid Rent (131); Office Equipment (163); Accounts Payable (201); Common Stock (307); Retained Earnings (318); Service Fees Earned (401); and Utilities Expense (690). Post journal entries from part 1 to the ledger accounts and enter the balance after each posting.

3. Prepare a trial balance (unadjusted) as of the end of this month's operations.

Check   (2) Ending balances: Cash, $21,520; Accounts Receivable, $9,800; Accounts Payable, $550

Check   (3) Total debits, $74,330

At the beginning of April, Brooke Wilson launched a custom computer programming company called Softways. The company had the following transactions during April:

a. Brooke Wilson invested $65,000 cash, office equipment with a value of $5,750, and $30,000 of computer equipment in the company in exchange for common stock.

b. Purchased land worth $22,000 for an office by paying $5,000 cash and signing a long-term note payable for $17,000.

c. Purchased a portable building with $34,500 cash and moved it onto the land acquired in *b*.

d. Paid $5,000 cash for the premium on a two-year insurance policy.

e. Provided services to a client and collected $4,600 cash.

f. Purchased $4,500 of additional computer equipment by paying $800 cash and signing a long-term note payable for $3,700.

g. Completed $4,250 of services for a client. This amount is to be received within 30 days.

h. Purchased $950 of additional office equipment on credit.

i. Completed client services for $10,200 on credit.

Problem 2-6B 🔁
Recording transactions in T-accounts; preparing a trial balance; computing a debt ratio

A1 A2 P2

j. Received a bill for rent of a computer testing device that was used on a recently completed job. The $580 rent must be paid within 30 days.

k. Collected $5,100 cash from the client described in transaction *i*.

l. Paid $1,800 cash for wages to an assistant.

m. Paid $950 cash to settle the account payable created in transaction *h*.

n. Paid $608 cash for minor repairs to the computer equipment.

o. Paid $6,230 cash for dividends.

p. Paid $1,800 cash for wages to an assistant.

q. Paid $750 cash for advertisements in the local newspaper during April.

Required

Check (1) Ending balances: Cash, $17,262; Accounts Receivable, $9,350; Accounts Payable, $580

1. Open the following T-accounts: Cash; Accounts Receivable; Prepaid Insurance; Office Equipment; Computer Equipment; Building; Land; Accounts Payable; Long-Term Notes Payable; Common Stock; Retained Earnings; Fees Earned; Wages Expense; Computer Rental Expense; Advertising Expense; and Repairs Expense.

Check (2) Trial balance totals, $141,080

2. Record the transactions by entering debits and credits directly in the T-accounts. Use the transaction letters to identify each debit and credit. Prepare a trial balance (unadjusted) as of April 30.

3. Calculate the company's debt ratio. Use $129,312 as its total assets amount. Are the company's assets financed more by debt or equity?

Problem 2-7B
Preparing and posting general journal entries; preparing a trial balance

A1 P1 P2

Shaw Management Services opens for business and completes these transactions in November:

Nov. 1   Ken Shaw, the owner, invested $30,000 cash along with $15,000 of office equipment in the business in exchange for common stock.

     2   Prepaid $4,500 cash for three months' rent for an office. (*Hint:* Debit Prepaid Rent for $4,500.)

     4   Made credit purchases of office equipment for $2,500 and of office supplies for $600.

     8   Completed work for a client and immediately received $3,400 cash.

     12   Completed a $10,200 project for a client, who will pay within 30 days.

     13   Paid $3,100 cash to settle the account payable created on November 4.

     19   Paid $1,800 cash for the premium on a 24-month insurance policy.

     22   Received $5,200 cash as partial payment for the work completed on November 12.

     24   Completed work for another client for $1,750 on credit.

     28   Paid $5,300 cash for dividends.

     29   Purchased $249 of additional office supplies on credit.

     30   Paid $831 cash for this month's utility bill.

Required

1. Prepare general journal entries to record these transactions (use account titles listed in part 2).

Check (2) Ending balances: Cash, $23,069; Accounts Receivable, $6,750; Accounts Payable, $249

2. Open the following accounts—their account numbers are in parentheses (use the balance column format): Cash (101); Accounts Receivable (106); Office Supplies (124); Prepaid Insurance (128); Prepaid Rent (131); Office Equipment (163); Accounts Payable (201); Common Stock (307); Retained Earnings (318); Services Revenue (403); and Utilities Expense (690). Post the journal entries from part 1 to the accounts and enter the balance after each posting.

Check (3) Total debits, $60,599

3. Prepare a trial balance (unadjusted) as of the end of this month's operations.

SERIAL PROBLEM

(This comprehensive problem starts in this chapter and continues in Chapter 3. It is most readily solved if you use the Working Papers that accompany this textbook.)

Sierra Systems

On October 1, 2002, Sela Solstise launched a computer services company called Sierra Systems, which is organized as a corporation and provides consulting services, computer system installations, and custom program development. Solstise adopts the calendar year for reporting purposes and expects to prepare the company's first set of financial statements on December 31, 2002. The initial chart of accounts for its accounting system includes these items:

Account	No.	Account	No.
Cash	101	Common Stock	307
Accounts Receivable	106	Retained Earnings	318
Computer Supplies	126	Computer Services Revenue	403
Prepaid Insurance	128	Wages Expense	623
Prepaid Rent	131	Advertising Expense	655
Office Equipment	163	Mileage Expense	676
Computer Equipment	167	Miscellaneous Expenses	677
Accounts Payable	201	Repairs Expense—Computer	684

Required

1. Prepare journal entries to record each of the following transactions for Sierra Systems.

Oct. 1   Sela Solstise invested $55,000 cash, a $20,000 computer system, and $8,000 of office equipment in the business in exchange for common stock.

2   Paid $3,300 cash for four months' rent. (*Hint:* Debit Prepaid Rent for $3,300.)

3   Purchased $1,420 of computer supplies on credit from Appier Office Products.

5   Paid $2,220 cash for one year's premium on a property and liability insurance policy. (*Hint:* Debit Prepaid Insurance for $2,220.)

6   Billed Prime Leasing $4,800 for services performed in installing a new Web server.

8   Paid $1,420 cash for the computer supplies purchased from Appier Office Products on October 3.

10   Hired Suzie Smith as a part-time assistant for $125 per day, as needed.

12   Billed Prime Leasing another $1,400 for services performed.

15   Received $4,800 cash from Prime Leasing on its account.

17   Paid $805 cash to repair computer equipment damaged when moving it.

20   Paid $1,940 cash for an advertisement in the local newspaper.

22   Received $1,400 cash from Prime Leasing on its account.

28   Billed Dade Company $5,208 for services performed.

31   Paid $875 cash for Suzie Smith's wages for seven days' work.

31   Paid $3,600 cash for dividends.

Nov. 1   Reimbursed Solstise in cash for business automobile mileage allowance (Solstise logged 1,000 miles at $0.32 per mile).

2   Received $4,633 cash from Elan Corporation for computer services performed.

5   Purchased computer supplies for $1,125 cash from Appier Office Products.

8   Billed Foster Co. $5,668 for services performed.

13   Received notification from Antonio's Engineering Co. that Sierra's bid of $3,950 for an upcoming project is accepted.

18   Received $2,208 cash from Dade Company as partial payment of the October 28 bill.

22   Donated $250 cash to the United Way in the company's name.

24   Completed work for Antonio's Engineering Co. and sent it a bill for $3,950.

25   Sent another bill to Dade Company for the past-due amount of $3,000.

28   Reimbursed Solstise in cash for business automobile mileage (1,200 miles at $0.32 per mile).

30   Paid $1,750 cash for Suzie Smith's wages for 14 days' work.

30   Paid $2,000 cash for dividends.

2. Open ledger accounts (in balance column format) and post the journal entries from part 1 to them.

BEYOND THE NUMBERS

BTN 2-1   Refer to Nike's financial statements in Appendix A to answer the following questions.

Required

1. Examine Nike's consolidated balance sheet. To what level are its dollar amounts rounded?

2. What is the reporting date of Nike's most recent annual reporting period?

3. What amount of net income did Nike earn for the fiscal year ended May 31, 2000?

4. How much cash (and equivalents) did Nike have at fiscal year-end May 31, 2000?

Reporting in Action

C5 A3 A4 𝒹

NIKE

5. What was the net amount of cash provided by its operating activities for the fiscal year ended May 31, 2000?

6. Did its investing activities for fiscal year ended May 31, 2000, create a net cash inflow or outflow? What was the amount of this net cash flow?

7. For the year ended May 31, 2000, how much cash is paid in dividends?

8. Compare fiscal year 2000's results to 1999's results to determine whether revenues increased or decreased. What was the amount of the increase or decrease?

9. What is the change in net income between fiscal years 2000 and 1999?

10. What amount is reported as total assets at fiscal year-end 2000?

11. What current assets are reported on Nike's consolidated balance sheet? (List items.)

12. What current liabilities are reported on its balance sheet? (List items.)

13. Calculate return on equity for fiscal year ended May 31, 2000.

14. What is Nike's debt ratio at May 31, 2000? (*Hint:* Use Liabilities = Assets − Shareholders' Equity.) How does this compare to its ratio at May 31, 1999?

Swoosh Ahead

15. Access Nike's financial statements (10-K) for a fiscal year ending after May 31, 2000, from its Web site (www.nike.com) or the SEC's EDGAR database (www.sec.gov). (*a*) Recompute Nike's return on equity with the new information. Compare the May 31, 2000, fiscal year-end return on equity to any subsequent year's return you are able to calculate. Also compare how Nike's total assets, total revenues, and net income have changed since May 31, 2000. (*b*) Recompute Nike's debt ratio with the new information. Compare the May 31, 2000, fiscal year-end debt ratio to any subsequent year's debt ratio that you are able to calculate.

Comparative Analysis

A3 A4

NIKE

Reebok

BTN 2-2   Key comparative figures ($ millions) for both Nike and Reebok follow:

Key Figures	Nike	Reebok
Ending liabilities	$2,720.9	$1,035.3
Beginning equity	3,334.6	524.4
Ending equity	3,136.0	528.8
Net income	579.1	11.05

Required

1. What is the return on equity for (*a*) Nike and (*b*) Reebok?

2. Is return on equity satisfactory for (*a*) Nike and (*b*) Reebok if competitors average a 10% return?

3. What are (ending) total assets for (*a*) Nike and (*b*) Reebok?

4. What is the debt ratio for (*a*) Nike and (*b*) Reebok?

5. Which of the two companies has the higher degree of financial leverage? What does this imply?

Ethics Challenge

C1 C2

BTN 2-3   Damara Crist is an entry-level accountant for a mail-order company that specializes in supplying skateboards and accessories. At the end of its fiscal period, Damara is advised by a supervisor to include as revenue for the period any orders that have been charged by phone but not yet shipped. Damara is also advised to include as revenue any orders received by mail with checks enclosed that are also pending shipment.

Required

1. Identify the most relevant accounting principle in assessing the supervisor's instructions.

2. What are the ethical factors in this situation?

3. Would you recommend that Damara follow the supervisor's directions?

4. What alternatives might be available to Damara other than following the supervisor's directions?

BTN 2-4 Divide the class into teams. Each team is to select an industry, and each team member is to select a different company in that industry. Each team member is to acquire the financial statements of the company selected. Financial statements can be obtained in many ways, including accessing the SEC's EDGAR database (www.sec.gov).

Communicating in Practice
A3 A4 🗗

Required

1. Each team member should use the financial statements to compute return on equity and the debt ratio.
2. Communicate with teammates via a meeting, e-mail, or telephone. The team must prepare a single memorandum reporting (*a*) the meaning of these ratios, (*b*) how different companies compare to each other, and (*c*) the industry norm. Identify any conclusions or consensus of opinion reached during the team's discussion. The memo is to be copied and distributed to the instructor and all classmates.

BTN 2-5 Visit the EDGAR database online at www.edgar-online.com. Alphabetically search for Fogdog Sports (ticker FOGD). Fogdog Sports is an online retailer of sports clothing and equipment. View Fogdog's 10-K405 report filed with the SEC on March 30, 2000. Search Fogdog's 10-K405 until you find the annual income statement that reports results for 1999, 1998, and 1997.

Taking It to the Net
C2 A2 🗗

Required

1. What is the net income trend (level and direction) for Fogdog during its most recent 3 years?
2. What expense reported on the income statement provides a clue that Fogdog is an Internet-based company?

BTN 2-6 Access EDGAR online (www.edgar-online.com) and locate the 10-K report of Amazon.com (ticker AMZN) filed on March 29, 2000. Review its cash flow statements reported for fiscal years ended 1997, 1998, and 1999 to answer the following questions:

A2 🗗

Required

1. What are the amounts of its net losses reported for each of these three years?
2. Does Amazon's operations provide cash or use cash for each of these three years?
3. If Amazon has a net loss and a use of cash provided by operations in 1999, how is it possible that the cash balance at December 31, 1999, shows an increase relative to the balance at January 1, 1999?

BTN 2-7 The expanded accounting equation consists of assets, liabilities, common stock, retained earnings, revenues, and expenses. It can be used to reveal information on changes in a company's financial position.

Teamwork in Action
C5 A1 A2

Required

1. Form *learning teams* of six (or more) members. Each team member must select one of the six components and each team must have at least one expert on each component: (*a*) assets, (*b*) liabilities, (*c*) common stock, (*d*) retained earnings, (*e*) revenues, and (*f*) expenses.
2. Form *expert teams* of individuals who selected the same component in part 1. Expert teams are to draft a report that each expert will present to his/her learning team addressing the following:
   a. Identify for its component the (i) increase and decrease side of the account and (ii) normal balance side of the account.
   b. Describe a transaction, with amounts, that increases its component.
   c. Using the transaction and amounts in (*b*), verify the equality of the accounting equation and then explain any effects on the income statement and statement of cash flows.
   d. Describe a transaction, with amounts, that decreases its component.
   e. Using the transaction and amounts in (*d*), verify the equality of the accounting equation and then explain any effects on the income statement and statement of cash flows.
3. Each expert should return to his/her learning team. In rotation, each member presents his/her expert team's report to the learning team. Team discussion is encouraged.

Business Week Activity
A3 🗗

BTN 2-8 *Business Week* periodically publishes a ranking of "Hot Growth Companies." It contains tables of selected accounting measures. Obtain the most recent issue on hot growth companies. (*Note:* May 29, 2000, was one such issue.)

Required

1. What company is ranked number 1 using return on equity (also called return on capital)?
2. What is the return on equity (capital) for the number 1 company?
3. Refer to the return on equity (capital) table and consider the relation between return and risk. Identify and discuss common risk characteristics for the top five companies.

Entrepreneurial Decision
A1 A2 A3 A4 P3
🖰 🗗

BTN 2-9 Liang Lu is a young entrepreneur who operates Lu Music Services, offering singing lessons and instruction on musical instruments. Lu wishes to expand but needs a loan. The bank requests Lu to prepare a balance sheet and key financial ratios. Lu has not kept formal records but is able to provide the following accounts and their amounts as of December 31, 2002:

Cash	$ 1,800	Accounts Receivable . . .	$4,800	Prepaid Insurance . .	$ 750
Prepaid Rent	4,700	Store Supplies	3,300	Equipment	25,000
Accounts Payable . .	1,100	Unearned Lesson Fees . .	7,800	Total Equity*	31,450
Annual net income . .	20,000				

* The total equity amount reflects all investments, revenues, expenses, and dividends as of Dec. 31, 2002.

Required

1. Prepare a balance sheet as of December 31, 2002, for Lu Music Services.
2. Compute Lu's debt ratio, return on equity, and return on assets (from Chapter 1). Assume average equity and average assets equal their respective ending balances.
3. Do you think the prospects of a $15,000 bank loan are good? Why or why not?

Hitting the Road
C1

BTN 2-10 Obtain a recent copy of the most prominent newspaper distributed in your area. Research the classified section and prepare a report answering the following questions (attach relevant classified clippings to your report). Alternatively, you may want to search the Web for the required job information. One suitable Web site is www.ajb.dni.us. For documentation, you should print copies of Web sites accessed.

1. Identify the number of listings for accounting positions and the various accounting job titles.
2. Identify the number of listings for other job titles, with examples, that require or prefer accounting knowledge/experience but are not specifically accounting positions.
3. Specify the salary range for the accounting and accounting-related positions if provided.
4. Indicate the job that appeals to you, the reason for its appeal, and its requirements.

Global Decision
A3 A4 🗗

BTN 2-11 Both Nike and Reebok compete with each other and with Adidas-Salomon (www.adidas.com/investor). Key financial ratios for Adidas-Salomon by segments for the 2000 calendar year follow:

Key Figure*	Europe	North America	Asia	Latin America
Return on equity . . .	52.3%	32.8%	53.8%	32.4%
Debt ratio	21.6	37.4	47.3	34.9

* Figures prepared in accordance with International Accounting Standards.

Required

1. Which segment is most profitable according to return on equity?
2. Which segment is most risky according to the debt ratio?
3. Which segment deserves increased investment based on a joint analysis of return on equity and the debt ratio?

3

Reporting and Preparing Financial Statements

1. ultra hairlights on a handbag
2. ultra hairlights on a card
3. hairlight on a handbag
4. hairlight on a card
5. hairbrights

6. bohemian
7. headbands
8. accessories
9. sparkles
10. press

MELLiES

"Stay focused and keep doing what you believe in"—Melody Kulp (far left)

A Look Back

Chapter 2 explained the analysis and recording of transactions. We showed how to work with source documents, T-accounts, double-entry accounting, ledgers, postings, and trial balances.

A Look at This Chapter

This chapter explains the timing of reports and the need to adjust accounts. We describe the adjusted trial balance and how it is used to prepare financial statements. We then explain the closing process, including use of a post-closing trial balance. A classified balance sheet is also described.

A Look Ahead

Chapter 4 looks at accounting for merchandising activities. We describe the sale and purchase of merchandise and its implications for preparing and analyzing financial statements of merchandisers.

Sparkling Financials

e EL SEGUNDO, CA—One afternoon 23-year-old Melody Kulp was playing outside with the young cousin of a friend when she placed yard-picked flowers in the girl's hair and thought how much prettier they looked than headbands or hair clips. The next day, with some silk flowers and Velcro she purchased, Kulp made similar hair accessories, called them *Sparkles,* and began wearing them. When a friend wore one to work at Fred Segal's, the shop's buyer asked to meet with Kulp about putting together a product line. Kulp quickly organized a business—dubbed **Mellies (www.Mellies.com)**—and then converted a 10' × 10' room into a minifactory. The rest is the stuff of Hollywood movies.

After only two years, Mellies is a $40 million accessories company. With her 25-year-old partner David Reinstein, Melody Kulp now manages 15 employees and plans to launch a cosmetics line. The young entrepreneurs learned a lot in a hurry. She had to meet creditors and bankers, set up a reliable accounting system, draw up financial statements, and analyze and interpret financial data. It was at times overwhelming, says Kulp, but "the key is to stay focused and keep doing what you believe in."

Kulp knows how important a timely and reliable accounting system is for Mellies' continued success. Historical and projected financial statements have enabled her company to obtain the necessary financing to propel it to new heights. This chapter focuses on the accounting system underlying financial statements. Says Kulp, "We've got the system set up where we can look ahead, rather than live day to day." That look ahead reveals sparkling financials. [Sources: Mellies Web site, January 2002; *Success Publishing*, 2000; *Entrepreneur*, November 2000.]

Learning Objectives

Conceptual

C1 Explain the importance of periodic reporting and the time period principle.

C2 Explain accrual accounting and how it makes financial statements more useful.

C3 Identify the types of adjustments and their purpose.

C4 Explain why temporary accounts are closed each period.

C5 Identify steps in the accounting cycle.

C6 Explain and prepare a classified balance sheet.

Analytical

A1 Explain how accounting adjustments link to financial statements.

A2 Compute profit margin and describe its use in analyzing company performance.

A3 Compute the current ratio and describe what it reveals about a company's financial condition.

Procedural

P1 Prepare and explain adjusting entries.

P2 Explain and prepare an adjusted trial balance.

P3 Prepare financial statements from an adjusted trial balance.

P4 Describe and prepare closing entries.

P5 Explain and prepare a post-closing trial balance.

Chapter Preview

Financial statements reflect revenues when earned and expenses when incurred. This is known as *accrual accounting*. Accrual accounting requires several steps. We described many of these steps in Chapter 2. We showed how companies use accounting systems to collect information about *external* transactions and events. We also explained how journals, ledgers, and other tools are useful in preparing financial statements. This chapter describes the accounting process for producing useful information involving *internal* transactions and events. An important part of this process is adjusting the account balances so that financial statements at the end of a reporting period reflect the effects of all transactions. We then explain the important steps in preparing financial statements, describe the classified balance sheet, and discuss the closing process that prepares accounts for the next period. We also identify and explain an important measure of company performance (profit margin), along with a measure of a company's ability to pay its short-term liabilities (current ratio).

Timing and Reporting

Regular, or periodic, reporting is an important part of the accounting process. This section describes the impact on the accounting process of the point in time or the period of time that a report refers to.

The Accounting Period

C1 Explain the importance of periodic reporting and the time period principle.

The value of information is often linked to its timeliness. Useful information must reach decision makers frequently and promptly. To provide timely information, accounting systems prepare reports at regular intervals. This results in an accounting process impacted by the time period (or periodicity) principle. The **time period principle** assumes that an organization's activities can be divided into specific time periods such as a month, a three-month quarter, or a year. Exhibit 3.1 shows various **accounting,** or *reporting,* **periods.** Most organizations use a year as their primary accounting period. Reports covering a one-year period are known as **annual financial statements.** Many organizations also prepare **interim financial statements** covering one, three, or six months of activity.

"Nike announces earnings per share of . . ."

The annual reporting period is not always a calendar year ending on December 31. An organization can adopt a **fiscal year** consisting of any 12 consecutive months. It is also acceptable to adopt an annual reporting period of 52 weeks. For example, **Gap**'s

Exhibit 3.1
Accounting Periods

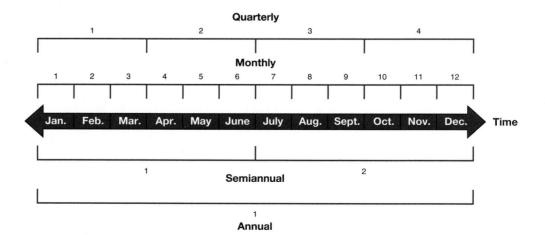

fiscal year consistently ends the final week of January or the first week of February each year.

Companies with little seasonal variation in sales during the year often choose the calendar year as their fiscal year. For example, the financial statements of Alcoa reflect a fiscal year that ends on December 31. Companies experiencing seasonal variations in sales often choose a fiscal year corresponding to their natural business year. The **natural business year** ends when sales activities are at their lowest point during the year. The natural business year for retailers usually ends around January 31, after the holiday season. Examples of these companies include Wal-Mart, Kmart, Dell, and FUBU. Most start their annual accounting periods on or near February 1.

Purpose of Adjusting

The usual accounting process is to record external transactions and events (with outside parties) during an accounting period. After external transactions have been recorded, several accounts in the ledger need adjustments before their balances appear in financial statements. This need arises because internal transactions and events remain unrecorded.

An example is the cost of certain assets that expire as time passes. The Prepaid Insurance account of FastForward is one of these. FastForward's trial balance (in Exhibit 2.18) shows Prepaid Insurance (asset) with a balance of $2,400. This amount is the premium for *two years* of insurance benefits beginning on December 1. By December 31, one month's coverage is used up. Because these benefits cost an average of $100 per month ($2,400/24 months), the Prepaid Insurance account balance must be reduced by one month's cost. The December income statement must report a $100 cost as insurance expense, and the December 31 balance sheet must report the Prepaid Insurance asset account adjusted to a balance of $2,300. This adjusted balance reflects the remaining 23 months of insurance benefits.

Another example is FastForward's $9,720 balance in Supplies. This balance includes the costs of all supplies that FastForward purchased in December. At December 31, many of these supplies have been used up. The costs of supplies used must be reported as an expense on the December income statement and the Supplies asset account balance must be adjusted to include the costs of only the remaining unused supplies. Other accounts also require adjustments to prepare financial statements. We explain in the next section how this adjusting process is carried out.

Point: Many companies record adjusting entries only at the end of each year because of the time and cost necessary. For interim financial statements, adjustments sometimes are omitted.

Recognizing Revenues and Expenses

We use the time period principle to divide a company's activities into specific time periods, but not all activities are complete when financial statements are prepared. Thus, to avoid misleading decision makers, we must make some adjustments in reporting.

We rely on two principles in the adjusting process: revenue recognition and matching. Chapter 2 explained that the *revenue recognition principle* requires that revenue be recorded when earned, not before and not after. Most companies earn revenue when they provide services and products to customers. If FastForward provides consulting to a client in December, the revenue is earned in December. This means it must be reported on the December income statement, even if the client paid for the services in a month other than December. A major goal of the adjusting process is to have revenue recognized (reported) in the time period when it is earned.

Point: IBM's revenues from services to customers are recorded when services are performed. Its revenues from product sales are recorded when products are shipped.

Decision Track 3.1		*d*
Decision Point	**Information Search**	**Analyze & Evaluate**
When is revenue recorded?	Transaction or event details: Revenue is recorded when earned, such as when products or services are delivered.	Recording revenue early overstates current-period revenue and income; recording it late understates current-period revenue and income.

Global: Some countries allow *income smoothing.* This means that balance sheet reserves can be set up by reducing income in good years and drawing down those reserves in bad years to increase income.

The **matching principle** aims to record expenses in the same accounting period as the revenues that are earned as a result of these expenses. This matching of costs (expenses) with benefits (revenues) is a major part of the adjusting process. FastForward earns monthly revenues while operating in rented store space. The earning of revenues requires rented space. The matching principle tells us that rent must be reported on the income statement for December, even if FastForward pays rent in a month either before or after December. This ensures that rent expense for December is matched with December's revenues.

Decision Track 3.2		d
Decision Point	**Information Search**	**Analyze & Evaluate**
When is expense recorded?	Transaction or event details: Expense is recorded (matched) with the revenue it helped generate—expense should "track" revenue.	Recording expense early overstates current-period expense and understates current-period income; recording it late understates current-period expense and overstates current-period income.

Matching expenses with revenues often requires us to predict certain events. When we use financial statements, we must understand that they require estimates and therefore include measures that are not precise. Walt Disney's annual report explains that its production costs from movies such as *Dinosaur* and *Atlantis* are matched to revenues based on a ratio of current revenues from the movie divided by its predicted total revenues.

C2   Explain accrual accounting and how it makes financial statements more useful.

Accrual Basis versus Cash Basis

Accrual basis accounting uses the adjusting process to recognize revenues when earned and to match expenses with revenues. This means that the economic effects of revenues and expenses are recorded when earned or incurred, not when cash is received or paid.

Cash basis accounting recognizes revenues when cash is received and records expenses when cash is paid. For example, if a business provides services in December but does not receive cash from clients until January, then cash basis accounting reports this revenue in January. This means that cash basis net income for a period is the difference between cash receipts and cash payments (disbursements). Cash basis accounting for the income statement, balance sheet, and statement of retained earnings is not consistent with generally accepted accounting principles. It is commonly held that accrual accounting better indicates business performance than information about cash receipts and payments. Accrual accounting also increases the *comparability* of financial statements from one period to another. Yet many companies and users of statements still find cash basis accounting useful for several business decisions. While accrual basis accounting is generally accepted for external reporting, information about cash flows is also useful—which is the reason companies must report a statement of cash flows.

Point: Cash basis accounting is generally used for tax returns.

Decision Insight

Doing Accounting Time   Like many companies, Centennial Technologies, a computer memory manufacturer, recognizes revenue when it ships products. What is not common is that Centennial's CEO shipped products to the warehouses of friends and reported it as revenue. In another case, Informix, a software maker, recorded revenue when products were passed to distributors. It admits now that there were "errors in the way revenues had been recorded," and its CEO is in jail. Such risky revenue recognition practices are often revealed by a large increase in the *accounts receivable to sales* ratio.

To see the impact of these different accounting systems, let's consider FastForward's Prepaid Insurance account. FastForward paid $2,400 for two years of insurance coverage beginning on December 1, 2001. Accrual accounting says that $100 of insurance expense is reported on December's income statement. Another $1,200 of expense is reported in year 2002, and the remaining $1,100 is reported as expense in the first 11 months of 2003. Exhibit 3.2 illustrates this allocation of insurance cost across these three years.

Exhibit 3.2

Accrual Basis Accounting for Prepaid Insurance

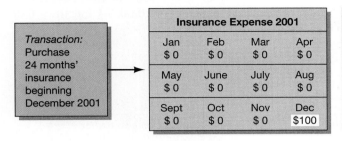

A cash basis income statement for December 2001 reports insurance expense of $2,400, as shown in Exhibit 3.3. The cash basis income statements for years 2002 and 2003 report no insurance expense from this policy.

Exhibit 3.3

Cash Basis Accounting for Prepaid Insurance

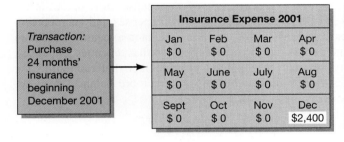

The accrual basis balance sheet reports the remaining unexpired premium as a Prepaid Insurance asset. The cash basis never reports this asset. The cash basis information is less useful for most business decisions because reported income for 2001–2003 fails to match the cost of insurance with the insurance benefits received for those years and months.

Quick Check

1. Describe a company's annual reporting period.
2. Why do companies prepare interim financial statements?
3. What two accounting principles most directly drive the adjusting process?
4. Is cash basis accounting consistent with the matching principle? Why or why not?
5. If your company pays a $4,800 premium on April 1, 2002, for two years' insurance coverage, how much insurance expense is reported in 2003 using cash basis accounting?

Answers—p. 138

Adjusting Accounts

The process of adjusting accounts involves analyzing each account balance, and the transactions and events that affect it, to determine any needed adjustments. An **adjusting entry** is recorded to bring an asset or liability account balance to its proper amount when an adjustment is needed. This entry also updates the related expense or revenue account. This section explains why adjusting entries are important. It also shows the mechanics of adjusting entries and their links to financial statements.

C3 Identify the types of adjustments and their purpose.

Topic Tackler 3-1

Exhibit 3.4

Framework for Adjustments

Framework for Adjustments

Adjustments are necessary for transactions and events that extend over more than one period. It is helpful to group adjustments by the timing of cash receipt or cash payment in relation to the recognition of the related revenues or expenses. Exhibit 3.4 identifies four types of adjustments that involve both expenses and revenues.

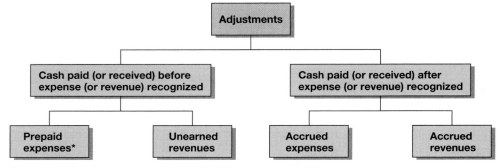

*Includes depreciation.

Both prepaid expenses (including depreciation) and unearned revenues reflect transactions when cash is paid or received *before* a related expense or revenue is recognized. Prepaids are also called *deferrals* because the recognition of an expense (or revenue) is *deferred* until after the related cash is paid (or received). Accrued expenses and accrued revenues reflect transactions when cash is paid or received *after* a related expense or revenue is recognized. Adjusting entries are necessary for each of these so that revenues, expenses, assets, and liabilities are correctly reported. It is helpful to remember that each adjusting entry affects one or more income statement accounts *and* one or more balance sheet accounts. An adjusting entry *never* involves the Cash account.

Point: Source documents provide information for daily transactions, and in many businesses the recordkeepers record them. Adjustments often require more knowledge and are usually handled by senior accounting professionals.

P1 Prepare and explain adjusting entries.

Adjusting Prepaid Expenses

Prepaid expenses refer to items *paid for* in advance of receiving their benefits. Prepaid expenses are assets. When these assets are used, their costs become expenses. Adjusting entries for prepaids involve increasing (debiting) expenses and decreasing (crediting) assets as shown in the T-accounts of Exhibit 3.5. Adjustments are made to reflect transactions and events that impact the amount of prepaid expenses (including passage of time). To illustrate the accounting for prepaid expenses, this section focuses on prepaid insurance, supplies, and depreciation.

"Here is the first 24 months' insurance in advance."

Exhibit 3.5

Adjusting for Prepaid Expenses

Prepaid Insurance

We illustrate prepaid insurance using FastForward's payment of $2,400 for 24 months of insurance benefits beginning on December 1, 2001. With the passage of time, the benefits of the insurance gradually expire and a portion of the Prepaid Insurance asset becomes expense. For instance, one month's insurance coverage expires by December 31, 2001. This expense is $100, or 1/24 of $2,400. The adjusting entry to record this expense and reduce the asset follows:

Asset — Unadjusted balance — Credit adjustment

Expense — Debit adjustment

Assets = Liabilities + Equity
−100   −100

	Adjustment (a)		
Dec. 31	Insurance Expense	100	
	Prepaid Insurance		100
	To record first month's expired insurance.		

Prepaid Insurance			128
Dec. 6	2,400	Dec. 31	100
Balance	2,300		

Insurance Expense		637
Dec. 31	100	

Exhibit 3.6

Insurance Accounts after Adjusting for Prepaids

Posting this adjusting entry affects the accounts as shown in Exhibit 3.6.

After adjusting and posting, the $100 balance in Insurance Expense and the $2,300 balance in Prepaid Insurance are ready for reporting in financial statements. *Not* making the adjustment on or before December 31 would (1) understate expenses by $100 and overstate net income by $100 for the December income statement and (2) overstate both Prepaid Insurance (assets) and equity (because of net income) by $100 in the December 31 balance sheet. It is also evident from Exhibit 3.2 that year 2002's adjustments must transfer a total of $1,200 from Prepaid Insurance to Insurance Expense, and year 2003's adjustments must transfer the remaining $1,100 to Insurance Expense.

Point: An alternative method to record prepaids is to initially debit expense for the total amount. We discuss this alternative in the appendix to this chapter. The adjusted financial statement information is identical under either method.

Supplies

Supplies are another prepaid expense often requiring adjustment. FastForward purchased $9,720 of supplies in December and used some of them during that month. Use of supplies creates expenses equal to their cost. Daily usage of supplies is not recorded in FastForward's accounts because this information is not needed. Making only one adjusting entry when financial statements are prepared can reduce recordkeeping costs. Since the income statement is for December, the cost of supplies used during December must be recognized in it. FastForward computes (takes inventory of) its remaining unused supplies at December 31. The amount of these remaining supplies is then deducted from the total unadjusted amount of supplies to obtain the amount used. FastForward has $8,670 of supplies remaining of the $9,720 total supplies in December. The $1,050 difference between these two amounts is the cost of the supplies used. This amount is December's supplies expense. The adjusting entry to record this expense and reduce the Supplies asset account follows:

Point: Some assets, liabilities, revenues, and expenses are so small in amount they do not affect analysis of financial statements. For example, office supplies are sometimes immaterial and immediately recorded as expenses. Management must still set controls over their use.

	Adjustment (b)		
Dec. 31	Supplies Expense	1,050	
	Supplies		1,050
	To record supplies used.		

Assets = Liabilities + Equity
−1,050   −1,050

Posting this adjusting entry affects the accounts as shown in Exhibit 3.7. The balance of the Supplies account is $8,670 after posting—equaling the cost of remaining supplies. *Not* making the adjustment on or before December 31 would (1) understate expenses by $1,050 and overstate net income by $1,050 for the December income statement and (2) overstate both Supplies and equity (because of net income) by $1,050 in the December 31 balance sheet.

Supplies			126
Dec. 2	2,500	Dec. 31	1,050
6	7,100		
26	120		
Balance	8,670		

Supplies Expense		652
Dec. 31	1,050	

Exhibit 3.7

Supplies Accounts after Adjusting for Prepaids

Other Prepaid Expenses

Other prepaid expenses, such as Prepaid Rent, are accounted for exactly as Insurance and Supplies are. We should also note that some prepaid expenses are both paid for and fully used up within a single accounting period. One example is when a company pays monthly rent on the first day of each month. This payment creates a prepaid expense on the first day of each month that fully expires by the end of the month. In these special cases, we can record the cash paid with a debit to the expense account instead of an asset account. This practice is described more completely later in the chapter.

Adjusting for Depreciation

A special category of prepaid expenses involves **plant assets,** which refers to long-term tangible assets used to produce and sell products and services. Plant assets are expected to provide benefits for more than one period. Examples of plant assets are buildings, machines, vehicles, and fixtures. All plant assets, with a general exception for land, eventually wear out or decline in usefulness. The costs of these assets are deferred but are gradually reported as expenses in the income statement over the assets' useful lives (benefit periods). **Depreciation** is the process of allocating the costs of these assets over their expected useful lives. Depreciation expense is recorded with an adjusting entry similar to that for other prepaid expenses.

Recall that FastForward purchased equipment for $26,000 in early December to use in earning revenue. This equipment's cost must be depreciated. Chuck Taylor expects this equipment to have a useful life (benefit period) of four years. He expects to sell the equipment for about $8,000 at the end of four years. This means the *net* cost of this equipment over its useful life is $18,000 ($26,000 − $8,000). We can use any of several methods to allocate this $18,000 net cost to expense. FastForward uses a method called *straight-line depreciation.* (Depreciation methods are explained in Chapter 8, but we briefly describe the straight-line method here to help explain the adjusting process.) **Straight-line depreciation** allocates equal amounts of an asset's net cost to depreciation during its useful life. Dividing the $18,000 net cost by the 48 months in the asset's useful life gives an average monthly cost of $375 ($18,000/48). The adjusting entry to record monthly depreciation expense follows:

Point: Depreciation does not necessarily measure the decline in market value.

Point: We use straight-line depreciation in the early chapters of the book when necessary to explain accounting for plant assets.

Assets = Liabilities + Equity
−375   −375

	Adjustment (c)		
Dec. 31	Depreciation Expense	375	
	Accumulated Depreciation—Equipment . . .		375
	To record monthly equipment depreciation.		

Posting this adjusting entry affects the accounts as shown in Exhibit 3.8. After posting the adjustment, the Equipment account ($26,000) less its Accumulated Depreciation ($375) account equals the $25,625 net cost of the 47 remaining months in the benefit period. The $375 balance in the Depreciation Expense account is reported in the December income statement. *Not* making the adjustment at December 31 would (1) understate expenses by $375 and overstate net income by $375 for the December income statement and (2) overstate both assets and equity (because of income) by $375 in the December 31 balance sheet.

Exhibit 3.8

Accounts after Depreciation Adjustments

Equipment	**167**		**Accumulated** **Depreciation — Equipment**	**168**		**Depreciation** **Expense — Equipment**	**612**
Dec. 3 26,000							
			Dec. 31 375			Dec. 31 375	

Decreases in an asset account are commonly recorded with a credit to the account, but this procedure is *not* followed when recording depreciation. Instead, depreciation is recorded in a separate contra account. A **contra account** is an account linked with another account and having an opposite normal balance. It is reported as a subtraction from the other account's balance. For instance, FastForward's contra account of Accumulated Depreciation— Equipment is subtracted from the Equipment account in the balance sheet (see Exhibit 3.21).

Use of a contra account allows balance sheet readers to know both the full costs of assets and the total amount of depreciation charged to expense. By knowing both these amounts, decision makers can better assess a company's capacity and its need to replace assets. For example, FastForward's balance sheet shows both the $26,000 original cost of equipment and the $375 balance in the accumulated depreciation contra account. This information reveals that the equipment is close to new. If FastForward reports equipment only at its net amount of $25,625, users cannot assess the equipment's age or its need for replacement. The title of the contra account, *Accumulated Depreciation,* indicates that this account includes total depreciation expense for all prior periods for which the asset was used. For instance, the Equipment and the Accumulated Depreciation accounts appear as shown in Exhibit 3.9 on February 28, 2002, after three months of adjusting entries.

> ### Decision Maker   *e*
>
> **Entrepreneur**   You are preparing an offer to purchase a family-run restaurant. The depreciation schedule for the restaurant's building and equipment shows costs of $175,000 and accumulated depreciation of $155,000. This leaves a net for building and equipment of $20,000. Is this information useful in helping you decide on a purchase offer?
>
> Answer—p. 138

Point: The cost principle requires an asset to be initially recorded at acquisition cost. Depreciation causes the asset's book value to decline over time.

Equipment	167		Accumulated Depreciation – Equipment	168
Dec. 3 26,000			Dec. 31	375
			Jan. 31	375
			Feb. 28	375
			Balance	1,125

Exhibit 3.9

Accounts after Three Months of Depreciation Adjustments

These account balances would be reported in the assets section of the February 28 balance sheet as shown in Exhibit 3.10. The net amount is called *book value*. **Book value** equals this asset's acquisition costs less its accumulated depreciation.

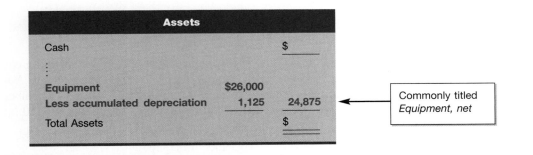

Assets		
Cash		$ _____
⋮		
Equipment	$26,000	
Less accumulated depreciation	1,125	24,875
Total Assets		$ _____

Commonly titled *Equipment, net*

Exhibit 3.10

Equipment and Accumulated Depreciation in the February 28 Balance Sheet

Adjusting Unearned Revenues

The term **unearned revenues** refers to cash received in advance of providing products and services. Unearned revenues, also called *deferred revenues,* are liabilities. When cash is accepted, an obligation to provide products or services is accepted. As products or services are provided, the unearned revenues become *earned* revenues. Adjusting entries for unearned revenues involve increasing (crediting) revenues and decreasing (debiting) unearned revenues, as shown in Exhibit 3.11. These adjustments reflect transactions and events that impact unearned revenues (including passage of time).

An example of unearned revenues is from **The New York Times Company,** which reports unexpired (unearned) subscriptions of more than $80 million: "Proceeds from subscriptions . . . are deferred at the time of sale and are included

Point: *To defer* is to postpone. We postpone reporting amounts received as revenues until they are earned.

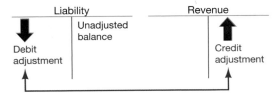

Exhibit 3.11

Adjusting for Unearned Revenues

in . . . income on a pro rata basis over the terms of the subscription." Unearned revenues are more than 10% of total current liabilities for the Times. Another example comes from the Boston Celtics. When the Celtics receive cash from advance ticket sales and broadcast fees, they record it in an unearned revenue account called *Deferred Game Revenues*. The Celtics recognize this unearned revenue with adjusting entries on a game-by-game basis. Since the NBA regular season begins in October and ends in April, revenue recognition is mainly limited to this period. For a recent season, the Celtics' quarterly revenues were $0 million for July–September; $25 for October–December; $40 million for January–March; and $11 million for April–June.

FastForward has unearned revenues. It agreed on December 26 to provide consulting services to a client for a fixed fee of $3,000 for 60 days. On that same day, this client paid the 60-day fee in advance, covering the period December 27 to February 24. The entry to record the cash received in advance is

Assets = Liabilities + Equity
+3,000   +3,000

Dec. 26	Cash	3,000	
	Unearned Consulting Revenue		3,000
	Received advance payment for services		
	over the next 60 days.		

This advance payment increases cash and creates an obligation to do consulting work over the next 60 days. As time passes, FastForward will earn this payment through consulting. By December 31, it has provided five days' service and earned 5/60 of the $3,000 unearned revenue. This amounts to $250 ($3,000 × 5/60). The *revenue recognition principle* implies that $250 of unearned revenue must be reported as revenue on the December income statement. The adjusting entry to reduce the liability account and recognize earned revenue is

Assets = Liabilities + Equity
           −250   +250

	Adjustment (d)		
Dec. 31	Unearned Consulting Revenue	250	
	Consulting Revenue		250
	To record earned revenue that was received		
	in advance ($3,000 × 5/60).		

After posting the adjusting entry, the accounts appear as in Exhibit 3.12. The adjusting entry transfers $250 from unearned revenue (a liability account) to a revenue account. *Not* making the adjustment (1) understates revenue and net income by $250 in the December income statement and (2) overstates unearned revenue and understates equity by $250 on the December 31 balance sheet.

Exhibit 3.12

Revenue Accounts after Adjusting for Prepaids

Unearned Consulting Revenue		236		
Dec. 31	250	Dec. 26	3,000
		Balance	2,750

Consulting Revenue		403
	Dec. 5	4,200
	12	1,600
	31	250
	Balance	6,050

Adjusting Accrued Expenses

Accrued expenses refer to costs that are incurred in a period but are both unpaid and unrecorded. Accrued expenses must be reported on the income statement of the period when incurred. Adjusting entries for recording accrued expenses involves increasing (debiting) expenses and increasing (crediting) liabilities as shown in Exhibit 3.13. This adjustment recognizes expenses

Exhibit 3.13

Adjusting for Accrued Expenses

Expense

Debit adjustment

Liability

Credit adjustment

incurred in a period but not yet paid. Common examples of accrued expenses are salaries, interest, rent, and taxes. We use salaries and interest to show how to adjust accounts for accrued expenses.

Accrued Salaries Expense

FastForward's employee earns $70 per day, or $350 for a five-day workweek beginning on Monday and ending on Friday. This employee is paid every two weeks on Friday. On December 12 and 26, the wages are paid, recorded in the journal, and posted to the ledger. The calendar in Exhibit 3.14 shows three working days after the December 26 payday (29, 30, and 31). This means the employee has earned three days' salary by the close of business on Wednesday, December 31, yet this salary cost is not paid or recorded.

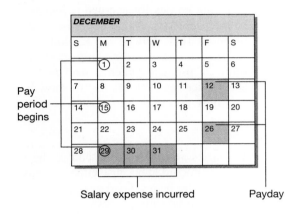

Salary expense incurred   Payday   Payday

Exhibit 3.14

Salary Accrual and Paydays

The financial statements would be incomplete if FastForward fails to report the added expense and liability to the employee for unpaid salary from December 29–31. The adjusting entry to account for accrued salaries is

	Adjustment (e)		
Dec. 31	Salaries Expense	210	
	Salaries Payable		210
	To record three days' accrued salary (3 × $70).		

$$\text{Assets} = \text{Liabilities} + \text{Equity}$$
$$+210 \qquad -210$$

After the adjusting entry is posted, the expense and liability accounts appear as shown in Exhibit 3.15. This means that $1,610 of salaries expense is reported on the December income statement and a $210 salaries payable (liability) is reported in the balance sheet. *Not* making the adjustment (1) understates Salaries Expense and overstates net income by $210 in the December income statement and (2) understates Salaries Payable (liabilities) and overstates equity by $210 on the December 31 balance sheet.

Point: An employer records salaries expense and a vacation pay liability when employees earn vacation pay.

Salaries Expense	**622**		
Dec. 12	700		
26	700		
31	210		
Balance	1,610		

Salaries Payable	**209**
Dec. 31	210

Exhibit 3.15

Salary Accounts after Accrual Adjustments

Accrued Interest Expense

Companies commonly have accrued interest expense on notes payable and other long-term liabilities at the end of a period. Interest expense is incurred with the passage of time. Unless interest is paid on the last day of an accounting period, we need to adjust accounts for interest expense incurred but not yet paid. This means we must accrue interest cost from the most recent payment date up to the end of the period. (The formula for computing accrued interest is: *Payable amount owed* × *Annual interest rate* × *Fraction of year since last payment date*.) The adjusting entry debits Interest Expense and credits Interest Payable.

Adjusting Accrued Revenues

The term **accrued revenues** refers to revenues earned in a period that are both unrecorded and not yet received in cash (or other assets). Accrued revenues are earned revenues that must be reported on the income statement. An example is a technician who bills customers only when the job is done. If one-third of a job is complete by the end of a period, then the technician must record one-third of the expected billing as revenue in that period—even though there is no billing or collection. The adjusting entries for accrued revenues increase (debit) assets and increase (credit) revenues as shown in Exhibit 3.16. Accrued revenues commonly arise from services, products, interest, and rent. We use service fees and interest to show how to adjust accounts for accrued revenues.

Exhibit 3.16

Adjusting for Accrued Revenues

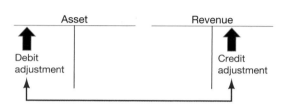

Accrued Services Revenue

Accrued revenues are not recorded until adjusting entries are made at the end of the accounting period. These accrued revenues are earned but unrecorded because either the buyer has not yet paid for them or the seller has not yet billed the buyer. FastForward provides an example. In the second week of December, it agreed to provide 30 days of consulting services to a local sports club for a fixed fee of $2,700. The terms of the initial agreement call for FastForward to provide services from December 12, 2001, through January 10, 2002, or 30 days of service. The club agrees to pay FastForward $2,700 on January 10, 2002, when the service period is complete. At December 31, 2001, 20 days of services have already been provided. Since the contracted services are not yet entirely provided, FastForward has neither billed the club nor recorded the services already provided. Still, FastForward has earned two-thirds of the 30-day fee, or $1,800 ($2,700 × 20/30). The *revenue recognition principle* implies that we must report the $1,800 on the December income statement because it was earned in December. The balance sheet also must report that the club owes FastForward $1,800. The year-end adjusting entry to account for accrued services revenue is

	Adjustment (f)		
Assets = Liabilities + Equity			
+1,800 +1,800	Dec. 31	Accounts Receivable	1,800	
		Consulting Revenue		1,800
		To record 20 days' accrued revenue.		

The debit to accounts receivable reflects the amount the club owes FastForward for consulting services already provided. After the adjusting entry is posted, the affected accounts appear as shown in Exhibit 3.17.

Exhibit 3.17

Receivable and Revenue Accounts after Accrual Adjustments

Accounts Receivable			**106**
Dec. 12	1,900	Dec. 22	1,900
31	1,800		
Balance	1,800		

Consulting Revenue			**403**
		Dec. 5	4,200
		12	1,600
		31	250
		31	1,800
		Balance	7,850

Accounts receivable are reported on the balance sheet at $1,800, and the $7,850 of consulting revenue is reported on the income statement. *Not* making the adjustment would understate (1) both Consulting Revenue and net income by $1,800 in the December income statement and (b) both Accounts Receivable (assets) and equity by $1,800 on the December 31 balance sheet.

Example: What is the adjusting entry if the 30-day consulting period began on December 22? *Answer:* One-third of the fee is earned:
Accounts Receivable . . . 900
Consulting Revenue . . . 900

Accrued Interest Revenue

In addition to the accrued interest expense we described earlier, interest can yield an accrued revenue when a debtor owes money (or other assets) to a company. If a company is holding notes or accounts receivable that produce interest revenue, we must adjust the accounts to record any earned and yet uncollected interest revenue. The adjusting entry is similar to the one for accruing services revenue. Specifically, we debit Interest Receivable (asset) and credit Interest Revenue.

Decision Maker

Loan Officer   The owner of an electronics store applies for a business loan. The store's financial statements reveal large increases in current-year revenues and income. Analysis shows that these increases are due to a promotion that let consumers buy now and pay nothing until January 1 of next year. The store recorded these sales as accrued revenue. Does your analysis raise any concerns?

Answer—p. 138

Links to Financial Statements

The process of adjusting accounts is intended to bring an asset or liability account balance to its correct amount. The adjusting entry also updates a related expense or revenue account. These adjustments are necessary for transactions and events that extend over more than one period. Adjusting entries are posted like any other entry. Exhibit 3.18 summarizes the four types of transactions requiring adjustment.Understanding this exhibit is important to understanding the adjusting process and its importance to financial statements. Remember that each adjusting entry affects one or more income statement accounts *and* one or more balance sheet accounts. An adjusting entry never affects cash.

A1   Explain how accounting adjustments link to financial statements.

Decision Ethics

Financial Officer   At year-end, the president instructs you, the financial officer, not to record accrued expenses until next year since they will not be paid until then. The president also directs you to record a recent purchase order from a customer that requires merchandise to be delivered 2 weeks after the year-end in current-year sales. Your company would report a net income instead of a net loss if you carry out these instructions. What do you do?

Answer—p. 138

	Before Adjusting		
Category	**Balance Sheet**	**Income Statement**	**Adjusting Entry**
Prepaid expense	Asset overstated	Expense understated	Dr. Expense Cr. Asset*
Unearned revenues	Liability overstated	Revenue understated	Dr. Liability Cr. Revenue
Accrued expenses	Liability understated	Expense understated	Dr. Expense Cr. Liability
Accrued revenues	Asset understated	Revenue understated	Dr. Asset Cr. Revenue

* For depreciation, the credit is to Accumulated Depreciation (contra asset).

Exhibit 3.18

Summary of Adjustments and Financial Statement Links

Quick Check

6. If you omit an adjusting entry for accrued revenues of $200 at year-end, what is this error's effect on the year-end income statement and balance sheet?

7. What is a contra account? Explain its purpose.

8. What is an accrued expense? Give an example.

9. Describe how an unearned revenue arises. Give an example.

Answers—p. 139

Adjusted Trial Balance

P2 Explain and prepare an adjusted trial balance.

An **unadjusted trial balance** is a list of accounts and balances prepared *before* adjustments are recorded. An **adjusted trial balance** is a list of accounts and balances prepared *after* adjusting entries have been recorded and posted to the ledger. Exhibit 3.19 shows both the unadjusted and the adjusted trial balances for FastForward at December 31, 2001. Notice that several new accounts arise from the adjusting entries. Also, the order of accounts in the trial balance is usually set up to match the order in the chart of accounts.

Exhibit 3.19

Unadjusted and Adjusted Trial Balances

FASTFORWARD
Trial Balances
December 31, 2001

	Unadjusted Trial Balance		Adjustments		Adjusted Trial Balance	
	Dr.	Cr.	Dr.	Cr.	Dr.	Cr.
Cash	$ 3,950				$ 3,950	
Accounts receivable	0		*(f)* 1,800		1,800	
Supplies	9,720			*(b)* 1,050	8,670	
Prepaid insurance	2,400			*(a)* 100	2,300	
Equipment	26,000				26,000	
Accumulated depreciation—Equip.		$ 0		*(c)* 375		$ 375
Accounts payable		6,200				6,200
Salaries payable		0		*(e)* 210		210
Unearned consulting revenue		3,000	*(d)* 250			2,750
Common stock		30,000				30,000
Retained earnings	600				600	
Consulting revenue		5,800		*(d)* 250		7,850
				(f) 1,800		
Rental revenue		300				300
Depreciation expense—Equip.	0		*(c)* 375		375	
Salaries expense	1,400		*(e)* 210		1,610	
Insurance expense	0		*(a)* 100		100	
Rent expense	1,000				1,000	
Supplies expense	0		*(b)* 1,050		1,050	
Utilities expense	230				230	
Totals	$ 45,300	$ 45,300	$ 3,785	$ 3,785	$ 47,685	$ 47,685

Exhibit 3.19 shows all the accounts, their adjustments, and their final adjusted balances. Each adjustment is identified by a letter in parentheses that links it to an adjusting entry explained earlier. Each amount in the Adjusted Trial Balance columns is computed by taking that account's amount from the Unadjusted Trial Balance columns and adding or subtracting any adjustment(s). To illustrate, Supplies has a $9,720 Dr. balance in the unadjusted columns. Subtracting the $1,050 Cr. amount shown in the adjustments columns yields an adjusted $8,670 Dr. balance for Supplies. An account can have more than one adjustment, such as for Consulting Revenue. Also, some accounts might not require adjustments for this period, such as Accounts Payable.

Accrual Reversals in Future Periods

The adjusting entries for both accrued expenses and accrued revenues foretell cash transactions in future periods. For example, accrued expenses at the end of one accounting period result in *cash payments* in a *future* period(s). Also, accrued revenues at the end of one accounting period result in *cash receipts* in a *future* period(s). This section explains how we account for these cash payments and cash receipts in future periods.

Paying Accrued Expenses

Recall that FastForward recorded accrued salaries with this adjusting entry:

(e) Dec. 31	Salaries Expense	210	
	Salaries Payable		210
	To record three days' accrued salary (3 × $70).		

Assets = Liabilities + Equity
          +210   −210

On January 9, the first payday of the next period, the following entry settles the accrued liability (salaries payable) and records salaries expense for seven days of work in January:

Jan. 9	Salaries Payable (3 days at $70)	210	
	Salaries Expense (7 days at $70)	490	
	Cash		700
	Paid two weeks' salary including three days accrued in December.		

Assets = Liabilities + Equity
−700   −210   −490

The $210 debit in the January 9 entry records the payment of the liability for the three days' salary accrued on December 31. The $490 debit records the salary for January's first seven working days (including the New Year's Day holiday) as an expense of the new accounting period. The $700 credit records the total amount of cash paid to the employee.

Receiving Accrued Revenues

Recall that FastForward made the following adjusting entry to record 20 days' accrued revenue earned from its consulting contract:

(f) Dec. 31	Accounts Receivable	1,800	
	Consulting Revenue		1,800
	To record 20 days' accrued revenue.		

Assets = Liabilities + Equity
+1,800   +1,800

When FastForward receives the cash on January 10, it makes the following entry to remove the accrued asset (accounts receivable) and recognize the revenue earned in January:

Jan. 10	Cash	2,700	
	Accounts Receivable		1,800
	Consulting Revenue		900
	Received cash for accrued asset and recorded earned consulting revenue.		

Assets = Liabilities + Equity
+2,700   +900
−1,800

The $2,700 debit reflects the cash received. The $1,800 credit reflects the removal of the receivable, and the $900 credit records the revenue earned in January.

We can prepare financial statements directly from information in the *adjusted* trial balance. An adjusted trial balance (see the right-most columns in Exhibit 3.19) includes all accounts and balances appearing in financial statements, and is easier to work from than the entire ledger when preparing financial statements.

Exhibit 3.20 shows how FastForward's revenue and expense balances are transferred from the adjusted trial balance to (1) the income statement and (2) the statement of retained earnings. Notice that we use the net income amount to prepare the statement of retained earnings.

Exhibit 3.21 shows how FastForward's asset and liability balances on the adjusted trial balance are transferred to the balance sheet. The ending retained earnings are determined on the statement of retained earnings and transferred to the balance sheet. The balance sheet in Exhibit 3.21 is in report form. The **report form balance sheet** lists assets, liabilities, and equity in

Preparing Financial Statements

P3 Prepare financial statements from an adjusted trial balance.

Exhibit 3.20

Preparing the Income Statement and Statement of Retained Earnings

From Exhibit 3.19

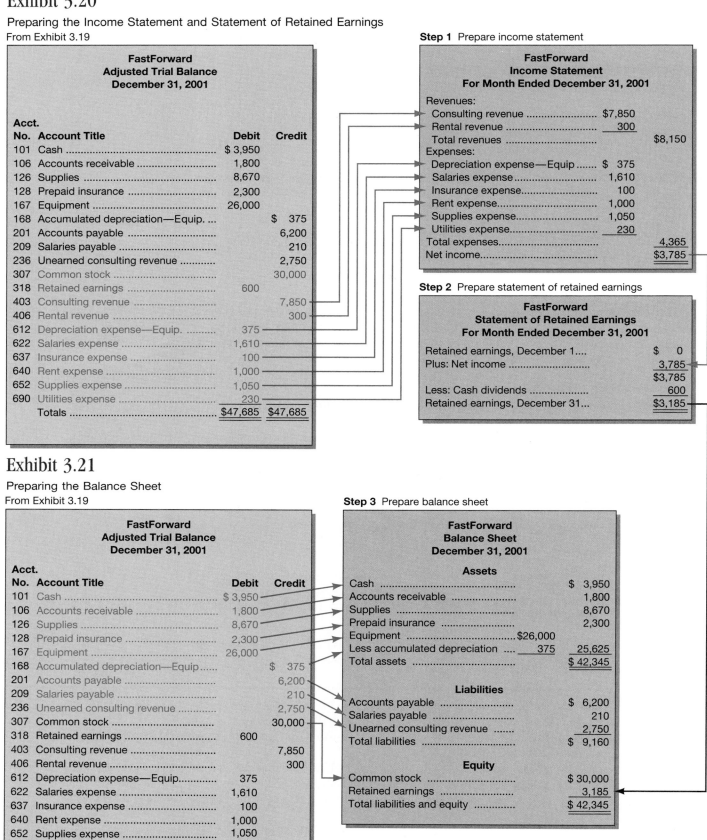

FastForward
Adjusted Trial Balance
December 31, 2001

Acct. No.	Account Title	Debit	Credit
101	Cash	$ 3,950	
106	Accounts receivable	1,800	
126	Supplies	8,670	
128	Prepaid insurance	2,300	
167	Equipment	26,000	
168	Accumulated depreciation—Equip.		$ 375
201	Accounts payable		6,200
209	Salaries payable		210
236	Unearned consulting revenue		2,750
307	Common stock		30,000
318	Retained earnings	600	
403	Consulting revenue		7,850
406	Rental revenue		300
612	Depreciation expense—Equip.	375	
622	Salaries expense	1,610	
637	Insurance expense	100	
640	Rent expense	1,000	
652	Supplies expense	1,050	
690	Utilities expense	230	
	Totals	$47,685	$47,685

Step 1 Prepare income statement

FastForward
Income Statement
For Month Ended December 31, 2001

Revenues:
Consulting revenue $7,850
Rental revenue 300
Total revenues $8,150
Expenses:
Depreciation expense—Equip .... $ 375
Salaries expense........................... 1,610
Insurance expense......................... 100
Rent expense................................ 1,000
Supplies expense.......................... 1,050
Utilities expense........................... 230
Total expenses.............................. 4,365
Net income..................................... $3,785

Step 2 Prepare statement of retained earnings

FastForward
Statement of Retained Earnings
For Month Ended December 31, 2001

Retained earnings, December 1.... $ 0
Plus: Net income 3,785
$3,785
Less: Cash dividends 600
Retained earnings, December 31... $3,185

Exhibit 3.21

Preparing the Balance Sheet

From Exhibit 3.19

FastForward
Adjusted Trial Balance
December 31, 2001

Acct. No.	Account Title	Debit	Credit
101	Cash	$ 3,950	
106	Accounts receivable	1,800	
126	Supplies	8,670	
128	Prepaid insurance	2,300	
167	Equipment	26,000	
168	Accumulated depreciation—Equip.		$ 375
201	Accounts payable		6,200
209	Salaries payable		210
236	Unearned consulting revenue		2,750
307	Common stock		30,000
318	Retained earnings	600	
403	Consulting revenue		7,850
406	Rental revenue		300
612	Depreciation expense—Equip.	375	
622	Salaries expense	1,610	
637	Insurance expense	100	
640	Rent expense	1,000	
652	Supplies expense	1,050	
690	Utilities expense	230	
	Totals	$47,685	$47,685

Step 3 Prepare balance sheet

FastForward
Balance Sheet
December 31, 2001

Assets
Cash .... $ 3,950
Accounts receivable 1,800
Supplies 8,670
Prepaid insurance 2,300
Equipment $26,000
Less accumulated depreciation 375 25,625
Total assets .... $ 42,345

Liabilities
Accounts payable .... $ 6,200
Salaries payable 210
Unearned consulting revenue 2,750
Total liabilities .... $ 9,160

Equity
Common stock .... $ 30,000
Retained earnings 3,185
Total liabilities and equity .... $ 42,345

vertical order. Nike also uses a report form—see Appendix A. The **account form balance sheet** lists assets on the left and liabilities and equity on the right side. Its name comes from its link to the accounting equation, Assets = Liabilities + Equity. The balance sheet in Exhibit 2.19 is in account form. Both forms are widely used and are considered equally helpful to users.

We usually prepare financial statements in the following order: income statement, statement of retained earnings, and balance sheet. This order makes sense since the balance sheet uses information from the statement of retained earnings, which in turn uses information from the income statement.

The statement of cash flows is usually the final statement prepared. All of FastForward's cash receipts and cash payments are recorded in its Cash account in the ledger. This Cash account holds information about cash flows from operating, investing, and financing activities and is summarized in Exhibit 3.22. It reports individual cash transactions that are keyed to the transactions numbered (1) through (16) from Chapter 2.

Cash			
Investment by owner (1)	30,000	Purchase of supplies (2)	2,500
Consulting revenue receipts (5)	4,200	Purchase of equipment (3)	26,000
Collection of account receivable (9)	1,900	Payment of rent (6)	1,000
Receipts for future services (12)	3,000	Payment of salary (7)	700
		Payment of account payable (10)	900
		Payment of dividend (11)	600
		Payment of insurance (13)	2,400
		Purchase of supplies (14)	120
		Payment of utilities (15)	230
		Payment of salary (16)	700
Balance	**3,950**		

Exhibit 3.22

Cash Account of FastForward

To prepare the statement of cash flows, we must determine whether a cash flow reflects an operating, investing, or financing activity. We then report amounts in their proper category on the statement of cash flows. FastForward's statement of cash flows is shown in Exhibit 3.23.

Exhibit 3.23

Statement of Cash Flows*

FAST*Forward*

FastForward Statement of Cash Flows For Month Ended December 31, 2001		
Cash flows from operating activities		
Cash received from clients (5 + 9 + 12)	$ 9,100	
Cash paid for supplies (2 + 10 + 14)	(3,520)	
Cash paid for rent (6)	(1,000)	
Cash paid for insurance (13)	(2,400)	
Cash paid for utilities (15)	(230)	
Cash paid to employee (7 + 16)	(1,400)	
Net cash provided by operating activities		$ 550
Cash flows from investing activities		
Purchase of equipment (3)	(26,000)	
Net cash used by investing activities		(26,000)
Cash flows from financing activities		
Investment by owner (1)	30,000	
Dividend to owner (11)	(600)	
Net cash provided by financing activities		29,400
Net increase in cash		$ 3,950
Cash balance, December 1		0
Cash balance, December 31		$ 3,950

*Transaction numbers from Exhibit 3.22 are shown in parentheses.

Analysis of the Cash account provides a direct means to prepare the statement of cash flows, but this method has two limitations. First, companies often have so many individual cash receipts and disbursements that it is difficult to review them all. Second, the Cash account often does not contain a description of each cash transaction. Chapter 12 explains how to prepare the statement of cash flows when facing these limitations.

Global: Both U.S. and international standards require that cash flows be classified as operating, investing, or financing.

Answers—p. 139

Closing Process

C4 Explain why temporary accounts are closed each period.

Temporary Accounts

Revenues
Expenses
Income Summary

Permanent Accounts

Assets
Liabilities
Equity

Topic Tackler 3-2

Point: To understand the closing process, it can help to focus on its *outcomes—updating* the retained earnings account balance to its proper ending balance, and getting *temporary accounts* to show *zero balances* for purposes of accumulating data for the next period.

The **closing process** is an important step at the end of an accounting period *after* financial statements have been completed. It prepares accounts for recording the transactions and the events of the *next* period. In the closing process we must (1) identify accounts for closing, (2) record and post the closing entries, and (3) prepare a post-closing trial balance. The purpose of the closing process is twofold. First, it resets revenue and expense account balances to zero at the end of each period. This is done so that these accounts can properly measure income for the next period. Second, it helps in summarizing a period's revenues and expenses. This section explains the closing process.

Temporary and Permanent Accounts

Temporary (or *nominal*) **accounts** accumulate data related to one accounting period. They include all income statement accounts and the Income Summary account. They are temporary because the accounts are opened at the beginning of a period, used to record transactions and events for that period, and then closed at the end of the period. *The closing process applies only to temporary accounts.* **Permanent** (or *real*) **accounts** report on activities related to one or more future accounting periods. They carry their ending balances into the next period and include all balance sheet accounts. These asset, liability, and equity accounts are not closed as long as a company continues to own the assets, owe the liabilities, and have equity.

Recording Closing Entries

To record and post **closing entries** is to transfer the end-of-period balances in revenue and expense accounts to the permanent retained earnings account. Closing entries are necessary at the end of each period after financial statements are prepared because

- Revenue and expense accounts must begin each period with zero balances.
- Retained earnings must reflect increases from revenues and decreases from expenses.

An income statement aims to report revenues (and gains) earned and expenses (and losses) incurred for a specific accounting period. The statement of retained earnings uses similar information. Since revenue and expense accounts must accumulate information separately for each period, they must start each period with zero balances. To close these accounts, we transfer their balances first to an account called *Income Summary*. **Income Summary** is a temporary account that contains a credit for the sum of all revenues (and gains) and a debit for the sum of all expenses (and losses). Its balance equals net income or net loss and is transferred to the retained earnings account. After these closing entries are posted, the

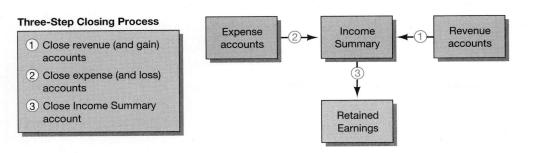

Exhibit 3.24

Closing Process

revenue, gain, expense, loss, and Income Summary accounts have zero balances. These accounts are then said to be *closed* or *cleared*. This process is illustrated in Exhibit 3.24.

Exhibit 3.25 uses the adjusted account balances of FastForward from Exhibit 3.19 to show the three steps necessary to close its temporary accounts. We explain each of these steps below.

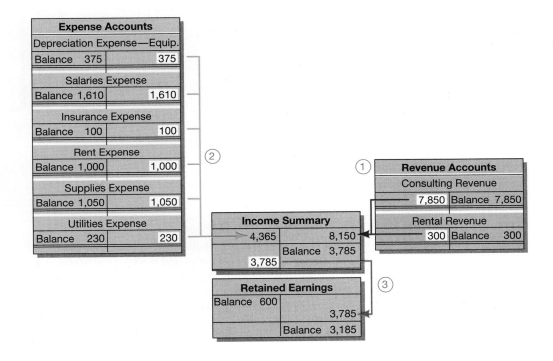

Exhibit 3.25

Closing Entries for FastForward

Step 1: Close Credit Balances in Revenue Accounts to Income Summary

The first closing entry transfers credit balances in revenue (and gain) accounts to the Income Summary account. We bring accounts with credit balances to zero by debiting them. For FastForward, this journal entry is step 1 in Exhibit 3.26. This entry closes revenue accounts and leaves them with zero balances. They are now ready to record revenues for the next period. The Income Summary account is created and used *only* for the closing process. The current $8,150 credit balance in Income Summary equals total revenues for the period.

P4 Describe and prepare closing entries.

Step 2: Close Debit Balances in Expense Accounts to Income Summary

The second closing entry transfers debit balances in expense (and loss) accounts to the Income Summary account. We bring expense accounts' debit balances to zero by crediting them. With a balance of zero, these accounts are ready to accumulate a record of expenses for the next period. This second closing entry for FastForward is step 2 in Exhibit 3.26. Exhibit 3.25 shows that posting this entry gives each expense account a zero balance. The entry also makes the balance of Income Summary equal to December's net income of $3,785.

Exhibit 3.26

Preparing Closing Entries

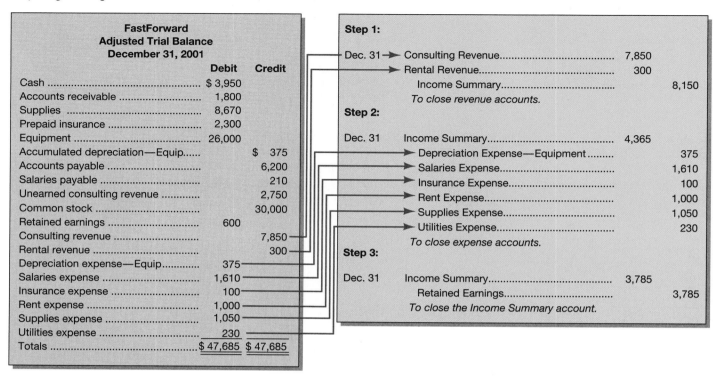

FastForward Adjusted Trial Balance December 31, 2001		
	Debit	Credit
Cash	$ 3,950	
Accounts receivable	1,800	
Supplies	8,670	
Prepaid insurance	2,300	
Equipment	26,000	
Accumulated depreciation—Equip.		$ 375
Accounts payable		6,200
Salaries payable		210
Unearned consulting revenue		2,750
Common stock		30,000
Retained earnings	600	
Consulting revenue		7,850
Rental revenue		300
Depreciation expense—Equip.	375	
Salaries expense	1,610	
Insurance expense	100	
Rent expense	1,000	
Supplies expense	1,050	
Utilities expense	230	
Totals	$ 47,685	$ 47,685

Step 1:

Dec. 31   Consulting Revenue... 7,850
          Rental Revenue... 300
              Income Summary..   8,150
              To close revenue accounts.

Step 2:

Dec. 31   Income Summary.. 4,365
            Depreciation Expense—Equipment........   375
            Salaries Expense...................................   1,610
            Insurance Expense.................................   100
            Rent Expense..   1,000
            Supplies Expense..................................   1,050
            Utilities Expense....................................   230
             To close expense accounts.

Step 3:

Dec. 31   Income Summary.. 3,785
            Retained Earnings....................................   3,785
           To close the Income Summary account.

All debit and credit balances related to expense and revenue accounts are now collected in the Income Summary account.

Step 3: Close Income Summary to Retained Earnings

The third closing entry transfers the balance of the Income Summary account to the Retained Earnings account. This entry closes the Income Summary account and is step 3 in Exhibit 3.26. The Income Summary account has a zero balance after posting this entry. It continues to have a zero balance until the closing process occurs at the end of the next period. The Retained Earnings account has now been increased by the amount of net income. Increases to retained earnings from net income are credits.

Notice that we can select the accounts and amounts needing to be closed by identifying individual revenue (and gain) and expense (and loss) accounts in the ledger. If we prepare an adjusted trial balance after the adjusting process, the information for closing entries is readily taken from it. This is illustrated in Exhibit 3.26 where we prepare closing entries using only the adjusted trial balance.

Information about some transactions and events that require adjusting is not always available until several days or even weeks after the period-end. This means that some adjusting and closing entries are recorded later than, but dated as of, the last day of the period. One example is a company that receives a utility bill on January 10 for costs incurred for the month of December. When it receives the bill, the company records the expense and the payable as of December 31. Other examples include long-distance phone usage and costs of many Web billings. The December income statement reflects these additional expenses

Decision Insight

Virtual Financial Statements

Quantum leaps in computing technology are increasing the importance of accounting analysis and interpretation. We are moving toward what the chief financial officer of Johnson & Johnson calls the "virtual financial statement"— where we can get up-to-date financials with the click of a mouse.

incurred, and the December 31 balance sheet includes these payables, although the amounts were not actually known on December 31.

Post-Closing Trial Balance

A **post-closing trial balance** is a list of permanent accounts and their balances from the ledger after all closing entries have been journalized and posted. It lists the balances for all accounts not closed. These accounts are a company's assets, liabilities, and equity, and they are identical to those in the balance sheet. The aim of a post-closing trial balance is to verify that (1) total debits equal total credits for permanent accounts and (2) all temporary accounts have zero balances. FastForward's post-closing trial balance is shown in Exhibit 3.27. The post-closing trial balance usually is the last step in the accounting process. Like the unadjusted and adjusted trial balances, the post-closing trial balance does not necessarily tell us that all transactions are recorded or that the ledger is correct.

P5 Explain and prepare a post-closing trial balance.

FASTFORWARD Post-Closing Trial Balance December 31, 2001		
	Debit	Credit
Cash	$ 3,950	
Accounts receivable	1,800	
Supplies	8,670	
Prepaid insurance	2,300	
Equipment	26,000	
Accumulated depreciation—Equipment		$ 375
Accounts payable		6,200
Salaries payable		210
Unearned consulting revenue		2,750
Common stock		30,000
Retained earnings		3,185
Totals	$42,720	$42,720

Exhibit 3.27

Post-Closing Trial Balance

Exhibit 3.28 shows the entire ledger of FastForward as of December 31 after adjusting and closing entries are posted. Note that the temporary accounts (revenues and expenses) have balances equal to zero.

Quick Check

14. What are the three major steps in preparing closing entries?

15. Why are revenue and expense accounts called *temporary*? Are there other temporary accounts?

16. What accounts are listed on the post-closing trial balance?

Answers—p. 139

Reviewing the Accounting Cycle

The term **accounting cycle** refers to the steps in preparing financial statements. It is called a *cycle* because the steps are repeated each reporting period. Exhibit 3.29 shows the 10 steps in the cycle, beginning with analyzing transactions and ending with a post-closing trial balance or reversing entries. Steps 1 through 3 usually occur regularly as a company enters into transactions. Steps 4 through 9 are done at the end of a period. Reversing entries in step 10 are optional and are explained in Appendix 3C. Detailed descriptions of these steps are in Chapters 2 and 3.

C5 Identify steps in the accounting cycle.

Decision Insight

Data Speedway Five years ago, Sun Microsystems took a month to prepare statements after its year-end. Today, it takes only 24 hours to deliver preliminary figures to key decision makers. What is Sun's secret? Transactions are entered into a network of computers so everyone can share and quickly manage data.

Exhibit 3.28

Ledger after the Closing Process for FastForward

General Ledger

Asset Accounts

Cash   Acct. No. 101

Date	Explan.	PR	Debit	Credit	Balance
2001					
Dec. 1		G1	30,000		30,000
2		G1		2,500	27,500
3		G1		26,000	1,500
5		G1	4,200		5,700
6		G1		2,400	3,300
12		G1		1,000	2,300
12		G1		700	1,600
22		G1	1,900		3,500
24		G1		900	2,600
24		G1		600	2,000
26		G1	3,000		5,000
26		G1		120	4,880
26		G1		230	4,650
26		G1		700	**3,950**

Accounts Receivable   Acct. No. 106

Date	Explan.	PR	Debit	Credit	Balance
2001					
Dec.12		G1	1,900		1,900
22		G1		1,900	0
31	Adj.	G1	1,800		**1,800**

Supplies   Acct. No. 126

Date	Explan.	PR	Debit	Credit	Balance
2001					
Dec. 2		G1	2,500		2,500
6		G1	7,100		9,600
26		G1	120		9,720
31	Adj.	G1		1,050	**8,670**

Prepaid Insurance   Acct. No. 128

Date	Explan.	PR	Debit	Credit	Balance
2001					
Dec. 6		G1	2,400		2,400
31	Adj.	G1		100	**2,300**

Equipment   Acct. No. 167

Date	Explan.	PR	Debit	Credit	Balance
2001					
Dec. 3		G1	26,000		**26,000**

Accumulated Depreciation— Equipment   Acct. No. 168

Date	Explan.	PR	Debit	Credit	Balance
2001					
Dec. 31	Adj.	G1		375	**375**

Liability and Equity Accounts

Accounts Payable   Acct. No. 201

Date	Explan.	PR	Debit	Credit	Balance
2001					
Dec. 6		G1		7,100	7,100
24		G1	900		**6,200**

Salaries Payable   Acct. No. 209

Date	Explan.	PR	Debit	Credit	Balance
2001					
Dec. 31	Adj.	G1		210	**210**

Unearned Consulting Revenue   Acct. No. 236

Date	Explan.	PR	Debit	Credit	Balance
2001					
Dec. 26		G1		3,000	3,000
31	Adj.	G1	250		**2,750**

Common Stock   Acct. No. 307

Date	Explan.	PR	Debit	Credit	Balance
2001					
Dec. 1		G1		30,000	**30,000**

Retained Earnings   Acct. No. 318

Date	Explan.	PR	Debit	Credit	Balance
2001					
Dec. 24		G1	600		600
31	Closing	G1		3,785	3,185

Revenue and Expense Accounts (including Income Summary)

Consulting Revenue   Acct. No. 403

Date	Explan.	PR	Debit	Credit	Balance
2001					
Dec. 5		G1		4,200	4,200
12		G1		1,600	5,800
31	Adj.	G1		250	6,050
31	Adj.	G1		1,800	7,850
31	Closing	G1	7,850		0

Rental Revenue   Acct. No. 406

Date	Explan.	PR	Debit	Credit	Balance
2001					
Dec.12		G1		300	300
31	Closing	G1	300		0

Depreciation Expense— Equipment   Acct. No. 612

Date	Explan.	PR	Debit	Credit	Balance
2001					
Dec.31	Adj.	G1	375		375
31	Closing	G1		375	0

Salaries Expense   Acct. No. 622

Date	Explan.	PR	Debit	Credit	Balance
2001					
Dec.12		G1	700		700
26		G1	700		1,400
31	Adj.	G1	210		1,610
31	Closing	G1		1,610	0

Insurance Expense   Acct. No. 637

Date	Explan.	PR	Debit	Credit	Balance
2001					
Dec.31	Adj.	G1	100		100
31	Closing	G1		100	0

Rent Expense   Acct. No. 640

Date	Explan.	PR	Debit	Credit	Balance
2001					
Dec.12		G1	1,000		1,000
31	Closing	G1		1,000	0

Supplies Expense   Acct. No. 652

Date	Explan.	PR	Debit	Credit	Balance
2001					
Dec. 31	Adj.	G1	1,050		1,050
31	Closing	G1		1,050	0

Utilities Expense   Acct. No. 690

Date	Explan.	PR	Debit	Credit	Balance
2001					
Dec. 26		G1	230		230
31	Closing	G1		230	0

Income Summary   Acct. No. 901

Date	Explan.	PR	Debit	Credit	Balance
2001					
Dec. 31	Closing	G1		8,150	8,150
31	Closing	G1	4,365		3,785
31	Closing	G1	3,785		0

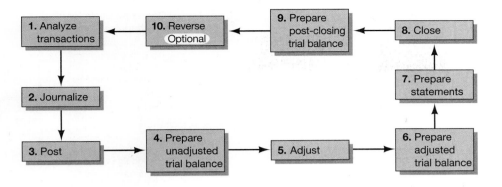

Exhibit 3.29
Steps in the
Accounting Cycle*

Explanations

1. Analyze transaction	Analyze transactions to prepare for journalizing.
2. Journalize	Record accounts, including debits and credits, in a journal.
3. Post	Transfer debits and credits from the journal to the ledger.
4. Prepare unadjusted trial balance	Summarize unadjusted ledger accounts and amounts.
5. Adjust	Record adjustments to bring account balances up to date; journalize and post adjusting entries.
6. Prepare adjusted trial balance	Summarize adjusted ledger accounts and amounts.
7. Prepare statements	Use adjusted trial balance to prepare statements.
8. Close	Journalize and post entries to close temporary accounts.
9. Prepare post-closing trial balance	Test clerical accuracy of the closing procedures.
10. Reverse (optional)	Reverse certain adjustments in the next period—see Appendix 3C.

*Steps 4, 6, and 9 can be done on a work sheet, but adjustments (step 5) and closings (step 8) must always be journalized and posted.

Classified Balance Sheet

Our discussion to this point has been limited to unclassified financial statements. Companies also prepare classified financial statements. This section focuses on a classified balance sheet. Chapter 4 describes a classified income statement. An **unclassified balance sheet** is one whose items are broadly grouped into assets, liabilities, and equity. One example is FastForward's balance sheet in Exhibit 3.21. A **classified balance sheet** organizes assets and liabilities into important subgroups that provide more useful information to decision makers. One example is information to distinguish liabilities that are due soon from those not due for several years. This information helps us better assess a company's ability to meet liabilities when they come due.

C6 Explain and prepare a classified balance sheet.

Classification Structure

A classified balance sheet has no required layout, but it usually contains the categories in Exhibit 3.30. One of the more important classifications is the separation between current and noncurrent items for both assets and liabilities. Current items are those expected to come due (either collected or owed) within one year or the company's operating cycle, whichever is longer. An **operating cycle** is the length of time between (1) purchases of services or products from suppliers and (2) cash receipts from the sale of services or products to customers. The length of a company's operating cycle depends on its activities. Exhibit 3.31 shows key points in the operating cycle for both a service company and a merchandising company. For a service company, the operating cycle is the normal time between (1) paying employees who perform the services and (2) receiving cash from customers. For a merchandiser selling products, the

Topic Tackler 3-3

Assets	Liabilities and Equity
Current assets	Current liabilities
Noncurrent assets	Noncurrent liabilities
Long-term investments	Equity
Plant assets	
Intangible assets	

Exhibit 3.30

Typical Categories in a Classified Balance Sheet

Exhibit 3.31

Operating Cycles for a Service Company and a Merchandise Company

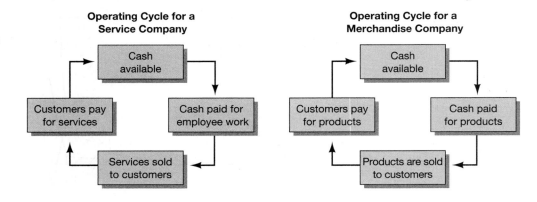

Operating Cycle for a Service Company

Cash available → Cash paid for employee work → Services sold to customers → Customers pay for services → Cash available

Operating Cycle for a Merchandise Company

Cash available → Cash paid for products → Products are sold to customers → Customers pay for products → Cash available

Point: Current is also called *short term,* and noncurrent is also called *long term.*

Point: Short-term investments maturing within three months are combined with cash on both the balance sheet and cash flow statement. This combination is called *cash and cash equivalents.*

Global: In the U.K. and many countries influenced by U.K. reporting, noncurrent assets are listed first and current assets are listed second.

operating cycle is the normal time between (1) paying suppliers for merchandise and (2) receiving cash from customers.

Most operating cycles are less than one year. This means most companies use a one-year period in deciding which assets and liabilities are current. Other companies have an operating cycle longer than one year. For instance, producers of certain beverages (wine) and products (ginseng) that require aging for several years have operating cycles longer than one year. These companies use their multiyear operating cycles in deciding which balance sheet items are current or noncurrent. A balance sheet usually lists current assets before noncurrent assets and current liabilities before noncurrent liabilities. This consistency in presentation allows users to quickly identify current assets that are most easily converted to cash and current liabilities that are shortly coming due. Items in the current group are usually listed in the order of how quickly they will be converted to, or paid in, cash.

Classification Categories

This section describes the most common categories in a classified balance sheet. The balance sheet for **Music Components** in Exhibit 3.32 shows these typical categories. Its assets are classified as either current or noncurrent. Its noncurrent assets include three main categories: long-term investments, plant assets, and intangible assets. Its liabilities are classified as either current or long term. Not all companies use the same categories of assets and liabilities for their balance sheets. **K2**'s balance sheet lists only three asset classes: current assets; property, plant and equipment; and other assets.

Current Assets

Current assets are cash and other resources that are expected to be sold, collected, or used within one year or the company's operating cycle, whichever is longer. Examples are cash, short-term investments, accounts receivable, short-term notes receivable, goods for sale (called *merchandise* or *inventory*), and prepaid expenses. A company's prepaid expenses are usually small in amount compared to many other assets and are often combined and shown as a single item. The prepaid expenses in Exhibit 3.32 likely include items such as prepaid insurance, prepaid rent, office supplies, and store supplies. Prepaid expenses are usually listed last because they will not be converted to cash (instead, they are used).

Long-Term Investments

A second major balance sheet classification is **long-term** (or *noncurrent*) **investments.** Notes receivable and investments in stocks and bonds are long-term assets when they are expected to be held for more than the longer of one year or the operating cycle. We further explain the differences between short- and long-term investments later in the book.

Plant Assets

Plant assets are tangible long-lived assets used to help produce or sell products and services. Items in this category are both *long lived* and *used to produce* or *sell products and services.*

Exhibit 3.32

Example of a Classified
Balance Sheet

MUSIC COMPONENTS Balance Sheet January 31, 2002		
Assets		
Current assets		
Cash	$ 6,500	
Short-term investments	2,100	
Accounts receivable	4,400	
Merchandise inventory	27,500	
Prepaid expenses	2,400	
Total current assets		$ 42,900
Long-term investments		
Notes receivable	1,500	
Investments in stocks and bonds	18,000	
Land held for future expansion	48,000	
Total long-term investments		67,500
Plant assets		
Store equipment	$ 33,200	
Less accumulated depreciation	8,000	25,200
Buildings	170,000	
Less accumulated depreciation	45,000	125,000
Land		73,200
Total plant assets		223,400
Intangible assets		10,000
Total assets		$343,800
Liabilities		
Current liabilities		
Accounts payable	$15,300	
Wages payable	3,200	
Notes payable	3,000	
Current portion of long-term liabilities	7,500	
Total current liabilities		$ 29,000
Long-term liabilities (net of current portion)		150,000
Total liabilities		$179,000
Equity		
Common stock		50,000
Retained earnings		114,800
Total liabilities and equity		$343,800

For example, land held for future expansion is *not* a plant asset because it is not used to produce or sell products and services. The order of listing plant assets is usually from most liquid to least liquid such as equipment and machinery to buildings and land.

Point: Plant assets are also called **fixed assets; property, plant and equipment;** or **long-lived assets.**

Intangible Assets

Intangible assets are long-term resources used to produce or sell products and services. They usually lack physical form and have uncertain benefits. Examples are patents, trademarks, copyrights, franchises, and goodwill. Their value comes from the privileges or rights granted to or held by the owner. **Outboard Marine** reports intangible assets of $79.3 million, which is nearly 10 percent of its total assets. Its intangibles include trademarks, patents, and its dealer network.

Point: Companies sometimes have intangible assets, but because of materiality or cost principles these assets are not reported.

Current Liabilities

Point: Many financial ratios are distorted if accounts are not classified correctly. We must be especially careful when analyzing accounts whose balances are separated into short and long term.

Current liabilities are obligations due to be paid or settled within one year or the operating cycle, whichever is longer. They are usually settled by paying out current assets such as cash. Current liabilities often include accounts payable, notes payable, wages payable, taxes payable, interest payable, and unearned revenues. Also, any portion of a long-term liability due to be paid within one year or the operating cycle, whichever is longer, is a current liability—see Exhibit 3.32. Unearned revenues are current liabilities when they will be settled by delivering products or services within one year or the operating cycle, whichever is longer. Current liabilities are often reported in the order of those to be settled first.

Long-Term Liabilities

Point: Many companies report two or more subgroups for long-term liabilities. See the balance sheets in Appendix A for examples.

Long-term liabilities are obligations *not* due within one year or the operating cycle, whichever is longer. Notes payable, mortgages payable, bonds payable, and lease obligations are common long-term liabilities. If a company has both short- and long-term items in each of these categories, they are commonly separated into two accounts in the ledger.

Equity

Point: For noncorporations, the equity section reports a capital account for each owner.

Equity is the owners' claim on assets. The equity section is divided into two main subsections, common stock and retained earnings. Investments of assets in the business by the owners in exchange for stock are recorded as common stock. Income retained for use in the business is recorded as retained earnings.

Quick Check

17. Identify which of the following assets are classified as (1) current assets or (2) plant assets: (*a*) land used in operations, (*b*) office supplies, (*c*) receivables from customers due in 10 months, (*d*) insurance protection for the next nine months, (*e*) trucks used to provide services to customers, (*f*) trademarks.

18. Cite two examples of assets classified as investments on the balance sheet.

19. Explain the operating cycle for a service company.

Answers—p. 139

Decision Analysis   *d*   Profit Margin and Current Ratio

This section describes and illustrates a measure of profitability (profit margin) and a measure of liquidity (current ratio).

A2 Compute profit margin and describe its use in analyzing company performance.

Profit Margin

A useful measure of a company's operating results is the ratio of its net income to net sales. This ratio is called **profit margin,** also called *return on sales,* and is computed as shown in Exhibit 3.33.

Exhibit 3.33
Profit Margin

$$\text{Profit margin} = \frac{\text{Net income}}{\text{Net sales}}$$

This ratio is interpreted as reflecting the percent of profit in each dollar of sales. To illustrate how we compute and use profit margin, let's look at the results of Ben & Jerry's Homemade, Inc., in Exhibit 3.34. Profit margin is one measure we can use to help evaluate Ben & Jerry's performance.

	1999	1998	1997	1996
Net income (in mil.)	$ 3.4	$ 6.2	$ 3.9	$ 3.9
Net sales (in mil.)	$237.0	$209.2	$174.2	$167.2
Profit margin	1.4%	3.0%	2.2%	2.3%
Industry profit margin	2.2%	1.6%	2.0%	2.1%

Exhibit 3.34
Ben & Jerry's Profit Margin

Ben & Jerry's average profit margin is 2.2% over this period. Year 1999 stands out as especially poor. This is partly due to special charges tied to the discontinuance of a manufacturing plant. During this period there is a steady increase in Ben & Jerry's sales, from less than $170 million in 1996 to more than $237 million in 1999. We also compare its profit margin to that of competitors (last row of Exhibit 3.34). Ben & Jerry's is a relatively small competitor in the superpremium ice cream industry, but its historical profit margins tended to be at or better than those of its competitors. Still, competition from larger superpremium companies kept Ben & Jerry's from enjoying a higher margin, and played a part in its recent purchase by Dutch conglomerate Unilever.

Current Ratio

Another important use of financial statements is to help assess a company's ability to pay its debts in the near future. This type of analysis affects decisions by suppliers when allowing a company to buy on credit. It also affects decisions by creditors when lending money to a company, including loan terms such as interest rate, due date, and collateral requirements. It can also affect a manager's decisions about using cash to pay existing debts when they come due. The **current ratio** is an important measure of a company's ability to pay its short-term obligations. It is defined in Exhibit 3.35 as current assets divided by current liabilities:

A3   Compute the current ratio and describe what it reveals about a company's financial condition.

$$\text{Current ratio} = \frac{\text{Current assets}}{\text{Current liabilities}}$$

Exhibit 3.35
Current Ratio

Using financial information from Ben & Jerry's, we compute its current ratio for the recent four-year period. The results are shown in Exhibit 3.36.

($ in Millions)	1999	1998	1997	1996
Current assets	$87.3	$82.3	$80.1	$68.1
Current liabilities	$44.5	$33.9	$28.7	$18.1
Current ratio	2.0	2.4	2.8	3.8
Industry current ratio	1.8	2.1	2.3	2.2

Exhibit 3.36
Ben & Jerry's Current Ratio

Ben & Jerry's current ratio dipped to 2.0 in 1999 compared to higher ratios for prior years. Still, the current ratio for each of these years exceeds the industry norm and suggests that the company's short-term obligations can be covered with its short-term assets. However, if its ratio approached 1, Ben & Jerry's would expect to face more challenges in covering liabilities. If the ratio were *less* than 1, Ben & Jerry's current liabilities would exceed its current assets, and its ability to pay short-term obligations would be in doubt.

Decision Maker   *d*

Analyst   You are analyzing the financial condition of a fitness club to assess its ability to meet upcoming loan payments. You compute its current ratio as 1.2. You also find that a major portion of accounts receivable is due from one client who has not made any payments in the past 12 months. Removing this receivable from current assets drops the current ratio to 0.7. What do you conclude?

Answer—p. 138

Demonstration Problem 1

The following information relates to Fanning's Electronics on December 31, 2002. The company, which uses the calendar year as its annual reporting period, initially records prepaid and unearned items in balance sheet accounts (assets and liabilities, respectively).

a. The company's weekly payroll is $8,750, paid each Friday for a five-day workweek. December 31, 2002 falls on a Monday, but the employees will not be paid their wages until Friday, January 4, 2003.

b. Eighteen months earlier, on July 1, 2001, the company purchased equipment that cost $20,000 and had no salvage value. Its useful life is predicted to be five years.

c. On October 1, 2002, the company agreed to work on a new housing development. The company is paid $120,000 on October 1 in advance of future installation of similar alarm systems in 24 new homes. That amount was credited to the Unearned Services Revenue account. Between October 1 and December 31, work on 20 homes was completed.

d. On September 1, 2002, the company purchased a 12-month insurance policy for $1,800. The transaction was recorded with an $1,800 debit to Prepaid Insurance.

e. On December 29, 2002, the company performed a $7,000 service that has not been billed as of December 31, 2002.

Required

1. Prepare any necessary adjusting entries on December 31, 2002, in relation to transactions and events *a* through *e*.

2. Prepare T-accounts for the accounts affected by adjusting entries, and post the adjusting entries. Determine the adjusted balances for the Unearned Revenue and the Prepaid Insurance accounts.

3. Complete the following table and determine the amounts and effects of your adjusting entries on the year 2002 income statement and the December 31, 2002, balance sheet. Use up (down) arrows to indicate an increase (decrease) in the Effect columns.

Entry	Amount in the Entry	Effect on Net Income	Effect on Total Assets	Effect on Total Liabilities	Effect on Equity

Planning the Solution

- Analyze each situation to determine which accounts need to be updated with an adjustment.
- Calculate the amount of each adjustment and prepare the necessary journal entries.
- Show the amount of each adjustment in the designated accounts, determine the adjusted balance, and identify the balance sheet classification of the account.
- Determine each entry's effect on net income for the year and on total assets, total liabilities, and equity at the end of the year.

Solution to Demonstration Problem

1. Adjusting journal entries.

(a) Dec. 31	Wages Expense	1,750	
	Wages Payable		1,750
	To accrue wages for the last day of the year ($8,750 × 1/5).		
(b) Dec. 31	Depreciation Expense—Equipment	4,000	
	Accumulated Depreciation—Equipment ...		4,000
	To record depreciation expense for the year ($20,000/5 years = $4,000 per year).		
(c) Dec. 31	Unearned Services Revenue	100,000	
	Services Revenue		100,000
	To recognize services revenue earned ($120,000 × 20/24).		
(d) Dec. 31	Insurance Expense	600	
	Prepaid Insurance		600
	To adjust for expired portion of insurance ($1,800 × 4/12).		
(e) Dec. 31	Accounts Receivable	7,000	
	Services Revenue		7,000
	To record services revenue earned.		

2. T-accounts for adjusting journal entries *a* through *e*.

Wages Expense				Wages Payable	
(a)	1,750			(a)	1,750

Depreciation Expense—Equipment				Accumulated Depreciation—Equipment	
(b)	4,000			(b)	4,000

Unearned Revenue				Services Revenue	
		Unadj. Bal.	120,000	(c)	100,000
(c)	100,000			(e)	7,000
		Adj. Bal.	20,000	Adj. Bal.	107,000

Insurance Expense				Prepaid Insurance	
(d)	600		Unadj. Bal.	1,800	
				(d)	600

Accounts Receivable					
			Adj. Bal.	1,200	
(e)	7,000				

3. Financial statement effects of adjusting journal entries.

Entry	Amount in the Entry	Effect on Net Income	Effect on Total Assets	Effect on Total Liabilities	Effect on Equity
a	$ 1,750	$ 1,750 ↓	No effect	$ 1,750 ↑	$ 1,750 ↓
b	4,000	4,000 ↓	$4,000 ↓	No effect	4,000 ↓
c	100,000	100,000 ↑	No effect	$100,000 ↓	100,000 ↑
d	600	600 ↓	$ 600 ↓	No effect	600 ↓
e	7,000	7,000 ↑	$7,000 ↑	No effect	7,000 ↑

Following is the adjusted trial balance of Midtown Repair Company at December 31, 2002:

Demonstration Problem 2

Midtown Repair Company Adjusted Trial Balance December 31, 2002		
	Debit	Credit
Cash	$ 95,600	
Notes receivable	50,000	
Prepaid insurance	16,000	
Prepaid rent	4,000	
Equipment	170,000	
Accumulated depreciation—Equipment		$ 57,000
Accounts payable		52,000
Long-term notes payable		63,000
Common stock		118,500
Retained earnings		30,000
Repair services revenue		180,800
Interest revenue		7,500
Depreciation expense—Equipment	28,500	
Wages expense	85,000	
Rent expense	48,000	
Insurance expense	6,000	
Interest expense	5,700	
Totals	$508,800	$508,800

Required

1. Prepare closing entries for Midtown Repair Company.
2. Set up the Income Summary and the Retained Earnings accounts in the general ledger (in balance column format), and post the closing entries to these accounts.
3. Determine the balance of the Retained Earnings account to be reported on the December 31, 2002, balance sheet.

Planning the Solution

- Prepare entries to close the revenue accounts to Income Summary, to close the expense accounts to Income Summary, and to close Income Summary to the Retained Earnings account.
- Post the closing entries.

Solution to Demonstration Problem

1. Closing entries:

Dec. 31	Repair Services Revenue	180,800	
	Interest Revenue	7,500	
	Income Summary		188,300
	To close revenue accounts.		
Dec. 31	Income Summary	173,200	
	Depreciation Expense—Equipment		28,500
	Wages Expense		85,000
	Rent Expense		48,000
	Insurance Expense		6,000
	Interest Expense		5,700
	To close expense accounts.		
Dec. 31	Income Summary	15,100	
	Retained Earnings		15,100
	To close the Income Summary account.		

2. Set up the Income Summary and Retained Earnings ledger accounts, and post the closing entries.

Income Summary					Account No. 901
Date	**Explanation**	**PR**	**Debit**	**Credit**	**Balance**
2002					
Jan. 1	Beginning balance				0
Dec. 31	Close revenue accounts			188,300	188,300
31	Close expense accounts		173,200		15,100
31	Close income summary		15,100		0

Retained Earnings					Account No. 318
Date	**Explanation**	**PR**	**Debit**	**Credit**	**Balance**
2002					
Jan. 1	Unadjusted balance			30,000	30,000
Dec. 31	Close Income Summary			15,100	45,100

3. The final retained earnings balance of $45,100 (from part 2) will be reported on the December 31, 2002, balance sheet.

Alternative Accounting for Prepaids

3A

This appendix explains an alternative in accounting for prepaid expenses and for unearned (prepaid) revenues.

Recording Prepaid Expenses in Expense Accounts

An alternative method is to record *all* prepaid expenses with debits to expense accounts. If any prepaids remain unused or unexpired at the end of an accounting period, then adjusting entries must transfer the cost of the unused portions from expense accounts to prepaid expense (asset) accounts. This alternative method is acceptable. The financial statements are identical under either method, but the adjusting entries are different. To illustrate the differences between these two methods, let's look at FastForward's cash payment of December 6 for 24 months of insurance coverage beginning on December 1. FastForward recorded that payment with a debit to an asset account, but it could have recorded a debit to an expense account. These alternatives are shown in Exhibit 3A.1.

P6 Identify and explain alternatives in accounting for prepaids.

		Payment Recorded as Asset		Payment Recorded as Expense	
Dec. 6	Prepaid Insurance	2,400			
	Cash		2,400		
Dec. 6	Insurance Expense			2,400	
	Cash				2,400

Exhibit 3A.1

Alternative Initial Entries for Prepaid Expenses

At the end of its accounting period on December 31, insurance protection for one month has expired. This means $100 ($2,400/24) of insurance coverage expires and is an expense for December. The adjusting entry depends on how the original payment was recorded. This is shown in Exhibit 3A.2.

		Payment Recorded as Asset		Payment Recorded as Expense	
Dec. 31	Insurance Expense	100			
	Prepaid Insurance		100		
Dec. 31	Prepaid Insurance			2,300	
	Insurance Expense				2,300

Exhibit 3A.2

Adjusting Entry for Prepaid Expenses for the Two Alternatives

When these entries are posted to the accounts in the ledger, we can see that these two methods give identical results. The December 31 adjusted account balances in Exhibit 3A.3 show Prepaid Insurance of $2,300 and Insurance Expense of $100 for both methods.

Recording Unearned Revenues in Revenue Accounts

As with prepaid expenses, an alternative method is to record *all* unearned revenues with credits to revenue accounts. If any revenues are unearned at the end of an accounting period, then adjusting entries must transfer the unearned portions from revenue accounts to unearned revenue (liability) accounts. This alternative method is acceptable. While the adjusting entries are different for these two alternatives, the financial statements are identical. To illustrate the accounting differences between

Exhibit 3A.3

Account Balances under Two
Alternatives for Recording
Prepaid Expenses

Payment Recorded as Asset			
Prepaid Insurance			**128**
Dec. 6	2,400	Dec. 31	100
Balance	2,300		

Insurance Expense			**637**
Dec. 31	100		

Payment Recorded as Expense			
Prepaid Insurance			**128**
Dec. 31	2,300		

Insurance Expense			**637**
Dec. 6	2,400	Dec. 31	2,300
Balance	100		

these two methods, let's look at FastForward's December 26 receipt of $3,000 for consulting services covering the period December 27 to February 24. FastForward recorded this transaction with a credit to a liability account. The alternative is to record it with a credit to a revenue account, as shown in Exhibit 3A.4.

Exhibit 3A.4

Alternative Initial Entries
for Unearned Revenues

			Receipt Recorded as Liability	Receipt Recorded as Revenue
Dec. 26	Cash	3,000		
	Unearned Consulting Revenue		3,000	
Dec. 26	Cash		3,000	
	Consulting Revenue			3,000

By the end of its accounting period on December 31, FastForward has earned $250 of this revenue. This means $250 of the liability has been satisfied. Depending on how the initial receipt is recorded, the adjusting entry is as shown in Exhibit 3A.5.

Exhibit 3A.5

Adjusting Entry for
Unearned Revenues for
the Two Alternatives

			Receipt Recorded as Liability	Receipt Recorded as Revenue
Dec. 31	Unearned Consulting Revenue	250		
	Consulting Revenue		250	
Dec. 31	Consulting Revenue		2,750	
	Unearned Consulting Revenue			2,750

After adjusting entries are posted, the two alternatives give identical results. The December 31 adjusted account balances in Exhibit 3A.6 show unearned consulting revenue of $2,750 and consulting revenue of $250 for both methods.

Exhibit 3A.6

Account Balances under Two
Alternatives for Recording
Unearned Revenues

Receipt Recorded as Liability			
Unearned Consulting Revenue			**236**
Dec. 31	250	Dec. 26	3,000
		Balance	2,750

Consulting Revenue			**403**
		Dec. 31	250

Receipt Recorded as Revenue			
Unearned Consulting Revenue			**236**
		Dec. 31	2,750

Consulting Revenue			**403**
Dec. 31	2,750	Dec. 26	3,000
		Balance	250

Work Sheet as a Tool

3B

Information preparers use various analyses and internal documents when organizing information for reports to internal and external decision makers. Internal documents are important and are often called **working papers.** One widely used working paper is the **work sheet,** which is a useful tool for preparers in working with accounting information. It is usually not available to external decision makers.

Benefits of a Work Sheet

A work sheet is *not* a required financial report, yet using a manual or electronic work sheet has several potential benefits: it (1) reduces errors when working with systems involving many accounts and adjustments, (2) links accounts and adjustments to their impacts in financial statements, (3) assists in planning and organizing an audit of financial statements—it can be used to reflect any adjustments necessary, (4) is useful in preparing interim (monthly or quarterly) financial statements when the journalizing and posting of adjusting entries are postponed until the year-end, and (5) is helpful in showing the effects of proposed or "what if" transactions.

P7   Prepare a work sheet and explain its usefulness.

Decision Insight

Silicon Accounting   An electronic work sheet using spreadsheet software such as Excel allows us to easily change numbers, assess the impact of alternative strategies, and quickly prepare financial statements at lower cost. It can also decrease the time devoted to the accounting process and increase the time for analysis and interpretation.

Using a Work Sheet

When a work sheet is used to prepare financial statements, it is constructed at the end of a period before the adjusting process. The work sheet includes a listing of the accounts, their balances and adjustments, and their sorting into financial statement columns. It provides two columns each for the unadjusted trial balance, the adjustments, the adjusted trial balance, the income statement, and the balance sheet (including the statement of retained earnings). To describe and interpret the work sheet, we use the information from FastForward. Preparing the work sheet has five important steps. Each step, 1 through 5, is color-coded and explained with reference to Exhibit 3B.1.

① Step 1. Enter Unadjusted Trial Balance

The first step in preparing a work sheet is to list the title of every account that is expected to appear on the company's financial statements.[1] The unadjusted balance for each account in the ledger is recorded in the appropriate Debit or Credit column of the unadjusted trial balance. The totals of these two columns must be equal. The unadjusted trial balance reflects the account balances after the December transactions are recorded but *before any adjusting entries are journalized and posted.* Sometimes blank lines are left on the work sheet based on past experience to indicate where lines will be needed for adjustments to certain accounts. Exhibit 3B.1 shows Consulting Revenue as one example. An alternative is to squeeze adjustments on one line or to combine the effects of two or more adjustments in one amount.

---

[1] This includes all ledger accounts plus any expected ones from adjusting entries. Most adjusting entries—including expenses from salaries, supplies, depreciation, and insurance—are predictable and recurring. In the unusual case when an account is not predicted, we can add a new line for such an account following the *Totals* line.

Exhibit 3B.1

Work Sheet

No.	Account	Unadjusted Trial Balance Dr.	Cr.	Adjustments Dr.	Cr.	Adjusted Trial Balance Dr.	Cr.	Income Statement Dr.	Cr.	Balance Sheet Dr.	Cr.

FastForward
Work Sheet
For Month Ended December 31, 2001

No.	Account	Unadjusted Trial Balance		Adjustments		Adjusted Trial Balance		Income Statement		Balance Sheet	
		Dr.	Cr.	Dr.	Cr.	Dr.	Cr.	Dr.	Cr.	Dr.	Cr.
101	Cash	3,950				3,950				3,950	
106	Accounts receivable	0		(f) 1,800		1,800				1,800	
126	Supplies	9,720			(b) 1,050	8,670				8,670	
128	Prepaid insurance	2,400			(a) 100	2,300				2,300	
167	Equipment	26,000				26,000				26,000	
168	Accumulated depreciation—Equip.		0		(c) 375		375				375
201	Accounts payable		6,200				6,200				6,200
209	Salaries payable		0		(e) 210		210				210
236	Unearned consulting revenue		3,000	(d) 250			2,750				2,750
307	Common stock		30,000				30,000				30,000
318	Retained earnings	600				600				600	
403	Consulting revenue		5,800		(d) 250		7,850		7,850		
					(f) 1,800						
406	Rental revenue		300				300		300		
612	Depreciation expense—Equip.	0		(c) 375		375		375			
622	Salaries expense	1,400		(e) 210		1,610		1,610			
637	Insurance expense	0		(a) 100		100		100			
640	Rent expense	1,000				1,000		1,000			
652	Supplies expense	0		(b) 1,050		1,050		1,050			
690	Utilities expense	230				230		230			
	Totals	45,300	45,300	3,785	3,785	47,685	47,685	4,365	8,150	43,320	39,535
	Net income							3,785			3,785
	Totals							8,150	8,150	43,320	43,320

① ② ③ ④ ⑤

② Step 2. Enter Adjustments

Point: A recordkeeper often can complete the procedural task of journalizing and posting adjusting entries by using a work sheet and the guidance that *keying* provides.

The second step in preparing a work sheet is to enter adjustments in the Adjustments columns. The adjustments shown are the same ones we explained in the chapter. An identifying letter links the debit and credit of each adjusting entry. This is called *keying* the adjustments. After preparing a work sheet, we still must enter adjusting entries in the journal and post them to the ledger.

③ Step 3. Prepare Adjusted Trial Balance

Point: To avoid omitting the transfer of an account balance, start with the first line (cash) and continue in account order.

The adjusted trial balance is prepared by combining the adjustments with the unadjusted balances for each account. As an example, the Prepaid Insurance account has a $2,400 debit balance in the Unadjusted Trial Balance columns. This $2,400 debit is combined with the $100 credit in the Adjustments columns to give Prepaid Insurance a $2,300 debit in the Adjusted Trial Balance columns. The totals of the Adjusted Trial Balance columns confirm the equality of debits and credits.

④ Step 4. Sort Adjusted Trial Balance Amounts to Financial Statements

This step involves sorting account balances in the adjusted trial balance to their proper financial statement columns. Expenses go to the Income Statement Debit column and revenues to the Income Statement Credit column. Assets go to the Balance Sheet Debit column. Liabilities and equity go to the Balance Sheet Credit column.

⑤ Step 5. Total Statement Columns, Compute Income or Loss, and Balance Columns

Each financial statement column (from Step 4) is totaled. The difference between the totals of the Income Statement columns is net income or net loss. This occurs because revenues are entered in the Credit column and expenses in the Debit column. If the Credit total exceeds the Debit total, there is net income. If the Debit total exceeds the Credit total, there is a net loss. For FastForward, the Credit total exceeds the Debit total, giving a $3,785 net income.

The net income from the Income Statement columns is then entered in the Balance Sheet Credit column. Adding net income to the last Credit column implies that it is to be added to retained earnings. If a loss occurs, it is entered in the Debit column. This implies that it is to be subtracted from retained earnings. The ending balance of retained earnings does not appear in the last two columns as a single amount, but it is computed as the beginning Retained Earnings account balance *plus* net income (or minus net loss) and *minus* any dividends. When net income or net loss is added to the proper Balance Sheet column, the totals of the last two columns must balance. If they do not, one or more errors have been made. The error can either be mathematical or involve sorting one or more amounts to incorrect columns. A balance in the last two columns is not proof of no errors.

Entering adjustments in the Adjustments columns of a work sheet does not adjust the ledger accounts. Adjusting entries still must be entered in the general journal and posted to ledger accounts. The Adjustments columns provide the information for these entries. The adjustments match the adjusting entries we described in the chapter. Also, all items in the Income Statement columns must be closed to Income Summary. The resulting net income or loss shown in the Income Summary must be closed to retained earnings.

Work Sheet Application and Analysis

A work sheet does not substitute for financial statements; it is a tool we can use at the end of an accounting period to help organize data and prepare financial statements. FastForward's financial statements are shown in Exhibits 3.20 and 3.21. Its income statement amounts are taken from the Income Statement columns of the work sheet. Similarly, amounts for its balance sheet are taken from the Balance Sheet columns of the work sheet. Work sheets are also useful in analyzing the effects of proposed, or what-if, transactions. This is done by entering financial statement amounts in the Unadjusted (what-if) columns. Proposed transactions are then entered in the Adjustments columns. We then compute "adjusted" amounts from these proposed transactions. The extended amounts in the financial statement columns show the effects of these proposed transactions. These financial statement columns yield **pro forma financial statements** because they show the statements *as if* the proposed transactions occurred.

Reversing Entries

This appendix describes the use of reversing entries in accounting.

Reversing Entries

Reversing entries are optional. They are linked to accrued assets and liabilities that were created by adjusting entries at the end of a reporting period. The purpose of reversing entries is to simplify a company's recordkeeping. Exhibit 3C.1 shows how reversing entries work for FastForward. The top of the exhibit shows the adjusting entry FastForward recorded on December 31 for its employee's

Point: As a general rule, adjusting entries that create new asset or liability accounts are likely candidates for reversing.

Exhibit 3C.1

Reversing Entries for
Accrued Expenses

Accrue salaries expense on December 31, 2001

Salaries Expense 210
    Salaries Payable 210

Salaries Expense

Date	Expl.	Debit	Credit	Balance
2001				
Dec. 12	(7)	700		700
26	(16)	700		1,400
31	(e)	210		1,610

Salaries Payable

Date	Expl.	Debit	Credit	Balance
2001				
Dec. 31	(e)		210	210

— OR —

*No reversing entry recorded on
January 1, 2002*

NO ENTRY

Salaries Expense

Date	Expl.	Debit	Credit	Balance
2002				

Salaries Payable

Date	Expl.	Debit	Credit	Balance
2001				
Dec. 31	(e)		210	210
2002				

*Reversing entry recorded on
January 1, 2002*

Salaries Payable 210
    Salaries Expense 210

Salaries Expense*

Date	Expl.	Debit	Credit	Balance
2002				
Jan. 1			210	(210)

Salaries Payable

Date	Expl.	Debit	Credit	Balance
2001				
Dec. 31	(e)		210	210
2002				
Jan. 1		210		0

Pay the accrued and current salaries on January 9, the first payday in 2002

Salaries Expense 490
Salaries Payable 210
    Cash 700

Salaries Expense

Date	Expl.	Debit	Credit	Balance
2002				
Jan. 9		490		490

Salaries Payable

Date	Expl.	Debit	Credit	Balance
2001				
Dec. 31	(e)		210	210
2002				
Jan. 9		210		0

Salaries Expense 700
    Cash 700

Salaries Expense*

Date	Expl.	Debit	Credit	Balance
2002				
Jan. 1			210	(210)
Jan. 9		700		490

Salaries Payable

Date	Expl.	Debit	Credit	Balance
2001				
Dec. 31	(e)		210	210
2002				
Jan. 1		210		0

Under both approaches, the expense and liability accounts have
identical balances after the cash payment on January 9.

Salaries Expense $490
Salaries Payable .... $ 0

*Circled numbers in the *Balance* column indicate abnormal balances.

earned but unpaid salary. The entry recorded three days' salary of $210, which increased December's total salary expense to $1,610. The entry also recognized a liability of $210. The expense is reported on December's income statement. The expense account is then closed. The ledger on January 1, 2002, shows a $210 liability and a zero balance in the Salaries Expense account. At this point, the choice is made between using or not using reversing entries.

Accounting *without* Reversing Entries

The path down the left side of Exhibit 3C.1 is described in the chapter. To summarize here, when the next payday occurs on January 9, we record payment with a compound entry that debits both the expense and liability accounts and credits Cash. Posting that entry creates a $490 balance in the expense account and reduces the liability account balance to zero because the debt has been settled. The disadvantage of this approach is the slightly more complex entry required on January 9. Paying the accrued liability means that this entry differs from the routine entries made on all other paydays. To construct the proper entry on January 9, we must recall the effect of the December 31 adjusting entry. Reversing entries overcome this disadvantage.

Accounting *with* Reversing Entries

The right side of Exhibit 3C.1 shows how a reversing entry on January 1 overcomes the disadvantage of the January 9 entry when not using reversing entries. A reversing entry is the exact opposite of an adjusting entry. For FastForward, the Salaries Payable liability account is debited for $210, meaning that this account now has a zero balance after the entry is posted. The Salaries Payable account temporarily understates the liability, but this is not a problem since financial statements are not prepared before the liability is settled on January 9. The credit to the Salaries Expense account is unusual because it gives the account an *abnormal credit balance*. We highlight an abnormal balance by circling it. Because of the reversing entry, the January 9 entry to record payment is straightforward. This entry debits the Salaries Expense account and credits Cash for the full $700 paid. It is the same as all other entries made to record 10 days' salary for the employee. Notice that after the payment entry is posted, the Salaries Expense account has a $490 balance that reflects seven days' salary of $70 per day (see the lower right side of Exhibit 3C.1). The zero balance in the Salaries Payable account is now correct. The lower section of Exhibit 3C.1 shows that the expense and liability accounts have exactly the same balances whether reversing entries are used or not. This means that both approaches yield identical results.

P8 Prepare reversing entries and explain their purpose.

Summary

C1 **Explain the importance of periodic reporting and the time period principle.** The value of information is often linked to its timeliness. To provide timely information, accounting systems prepare periodic reports at regular intervals. The time period principle assumes that an organization's activities can be divided into specific time periods for periodic reporting.

C2 **Explain accrual accounting and how it makes financial statements more useful.** Accrual accounting recognizes revenue when earned and expenses when incurred—not necessarily when cash inflows and outflows occur. This information is valuable in assessing a company's financial position and performance.

C3 **Identify the types of adjustments and their purpose.** Adjustments can be grouped according to the timing of cash receipts and cash payments relative to when they are recognized as revenues or expenses as follows: prepaid expenses, unearned revenues, accrued expenses, and accrued revenues. Adjusting entries are necessary so that revenues, expenses, assets, and liabilities are correctly reported.

C4 **Explain why temporary accounts are closed each period.** Temporary accounts are closed at the end of each accounting period for two main reasons. First, the closing process updates the retained earnings account to include the effects of all transactions and events recorded for the period. Second, it prepares revenue and expense accounts for the next reporting period by giving them zero balances.

C5 **Identify steps in the accounting cycle.** The accounting cycle consists of 10 steps: (1) analyze transactions, (2) journalize, (3) post, (4) prepare an unadjusted trial balance, (5) adjust accounts, (6) prepare an adjusted trial balance, (7) prepare statements, (8) close, (9) prepare a post-closing trial balance, and (10) prepare (optional) reversing entries.

C6 **Explain and prepare a classified balance sheet.** Classified balance sheets report assets and liabilities in two categories: current and noncurrent. Noncurrent assets often include long-term investments, plant assets, and intangible assets. A corporation separates equity into common stock and retained earnings.

A1 **Explain how accounting adjustments link to financial statements.** Accounting adjustments bring an asset or liability account balance to its correct amount. They also update related expense or revenue accounts. Every adjusting entry affects one or more income statement accounts *and* one or more balance sheet accounts. An adjusting entry never affects cash.

A2 **Compute profit margin and describe its use in analyzing company performance.** *Profit margin* is defined as the reporting period's net income divided by net sales for the same period. Profit margin reflects on a company's earnings activities by showing how much income is in each dollar of sales.

A3 **Compute the current ratio and describe what it reveals about a company's financial condition.** A company's current ratio is defined as current assets divided by current liabilities. We use it to evaluate a company's ability to pay its current liabilities out of current assets.

P1 **Prepare and explain adjusting entries.** *Prepaid expenses* refer to items paid for in advance of receiving their benefits. Prepaid expenses are assets. Adjusting entries for prepaids involve increasing (debiting) expenses and decreasing (crediting) assets. *Unearned* (or *prepaid*) *revenues* refer to cash received in advance of providing products and services. Unearned revenues are liabilities. Adjusting entries for unearned revenues involves increasing (crediting) revenues and decreasing (debiting) unearned revenues. *Accrued expenses* refer to costs incurred in a period that are both unpaid and unrecorded. Adjusting entries for recording accrued expenses involves increasing (debiting) expenses and increasing (crediting) liabilities. *Accrued revenues* refer to revenues earned in a period that are both unrecorded and not yet received in cash. Adjusting entries for recording accrued revenues involves increasing (debiting) assets and increasing (crediting) revenues.

P2   **Explain and prepare an adjusted trial balance.** An adjusted trial balance is a list of accounts and balances prepared after recording and posting adjusting entries. Financial statements are often prepared from the adjusted trial balance.

P3   **Prepare financial statements from an adjusted trial balance.** Revenue and expense balances are reported on the income statement. Asset, liability, and equity balances are reported on the balance sheet. We usually prepare statements in the following order: income statement, statement of retained earnings, balance sheet, and statement of cash flows.

P4   **Describe and prepare closing entries.** Closing entries involve three steps: (1) close credit balances in revenue (and gain) accounts to Income Summary, (2) close debit balances in expense (and loss) accounts to Income Summary, and (3) close Income Summary to Retained Earnings.

P5   **Explain and prepare a post-closing trial balance.** A post-closing trial balance is a list of permanent accounts and their balances after all closing entries have been journalized and posted. Its purpose is to verify that (1) total debits equal total

credits for permanent accounts and (2) all temporary accounts have zero balances.

P6   **Identify and explain alternatives in accounting for prepaids.** Charging all prepaid expenses to expense accounts when they are purchased is acceptable. When this is done, adjusting entries must transfer any unexpired amounts from expense accounts to asset accounts. Crediting all unearned revenues to revenue accounts when cash is received is also acceptable. In this case, the adjusting entries must transfer any unearned amounts from revenue accounts to unearned revenue accounts.

P7   **Prepare a work sheet and explain its usefulness.** A work sheet can be a useful tool in preparing and analyzing financial statements. It is helpful at the end of a period in preparing adjusting entries, an adjusted trial balance, and financial statements. A work sheet usually contains five pairs of columns: Unadjusted Trial Balance, Adjustments, Adjusted Trial Balance, Income Statement, and Balance Sheet.

P8   **Prepare reversing entries and explain their purpose.** Reversing entries are an optional step. They are applied to accrued assets and liabilities. The purpose of reversing entries is to simplify subsequent journal entries. Financial statements are unaffected by the choice to use or not use reversing entries.

Guidance Answers to **Decision Maker** and **Decision Ethics**

Investor   Prepaid expenses are items paid for in advance of receiving their benefits. They are assets and are expensed as they are used up. The publishing company's treatment of the signing bonus is acceptable provided future book sales can at least match the $500,000 expense. As an investor, you are concerned about the risk of future book sales. The riskier the likelihood of future book sales is, the more likely your analysis is to treat the $500,000, or a portion of it, as an expense, not a prepaid expense (asset).

Entrepreneur   Depreciation is a process of cost allocation, not asset valuation. Knowing the depreciation schedule is not especially useful in your estimation of what the building and equipment are currently worth. Your own assessment of the age, quality, and usefulness of the building and equipment is more important.

Loan Officer   Your concern in lending to this store arises from analysis of current-year sales. While increased revenues and income are fine, your concern is with collectibility of these promotional sales. If the owner sold products to customers with poor records of

paying bills, then collectibility of these sales is low. Your analysis must assess this possibility and recognize any expected losses.

Financial Officer   Omitting accrued expenses and recognizing revenue early can mislead financial statement users. One action is to request a second meeting with the president so you can explain that accruing expenses when incurred and recognizing revenue when earned are required practices. If the president persists, you might discuss the situation with legal counsel and any auditors involved. Your ethical action might cost you this job, but the potential pitfalls for falsification of statements, reputation loss, personal integrity, and other costs are too great.

Analyst   A current ratio of 1.2 suggests that current assets are sufficient to cover current liabilities—but it implies a minimal buffer in case of errors in measuring current assets or current liabilities. Removing tardy receivables reduces the current ratio to 0.7. Your assessment is that the club will have some difficulty meeting its loan payments.

Guidance Answers to **Quick Checks**

1. An annual reporting (or accounting) period covers one year and refers to the preparation of annual financial statements. The annual reporting period is not always a calendar year that ends on December 31. An organization can adopt a fiscal year consisting of any consecutive 12 months or 52 weeks.

2. Interim financial statements (covering less than one year) are prepared to provide timely information to decision makers.

3. The revenue recognition principle and the matching principle lead most directly to the adjusting process.

4. No. Cash basis accounting is not consistent with the matching principle because it reports expenses when paid, not in the period when revenue is earned as a result of those expenses.

5. No expense is reported in 2003. Under cash basis accounting the entire $4,800 is reported as expense in April 2002 when the premium is paid.

6. If the accrued revenues adjustment of $200 is not made, then both revenues and net income are understated by $200 on the current year's income statement, and both assets and equity are understated by $200 on the balance sheet.

7. A contra account is an account that is subtracted from the balance of a related account. Use of a contra account provides more information than simply reporting a net amount.

8. An accrued expense is a cost incurred in a period that is both unpaid and unrecorded prior to adjusting entries. One example is salaries earned but not yet paid at period-end.

9. An unearned revenue arises when a firm receives cash (or other assets) from a customer before providing the services or products to the customer. A magazine subscription paid in advance is one example; season ticket sales is another.

10.

Salaries Payable	1,000	
Salaries Expense	6,000	
Cash		7,000

Paid salary including accrual from December.

11. The probable adjusting entries of Jordan Air are:

Insurance Expense	300	
Prepaid Insurance		300

To record insurance expired.

Salaries Expense	1,400	
Salaries Payable		1,400

To record accrued salaries.

12. Revenue accounts and expense accounts.

13. Statement of retained earnings.

14. The major steps in preparing closing entries are to close (1) credit balances in revenue accounts to Income Summary, (2) debit balances in expense accounts to Income Summary, and (3) Income Summary to retained earnings.

15. Revenue (and gain) and expense (and loss) accounts are called *temporary* because they are opened and closed each period. The Income Summary account is also temporary.

16. Permanent accounts make up the post-closing trial balance. These accounts are asset, liability, and equity accounts.

17. Current assets: (*b*), (*c*), (*d*). Plant assets: (*a*), (*e*). Item (*f*) is an intangible asset.

18. Investment in common stock, investment in bonds, and land held for future expansion.

19. For a service company, the operating cycle is the usual time between (1) paying employees who do the services and (2) receiving cash from customers for services provided.

Glossary

Account form balance sheet Balance sheet that lists assets on the left side and liabilities and equity on the right. (p. 117)

Accounting cycle Recurring steps performed each accounting period, starting with analyzing transactions and continuing through the post-closing trial balance (or reversing entries). (p. 121)

Accounting period Length of time covered by financial statements; also called *reporting period.* (p. 102)

Accrual basis accounting Accounting system that recognizes revenues when earned and expenses when incurred; the basis for GAAP. (p. 104)

Accrued expenses Costs incurred in a period that are both unpaid and unrecorded; adjusting entries for recording accrued expenses involve increasing (debiting) expenses and increasing (crediting) liabilities. (p. 110)

Accrued revenues Revenues earned in a period that are both unrecorded and not yet received in cash (or other assets); adjusting entries for recording accrued revenues involve increasing (debiting) assets and increasing (crediting) revenues. (p. 112)

Adjusted trial balance List of accounts and balances prepared after adjustments are recorded and posted. (p. 114)

Adjusting entry Journal entry at the end of an accounting period to bring an asset or liability account to its proper amount and update the related expense or revenue account. (p. 105)

Annual financial statements Financial statements covering a one-year period; often based on a calendar year, but any consecutive 12-month (or 52-week) period is acceptable. (p. 102)

Book value An asset's acquisition costs less its accumulated depreciation. (p. 109)

Cash basis accounting Accounting system that recognizes revenues when cash is received and records expenses when cash is paid. (p. 104)

Classified balance sheet Balance sheet that presents assets and liabilities in relevant subgroups. (p. 123)

Closing entries Entries recorded at the end of each accounting period to transfer end-of-period balances in revenue (and gain) and expense (and loss) accounts to the retained earnings account. (p. 118)

Closing process Necessary steps to prepare the accounts for recording the transactions of the next period. (p. 118)

Contra account Account linked with another account and having an opposite normal balance; reported as a subtraction from the other account's balance. (p. 108)

Current assets Cash or other assets that are expected to be sold, collected, or used

within one year or the company's operating cycle, whichever is longer. (p. 124)

Current liabilities Obligations due to be paid or settled within one year or the operating cycle, whichever is longer. (p. 126)

Current ratio Ratio used to evaluate a company's ability to pay its short-term obligations, calculated by dividing current assets by current liabilities. (p. 127)

Depreciation Expense created by allocating the cost of plant and equipment to periods in which they are used. (p. 108)

Equity Owners' claim on a company's assets. (p. 126)

Fiscal year Consecutive 12 month (or 52 week) period chosen as the organization's annual accounting period. (p. 102)

Income Summary Temporary account used only in the closing process to which the balances of revenue and expense accounts are transferred; its balance is transferred to the Retained Earnings account. (p. 118)

Intangible assets Long-term assets used to produce or sell products or services; they usually lack physical form and their benefits are uncertain. (p. 125)

Interim financial statements Financial statements covering periods of less than one year; usually based on one-, three-, or six-month periods. (p. 102)

Long-term investments Long-term assets such as notes receivable and investments in stocks and bonds. (p. 124)

Long-term liabilities Obligations that are not due to be paid within one year or the operating cycle, whichever is longer. (p. 126)

Matching principle Requires expenses to be reported in the same period as the revenues that were earned as a result of the expenses. (p. 104)

Natural business year The 12-month period that ends when a company's sales activities are at their lowest point. (p. 103)

Operating cycle Normal time between paying cash for merchandise or employee services and receiving cash from customers. (p. 123)

Permanent accounts Accounts that reflect activities related to one or more future periods; balance sheet accounts whose balances are not closed; also called *real accounts*. (p. 118)

Plant assets Tangible long-lived assets used to produce or sell products and services; also called *property, plant and equipment* or *fixed assets*. (p. 108)

Post-closing trial balance List of permanent accounts and their balances from the ledger after all closing entries are journalized and posted. (p. 121)

Prepaid expenses Items paid for in advance of receiving their benefits; classified as assets. (p. 106)

Profit margin Ratio of a company's net income to its net sales; the percent of income in each dollar of revenue. (p. 126)

Pro forma financial statements Statements that show the effects of proposed transactions as if they occurred. (p. 135)

Report form balance sheet Balance sheet that lists accounts vertically in the order of assets, liabilities, and equity. (p. 115)

Reversing entries Optional entries recorded at the beginning of a new period that prepare the accounts for the usual journal entries as if adjusting entries had not occurred. (p. 135)

Straight-line depreciation method Allocates equal amounts of an asset's cost (less any salvage value) to depreciation expense during its useful life. (p. 108)

Temporary accounts Accounts used to record revenues and expenses; they are closed at the end of each period; also called *nominal accounts*. (p. 118)

Time period principle Assumes an organization's activities can be divided into specific time periods such as months, quarters, or years. (p. 102)

Unadjusted trial balance List of accounts and balances prepared before adjustments are recorded and posted. (p. 114)

Unclassified balance sheet Balance sheet that broadly groups assets, liabilities, and equity accounts. (p. 123)

Unearned revenues Reflects cash (or other assets) received in advance of providing products or services; a liability. (p. 109)

Working papers Analyses and other informal reports prepared by accountants when organizing information for formal reports and financial statements. (p. 133)

Work sheet Spreadsheet used to draft an unadjusted trial balance, adjusting entries, adjusted trial balance, and financial statements; an optional procedure. (p. 133)

Superscript letters ^{A}, ^{B}, and ^{C} denote assignments based on Appendixes 3A, 3B, and 3C.

Questions

1. What is the difference between the cash basis and the accrual basis of accounting?

2. 🔲 Why is the accrual basis of accounting generally preferred over the cash basis?

3. What type of business is most likely to select a fiscal year that corresponds to its natural business year instead of the calendar year?

4. Where is a prepaid expense reported in the financial statements?

5. 🔲 What type of asset(s) requires adjusting entries to record depreciation?

6. 🔲 What contra account is used when recording and reporting the effects of depreciation? Why is it used?

7. Where is unearned revenue reported in financial statements?

8. What is an accrued revenue? Give an example.

9.^{A} If a company initially records prepaid expenses with debits to expense accounts, what type of account is debited in the adjusting entries for prepaid expenses?

10. 🔲 Review the balance sheet of **Nike** in **NIKE** Appendix A. Identify two asset accounts that require adjustment before annual financial statements can be

prepared. What would be the effect on the income statement if these two asset accounts were not adjusted?

11. 🔲 Review the balance sheet of **Reebok** in **Reebok** Appendix A. In addition to prepaid expenses and property and equipment, identify two accounts (either assets or liabilities) requiring adjusting entries.

12. 🔲 Refer to **Gap**'s balance sheet in Appendix **GAP** A. Identify three types of property and equipment that it must depreciate.

13. What accounts are affected by closing entries? What accounts are not affected?

14. 🔲 What two purposes are accomplished by recording closing entries?

15. What are the steps in recording closing entries?

16. What is the purpose of the Income Summary account?

17. 🔲 Explain whether an error has occurred if a post-closing trial balance includes a Depreciation Expense account.

18.^{B} What tasks are aided by a work sheet?

19.^{B} Why are the debit and credit entries in the Adjustments columns of the work sheet identified with letters?

20. What is a company's operating cycle?

21. What classes of assets and liabilities are shown on a typical classified balance sheet?

22. How is unearned revenue classified on the balance sheet?

23. What are the characteristics of plant assets?

24.ᶜ How do reversing entries simplify recordkeeping?

25.ᶜ If a company accrued unpaid salaries expense of $500 at the end of a fiscal year, what reversing entry could be made? When would it be made?

26. 🗗 Refer to the balance sheet for Nike in Appendix A. What percent of Nike's long-term debt is coming due before May 31, 2001?

27. 🗗 Refer to Reebok's balance sheet in Appendix A. Identify the accounts listed as current liabilities.

28. 🗗 Refer to Gap's financial statements in Appendix A. What journal entry was likely recorded as of Jan. 29, 2000, to close the company's Income Summary account?

---

a. On July 1, 2002, McCay Company paid $1,200 for six months of insurance coverage. No adjustments have been made to the Prepaid Insurance account, and it is now December 31, 2002. Prepare the journal entry to reflect expiration of the insurance as of December 31, 2002.

b. Taylor Company has a supplies balance of $500 on January 1, 2002. During 2002, it purchased $2,000 of supplies. As of December 31, 2002, a supplies inventory shows $800 of supplies available. Prepare the adjusting journal entry to correctly state the balance of the Supplies account and the Supplies Expense account as of December 31, 2002.

QUICK STUDY

QS 3-1
Adjusting prepaid expenses

P1

---

a. Decker Company purchases $20,000 of equipment on January 1, 2002. The equipment is expected to last five years and be worth $2,000 at the end of that time. Prepare the entry to record one year's depreciation expense for Decker's equipment as of December 31, 2002.

b. Decker Company purchases $10,000 of land on January 1, 2002. The land is expected to last indefinitely. What depreciation adjustment, if any, should Decker Company make with respect to the Land account as of December 31, 2002?

QS 3-2
Adjusting for depreciation

P1

---

a. W. Nelson has a client that paid $10,000 cash in advance for legal work. He will work on this client's case over a four-month period. Nelson receives the cash advance on October 1, 2002, and records it by debiting Cash and crediting Unearned Revenue for $10,000. It is now December 31, 2002, and Nelson has worked as planned on the client's case. What adjusting entry should Nelson make to account for the work performed from October 1 through December 31, 2002?

b. P. Tidwell started a new publication called *Contest News*. Her subscribers pay $24 to receive 12 issues. With every new subscriber, Patty debits Cash and credits Unearned Subscription Revenue for the amounts received. Patty has 100 subscribers as of July 1, 2002. She sends *Contest News* to each of these subscribers every month from July through December. Assuming no changes in subscribers, prepare the journal entry that Patty must make as of December 31, 2002, to adjust the Subscription Revenue account and the Unearned Subscription Revenue account.

QS 3-3 🗗
Adjusting for unearned revenues

A1 P1

Robin Fischer employs three college students every summer in her coffee shop. The students work the five weekdays and are paid on the following Monday. (For example, a student who works Monday through Friday, June 1 through June 5, is paid for that work on Monday, June 8.) Robin adjusts her books monthly, if needed, to show salaries earned but unpaid at month-end. All three students work the last week of July—Friday is August 1. If each student earns $100 per day, what adjusting entry must Robin make on July 31 to correctly record salaries expense for July?

QS 3-4
Accruing salaries

A1 P1

Adjusting entries affect at least one balance sheet account and at least one income statement account. For the following entries, identify the account to be debited and the account to be credited. Indicate which of the accounts is the income statement account and which is the balance sheet account.

a. Entry to record revenue earned that was previously received as cash in advance.

b. Entry to record annual depreciation expense.

c. Entry to record wage expenses incurred but not yet paid (nor recorded).

d. Entry to record revenue earned but not yet billed (nor recorded).

e. Entry to record expiration of prepaid insurance.

QS 3-5
Recording and analyzing adjusting entries

A1

QS 3-6

Computing accrual and cash income   **C2**

In its first year of operations, Heyer Co. earned $42,000 in revenues and received $37,000 cash from these customers. The company incurred expenses of $25,500 but had not paid $5,250 of them at year-end. Heyer also prepaid $6,750 cash for expenses that would be incurred the next year. Calculate the first year's net income under both the cash basis and the accrual basis of accounting.

QS 3-7 🗹

Determining effects of adjusting entries

C3 A1

In making adjusting entries at the end of its accounting period, Malson Consulting Agency failed to record $1,600 of insurance coverage that had expired. This $1,600 cost had been initially debited to the Prepaid Insurance account. The company also failed to record accrued salaries payable of $1,000. As a result of these two oversights, the financial statements for the reporting period will [choose one] (1) understate assets by $1,600; (2) understate expenses by $2,600; (3) understate net income by $1,000; or (4) overstate liabilities by $1,000.

QS 3-8 🗹

Determining effects of closing entries

C4 P4

Argosy Company began the current period with a $15,000 balance in its Retained Earnings account. At the end of the period, the company's adjusted account balances include the following temporary accounts with normal balances:

Service fees earned	$36,000	Interest revenue	$4,500
Salaries expense	20,000	Rent expense	7,000
Depreciation expense	5,000	Utilities expense	3,300

After closing revenue and expense accounts, what will be the balance of the Income Summary account? After all closing entries are journalized and posted, what will be the balance of the Retained Earnings account (assume no dividends)?

QS 3-9

Identifying the accounting cycle

C5

List the following steps of the accounting cycle in their proper order:
a. Preparing the post-closing trial balance.   9
b. Posting the journal entries.   3
c. Journalizing and posting adjusting entries.   5
d. Preparing the adjusted trial balance.   6
e. Journalizing and posting closing entries.   8
f. Analyzing transactions and events.   1
g. Preparing the financial statements.   7
h. Preparing the unadjusted trial balance.   4
i. Journalizing transactions and events.   2

QS 3-10

Classifying balance sheet items

C6

The following are common categories on a classified balance sheet:
A. Current assets   **D.** Intangible assets
B. Long-term investments   **E.** Current liabilities
C. Plant assets   **F.** Long-term liabilities

For each of the following items, select the letter that identifies the balance sheet category where the item typically would appear.
   D   **1.** Trademarks   A   **5.** Cash
   A   **2.** Accounts receivable   E   **6.** Wages payable
   B   **3.** Land not currently used in operations   C   **7.** Store equipment
   E   **4.** Notes payable (due in three years)   E   **8.** Accounts payable

---

QS 3-11 🗹

Analyzing profit margin   **A2**

Hao Company reported net income of $48,152 and net sales of $425,000 for the current year. Calculate Hao's profit margin and interpret the result.

QS 3-12

Computing current ratio

A3

Compute Neon Company's current ratio using the following information:

Accounts receivable	$16,000	Long-term notes payable	$21,000
Accounts payable	11,000	Office supplies	2,800
Buildings	43,000	Prepaid insurance	3,500
Cash	7,000	Unearned services revenue	5,000

QS 3-13^C

Reversing entries

P8

On December 31, 2002, Yates Co. prepared an adjusting entry for $7,600 of earned but unrecorded management fees. On January 16, 2003, Yates received $25,500 of management fees, which included the accrued fees earned in 2002. Assuming the company uses reversing entries, prepare the January 1, 2003, reversing entry and the January 16, 2003, cash receipt entry.

For each of the following separate cases, prepare adjusting entries required for financial statements for the year ended (or date of) December 31, 2002. (Assume that prepaid expenses are initially recorded in asset accounts and that fees collected in advance of work are initially recorded as liabilities.)

a. One-third of the work related to $15,000 cash received in advance is performed this period.

b. Wages of $8,000 are earned by workers but not paid as of December 31, 2002.

c. Depreciation on the company's equipment for 2002 is $18,534.

d. The Office Supplies account had a $240 debit balance on December 31, 2001. During 2002, $5,239 of office supplies are purchased. A physical count of supplies at December 31, 2002, shows $487 of supplies available.

e. The Prepaid Insurance account had a $4,000 balance on December 31, 2001. An analysis of insurance policies shows that $1,200 of unexpired insurance benefits remain at December 31, 2002.

f. The company has earned (but not recorded) $1,000 of interest from investments in CDs for the year ended December 31, 2002. The interest revenue will be received on January 10, 2003.

g. The company has a bank loan and has incurred (but not recorded) interest expenses of $2,500 for the year ended December 31, 2002. The company must pay the interest on January 2, 2003.

EXERCISES

Exercise 3-1
Preparing adjusting entries

P1

Check (e) Dr. Insurance expense, $2,800; (f) Cr. Interest revenue, $1,000

Prepare adjusting journal entries for the year ended (or date of) December 31, 2002, for each of these independent situations. Assume that prepaid expenses are initially recorded in asset accounts. Also assume that fees collected in advance of work are initially recorded as liabilities.

a. Depreciation on the company's equipment for 2002 is computed to be $18,000.

b. The Prepaid Insurance account had a $6,000 debit balance at December 31, 2002, before adjusting for the costs of any expired coverage. An analysis of the company's insurance policies showed that $1,100 of unexpired insurance remained in effect.

c. The Office Supplies account had a $700 debit balance on December 31, 2001; $3,480 of office supplies were purchased during the year; and the December 31, 2002, physical count showed $298 of supplies available.

d. One-half of the work related to $15,000 cash received in advance was performed this period.

e. The Prepaid Insurance account had a $6,800 debit balance at December 31, 2002, before adjusting for the costs of any expired coverage. An analysis of insurance policies showed that $5,800 of coverage had expired.

f. Wage expenses of $3,200 have been incurred but are not paid as of December 31, 2002.

Exercise 3-2
Preparing adjusting entries

P1

Check (c) Dr. Office supplies expense, $3,882; (e) Dr. Insurance expense, $5,800

Asset Management has five part-time employees, each of whom earns $250 per day. They are normally paid on Fridays for work completed Monday through Friday of the same week. They were paid in full on Friday, December 28, 2002. The next week, the five employees worked only four days because New Year's Day was an unpaid holiday. Show the adjusting entry that would be recorded on Monday, December 31, 2002, and the journal entry that would be made to record payment of the employees' wages on Friday, January 4, 2003.

Exercise 3-3
Adjusting and paying accrued wages

P1

Determine the missing amounts in each of these four separate situations *a* through *d*:

	a	b	c	d
Supplies available—prior year-end	$ 400	$1,200	$1,260	?
Supplies purchased during the current year	2,800	6,500	?	$3,000
Supplies available—current year-end	650	?	1,350	700
Supplies expense for the current year	?	1,200	8,400	4,588

Exercise 3-4
Determining cost flows through accounts

A1 P1

The following three situations require adjusting journal entries to prepare financial statements as of April 30. For each situation, present both the April 30 adjusting entry and the subsequent entry during May to record the payment of the accrued liability.

a. On April 1, the company retained an attorney at a flat monthly fee of $3,500. This amount is payable on the 12th of the following month.

b. An $800,000 note payable requires 1.0% interest to be paid every 30 days. The interest was last paid on April 20 and the next payment is due on May 20. $8000 \times 10/30 = 266\overline{7}$

c. Total weekly salaries expense for all employees is $10,000. This amount is paid at the end of the day on Friday of each 5-day workweek. April 30 falls on Tuesday of this year, which means that the employees had worked two days since the last payday. The next payday is May 3.

$10000 / week \times 2/5 = 4000$

Exercise 3-5
Adjusting and paying accrued expenses

A1 P1

Check (b) May 20 Dr. Interest Expense, $5,333

Exercise 3-6

Determining assets and expenses for accrual and cash accounting

C2

Check 2003 insurance expense: Accrual, $6,000; Cash, $0. Dec. 31, 2003, asset: Accrual, $1,000; Cash, $0.

On March 1, 2001, a company paid an $18,000 premium on a three-year insurance policy for coverage beginning on that date. Refer to that policy and fill in the blanks in the following table:

| | Balance Sheet Asset Using | | | Insurance Expense Using | |
	Accrual Basis	Cash Basis		Accrual Basis	Cash Basis
Dec. 31, 2001	$_____	$_____	2001	$_____	$_____
Dec. 31, 2002	_____	_____	2002	_____	_____
Dec. 31, 2003	_____	_____	2003	_____	_____
Dec. 31, 2004	_____	_____	2004	_____	_____
			Total	$_____	$_____

Exercise 3-7

Preparing closing entries and a post-closing trial balance

C4 P4 P5

Check (1) Cr. Retained Earnings, $10,900; (2) Total debits, $59,000

The following adjusted trial balance contains the accounts and balances of Clover Company as of December 31, 2002, the end of its fiscal year. (1) Prepare the December 31, 2002, closing entries for Clover Company. (2) Prepare the December 31, 2002, post-closing trial balance for Clover Company.

No.	Account Title	Debit	Credit
101	Cash	$19,000	
126	Supplies	13,000	
128	Prepaid insurance	3,000	
167	Equipment	24,000	
168	Accumulated depreciation—Equipment		$ 7,500
307	Common stock		30,000
318	Retained earnings		10,600
404	Services revenue		44,000
612	Depreciation expense—Equipment	3,000	
622	Salaries expense	22,000	
637	Insurance expense	2,500	
640	Rent expense	3,400	
652	Supplies expense	2,200	
	Totals	$92,100	$92,100

Exercise 3-8

Preparing a classified balance sheet

C6

Check Total assets, $249,500; Total equity, $180,500

Use the following adjusted trial balance of Webb Trucking Company to prepare a classified balance sheet as of December 31, 2002. (The company paid no dividends during 2002.)

Account Title	Debit	Credit
Cash	$ 8,000	
Accounts receivable	17,500	
Office supplies	3,000	
Trucks	172,000	
Accumulated depreciation—Trucks		$ 36,000
Land	85,000	
Accounts payable		12,000
Interest payable		4,000
Long-term notes payable		53,000
Common stock		100,000
Retained earnings		55,000
Trucking fees earned		130,000
Depreciation expense—Trucks	23,500	
Salaries expense	61,000	
Office supplies expense	8,000	
Repairs expense—Trucks	12,000	
Total	$390,000	$390,000

Use the information in the adjusted trial balance reported in Exercise 3-8 to prepare Webb Trucking Company's (1) income statement, and (2) statement of retained earnings.

Exercise 3-9
Preparing financial statements **P3**

Use the information in the adjusted trial balance reported in Exercise 3-8 to compute the current ratio as of the balance sheet date. Interpret the current ratio for this company. (Assume that the industry norm for the current ratio is 1.5.)

Exercise 3-10 🖸
Computing current ratio **A3**

Use the following information to compute profit margin for each separate company *a* through *e*:

	Net Income	Net Sales			Net Income	Net Sales
a.	$ 4,390	$ 44,830		d.	$65,234	$1,458,999
b.	97,644	398,954		e.	80,158	435,925
c.	111,385	257,082				

Which of the five companies is the most profitable according to the profit margin ratio? Interpret that company's profit margin ratio.

Exercise 3-11 🖸
Computing and interpreting profit margin

A2

Calculate the current ratio in each of the following separate cases. Identify the company case with the strongest liquidity position. (All of these cases represent competing companies in the same industry.)

Exercise 3-12 🖸
Computing and analyzing the current ratio

A3

	Current Assets	Current Liabilities
Case 1	$ 79,000	$ 32,000
Case 2	105,000	76,000
Case 3	45,000	49,000
Case 4	85,500	81,600
Case 5	61,000	100,000

Tri-Mark Construction began operations on December 1. In setting up its accounting procedures, the company decided to debit expense accounts when it prepays its expenses and to credit revenue accounts when customers pay for services in advance. Prepare journal entries for items *a* through *d* and the adjusting entries as of December 31 for items *e* through *g*.

a. Supplies are purchased on December 1 for $2,000 cash.

b. The company prepaid its insurance premiums for $1,540 cash on December 2.

c. On December 15, the company receives an advance payment of $13,000 cash from a customer for remodeling work.

d. On December 28, the company receives $3,700 cash from another customer for remodeling work to be performed in January.

e. A physical count on December 31 indicates that Tri-Mark has $1,840 of supplies available.

f. An analysis of the insurance policies in effect on December 31 shows that $340 of insurance coverage had expired.

g. As of December 31, only one project has been worked on and completed. The $5,570 fee for this project had been received in advance.

Exercise 3-13ᴬ
Adjusting for prepaids recorded as expenses and unearned revenues recorded as revenues

P6

Check (*f*) Cr. Insurance expense, $1,200; (*g*) Dr. Remodeling fees earned, $11,130

Globus Company experienced the following events and transactions during July:

July	1	Received $3,000 cash in advance of performing work for Nicole Renker.
	6	Received $7,500 cash in advance of performing work for Lisa Gardner.
	12	Completed the job for Nicole Renker.
	18	Received $8,500 cash in advance of performing work for Drew Hanson.
	27	Completed the job for Lisa Gardner.
	31	None of the work for Drew Hanson has been performed.

a. Prepare journal entries (including any adjusting entries as of the end of the month) to record these events using the procedure of initially crediting the Unearned Fees account when payment is received from a customer in advance of performing services.

b. Prepare journal entries (including any adjusting entries as of the end of the month) to record these events using the procedure of initially crediting the Fees Earned account when payment is received from a customer in advance of performing services.

c. Under each method, determine the amount of earned fees reported on the income statement for July and the amount of unearned fees reported on the balance sheet as of July 31.

Exercise 3-14ᴬ
Recording and reporting revenues received in advance

P6

Exercise 3-15ᴮ

Preparing a work sheet and recording closing entries

P4 P7

The following unadjusted trial balance contains the accounts and balances of the Dalton Delivery Company as of December 31, 2002, its first year of operations. Use the following information about the company's adjustments to complete a 10-column work sheet for Dalton.

a. Unrecorded depreciation on the trucks at the end of the year is $40,000.

b. The total amount of incurred but unpaid interest at year-end is $6,000.

c. The cost of unused office supplies still available at the end of the year is $2,000.

Also prepare the year-end closing entries for Dalton (current year dividends total $39,000), and determine the retained earnings amount to be reported on the year-end balance sheet.

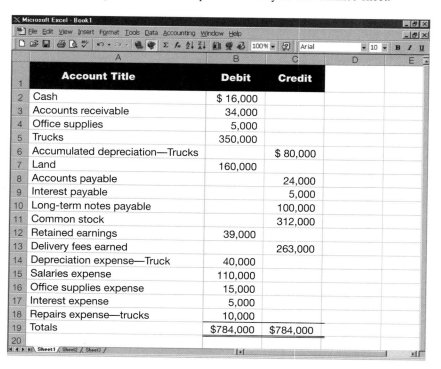

Account Title	Debit	Credit
Cash	$ 16,000	
Accounts receivable	34,000	
Office supplies	5,000	
Trucks	350,000	
Accumulated depreciation—Trucks		$ 80,000
Land	160,000	
Accounts payable		24,000
Interest payable		5,000
Long-term notes payable		100,000
Common stock		312,000
Retained earnings	39,000	
Delivery fees earned		263,000
Depreciation expense—Truck	40,000	
Salaries expense	110,000	
Office supplies expense	15,000	
Interest expense	5,000	
Repairs expense—trucks	10,000	
Totals	$784,000	$784,000

Check Adj. trial balance totals, $825,000; Net income, $39,000

Exercise 3-16ᴬ

Preparing reversing entries

P8

The following two events occurred for Totten Co. on October 31, 2002, the end of its fiscal year:

a. Totten rents a building from its owner for $2,800 per month. By a prearrangement, the company delayed paying October's rent until November 5. On this date, the company paid the rent for both October and November.

b. Totten rents space in a building it owns to a tenant for $850 per month. By prearrangement, the tenant delayed paying the October rent until November 8. On this date, the tenant paid the rent for both October and November.

Required

1. Prepare adjusting entries that Totten must record for these events as of October 31.

2. Assuming Totten does *not* use reversing entries, prepare journal entries to record Totten's payment of rent on November 5 and the collection of rent on November 8 from Totten's tenant.

3. Assuming that Totten uses reversing entries, prepare reversing entries on November 1 and the journal entries to record Totten's payment of rent on November 5 and the collection of rent on November 8 from Totten's tenant.

PROBLEM SET A

Problem 3-1A

Preparing adjusting and subsequent journal entries

A1 P1

Feinman Co. follows the practice of recording prepaid expenses and unearned revenues in balance sheet accounts. Feinman's annual accounting period ends on December 31, 2003. The following information concerns the adjusting entries to be recorded as of that date:

a. The Office Supplies account started the year with a $4,000 balance. During 2003, the company purchased supplies for $13,400, which was added to the Office Supplies account. The inventory of supplies available at December 31, 2003, totaled $2,554.

b. An analysis of the company's insurance policies provided these facts:

Policy	Date of Purchase	Months of Coverage	Cost
A	April 1, 2002	24	$14,400
B	April 1, 2003	36	12,960
C	August 1, 2003	12	2,400

The total premium for each policy was paid in full (for all months) at the purchase date, and the Prepaid Insurance account was debited for the full cost.

c. The company has 14 employees, who earn a total of $1,960 in salaries each working day. They are paid each Monday for their work in the five-day workweek ending on the previous Friday. December 31, 2003, falls on Tuesday, and all 14 employees worked the first two days of that week. Because New Year's Day is a paid holiday, they will be paid salaries for five full days on Monday, January 6, 2004.

d. The company purchased a building on January 1, 2003. It cost $960,000 and is expected to have a $45,000 salvage value at the end of its predicted 30-year life.

e. Since the company is not large enough to occupy the entire building, it rented some space to a tenant at $3,000 per month, starting on November 1, 2003. The rent was paid on time on November 1, and the amount received was credited to the Rent Earned account. However, the tenant has not paid the December rent. The company has worked out an agreement with the tenant, who has promised to pay both December and January rent in full on January 15. The tenant has agreed not to fall behind again.

f. On November 1, the company rented space to another tenant for $2,800 per month. The tenant paid five months' rent in advance on that date. The payment was recorded with a credit to the Unearned Rent account.

Required

1. Use the information to prepare adjusting entries as of December 31, 2003.

2. Prepare journal entries to record the first subsequent cash transaction in 2004 for parts *c* and *e*.

Thomas Technical Institute, a school owned by Joshua Thomas, provides training to individuals who pay tuition directly to the school. The school also offers training to groups in off-site locations. The school's unadjusted trial balance as of December 31, 2002, follows. Thomas Technical Institute initially records prepaid expenses and unearned revenues in balance sheet accounts. Items *a* through *h* that require adjusting entries on December 31, 2002, are described below.

Problem 3-2A
Making adjusting entries, preparing financial statements, and calculating profit margin

A1 A2 P1 P3

Additional Information Items

a. An analysis of the company's insurance policies shows that $2,400 of coverage has expired.

b. An inventory shows that teaching supplies costing $2,800 are available at year-end 2002.

c. Annual depreciation on the equipment is $13,200.

d. Annual depreciation on the professional library is $7,200.

e. On November 1, the company agreed to do a special six-month course (starting immediately) for a client. The contract calls for a monthly fee of $2,500, and the client paid the first five months' fees in advance. When the cash was received, the Unearned Training Fees account was credited. The fee for the sixth month will be recorded when it is collected in 2003.

f. On October 15, the school agreed to teach a four-month class (beginning immediately) for an individual for $3,000 tuition per month payable at the end of the class. The services are being provided as agreed, and no payment has been received.

g. The school's two employees are paid weekly. As of the end of the year, two days' wages have accrued at the rate of $100 per day for each employee. $100 (2)(2) =$400

h. The balance in the Prepaid Rent account represents rent for December.

Required

1. Prepare T-accounts with the balances from the unadjusted trial balance.

2. Prepare the necessary adjusting journal entries for items *a* through *h* and post them to the T-accounts. Assume that adjusting entries are made only at year-end.

THOMAS TECHNICAL INSTITUTE Unadjusted Trial Balance December 31, 2002		
	B	C
Cash	$ 34,000	
Accounts receivable	0	
Teaching supplies	8,000	
Prepaid insurance	12,000	
Prepaid rent	3,000	
Professional library	35,000	
Accumulated depreciation—Professional library		$ 10,000
Equipment	80,000	
Accumulated depreciation—Equipment		15,000
Accounts payable		26,000
Salaries payable		0
Unearned training fees		12,500
Common stock		30,000
Retained earnings		10,000
Tuition fees earned		123,900
Training fees earned		40,000
Depreciation expense—Professional library	0	
Depreciation expense—Equipment	0	
Salaries expense	50,000	
Insurance expense	0	
Rent expense	33,000	
Teaching supplies expense	0	
Advertising expense	6,000	
Utilities expense	6,400	
Totals	$ 267,400	$ 267,400

3. Update balances in the T-accounts for the adjusting entries and prepare an adjusted trial balance.

4. Prepare Thomas Technical Institute's income statement and statement of retained earnings for the year 2002 and prepare its balance sheet as of December 31, 2002. (The company paid no dividends in 2002.)

5. Calculate the company's profit margin for the year.

Problem 3-3A

Interpreting unadjusted and adjusted trial balances, preparing financial statements, and calculating profit margin

A1 A2 **P1 P3**

Check   (2) Net income, $4,960; Retained earnings (7/31/02), $29,960; Total assets, $124,960

Check   (3) Profit margin, 3.7%

A six-column table for JLK Company follows. The first two columns contain the unadjusted trial balance for the company as of July 31, 2002. The last two columns contain the adjusted trial balance as of the same date.

Required

Analysis Component

1. Analyze the differences between the unadjusted and adjusted trial balances to determine the adjustments that must have been made. Show the results of your analysis by inserting these adjustment amounts in the table's two middle columns. Label each adjustment with a letter and provide a short description of it.

Preparation Component

2. Use the information in the adjusted trial balance to prepare the company's (*a*) income statement and its statement of retained earnings for the year ended July 31, 2002 (*note:* retained earnings at July 31, 2001, were $30,000, and the current-year dividends were $5,000), and (*b*) the balance sheet as of July 31, 2002.

3. Calculate the company's profit margin for the year ended July 31, 2002.

	Unadjusted Trial Balance		Adjustments		Adjusted Trial Balance	
Cash	$ 34,000				$ 34,000	
Accounts receivable	14,000				22,000	
Office supplies	16,000				2,000	
Prepaid insurance	8,540				2,960	
Office equipment	84,000				84,000	
Accum. depreciation— Office equip.		$ 14,000				$ 20,000
Accounts payable		9,100				10,000
Interest payable		0				1,000
Salaries payable		0				7,000
Unearned consulting fees .		18,000				15,000
Long-term notes payable ..		52,000				52,000
Common stock		10,000				10,000
Retained earnings		25,000				25,000
Consulting fees earned ...		123,240				134,240
Depreciation expense— Office equip.	0				6,000	
Salaries expense	67,000				74,000	
Interest expense	1,200				2,200	
Insurance expense	0				5,580	
Rent expense	14,500				14,500	
Office supplies expense ...	0				14,000	
Advertising expense	12,100				13,000	
Totals	$251,340	$251,340			$274,240	$274,240

The records for Turf's Up Landscape Co. are kept on the cash basis instead of the accrual basis. The company is now applying for a loan and the bank wants to know what its net income for year 2002 is under the accrual basis. Its income statement for year 2002 under the cash basis follows:

Problem 3-4A
Computing accrual income from cash income

C3

TURF'S UP LANDSCAPE CO.
Income Statement (Cash Basis)
For Year Ended December 31, 2002

Revenues	$625,000
Expenses	440,000
Net income	$185,000

Additional information was gathered to help convert the income statement to the accrual basis:

	As of 12/31/2001	As of 12/31/2002
Accrued revenues	$13,000	$17,500
Unearned revenues	67,000	22,000
Accrued expenses	15,700	10,000
Prepaid expenses	28,000	21,700

Hint
Cash inflows 2002
+ Accrued revenues 2002
+ Unearned revenues 2001
− Accrued revenues 2001
− Unearned revenues 2002
Accrual revenues 2002

All prepaid expenses from the beginning of the year have been used or expired, all unearned revenues from the beginning of the year have been earned, and all accrued expenses and accrued revenues from the beginning of the year have been paid or collected.

Required

Prepare the accrual basis income statement for year 2002. Provide calculations that explain how you converted from cash revenues and cash expenses to accrual revenues and accrual expenses.

Check   Net income, $233,900

Problem 3-5A^A

Recording prepaid expenses and unearned revenues

P1 P6

Quisp Co. had the following transactions in the last two months of its year ended December 31:

Nov. 1 Paid $1,800 cash for future newspaper advertising.

1 Paid $2,460 cash for 12 months of insurance through October 31 of the following year.

30 Received $3,600 cash for future services to be provided to a customer.

Dec. 1 Paid $3,000 cash for a consultant's services to be received over the next three months.

15 Received $7,950 cash for future services to be provided to a customer.

31 Of the advertising paid for on November 1, $1,200 worth is yet to be used.

31 A portion of the insurance paid for on November 1 has expired.

31 Services worth $1,500 are not yet provided to the customer who paid on November 30.

31 One-third of the consulting services paid for on December 1 have been received.

31 The company has performed $3,300 of services that the customer paid for on December 15.

Required

1. Prepare entries for these transactions under the method that records prepaid expenses as assets and records unearned revenues as liabilities. Also prepare adjusting entries at the end of the year.

2. Prepare entries for these transactions under the method that records prepaid expenses as expenses and records unearned revenues as revenues. Also prepare adjusting entries at the end of the year.

Analysis Component

3. Explain why the alternative sets of entries in requirements 1 and 2 do not result in different financial statement amounts.

Problem 3-6A

Applying the accounting cycle

C5 A1 P1 P4 P5

E_x

On April 1, 2002, Jennifer Stafford created a new travel agency, Ambassador Travel. The following transactions occurred during the company's first month:

April 1 Stafford invested $30,000 cash and computer equipment worth $20,000 in the business in exchange for common stock.

2 Rented furnished office space by paying $1,800 cash for the first month's rent.

3 Purchased $1,000 of office supplies for cash.

10 Paid $2,400 cash for the premium on a 12-month insurance policy. Coverage began on April 11.

14 Paid $1,600 cash for two weeks' salaries earned by employees.

24 Collected $8,000 cash on commissions from airlines on tickets obtained for customers.

28 Paid another $1,600 cash for two weeks' salaries earned by employees.

29 Paid $350 cash for minor repairs to the company's computer.

30 Paid this month's $750 telephone bill in cash.

30 Paid $1,500 cash for dividends.

The company's chart of accounts included the following:

101 Cash	405 Commissions Earned
106 Accounts Receivable	612 Depreciation Expense—Computer Equip.
124 Office Supplies	622 Salaries Expense
128 Prepaid Insurance	637 Insurance Expense
167 Computer Equipment	640 Rent Expense
168 Accumulated Depreciation—Computer Equip.	650 Office Supplies Expense
209 Salaries Payable	684 Repairs Expense
307 Common Stock	688 Telephone Expense
318 Retained Earnings	901 Income Summary

Required

1. Use the balance column format to set up each account listed in its chart of accounts.

2. Prepare journal entries to record the transactions for April and post them to the accounts. The company records prepaid and unearned items in balance sheet accounts.

3. Prepare an unadjusted trial balance as of April 30.

Check (3) Unadj. trial balance totals, $58,000

4. Use the following information to journalize and post adjusting entries for the month:
  a. Two-thirds of one month's insurance coverage has expired.
  b. There are $600 of office supplies available at the end of the month.
  c. Depreciation on the computer equipment is $500.
  d. Employees earned $420 of unpaid and unrecorded salaries.
  e. The company earned $1,750 of commissions that are not yet billed.

5. Prepare the income statement and the statement of retained earnings for April, and the balance sheet at April 30, 2002.

6. Prepare journal entries to close the temporary accounts and post these entries to the accounts.

7. Prepare a post-closing trial balance.

Check (4a) Dr. Insurance expense, $133

Check (5) Net income, $2,197; Retained earnings (4/30/02), $697; Total assets, $51,117

Check (7) P-C trial balance totals, $51,617

In the blank space beside each numbered balance sheet item, enter the letter of its balance sheet classification. If the item should not appear on the balance sheet, enter a Z in the blank.

Problem 3-7A
Determining balance sheet classifications

C6

A. Current assets   **D.** Intangible assets   **F.** Long-term liabilities
B. Long-term investments   **E.** Current liabilities   **G.** Equity
C. Plant assets

____ **1.** Accumulated depreciation—Trucks
____ **2.** Cash
____ **3.** Buildings
____ **4.** Retained earnings
____ **5.** Office equipment
____ **6.** Land (used in operations)
____ **7.** Repairs expense
____ **8.** Prepaid property taxes
____ **9.** Current portion of long-term note payable
____ **10.** Long-term investment in stock
____ **11.** Depreciation expense—Trucks
____ **12.** Prepaid rent
____ **13.** Interest receivable
____ **14.** Taxes payable
____ **15.** Automobiles
____ **16.** Notes payable (due in 3 years)
____ **17.** Accounts payable
____ **18.** Prepaid insurance
____ **19.** Common stock
____ **20.** Unearned services revenue

Sanuk Co. follows the practice of recording prepaid expenses and unearned revenues in balance sheet accounts. Sanuk's annual accounting period ends on October 31, 2003. The following information concerns the adjusting entries that need to be recorded as of that date:

a. The Office Supplies account started the fiscal year with a $600 balance. During the fiscal year, the company purchased supplies for $4,570, which was added to the Office Supplies account. The supplies available at October 31, 2003, totaled $800.

b. An analysis of the company's insurance policies provided these facts:

PROBLEM SET B

Problem 3-1B
Preparing adjusting and subsequent journal entries

A1 P1

Policy	Date of Purchase	Months of Coverage	Cost
A	April 1, 2002	24	$6,000
B	April 1, 2003	36	7,200
C	August 1, 2003	12	1,320

The total premium for each policy was paid in full (for all months) at the purchase date, and the Prepaid Insurance account was debited for the full cost.

c. The company has five employees, who earn a total of $1,000 for each workday. They are paid each Monday for their work in the five-day workweek ending on the previous Friday. October 31, 2003, falls on Monday, and all five employees worked the first day of that week. They will be paid salaries for five full days on Monday, November 7, 2003.

d. The company purchased a building on November 1, 2002, that cost $175,000 and is expected to have a $40,000 salvage value at the end of its predicted 25-year life.

e. Since the company is not large enough to occupy the entire building, it rented some space to a tenant at $1,000 per month, starting on September 1, 2003. The rent was paid on time on September 1, and the amount received was credited to the Rent Earned account. However, the October rent has not been paid. The company has worked out an agreement with the tenant, who has promised to pay both October and November rent in full on November 15. The tenant has agreed not to fall behind again.

f. On September 1, the company rented space to another tenant for $725 per month. The tenant paid five months' rent in advance on that date. The payment was recorded with a credit to the Unearned Rent account.

Check   (*1b*) Dr. Insurance expense, $4,730; (*1d*) Dr. Depreciation expense, $5,400

Required

1. Use the information to prepare adjusting entries as of October 31, 2003.
2. Prepare journal entries to record the first subsequent cash transaction in 2004 for parts *c* and *e*.

Problem 3-2B

Preparing adjusting entries, preparing financial statements, and calculating profit margin

A1 A2 P1 P3

Following is the unadjusted trial balance for Triangle Institute as of December 31, 2002, which initially records prepaid expenses and unearned revenues in balance sheet accounts. The institute provides one-on-one training to individuals who pay tuition directly to the business and offers extension training to groups in off-site locations. Shown after the trial balance are items *a* through *h* that require adjusting entries as of December 31, 2002.

TRIANGLE INSTITUTE Unadjusted Trial Balance December 31, 2002		
Cash	$ 60,000	
Accounts receivable	0	
Teaching supplies	70,000	
Prepaid insurance	19,000	
Prepaid rent	3,800	
Professional library	12,000	
Accumulated depreciation—Professional library		$ 2,500
Equipment	40,000	
Accumulated depreciation—Equipment		20,000
Accounts payable		11,200
Salaries payable		0
Unearned training fees		28,600
Common stock		40,000
Retained earnings		11,500
Tuition fees earned		129,200
Training fees earned		68,000
Depreciation expense—Professional library	0	
Depreciation expense—Equipment	0	
Salaries expense	44,200	
Insurance expense	0	
Rent expense	29,600	
Teaching supplies expense	0	
Advertising expense	19,000	
Utilities expense	13,400	
Totals	$ 311,000	$ 311,000

Additional Information Items

a. An analysis of the institute's insurance policies shows that $9,500 of coverage has expired.
b. An inventory shows that teaching supplies costing $20,000 are available at year-end 2002.
c. Annual depreciation on the equipment is $5,000.
d. Annual depreciation on the professional library is $2,400.
e. On November 1, the institute agreed to do a special four-month course (starting immediately) for a client. The contract calls for a $5,600 monthly fee, and the client paid the first two months' fees in advance. When the cash was received, the Unearned Training Fees account was credited. The last two months' fees will be recorded when collected in 2003.

f. On October 15, the institute agreed to teach a four-month class (beginning immediately) to an individual for $2,300 tuition per month payable at the end of the class. The class started on October 15, but no payment has been received.

g. The institute's only employee is paid weekly. As of the end of the year, three days' wages have accrued at the rate of $150 per day.

h. The balance in the Prepaid Rent account represents rent for December.

Required

1. Prepare T-accounts with the balances from the unadjusted trial balance.

2. Prepare the necessary adjusting journal entries for items *a* through *h*, and post them to the T-accounts. Assume that adjusting entries are made only at year-end.

3. Update balances in the T-accounts for the adjusting entries and prepare an adjusted trial balance.

4. Prepare Triangle Institute's income statement and statement of retained earnings for the year 2002, and prepare its balance sheet as of December 31, 2002. (The company paid no dividends in 2002.)

5. Compute the company's profit margin for the year.

Check (2e) Cr. Training fees earned, $11,200; (2f) Cr. Tuition fees earned, $5,750; (3) Adj. trial balance totals, $324,600; (4) Net income, $36,800; Ending retained earnings, $48,300

A six-column table for Daxu Consulting Company follows. The first two columns contain the unadjusted trial balance for the company as of December 31, 2002, and the last two columns contain the adjusted trial balance as of the same date.

Problem 3-3B
Interpreting unadjusted and adjusted trial balances, preparing financial statements, and calculating profit margin

A1 A2 P1 P3

	Unadjusted Trial Balance		Adjustments		Adjusted Trial Balance	
Cash	$ 45,000				$ 45,000	
Accounts receivable	60,000				66,660	
Office supplies	40,000				17,000	
Prepaid insurance	8,200				3,600	
Office equipment	120,000				120,000	
Accumulated depreciation—Office equip.		$ 20,000				$ 30,000
Accounts payable		26,000				32,000
Interest payable		0				2,150
Salaries payable		0				16,000
Unearned consulting fees		40,000				27,800
Long-term notes payable		75,000				75,000
Common stock		20,000				20,000
Retained earnings		40,200				40,200
Consulting fees earned		234,600				253,460
Depreciation expense—Office equip.	0				10,000	
Salaries expense	112,000				128,000	
Interest expense	8,600				10,750	
Insurance expense	0				4,600	
Rent expense	20,000				20,000	
Office supplies expense	0				23,000	
Advertising expense	42,000				48,000	
Totals	$455,800	$455,800			$496,610	$496,610

Required

Analysis Component

1. Analyze the differences between the unadjusted and adjusted trial balances to determine the adjustments that must have been made. Show the results of your analysis by inserting these adjustment amounts in the table's two middle columns. Label each adjustment with a letter and provide a short description of it.

Check   (2) Net income, $9,110;
Retained earnings (12/31/02),
$49,310; Total assets, $222,260

Check   (3) Profit margin, 3.6%

Preparation Component

2. Use the information in the adjusted trial balance to prepare this company's (*a*) income statement and its statement of retained earnings for the year ended December 31, 2002 (*note:* retained earnings at December 31, 2001, were $60,200, and the current-year dividends were $20,000), and (*b*) the balance sheet as of December 31, 2002.

3. Calculate the company's profit margin for the year ended December 31, 2002.

Problem 3-4B
Computing accrual income from cash income

C3

The records for Web Products are kept on the cash basis instead of the accrual basis. The company is now applying for a loan and the bank wants to know what its net income for year 2002 is under the accrual basis. Its income statement for year 2002 under the cash basis follows:

WEB PRODUCTS
Income Statement (Cash Basis)
For Year Ended December 31, 2002

Revenues	$185,000
Expenses	86,000
Net income	$ 99,000

Additional information was gathered to help convert the income statement to the accrual basis:

Hint
Cash outflows 2002
+ Accrued expenses 2002
+ Prepaid expenses 2001
− Accrued expenses 2001
− Prepaid expenses 2002
‾‾‾‾‾‾‾‾‾‾‾‾‾‾‾‾‾‾‾‾‾‾
Accrual expenses 2002

	As of 12/31/2001	As of 12/31/2002
Accrued revenues	$13,100	$ 5,600
Unearned revenues	9,050	9,800
Accrued expenses	6,800	13,400
Prepaid expenses	8,300	5,300

All prepaid expenses from the beginning of the year are used or expired, all unearned revenues from the beginning of the year are earned, and all accrued expenses and accrued revenues from the beginning of the year are paid or collected.

Required

Check   Net income, $81,150

Prepare the accrual basis income statement for year 2002. Provide calculations that explain how you converted from cash revenues and cash expenses to accrual revenues and accrual expenses.

Problem 3-5B[A]
Recording prepaid expenses and unearned revenues

P1 P6

Quake Co. had the following transactions in the last two months of its fiscal year ended May 31:

Apr. 1   Paid $2,450 cash for future consulting services.
       1   Paid $3,600 cash for 12 months of insurance through March 31 of the following year.
      30   Received $8,500 cash for future services to be provided to a customer.
May 1   Paid $4,450 cash for future newspaper advertising.
      23   Received $10,450 cash for future services to be provided to a customer.
      31   Of the consulting services paid for on April 1, $2,000 worth has been received.
      31   A portion of the insurance paid for on April 1 has expired. No adjustment was made in April to Prepaid Insurance.
      31   Services worth $4,600 are not yet provided to the customer who paid on April 30.
      31   Of the advertising paid for on May 1, $2,050 worth is not yet used.
      31   The company has performed $5,500 of services that the customer paid for on May 23.

Required

1. Prepare entries for these transactions under the method that records prepaid expenses and unearned revenues in balance sheet accounts. Also prepare adjusting entries at the end of the year.

2. Prepare entries for these transactions under the method that records prepaid expenses and unearned revenues in income statement accounts. Also prepare adjusting entries at the end of the year.

Analysis Component

3. Explain why the alternative sets of entries in parts 1 and 2 do not result in different financial statement amounts.

On July 1, 2002, Lucinda Fogle created a new self-storage business, SafeStore Co. The following transactions occurred during the company's first month:

July   1   Fogle invested $30,000 cash and buildings worth $150,000 in the business in exchange for common stock.

2   Rented equipment by paying $2,000 cash for the first month's (July) rent.

5   Purchased $2,400 of office supplies for cash.

10   Paid $7,200 cash for the premium on a 12-month insurance policy. Coverage begins on July 11.

14   Paid an employee $1,000 cash for two weeks' salary earned.

24   Collected $9,800 cash for storage fees from customers.

28   Paid another $1,000 cash for two weeks' salary earned by an employee.

29   Paid $950 cash for minor repairs to a leaking roof.

30   Paid this month's $400 telephone bill in cash.

31   Paid $2,000 cash for dividends.

The company's chart of accounts included the following:

101	Cash	401	Storage Fees Earned
106	Accounts Receivable	606	Depreciation Expense—Buildings
124	Office Supplies	622	Salaries Expense
128	Prepaid Insurance	637	Insurance Expense
173	Buildings	640	Rent Expense
174	Accumulated Depreciation—Buildings	650	Office Supplies Expense
209	Salaries Payable	684	Repairs Expense
307	Common Stock	688	Telephone Expense
318	Retained Earnings	901	Income Summary

Problem 3-6B
Applying the accounting cycle

C5 A1 P1 P4 P5

Required

1. Use the balance column format to set up each account listed in its chart of accounts.

2. Prepare journal entries to record the transactions for July and post them to the accounts. Record prepaid and unearned items in balance sheet accounts.

3. Prepare an unadjusted trial balance as of July 31.

4. Use the following information to journalize and post adjusting entries for the month:

   a. Two-thirds of one month's insurance coverage has expired.

   b. There are $1,525 of office supplies available at the end of the month.

   c. Depreciation on the buildings is $1,500.

   d. An employee earned $100 of unpaid and unrecorded salary.

   e. The company earned $1,150 of storage fees that are not yet billed.

5. Prepare the income statement and the statement of retained earnings for July, and the balance sheet at July 31, 2002.

6. Prepare journal entries to close the temporary accounts and post these entries to the accounts.

7. Prepare a post-closing trial balance.

Check   (3) Unadj. trial balance totals, $189,800

Check   (4a) Dr. Insurance expense, $400

Check   (5) Net income, $2,725; Retained earnings (7/31/02), $725; Total assets, $180,825

Check   (7) P-C trial balance totals, $182,325

In the blank space beside each numbered balance sheet item, enter the letter of its balance sheet classification. If the item should not appear on the balance sheet, enter a Z in the blank.

A. Current assets

B. Long-term investments

C. Plant assets

D. Intangible assets

E. Current liabilities

F. Long-term liabilities

G. Equity

Problem 3-7B
Determining balance sheet classifications

C6

———— **1.** Buildings

———— **2.** Prepaid insurance

———— **3.** Current portion of long-term note payable

———— **4.** Interest receivable

———— **5.** Short-term investments

———— **6.** Land (used in operations)

———— **7.** Copyrights

———— **8.** Rent earned

———— **9.** Depreciation expense—Trucks

———— **10.** Long-term investment in stock

———— **11.** Office supplies

———— **12.** Interest payable

———— **13.** Common stock

———— **14.** Notes receivable (due in 120 days)

———— **15.** Accumulated depreciation— Trucks

———— **16.** Salaries payable

———— **17.** Commissions earned

———— **18.** Retained earnings

———— **19.** Office equipment

———— **20.** Notes payable (due in 5 years)

SERIAL PROBLEM

Sierra Systems

(This serial problem involving Sierra Systems was introduced in Chapter 2 and continues in Chapter 4. If the Chapter 2 segment has not been completed, the assignment can begin at this point. You need to use the facts for the serial problem at the end of Chapter 2. This problem is best solved if you use the Working Papers that accompany this book.)

After the success of the company's first two months, Sela Solstise decides to continue operating Sierra Systems. (Transactions that occurred in these first two months are described in Chapter 2.) On December 1, Solstise adds these new accounts to its chart of accounts:

Account	No.
Accumulated Depreciation—Office equipment	164
Accumulated Depreciation—Computer equipment	168
Wages Payable	210
Unearned Computer Services Revenue	236
Depreciation Expense—Office equipment	612
Depreciation Expense—Computer equipment	613
Insurance Expense	637
Rent Expense	640
Computer Supplies Expense	652
Income Summary	901

Sierra Systems had the following transactions and events in December 2002:

Dec. 2   Paid $1,025 cash to Hilldale Mall for Sierra Systems' share of mall advertising costs.

   3   Paid $500 cash for minor repairs to the company's computer.

   4   Received $3,950 cash from Antonio's Engineering Co. for the receivable from November.

   10 Paid cash to Suzie Smith for six days of work at the rate of $125 per day.

   14 Notified by Antonio's Engineering Co. that Sierra's bid of $7,000 on a proposed project has been accepted. Antonio's paid an advance of $1,500 cash to Sierra Systems.

   15 Purchased $1,100 of computer supplies on credit from Appier Office Products.

   16 Sent a reminder to Foster Co. to pay the fee for services recorded on November 8.

   20 Completed a project for Elan Corporation and received $5,625 cash.

22–26 Took the week off for the holidays.

   28 Received $3,000 cash from Foster Co. on its receivable.

   29 Reimbursed Solstise's business automobile mileage (600 miles at $0.32 per mile).

   31 Paid $1,500 cash for dividends.

The following additional facts are collected for use in making adjusting entries prior to preparing financial statements for the company's first three months:

a. The December 31 inventory of computer supplies is $580.

b. Three months have expired since the annual insurance premium was paid in advance.

c. As of December 31, Suzie Smith has not been paid for four days of work at $125 per day.

d. The company's computer is expected to have a four-year life with no salvage value.

e. The office equipment is expected to have a five-year life with no salvage value.

f. Prepaid rent for three of the four months has expired.

Required

1. Prepare journal entries to record each of the December transactions and events for Sierra Systems. Post these entries to the accounts in the ledger.

2. Prepare all necessary adjusting entries. Post these entries to the accounts in the ledger.

3. Prepare an adjusted trial balance as of December 31, 2002.   **Check**   (3) Adjusted trial balance

4. Prepare an income statement for the three months ended December 31, 2002.   totals, $119,034

5. Prepare a statement of retained earnings for the three months ended December 31, 2002.

6. Prepare a balance sheet as of December 31, 2002.

7. Record and post the necessary closing entries for Sierra Systems.

8. Prepare a post-closing trial balance as of December 31, 2002.

BEYOND THE NUMBERS

BTN 3-1   Refer to Nike's financial statements in Appendix A to answer the following:

1. What are the major items making up Nike's prepaid expenses listed in its balance sheet?

2. When does Nike recognize its prepaid advertising costs as expenses?

3. What is Nike's profit margin for 2000 and 1999?

4. For the fiscal year ended May 31, 2000, what amount will be credited to Income Summary to summarize Nike's revenues earned?

5. For the fiscal year ended May 31, 2000, what amount will be debited to Income Summary to summarize Nike's expenses incurred?

6. For the fiscal year ended May 31, 2000, what will be the balance of the Income Summary account before it is closed?

7. In its statement of cash flows for the year ended May 31, 2000, what amount of cash is paid in dividends to common and preferred stockholders?

Swoosh Ahead

8. Access Nike's financial statements (10-K) for fiscal years ending after May 31, 2000, at its Web site (www.nike.com) or the SEC's EDGAR database (www.sec.gov). Compare the May 31, 2000, fiscal year profit margin to any subsequent year's profit margin that you are able to calculate. How has the amount of cash paid as dividends changed in the fiscal years ending after May 31, 2000?

Reporting in Action

C4 A1 A2 P4

NIKE

BTN 3-2   Key figures ($ millions) for the recent two years of both Nike and Reebok follow:

Key Figures	Nike		Reebok	
	Current Year	Prior Year	Current Year	Prior Year
Net income ..	$ 579	$ 451	$ 11	$ 24
Net sales ...	8,995	8,777	2,900	3,225
Current assets	3,596	3,265	1,243	1,363
Current liabilities	2,140	1,447	624	543

Comparative Analysis

A2 A3

NIKE

Reebok

Required

1. Compute profit margins for (*a*) Nike and (*b*) Reebok for the two years of data shown.

2. Which company is more successful on the basis of profit margin?

3. Compute the current ratio for both years and both companies.

4. Which has the better ability to pay short-term obligations according to the current ratio?

5. Analyze and comment on each company's current ratios for the past two years.

6. How do Nike's and Reebok's current ratios compare to their industry average ratio of about 1.6?

Ethics Challenge
A1

BTN 3-3   Jackie Houston works for Seitzer Co. She and Bob Welch, her manager, are preparing adjusting entries for annual financial statements. Jackie computes depreciation and records it as

Depreciation Expense—Equipment	123,000
Accumulated Depreciation—Equipment	123,000

Bob agrees with her computation but says the credit entry should be directly to the Equipment account. He argues that while accumulated depreciation is technically correct, "it is less hassle not to use a contra account and just credit the Equipment account directly. And besides, the balance sheet shows the same amount for total assets under either method."

Required

1. How should depreciation be recorded? Do you support Jackie or Bob?

2. Evaluate the strengths and weaknesses of Bob's reasons for preferring his method.

3. Indicate whether the situation Jackie faces is an ethical problem.

Communicating in Practice
C1

BTN 3-4   Assume that one of your classmates said that the *going-concern principle* states that a company's books should be ongoing and therefore not closed until that business is terminated. This classmate does not understand the objective of the closing process or the meaning of the going-concern principle. Write a half-page memo to this classmate explaining the concept of the closing process by drawing analogies between (1) a scoreboard for an athletic event and the revenue and expense accounts of a business or (2) a sports team's record book and the retained earnings account. (*Hint:* Think about what would happen if the scoreboard is not cleared before the start of a new game.) Your memo should also clarify the meaning of the going-concern principle.

Taking It to the Net
C1 A2 🖉

BTN 3-5   Access the Cannondale promotional Web site (www.cannondale.com).

1. What is the primary product that Cannondale sells?

2. Review its form 10-K. You can access this from the EDGAR system (www.sec.gov). You must scroll down the form to find the financial statements.

3. What is Cannondale's fiscal year-end?

4. What are Cannondale's net sales for the annual period ended July 3, 1999?

5. What is Cannondale's net income for the annual period ended July 3, 1999?

6. Compute Cannondale's profit margin ratio for the annual period ended July 3, 1999.

7. Do you think its decision to use a year-end of late June or early July relates to its natural business year?

Teamwork in Action
C2 A1 P1 🖉

BTN 3-6   Four types of adjustments are described in the chapter: (1) prepaid expenses, (2) unearned revenues, (3) accrued expenses, and (4) accrued revenues.

Required

1. Form *learning teams* of four (or more) members. Each team member must select one of the four adjustments as an area of expertise (each team must have at least one expert in each area).

2. Form *expert teams* from the individuals who have selected the same area of expertise. Expert teams are to discuss and write a report that each expert will present to his or her learning team addressing the following:

a. Description of the adjustment and why it's necessary.

b. Example of a transaction or event, with dates and amounts, that requires adjustment.

c. Adjusting entry(ies) for the example in requirement *b*.

d. Status of the affected account(s) before and after the adjustment in requirement *c*.

e. Effects on financial statements of not making the adjustment.

3. Each expert should return to his or her learning team. In rotation, each member should present his or her expert team's report to the learning team. Team discussion is encouraged.

BTN 3-7   Read "Computer Learning Centers: School for Scandal?" in the May 4, 1998, issue of *Business Week*. (Access the book's Web site for a free link.)

Business Week Activity

C3 🗹

Required

1. What type of school is CLC?

2. What three revenue accounting issues does the article discuss?

3. Discuss the effects of each of the revenue accounting issues on CLC's financial statements.

BTN 3-8   Robin Drucker operates a collection agency. For a 50% commission, she collects on accounts receivables from her clients' customers who are delinquent in their payments. For example, a company turns over a $100 accounts receivable to Robin. If she can collect the $100 from the customer, then she keeps $50 and remits the other $50 to her client. Robin now has more than 100 clients, and manually accounting for her business activities is becoming increasingly challenging.

Entrepreneurial Decision

C3 🄮 🗹

Required

1. Why would a company hire a collection agency to pursue its accounts?

2. Robin is trying to decide whether to buy preprogrammed collection software from a major vendor in her industry or hire a programmer to write specialized software tailored exactly to her needs. Identify advantages and disadvantages of packaged versus proprietary software.

BTN 3-9   Select a company that you can visit in person or interview on the telephone. Call ahead to the company to arrange a time when you can interview an employee (preferably an accountant) who helps prepare the annual financial statements. Inquire about the following aspects of its accounting cycle:

Hitting the Road

C2

1. Does it prepare interim financial statements? What time period(s) is used for interim statements?

2. Does the company use the cash or accrual basis of accounting?

3. Does the company use a work sheet in preparing financial statements? Why or why not?

4. Does the company use a spreadsheet program? If so, which software program is used?

5. How long does it take after the end of its reporting period to complete annual statements?

BTN 3-10   Read the article, "Porsche Is Back—and Then Some," in the September 15, 1997, issue of *Business Week*.

Global Decision

A2 🗹

Required

1. Contrast the profitability of **Porsche** in 1992 to five years later in 1997.

2. When does Porsche's fiscal year end?

3. What is the amount of sales for Porsche in the 1997 fiscal year?

4. Calculate Porsche's profit margin ratio for the 1997 fiscal year.

5. Despite its recent profitability, what does the article identify as Porsche's weaknesses?

4

Reporting and Analyzing Merchandising Activities

A Look Back

Chapter 3 focused on the final steps of the accounting process. We explained the importance of proper revenue and expense recognition and described the closing process. We also showed how to prepare financial statements from accounting records.

A Look at This Chapter

This chapter emphasizes merchandising activities. We explain how reporting merchandising activities differs from reporting service activities. We also analyze and record merchandise purchases and sales transactions and explain the adjustments and closing process for merchandisers.

A Look Ahead

Chapter 5 extends our analysis of merchandising activities and focuses on the valuation of inventory. Topics include the items in inventory, costs assigned, costing methods used, and inventory estimation techniques.

"I felt we should go into something that we had some connection to."
Dwayne Lewis

Dada's Hip

e EL SEGUNDO, CA—Dwayne Lewis and Michael Cherry had a dream—a dream to own and run a company. With one lone product (a five-panel polo hat) and $1,000 in pooled paychecks, they launched **Damani Dada (www.DamaniDada.com).** The two dreamed that Damani Dada would bring an ultra-hip style to the urban fashion scene. A mere six years after its launch, Dada projects annual sales of more than $50 million.

The early days, however, were far from easy as Lewis and Cherry struggled alone against long odds. "It was very tricky to try and learn the business without a mentor," recalls Lewis. "We always struggled with the task of maintaining a strong financial backing, and we had to learn a lot by making mistakes." Among those struggles was implementing and learning a merchandising system—one that could capture and communicate the costs and sales information so desperately needed by the young entrepreneurs. A crucial part of their success was tracking merchandising activities. This was necessary for setting prices and making policies for everything from discounts and allowances to returns on both sales and purchases. Also, use of a perpetual inventory system enabled them to stock the right type and amount of merchandise, and to avoid the costs of out-of-stock and excess inventory. This chapter describes how the accounting system captures merchandising information for these and other business decisions. It also introduces analysis tools for assessing the financial condition and performance of merchandisers.

Damani Dada successfully weathered the storm and has expanded to offer a full line of both men's and women's apparel. "Business is war," says Lewis. "You have to be mentally strong, willing to sacrifice, and willing to accept delayed gratification." [Sources: Damani Dada Web site, January 2002; *Entrepreneur,* November 2000.]

Learning Objectives

Conceptual

C1 Describe merchandising activities and identify business examples.

C2 Identify and explain the components of income for a merchandising company.

C3 Identify and explain the inventory asset of a merchandising company.

C4 Describe both perpetual and periodic inventory systems.

C5 Analyze and interpret cost flows and operating activities of a merchandising company.

Analytical

A1 Analyze and interpret accruals and cash flows for merchandising activities.

A2 Compute the acid-test ratio and explain its use to assess liquidity.

A3 Compute the gross margin ratio and explain its use to assess profitability.

Procedural

P1 Analyze and record transactions for merchandise purchases using a perpetual system.

P2 Analyze and record transactions for sales of merchandise using a perpetual system.

P3 Prepare adjustments and close accounts for a merchandising company.

P4 Define and prepare multiple-step and single-step income statements.

Chapter Preview

Merchandising activities are a major part of modern business. Consumers expect a wealth of products, discount prices, inventory on demand, and high quality. This chapter introduces the business and accounting practices used by companies engaged in merchandising activities. These companies buy products and then resell them to customers. We show how financial statements reflect these merchandising activities and explain the new financial statement elements created by merchandising activities. We also analyze and record merchandise purchases and sales, and explain the adjustments and the closing process for merchandising companies.

Merchandising Activities

C1 Describe merchandising activities and identify business examples.

Previous chapters emphasized the accounting and reporting activities of service companies. In return for services provided to its customers, a service company receives commissions, fares, or fees as revenue. Its net income is the difference between its revenues and the expenses incurred in providing those services.

A merchandising company's activities differ from those of a service company. A **merchandiser** earns net income by buying and selling merchandise. **Merchandise** consists of products, also called *goods,* that a company acquires to resell to customers. Merchandisers are often identified as either wholesalers or retailers. A **wholesaler** is an *intermediary* that buys products from manufacturers or other wholesalers and sells them to retailers or other wholesalers. Wholesalers provide promotion, market information, and financial assistance to retailers. They also provide a sales force, savings on inventory costs, risk reductions, and market information to manufacturers. Wholesalers include such companies as Fleming, SuperValu, McKesson, and SYSCO. Another type of intermediary is a **retailer,** which buys products from manufacturers or wholesalers and sells them to consumers. Examples of retailers include Gap, Oakley, CompUSA, Wal-Mart, and Musicland. Many retailers sell both products and services.

Reporting Financial Performance

C2 Identify and explain the components of income for a merchandising company.

Net income to a merchandiser equals revenues from selling merchandise minus both the cost of merchandise sold to customers and the cost of other expenses for the period (see Exhibit 4.1). The usual accounting term for revenues from selling merchandise is *sales,* and the term used for the cost of buying and preparing the merchandise is *cost of goods sold.* (Many service companies also use the term *sales* in their income statements to identify revenues. Marriott is one example. Cost of goods sold is also called *cost of sales.*)

Exhibit 4.1

Computing Income for a Merchandising Company versus a Service Company

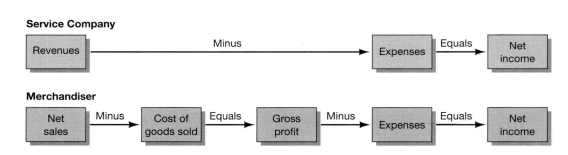

The condensed income statement for Z-Mart in Exhibit 4.2 shows important components of net income. This statement shows that Z-Mart acquired products at a cost of $230,400 and sold them to customers for $314,700. This yields an $84,300 gross profit. **Gross profit,** also called **gross margin,** equals net sales less cost of goods sold. Gross profit is important to merchandisers' profitability. Changes in gross profit often greatly impact a merchandiser's operations since gross profit must cover all other expenses plus yield a return for the owner. Z-Mart, for instance, used its gross profit to cover $71,400 of other expenses. This left $12,900 in net income.

Point: Analysis of gross profit is important to effective business decisions. We describe such analysis later in this chapter.

Reporting Financial Condition

A merchandising company's balance sheet includes a current asset called *merchandise inventory,* an item not on a service company's balance sheet. **Merchandise inventory** refers to products that a company owns and intends to sell to customers. Exhibit 4.3 shows the classified balance sheet for Z-Mart, including merchandise inventory of $21,000. The cost of this asset includes the cost incurred to buy the goods, ship them to the store, and make them ready for sale.

Z-MART Condensed Income Statement For Year Ended December 31, 2002	
Net sales	$314,700
Cost of goods sold	(230,400)
Gross profit	$ 84,300
Expenses	(71,400)
Net income	$ 12,900

Exhibit 4.2

Condensed Income Statement for a Merchandiser

C3 Identify and explain the inventory asset of a merchandising company.

Exhibit 4.3

Classified Balance Sheet for a Merchandiser

Point: Many companies simply refer to merchandise inventory as *inventory.*

Z-MART Balance Sheet December 31, 2002			
Assets			
Current assets			
Cash		$ 8,200	
Accounts receivable		11,200	
Merchandise inventory		21,000	
Office supplies		550	
Store supplies		250	
Prepaid insurance		300	
Total current assets			$41,500
Plant assets			
Office equipment	$ 4,200		
Less accumulated depreciation	1,400	2,800	
Store equipment	30,000		
Less accumulated depreciation	6,000	24,000	
Total plant assets			26,800
Total assets			$68,300
Liabilities			
Current liabilities			
Accounts payable		$ 6,000	
Salaries payable		800	
Total current liabilities			$ 6,800
Long-term note payable			10,000
Equity			
Common stock			$20,000
Retained earnings			31,500
Total liabilities and equity			$68,300

Operating Cycle

A merchandising company's operating cycle begins by purchasing merchandise and ends by collecting cash from selling the merchandise. An example is a merchandiser that buys products at wholesale and sells them to consumers at retail. The length of an operating cycle differs across the types of businesses. Department stores such as **The Limited** and **Dayton Hudson** commonly have operating cycles of three to five months. Operating cycles for grocery merchants such as **Kroger** and **Safeway** usually range from three to eight weeks.

Exhibit 4.4 illustrates an operating cycle for a merchandiser with cash sales and another with credit sales. The cash sales cycle moves from (*a*) merchandise purchases to (*b*) inventory for sale to (*c*) cash sales. The credit sales cycle moves from (*a*) merchandise purchases to (*b*) inventory for sale to (*c*) credit sales to (*d*) accounts receivable to (*e*) cash. Credit sales delay the receipt of cash until the receivable is paid by the customer. Companies try to keep their operating cycles as short as possible because assets tied up in inventory and receivables are not productive.

Exhibit 4.4

Operating Cycle of a Merchandiser*

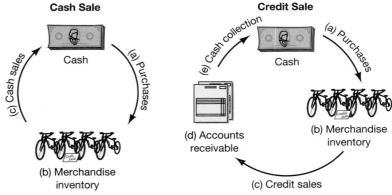

* This exhibit assumes cash purchases. Credit purchases would involve inserting into the cycle (*a*) credit purchases, (*b*) accounts payable, and (*c*) cash payment.

Inventory Systems

We explained that a merchandising company's income statement includes an item called *cost of goods sold* and its balance sheet includes a current asset called *inventory*. **Cost of goods sold** is the cost of merchandise sold to customers during a period. It is often the largest single deduction on a merchandiser's income statement. **Inventory** refers to products a company owns and expects to sell in its normal operations. Inventory items are part of merchandising activities as reflected in Exhibit 4.5. This exhibit shows that a company's merchandise available for sale is a combination of what it begins with (beginning inventory) and what it purchases (net cost of purchases). The merchandise available is either sold (cost of goods sold) or kept for future sales (ending inventory).

Exhibit 4.5

Merchandising Cost Flow

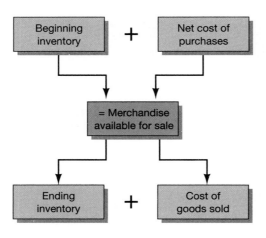

Two alternative inventory accounting systems can be used to collect information about cost of goods sold and cost of inventory available: *periodic system* or *perpetual system*.

Periodic Inventory System

C4   Describe both perpetual and periodic inventory systems.

A **periodic inventory system** requires updating the inventory account only at the *end of a period* to reflect the quantity and cost of both the goods available and the goods sold. It does not require continual updating of the inventory account. The cost of merchandise is recorded in a temporary *Purchases* account. When a company sells merchandise, it records revenue but not the cost of the merchandise sold. Instead, when it prepares financial statements, the company takes a *physical count of inventory* by counting the quantities of merchandise available. The cost of merchandise available is computed by linking the quantities counted to the purchase records that show cost. The cost of merchandise available is used to compute cost of goods sold. The inventory account is then adjusted to reflect the amount computed from the physical count of inventory. Companies such as hardware, drug, and department stores that sell large quantities of low-value items historically used periodic systems. Without today's computers and scanners, it was not feasible for accounting systems to track numerous low-cost items such as pens, candy bars, socks, and magazines through inventory and into customers' hands.

Perpetual Inventory System

A **perpetual inventory system** keeps a continual record of the amount of inventory both available and sold. A perpetual system accumulates the net cost of merchandise purchases in the inventory account and subtracts the cost of each sale from the same inventory account. When a company sells an item, it records its cost in the *Cost of Goods Sold* account. With a perpetual system we know the cost of merchandise available at any time by looking at the balance of the inventory account. We also know the current balance of cost of goods sold anytime during a period by looking in the Cost of Goods Sold account.

> **Point:** Growth of superstores such as Price Club and Costco is fed by the efficient use of perpetual inventory techniques and technology.

Before advancements in computing technology, a perpetual system was often limited to businesses making a small number of daily sales such as automobile dealers and major appliance stores. A perpetual system was feasible because transactions were relatively few. In today's information age, with widespread use of computing technology, the use of a perpetual system has dramatically increased. A perpetual inventory system gives users timely information. Accordingly, this chapter emphasizes a perpetual system. However, we analyze and record merchandising transactions using *both* periodic and perpetual inventory systems in the appendix to this chapter.

Decision Insight

Perpetual Info Technology and perpetual inventory systems are taking the guesswork out of purchasing, slashing inventory cycles, keeping popular items in stock, and cutting return rates. Technology "totally changed the industry from a push industry to a pull industry," says the chairman of Western Merchandisers, a supplier to more than 1,000 Wal-Marts. A recent study says grocers can cut prices by 11% or more with similar changes.

Decision Track 4.1 *d*

Decision Point	Information Search	Analyze & Evaluate
What inventory system should a company adopt?	Merchandise type, volume, and cost	A perpetual inventory system is preferred; possible exceptions are companies that can visibly monitor low-cost inventory.

Quick Check

1. Describe a merchandiser's cost of goods sold.

2. What is gross profit for a merchandising company?

3. Explain why use of the perpetual inventory system has dramatically increased.

Answers—p. 192

With a perpetual inventory system, the cost of merchandise bought for resale is recorded in the Merchandise Inventory asset account. To illustrate, Z-Mart records a $1,200 cash purchase of merchandise on November 2 with this entry:

Nov. 2	Merchandise Inventory	1,200	
	Cash		1,200
	Purchased merchandise for cash.		

Merchandise Purchases

Assets = Liabilities + Equity
+1,200
−1,200

The invoice for this merchandise is shown in Exhibit 4.6. The buyer usually receives the original invoice, and the seller keeps a copy. This *source document* serves as the purchase invoice of Z-Mart (buyer) and the sales invoice for Trex (seller). The amount recorded for merchandise inventory includes its purchase cost, shipping fees, taxes, and any other costs

P1 Analyze and record transactions for merchandise purchases using a perpetual system.

Exhibit 4.6

Invoice

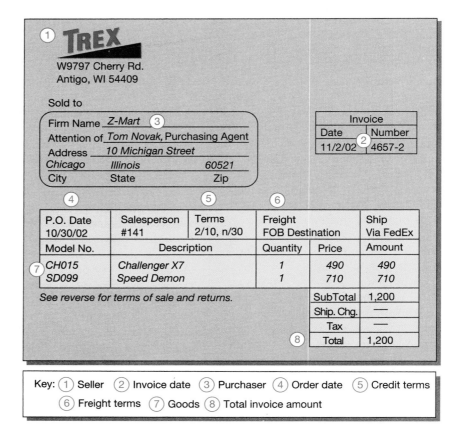

Key: (1) Seller (2) Invoice date (3) Purchaser (4) Order date (5) Credit terms
(6) Freight terms (7) Goods (8) Total invoice amount

Topic Tackler 4-1

necessary to make it ready for sale. For example, to compute the total cost of merchandise purchases, we must adjust the invoice cost for (1) any discounts a supplier gives a purchaser, (2) any returns and allowances for unsatisfactory items received from a supplier, and (3) any required freight costs paid by a purchaser. This section explains how these items affect the recorded cost of merchandise purchases.

Trade Discounts

When a manufacturer or wholesaler prepares a catalog of items it has for sale, it usually gives each item a **list price,** also called a *catalog price.* List price usually is not the item's intended selling price. Instead, its intended selling price equals list price minus a given percent called a **trade discount.** The amount of trade discount usually depends on whether a buyer is a wholesaler, retailer, or final consumer. A wholesaler buying in large quantities is often granted a larger discount than a retailer buying in smaller quantities. Manufacturers and wholesalers commonly use trade discounts to change selling prices without republishing their catalogs. When a seller wants to change selling prices, it can notify its customers merely by sending them a new table of trade discounts.

Point: The Merchandise Inventory account reflects the cost of goods available for resale.

A buyer does *not* enter list prices and trade discounts in its accounts. Instead, a buyer records the net amount of list price minus trade discount. For example, in the November 2 purchase of merchandise by Z-Mart, the merchandise was listed in the seller's catalog at $2,000 and Z-Mart received a 40% trade discount. This means that Z-Mart's purchase price is $1,200, computed as $2,000 - (40% \times $2,000).

Purchase Discounts

The purchase of goods on credit requires a clear statement of expected future payments and dates to avoid misunderstandings. **Credit terms** for a purchase include the amounts and timing of payments from a buyer to a seller. Credit terms usually reflect an industry's practices. In some industries, sellers require payment within 10 days after the end of the month

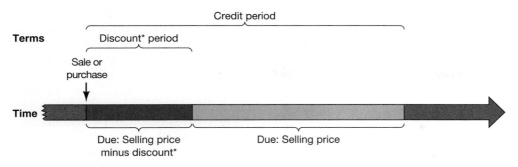

Exhibit 4.7

Credit Terms

*Discount refers to either purchase or sales discounts.

in which the purchase occurs. The sales invoice will carry the credit terms as "n/10 **EOM**," which stands for net 10 days after end of month. In some other industries, sellers require payment within 30 calendar days after the invoice date. These terms appear on the invoice as "n/30," which stands for *net 30 days*. Whatever the terms, the amount of time allowed before full payment is due is called the **credit period.** Exhibit 4.7 portrays credit terms.

Point: Since both the buyer and seller know the invoice date, this date is used in determining the end of the credit period.

When the credit period is long, sellers often grant a **cash discount** to encourage buyers to pay within an earlier period. A buyer views a cash discount as a **purchase discount.** A seller views a cash discount as a **sales discount.** If cash discounts for early payment exist, they are described as credit terms on the invoice. For example, credit terms of "2/10, n/60" imply that a 60-day credit period occurs before full payment is due. The seller allows the buyer to deduct 2% of the invoice amount if payment is made within 10 days of the invoice date. The reduced payment applies only during the **discount period.**

To illustrate how a buyer accounts for a purchase discount, let's assume that Z-Mart's purchase of merchandise for $1,200 is on credit with terms of 2/10, n/30. Z-Mart's entry to record this credit purchase is

Point: Appendix 4A repeats journal entries *a* through *f* using a periodic inventory system.

(*a*) Nov. 2	Merchandise Inventory	1,200	
	Accounts Payable		1,200
	Purchased merchandise on credit, invoice		
	dated Nov. 2, terms 2/10, n/30.		

Assets = Liabilities + Equity
+1,200   +1,200

If Z-Mart takes advantage of the discount and pays the amount due on November 12, the entry to record payment is

(*b*) Nov. 12	Accounts Payable	1,200	
	Merchandise Inventory		24
	Cash		1,176
	Paid for the $1,200 purchase of Nov. 2		
	less the discount of $24 (2% × $1,200).		

Assets = Liabilities + Equity
−24   −1,200
−1,176

Z-Mart's Merchandise Inventory account after this entry reflects the net cost of merchandise purchased. Its Accounts Payable account shows a zero balance, meaning that the debt is satisfied. Both accounts, in T-account form, follow:

Merchandise Inventory					Accounts Payable				
Nov. 2	1,200	Nov. 12	24		Nov. 12	1,200	Nov. 2	1,200
Balance	1,176						Balance	0

Managing Discounts

A buyer's failure to pay within a discount period can be expensive. In the preceding example, if Z-Mart does not pay within the 10-day discount period, it can delay payment by 20

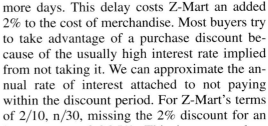

Decision Maker

Entrepreneur   You purchase a batch of products on terms of 3/10, n/90, but your company has limited cash and you must borrow funds at an 11% annual rate if you are to pay within the discount period. Do you take advantage of the purchase discount?

Answer—p. 191

Decision Insight

Clout!   Merchandising companies are unleashing a barrage of demands on suppliers. These include special discounts for new stores, payment of fines for shipping errors, and free samples. One merchandiser warned Totes it would impose a $30,000 fine for errors in bar-coding on products Totes shipped. Merchandisers' goals are to slash inventories, shorten lead times, and eliminate errors.

more days. This delay costs Z-Mart an added 2% to the cost of merchandise. Most buyers try to take advantage of a purchase discount because of the usually high interest rate implied from not taking it. We can approximate the annual rate of interest attached to not paying within the discount period. For Z-Mart's terms of 2/10, n/30, missing the 2% discount for an additional 20 days is equal to an annual interest rate of 36.5%. This is computed as (365 days/20 additional days) × 2% discount rate. More generally, the implied interest rate formula is: (365 days ÷ [Credit period − Discount period]) × Cash discount rate.

Most companies set up a system to pay invoices with favorable discounts within the discount period. Careful cash management means that no invoice is paid until the last day of a discount period. One technique to achieve this goal is to file each invoice so that it automatically comes up for payment on the last day of its discount period. A simple filing system uses up to 31 folders, one for each day in a month. After an invoice is recorded, it is entered in the folder matching the last day of its discount period. If the last day of an invoice's discount period is November 12, it is entered in folder 12. This and other invoices in the same folder are retrieved and paid on November 12.

Decision Track 4.2		
Decision Point	**Information Search**	**Analyze & Evaluate**
When should a company take advantage of purchase or sales discounts?	Transaction details: Reveals credit term for each purchase and sales transaction.	Favorable discounts are those with annualized rates exceeding the company's annual rate of borrowing money.

Purchase Returns and Allowances

Purchase returns refer to merchandise a purchaser receives but then returns to the supplier. A *purchase allowance* is a reduction in the cost of defective or unacceptable merchandise that a purchaser receives from a supplier. Purchasers often keep defective but still marketable merchandise if the supplier grants an acceptable allowance.

The purchaser usually informs the supplier in writing of any returns and allowances, often with a **debit memorandum,** a document the purchaser issues to inform the supplier of a debit made to the supplier's account in the purchaser's records, including the reason for the return or allowance. Exhibit 4.8 shows a debit memorandum prepared by Z-Mart requesting an allowance from Trex for the defective Speed Demon mountain bike. The November 15 entry by Z-Mart to update the Merchandise Inventory account to reflect the purchase allowance requested in the debit memorandum is

Point: The sender of a debit memorandum will debit the account of the receiver. The receiver of a debit memorandum will credit the account of the sender.

Assets = Liabilities + Equity
−300   −300

(c) Nov. 15	Accounts Payable	300	
	Merchandise Inventory		300
	Allowance for defective merchandise.		

If this had been a return, then the total *recorded cost* (all costs less any discounts) of the defective merchandise would have been entered. Z-Mart's agreement with this supplier says the cost of returned and defective merchandise is offset against Z-Mart's next purchase or its current account payable balance. Some agreements with suppliers involve refunding the cost to a buyer. When cash is refunded, the Cash account is debited instead of Accounts Payable.

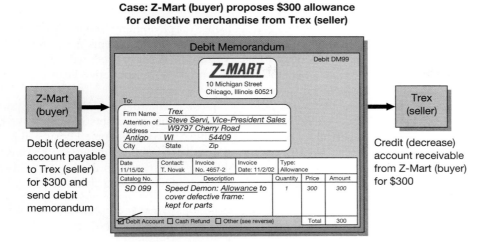

Case: Z-Mart (buyer) proposes $300 allowance for defective merchandise from Trex (seller)

Z-Mart (buyer)

Debit (decrease) account payable to Trex (seller) for $300 and send debit memorandum

Trex (seller)

Credit (decrease) account receivable from Z-Mart (buyer) for $300

Exhibit 4.8

Debit Memorandum

Discounts and Returns

When goods are returned within the discount period, a buyer can take the discount on only the remaining balance of the invoice. As an example, suppose Z-Mart purchases $1,000 of merchandise offered with a 2% cash discount. Two days later, Z-Mart returns $100 of goods before paying the invoice. When Z-Mart later pays within the discount period, it can take the 2% discount only on the $900 remaining balance. The discount is $18 (2% × $900), and the cash payment is $882 ($900 − $18).

Decision Ethics

Credit Manager   As the new credit manager, you are being trained by the outgoing manager. She explains that the system prepares checks for amounts net of favorable cash discounts, and the checks are dated the last day of the discount period. She also tells you that checks are not mailed until five days later, adding that "the company gets free use of cash for an extra five days, and our department looks better. When a supplier complains, we blame the computer system and the mailroom." Do you continue this payment policy?

Answer—p. 191

Transportation Costs

Depending on terms negotiated with suppliers, a merchandiser is sometimes responsible for paying shipping costs on purchases, often called *transportation-in* or *freight-in* costs. Z-Mart's $1,200 purchase on November 2 is on terms of **FOB** (*free on board*) destination. This means Z-Mart is not responsible for paying transportation costs. When a buyer is responsible for paying transportation costs, they usually are made to an independent carrier or directly to the seller. Transportation costs are often included on the invoice when owed to the seller, whereas transportation costs owed to an independent carrier usually are not included on the invoice. The cost principle requires that any necessary transportation costs be included as part of the cost of purchased merchandise. This means a separate entry is necessary when they are *not* listed on the invoice. For example, Z-Mart's entry to record a $75 freight charge from an independent carrier for merchandise purchased FOB shipping point would be

(d) Nov. 24	Merchandise Inventory	75	
	Cash		75
	Paid freight costs on purchased merchandise.		

Example: Z-Mart pays cash for $1,000 of merchandise purchased within the discount period and receives a 2% discount. Later, Z-Mart returns $100 of the original $1,000 merchandise. What amount of cash refund does it receive? How are the return and cash receipt recorded? *Answers:* Cash refund = Cash paid for $100 of goods = 98% × $100 = $98. The entry to record this is
Cash 98
   Merchandise Inventory .   98

Assets = Liabilities + Equity
+75
−75

Transportation-in costs differ from the costs of shipping goods to customers. Transportation-in costs are included in the buyer's cost of merchandise inventory, but the costs of shipping goods to customers are not. The costs of shipping goods to customers are recorded in a Delivery Expense account when the merchandiser (seller in this case) is responsible for these costs. Delivery expense, also called *freight-out* or *transportation-out,* is reported as a selling expense in the income statement.

Point: When CompUSA purchases merchandise and then distributes it among its stores, the cost of shipping merchandise to the stores is included in the costs of the store inventories as required by the cost principle.

Transfer of Ownership

The buyer and seller must agree on who is responsible for paying any freight costs and who bears the risk of loss during transit for merchandising transactions. This is essentially the same as asking at what point ownership transfers from the seller to the buyer. The point of transfer is called the FOB point, which determines who pays transportation costs (and other incidental costs of transit such as insurance).

Exhibit 4.9 identifies two alternative points of transfer. The first is FOB shipping point. *FOB shipping point,* also called *FOB factory,* means the buyer accepts ownership at the seller's place of business. The buyer is then responsible for paying shipping costs and bearing the risk of damage or loss when goods are in transit. The goods are part of the buyer's inventory when they are in transit since ownership has transferred to the buyer. Midway Games, a leading seller in entertainment software, uses FOB shipping point.

Exhibit 4.9

Identifying Transfer of Ownership

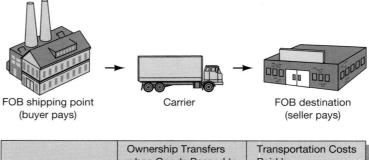

FOB shipping point
(buyer pays)

Carrier

FOB destination
(seller pays)

	Ownership Transfers when Goods Passed to	Transportation Costs Paid by
FOB shipping point	Carrier	Buyer
FOB destination	Buyer	Seller

The second means of transfer is *FOB destination,* which means ownership of the goods transfers to the buyer at the buyer's place of business. The seller is responsible for paying shipping charges and bears the risk of damage or loss in transit. The seller does not record revenue from this sale until the goods arrive at the destination because this transaction is not complete before that point. Compaq Computer at one time shipped its products FOB shipping point, but it found delivery companies to be unreliable in picking up shipments at scheduled times. The resulting backups and missing deliveries made consumers unhappy. Compaq then changed its agreements to FOB destination, took control of shipping, and eliminated its problems.

In some situations, the party not responsible for shipping costs pays the carrier. In these cases, the party paying these costs either bills the party responsible or, more commonly, adjusts its account payable or account receivable with the other party. For example, a buyer paying a carrier when terms are FOB destination can decrease its account payable to the seller by the amount of shipping cost. Similarly, a seller who pays a carrier when terms are FOB shipping point can increase its account receivable from the buyer by the amount of shipping cost.

Recording Purchases Information

We explained that purchase discounts, purchase returns and allowances, and transportation-in are included in computing the cost of merchandise inventory. Purchases are initially recorded as debits to Merchandise Inventory. Any later purchase discounts, returns, and allowances are credited (decreases) to Merchandise Inventory. Transportation-in is debited (added) to Merchandise Inventory. Z-Mart's itemized costs of merchandise purchases for year 2002 are in Exhibit 4.10. The Merchandise Inventory account reflects the net cost of purchased merchandise according to the *cost principle.* Recall that the Merchandise Inventory account (under a perpetual inventory system) is updated after each transaction that affects the cost of goods either purchased or sold.

Exhibit 4.10
Itemized Costs of Merchandise Purchases

Z-MART Itemized Costs of Merchandise Purchases For Year Ended December 31, 2002	
Invoice cost of merchandise purchases................................	$235,800
Less: Purchase discounts received	(4,200)
Purchase returns and allowances................................	(1,500)
Add: Costs of transportation-in....................................	2,300
Total cost of merchandise purchases................................	$232,400

The accounting system described here does not provide separate records for total purchases, total purchase discounts, total purchase returns and allowances, and total transportation-in. Managers usually need this information, however, to evaluate and control each of these cost elements. Nearly all companies collect this information in supplementary records. **Supplementary records,** also called *supplemental records,* refer to information outside the usual accounting ledger accounts.

Point: Some companies have separate accounts for purchase discounts, returns and allowances, and transportation-in. Balances of these accounts are then transferred to Merchandise Inventory at the end of each period. This is a hybrid system of perpetual and periodic. That is, Merchandise Inventory is updated on a perpetual basis but only for purchases and cost of goods sold.

Quick Check

4. How long are the credit and discount periods when credit terms are 2/10, n/60?

5. Identify which items are subtracted from the *list* amount and not recorded when computing purchase price: (*a*) freight-in; (*b*) trade discount; (*c*) purchase discount; (*d*) purchase return.

6. What does *FOB* mean? What does *FOB destination* mean?

Answers—p. 192

Merchandise Sales

We explained that companies buying merchandise for resale need to account for its cost. Merchandising companies also must account for sales, sales discounts, sales returns and allowances, and cost of goods sold. A merchandising company such as Z-Mart reports these items in the gross profit section of its income statement, as shown in Exhibit 4.11. This section explains how information in this computation is derived from transactions involving sales, sales discounts, and sales returns and allowances.

Exhibit 4.11
Gross Profit Section of Income Statement

Z-MART Computation of Gross Profit For Year Ended December 31, 2002		
Sales		$321,000
Less: Sales discounts	$4,300	
Sales returns and allowances	2,000	6,300
Net sales		$314,700
Cost of goods sold		(230,400)
Gross profit		$ 84,300

Sales Transactions

Each sales transaction for a seller of merchandise involves two parts. One part is the revenue received in the form of an asset from a customer. The second part is the recognition

P2 Analyze and record transactions for sales of merchandise using a perpetual system.

Topic Tackler 4-2

Assets = Liabilities + Equity
+2,400   +2,400

of the cost of merchandise sold to a customer. Accounting for a sales transaction means capturing information about both parts. This means that each sales transaction for merchandisers, whether for cash or on credit, requires two entries: one for revenue and one for cost. Suppose that Z-Mart sold $2,400 of merchandise on credit on November 3. The revenue part of this transaction is recorded as

(e) Nov. 3	Accounts Receivable	2,400	
	Sales		2,400
	Sold merchandise on credit.		

This entry reflects an increase in Z-Mart's assets in the form of an account receivable. It also shows the increase in revenue (Sales). If the sale is for cash, the debit is to Cash instead of Accounts Receivable. (We describe in Chapter 7 the accounting for sales to customers who use third-party credit cards such as those issued by banks.)

The cost of the merchandise Z-Mart sold on November 3 is $1,600. (In Chapter 5 we explain the computation of this cost.) The entry to record the cost part of this sales transaction (under a perpetual inventory system) is

Assets = Liabilities + Equity
−1,600   −1,600

(e) Nov. 3	Cost of Goods Sold	1,600	
	Merchandise Inventory		1,600
	To record the cost of Nov. 3 sale.		

Since the cost part is recorded each time a sale occurs, the Merchandise Inventory account will reflect the cost of the remaining merchandise available for sale.

Sales Discounts

Selling goods on credit demands that the future payments and dates be made clear to avoid misunderstandings. We explained earlier in this chapter that credit terms often include a discount to encourage early payment. Companies granting cash discounts to customers refer to these as *sales discounts*. Sales discounts can benefit a seller by decreasing the delay in receiving cash. Prompt payments also reduce future efforts and costs of billing customers.

At the time of a credit sale, a seller does not know whether a customer will pay within the discount period and take advantage of a cash discount. This means the seller usually does not record a sales discount until a customer actually pays within the discount period. Suppose that Z-Mart completes a credit sale for $1,000 on November 12, subject to terms of 2/10, n/60. The entry to record the revenue part of this sale is

Assets = Liabilities + Equity
+1,000   +1,000

Nov. 12	Accounts Receivable	1,000	
	Sales		1,000
	Sold merchandise under terms of 2/10, n/60.		

This entry records the receivable and the revenue as if the customer will pay the full amount. The customer has two options, however. One option is to wait 60 days until January 11 and pay the full $1,000. In this case, Z-Mart records the payment as

Assets = Liabilities + Equity
+1,000
−1,000

Jan. 11	Cash	1,000	
	Accounts Receivable		1,000
	Received payment for Nov. 12 sale.		

The customer's second option is to pay $980 within a 10-day period ending November 22. If the customer pays on or before November 22, Z-Mart records the payment as

Nov. 22	Cash	980	
	Sales Discounts	20	
	Accounts Receivable		1,000
	Received payment for Nov. 12 sale less the discount.		

Assets = Liabilities + Equity
+980   −20
−1,000

Sales Discounts is a contra revenue account. Management monitors Sales Discounts to assess the effectiveness and cost of its discount program. The Sales Discounts account is deducted from the Sales account when computing a company's net sales (see Exhibit 4.11). Information about sales discounts is seldom reported on income statements distributed to external users.

Decision Insight

Discount Targeting Catalina Supermarkets uses bar codes, software, and the Web to help execs keep tabs on who buys what foods, how often, and at what price. Its high-profit customer rate is up because most discounts and services, such as coupons and free delivery, are given almost exclusively to its best customers.

Sales Returns and Allowances

Sales returns refer to merchandise that customers return to the seller after a sale. Many companies allow customers to return merchandise for a full refund. *Sales allowances* refer to reductions in the selling price of merchandise sold to customers. This can occur with damaged merchandise that a customer is willing to purchase with a decrease in selling price. Sales returns and allowances involve dissatisfied customers and the possibility of lost future sales, and managers need information about returns and allowances to monitor these problems. Many accounting systems record returns and allowances in a separate contra revenue account.

Recall Z-Mart's sale of merchandise on November 3 for $2,400 that had cost $1,600. Assume that the customer returns part of the merchandise on November 6, and the returned items sell for $800 and cost $600. The revenue part of this transaction must reflect the decrease in sales from the customer's return of merchandise as follows:

(f) Nov. 6	Sales Returns and Allowances	800	
	Accounts Receivable		800
	Customer returns merchandise of Nov. 3 sale.		

Assets = Liabilities + Equity
−800   −800

Managers monitor the Sales Returns and Allowances contra account, but published income statements usually omit this detail and show only net sales.

If the merchandise returned to Z-Mart is not defective and can be resold to another customer, Z-Mart returns these goods to its inventory. The entry to restore the cost of these goods to the Merchandise Inventory account is

Decision Insight

MegaReturns Book merchandisers such as Barnes & Noble and Borders Books can return unsold books to publishers at purchase price. Publishers say returns of new hardcover books run between 35% and 50%. This compares with 15% to 25% ten years ago.

Nov. 6	Merchandise Inventory	600	
	Cost of Goods Sold		600
	Returned goods added to inventory.		

Assets = Liabilities + Equity
+600   +600

However, if the merchandise returned is defective, the seller might decide to discard it. In this case, the cost of returned merchandise is not restored to the Merchandise Inventory account but is left in the Cost of Goods Sold account.[1] Alternatively, the seller might offer a

[1] When managers want to monitor the cost of defective merchandise, a better method is to remove (credit) the cost from Cost of Goods Sold and charge (debit) it to the Loss from Defective Merchandise account.

price reduction. For example, suppose that $800 of the merchandise Z-Mart sold on November 3 is defective but the buyer decides to keep it because Z-Mart offers a $500 price reduction. The entry Z-Mart must make in this case is to record the allowance and decrease expected assets:

Assets = Liabilities + Equity
−500   −500

Nov. 6	Sales Returns and Allowances	500	
	Accounts Receivable		500
	To record sales allowance on Nov. 3 sale.		

Point: The sender of a credit memorandum will credit the account of the receiver. The receiver of a credit memorandum will debit the account of the sender.

The seller usually prepares a credit memorandum to confirm a buyer's return or allowance. A **credit memorandum** informs a buyer of a credit to its Account Receivable account from a sales return or allowance. Z-Mart's credit memorandum issued to the buyer for the $500 sales allowance on November 6 is shown in Exhibit 4.12.

Exhibit 4.12

Credit Memorandum

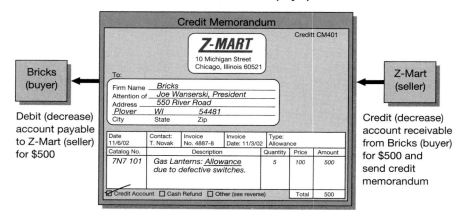

Quick Check

7. Why are sales discounts and sales returns and allowances recorded in contra revenue accounts instead of directly in the Sales account?

8. Under what conditions are two entries necessary to record a sales return?

9. When merchandise is sold on credit and the seller notifies the buyer of a price reduction, does the seller send a credit memorandum or a debit memorandum?

Answers—p. 192

Additional Merchandising Issues

This section explains the impacts of merchandising activities on other accounting processes. We address cost and price adjustments, preparation of adjusting and closing entries, and relations between important accounts.

Cost and Price Adjustments

Buyers and sellers sometimes need to adjust the amounts they owe each other. Such adjustments can occur when purchased merchandise does not meet specifications, unordered goods are received, quantities received are different from those ordered and billed, or errors occur in billing. The buyer can sometimes adjust the balance without negotiation. For example, when a seller makes an error on an invoice and the buyer discovers it, the buyer can make an adjustment and notify the seller by sending a debit or a credit memorandum. Sometimes, such as when a buyer claims that some merchandise does not meet specifications, adjustments can be made only after negotiations between the buyer and seller.

Adjusting Entries

Most adjusting entries are the same for merchandising companies and service companies. In all cases, the adjustments are limited to prepaid expenses (including depreciation), accrued expenses, unearned revenues, and accrued revenues. However, a merchandising company using a perpetual inventory system is usually required to make a special adjustment to update the Merchandise Inventory account to reflect any loss of merchandise. Companies can lose merchandise in several ways, including theft and deterioration. **Shrinkage** is the term used to refer to the loss of inventory. While a perpetual inventory system tracks all goods as they move in and out of the company, it is unable to directly measure shrinkage. Instead, we compute shrinkage by comparing a physical count of inventory with recorded amounts. A physical count is usually performed at least once annually. Most companies record shrinkage by charging it to Cost of Goods Sold, provided that the shrinkage is not abnormally large.

P3 Prepare adjustments and close accounts for a merchandising company.

Decision Insight

Wanted for Shrinkage   Shrinkage can be a sizable cost for many merchandisers. Recent annual losses due to shrinkage are

Musicland	$22 million
Sports Authority	9 million

Companies often invest considerable resources to reduce shrinkage.

Suppose that Z-Mart's Merchandise Inventory account at the end of year 2002 has a balance of $21,250, but that a physical count reveals that only $21,000 of inventory exists. The adjusting entry to record this $250 shrinkage is (see top of next page)

Point: Two-thirds of shoplifting losses are thefts by employees.

Exhibit 4.13
Adjusted Trial Balance for a Merchandiser

Z-MART
Adjusted Trial Balance
December 31, 2002

	Debit	Credit
Cash	$ 8,200	
Accounts receivable	11,200	
Merchandise inventory	21,000	
Office supplies	550	
Store supplies	250	
Prepaid insurance	300	
Office equipment	4,200	
Accumulated depreciation—Office equipment		$ 1,400
Store equipment	30,000	
Accumulated depreciation—Store equipment		6,000
Accounts payable		6,000
Salaries payable		800
Long-term note payable		10,000
Common stock		20,000
Retained earnings		18,600
Sales		321,000
Sales discounts	4,300	
Sales returns and allowances	2,000	
Cost of goods sold	230,400	
Depreciation expense—Store equipment	3,000	
Depreciation expense—Office equipment	700	
Office salaries expense	25,300	
Sales salaries expense	18,500	
Insurance expense	600	
Rent expense—Office space	900	
Rent expense—Selling space	8,100	
Office supplies expense	1,800	
Store supplies expense	1,200	
Advertising expense	11,300	
Totals	$383,800	$383,800

Assets = Liabilities + Equity
−250   −250

Dec. 31	Cost of Goods Sold	250	
	Merchandise Inventory		250
	To adjust for $250 shrinkage revealed by a physical count of inventory.		

Closing Entries

Closing entries are similar for service companies and merchandising companies using a perpetual system. One difference is that we must close some new temporary accounts that arise from merchandising activities. We use Z-Mart's adjusted trial balance in Exhibit 4.13 to show its closing process in Exhibit 4.14.

Exhibit 4.14

Closing Entries for a
Merchandiser

Step 1: Close Credit Balances in Temporary Accounts to Income Summary.

Z-Mart has one temporary account with a credit balance; it is closed with this entry:

Dec. 31	Sales	321,000	
	Income Summary		321,000
	To close credit balances in temporary accounts.		

Step 2: Close Debit Balances in Temporary Accounts to Income Summary.

The second entry closes temporary accounts having debit balances such as Cost of Goods Sold, Sales Discounts, and Sales Returns and Allowances and is shown here:

Dec. 31	Income Summary	308,100	
	Sales Discounts		**4,300**
	Sales Returns and Allowances		**2,000**
	Cost of Goods Sold		**230,400**
	Depreciation Expense—Store Equipment . . .		3,000
	Depreciation Expense—Office Equipment . .		700
	Office Salaries Expense		25,300
	Sales Salaries Expense		18,500
	Insurance Expense		600
	Rent Expense—Office Space		900
	Rent Expense—Selling Space		8,100
	Office Supplies Expense		1,800
	Store Supplies Expense		1,200
	Advertising Expense		11,300
	To close debit balances in temporary accounts.		

Step 3: Close Income Summary to Retained Earnings.

The third closing entry is exactly the same for a merchandising company and a service company. It updates the retained earnings account for the net income or loss and is shown here:

Dec. 31	Income Summary	12,900	
	Retained Earnings		12,900
	To close the Income Summary account.		

The $12,900 amount in the entry is net income reported on the income statement in Exhibit 4.2. When these entries are posted, all temporary accounts are set to zero and are ready to record events for next year.

Z-Mart's trial balance includes several accounts unique to merchandising companies: Merchandise Inventory, Sales (of goods), Sales Discounts, Sales Returns and Allowances, and Cost of Goods Sold. Their existence in the ledger means that the first two closing entries for a merchandiser are slightly different from the ones described in Chapter 3 for a service company. These differences are set in boldface in the closing entries of Exhibit 4.14.

C5 Analyze and interpret cost flows and operating activities of a merchandising company.

Merchandising Cost Flows

Exhibit 4.15 shows the relations between inventory, merchandise purchases, and cost of goods sold across periods. We already explained that the net cost of purchases reflects trade discounts, purchase discounts, and purchase returns and allowances. These items constituting the cost of purchases are recorded in the Merchandise Inventory account under a perpetual system. When each sale occurs, the cost of items sold is transferred from Merchandise Inventory to the Cost of Goods Sold account. Cost of goods sold is reported on the income statement. The ending balance in Merchandise Inventory is reported on the balance sheet. Note that the Merchandise Inventory account balance at the end of one period is the beginning inventory for the next period.

Merchandising Cost Accounts

To explain how merchandising transactions affect the Merchandise Inventory and Cost of Goods Sold accounts, we summarize Z-Mart's merchandising activities for year 2002 using T-accounts in Exhibit 4.16. Most amounts are summary representations of several entries made during the year.

We explained that the perpetual inventory accounting system does not include separate accounts for purchases, purchase discounts, purchase returns and allowances, and transportation-in. Like most companies, however, Z-Mart keeps supplementary records of these items. These supplementary records are used to accumulate the information in Exhibit 4.16. Z-Mart also keeps a separate record for the cost of merchandise returned by customers and restored in inventory. The Cost of Goods Sold ending balance of $230,400 is the amount reported on the income statement in Exhibit 4.2. The Merchandise Inventory ending balance of $21,000 is the amount reported as a current asset on the balance sheet in Exhibit 4.3. These amounts also appear on Z-Mart's adjusted trial balance in Exhibit 4.13.

Exhibit 4.15

Merchandising Cost Flow Across Periods

Exhibit 4.16

Merchandising Transactions Reflected in T-Accounts

Merchandise Inventory			
Jan. 1, balance	19,000		
Purchases of merchandise	235,800	Purchase discounts received	4,200
Merchandise returned by customers and restored to inventory	1,400	Purchase returns and allowances	1,500
Transportation-in costs	2,300	Cost of sales to customers	231,550
Dec. 31, unadjusted balance	21,250		
		Dec. 31, shrinkage	250
Dec. 31, adjusted balance	21,000		

Cost of Goods Sold			
Cost of sales	231,550	Merchandise returned by customers and restored to inventory	1,400
Inventory shrinkage adjusting entry	250		
Dec. 31, balance (before closing)	230,400		

Quick Check

10. When a merchandiser uses a perpetual inventory system, why is it sometimes necessary to adjust the Merchandise Inventory balance with an adjusting entry?

11. What temporary accounts do you expect to find in a merchandising business but not in a service business?

12. Describe the closing entries normally made by a merchandising company.

Answers—p. 192

Income Statement Formats

Generally accepted accounting principles do not require companies to use any one presentation format for financial statements, and we see many different formats in practice. The first part of this section describes two common income statement formats using Z-Mart's data: multiple-step and single-step. The final part of this section compares accrual and cash flow measures of gross profit.

Multiple-Step Income Statement

P4 Define and prepare multiple-step and single-step income statements.

A **multiple-step income statement** contains more detail than simply a list of revenues and expenses. Exhibit 4.17 shows a multiple-step income statement for Z-Mart. This format shows detailed computations of net sales and other costs and expenses, and reports subtotals for various classes of items. Z-Mart's sales section is the same as shown earlier in the chapter. The cost of goods sold section draws on Exhibit 4.16. The difference between net sales and cost of goods sold is Z-Mart's gross profit. Its expenses are classified into two categories. **Selling expenses** include the expenses of promoting sales by displaying and advertising merchandise, making sales, and delivering goods to customers. **General and administrative expenses** support a company's overall operations and include expenses related to accounting, human resource management, and financial management. Expenses are often allocated between categories when they contribute to more than one activity. Exhibit 4.17 shows that Z-Mart allocates rent expense of $9,000 from its store building between two categories: $8,100 to selling expense and $900 to general and administrative expense.

Exhibit 4.17

Multiple-Step Income Statement

Z-MART
Income Statement
For Year Ended December 31, 2002

Sales			$321,000
Less: Sales discounts		$ 4,300	
Sales returns and allowances		2,000	6,300
Net sales			$314,700
Cost of goods sold			230,400
Gross profit			$ 84,300
Expenses			
Selling expenses			
Depreciation expense—Store equipment	$ 3,000		
Sales salaries expense	18,500		
Rent expense—Selling space	8,100		
Store supplies expense	1,200		
Advertising expense	11,300		
Total selling expenses		$42,100	
General and administrative expenses			
Depreciation expense—Office equipment	700		
Office salaries expense	25,300		
Insurance expense	600		
Rent expense—Office space	900		
Office supplies expense	1,800		
Total general and administrative expenses		29,300	
Total expenses			71,400
Net income			$ 12,900

Single-Step Income Statement

A **single-step income statement** is another widely used format, and is shown in Exhibit 4.18 for Z-Mart. It includes cost of goods sold as another expense and shows only one subtotal for total expenses. Expenses are grouped into very few categories. As another example, **Reebok**'s income statement in Appendix A shows a single line item titled *Selling, general and administrative expenses*. Its annual report does, however, include management's discussion and analysis on details of these expenses. Many companies use formats that combine features of both the single- and multiple-step statements. Provided that income statement items are shown sensibly, management can choose the format. (In later chapters, we describe some items, such as extraordinary gains and losses, that must be reported in certain locations on the income statement.) Similar presentation options are available for the statement of retained earnings and statement of cash flows.

Point: Many companies report interest expense and interest income in a separate category after income from operations and before subtracting income taxes expense. As one example, see Gap's income statement in Appendix A.

Z-MART Income Statement For Year Ended December 31, 2002		
Net sales		$314,700
Cost of goods sold	$230,400	
Selling expenses	42,100	
General and administrative expenses	29,300	
Total expenses		301,800
Net income		$ 12,900

Exhibit 4.18

Single-Step Income Statement

Merchandising Cash Flows

Another aspect of merchandising activities relates to their cash flow impacts. Merchandising sales and costs reported in the income statement usually differ from their cash receipts and cash payments for a specific period. This is because an income statement is prepared using accrual accounting, not cash flows. Recognition of sales earned rarely equals cash received from customers. Also, recognition of cost of goods sold rarely equals cash paid to suppliers for a given period.

We use Z-Mart's data in Exhibit 4.19 to illustrate this point. Z-Mart's net sales are $314,700, yet cash receipts from customers are only $309,200 (shown on the right side of Exhibit 4.19). This difference reflects a $5,500 *increase* in the Accounts Receivable balance during this period for Z-Mart.

A1 Analyze and interpret accruals and cash flows for merchandising activities.

Z-MART For Year Ended December 31, 2002			
Income Statement		**Statement of Cash Flows**	
Net sales	$314,700	Receipts from customers	$309,200
Cost of goods sold	230,400	Payments to suppliers	240,900
Gross profit	$ 84,300	Net cash flows from customers and suppliers	$ 68,300

Exhibit 4.19

Analysis of Merchandising Cash Flows

An increase in accounts receivable means a delay in receipt of cash from customers, and therefore cash received from customers this period is less than net sales. To see this, recall that net sales and cash received are the same if all net sales are cash sales. But when some or all net sales are credit sales, the amounts for net sales and cash sales likely differ. Since Accounts Receivable increased during the period, we know cash received is less than net sales. If Accounts Receivable had decreased, then cash received would be greater

Point: Cash paid to suppliers = Cost of goods sold + Increase (or − decrease) in Inventory + Decrease (or − increase) in accounts payable

than net sales. We apply similar analysis to cost of goods sold. Z-Mart's cost of goods sold reported in its income statement totals $230,400, but cash paid to suppliers is $240,900. The difference between cost of goods sold and cash paid to suppliers reflects *two* items: (1) change in inventory and (2) change in accounts payable.

Decision Insight

Entrepreneur Incubators Incubators provide start-ups a space plus services for a fee. Services typically include management advice, office support, and financial, legal, and technical help. Entrepreneurs usually leave an incubator after two to three years. Nearly 90% of entrepreneurs that "hatch" from incubators are still in business six years later, which is more than double the usual success rate.

Buying and selling merchandise is the most important activity for a merchandiser such as Z-Mart. We need to analyze both accrual measures and cash flows of this activity for signs of opportunities or problems. Z-Mart is trying to expand its sales by extending credit to more customers. However, extending credit to customers who do not pay their bills can backfire. For effective decision making, we must always analyze important differences in accrual and cash flow figures and assess their future implications. We further analyze the relation between accrual measures and cash flows in Chapter 12.

Decision Analysis   Acid-Test and Gross Margin Ratios

Companies with merchandising activities have at least two major differences from service companies. First, merchandise inventory often makes up a large part of a merchandiser's assets, especially current assets. Second, merchandising activities result in cost of goods sold, which is often the largest cost for these companies. These differences alter our ratio analysis. This is especially the case with the current ratio and the profit margin ratio (see Chapter 3). This section describes adjustments to these ratios to help analyze merchandisers.

Acid-Test Ratio

A2 **Compute the acid-test ratio and explain its use** to assess liquidity.

For many merchandisers, inventory makes up a large portion of current assets. The inventory must be sold and any resulting accounts receivable must be collected before cash is available for activities such as paying liabilities. We explained in Chapter 3 that the current ratio, defined as current assets divided by current liabilities, is useful in assessing a company's ability to pay current liabilities. Since it is sometimes unreasonable to assume that inventories are a source of payment for current liabilities, we look to other measures.

One measure to help us assess a merchandiser's ability (its *liquidity*) to pay its current liabilities is the acid-test ratio. It differs from the current ratio by excluding less liquid current assets such as inventory and prepaid expenses. The less liquid assets are those that will take longer to be converted to cash. The **acid-test ratio,** also called *quick ratio,* is defined as *quick assets* (cash, short-term investments, and current receivables) divided by current liabilities—see Exhibit 4.20.

Exhibit 4.20

Acid-Test (Quick) Ratio

$$\text{Acid-test ratio} = \frac{\text{Cash and equivalents} + \text{Short-term investments} + \text{Current receivables}}{\text{Current liabilities}}$$

Point: Successful use of a just-in-time inventory system can narrow the gap between the acid-test ratio and the current ratio.

Exhibit 4.21 shows both the acid-test and current ratios of retailer JCPenney for 1998 through 2000. JCPenney's acid-test ratio reveals a recent decline that exceeds the decline in the retailing industry's acid-test ratio. JCPenney's current ratio suggests that its short-term obligations can be covered with short-term assets, but the acid-test ratio raises some concerns. Specifically, an acid-test ratio less than 1.0 (0.53 for JCPenney) means that current liabilities exceed quick assets. A rule of thumb is that the acid-test ratio should have a value of at least 1.0 to conclude that a company is unlikely to face liquidity problems in the near future. A value less than 1.0 suggests a liquidity problem unless a company can generate enough cash from sales or if much of its liabilities are not due until late in the next period. Similarly, a value greater than 1.0 can hide a liquidity problem if payables are due shortly and receivables will not be collected until late in the next period. Our analysis of JCPenney reveals a concern with its liquidity, especially when benchmarked against the industry ratio of 0.7.

Decision Maker *d*

Supplier   A retailer requests to purchase supplies on credit from your company. You have no prior experience with this retailer. The retailer's current ratio is 2.1, its acid-test ratio is 0.5, and inventory makes up most of its current assets. Do you extend credit?

Answer—p. 191

($ in millions)	2000	1999	1998
Total quick assets	$2,371	$ 4,779	$ 5,179
Total current assets	$8,472	$11,007	$11,484
Total current liabilities	$4,465	$ 5,912	$ 6,137
Acid-test ratio	0.53	0.81	0.84
Current ratio	1.90	1.86	1.87
Industry acid-test ratio	0.7	0.8	1.0
Industry current ratio	3.0	3.1	3.5

Exhibit 4.21
JCPenney's Acid-Test and Current Ratios

Gross Margin Ratio

The cost of goods sold makes up much of the costs for merchandisers. This means that success for merchandisers often depends on the relation between sales and cost of goods sold. Without sufficient gross profit, a merchandiser will likely fail. Users often compute the gross margin ratio to help understand this relation. It differs from the profit margin ratio in that it excludes all costs except cost of goods sold. The **gross margin ratio** is defined as *gross margin* (net sales minus cost of goods sold) divided by net sales—see Exhibit 4.22.

A3 Compute the gross margin ratio and explain its use to assess profitability.

$$\text{Gross margin ratio} = \frac{\text{Net sales} - \text{Cost of goods sold}}{\text{Net sales}}$$

Exhibit 4.22
Gross Margin Ratio

Exhibit 4.23 shows the gross margin ratio of JCPenney for 1998–2000. For JCPenney, each $1 of sales in 2000 yielded about 28¢ in gross margin to cover all other expenses and still produce a profit. This 28¢ margin is down from 29¢ in 1999 and from 30¢ in 1998. This decline is an important (and negative) development. Success for merchandisers such as JCPenney depends on maintaining an adequate gross margin. Moreover, data in this exhibit reveal that JCPenney's net sales increased over this period while its gross margin ratio decreased. Overall, both the acid-test ratio and the gross margin ratio raise serious concerns about the financial condition and performance of JCPenney.

Point: The power of a ratio is often its ability to identify areas for more detailed analysis.

Decision Maker *d*

Financial Officer   Your company has a 36% gross margin ratio and a 17% net profit margin ratio. Industry averages are 44% for gross margin and 16% for net profit margin. Do these results concern you?

Answer—p. 191

($ in millions)	2000	1999	1998
Gross margin	$ 9,136	$ 8,819	$ 9,116
Net sales	$32,510	$30,461	$30,410
Gross margin ratio	28.1%	29.0%	30.0%

Exhibit 4.23
JCPenney's Gross Margin Ratio

Demonstration Problem

Use the following adjusted trial balance and additional information to complete the requirements:

KC ANTIQUES Adjusted Trial Balance December 31, 2002	Debit	Credit
Cash	$ 20,000	
Merchandise inventory	60,000	
Store supplies	1,500	
Equipment	45,600	
Accumulated depreciation—Equipment		$ 16,600
Accounts payable		9,000
Salaries payable		2,000
Common stock		20,000
Retained earnings		49,000
Sales		343,250
Sales discounts	5,000	
Sales returns and allowances	6,000	
Cost of goods sold	159,900	
Depreciation expense—Store equipment	4,100	
Depreciation expense—Office equipment	1,600	
Sales salaries expense	30,000	
Office salaries expense	34,000	
Insurance expense	11,000	
Rent expense (70% is store, 30% is office)	24,000	
Store supplies expense	5,750	
Advertising expense	31,400	
Totals	$439,850	$439,850

KC Antiques' *supplementary records* for 2002 reveal the following itemized costs for merchandising activities:

Invoice cost of merchandise purchases	$150,000
Purchase discounts received	2,500
Purchase returns and allowances	2,700
Cost of transportation-in	5,000

Required

1. Use the supplementary records to compute the total cost of merchandise purchases for 2002.
2. Prepare a 2002 multiple-step income statement. (Inventory at December 31, 2001, is $70,100.)
3. Prepare a single-step income statement for 2002.
4. Prepare closing entries for KC Antiques at December 31, 2002.
5. Compute the acid-test ratio and the gross margin ratio. Explain the meaning of each ratio and interpret them for KC Antiques.

Planning the Solution

- Compute the total cost of merchandise purchases for 2002.
- To prepare the multiple-step statement, first compute net sales. Then, to compute cost of goods sold, add the net cost of merchandise purchases for the year to beginning inventory and subtract the cost of ending inventory. Subtract cost of goods sold from net sales to get gross profit. Then classify expenses as selling expenses or general and administrative expenses.
- To prepare the single-step income statement, begin with net sales. Then list and subtract the expenses.

- The first closing entry debits all temporary accounts with credit balances and opens the Income Summary account. The second closing entry credits all temporary accounts with debit balances. The third entry closes the Income Summary account to the Retained Earnings account.
- Identify the quick assets on the adjusted trial balance. Compute the acid-test ratio by dividing quick assets by current liabilities. Compute the gross margin ratio by dividing gross profit by net sales.

Solution to Demonstration Problem

1.

Invoice cost of merchandise purchases	$150,000
Less: Purchases discounts received	(2,500)
Purchase returns and allowances	(2,700)
Add: Cost of transportation-in	5,000
Total cost of merchandise purchases	$149,800

2. Multiple-step income statement

KC ANTIQUES Income Statement For Year Ended December 31, 2002			
Sales			$343,250
Less: Sales discounts		$ 5,000	
Sales returns and allowances		6,000	11,000
Net sales			$332,250
Cost of goods sold*			159,900
Gross profit			$172,350
Expenses			
Selling expenses			
Depreciation expense—Store equipment	$ 4,100		
Sales salaries expense	30,000		
Rent expense—Selling space	16,800		
Store supplies expense	5,750		
Advertising expense	31,400		
Total selling expenses		$88,050	
General and administrative expenses			
Depreciation expense—Office equipment	$ 1,600		
Office salaries expense	34,000		
Insurance expense	11,000		
Rent expense—Office space	7,200		
Total general and administrative expenses		53,800	
Total operating expenses			141,850
Net income			$ 30,500

* Cost of goods sold can also be directly computed (apply concepts from Exhibit 4.5):

Merchandise inventory, December 31, 2001	$ 70,100
Total cost of merchandise purchases (from part 1)	149,800
Goods available for sale	$219,900
Merchandise inventory, December 31, 2002	60,000
Cost of goods sold	$159,900

3. Single-step income statement

KC ANTIQUES Income Statement For Year Ended December 31, 2002		
Net sales		$332,250
Cost of goods sold	$159,900	
Selling expenses	88,050	
General and administrative expenses	53,800	301,750
Net income		$ 30,500

4.

Dec. 31	Sales	343,250	
	Income Summary		343,250
	To close credit balances in temporary accounts.		
Dec. 31	Income Summary	312,750	
	Sales Discounts		5,000
	Sales Returns and Allowances		6,000
	Cost of Goods Sold		159,900
	Depreciation Expense—Store Equipment ..		4,100
	Depreciation Expense—Office Equipment ..		1,600
	Sales Salaries Expense		30,000
	Office Salaries Expense		34,000
	Insurance Expense		11,000
	Rent Expense		24,000
	Store Supplies Expense		5,750
	Advertising Expense		31,400
	To close debit balances in temporary accounts.		
Dec. 31	Income Summary	30,500	
	Retained Earnings		30,500
	To close the Income Summary account.		

5. Acid-test ratio = (Cash and equivalents + Short-term investments + Current receivables)/ Current liabilities

= Cash/(Accounts payable + Salaries payable)

= $20,000/$9,000 + $2,000) = $20,000/$11,000 = 1.82

Gross margin ratio = Gross profit/Net sales = $172,350/$332,250 = 0.52

KC Antiques has a healthy acid-test ratio of 1.82. This means it has more than $1.80 in liquid assets to satisfy each $1.00 in current liabilities. The gross margin of 0.52 shows that KC Antiques spends 48¢ ($1.00 − $0.52) of every dollar of net sales on the costs of acquiring the merchandise it sells. This leaves 52¢ of every dollar of net sales to cover other expenses incurred in the business and to provide a profit.

Comparing Periodic and Perpetual Inventory Systems

4A

Recall that under a perpetual system, the Merchandise Inventory account is updated after each purchase and each sale. The Cost of Goods Sold account also is updated after each sale so that during the period its account balance reflects the period's total cost of goods sold to date. Under a periodic inventory system, the Merchandise Inventory account is updated only once each accounting period. This update occurs at the *end* of the period. Also during the period, the Merchandise Inventory balance remains unchanged. It reflects the beginning inventory balance until it is updated at the end of the period. Similarly, in a periodic inventory system, cost of goods sold is not recorded as each sale occurs. Instead, cost of goods sold for the period is computed at the end of the period.

Under a perpetual system, each purchase, purchase return and allowance, purchase discount, and transportation-in transaction is recorded in the Merchandise Inventory account. Under a periodic system, a separate temporary account is set up for *each* of these items. At period-end, each of these temporary accounts is closed and the Merchandise Inventory account is updated. To illustrate the differences, we use parallel columns to show journal entries for the most common transactions using both periodic and perpetual inventory systems (codes *a* through *f* link these transactions to those in the chapter, and we drop explanations for simplicity).

Recording Merchandise Transactions

P5 Record and compare merchandising transactions using both periodic and perpetual inventory systems.

Purchases

The periodic system uses a temporary *Purchases* account that accumulates the cost of all purchase transactions during the period. Z-Mart's entry to record the purchase of merchandise for $1,200 on credit with terms of 2/10, n/30 is

(a)

Periodic				Perpetual		
Purchases	1,200			Merchandise Inventory	1,200	
Accounts Payable		1,200		Accounts Payable		1,200

Purchase Discounts

The periodic system uses a temporary *Purchase Discounts* account that accumulates discounts taken on purchase transactions during the period. If payment in (*a*) is delayed until after the discount period expires, the entry under both methods is to debit Accounts Payable and credit Cash for $1,200 each. However, when Z-Mart pays the supplier for the previous purchase in (*a*) within the discount period, the required payment is $1,176 ($1,200 × 98%) and is recorded as

(b)

Periodic				Perpetual		
Accounts Payable	1,200			Accounts Payable	1,200	
Purchase Discounts		24		Merchandise Inventory		24
Cash		1,176		Cash		1,176

Purchase Returns and Allowances

Z-Mart returned merchandise purchased on November 2 because of defects. In the periodic system, the temporary *Purchase Returns and Allowances* account accumulates the cost of all returns and allowances during a period. The recorded cost (including discounts) of the defective merchandise is $300, and Z-Mart records the return with this entry:

(c)   *Periodic*   *Perpetual*

Accounts Payable	300		Accounts Payable	300	
Purchase Returns			Merchandise Inventory .		300
and Allowances . .		300			

Transportation-In

Z-Mart paid a $75 freight charge to haul merchandise to its store. In the periodic system, this cost is charged to a temporary *Transportation-In* account.

(d)   *Periodic*   *Perpetual*

| Transportation-In . . . . . . | 75 | | Merchandise Inventory . . . . | 75 | |
| Cash . . . . | | 75 | Cash . . . . | | 75 |

Sales

Under the periodic system, the cost of goods sold is not recorded at the time of each sale. (We later show how to compute total cost of goods sold at the end of a period.) Z-Mart's entry to record sales of $2,400 in merchandise on credit (when its cost is $1,600) is:

(e)   *Periodic*   *Perpetual*

Accounts Receivable . . .	2,400		Accounts Receivable	2,400	
Sales		2,400	Sales		2,400
			Cost of Goods Sold	1,600	
			Merchandise Inventory .		1,600

Sales Returns

A customer returned part of the merchandise from the transaction in (*e*), where the returned items sell for $800 and cost $600. (*Recall:* The periodic system records only the revenue effect, not the cost effect, for sales transactions.) Z-Mart restores the merchandise to inventory and records the return as

(f)   *Periodic*   *Perpetual*

Sales Returns and			Sales Returns and		
Allowances	800		Allowances	800	
Accounts Receivable		800	Accounts Receivable . .		800
			Merchandise Inventory	600	
			Cost of Goods Sold . . .		600

Adjusting and Closing Entries

The periodic and perpetual inventory systems have slight differences in adjusting and closing entries. Z-Mart's adjusted trial balance (except for shrinkage) under each system is shown in Exhibit 4A.1.

The Merchandise Inventory balance is $19,000 under the periodic system and $21,250 under the perpetual system. Since the periodic system does not revise the Merchandise Inventory balance during the period, the $19,000 amount is the beginning inventory. However, the $21,250 balance under the perpetual system is the recorded ending inventory before adjusting for any inventory shrinkage.

Exhibit 4A.1

Comparison of Adjusted Trial Balances (absent shrinkage)—Periodic and Perpetual

Z-MART — Adjusted Trial Balance (Periodic System) December 31, 2002	Debit	Credit
Cash	$ 8,200	
Accounts receivable	11,200	
Merchandise inventory	19,000	
Office supplies	550	
Store supplies	250	
Prepaid insurance	300	
Office equipment	4,200	
Accum. depreciation—Office eq.		$ 1,400
Store equipment	30,000	
Accum. depreciation—Store eq.		6,000
Accounts payable		6,000
Salaries payable		800
Long-term note payable		10,000
Common stock		20,000
Retained earnings		18,600
Sales		321,000
Sales discounts	4,300	
Sales returns and allowances	2,000	
Purchases	235,800	
Purchase discounts		4,200
Purchase returns and allowances		1,500
Transportation-in	2,300	
Depreciation expense—Store eq.	3,000	
Depreciation expense—Office eq.	700	
Office salaries expense	25,300	
Sales salaries expense	18,500	
Insurance expense	600	
Rent expense—Office space	900	
Rent expense—Selling space	8,100	
Office supplies expense	1,800	
Store supplies expense	1,200	
Advertising expense	11,300	
Totals	$389,500	$389,500

Z-MART — Adjusted Trial Balance (Perpetual System) December 31, 2002	Debit	Credit
Cash	$ 8,200	
Accounts receivable	11,200	
Merchandise inventory	21,250	
Office supplies	550	
Store supplies	250	
Prepaid insurance	300	
Office equipment	4,200	
Accum. depreciation—Office eq.		$ 1,400
Store equipment	30,000	
Accum. depreciation—Store eq.		6,000
Accounts payable		6,000
Salaries payable		800
Long-term note payable		10,000
Common stock		20,000
Retained earnings		18,600
Sales		321,000
Sales discounts	4,300	
Sales returns and allowances	2,000	
Cost of goods sold	230,150	
Depreciation expense—Store eq.	3,000	
Depreciation expense—Office eq.	700	
Office salaries expense	25,300	
Sales salaries expense	18,500	
Insurance expense	600	
Rent expense—Office space	900	
Rent expense—Selling space	8,100	
Office supplies expense	1,800	
Store supplies expense	1,200	
Advertising expense	11,300	
Totals	$383,800	$383,800

A physical count of inventory taken at the end of the period reveals $21,000 of merchandise available (revealing inventory shrinkage of $21,250 − $21,000 = $250).

The adjusting entry for shrinkage and the closing entries for the two systems are shown in Exhibit 4A.2. The periodic system does not make an adjusting entry to record inventory shrinkage. Instead, it puts the ending inventory of $21,000 in the Merchandise Inventory account (which is net of shrinkage) in the first closing entry and removes the $19,000 beginning inventory balance from the account in the second closing entry.

By updating Merchandise Inventory and closing Purchases, Purchase Discounts, Purchase Returns and Allowances, and Transportation-In, the periodic system transfers the cost of goods sold amount to Income Summary. Review the periodic side of Exhibit 4A.2 and notice that the boldface items affect Income Summary as follows:

Credited to Income Summary in the first closing entry	
Merchandise inventory (ending)	$ 21,000
Purchase discounts	4,200
Purchase returns and allowances	1,500
Debited to Income Summary in the second closing entry	
Merchandise inventory (beginning)	(19,000)
Purchases	(235,800)
Transportation-in	(2,300)
Net effect on Income Summary	**$(230,400)**

This $230,400 effect on Income Summary is the cost of goods sold amount. The periodic system transfers cost of goods sold to the Income Summary account but without using a Cost of Goods Sold account. Also, the periodic system does not separately measure shrinkage. Instead, it computes cost of goods available for sale, subtracts the cost of ending inventory, and defines the difference as cost of goods sold. This difference includes shrinkage.

Exhibit 4A.2

Comparison of Adjusting and Closing Entries—Periodic and Perpetual

Periodic			**Perpetual**		
Adjusting Entry — Shrinkage			**Adjusting Entry — Shrinkage**		
None			Cost of Goods Sold	250	
			Merchandise Inventory		250
Closing Entries			**Closing Entries**		
(1) Sales	321,000		**(1)** Sales	321,000	
Merchandise Inventory	21,000		Income Summary		321,000
Purchase Discounts	4,200				
Purchase Returns and Allowances . . .	1,500				
Income Summary		347,700			
(2) Income Summary	334,800		**(2)** Income Summary	308,100	
Sales Discounts		4,300	Sales Discounts		4,300
Sales Returns and Allowances		2,000	Sales Returns and Allowances		2,000
Merchandise Inventory		19,000			
Purchases		235,800	Cost of Goods Sold		230,400
Transportation-In		2,300			
Depreciation Expense—Store eq.		3,000	Depreciation Expense—Store eq.		3,000
Depreciation Expense—Office eq. . .		700	Depreciation Expense—Office eq. . .		700
Office Salaries Expense		25,300	Office Salaries Expense		25,300
Sales Salaries Expense		18,500	Sales Salaries Expense		18,500
Insurance Expense		600	Insurance Expense		600
Rent Expense—Office space		900	Rent Expense—Office space		900
Rent Expense—Selling space		8,100	Rent Expense—Selling space		8,100
Office Supplies Expense		1,800	Office Supplies Expense		1,800
Store Supplies Expense		1,200	Store Supplies Expense		1,200
Advertising Expense		11,300	Advertising Expense		11,300
(3) Income Summary	12,900		**(3)** Income Summary	12,900	
Retained Earnings		12,900	Retained Earnings		12,900

Exhibit 4A.3 shows the work sheet for preparing financial statements. It differs slightly from the work sheet layout in Chapter 3—the differences are in bold. Also, the adjustments in the work sheet reflect the following: (*a*) Expiration of $600 of prepaid insurance. (*b*) Use of $1,200 of store supplies. (*c*) Use of $1,800 of office supplies. (*d*) Depreciation of $3,000 for store equipment. (*e*) Depreciation of $700 for office equipment. (*f*) Accrual of $300 of unpaid office salaries and $500 of unpaid store salaries. (*g*) Inventory shrinkage of $250. Once the adjusted amounts are extended into the financial statement columns, the information is used to develop financial statements.

Work Sheet for a Merchandiser— Perpetual System

Exhibit 4A.3

Work Sheet for Merchandiser (using a perpetual system)

No.	Account	Unadjusted Trial Balance Dr.	Cr.	Adjustments Dr.	Cr.	Adjusted Trial Balance Dr.	Cr.	Income Statement Dr.	Cr.	Balance Sheet Dr.	Cr.
101	Cash	8,200				8,200				8,200	
106	Accounts receivable	11,200				11,200				11,200	
119	**Merchandise Inventory**	**21,250**			(g) 250	**21,000**				**21,000**	
124	Office supplies	2,350			(c) 1,800	550				550	
125	Store supplies	1,450			(b) 1,200	250				250	
128	Prepaid insurance	900			(a) 600	300				300	
163	Office equipment	4,200				4,200				4,200	
164	Accum. depr.—Office equip.		700		(e) 700		1,400				1,400
165	Store equipment	30,000				30,000				30,000	
166	Accum. depr.—Store equip.		3,000		(d) 3,000		6,000				6,000
201	Accounts payable		16,000				16,000				16,000
209	Salaries payable				(f) 800		800				800
307	Common stock		20,000				20,000				20,000
318	Retained earnings		18,600				18,600				18,600
413	**Sales**		**321,000**				**321,000**		**321,000**		
414	**Sales returns and allowances**	**2,000**				**2,000**		**2,000**			
415	**Sales discounts**	**4,300**				**4,300**		**4,300**			
502	**Cost of goods sold**	**230,150**		(g) 250		**230,400**		**230,400**			
612	Depr. expense—Store equip.			(d) 3,000		3,000		3,000			
613	Depr. expense—Office equip.			(e) 700		700		700			
620	Office salaries expense	25,000		(f) 300		25,300		25,300			
621	Sales salaries expense	18,000		(f) 500		18,500		18,500			
637	Insurance expense			(a) 600		600		600			
641	Rent expense—Office space	900				900		900			
642	Rent expense—Selling space	8,100				8,100		8,100			
650	Office supplies expense			(c) 1,800		1,800		1,800			
651	Store supplies expense			(b) 1,200		1,200		1,200			
655	Advertising expense	11,300				11,300		11,300			
	Totals	379,300	379,300	8,350	8,350	383,800	383,800	308,100	321,000	75,700	62,800
	Net income							12,900			12,900
	Totals							321,000	321,000	75,700	75,700

In our discussion of the periodic system, the change in the Merchandise Inventory account is recorded as part of the closing process. This *closing entry method* is common. An alternative method, called the *adjusting entry method*, also is used. The *adjusting entry method* records the change in the Merchandise Inventory account with adjusting entries. Under this method, the first two closing entries (see Exhibit 4A.2) do not include the Merchandise Inventory account.

Adjusting Entry Method—Periodic System

Adjusting Entries—Alternative Periodic Method

Under the adjusting entry method of the periodic system, Z-Mart removes the beginning balance from the Merchandise Inventory account by recording this adjusting entry at the end of the period:

Dec. 31	Income Summary	19,000	
	Merchandise Inventory		19,000
	To remove the beginning balance from the Merchandise Inventory account.		

A second adjusting entry inserts the ending balance in the inventory account:

Dec. 31	Merchandise Inventory	21,000	
	Income Summary		21,000
	To insert the ending balance in the Merchandise Inventory account.		

After these entries are posted, the Merchandise Inventory account appears as follows:

Merchandise Inventory			
Beg. balance	19,000	Adjustment	19,000
Adjustment	21,000		
End. balance	21,000		

Closing Entries—Alternative Periodic Method

If the adjusting entry method for inventory is used, the closing entries do not include the Merchandise Inventory account. In particular, entries (1) and (2) in Exhibit 4A.2 are the same except for removing the Merchandise Inventory account and its balance from both entries (including its amount from Income Summary). Entry (3) to close Income Summary is unchanged. The adjusting entry method took four entries instead of two to get net income of $12,900 into Income Summary.

Quick Check

13. What account is used in a perpetual inventory system but not in a periodic system?

14. Which of the following accounts are temporary accounts under a periodic system? (a) Merchandise Inventory; (b) Purchases; (c) Transportation-In.

15. How is cost of goods sold computed under a periodic inventory system?

16. Do reported amounts of ending inventory and net income differ if the adjusting entry method of recording the change in inventory is used instead of the closing entry method?

Answer—p. 192

Summary

C1   Describe merchandising activities and identify business examples. Operations of merchandisers involve buying products and reselling them. Examples of merchandisers include Wal-Mart, Home Depot, The Limited, and Barnes & Noble.

C2   Identify and explain the components of income for a merchandising company. A merchandiser's costs on an income statement include an amount for cost of goods sold. Gross profit, or gross margin, equals sales minus cost of goods sold.

C3   Identify and explain the inventory asset of a merchandising company. The current asset section of a merchandising company's balance sheet includes *merchandise inventory*, which refers to the products a merchandiser sells and are available for sale at the balance sheet date.

C4   Describe both perpetual and periodic inventory systems. A perpetual inventory system continuously tracks the cost of goods available for sale and the cost of goods sold. A periodic system accumulates the cost of goods purchased during the period and does not compute the amount of inventory or the cost of goods sold until the end of a period.

C5 **Analyze and interpret cost flows and operating activities of a merchandising company.** Cost of merchandise purchases flows into Merchandise Inventory and from there to Cost of Goods Sold on the income statement. Any remaining inventory is reported as a current asset on the balance sheet.

A1 **Analyze and interpret accruals and cash flows for merchandising activities.** Merchandising sales and costs of sales reported in the income statement usually differ from their corresponding cash receipts and cash payments. Cash received from customers equals net sales less the increase (or plus the decrease) in Accounts Receivable during the period. Cash paid to suppliers equals cost of goods sold less the increase (or plus the decrease) in Accounts Payable and less the decrease (or plus the increase) in Inventory during the period.

A2 **Compute the acid-test ratio and explain its use to assess liquidity.** The acid-test ratio is computed as quick assets (cash, short-term investments, and current receivables) divided by current liabilities. It indicates a company's ability to pay its current liabilities with its existing quick assets. A ratio equal to or greater than 1.0 is often adequate.

A3 **Compute the gross margin ratio and explain its use to assess profitability.** The gross margin ratio is computed as gross margin (net sales minus cost of goods sold) divided by net sales. It indicates a company's profitability before considering other expenses.

P1 **Analyze and record transactions for merchandise purchases using a perpetual system.** For a perpetual inventory system, purchases of inventory (net of trade discounts) are added (debited) to the Merchandise Inventory account. Purchase discounts and purchase returns and allowances are subtracted (credited) from Merchandise Inventory, and transportation-in costs are added (debited) to Merchandise Inventory.

P2 **Analyze and record transactions for sales of merchandise using a perpetual system.** A merchandiser records sales at list price less any trade discounts. The cost of items sold is transferred from Merchandise Inventory to Cost of Goods Sold. Refunds or credits given to customers for unsatisfactory merchandise are recorded (debited) in Sales Returns and Allowances, a contra account to Sales. If merchandise is returned and restored to inventory, the cost of this merchandise is removed from Cost of Goods Sold and transferred back to Merchandise Inventory. When cash discounts from the sales price are offered and customers pay within the discount period, the seller records (debits) Sales Discounts, a contra account to Sales.

P3 **Prepare adjustments and close accounts for a merchandising company.** With a perpetual system, it is often necessary to make an adjustment for inventory shrinkage. This is computed by comparing a physical count of inventory with the Merchandise Inventory balance. Shrinkage is normally charged to Cost of Goods Sold. Temporary accounts closed to Income Summary for a merchandiser include Sales, Sales Discounts, Sales Returns and Allowances, and Cost of Goods Sold.

P4 **Define and prepare multiple-step and single-step income statements.** Multiple-step income statements include greater detail for sales and expenses than do single-step income statements. They also show details of net sales and report expenses in categories reflecting different activities.

P5 **Record and compare merchandising transactions using both periodic and perpetual inventory systems.** Transactions involving the sale and purchase of merchandise are recorded and analyzed under both the periodic and perpetual inventory systems. Adjusting and closing entries for both inventory systems are illustrated and explained.

Guidance Answers to **Decision Maker** and **Decision Ethics**

Entrepreneur For terms of 3/10, n/90, missing the 3% discount for an additional 80 days equals an annual interest rate of 13.69% computed as (365 days ÷ 80 days) × 3%. Since you can borrow funds at 11% (assuming no other processing costs), it is better to borrow and pay within the discount period. You save 2.69% (13.69% − 11%) in interest costs by paying early.

Credit Manager Your decision is whether to comply with prior policy or to create a new policy and not abuse discounts offered by suppliers. Your first step should be to meet with your superior to find out if the late payment policy is the actual policy and, if so, its rationale. If it is the policy to pay late, you must apply your own sense of ethics. One point of view is that the late payment policy is unethical. A deliberate plan to make late payments means the company lies when it pretends to make purchases within the credit terms. Another view is that the late payment policy is acceptable. In some markets, attempts to take discounts through late payments are accepted as a continued phase of "price negotiation." Also, your company's suppliers can respond by billing your company for the discounts not accepted because of late payments. However, this is a dubious viewpoint, especially since the prior manager proposes that you explain late payments as computer or mail problems and since some suppliers have complained.

Supplier A current ratio of 2.1 suggests sufficient current assets to cover current liabilities. An acid-test ratio of 0.5 suggests, however, that quick assets can cover only about one-half of current liabilities. This implies that the retailer depends on profits from sales of inventory to pay current liabilities. If sales of inventory decline or profit margins decrease, the likelihood that this retailer will default on its payments increases. Your decision is probably not to extend credit. If you do extend credit, you are likely to closely monitor the retailer's financial condition.

Financial Officer Your company's net profit margin is about equal to the industry average and suggests typical industry performance. However, gross margin reveals that your company is paying far more in cost of goods sold or receiving far less in sales price than competitors. Your attention must be directed to finding the problem with cost of goods sold, sales, or both. One positive note is that your company's expenses make up 19% of sales (36% − 17%). This favorably compares with competitors' expenses that make up 28% of sales (44% − 16%).

Guidance Answers to **Quick Checks**

1. Cost of goods sold is the cost of merchandise purchased from a supplier that is sold to customers during a specific period.

2. Gross profit (or gross margin) is the difference between net sales and cost of goods sold.

3. Widespread use of computing and related technology has dramatically increased the use of the perpetual inventory system.

4. Under credit terms of 2/10, n/60, the credit period is 60 days and the discount period is 10 days.

5. (b) trade discount.

6. *FOB* means "free on board." It is used in identifying the point when ownership transfers from seller to buyer. *FOB destination* means that the seller transfers ownership of goods to the buyer when they arrive at the buyer's place of business. It also means that the seller is responsible for paying shipping charges and bears the risk of damage or loss during shipment.

7. Recording sales discounts and sales returns and allowances separately from sales gives useful information to managers for internal monitoring and decision making.

8. When a customer returns merchandise *and* the seller restores the merchandise to inventory, two entries are necessary. One entry records the decrease in revenue and credits the customer's account. The second entry debits inventory and reduces cost of goods sold.

9. Credit memorandum—seller credits accounts receivable from buyer.

10. Merchandise Inventory may need adjusting to reflect shrinkage.

11. Sales (of goods), Sales Discounts, Sales Returns and Allowances, and Cost of Goods Sold.

12. Three closing entries: (1) close credit balances in temporary accounts to Income Summary, (2) close debit balances in temporary accounts to Income Summary, and (3) close Income Summary to Retained Earnings.

13. Cost of Goods Sold.

14. (b) Purchases and (c) Transportation-In.

15. Under a periodic inventory system, the cost of goods sold is determined at the end of an accounting period by adding the net cost of goods purchased to the beginning inventory and subtracting the ending inventory.

16. Both methods report the same ending inventory and income.

Glossary

Acid-test ratio Ratio used to assess a company's ability to settle its current debts with its most liquid assets; defined as quick assets (cash, short-term investments, and current receivables) over current liabilities. (p. 180)

Cash discount Reduction in the price of merchandise granted by a seller to a buyer when payment is made within the discount period. (p. 167)

Cost of goods sold Cost of inventory sold to customers during a period. (p. 164)

Credit memorandum Notification that the sender has credited the recipient's account in the sender's records. (p. 174)

Credit period Time period that can pass before a customer's payment is due. (p. 167).

Credit terms Description of the amounts and timing of payments that a buyer agrees to make in the future. (p. 166)

Debit memorandum Notification that the sender has debited the recipient's account in the sender's records. (p. 168)

Discount period Time period in which a cash discount is available and the buyer can make a reduced payment. (p. 167)

EOM Abbreviation for *end of month;* used to describe credit terms for some transactions. (p. 167)

FOB Abbreviation for *free on board;* the point when ownership of goods passes to the buyer; *FOB shipping point* (or *factory*) means the buyer pays shipping costs and accepts ownership of goods when the seller transfers goods to carrier; *FOB destination* means the seller pays shipping costs and buyer accepts ownership of goods at the buyer's place of business. (p. 169)

General and administrative expenses Expenses that support the operating activities of a business. (p. 178)

Gross margin (See *gross profit.*) (p. 162)

Gross margin ratio Gross margin (net sales minus cost of goods sold) divided by net sales; also called *gross profit ratio.* (p. 181)

Gross profit Net sales minus cost of goods sold; also called *gross margin.* (p. 162)

Inventory Merchandise a company owns and expects to sell in its normal operations. (p. 164)

List price Catalog price of an item before any trade discount is deducted. (p. 166)

Merchandise (See *merchandise inventory.*) (p. 162)

Merchandise inventory Products that a company owns and expects to sell to customers; also called *merchandise.* (p. 163)

Merchandiser Entity that earns net income by buying and selling merchandise. (p. 162)

Multiple-step income statement Income statement format that shows subtotals between sales and net income and the details of net sales and expenses. (p. 178)

Periodic inventory system Method that records the cost of inventory purchased but does not track the quantity available or sold to customers; records are updated at the end of each period to reflect the physical count of goods available. (p. 164)

Perpetual inventory system Method that maintains continuous records of the cost of inventory available and the cost of goods sold. (p. 165)

Purchase discount Term used by a purchaser to describe a cash discount granted to the purchaser for paying within the discount period. (p. 167)

Retailer Intermediary that buys products from manufacturers or wholesalers and sells them to consumers. (p. 162)

Sales discount Term used by a seller to describe a cash discount granted to buyers who pay within the discount period. (p. 167)

Selling expenses Expenses of promoting sales, such as displaying and advertising merchandise, making sales, and delivering goods to customers. (p. 178)

Shrinkage Inventory losses that occur as a result of theft or deterioration. (p. 175)

Single-step income statement Income statement format that includes cost of goods sold as an expense and shows only one subtotal for total expenses. (p. 179)

Supplementary records Information outside the usual accounting records; also called *supplemental records*. (p. 171)

Trade discount Reduction from a list or catalog price that can vary for wholesalers, retailers, and consumers. (p. 166)

Wholesaler Intermediary that buys products from manufacturers or other wholesalers and sells them to retailers or other wholesalers. (p. 162)

The superscript letter ^{A} denotes assignments based on Appendix 4A.

Questions

1. In comparing the accounts of a merchandising company with those of a service company, what additional accounts would the merchandising company likely use, assuming it employs a perpetual inventory system?

2. What items appear in financial statements of merchandising companies but not in the statements of service companies?

3. 𝒹 Explain how a business can earn a positive gross profit on its sales and still have a net loss.

4. 𝒹 Why do companies offer a cash discount?

5. How does a company that uses a perpetual inventory system determine the amount of inventory shrinkage?

6. Distinguish between cash discounts and trade discounts. Is the amount of a trade discount on purchased merchandise recorded in the accounts?

7. What is the difference between a sales discount and a purchase discount?

8. 𝒹 Why would a company's manager be concerned about the quantity of its purchase returns if its suppliers allow unlimited returns?

9. Does the sender of a debit memorandum record a debit or a credit in the recipient's account? Which (debit or credit) does the recipient record?

10. What is the difference between single-step and multiple-step income statement formats?

11. Refer to the income statement for Nike in Appendix A. What term is used instead of cost of goods sold? Does the company present a detailed calculation of its cost of goods sold?

12. Refer to the balance sheet for Reebok in Appendix A. What does Reebok call its inventory account? What alternate name could it use?

13. Refer to the income statement of Gap in Appendix A. Does its income statement report a gross profit figure?

14. 𝒹 Buyers negotiate purchase contracts with suppliers. What type of shipping terms should a buyer attempt to negotiate to minimize freight-in costs?

Prepare journal entries to record each of the following purchases transactions of a merchandising company. Show any supporting calculations. Assume a perpetual inventory system.

Mar. 5   Purchased 600 units of product with a list price of $10 per unit. The purchaser is granted a trade discount of 20%; terms of the sale are 2/10, n/60; and invoice dated March 5.
Mar. 7   Returned 25 defective units from the March 5 purchase and received full credit.
Mar. 15 Paid the amount due from the March 5 purchase, less the return on March 7.

QUICK STUDY

QS 4-1
Recording purchases—perpetual system   **P1**

Prepare journal entries to record each of the following sales transactions of a merchandising company. Show any supporting calculations. Assume a perpetual inventory system.

Apr. 1   Sold merchandise for $3,000, granting the customer terms of 2/10, EOM; invoice dated April 1. The cost of the merchandise is $1,800.
Apr. 4   The customer in the April 1 sale returned merchandise and received credit for $600. The merchandise, which had cost $360, is returned to inventory.
Apr. 11 Received payment for the amount due from the April 1 sale less the return on April 4.

QS 4-2
Recording sales—perpetual system
P2

Compute net sales, gross profit, and the gross margin ratio for each situation *a* through *d:*

QS 4-3 𝒹
Computing and analyzing gross margin
C2 A3

	a	b	c	d
Sales	$150,000	$550,000	$38,700	$255,700
Sales discounts	5,200	17,500	600	4,200
Sales returns and allowances	20,000	6,000	5,300	900
Cost of goods sold	79,600	329,700	24,300	128,900

Interpret the gross margin ratio for situation *a.*

QS 4-4
Accounting for shrinkage—
perpetual system
P3

Bemis Company's ledger on July 31, its fiscal year-end, includes the following accounts that have normal balances (Bemis uses the perpetual inventory system):

Merchandise inventory	$ 37,800	Sales returns and allowances . .	$ 6,500
Common stock	118,300	Cost of goods sold	105,000
Retained earnings	7,000	Depreciation expense	10,300
Sales	160,200	Salaries expense	32,500
Sales discounts	4,700	Miscellaneous expenses	5,000

A physical count of its July 31 year-end inventory discloses that the cost of the merchandise available for sale is $35,900. Prepare the entry to record any inventory shrinkage.

QS 4-5
Closing entries **P3**

Refer to QS 4-4 and prepare journal entries to close the balances in temporary accounts. Remember to consider the entry that is made to solve QS 4-4.

QS 4-6
Acid-test ratio

A2

Use the following information on current assets and current liabilities to compute and interpret the acid-test ratio. Also explain what the acid-test ratio of a company measures.

Cash	$1,500	Prepaid expenses	$ 700
Accounts receivable	2,800	Accounts payable	5,750
Inventory	6,000	Other current liabilities	850

QS 4-7 🗹
Contrasting liquidity **A2**
ratios

Identify similarities and differences between the acid-test ratio and the current ratio. Compare and describe how the two ratios reflect a company's ability to meet its current obligations.

QS 4-8ᴬ 🗹
Contrasting periodic and
perpetual systems

C4

Identify whether each description best applies to a periodic or a perpetual inventory system.
a. Provides more timely information to managers.
b. Requires an adjusting entry to record inventory shrinkage.
c. Markedly increased in frequency and popularity in business within the past decade.
d. Records cost of goods sold each time a sales transaction occurs.

EXERCISES

Exercise 4-1
Recording entries for
merchandise purchases

P1

Prepare journal entries to record the following transactions for a retail store. Assume a perpetual inventory system.

Apr. 2   Purchased merchandise from Blass Company under the following terms: $4,600 price, invoice dated April 2, 2/15, n/60 credit terms, FOB shipping point.
    3   Paid $300 for shipping charges on the April 2 purchase.
    4   Returned to Blass Company unacceptable merchandise that had an invoice price of $600.
   17   Sent a check to Blass Company for the April 2 purchase, net of the discount and the returned merchandise.
   18   Purchased merchandise from Flow Corp. under the following terms: $8,500 price, invoice dated April 18, 2/10, n/30 credit terms, FOB destination.
   21   After negotiations, received from Flow an $1,100 allowance on the April 18 purchase.
   28   Sent a check to Flow paying for the April 18 purchase, net of the discount and allowance.

Check April 28, Cr. Cash $7,252

Exercise 4-2 🗹
Analyzing and recording
merchandise transactions—
both buyer and seller

P1 P2

Sundance Company purchased merchandise for resale from Phoenix with an invoice price of $24,000 and credit terms of 3/10, n/60. The merchandise had cost Phoenix $16,000. Sundance paid within the discount period. Assume that both buyer and seller use a perpetual inventory system.

1. Prepare entries that the buyer should record for the purchase and the cash payment.
2. Prepare entries that the seller should record for the sale and the cash collection.

3. Assume that the buyer borrowed enough cash to pay the balance on the last day of the discount period at an annual interest rate of 8% and paid it back on the last day of the credit period. Compute how much the buyer saved by following this strategy. (Assume a 365-day year.)

Check (3) $465 savings

Insert the letter for each term in the blank space beside the definition that it most closely matches:

A. Cash discount   **E.** FOB shipping point   **H.** Purchase discount
B. Credit period   **F.** Gross profit   **I.** Sales discount
C. Discount period   **G.** Merchandise inventory   **J.** Trade discount
D. FOB destination

Exercise 4-3
Applying merchandising terms

C1 C2

_____ **1.** Ownership of goods is transferred when the seller delivers goods to the carrier.
_____ **2.** Reduction below list or catalog price that is negotiated in setting the price of goods.
_____ **3.** Seller's description of a cash discount granted to buyers in return for early payment.
_____ **4.** Time period that can pass before a customer's payment is due.
_____ **5.** Goods a company owns and expects to sell to its customers.
_____ **6.** Ownership of goods is transferred when delivered to the buyer's place of business.
_____ **7.** Time period in which a cash discount is available.
_____ **8.** Difference between net sales and the cost of goods sold.
_____ **9.** Reduction in a receivable or payable if it is paid within the discount period.
_____ **10.** Purchaser's description of a cash discount received from a supplier of goods.

A1 Parts is organized on May 1, 2002, and made its first purchase of merchandise on May 3. The purchase is for 2,000 units at a price of $10 per unit. On May 5, A1 Parts sold 600 of the units for $14 per unit to Dean Co. Terms of the sale are 2/10, n/60. Prepare entries for A1 Parts to record the May 5 sale and each of the following separate transactions using a perpetual inventory system.

a. On May 7, Dean returns 200 units because they did not fit the customer's needs. A1 Parts restores the units to its inventory.
b. On May 8, Dean discovers that 300 units are damaged but of some use and, therefore, keeps the units. A1 Parts sends Dean a credit memorandum for $600 to compensate for the damage.
c. On May 15, Dean returns 20 defective units and A1 Parts concludes that these units cannot be resold. As a result, A1 Parts discards them.

Exercise 4-4
Recording sales returns and allowances

P2

Refer to Exercise 4-4 and prepare the appropriate journal entries for Dean Co. to record the May 5 purchase and each of the three separate transactions *a* through *c*. Dean is a retailer that uses a perpetual inventory system and purchases these units for resale.

Exercise 4-5
Recording purchase returns and allowances   P1

On May 11, Sanuk Co. accepts delivery of $40,000 of merchandise it purchases for resale from Hoak Corporation. With the merchandise is an invoice dated May 11, with terms of 3/10, n/90, FOB factory. The cost of the goods for Hoak is $30,000. When the goods are delivered, Sanuk pays $345 to Express Shipping for delivery charges on the merchandise. On May 12, Sanuk returns $1,400 of goods to Hoak, who receives them one day later and restores them to inventory. The returned goods had cost Hoak $800. On May 20, Sanuk mails a check to Hoak Corporation for the amount owed. Hoak receives it the following day. (Both Sanuk and Hoak use a perpetual inventory system)

1. Prepare journal entries that Sanuk Co. records for these transactions.
2. Prepare journal entries that Hoak Corporation records for these transactions.

Exercise 4-6
Analyzing and recording merchandise transactions—both buyer and seller

P1 P2

Check (1) May 20, Cr. Cash $37,442

Explain why a company's manager wants the accounting system to record customers' returns of unsatisfactory goods in the Sales Returns and Allowances account instead of the Sales account. In addition, explain whether this information would be useful for external decision makers.

Exercise 4-7
Sales returns and allowances   C2 P2

Exercise 4-8
Recording effects of merchandising activities

C5

The following supplementary records summarize Duncan Company's merchandising activities for year 2002. Set up T-accounts for Merchandise Inventory and Cost of Goods Sold. Then record the summarized activities in the T-accounts and compute account balances. (*Hint:* See Exhibit 4.16.)

Cost of merchandise sold to customers in sales transactions	$196,000
Merchandise inventory, December 31, 2001	25,000
Invoice cost of merchandise purchases	192,500
Shrinkage determined on December 31, 2002	800
Cost of transportation-in	2,900
Cost of merchandise returned by customers and restored to inventory	2,100
Purchase discounts received	1,700
Purchase returns and allowances	4,000

Exercise 4-9
Calculating revenues, expenses, and income

C2 C5

Fill in the blanks in the following separate income statements *a* through *e*. Identify any negative amount by putting it in parentheses.

	a	b	c	d	e
Sales	$62,000	$43,500	$46,000	$?	$25,600
Cost of goods sold					
Merchandise inventory (beginning)	8,000	17,050	7,500	8,000	4,560
Total cost of merchandise purchases	38,000	?	?	32,000	6,600
Merchandise inventory (ending)	?	(2,700)	(9,000)	(6,600)	?
Cost of goods sold	$34,050	$15,900	$?	$?	$ 6,600
Gross profit	$?	$?	$ 3,750	$45,600	$?
Expenses	10,000	10,650	12,150	3,600	6,000
Net income (loss)	$?	$16,950	$(8,400)	$42,000	$?

Exercise 4-10
Preparing adjusting and closing entries for a merchandiser

P3

The following list includes some permanent accounts and all of the temporary accounts from the December 31, 2002, unadjusted trial balance of Davis Co., a business owned by Julie Davis. Use these account balances along with the additional information to journalize (*a*) adjusting entries and (*b*) closing entries. Davis Co. uses a perpetual inventory system.

	Debit	Credit
Merchandise inventory	$ 30,000	
Prepaid selling expenses	5,500	
Sales		$529,000
Sales returns and allowances	17,500	
Sales discounts	5,000	
Cost of goods sold	212,000	
Sales salaries expense	48,000	
Utilities expense	15,000	
Selling expenses	36,000	
Administrative expenses	105,000	

Check Dec. 31 closing entry, Cr.
Retained Earnings $84,250

Additional Information

Accrued sales salaries amount to $1,700. Prepaid selling expenses of $3,000 have expired. A physical count of merchandise inventory discloses $28,450 of goods available.

Exercise 4-11
Interpreting physical count error as inventory shrinkage

A2 A3 P3

A retail company recently completed a physical count of ending merchandise inventory to use in preparing adjusting entries. In determining the cost of the counted inventory, company employees failed to consider that $3,000 of incoming goods had been shipped by a supplier on December 31 under an FOB shipping point agreement. These goods had been recorded in Merchandise Inventory as a purchase, but they were not included in the physical count because they were in transit. Explain how this overlooked fact affects the company's financial statements and the following ratios: return on equity, debt ratio, current ratio, profit margin ratio, and acid-test ratio.

BMX Company reports the following balances and activities at the current year-end:

Net sales	$1,010,000
Cost of goods sold	565,000
Increase in accounts receivable for the period	45,000
Cash payments to suppliers of goods	515,000

1. Calculate gross profit.

2. Calculate cash received from customers.

3. Calculate cash flows from customers less cash flows paid to suppliers.

Exercise 4-12
Computing profitability and merchandising cash flows

A1

Calculate the current ratio and acid-test ratio for each of the following separate cases. Which company case is in the best position to meet short-term obligations? Explain your choice.

	Case X	Case Y	Case Z
Cash	$ 900	$ 810	$1,000
Short-term investments	0	0	600
Current receivables	0	1,090	700
Inventory	3,000	1,100	4,100
Prepaid expenses	1,300	500	900
Total current assets	$5,200	$3,500	$7,300
Current liabilities	$2,200	$1,200	$3,750

Exercise 4-13 🄳
Computing and analyzing acid-test and current ratios

A2

Journalize the following merchandising transactions for Texas Systems assuming it uses (*a*) a periodic inventory system and (*b*) a perpetual inventory system.

1. On November 1, Texas Systems purchases merchandise for $1,500 on credit with terms of 2/5, n/30, FOB shipping point; invoice dated November 1.

2. On November 5, Texas Systems pays cash for the November 1 purchase.

3. On November 7, Texas Systems discovers and returns $200 of defective merchandise purchased on November 1 for a cash refund.

4. On November 10, Texas Systems pays $90 cash for transportation costs with the November 1 purchase.

5. On November 13, Texas Systems sells merchandise for $1,600 on credit. The cost of the merchandise is $800.

6. On November 16, the customer returns merchandise from the November 13 transaction. The returned items sell for $300 and cost $150.

Exercise 4-14ᴬ
Preparing journal entries for both the periodic and perpetual systems

P1 P2 P5

Prepare journal entries to record the following merchandising transactions of Heflin Company, which applies the perpetual inventory system. (Use a separate account for each receivable and payable; for example, record the purchase on August 1 in Accounts Payable—Chapman Co.)

Aug. 1   Purchased merchandise from Chapman Company for $7,500 under credit terms of 1/10, n/30, FOB destination.

4   At Chapman's request, Heflin paid $200 cash for freight charges on the August 1 purchase, reducing the amount owed to Chapman.

5   Sold merchandise to Griffin Corp. for $5,200 under credit terms of 2/10, n/60, FOB destination. The merchandise had cost $4,000.

8   Purchased merchandise from Follmer Corporation for $5,400 under credit terms of 1/10, n/45, FOB shipping point. The invoice showed that at Heflin's request, Follmer paid the $140 shipping charges and added that amount to the bill.

9   Paid $125 cash for shipping charges related to the August 5 sale to Griffin Corp.

10   Griffin returned merchandise from the August 5 sale that had cost $400 and been sold for $600. The merchandise was restored to inventory.

12   After negotiations with Follmer Corporation concerning problems with the merchandise purchased on August 8, Heflin received a credit memorandum from Follmer granting a price reduction of $700.

15   Received balance due from Griffin Corp. for the August 5 sale less the return on August 10.

18   Paid the amount due Follmer Corporation for the August 8 purchase less the price reduction granted.

PROBLEM SET A

Problem 4-1A
Preparing journal entries for merchandising activities (perpetual system)

P1 P2

Check Aug. 9, Dr. Delivery Expense, $125

Check Aug. 18, Cr. Cash $4,793

19   Sold merchandise to Trigger for $4,800 under credit terms of 1/10, n/30, FOB shipping point. The merchandise had cost $2,400.

22   Trigger requested a price reduction on the August 19 sale because the merchandise did not meet specifications. Sent Trigger a credit memorandum for $500 to resolve the issue.

Check Aug. 29, Dr. Cash $4,257

29   Received Trigger's cash payment for the amount due from the August 19 purchase.

30   Paid Chapman Company the amount due from the August 1 purchase.

Problem 4-2A
Preparing journal entries for merchandising activities (perpetual system)

P1 P2 G

Prepare journal entries to record the following merchandising transactions of Beltran Company, which applies the perpetual inventory system. (Use a separate account for each receivable and payable; for example, record the purchase on July 1 in Accounts Payable—White Co.)

July 1   Purchased merchandise from White Company for $6,000 under credit terms of 1/15, n/30, FOB shipping point.

2   Sold merchandise to Terry Co. for $900 under credit terms of 2/10, n/60, FOB shipping point. The merchandise had cost $500.

3   Paid $125 cash for freight charges on the purchase of July 1.

8   Sold merchandise that had cost $1,300 for $1,700 cash.

9   Purchased merchandise from Kane Co. for $2,200 under credit terms of 2/15, n/60, FOB destination.

11   Received a $200 credit memorandum from Kane Co. for the return of some of the merchandise purchased on July 9.

Check July 12, Dr. Cash $882
          July 16, Cr. Cash $5,940

12   Received the balance due from Terry Co. for the credit sale dated July 2, net of the discount.

16   Paid the balance due to White Company within the discount period.

19   Sold merchandise that cost $800 to Jolie Co. for $1,200 under credit terms of 2/15, n/60, FOB shipping point.

21   Issued a $200 credit memorandum to Jolie Co. for an allowance on goods sold on July 19.

Check July 24, Cr. Cash $1,960
          July 30, Dr. Cash $980

24   Paid Kane Co. the balance due after deducting the discount.

30   Received the balance due from Jolie Co. for the credit sale dated July 19, net of discount.

31   Sold merchandise that cost $4,800 to Terry Co. for $7,000 under credit terms of 2/10, n/60, FOB shipping point.

Problem 4-3A
Preparing adjusting entries and income statements, and computing gross margin, acid-test, and current ratios

A2 A3 P3 P4

The following unadjusted trial balance is prepared at fiscal year-end for Tioga Company:

TIOGA COMPANY
Unadjusted Trial Balance
January 31, 2002

	Debit	Credit
Cash	$ 5,200	
Merchandise inventory	12,500	
Store supplies	5,800	
Prepaid insurance	2,400	
Store equipment	42,900	
Accumulated depreciation—Store equipment		$ 15,250
Accounts payable		10,000
Common stock		14,000
Retained earnings		18,000
Sales		111,950
Sales discounts	2,000	
Sales returns and allowances	2,200	
Cost of good sold	38,400	
Depreciation expense—Store equipment	0	
Salaries expense	33,000	
Insurance expense	0	
Rent expense	15,000	
Store supplies expense	0	
Advertising expense	9,800	
Totals	$ 169,200	$ 169,200

Rent and salaries expenses are equally divided between selling activities and the general and administrative activities. Tioga Company uses a perpetual inventory system.

Required

1. Prepare adjusting journal entries to reflect the following:
   a. Store supplies available at fiscal year-end amount to $1,750.
   b. Expired insurance, an administrative expense, for the fiscal year is $1,400.
   c. Depreciation expense on store equipment, a selling expense, is $1,525 for the fiscal year.
   d. To estimate shrinkage, a physical count of ending merchandise inventory is taken. It shows $10,900 of goods are available for sale.
2. Prepare a multiple-step income statement for fiscal year 2002.
3. Prepare a single-step income statement for fiscal year 2002.
4. Compute the current ratio, acid-test ratio, and gross margin ratio as of January 31, 2002.

Check   (2) Gross profit, $67,750; (3) Total expenses, $104,775; Net income, $2,975

Big Star Company's adjusted trial balance on August 31, 2002, its fiscal year-end, follows:

Problem 4-4A
Computing merchandising amounts and formatting an income statement

C5 A1 P4

$\mathbf{E_x}$

	Debit	Credit
Merchandise inventory	$ 41,000	
Other (noninventory) assets	130,400	
Liabilities		$ 25,000
Common stock		40,000
Retained earnings		56,550
Sales		225,600
Sales discounts	2,250	
Sales returns and allowances	12,000	
Cost of goods sold	74,500	
Sales salaries expense	32,000	
Rent expense—selling space	8,000	
Store supplies expense	1,500	
Advertising expense	13,000	
Office salaries expense	28,500	
Rent expense—office space	3,600	
Office supplies expense	400	
Totals	$347,150	$347,150

On August 31, 2001, merchandise inventory was $26,000. Supplementary records of merchandising activities for the year ended August 31, 2002, reveal the following itemized costs:

Invoice cost of merchandise purchases	$92,000
Purchase discounts received	2,000
Purchase returns and allowances	4,500
Costs of transportation-in	4,000

Required

1. Compute the company's net sales for the year.
2. Compute the company's total cost of merchandise purchased for the year.
3. Prepare a multiple-step income statement that lists the company's net sales, cost of goods sold, and gross profit, as well as the components and amounts of selling expenses and of general and administrative expenses.
4. Prepare a single-step income statement that lists these costs: cost of goods sold, selling expenses, and general and administrative expenses.
5. Accounts receivable decreased during the period by $30,000. Compute cash received from customers.

Check   (2) $89,500; (3) Gross profit, $136,850; Net income, $49,850; (4) Total expenses, $161,500

Problem 4-5A

Preparing closing entries and interpreting information about discounts and returns

C5 P3 Ⓖ

Check (1) $49,850 Dr. to close Income Summary

Check (3) Current-year rate, 5.3%

Use the data for Big Star Company in Problem 4-4A to complete the following requirements:

Required

Preparation Component

1. Prepare closing entries as of August 31, 2002 (the perpetual inventory system is used).

Analysis Component

2. The company makes all purchases on credit, and its suppliers uniformly offer a 3% sales discount. Does it appear that the company's cash management system is accomplishing the goal of taking all available discounts? Explain.

3. In prior years, the company experienced a 4% returns and allowance rate on its sales, which means approximately 4% of its gross sales were eventually returned outright or caused the company to grant allowances to customers. How do this year's results compare to prior years' results?

PROBLEM SET B

Problem 4-1B

Preparing journal entries for merchandising activities (perpetual system)

P1 P2

Check July 17, Dr. Cash $9,457
July 20, Cr. Cash $12,578

Check July 30, Dr. Cash $9,603

Prepare journal entries to record the following merchandising transactions of Whitecap Company, which applies the perpetual inventory system. (Use a separate account for each receivable and payable; for example, record the purchase on July 3 in Accounts Payable—MAP Corp.)

July 3 Purchased merchandise from MAP Corp. for $15,000 under credit terms of 1/10, n/30, FOB destination.

4 At MAP's request, Whitecap paid $150 cash for freight charges on the July 3 purchase, reducing the amount owed to MAP.

7 Sold merchandise to Bergez Co. for $11,500 under credit terms of 2/10, n/60, FOB destination. The merchandise had cost $7,750.

10 Purchased merchandise from McFarland Corporation for $14,200 under credit terms of 1/10, n/45, FOB shipping point. The invoice showed that at Whitecap's request, McFarland paid the $500 shipping charges and added that amount to the bill.

11 Paid $300 cash for shipping charges related to the July 7 sale to Bergez Co.

12 Bergez returned merchandise from the July 7 sale that had cost $1,450 and been sold for $1,850. The merchandise was restored to inventory.

14 After negotiations with McFarland Corporation concerning problems with the merchandise purchased on July 10, Whitecap received a credit memorandum from McFarland granting a price reduction of $2,000.

17 Received balance due from Bergez Co. for the July 7 sale less the return on July 12.

20 Paid the amount due McFarland Corporation for the July 10 purchase less the price reduction granted.

21 Sold merchandise to Harden for $11,000 under credit terms of 1/10, n/30, FOB shipping point. The merchandise had cost $7,000.

24 Harden requested a price reduction on the July 21 sale because the merchandise did not meet specifications. Sent Harden a credit memorandum for $1,300 to resolve the issue.

30 Received Harden's cash payment for the amount due from the July 21 purchase.

31 Paid MAP Corp. the amount due from the July 3 purchase.

Problem 4-2B

Preparing journal entries for merchandising activities (perpetual system)

P1 P2

Check May 14, Dr. Cash $10,780

Check May 17, Cr. Cash $9,900

Prepare journal entries to record the following merchandising transactions of Chang Company, which applies the perpetual inventory system. (Use a separate account for each receivable and payable; for example, record the purchase on May 2 in Accounts Payable—McManus Co.)

May 2 Purchased merchandise from McManus Co. for $10,000 under credit terms of 1/15, n/30, FOB shipping point.

4 Sold merchandise to Four Winds Co. for $11,000 under credit terms of 2/10, n/60, FOB shipping point. The merchandise had cost $5,600.

5 Paid $250 cash for freight charges on the purchase of May 2.

9 Sold merchandise that had cost $2,000 for $2,500 cash.

10 Purchased merchandise from Alvarez Co. for $3,650 under credit terms of 2/15, n/60, FOB destination.

12 Received a $400 credit memorandum from Alvarez Co. for the return of some of the merchandise purchased on May 10.

14 Received the balance due from Four Winds Co. for the credit sale dated May 4, net of the discount.

17 Paid the balance due to McManus Co. within the discount period.

20 Sold merchandise that cost $1,450 to Wickham Co. for $2,800 under credit terms of 2/15, n/60, FOB shipping point.

22 Issued a $400 credit memorandum to Wickham Co. for an allowance on goods sold from May 20.

25 Paid Alvarez Co. the balance due after deducting the discount.

30 Received the balance due from Wickham Co. for the credit sale dated May 20, net of discount (and corrected for the error).

Check May 30, Dr. Cash $2,352

31 Sold merchandise that cost $3,600 to Four Winds Co. for $7,200 under credit terms of 2/10, n/60, FOB shipping point.

The following unadjusted trial balance is prepared at fiscal year-end for Durable Products Co.:

Problem 4-3B

Preparing adjusting entries and income statements, and computing gross margin, acid-test, and current ratios

A2 A3 **P3 P4**

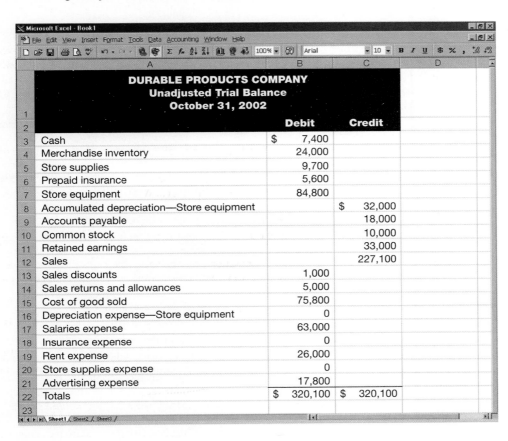

DURABLE PRODUCTS COMPANY
Unadjusted Trial Balance
October 31, 2002

	Debit	Credit
Cash	$ 7,400	
Merchandise inventory	24,000	
Store supplies	9,700	
Prepaid insurance	5,600	
Store equipment	84,800	
Accumulated depreciation—Store equipment		$ 32,000
Accounts payable		18,000
Common stock		10,000
Retained earnings		33,000
Sales		227,100
Sales discounts	1,000	
Sales returns and allowances	5,000	
Cost of good sold	75,800	
Depreciation expense—Store equipment	0	
Salaries expense	63,000	
Insurance expense	0	
Rent expense	26,000	
Store supplies expense	0	
Advertising expense	17,800	
Totals	$ 320,100	$ 320,100

Rent and salaries expenses are equally divided between the selling activities and the general and administrative activities. Durable Products Company uses a perpetual inventory system.

Required

1. Prepare adjusting journal entries to reflect the following:

   a. Store supplies available at fiscal year-end amount to $3,700.

   b. Expired insurance, an administrative expense, for the fiscal year is $2,800.

   c. Depreciation expense on store equipment, a selling expense, is $3,000 for the fiscal year.

   d. To estimate shrinkage, a physical count of ending merchandise inventory is taken. It shows $21,300 of goods are available for sale.

2. Prepare a multiple-step income statement for fiscal year 2002.

3. Prepare a single-step income statement for fiscal year 2002.

4. Compute the current ratio, acid-test ratio, and gross margin ratio as of October 31, 2002.

Check (2) Gross profit, $142,600; (3) Total expenses, $197,100; Net income, $24,000

Problem 4-4B

Computing merchandising amounts and formatting an income statement

C5 A1 P4

Ryan Company's adjusted trial balance on March 31, 2002, its fiscal year-end, follows:

	Debit	Credit
Merchandise inventory..................	$ 56,500	
Other (noninventory) assets.............	202,600	
Liabilities		$ 42,500
Common stock.......................		25,000
Retained earnings....................		136,425
Sales................................		332,650
Sales discounts	5,875	
Sales returns and allowances...........	20,000	
Cost of goods sold...................	115,600	
Sales salaries expense	44,500	
Rent expense—Selling space	16,000	
Store supplies expense................	3,850	
Advertising expense	26,000	
Office salaries expense...............	40,750	
Rent expense—Office space............	3,800	
Office supplies expense...............	1,100	
Totals............................	$536,575	$536,575

On March 31, 2001, merchandise inventory was $37,500. Supplementary records of merchandising activities for the year ended March 31, 2002, reveal the following itemized costs:

Invoice cost of merchandise purchases	$138,500
Purchase discounts received	2,950
Purchase returns and allowances	6,700
Costs of transportation-in	5,750

Required

1. Calculate the company's net sales for the year.

Check (2) $134,600; (3) Gross profit, $191,175; Net income, $55,175; (4) Total expenses, $251,600

2. Calculate the company's total cost of merchandise purchased for the year.

3. Prepare a multiple-step income statement that lists the company's net sales, cost of goods sold, and gross profit, as well as the components and amounts of selling expenses and of general and administrative expenses.

4. Prepare a single-step income statement that lists these costs: cost of goods sold, selling expenses, and general and administrative expenses.

5. Accounts receivable increased by $50,000 during the period. Calculate cash received from customers.

Problem 4-5B

Preparing closing entries and interpreting information about discounts and returns

C5 P3

Check (1) $55,175 Dr. to close Income Summary

Check (3) Current-year rate, 6.0%

Use the data for Ryan Company in Problem 4-4B to complete the following requirements:

Required

Preparation Component

1. Prepare closing entries as of March 31, 2002 (the perpetual inventory system is used).

Analysis Component

2. The company makes all purchases on credit, and its suppliers uniformly offer a 3% sales discount. Does it appear that the company's cash management system is accomplishing the goal of taking all available discounts? Explain.

3. In prior years, the company experienced a 4% returns and allowance rate on its sales, which means approximately 4% of its gross sales were eventually returned outright or caused the company to grant allowances to customers. How do this year's results compare to prior years' results?

(The first two segments of this serial problem were presented in Chapters 2 and 3. If those segments have not been completed, the assignment can begin at this point. You should use the Working Papers that accompany this text because they reflect the account balances that resulted from posting the entries required in Chapters 2 and 3.)

SERIAL PROBLEM

Sierra Systems

Earlier segments of this problem have described how Sela Solstise created Sierra Systems on October 1, 2002. The company has been successful, and its list of customers has grown. To accommodate the growth, the accounting system is modified to set up separate accounts for each customer. The following list of customers includes the account number used for each account and any balance as of December 31, 2002. Solstise decided to add a fourth digit with a decimal point to the 106 account number that had been used for the single Accounts Receivable account. This modification allows the company to continue using the existing chart of accounts.

Customer Account	No.	12/31/02 Balance
Antonio's Engineering Co.	106.1	$ 0
Alexander Services	106.2	0
Prime Leasing	106.3	0
Dade Co.	106.4	3,000
Elan Corporation	106.5	0
Foster Co.	106.6	2,668
Olathe Co.	106.7	0
Taos, Inc.	106.8	0
Imagine, Inc.	106.9	0

In response to requests from customers, Solstise has decided to begin selling computer software. The company also will extend credit terms of 1/10, n/30 to all customers who purchase this merchandise. No cash discount will be available on consulting fees. The following additional accounts are added to the general ledger to allow the system to account for the company's new merchandising activities:

Account	No.
Merchandise Inventory	119
Sales	413
Sales Returns and Allowances	414
Sales Discounts	415
Cost of Goods Sold	502

Sierra Systems does not use reversing entries and, therefore, all revenue and expense accounts have zero balances as of January 1, 2003. Its transactions for January through March follow:

Jan. 4   Paid cash to Suzie Smith for five days' work at the rate of $125 per day. Four of the five days relate to wages payable that were accrued in the prior year.

5   Sela Solstise invested an additional $25,000 cash in the business in exchange for stock.

7   Purchased $5,800 of merchandise from Jersey Corp. with terms of 1/10, n/30, FOB shipping point.

9   Received $2,668 cash from Foster Co. as full payment on its account.

11   Completed a five-day project for Antonio's Engineering Co. and billed it $5,500, which is the total price of $7,000 less the advance payment of $1,500.

13   Sold merchandise with a retail value of $5,200 and a cost of $3,560 to Elan Corporation with terms of 1/10, n/30, FOB shipping point.

15   Paid $600 cash for freight charges on the merchandise purchased on January 7.

16   Received $4,000 cash from Olathe Co. for computer services provided.

17   Paid Jersey Corp. for the purchase on January 7, net of the discount.

20   Elan Corporation returned $500 of defective merchandise from its purchase on January 13. The returned merchandise, which had a $320 cost, is discarded.

22   Received the balance due from Elan Corporation, net of both the discount and the credit for the returned merchandise.

24   Returned defective merchandise to Jersey Corp. and accepted a credit against future purchases. Its cost, net of the discount, was $496.

26   Purchased $9,000 of merchandise from Jersey Corp. with terms of 1/10, n/30, FOB destination.

26   Sold merchandise with a $4,640 cost for $5,800 on credit to Taos, Inc.

29   Received a $496 credit memorandum from Jersey Corp. concerning the merchandise re-
turned on January 24.
31   Paid cash to Suzie Smith for 10 days' work at $125 per day.
Feb. 1   Paid $2,475 cash to Hilldale Mall for another three months' rent in advance.
3   Paid Jersey Corp. for the balance due, net of the cash discount, less the $496 amount in
the credit memorandum.
5   Paid $600 cash to the local newspaper for an advertising insert in today's paper.
11   Received the balance due from Antonio's Engineering Co. for fees billed on January 11.
15   Paid $4,800 cash in dividends.
23   Sold merchandise with a $2,660 cost for $3,220 on credit to Olathe Co.
26   Paid cash to Suzie Smith for eight days' work at $125 per day.
27   Reimbursed Sela Solstise for business automobile mileage (600 miles at $0.32 per mile).
Mar. 8   Purchased $2,730 of computer supplies from Appier Office Products on credit.
9   Received the balance due from Olathe Co. for merchandise sold on February 23.
11   Paid $960 cash for minor repairs to the company's computer.
16   Received $5,260 cash from Imagine, Inc., for computing services provided.
19   Paid the full amount due to Appier Office Products, including amounts created on December
15 and March 8.
24   Billed Prime Leasing for $8,900 of computing services provided.
25   Sold merchandise with a $2,002 cost for $2,800 on credit to Alexander Services.
30   Sold merchandise with a $1,100 cost for $2,220 on credit to Dade Company.
31   Reimbursed Sela Solstise for business automobile mileage (400 miles at $0.32 per mile).

The following additional facts are available for preparing adjustments on March 31 prior to financial
statement preparation:

a. The March 31 inventory of computer supplies totals $2,005.
b. Three more months have expired since the company purchased its annual insurance policy at a
$2,220 cost for 12 months of coverage.
c. Suzie Smith has not been paid for seven days of work.
d. Three months have passed since any prepaid rent has been transferred to expense. The monthly
rent is $825.
e. Depreciation on the computer equipment for January 1 through March 31 is $1,250.
f. Depreciation on the office equipment for January 1 through March 31 is $400.
g. The March 31 amount of merchandise inventory totals $704.

Required

1. Prepare journal entries to record each of the January through March transactions.

Check (2) Ending balances: Cash,
$77,845; Inventory, $794; Sales,
$19,240; (3) Unadj. totals, $156,398;
Adj. totals, $158,923; (4) Net
income, $18,686; (5) R.E. (3/31/03),
$21,034; (6) Total assets, $129,909

2. Post the journal entries in part 1 to the accounts in the company's general ledger. (*Note:* Begin
with the ledger's post-closing adjusted balances as of December 31, 2002.)
3. Prepare a partial work sheet consisting of the first six columns (similar to the one shown in Exhibit
4A.3) that includes the unadjusted trial balance, the March 31 adjustments (*a*) through (*g*), and
the adjusted trial balance. Do not prepare closing entries and do not journalize the adjustments or
post them to the ledger.
4. Prepare an income statement (from the adjusted trial balance in part 3) for the three months ended
March 31, 2003. Use a single-step format. List all expenses without differentiating between selling expenses and general and administrative expenses.
5. Prepare a statement of retained earnings (from the adjusted trial balance in part 3) for the three
months ended March 31, 2003.
6. Prepare a balance sheet (from the adjusted trial balance in part 3) as of March 31, 2003.

BEYOND THE NUMBERS

Reporting in Action

C5 A2 🔼

NIKE

BTN 4-1   Refer to Nike's financial statements in Appendix A to answer the following.

Required

1. Assume that the amounts reported for inventories and cost of sales reflect items purchased in a form
ready for resale. Compute the net cost of goods purchased for the fiscal year ended May 31, 2000.
2. Compute the current ratio and acid-test ratio as of May 31, 2000, and May 31, 1999. Interpret and
comment on the ratio results.

Swoosh Ahead

3. Access Nike's financial statements (form 10-K) for fiscal years ending after May 31, 2000, from its Web site (www.nike.com) or the SEC's EDGAR database (www.sec.gov). Recompute and interpret the current ratio and acid-test ratio for these fiscal years.

BTN 4-2   Key comparative figures ($ millions) for both Nike and Reebok follow:

Key Figures	Nike Current Year	Nike Prior Year	Reebok Current Year	Reebok Prior Year
Revenues (net sales)	$8,995.1	$8,776.9	$2,899.9	$3,224.6
Cost of sales	5,403.8	5,493.5	1,783.9	2,037.5

Comparative Analysis

A3 🗗

Reebok

NIKE

Required

1. Compute the dollar amount of gross margin and the gross margin ratio for the two years shown for both companies.

2. Which company earns more in gross margin for each dollar of net sales?

3. Did the gross margin ratios improve or decline for these companies?

BTN 4-3   Helen Gaines is a student who plans to attend approximately four professional events a year at her college. Each event necessitates a financial outlay of $100–$200 for a new suit and accessories. After incurring a major hit to her savings for the first event, Helen developed a different approach. She buys the suit on credit the week before the event, wears it to the event, and returns it the next week to the store for a full refund on her charge card.

Ethics Challenge

P2

Required

1. Comment on the ethics exhibited by Helen and possible consequences of her actions.

2. How does the merchandising company account for the suits that Helen returns?

BTN 4-4   You are the financial officer for Music and More, a retailer that sells goods for home entertainment needs. The business owner, Mr. U. Paah, recently reviewed the annual financial statements you prepared and sent you an e-mail stating that he thinks you overstated net income. He explains that although he has invested a great deal in security, he is sure shoplifting and other forms of inventory shrinkage have occurred, but he does not see any deduction for shrinkage on the income statement. The store uses a perpetual inventory system.

Communicating in Practice

C4 C5 P3 🗗 ℯ

Required

Prepare a brief memorandum that responds to the owner's concerns in paper or e-mail format. If the response is made via e-mail, assume that your instructor is the owner instead of Mr. U. Paah.

BTN 4-5   Access the SEC's EDGAR database (www.sec.gov) and obtain the June 2, 2000, filing of its 10-K report (for the year ended March 31, 2000) for eToys.com Inc. (ticker ETYS). Construct a three-year trend of gross margin ratios for eToys using the net sales and cost of goods sold data from eToys' income statement. Analyze and comment on the trend.

Taking It to the Net

C1 🗗 ℯ

BTN 4-6   World Brands' general ledger and supplementary records at the end of its current period reveal the following:

Teamwork in Action

C2 C5 A3

Sales	$430,000	Merchandise inventory (beginning of period) ..	$ 49,000
Sales returns	18,000	Invoice cost of merchandise purchases	180,000
Sales discounts	6,600	Purchase discounts received	4,500
Cost of transportation-in ...	11,000	Purchase returns and allowances	5,500
Operating expenses	20,000	Merchandise inventory (end of period)	42,000

Required

Point: In teams of four, assign the same student *a* and *e*. Rotate teams for reporting on a different computation and the analysis in step 3.

1. *Each* member of the team is to assume responsibility for computing *one* of the following items. You are not to duplicate your teammates' work. Get any necessary amounts to compute your item from the appropriate teammate. Each member is to explain his or her computation to the team in preparation for reporting to the class.

   a. Net sales   **d.** Gross profit

   b. Total cost of merchandise purchases   **e.** Net income

   c. Cost of goods sold

2. Check your net income with the instructor. If correct, proceed to step 3.

3. Assume that a physical inventory count finds that actual ending inventory is $38,000. Discuss how this affects previously computed amounts in step 1.

Business Week Activity

P4 𝒹

BTN 4-7   Read the article, "You Can Survive Online Shopping" in the December 6, 1999, issue of *Business Week*. (Access the book's Web site for a free link.)

Required

1. How does the 1999 projected dollar volume of online November and December shopping compare to the 1998 figure?

2. Return policies for e-merchants vary widely. Discuss the variety of return policies implemented by online retailers.

3. What account title would you recommend an online retailer use to record goods returned that were purchased online? Would you record these returns in a separate account from goods that were purchased in a store and returned (assuming the retailer operates a "brick-and-mortar" storefront as well as online retailing)? Explain your answer.

Entrepreneurial Decision

C1 C5 P4

𝑒 𝒹

BTN 4-8   Steve Miller is an entrepreneur who buys and sells new and used musical instruments to small retail outlets that offer musical instruments and training to customers. He recently completed his first year of operations. His income statement follows:

MUSICAL NIRVANA Income Statement For Year Ended January 31, 2002	
Net sales	$ 250,000
Cost of sales	(175,000)
Expenses	(20,000)
Net income	$ 55,000

To increase income, Miller is proposing to offer sales discounts of 3/10, n/30, and to ship all merchandise FOB shipping point. He presently offers no discounts and ships merchandise FOB destination. The discounts are predicted to increase net sales by 14%; and the ratio of cost of sales divided by net sales is expected to remain unchanged. Since delivery expenses are zero under this proposal, the expenses are predicted to increase by only 10%.

Required

1. Prepare a forecasted income statement for the year ended January 31, 2003, based on Miller's proposal.

2. Do you recommend that Miller implement his proposal given your analysis in part 1?

3. Identify any concerns you might express to Miller regarding his proposal.

Hitting the Road

C1 𝒹 𝑒

BTN 4-9   Arrange an interview (in person or by phone) with the manager of a retail shop in a mall or in the downtown area of your community. Explain to the manager that you are a student studying merchandising activities and the accounting for sales returns and sales allowances. Ask the manager what the store policy is regarding returns. Also find out if the sales allowances are ever negotiated with customers. Inquire whether management perceives that customers are abusing return policies and what actions management takes to counter potential abuses. Be prepared to discuss your findings in class.

Point: This activity complements the Ethics Challenge assignment.

BTN 4-10   Read the article "An Adrenalin Rush at Adidas," in the September 29, 1997, issue of *Business Week*. (Access the book's Web site for a free link.)

Global Decision
P4

Required

1. The article identifies Adidas (www.adidas.com/investor) as the number two company in the sporting goods market. What companies are numbers one and three respectively?
2. What strategy is Adidas using to compete more effectively against its number one rival?
3. After reading the article, do you think the strategy of Adidas will be effective? Explain.
4. Consult the notes of the annual report of Nike in Appendix A. Identify the advertising and promotion expenses incurred by Nike. Compare advertising expenses of Nike to those incurred by Adidas.
5. Identify where advertising expenses are reported in the financial statements of Nike.

5

Reporting and Analyzing Inventories

A Look Back

Chapter 4 focused on merchandising activities and how they are reported and analyzed. We also analyzed and recorded merchandise purchases and sales and explained accounting adjustments and the closing process for merchandising companies.

A Look at This Chapter

This chapter emphasizes accounting for inventory. We describe the methods available for assigning costs to inventory and explain the items and costs making up merchandise inventory. We also analyze the effects of inventory on both financial and tax reporting, and we discuss other methods of estimating and measuring inventory.

A Look Ahead

Chapter 6 focuses on internal controls and accounting for cash and cash equivalents. We explain good internal control procedures and their importance for accounting and analysis.

"I'm making babies smile . . . this is beautiful stuff!"—Julie Aigner-Clark

Conceptual

C1 Identify the items making up merchandise inventory.

C2 Identify the costs of merchandise inventory.

Analytical

A1 Analyze the effects of inventory methods for both financial and tax reporting.

A2 Analyze the effects of inventory errors on current and future financial statements.

A3 Assess inventory management using both inventory turnover and days' sales in inventory.

Procedural

P1 Compute inventory in a perpetual system using the methods of specific identification, FIFO, LIFO, and weighted average.

P2 Compute the lower of cost or market amount of inventory.

P3 Apply both the retail inventory and gross profit methods to estimate inventory.

Decision Feature

Mother of Invention

e LITTLETON, CO—While pregnant with her first child, Julie Aigner-Clark ran across articles showing that exposure to a variety of language sounds in infancy helps children learn languages later on. Yet Aigner-Clark found nothing in stores that could provide infants with such exposure, so she decided to create a video that would do so. Dubbed *Baby Einstein,* it featured various images with an audio backdrop of mothers singing songs and reciting nursery rhymes in different languages. Aigner-Clark hired the women from a language school and instructed them to speak in "motherese," that high-pitched tone that most mothers use when talking to infants. Says Aigner-Clark, "I wanted something that was not only entertaining but stimulating and engaging."

Right Start, a children's retail and catalog company, agreed to sell the video, which quickly became the store's fastest-moving item. Aigner-Clark soon formed a company, **Baby Einstein (www.BabyEinstein.com),** and followed up with more videos as well as CDs, DVDs, multilingual flash cards, books, and puppets. Now, five years later, her annual sales are a projected $10 million. One of her biggest obstacles, and continuing challenges, is maintaining the right inventories and controlling costs of sales. Success is more than having good products, says Aigner-Clark; it also depends on assigning and monitoring costs of inventory and applying sound inventory management procedures. With business booming, she notes, inventory costs must be kept in check to avoid a downturn. Moreover, she keeps watch over inventory turnover and days' sales in inventory. This chapter focuses on measuring, monitoring, and managing inventories. But Aigner-Clark keeps it all in perspective: "I'm making babies smile. Can you think of anything more wonderful?" By the looks of it, we'd say Aigner-Clark is smiling with them. [Sources: Baby Einstein Web site, January 2002; *Entrepreneur,* November 2000; *Time,* March 20, 2000.]

Merchandisers' activities include purchasing and reselling of merchandise. We explained accounting for merchandisers in Chapter 4, including that for sales and purchases. In this chapter, we extend the study and analysis of inventory by explaining the methods used to assign costs to merchandise inventory *and* to cost of goods sold. Many retailers, wholesalers, and other merchandising companies that purchase products for resale use the principles and methods we describe. These principles and methods affect reported amounts of income, assets, equity, revenues, and expenses. Understanding fundamental concepts of inventory accounting increases our ability to analyze and interpret financial statements. An understanding of these topics also helps people run their own businesses.

Assigning Costs to Inventory

Accounting for inventory affects both the balance sheet and the income statement. A major goal in accounting for inventory is to match relevant costs against revenues. This is important to properly compute income. We use the *matching principle* to decide how much of the cost of the goods available for sale is deducted from sales and how much is carried forward as inventory and matched against future sales. Management must make this decision and several others when accounting for inventory. These decisions include selecting the

- Costing method (specific identification, FIFO, LIFO, or weighted average).
- Inventory system (perpetual or periodic).
- Items included in inventory and their costs.
- Use of market values or other estimates.

P1 Compute inventory in a perpetual system using the methods of specific identification, FIFO, LIFO, and weighted average.

Decisions on these points affect the reported amounts for inventory, cost of goods sold, gross profit, income, current assets, and other accounts. This chapter discusses all of these important issues and their effects on accounting reports and analysis.

One of the most important decisions in accounting for inventory is determining the per unit costs assigned to inventory items. When all units are purchased at the same unit cost, this process is simple. When identical items are purchased at different costs, however, a question arises as to which amounts to record in cost of goods sold when sales occur and which amounts remain in inventory. How we assign these costs to inventory and cost of goods sold affects the financial statements and their analysis.

Four methods are commonly used to assign costs to inventory and cost of goods sold: (1) specific identification; (2) first-in, first-out; (3) last-in, first-out; and (4) weighted average. Each method assumes a particular pattern for how costs flow through inventory. Each of these four methods is acceptable whether or not the actual physical flow of goods follows the cost flow assumption.[1] Exhibit 5.1 shows the frequency in the use of these methods.

Exhibit 5.1

Frequency in Use of Inventory Methods

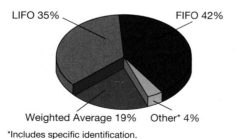

LIFO 35% FIFO 42%

Weighted Average 19% Other* 4%

*Includes specific identification.

We use information from Trekking, a sporting goods store, to describe the four methods. Among its many products, Trekking carries one type of mountain bike whose sales are directed at biking clubs. Its customers usually purchase in amounts of 10 or more bikes. We use data from Trekking's August 2002. Its mountain bike (unit) inventory at the beginning of August and its purchases during August are shown in Exhibit 5.2.

---

[1] Physical flow of goods depends on the type of product and the way it is stored. Perishable goods such as fresh fruit demand that a business attempt to sell them in a first-in, first-out physical flow pattern. Other products such as lanterns or grills can often be sold in a last-in, first-out physical flow pattern. Physical flow and cost flow need not be the same.

Aug.	1	Beginning inventory	10 units @ $ 91 = $ 910
Aug.	3	Purchases	15 units @ $106 = 1,590
Aug.	17	Purchases	20 units @ $115 = 2,300
Aug.	28	Purchases	10 units @ $119 = 1,190
		Totals	55 units $5,990

Exhibit 5.2

Cost of Goods Available for Sale

Trekking had two large sales of mountain bikes to two different biking clubs in August as shown in Exhibit 5.3. It ends August with 12 bikes remaining in inventory.

Aug. 14	Sales	20 units @ $130 = $2,600
Aug. 31	Sales	23 units @ $150 = 3,450
	Totals	43 units $6,050

Exhibit 5.3

Retail Sales of Goods

Trekking uses the perpetual inventory system. We explained in Chapter 4 that use of the perpetual inventory system is increasing as a result of advances in information and computing technology. Widespread use of electronic scanners and product bar codes encourages a perpetual inventory system. **(In Appendix 5A, we describe the assignment of costs to inventory using a periodic system.)** Regardless of what inventory method or system is used, cost of goods available for sale is allocated between cost of goods sold and ending inventory.

Point: Cost of goods sold plus ending inventory equals cost of goods available for sale.

Trekking's use of a perpetual inventory system means that its merchandise inventory account is continually updated to reflect purchases and sales. As described in Chapter 4, the important accounting aspects of a perpetual system are:

■ Each purchase of merchandise for resale increases (debits) inventory.
■ Each sale of merchandise decreases (credits) inventory and increases (debits) costs of goods sold.
■ Necessary costs of merchandise such as transportation-in increase (debit) inventory, and cost reductions such as purchase discounts and purchase returns and allowances decrease (credit) inventory.

Point: Three key variables determine the dollar value of ending inventory: (1) inventory quantity, (2) costs of inventory, and (3) cost flow assumption.

Except for any inventory shrinkage, the balance in the Merchandise Inventory account reflects the cost of merchandise available for sale at all times.

Specific Identification

When each item in inventory can be identified with a specific purchase and its invoice, we can use **specific identification** (also called *specific invoice inventory pricing*) to assign costs. We also need sales records that identify exactly which items were sold and when. Trekking's internal documents reveal that 7 of the 12 unsold units were from the August 28 purchase and 5 were from the August 17 purchase. We use this information and the specific identification method to assign costs to the 12 units in ending inventory and to the 43 units sold as shown in Exhibit 5.4. Notice that each unit, whether sold or remaining in inventory, has its own specific cost attached to it.

Point: Inventories are a large portion of current asset for most wholesalers, retailers, and manufacturers. Accounting for inventories is key to determining cost of goods sold and gross profit.

When using specific identification, Trekking's cost of goods sold reported on the income statement totals **$4,582**, the sum of $2,000 and $2,582 from the third column of Exhibit 5.4. Trekking's ending inventory reported on the balance sheet is **$1,408**, which is the final inventory balance from the fourth column of Exhibit 5.4. *The assignment of costs to the goods sold and to inventory using specific identification is the same for both the perpetual and periodic systems.*

Point: Companies with expensive, custom-made inventory often use specific identification.

Exhibit 5.4

Specific Identification
Computations

For the 20 units sold on Aug. 14, the company specifically identified that 8 of those had cost $91 and 12 had cost $106.

For the 23 units sold on Aug. 31, the company specifically identified each bike sold and its acquisition cost.

	"goods in"	"goods out"	"what's left"

Date	Purchases	Cost of Goods Sold	Inventory Balance
Aug. 1	Beginning balance		10 @ $ 91 = $ 910
Aug. 3	15 @ $106 = $1,590		10 @ $ 91 15 @ $106 } = $2,500
Aug. 14		8 @ $ 91 = $ 728 12 @ $106 = $1,272 } = $2,000*	2 @ $ 91 3 @ $106 } = $ 500
Aug. 17	20 @ $115 = $2,300		2 @ $ 91 3 @ $106 20 @ $115 } = $2,800
Aug. 28	10 @ $119 = $1,190		2 @ $ 91 3 @ $106 20 @ $115 10 @ $119 } = $3,990
Aug. 31		2 @ $ 91 = $ 182 3 @ $106 = $ 318 15 @ $115 = $1,725 3 @ $119 = $ 357 } = $2,582*	5 @ $115 7 @ $119 } = $1,408

* Identification of items sold (and their costs) is obtained from internal documents that track each unit from its purchase to its sale.

First-In, First-Out

Point: The "Purchases" column is identical across all methods. The data are taken from Exhibit 5.2.

The **first-in, first-out (FIFO)** method of assigning costs to both inventory and cost of goods sold assumes that inventory items are sold in the order acquired. When sales occur, the costs of the earliest units acquired are charged to cost of goods sold. This leaves the costs from the most recent purchases in ending inventory. Use of FIFO for computing the cost of inventory and cost of goods sold is shown in Exhibit 5.5.

Exhibit 5.5

FIFO Computations—
Perpetual System

For the 20 units sold on Aug. 14, the first 10 sold are assigned the earliest cost of $91 (from beg. bal.). The next 10 sold are assigned the next earliest cost of $106.

For the 23 units sold on Aug. 31, the first 5 sold are assigned the earliest available cost of $106 (from Aug. 3 purchase). The next 18 sold are assigned the next earliest cost of $115 (from Aug. 17 purchase).

Date	Purchases	Cost of Goods Sold	Inventory Balance
Aug. 1	Beginning balance		10 @ $ 91 = $ 910
Aug. 3	15 @ $106 = $1,590		10 @ $ 91 15 @ $106 } = $2,500
Aug. 14		10 @ $ 91 = $ 910 10 @ $106 = $1,060 } = $1,970	5 @ $106 = $ 530
Aug. 17	20 @ $115 = $2,300		5 @ $106 20 @ $115 } = $2,830
Aug. 28	10 @ $119 = $1,190		5 @ $106 20 @ $115 10 @ $119 } = $4,020
Aug. 31		5 @ $106 = $ 530 18 @ $115 = $2,070 } = $2,600	2 @ $115 10 @ $119 } = $1,420

Point: Under FIFO, a unit sold is assigned the earliest (oldest) cost from inventory. This leaves the most recent costs in ending inventory.

Trekking's FIFO cost of goods sold reported on the income statement (reflecting the 43 units sold) is **$4,570** ($1,970 + $2,600), and its ending inventory reported on the balance sheet (reflecting the 12 units unsold) is **$1,420**. *The assignment of costs to the goods sold and to inventory using FIFO is the same for both the perpetual and periodic systems.*

Last-In, First-Out

The **last-in, first-out (LIFO)** method of assigning costs assumes that the most recent purchases are sold first. These more recent costs are charged to the goods sold, and the costs of the earliest purchases are assigned to inventory. As with other methods, LIFO is acceptable even when the physical flow of goods does not follow a last-in, first-out pattern. One appeal of LIFO is that by assigning costs from the most recent purchases to cost of goods sold, LIFO comes closest to matching current replacement costs with revenues (compared to FIFO or weighted average). While costs for the most recent purchases are not exactly replacement costs, they usually are close approximations. Exhibit 5.6 shows how LIFO assigns the costs of mountain bikes to the 12 units in ending inventory and to the 43 units sold.

Topic Tackler 5-1

Point: Under LIFO, a unit sold is assigned the most recent (latest) cost from inventory. This leaves the oldest costs in inventory.

Date	Purchases	Cost of Goods Sold	Inventory Balance
Aug. 1	Beginning balance		10 @ $ 91 = $ 910
Aug. 3	15 @ $106 = $1,590		10 @ $ 91 } 15 @ $106 } = $2,500
Aug. 14		15 @ $106 = $1,590 } 5 @ $ 91 = $ 455 } = $2,045	5 @ $ 91 = $ 455
Aug. 17	20 @ $115 = $2,300		5 @ $ 91 } 20 @ $115 } = $2,755
Aug. 28	10 @ $119 = $1,190		5 @ $ 91 } 20 @ $115 } = $3,945 10 @ $119 }
Aug. 31		10 @ $119 = $1,190 } 13 @ $115 = $1,495 } = $2,685	5 @ $ 91 } 7 @ $115 } = $1,260

Exhibit 5.6

LIFO Computations—
Perpetual System

For the 20 units sold on Aug. 14, the first 15 sold are assigned the most recent cost of $106. The next 5 sold are assigned the next most recent cost of $91.

For the 23 units sold on Aug. 31, the first 10 sold are assigned the most recent cost of $119. The next 13 sold are assigned the next most recent cost of $115.

Trekking's LIFO cost of goods sold reported on the income statement is $4,730 ($2,045 + $2,685), and its ending inventory reported on the balance sheet is $1,260. The assignment of costs to cost of goods sold and to inventory using LIFO usually gives different results between the perpetual and the periodic systems. This is so because LIFO under a perpetual system assigns the most recent costs to goods sold at the time of each sale, whereas the periodic system waits to assign costs until the end of a period.

Global: LIFO is mainly used in the U.S. In some countries, such as Australia, Ireland, and the United Kingdom, the use of LIFO is rare.

Weighted Average

The **weighted average** (also called **average cost**) method of assigning cost requires that we compute the weighted average cost per unit of inventory at the time of each sale. Weighted average cost per unit at the time of each sale equals the cost of goods available for sale divided by the units available. The results using weighted average for Trekking are shown in Exhibit 5.7.

Trekking's cost of goods sold reported on the income statement (reflecting the 43 units sold) is $4,622 ($2,000 + $2,622), and its ending inventory reported on the balance sheet (reflecting the 12 units unsold) is $1,368. The assignment of costs to cost of goods sold and to inventory using weighted average usually yields different results between the perpetual and the periodic systems. This is so because weighted average under a perpetual system recomputes the per unit cost at the time of each sale, whereas under the periodic system, the per unit cost is computed only at the end of a period.

Point: Under weighted average, a unit sold is assigned the average cost of all items currently available for sale at the date of each sale.

Inventory Costing and Technology

A perpetual inventory system can be kept in either electronic or manual form. Using a manual form can make a perpetual inventory system too costly for some businesses, especially those with many purchases and sales and with many units in inventory. Advances in information and computing technology have greatly reduced the cost of a perpetual inventory system. Many companies are now asking whether they can afford *not* to have a perpetual inventory system

Point: Inventory methods of assigning costs need not follow the physical flow of inventory.

Exhibit 5.7

Weighted Average
Computations—Perpetual
System

For the 20 units sold on Aug. 14,
the cost assigned is the most
recent *average cost* per unit from
the inventory balance column.

Date	Purchases	Cost of Goods Sold	Inventory Balance
Aug. 1	Beginning balance		10 @ $ 91 = $ 910
Aug. 3	15 @ $106 = $1,590		10 @ $ 91 ⎫ = $2,500 (or $100 per unit)[a] 15 @ $106 ⎭
Aug. 14		20 @ $100 = **$2,000**	5 @ $100 = $ 500 (or $100 per unit)[b]
Aug. 17	20 @ $115 = $2,300		5 @ $100 ⎫ = $2,800 (or $112 per unit)[c] 20 @ $115 ⎭
Aug. 28	10 @ $119 = $1,190		5 @ $100 ⎫ 20 @ $115 ⎬ = $3,990 (or $114 per unit)[d] 10 @ $119 ⎭
Aug. 31		23 @ $114 = **$2,622**	12 @ $114 = **$1,368** (or $114 per unit)[e]

[a] $100 per unit = ($2,500 inventory balance ÷ 25 units in inventory).
[b] $100 per unit = ($500 inventory balance ÷ 5 units in inventory).
[c] $112 per unit = ($2,800 inventory balance ÷ 25 units in inventory).
[d] $114 per unit = ($3,990 inventory balance ÷ 35 units in inventory).
[e] $114 per unit = ($1,368 inventory balance ÷ 12 units in inventory).

Decision Insight

Battle of Inventory   The Pentagon applies accounting skills to
shrink inventories and speed deliveries. Use of bar codes, laser cards,
radio tags, and accounting databases to track supplies speeds
delivery from factory to foxhole.

because timely access to inventory information
is a competitive advantage. Scanned sales data,
for instance, can reveal crucial information on
buying patterns. It can also help companies target promotional and advertising activities. These
and other applications have greatly increased the
use of the perpetual inventory system.

Decision Track 5.1   *d*

Decision Point	Information Search	Analyze & Evaluate
What inventory costing method should a company adopt?	Business operations, cost trends, and financial statements.	Depends on goals. When costs are rising, inventory and income are lower and cash flow is higher using LIFO; FIFO yields opposite results. The weighted average method usually yields results between LIFO and FIFO.

Inventory Analysis and Effects

This section analyzes and compares the alternative inventory costing methods. We also analyze the tax effects of inventory methods, examine managers' preferences for an inventory
method, and consider the effects of inventory errors.

Financial Reporting

A1   Analyze the effects of inventory methods for both financial and tax reporting.

When purchase prices do not change, each inventory costing method assigns the same cost
amounts to inventory and to cost of goods sold. When purchase prices are different, however, the methods are likely to assign different cost amounts. We show these differences in
Exhibit 5.8 using Trekking's segment income statement for its mountain bike operations.
The different inventory costing methods show different results for net income. Since Trekking's
purchase costs rose in August, FIFO assigned the least amount to cost of goods sold. This led
to the highest gross profit and the highest net income. In contrast, LIFO assigned the highest
amount to cost of goods sold. This yielded the lowest gross profit and the lowest net income.
As expected, amounts from using the weighted average method fell between FIFO and LIFO.
(The weighted average amount can be outside the FIFO or LIFO amounts if costs do not

TREKKING COMPANY Segment Income Statement — Mountain Bikes For Month Ended August 31				
	Specific Identification	FIFO	LIFO	Weighted Average
Sales	$6,050	$6,050	$6,050	$6,050
Cost of goods sold	4,582	4,570	4,730	4,622
Gross profit	$1,468	$1,480	$1,320	$1,428
Expenses	450	450	450	450
Income before taxes	$1,018	$1,030	$ 870	$ 978
Income tax expense (30%)	305	309	261	293
Net income	$ 713	$ 721	$ 609	$ 685

Exhibit 5.8

Income Statement Effects of Inventory Costing Methods

steadily increase or decrease but exhibit a cyclical pattern.) The amounts from using specific identification depend on which units are actually sold.

All four inventory costing methods are acceptable in practice. Each method offers certain advantages. One advantage of specific identification is that it exactly matches costs and revenues. This is important when each unit has unique features affecting its cost. An advantage of weighted average is that it tends to smooth out changes in costs. An advantage of FIFO is that it assigns an amount to inventory on the balance sheet that closely approximates current replacement cost. An advantage of LIFO is that it assigns the most recent costs incurred to cost of goods sold and likely better matches current costs with revenues on the income statement. The choice of an inventory costing method can greatly impact amounts on financial statements. In its financial statements or notes, a company must disclose the inventory method it uses.

It is important to understand inventory costing for analysis of financial statements. Some companies' financial statements help in our analysis by reporting what the difference would be if another costing method were used. **Kmart**, for instance, reports in a recent annual report: "Inventories valued on LIFO were $194, $202 and $249 [$ millions] lower than amounts that would have been reported using the first-in, first-out (FIFO) method at year end . . . [for the most recent 3 years], respectively." Companies using LIFO must always disclose the amount that inventory would increase or decrease if FIFO were used. This amount is called the *LIFO reserve*. To adjust LIFO inventory and LIFO cost of goods sold (COGS) to FIFO amounts, we use these adjustments:

Global: Swiss standards require no disclosures related to inventory.

Point: LIFO inventory often understates the inventory's replacement cost because LIFO inventory is valued using the oldest inventory purchase costs.

Point: *LIFO reserve* is the amount by which FIFO (replacement cost) inventory exceeds the LIFO inventory amount.

Decision Maker

Financial Planner   One of your clients asks if the inventory account of a company using FIFO needs any "adjustments" for analysis purposes in light of recent inflation. What is your advice? Does your advice depend on changes in the costs of these inventories?

Answer—p. 232

$$\textbf{FIFO inventory} = \textbf{LIFO inventory} + \textbf{LIFO reserve}$$

$$\textbf{FIFO COGS} = \textbf{LIFO COGS} - \textbf{Increase (or + Decrease) in LIFO reserve}$$

When a company is using LIFO, these adjustments are potentially important for analyses that use ratios such as the current ratio, inventory turnover, and days' sales in inventory.[2]

Point: Analysts often adjust LIFO inventory to approximate FIFO inventory for ratios based on reported LIFO inventory figures because FIFO inventory better reflects current costs. It also helps in comparing companies using LIFO to those using FIFO.

---

[2] To illustrate, Z-Mart uses LIFO and reports the following year-end financial data ($ thousands):

	2002	**2001**
LIFO inventory	$160	$110
LIFO cost of goods sold	740	680
LIFO reserve	80	35

We compute its FIFO numbers for 2002 as follows:
FIFO inventory = $160 + $80 = $240
FIFO COGS = $740 − ($80 − $35) = $695

Decision Track 5.2

Decision Point	Information Search	Analyze & Evaluate
How is reported inventory impacted by use of LIFO?	Balance sheet, income statement, and LIFO reserve disclosures.	Restate key financials to assess impact: FIFO inventory = LIFO inventory + LIFO reserve; and FIFO COGS = LIFO COGS − Increase (or + Decrease) in LIFO reserve.

Tax Reporting

Trekking's segment income statement in Exhibit 5.8 includes income tax expense (at a rate of 30%). Since inventory costs affect net income, they have potential tax effects for corporations. Trekking gains a temporary tax advantage by using LIFO. This advantage occurs because LIFO assigns a larger dollar amount to cost of goods sold when purchase costs are increasing, as in the case of Trekking. This means that less income is reported when LIFO is used *and* purchase costs are rising. This in turn results in less income tax expense.

The Internal Revenue Service (IRS) identifies several acceptable methods for inventory costing in reporting taxable income for corporations. It is important to know that companies can and often do use different costing methods for financial reporting and tax reporting. *The only exception is when LIFO is used for tax purposes; in this case, the IRS requires that it be used in financial statements.* Since costs tend to rise, LIFO usually gives a lower taxable income and a tax advantage. Many companies use LIFO for this reason. Yet managers often have incentives to report higher net income for reasons such as bonus plans, job security, and reputation. FIFO is sometimes preferred in these cases because it tends to report a higher income when costs are rising.

Global: Countries allowing LIFO for tax reporting include Germany, Belgium, Japan, Taiwan, and South Korea.

Decision Insight

Entrepreneurial Giving Many entrepreneurs donate 10% or more of their pretax income to charities. Consultants cite evidence that socially conscious behavior brings tangible financial rewards. A recent survey found 76% of buyers saying they'd switch from their current store to one with a good cause if price and quality are equal.

Consistency in Reporting

Inventory costing methods can affect amounts on financial statements, and some managers are inclined to choose a method most consistent with their hoped-for results each period. One objective might be to pick the method giving the most favorable financial statement amounts. Managers might also be inclined to pick the method giving them the highest bonus since many management bonus plans are based on net income. If managers were allowed to pick the method *each* period, users of financial statements would have more difficulty comparing a company's financial statements from one period to the next. If income increased, for instance, a user would need to assess whether it resulted from successful operations or from an accounting method change. Using the consistency principle helps a company avoid this problem.

Global: LIFO is acceptable under international accounting standards.

The **consistency principle** requires a company to use the same accounting methods period after period so that financial statements are comparable across periods. The consistency principle applies to all accounting methods. When a company must choose between alternative methods, consistency requires that the company continue to use the selected method period after period. Users of financial statements can then make comparisons of a company's statements across periods.

The consistency principle does *not* require a company to use one method exclusively. It can use different methods to value different categories of inventory. Harley-Davidson, for instance, reports the following: "Inventories located in the United States are valued using the last-in, first-out (LIFO) method. Other inventories . . . are valued at the lower of cost or market using the first-in, first-out (FIFO) method." Also, the consistency principle does not

imply that a company can never change from one accounting method to another. Instead it means that a company must argue that the method to which it is changing will improve its financial reporting. When an alternative method will improve its reporting, a change is acceptable. The *full-disclosure principle* requires that the notes to the statements report this type of change, its justification, and its effect on net income.

Decision Ethics

Inventory Manager Your compensation as inventory manager includes a bonus plan based on gross profit. Your superior asks your opinion on changing the inventory costing method from FIFO to LIFO. Since costs are expected to continue to rise, your superior predicts that LIFO would match higher current costs against sales, thereby lowering taxable income (and gross profit). What do you recommend?

Answer—p. 232

Errors in Reporting Inventory

Companies must take care in both computing and taking a physical count of inventory. An inventory error causes misstatements in cost of goods sold, gross profit, net income, current assets, and equity. It also causes misstatements in the next period's statements because ending inventory of one period is the beginning inventory of the next. An error carried forward causes misstatements in the next period's cost of goods sold, gross profit, and net income. Such misstatements can reduce the usefulness of financial statements.

A2 Analyze the effects of inventory errors on current and future financial statements.

Income Statement Effects

The income statement effects of an inventory error are evident by reviewing the components of cost of goods sold as shown in Exhibit 5.9—this relation applies to both the perpetual and periodic systems. The effect of an inventory error on cost of goods sold can be determined by computing it with the incorrect amount and comparing it to cost of goods sold when using the correct amount.

Topic Tackler 5-2

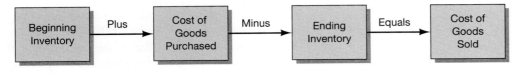

Exhibit 5.9

Cost of Goods Sold Components

We can see, for example, that understating ending inventory in a physical count overstates cost of goods sold. An overstatement in cost of goods sold yields an understatement in net income. We can do the same analysis with overstating ending inventory and for errors in beginning inventory. Exhibit 5.10 shows the effects of inventory errors on the current period's income statement amounts. Notice that inventory errors yield opposite effects in cost of goods sold and net income. Inventory errors also carry over to the next period, yielding reverse effects.

Inventory Error	Cost of Goods Sold	Net Income
Understate ending inventory	Overstated	Understated
Understate beginning inventory	Understated	Overstated
Overstate ending inventory*	Understated	Overstated
Overstate beginning inventory*	Overstated	Understated

Exhibit 5.10

Effects of Inventory Errors on the Current Period's Income Statement

*These errors are less likely under a perpetual system because they suggest more inventory than is recorded (or less shrinkage than expected). Thus, management will normally follow up and discover and correct these errors before they impact any accounts.

To show these effects, consider an inventory error for a company with $100,000 in sales for years 2001, 2002, and 2003. If this company maintains a steady $20,000 inventory level during this period and makes $60,000 in purchases in each of these years, its cost of goods sold is $60,000 and its gross profit is $40,000 each year. But what if this company errs in computing its 2001 ending inventory and reports $16,000 instead of the correct amount of $20,000? The effects of this error are shown in Exhibit 5.11. The $4,000 understatement of the year 2001 ending inventory causes a $4,000 overstatement in year 2001 cost of goods

Exhibit 5.11

Effects of Inventory Errors on Three Periods' Income Statements

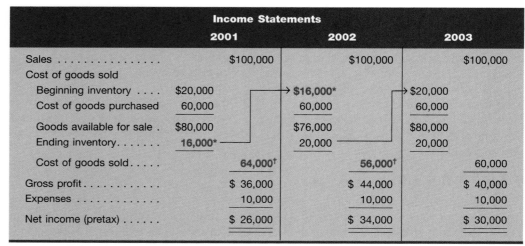

	Income Statements					
		2001		**2002**		**2003**
Sales		$100,000		$100,000		$100,000
Cost of goods sold						
Beginning inventory	$20,000		$16,000*		$20,000	
Cost of goods purchased	60,000		60,000		60,000	
Goods available for sale	$80,000		$76,000		$80,000	
Ending inventory	16,000*		20,000		20,000	
Cost of goods sold		64,000†		56,000†		60,000
Gross profit		$ 36,000		$ 44,000		$ 40,000
Expenses		10,000		10,000		10,000
Net income (pretax)		$ 26,000		$ 34,000		$ 30,000

* Correct amount is $20,000.   † Correct amount is $60,000.

Example: If year 2001 ending inventory in Exhibit 5.11 is overstated by $3,000, what is the effect on cost of goods sold, gross profit, assets, and equity?
Answer: Cost of goods sold is understated by $3,000 in 2001 and overstated by $3,000 in 2002. Gross profit and net income are overstated in 2001 and understated in 2002. Assets and equity are overstated in 2001.

sold and a $4,000 understatement in both gross profit and net income for year 2001. Since year 2001 ending inventory becomes year 2002 beginning inventory, this error causes an understatement in 2002 cost of goods sold and a $4,000 overstatement in both gross profit and net income for year 2002. Notice that an inventory error in one period does not affect the third period, year 2003. Also, an inventory error is said to be *self-correcting* because it always yields an offsetting error in the next period. This, however, does not make inventory errors less serious. Managers, lenders, owners, and other users make important decisions from analysis of changes in net income and cost of goods sold.

Balance Sheet Effects

Balance sheet effects of an inventory error are evident by considering the components of the accounting equation: Assets = Liabilities + Equity. For example, understating ending inventory understates both current and total assets. An understatement in ending inventory also yields an understatement in equity because of the understatement in net income. Exhibit 5.12 shows the effects of inventory errors on the current period's balance sheet amounts. Errors in *beginning* inventory do not yield misstatements in the end-of-period balance sheet, but they do affect the current period's income statement.

Exhibit 5.12

Effects of Inventory Errors on Current Period's Balance Sheet

Inventory Error	Assets	Equity
Understate ending inventory	Understated	Understated
Overstate ending inventory	Overstated	Overstated

Quick Check

1. Describe one advantage for each of the inventory costing methods: specific identification, FIFO, LIFO, and weighted average.
2. When costs are rising, which method reports higher net income—LIFO or FIFO?
3. When costs are rising, what effect does LIFO have on a balance sheet compared to FIFO?
4. A company takes a physical count of inventory at the end of 2002 and finds that ending inventory is understated by $10,000. Would this error cause cost of goods sold to be overstated or understated in 2002? In year 2003? If so, by how much?

Answers—p. 233

This section identifies the items and costs making up merchandise inventory. This identification is important given the major impact of inventory in financial statements. We also describe the importance of and the method used in taking a physical count of inventory.

Items in Merchandise Inventory

Merchandise inventory includes all goods that a company owns and holds for sale. This rule holds regardless of where the goods are located when inventory is counted. Certain inventory items require special attention, including goods in transit, goods on consignment, and goods that are damaged or obsolete.

C1 Identify the items making up merchandise inventory.

Goods in Transit

Does a purchaser's inventory include goods in transit from a supplier? The answer is that if ownership has passed to the purchaser, the goods are included in the purchaser's inventory. Chapter 4 explained how we determine this by reviewing the shipping terms—*FOB destination* or *FOB shipping point*. If the purchaser is responsible for paying freight, ownership passes when goods are loaded on the transport vehicle. If the seller is responsible for paying freight, ownership passes when goods arrive at their destination.

Point: Ownership of merchandise held for resale determines whether or not it is included in inventory. This is consistent with the definition of assets in Chapter 1.

Goods on Consignment

Goods on consignment are goods shipped by the owner, called the **consignor,** to another party, the **consignee.** A consignee sells goods for the owner. The consignor owns consigned goods and reports them in its inventory. Score Board, Tri Star, and Upper Deck, for instance, pay sports celebrities such as Tiger Woods and Ken Griffey, Jr., to sign memorabilia. These autographed items (footballs, baseballs, jerseys, photos) are offered to shopping networks on consignment and are sold through catalogs and dealers. The consignor must report these items in its inventory until sold.

Goods Damaged or Obsolete

Damaged goods and obsolete (or deteriorated) goods are not counted in inventory if they are unsalable. If these goods are salable at a reduced price, they are included in inventory at a conservative estimate of their **net realizable value.** Net realizable value is sales price minus the cost of making the sale. The period when damage or obsolescence (or deterioration) occurs is the period when the loss in value is reported.

Costs of Merchandise Inventory

Merchandise inventory includes costs of expenditures necessary, directly or indirectly, to bring an item to a salable condition and location. This means that the cost of an inventory item includes its invoice cost minus any discount, and plus any added or incidental costs necessary to put it in a place and condition for sale. Added or incidental costs can include import duties, transportation-in, storage, insurance, and costs incurred in an aging process (for example, aging wine or cheese).

Accounting principles require that incidental costs be assigned to the units purchased. The purpose is to properly match all inventory costs against revenue in the period when inventory is sold. Some companies use the *materiality principle* or the *cost-to-benefit constraint* to avoid assigning incidental costs of acquiring merchandise to inventory. These companies argue either that incidental costs are immaterial or that the effort in assigning these costs to inventory outweighs the benefit. Such

> ### Decision Insight
>
> **Inventory Online** Warehouse clerks can quickly record inventory by scanning bar codes. Thanks to Motorola, a wireless portable computer with a two-way radio allows clerks to send and receive data instantly. It gives managers immediate access to up-to-date information on inventory and its location.

C2 Identify the costs of merchandise inventory.

> ### Decision Insight
>
> **Express Lane Shopping** Some retailers are adding bar code readers on shopping carts for customers to swipe the product over the reader, automatically charging it to a credit card. There is no need to stand in a checkout line. Customers simply pass through a gate that verifies that everything in the cart has been scanned.

companies often value inventory using invoice costs only. When this is done, the incidental costs are allocated to cost of goods sold in the period when they are incurred.

Physical Count of Merchandise Inventory

The Inventory account under a perpetual system is updated for each purchase and sale, but events can cause the account balance to be different from the actual inventory available. Such events include theft, loss, damage, and errors. Thus, nearly all companies take a *physical count of inventory* at least once each year, the process informally called *taking an inventory.* This often occurs at the end of a fiscal year or when inventory amounts are low. This physical count is used to adjust the Inventory account balance to the actual inventory available.

We determine a dollar amount for the physical count of inventory available by (1) counting the units of each product, (2) multiplying the count for each product by its cost per unit, and (3) adding the costs for all products. When taking a count, items are less likely to be counted more than once or omitted if prenumbered inventory tickets are used. We show a typical inventory ticket in Exhibit 5.13. Conducting a physical count is a fairly standard procedure. We first prepare at least one inventory ticket for each product. These tickets are issued to employees doing the count. An employee counts the quantity of a product and obtains information on its purchase date, selling price, and cost. This information is sometimes included with the product but often must be obtained from accounting records or invoices. The employee enters the findings on the inventory ticket and signs it. The inventory ticket is then attached to the counted inventory. Another employee often re-counts the product and rechecks the ticket, signs it, and returns it to the manager. To ensure that no ticket is lost or missed, internal control procedures verify that all prenumbered tickets are returned. The unit and cost data on inventory tickets are aggregated by multiplying the number of units for each product by its unit cost. The sum total of all product costs is the amount reported for inventory on the balance sheet.

Point: The Merchandise Inventory account is a controlling account for the merchandise inventory subsidiary ledger. This *subsidiary ledger* contains a separate record (units and costs) for each separate product, and it can be in electronic or paper form. Subsidiary records assist managers in planning and monitoring inventory.

Exhibit 5.13
Inventory Ticket

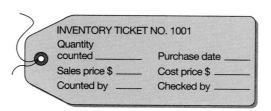

Quick Check

5. What accounting principle most guides the allocation of cost of goods available for sale between ending inventory and cost of goods sold?

6. If Nike sells goods to Target with terms FOB shipping point, which company reports these goods in its inventory while they are in transit?

7. An art gallery purchases a painting for $11,400 on terms FOB shipping point. Additional costs in obtaining and offering the artwork for sale include $130 for transportation-in, $150 for import duties, $100 for insurance during shipment, $180 for advertising, $400 for framing, and $800 for office salaries. For computing inventory, what cost is assigned to the painting?

Answers—p. 233

Other Inventory Valuations

This section describes other methods to value inventory. Knowledge of these methods is important for understanding and analyzing financial statements.

Lower of Cost or Market

We explained how to assign costs to ending inventory and cost of goods sold using one of four costing methods (FIFO, LIFO, weighted average, or specific identification). However, *accounting principles require that inventory be reported at the market value (cost) of replacing inventory when market value is lower than cost.* Merchandise inventory is then said to be reported on the balance sheet at the **lower of cost or market (LCM).**

P2 Compute the lower of cost or market amount of inventory.

Computing the Lower of Cost or Market

Market in the term LCM is defined as the current replacement cost of purchasing the same inventory items in the usual manner. A decline in replacement cost reflects a loss of value in inventory. When the recorded cost of inventory is higher than the replacement cost, a loss is recognized. LCM is applied in one of three ways: (1) to each individual item separately, (2) to major categories of items, or (3) to the entire inventory. The less similar the items that make up inventory, the more likely companies are to apply LCM to individual items. Advances in technology further encourage the individual-item approach. To illustrate, we apply LCM to the ending inventory of a motorsports retailer. Inventory data for this retailer and LCM computations are shown in Exhibit 5.14.

Inventory Items	Units	Per Unit Cost	Per Unit Market	Total Cost	Total Market	LCM Applied to Items	LCM Applied to Categories	LCM Applied to Whole
Cycles								
Roadster	20	$8,000	$7,000	$160,000	$140,000	$140,000		
Sprint	10	5,000	6,000	50,000	60,000	50,000		
Category subtotal				210,000	200,000		$200,000	
Off-Road								
Trax-4	8	5,000	6,500	40,000	52,000	40,000		
Blazer	5	9,000	7,000	45,000	35,000	35,000		
Category subtotal				85,000	87,000		85,000	
Totals				$295,000	$287,000	$265,000	$285,000	$287,000

Exhibit 5.14

Lower of Cost or Market Computations

When LCM is applied to the *entire* inventory, the market cost is $287,000. Since this market cost is $8,000 lower than the $295,000 recorded cost, it is the amount reported for inventory on the balance sheet. When LCM is applied to the major *categories* of inventory, the market cost is $285,000. When LCM is applied to individual *items* of inventory, the market cost is $265,000. Since market cost for these cases is less than the $295,000 recorded cost, market cost is the amount reported for inventory. Any one of these three applications of LCM is acceptable. The retailer **Best Buy** applies LCM and reports that its "merchandise inventories are recorded at the lower of average cost or market."

Global: In Canada, the Netherlands, and the United Kingdom, the *market* in LCM is defined as "net realizable value" (selling price less costs to complete and sell).

The *direct method* is a common way to record inventory at LCM—it substitutes market cost (when lower) for recorded cost in the inventory account. Using LCM applied to individual *items* of inventory in Exhibit 5.14, we would make the following entry: Cost of Goods Sold, Dr. $30,000; Merchandise Inventory, Cr. $30,000. The Merchandise Inventory account balance would then be $265,000, computed as $295,000 minus $30,000.

Conservatism Principle

Accounting rules require recording inventory down to market cost when market cost is less than recorded cost, but inventory usually cannot be written up to market cost when market exceeds recorded cost. If recording inventory down to market is acceptable, why are companies not allowed to record inventory up to market? One reason is the view that any gain from a market increase not be realized until a sales transaction verifies the gain. However, this problem also applies when market is less than recorded cost. The second and primary reason is the **conservatism principle,** which requires the use of the less optimistic amount when more than one estimate of the amount to be received or paid in the future exists and these estimates are about equally likely.

P3   Apply both the retail inventory and gross profit methods to estimate inventory.

Retail Inventory Method

Many companies prepare quarterly or monthly financial statements, called **interim statements** because they are prepared between the traditional annual statements. The cost of goods sold information needed to prepare interim statements is readily available if the company uses a perpetual inventory system but requires a physical inventory if the company uses a periodic system. To avoid the time-consuming and expensive process of taking a physical inventory each month or quarter, some companies use the **retail inventory method** to estimate cost of goods sold and ending inventory. Some companies even use the retail inventory method to prepare the annual statements. Home Depot, for instance, says in its recent annual report: "Inventories are stated at the lower of cost (first-in, first-out) or market, as determined by the retail inventory method." A company may also estimate inventory for audit purposes or when inventory is damaged or destroyed.

The retail inventory method uses a three-step process to estimate ending inventory. We need to know the amount of inventory a company had at the beginning of the period in both *cost* and *retail* amounts. We already explained how to compute the cost of inventory. The retail amount of inventory refers to its dollar amount measured using selling prices of inventory items. We also need to know the net amount of goods purchased (minus returns, allowances, and discounts) in the period, both at cost and at retail. The amount of net sales at retail is also needed. The process is shown in Exhibit 5.15.

The reasoning behind the retail inventory method is that if we can get a good estimate of the cost-to-retail ratio, we can multiply ending inventory at retail by this ratio to estimate ending inventory at cost. We show in Exhibit 5.16 how these steps are applied to estimate ending inventory for a typical company. First, we find that $100,000 of goods (at retail selling prices) were available for sale. We see that $70,000 of these goods were sold, leaving $30,000 (retail value) of merchandise in ending inventory. Second, the cost of these goods is 60% of the $100,000 retail value. Third, since cost for these goods is 60% of retail, the estimated cost of ending inventory is $18,000.

Exhibit 5.15

Retail Inventory Method of Inventory Estimation

Step 1: Goods Available for Sale at Retail − Net Sales at Retail = Ending Inventory at Retail

Step 2: Goods Available for Sale at Cost ÷ Goods Available for Sale at Retail = Cost to Retail Ratio

Step 3: Ending Inventory at Retail × Cost-to-Retail Ratio = Estimated Ending Inventory at Cost

Point: When a retailer takes a physical inventory, it can restate the retail value of inventory to a cost basis by applying the cost-to-retail ratio. It can also estimate the amount of shrinkage by comparing the inventory computed with the amount from a physical inventory.

Exhibit 5.16

Estimated Inventory Using the Retail Inventory Method

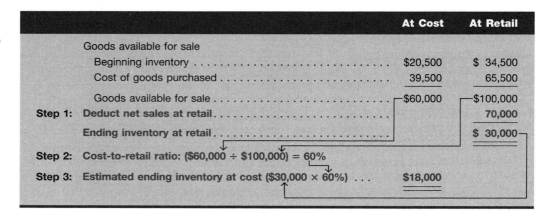

		At Cost	At Retail
Goods available for sale			
Beginning inventory		$20,500	$ 34,500
Cost of goods purchased		39,500	65,500
Goods available for sale		$60,000	$100,000
Step 1:	Deduct net sales at retail		70,000
	Ending inventory at retail		$ 30,000
Step 2:	Cost-to-retail ratio: ($60,000 ÷ $100,000) = 60%		
Step 3:	Estimated ending inventory at cost ($30,000 × 60%)	$18,000	

Example: What is the cost of ending inventory in Exhibit 5.16 if the cost of beginning inventory is $22,500 and its retail value is $34,500? *Answer:* $30,000 × 62% = $18,600

Gross Profit Method

The **gross profit method** estimates the cost of ending inventory by applying the gross profit ratio to net sales (at retail). This type of estimate often is needed when inventory is destroyed, lost, or stolen. These cases require an inventory estimate so that a company can file a claim with its insurer. Users also apply this method to see whether inventory amounts from a physical count are reasonable. This method uses the historical relation between cost of goods sold and net sales to estimate the proportion of cost of goods sold making up current sales. This cost of goods sold estimate is then subtracted from cost of goods available for sale to estimate the ending inventory at cost. These two steps are shown in Exhibit 5.17.

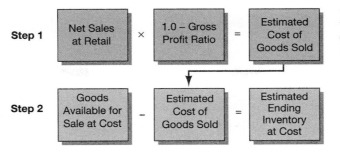

Exhibit 5.17
Gross Profit Method of Inventory Estimation

To illustrate, assume that a company's inventory is destroyed by fire in March 2002. When the fire occurs, the company's accounts show the following balances for January through March: sales, $31,500; sales returns, $1,500; inventory (January 1, 2002), $12,000; and cost of goods purchased, $20,500. If this company's gross profit ratio is 30%, then 30% of each net sales dollar is gross profit and 70% is cost of goods sold. We show in Exhibit 5.18 how this 70% is used to estimate lost inventory of $11,500. To understand this exhibit, think of subtracting cost of goods sold from the goods available for sale to get ending inventory.

Point: A fire or other catastrophe can result in an insurance claim for lost inventory or income. Backup procedures for financial data and off-site storage of data help ensure coverage for such losses.

Point: Reliability of the gross profit method depends on a good estimate of the gross profit ratio.

Goods available for sale	
Inventory, January 1, 2002	$12,000
Cost of goods purchased	20,500
Goods available for sale (at cost)	32,500
Net sales at retail ($31,500 − $1,500)	$30,000
Step 1: Estimated cost of goods sold ($30,000 × 70%)	(21,000) ← × 0.70
Step 2: Estimated March inventory at cost	$11,500

Exhibit 5.18
Estimated Inventory Using the Gross Profit Method

Quick Check

8. Use LCM applied separately to individual items to compute this company's ending inventory if the data are as follows:

Product	Units	Unit Recorded Cost	Unit Market Cost
A	20	$ 6	$ 5
B	40	9	8
C	10	12	15

9. Using the retail method and the following data, estimate the cost of ending inventory.

	Cost	Retail
Beginning inventory	$324,000	$530,000
Cost of goods purchased	195,000	335,000
Net sales		320,000

Answers—p. 233

Decision Analysis Inventory Turnover and Days' Sales in Inventory

This section describes how we use information about inventory to assess a company's short-term liquidity (ability to pay) and its management of inventory.

Inventory Turnover

A3 Assess inventory management using both inventory turnover and days' sales in inventory.

We described in earlier chapters two important ratios useful in evaluating a company's short-term liquidity: current ratio and acid-test ratio. A merchandiser's ability to pay its short-term obligations also depends on how quickly it sells its merchandise inventory. **Inventory turnover,** also called *merchandise inventory turnover,* is one ratio used to assess this. It is computed as shown in Exhibit 5.19.

Exhibit 5.19
Inventory Turnover

$$\text{Inventory turnover} = \frac{\text{Cost of goods sold}}{\text{Average inventory}}$$

This ratio reveals how many *times* a company turns over its inventory during a period. Average inventory is usually computed by adding a period's beginning and ending inventory amounts and dividing the total by two. If a company's inventory greatly varies within a year, it is often better to average inventory amounts from the end of each quarter or month.

Point: We must take care when comparing turnover ratios across companies that use different costing methods (such as FIFO and LIFO).

Users apply inventory turnover to help analyze short-term liquidity and to assess whether management is doing a good job controlling the amount of inventory available. A low ratio compared to that of competitors suggests inefficient use of assets. The company may be holding more inventory than it needs to support its sales volume. Similarly, a very high ratio compared to that of competitors suggests inventory might be too low. This can cause lost sales because customers must back order merchandise. Inventory turnover has no simple rule except to say *a high ratio is preferable provided inventory is adequate to meet demand.*

Decision Insight

Dell-ocity   From its roots in a college dorm room, Dell now sells 50 million dollars' worth of computers each day from its Web site. The speed of Web technology has allowed Dell to slash inventories. Dell's operating cycle is less than 15 hours and its days' sales in inventory is 3 days. Michael Dell asserts, "Speed is everything in this business."

Days' Sales in Inventory

To better interpret inventory turnover, many users measure the adequacy of inventory to meet sales demand. **Days' sales in inventory,** also called *days' stock on hand,* is a ratio that reveals how much inventory is available in terms of the number of days' sales. It can be interpreted as the number of days one can sell from inventory if no new items are purchased. This ratio is often viewed as a measure of the buffer against out-of-stock inventory and is useful in evaluating liquidity of inventory. Days' sales in inventory is computed as shown in Exhibit 5.20.

Exhibit 5.20
Days' Sales in Inventory

$$\text{Days' sales in inventory} = \frac{\text{Ending inventory}}{\text{Cost of goods sold}} \times 365$$

Days' sales in inventory focuses on ending inventory and it estimates how many days it will take to convert inventory at the end of a period into accounts receivable or cash. Notice that days' sales in inventory focuses on *ending* inventory whereas inventory turnover focuses on *average* inventory.

Analysis of Inventory Management

Inventory management is a major emphasis for most merchandisers. They must both plan and control inventory purchases and sales. Toys "R" Us is one of those merchandisers. Its merchandise inventory in 2000 was $2,027 million. This inventory constituted 70% of its current assets and 24% of its total assets. We apply the analysis tools in this section to Toys "R" Us, as shown in Exhibit 5.21.

($ in millions)	2000	1999	1998
Cost of goods sold	$8,321	$8,191	$7,710
Ending merchandise inventory	$2,027	$1,902	$2,464
Inventory turnover	4.24 times	3.75 times	3.30 times
Industry inventory turnover	3.01 times	2.88 times	2.76 times
Days' sales in inventory	88.9 days	84.8 days	116.6 days
Industry days' sales in inventory	121.3 days	126.7 days	129.7 days

Exhibit 5.21

Inventory Turnover and Days' Sales in Inventory for Toys "R" Us

Its 2000 inventory turnover of 4.24 is computed as $8,321 ÷ [($2,027 + $1,902) ÷ 2]. This means that Toys "R" Us turns over its inventory 4.24 times per year, or once every 86 days (365 days ÷ 4.24). We prefer inventory turnover to be high provided inventory is not out of stock and the company is not losing customers. The 2000 days' sales in inventory of 88.9 for Toys "R" Us helps us assess this likelihood and is computed as ($2,027 ÷ $8,321) × 365. This tells us it is carrying 88.9 days of sales in inventory. This inventory buffer seems more than adequate. Toys "R" Us might benefit from further management efforts to increase inventory turnover.

Decision Maker

Entrepreneur Analysis of your retail store yields an inventory turnover of 5.0 and a days' sales in inventory of 73 days. The industry norm for inventory turnover is 4.4 and for days' sales in inventory is 74 days. What is your assessment of inventory management?

Answer—p. 233

Demonstration Problem

Mozart Company uses a perpetual inventory system for its one product. Its beginning inventory and purchases during year 2002 follow:

Date		Units	Unit Cost
Jan. 1	Beg. Inventory . . .	400	$14
March 10	Purchase	200	15
May 9	Purchase	300	16
Sept. 22	Purchase	250	20
Nov. 28	Purchase	100	21

At December 31, 2002, 550 units remain in inventory. Sales in year 2002 are as follows:

Jan. 15	200 units at $30
April 1	200 units at $30
Nov. 1	300 units at $35

Additional tracking data for applying specific identification: (1) January 15 sale—200 units @ $14, (2) April 1 sale—200 units @ $15, and (3) November 1 sale—200 units @ $14 and 100 units @ $20.

Required

1. Calculate the cost of goods available for sale.
2. Apply the four different methods of inventory costing (FIFO, LIFO, weighted average, and specific identification) to calculate ending inventory and cost of goods sold under each method.
3. In preparing financial statements for year 2002, the financial officer was instructed to use FIFO but failed to do so and instead computed cost of goods sold according to LIFO. Determine the impact on year 2002's income from the error. Also determine the effect of this error on year 2003's income. Assume no income taxes.
4. Management wants a report that shows how changing from FIFO to another method would change net income. Prepare a table showing (1) the cost of goods sold amount under each of the four methods, (2) the amount by which each cost of goods sold total is different from the FIFO cost of goods sold, and (3) the effect on net income if another method is used instead of FIFO.

Planning the Solution

- Compute cost of goods available for sale by multiplying the units of beginning inventory and each purchase by their unit costs to determine the total cost of goods available for sale.
- Prepare a perpetual FIFO table starting with beginning inventory and showing how inventory changes after each purchase and after each sale (see Exhibit 5.5).
- Prepare a perpetual LIFO table starting with beginning inventory and showing how inventory changes after each purchase and after each sale (see Exhibit 5.6).
- Make a table of purchases and sales recalculating the average cost of inventory after each purchase to arrive at the weighted average cost of ending inventory. Total the average costs associated with each sale to determine cost of goods sold (see Exhibit 5.7).
- Prepare a table showing the computation of cost of goods sold and ending inventory using the specific identification method (see Exhibit 5.4).
- Compare the year-end 2002 inventory amounts under FIFO and LIFO to determine the misstatement of year 2002 income that results from using LIFO. The errors for year 2002 and 2003 are equal in amount but opposite in effect.
- Create a table showing cost of goods sold under each method and how net income would differ from FIFO net income if an alternate method is adopted.

Solution to Demonstration Problem

1. Cost of goods available for sale (this amount is the same for all methods):

Date		Units	Unit Cost	Total Cost
Jan. 1	Beg. Inventory	400	$14	$ 5,600
March 10	Purchase	200	15	3,000
May 9	Purchase	300	16	4,800
Sept. 22	Purchase	250	20	5,000
Nov. 28	Purchase	100	21	2,100
Total cost of goods available for sale				$20,500

2a. FIFO perpetual method:

Date	Purchases	Cost of Goods Sold	Inventory Balance
Jan. 1	Beginning balance		400 @ $14 = $ 5,600
Jan. 15		200 @ $14 = $2,800	200 @ $14 = $ 2,800
Mar. 10	200 @ $15 = $3,000		200 @ $14 200 @ $15 } = $ 5,800
April 1		200 @ $14 = $2,800	200 @ $15 = $ 3,000
May 9	300 @ $16 = $4,800		200 @ $15 300 @ $16 } = $ 7,800
Sept. 22	250 @ $20 = $5,000		200 @ $15 300 @ $16 250 @ $20 } = $12,800
Nov. 1		200 @ $15 = $3,000 100 @ $16 = $1,600	200 @ $16 250 @ $20 } = $ 8,200
Nov. 28	100 @ $21 = $2,100		200 @ $16 250 @ $20 100 @ $21 } = $10,300
Total cost of goods sold		$10,200	

Note to students: **In a classroom situation,** once we compute cost of goods available for sale, we can compute the amount for either cost of goods sold or ending inventory—it is a matter of preference. **In practice,** the costs of items sold are identified as sales are made and immediately transferred from the inventory account to the cost of goods sold account. The previous solution showing the line-by-line approach illustrates actual application in practice. The following alternate solutions illustrate that, once the concepts are understood, other solution approaches are available.

Alternate Methods to Compute FIFO Perpetual Numbers

[FIFO Alternate No. 1: Computing cost of goods sold first]

Cost of goods available for sale (from part 1)		$20,500
Cost of goods sold		
Jan. 15 Sold (200 @ $14)	$ 2,800	
April 1 Sold (200 @ $14)	2,800	
Nov. 1 Sold (200 @ $15 and 100 @ $16)	4,600	10,200
Ending inventory		**$10,300**

[FIFO Alternate No. 2: Computing ending inventory first]

Cost of goods available for sale (from part 1)		$20,500
Ending inventory*		
Nov. 28 Purchase (100 @ $21)	$2,100	
Sept. 22 Purchase (250 @ $20)	5,000	
May 9 Purchase (200 @ $16)	3,200	
Ending inventory		10,300
Cost of goods sold		**$10,200**

* Since FIFO assumes that the earlier costs are the first to flow out, we determine ending inventory by assigning the most recent costs to the remaining items.

2b. LIFO perpetual method:

Date	Purchases	Cost of Goods Sold	Inventory Balance
Jan. 1	Beginning balance		400 @ $14 = $ 5,600
Jan. 15		200 @ $14 = $2,800	200 @ $14 = $ 2,800
Mar. 10	200 @ $15 = $3,000		200 @ $14 200 @ $15 } = $ 5,800
April 1		200 @ $15 = $3,000	200 @ $14 = $ 2,800
May 9	300 @ $16 = $4,800		200 @ $14 300 @ $16 } = $ 7,600
Sept. 22	250 @ $20 = $5,000		200 @ $14 300 @ $16 250 @ $20 } = $12,600
Nov. 1		250 @ $20 = $5,000 50 @ $16 = $ 800	200 @ $14 250 @ $16 } = $ 6,800
Nov. 28	100 @ $21 = $2,100		200 @ $14 250 @ $16 100 @ $21 } = $ 8,900
Total cost of goods sold		**$11,600**	

Alternate Methods to Compute LIFO Perpetual Numbers

[LIFO Alternate No. 1: Computing cost of goods sold first]

Cost of goods available for sale (from part 1)		$20,500
Cost of goods sold with LIFO perpetual		
Jan. 15 200 units @ $14	$2,800	
April 1 200 units @ $15	3,000	
Nov. 1 { 250 units @ $20	5,000	
{ 50 units @ $16	800	
Cost of goods sold		11,600
Ending inventory		$ 8,900

[LIFO Alternate No. 2: Computing ending inventory first]

Cost of goods available for sale (from part 1)		$20,500
Ending inventory with LIFO perpetual		
Jan. 1 Inventory (200 @ $14)	$2,800	
May 9 Purchase (250 @ $16)	4,000	
Nov. 28 Purchase (100 @ $21)	2,100	
Ending inventory		8,900
Cost of goods sold		$11,600

2c. Weighted average perpetual method:

Date	Purchases	Cost of Goods Sold	Inventory Balance
Jan. 1	Beginning balance		400 @ $14 = $ 5,600
Jan. 15		200 @ $14 = $2,800	200 @ $14 = $ 2,800
Mar. 10	200 @ $15 = $3,000		200 @ $14 } 200 @ $15 } = $ 5,800 (avg. cost is $14.5)
April 1		200 @ $14.5 = $2,900	200 @ $14.5 = $ 2,900
May 9	300 @ $16 = $4,800		200 @ $14.5 } 300 @ $16 } = $ 7,700 (avg. cost is $15.4)
Sept. 22	250 @ $20 = $5,000		200 @ $14.5 } 300 @ $16 } = $12,700 250 @ $20 } (avg. cost is $16.93)
Nov. 1		300 @ $16.93 = $5,079	450 @ $16.93 = $7,618.5
Nov. 28	100 @ $21 = $2,100		450 @ $16.93 } = $9,718.5 100 @ $21 }
Total cost of goods sold*		**$10,779**	

* The cost of goods sold ($10,779) plus ending inventory ($9,718.5) is $2.5 less than the cost of goods available for sale ($20,500) due to rounding.

2d. Specific identification method:

Date	Purchases	Cost of Goods Sold	Inventory Balance
Jan. 1	Beginning balance		400 @ $14 = $ 5,600
Jan. 15		200 @ $14 = $2,800	200 @ $14 = $ 2,800
Mar. 10	200 @ $15 = $3,000		200 @ $14 } 200 @ $15 } = $ 5,800
April 1		200 @ $15 = $3,000	200 @ $14 = $ 2,800
May 9	300 @ $16 = $4,800		200 @ $14 } 300 @ $16 } = $ 7,600
Sept. 22	250 @ $20 = $5,000		200 @ $14 } 300 @ $16 } = $12,600 250 @ $20 }
Nov. 1		200 @ $14 = $2,800 100 @ $20 = $2,000	300 @ $16 } 150 @ $20 } = $ 7,800
Nov. 28	100 @ $21 = $2,100		300 @ $16 } 150 @ $20 } = $ 9,900 100 @ $21 }
Total cost of goods sold		**$10,600**	

[Specific Identification Alternate No. 1: Computing cost of goods sold first]

Cost of goods available for sale (from part 1)			$20,500
Cost of goods sold			
Jan. 1	Purchase (400 @ $14)	$5,600	
March 10	Purchase (200 @ $15)	3,000	
Nov. 28	Purchase (100 @ $20)	2,000	
Total cost of goods sold			**10,600**
Ending inventory			**$ 9,900**

[Specific Identification Alternate No. 2: Computing ending inventory first]

Cost of goods available for sale (from part 1)			$20,500
Ending inventory			
May 9	Purchase (300 @ $16)	$4,800	
Sept. 22	Purchase (150 @ $20)	3,000	
Nov. 28	Purchase (100 @ $21)	2,100	
Total ending inventory			**9,900**
Cost of goods sold			**$10,600**

3. Mistakenly using LIFO when FIFO should have been used overstates cost of goods sold in year 2002 by $1,400, which is the difference between the FIFO and LIFO amounts of ending inventory. It understates income in 2002 by $1,400. In year 2003, income is overstated by $1,400 because of the understatement in beginning inventory.

4. Analysis of the effects of alternative inventory methods:

	Cost of Goods Sold	Difference from FIFO Cost of Goods Sold	Effect on Net Income if Adopted Instead of FIFO
FIFO	$10,200	—	—
LIFO	11,600	+$1,400	$1,400 lower
Weighted average	10,779	+ 579	579 lower
Specific identification	10,600	+ 400	400 lower

APPENDIX

5A Assigning Costs to Inventory—Periodic System

The basic aim of the periodic system and the perpetual system is the same: to assign costs to inventory and cost of goods sold. The same four methods are used to assign costs under both systems—specific identification; first-in, first-out; last-in, first-out; and weighted average. We use information from Trekking to show how we assign costs using these four methods with a periodic system. Data for sales and purchases are reported in the chapter (see Exhibits 5.2 and 5.3). Also recall that we explained the accounting under a periodic system in Appendix 4A, including the following important elements:

P4 Compute inventory in a periodic system using the methods of specific identification, FIFO, LIFO, and weighted average.

■ Each purchase of merchandise for resale increases (debits) the Purchases account.
■ Cost of merchandise sold is *not* recorded at the time of each sale. A physical count of inventory at the end of the period is used to compute cost of goods sold and inventory amounts.
■ Necessary costs of merchandise such as transportation-in and cost reductions such as purchase discounts and purchase returns and allowances are recorded in *separate* accounts.

Specific Identification

The amount of costs assigned to inventory and cost of goods sold is the same under the perpetual and periodic systems when using specific identification. This is so because specific identification precisely tracks (identifies) which units are in inventory and which have been sold.

First-In, First-Out

The first-in, first-out (FIFO) method of assigning cost to both inventory and cost of goods sold using the periodic system is shown in Exhibit 5A.1.

Exhibit 5A.1

FIFO Computations—Periodic System

Total cost of 55 units available for sale		$5,990
Less ending inventory priced using FIFO		
10 units from August 28 purchase at $119 each	$1,190	
2 units from August 17 purchase at $115 each	230	
Ending inventory		1,420
Cost of goods sold		$4,570

Trekking's ending inventory reported on the balance sheet is $1,420, and its cost of goods sold reported on the income statement is $4,570. These amounts are the same as those computed using the perpetual system. This always occurs because the most recent purchases are in ending inventory under both systems.

Last-In, First-Out

The last-in, first-out (LIFO) method of assigning costs to the 12 remaining units in inventory (and to the 43 units in cost of goods sold) using the periodic system is shown in Exhibit 5A.2.

Total cost of 55 units available for sale		$5,990
Less ending inventory priced using LIFO		
10 units in beginning inventory at $91 each	$ 910	
2 units from August 3 purchase at $106 each	212	
Ending inventory		1,122
Cost of goods sold		$4,868

Exhibit 5A.2

LIFO Computations—
Periodic System

Trekking's ending inventory reported on the balance sheet is **$1,122**, and its cost of goods sold reported on the income statement is **$4,868**. When LIFO is used with the periodic system, cost of goods sold is assigned costs from the most recent purchases for the period. With a perpetual system, cost of goods sold is assigned costs from the most recent purchases at the point of *each sale*.

Weighted Average

The weighted average method of assigning cost involves three important steps. The first two steps are shown in Exhibit 5A.3. First, multiply the per unit cost for beginning inventory and each particular purchase by the corresponding number of units. Second, add these amounts and divide by the total number of units available for sale to find the weighted average cost per unit.

Step 1:	10 units @ $91 =	$ 910
	15 units @ $106 =	1,590
	20 units @ $115 =	2,300
	10 units @ $119 =	1,190
	55	$5,990
Step 2:	$5,990/55 units = **$108.91** weighted average cost per unit	

Exhibit 5A.3

Weighted Average Cost
per Unit

Example: In Exhibit 5A.3, if 5 more units had been purchased at $120 each, what would be the weighted average cost per unit?
Answer: $109.83 ($6,590/60)

The third step is to use the weighted average cost per unit to assign costs to inventory and to the units sold as shown in Exhibit 5A.4.

Step 3:	Total cost of 55 units available for sale	$5,990
	Less **ending inventory** priced on a weighted average	
	cost basis: 12 units at $108.91 each (from Exhibit 5A.3)	1,307
	Cost of goods sold	$4,683

Exhibit 5A.4

Weighted Average
Computations—Periodic

Trekking's ending inventory reported on the balance sheet is **$1,307**, and its cost of goods sold reported on the income statement is **$4,683** when using the weighted average (periodic) method.

Quick Check

10. A company reports the following beginning inventory and purchases, and it ends the period with 30 units in inventory.

Beginning Inventory	100 units at $10 cost per unit
Purchase 1	40 units at $12 cost per unit
Purchase 2	20 units at $14 cost per unit

a. Compute ending inventory using the FIFO periodic system.
b. Compute cost of goods sold using the LIFO periodic system.

Answers—p. 233

Summary

C1 **Identify the items making up merchandise inventory.**
Merchandise inventory refers to goods owned by a company and held for resale. Three special cases merit our attention. Goods in transit are reported in inventory of the company that holds ownership rights. Goods on consignment are reported in the consignor's inventory. Goods damaged or obsolete are reported in inventory at their net realizable value.

C2 **Identify the costs of merchandise inventory.** Costs of merchandise inventory include expenditures necessary to bring an item to a salable condition and location. This includes its invoice cost minus any discount plus any added or incidental costs necessary to put it in a place and condition for sale.

A1 **Analyze the effects of inventory methods for both financial and tax reporting.** When purchase costs are rising or falling, the inventory costing methods are likely to assign different costs to inventory. Specific identification exactly matches costs and revenues. Weighted average smooths out cost changes. FIFO assigns an amount to inventory closely approximating current replacement cost. LIFO assigns the most recent costs incurred to cost of goods sold and likely better matches current costs with revenues.

A2 **Analyze the effects of inventory errors on current and future financial statements.** An error in the amount of ending inventory affects assets (inventory), net income (cost of goods sold), and equity for that period. Since ending inventory is next period's beginning inventory, an error in ending inventory affects next period's cost of goods sold and net income. Inventory errors in one period are offset in the next period.

A3 **Assess inventory management using both inventory turnover and days' sales in inventory.** We prefer a high inventory turnover, provided that goods are not out of stock and customers are not turned away. We use days' sales in inventory to assess the likelihood of goods being out of stock. We prefer a small number of days' sales in inventory if we can serve customer needs and provide a buffer for uncertainties.

P1 **Compute inventory in a perpetual system using the methods of specific identification, FIFO, LIFO, and weighted average.** Costs are assigned to the cost of goods sold account *each time* a sale occurs in a perpetual system. Specific

identification assigns a cost to each item sold by referring to its actual cost (for example, its net invoice cost). Weighted average assigns a cost to items sold by dividing the current balance in the inventory account by the total items available for sale to determine cost per unit. We then multiply the number of units sold by this cost per unit to get the cost of each sale. FIFO assigns cost to items sold assuming that the earliest units purchased are the first units sold. LIFO assigns cost to items sold assuming that the most recent units purchased are the first units sold.

P2 **Compute the lower of cost or market amount of inventory.** Inventory is reported at market cost when market is *lower* than recorded cost, called the *lower of cost or market* (*LCM*) *inventory.* Market is typically measured as replacement cost. Lower of cost or market can be applied separately to each item, to major categories of items, or to the entire inventory.

P3 **Apply both the retail inventory and gross profit methods to estimate inventory.** The retail inventory method involves three steps: (1) goods available at retail minus net sales at retail equals ending inventory at retail, (2) goods available at cost divided by goods available at retail equals the cost-to-retail ratio, and (3) ending inventory at retail multiplied by the cost-to-retail ratio equals estimated ending inventory at cost. The gross profit method involves two steps: (1) net sales at retail multiplied by 1 minus the gross profit ratio equals estimated cost of goods sold, and (2) goods available at cost minus estimated cost of goods sold equals estimated ending inventory at cost.

P4 **Compute inventory in a periodic system using the methods of specific identification, FIFO, LIFO, and weighted average.** Periodic inventory systems allocate the cost of goods available for sale between cost of goods sold and ending inventory *at the end of a period.* Specific identification and FIFO give identical results whether the periodic or perpetual system is used. LIFO assigns costs to cost of goods sold assuming the last units purchased for the period are the first units sold. The weighted average cost per unit is computed by dividing the total cost of beginning inventory and net purchases for the period by the total number of units available. Then, it multiplies cost per unit by the number of units sold to give cost of goods sold.

Guidance Answers to **Decision Maker** and **Decision Ethics**

Financial Planner The FIFO method implies that the oldest costs are the first ones assigned to cost of goods sold. This leaves the most recent costs in ending inventory. You report this to your client and note that in most cases, the ending inventory of a company using FIFO is reported at or near its replacement cost. This means that your client need not in most cases adjust the reported value of inventory. Your answer changes only if there are major increases in replacement cost compared to the cost of recent purchases reported in inventory. When major increases in costs occur, your client might wish to adjust inventory (for

internal reports) for the difference between the reported cost of inventory and its replacement cost. (*Note:* Decreases in costs of purchases are recognized under the lower of cost or market adjustment.)

Inventory Manager It seems your company can save (or at least postpone) taxes by switching to LIFO, but the switch is likely to reduce bonus money that you think you have earned and deserve. Since the U.S. tax code requires companies that use LIFO for tax reporting also to use it for financial reporting, your options are further constrained. Your best decision is to tell your superior about the tax savings with LIFO. You also should discuss your bonus plan and how this is likely to hurt you unfairly. You might propose to compute inventory under the LIFO method for reporting purposes but use the FIFO method for your bonus calculations. Another solution is to revise the bonus plan to reflect the company's use of the LIFO method.

Entrepreneur Your inventory turnover is markedly higher than the norm, whereas days' sales in inventory approximates the norm. Since your turnover is already 14% better than average, you are probably best served by directing attention to days' sales in inventory. You should see whether you can reduce the level of inventory while maintaining service to customers. Given your higher turnover, you should be able to hold less inventory.

Guidance Answers to **Quick Checks**

1. Specific identification exactly matches costs and revenues. Weighted average tends to smooth out cost changes. FIFO assigns an amount to inventory that closely approximates current replacement cost. LIFO assigns the most recent costs incurred to cost of goods sold and likely better matches current costs with revenues.

2. FIFO—it gives a lower cost of goods sold, a higher gross profit, and a higher net income when costs are rising.

3. When costs are rising, LIFO gives a lower inventory figure on the balance sheet as compared to FIFO. FIFO's inventory amount approximates current replacement costs.

4. Cost of goods sold is overstated by $10,000 in 2002 and understated by $10,000 in year 2003.

5. The matching principle.

6. Target reports these goods in its inventory.

7. Total cost assigned to the painting is $12,180, computed as $11,400 + $130 + $150 + $100 + $400.

8. The reported LCM inventory amount (using items) is $540, computed as $[(20 \times \$5) + (40 \times \$8) + (10 \times \$12)]$.

9. Estimated ending inventory (at cost) is $327,000. It is computed as follows:

Step 1: $(\$530,000 + \$335,000) - \$320,000 = \$545,000$

Step 2: $\dfrac{\$324,000 + \$195,000}{\$530,000 + \$335,000} = 60\%$

Step 3: $\$545,000 \times 60\% = \$327,000$

10. a. FIFO periodic inventory $= (20 \times \$14) + (10 \times \$12)$
$$= \$400$$

b. LIFO periodic cost of goods sold
$$= (20 \times \$14) + (40 \times \$12) + (70 \times \$10)$$
$$= \$1,460$$

Glossary

Average cost (See *weighted average.*) (p. 213)

Conservatism principle Principle that seeks to select the less optimistic estimate when two estimates are about equally likely. (p. 221)

Consignee One who receives and holds goods owned by another for purposes of selling the goods for the owner. (p. 219)

Consignor Owner of goods who ships them to another party who will sell them for the owner. (p. 219)

Consistency principle Principle encouraging use of the same accounting methods over time so that financial statements are comparable across periods. (p. 216)

Days' sales in inventory Estimate of days needed to convert inventory into receivables or cash; equals ending inventory divided by cost of goods sold and then multiplied by 365; also called *days' stock on hand.* (p. 224)

First-in, first-out (FIFO) Method to assign cost to inventory that assumes items are sold in the order acquired; earliest items purchased are the first sold. (p. 212)

Gross profit method Procedure to estimate inventory when the past gross profit rate is used to estimate cost of goods sold, which is then subtracted from the cost of goods available for sale. (p. 222)

Interim statements Financial statements for periods of less than one year. (p. 222)

Inventory turnover Number of times a company's average inventory is sold during a period; computed by dividing cost of goods sold by average inventory; also called *merchandise turnover.* (p. 224)

Last-in, first-out (LIFO) Method to assign cost to inventory that assumes costs for the most recent items purchased are sold first and charged to cost of goods sold. (p. 213)

Lower of cost or market (LCM) Required method to report inventory at market replacement cost when that market cost is lower than recorded cost. (p. 221)

Net realizable value Expected selling price of an item minus the cost of making the sale. (p. 219)

Retail inventory method Method to estimate ending inventory based on the ratio of the amount of goods for sale at cost to the amount of goods for sale at retail. (p. 222)

Specific identification Method to assign cost to inventory when the purchase cost of each item in inventory is identified and used to compute cost of inventory. (p. 211)

Weighted average Method to assign cost to inventory where the cost of goods available for sale is divided by the number of units available to get per unit cost that is then multiplied by the units in inventory after each sale. (p. 213)

The superscript letter ^{A} denotes assignments based on Appendix 5A.

Questions

1. Describe the flow of costs for the following methods when applied to inventory: (*a*) FIFO and (*b*) LIFO.
2. Where is merchandise inventory disclosed in the financial statements?
3. Why are incidental costs sometimes ignored in inventory costing? Under what principle is this permitted?
4. 🔲 If costs are declining, will the LIFO or FIFO method of inventory valuation result in the lower cost of goods sold?
5. What does the full-disclosure principle require if a company changes from one acceptable accounting method to another?
6. Can a company change its inventory method each accounting period? Explain.
7. 🔲 Does the accounting principle of consistency preclude any changes from one accounting method to another?
8. 🔲 If inventory errors are said to correct themselves, why are users concerned when such errors are made?
9. Explain the following statement: "Inventory errors correct themselves."
10. What is the meaning of *market* as it is used in determining the lower of cost or market for inventory?
11. 🔲 What guidance does the principle of conservatism offer?
12. When preparing interim financial statements, what two methods can companies utilize to estimate cost of goods sold and ending inventory?
13. What factors contribute to (or cause) inventory shrinkage?
14. Refer to **Nike**'s financial statements in Appendix A. On May 31, 2000, what percent of current assets are represented by inventory? **NIKE**
15. Refer to **Reebok**'s financial statements in Appendix A. Compute Reebok's cost of goods available for sale for the year ended December 31, 1999. **Reebok**
16. What percent of **Gap**'s current assets are inventory as of January 29, 2000, and as of January 30, 1999? **GAP**
17.^{A} What accounts are used in a periodic inventory system but not in a perpetual inventory system?

QUICK STUDY

Stein Row starts a merchandising business on December 1 and enters into three inventory purchases:

QS 5-1
Assigning costs to inventory

P1

December 7	10 units @	$7
December 14	20 units @	$8
December 21	15 units @	$10

Stein sells 15 units for $25 each on December 15. Eight of the sold units are from the December 7 purchase and seven are from the December 14 purchase. Stein uses a perpetual inventory system. Determine the costs assigned to the December 31 ending inventory when costs are assigned based on (*a*) FIFO, (*b*) LIFO, (*c*) weighted average, and (*d*) specific identification.

QS 5-2
Computing goods available for sale **P1**

A company has beginning inventory of 10 units at $60 each. Every week for four weeks it purchases an additional 10 units at respective costs of $61, $62, $65, and $70 per unit for weeks 1 through 4. Calculate the cost of goods available for sale and the units available for sale for this four-week period.

QS 5-3
Inventory costing methods

P1

A company had the following beginning inventory and purchases for January. On January 26, 355 units were sold. What is the cost of the 160 units that remain in ending inventory, assuming (*a*) FIFO, (*b*) LIFO, and (*c*) weighted average? (Round unit costs to the nearest cent.)

	Units	Unit Cost
Beginning inventory on January 1	320	$3.00
Purchase on January 9	85	3.20
Purchase on January 25	110	3.35

QS 5-4 🔲
Contrasting inventory costing methods **A1**

Identify the inventory costing method best described by each of the following separate statements. Assume a period of increasing costs.
1. The preferred method when each unit of product has unique features that markedly affect cost.
2. Matches recent costs against net sales.

3. Provides a tax advantage (deferral) to a corporation.

4. Understates the market replacement cost of inventory on the balance sheet.

5. Results in a balance sheet inventory amount approximating replacement cost.

---

1. At year-end, Damon Co. had shipped $750 of merchandise FOB destination to Wagner Co. Which company should include the $750 of merchandise in transit as part of its year-end inventory?

2. Damon Company has shipped $600 of goods to Wagner. Wagner has arranged to sell the goods for Damon. Identify the consignor and the consignee. Which company should include any unsold goods as part of its inventory?

QS 5-5
Inventory ownership

C1

Hobby Crafts, a distributor of handmade gifts, operates out of owner Tina Larsen's house. At the end of the current period, Tina reports she has 1,300 units (products) in her basement, 20 of which were damaged by water and cannot be sold. She also has another 350 units in her van, ready to deliver per a customer order, terms FOB destination, and another 80 units out on consignment to a friend who owns a retail store. How many units should Tina include in her company's period-end inventory?

QS 5-6
Inventory ownership

C1

A car dealer acquires a used car for $14,000, terms FOB shipping point. Additional costs in obtaining and offering the car for sale include $500 for transportation-in, $900 for import duties, $300 for insurance during shipment, $150 for advertising, and $1,250 for sales staff salaries. For computing inventory, what cost is assigned to the used car?

QS 5-7
Inventory costs

C2

Bixby & Son, antique dealers, purchased the contents of an estate for $38,500. Terms of the purchase were FOB shipping point, and the cost of transporting the goods to Bixby & Son's warehouse was $1,100. Bixby & Son insured the shipment at a cost of $250. Prior to putting the goods up for sale, they cleaned and refurbished them at a cost of $800. Determine the cost of the inventory acquired from the estate.

QS 5-8
Inventory costs

C2

Tiffany Trading Co. has the following products in its ending inventory. Compute lower of cost or market for inventory (*a*) as a whole and (*b*) applied separately to each product.

QS 5-9
Applying LCM to inventories

P2

Product	Quantity	Cost per Unit	Market per Unit
Mountain bikes	11	$600	$550
Skateboards	13	350	425
Gliders	26	800	700

Dell Store's inventory is destroyed by a fire on September 5, 2002. The following data for year 2002 are available from the accounting records. Estimate the cost of the inventory destroyed.

QS 5-10
Estimating inventories

P3

Jan. 1 inventory	$190,000
Jan. 1 through Sept. 5 purchases (net)	$352,000
Jan. 1 through Sept. 5 sales (net)	$685,000
Year 2002 estimated gross profit rate	44%

In taking a physical inventory at the end of year 2002, Summit Company erroneously forgot to count certain units. Explain how this error affects the following: (*a*) 2002 cost of goods sold, (*b*) 2002 gross profit, (*c*) 2002 net income, (*d*) 2003 net income, (*e*) the combined two-year income, and (*f*) income for years after 2003.

QS 5-11
Inventory errors

A2

Mercantile Company begins the year with $150,000 of goods in inventory. At year-end, the amount in inventory has increased to $180,000. Cost of goods sold for the year is $1,200,000. Compute Mercantile's inventory turnover and days' sales in inventory.

QS 5-12
Analyzing inventory   **A3**

EXERCISES

Foor Corporation reported the following current-year data for its only product:

Exercise 5-1

Inventory costing
methods—perpetual

P1

Jan. 1	Beginning inventory ..	140 units @ $6.00 =	$ 840
Mar. 7	Purchase	300 units @ $5.60 =	1,680
July 28	Purchase	550 units @ $5.00 =	2,750
Oct. 3	Purchase	350 units @ $4.60 =	1,610
Dec. 19	Purchase	50 units @ $4.10 =	205
	Totals	1,390 units	$7,085

Foor Corporation resold its product at $15 per unit on the following dates:

Jan. 10	Sales ...	100 units
Mar. 15	Sales ...	225 units
Oct. 5	Sales ...	700 units
Total	....	1,025 units

Check Ending inventory: LIFO,
$1,865; WA, $1,761

Foor uses a perpetual inventory system. Ending inventory consists of 365 units, 315 from the July 28 purchase and 50 from the December 19 purchase. Determine the cost assigned to ending inventory and to cost of goods sold using (*a*) specific identification, (*b*) weighted average, (*c*) FIFO, and (*d*) LIFO.

Exercise 5-2

Income effects of inventory
methods

A1

Use the data in Exercise 5-1 to prepare comparative income statements for Foor Corporation (calendar year-end 2002) similar to those shown in Exhibit 5.8 for the four inventory methods. Assume expenses are $1,250. The applicable income tax rate is 30%.

1. Which method yields the highest net income?
2. Does net income using weighted average fall between that using FIFO and LIFO?
3. If costs are rising instead of declining, which method would yield the highest net income?

Exercise 5-3

Inventory costing methods
(perpetual)—FIFO and LIFO

P1

Hingus Co. reported the following current-year data for its only product:

Jan. 1	Beginning inventory	200 units @ $10 =	$ 2,000
Mar. 14	Purchase	350 units @ $15 =	5,250
July 30	Purchase	450 units @ $20 =	9,000
Oct. 26	Purchase	700 units @ $25 =	17,500
Units available	1,700 units		
Cost of goods available for sale			$33,750

Hingus resold its product at $40 per unit on the following dates:

Jan. 10	Sales	100 units
Mar. 15	Sales	150 units
Oct. 5	Sales	310 units
Total sales	....	560 units

Check Ending inventory: LIFO,
$24,300

Hingus uses a perpetual inventory system. Determine the costs assigned to ending inventory and to cost of goods sold using (*a*) FIFO and (*b*) LIFO. Compute the gross margin for each method.

Exercise 5-4

Specific Identification

P1

Refer to the data in Exercise 5-3. Assume that ending inventory is made up of 100 units from the March 14 purchase, 340 units from the July 30 purchase, and all the units of the October 26 purchase. Using the specific identification method, calculate (*a*) the cost of goods sold and (*b*) the gross margin.

Legacy Company's ending inventory includes the following items. Compute the lower of cost or market for ending inventory (*a*) as a whole and (*b*) applied separately to each product.

Product	Units	Recorded Cost per Unit	Market Cost per Unit
Helmets	24	$50	$54
Sticks	17	78	72
Skates	38	95	91
Pads	42	36	36

Exercise 5-5
Lower of cost or market

P2

Check (*b*) $7,394

Harrison Company had $850,000 of sales in each of three consecutive years 2002–2004, and it purchased merchandise costing $500,000 in each of those years. It also maintained a $250,000 inventory from the beginning to the end of the three-year period. In accounting for inventory, it made an error at the end of year 2002 that caused its year-end 2002 inventory to appear on its statements as $230,000 rather than the correct $250,000.

1. Determine the correct amount of the company's gross profit in each of the years 2002–2004.

2. Prepare comparative income statements as in Exhibit 5.11 to show the effect of this error on the company's cost of goods sold and gross profit in years 2002–2004.

Exercise 5-6
Analysis of inventory errors

A2

Check 2002 gross profit, $330,000

In 2002, Hayden Company had retail sales (net) of $140,000. The following additional information is available from its records at the end of 2002. Use the retail inventory method to estimate Hayden's 2002 ending inventory at cost.

	At Cost	At Retail
Beginning inventory	$32,900	$63,400
Cost of goods purchased	56,700	96,600

Exercise 5-7
Estimating ending inventory—retail method

P3

Check End Inventory, $11,200

On January 1, The Fun Store had $550,000 of inventory at cost. In the first quarter of the year, it purchased $1,690,000 of merchandise, returned $22,200, and paid freight charges of $27,600 on purchased merchandise, terms FOB shipping point. The store's gross profit averages 28%. The store had $2,000,000 of retail sales (net) in the first quarter of the year. Use the gross profit method to estimate its cost of inventory at the end of the first quarter.

Exercise 5-8
Estimating ending inventory—gross profit method

P3

Use the following information for Costner Co. to compute inventory turnover for 2003 and 2002 and days' sales in inventory at December 31, 2003 and 2002. (Round answers to the tenths place.) Comment on Costner's efficiency in using its assets to increase sales from 2002 to 2003.

	2003	2002	2001
Cost of goods sold	$643,825	$426,650	$391,300
Inventory (Dec. 31)	97,400	87,750	92,500

Exercise 5-9
Inventory turnover and days' sales in inventory

A3

Z-Mart uses LIFO for inventory costing and reports the following financial data:

	2002	2001
LIFO inventory	$160	$110
LIFO cost of goods sold	740	680
LIFO reserve	80	35
Current assets	220	190
Current liabilities	200	180

1. Compute its FIFO inventory for 2002 and 2001 and its FIFO cost of goods sold for 2002.

2. Compute its current ratio, inventory turnover, and days' sales in inventory for 2002 using (*a*) LIFO numbers and (*b*) FIFO numbers.

3. Comment on and interpret the results of parts 1 and 2.

Exercise 5-10
Restating LIFO numbers to FIFO numbers; ratio analysis

A1 A3

Check (1) 2002 FIFO: Inventory, $240; Cost of goods sold, $695; (2) FIFO: Current ratio, 1.5; Inventory turnover, 3.6

Exercise 5-11^A

Alternative cost flow assumptions—periodic

P4

Rasure & Roney Co. reported the following current-year data for its only product. The company uses a periodic inventory system, and its ending inventory consists of 150 units, 50 from each of the last three purchases. Determine the cost assigned to ending inventory and to cost of goods sold using (*a*) specific identification, (*b*) weighted average, (*c*) FIFO, and (*d*) LIFO. Which method yields the highest net income?

Jan. 1	Beginning inventory	100 units @ $2.00 =	$ 200
Mar. 7	Purchase	220 units @ $2.25 =	495
July 28	Purchase	540 units @ $2.50 =	1,350
Oct. 3	Purchase	480 units @ $2.80 =	1,344
Dec. 19	Purchase	160 units @ $2.90 =	464
	Totals	1,500 units	$3,853

Check Inventory: LIFO, $312.5; FIFO, $435

Exercise 5-12^A

Alternative cost flow assumptions—periodic

P4

Erikson Gifts reported the following current-year data for its only product. The company uses a periodic inventory system, and its ending inventory consists of 150 units, 50 from each of the last three purchases. Determine the cost assigned to ending inventory and to cost of goods sold using (*a*) specific identification, (*b*) weighted average, (*c*) FIFO, and (*d*) LIFO. Which method yields the lowest net income?

Jan. 1	Beginning inventory	140 units @ $3.00 =	$ 420
Mar. 7	Purchase	300 units @ $2.80 =	840
July 28	Purchase	400 units @ $2.50 =	1,000
Oct. 3	Purchase	550 units @ $2.30 =	1,265
Dec. 19	Purchase	125 units @ $2.00 =	250
	Totals	1,515 units	$3,775

Check Inventory: LIFO, $448; FIFO, $307.5

PROBLEM SET A

Problem 5-1A

Alternative cost flows—perpetual

P1

Helton Company's inventory transactions in the fiscal year ended December 31, 2002, follow:

Jan. 1	Beginning inventory	600 units @ $45/unit
Feb. 10	Purchase	350 units @ $42/unit
Mar. 13	Purchase	200 units @ $29/unit
Aug. 21	Purchase	150 units @ $50/unit
Sept. 5	Purchase	545 units @ $48/unit

Helton Company uses a perpetual inventory system. Its inventory had a selling price of $75 per unit, and it entered into the following current-year sales transactions:

Mar. 15	Sales	600 units @ $75/unit
Sept. 10	Sales	100 units @ $75/unit

Required

1. Compute cost of goods available for sale and the number of units available for sale.

2. Compute the number of units in ending inventory.

Check (3) Ending inventory: FIFO, $49,960; LIFO, $53,610; WA, $51,846; (4) LIFO gross profit, $24,950

3. Compute the cost assigned to ending inventory using (*a*) FIFO, (*b*) LIFO, (*c*) specific identification (*note:* 600 units from beginning inventory and 100 units from the March 13 purchase were sold), and (*d*) weighted average.

4. Compute the gross profit earned by the company for each of the costing methods in part 3.

Analysis Component

5. If Helton Company's manager earns a bonus based on a percent of gross profit, which method of inventory costing will the manager likely prefer?

Stokeley Company's financial statements report the following. Stokeley recently discovered that in making physical counts of inventory, it had made the following errors: Inventory on December 31, 2000, is understated by $56,000, and inventory on December 31, 2001, is overstated by $20,000.

Problem 5-2A
Analysis of inventory errors

A2

E_X

Key Figures	For Year Ended December 31		
	2000	**2001**	**2002**
(a) Cost of goods sold	$ 815,000	$ 957,000	$ 780,000
(b) Net income	230,000	285,000	241,000
(c) Total current assets	1,255,000	1,365,000	1,200,000
(d) Equity	1,387,000	1,530,000	1,242,000

Required

1. For each key financial statement figure—(a), (b), (c), and (d) above—prepare a table similar to the following to show the adjustments necessary to correct the reported amounts.

Figure: _____	**2000**	**2001**	**2002**
Reported amount	_____	_____	_____
Adjustments: 12/31/2000 error	_____	_____	_____
12/31/2001 error	_____	_____	_____
Corrected amount	_____	_____	_____

Check (1) Corrected net income: 2000, $286,000; 2001, $209,000; 2002, $261,000

Analysis Component

2. What is the error in total net income for the combined three-year period resulting from the inventory errors? Explain.

3. Explain why the understatement of inventory by $56,000 at the end of 2000 results in an understatement of equity by the same amount in that year.

A physical inventory of Rap Unlimited taken at December 31 reveals the following:

Problem 5-3A
Lower of cost or market

P2

Item	Units	Per Unit	
		Cost	Market
Audio equipment			
Receivers	345	$ 90	$ 98
CD players	260	111	100
DVD players	326	86	95
Speakers	204	52	41
Video equipment			
Televisions	480	150	125
VCRs	291	93	84
Video cameras	212	310	322
Car audio equipment			
DVD radios	185	70	84
CD radios	170	97	105

Required

Calculate the lower of cost or market for the inventory (a) as a whole, (b) by major category, and (c) applied separately to each item.

Check (b) $280,702; (c) $273,054

Problem 5-4A
Retail inventory method

P3

The records of Livingston Company provide the following information for the year ended December 31:

	At Cost	At Retail
January 1 beginning inventory	$ 469,010	$ 928,950
Cost of goods purchased	3,376,050	6,381,050
Sales		5,595,800
Sales returns		42,800

Check (1) Inventory, $924,182 cost; (2) Inventory shortage at cost, $36,873

Required

1. Use the retail inventory method to estimate the company's year-end inventory.
2. A year-end physical inventory at retail prices yields a total inventory of $1,686,900. Prepare a calculation showing the company's loss from shrinkage at cost and at retail.

Problem 5-5A
Gross profit method

P3

Geiger Company wants to prepare interim financial statements for the first quarter. The company wishes to avoid making a physical count of inventory. Geiger's gross profit rate averages 34%. The following information for the first quarter is available from its records:

January 1 beginning inventory	$ 302,580
Cost of goods purchased	941,040
Sales	1,211,160
Sales returns	8,398

Check Estimated ending inventory, $449,797

Required

Use the gross profit method to estimate the company's first-quarter ending inventory.

Problem 5-6A[A]
Alternative cost flows—periodic

P4

G Eₓ

Vandenburg Company began year 2002 with 25,000 units of product in its January 1 inventory costing $15 each. It made successive purchases of its product in year 2002 as follows:

Mar. 7	30,000 units @ $18 each
May 25	32,000 units @ $22 each
Aug. 1	22,000 units @ $24 each
Nov. 10	35,000 units @ $27 each

The company uses a periodic inventory system. On December 31, 2002, a physical count reveals that 40,000 units of its product remain in inventory.

Required

Check (2) Cost of goods sold: FIFO, $2,027,000; LIFO, $2,447,000; WA, $2,233,111

1. Compute the number and total cost of the units available for sale in year 2002.
2. Compute the amounts assigned to the 2002 ending inventory and the cost of goods sold using (*a*) FIFO, (*b*) LIFO, and (*c*) weighted average.

Problem 5-7A[A]
Income comparisons and cost flows—periodic

A1 P4

New Navy Corp. sold 6,500 units of its product at $50 per unit in year 2002 and incurred operating expenses of $5 per unit in selling the units. It began the year with 700 units in inventory and made successive purchases of its product as follows:

Jan. 1	Beginning inventory	700 units @ $18 per unit
Feb. 20	Purchase	1,600 units @ $19 per unit
May 16	Purchase	800 units @ $20 per unit
Oct. 3	Purchase	500 units @ $21 per unit
Dec. 11	Purchase	3,500 units @ $22 per unit
	Total	7,100 units

Required

1. Prepare comparative income statements similar to Exhibit 5.8 for the three inventory costing methods of FIFO, LIFO, and weighted average. Include a detailed cost of goods sold section as part of each statement. The company uses a periodic inventory system, and its income tax rate is 28%.

2. How would the financial results from using the three alternative inventory costing methods change if New Navy had been experiencing declining costs in its purchases of inventory?

3. What advantages and disadvantages are offered by using (*a*) LIFO and (*b*) FIFO? Assume the continuing trend of increasing costs.

Check (1) Net income: LIFO, $112,896; FIFO, $114,624; WA, $114,034

Mercado Company's inventory transactions in the fiscal year ended December 31, 2002, follow:

Jan. 1	Beginning inventory	700 units @ $55/unit
Jan. 10	Purchase	550 units @ $56/unit
Feb. 13	Purchase	220 units @ $57/unit
July 21	Purchase	270 units @ $58/unit
Aug. 5	Purchase	445 units @ $59/unit

Mercado Company uses a perpetual inventory system. Its inventory had a selling price of $100 per unit, and it entered into the following current-year sales transactions:

Feb. 15	Sales	530 units @ $100/unit
Aug. 10	Sales	235 units @ $100/unit

Required

1. Compute cost of goods available for sale and the number of units available for sale.

2. Compute the number of units in ending inventory.

3. Compute the cost assigned to ending inventory using (*a*) FIFO, (*b*) LIFO, (*c*) specific identification (*note:* 700 units from beginning inventory and 65 units from the February 13 purchase were sold), and (*d*) weighted average.

4. Compute the gross profit earned by the company for each of the costing methods in part 3.

Analysis Component

5. If Mercado Company's manager earns a bonus based on a percent of gross profit, which method of inventory costing will the manager likely prefer?

PROBLEM SET B

Problem 5-1B
Alternative cost flows—perpetual

P1

Check (3) Ending inventory: FIFO, $81,615; LIFO, $79,990; WA, $80,869; (4) LIFO gross profit, $32,735

Secado Company's financial statements report the following. Secado recently discovered that in making physical counts of inventory, it had made the following errors: Inventory on December 31, 2000, is overstated by $18,000, and inventory on December 31, 2001, is understated by $26,000.

Problem 5-2B
Analysis of inventory errors

A2

	For Year Ended December 31		
Key Figures	**2000**	**2001**	**2002**
(a) Cost of goods sold	$207,200	$213,800	$197,060
(b) Net income	175,800	212,270	184,810
(c) Total current assets ...	276,000	277,500	272,950
(d) Equity	314,000	315,000	346,000

Required

1. For each key financial statement figure—(*a*), (*b*), (*c*), and (*d*) above—prepare a table similar to the following to show the adjustments necessary to correct the reported amounts.

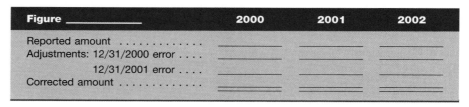

Figure _____	2000	2001	2002
Reported amount			
Adjustments: 12/31/2000 error			
12/31/2001 error			
Corrected amount			

Check (1) Corrected net income: 2000, $157,800; 2001, $256,270; 2002, $158,810

Analysis Component

2. What is the error in total net income for the combined three-year period resulting from the inventory errors? Explain.

3. Explain why the overstatement of inventory by $18,000 at the end of 2000 results in an overstatement of equity by the same amount in that year.

Problem 5-3B

Lower of cost or market

P2

A physical inventory of Office Outlet taken at December 31 reveals the following:

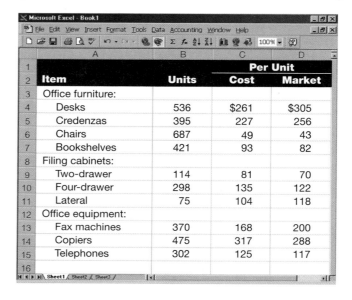

Item	Units	Per Unit Cost	Per Unit Market
Office furniture:			
Desks	536	$261	$305
Credenzas	395	227	256
Chairs	687	49	43
Bookshelves	421	93	82
Filing cabinets:			
Two-drawer	114	81	70
Four-drawer	298	135	122
Lateral	75	104	118
Office equipment:			
Fax machines	370	168	200
Copiers	475	317	288
Telephones	302	125	117

Required

Check (*b*) $601,697; (*c*) $580,054

Calculate the lower of cost or market for the inventory (*a*) as a whole, (*b*) by major category, and (*c*) applied separately to each item.

Problem 5-4B

Retail inventory method

P3

The records of R. U. MacBeth Co. provide the following information for the year ended December 31:

	At Cost	At Retail
January 1 beginning inventory	$ 90,022	$ 115,610
Cost of goods purchased	502,250	761,830
Sales		782,300
Sales returns		3,460

Required

Check (1) Inventory, $66,555 cost; (2) Inventory shortage at cost, $12,251

1. Use the retail inventory method to estimate the company's year-end inventory.

2. A year-end physical inventory at retail prices yields a total inventory of $80,450. Prepare a calculation showing the company's loss from shrinkage at cost and at retail.

Eck Equipment Co. wants to prepare interim financial statements for the first quarter. The company wishes to avoid making a physical count of inventory. Eck's gross profit rate averages 35%. The following information for the first quarter is available from its records:

Problem 5-5B
Gross profit method
P3

January 1 beginning inventory	$ 802,880
Cost of goods purchased	2,209,630
Sales	3,760,250
Sales returns	79,300

Required

Use the gross profit method to estimate the company's first quarter ending inventory.

Check Estim. ending inventory, $619,892

Blue View Co. began year 2002 with 6,500 units of product in its January 1 inventory costing $35 each. It made successive purchases of its product in year 2002 as follows:

Problem 5-6B[A]
Alternative cost flows—periodic
P4

Jan. 4	11,500 units @ $33 each
May 18	13,400 units @ $32 each
July 9	11,000 units @ $29 each
Nov. 21	16,500 units @ $26 each

The company uses a periodic inventory system. On December 31, 2002, a physical count reveals that 18,500 units of its product remain in inventory.

Required

1. Compute the number and total cost of the units available for sale in year 2002.
2. Compute the amounts assigned to the 2002 ending inventory and the cost of goods sold using (a) FIFO, (b) LIFO, and (c) weighted average.

Check (2) Cost of goods sold: FIFO, $1,296,800; LIFO, $1,160,800; WA, $1,223,523

McKray Corp. sold 2,000 units of its product at $108 per unit in year 2002 and incurred operating expenses of $14 per unit in selling the units. It began the year with 840 units in inventory and made successive purchases of its product as follows:

Problem 5-7B[A]
Income comparisons and cost flows—periodic
A1 P4

Jan. 1	Beginning inventory	840 units @ $58 per unit
April 2	Purchase	600 units @ $59 per unit
June 14	Purchase	500 units @ $61 per unit
Aug. 29	Purchase	700 units @ $64 per unit
Nov. 18	Purchase	900 units @ $65 per unit
	Total	3,540 units

Required

1. Prepare comparative income statements similar to Exhibit 5.8 for the three inventory costing methods of FIFO, LIFO, and weighted average. Include a detailed cost of goods sold section as part of each statement. The company uses a periodic inventory system, and its income tax rate is 30%.
2. How would the financial results from using the three alternative inventory costing methods change if McKray had been experiencing decreasing prices in its purchases of inventory?
3. What advantages and disadvantages are offered by using (a) LIFO and (b) FIFO? Assume the continuing trend of increasing costs.

Check (1) Net income: LIFO, $42,210; FIFO, $48,678; WA, $45,417

BEYOND THE NUMBERS

Reporting in Action

C2 A3

NIKE

BTN 5-1 Refer to the financial statements of Nike in Appendix A to answer the following:

Required

1. What amount of inventories did Nike hold as a current asset on May 31, 2000? On May 31, 1999?
2. Inventories represent what percent of total assets on May 31, 2000? On May 31, 1999?
3. Comment on the relative size of Nike's inventories compared to its other types of assets.
4. What accounting method did Nike use to compute inventory amounts on its balance sheet?
5. Calculate inventory turnover for fiscal year ended May 31, 2000, and days' sales in inventory as of May 31, 2000. (*Note:* Cost of sales is cost of goods sold.)

Swoosh Ahead

6. Access Nike's financial statements for fiscal years ended after May 31, 2000, from its Web site (www.nike.com) or the SEC's EDGAR database (www.sec.gov). Answer questions 1 through 5 using the current Nike information and compare results to those prior years.

Comparative Analysis

A3

NIKE Reebok

BTN 5-2 Key comparative figures ($ millions) for both Nike and Reebok follow:

| | Nike | | | Reebok | | |
Key Figures	Current Year	One Year Prior	Two Years Prior	Current Year	One Year Prior	Two Years Prior
Inventory	$1,446.0	$1,170.6	$1,396.6	$ 414.6	$ 535.1	$ 563.7
Cost of sales	5,403.8	5,493.5	6,065.5	1,783.9	2,037.5	2,294.0

Required

1. Calculate inventory turnover for both companies for the most recent two years shown.
2. Calculate days' sales in inventory for both companies for the three years shown.
3. Comment on and interpret your findings from parts 1 and 2.

Ethics Challenge

A1 e d

BTN 5-3 U-Golf Corp. is a retail sports store carrying golf apparel and equipment. The store is at the end of its second year of operation and is struggling. A major problem is that its cost of inventory has continually increased in the past two years. In the first year of operations, the store assigned inventory costs using LIFO. A loan agreement the store has with its bank, its prime source of financing, requires the store to maintain a certain profit margin and current ratio. The store's owner is currently looking over U-Golf's preliminary financial statements for its second year. The numbers are not favorable. The only way the store can meet the required financial ratios agreed on with the bank is to change from LIFO to FIFO. The store originally decided on LIFO because of its tax advantages. The owner recalculates ending inventory using FIFO and submits the statements to the loan officer at the bank for the required bank review. The owner thankfully reflects on the available latitude in choosing the inventory costing method.

Required

1. How does U-Golf's use of FIFO improve its net profit margin and current ratio?
2. Is the action by U-Golf's owner ethical? Explain.

Communicating in Practice

A1 e d

BTN 5-4 You are a financial adviser with a client in the wholesale produce business that just completed its first year of operations. Due to weather conditions, the cost of acquiring produce to resell has escalated during the later part of this period. Your client, Juana Peabody, mentions that because the business sells perishable goods, she has striven to maintain a FIFO flow of goods. Although sales are good, the increasing cost of inventory has put the business in a tight cash position. Juana has expressed concern regarding the ability of the business to meet income tax obligations.

Required

Prepare a memorandum or send an e-mail that identifies, explains, and justifies the inventory method you recommend your client, Ms. Peabody, adopt. If the response is to be made via e-mail, you can assume that your instructor is your client.

Point: If an e-mail response is preferred, students need an e-mail address.

BTN 5-5 Access the March 30, 2000, filing of the 1999 annual 10-K report for Oakley, Inc. (Ticker OO), from www.edgar-online.com.

Required

1. What product does Oakley sell that is especially popular with college students?
2. What inventory method does Oakley use? (*Hint:* See the notes to its financial statements.)
3. Compute Oakley's gross margin and gross margin ratio for the current year.
4. Compute Oakley's inventory turnover and days' sales in inventory for the current year.

Taking It to the Net

A3

BTN 5-6 Each team member has the responsibility to become an expert on an inventory method. This expertise will be used to facilitate teammates' understanding of the concepts relevant to that method.

1. Each learning team member should select an area for expertise by choosing one of the following inventory methods: specific identification, LIFO, FIFO, or weighted average.
2. Form expert teams made up of students who have selected the same area of expertise. The instructor will identify where each expert team will meet.
3. Using the following data, each expert team must collaborate to develop a presentation that illustrates the relevant concepts and procedures for its inventory method. Each team member must write the presentation in a format that can be shown to the learning team.

Teamwork in Action

A1 P1

Point: Step 1 allows four choices or areas for expertise. Larger teams will have some duplication of choice, but the specific identification method should not be duplicated.

Data

Sunmann Corp. uses a perpetual inventory system. It had the following beginning inventory and current year purchases of its product:

Jan. 1	Beginning inventory	50 units @ $10 =	$ 500
Jan. 14	Purchase	150 units @ $12 =	1,800
Apr. 30	Purchase	200 units @ $15 =	3,000
Sept. 26	Purchase	300 units @ $20 =	6,000

Sunmann Corp. transacted sales on the following dates at a $35 per unit sales price:

Jan. 10	30 units	(specific cost: 30 @ $10)
Feb. 15	100 units	(specific cost: 100 @ $12)
Oct. 5	350 units	(specific cost: 100 @ $15 and 250 @ $20)

Concepts and Procedures to Illustrate in Expert Presentation

a. Identify and compute the costs to assign to the units sold.
b. Identify and compute the costs to assign to the units in ending inventory.
c. How likely is it that this inventory costing method will reflect the actual physical flow of goods? How relevant is that factor in determining whether this is an acceptable method to use?
d. What is the impact of this method versus others in determining net income and income taxes?
e. How closely does the ending inventory amount reflect replacement cost?

4. Re-form learning teams. In rotation, each expert is to present to the team the presentation developed in part 3. Experts are to encourage and respond to questions.

Business Week Activity

A3 🄳

BTN 5-7   Read the article "Yes, Steve, You Fixed It. Congrats! Now What's Act Two?" from the July 31, 2000, issue of *Business Week*. (The book's Web site provides a free link.)

Required

1. What percent of the U.S. home computer market does Apple have? What is Apple's overall world-wide market share? Has Apple's worldwide market share grown or declined from 1993?

2. How many days' worth of parts are in its computer parts inventory? How were efficiencies achieved in the computer parts inventory?

3. Do critics think that the days' parts in inventory figure is reliable? Explain.

Entrepreneurial Decision

A3

🄴 🄳

BTN 5-8   Brad Eldridge is an entrepreneur and owner of Home Security, which designs, sells, and installs home security equipment. The company consistently maintains an inventory level of $50,000, meaning that its average and ending inventory levels are the same. Its cost of sales is $190,000. To cut costs, Brad proposes to slash inventory to a constant level of $25,000 with no impact on cost of sales.

Required

1. Compute the company's inventory turnover and its days' sales in inventory under (*a*) current conditions and (*b*) proposed conditions.

2. Evaluate and comment on the merits of Brad's proposal given your analysis in part 1. Identify any concerns you would express about the proposal.

Hitting the Road

C1 C2

BTN 5-9   Visit four retail stores with another classmate. In each store, identify whether the store uses a bar-coding system to help manage its inventory. Try to find at least one store that does not use bar-coding. If a store does not use bar-coding, ask the store's manager or clerk whether he or she knows which type of inventory method the store employs. Create a table that shows columns for the name of store visited, type of merchandise sold, use or nonuse of bar-coding, and the inventory method used if bar-coding is not employed. You might also inquire as to what the store's merchandise turnover is and how often physical inventory is taken.

Global Decision

A3 🄳

BTN 5-10   Key figures (euros millions) for **Adidas-Salomon** (www.adidas.com/investor) follow:

Key Figures	Current Year	One Year Prior	Two Years Prior
Inventory	1,294	1,045	975
Cost of sales	3,307	3,002	2,941

Required

1. Use these data and those from BTN 5-2 to compute (*a*) inventory turnover and (*b*) days' sales in inventory for the most recent two years shown for Adidas, Nike, and Reebok.

2. Comment on and interpret your findings from part 1.

6

Reporting and Analyzing Cash and Internal Controls

"We have created one of the strongest companies in recent times"—Meg Whitman

A Look Back

Chapters 4 and 5 focused on merchandising activities and the accounting for and analysis of inventory. We explained the inventory system, the accounting for inventory transactions, and the methods for assigning costs to inventory.

A Look at This Chapter

This chapter extends our study of accounting to the area of internal control and the analysis of cash. We describe procedures that are good for internal control. We also explain the control of and the accounting for cash.

A Look Ahead

Chapter 7 focuses on receivables and short-term investments. These items are the most liquid assets other than cash. We explain how to account and report for these assets.

Learning Objectives

Conceptual

C1 Define internal control and its purpose.

C2 Identify principles of internal control.

C3 Define cash and cash equivalents and explain how to report them.

C4 Identify control features of banking activities.

Analytical

A1 Compute the days' sales uncollected ratio and use it to analyze liquidity.

Procedural

P1 Apply internal control to cash receipts.

P2 Apply the voucher system to control cash disbursements.

P3 Explain and record petty cash fund transactions.

P4 Apply the net method to control purchase discounts.

P5 Prepare a bank reconciliation.

Decision Feature

Flea Market in Cyberspace

e   SAN JOSE, CA—Who ever thought a flea market could be worth $12 billion? Meg Whitman and Pierre Omidyar started their Net auction service, **eBay** (a combination of the words *electronic* and *Bay Area*), (**www.ebay.com**) because they saw a need for a Web site where people could buy and sell all kinds of items. eBay is now the largest person-to-person auction site on the Web. It creates the marketplace, but buyers and sellers do their own work. eBay never touches the goods or the money. Its earnings derive from commissions, between 1% and 5%, depending on the item's value.

Whitman and Omidyar call eBay an experiment in e-commerce. But how do they persuade strangers to trust one another enough to hand over merchandise or cash? "Most people are honest, trustworthy people," says Omidyar. Still, they set up basic controls to establish responsibilities of each party to a trade and to monitor and record transactions. When complications still arose between buyers and sellers, they had to install a better control system. First, they devised a control system whereby buyers and sellers rate their experiences with the other party. This *Feedback Forum* is a public record of past eBay dealings of buyers and sellers. Omidyar says, "It's become a kind of virtuous cycle that's encouraged good behavior." Second, they brought in escrow services to assist traders in making deals. Buyers can have their goods delivered to an escrow service before their money is sent to the seller. Likewise, sellers can require that a buyer send money to the escrow service before sending the goods. Third, they gave traders free insurance against fraud or the mislabeling of goods. Finally, they set up SafeHarbor™, a customer-support team dedicated to providing regular, independent reviews of transactions and users.

Whitman and Omidyar are confident the new controls will deter fraud. "By creating an open market that encourages honest dealings," says Omidyar, "we hope to make it easier to conduct business with strangers over the Net." If eBay's record of success is any indication, they've made Internet *strangers* feel like *bosom buddies!* [Sources: *Business Week*, June 4 and May 14, 2001; eBay Web site, March 2002.]

Chapter Preview

We all are aware of reports and experiences involving theft and fraud. These occurrences affect us in several ways: we lock doors, chain bikes, review sales receipts, and acquire alarm systems. A company also takes actions to safeguard, control, and manage what it owns. Experience tells us that small companies are most vulnerable, usually due to weak internal controls. It is management's responsibility to set up policies and procedures to safeguard a company's assets, especially cash. To do so, management and employees must understand and apply principles of internal control. This chapter describes these principles and how to apply them. We focus special attention on cash because it is easily transferable and often at high risk of loss. Several controls for cash are explained. Our understanding of these controls and procedures makes us more secure in carrying out business activities and in assessing the activities of other companies.

Internal Control

This section describes internal control and its fundamental principles. We also discuss the impact of technology on internal control and the limitations of control procedures.

Purpose of Internal Control

C1 Define internal control and its purpose.

Topic Tackler 6-1

Managers (or owners) of small businesses often control the entire operation. They supervise workers, participate in all activities, and make major decisions. These managers usually purchase all assets, hire and manage employees, negotiate all contracts, and sign all checks. They know from personal contact and observation whether the business is actually receiving the assets and services paid for. Most companies, however, cannot maintain this close personal supervision. They must delegate responsibilities and rely on formal procedures rather than personal contact in controlling business activities.

Managers use an internal control system to monitor and control business activities. An **internal control system** consists of the policies and procedures managers use to

- Protect assets.
- Ensure reliable accounting.
- Promote efficient operations.
- Urge adherence to company policies.

A properly designed internal control system is a key part of systems design, analysis, and performance. Managers place a high priority on internal control systems because they can prevent avoidable losses, help managers plan operations, and monitor company and employee performance. While internal controls do not provide guarantees, they lower the company's risk of loss.

Decision Insight

Restricted Access Good internal control prevents unauthorized access to assets and accounting records by requiring passwords. It takes a password, for instance, to boot up most office PCs, log onto a network, and access voice mail, e-mail, and online services—not to mention personal ID numbers on credit and cash cards. Preventing unauthorized access is a crucial goal of internal control.

Principles of Internal Control

C2 Identify principles of internal control.

Internal control policies and procedures vary from company to company according to such factors as the nature of the business and its size. Certain fundamental internal control principles apply to all companies. The **principles of internal control** are to

1. Establish responsibilities.
2. Maintain adequate records.
3. Insure assets and bond key employees.
4. Separate recordkeeping from custody of assets.
5. Divide responsibility for related transactions.
6. Apply technological controls.
7. Perform regular and independent reviews.

In this section, we explain these seven principles and describe how internal control procedures minimize the risk of fraud and theft. These procedures also increase the reliability and accuracy of accounting records.

Establish Responsibilities

Proper internal control means that responsibility for a task is clearly established and assigned to one person. When a problem occurs in a company where responsibility is not identified, determining who is at fault is difficult. For instance, if two salesclerks share the same cash register and there is a cash shortage, neither clerk can be held accountable. To prevent this problem, one clerk might be given responsibility for handling all cash sales. Alternately, a company can use a register with separate cash drawers for each clerk. Most of us have waited in line at a retail counter during a change of shift while employees swap cash drawers.

Point: Many companies have a mandatory vacation policy for employees who handle cash.

Maintain Adequate Records

Good recordkeeping is part of an internal control system. It helps protect assets and ensures that employees use prescribed procedures. Reliable records are also a source of information that managers use to monitor company activities. When detailed records of equipment are kept, for instance, items are unlikely to be lost or stolen without detection. Similarly, transactions are less likely to be entered in wrong accounts if a chart of accounts is set up and carefully used. Many preprinted forms and internal documents are also designed for use in a good internal control system. When sales slips are properly designed, for instance, sales personnel can record needed information efficiently with less chance of errors or delays to customers. When sales slips are prenumbered and controlled, each one issued is the responsibility of one salesperson, preventing the salesperson from pocketing cash by making a sale and destroying the sales slip. Computerized point-of-sale systems achieve the same control results.

Point: The association of Certified Fraud Examiners (www.cfenet.com) estimates that employee fraud costs small companies an average of $120,000 per incident.

Insure Assets and Bond Key Employees

Good internal control means that assets are adequately insured against casualty and that employees handling cash and negotiable assets are bonded. An employee is *bonded* when a company purchases an insurance policy, or a bond, against losses from theft by that employee. Bonding reduces the risk of loss suffered from theft. It also discourages theft because bonded employees know an independent bonding company will be involved when theft is uncovered and is unlikely to be sympathetic with an employee involved in theft.

> **Decision Insight**
>
> **Employee Control**   Do you know what lurks behind that spiffy résumé you recently reviewed? The Fraud Defense Network's Fraud Tools page (www.frauddefense.com) provides links to free search engines to verify Social Security numbers, addresses, and phone numbers. For under $10, KnowX.com lets you check lawsuits and bankruptcies. For under $100, Employeescreen.com offers full background searches, including employment verification.

Separate Recordkeeping from Custody of Assets

A person who controls or has access to an asset must not keep that asset's accounting records. This principle reduces the risk of theft or waste of an asset because the person with control over it knows that another person keeps its records. Also, a recordkeeper who does not have access to the asset has no reason to falsify records. This means that, to steal an asset and hide the theft from the records, two or more people must *collude*—or agree in secret to commit the fraud. Since collusion is difficult, the separation of recordkeeping from custody of assets is an important principle of internal control.

> **Decision Insight**
>
> **High-Tech Threads**   Tracer Detection Technology has developed a technique for permanently marking all physical assets. Its technique involves embedding a one-inch-square tag of nylon fibers with different light-absorbing properties. Each pattern of fibers creates a unique optical signature recordable by scanners. The company hopes to embed tags in everything from compact discs and credit cards to designer clothes.

Divide Responsibility for Related Transactions

Good internal control divides responsibility for a transaction or a series of related transactions between two or more individuals or departments. This is to ensure that the work of one individual acts as a check on the other. This principle, often called *separation of duties*, is not a call for duplication of work. Each employee or department should perform unduplicated effort. Examples of transactions with divided responsibility are placing purchase orders, receiving merchandise, and paying vendors. These tasks should not be given to one individual or department. Assigning responsibility for two or more of these tasks to one party increases mistakes and perhaps fraud. Having an independent person, for example, check incoming goods for quality and quantity encourages more care and attention to detail than having the person who placed the order do the checking. Added protection can result from identifying a third person to approve payment of the invoice. A company can even designate a fourth person with authority to write checks as another protective measure.

Apply Technological Controls

Cash registers, check protectors, time clocks, and personal identification scanners are examples of devices that can improve internal control. Technology often improves the effectiveness of controls. A cash register with a locked-in tape or electronic file makes a record of each cash sale. A check protector perforates the amount of a check into its face and makes it difficult to alter the amount. A time clock registers the exact time an employee both arrives at and departs from the job. Mechanical change and currency counters quickly and accurately count amounts, and personal scanners limit access to only authorized individuals. Each of these and other technological controls are an effective part of many internal control systems.

Decision Insight

Face Code   Viisage Technology has licensed a powerful face-recognition program from MIT. It snaps a digital picture of the face and converts key facial features—say, the distance between the eyes—into a series of numerical values. These can be stored on an ID or ATM card as a simple bar code. Welfare agencies in Massachusetts already use the system.

Perform Regular and Independent Reviews

No internal control system is perfect. Changes in personnel and technological advances present opportunities for shortcuts and lapses. So does the stress of time pressures. To counter these factors, regular reviews of internal control systems are needed to ensure that procedures are followed. These reviews are preferably done by internal auditors not directly involved in the activities. Their impartial perspective encourages an evaluation of the efficiency as well as the effectiveness of the internal control system. Many companies also pay for audits by independent, external auditors. These external auditors test the company's financial records to give an opinion as to whether its financial statements are presented fairly.

Decision Maker   *e*

Entrepreneur   As owner of a start-up information services company, you hire a systems analyst. One of her first recommendations is to require all employees to take at least one week of vacation per year. Why would she recommend a "forced vacation" policy?

Answer—p. 275

Before external auditors decide on how much testing is needed, they evaluate the effectiveness of the internal control system. This evaluation is often helpful to a client.

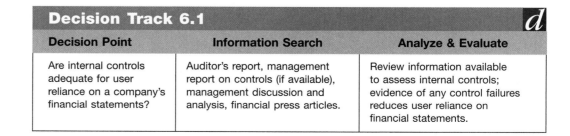

Decision Track 6.1   *d*

Decision Point	Information Search	Analyze & Evaluate
Are internal controls adequate for user reliance on a company's financial statements?	Auditor's report, management report on controls (if available), management discussion and analysis, financial press articles.	Review information available to assess internal controls; evidence of any control failures reduces user reliance on financial statements.

Technology and Internal Control

The fundamental principles of internal control are relevant no matter what the technological state of the accounting system, from purely manual to fully automated systems. Technology impacts an internal control system in several important ways. Perhaps the most obvious is that technology allows us quicker access to databases and information. Used effectively, technology greatly improves managers' abilities to monitor and control business activities. This section describes some technological impacts we must be alert to.

Point: Information on Internet fraud can be found at these sites:
www.ftc.gov/ftc/consumer.htm
www.sec.gov/investor/pubs/cyberfraud.htm
www.fraud.org

Reduced Processing Errors

Technologically advanced systems reduce the number of errors in processing information. Provided the software and data entry are correct, the risk of mechanical and mathematical errors is nearly eliminated. However, we must remember that erroneous software or data entry does exist. Also, less human involvement in data processing can cause data entry errors to go undiscovered. Moreover, errors in software can produce consistent but erroneous processing of transactions. Continually checking and monitoring all types of systems are important.

> **Decision Insight**
>
> **Shredder or Spy?** A Web site that specializes in high-tech spy tools sold several $5,000 paper shredders fitted with scanners and wireless transmitters, say law-enforcement sources. As unsuspecting companies feed in confidential documents, the info is sent to the spy's e-mail address.

More Extensive Testing of Records

A company's review and audit of electronic records can include more extensive testing when information is easily and rapidly accessed. When accounting records are kept manually, auditors and others likely select only small samples of data to test. When data are accessible with computer technology, however, auditors can quickly analyze large samples or even complete data files.

Limited Evidence of Processing

Many data processing steps are increasingly done by computer. Accordingly, fewer hard-copy items of documentary evidence are available for review. Yet technologically advanced systems can provide new evidence. They can, for instance, record who made the entries, the date and time, the source of the entry, and so on. Technology can also be designed to require the use of passwords or other identification before access to the system is granted. This means that internal control depends more on the design and operation of the information system and less on the analysis of its resulting documents.

Crucial Separation of Duties

Technological advances in accounting information systems often yield some job eliminations or consolidations. While those who remain have the special skills necessary to operate advanced programs and equipment, a company with a reduced workforce risks losing its crucial separation of duties. The company must establish ways to control and monitor employees to minimize risk of error and fraud. For instance, the person who designs and programs the information system must not be the one who operates it. The company must also separate control over programs and files related to cash receipts and disbursements. For instance, a computer operator should not control check-writing activities. Achieving acceptable separation of duties can be especially difficult and costly in small companies with few employees.

> **Decision Insight**
>
> **Accounting Techies** A recent study estimates that 200,000 jobs in accounting information technology are vacant. Demand far outstrips supply, producing a bidding war for digital talent in accounting. The most prized recruits are adept at enterprise software, the Web, intranets, and accounting. A recent survey cited the shortage of accounting techies as one of the greatest barriers to company growth.

Limitations of Internal Control

Point: When the electronic equipment maker Casio started an e-commerce site (**www.Casio.com**), 13% of its first-year purchases were fraudulent.

All internal control policies and procedures have limitations. Probably the most serious limitation is that internal control policies and procedures are applied by people and often impact other people. This human element creates several potential limitations that we can categorize as either (1) human error or (2) human fraud. *Human error* can occur from negligence, fatigue, misjudgment, or confusion. It is a factor when people carry out internal control policies and procedures. *Human fraud* involves intent by people to defeat internal controls for personal gain. Fraud includes collusion to thwart the separation of duties. The human element highlights the importance of establishing an *internal control environment* to convey management's commitment to internal control policies and procedures.

Another important limitation on internal control is the *cost-benefit principle*. This means that the costs of internal controls must not exceed their benefits. Analysis of costs and benefits must consider all factors, including the impact on morale. Most companies, for instance, have a legal right to read employees' e-mails, yet companies seldom exercise that right unless they are confronted with evidence of potential harm to the company. The same holds for drug testing, phone tapping, and hidden camera monitoring. The bottom line is that no internal control system is perfect and that managers must establish internal control policies and procedures with a net benefit to the company.

Quick Check

1. Fundamental principles of internal control suggest which of the following:
(a) Responsibility for a series of related transactions (such as placing orders, receiving and paying for merchandise) should be assigned to one employee;
(b) Responsibility for individual tasks should be shared by more than one employee so that one serves as a check on the other; or (c) Employees who handle cash and easily transferable assets should be bonded.

2. What are some impacts of computing technology on internal control?

Answers—p. 276

Control of Cash

Cash is a necessary asset of every company. Most companies include *cash equivalents*, which are similar to cash, as part of cash. Applying principles of internal control to both cash and cash equivalents is important. Cash and cash equivalents are the most liquid of all assets and are easily hidden and moved. An effective system of internal controls protects both cash receipts and cash disbursements and should meet three basic guidelines:

1. Handling cash is separate from recordkeeping of cash.
2. Cash receipts are promptly deposited in a bank.
3. Cash disbursements are made by check.

The first guideline applies separation of duties to minimize errors and fraud. As noted earlier, when duties are separated, two or more people must collude to steal cash and conceal this action in the accounting records. The second guideline uses immediate (say, daily) deposits of all cash receipts to produce a timely independent record of the cash received. It also reduces the likelihood of cash theft (or loss) and the risk that an employee could personally use the money before depositing it. The third guideline uses payments by check to develop an independent bank record of cash disbursements. This guideline also reduces the risk of cash theft (or loss).

This section begins with definitions of cash and cash equivalents. Discussion then focuses on controls and accounting for both cash receipts and disbursements. The exact procedures used to achieve control over cash vary across companies. They depend on factors such as company size, number of employees, volume of cash transactions, and sources of cash. We must therefore view the procedures described in this section as illustrative.

Cash, Cash Equivalents, and Liquidity

Cash must be managed and controlled. Good accounting systems both help manage the amount of cash and control who has access to it. The importance of accounting for cash is highlighted by the inclusion of a statement of cash flows in a complete set of financial statements. That statement identifies activities affecting cash.

Cash includes currency and coins along with the amounts on deposit in bank accounts, checking accounts (called *demand deposits*), and many savings accounts (called *time deposits*). Cash also includes items that are acceptable for deposit in these accounts such as customers' checks, cashier checks, certified checks, and money orders. **Cash equivalents** are short-term, highly liquid investment assets meeting two criteria: (1) readily convertible to a known cash amount and (2) sufficiently close to their maturity date so that their market value is not sensitive to interest rate changes. Only investments purchased within three months of their maturity date usually satisfy these criteria. Examples of cash equivalents are short-term investments in assets such as U.S. Treasury bills, money market funds, and commercial paper (such as short-term corporate notes). To increase their return on investment in cash, many companies invest idle cash in cash equivalents. Most companies combine cash equivalents with cash as a single item on the balance sheet. For example, the toymaker **Mattel** reports a single cash balance and states: "Cash includes cash equivalents, which are highly liquid investments with maturities of three months or less when purchased. Because of the short maturities of these instruments, the carrying amount is a reasonable estimate of fair value."

Cash is the usual means of payment when paying for other assets, services, or liabilities. **Liquidity** refers to a company's ability to pay for its near-term obligations. Cash and similar assets are called **liquid assets** because they can be readily used to settle such obligations. A company needs liquid assets to effectively operate.

C3 Define cash and cash equivalents and explain how to report them.

Point: The most liquid assets are usually reported first on a balance sheet; the least liquid assets are reported last.

Point: The e-commerce company i2 Technologies reports cash and cash equivalents of $455 million in its recent balance sheet. This amount makes up more than one-half of its total assets.

Decision Insight

Cybersleuths   Lawyers at the FTC are on the cutting edge of cybersleuthing. Opportunists in search of easy money are lured to **www.wemarket4u.net/netops**, where a banner proclaims: "The Internet is a GOLD MINE!!!" It says you can get rich quick—as an "Internet Con$ultant." Take the bait and you get warned—and probably targeted.

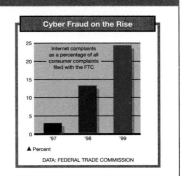

Decision Track 6.2

Decision Point	Information Search	Analyze & Evaluate
Is the reported cash (and cash equivalents) balance available for company use?	Balance sheet and financial statement notes; disclosure of any cash restrictions.	Analyze evidence for restrictions that limit the use of cash and would reduce a company's liquidity.

Control of Cash Receipts

Internal control of cash receipts ensures that cash received is properly recorded and deposited. Cash receipts arise from transactions such as cash sales, collections of customers' accounts, receipts of interest earned, bank loans, sales of assets, and owner investments. The principles of internal control apply to all cash receipts. This section explains internal control over two important types of cash receipts: over-the-counter and by mail.

P1 Apply internal control to cash receipts.

Over-the-Counter Cash Receipts

For purposes of internal control, over-the-counter cash receipts from sales should be recorded on a cash register at the time of each sale. To help ensure that correct amounts are entered, each register should be located so customers can read the amounts entered. Clerks also should be required to enter each sale before wrapping merchandise and to give the customer

Point: Retailers often require cashiers to restrictively endorse checks immediately on receipt by stamping them "For deposit only."

a receipt for each sale. The design of each cash register should provide a permanent, locked-in record of each transaction. In many systems, the register is directly linked with computing and accounting services. Less advanced registers simply print a record of each transaction on a paper tape or electronic file locked inside the register.

One principle of internal control states that custody over cash should be separate from its recordkeeping. For over-the-counter cash receipts, this separation begins with the cash sale. The clerk who has access to cash in the register should not have access to its locked-in record. At the end of the clerk's work period, the clerk should count the cash in the register, record the amount, and turn over the cash and a record of its amount to the company's cashier. The cashier, like the clerk, has access to the cash but should not have access to accounting records (or the register tape or file). A third employee compares the record of total register transactions (or the register tape or file) with the cash receipts reported by the cashier. This record (or register tape or file) is the basis for a journal entry recording over-the-counter cash receipts. The third employee has access to the records for cash but not to the actual cash. The clerk and the cashier have access to cash but not to the accounting records. None of them can make a mistake or divert cash without the difference being revealed.

Cash over and short. Sometimes errors in making change are discovered from differences between the cash in a cash register and the record of the amount of cash receipts. Although a clerk is careful, one or more customers can be given too much or too little change. This means that at the end of a work period, the cash in a cash register might not equal the cash receipts entered. This difference is reported in the **Cash Over and Short** account, which is an income statement account recording the income effects of cash overages and cash shortages. To illustrate, if a cash register shows cash receipts of $550 but the count of cash in the register is $555, the entry to record cash sales and its overage is

Assets = Liabilities + Equity
+555   +   5
                        +550

Cash	555	
Cash Over and Short		5
Sales		550
To record cash sales and an overage.		

On the other hand, if a cash register shows cash receipts of $625 but the count of cash in the register is $621, the entry to record cash sales and its shortage is:

Assets = Liabilities + Equity
+621   −   4
                        +625

Cash	621	
Cash Over and Short	4	
Sales		625
To record cash sales and a shortage.		

Since customers are more likely to dispute being shortchanged than being given too much change, the Cash Over and Short account usually has a debit balance at the end of an accounting period. A debit balance reflects an expense. It can be shown on the income statement as part of general and administrative expenses. But since the amount is usually small, it is often combined with other small expenses and reported as part of *miscellaneous expenses*. If Cash Over and Short has a credit balance at the end of the period, it usually is shown on the income statement as part of *miscellaneous revenues*.

Cash Receipts by Mail

Control of cash receipts that arrive through the mail starts with the person who opens the mail. Preferably, two people are assigned the task of, and are present for, opening the mail. In this case, theft of cash receipts by mail requires collusion between these two employees. Specifically, the person(s) opening the mail enters a list (in triplicate) of money received. This list should contain a record of each sender's name, the amount, and an explanation of why the money is sent. The first copy is sent with the money to the cashier. A second copy is sent to the recordkeeper in the accounting area. A third copy is kept by the clerks who opened the mail. The cashier deposits the money in a bank, and the recordkeeper records the amounts received in the accounting records.

Point: A complete set of financial statements includes a statement of cash flows, which provides useful information about a company's sources and uses of cash and cash equivalents during a period of time.

This process reflects good internal control. That is, when the bank balance is reconciled by another person (explained later in the chapter), errors or acts of fraud by the mail clerks, the cashier, or the recordkeeper are revealed. They are revealed because the bank's record of cash deposited must agree with the records from each of the three. Moreover, if the mail clerks do not report all receipts correctly, customers will question their account balances. If the cashier does not deposit all receipts, the bank balance does not agree with the recordkeeper's cash balance. The recordkeeper and the person who reconciles the bank balance do not have access to cash and therefore have no opportunity to divert cash to themselves. This system makes errors and fraud highly unlikely. The exception is when employees collude.

Decision Insight

Entrepreneurs, Head West! In a recent survey by the Small Business Survival Foundation (www.SBSC.org), 5 of the top 6 states ranked as most entrepreneur friendly are west of the Mississippi. The top six are (1) South Dakota, (2) Wyoming, (3) Nevada, (4) New Hampshire, (5) Texas, and (6) Washington. The index is based on several factors including taxes, regulations, compensation costs, and crime.

Control of Cash Disbursements

Control of cash disbursements is especially important for companies. Most large thefts occur from payment of fictitious invoices. One key to controlling cash disbursements is to require all expenditures to be made by check. The only exception is small payments made from petty cash. Another key is to deny access to the accounting records to anyone other than the owner who has the authority to sign checks. The owner of a small business often signs checks and knows from personal contact that the items being paid for are actually received. This arrangement is impossible in large businesses. Instead, internal control procedures must be substituted for personal contact. Such procedures are designed to assure the check

Decision Insight

Paper Chase The basic purposes of most paper and electronic documents are the same. However, the internal control system must change to reflect different risks, including confidential and competitive-sensitive information that is at greater risk in electronic systems.

signer that the obligations recorded are properly incurred and should be paid. This section describes these and other internal control procedures. They include the voucher system, petty cash system, and the management of cash disbursements for purchases.

Voucher System of Control

A **voucher system** is a set of procedures and approvals designed to control cash disbursements and the acceptance of obligations. The voucher system of control establishes procedures for

P2 Apply the voucher system to control cash disbursements.

■ Verifying, approving, and recording obligations for eventual cash disbursement.
■ Issuing checks for payment of verified, approved, and recorded obligations.

A reliable voucher system follows standard procedures for every transaction. This applies even when multiple purchases are made from the same supplier.

A voucher system's control over cash disbursements begins when a company incurs an obligation that will result in payment of cash. A key factor in this system is that only approved departments and individuals are authorized to incur such obligations. The system often limits the type of obligations that a department or individual can incur. In a large retail store, for instance, only a purchasing department should be authorized to incur obligations for merchandise inventory. Another key factor is that procedures for purchasing, receiving, and paying for merchandise are divided among several departments (or individuals). These departments include the one requesting the purchase, the purchasing department, the receiving department, and the accounting department. To coordinate and control responsibilities of these departments, a company uses several different business documents. Exhibit 6.1 shows how documents are accumulated in a **voucher,** which is an internal document (or file) used to accumulate information to control cash disbursements and to ensure that a transaction is properly recorded. This specific example begins with a *purchase requisition* and concludes with a *check* drawn against cash. Appendix 6A describes each document entering and leaving a voucher system. It also describes the internal control objective served by each document.

Exhibit 6.1

Document Flow in a Voucher System

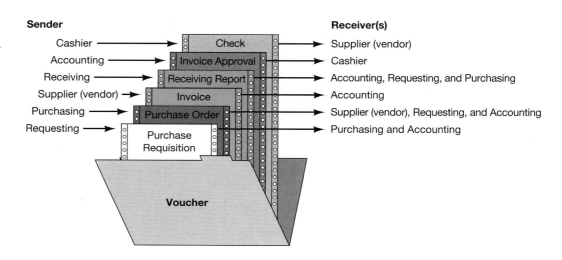

A voucher system should be applied not only to purchases but to all expenses. To illustrate, when a company receives a monthly telephone bill, it should review and verify the charges, prepare a voucher (file), and insert the bill. This transaction is then recorded with a journal entry. If the amount is due at once, a check is issued. If not, the voucher is filed for payment on its due date.

Vouchers should be prepared for all incurred expenses, whether cash payment occurs now or later. This is so because many invoices or bills are often not received until weeks after work is done. If no expense (voucher) records exist, verifying the invoice and its amount can be difficult. Also, without records, a dishonest employee could collude with a dishonest supplier to get more than one payment for an obligation, payment for excessive amounts, or payment for goods and services not received. An effective voucher system helps prevent such frauds.

Point: A voucher is an internal document (or file).

Quick Check

3. Why must a company hold liquid assets?

4. Why does a company hold cash equivalent assets in addition to cash?

5. Identify at least two assets that are classified as cash equivalents.

6. Good internal control procedures for cash include which of the following? (a) All cash disbursements, other than those for very small amounts, are made by check; (b) One employee should count cash received from sales and promptly deposit cash receipts; or (c) Cash receipts by mail should be opened by one employee who is then responsible for recording and depositing receipts.

7. Do all companies require a voucher system? At what point in a company's growth would you recommend a voucher system?

Answers—p. 276

Petty Cash System of Control

A basic principle for controlling cash disbursements is that all payments must be made by check. An exception to this rule is made for *petty cash disbursements,* which are the small payments required for items such as postage, courier fees, repairs, and low-cost supplies. To avoid the time and cost of writing checks for small amounts, a company sets up a petty cash fund to make small payments.

P3 Explain and record petty cash fund transactions.

Operating a petty cash fund. Establishing a petty cash fund requires estimating the total amount of small payments likely to be made during a short period such as a week or month. A check is then drawn by the company cashier for an amount slightly in excess of this estimate. This check is recorded with a debit to the Petty Cash account (an asset) and a credit to Cash. The check is cashed, and the currency is given to an employee designated as the *petty cashier* or *petty cash custodian.* The petty cashier is responsible for keeping this cash safe, making payments from the fund, and keeping records of it. The petty cashier keeps petty cash and its records in a secure place referred to as the *petty cashbox.*

To illustrate, when each cash disbursement is made, the person receiving payment should sign a *petty cash receipt,* also called *petty cash ticket*—see Exhibit 6.2. The petty cash receipt is then placed in the petty cashbox with the remaining money. Under this system, the sum of all receipts plus the remaining cash equals the total fund amount. A $100 petty cash fund, for instance, contains any combination of cash and petty cash receipts that total $100 (examples are $80 cash plus $20 in receipts, or $10 cash plus $90 in receipts). Each disbursement reduces cash and increases the amount of receipts in the petty cashbox.

Point: A petty cash fund is used only for business expenses.

Petty Cash Receipt	No. 9
Z-Mart	
For ____Freight charges____	Date ____11/5/02____
Charge to ____Merchandise Inventory____	Amount ____$6.75____
Approved by ____*Jim Gibbs*____	Received by ____*Dick Fitch*____

Exhibit 6.2

Petty Cash Receipt

When the petty cash is nearing zero, it should be reimbursed. The petty cashier first sorts the paid receipts by the type of expense or account and then totals the receipts. The petty cashier presents all paid receipts to the company cashier, who stamps all receipts *paid* so they cannot be reused, files them for recordkeeping, and gives the petty cashier a check for their sum. When this check is cashed and the money placed in the cashbox, the total money in the cashbox is restored to its original amount. The fund is now ready for a new cycle of petty cash payments.

Point: Auditors often find misuse of petty cash when petty cash receipts have either no signature or a forged signature. Companies respond with surprise petty cash counts for verification.

Illustration of a petty cash fund. Z-Mart uses a petty cash fund to avoid writing an excessive number of checks for small amounts. To illustrate, assume that it establishes the fund on November 1 and designates one of its office employees as the petty cashier. A $75 check is drawn, cashed, and the proceeds given to the petty cashier. The entry to record the setup of this petty cash fund is

Assets = Liabilities + Equity
+75
−75

Nov. 1	Petty Cash	75	
	Cash		75
	To establish a petty cash fund.		

This entry transfers $75 from the regular Cash account to the Petty Cash account. After the petty cash fund is established, the Petty Cash account is not debited or credited again unless the amount of the fund is changed. A fund probably should be increased if it is being used and reimbursed too frequently. If the fund is too large, some of its money should be redeposited in the Cash account.

During November, Z-Mart's petty cashier makes several payments from petty cash. Each person who received payment is required to sign a receipt. On November 27, after making a $26.50 cash payment for a printer cartridge, only $3.70 cash remains in the fund. The petty cashier then summarizes and totals the petty cash receipts as shown in Exhibit 6.3. This summary and all petty cash receipts are given to the company cashier in exchange for a $71.30 check to reimburse the fund. The petty cashier cashes the check and puts the $71.30 cash in the petty cashbox. The company records this reimbursement as follows:

Point: Although *individual* petty cash disbursements are not evidenced by a check, the initial petty cash fund is evidenced by a check, and later petty cash expenditures are evidenced by a check to replenish them *in total*.

Assets = Liabilities + Equity
−71.30   −46.50
                         −15.05
                         − 5.00
                         − 4.75

Nov. 27	Miscellaneous Expenses	46.50	
	Merchandise Inventory	15.05	
	Delivery Expense	5.00	
	Office Expense	4.75	
	Cash		71.30
	To reimburse petty cash.		

Information for this entry is taken from the petty cashier's summary of payments in Exhibit 6.3. The debits in this entry reflect the petty cash payments.

Exhibit 6.3

Petty Cash Payments Report

Z-MART		
Petty Cash Payments Report		
Miscellaneous Expenses		
Nov. 2 Washing windows	$20.00	
Nov. 27 Printer cartridge	26.50	$46.50
Merchandise Inventory (transportation-in)		
Nov. 5 Transport of merchandise purchased	6.75	
Nov. 20 Transport of merchandise purchased	8.30	15.05
Delivery Expense		
Nov. 18 Customer's package delivered		5.00
Office Supplies Expense		
Nov. 15 Purchase of office supplies immediately used		4.75
Total		$71.30

Point: To avoid errors in recording petty cash reimbursement, follow these steps: (1) prepare payments report, (2) compute cash needed by subtracting cash remaining from total fund amount, (3) record entry, and (4) check "Dr. = Cr." in entry—any difference is Cash Over and Short.

A petty cash fund is often reimbursed at the end of an accounting period even if it is not low on money. This is done to record expenses in the proper period. If the fund is not reimbursed at the end of a period, the financial statements show both an overstated petty cash asset and understated expenses (or assets) that were paid out of petty cash. Some companies do not reimburse the petty cash fund at the end of each period under the assumption that this amount is immaterial to users of financial statements.

Increasing or decreasing a petty cash fund. A decision to increase or decrease a petty cash fund is often made when reimbursing it. To illustrate, let's assume Z-Mart decides to *increase* its petty cash fund to $100 on November 27 when it reimburses the fund. The entry to do this is identical to the preceding one except that it includes a (1) debit to Petty Cash for $25 (increasing the fund from $75 to $100) and (2) credit to Cash for $96.30 ($71.30 reimbursement of expenses plus $25 increase in the fund). Alternatively, if Z-Mart *decreases* the petty cash fund from $75 to $55 on November 27, the changes required for the entry on this date include a (1) credit to Petty Cash for $20 (decreasing the fund from $75 to $55) and (2) credit to Cash for $51.30 ($71.30 reimbursement of expense minus $20 decrease in the fund).

Decision Ethics

Internal Auditor You are making a surprise count of a $300 petty cash fund. You arrive at the petty cashier when she is on the telephone. She politely asks that you return after lunch so that she can finish her business on the telephone. You agree and return after lunch. In the petty cashbox, you find 14 new $20 bills with consecutive serial numbers plus receipts totaling $20. What is your evaluation?

Answer—p. 275

Cash over and short. Sometimes a petty cashier fails to get a receipt for payment or overpays for the amount due. When this occurs and the fund is later reimbursed, the petty cash payments report plus the cash remaining will not total to the fund balance. This mistake causes the fund to be *short*. This shortage is recorded as an expense in the reimbursing entry with a debit to the Cash Over and Short account. (An overage in the petty cash fund is recorded with a credit to Cash Over and Short in the reimbursing entry.)

Example: Prepare the entry to reimburse a $200 petty cash fund when its payments report shows $178 in miscellaneous expenses and $15 cash remains.
Miscel. Expenses 178
Cash Over & Short 7
        Cash   185

Quick Check

8. Why are some cash payments made from a petty cash fund, and not by check?

9. Why should a petty cash fund be reimbursed at the end of an accounting period?

10. Identify at least two results of reimbursing a petty cash fund.

Answers—p. 276

Control of Purchase Discounts

This section explains how a company can gain more control over cash *disbursements* to take advantage of favorable purchase discounts. Chapter 4 described the entries to record the receipt and payment of an invoice for a purchase of merchandise. When Z-Mart purchases merchandise at a $1,200 invoice price with terms of 2/10, n/30, it makes this entry:

P4 Apply the net method to control purchase discounts.

Nov. 2	Merchandise Inventory	1,200	
	Accounts Payable		1,200
	Purchased merchandise on credit, invoice dated Nov. 2, terms 2/10, n/30.		

Assets = Liabilities + Equity
+1,200   +1,200

If Z-Mart takes advantage of the discount and pays the amount due on November 12, the entry is

Nov. 12	Accounts Payable	1,200	
	Merchandise Inventory		24
	Cash		1,176
	Paid for the purchase of Nov. 2 less the discount (2% × $1,200).		

Assets = Liabilities + Equity
−24   −1,200
−1,176

These entries reflect the **gross method** of recording purchases, which records the invoice at its *gross* amount of $1,200 *before* recognizing the cash discount.

Another method of recording purchases is the **net method,** which records the invoice at its *net* amount *after* recognizing the cash discount. If Z-Mart uses the net method of recording purchases, it deducts the potential $24 cash discount from the gross amount and records the initial purchase at the $1,176 net amount:

Assets = Liabilities + Equity
+1,176   +1,176

Nov. 2	Merchandise Inventory	1,176	
	Accounts Payable		1,176
	Purchased merchandise on credit, invoice dated Nov. 2, terms 2/10, n/30.		

If the invoice for this purchase is paid within the discount period, the entry debits Accounts Payable and credits Cash for $1,176. However, if payment is not made within the discount period and the discount is *lost,* the following additional entry must be made either on the date the discount is lost or later when the invoice is paid:

Assets = Liabilities + Equity
            +24   −24

Nov. 13	Discounts Lost	24	
	Accounts Payable		24
	To record the discount lost.		

When payment is later made, a check for the full $1,200 invoice amount must be written, recorded, and sent to the creditor.[1] The net method gives management an advantage in controlling and monitoring cash payments involving purchase discounts. When invoices are recorded at *gross* amounts, the amount of any discounts taken is deducted from the balance of the Merchandise Inventory account when cash payment is made. This means that the amount of any discounts lost is not reported in any account or on the income statement. Lost discounts recorded in this way are unlikely to come to the attention of management. However, when purchases are recorded at *net* amounts, a **Discounts Lost** expense account is recorded and brought to management's attention. Management can then seek to identify the reason for discounts lost such as oversight, carelessness, or unfavorable terms.[2]

Banking Activities as Controls

Banks (and other financial institutions) provide many different services, including helping companies control cash. Banks safeguard cash, provide detailed and independent records of cash transactions, and are a source of cash financing. This section describes these services and the documents provided by banking activities that increase managers' control over cash.

Basic Bank Services

C4 Identify control features of banking activities.

This section explains basic bank services—such as the bank account, the bank deposit, and checking—that contribute to the control of cash.

Bank Account, Deposit, and Check

A *bank account* is a record set up by a bank for a customer. It permits a customer to deposit money for safekeeping and helps control withdrawals. To limit access to a bank account, all persons authorized to write checks on the account must sign a **signature card,** which bank employees use to verify signatures on checks. Many companies have more than

---

[1] The discount lost can be recorded when the cash payment is made with a single entry. However, when financial statements are prepared after a discount is lost and before the cash payment is made, an adjusting entry is required to recognize any unrecorded discount lost in the period when incurred.

[2] To help managers assess whether a discount is favorable or not, we compute the *implied interest rate* of not taking the discount: (365 days/[Credit period − Discount period]) × Cash discount percent. For example, if terms are 2/10, n/30, then missing the 2% discount for an additional 20 days implies an annual interest rate of 36.5%, computed as (365 days/[30 days − 10 days]) × 2%. This suggests that if money can be borrowed for less than 36.5%, an entity should take advantage of the discount offered.

one bank account to serve different needs and to handle special transactions such as payroll.

Each bank deposit is supported by a **deposit ticket,** which lists items such as currency, coins, and checks deposited along with their corresponding dollar amounts. The bank gives the customer a copy of the deposit ticket or a deposit receipt as proof of the deposit. Exhibit 6.4 shows one type of deposit ticket.

Exhibit 6.4

Deposit Ticket

Front

Back

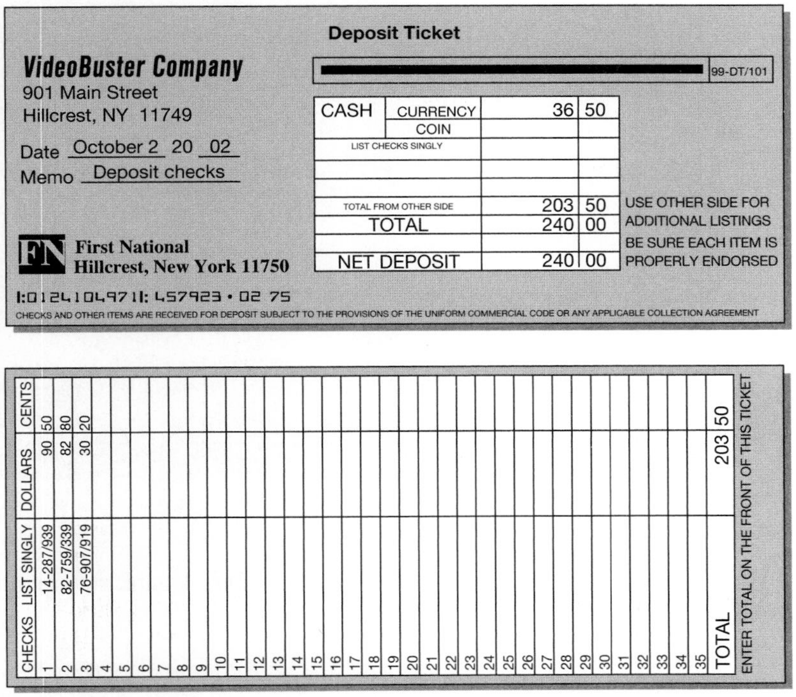

Deposit Ticket

VideoBuster Company
901 Main Street
Hillcrest, NY 11749

Date October 2 20 02
Memo Deposit checks

CASH	CURRENCY	36	50
	COIN		
LIST CHECKS SINGLY			
TOTAL FROM OTHER SIDE		203	50
TOTAL		240	00
NET DEPOSIT		240	00

99-DT/101

USE OTHER SIDE FOR ADDITIONAL LISTINGS
BE SURE EACH ITEM IS PROPERLY ENDORSED

First National
Hillcrest, New York 11750

I:012410497 I: 457923 • 02 75

CHECKS AND OTHER ITEMS ARE RECEIVED FOR DEPOSIT SUBJECT TO THE PROVISIONS OF THE UNIFORM COMMERCIAL CODE OR ANY APPLICABLE COLLECTION AGREEMENT

CHECKS	LIST SINGLY	DOLLARS	CENTS
1	14-287/939	90	50
2	82-759/339	82	80
3	76-907/919	30	20
4			
5			
6			
7			
8			
9			
10			
11			
12			
13			
14			
15			
16			
17			
18			
19			
20			
21			
22			
23			
24			
25			
26			
27			
28			
29			
30			
31			
32			
33			
34			
35			
TOTAL		203	50

ENTER TOTAL ON THE FRONT OF THIS TICKET

To withdraw money from an account, the depositor uses a **check,** which is a document signed by the depositor instructing the bank to pay a specified amount of money to a designated recipient. A check involves three parties: a *maker* who signs the check, a *payee* who is the recipient, and a *bank* (or *payer*) on which the check is drawn. The bank provides a depositor the checks that are serially numbered and imprinted with the name and address of both the depositor and bank. Both checks and deposit tickets are imprinted with identification codes in magnetic ink for computer processing. Exhibit 6.5 shows one type of check. It is accompanied with an optional *remittance advice* explaining the payment. When a remittance advice is unavailable, the *memo* line is often used for a brief explanation.

Decision Insight

Booting Up Your Banker Many companies balance checkbooks and pay bills via the Web. The convenience and low cost of banking services anytime, anywhere, are attracting customers. Services include the ability to stop payment on a check, move money between accounts, get up-to-date account balances, and identify checks and deposits that have cleared.

Electronic Funds Transfer

Electronic funds transfer (EFT) is the electronic communication transfer of cash from one party to another. No paper documents are necessary. Banks simply transfer cash from one account to another with a journal entry. Companies are increasingly using EFT because of its convenience and low cost. For instance, it can cost up to 50 cents to process a check through the banking system, whereas EFT cost is near zero. We now commonly see items such as payroll, rent, utilities, insurance, and interest payments being handled by EFT. The bank statement lists cash withdrawals by EFT with checks and other deductions. Cash

Global: If cash is in more than one currency, a company usually translates these amounts into U.S. dollars using the exchange rate as of the balance sheet date.

Exhibit 6.5

Check with Remittance Advice

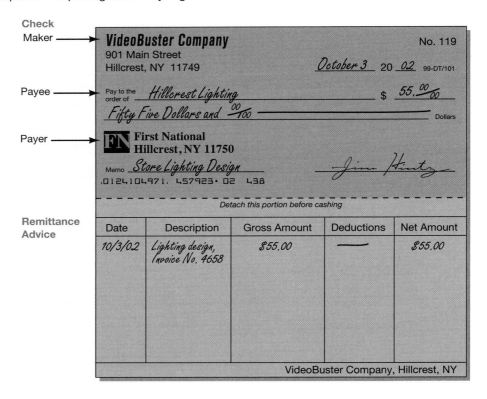

Check Maker →

Payee →

Payer →

Remittance Advice

---

receipts by EFT are listed with deposits and other additions. A bank statement is sometimes a depositor's only notice of an EFT.

Bank Statement

Usually once a month, the bank sends each depositor a bank statement showing the activity in the account. Different banks use different formats for their bank statements, but all of them include the following items of information:

1. Beginning-of-period balance of the depositor's account.
2. Checks and other debits decreasing the account during the period.
3. Deposits and other credits increasing the account during the period.
4. End-of-period balance of the depositor's account.

This information reflects the bank's records. Exhibit 6.6 shows one type of bank statement. Identify each of these four items in that statement. Part A of Exhibit 6.6 summarizes changes in the account. Part B lists paid checks along with other debits. Part C lists deposits and credits to the account, and part D shows the daily account balances.

Enclosed with a bank statement is a list of the depositor's canceled checks or the actual canceled checks along with any debit or credit memoranda affecting the account. **Canceled checks** are checks the bank has paid and deducted from the customer's account during the period. Other deductions that can appear on a bank statement include (1) service charges and fees assessed by the bank, (2) checks deposited that are uncollectible, (3) corrections of previous errors, (4) withdrawals through automated teller machines (ATMs), and (5) periodic payments arranged in advance by a depositor.[3] Except for service charges, the bank

Point: Good internal control is to deposit all cash receipts daily and make all payments for goods and services by check. This controls access to cash and creates an independent record of all cash activities.

---

[3] Most business checking accounts do not allow ATM withdrawals because of a desire to make all disbursements by check.

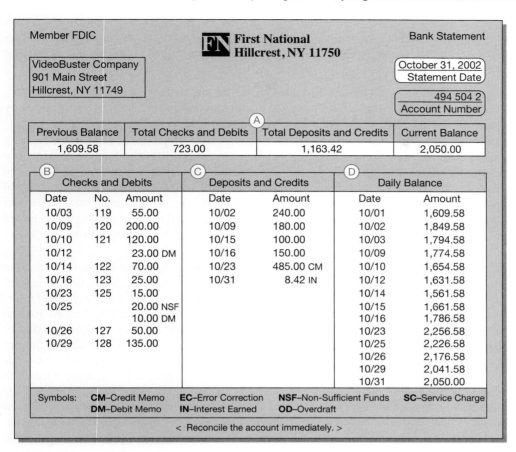

Member FDIC	**First National** **Hillcrest, NY 11750**	Bank Statement

VideoBuster Company
901 Main Street
Hillcrest, NY 11749

October 31, 2002
Statement Date

494 504 2
Account Number

(A)

Previous Balance	Total Checks and Debits	Total Deposits and Credits	Current Balance
1,609.58	723.00	1,163.42	2,050.00

(B)   (C)   (D)

Checks and Debits			Deposits and Credits		Daily Balance	
Date	No.	Amount	Date	Amount	Date	Amount
10/03	119	55.00	10/02	240.00	10/01	1,609.58
10/09	120	200.00	10/09	180.00	10/02	1,849.58
10/10	121	120.00	10/15	100.00	10/03	1,794.58
10/12		23.00 DM	10/16	150.00	10/09	1,774.58
10/14	122	70.00	10/23	485.00 CM	10/10	1,654.58
10/16	123	25.00	10/31	8.42 IN	10/12	1,631.58
10/23	125	15.00			10/14	1,561.58
10/25		20.00 NSF			10/15	1,661.58
		10.00 DM			10/16	1,786.58
10/26	127	50.00			10/23	2,256.58
10/29	128	135.00			10/25	2,226.58
					10/26	2,176.58
					10/29	2,041.58
					10/31	2,050.00

Symbols:	**CM**–Credit Memo	**EC**–Error Correction	**NSF**–Non-Sufficient Funds	**SC**–Service Charge
	DM–Debit Memo	**IN**–Interest Earned	**OD**–Overdraft	

< Reconcile the account immediately. >

Exhibit 6.6

Bank Statement

notifies the depositor of each deduction with a debit memorandum when the bank reduces the balance. A copy of each debit memorandum is usually sent with the statement.[4]

Transactions that increase the depositor's account include amounts the bank collects on behalf of the depositor and the corrections of previous errors. Credit memoranda notify the depositor of all increases when they are recorded. A copy of each credit memorandum is often sent with the bank statement. Another item sometimes added to the bank balance is interest earned by the depositor. Banks that pay interest on checking accounts often compute the amount of interest earned on the average cash balance and credit it to the depositor's account each period. In Exhibit 6.6, the bank credits $8.42 of interest to the account.

Global: A company must disclose any restrictions on cash accounts located outside the United States.

Bank Reconciliation

When a company deposits all cash receipts and makes all cash payments (except petty cash) by check, it can use the bank statement for proving the accuracy of its cash records. This is done using a **bank reconciliation,** which is a report explaining any differences between the checking account balance according to the depositor's records and the balance reported on the bank statement.

P5 Prepare a bank reconciliation.

Purpose of Bank Reconciliation

The balance of a checking account reported on the bank statement rarely equals the balance in the depositor's accounting records. This is usually due to information that one party has

---

[4] A depositor's account is a liability on the bank's records. This is so because the money belongs to the depositor, not the bank. When a depositor increases the account balance, the bank records it with a *credit* to the account. This means that debit memos from the bank produce *credits* on the depositor's books, and credit memos from the bank produce *debits* on the depositor's books.

Topic Tackler 6-2

that the other does not. We must therefore prove the accuracy of both the depositor's records and those of the bank. This means we must *reconcile* the two balances and explain or account for any differences in them. Among the factors causing the bank statement balance to differ from the depositor's book balance are these:

1. **Outstanding checks. Outstanding checks** are checks written (or drawn) by the depositor, deducted on the depositor's records, and sent to the payees but not yet received by the bank for payment at the bank statement date.

2. **Deposits in transit** (also called **outstanding deposits**). **Deposits in transit** are deposits made and recorded by the depositor but not yet recorded on the bank statement. For example, companies can make deposits (in the night depository) at the end of a business day after the bank is closed. If such a deposit occurred on a bank statement date, it would not appear on this period's statement. The bank would record such a deposit on the next business day, and it would appear on the next period's bank statement. Deposits mailed to the bank near the end of a period also can be in transit and unrecorded when the statement is prepared.

3. **Deductions for uncollectible items and for services.** A company sometimes deposits another party's check that is uncollectible (usually meaning the balance in such an account is not large enough to cover the check). This check is called a *non-sufficient funds (NSF)* check. The bank would have initially credited the depositor's account for the amount of the check. When the bank learns the check is uncollectible, it debits (reduces) the depositor's account for the amount of that check. The bank may also charge the depositor a fee for processing an uncollectible check and notify the depositor of the deduction by sending a debit memorandum. Each deduction should be recorded by the depositor when a debit memorandum is received, but an entry is sometimes not made until the bank reconciliation is prepared. Other possible bank charges to a depositor's account that are first reported on a bank statement include printing new checks and service fees.

4. **Additions for collections and for interest.** Banks sometimes act as collection agents for their depositors by collecting notes and other items. Banks can also receive electronic funds transfers to the depositor's account. When a bank collects an item, it is added to the depositor's account, less any service fee. The bank also sends a credit memorandum to notify the depositor of the transaction. When the memorandum is received, the depositor should record it; yet it sometimes remains unrecorded until the bank reconciliation is prepared. The bank statement also includes a credit for any interest earned.

5. **Errors.** Both banks and depositors can make errors. Bank errors might not be discovered until the depositor prepares the bank reconciliation. Also, depositor errors are sometimes discovered when the bank balance is reconciled.

Reconciling a Bank Balance

The person preparing the bank reconciliation should not be responsible for processing cash receipts, managing checks, or maintaining cash records. A reconciliation requires this person to

- Compare deposits on the bank statement with deposits in the accounting records. Identify any discrepancies, determine which is correct, and list any unrecorded deposits.

- Inspect all credits on the bank statement and determine whether each is recorded. Examples are collections by the bank, correction of previous bank statement errors, and interest earned by the depositor. List any unrecorded credits.

- Compare canceled checks on the bank statement with actual checks returned (if provided) with the statement. For each check, make sure the bank deducts the correct amount and properly charges it to the account. List any discrepancies.

- Compare canceled checks on the bank statement with checks recorded. List any outstanding checks. Inspect and list any canceled checks unrecorded.

- Identify any outstanding checks listed on the previous period's bank reconciliation that are not included in the canceled checks on this period's bank statement. List those checks that still remain outstanding. Send the list to the cashier for follow-up with payees to see if the checks were received.

■ Inspect all debits on the bank statement and determine whether each is recorded. Examples are bank charges for newly printed checks, NSF checks, and monthly service charges. List any unrecorded debits.

Point: Small businesses with few employees often allow recordkeepers to both write checks and keep the general ledger. If this is done, it is essential that the owner do the bank reconciliation.

When these tasks are complete, the employee can prepare the bank reconciliation report.

Illustrating a Bank Reconciliation

We follow nine steps in preparing the bank reconciliation. It is helpful to refer to the bank reconciliation in Exhibit 6.7 when studying steps ① through ⑨.

① Identify the bank statement balance of the cash account (*balance per bank*).

② Identify and list any unrecorded deposits and any bank errors understating the bank balance. Add them to the bank balance.

③ Identify and list any outstanding checks and any bank errors overstating the bank balance. Deduct them from the bank balance.

④ Compute the *adjusted bank balance,* also called the *corrected* or *reconciled balance.*

⑤ Identify the company's book balance of the cash account (*balance per book*).

⑥ Identify and list any unrecorded credit memoranda from the bank, interest earned, and errors understating the book balance. Add them to the book balance.

⑦ Identify and list any unrecorded debit memoranda from the bank, service charges, and errors overstating the book balance. Deduct them from the book balance.

⑧ Compute the *adjusted book balance,* also called *corrected* or *reconciled balance.*

⑨ Verify that the two adjusted balances from steps 4 and 8 are equal. If so, they are reconciled. If not, check for accuracy and missing data to achieve reconciliation.

In reconciling its bank account, VideoBuster gathered the following data:

■ Bank balance shown on the bank statement is $2,050.

■ Book balance shown in the accounting records is $1,404.58.

■ A $145 deposit placed in the bank's night depository on October 31 is not recorded on the bank statement.

■ A comparison of canceled checks with the company's books showed two checks outstanding—No. 124 for $150 and No. 126 for $200.

■ Enclosed with the bank statement is a credit memorandum showing the bank collected a note receivable for the company on October 23. The note's proceeds of $500 (minus a $15 collection fee) are credited to the company's account. The company has not yet recorded this credit memorandum.

■ The bank statement shows a credit of $8.42 for interest earned on the average cash balance. There was no prior notification of this item, and it is not yet recorded.

■ Other debits on the bank statement that are not recorded include (1) a $23 charge for check printing and (2) an NSF check for $20 plus a related $10 processing fee. (The NSF check is dated October 16 and was included in the book balance.)

Decision Insight

Days' Cash Expense Coverage The ratio of *cash (and cash equivalents) to average daily cash expenses* reflects the number of days a company can operate without additional cash inflows. It reflects on company liquidity.

The bank reconciliation in Exhibit 6.7 reflects these items. The circled numbers in this reconciliation correspond to the nine steps listed.

Recording Adjusting Entries from a Bank Reconciliation

A bank reconciliation identifies unrecorded items that need recording by the company. In VideoBuster's reconciliation, the adjusted balance of $1,845 is the correct balance as of

\$2,050.00		**VIDEOBUSTER**				
		Bank Reconciliation				
		October 31, 2002				

①	Bank statement balance		$2,050.00	⑤	Book balance		$1,404.58
②	Add			⑥	Add		
	Deposit of Oct. 31 in transit		145.00		Collect $500 note less $15 fee . .	$485.00	
			2,195.00		Interest earned	8.42	493.42
③	Deduct						1,898.00
	Outstanding checks			⑦	Deduct		
	No. 124	$150.00			Check printing charge	23.00	
	No. 126	200.00	350.00		NSF check plus service fee	30.00	53.00
④	**Adjusted bank balance**		**$1,845.00**	⑧	Adjusted book balance		**$1,845.00**
			⬆	⑨ Balances are equal (reconciled)			⬆

Exhibit 6.7

Bank Reconciliation

October 31. But the company's accounting records show a $1,404.58 balance. We must prepare journal entries to adjust the book balance to the correct balance. *It is important to remember that only the items reconciling the book balance require adjustment.* A review of Exhibit 6.7 indicates that four entries are required for VideoBuster.

Collection of note. The first entry is to record the proceeds of its note receivable collected by the bank less the expense of having the bank perform that service:

Assets = Liabilities + Equity
+485   −15
−500

Oct. 31	Cash	485	
	Collection Expense	15	
	Notes Receivable		500
	To record the collection fee and proceeds for a note collected by the bank.		

Interest earned. The second entry records interest credited to its account by the bank:

Assets = Liabilities + Equity
+8.42   +8.42

Oct. 31	Cash	8.42	
	Interest Revenue		8.42
	To record interest earned on the cash balance in the checking account.		

Check printing. The third entry records expenses for the check printing charge:

Assets = Liabilities + Equity
−23   −23

Oct. 31	Miscellaneous Expenses	23	
	Cash		23
	Check printing charge.		

NSF check. The fourth entry records the NSF check that is returned as uncollectible. The $20 check was originally received from F. Heflin in payment of his account and then deposited. The bank charged $10 for handling the NSF check and deducted $30 total from VideoBuster's account. This means the entry must reverse the effects of the original entry made when the check was received and also must record (add) the $10 bank fee:

Point: The company will try to collect the entire NSF amount ($30).

Assets = Liabilities + Equity
+30
−30

Oct. 31	Accounts Receivable—F. Heflin	30	
	Cash		30
	To charge Heflin's account for $20 NSF check and $10 bank fee.		

After these four entries are recorded, the book balance of cash is adjusted to the correct amount of $1,845 ($1,404.58 + $485 + $8.42 − $23 − $30).

Quick Check

11. What is a bank statement?

12. What is the meaning of the phrase *to reconcile a bank balance?*

13. Why do we reconcile the bank statement balance of cash and the depositor's book balance of cash?

14. List at least two items affecting the bank balance side of a bank reconciliation and indicate whether the items are added or subtracted.

15. List at least three items affecting the book balance side of a bank reconciliation and indicate whether the items are added or subtracted.

Answers—p. 276

Days' Sales Uncollected

Decision Analysis

Many companies attract customers by selling to them on credit. This means that cash receipts from customers are delayed until accounts receivable are collected. Users of accounting information often want to know how quickly a company can convert its accounts receivable into cash. This is important for evaluating a company's liquidity. One measure of the receivables' nearness to cash is the **days' sales uncollected,** also called *days' sales in receivables.* This measure is computed by dividing the current balance of receivables by net credit sales over the year just completed and then multiplying by 365 (number of days in a year). Since net credit sales usually are not reported to external users, the net sales (or revenues) figure is commonly used in the computation as shown in Exhibit 6.8.

A1 Compute the days' sales uncollected ratio and use it to analyze liquidity.

$$\text{Days' sales uncollected} = \frac{\text{Accounts receivable}}{\text{Net sales}} \times 365$$

Exhibit 6.8
Days' Sales Uncollected

We use days' sales uncollected to estimate how much time is likely to pass before the current amount of accounts receivable is received in cash. For evaluation purposes, we need to compare this estimate to that for other companies in the same industry. We also make comparisons between current and prior periods.

To illustrate, we select data from the annual reports of two toy manufacturers, Hasbro and Mattel. Their days' sales uncollected figures are shown in Exhibit 6.9.

Company	Figure ($ millions)	2000	1999
Hasbro	Accounts receivable	$686	$1,084
	Net sales	$3,787	$4,232
	Days' sales uncollected	**66 days**	**93 days**
Mattel	Accounts receivable	$840	$1,002
	Net sales	$4,670	$4,595
	Days' sales uncollected	**66 days**	**80 days**

Exhibit 6.9
Analysis using Days' Sales Uncollected

Decision Maker

Sales Representative   The sales staff is told to take action to help reduce days' sales uncollected. What can you, a salesperson, do to reduce days' sales uncollected?

Answer—p. 275

Days' sales uncollected for Hasbro in 2000 is computed as ($686/$3,787) × 365 days = 66 days. This means that it will take about 66 days to collect cash from ending accounts receivable. This number reflects one or more of the following factors: a company's ability to collect receivables, customer financial health, customer payment strategies, and discount terms. To further assess days' sales uncollected for Hasbro, we compare it to the prior year and to those of Mattel. We see that Hasbro's days' sales uncollected has declined (improved) from 93 to 66 days. In comparison to Mattel, Hasbro is competitive on this factor. Specifically, days' sales uncollected for Mattel has declined from 80 days to 66 days. The less time money is tied up in receivables often translates into increased profitability.

Demonstration Problem

Prepare a bank reconciliation for Jamboree Enterprises for the month ended November 30, 2002. The following information is available to reconcile Jamboree Enterprises' book balance of cash with its bank statement balance as of November 30, 2002:

a. After all posting is complete on November 30, the company's book balance of Cash has a $16,380 debit balance, but its bank statement shows a $38,520 balance.

b. Checks No. 2024 for $4,810 and No. 2036 for $5,000 are outstanding.

c. In comparing the canceled checks on the bank statement with the entries in the accounting records, it is found that Check No. 2025 in payment of rent is correctly drawn for $1,000 but is erroneously entered in the accounting records as $880.

d. The November 30 deposit of $17,150 was placed in the night depository after banking hours on that date, and this amount does not appear on the bank statement.

e. In reviewing the bank statement, a check written by Jumbo Enterprises in the amount of $160 was erroneously drawn against Jamboree's account.

f. A credit memorandum enclosed with the bank statement indicates that the bank collected a $30,000 note and $900 of related interest on Jamboree's behalf. This transaction was not recorded by Jamboree prior to receiving the statement.

g. A debit memorandum for $1,100 lists a $1,100 NSF check received from a customer, Marilyn Welch. Jamboree had not recorded the return of this check before receiving the statement.

h. Bank service charges for November total $40. These charges were not recorded by Jamboree before receiving the statement.

Planning the Solution

● Set up a bank reconciliation with a bank side and a book side (as in Exhibit 6.7). Leave room to both add and deduct items. Each column will result in a reconciled, equal balance.

● Examine each item *a* through *h* to determine whether it affects the book or the bank balance and whether it should be added or deducted from the bank or book balance.

● After all items are analyzed, complete the reconciliation and arrive at a reconciled balance between the bank side and the book side.

● For each reconciling item on the book side, prepare an adjusting entry. Additions to the book side require an adjusting entry that debits Cash. Deductions on the book side require an adjusting entry that credits Cash.

Solution to Demonstration Problem

JAMBOREE ENTERPRISES
Bank Reconciliation
November 30, 2002

Bank statement balance		$38,520	Book balance		$16,380	
Add			Add			
Deposit of Nov. 30. . . .	$17,150		Collection of note . .	$30,000		
Bank error.	160	17,310	Interest earned	900	30,900	
		55,830			47,280	
Deduct			Deduct			
Outstanding checks		9,810	NSF check	1,100		
			Recording error	120		
			Service charge	40	1,260	
Adjusted bank balance		**$46,020**	**Adjusted book balance**		**$46,020**	

Required Adjusting Entries for Jamboree

Nov. 30	Cash	30,900	
	Notes Receivable		30,000
	Interest Earned		900
	To record collection of note with interest.		
Nov. 30	Accounts Receivable—M. Welch	1,100	
	Cash		1,100
	To reinstate account due from an NSF check.		
Nov. 30	Rent Expense	120	
	Cash		120
	To correct recording error on check no. 2025.		
Nov. 30	Bank Service Charges	40	
	Cash		40
	To record bank service charges.		

Documents in a Voucher System

This appendix describes the important business documents of a voucher system of control.

Purchase Requisition

Department managers are usually not allowed to place orders directly with suppliers. If each manager were allowed to deal directly with suppliers, the merchandise purchased and the resulting liabilities would not be well controlled. To gain control over purchases, department managers are usually required to place all orders through a purchasing department. When merchandise is needed, a

Exhibit 6A.1
Purchase Requisition

Purchase Requisition		No. 917

Z-Mart

From ___ Sporting Goods Department __   **Date** _____ October 28, 2002 _____
To ____ Purchasing Department _____   **Preferred Vendor** ___ Trex ___

Request purchase of the following item(s):

Model No.	Description	Quantity
CH 015	Challenger X7	1
SD 099	SpeedDemon	1

Reason for Request _____ Replenish inventory _____
Approval for Request _____   *J.Z.* _____

For Purchasing Department use only: Order Date _10/30/02_   P.O. No. ____P98____

department manager must inform the purchasing department of its needs by preparing and signing a **purchase requisition,** which lists the merchandise needed and requests that it be purchased—see Exhibit 6A.1. Two copies of the purchase requisition are sent to the purchasing department. The purchasing department then sends one copy to the accounting department. When the accounting department receives a purchase requisition, it creates and maintains a voucher for this transaction. A third copy of the requisition is kept by the requesting department as backup.

Purchase Order

A **purchase order** is a document the purchasing department uses to place an order with a **vendor** (seller or supplier). A vendor usually is a manufacturer or wholesaler. A purchase order authorizes a vendor to ship ordered merchandise at the stated price and terms—see Exhibit 6A.2. When the purchasing department receives a purchase requisition, it prepares at least four copies of a purchase order. The copies are distributed as follows: *copy 1* is sent to the vendor as a purchase request and as authority to ship merchandise; *copy 2* is sent, along with a copy of the purchase requisition, to the accounting department, where it is entered in the voucher and used in approving payment of the invoice; *copy 3* is sent to the requesting department to inform its manager that action is being taken; and *copy 4* is retained on file by the purchasing department.

Exhibit 6A.2
Purchase Order

Purchase Order		No. P98

Z-Mart
10 Michigan Street
Chicago, Illinois 60521

To: Trex
W9797 Cherry Road
Antigo, Wisconsin 54409

Date _____ 10/30/02 _____
FOB _____ Destination _____
Ship by As soon as possible ____
Terms _____ 2/15, n/30 _____

Request shipment of the following item(s):

Model No.	Description	Quantity	Price	Amount
CH 015	Challenger X7	1	490	490
SD 099	SpeedDemon	1	710	710

All shipments and invoices must include purchase order number

Ordered by

J.W.

Invoice

An **invoice** is an itemized statement of goods prepared by the vendor listing the customer's name, items sold, sales prices, and terms of sale. An invoice is also a bill sent to the buyer from the supplier. From the vendor's point of view, it is a *sales invoice*. The vendor sends the invoice to a buyer, or **vendee,** who treats it as a *purchase invoice*. When receiving a purchase order, the vendor ships the ordered merchandise to the buyer and includes or mails a copy of the invoice covering the shipment to the buyer. The invoice is sent to the buyer's accounting department where it is placed in the voucher. (Refer back to Exhibit 4.6, which shows Z-Mart's purchase invoice.)

Receiving Report

Many companies maintain a separate department to receive all merchandise and purchased assets. When each shipment arrives, this receiving department counts the goods and checks them for damage and agreement with the purchase order. It then prepares four or more copies of a **receiving report,** which is used within the company to notify the appropriate persons that ordered goods have been received and to describe the quantities and condition of the goods. One copy is placed in the voucher. Copies are also sent to the requesting department and the purchasing department to notify them that the goods have arrived. The receiving department retains a copy in its files.

Invoice Approval

When a receiving report arrives, the accounting department should have copies of the following documents in the voucher: purchase requisition, purchase order, and invoice. With the information in these documents, the accounting department can record the purchase and approve its payment. In approving an invoice for payment, the department checks and compares information across all documents. To facilitate this checking and to ensure that no step is omitted, the department often uses an **invoice approval,** also called *check authorization*—see Exhibit 6A.3. An invoice approval is a checklist of steps necessary for approving an invoice for recording and payment. It is a separate document either filed in the voucher or preprinted (or stamped) on the voucher.

Invoice Approval			
Document		By	Date
Purchase requisition	917	72	10/28/02
Purchase order	P98	9w	10/30/02
Receiving report	R85	SK	11/3/02
Invoice	4657		11/12/02
Price		9K	11/12/02
Calculations		9K	11/12/02
Terms		9K	11/12/02
Approved for payment		BC	

Exhibit 6A.3

Invoice Approval

As each step in the checklist is approved, the person initials the invoice approval and records the current date. Final approval implies the following steps have occurred:

1. **Requisition check:** Items on invoice are requested per purchase requisition.
2. **Purchase order check:** Items on invoice are ordered per purchase order.
3. **Receiving report check:** Items on invoice are received, per receiving report.
4. **Invoice check: Price:** Invoice prices are as agreed with the vendor.
   Calculations: Invoice has no mathematical errors.
   Terms: Terms are as agreed with the vendor.

Point: Recording a purchase is initiated by an invoice approval, not an invoice. An invoice approval verifies that the amount is consistent with that requested, ordered, and received. This controls and verifies purchases and related liabilities.

Voucher

Once an invoice has been checked and approved, the voucher is complete. A complete voucher is a record summarizing a transaction. Once the voucher certifies a transaction as correct, it authorizes recording an obligation. A voucher also contains approval for paying the obligation on an appropriate date. The physical form of a voucher varies across companies. Many are designed so that the invoice and other related source documents are placed inside the voucher, which is often a folder.

Completion of a voucher usually requires a person to enter certain information on both the inside and outside of the voucher. Typical information required on the inside of a voucher is shown in Exhibit 6A.4, and that for the outside is shown in Exhibit 6A.5. This information is taken from the

Exhibit 6A.4

Inside of a Voucher

		Z-Mart	Voucher No. 4657
		Chicago, Illinois	

Date ___ Oct. 28, 2002 _____

Pay to __ Trex _____

City ____ Antigo _____ State Wisconsin _____

For the following: (attach all invoices and supporting documents)

Date of Invoice	Terms	Invoice Number and Other Details	Terms
Nov. 2, 2002	2/15, n/30	Invoice No. 4657	1,200
		Less discount	24
		Net amount payable	1,176

Payment approved

N. O. Neal

Auditor

invoice and the supporting documents filed in the voucher. A complete voucher is sent to an authorized individual (often called an *auditor*). This person performs a final review, approves the accounts and amounts for debiting (called the *accounting distribution*), and authorizes recording of the voucher.

After a voucher is approved and recorded, it is filed until its due date, when it is sent to the cashier for payment. The person issuing checks relies on the approved voucher and its signed supporting documents as proof that an obligation has been incurred and must be paid. The purchase requisition and purchase order confirm the purchase was authorized. The receiving report shows that items have been received, and the invoice approval form verifies that the invoice has been checked for errors. There is little chance for error and even less chance for fraud without collusion unless all the documents and signatures are forged.

Exhibit 6A.5

Outside of a Voucher

Voucher No. 4657

Accounting Distribution

Account Debited	Amount
Merch. Inventory	1,200
Store Supplies	
Office Supplies	
Sales Salaries	
Other	
Total Vouch. Pay. Cr.	1,200

Due Date _____ November 12, 2002 ____

Pay to _____ Trex _____

City _____ Antigo _____

State _____ Wisconsin ____

Summary of charges:

Total charges _____ 1,200

Discount _____ 24

Net payment _____ 1,176

Record of payment:

Paid _____

Check No. _____

Summary

C1 Define internal control and its purpose. An internal control system consists of the policies and procedures managers use to protect assets, ensure reliable accounting, promote efficient operations, and urge adherence to company policies. It can prevent avoidable losses and help managers both plan operations and monitor company and human performance.

C2 Identify principles of internal control. Principles of good internal control include establishing responsibilities, maintaining adequate records, insuring assets and bonding employees, separating recordkeeping from custody of assets, dividing responsibilities for related transactions, applying technological controls, and performing regular independent reviews.

C3 **Define cash and cash equivalents and explain how to report them.** Cash includes currency, coins, and amounts on (or acceptable for) deposit in checking and savings accounts. Cash equivalents are short-term, highly liquid investment assets readily convertible to a known cash amount and sufficiently close to their maturity date so that market value is not sensitive to interest rate changes. Cash and cash equivalents are liquid assets because they are readily converted into other assets or can be used to pay for goods, services, or liabilities.

C4 **Identify control features of banking activities.** Banks offer several services that promote the control and safeguarding of cash. A bank account is a record set up by a bank permitting a customer to deposit money for safekeeping and to draw checks on it. A bank deposit is money contributed to the account with a deposit ticket as proof. A check is a document signed by the depositor instructing the bank to pay a specified amount of money to a designated recipient.

A1 **Compute the days' sales uncollected ratio and use it to analyze liquidity.** Many companies attract customers by selling to them on credit. This means that cash flows from customers are delayed until accounts receivable are collected. Users want to know how quickly a company can convert its accounts receivable into cash. This is important for evaluating a company's liquidity. The days' sales uncollected ratio, one measure reflecting liquidity, is computed by dividing the ending balance of receivables by annual net sales, and then multiplying by 365.

P1 **Apply internal control to cash receipts.** Internal control of cash receipts ensures all cash received is properly recorded and deposited. Attention is focused on two important types of cash receipts: over-the-counter and by mail. Good internal control for over-the-counter cash receipts includes use of a cash register, customer review, use of receipts, a permanent transaction record, and separation of the custody of cash from its recordkeeping. Good internal control for cash receipts by mail includes at least two people assigned to open mail and a listing of each sender's name, amount, and explanation.

P2 **Apply the voucher system to control cash disbursements.** A voucher system is a set of procedures and approvals designed to control cash disbursements and acceptance of obligations. The voucher system of control relies on several important documents, including the voucher and its supporting files. A key factor in this system is that only approved departments and individuals are authorized to incur certain obligations.

P3 **Explain and record petty cash fund transactions.** Petty cash disbursements are payments of small amounts for items such as postage, courier fees, repairs, and supplies. A company usually sets up one or more petty cash funds. A petty fund cashier is responsible for safekeeping the cash, making payments from this fund, and keeping receipts and records. A Petty Cash account is debited only when the fund is established or increased in amount. When the fund is replenished, petty cash disbursements are recorded with debits to expense (or asset) accounts and a credit to cash.

P4 **Apply the net method to control purchase discounts.** The net method aids management in monitoring and controlling purchase discounts. When invoices are recorded at gross amounts, the amount of discounts taken is deducted from the balance of the Merchandise Inventory account. This means that the amount of any discounts lost is not reported in any account and is unlikely to come to the attention of management. When purchases are recorded at net amounts, a Discounts Lost account is brought to management's attention as an operating expense. Management can then seek to identify the reason for discounts lost, such as oversight, carelessness, or unfavorable terms.

P5 **Prepare a bank reconciliation.** A bank reconciliation proves the accuracy of the depositor's and the bank's records. The bank statement balance is adjusted for items such as outstanding checks and unrecorded deposits made on or before the bank statement date but not reflected on the statement. The book balance is adjusted for items such as service charges, bank collections for the depositor, and interest earned on the account.

Guidance Answers to **Decision Maker** and **Decision Ethics**

Entrepreneur A forced vacation policy is part of a good system of internal controls. When employees are forced to take vacations, their ability to hide any fraudulent behavior decreases because others must perform the duties of the people on vacation. A replacement employee potentially can uncover fraudulent behavior or falsified records. A forced vacation policy is especially important for employees in sensitive positions of handling money or in control of easily transferable assets.

Internal Auditor Since you were asked to postpone your count, along with the fact the fund consists of 14 new $20 bills, you have legitimate concerns about whether money is being used for personal use. It is possible the most recent reimbursement of the fund was for $280 (14 × $20) or more. In that case, this reimbursement can leave the fund with sequentially numbered $20 bills. But if the most recent reimbursement was for less than $280, the presence of 14

sequentially numbered $20 bills suggests that the new bills were obtained from a bank as replacement for bills that had been removed. Neither situation shows that the cashier is stealing money, but the second case indicates that the cashier "borrowed" the cash and later replaced it after the auditor showed up. In writing your report, you must not conclude that the cashier is unethical unless other evidence supports it. You should consider additional surprise counts of this petty cashier over the next few weeks.

Sales Representative A salesperson can take several steps to reduce days' sales uncollected. These include (1) decreasing the ratio of sales on account to total sales by encouraging more cash sales, (2) identifying customers most delayed in their payments and encouraging earlier payments or cash sales, and (3) applying stricter credit policies to eliminate credit sales to customers that never pay.

Guidance Answers to **Quick Checks**

1. (*c*)

2. Technology reduces processing errors. It also allows more extensive testing of records, limits the amount of hard evidence, and highlights the importance of separation of duties.

3. A company holds liquid assets so that it can purchase other assets, buy services, and pay obligations.

4. It owns cash equivalents because they yield a return greater than what cash earns (and are readily exchanged for cash).

5. Examples of cash equivalents are 90-day U.S. Treasury bills, money market funds, and commercial paper (notes).

6. (*a*)

7. A voucher system is used when an owner/manager can no longer control purchasing procedures through personal supervision and direct participation.

8. If all cash payments are made by check, numerous checks for small amounts must be written. Since this practice is expensive and time-consuming, a petty cash fund is often established for making small (immaterial) cash payments.

9. If the petty cash fund is not reimbursed at the end of an accounting period, the transactions involving petty cash are not yet recorded and the petty cash asset is overstated.

10. First, when the petty cash fund is reimbursed, the petty cash transactions are recorded. Second, reimbursement provides cash to allow the fund to continue being used. Third, reimbursement identifies any cash shortage or overage in the fund.

11. A bank statement is a report prepared by the bank describing the activities in a depositor's account.

12. To reconcile a bank balance means to explain the difference between the cash balance in the depositor's accounting records and the cash balance on the bank statement.

13. The purpose of the bank reconciliation is to determine whether the bank or the depositor has made any errors and whether the bank has entered any transactions affecting the account that the depositor has not recorded.

14. Outstanding checks—subtracted
    Unrecorded deposits—added

15. Debit memos—subtracted   Interest earned—added
    NSF checks—subtracted   Credit memos—added
    Bank service charges—subtracted

Glossary

Bank reconciliation Report that explains the difference between the book balance of cash and the cash balance reported on the bank statement. (p. 265)

Canceled checks Checks that the bank has paid and deducted from the depositor's account. (p. 264)

Cash Includes currency, coins, and amounts on deposit in bank checking or savings accounts. (p. 255)

Cash equivalents Short-term, investment assets that are readily convertible to a known cash amount and sufficiently close to their maturity date so that market value is not sensitive to interest rate changes. (p. 255)

Cash Over and Short Income statement account used to record cash overages and cash shortages arising from errors in cash receipts or payments. (p. 256)

Check Document signed by the depositor instructing the bank to pay a specified amount to a designated recipient. (p. 263)

Days' sales uncollected Measure of the liquidity of receivables computed by dividing the current balance of receivables by the annual credit (or net) sales, and then multiplying by 365; also called *days' sales in receivables*. (p. 269)

Deposits in transit Deposits recorded by the company but not yet by its bank. (p. 266)

Deposit ticket Lists items such as currency, coins, and checks deposited and their corresponding dollar amounts. (p. 263)

Discounts Lost Expense resulting from a failure to take advantage of cash discounts on purchases. (p. 262)

Electronic funds transfer (EFT) Use of electronic communication to transfer cash from one party to another. (p. 263)

Gross method Method of recording purchases at the full invoice price without deducting any cash discounts. (p. 261)

Internal control system All policies and procedures used to protect assets, ensure reliable accounting, promote efficient operations, and urge adherence to company policies. (p. 250)

Invoice Itemized record of goods prepared by the vendor that lists the customer's name, the items sold, the sales prices, and the terms of sale. (p. 273)

Invoice approval Document containing a checklist of steps necessary for approving an invoice for recording and payment; also called *check authorization*. (p. 273)

Liquid assets Resources such as cash that are easily converted into other assets or used to pay for goods, services, or liabilities. (p. 255)

Liquidity Company's ability to pay for its short-term obligations. (p. 255)

Net method Method of recording purchases at the full invoice price less any cash discounts. (p. 262)

Outstanding checks Checks written and recorded by the depositor but not yet paid by the bank at the bank statement date. (p. 266)

Principles of internal control Principles requiring management to establish responsibility, maintain records, insure assets, separate recordkeeping from custody of assets, divide responsibility for related transactions, apply technological controls, and perform reviews. (p. 250)

Purchase order Document used by the purchasing department to place an order with a seller (vendor). (p. 272)

Purchase requisition Document listing merchandise needed by a department and requesting it be purchased. (p. 272)

Receiving report Form used to report that ordered goods are received and to describe their quantity and condition. (p. 273)

Signature card Includes the signatures of each person authorized to sign checks on the account. (p. 262)

Vendee Buyer or purchaser of goods or services. (p. 273)

Vendor Seller of goods or services. (p. 272)

Voucher Internal file used to store documents and information to control cash disbursements and to ensure that a transaction is properly recorded. (p. 258)

Voucher system Procedures and approvals designed to control cash disbursements and acceptance of obligations. (p. 257)

The superscript letter ^A denotes assignments based on Appendix 6A.

Questions

1. List the seven broad principles of internal control.

2. 🖉 Why should responsibility for related transactions be divided among different departments or individuals?

3. 🖉 Internal control procedures are important in every business, but at what stage in the development of a business do they become especially critical?

4. Which of the following assets is most liquid? Which is least liquid? Inventory, building, accounts receivable or cash.

5. 🖉 Why should the person who keeps the records of an asset not be the person responsible for its custody?

6. 🖉 When a store purchases merchandise, why are individual departments not allowed to directly deal with suppliers?

7. What is a petty cash receipt? Who should sign it?

8. Why should cash receipts be deposited on the day of receipt?

9. **Nike**'s statement of cash flows in Appendix A describes changes in cash and cash equivalents for the year ended May 31, 2000. What amount is provided (used) by investing activities? What amount is provided (used) by financing activities?   **NIKE**

10. 🖉 **Reebok**'s balance sheet in Appendix A reports cash and cash equivalents as of December 31, 1999 and 1998. Compare and discuss the amount of cash and cash equivalents with the other current assets as of December 31, 1999. Compare and assess the amount of cash and cash equivalents as of December 31, 1999 with its amount at December 31, 1998.   **Reebok**

11. 🖉 **Gap**'s balance sheet in Appendix A reports that cash and equivalents decreased during the fiscal year ended Jan. 29, 2000. Identify at least three major sources of this change in cash and equivalents.   **GAP**

QUICK STUDY

An internal control system consists of all policies and procedures used to protect assets, ensure reliable accounting, promote efficient operations, and urge adherence to company policies.

1. What is the main objective of internal control procedures, and how is it achieved?

2. Why should recordkeeping for assets be separated from custody over the assets?

QS 6-1 🖉
Internal control objectives   C1 C2

A good system of internal control for cash provides adequate procedures for protecting both cash receipts and cash disbursements. What are three basic guidelines that help achieve this protection?

QS 6-2 🖉
Internal control for cash   P1

Define and contrast the terms *liquid asset* and *cash equivalent*.

QS 6-3
Terminology   C1

Which accounting method uses a Discounts Lost account? What is the advantage of this method for management?

QS 6-4 🖉
Purchase discounts   P4

---

1. The petty cash fund of the Roberts Agency is established at $85. At the end of the current period, the fund contained $14.80 and had the following receipts: film rentals, $21.30, and refreshments for meetings, $30.85 (both expenditures to be classified as Entertainment Expense); postage, $8.95; and printing, $9.10. Prepare journal entries to record (*a*) establishment of the fund and (*b*) reimbursement of the fund at the end of the current period.

2. Identify the two events that cause a Petty Cash account to be credited in a journal entry.

QS 6-5
Petty cash accounting

P3

QS 6-6
Bank reconciliation
P5

1. For each of the following items indicate whether its amount (i) affects the bank or book side of a bank reconciliation and (ii) represents an addition or a subtraction in a bank reconciliation:

   a. Outstanding checks   **d.** Unrecorded deposits   **g.** Bank service charges
   b. Debit memos   **e.** Interest on cash balance
   c. NSF checks   **f.** Credit memos

2. Which of the items in part 1 require an adjusting journal entry?

QS 6-7
Days' sales uncollected
A1

The following annual account balances are taken from Daredevil Sports at December 31:

	2002	2001
Accounts receivable	$ 85,692	$ 80,485
Net sales	2,691,855	2,396,858

What is the change in the number of days' sales uncollected between years 2002 and 2001? According to this analysis, is the company's collection of receivables improving? Explain your answer.

EXERCISES

Exercise 6-1
Recommend internal control procedures **C2**

What internal control procedures would you recommend in each of the following situations?

1. A concession company has one employee who sells T-shirts and sunglasses at the beach. Each day, the employee is given enough shirts and sunglasses to last through the day and enough cash to make change. The money is kept in a box at the stand.

2. An antique store has one employee who is given cash and sent to garage sales each weekend. The employee pays cash for this merchandise that the antique store resells.

Exercise 6-2
Internal control of cash **P1**
receipts by mail

Some of O'Hara Co.'s cash receipts from customers are sent to the company with the regular mail. O'Hara's recordkeeper opens these letters and deposits the cash received each day. Identify any internal control problem(s) in this arrangement. What changes do you recommend?

Exercise 6-3
Analyzing internal control
C2

Folkerts Company is a rapidly growing start-up business. Its recordkeeper, who was hired one year ago, left town after the company's manager discovered that a large sum of money had disappeared over the past six months. An audit disclosed that the recordkeeper had written and signed several checks made payable to her fiancé and then recorded the checks as salaries expense. The fiancé, who cashed the checks but never worked for the company, left town with the recordkeeper. As a result, the company incurred an uninsured loss of $184,000. Evaluate Folkerts's internal control system and indicate which principles of internal control appear to have been ignored.

Exercise 6-4
Petty cash fund **P3**
with a shortage

Brady Company establishes a $350 petty cash fund on September 9. On September 30, the fund shows $103.25 in cash along with receipts for the following expenditures: transportation-in, $39.85; postage expenses, $123.55; and miscellaneous expenses, $80.00. The petty cashier could not account for a $3.35 shortage in the fund. Brady uses the perpetual system in accounting for merchandise inventory. Prepare (1) the September 9 entry to establish the fund and (2) the September 30 entry to reimburse the fund and reduce it to $250.

Check (2) Cr. Cash $146.75

Exercise 6-5
Petty cash fund
P3

Eanes Co. establishes a $200 petty cash fund on January 1. One week later, the fund shows $38 in cash along with receipts for the following expenditures: postage, $74; transportation-in, $29; delivery expenses, $16; and miscellaneous expenses, $43. Eanes uses the perpetual system in accounting for merchandise inventory. Prepare journal entries to (1) establish the fund on January 1, (2) reimburse it on January 8, and (3) reimburse the fund and increase it to $400 on January 8 assuming no entry in part 2.

Check (3) Cr. Cash $362

Exercise 6-6
Bank reconciliation and adjusting entries
P5

Prepare a table with the following headings for a monthly bank reconciliation dated September 30:

Bank Balance		Book Balance			Not Shown on the Reconciliation
Add	Deduct	Add	Deduct	Adjust	

For each item 1 through 12, place an *x* in the appropriate column to indicate whether the item should be added to or deducted from the book or bank balance, or whether it should not appear on the reconciliation. If the book balance is to be adjusted, place a *Dr.* or *Cr.* in the Adjust column to indicate whether the Cash balance should be debited or credited. At the left side of your table, number the items to correspond to the following list.

1. Bank service charge.
2. Checks written and mailed to payees on October 2.
3. Checks written by another depositor but charged against this company's account.
4. Principal and interest on a note collected by the bank but not yet recorded by the company.
5. Special bank charge for collection of note in part 4 on this company's behalf.
6. Check written against the company's account and cleared by the bank; erroneously not recorded by the company's recordkeeper.
7. Interest earned on the cash balance in the bank.
8. Night deposit made on September 30 after the bank closed.
9. Checks outstanding on August 31 that cleared the bank in September.
10. NSF check from customer returned on September 25 but not yet recorded by this company.
11. Checks written by the company and mailed to payees on September 30.
12. Deposit made on September 5 and processed on September 6.

Ashley Clinic deposits all cash receipts on the day when they are received and makes all cash payments by check. At the close of business on June 30, 2002, its Cash account shows an $11,589 debit balance. Ashley Clinic's June 30 bank statement shows $10,555 on deposit in the bank on that day. Prepare a bank reconciliation for Ashley Clinic using the following information:

a. Outstanding checks as of June 30 total $1,829.
b. The June 30 bank statement included a $16 debit memorandum for bank services.
c. Check No. 919, listed with the canceled checks, was correctly drawn for $467 in payment of a utility bill on June 15. Ashley Clinic mistakenly recorded it with a debit to Utilities Expense and a credit to Cash in the amount of $476.
d. The June 30 cash receipts of $2,856 were placed in the bank's night depository after banking hours and were not recorded on the June 30 bank statement.

Exercise 6-7
Bank reconciliation
P5

Check Reconciled bal., $11,582

Prepare the adjusting journal entries that Ashley Clinic must record as a result of preparing the bank reconciliation in Exercise 6-7.

Exercise 6-8
Adjusting entries from **P5**
bank reconciliation

Fresh Jive Co. reported annual net sales for 2001 and 2002 of $665,000 and $747,000, respectively. Its year-end balances of accounts receivable were as follows: December 31, 2001, $61,000; and December 31, 2002, $93,000. Calculate its days' sales uncollected at the end of each year and comment on any changes in the amount of liquid assets tied up in receivables.

Exercise 6-9
Liquid assets and **A1**
accounts receivable

Pelkner's Imports uses the perpetual system in accounting for merchandise inventory and had the following transactions during the month of October. Prepare entries to record these transactions assuming Pelkner's records invoices (*a*) at gross amounts and (*b*) at net amounts.

Oct. 2 Received merchandise purchased at a $3,000 invoice price, invoice dated October 2, terms 2/10, n/30.
10 Received a $500 credit memorandum (at full invoice price) for merchandise received on October 2 and returned for credit.
17 Received merchandise purchased at a $5,400 invoice price, invoice dated October 16, terms 2/10, n/30.
26 Paid for the merchandise received on October 17, less the discount.
31 Paid for the merchandise received on October 2. Payment was delayed because the invoice was mistakenly filed for payment today. This error caused the discount to be lost.

Exercise 6-10
Record invoices at gross or net amounts
P4

Management uses a voucher system to help control and monitor cash disbursements. Identify at least four key documents that are part of a voucher system of control. Explain each document's purpose, where it originates, and how it flows through the voucher system (including its copies).

Exercise 6-11^A
Documents in a **P2**
voucher system

PROBLEM SET A

Problem 6-1A
Analyzing internal control

C2

For each of these five separate cases, identify the principle of internal control that is violated. Recommend what the business should do to ensure adherence to principles of internal control.

1. Heather Hawthorne records all incoming customer cash receipts for her employer and posts the customer payments to their respective accounts.
2. At Cunningham Company, John and Jo alternate lunch hours. John is the petty cash custodian, but if someone needs petty cash when he is at lunch, Jo fills in as custodian.
3. Marcia Diamond does all the posting of patient charges and payments at the Provincetown Medical Clinic. Each night Marcia backs up the computerized accounting system to a tape and stores the tape in a locked file at her desk.
4. Bob Magee prides himself on hiring quality workers who require little supervision. As office manager, Bob gives his employees full discretion over their tasks and for years has seen no reason to perform independent reviews of their work.
5. Susan Smith's manager has told her to reduce costs. Susan decides to raise the deductible on the plant's property insurance from $5,000 to $10,000. This cuts the property insurance premium in half. In a related move, she decides that bonding the plant's employees is a waste of money since the company has not experienced any losses due to employee theft. Susan saves the entire amount of the bonding insurance premium by dropping the bonding insurance.

Problem 6-2A
Establish, reimburse, and adjust petty cash

P3

G

Roosevelt Co. set up a petty cash fund for payments of small amounts. The following transactions involving the petty cash fund occurred in May (the last month of the company's fiscal year):

May 1   Prepared a company check for $250 to establish the petty cash fund.
    15   Prepared a company check to replenish the fund for the following expenditures made since May 1 and to increase the fund to $500.
         a. Paid $88 for janitorial services.
         b. Paid $53.68 for miscellaneous expenses.
         c. Paid postage expenses of $53.50.
         d. Paid $47.15 to *The County Crier* (the local newspaper) for an advertisement.
         e. Counted $11.15 remaining in the petty cash box.
    31   The petty cashier reports that $293.39 cash remains in the fund and decides that the May 15 increase in the fund was too large. A company check is drawn to replenish the fund for the following expenditures made since May 15 and to reduce the fund to $400.
         f. Paid postage expenses of $147.36.
         g. Reimbursed the office manager for business mileage, $23.50.
         h. Paid $34.75 to deliver merchandise to a customer, terms FOB destination.

Required

Check (1) Cr. Cash: May 15, $488.85; May 31, $106.61

1. Prepare journal entries to establish the fund on May 1 and to replenish it on May 15 and on May 31 along with any increase or decrease in the fund balance on those dates.

Analysis Component

2. Explain how the company's financial statements are affected if the petty cash fund is not replenished and no entry is made on May 31.

Problem 6-3A
Establish, reimburse, and increase petty cash

P3

Metro Gallery had the following petty cash transactions in February of the current year:

Feb. 2   Wrote a $400 check, cashed it, and gave the proceeds and the petty cashbox to Kareena White, the petty cashier.
     5   Purchased bond paper for the copier for $14.15 that is immediately used.
     9   Paid $32.50 COD shipping charges on merchandise purchased for resale, terms FOB shipping point. Metro uses the perpetual system to account for merchandise inventory.
    12   Paid $7.95 postage to express mail a contract to a client.
    14   Reimbursed Liz Walcotte, the manager, $68 for business mileage on her car.

20   Purchased stationery for $67.77 that is immediately used.

23   Paid a courier $20 to deliver merchandise sold to a customer, terms FOB destination.

25   Paid $13.10 COD shipping charges on merchandise purchased for resale, terms FOB shipping point.

27   Paid $54 for postage expenses.

28   Sorted the petty cash receipts by accounts affected and exchanged them for a check to both reimburse the fund for expenditures and increase the amount of the fund to $500. There was $121.53 cash in the fund.

Required

1. Prepare the journal entry to establish the petty cash fund.

2. Prepare a petty cash payments report for February with these categories: delivery expense, mileage expense, postage expense, merchandise inventory (for transportation-in), and office supplies expense. Sort the payments into the appropriate categories and total the expenditures in each category.

3. Prepare the journal entry to both reimburse and increase the amount in the fund.

Check   (3) Cr. Cash $378.47

The following information is available to reconcile Colin Company's book balance of cash with its bank statement cash balance as of July 31, 2002:

Problem 6-4A

Prepare a bank reconciliation and record adjustments

P5

E𝐱

a. After all posting is complete on July 31, the company's Cash account has a $27,497 debit balance, but its July bank statement shows a $27,233 balance.

b. Check No. 3031 for $1,482 and Check No. 3040 for $558 were outstanding on the June 30 bank reconciliation. Check No. 3040 is listed with the July canceled checks, but Check No. 3031 is not. Also, Check No. 3065 for $382 and Check No. 3069 for $2,281, both written in July, are not among the canceled checks on the July 31 statement.

c. In comparing the canceled checks on the bank statement with the entries in the accounting records, it is found that Check No. 3056 for July rent was correctly written and drawn for $1,270 but was erroneously entered in the accounting records as $1,250.

d. A credit memorandum enclosed with the July bank statement indicates the bank collected $8,000 cash on a noninterest-bearing note for Colin, deducted a $45 collection fee, and credited the remainder to its account. Colin had not recorded this event before receiving the statement.

e. A debit memorandum for $805 lists a $795 NSF check plus a $10 NSF charge. The check had been received from a customer, Jason White. Colin has not yet recorded this check as NSF.

f. Enclosed with the July statement is a $25 debit memorandum for bank services. It has not yet been recorded because no previous notification had been received.

g. Colin's July 31 daily cash receipts of $11,514 were placed in the bank's night depository on that date and do not appear on the July 31 bank statement.

Required

1. Prepare the bank reconciliation for this company as of July 31, 2002.

2. Prepare the journal entries necessary to bring the company's book balance of cash into conformity with the reconciled cash balance as of July 31, 2002.

Check   (1) Reconciled balance, $34,602; (2) Cr. Note Receivable $8,000

Analysis Component

3. Assume that the July 31, 2002, bank reconciliation for this company is prepared and some items are treated incorrectly. For each of the following errors, explain the effect of the error on (i) the adjusted bank statement cash balance and (ii) the adjusted cash account book balance.

a. The company's unadjusted cash account balance of $27,497 is listed on the reconciliation as $27,947.

b. The bank's collection of the $8,000 note less the $45 collection fee is added to the bank statement cash balance on the reconciliation.

Problem 6-5A

Prepare a bank reconciliation
and record adjustments

P5

Clarke Company most recently reconciled its bank statement and book balances of cash on August
31 and it reported two checks outstanding, No. 5888 for $1,028.05 and No. 5893 for $493.95. The
following information is available for its September 30, 2002, reconciliation:

From the September 30 Bank Statement

Previous Balance	Total Checks and Debits	Total Deposits and Credits	Current Balance
16,800.45	9,620.05	11,272.85	18,453.25

Checks and Debits			Deposits and Credits		Daily Balance	
Date	No.	Amount	Date	Amount	Date	Amount
09/03	5888	1,028.05	09/05	1,103.75	08/31	16,800.45
09/04	5902	719.90	09/12	2,226.90	09/03	15,772.40
09/07	5901	1,824.25	09/21	4,093.00	09/04	15,052.50
09/17		600.25 NSF	09/25	2,351.70	09/05	16,156.25
09/20	5905	937.00	09/30	12.50 IN	09/07	14,332.00
09/22	5903	399.10	09/30	1,485.00 CM	09/12	16,558.90
09/22	5904	2,090.00			09/17	15,958.65
09/28	5907	213.85			09/20	15,021.65
09/29	5909	1,807.65			09/21	19,114.65
					09/22	16,625.55
					09/25	18,977.25
					09/28	18,763.40
					09/29	16,955.75
					09/30	18,453.25

From Clarke Company's Accounting Records

Cash Receipts Deposited		
Date		**Cash Debit**
Sept. 5		1,103.75
12		2,226.90
21		4,093.00
25		2,351.70
30		1,682.75
		11,458.10

Cash Disbursements		
Check No.		**Cash Credit**
5901		1,824.25
5902		719.90
5903		399.10
5904		2,060.00
5905		937.00
5906		982.30
5907		213.85
5908		388.00
5909		1,807.65
		9,332.05

Cash						Acct. No. 101
Date		**Explanation**	**PR**	**Debit**	**Credit**	**Balance**
Aug. 31		Balance				15,278.45
Sept. 30		Total receipts	R12	11,458.10		26,736.55
30		Total disbursements	D23		9,332.05	17,404.50

Additional Information

Check No. 5904 is correctly drawn for $2,090 to pay for computer equipment; however, the record-
keeper misread the amount and entered it in the accounting records with a debit to Computer Equipment
and a credit to Cash of $2,060. The NSF check shown in the statement was originally received from
a customer, S. Nilson, in payment of her account. Its return has not yet been recorded by the company. The credit memorandum is from the collection of a $1,500 note for Clarke Company by the
bank. The bank deducted a $15 collection fee. The collection and fee are not yet recorded.

Required

1. Prepare the September 30, 2002, bank reconciliation for this company.
2. Prepare the journal entries to adjust the book balance of cash to the reconciled balance.

Analysis Component

3. The bank statement reveals that some of the prenumbered checks in the sequence are missing. Describe three possible situations that could explain this.

Check (1) Reconciled balance, $18,271.75 (2) Cr. Note Receivable $1,500

For each of these five separate cases, identify the principle of internal control that is violated. Recommend what the business should do to ensure adherence to principles of internal control.

1. Sue Stanley is the company's computer specialist and oversees the company's computerized payroll system. Her boss recently asked her to put password protection on all office computers. Sue has put a password in place that allows only the boss access to the file where pay rates are changed and personnel are added or deleted from the payroll.
2. Park Theater has a computerized order-taking system for its tickets. The system is active all week and backed up every Friday night.
3. B2B Company has two employees handling acquisitions of inventory. One employee places purchase orders and pays vendors. The second employee receives the merchandise.
4. The owner of Rite-Aid uses a check protector to perforate checks, making it difficult for anyone to alter the amount of the check. The check protector sits on the owner's desk in an office that contains company checks and is often unlocked.
5. Rison Company is a small company that has separated the duties of cash receipts and cash disbursements. The employee responsible for cash disbursements reconciles the bank account monthly.

PROBLEM SET B

Problem 6-1B 🖉
Analyzing internal control

C2

Cashco Co. establishes a petty cash fund for payments of small amounts. The following transactions involving the petty cash fund occurred in January (the last month of the company's fiscal year).

Jan. 3   A company check for $150 is written and made payable to the petty cashier to establish the petty cash fund.

    14   A company check is written to replenish the fund for the following expenditures made since January 3 and to increase the fund to $200.
- a. Purchased office supplies for $14.29 that are immediately used up.
- b. Paid $19.60 COD shipping charges on merchandise purchased for resale, terms FOB shipping point. Cashco uses the perpetual system to account for inventory.
- c. Paid $38.57 to All-Tech for minor repairs to a computer.
- d. Paid $12.82 for items classified as miscellaneous expenses.
- e. Counted $62.28 remaining in the petty cash box.

    31   The petty cashier reports that $17.35 remains in the fund and decides that the February 14 increase in the fund was not large enough. A company check is written to replenish the fund for the following expenditures made since January 14 and to increase it to $250.
- f. Paid $50 to The Smart Saver for an advertisement in January's newsletter.
- g. Paid $48.19 for postage expenses.
- h. Paid $78 to *3 Men and a Truck* for delivery of merchandise, terms FOB destination.

Problem 6-2B
Establishing, reimbursing, and adjusting petty cash

P3

Required

1. Prepare journal entries to establish the fund on January 3 and to replenish it on January 14 and January 31 along with any increase or decrease in the fund balance on those dates.

Check (1) Cr. Cash: Jan. 14, $137.72; Jan. 31, $232.65

Analysis Component

2. Explain how the company's financial statements are affected if the petty cash fund is not replenished and no entry is made on January 31.

Carousel Music Center had the following petty cash transactions in March of the current year:

March 5   Wrote a $250 check, cashed it, and gave the proceeds and the petty cashbox to Claire Mane, the petty cashier.

    6   Paid $12.50 COD shipping charges on merchandise purchased for resale, terms FOB shipping point. Carousel uses the perpetual system to account for merchandise inventory.

Problem 6-3B
Establish, reimburse, and increase petty cash

P3

11   Paid $10.75 delivery charges on merchandise sold to a customer, terms FOB destination.

12   Purchased file folders for $14.13 that are immediately used.

14   Reimbursed Trisha Cox, the manager, $11.65 for office supplies purchased and used.

18   Purchased paper for printer for $20.54 that is immediately used.

27   Paid $45.10 COD shipping charges on merchandise purchased for resale, terms FOB shipping point.

28   Paid postage expenses of $18.

30   Reimbursed Trisha Cox $56.80 for business car mileage.

31   Sorted the petty cash receipts by accounts affected and exchanged them for a check to both reimburse the fund for expenditures and increase the amount of the fund to $300. There was $61.53 cash remaining in the fund.

Required

1. Prepare the journal entry to establish the petty cash fund.

Check   (2) Total expenses $189.47

2. Prepare a petty cash payments report for March with these categories: delivery expense, mileage expense, postage expense, merchandise inventory (for transportation-in), and office supplies expense. Sort the payments into the appropriate categories and total the expenses in each category.

(3) Cr. Cash $238.47

3. Prepare the journal entry to both reimburse and increase the amount in the fund.

Problem 6-4B

Prepare a bank reconciliation and record adjustments

P5

The following information is available to reconcile Steele Co.'s book balance of cash with its bank statement cash balance as of December 31, 2002:

a. After posting is complete, the December 31 cash balance according to the accounting records is $32,878.30, and the bank statement cash balance for that date is $46,822.40.

b. Check No. 1273 for $4,589.30 and Check No. 1282 for $400.00, both written and entered in the accounting records in December, are not among the canceled checks. Two checks, No. 1231 for $2,289.00 and No. 1242 for $410.40, were outstanding on the most recent November 30 reconciliation. Check No. 1231 is listed with the December canceled checks, but Check No. 1242 is not.

c. When the December checks are compared with entries in the accounting records, it is found that Check No. 1267 had been correctly drawn for $3,456 to pay for office supplies but was erroneously entered in the accounting records as $3,465.

d. Two debit memoranda are enclosed with the statement and are unrecorded at the time of the reconciliation. One of the debit memoranda is for $762.50 and dealt with an NSF check for $745.00 that had been received from a customer, Tidwell Industries, in payment of its account. The bank assessed a $17.50 fee for processing it. The second debit memorandum is a $99.00 charge for check printing. Steele did not record these transactions before receiving the statement.

e. A credit memorandum indicates that the bank collected $19,000 cash on a note receivable for the company, deducted a $20 collection fee, and credited the balance to the company's cash account. Steele did not record this transaction before receiving the statement.

f. Steele's December 31 daily cash receipts of $9,583.10 were placed in the bank's night depository on that date and do not appear on the December 31 bank statement.

Required

Check   (1) Reconciled balance, $51,005.80; (2) Cr. Note Receivable $19,000

1. Prepare the bank reconciliation for this company as of December 31, 2002.

2. Prepare the journal entries necessary to bring the company's book balance of cash into conformity with the reconciled cash balance as of December 31, 2002.

Analysis Component

3. Explain the nature of the communications conveyed by a bank when the bank sends the depositor (*a*) a debit memorandum and (*b*) a credit memorandum.

Problem 6-5B

Prepare a bank reconciliation and record adjustments

P5

Sure Systems Co. most recently reconciled its bank balance on April 30 and reported two checks outstanding at that time, No. 1771 for $781.00 and No. 1780 for $1,425.90. The following information is available for its May 31, 2002, reconciliation:

From the May 31 Bank Statement

Previous Balance	Total Checks and Debits	Total Deposits and Credits	Current Balance
18,290.70	13,094.80	16,566.80	21,762.70

Checks and Debits			Deposits and Credits		Daily Balance	
Date	No.	Amount	Date	Amount	Date	Amount
05/01	1771	781.00	05/04	2,438.00	04/30	18,290.70
05/02	1783	382.50	05/14	2,898.00	05/01	17,509.70
05/04	1782	1,285.50	05/22	1,801.80	05/02	17,127.20
05/11	1784	1,449.60	05/25	7,350.00 CM	05/04	18,279.70
05/18		431.80 NSF	05/26	2,079.00	05/11	16,830.10
05/25	1787	8,032.50			05/14	19,728.10
05/26	1785	63.90			05/18	19,296.30
05/29	1788	654.00			05/22	21,098.10
05/31		14.00 SC			05/25	20,415.60
					05/26	22,430.70
					05/29	21,776.70
					05/31	21,762.70

From Sure Systems' Accounting Records

Cash Receipts Deposited		Cash Debit
Date		
May	4	2,438.00
	14	2,898.00
	22	1,801.80
	26	2,079.00
	31	2,727.30
		11,944.10

Cash Disbursements	
Check No.	Cash Credit
1782	1,285.50
1783	382.50
1784	1,449.60
1785	63.90
1786	353.10
1787	8,032.50
1788	644.00
1789	639.50
	12,850.60

Cash					Acct. No. 101
Date	Explanation	PR	Debit	Credit	Balance
Apr. 30	Balance				16,083.80
May 31	Total receipts	R7	11,944.10		28,027.90
31	Total disbursements	D8		12,850.60	15,177.30

Additional Information

Check No. 1788 is correctly drawn for $654 to pay for May utilities; however, the recordkeeper misread the amount and entered it in the accounting records with a debit to Utilities Expense and a credit to Cash for $644. The bank paid and deducted the correct amount. The NSF check shown in the statement was originally received from a customer, D. Hunt, in payment of her account. Its return has not yet been recorded by the company. The credit memorandum is from a $7,400 note that the bank collected for the company. The bank deducted a $50 collection fee and deposited the remainder in the company's account. The collection and fee are not yet recorded.

Required

1. Prepare the May 31, 2002, bank reconciliation for Sure Systems.
2. Prepare the journal entries to adjust the book balance of cash to the reconciled balance.

Analysis Component

3. The bank statement reveals that some of the prenumbered checks in the sequence are missing. Describe three possible situations that might explain this.

Check (1) Reconciled balance, $22,071.50; (2) Cr. Note Receivable $7,400

BEYOND THE NUMBERS

Reporting in Action

C3 A1 *a*

NIKE

BTN 6-1 Refer to the financial statements for Nike in Appendix A to answer the following:

1. For both fiscal year-end 2000 and 1999, identify the total amount of cash and cash equivalents. Determine the percent this amount represents of total current assets, total current liabilities, total shareholders' equity, and total assets for both years. Comment on any trends.
2. For both fiscal 2000 and 1999, use the information in the statement of cash flows to determine the percent change between the beginning and ending year amounts of cash and cash equivalents.
3. Compute the days' sales uncollected as of May 31, 2000, and May 31, 1999. Has the collection of receivables improved?

Swoosh Ahead

4. Access Nike's financial statements for fiscal years ending after May 31, 2000, from its Web site (www.nike.com) or the SEC's EDGAR database (www.sec.gov). Recompute the days' sales uncollected for fiscal years ending after May 31, 2000. Compare this to the days' sales uncollected for 2000 and 1999.

Comparative Analysis

A1 *a*

NIKE  Reebok

BTN 6-2 Key comparative figures ($ in millions) for both Nike and Reebok follow:

Key Figures	Nike Current Year	Nike Prior Year	Reebok Current Year	Reebok Prior Year
Accounts receivable	$1,567.2	$1,540.1	$ 417.4	$ 517.8
Net sales	8,995.1	8,776.9	2,899.9	3,224.6

Required

Compute days' sales uncollected for both companies for the two years shown. Comment on any trends for both companies. Which company has the larger percent change in days' sales uncollected?

Ethics Challenge

C2 *a* *e*

BTN 6-3 Susie Martin, Dot Night, and Colleen Walker work for a family physician, Dr. Gillbanks, who is in private practice. Dr. Gillbanks is knowledgeable about office management practices and has segregated the cash receipt duties as follows. Susie opens the mail and prepares a triplicate list of money received. She sends one copy of the list to Dot, the cashier, who deposits the receipts daily in the bank. Colleen, the recordkeeper, receives a copy of the list and posts payments to patients' accounts. About once a month the office clerks have an expensive lunch they pay for as follows. First, Dot endorses a patient's check in Dr. Gillbanks's name and cashes it at the bank. Susie then destroys the remittance advice accompaying the check. Finally, Colleen posts payment to the customer's account as a miscellaneous credit. The three justify their actions by their relatively low pay and knowledge that Dr. Gillbanks will likely never miss the money.

Required

1. Who is the best person in Dr. Gillbanks's office to reconcile the bank statement?
2. Would a bank reconciliation uncover this office fraud?
3. What are some ways to detect this type of fraud?
4. Suggest additional internal controls that Dr. Gillbanks may want to implement.

BTN 6-4   Assume you are a business consultant. The owner of a company sends you an e-mail expressing concern that the company is not taking advantage of discounts offered by vendors. The company currently uses the gross method of recording purchases. The owner is considering a review of all invoices and payments from the previous period. Due to the volume of purchases, however, the owner recognizes this is time consuming and costly. The owner seeks your advice about monitoring purchase discounts in the future. Provide a response in memorandum form.

Communicating in Practice

P4 🖉 🄲

BTN 6-5   Visit the Association of Certified Fraud Examiners Web site at **www.cfenet.com**. Research the fraud facts presented at this site and fill in the blanks in the following factual statements.

   1. Fraud and abuse cost U.S. organizations more than $_____ billion annually.
   2. The average organization loses more than $_____ per day per employee to fraud and abuse.
   3. The average organization loses about _____% of its total annual revenue to fraud and abuse committed by its own employees.
   4. The median fraud loss by males is about $_____; by females, about $_____.
   5. Men commit nearly _____% of the offenses.
   6. Losses caused by managers are _____ times those caused by employees.
   7. Median fraud losses caused by executives are _____ times those of their employees.
   8. The most costly abuses occur in organizations with less than _____ employees.
   9. The _____ industry experiences the lowest median losses.
   10. Occupational fraud and abuse fall into three main categories: _____.

Taking It to the Net

C1 C2 🄲

BTN 6-6   Each team must prepare a list of 10 internal controls a consumer could observe in a typical retail department store. When called upon, the team's spokesperson must be prepared to share controls identified by the team that have not been shared by another team's spokesperson.

Teamwork in Action C1 C2

BTN 6-7   Read the article "Fraud on the Net" in the April 3, 2000, issue of *Business Week*. (The book's Web site provides a free link.)

Required

   1. In 1997, 3% of all consumer complaints were about the Internet. How large is the percent now?
   2. What percentage of Nike.com's purchase requests are estimated to be fraudulent?
   3. Is the government making progress in detecting Internet fraud? Explain.
   4. What are 5 of the top 10 scams on the Net?

Business Week Activity

C1 🖉

BTN 6-8   Steffi Kraff is setting up operations for her new carry-out business to sell subs and salads to mainly college students. Customers will order and receive their food at the counter, where a cashier will exchange food for cash. From the counter, customers will be able to see other employees making subs and salads.

Required

List the seven principles of internal control. For each principle, identify how the owner of this business could implement it.

Entrepreneurial Decision

C2 P1

🄲 🖉

BTN 6-9   Visit a part of your college that serves the student community with either products or services. Some examples are food services, libraries, and book stores. Identify and describe between four and eight internal controls that are being implemented.

Hitting the Road

C1 🖉

7

Reporting and Analyzing Receivables and Investments

"Being able to visualize my success as an entrepreneur was the catapult"—Laura Tidwell

A Look Back

Chapter 6 focused on internal control and reporting for cash. We described procedures that are good for internal control, and we explained the accounting for and management of cash.

A Look at This Chapter

This chapter emphasizes receivables and short-term investments. We explain that they are liquid assets and describe how companies account for and report them. We also discuss the importance of estimating uncollectibles and the role of market values in analyzing liquid assets.

A Look Ahead

Chapter 8 focuses on plant assets, natural resources, and intangible assets. We explain how to account for, report, and analyze these long-term assets.

Decision Feature

The Engine That Could

e TROY, AL—Laura Tidwell's venture into business was of necessity. "I had no clients, no money, a one-bedroom apartment, and a little girl," recalls Tidwell. "I knew I had to make something happen." Making something happen is what Tidwell did when she started her ad agency, dubbed **Enginehouse Media (www.EnginehouseMedia.com).** "As a 22-year-old woman, I had to make the world think I was a huge company . . . without being dishonest." Landing a few big accounts in the early days, such as Encyclopedia Britannica, proved invaluable: "I always wondered back then what my clients would think if they knew that . . . [it] was just me and my little girl alone in that small apartment." But what clients care about are results, and results are what Tidwell delivered.

With projected annual sales exceeding $25 million, Tidwell no longer worries about perception. Now 30 employees strong, Enginehouse recently acquired a former bank building with 24 offices for expansion. Tidwell says that an important part of her business is keeping control over receivables. Do we sell on credit or not? What are our policies and criteria for extending credit? Do we offer cash discounts? Is our accounts receivable turnover reasonable? This chapter focuses on these and related issues. According to Tidwell, those factors are crucial to continued success as Enginehouse expands into new marketing media. This includes the monitoring of her company's investments. "We plan to give our clients an edge over their competition by offering them the most aggressive array of advertising and public relations," Tidwell says. Given the odds she has already overcome, no one underestimates her. [Sources: Enginehouse Media Web site, January 2002; *Entrepreneur*, April 2001; DiversityInc.com, June 23, 2000.]

Chapter Preview

This chapter focuses on accounts receivable, short-term notes receivable, and short-term investments. We describe each of these assets, their uses, and how they are accounted for and reported in financial statements. This knowledge helps us use accounting information to make better decisions. It can also help in predicting future company performance and financial condition, and in managing one's own business.

Accounts Receivable

A *receivable* is an amount due from another party. The two most common receivables are accounts receivable and notes receivable. Other receivables include interest receivable, rent receivable, tax refund receivable, and receivables from officers and employees. **Accounts receivable** are amounts due from customers for credit sales. This section begins by describing how accounts receivable occur. It includes receivables that occur when customers use credit cards issued by third parties and when a company gives credit directly to customers. When a company does extend credit directly to customers, it must (1) maintain a separate account receivable for each customer and (2) account for bad debts from credit sales.

Recognizing Accounts Receivable

C1 Describe accounts receivable and how they occur and are recorded.

Accounts receivable occur from credit sales to customers. The amount of credit sales has increased in recent years, reflecting several factors including an efficient financial system. Retailers such as **The Limited, Chic by H.I.S., Best Buy,** and **CompUSA** hold millions of dollars in accounts receivable. Similar amounts are held by wholesalers such as **Nike, Reebok, SUPERVALU, SYSCO,** and **Ace Hardware**. Exhibit 7.1 shows recent dollar amounts of accounts receivable and their percent of total assets for four well-known companies.

Exhibit 7.1

Accounts Receivable for Selected Companies

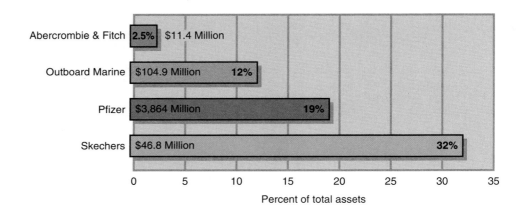

Sales on Credit

Credit sales are recorded by increasing (debiting) Accounts Receivable. A company must also maintain a separate account for each customer that tracks how much that customer purchases, has already paid, and still owes. This information provides the basis for sending bills to customers and for other business analyses. To maintain this information, companies that extend credit directly to their customers keep a separate account receivable for each one of them. The general ledger continues to have a single Accounts Receivable account along with the other financial statement accounts, but a supplementary record is created to maintain a separate account for each customer. This supplementary record is called the *accounts receivable ledger*.

Exhibit 7.2 shows the relation between the Accounts Receivable account in the general ledger and its individual customer accounts in the accounts receivable ledger for TechCom, a small electronics wholesaler. This exhibit reports a $3,000 ending balance of TechCom's accounts receivable for June 30. TechCom's transactions are mainly in cash, but it has two major credit customers: CompStore and RDA Electronics. Its *schedule of accounts receiv-*

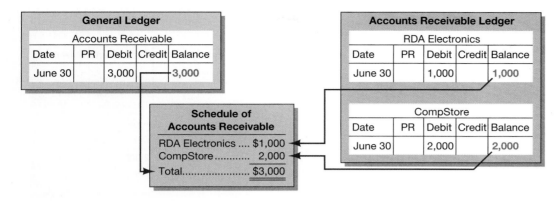

Exhibit 7.2

General Ledger and the Accounts Receivable Ledger (before July 1 transactions)

able shows that the $3,000 balance of the Accounts Receivable account in the general ledger equals the total of its two customers' balances in the accounts receivable ledger.

To see how accounts receivable from credit sales are recognized in the accounting records, we look at two transactions on July 1 between TechCom and its credit customers—see Exhibit 7.3. The first is a credit sale of $950 to CompStore. A credit sale is posted with both a debit to the Accounts Receivable account in the general ledger and a debit to the customer account in the accounts receivable ledger. The second transaction is a collection of $720 from RDA Electronics from a prior credit sale. Cash receipts from a credit customer are posted with a credit to both the Accounts Receivable account in the general ledger and to the customer account in the accounts receivable ledger. (Posting debits or credits to Accounts Receivable in two separate ledgers does not violate the requirement that debits equal credits. The equality of debits and credits is maintained in the general ledger. The accounts receivable ledger is a supplementary record providing information on each customer.)

July 1	Accounts Receivable—CompStore	950	
	Sales		950
	To record credit sales*		
July 1	Cash	720	
	Accounts Receivable—RDA Electronics . . .		720
	To record collection of credit sales.		

Exhibit 7.3

Accounts Receivable Transactions

* We omit the entry to Dr. Cost of Sales and Cr. Merchandise Inventory to focus on sales and receivables.

Exhibit 7.4 shows the general ledger and the accounts receivable ledger after recording the two July 1 transactions. The general ledger shows the effects of the sale, the collection, and the resulting balance of $3,230. These events are also reflected in the individual customer accounts: RDA Electronics has an ending balance of $280, and CompStore's ending balance is $2,950. The $3,230 sum of the individual accounts equals the debit balance of the Accounts Receivable account in the general ledger.

Like TechCom, many large retailers such as **Sears** and **JCPenney** sell on credit. Many also maintain their own credit cards to grant credit to approved customers and to earn interest on any balance not paid within a specified period of time. This allows them to avoid the fee charged by credit card companies. The entries in this case are the same as those for TechCom except for the possibility of added interest revenue. If a customer owes interest on a bill, we debit Interest Receivable and credit Interest Revenue for that amount.

Point: Software helps merchants build Web storefronts quickly and easily. Merchants simply enter product details such as names and prices, and out comes a respectable-looking Web site complete with order forms. They also offer security with credit card orders and can track sales and site visits.

Credit Card Sales

Many companies allow their customers to pay for products and services using third-party credit cards and bankcards such as **Visa**, **MasterCard**, or **American Express**. This practice gives customers the ability to make purchases without cash or checks. Once credit is established with a credit card company or bank, the customer does not have to open an

Exhibit 7.4

General Ledger and
the Accounts Receivable
Ledger (after July 1
transactions)

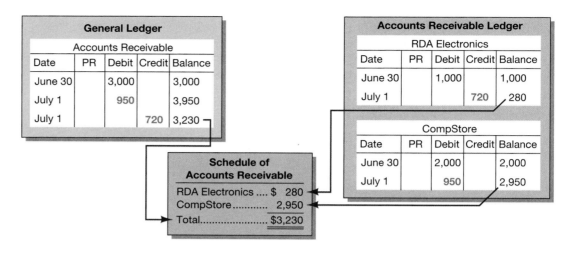

account with each store. Customers using these cards can make single monthly payments instead of several payments to different creditors, and can defer their payments.

There are several reasons why sellers allow customers to use third-party credit cards and bankcards instead of granting credit directly. First, the seller does not have to evaluate each customer's credit standing or make decisions about who gets credit and how much. Second, the seller avoids the risk of extending credit to customers who cannot or do not pay. This risk is transferred to the card company. Third, the seller typically receives cash from the credit card company sooner than had it granted credit directly to customers. Fourth, a variety of credit options for customers offers a potential increase in sales volume. **Sears** historically offered credit only to customers using a Sears card, but later changed its policy to permit customers to charge purchases to third-party credit card companies in a desire to increase sales. It reported that: "SearsCharge increased its share of Sears retail sales even as the company expanded the payment options available to its customers with the acceptance . . . of [Visa,] MasterCard, and American Express in addition to the Discover Card."

There are guidelines in how companies account for credit card and bankcard sales. Some credit cards, but mostly bankcards, credit a seller's Cash account immediately upon deposit. In this case the seller deposits a copy of each credit card sales receipt in its bank account just as it deposits a customer's check. Some other credit cards require the seller to remit a copy (often electronically) of each receipt to the credit card company. Until payment is received, the seller has an account receivable from the credit card company. In both cases, the seller pays a fee for services provided by the card company, often ranging from 1% to 5% of card sales. This charge is deducted from the credit to the seller's account or the cash payment to the seller.

The procedures used in accounting for credit card sales depend on whether cash is received immediately on deposit or cash receipt is delayed until the credit card company makes the payment. To illustrate, if TechCom has $100 of credit card sales with a 4% fee, and its cash is received immediately on deposit, the entry is

July 15	Cash	96	
	Credit Card Expense	4	
	Sales		100
	*To record credit card sales less a 4% credit card expense.**		

Assets = Liabilities + Equity
+96   −4
                          +100

* We omit the entry to Dr. Cost of Sales and Cr. Merchandise Inventory to focus on credit card expense.

However, if instead TechCom must remit the credit card sales receipts to the credit card company and wait for payment, the entry on the date of sale is

July 15	Accounts Receivable—Credit Card Co.	96	
	Credit Card Expense	4	
	Sales		100
	*To record credit card sales less 4% credit card expense.**		

Assets = Liabilities + Equity
+96   +100
                          −4

* We omit the entry to Dr. Cost of Sales and Cr. Merchandise Inventory to focus on credit card expense.

When cash is later received from the credit card company, the entry is

July 25	Cash	96	
	Accounts Receivable—Credit Card Co.		96
	To record cash receipt.		

Assets = Liabilities + Equity
+96
−96

Some firms report credit card expense in the income statement as a type of discount deducted from sales to get net sales. Other companies classify it as a selling expense or even as an administrative expense. Arguments can be made for each alternative.

Point: Third-party credit card costs can be large. JCPenney recently reported sales of $32,510 million along with third-party credit card costs of nearly $100 million.

Quick Check

1. In recording credit card sales, when do you debit Accounts Receivable and when do you debit Cash?

2. A company accumulates sales receipts and remits them to the credit card company for payment. When are the credit card expenses recorded? When are these expenses incurred?

Answers—p. 315

Valuing Accounts Receivable

When a company directly grants credit to its customers, it expects that some customers will not pay what they promised. The accounts of these customers are *uncollectible accounts,* commonly called **bad debts.** The total amount of uncollectible accounts is an expense of selling on credit. Why do companies sell on credit if they expect some accounts to be uncollectible? The answer is that companies believe that granting credit will increase total sales and net income enough to offset bad debts. Companies use two methods to account for uncollectible accounts: (1) direct write-off method and (2) allowance method. We describe both.

Decision Insight

Bad Debts Costs are rising for credit card issuers owing to default rates. Much of this is the fault of issuers who offer credit cards with low "teaser" rates. In response, credit card users have increased their debts, and many are unable to pay them.

Credit Card Default Rates

Banc One	6.8%
First Chicago	6.7
Discover	6.1
Citicorp	5.5
Chase	5.1
Capital One	5.1
Advanta	5.1

Direct Write-Off Method

The **direct write-off method** of accounting for bad debts records the loss from an uncollectible account receivable when it is determined to be uncollectible. No attempt is made to

P1 Apply the direct write-off and allowance methods to account for accounts receivable.

predict bad debts expense. Bad debts expense is recorded when specific accounts are written off as uncollectible. To illustrate, if TechCom determines on January 23 that it cannot collect $520 owed to it by its customer J. Kent, it recognizes the loss using the direct write-off method as follows:

<table>
<tr><td>Jan. 23</td><td>Bad Debts Expense . . . .</td><td>520</td><td></td></tr>
<tr><td></td><td>   Accounts Receivable—J. Kent . . . .</td><td></td><td>520</td></tr>
<tr><td></td><td colspan="3">*To write off an uncollectible account.*</td></tr>
</table>

Assets = Liabilities + Equity
−520   −520

The debit in this entry charges the uncollectible amount directly to the current period's Bad Debts Expense account. The credit removes its balance from the Accounts Receivable account in the general ledger (and its subsidiary ledger).

Sometimes an account written off is later collected. This can be due to factors such as continual collection efforts or a customer's good fortune. If the account of J. Kent that was written off directly to Bad Debts Expense is later collected in full, the following two entries record this recovery:

<table>
<tr><td>Mar. 11</td><td>Accounts Receivable—J. Kent . . . .</td><td>520</td><td></td></tr>
<tr><td></td><td>   Bad Debts Expense . . . .</td><td></td><td>520</td></tr>
<tr><td></td><td colspan="3">*To reinstate account previously written off.*</td></tr>
<tr><td>Mar. 11</td><td>Cash . . . .</td><td>520</td><td></td></tr>
<tr><td></td><td>   Accounts Receivable—J. Kent . . . .</td><td></td><td>520</td></tr>
<tr><td></td><td colspan="3">*To record full payment of account.*</td></tr>
</table>

Assets = Liabilities + Equity
+520   +520

Assets = Liabilities + Equity
+520
−520

Companies must weigh at least two accounting principles when considering the use of the direct write-off method: the (1) matching principle and (2) materiality principle.

Matching principle applied to bad debts. The **matching principle** requires expenses to be reported in the same accounting period as the sales they helped produce. This means that if extending credit to customers helped produce sales, the bad debts expense linked to those sales is matched and reported in the same period. The direct write-off method usually does not best match sales and expenses because bad debts expense is not recorded until an account becomes uncollectible, which often does not occur in the same period as the credit sale. However, applying the matching principle to bad debts presents challenges. Managers realize that some portion of credit sales will be uncollectible, but which credit sales are uncollectible is unknown. If a customer fails to pay within the credit period, most companies send out repeated billings and make other efforts to collect. They do not accept that a customer is not going to pay until they take every reasonable means of collection. This decision point may not be reached until one or more accounting periods after the sale is made. Matching bad debts expense with the sales it produces therefore requires a company to estimate uncollectibles.

Point: Pier 1 Imports reports $4.7 million of bad debts expense matched against $300.5 million of credit sales in a recent fiscal year.

Materiality principle applied to bad debts. The **materiality principle** states that an amount can be ignored if its effect on the financial statements is unimportant to users' business decisions. The materiality principle permits the use of the direct write-off method when bad debts expenses are very small in relation to a company's other financial statement items such as sales and net income.

Allowance Method

Point: Under the direct write-off method, expense is recorded each time an account is written off. Under the allowance method, expense is recorded with an adjusting entry equal to the total estimated uncollectibles for that period's sales.

The **allowance method** of accounting for bad debts matches the *expected* loss from uncollectible accounts receivable against the sales they helped produce. We must use expected losses since management cannot exactly identify the customers who will not pay their bills at the time of sale. This means that at the end of each period, the allowance method requires an estimate of the total bad debts expected to result from that period's sales. An allowance is then recorded for this expected loss. This method has two advantages over the direct write-off method: (1) it charges expected bad debts expense to the period when it recognizes the

Topic Tackler 7-1

related sales and (2) it reports accounts receivable on the balance sheet at the estimated amount of cash to be collected.

Recording Bad Debts Expense

The allowance method estimates bad debts expense at the end of each accounting period and records it with an adjusting entry. TechCom, for instance, had credit sales of approximately $300,000 during its first year of operations. At the end of the first year, $20,000 of credit sales remained uncollected. Based on the experience of similar businesses, TechCom estimated that $1,500 of its accounts receivable would be uncollectible. This estimated expense is recorded with the following adjusting entry:

Point: The Office of the Comptroller of the Currency reported that losses from bad debts contributed to the collapse of 98% of failed banks.

Dec. 31	Bad Debts Expense	1,500	
	Allowance for Doubtful Accounts		1,500
	To record estimated bad debts.		

Assets = Liabilities + Equity
−1,500   −1,500

The estimated Bad Debts Expense of $1,500 is reported on the income statement (as either a selling expense or an administrative expense) and offsets the $300,000 credit sales it helped produce. The **Allowance for Doubtful Accounts** is a contra asset account. A contra account is used instead of accounts receivable because at the time of the adjusting entry, the company does not know which customers will not pay. After the bad debts adjusting entry is posted, TechCom's account balances for Accounts Receivable and its Allowance for Doubtful Accounts are as shown in Exhibit 7.5.

Point: The process of evaluating and approving customers for credit is usually not assigned to the selling department because its main goal is to increase sales, and it may approve customers for credit at the expense of increased bad debts. Instead, responsibility for granting credit is assigned to a separate credit-granting or other administrative department.

Accounts Receivable			Allowance for Doubtful Accounts	
Dec. 31	20,000		Dec. 31	1,500

Exhibit 7.5

General Ledger Balances after Bad Debts Adjusting Entry

The Allowance for Doubtful Accounts credit balance of $1,500 has the effect of reducing accounts receivable to its estimated realizable value. **Realizable value** is the expected proceeds from converting an asset into cash. Although credit customers owe $20,000 to TechCom, only $18,500 is expected to be realized in cash collections from these customers. In the balance sheet, the Allowance for Doubtful Accounts is subtracted from Accounts Receivable to show the amount expected to be realized. This information is often reported as shown in Exhibit 7.6.

Point: Bad Debts Expense is also called *Uncollectible Accounts Expense.* The Allowance for Doubtful Accounts is also called *Allowance for Uncollectible Accounts.*

Current assets		
Accounts receivable	$20,000	
Less allowance for doubtful accounts	1,500	$18,500

Exhibit 7.6

Balance Sheet Presentation of the Allowance for Doubtful Accounts

Sometimes the Allowance for Doubtful Accounts is not reported separately. This alternative presentation is shown in Exhibit 7.7.

Current assets	
Accounts receivable (net of $1,500 estimated doubtful accounts)	$18,500

Exhibit 7.7

Alternative Presentation of the Allowance for Doubtful Accounts

Writing Off a Bad Debt

When specific accounts are identified as uncollectible, they are written off against the Allowance for Doubtful Accounts. To illustrate, after spending some time trying to collect from J. Kent, TechCom decides that Kent's $520 account is uncollectible and makes the following entry to write it off:

Jan. 23	Allowance for Doubtful Accounts	520	
	Accounts Receivable—J. Kent		520
	To write off an uncollectible account.		

Posting this write-off entry to the Accounts Receivable account removes the amount of the bad debt from the general ledger. Also, posting it to Kent's individual account removes the amount of the bad debt from the subsidiary ledger. The general ledger accounts now appear as in Exhibit 7.8 (assuming no other transactions affecting these accounts).

Exhibit 7.8

General Ledger Balances after Write-Off

Accounts Receivable					Allowance for Doubtful Accounts			
Dec. 31	20,000						Dec. 31	1,500
		Jan. 23	520		Jan. 23	520		

Note two points with the write-off entry. First, the bad debts expense account is not debited because bad debts expense is previously estimated and recorded with an adjusting entry in the period when the sales occurred. Second, while the write-off removes the uncollectible account receivable from the ledger, it does not affect the realizable value of accounts receivable as shown in Exhibit 7.9. Neither total assets nor net income is affected by the write-off of a specific account. Instead, both assets and net income are affected in the period when bad debts expense is recorded with an adjusting entry.

Exhibit 7.9

Realizable Value before and after Write-Off of a Bad Debt

	Before Write-Off	After Write-Off
Accounts receivable	$20,000	$19,480
Less allowance for doubtful accounts	1,500	980
Estimated realizable accounts receivable	**$18,500**	**$18,500**

Recovery of a Bad Debt

When a customer fails to pay and the account is written off as uncollectible, his or her credit standing is jeopardized. To help restore credit standing, a customer sometimes volunteers to pay all or part of the amount owed. A company makes two entries when collecting an account previously written off by the allowance method. The first is to reverse the write-off and reinstate the customer's account. The second entry records the collection of the reinstated account. To illustrate, if on March 11 Kent pays in full his account previously written off, the entries to record this recovery are

Mar. 11	Accounts Receivable—J. Kent	520	
	Allowance for Doubtful Accounts		520
	To reinstate account previously written off.		
Mar. 11	Cash	520	
	Accounts Receivable—J. Kent		520
	To record full payment of account.		

In this illustration, Kent paid the entire amount previously written off, but sometimes a customer pays only a portion of the amount owed. A question then arises as to whether the entire balance of the account is returned to accounts receivable or just the amount paid. This is a matter of judgment. If we believe this customer will later pay in full, we return the entire amount owed to accounts receivable, but if we expect no further collection, we return only the amount paid.

Decision Track 7.1		*d*
Decision Point	**Information Search**	**Analyze & Evaluate**
What is the level of a company's credit risk?	Balance sheet; compute the **credit risk ratio** by dividing the Allowance for Doubtful Accounts by Accounts Receivable.	The higher the Allowance for Doubtful Accounts to Accounts Receivable ratio, the higher is credit risk.

Estimating Bad Debts Expense

Companies with direct credit sales must attempt to estimate bad debts expense. They do this to help them manage their receivables and to set credit policies. The allowance method also requires an estimate of bad debts expense to prepare an adjusting entry at the end of each accounting period. There are two common methods to estimate bad debts expense. One is based on the income statement relation between bad debts expense and sales. The second is based on the balance sheet relation between accounts receivable and the allowance for doubtful accounts. Both methods require an analysis of past experience.

P2 Estimate uncollectibles using methods based on sales and accounts receivable.

Percent of Sales Method

The *percent of sales method* uses income statement relations to estimate bad debts. It is based on the idea that a given percent of a company's credit sales for the period are uncollectible. (The focus is on *credit* sales because cash sales do not produce bad debts. If cash sales are a small or stable percent of credit sales, they are often included in the analysis.) The income statement would then report a percent of sales as the amount of bad debts expense. To illustrate, assume that Musicland has credit sales of $400,000 in year 2002. Based on past experience, Musicland estimates 0.6% of credit sales to be uncollectible. This implies that Musicland expects $2,400 of bad debts expense from its sales (computed as $400,000 \times 0.006 = $2,400). The adjusting entry to record this estimated expense is

Point: When using the *percent of sales method* for estimating uncollectibles, the amount of the bad debts estimate is the number used in the adjusting entry.

Dec. 31	Bad Debts Expense	2,400	
	Allowance for Doubtful Accounts.		2,400
	To record estimated bad debts.		

Assets = Liabilities + Equity
−2,400   −2,400

This entry does not mean that the December 31, 2002, balance in Allowance for Doubtful Accounts will be $2,400. A $2,400 balance occurs only if the account had a zero balance prior to posting the adjusting entry. Unless a company is in its first period of operations, its allowance account has a zero balance only if the prior amounts written off as uncollectible *exactly* equal the prior estimated bad debts expenses. This means the allowance account balance reported on the balance sheet would rarely equal the amount of expense reported on the income statement. Note that expressing bad debts expense as a percent of sales is based on past experience. As new experience is obtained, we often find the percent to be too high or too low. When this happens, we adjust the percent for future periods.

Accounts Receivable Methods

The *accounts receivable methods* use balance sheet relations to estimate bad debts—mainly the relation between accounts receivable and the allowance amount. The objective of the bad debts adjusting entry for these methods is to make the Allowance for Doubtful Accounts balance equal to the portion of accounts

Point: When using an accounts receivable method for estimating uncollectibles, the allowance account balance is adjusted so as to equal the estimate of uncollectibles when recording the adjusting entry.

receivable estimated as uncollectible. The estimated balance for the allowance account is obtained in one of two ways: (1) computing the percent uncollectible from the total accounts receivable or (2) aging accounts receivable.

Percent of accounts receivable method. The *percent of accounts receivable method* assumes that a given percent of a company's receivables is uncollectible. This percent is based on past experience and is impacted by current conditions such as economic trends and difficulties faced by customers. The total dollar amount of all receivables is multiplied by this percent to get the estimated dollar amount of uncollectible accounts. This amount is reported in the balance sheet as the Allowance for Doubtful Accounts. To achieve this result, we prepare an adjusting entry debiting Bad Debts Expense and crediting Allowance for Doubtful Accounts. The amount of the adjustment is the amount necessary to yield a credit balance in the Allowance for Doubtful Accounts that equals the estimated amount of uncollectibles.

Global: In China, government regulation constrains the *percents* used to estimate bad debts.

To illustrate, assume that Musicland has $50,000 of accounts receivable on December 31, 2002. Past experience suggests 5% of receivables are uncollectible. This means that after the adjusting entry is posted, we want the Allowance for Doubtful Accounts to show a $2,500 credit balance (computed as 5% of $50,000). Before the adjustment the account appears as follows

Allowance for Doubtful Accounts			
		Dec. 31, 2001, bal.	2,200
Feb. 6	800		
July 10	700		
Nov. 20	500		
		Unadjusted bal.	200

The $2,200 beginning balance is from the December 31, 2001, balance sheet. During 2002, accounts of customers are written off on February 6, July 10, and November 20. The account has a $200 credit balance prior to the December 31, 2002, adjustment. The adjusting entry to give the allowance account the estimated $2,500 balance is

Assets = Liabilities + Equity
−2,300   −2,300

Dec. 31	Bad Debts Expense	2,300	
	Allowance for Doubtful Accounts		2,300
	To record estimated bad debts.		

After this entry the allowance has a $2,500 credit balance, as shown in Exhibit 7.10.

Exhibit 7.10

Allowance for Doubtful Accounts after Bad Debts Adjusting Entry

Allowance for Doubtful Accounts			
		Dec. 31, 2001, bal.	2,200
Feb. 6	800		
July 10	700		
Nov. 20	500		
		Unadjusted bal.	200
		Dec. 31 adjustment	2,300
		Dec. 31, 2002, bal.	2,500

Aging of accounts receivable method. Both the percent of sales (income statement) method and the percent of accounts receivable (balance sheet) method use information from *past* experience to estimate the amount of bad debts expense. Another balance sheet method, called the **aging of accounts receivable** method, uses both past and current receivables information to produce a more precise estimate. Specifically, each receivable is classified by how long it is past its due date. Then estimates of uncollectible amounts are made assuming that the longer an amount is past due, the more likely it is to be uncollectible. Classifications are often based on 30-day periods. After the amounts are classified (or aged), past experience is used to estimate the percent of each class that is uncollectible. These percents are applied to the amounts in each class to get the estimated balance of the Allowance for Doubtful Accounts. This computation is performed by setting up a schedule such as Exhibit 7.11 for Musicland.

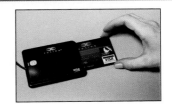

Decision Insight

Smart e-Commerce When you buy online with a credit card, you put your account number at risk. If, however, you slide a smart card into a reader on your PC and enter your password, the merchant never gets your account number but only a code authorizing the sale. Since American Express launched the first major U.S. smart card, millions of consumers have signed up.

Exhibit 7.11

Aging of Accounts Receivable

MUSICLAND
Schedule of Accounts Receivable by Age

Customer	Totals	Not Yet Due	1 to 30 Days Past Due	31 to 60 Days Past Due	61 to 90 Days Past Due	Over 90 Days Past Due
Charles Abbot	$ 450	$ 450				
Frank Allen	710			$ 710		
George Arden	500	300	$ 200			
Paul Baum	740				$ 100	$ 640
ZZ Services	1,000	810	190			
Totals	$ 49,900	$ 37,000	$ 6,500	$ 3,500	$ 1,900	$ 1,000
Percent uncollectible		x 2%	x 5%	x 10%	x 25%	x 40%
Estimated uncollectible	$ 2,290	$ 740	$ 325	$ 350	$ 475	$ 400

Exhibit 7.11 lists each customer's total account balance. Then each individual balance is assigned to one of five classes based on its days past due. When all accounts are aged, the amounts in each class are totaled and multiplied by the estimated percent of uncollectible accounts for each class. The reasonableness of the percents used is regularly reviewed to reflect changes in the company and economy.

To illustrate the aging method, notice that Musicland has $3,500 in accounts receivable that are 31 to 60 days past due. Its management estimates 10% of the amounts in this age class are uncollectible, or a total of $350 (computed as $3,500 × 10%). Similar analysis is done for each of the other four classes. The final total of $2,290 ($740 + $325 + $350 + $475 + $400) shown in the first column is the estimated balance for the Allowance for Doubtful Accounts. Since the allowance account has an unadjusted credit balance of $200, the required adjustment to the Allowance for Doubtful Accounts is $2,090. This computation is shown in Exhibit 7.12. Musicland then prepares the following end-of-period adjusting entry:

Point: Experience shows the longer a receivable is past due, the lower is the likelihood of collection. An aging schedule exploits this relation and yields useful information to evaluate credit policies.

Point: Spreadsheet software is especially useful for estimating bad debts. Using both current and past data, estimates of bad debts are obtained under different assumptions and economic trends.

Exhibit 7.12

Computation of the Required Adjustment for an Accounts Receivable Method

Unadjusted balance	$ 200 credit
Estimated balance	2,290 credit
Required adjustment	**$2,090 credit**

Dec. 31	Bad Debts Expense	2,090	
	Allowance for Doubtful Accounts		2,090
	To record estimated bad debts.		

Assets = Liabilities + Equity
−2,090   −2,090

Alternatively, if the allowance account had an unadjusted *debit* balance of $500 (instead of the $200 credit balance), its required adjustment would be computed as follows:

Unadjusted balance	$ 500 debit
Estimated balance	2,290 credit
Required adjustment	**$ 2,790 credit**

The entry to record the end-of-period adjustment for this alternative case is

Assets = Liabilities + Equity
−2,790   −2,790

Dec. 31	Bad Debts Expense	2,790	
	Allowance for Doubtful Accounts		2,790
	To record estimated bad debts.		

Global: International practices vary as to when receivables are written off. Some do not write off an account until it is 1 to 2 years past due.

To sum up the Musicland case, when the percent of sales (income statement) method is used, Musicland's bad debts expense is estimated at $2,400. When the percent of accounts receivable method is used, the expense is $2,300. When the aging of accounts receivable method is used, the expense is $2,090. We expect these amounts to differ since each method gives only an estimate of future payments. The aging of accounts receivable method is a more detailed examination of specific accounts and is usually the most reliable. (Aging analysis often is supplemented with information about specific customers, allowing management to better estimate which accounts are uncollectible.) Exhibit 7.13 summarizes the principles guiding all three estimation methods and their focus of analysis.

Exhibit 7.13

Methods to Estimate Bad Debts

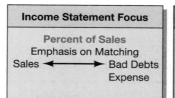
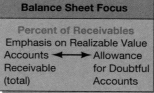
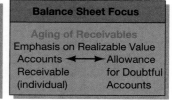

Income Statement Focus	Balance Sheet Focus	Balance Sheet Focus
Percent of Sales Emphasis on Matching Sales ⟷ Bad Debts Expense	**Percent of Receivables** Emphasis on Realizable Value Accounts Receivable (total) ⟷ Allowance for Doubtful Accounts	**Aging of Receivables** Emphasis on Realizable Value Accounts Receivable (individual) ⟷ Allowance for Doubtful Accounts

Quick Check

3. Why must bad debts expense be estimated if such an estimate is possible?

4. What term describes the balance sheet valuation of Accounts Receivable less the Allowance for Doubtful Accounts?

5. Why is estimated bad debts expense credited to a contra account (Allowance for Doubtful Accounts) rather than to the Accounts Receivable account?

6. SnoBoard Company's year-end balance in its Allowance for Doubtful Accounts is a credit of $440. By aging accounts receivable, it estimates that $6,142 is uncollectible. Prepare SnoBoard's year-end adjusting entry for bad debts.

7. Record entries for these transactions assuming the allowance method is used:

Jan. 10   The $300 account of customer Cool Jam is determined uncollectible.

April 12   Cool Jam unexpectedly pays in full the account that was deemed uncollectible on January 10.

Answers—p. 315

Installment Accounts Receivable

Many companies allow their credit customers to make periodic payments over several months. For example, **Harley-Davidson** holds more than $400 million in installment receivables. The seller refers to such assets as *installment accounts receivable,* which are amounts owed by customers from credit sales for which payment is required in periodic amounts over an extended time period. Source documents for installment accounts receivable include sales slips or invoices describing the sales transactions. The customer is usually charged interest. Although installment accounts receivable may have credit periods of more than one year, they are classified as current assets if the seller regularly offers customers such terms.

Decision Maker *d*

Labor Union Chief One week prior to labor contract negotiations, financial statements are released showing no growth in income. A 10% growth was predicted. In your analysis, you find that the company increased its allowance for uncollectibles from 1.5% to 4.5% of accounts receivable. Without this change, income would show a 9% growth. Does this analysis impact your negotiations?

Answer—p. 315

Decision Track 7.2 *d*

Decision Point	Information Search	Analyze & Evaluate
Are past due accounts receivable increasing? Which customers are least creditworthy?	Aging schedule and credit check; list individual customers' receivables by days past due.	The more past due the receivable, the less likely is its cash collection; collection efforts are directed at customers that are more past due.

Notes Receivable

A **promissory note** is a written promise to pay a specified amount of money either on demand or at a definite future date. Promissory notes are used in many transactions, including paying for products and services, lending and borrowing money, and paying for accounts receivable. Sellers sometimes allow customers to sign a note for sales. Sellers also sometimes ask for a note to replace an account receivable when a customer requests additional time to pay a past-due account. Most notes include interest charges. If a seller regularly offers customers this option, such notes are classified as current assets even when their credit period is longer than one year. For legal reasons, sellers generally prefer to receive notes when the credit period is long and when the receivable is for a large amount. If a lawsuit is needed to collect from a customer, a note is the buyer's written acknowledgment of the debt, its amount, and its terms.

Exhibit 7.14 shows a simple promissory note dated July 10, 2002. For this note, Julia Browne promises to pay TechCom or to its order (according to TechCom's instructions) a specified amount of money ($1,000), called the **principal of a note,** at a definite future date (October 8, 2002). As the one who signed the note and promised to pay it at maturity, Browne is the **maker of the note.** As the person to whom the note is payable, TechCom is the **payee of the note.** To Browne, the note is a liability called a *note payable.* To TechCom, the same note is an asset called a *note receivable.* This note bears interest at 12%, as written on the note. **Interest** is the charge for using (not paying) the money until a later date. To a borrower, interest is an expense. To a lender, it is revenue.

C2 Describe a note receivable and the computation of its maturity date and interest.

Topic Tackler 7-2

Exhibit 7.14

Promissory Note

Promissory Note

$1,000	July 10, 2002
Amount	**Date**

Ninety days after date ___I___ promise to pay to the order of

TechCom Company
Los Angeles, CA

One thousand and no/100 - Dollars

for value received with interest at the annual rate of _12%_

payable at First National Bank of Los Angeles, CA

Julia Browne

— Principal
— Date of note
— Due date
— Payee
— Interest rate
— Maker

Computations for Notes

This section describes key computations for notes including the determination of maturity date, period covered, and interest computation.

Maturity Date and Period

The **maturity date of a note** is the day the note (principal and interest) must be repaid. The *period* of a note is the time from the note's (contract) date to its maturity date. Many notes mature in less than a full year, and the period they cover is often expressed in days. When the time of a note is expressed in days, its maturity date is the specified number of days after the note's date. As an example, a five-day note dated June 15 matures and is due on June 20. A 90-day note dated July 10 matures on October 8. This October 8 due date is computed as shown in Exhibit 7.15. The period of a note is sometimes expressed in months or years. When months are used, the note matures and is payable in the month of its maturity on the *same day of the month* as its original date. A nine-month note dated July 10, for instance, is payable on April 10. The same analysis applies when years are used.

Exhibit 7.15

Maturity Date Computation

Days in July	31
Minus the date of the note	10
Days remaining in July	21
Add days in August	31
Add days in September	30
Days to equal 90 days, or **maturity date of October 8**	8
Period of the note in days	90

Interest Computation

Interest is the cost of borrowing money for the borrower or, alternatively, the profit from lending money for the lender. Unless otherwise stated, the rate of interest on a note is the rate charged for the use of the principal for one year. The formula for computing interest on a note is shown in Exhibit 7.16.

Exhibit 7.16

Computation of Interest Formula

$$\begin{array}{c} \text{Principal} \\ \text{of the} \\ \text{note} \end{array} \times \begin{array}{c} \text{Annual} \\ \text{interest} \\ \text{rate} \end{array} \times \begin{array}{c} \text{Time} \\ \text{expressed} \\ \text{in years} \end{array} = \text{Interest}$$

To simplify interest computations, a year is commonly treated as having 360 days (called the *banker's rule*). **We treat a year as having 360 days for interest computations in the examples and assignments.** Using the promissory note in Exhibit 7.14 where we have a 90-day, 12%, $1,000 note, the total interest is computed as follows:

$$\$1,000 \times 12\% \times \frac{90}{360} = \$1,000 \times .12 \times .25 = \$30$$

Receipt of a Note

P3 Record the receipt of a note receivable.

Notes receivable are usually recorded in a single Notes Receivable account to simplify recordkeeping. We need only one account because the original notes are kept on file. This means the maker, rate of interest, due date, and other information are available by examining the actual note. (When a company holds a large number of notes, it sometimes sets up a controlling account and a subsidiary ledger for notes. This is similar to the handling of accounts receivable.) To illustrate the recording for the receipt of a note, we use the $1,000, 90-day, 12% promissory note in Exhibit 7.14. TechCom received this note at the time of a product sale to Julia Browne. This transaction is recorded as follows:

July 10	Notes Receivable	1,000	
	Sales		1,000
	Sold goods in exchange for a 90-day, 12% note.		

Assets = Liabilities + Equity
+1,000   +1,000

* We omit the entry to Dr. Cost of Sales and Cr. Merchandise Inventory to focus on sales and receivables.

Companies also sometimes accept a note from an overdue customer as a way to grant a time extension on a past-due account receivable. When this occurs, a company might collect part of the past-due balance in cash. This partial payment forces a concession from the customer, reduces the customer's debt (and the seller's risk), and produces a note for a smaller amount. To illustrate, assume that TechCom agreed to accept $232 in cash along with a $600, 60-day, 15% note from Jo Cook to settle her $832 past-due account. TechCom made the following entry to record receipt of this cash and note:

Oct. 5	Cash	232	
	Notes Receivable	600	
	Accounts Receivable—J. Cook		832
	Received cash and note to settle account.		

Assets = Liabilities + Equity
+232
+600
−832

Honoring and Dishonoring a Note

The principal and interest of a note are due on its maturity date. The maker of the note usually *honors* the note and pays it in full. However, sometimes a maker *dishonors* the note and does not pay it at maturity.

P4 Record the honoring and dishonoring of a note and adjustments for interest on a note.

Recording an Honored Note

We use the preceding TechCom note transaction to illustrate the honoring of a note. When J. Cook pays the note on its due date, TechCom records it as follows:

Dec. 4	Cash	615	
	Notes Receivable		600
	Interest Revenue		15
	Collect note with interest of $600 × 15% × 60/360.		

Assets = Liabilities + Equity
+615   +15
−600

Interest Revenue, also called Interest Earned, is reported on the income statement.

Recording a Dishonored Note

When a note's maker is unable or refuses to pay at maturity, the note is *dishonored*. The act of dishonoring a note does not relieve the maker of the obligation to pay. The payee should use every legitimate means to collect. But how do companies report this event? The balance of the Notes Receivable account should include only those notes that have not matured. Thus, when a note is dishonored, we remove the amount of this note from the Notes Receivable account and charge it back to an account receivable from its maker. To illustrate, TechCom holds an $800, 12%, 60-day note of Greg Hart. At maturity, Hart dishonors the note. TechCom records this dishonoring of the note as follows:

Point: When posting a dishonored note to a customer's account, an explanation is included. Otherwise, a later review of the account might misinterpret the debit as a sale on account.

Oct. 14	Accounts Receivable—G. Hart	816	
	Interest Revenue		16
	Notes Receivable		800
	To charge account of G. Hart for a dishonored note and interest of $800 × 12% × 60/360.		

Assets = Liabilities + Equity
+816   +16
−800

Charging a dishonored note back to the account of its maker serves two purposes. First, it removes the amount of the note from the Notes Receivable account and records the dishonored note in the maker's account. Second, and more important, if the maker of the dishonored note applies for credit in the future, his or her account will reveal all past dealings, including the dishonored note. Restoring the account also reminds the company to continue collection efforts from Hart for both principal and interest. The entry records the full amount, including interest, to ensure that it is included in collection efforts.

End-of-Period Interest Adjustment

When notes receivable are outstanding at the end of a period, accrued interest is computed and recorded. This recognizes the interest earned by the note's holder. To illustrate, on December 16, TechCom accepts a $3,000, 60-day, 12% note from a customer in granting an extension on a past-due account. When TechCom's accounting period ends on December 31, $15 of interest has accrued on this note ($3,000 $\times$ 12% $\times$ 15/360). The following adjusting entry records this revenue:

Assets = Liabilities + Equity
+15   +15

Dec. 31	Interest Receivable	15	
	Interest Revenue		15
	To record accrued interest earned.		

Interest Revenue then appears on the income statement for the period when it is earned, and Interest Receivable appears on the balance sheet as a current asset. When the December 16 note is collected on February 14, TechCom's entry to record the cash receipt is

Assets   = Liabilities + Equity
+3,060   +45
−15
−3,000

Feb. 14	Cash	3,060	
	Interest Revenue		45
	Interest Receivable		15
	Notes Receivable		3,000
	Received payment of note and its interest.		

Total interest earned on the 60-day note is $60. The $15 credit to Interest Receivable on February 14 reflects the collection of the interest accrued from the December 31 adjusting entry. The $45 interest earned reflects TechCom's revenue from holding the note from January 1 to February 14 of the current period.

Quick Check

8. Irwin purchases $7,000 of merchandise from Stamford on December 16, 2002. Stamford accepts Irwin's $7,000, 90-day, 12% note as payment. Stamford's accounting period ends on December 31, and it does not make reversing entries. Prepare entries for Stamford on December 16, 2002, and December 31, 2002.

9. Using the information in Quick Check 8, prepare Stamford's March 16, 2003, entry if Irwin dishonors the note.

Answers—p. 316

Converting Receivables to Cash before Maturity

Sometimes companies convert receivables to cash before they are due. Reasons for this include the need for cash or the desire not to be involved in collection activities. Converting receivables is usually done either by (1) selling them or (2) using them as security for a loan. A recent survey shows that about 20% of large companies obtain cash from either selling receivables or pledging them as security. In some industries such as textiles and furniture, this is common practice. Recently, this practice has become common for other industries, especially the apparel industry.

Selling Accounts Receivable

A company can sell all or a portion of its accounts receivable to a finance company or bank. The buyer, called a *factor,* charges the seller a *factoring fee* and then receives cash from the receivables as they come due. By incurring a factoring fee, the seller receives cash earlier and can pass the risk of bad debts to the factor. The seller can also choose to avoid costs of billing and accounting for the receivables. To illustrate, if TechCom sells $20,000 of its accounts receivable and is charged a 4% factoring fee, it records this sale as follows:

C3 Explain how receivables can be converted to cash before maturity.

Aug. 15	Cash.	19,200	
	Factoring Fee Expense.	800	
	Accounts Receivable		20,000
	Sold accounts receivable for cash, less a 4% factoring fee.		

Assets = Liabilities + Equity
+19,200   −800
−20,000

Factoring is a major business today. **CIT Group** is a large factoring firm with annual volume of about $8 billion. Interestingly, about 90% of the factoring industry's business comes from textile, furniture, and apparel businesses.

Global: Companies in export sales increasingly sell their receivables to factors.

Pledging Accounts Receivable

A company can also raise cash by borrowing money and *pledging* its accounts receivable as security for the loan. Pledging receivables does not transfer the risk of bad debts to the lender because the borrower retains ownership of the receivables. If the borrower defaults on the loan, the lender has a right to be paid from the cash receipts of the accounts receivable when collected. To illustrate, when TechCom borrows $35,000 and pledges its receivables as security, it records this transaction as follows:

Point: When accounts receivable are sold, each subsidiary ledger account is credited along with the controlling account for the total.

Aug. 20	Cash.	35,000	
	Notes Payable.		35,000
	Borrowed money with a note secured by pledging accounts receivable.		

Assets = Liabilities + Equity
+35,000   +35,000

Since pledged receivables are committed as security for a specific loan, the borrower's financial statements should disclose the pledging of accounts receivable. TechCom, for instance, includes the following note with its financial statements: *Accounts receivable in the amount of $40,000 are pledged as security for a $35,000 note payable.* Another example is from the notes of **Chock Full O'Nuts**: "Outstanding borrowings . . . are collateralized by, among other things, the trade accounts receivable."

Discounting Notes Receivable

Notes receivable can be converted to cash before they mature. This can be done by discounting them at a financial institution. To illustrate, TechCom discounts a $3,000, 90-day, 10% note receivable at National Bank. TechCom

Decision Insight

Cash Poor? Both Zenith and Packard Bell used receivables to get much-needed cash. Zenith obtained a three-year, $60 million credit agreement by pledging accounts receivable as collateral. Intel converted accounts receivable to a note receivable for a customer—widely assumed to be Packard Bell.

had held the note for 50 of its 90 days before discounting it. The bank applies a 12% rate in discounting the note, and TechCom receives proceeds of $3,034 cash from the bank. It recorded the discounting of this note as follows:[1]

Aug. 25	Cash....................................	3,034	
	Interest Revenue*.......................		34
	Notes Receivable.......................		3,000
	Discounted a note receivable.		

* If the cash proceeds are less than the Note Receivable balance, the difference (a debit) is recorded as Interest Expense.

Point: Notes receivable often are a major part of a company's assets. Likewise, notes payable often are a large part of a company's liabilities.

Point: Much of the information required by the full disclosure principle is in notes to financial statements. This information is critical to financial analysis.

Notes receivable are discounted without recourse or with recourse. When a note is discounted *without recourse,* the bank assumes the risk of a bad debt loss, and the original payee does not have a contingent liability. A **contingent liability** is an obligation to make a future payment if, and only if, an uncertain future event occurs. Examples are potential tax assessments, debts of others guaranteed by the company, and outstanding lawsuits against the company. If a note is discounted *with recourse* and the original maker of the note fails to pay the bank when it matures, the original payee of the note must pay for it. This means that a company discounting a note with recourse has a contingent liability until the bank is paid. A company should disclose contingent liabilities in notes to its financial statements. TechCom included the following note: "The Company is contingently liable for a $3,000 note receivable discounted with recourse." A similar example of a receivables sale with recourse is from the notes of Tyco: "The Company entered into an agreement pursuant to which it sold . . . receivables. The Company has retained substantially the same risk of credit loss as if the receivables had not been sold."

The disclosure of contingencies in notes is consistent with the **full disclosure principle,** which requires financial statements (including notes) to report all relevant information about a company's operations and financial position. Relevance is judged by whether a company's disclosure impacts users' business decisions.

Decision Insight

No Place Like Home Home is where the business is—that according to nearly one-half (49%) of entrepreneurs in a recent survey with annual sales between $50,000 to $500,000. More similarities exist between home-based and non-home-based entrepreneurships than commonly assumed—see the table here.

	Home-Based	Non-Home-Based
Similarities		
Years in		
business. . . .	13.9 yrs.	14.5 yrs.
Checking		
acct. bal. . . .	$ 14,700	$ 15,200
Household		
income.	$108,400	$113,200
Differences		
Importance		
of growth . . .	11%	21%
Proprietorship .	72%	52%

Short-Term Investments

Recall from Chapter 6 that cash equivalents are investments readily converted to known amounts of cash and that mature within three months. Many investments, however, mature between 3 and 12 months. These investments are **short-term investments,** also called *temporary investments* or *marketable securities*. Specifically, short-term investments are secu-

---

[1] Cash proceeds from the bank are computed as follows:

Principal of note	$3,000
+ Interest from note ($3,000 × 10% × 90/360) ...	+ 75
= Maturity value of note	$3,075
− Bank discount ($3,075 × 12% × 40/360)	− (41)
= Cash proceeds	$3,034

The net Interest Revenue ($34) equals the total interest from the note ($75) less the bank's discount ($41). If the bank's discount exceeds the note's total interest, Interest Expense is debited for the difference.

rities that (1) management intends to convert to cash within one year or the operating cycle, whichever is longer, and (2) are readily convertible to cash. Short-term investments are current assets and serve a purpose similar to cash equivalents. Short-term investments can include both debt and equity securities. *Debt securities* reflect a creditor relationship such as investments in notes, bonds, and certificates of deposit. Debt securities are issued by governments, companies, and individuals. *Equity securities* reflect an owner relationship such as shares of stock issued by companies.

C4 Describe short-term investments in debt and equity securities.

Accounting for Short-Term Investments

This section explains the basics of accounting for short-term investments in both debt and equity securities. Appendix C (page *C1*) further expands on the accounting for investments.

Debt Securities

Short-term investments in debt (and equity) securities are recorded at cost when purchased. To illustrate, TechCom purchases **Intel** short-term notes payable for $4,000 on January 10. TechCom's entry to record this purchase is

Jan. 10	Short-Term Investments	4,000	
	Cash		4,000
	Bought $4,000 of Intel notes maturing May 10.		

Assets = Liabilities + Equity
+4,000
−4,000

These notes mature on May 10. When the cash proceeds of $4,000 plus the $120 interest ($4,000 × 9% × $\frac{120}{360}$) are received at maturity, TechCom records this as:

May 10	Cash.	4,120	
	Short-Term Investments		4,000
	Interest Revenue		120
	Received cash proceeds from matured notes.		

Assets = Liabilities + Equity
+4,120   +120
−4,000

Equity Securities

The cost of a short-term investment in equity securities includes all necessary costs to acquire it, including commissions paid. To illustrate, TechCom purchases 100 shares of **Nike** common stock as a short-term investment for $50 per share plus $100 in commissions. The entry to record this purchase is

Example: What is cost per share? *Answer:* Cost per share is the total cost of acquisition, inclusive of fees, divided by number of shares acquired.

June 2	Short-Term Investments	5,100	
	Cash		5,100
	Bought 100 shares of Nike stock at $50 per share plus $100 commission.		

Assets = Liabilities + Equity
+5,100
−5,100

TechCom receives a $0.40 per share cash dividend on its Nike stock during the current period. This dividend is recorded in a revenue account as follows:

Dec. 12	Cash.	40	
	Dividend Revenue		40
	Received dividend of $0.40 per share on 100 shares of Nike stock.		

Assets = Liabilities + Equity
+40   +40

Valuing and Reporting Short-Term Investments

Companies must value and report most short-term investments at their *fair market value,* or simply *market value.* Accounting requirements vary depending on whether short-term investments are classified as (1) held-to-maturity, (2) trading, or (3) available-for-sale securities.

P5 Record short-term investment transactions.

Held-to-Maturity Securities

Held-to-maturity securities are *debt securities* that the company has the intent and ability to hold until they mature. **Dairy Queen**, for instance, in notes to its financial statements, states: "Management determines the appropriate classification of debt securities at the time of purchase and reevaluates such designation as of each balance sheet date. Debt securities are classified as held-to-maturity because the Company has the positive intent and ability to hold such securities to maturity." Held-to-maturity securities are reported in current assets if their maturity dates are within the longer of one year or the operating cycle. Short-term held-to-maturity securities are reported at cost.

Trading Securities

Trading securities are *debt and equity securities* that the company intends to actively manage and trade for profit. This means that frequent purchases and sales are made to earn profits on short-term price changes. Trading securities are especially common with financial institutions such as banks and insurance companies.

Valuing and reporting trading securities. The entire portfolio of trading securities is reported at its market value with a "market adjustment" from the cost of the portfolio. The term *portfolio* refers to a group of securities. Any **unrealized gain (or loss)** from a change in the market value of the portfolio of trading securities during a period is reported on the income statement. Most users believe accounting reports are more useful when changes in market value for a portfolio of trading securities are reported in income. To illustrate, TechCom's portfolio of trading securities has a total cost of $11,500 and a market value of $13,000 on December 31, 2002 (this is the first year it held trading securities). The difference between the $11,500 cost and the $13,000 market value reflects a $1,500 gain. This gain is an unrealized gain because it is not yet confirmed by actual sales of these securities. TechCom records this gain as:

Dec. 31	Market Adjustment—Trading	1,500	
	Unrealized Gain—Income		1,500
	To reflect an unrealized gain in market values of trading securities.		

The Unrealized Gain (or Loss) is reported in the Other Revenues and Gains (or Expenses and Losses) section on the income statement. TechCom's investment in trading securities is reported in the current assets section of its balance sheet as follows:

Current Assets	
Short-Term Investments—Trading (at cost)	$11,500
Market Adjustment—Trading	1,500
Short-Term Investments—Trading (at market)	$13,000

The total cost of the portfolio of trading securities is maintained in one account and the market adjustment is recorded in a separate account. The market adjustment for trading securities is revised with an adjusting entry at the end of each period to equal the difference between the portfolio's cost and its market value.

Selling trading securities. When individual trading securities are sold, the difference between the net proceeds from the sale (sale price less fees) and the cost of the individual trading securities that are sold is recognized as a gain or a loss. To illustrate, when TechCom sells its $5,100 short-term investment in Nike stock on December 15 for net proceeds of $5,400, it recognizes a gain of $300. The entry to record this sale is

Dec. 15	Cash	5,400		Assets = Liabilities + Equity
	Gain on Sale of Short-Term Investments		300	+5,400 +300
	Short-Term Investments		5,100	−5,100
	To record sale of 100 shares of Nike stock.			

This gain is reported in the Other Revenues and Gains section on the income statement. If a loss is recorded, it is shown in Other Expenses and Losses. When TechCom computes its market adjustment for trading securities at the end of the period, it excludes the cost and market value of the Nike stock since it has been sold.

Available-for-Sale Securities

Available-for-sale securities are *debt and equity securities* not classified as trading or held-to-maturity securities. Available-for-sale securities are purchased to yield interest, dividends, or increases in market value. They are not actively managed like trading securities.

Valuing and reporting available-for-sale securities. Similar to trading securities, companies adjust the cost of the portfolio of available-for-sale securities to reflect changes in market value. This is done with a market adjustment to its total portfolio cost. However, any unrealized gain or loss for the portfolio of available-for-sale securities is *not* reported on the income statement. Instead, it is reported in the equity section of the balance sheet (and is part of comprehensive income—explained in Appendix C). To illustrate, TechCom's portfolio of available-for-sale securities had a total cost of $15,400 and a market value of $14,500 on December 31, 2002 (this is the first year it held such securities). The difference between the $15,400 cost and the $14,500 market value reflects a $900 unrealized loss. TechCom records this loss as follows:

Dec. 31	Unrealized Loss—Equity	900		Assets = Liabilities + Equity
	Market Adjustment—Available-for-Sale		900	−900 −900
	To reflect an unrealized loss in market values			
	of available-for-sale securities.			

TechCom's current asset and equity sections of its balance sheet appears as follows:

Current Assets		
Short-Term Investments—Available-for-sale (at cost)	$15,400	
Market Adjustment—Available-for-sale	(900)	
Short-Term Investments—Available-for-sale (at market)		$14,500
Equity		
... *usual equity accounts* ...		
Less: Unrealized loss on available-for-sale securities		$ 900

Selling available-for-sale securities. Accounting for the sale of individual available-for-sale securities is identical to that described for the sale of trading securities. When individual available-for-sale securities are sold, the difference between the cost of the individual securities sold and the net proceeds from the sale (sale price less fees) is recognized as a gain or loss.

Decision Insight

Back to the Future About 70 years ago banks switched from reporting market values for their short-term investments to reporting them at cost. We now see a return to market value reporting for most short-term investments. This is driven by S&L and other banking failures in disclosing market value changes. Ironically, the Great Depression fueled the conversion from market values to costs out of concern for the lack of reliability with market values.

Point: Many users believe that since available-for-sale securities are not actively traded, reporting changes in market value in income would unnecessarily increase the variability of income and decrease its usefulness.

Point: Unrealized Gain (or Loss)—Equity is a permanent account reported in the equity section.

Example: If TechCom's portfolio of available-for-sale securities has a cost of $7,500 and a market value of $8,500 at December 31, 2003, its adjusting entry is

Mkt. Adj.—AFS 1,900
  Unreal. Loss—Equity 900
  Unreal. Gain—Equity 1,000

This entry revises the balance in the market adjustment account. It also removes the unrealized loss and records the unrealized gain.

Point: Market Adjustment—Available-for-Sale is a permanent account, shown as a deduction or addition to Short-Term Investment—Available-for-Sale.

Decision Track 7.3   *d*

Decision Point	Information Search	Analyze & Evaluate
Is a company "window-dressing" its income with sales of securities?	Income statement, balance sheet, and financial statement notes on unrealized gains and losses for securities.	Income can be window-dressed upward by selling available-for-sale securities with unrealized gains; income is reduced by selling those with unrealized losses.

Summary of Accounting for Short-Term Investments

Exhibit 7.17 summarizes the accounting for short-term investments in securities.

Exhibit 7.17

Accounting for Short-Term Investments in Securities

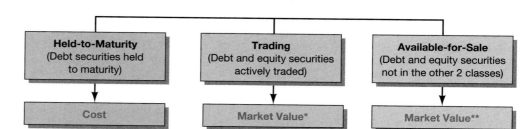

*Unrealized gains or losses reported on income statement.
**Unrealized gains or losses reported in equity section on balance sheet and in comprehensive income.

Point: Reporting securities at market value is referred to as *mark-to-market* accounting.

Point: The Other Revenues and Gains (and Expenses and Losses) section on the income statement is located after operating expenses.

The balance sheet presentation of short-term investments usually reports the market value for the sum *total* of all three classes of securities instead of each individual class. The cost is also usually reported and the details are sometimes disclosed in the notes. A typical presentation of short-term investments is shown in Exhibit 7.18. Although the contra account to Short-Term Investments is not shown, we can determine its balance as $1,700 by comparing the $16,200 cost with the $14,500 market value.

Exhibit 7.18

Statement Presentation of Short-Term Investments

Current assets
    Short-term investments, at market value (cost is $16,200) **$14,500**

Quick Check

10. How are current held-to-maturity securities reported (valued) on the balance sheet?

11. How are trading securities reported (valued) on the balance sheet?

12. Where are unrealized gains and losses on available-for-sale securities reported?

13. Where are unrealized gains and losses on trading securities reported?

14. A company has substantial accounts receivable but needs cash. What alternatives are available for getting cash from its accounts receivable prior to receiving payments from credit customers? Show the entry made for each alternative.

Answers—p. 316

Decision Analysis *d*   **Accounts Receivable Turnover**

A1 Compute accounts receivable turnover and use it to help assess financial condition.

For a company selling on credit, we want to assess both the quality and liquidness of its accounts receivable. *Quality* of receivables refers to the likelihood of collection without loss. Experience shows that the longer receivables are outstanding beyond their due date, the lower the likelihood of collection. *Liquidness* of receivables refers to the speed of collection. **Accounts receivable turnover** is a measure of both the quality and liquidness of accounts receivable. It indicates how often, on average, receivables are received and collected during the period. The formula for this ratio is shown in Exhibit 7.19.

$$\text{Accounts receivable turnover} = \frac{\text{Net sales}}{\text{Average accounts receivable}}$$

Exhibit 7.19

Accounts Receivable Turnover

We prefer to use net *credit* sales in the numerator because cash sales do not create receivables. However, since financial statements rarely report net credit sales, our analysis uses net sales. The denominator is the *average* accounts receivable balance, computed as (Beginning balance + Ending balance) ÷ 2. TechCom has an accounts receivable turnover of 5.1. This indicates its average accounts receivable balance is converted into cash 5.1 times during the period. Exhibit 7.20 shows graphically this turnover activity for TechCom.

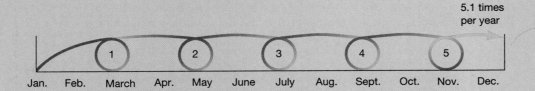

Exhibit 7.20

Rate of Accounts Receivable Turnover for TechCom

Accounts receivable turnover also reflects how well management is doing in granting credit to customers in a desire to increase sales. A high turnover in comparison with competitors suggests that management should consider using more liberal credit terms to increase sales. A low turnover suggests management should consider stricter credit terms and more aggressive collection efforts to avoid having its resources tied up in accounts receivable.

To illustrate its application, we take data from two competitors: Dell Computer and Apple Computer. Exhibit 7.21 shows accounts receivable turnover for both companies.

Company	Figure ($ in millions)	2000	1999	1998
Dell	Net sales	$31,888	$25,265	$18,243
	Average accounts receivable	$ 2,752	$ 2,351	$ 1,790
	Accounts receivable turnover	11.6	10.7	10.2
Apple	Net sales	$ 7,983	$ 6,134	$ 5,941
	Average accounts receivable	$ 817	$ 818	$ 995
	Accounts receivable turnover	9.8	7.5	6.0

Exhibit 7.21

Analysis Using Accounts Receivable Turnover

Dell's 2000 turnover is computed ($ in millions) as $31,888/$2,752 = 11.6. This means that Dell's average accounts receivable balance was converted into cash 11.6 times in 2000. Also, its turnover improved in 2000 (versus its prior two years), and it is superior to Apple. Is Dell's turnover too high? Since sales are markedly growing over this time period, Dell's turnover does not appear to be too high. Instead, its management seems to be doing a good job managing receivables. Similarly, Apple has improved its management of receivables during this period. Turnover for competitors is generally in the range of 6 to 9 for this same period.[2]

> **Decision Maker**   *d*
>
> **Family Physician**   Your practice has turned less profitable, so you hire a health care analyst. The analyst highlights several points including the following: *"Accounts receivable turnover is too low. Tighter credit policies are recommended along with discontinuing service to those most delayed in payments."* How do you interpret these recommendations? What actions do you take? .
>
> Answer—p. 315

[2] As an approximation of *average days' sales uncollected* (see Chapter 6), we can estimate how many days (*on average*) it takes to collect receivables as follows: 365 days ÷ accounts receivable turnover. An increase in this *average collection period* can reflect a decline in customers' financial condition.

Demonstration Problem

Garden Company completes the following selected transactions during year 2002:

May	8	Purchases 300 shares of Federal Express stock as a short-term investment in available-for-sale securities at a cost of $40 per share plus $975 in broker fees.
July	14	Writes off a $750 account receivable arising from a sale to Briggs Company that dates to 10 months ago. (Garden Company uses the allowance method.)
	30	Garden Company receives a $1,000, 90-day, 10% note in exchange for merchandise sold to Sumrell Company (the merchandise cost $600).
Aug.	15	Receives $2,000 cash plus a $10,000 note from JT Co. in exchange for merchandise that sells for $12,000 (its cost is $8,000). The note is dated August 15, bears 12% interest, and matures in 180 days.
Sept.	2	Sells 100 shares of its investment in Federal Express stock at $47 per share and holds the remaining 200 shares. The broker's commission on this sale is $225.
	15	Receives $9,850 cash in exchange for discounting without recourse the $10,000 note (dated August 15) at the local bank.
Oct.	2	Purchases 400 shares of McDonald's stock for $60 per share plus $1,600 in commissions. The stock is held as a short-term investment in available-for-sale securities.
Nov.	1	Completed a $200 credit card sale with a 4% fee (the cost of sales is $150). The cash is received immediately from the credit card company.
	3	Sumrell Company refuses to pay the note that was due to Garden Company on October 28. Prepare the journal entry to charge the dishonored note plus accrued interest to Sumrell Company's accounts receivable.
	5	Completed a $500 credit card sale with a 5% fee (the cost of sales is $300) . The payment from the credit card company is received on Nov. 7.
	15	Received the full amount of $750 from Briggs Company that was previously written off on July 14. Record the bad debts recovery.

Required

1. Prepare journal entries to record these transactions on Garden Company's books.

2. Prepare an adjusting journal entry as of December 31, 2002, assuming the following:

   a. Bad debts expense is estimated to be $20,400 by aging accounts receivable. The unadjusted balance of the Allowance for Doubtful Accounts is $1,000 debit.

   b. Alternatively, assume that bad debts expense is estimated using the percent of sales method. The Allowance for Doubtful Accounts had a $1,000 debit balance before adjustment, and the company estimates bad debts to be 1% of its credit sales of $2,000,000.

3. Prepare an adjusting journal entry as of December 31, 2002, if the market prices of the equity securities held by Garden Company are $48 per share for Federal Express and $55 per share for McDonald's. (Year 2002 is the first year Garden Co. acquired short-term investments.)

Planning the Solution

- Examine each transaction to determine the accounts affected and then record the entries.
- For the year-end adjustment, record the bad debts expense for the two approaches.

Solution to Demonstration Problem

1.

May 8	Short-Term Investments	12,975	
	Cash		12,975
	Purchased 300 shares of Federal Express stock (300 × $40) + $975.		
July 14	Allowance for Doubtful Accounts	750	
	Accounts Receivable—Briggs Co.		750
	Wrote off an uncollectible account.		
July 30	Notes Receivable—Sumrell Co.	1,000	
	Sales		1,000
	Sold merchandise for a 90-day, 10% note.		
July 30	Cost of Goods Sold.	600	
	Merchandise Inventory.		600
	To record the cost of July 30 sale.		

Aug. 15	Cash	2,000	
	Notes Receivable—JT Co.	10,000	
	Sales		12,000
	Sold merchandise to customer for $2,000 cash and $10,000 note.		
Aug. 15	Cost of Goods Sold	800	
	Merchandise Inventory..................		800
	To record the cost of Aug. 15 sale.		
Sept. 2	Cash	4,475	
	Gain on Sale of Short-term Investment		150
	Short-Term Investments		4,325
	Sold 100 shares of Federal Express for $47 per share less a $225 commission. The original cost is ($12,975 × 100/300).		
Sept. 15	Cash	9,850	
	Interest Expense	150	
	Notes Receivable—JT Co.		10,000
	Discounted note receivable dated August 15.		
Oct. 2	Short-Term Investments	25,600	
	Cash		25,600
	Purchased 400 shares of McDonald's for $60 per share plus $1,600 in commissions.		
Nov. 1	Cash	192	
	Credit Card Expense	8	
	Sales		200
	To record credit card sale less a 4% credit card expense.		
Nov. 1	Cost of Goods Sold	150	
	Merchandise Inventory..................		150
	To record the cost of Nov. 1 sale.		
Nov. 3	Accounts Receivable—Sumrell Co..............	1,025	
	Interest Revenue		25
	Notes Receivable—Sumrell Co.		1,000
	To charge account of Sumrell Company for a $1,000 dishonored note and interest of $1,000 × 10% × 90/360.		
Nov. 5	Accounts Receivable—Credit Card Co...........	475	
	Credit Card Expense	25	
	Sales		500
	To record credit card sale less a 5% credit card expense.		
Nov. 5	Cost of Goods Sold.......................	300	
	Merchandise Inventory...................		300
	To record the cost of Nov. 5 sale.		
Nov. 7	Cash....................................	475	
	Accounts Receivable—Credit Card Co.........		475
	To record cash receipt from Nov. 5 sale.		
Nov. 15	Accounts Receivable—Briggs Co..............	750	
	Allowance for Doubtful Accounts		750
	To reinstate the account of Briggs Company previously written off.		
Nov. 15	Cash....................................	750	
	Accounts Receivable—Briggs Co.		750
	Cash received in full payment of account.		

> Interest Expense of $150 is the *net* of interest revenue from holding the note *less* the bank discounting charge.

2a. Aging of accounts receivable method:

Dec. 31	Bad Debts Expense........................	21,400	
	Allowance for Doubtful Accounts		21,400
	To adjust allowance account from a $1,000 debit balance to a $20,400 credit balance.		

2b. Percent of sales method:

Dec. 31	Bad Debts Expense.	20,000	
	Allowance for Doubtful Accounts		20,000
	To provide for bad debts as 1% × $2,000,000		
	in credit sales.		

(*Note:* For the income statement approach, which requires estimating bad debts as a percent of sales or credit sales, the Allowance account balance is *not* considered when making the adjusting entry.)

3. Computation of unrealized gain or loss:

Short-Term Investments in Available-for-Sale Securities	Shares	Cost per Share	Total Cost	Market Value per Share	Total Market Value	Unrealized Gain (Loss)
Federal Express	200	$43.25	$ 8,650	$ 48.00	$ 9,600	
McDonald's	400	64.00	25,600	55.00	22,000	
Total			$ 34,250		$31,600	$(2,650)

Adjusting entry:

Dec. 31	Unrealized Loss—Equity	2,650	
	Market Adjustment—Available-for-Sale		2,650
	To reflect an unrealized loss in market values		
	of available-for-sale securities.		

Summary

C1 **Describe accounts receivable and how they occur and are recorded.** Accounts receivable are amounts due from customers for credit sales. A subsidiary ledger lists amounts owed by each customer. Credit sales arise from at least two sources: (1) sales on credit and (2) credit card sales. Sales on credit refer to a company's granting credit directly to customers. Credit card sales involve customers' use of third-party credit cards.

C2 **Describe a note receivable and the computation of its maturity date and interest.** A note receivable is a written promise to pay a specified amount of money at a definite future date. The maturity date is the day the note (principal and interest) must be repaid. Interest rates are normally stated in annual terms. The amount of interest on the note is computed by expressing time as a fraction of one year and multiplying the note's principal by this fraction and the annual interest rate.

C3 **Explain how receivables can be converted to cash before maturity.** Receivables can be converted to cash before maturity in three ways. First, a company can sell accounts receivable to a factor, who charges a factoring fee. Second, a company can borrow money by signing a note payable that is secured by pledging the accounts receivable. Third, notes receivable can be discounted at a bank, with or without recourse.

C4 **Describe short-term investments in debt and equity securities.** Short-term investments can include both debt and equity securities. *Debt securities* reflect a creditor relationship and include investments in notes, bonds, and certificates of deposit. *Equity securities* reflect an owner relationship and include shares of stock issued by other companies.

A1 **Compute accounts receivable turnover and use it to help assess financial condition.** Accounts receivable turnover is a measure of both the quality and liquidness of accounts receivable. The accounts receivable turnover measure indicates how often, on average, receivables are received and collected during the period. Accounts receivable turnover is computed as net sales divided by average accounts receivable.

P1 **Apply the direct write-off and allowance methods to account for accounts receivable.** The direct write-off method charges Bad Debts Expense when accounts are written off as uncollectible. This method is acceptable only when the amount of bad debts expense is immaterial. Under the allowance method, bad debts expense is recorded with an adjustment at the end of each accounting period that debits the Bad Debts Expense account and credits the Allowance for Doubtful Accounts. The uncollectible accounts are later written off with a debit to the Allowance for Doubtful Accounts.

P2 **Estimate uncollectibles using methods based on sales and accounts receivable.** Uncollectibles are estimated by focusing on either (1) the income statement relation between bad debts expense and credit sales or (2) the balance sheet relation between accounts receivable and the allowance for doubtful accounts. The first approach emphasizes the matching principle using the income statement. The second approach emphasizes realizable value of accounts receivable using the balance sheet.

P3 **Record the receipt of a note receivable.** A note received is recorded at its principal amount by debiting the Notes Receivable account. The credit amount is to the asset, product, or service provided in return for the note.

P4 **Record the honoring and dishonoring of a note and adjustments for interest on a note.** When a note is honored, the payee debits the money received and credits both Notes Receivable and Interest Revenue. Dishonored notes are credited to Notes Receivable and debited to Accounts Receivable (to the account of the maker in an attempt to collect). Interest Revenue from holding a note is recorded for the time the note is held.

P5 **Record short-term investment transactions.** Short-term investments are initially recorded at cost, and any dividends or interest from these investments is recorded in the income statement. Short-term investments are classified as held-to-maturity securities, trading securities, or available-for-sale securities. Held-to-maturity securities are reported at cost on the balance sheet. Trading securities and available-for-sale securities are reported at their market values. Unrealized gains and losses on trading securities are reported in income. Unrealized gains and losses on available-for-sale securities are reported in the equity section of the balance sheet. When short-term investments are sold, the difference between the net proceeds from the sale and the cost of the securities is recognized as a gain or loss.

Guidance Answers to **Decision Maker** and **Decision Ethics**

Entrepreneur   Analysis of credit card sales should weigh the benefits against the costs. The primary benefit is the potential to increase sales by attracting customers who prefer the convenience of credit cards. The primary cost is the fee charged by the credit card company for providing this service. Analysis should therefore estimate the expected increase in dollar sales from allowing credit card sales and then subtract (1) the normal costs and expenses and (2) the credit card fees associated with this expected increase in dollar sales. If your analysis shows an increase in profit from allowing credit card sales, your store should probably accept them.

Labor Union Chief   Yes, this information is likely to impact your negotiations. The obvious question is why the company markedly increased this allowance. The large increase in this allowance means a substantial increase in bad debts expense *and* a decrease in earnings. This change (coming immediately prior to labor contract discussions) also raises concerns since it reduces the union's bargaining power for increased compensation. You want to ask management for supporting documentation justifying this increase. You also want data for two or three prior years and similar data from competitors. These data should give you some sense of whether the change in the allowance for uncollectibles is justified.

Family Physician   The recommendations are twofold. First, the analyst suggests more stringent screening of patients' credit standing. Second, the analyst suggests dropping patients who are most overdue in payments. You are likely bothered by both suggestions. While they are probably financially wise recommendations, you are troubled by eliminating services to those less able to pay. One alternative is to follow the recommendations while implementing a care program directed at patients less able to pay for services. This allows you to continue services to patients less able to pay and lets you discontinue services to patients able but unwilling to pay.

Guidance Answers to **Quick Checks**

1. If cash is received when credit card sales receipts are deposited in the bank, the company debits Cash at the time of sale. If the company does not receive payment until after it submits receipts to the credit card company, it debits Accounts Receivable at the time of sale. (Cash is later debited when payment is received from the credit card company.)

2. Credit card expenses are usually *recorded* and *incurred* at the time of their related sales, not when cash is received from the credit card company.

3. If possible, bad debts expense must be matched with the sales that gave rise to the accounts receivable. This requires that companies estimate future bad debts at the end of each period before they learn which accounts are uncollectible.

4. Realizable value (also called *net realizable value*).

5. The estimated amount of bad debts expense cannot be credited to the Accounts Receivable account because the specific customer accounts that will prove uncollectible cannot yet be identified and removed from the subsidiary accounts receivable ledger. Moreover, if only the Accounts Receivable account is credited, its balance would not equal the sum of its subsidiary account balances.

6.

Dec. 31	Bad Debts Expense	5,702	
	Allowance for Doubtful Accounts		5,702

7.

Jan. 10	Allowance for Doubtful Accounts	300	
	Accounts Receivable—Cool Jam		300
Apr. 12	Accounts Receivable—Cool Jam. . . .	300	
	Allowance for Doubtful Accounts.		300
Apr. 12	Cash	300	
	Accounts Receivable—Cool Jam		300

8.

Dec. 16	Note Receivable—Irwin	7,000	
	Sales		7,000
Dec. 31	Interest Receivable	35	
	Interest Revenue		35
	($7,000 × 12% × 15/360)		

9.

Mar. 16	Accounts Receivable—Irwin	7,210	
	Interest Revenue		175
	Interest Receivable		35
	Notes Receivable—Irwin . . .		7,000

10. Short-term held-to-maturity securities are reported at cost.

11. Trading securities are reported at market value.

12. The equity section of the balance sheet (and in comprehensive income).

13. The income statement.

14. Alternatives are (1) selling their accounts receivable to a factor and (2) pledging accounts receivable as loan security. The entries to record these transactions take the following form:

(1) Cash	#	
Factoring Fee Expense	#	
Accounts Receivable		#
(2) Cash	#	
Notes Payable		#

Glossary

Accounts receivable Amounts due from customers for credit sales. (p. 290)

Accounts receivable turnover Measure of both the quality and liquidness of accounts receivable; indicates how often receivables are received and collected during the period; computed by dividing net sales by average accounts receivable. (p. 310)

Aging of accounts receivable Process of classifying accounts receivable by how long they are past due for purposes of estimating uncollectible accounts. (p. 298)

Allowance for Doubtful Accounts Contra asset account with a balance approximating uncollectible accounts receivable; also called *Allowance for Uncollectible Accounts*. (p. 295)

Allowance method Procedure that (1) estimates and matches bad debts expense with its sales for the period and (2) reports accounts receivable at estimated realizable value. (p. 294)

Available-for-sale securities Investments in debt and equity securities that are not classified as trading securities or held-to-maturity securities. (p. 309)

Bad debts Accounts of customers who do not pay what they have promised to pay;

an expense of selling on credit; also called *uncollectible accounts*. (p. 293)

Contingent liability Obligation to make a future payment if, and only if, an uncertain future event occurs. (p. 306)

Direct write-off method Method that records the loss from an uncollectible account receivable at the time it is determined to be uncollectible; no attempt is made to estimate bad debts. (p. 293)

Full disclosure principle Principle that requires financial statements (including notes) to report all relevant information about an entity's operations and financial condition. (p. 306)

Held-to-maturity securities Debt securities that a company has the intent and ability to hold until they mature. (p. 308)

Interest Charge for using money (or other assets) until repaid at a future date. (p. 301)

Maker of a note Entity who signs a note and promises to pay it at maturity. (p. 301)

Matching principle Requires expenses to be reported in the same period as the sales they helped produce. (p. 294)

Materiality principle Implies that an amount can be ignored if its effect on fi-

nancial statements is unimportant to users. (p. 294)

Maturity date of a note Date when principal and interest of a note are due. (p. 302)

Payee of a note Entity to whom a note is made payable. (p. 301)

Principal of a note Amount that the signer of a note agrees to pay back when it matures, not including interest. (p. 301)

Promissory note (or **note**) Written promise to pay a specified amount either on demand or at a definite future date. (p. 301)

Realizable value Expected proceeds from converting an asset into cash. (p. 295)

Short-term investments Debt and equity securities that management expects to convert to cash within the next 3 to 12 months (or the operating cycle if longer); also called *temporary investments*. (p. 306)

Trading securities Investments in debt and equity securities that the company intends to actively trade for profit. (p. 308)

Unrealized gain (loss) Gain (loss) not yet realized by an actual transaction or event such as a sale. (p. 308)

Questions

1. How do sellers benefit from allowing their customers to use credit cards?

2. Why does the direct write-off method of accounting for bad debts usually fail to match revenues and expenses?

3. Explain the accounting principle of materiality.

4. Explain why writing off a bad debt against the Allowance for Doubtful Accounts does not reduce the estimated realizable value of a company's accounts receivable.

5. Why does the Bad Debts Expense account usually not have the same adjusted balance as the Allowance for Doubtful Accounts?

6. Why might a business prefer a note receivable to an account receivable?

7. What does it mean to sell a receivable without recourse?

8. Under what two conditions should investments be classified as current assets?

9. On a balance sheet, what valuation must be reported for short-term investments in trading securities?

10. If a short-term investment in available-for-sale securities costs $6,780 and is sold for $7,500, how should the difference between these two amounts be recorded?

11. Refer to Nike's balance sheet in Appendix A. What percent of accounts receivable at May 31, **NIKE**

2000, has been set aside as an allowance for doubtful accounts? How does this percent compare to the prior year?

12. Refer to the balance sheet of Reebok in Appendix A. Does it use the direct write-off method or allowance method to account for doubtful accounts? What is the realizable value of its accounts receivable as of December 31, 1999? What is another name for the Allowance for Doubtful Accounts?

13. Refer to the balance sheet of Gap in Appendix A. Why does it not show any accounts receivable in its current asset section? **GAP**

Prepare journal entries for the following sales transactions involving credit cards (the company uses the perpetual inventory system):

1. Sold merchandise that cost $15,000 for $20,000 on MasterCard credit cards. The net cash receipts from sales are immediately deposited in the seller's bank account. MasterCard charges a 5% fee.

2. Sold $5,000 in merchandise (that had cost $3,000) on an assortment of credit cards. Net cash receipts are received 10 days later, and a 4% fee is charged.

QUICK STUDY

QS 7-1
Credit card sales
C1

Fortune Corp. uses the allowance method to account for uncollectibles. On October 31, it wrote off an $800 account of a customer, C. Rowland. On December 9, it receives a $300 payment from Rowland.

1. Prepare the journal entry or entries for October 31.

2. Prepare the journal entry or entries for December 9—assume no additional money is expected from Rowland.

QS 7-2
Allowance method **P1**
for bad debts

Blazek Company's year-end unadjusted trial balance shows accounts receivable of $99,000, allowance for doubtful accounts of $600 (credit), and sales of $280,000. Uncollectibles are estimated to be 1.5% of accounts receivable.

1. Prepare the December 31 year-end adjusting entry for uncollectibles.

2. What amount would have been used in the year-end adjusting entry if the allowance account had a year-end unadjusted debit balance of $300?

3. Assume the same facts as in part 1, except that Blazek estimates uncollectibles as 0.5% of sales. Prepare the December 31 year-end adjusting entry for uncollectibles.

QS 7-3
Percent of accounts receivable and percent of sales methods
P1 P2

On August 2, 2002, PSI Co. receives a $6,000, 90-day, 12% note from customer Tom Cather as payment on his $6,000 account. Prepare PSI's journal entries for August 2 and for the note's maturity date assuming the note is honored by Cather.

QS 7-4 **P3 P4**
Note receivable

Snyder Company's December 31 year-end unadjusted trial balance shows a $10,000 balance in Notes Receivable. This balance is from one 6% note dated December 1, with a period of 45 days. Prepare journal entries for December 31 and for the note's maturity date assuming it is honored.

QS 7-5 **C2 P4**
Note receivable

On April 18, Derek Co. made a short-term investment in 300 shares of Computer Advantage common stock. Their purchase price is $42.5 per share and the broker's fee is $250. The intent is to actively manage these shares for profit. On May 30, Derek Co. receives $1 per share from Computer Advantage in dividends. Prepare the April 18 and May 30 journal entries.

QS 7-6
Short-term equity **C4 P5**
investments

Cooper Co. purchases short-term investments in available-for-sale securities at a cost of $50,000 on November 25, 2002. At December 31, 2002, these securities had a market value of $47,000. This is the first and only time the company has purchased such securities.

1. Prepare the December 31, 2002, year-end adjusting entry for these securities' portfolio.

2. For each account in the entry for part 1, explain how it is reported in financial statements.

3. Prepare the April 6, 2003, entry when Cooper sells one-half of these securities for $26,000.

QS 7-7
Available-for-sale securities
C4 P5

QS 7-8 *[icon]*
Accounts receivable turnover

A1

The following data are taken from the comparative balance sheets of Fuqua Company Compute and interpret the accounts receivable turnover for year 2002.

	2002	2001
Accounts receivable.......	$153,400	$138,500
Net sales.............	854,200	910,600

EXERCISES

Exercise 7-1
Accounting for credit card sales

C1

Busch Company allows customers to use two credit cards in charging purchases. With the NuWay Card, Busch receives an immediate credit when it deposits sales receipts in its checking account. NuWay Card assesses a 4% service charge for credit card sales. The second credit card that Busch accepts is the Continental Bank Card. Busch sends its accumulated receipts to Continental Bank on a weekly basis and is paid by Continental about 10 days later. Continental Bank charges 2.5% of sales for using its card. Prepare journal entries to record the following selected credit card transactions of Busch Company:

Apr. 8 Sold merchandise for $8,400 (that had cost $6,000) and accepted the customer's NuWay Card. The NuWay receipts are immediately deposited in Busch's bank account.
  12 Sold merchandise for $5,602 (that had cost $3,500) and accepted the customer's Continental Bank Card. Transferred $5,602 of credit card receipts to Continental Bank, requesting payment.
  20 Received Continental Bank's check for the April 12 billing, less the service charge.

Exercise 7-2
Accounts receivable subsidiary ledger; schedule of accounts receivable

C1

Taku Company recorded the following selected transactions during November 2002:

Nov. 5	Accounts Receivable—Paint Shop	4,615	
	Sales		4,615
10	Accounts Receivable—Cool Enterprises	1,350	
	Sales		1,350
13	Accounts Receivable—Matt Mahoney	832	
	Sales		832
21	Sales Returns and Allowances	209	
	Accounts Receivable—Matt Mahoney		209
30	Accounts Receivable—Paint Shop	2,713	
	Sales		2,713

1. Open a general ledger having T-accounts for Accounts Receivable, Sales, and Sales Returns and Allowances. Also open a subsidiary accounts receivable ledger having a T-account for each customer. Post these entries to both the general ledger and the accounts receivable ledger.

2. Prepare a schedule of accounts receivable (see Exhibit 7.4) and compare its total with the balance of the Accounts Receivable controlling account as of November 30.

Exercise 7-3
Percent of sales method; write-off

P1 P2

At year-end (December 31), Cayman Company estimates its bad debts as 0.5% of its annual credit sales of $975,000. Cayman adjusts its Allowance for Doubtful Accounts for that estimate. On the following February 1, Cayman decides that the $580 account of P. Snoop is uncollectible and writes it off as a bad debt. On June 5, Snoop unexpectedly pays the amount previously written off. Prepare the journal entries of Cayman to record these transactions and events of December 31, February 1, and June 5.

Exercise 7-4
Percent of accounts receivable method

P1 P2

At each calendar year-end, Bayoo Supply Co. uses the percent of accounts receivable method to estimate bad debts. On December 31, 2002, it has outstanding accounts receivable of $55,000, and it estimates that 2% will be uncollectible. Prepare the adjusting entry to record bad debts expense for year 2002 under the assumption that the Allowance for Doubtful Accounts has (1) a $415 credit balance before the adjustment and (2) a $291 debit balance before the adjustment.

On June 30, Koby Co. has $128,700 of accounts receivable. Prepare journal entries to record the following selected July transactions. Also prepare any footnotes to the July 31 financial statements that result from these transactions. (The company uses the perpetual inventory system.)

July   4   Sold $7,245 of merchandise (that had cost $5,000) to customers on credit.
      9   Sold $20,000 of accounts receivable to NBD Bank. NBD charges a 4% factoring fee.
    17   Received $5,859 cash from customers in payment on their accounts.
    27   Borrowed $10,000 cash from NBD Bank, pledging $12,500 of accounts receivable as security for the loan.

Exercise 7-5
Selling and pledging accounts receivable
C3

Prepare journal entries to record these selected transactions for Venus Company:

Nov.   1   Accepted a $6,000, 180-day, 8% note dated November 1 from Shelia Denton in granting a time extension on her past-due account receivable.
Dec. 31   Adjusted the year-end accounts for the accrued interest earned on the Denton note.
Apr. 30   Denton honors her note when presented for payment.

Exercise 7-6
Honoring a note
P4

Prepare journal entries to record the following selected transactions of Warren Company:

Mar. 21   Accepted a $2,500, 180-day, 8% note dated March 21 from Tina Adams in granting a time extension on her past-due account receivable.
Sept. 17   Adams dishonors her note when it is presented for payment.
Dec. 31   After exhausting all legal means of collection, Warren Company writes off Adams's account against the Allowance for Doubtful Accounts.

Exercise 7-7
Dishonoring a note
P4

Prepare journal entries for the following selected transactions of Chandra Company:

2002

Dec. 13   Accepted a $9,500, 60-day, 8% note dated December 13 in granting Tom Alcox a time extension on his past-due account receivable.
    31   Prepared an adjusting entry to record the accrued interest on the Alcox note.
    31   Closed the Interest Revenue account to Income Summary.

2003

Feb. 11   Received Alcox's payment for principal and interest on the note dated December 13.
Mar.   3   Accepted a $5,000, 10%, 90-day note dated March 3 in granting a time extension on the past-due account receivable of BAX Company.
    17   Accepted a $2,000, 30-day, 9% note dated March 17 in granting Bill Connors a time extension on his past-due account receivable.
Apr. 16   Connors dishonors his note when presented for payment.
May   1   Wrote off the Connors account against the Allowance for Doubtful Accounts.
June   1   Received the BAX payment for principal and interest on the note dated March 3.

Exercise 7-8
Notes receivable transactions and entries
C2 P3 P4

Check   Dec. 31, Cr. Interest Revenue $38

Check   Feb. 11, Dr. Cash $9,626.67

Check   June 1, Dr. Cash $5,125

Prepare journal entries to record the following transactions involving the short-term investments of Morford Co., all of which occurred during year 2002:

a. On February 15, paid $120,000 cash to purchase MRI's 90-day short-term debt securities ($120,000 principal), which are dated February 15 and pay 8% interest (categorized as held-to-maturity securities).

b. On March 22, purchased 700 shares of GRE Company stock at $27.50 per share plus a $150 brokerage fee. These shares are categorized as trading securities

c. On May 16, received a check from MRI in payment of the principal and 90 days' interest on the debt securities purchased in transaction *a*.

d. On August 1, paid $80,000 cash to purchase Flash Electronics' 10% debt securities ($80,000 principal), dated July 30, 2002, and maturing January 30, 2003 (categorized as available-for-sale securities).

e. On September 1, received a $1.00 per share cash dividend on the GRE Company stock purchased in transaction *b*.

f. On October 8, sold 350 shares of GRE Co. stock for $34 per share, less a $140 brokerage fee.

g. On October 30, received a check from Flash Electronics for 90 days' interest on the debt securities purchased in transaction *d*.

Exercise 7-9
Accounting for short-term investment transactions
C4 P5

Check   (c) Dr. Cash $122,400

Check   (f) Dr. Cash $11,760

Exercise 7-10 🗐
Accounting for trading securities

C4 P5

Check (3) Gain, $2,000

Focus Co. purchases short-term investments in trading securities at a cost of $66,000 on December 27, 2002. (This is its first and only purchase of such securities.) At December 31, 2002, these securities had a market value of $72,000.

1. Prepare the December 31, 2002, year-end adjusting entry for the trading securities' portfolio.

2. For each account in the entry for part 1, explain how it is reported in financial statements.

3. Prepare the January 3, 2003, entry when Focus sells one-half of these securities for $35,000.

Exercise 7-11 🗐
Adjusting available-for-sale securities to market

C4 P5

Check Unrealized loss, $9,100

On December 31, 2002, Quaker Company held the following short-term investments in its portfolio of available-for-sale securities. Quaker had no short-term investments in its prior accounting periods. Prepare the December 31, 2002, adjusting entry to report these investments at market value.

	Cost	Market Value
Valdez Corporation bonds payable	$89,600	$91,600
Transunion Corporation notes payable	70,600	62,900
Lake Placid Company common stock	86,500	83,100

Exercise 7-12 🗐
Accounts receivable turnover

A1

The following information is from the annual financial statements of Whipple Company. Compute Whipple's accounts receivable turnover for 2002 and 2003. Compare the two results and give a possible explanation for any change.

	2003	2002	2001
Net sales	$405,000	$336,000	$388,000
Accounts receivable (December 31)	44,800	41,400	34,800

PROBLEM SET A

Problem 7-1A
Sales on credit and credit card sales

C1 Ⓖ

American Co. allows select customers to make purchases on credit. Its other customers can use either of two credit cards: Zip Bank or OneCharge. Zip Bank deducts a 3% service charge for sales on its credit card but credits the checking account of American immediately when credit card receipts are deposited. American deposits the Zip Bank credit card receipts each business day. When customers use OneCharge credit cards, American accumulates the receipts for several days before submitting them to OneCharge for payment. OneCharge deducts a 2% service charge and usually pays within one week of being billed. American completes the following transactions in June. (The terms of all credit sales are 2/15, n/30, and all sales are recorded at the gross price.)

June 4   Sold $650 of merchandise (that had cost $400) on credit to Anne Klein.
     5   Sold merchandise for $6,900 (that had cost $4,200) to customers who used their Zip Bank credit cards.
     6   Sold merchandise for $5,872 (that had cost $3,800) to customers who used their OneCharge credit cards.
     8   Sold merchandise for $4,335 (that had cost $2,900) to customers who used their OneCharge credit cards.
     10   Submitted OneCharge card receipts accumulated since June 6 to the credit card company for payment.
     13   Wrote off the account of Mandy Smith against the Allowance for Doubtful Accounts. The $429 balance in Smith's account stemmed from a credit sale in October of last year.

Check June 17, Dr. Cash $10,003

     17   Received the amount due from OneCharge.
     18   Received Klein's check paying for the purchase of June 4.

Required

Prepare journal entries to record the preceding transactions and events. (The company uses the perpetual inventory system.)

Problem 7-2A
Accounts receivable transactions and bad debts adjustments

C1 P1 P2

Heche Company began operations on January 1, 2002. During its first two years, the company completed a number of transactions involving sales on credit, accounts receivable collections, and bad debts. These transactions are summarized as follows:

2002

a. Sold $1,345,400 of merchandise (that had cost $975,000) on credit, terms n/30.

b. Wrote off $18,300 of uncollectible accounts receivable.

c. Received $669,200 cash in payment of accounts receivable.

d. In adjusting the accounts on December 31, the company estimated that 1.5% of accounts receivable will be uncollectible.

Check (*d*) Bad Debts Expense, $28,168.5 Dr.

2003

e. Sold $1,525,600 of merchandise (that had cost $1,250,000) on credit, terms n/30.

f. Wrote off $27,800 of uncollectible accounts receivable.

g. Received $1,204,666 cash in payment of accounts receivable.

h. In adjusting the accounts on December 31, the company estimated that 1.5% of accounts receivable will be uncollectible.

Check (*h*) Bad Debts Expense, $32,197 Dr.

Required

Prepare journal entries to record Heche's 2002 and 2003 summarized transactions and its year-end adjustments to record bad debts expense. (The company uses the perpetual inventory system.)

On December 31, 2002, MidComm's records show the following results for the calendar-year:

Cash sales	$1,905,000
Credit sales	5,682,000

In addition, its unadjusted trial balance includes the following items:

Accounts receivable	$1,270,100 debit
Allowance for doubtful accounts	16,580 debit

Problem 7-3A 𝑎
Estimating and reporting bad debts

P1 P2

Required

1. Prepare the adjusting entry for MidComm to recognize bad debts under each of the following independent assumptions:

    a. Bad debts are estimated to be 2% of credit sales.

    b. Bad debts are estimated to be 1% of total sales.

    c. An aging analysis estimates that 5% of year-end accounts receivable are uncollectible.

2. Show how Accounts Receivable and the Allowance for Doubtful Accounts appear on the December 31, 2002, balance sheet given the facts in part 1*a*.

3. Show how Accounts Receivable and the Allowance for Doubtful Accounts appear on the December 31, 2002, balance sheet given the facts in part 1*c*.

Check Bad Debts Expense: (1*a*) $113,640, (1*c*) $80,085

Hawkins Company has credit sales of $3.6 million for year 2002. On December 31, 2002, the company's Allowance for Doubtful Accounts has an unadjusted credit balance of $14,500. Hawkins prepares a schedule of its December 31, 2002, accounts receivable by age. On the basis of past experience, it estimates the percent of receivables in each age category that will become uncollectible. This information is summarized here:

Problem 7-4A 𝑎
Aging accounts receivable and accounting for bad debts

P1 P2

December 31, 2002 Accounts Receivable	Age of Accounts Receivable	Expected Percent Uncollectible
$830,000	Not yet due	1.25%
254,000	1 to 30 days past due	2.00
86,000	31 to 60 days past due	6.50
38,000	61 to 90 days past due	32.75
12,000	Over 90 days past due	68.00

Required

1. Estimate the required balance of the Allowance for Doubtful Accounts at December 31, 2002, using the aging of accounts receivable method.

2. Prepare the adjusting entry to record bad debts expense at December 31, 2002.

Check (2) Bad Debts Expense, $27,150 Dr.

Analysis Component

3. On June 30, 2003, Hawkins Company concludes that a customer's $4,750 receivable (created in 2002) is uncollectible and that the account should be written off. What effect will this action have on Hawkins' 2003 net income? Explain.

Problem 7-5A
Analyzing and journalizing notes receivable transactions

C2 C3 P3 P4

Ⓖ

The following selected transactions are from Van Dyken Company:

2002

Dec. 16   Accepted a $10,800, 60-day, 8% note dated this day in granting Roy Williams a time extension on his past-due account receivable.

31   Made an adjusting entry to record the accrued interest on the Williams note.

31   Closed the Interest Revenue account to Income Summary.

2003

Check Feb. 14, Cr. Interest Revenue $108

Feb. 14   Received Williams's payment of principal and interest on the note dated December 16.

Mar. 2   Accepted a $6,120, 8%, 90-day note dated this day in granting a time extension on the past-due account receivable from DST Co.

17   Accepted a $2,400, 30-day, 7% note dated this day in granting Penny Kleen a time extension on her past-due account receivable.

Apr. 16   Kleen dishonored her note when presented for payment.

Check April 21, Dr. Interest Expense $60

21   Discounted, with recourse, the DST Co. note at BancFirst at a net interest cost of $60 (the net of interest from the note less the bank discount) receiving cash proceeds of $6,060.

June 2   Received notice from BancFirst that DST Co. had dishonored the note due May 31. Paid the bank the principal plus interest due on the note. (*Hint:* Create an account receivable for the maturity value of the note.)

July 17   Received payment from DST Co. for the maturity value of its dishonored note plus interest for 46 days beyond maturity at 8%.

Aug. 7   Accepted a $7,450, 90-day, 10% note dated this day in granting a time extension on the past-due account receivable of Mentzer and Oak.

Sept. 3   Accepted a $2,120, 60-day, 10% note dated this day in granting Keva White a time extension on her past-due account receivable.

Check Sept. 18, Dr. Interest Expense $30

18   Discounted, without recourse, the White note at BancFirst at a net interest cost of $30 (the net of interest from the note less the bank discount) receiving cash proceeds of $2,090.

Nov. 5   Received payment of principal plus interest from Mentzer and Oak for the note of August 7.

Dec. 1   Wrote off the Penny Kleen account against Allowance for Doubtful Accounts.

Required

1. Prepare journal entries to record these transactions and events.

Analysis Component

2. What reporting is necessary when a business discounts notes receivable with recourse and these notes have not reached maturity by the end of the period? Explain the reason for this requirement and the accounting principle being satisfied.

Problem 7-6A
Short-term investment (trading securities) transactions and entries

C4 P5

Elliott Company, which began operations in 2002, invests its idle cash in trading securities. The following transactions are from the company's short-term investments in its trading securities:

2002

Jan. 20   Purchased 800 shares of Ford Motor Co. at $26 per share plus a $125 commission.

Feb. 9   Purchased 2,200 shares of Lucent at $44.25 per share plus a $578 commission.

Oct. 12   Purchased 750 shares of Z-Seven at $7.55 per share plus a $200 commission.

2003

Apr. 15   Sold 800 shares of Ford Motor Co. at $29 per share less a $285 commission.
July 5   Sold 750 shares of Z-Seven at $10.25 per share less a $102.50 commission.
      22   Purchased 1,600 shares of Hunt Corp. at $30 per share plus a $444 commission.
Aug. 19   Purchased 1,800 shares of Donna Karan at $8.15 per share plus a $290 commission.

2004

Feb. 27   Purchased 3,400 shares of HCA at $34 per share plus a $420 commission.
Mar. 3   Sold 1,600 shares of Hunt at $25 per share less a $250 commission.
June 21   Sold 2,200 shares of Lucent at $42 per share less a $420 commission.
      30   Purchased 1,200 shares of Black & Decker at $47.50 per share plus a $595 commission.
Nov. 1   Sold 1,800 shares of Donna Karan at $18.25 per share less a $309 commission.

Required

1. Prepare journal entries to record these short-term investment activities for the years shown. (Ignore any year-end adjusting entries.)

2. On December 31, 2004, prepare the adjusting entry to record the market value of these investments: HCA's share price was $36 and Black & Decker's share price was $43.50. (The Market Adjustment—Trading Account had an unadjusted balance of zero.)

Check   (2) Dr. Market Adjustment—Trading $985

Boca Company had no short-term investments prior to year 2002. It had the following transactions involving short-term investments in available-for-sale securities during 2002:

Apr. 16   Purchased 4,000 shares of Gem Co. stock at $24.25 per share plus a $180 brokerage fee.
May   1   Paid $100,000 to buy 90-day U.S. Treasury bills (debt securities): $100,000 principal amount, 6% interest, securities dated May 1.
July 7   Purchased 2,000 shares of PepsiCo stock at $49.25 per share plus a $175 brokerage fee.
      20   Purchased 1,000 shares of Xerox stock at $16.75 per share plus a $205 brokerage fee.
Aug. 3   Received a check for principal and accrued interest on the U.S. Treasury bills that matured on July 29.
      15   Received an $0.85 per share cash dividend on the Gem Co. stock.
      28   Sold 2,000 shares of Gem Co. stock at $30 per share less a $225 brokerage fee.
Oct. 1   Received a $1.90 per share cash dividend on the PepsiCo shares.
Dec. 15   Received a $1.05 per share cash dividend on the remaining Gem Co. shares.
      31   Received a $1.30 per share cash dividend on the PepsiCo shares.
      31   Market values per share are Gem Co., $26.50; PepsiCo, $46.50; and Xerox, $13.75.

Problem 7-7A
Short-term investment (available-for-sale securities) transactions and entries

C4 P5
G Eₓ

Required

1. Prepare journal entries to record these preceding transactions and events.

2. Prepare a table to compare the cost and market values of Boca's short-term investments in available-for-sale securities (for example, see part 3 of the Demonstration Problem).

3. Prepare an adjusting entry, if necessary, to record the market adjustment for the portfolio of short-term investments in available-for-sale securities.

Check   (2) Cost = $164,220
(3) Dr. Unrealized Loss—Equity $4,470

Analysis Component

4. Explain the balance sheet presentation of a market adjustment for these short-term investments.

5. How do these short-term investments affect Boca's income statement for year 2002 and the equity section of its balance sheet at the end of year 2002?

King Co. allows select customers to make purchases on credit. Its other customers can use either of two credit cards: Commerce Bank or Via. Commerce Bank deducts a 3% service charge for sales on its credit card but immediately credits the checking account of King when credit card receipts are deposited. King deposits the Commerce Bank credit card receipts each business day. When customers use the Via card, King accumulates the receipts for several days and then submits them to Via for payment. Via deducts a 2% service charge and usually pays within one week of being billed. King completed the following transactions in August (terms of all credit sales are 2/10, n/30; and all sales are recorded at the gross price).

PROBLEM SET B

Problem 7-1B
Sales on credit and credit card sales

C1

Aug. 4   Sold $3,700 of merchandise (that had cost $2,000) on credit to Tess Wright.
      10   Sold merchandise for $5,200 (that had cost $2,800) to customers who used their Commerce Bank credit cards.
      11   Sold merchandise for $1,250 (that had cost $900) to customers who used their Via cards.
      14   Received Wright's check paying for the purchase of August 4.
      15   Sold merchandise for $3,240 (that had cost $1,800) to customers who used their Via cards.
      18   Submitted Via card receipts accumulated since August 11 to the credit card company for payment.
      22   Wrote off the account of Silver City against the Allowance for Doubtful Accounts. The $498 balance in Silver City's account stemmed from a credit sale in November of last year.
      25   Received the amount due from Via.

Check Aug. 25, Dr. Cash $4,400.2

Required

Prepare journal entries to record the preceding transactions and events. (The company uses the perpetual inventory system.)

Problem 7-2B
Accounts receivable transactions and bad debts adjustments

C1 P1 P2

Wergeles Co. began operations on January 1, 2002, and completed several transactions during 2002 and 2003 that involved sales on credit, accounts receivable collections, and bad debts. These transactions are summarized as follows:

2002

a. Sold $685,320 of merchandise (that had cost $500,000) on credit, terms n/30.
b. Received $482,300 cash in payment of accounts receivable.
c. Wrote off $9,350 of uncollectible accounts receivable.

Check (d) Bad Debts Expense, $11,286.7 Dr.

d. In adjusting the accounts on December 31, the company estimated that 1% of accounts receivable will be uncollectible.

2003

e. Sold $870,200 of merchandise (that had cost $650,000) on credit, terms n/30.
f. Received $990,800 cash in payment of accounts receivable.
g. Wrote off $11,090 of uncollectible accounts receivable.

Check (h) Bad Debts Expense, $9,773.10 Dr.

h. In adjusting the accounts on December 31, the company estimated that 1% of accounts receivable will be uncollectible.

Required

Prepare journal entries to record Wergeles' 2002 and 2003 summarized transactions and its year-end adjusting entry to record bad debts expense. (The company uses the perpetual inventory system.)

Problem 7-3B
Estimating and reporting bad debts

P1 P2

On December 31, 2002, Sherman Co.'s records show the following results for the year:

Cash sales	$1,025,000
Credit sales	1,342,000

In addition, its unadjusted trial balance includes the following items:

Accounts receivable	$575,000 debit
Allowance for doubtful accounts	7,500 credit

Required

1. Prepare the adjusting entry for Sherman Co. to recognize bad debts under each of the following independent assumptions:
   a. Bad debts are estimated to be 2.5% of credit sales.
   b. Bad debts are estimated to be 1.5% of total sales.
   c. An aging analysis estimates that 6% of year-end accounts receivable are uncollectible.

Check Bad debts expense: (1b) $35,505, (1c) $27,000

2. Show how Accounts Receivable and the Allowance for Doubtful Accounts appear on the December 31, 2002, balance sheet given the facts in part 1*a*.

3. Show how Accounts Receivable and the Allowance for Doubtful Accounts appear on the December 31, 2002, balance sheet given the facts in part 1*c*.

Quest Company has credit sales of $4.5 million for year 2002. On December 31, 2002, the company's Allowance for Doubtful Accounts has an unadjusted debit balance of $3,400. Quest prepares a schedule of its December 31, 2002, accounts receivable by age. On the basis of past experience, it estimates the percent of receivables in each age category that will become uncollectible. This information is summarized here:

Problem 7-4B
Aging accounts receivable and accounting for bad debts

P1 P2

December 31, 2002 Accounts Receivable	Age of Accounts Receivable	Expected Percent Uncollectible
$396,400	Not yet due	2.0%
277,800	1 to 30 days past due	4.0
48,000	31 to 60 days past due	8.5
6,600	61 to 90 days past due	39.0
2,800	Over 90 days past due	82.0

Required

1. Compute the required balance of the Allowance for Doubtful Accounts at December 31, 2002, using the aging of accounts receivable method.

2. Prepare the adjusting entry to record bad debts expense at December 31, 2002.

Analysis Component

3. On July 31, 2003, Quest concludes that a customer's $3,455 receivable (created in 2002) is uncollectible and that the account should be written off. What effect will this action have on Quest's 2003 net income? Explain.

Check (2) Bad Debts Expense, $31,390 Dr.

The following selected transactions are from Cruiser Company:

Problem 7-5B
Analyzing and journalizing notes receivable transactions

C2 C3 P3 P4

2002

Nov. 1   Accepted a $4,800, 90-day, 10% note dated this day in granting Terry Mullen a time extension on her past-due account receivable.

Dec. 31   Made an adjusting entry to record the accrued interest on the Mullen note.

31   Closed the Interest Revenue account to Income Summary.

2003

Jan. 30   Received Mullen's payment for principal and interest on the note dated November 1.

Feb. 28   Accepted a $12,600, 8%, 30-day note dated this day in granting a time extension on the past-due account receivable from Coffey Co.

Mar. 1   Accepted a $6,200, 60-day, 12% note dated this day in granting Staci Case a time extension on her past-due account receivable.

23   Discounted, without recourse, the Case note at Firstar Bank at a net interest cost of $60 (the net of interest from note less the bank discount) receiving cash proceeds of $6,140.

30   The Coffey Co. dishonored its note when presented for payment.

June 15   Accepted a $2,000, 60-day, 8% note dated this day in granting a time extension on the past-due account receivable of Sarah Morris.

21   Accepted a $9,500, 90-day, 14% note dated this day in granting Vinnie May a time extension on his past-due account receivable.

Check Jan. 30, Cr. Interest Revenue $40

Check March 23, Dr. Interest Expense $60

July   5   Discounted, with recourse, the V. May note at Firstar Bank at a net interest cost of $200 (the net of interest from note less the bank discount) receiving cash proceeds of $9,300.

Aug. 14   Received payment of principal plus interest from Morris for the note of June 15.

Sept. 25   Received notice from Firstar Bank that the V. May note had been paid.

Nov. 30   Wrote off Coffey Co.'s account against Allowance for Doubtful Accounts.

Required

1. Prepare journal entries to record these transactions and events.

Analysis Component

2. What reporting is necessary when a business discounts notes receivable with recourse and these notes have not reached maturity by the end of the period? Explain the reason for this requirement and the accounting principle being satisfied.

Problem 7-6B

Short-term investment (trading securities) transactions and entries

C4 P5

Dryfus Co., which began operations in 2002, invests its idle cash in trading securities. The following transactions relate to the company's short-term investments in its trading securities.

2002

Mar. 10   Purchased 2,400 shares of AOL at $59.15 per share plus a $1,545 commission.

May   7   Purchased 5,000 shares of Motorola at $36.25 per share plus a $2,855 commission.

Sept. 1   Purchased 1,200 shares of UPS at $57.25 per share plus a $1,250 commission.

2003

Apr. 26   Sold 5,000 shares of Motorola at $34.50 per share less a $2,050 commission.

27   Sold 1,200 shares of UPS at $60.50 per share less a $1,788 commission.

June 2   Purchased 3,600 shares of SPW at $172 per share plus a $3,250 commission.

14   Purchased 900 shares of Wal-Mart at $50.25 per share plus a $1,082 commission.

2004

Jan. 28   Purchased 2,000 shares of PepsiCo at $43 per share plus a $2,890 commission.

31   Sold 3,600 shares of SPW at $168 per share less a $2,040 commission.

Aug. 22   Sold 2,400 shares of AOL at $56.75 per share less a $2,480 commission.

Sept. 3   Purchased 1,500 shares of Vodaphone at $40.50 per share plus a $1,680 commission.

Oct.   9   Sold 900 shares of Wal-Mart at $53.75 per share less a $1,220 commission.

Required

1. Prepare journal entries to record these short-term investment activities for the years shown. (Ignore any year-end adjusting entries.)

2. On December 31, 2004, prepare the adjusting entry to record the market value of these investments: PepsiCo's share price was $41 and Vodaphone's share price was $37. (The Market Adjustment—Trading account had an unadjusted balance of zero.)

Problem 7-7B

Short-term investment (available-for-sale securities) transactions and entries

C4 P5

Corbin Systems had no short-term investments on December 31, 2001. It had the following transactions involving short-term investments in available-for-sale securities during 2002.

Feb. 6   Purchased 3,400 shares of Nokia stock at $41.25 per share plus a $3,000 brokerage fee.

15   Paid $20,000 to buy six-month U.S. Treasury bills (debt securities): $20,000 principal amount, 6% interest, securities dated February 15.

Apr. 7   Purchased 1,200 shares of Dell Co. stock at $39.50 per share plus a $1,255 brokerage fee.

June 2   Purchased 2,500 shares of Merck stock at $72.50 per share plus a $3,890 brokerage fee.

30   Received a $0.19 per share cash dividend on the Nokia shares.

Aug. 11   Sold 850 shares of Nokia stock at $46 per share less a $1,050 brokerage fee.

16   Received a check for principal and accrued interest on the U.S. Treasury bills purchased February 15.

24   Received a $0.10 per share cash dividend on the Dell shares.

Nov. 9   Received a $0.20 per share cash dividend on the remaining Nokia shares.

Dec. 18   Received a $0.15 per share cash dividend on the Dell shares.

31   Market values per share are Nokia, $40.25; Dell, $40.50; and Merck, $59.

Required

1. Prepare journal entries to record these preceding transactions and events.

2. Prepare a table to compare the cost and market values of the short-term investments in available-for-sale securities (for example, see part 3 of the Demonstration Problem).

Check (2) Cost = $341,232.50

3. Prepare an adjusting entry, if necessary, to record the market adjustment for the portfolio of short-term investments in available-for-sale securities.

Check (3) Dr. Unrealized Loss—Equity, $42,495

Analysis Component

4. Explain the balance sheet presentation of a market adjustment to these short-term investments.

5. How do these short-term investments affect its income statement for year 2002 and the equity section of its balance sheet at the end of year 2002?

BEYOND THE NUMBERS

BTN 7-1   Refer to Nike's financial statements in Appendix A to answer the following:

1. What is the amount of accounts receivable (net) on May 31, 2000?

2. Nike's most liquid assets include "cash and equivalents" and "accounts receivable." Compute its most liquid assets as of May 31, 2000, as a percent of current liabilities. Do the same for May 31, 1999. Comment on the company's ability to satisfy current liabilities at the end of the fiscal year 2000 as compared to the end of fiscal year 1999.

3. What criteria did Nike use to classify items as cash equivalents?

4. Compute Nike's accounts receivable turnover as of May 31, 2000.

Reporting in Action

A1 𝑑

NIKE

Swoosh Ahead

5. Access Nike's financial statements for fiscal years ending after May 31, 2000, at its Web site (www.nike.com) or the SEC's EDGAR database (www.sec.gov). Recompute parts 2 and 4 and comment on any changes since May 31, 2000.

BTN 7-2   Key comparative figures ($ in millions) for both Nike and Reebok follow:

Comparative Analysis

A1 P2 𝑑

NIKE

Reebok

Key Figures	Nike			Reebok		
	Current Year	One-Year Prior	Two-Years Prior	Current Year	One-Year Prior	Two-Years Prior
Allowance for doubtful accounts	$ 65.4	$ 73.2	$ 71.4	$ 46.2	$ 47.4	$ 44.0
Accounts receivable, net ..	1,567.2	1,540.1	1,674.4	417.4	517.8	561.7
Net sales	8,995.1	8,776.9	9,553.1	2,891.2	3,205.4	3,643.6

Required

1. Compute the accounts receivable turnover for both Nike and Reebok for each of the two most recent years using the data shown.

2. Using results from part 1, compute how many days it takes each company, *on average,* to collect receivables.

3. Which company is more efficient in collecting its accounts receivable?

4. Which company estimates a higher percent of uncollectible accounts receivable?

BTN 7-3   Susie Norton is the manager of a medium-size company. A few years ago, Susie persuaded the owner to base a part of her compensation on the net income the company earns each year. Each December Susie estimates year-end financial figures in anticipation of the bonus she will receive. If the bonus is not as high as she would like, she offers several recommendations to the accountant for year-end adjustments. One of her favorite recommendations is for the controller to reduce the estimate of doubtful accounts.

Ethics Challenge

P1 P2 𝑑

Required

1. What effect does lowering the estimate for doubtful accounts have on the income statement and balance sheet?
2. Do you think Susie's recommendation to adjust the allowance for doubtful accounts is within her right as manager, or do you think this action is an ethics violation? Justify your response.
3. What type of internal control(s) might be useful for this company in overseeing the manager's recommendations for accounting changes?

Communicating in Practice

P1 P2 🖉

BTN 7-4   As the accountant for Bel-Air Distributing, you attend a sales managers' meeting devoted to a discussion of credit policies. At the meeting, you report that bad debts expense is estimated to be $59,000 and accounts receivable at year-end amount to $1,750,000 less a $43,000 allowance for doubtful accounts. Stan Waters, a sales manager, expresses confusion over why bad debts expense and the allowance for doubtful accounts are different amounts. Write a one-page memorandum to him explaining why a difference in bad debts expense and the allowance for doubtful accounts is not unusual. The company estimates bad debts expense as 2% of sales.

Taking It to the Net

C4 P5

BTN 7-5   Access the September 28, 1999, 10-K filing (for year-end June 30, 1999) of **Microsoft** (MSFT) at www.edgaronline.com. Identify Microsoft's "Equity and Other Investments" footnote.

Required

1. As of June 30, 1999, did Microsoft's debt securities that were recorded at market show a net unrealized gain or net unrealized loss? What was the amount of this net gain or loss?
2. As of June 30, 1999, did Microsoft's equity securities that were recorded at market show a net unrealized gain or net unrealized loss? What was the amount of this net gain or loss?
3. Identify two common stocks that Microsoft had in its investment portfolio as of June 30, 1999.

Teamwork in Action

P2

BTN 7-6   Each member of a team is to participate in estimating uncollectibles using the aging schedule and percents shown in Problem 7-4A. The division of labor is up to the team. Your goal is to accurately complete this task as soon as possible. After estimating uncollectibles, check your estimate with the instructor. If the team's estimate is correct, the team then should prepare the adjusting entry and the presentation of accounts receivable (net) for the December 31, 2002, balance sheet.

Business Week Activity

C1 P1

BTN 7-7   Read the article "For CFS, Bad Debts Are Sweet Profits" in the August 11, 1997, issue of *Business Week*. (The book's Web site provides a free link.)

Required

1. How does CFS make money by collecting bad debts for others?
2. What was CFS's net margin in 1996? Why was the margin so large?
3. Who are CFS's main competitors?
4. To what does CFS's CEO attribute the company's success?

Entrepreneurial Decision

C1

🅔 🖉

BTN 7-8   Kimberly Mills operates Musician Memorabilia, a merchandising business that buys and sells souvenirs and mementos linked with contemporary musicians. Mills accepts only cash from buyers. Her monthly cash sales are $25,000, with a net profit margin of 30%. However, buyers are increasingly requesting either to use credit cards with their purchases or to buy on credit. Therefore, Mills has decided to pursue one of two plans (neither plan will impact cash sales nor alter current costs as a percent of sales):

Plan A. *Mills accepts credit cards.* This plan is expected to yield new credit sales equal to 20% of current cash sales. Cost estimates of this plan as a percent of net credit sales are: credit card fee, 4.8%; recordkeeping, 1.2%.

Plan B. *Mills grants credit directly to qualified buyers.* This plan is expected to yield new credit sales equal to 24% of current cash sales. Cost estimates of this plan as a percent of net credit sales are: uncollectibles, 6.7%; collection expenses, 1.3%; recordkeeping, 2.0%.

Required

1. Compute the added monthly net income (loss) expected under (*a*) Plan A and (*b*) Plan B.

2. Should Mills pursue either plan? Discuss the financial and nonfinancial factors relevant to this decision.

BTN 7-9   Many commercials include comments similar to the following: "Bring your **VISA**" or "We do not accept **American Express**." Conduct your own research via interviews, phone calls, or the Internet to determine the reason(s) why companies discriminate in their use of credit cards.

Hitting the Road
C1 *a*

8

Reporting and Analyzing Long-Term Assets

A Look Back

Chapters 6 and 7 focused on short-term assets: cash, cash equivalents, receivables, and short-term investments. We explained why they are known as liquid assets and described how companies account and report for them.

A Look at This Chapter

This chapter introduces us to long-term assets, including plant assets, natural resource assets, and intangible assets. We explain how to record a long-term asset's cost, the allocation of an asset's cost to periods benefiting from the asset, the recording of additional asset costs after an asset is purchased, and the disposal of an asset.

A Look Ahead

Chapter 9 focuses on current liabilities. We explain how they are computed, recorded, and reported in financial statements. We also explain the accounting for payroll.

"We have greatly exceeded our sales projections"—Sheila McCann

Learning Objectives

Conceptual

C1 Describe plant assets and issues in accounting for them.

C2 Explain depreciation and the factors affecting its computation.

C3 Explain depreciation for partial years and changes in estimates.

C4 Identify cash flow impacts of long-term asset transactions.

Analytical

A1 Compare and analyze alternative depreciation methods.

A2 Compute total asset turnover and apply it to analyze a company's use of assets.

Procedural

P1 Apply the cost principle to compute the cost of plant assets.

P2 Compute and record depreciation using the straight-line, units-of-production, and declining-balance methods.

P3 Distinguish between revenue and capital expenditures, and account for these expenditures.

P4 Account for asset disposal through discarding, selling, and exchanging an asset.

P5 Account for natural resource assets and their depletion.

P6 Account for intangible assets.

Decision Feature

Making Dough

e SAN LUIS OBISPO, CA—Before Sheila McCann donned a baker's apron she didn't know much about baking bread. "I asked myself, What need in the community could I fill?" recalls McCann. "Then, I thought, we have no good bread." After experimenting with some bread recipes, she apprenticed without pay at local bakeries. McCann observed that "once people switch to the healthful whole grain breads, they are unable to return to the flavorless alternatives."

After nearly a year of research, McCann launched **House of Bread (www.HouseofBread.com)**. She made mistakes, but she did not let them stop her. One of the greatest challenges, says McCann, was gauging the type, size, and amount of plant assets required to launch and maintain the bakery. She estimates that plant asset costs for a single bakery can exceed $200,000—producing annual sales of about $400,000. McCann says that maintaining a strong sales-to-assets ratio is crucial to her success. This includes asset costs ranging from expensive ovens and baking equipment to building and land costs. To be successful, her sales must not only cover these plant asset costs but also yield a return adequate to pay other expenses and meet the owners' earnings expectations. This chapter focuses on these and other crucial issues related to long-term assets.

McCann says that her goal is "to provide customers with the most delicious and healthful bread products." Her annual sales are now projected to exceed $5 million. There aren't many bakeries with dough that rises like that! [Sources: House of Bread Web site, January 2002; *Entrepreneur,* November 2000; SBTV.com, 2000; *Modern Baking,* February 2000.]

Chapter Preview

This chapter focuses on long-term assets used in the operation of a company. These assets can be grouped into plant assets, natural resource assets, and intangible assets. Plant assets are a major investment for most companies. They make up a large part of assets on most balance sheets, and they yield depreciation, often one of the largest expenses on income statements. They also affect the statement of cash flows when cash is paid to acquire plant assets or is received from their sale. The acquisition or building of a plant asset is often referred to as a *capital expenditure.* Capital expenditures are important events because they impact both the short- and long-term success of a company. Natural resource assets and intangible assets have similar impacts. This chapter describes the purchase and use of these assets. We also explain what distinguishes these assets from other types of assets, how to determine their cost, how to allocate their costs to periods benefiting from their use, and how to dispose of them.

Section 1— Plant Assets

Plant assets are tangible assets used in a company's operations that have a useful life of more than one accounting period. Plant assets are also called *plant and equipment; property, plant, and equipment;* or *fixed assets.* For many companies, plant assets make up the single largest class of assets they own. Exhibit 8.1 shows plant assets as a percent of total assets for several companies. Not only do they make up a large percent of these companies' assets, but their dollar values are large. **McDonald's** plant assets, for instance, are reported at more than $16 billion, and **Wal-Mart** reports plant assets of more than $32 billion.

Exhibit 8.1

Plant Assets of Selected Companies

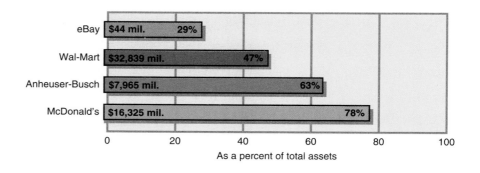

As a percent of total assets

C1 Describe plant assets and issues in accounting for them.

Point: Amazon.com's plant assets of $318 million make up 13% of its total assets, and Priceline.com's plant assets of $28 million make up 6% of its total assets.

Point: It often helps to view plant assets as prepaid expenses that benefit several future accounting periods.

Plant assets are set apart from other assets by two important features. First, *plant assets are used in operations.* This makes them different from, for instance, inventory that is held for sale and not used in operations. The distinctive feature here is use, not type of asset. A company that purchases a computer for purposes of reselling it reports it on the balance sheet as inventory. If the same company purchases this computer to use in operations, however, it is a plant asset. Another example is a long-term investment such as land held for future expansion. If this land holds a factory used in operations, the land is part of plant assets. Another example is equipment held for use in the event of a breakdown or for peak periods of production. This equipment is reported in plant assets. If this same equipment is removed from use and held for sale, however, it is not reported in plant assets.

The second important feature is that *plant assets have useful lives extending over more than one accounting period.* This makes plant assets different from current assets such as supplies that are usually consumed in a short time period after they are placed in use.

The accounting for plant assets reflects these two features. Since plant assets are used in operations, we try to match their costs against the revenues they generate. Also, since their useful lives extend over more than one period, our matching of costs and revenues must extend over several periods. Specifically, we value plant assets (balance sheet effect) and then allocate their costs to periods benefiting from their use (income statement effect).

Exhibit 8.2 shows four main issues in accounting for plant assets: (1) computing the costs of plant assets, (2) allocating the costs of plant assets (less any salvage amounts) against

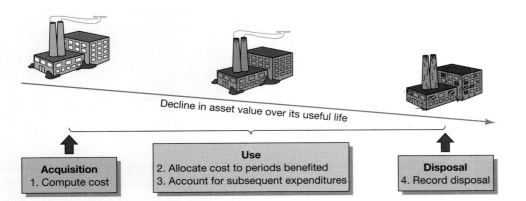

Exhibit 8.2

Issues in Accounting for Plant Assets

Decline in asset value over its useful life

Acquisition	**Use**	**Disposal**
1. Compute cost	2. Allocate cost to periods benefited 3. Account for subsequent expenditures	4. Record disposal

revenues for the periods they benefit, (3) accounting for expenditures such as repairs and improvements to plant assets, and (4) recording the disposal of plant assets. The following sections discuss the decisions and factors surrounding each of these four important issues.

Topic Tackler 8-1

Plant assets are recorded at cost when purchased. This is consistent with the *cost principle.* **Cost** includes all normal and reasonable expenditures necessary to get the asset in place and ready for its intended use. The cost of a factory machine, for instance, includes its invoice cost less any cash discount for early payment, plus any necessary freight, unpacking, and assembling costs. A plant asset's cost also includes any necessary costs to install and test it before placing it in use. Examples are the costs of building a base or foundation for a machine, providing electrical hook-ups, and adjusting the asset before using it in operations.

To be charged to and reported as part of the cost of a plant asset, an expenditure must be normal, reasonable, and necessary in preparing it for its intended use. If an asset is damaged during unpacking, the repairs are not added to its cost. Instead, they are charged to an expense account. Nor is a paid traffic fine for moving heavy machinery on city streets without a proper permit part of the machinery's cost; but payment for a proper permit is included in the cost of machinery. Charges in addition to the purchase price are sometimes incurred to modify or customize a new plant asset. These charges are added to the asset's cost. We explain in this section how to determine the cost of plant assets for each of four major classes of plant assets.

Cost of Plant Assets

Global: Many countries—including Switzerland, Brazil, the Netherlands, and the United Kingdom—permit asset revaluations under certain conditions. This is a deviation from the cost principle.

Land

When land is purchased for a building site, its cost includes the total amount paid for the land, including any real estate commissions. Its cost also includes fees for insuring the title, legal fees, and any accrued property taxes paid by the purchaser. Payments for surveying, clearing, grading, draining, and landscaping also are included in the cost of land. Other costs include local government assessments, whether incurred at the time of purchase or later, for items such as public roadways, sewers, and sidewalks. These assessments are included because they permanently add to the land's value. Land purchased as a building site sometimes includes structures that must be removed. In such cases, the total purchase price is charged to the Land account along with the cost of removing the structures, less any amounts recovered through sale of salvaged materials. To illustrate, assume **Gap** paid $167,000 cash to acquire land for a retail store. This land contains an old service garage that is removed at a net cost of $13,000 ($15,000 in costs less $2,000 proceeds from salvaged materials). Additional closing costs total $10,000, consisting of brokerage fees ($8,000), legal fees ($1,500), and title costs ($500). The cost of this land to Gap is $190,000 and is computed as shown in Exhibit 8.3.

P1 Apply the cost principle to compute the cost of plant assets.

Exhibit 8.3

Computing Cost of Land

Cash price of land	$167,000
Net cost of garage removal	13,000
Closing costs	10,000
Cost of land	**$190,000**

Land Improvements

Land is not depreciated because it has an unlimited life and is not usually used up over time. **Land improvements** such as parking lot surfaces, driveways, fences, and lighting systems, however, have limited useful lives and are used up. While the costs of these improvements increase the usefulness of the land, they are charged to a separate Land Improvement account so that their costs can be allocated to the periods they benefit.

Buildings

A Building account is charged for the costs of purchasing or constructing a building that is used in operations. When purchased, a building's costs usually include its purchase price, brokerage fees, taxes, title fees, and attorney costs. Its costs also include all expenditures to make it ready for its intended use, including any necessary repairs or renovations such as wiring, lighting, flooring, and wall coverings. When a company constructs a building or any plant asset for its own use, its costs include materials and labor plus a reasonable amount of indirect overhead cost. Overhead includes the costs of items such as heat, lighting, power, and depreciation on machinery used to construct the asset. Costs of construction also include design fees, building permits, and insurance during construction. However, costs such as insurance to cover the asset *after* it is placed in use are operating expenses.

Machinery and Equipment

The costs of machinery and equipment consist of all costs normal and necessary to purchase them and prepare them for their intended use. These include the purchase price, taxes, transportation charges, insurance while in transit, and installing, assembling, and testing machinery and equipment. **Sony**, for instance, disclosed in a recent annual report that "capital expenditures during the year under review increased . . . Sony intends to further increase its capital expenditures [for machinery and equipment]."

Example: If appraised values in Exhibit 8.4 are land, $24,000; land improvements, $12,000; and building, $84,000, what cost is assigned to the building? *Answer*:
(1) $24,000 + $12,000 + $84,000 = $120,000 (total appraisal)
(2) $84,000/$120,000 = 70% (building's percent of total)
(3) 70% × $90,000 = $63,000 (building's apportioned cost)

Lump-Sum Purchase

Plant assets sometimes are purchased as a group in a single transaction for a lump-sum price. This transaction is called a *lump-sum purchase,* or *group, bulk,* or *basket purchase.* When this occurs, we allocate the cost of the purchase among the different types of assets acquired based on their *relative market values.* Their market values can be estimated by appraisal or by using the tax-assessed valuations of the assets. Let's say that Cola Company paid $90,000 cash to acquire a group of items consisting of land appraised at $30,000, land improvements appraised at $10,000, and a building appraised at $60,000. The $90,000 cost is allocated on the basis of these appraised values as shown in Exhibit 8.4.

Exhibit 8.4

Computing Costs in a Lump-Sum Purchase

	Appraised Value	Percent of Total	Apportioned Cost
Land	$ 30,000	30% ($30,000/$100,000)	**$27,000** ($90,000 × 30%)
Land improvements. . . .	10,000	10 ($10,000/$100,000)	**9,000** ($90,000 × 10%)
Building	60,000	60 ($60,000/$100,000)	**54,000** ($90,000 × 60%)
Totals.	$100,000	100%	$90,000

Answers—p. 359

Depreciation

We explained at the beginning of the chapter that plant assets are tangible assets purchased for use in operations for more than one period. It is helpful to think of a plant asset as an amount of "usefulness" contributing to a company's operations throughout the asset's life. **Depreciation** is the process of allocating the cost of a plant asset to expense in the accounting periods benefiting from its use. For instance, when a company buys a delivery truck as a plant asset, it acquires an amount of usefulness (a quantity of transportation). The total cost of this transportation is the cost of the truck less the proceeds expected to be received when the truck is sold or traded in at the end of its useful life. This net cost is allocated to the periods that benefit from the truck's use. This allocation of cost is called depreciation. Depreciation does not measure the decline in the truck's market value each period, nor does it measure the truck's physical deterioration. Depreciation is a process of allocating a plant asset's cost to expense over its useful life, nothing more. Since depreciation reflects the cost of using a plant asset, we do not begin recording depreciation charges until the asset is actually put into service. This section describes the factors we must consider in computing depreciation, the depreciation methods used, revisions in depreciation, and depreciation for partial periods.

Topic Tackler 8-2

Global: International accounting standards encourage use of the cost principle for plant assets. Plant asset revaluation is permitted provided it is consistently applied across periods.

Factors in Computing Depreciation

Factors relevant in determining depreciation are: (1) cost, (2) salvage value, and (3) useful life.

C2 Explain depreciation and the factors affecting its computation.

Cost

The cost of a plant asset consists of all necessary and reasonable expenditures to acquire it and to prepare it for its intended use. We described the computation of cost earlier in this chapter.

Salvage Value

The total amount of depreciation to be charged off over an asset's benefit period equals the asset's cost minus its salvage value. **Salvage value,** also called *residual value* or *scrap value,* is an estimate of the asset's value at the end of its benefit period. This is the amount we expect to receive from disposing of the asset at the end of its benefit period. If we expect an asset to be traded in on a new asset, its salvage value is the expected trade-in value.

Point: If we expect additional costs in preparing a plant asset for disposal, the salvage value equals the expected amount from disposing of the asset less these disposal costs.

Useful Life

The **useful life** of a plant asset is the length of time it is productively used in a company's operations. Useful life, also called *service life,* might not be as long as the asset's total productive life. For example, the productive life of a computer can be eight years or more. Some companies, however, trade in old computers for new ones every two years. In this case, these computers have a two-year useful life, meaning the cost of these computers (less their expected trade-in values) is charged to depreciation expense over a two-year period.

Point: Useful life and salvage value are estimates. Estimates require judgment based on consideration of all available information.

Global: While accounting in the U.S. must consider inadequacy and obsolescence in estimating useful life, the accounting in many other countries does not.

Several variables often make the useful life of a plant asset difficult to predict. A major variable is the wear and tear from use in operations. Two other variables, inadequacy and obsolescence, also demand consideration. **Inadequacy** refers to the capacity of a company's plant assets that is unable to meet the company's growing productive demands. **Obsolescence** refers to a plant asset that is no longer useful in producing goods or services with a competitive advantage because of new inventions and improvements. Both inadequacy and obsolescence are difficult to predict because the timing of demand changes, new inventions, and improvements is unknown. A company usually disposes of an inadequate or obsolete asset before it wears out.

A company is often able to better predict a new asset's useful life when it has past experience with a similar asset. When it has no such experience, a company relies on the experience of others or on engineering studies and judgment. In note 4 of its annual report, **Coca-Cola Bottling** reports the following useful lives:

Estimated useful lives of property, plant and equipment were:	
Buildings	10–50 years
Machinery and equipment	5–20 years
Transportation equipment	4–10 years
Furniture and fixtures	7–10 years
Vending equipment	6–13 years

Decision Track 8.1   *d*

Decision Point	Information Search	Analyze & Evaluate
What is the estimated useful life of depreciable assets? Is the estimate reasonable?	Financial statement notes (**plant asset useful life** equals the plant asset cost divided by depreciation expense) and competitor data.	Income can be overstated (and depreciation understated) with a useful life that is too high; a useful life that is too low yields opposite results.

Depreciation Methods

Many *depreciation methods* are used to allocate a plant asset's cost over the accounting periods in its useful life. The most frequently used method of depreciation is the straight-line method. Another common depreciation method is the units-of-production method. We explain both of these methods in this section. This section also describes accelerated depreciation methods, with a focus on the declining-balance method.

Exhibit 8.5

Data for Athletic Shoe-Inspecting Machine

Cost	$10,000
Salvage value	1,000
Depreciable cost	$ 9,000
Useful life	
Accounting periods	5 years
Units inspected	36,000 shoes

The computations in this section use information from an athletic shoe manufacturer. In particular, we look at a machine used for inspecting athletic shoes before packaging. Manufacturers such as **Converse, Reebok, Adidas,** and **Fila** use this machine. Data for its depreciation are in Exhibit 8.5.

P2   Compute and record depreciation using the straight-line, units-of-production, and declining-balance methods.

Straight-Line Method

Straight-line depreciation charges the same amount of expense to each period of the asset's useful life. A two-step process is used. We first compute the *depreciable cost* of the asset; this amount is also called the *cost to be depreciated*. It is computed by subtracting the asset's salvage value from its total cost. Second, depreciable cost is divided by the number of accounting periods in the asset's useful life. The formula for straight-line depreciation, along with its computation for the inspection machine described above, is shown in Exhibit 8.6.

$$\frac{\text{Cost} - \text{Salvage value}}{\text{Useful life in periods}} = \frac{\$10,000 - \$1,000}{5 \text{ years}} = \$1,800 \text{ per year}$$

Exhibit 8.6

Straight-Line Depreciation Formula and Example

If this machine is purchased on December 31, 2000, and used throughout its predicted useful life of five years, the straight-line method allocates an equal amount of depreciation to each of the years 2001 through 2005. We make the following adjusting entry at the end of each of the five years to record straight-line depreciation of this machine:

Dec. 31	Depreciation Expense	1,800	
	Accumulated Depreciation—Machinery . . .		1,800
	To record annual depreciation.		

Assets $=$ Liabilities $+$ Equity
$-1,800$ $\qquad\qquad$ $-1,800$

The $1,800 Depreciation Expense is reported on the income statement among operating expenses. The $1,800 Accumulated Depreciation is a contra asset account to the Machinery account in the balance sheet. The graph on the left in Exhibit 8.7 shows the $1,800 per year expenses reported in each of the five years. The graph on the right shows the amounts reported on each of the six December 31 balance sheets while the company owns the asset.

Example: If salvage value of the machine is estimated to be $2,500, what is the annual depreciation expense? *Answer:*
($10,000 − $2,500)/5 years
= $1,500

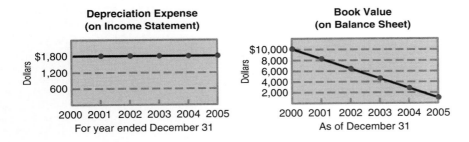

Exhibit 8.7

Financial Statement Effects of Straight-Line Depreciation

The net balance sheet amount is the asset's **book value** and is computed as the asset's total cost less its accumulated depreciation. For example, at the end of year 2 (December 31, 2002), its book value is $6,400 and is reported in the balance sheet as follows:

| Machinery . . . . | $10,000 | |
| Less accumulated depreciation . . . . . | 3,600 | $6,400 |

The book value of this machine declines by $1,800 each year due to depreciation. From the graphs in Exhibit 8.7 we can see why this method is called straight line.

We also can compute the *straight-line depreciation rate,* defined as 100% divided by the number of periods in the asset's useful life. For the inspection machine, this rate is 20% (100% ÷ 5 years). We use this rate, along with other information, to compute the machine's *straight-line depreciation schedule* shown in Exhibit 8.8. Note three points in Exhibit 8.8. First, depreciation expense is the same each period. Second, accumulated depreciation is the sum of current and prior periods' depreciation expense. Third, book value declines each period until it equals salvage value at the end of the machine's useful life.

Point: Depreciation requires estimates for salvage value and useful life. Decision ethics are relevant when managers might be tempted to choose estimates to achieve desired results on financial statements.

Units-of-Production Method

The straight-line method charges an equal share of an asset's cost to each period. If plant assets are used up in about equal amounts each accounting period, this method produces a reasonable matching of expenses with revenues. However, the use of some plant assets varies

Exhibit 8.8

Straight-Line Depreciation Schedule

| Annual Period | Depreciation for the Period | | | End of Period | |
	Depreciable Cost*	Depreciation Rate	Depreciation Expense	Accumulated Depreciation	Book Value†
2000	—	—	—	—	$10,000
2001	$9,000	20%	$1,800	$1,800	8,200
2002	9,000	20	1,800	3,600	6,400
2003	9,000	20	1,800	5,400	4,600
2004	9,000	20	1,800	7,200	2,800
2005	9,000	20	1,800	9,000	1,000

* $10,000 − $1,000.   † Book value is cost minus accumulated depreciation.

greatly from one period to the next. A builder, for instance, might use a piece of construction equipment for a month and then not use it again for several months. When equipment use varies from period to period, the units-of-production depreciation method can better match expenses with revenues. **Units-of-production depreciation** charges a varying amount to expense for each period of an asset's useful life depending on its usage.

A two-step process is used to compute units-of-production depreciation. We first compute *depreciation per unit* by subtracting the asset's salvage value from its total cost and then dividing by the total number of units expected to be produced during its useful life. Units of production can be expressed in product or other units such as hours used or miles driven. The second step is to compute depreciation expense for the period by multiplying the units produced in the period by the depreciation per unit. The formula for units-of-production depreciation, along with its computation for the machine described in Exhibit 8.5, is shown in Exhibit 8.9. (*Note:* 7,000 shoes are inspected and sold in its first year.)

Exhibit 8.9

Units-of-Production Depreciation Formula and Example

Step 1

$$\text{Depreciation per unit} = \frac{\text{Cost} - \text{Salvage value}}{\text{Total units of production}} = \frac{\$10,000 - \$1,000}{36,000 \text{ shoes}} = \$0.25 \text{ per shoe}$$

Step 2

$$\text{Depreciation expense} = \text{Depreciation per unit} \times \text{Units produced in period}$$

$$\$0.25 \text{ per shoe} \times 7,000 \text{ shoes} = \$1,750$$

Using data on the number of shoes inspected by the machine, we can compute the *units-of-production depreciation schedule* shown in Exhibit 8.10. For example, depreciation for the first year is $1,750 (7,000 shoes at $0.25 per shoe). Depreciation for the second year is $2,000 (8,000 shoes at $0.25 per shoe). Other years are similarly computed. Notice in Exhibit 8.10 that (1) depreciation expense depends on unit output, (2) accumulated depreciation is the sum of current and prior periods' depreciation expense, and (3) book value declines each period until it equals salvage value at the end of the asset's useful life. Boise Cascade is one of many companies using the units-of-production depreciation method. It reports that "substantially all of the Company's paper and wood products manufacturing facilities determine depreciation by the units-of-production method."

Example: Refer to Exhibit 8.10. If the number of shoes inspected in 2005 is 5,500, what is depreciation expense for that year? *Answer:* $1,250 (we never depreciate below salvage value)

Declining-Balance Method

An **accelerated depreciation method** yields larger depreciation expenses in the early years of an asset's life and smaller charges in later years. Of several accelerated methods, the most common is the **declining-balance method** of depreciation, which uses a depreciation rate that is a multiple of the straight-line rate and applies it to the asset's beginning-of-period

Global: German accounting permits accelerated depreciation of up to three times the straight-line rate.

| Annual Period | Depreciation for the Period | | | End of Period | |
	Number of Units	Depreciation per Unit	Depreciation Expense	Accumulated Depreciation	Book Value
2000	—	—	—	—	$10,000
2001	7,000	$0.25	$1,750	$1,750	8,250
2002	8,000	0.25	2,000	3,750	6,250
2003	9,000	0.25	2,250	6,000	4,000
2004	7,000	0.25	1,750	7,750	2,250
2005	5,000	0.25	1,250	9,000	1,000

Exhibit 8.10

Units-of-Production Depreciation Schedule

book value. The amount of depreciation declines each period because book value declines each period.

A common depreciation rate for the declining-balance method is double the straight-line rate. This is called the *double-declining-balance* (*DDB*) method. This method is applied in three steps: (1) compute the asset's straight-line depreciation rate, (2) double the straight-line rate, and (3) compute depreciation expense by multiplying this rate by the asset's beginning-of-period book value. To illustrate, let's return to the machine in Exhibit 8.5 and apply the double-declining-balance method to compute depreciation expense. Exhibit 8.11 shows the first-year depreciation computation for the machine. The three-step process is to (1) divide 100% by five years to determine the straight-line rate of 20% per year, (2) double this 20% rate to get the declining-balance rate of 40% per year, and (3) compute depreciation expense as 40% multiplied by the beginning-of-period book value.

Point: In the DDB method, *double* refers to the rate and *declining balance* refers to book value. The rate is applied to beginning book value each period.

Exhibit 8.11

Double-Declining-Balance Depreciation Formula

Step 1

Straight-line rate = 100% ÷ Useful life = 100% ÷ 5 years = 20%

Step 2

Double-declining-balance rate = 2 × Straight-line rate = 2 × 20% = 40%

Step 3

Depreciation expense = Double-declining-balance rate × Beginning-period book value

40% × $10,000 = $4,000 (for 2001)

The *double-declining-balance depreciation schedule* is shown in Exhibit 8.12. The schedule follows the formula except for year 2005, when depreciation expense is $296. This $296 is not equal to 40% × $1,296, or $518.40. If we had used the $518.40 for depreciation expense in 2005, ending book value would equal $777.60, which is less than the $1,000 salvage value. Instead, the $296 is computed by subtracting the $1,000 salvage value from the $1,296 book value at the beginning of the fifth year (the year when DDB depreciation cuts into salvage value).

Point: Graph and describe the asset's book value over its useful life using the DDB method for further insights.

Example: What is DDB depreciation expense in year 2004 if the salvage value is $2,000? *Answer:* $2,160 − $2,000 = $160

| Annual Period | Depreciation for the Period | | | End of Period | |
	Beginning of Period Book Value	Depreciation Rate	Depreciation Expense	Accumulated Depreciation	Book Value
2000	—	—	—	—	$10,000
2001	$10,000	40%	$4,000	$4,000	6,000
2002	6,000	40	2,400	6,400	3,600
2003	3,600	40	1,440	7,840	2,160
2004	2,160	40	864	8,704	1,296
2005	1,296	40	296*	9,000	**1,000**

Exhibit 8.12

Double-Declining-Balance Depreciation Schedule

* Year 2005 depreciation is $1,296 − $1,000 = $296 (never depreciate book value below salvage value).

Comparing Depreciation Methods

A1 Compare and analyze alternative depreciation methods.

Exhibit 8.13 shows depreciation expense for each year of the machine's useful life under each of the three depreciation methods.

Exhibit 8.13

Depreciation Expense for the Different Methods

Period	Straight-Line	Units-of-Production	Double-Declining-Balance
2001	$1,800	$1,750	$4,000
2002	1,800	2,000	2,400
2003	1,800	2,250	1,440
2004	1,800	1,750	864
2005	1,800	1,250	296
Totals	$9,000	$9,000	$9,000

While the amount of depreciation expense per period differs for different methods, total depreciation expense is the same over the machine's useful life. Each method starts with a total cost of $10,000 and ends with a salvage value of $1,000. The difference is the pattern in depreciation expense over the useful life. The book value of the asset when using straight-line is always greater than the book value from using double-declining-balance, except at the beginning and end of the asset's useful life, when it is the same. Also, the straight-line method yields a steady pattern of depreciation expense while the units-of-production depreciation depends on the number of units produced. Each of these methods is acceptable because it allocates cost in a systematic and rational manner.

Decision Insight

Trends Approximately 80% of companies use straight-line depreciation for their plant assets, 7% use units-of-production, and 4% use declining-balance. Another 9% use an unspecified accelerated method—most of these probably are declining-balance.

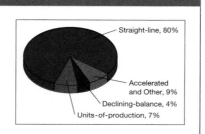

Straight-line, 80%
Accelerated and Other, 9%
Declining-balance, 4%
Units-of-production, 7%

Decision Track 8.2   *d*

Decision Point	Information Search	Analyze & Evaluate
What depreciation method should a company adopt?	Business operations, cost trends, asset benefits, and financial statements.	Depends on goals; depreciation is higher and income lower in the short run when using accelerated methods versus straight-line. Income measurement is served by methods that best match depreciation of the asset against its revenues.

Global: Some Canadian companies are permitted to use an "increasing charge" depreciation (the opposite of accelerated depreciation).

Point: Differences between financial accounting and tax accounting records are normal and expected.

Point: Understanding depreciation for financial accounting will help in learning MACRS for tax accounting. Rules for MACRS are available from www.IRS.com.

Depreciation for Tax Reporting

The records a company keeps for financial accounting purposes are usually separate from the records it keeps for tax accounting purposes. This is so because financial accounting aims to report useful information on financial performance and position, whereas tax accounting reflects government objectives in raising revenues. Differences between these two accounting systems are normal and expected. Depreciation is a common example of how the records differ. For example, many companies use accelerated depreciation in computing taxable income. Reporting higher depreciation expense in the early years of an asset's life reduces the company's taxable income in those years and increases it in later years, when the depreciation expense is lower. The company's goal here is to *postpone* its tax pay-

This means the company can use these resources now to earn additional income before payment is due.

The U.S. federal income tax law has rules for depreciating assets. These rules include the **Modified Accelerated Cost Recovery System (MACRS).** MACRS allows straight-line depreciation for some assets, but it requires accelerated depreciation for most kinds of assets. MACRS separates depreciable assets into different classes and defines the depreciable life and rate for each class. MACRS is not acceptable for financial reporting because it often allocates costs over an arbitrary period that is less than the asset's useful life. Details of MACRS are covered in tax accounting courses.

Global: Some countries require the depreciation method chosen for financial reporting to match the method chosen for tax reporting.

Decision Insight

Depreciation Technology   Computer technology greatly simplifies depreciation computations and revisions. Many inexpensive, off-the-shelf software packages and business calculators allow a user to choose from a variety of depreciation methods for each asset entered.

Partial-Year Depreciation

Plant assets are purchased and disposed of at various times. When an asset is purchased (or disposed of) at a time other than the beginning or end of an accounting period, depreciation is recorded for part of a year. This is done so that the year of purchase or the year of disposal is charged with its share of the asset's depreciation.

C3   Explain depreciation for partial years and changes in estimates.

To illustrate, let's return to the machine described in Exhibit 8.5. Assume that this machine is purchased and placed in service on October 8, 2000, and the annual accounting period ends on December 31. This machine costs $10,000, has a useful life of five years, and a salvage value of $1,000. Since this machine is purchased and used for nearly three months in 2000, the calendar-year income statement should report depreciation expense on the machine for that part of the year. Normally, the amount of depreciation is based on the assumption that the asset is purchased on the first day of the month nearest the actual date of purchase. In this case, since the purchase occurred on October 8, we assume an October 1 purchase date. This means that three months' depreciation is recorded in 2000. Using straight-line depreciation, we compute three months' depreciation of $450 as follows:

Example: If the machine's salvage value is zero and purchase occurs on Oct. 8, 2000, how much depreciation is recorded at Dec. 31, 2000?
Answer: $10,000/5 × 3/12 = $500

$$\frac{\$10,000 - \$1,000}{5 \text{ years}} \times \frac{3}{12} = \$450$$

A similar computation is necessary when an asset disposal occurs during a period. For example, let's suppose the machine is sold on June 24, 2005. Depreciation is recorded for the period January 1 through June 24 when it is disposed of. This partial year's depreciation, computed to the nearest whole month, is

$$\frac{\$10,000 - \$1,000}{5 \text{ years}} \times \frac{6}{12} = \$900$$

Revising Depreciation

Depreciation is based on estimates of salvage value and useful life. During the useful life of an asset, new information may indicate that these estimates are inaccurate. If our estimate of an asset's useful life and/or salvage value changes, what should we do? The answer is to use the new estimate to compute depreciation for current and future periods. This means that we revise depreciation expense computation by spreading the cost yet to be depreciated over the useful life remaining. This approach is used for all depreciation methods.

Point: Remaining depreciable cost equals book value less revised salvage value at the point of revision.

Let's return to our machine described in Exhibit 8.8 using straight-line depreciation. At the beginning of this asset's third year, its book value is $6,400, computed as $10,000 minus $3,600. Assume that at the beginning of its third year, the estimated number of years remaining in its useful life changes from three to four years *and* its estimate of salvage value changes from $1,000 to $400. Straight-line depreciation for each of the four remaining years is computed as shown in Exhibit 8.14.

Exhibit 8.14

Computing Revised
Straight-Line Depreciation

$$\frac{\text{Book value} - \text{Revised salvage value}}{\text{Revised remaining useful life}} = \frac{\$6,400 - \$400}{4 \text{ years}} = \$1,500 \text{ per year}$$

Example: If at the beginning of its second year the machine's remaining useful life changes from four to three years and salvage value from $1,000 to $400, how much straight-line depreciation is recorded in remaining years? *Answer:* Revised depreciation = ($8,200 − $400)/3 = $2,600.

Thus, $1,500 of depreciation expense is recorded for the machine at the end of the third through sixth years of its remaining useful life. Since this asset was depreciated at $1,800 per year for the first two years, it is tempting to conclude that depreciation expense was overstated in the first two years. However, these expenses reflected the best information available at that time. We do not go back and restate prior years' financial statements for this type of new information. Instead, we adjust the current and future periods' statements to reflect this new information. Revising an estimate of the useful life or salvage value of a plant asset is referred to as a **change in an accounting estimate** and is reflected in current and future financial statements, not in prior statements.

Reporting Depreciation

Both the cost and accumulated depreciation of plant assets are reported on the balance sheet or in its notes. **Arctic Cat**, for instance, reports the following in its balance sheet:

Property and equipment ($ thousands):	
Machinery, equipment, and tooling	$71,936
Land, buildings, and improvements	16,861
	$88,797
Less accumulated depreciation	(52,411)
Total	$36,386

Many companies also show plant assets on one line with the net amount of cost less accumulated depreciation. When this is done, the amount of accumulated depreciation is disclosed in a note. **Nike** reports only the net amount of its property, plant, and equipment in its balance sheet in Appendix A. To satisfy the *full-disclosure principle,* Nike describes its depreciation methods in its Note 1 and the amounts comprising plant assets in its Note 3.

Point: A company usually keeps records for each asset showing its cost and depreciation to date. The combined records for individual assets are a type of *subsidiary plant asset ledger.*

Reporting both the cost and accumulated depreciation of plant assets helps users compare the assets of different companies. For example, a company holding assets costing $50,000 and accumulated depreciation of $40,000 is likely in a situation different from a company with new assets costing $10,000. While the net undepreciated cost of $10,000 is the same in both cases, the first company may have more productive capacity available but likely is facing the need to replace older assets. These insights are not provided if the two balance sheets report only the $10,000 book values.

Plant assets are reported on a balance sheet at their undepreciated costs (book value), not at market values. This emphasis on costs rather than market values is based on the *going-concern principle* described in Chapter 2. This principle states that, unless there is evidence to the contrary, we assume that a company continues in business. This implies that plant assets are held and used long enough to recover their cost through the sale of products and services. Since plant assets are not for sale, their market values are not reported. Instead, plant assets are reported at cost less accumulated depreciation.

Accumulated depreciation is a contra asset account with a normal credit balance. It does not reflect funds accumulated to buy new assets when the assets currently owned are re-

Decision Ethics   *d*

Controller   You are the controller for a struggling company. Its operations require regular investments in equipment, and depreciation is its largest expense. Its competitors frequently replace equipment—typically depreciated over three years. The company president instructs you to revise useful lives of equipment from three to six years and to use a six-year life on all new equipment. What actions do you take?

Answer—p. 358

placed. If a company has funds available to buy assets, the funds are shown on the balance sheet among liquid assets such as Cash or Investments.

Quick Check

4. On January 1, 2002, a company pays $77,000 to purchase office furniture with a zero salvage value. The furniture's useful life is somewhere between 7 and 10 years. What is the year 2002 straight-line depreciation on the furniture using (a) a 7-year useful life and (b) a 10-year useful life?

5. What does the term *depreciation* mean in accounting?

6. A company purchases a machine for $96,000 on January 1, 2003. Its useful life is five years or 100,000 units of product, and its salvage value is $8,000. During 2003, 10,000 units of product are produced. Compute the book value of this machine on December 31, 2003, assuming (a) straight-line depreciation and (b) units-of-production depreciation.

7. In early January 2002, a company acquires equipment for $3,800. The company estimates this equipment to have a useful life of three years and a salvage value of $200. Early in 2004, the company changes its estimates to a total four-year useful life and zero salvage value. Using straight-line, what is depreciation for the year ended 2004?

Revenue and Capital Expenditures

After a company acquires a plant asset and puts it into service, it often faces additional expenditures for that asset's operation, maintenance, repair, and improvement. In recording these expenditures, we must decide whether to capitalize or expense them. To capitalize an expenditure is to debit the asset account. The issue is whether more useful information is provided by reporting these expenditures as current period expenses or by adding them to the plant asset's cost and depreciating them over its remaining useful life.

Revenue expenditures, also called *income statement expenditures,* are additional costs of plant assets that do not materially increase the asset's life or productive capabilities. They are recorded as expenses and deducted from revenues in the current period's income statement. Examples of revenue expenditures are cleaning, repainting, adjustments, and lubricants. **Capital expenditures,** also called *balance sheet expenditures,* are additional costs of plant assets that provide benefits extending beyond the current period. They are debited to asset accounts and reported on the balance sheet. Capital expenditures increase or improve the type or amount of service an asset provides. Examples are roofing replacement, plant expansion, and major overhauls of machinery and equipment.

Financial statements are affected for several years by the accounting choice of recording costs as either revenue expenditures or capital expenditures. Managers must be careful in classifying them. This classification decision is helped by identifying these expenditures as either ordinary repairs or as betterments and extraordinary repairs.

P3 Distinguish between revenue and capital expenditures, and account for these expenditures.

Point: When an amount is said to be *capitalized* to an account, the amount is added to the account's normal balance.

Ordinary Repairs

Ordinary repairs are expenditures to keep an asset in normal, good operating condition. They are necessary if an asset is to perform to expectations over its useful life. Ordinary repairs do not extend an asset's useful life beyond its original estimate or increase its productivity beyond original expectations. Examples are normal costs of cleaning, lubricating, adjusting, and replacing small parts of a machine. Ordinary repairs are treated as *revenue expenditures.* This means their costs are reported as expenses on the current period income statement. Following this rule, **America West Airlines** reports "routine maintenance and repairs are charged to expense as incurred."

Point: If a manager's compensation is tied to net income, evidence suggests that this can influence a manager's classification of expenditures.

	Financial Statement Effect		
Treatment	**Accounting**	**Expense**	**Current Income**
Revenue expenditure	Income stmt. account debited	Currently recognized	Lower
Capital expenditure	Balance sheet account debited	Deferred to future	Higher

Few companies keep records for assets costing less than some minimum amount such as $500. Instead, these *low-cost plant assets* are treated as revenue expenditures. This means their costs are charged to an expense account at the time of purchase. This practice is acceptable under the *materiality principle.* Treating immaterial capital expenditures as revenue expenditures is unlikely to mislead users of financial statements. As an example, **Coca-Cola Bottling** capitalizes only major, or material, asset replacements: "minor replacements are charged to expense when incurred."

Betterments and Extraordinary Repairs

Point: Expenditures for both extraordinary repairs and betterments require revision of depreciation schedules.

Betterments, also called *improvements,* are expenditures that make a plant asset more efficient or productive. A betterment often involves adding a component to an asset or replacing one of its old components with a better one. A betterment does not always increase an asset's useful life. An example is replacing manual controls on a machine with automatic controls to reduce labor costs. This machine will still wear out as fast as it would with manual controls. One special type of betterment is an *addition.* Examples are a new wing to a factory or a new dock to a warehouse. Since a betterment benefits future periods, it is debited to the asset account as a capital expenditure. The new book value (less salvage value) is then depreciated over the asset's remaining useful life. To illustrate, suppose a company pays $8,000 for a machine with an eight-year useful life and no salvage value. After three years and $3,000 of depreciation, it adds an automated system to the machine at a cost of $1,800. This results in reduced labor costs when operating the machine in future periods. The cost of this betterment is added to the Machinery account with this entry:

Example: Assume a company owns a Web server. Identify each item as a revenue or capital expenditure: (1) purchase price, (2) necessary wiring, (3) platform for operation, (4) circuits to increase capacity, (5) cleaning after each three months of use, (6) repair of a faulty connection, and (7) replaced a worn cooling fan. *Answer:* Capital expenditures: 1, 2, 3, 4; Revenue expenditures: 5, 6, 7.

Assets = Liabilities + Equity
+1,800
−1,800

Jan. 2	Machinery	1,800	
	Cash		1,800
	To record installation of automated system.		

After the betterment, the remaining cost to be depreciated is $6,800, computed as $8,000 − $3,000 + $1,800. Depreciation expense for the remaining five years is $1,360 per year, computed as $6,800/5 years.

Extraordinary repairs are expenditures extending the asset's useful life beyond its original estimate. Costs of extraordinary repairs are *capital expenditures* because they benefit future periods. As with betterments, they can be debited to the asset account. For example, **America West Airlines** reports: "the cost of major scheduled airframe, engine and certain component overhauls are capitalized (and expensed) . . . over the periods benefited."

Decision Maker *e*

Entrepreneur Your start-up Internet services company needs cash, and you are preparing financial statements to apply for a short-term loan. A friend suggests that you treat as many expenses as possible as capital expenditures. What are the impacts on financial statements of this suggestion? What do you think is the aim of this suggestion?

Answer—p. 358

Decision Track 8.3 *d*

Decision Point	Information Search	Analyze & Evaluate
What is the age of plant assets? Is replacement imminent?	Income statement and balance sheet (**plant asset age** is estimated by dividing accumulated depreciation by depreciation expense).	Aged plant assets can signal necessary asset replacements; it may also imply use of less efficient assets versus competitors.

Plant assets are disposed of for several reasons. Some assets are eventually discarded because they wear out or become obsolete. Other assets are sold because of changing business plans. Regardless of the reason, disposals of plant assets occur in one of three basic ways: discarding, sale, or exchange. The general steps in accounting for a disposal of plant assets is described in Exhibit 8.15.

Disposals of Plant Assets

1. Record depreciation up to the date of disposal—this also updates Accumulated Depreciation.
2. Remove account balances of the disposed asset—including its Accumulated Depreciation.
3. Record any cash (and/or other assets) received or paid in the disposal.
4. Record any gain or loss—computed by comparing the disposed asset's book value with the market value of any assets received.*

Exhibit 8.15
Accounting for Disposals of Plant Assets

* One exception to step 4 is the case of a gain on a similar asset exchange—it is described later in this section.

Discarding Plant Assets

A plant asset is *discarded* when it is no longer useful to the company and it has no market value. To illustrate, assume that a machine costing $9,000 with accumulated depreciation of $9,000 is discarded. When accumulated depreciation equals the asset's cost, it is said to be *fully depreciated* (zero book value). The entry to record the discarding of this asset is

P4 Account for asset disposal through discarding, selling, and exchanging an asset.

June 5	Accumulated Depreciation—Machinery	9,000	
	Machinery		9,000
	To discard fully depreciated machinery.		

Assets = Liabilities + Equity
+9,000
−9,000

This entry reflects all four steps of Exhibit 8.15. Step 1 is unnecessary since the machine is fully depreciated. Step 2 is reflected in the debit to Accumulated Depreciation and credit to Machinery. Since no other asset is involved, step 3 is irrelevant. Finally, since book value is zero and no other asset is involved, no gain or loss is recorded in step 4.

How do we account for discarding an asset that is not fully depreciated? Or one whose depreciation is not up-to-date? To answer this, consider equipment costing $8,000 with accumulated depreciation of $6,000 on December 31 of the prior fiscal year-end. This equipment is being depreciated using the straight-line method over eight years with zero salvage. On July 1 of the current year it is discarded. Step 1 is to bring depreciation up-to-date:

Point: Recording depreciation expense up-to-date gives an up-to-date book value for determining gain or loss.

July 1	Depreciation Expense	500	
	Accumulated Depreciation—Equipment		500
	To record 6 months' depreciation ($1,000 × 6/12).		

Assets = Liabilities + Equity
−500   −500

Steps 2 through 4 of Exhibit 8.15 are reflected in the second (and final) entry:

July 1	Accumulated Depreciation—Equipment	6,500	
	Loss on Disposal of Equipment	1,500	
	Equipment		8,000
	To discard equipment with a $1,500 book value.		

Assets = Liabilities + Equity
+6,500   −1,500
−8,000

The loss is computed by comparing the equipment's $1,500 book value ($8,000 − $6,000 − $500) with the zero net cash proceeds. This loss is reported in the Other Expenses and Losses section of the income statement. Discarding an asset can sometimes require a cash payment that would increase the loss. The income statement reports any gain or loss from discarding an asset, and the balance sheet reflects the changes in the asset and accumulated depreciation accounts.

Point: Gain or loss is determined by comparing "value given" (book value) to "value received."

Selling Plant Assets

Companies often sell plant assets when they restructure or downsize operations. To illustrate the accounting for selling plant assets, we consider BTO's March 31 sale of equipment that cost $16,000 and has accumulated depreciation of $12,000 at December 31 of the prior calendar year-end. Annual depreciation on this equipment is $4,000 computed using straight-line depreciation. Step 1 of this sale is to record depreciation expense and update accumulated depreciation to March 31 of the current year:

Assets = Liabilities + Equity
−1,000   −1,000

March 31	Depreciation Expense	1,000	
	Accumulated Depreciation—Equipment		1,000
	To record 3 months' depreciation ($4,000 × 3/12).		

Steps 2 through 4 of Exhibit 8.15 can be reflected in one final entry that depends on the amount received from the asset's sale. We consider three different possibilities.

Sale at Book Value

If BTO receives $3,000, an amount equal to the equipment's book value as of March 31, no gain or loss occurs on disposal. The accounting in this case is

Assets = Liabilities + Equity
+3,000
+13,000
−16,000

March 31	Cash	3,000	
	Accumulated Depreciation—Equipment	13,000	
	Equipment		16,000
	To record sale of equipment for no gain or loss.		

Sale above Book Value

If BTO receives $7,000, an amount that is $4,000 above the equipment's book value as of March 31, a gain on disposal occurs. The entry is

Assets = Liabilities + Equity
+7,000   +4,000
+13,000
−16,000

March 31	Cash	7,000	
	Accumulated Depreciation—Equipment	13,000	
	Gain on Disposal of Equipment		4,000
	Equipment		16,000
	To record sale of equipment for a $4,000 gain.		

Sale below Book Value

If BTO receives $2,500, an amount that is $500 below the equipment's book value as of March 31, a loss on disposal occurs. The entry is

Assets = Liabilities + Equity
+2,500   −500
+13,000
−16,000

March 31	Cash	2,500	
	Loss on Disposal of Equipment	500	
	Accumulated Depreciation—Equipment	13,000	
	Equipment		16,000
	To record sale of equipment for a $500 loss.		

Exchanging Plant Assets

Many plant assets such as machinery, automobiles, and office equipment are disposed of by exchanging them for newer assets. In a typical exchange of plant assets, a trade-in allowance is received on the old asset and the balance is paid in cash. Accounting for the exchange of assets is similar to any other disposal unless the old and the new assets are similar in the functions they perform. Trading an old truck for a new truck is an exchange of similar assets, whereas trading a truck for a machine is an exchange of dissimilar assets. This section describes the accounting for the exchange of similar assets. Similar asset exchanges are common, whereas dissimilar asset exchanges are not (the latter are discussed in advanced courses).

Accounting for exchanges of similar assets depends on whether the book value of the asset given up is less or more than the market value of the asset received. When the market value of the asset received is less than the book value of the asset given up, the difference is recognized as a loss. However, when the value of the asset received is more than the asset's book value given up, the gain is *not* recognized.

Receiving Less in Exchange: A Loss

Let's assume that a company exchanges both old equipment and $33,000 in cash for new equipment. The old equipment originally cost $36,000 and has accumulated depreciation of $20,000 at the time of exchange. The new equipment has a market value of $42,000. These details are reflected in the middle ("Loss") columns of Exhibit 8.16.

Point: Trade-in allowance minus book value equals gain (loss if negative) on exchange.

Similar Plant Asset Exchange	Loss		Gain	
Market value of assets received		$42,000		$52,000
Book value of assets given up:				
Equipment ($36,000 − $20,000)	$16,000		$16,000	
Cash	33,000	49,000	33,000	49,000
Gain (loss) on exchange		$ (7,000)		$ 3,000

Exhibit 8.16

Computing Gain or Loss on *Similar* Asset Exchange

The entry to record this similar asset exchange is

Jan. 3	Equipment (**new**)	42,000	
	Loss on Exchange of Assets	7,000	
	Accumulated Depreciation—Equipment (**old**) . . .	20,000	
	Equipment (**old**)		36,000
	Cash		33,000
	To record exchange of old equipment and cash for new equipment.		

Assets = Liabilities + Equity
+42,000   −7,000
+20,000
−36,000
−33,000

The book value of the assets given up is $49,000. This includes the $33,000 cash and the $16,000 ($36,000 − $20,000) book value of the old equipment. The $49,000 book value of assets given up is compared to the market value of the new equipment received ($42,000). This yields a loss of $7,000 ($42,000 − $49,000).

Point: Parenthetical journal entry notes to "new" and "old" equipment are for illustration only. Both the debit and credit are to the same Equipment account in the general ledger.

Receiving More in Exchange: A Gain

Let's assume the same facts as in the preceding similar asset exchange *except* that the new equipment received has a market value of $52,000 instead of $42,000. The entry to record this similar asset exchange is

Jan. 3	Equipment (**new**)	49,000	
	Accumulated Depreciation—Equipment (**old**) . . .	20,000	
	Equipment (**old**)		36,000
	Cash		33,000
	To record exchange of old equipment and cash for new equipment.		

Assets = Liabilities + Equity
+49,000
+20,000
−36,000
−33,000

We show how to compute the gain from this exchange in the far right ("Gain") columns of Exhibit 8.16. This gain is *not* recognized in the entry because of a rule prohibiting recognizing a gain on similar asset exchanges.[1] The $49,000 recorded for the new equipment

Point: No gain is recognized for similar asset exchanges.

---

[1] The reason a gain from a similar asset exchange is not recognized is that the earnings process is not considered complete for the exchanged asset. The decision to recognize a loss from a similar asset exchange is an application of *accounting conservatism* in measuring and recording asset values.

Exhibit 8.17

Cost Basis of New Asset
when Gain Not Recognized

Cost of old equipment	$36,000
Less accumulated depreciation . . .	20,000
Book value of old equipment	$16,000
Cash paid in the exchange	33,000
Cost recorded for new	
equipment	**$49,000**

equals its cash price ($52,000) less the un-recognized gain ($3,000) on the exchange. The $49,000 cost recorded is called the *cost basis* of the new machine. This cost basis is the amount we use to compute depreciation and its book value. The cost basis of the new asset also can be computed by summing the book values of the assets given up as shown in Exhibit 8.17.

Example: Assume this old equipment is sold for $19,000 and, in a separate transaction, new equipment is purchased for $52,000. Record both transactions. *Answer:*

Cash 19,000
Accum. Depr—Eq. . 20,000
   Equipment (old) 36,000
   Gain on Sale of Eq.   3,000
Equipment (new) . . . 52,000
   Cash 52,000

Quick Check

8. Early in the fifth year of a machine's six-year useful life, it is overhauled, and its useful life is extended to nine years. This machine originally cost $108,000 and the overhaul cost is $12,000. Prepare the entry to record the overhaul cost.

9. Explain the difference between revenue expenditures and capital expenditures and how both are recorded.

10. What is a betterment? How is a betterment recorded?

11. A company acquires equipment on January 10, 2002, at a cost of $42,000. Straight-line depreciation is used with a five-year life and $7,000 salvage value. On June 27, 2003, the company sells this equipment for $32,000. Prepare the entry(ies) for June 27, 2003.

12. A company trades an old Web server for a new one. The cost of the old server is $30,000, and its accumulated depreciation at the time of the trade is $23,400. The new server has a cash price of $45,000. Prepare entries to record the trade under two different assumptions: the company receives a trade-in allowance of (a) $3,000 and (b) $7,000.

Answers—p. 359

Section 2— Natural Resources

Natural resources are assets that are physically consumed when used. Examples are standing timber, mineral deposits, and oil and gas fields. Since they are consumed when used, they are often called *wasting assets*. These assets represent soon-to-be inventories of raw materials that will be converted into one or more products by cutting, mining, or pumping. Until that conversion takes place, they are noncurrent assets and are shown in a balance sheet using titles such as timberlands, mineral deposits, or oil reserves. Natural resources are reported under either plant assets or its own separate category. **Alcoa**, for instance, reports its natural resources under the balance sheet title *Properties, plants and equipment.* In a note to its financial statements, Alcoa reports a separate amount for *Land and land rights, including mines.* **Weyerhaeuser**, on the other hand, reports its timber holdings in a separate balance sheet category titled *Timber and timberlands.*

Acquisition Cost and Depletion

P5 Account for natural resource assets and their depletion.

Natural resources are recorded at cost, which includes all expenditures necessary to acquire the resource and prepare it for its intended use. **Depletion** is the process of allocating the cost of a natural resource to the period when it is consumed, known as the resource's *useful life.* Natural resources are reported on the balance sheet at cost less *accumulated depletion.* The depletion expense per period is usually based on units extracted from cutting, mining, or pumping. This is similar to units-of-production depreciation. **Exxon Mobil** uses this approach to amortize the costs of discovering and operating its oil wells.

To illustrate depletion of natural resources, let's consider a mineral deposit with an estimated 250,000 tons of available ore. It is purchased for $500,000, and we expect zero salvage value. The depletion charge per ton of ore mined is $2, computed as $500,000 ÷ 250,000 tons. If 85,000 tons are mined and sold in the first year, the depletion charge for that year is $170,000. These computations are detailed in Exhibit 8.18.

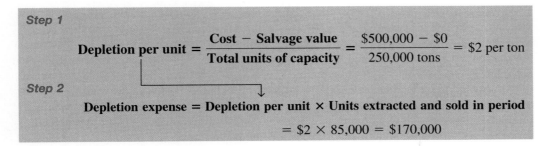

Exhibit 8.18

Depletion Formula and
Example

Depletion expense for the period is recorded as follows:

Dec. 31	Depletion Expense—Mineral Deposit	170,000	
	Accumulated Depletion—Mineral Deposit . .		170,000
	To record depletion of the mineral deposit.		

Assets	= Liabilities +	Equity
−170,000		−170,000

The period-end balance sheet reports the mineral deposit as shown in Exhibit 8.19.

Mineral deposit	$500,000	
Less accumulated depletion	170,000	$330,000

Exhibit 8.19

Balance Sheet Presentation of
Natural Resources

Since all 85,000 tons of the mined ore are sold during the year, the entire $170,000 of depletion is reported on the income statement. If some of the ore remains unsold at year-end, however, the depletion related to the unsold ore is carried forward on the balance sheet and reported as Ore Inventory, a current asset.

Plant Assets Used in Extracting Resources

The conversion of natural resources by mining, cutting, or pumping usually requires machinery, equipment, and buildings. When the usefulness of these plant assets is directly related to the depletion of a natural resource, their costs are depreciated over the useful life of the natural resource in proportion to its depletion. This means that depreciation is computed using the units-of-production method. For example, if a machine is permanently installed in a mine and 10% of the ore is mined and sold in the period, then 10% of the machine's cost (less any salvage value) is allocated to depreciation expense. The same procedure is used when a machine is abandoned once resources are extracted. If, however, a machine will be moved to and used at another site when extraction is complete, the machine is depreciated over its useful life.

Intangible assets are certain nonphysical assets (used in operations) that confer on their owners long-term rights, privileges, or competitive advantages. Examples are patents, copyrights, licenses, leaseholds, franchises, goodwill, and trademarks. Lack of physical substance does not necessarily make an asset intangible. Notes and accounts receivable, for instance, lack physical substance, but they are not intangibles. This section identifies the more common types of intangible assets and explains the accounting for them.

Accounting for Intangible Assets

An intangible asset is recorded at cost when purchased. Its cost is systematically allocated to expense over its estimated useful life through the process of **amortization.** If an intangible asset has an *indefinite useful life*—meaning that no legal, regulatory, contractual, competitive, economic, or other factors limit its useful life—it should not be amortized. (If an intangible with an indefinite useful life is later judged to have a limited useful life, it is

Section 3—
Intangible Assets

P6 Account for intangible assets.

Point: Goodwill is not amortized; instead, it is annually tested for impairment.

amortized over that limited useful life.) Amortization of intangible assets is similar to depreciation of plant assets and the depletion of natural resources in that it is a process of cost allocation. However, only the straight-line method is used for amortizing intangibles *unless* the company can show that another method is preferred. The effects of amortization are recorded in a contra account (Accumulated Amortization). This means that the gross acquisition cost of intangible assets is disclosed in the balance sheet along with their accumulated amortization (these disclosures are new per *SFAS 142*). The eventual disposal of an intangible asset involves removing its book value, recording any other asset(s) received or given up, and recognizing any gain or loss for the difference.

Many intangibles have limited useful lives due to laws, contracts, or other asset characteristics. Examples are patents, copyrights, and leaseholds. Other intangibles such as goodwill, trademarks, and trade names have useful lives that cannot be easily determined. The cost of intangible assets is amortized over the periods expected to benefit by their use, but in no case can this period be longer than the asset's legal existence. The values of some intangible assets such as goodwill continue indefinitely into the future and are not amortized. (An intangible asset that is not amortized is tested annually for *impairment*—if necessary, an impairment loss is recorded. Details for this test are in advanced courses.)

Intangible assets are often shown in a separate section of the balance sheet immediately after plant assets. **Callaway Golf**, for instance, follows this approach in reporting more than $100 million of intangible assets in its recent balance sheet. Companies usually disclose the amortization periods they apply to intangibles. **Corning**'s annual report, for instance, says the company amortizes intangible assets over a maximum of 15 years except for goodwill. The remainder of our discussion focuses on accounting for specific types of intangible assets.

Patents

The federal government grants patents to encourage the invention of new technology, mechanical devices, and production processes. A **patent** is an exclusive right granted to its owner to manufacture and sell a patented item, or to use a process, for 17 years. When patent rights are purchased, the cost to acquire the rights is debited to an account called *Patents*. If the owner engages in lawsuits to successfully defend a patent, the cost of lawsuits is debited to the Patents account. However, the costs of research and development leading to a new patent are expensed when incurred.

A patent gives its owner exclusive rights to it for 17 years, but its cost is amortized over its estimated useful life (not to exceed 17 years). If we purchase a patent costing $25,000 with a useful life of 10 years, we make the following adjusting entry at the end of each of the 10 years to amortize one-tenth of its cost:

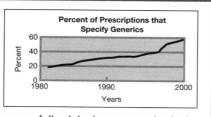

Assets = Liabilities + Equity
−2,500   −2,500

Dec. 31	Amortization Expense—Patents	2,500	
	Accumulated Amortization—Patents		2,500
	To amortize patent costs over its useful life.		

The $2,500 debit to Amortization Expense appears on the income statement as a cost of the product or service provided under protection of the patent. The Accumulated Amortization—Patents account is a contra asset account to Patents.

Copyrights

A **copyright** gives its owner the exclusive right to publish and sell a musical, literary, or artistic work during the life of the creator plus 50 years, although the useful life of most copyrights is much shorter. The costs of a copyright are amortized over its useful life. The only identifiable cost of many copyrights is the fee paid to the Copyright Office of the federal government or international agency granting the copyright. If this fee is immaterial, it is charged directly to an expense account, but if the identifiable costs of a copyright are material, they are capitalized (recorded in an asset account) and periodically amortized by debiting an account called *Amortization Expense—Copyrights.*

Decision Insight

Son of Napster   Music fans call it the next Napster: a Web-based tuner that can search some 10,000 Internet radio stations and allow listeners to record selected tunes on their hard drives. Start-up **Audio Mill**, which already has more than 100,000 users, expects to avoid Napster's copyright woes. The recording industry has yet to weigh in, but it has been filing lawsuits in similar cases. Stay tuned.

Leaseholds

Property is rented under a contract called a **lease.** The property's owner, called the **lessor,** grants the lease. The one who secures the right to possess and use the property is called the **lessee.** A **leasehold** refers to the rights the lessor grants to the lessee under the terms of the lease. A leasehold is an intangible asset for the lessee.

Certain leases require no advance payment from the lessee but require monthly rent payments. In this case, we do not set up a Leasehold account. Instead, the monthly payments are debited to a Rent Expense account. If a long-term lease requires the lessee to pay the final period's rent in advance when the lease is signed, the lessee records this advance payment with a debit to the Leasehold account. Since the advance payment is not used until the final period, the Leasehold account balance remains intact until that time. Then its balance is transferred to Rent Expense. (Some long-term leases give the lessee essentially the same rights as a purchaser. This results in tangible assets and liabilities reported by the lessee. Chapter 9 describes these so-called *capital leases.*)

Point: A leasehold account implies existence of future benefits that the lessee controls because of a prepayment. It also meets the definition of an asset.

Point: Capital leases are recorded by the lessee similar to a purchase; see Chapter 9.

A long-term lease can increase in value when current rental rates for similar property rise while the required payments under the lease remain constant. This increase in value of a lease is not reported on the lessee's balance sheet since no extra cost is incurred to acquire it. However, if the property is subleased and the new tenant makes a cash payment to the original lessee for the rights under the old lease, the new tenant debits this payment to a Leasehold account. The balance of this Leasehold account is amortized to Rent Expense of the new tenant over the remaining life of the lease. To illustrate how the changing value of a lease can affect business decisions, consider **La Côte Basque**, a historic restaurant in New York. A few years ago, it sold the two years remaining on its lease to **Walt Disney Company**. La Côte Basque already knew it could not renew the lease when it expired because Disney had negotiated a long-term lease of the property with the building owner, **Coca-Cola Company**. La Côte Basque had been operating in this location for 36 years but could not compete with Disney's offer. The restaurant sold the remainder of its lease for a sizable amount and relocated earlier than required.

Leasehold Improvements

Long-term leases sometimes require the lessee to pay for alterations or improvements to the leased property such as partitions, painting, and storefronts. These alterations and improvements are called **leasehold improvements,** and their costs are debited to a *Leasehold Improvements* account. Since leasehold improvements become part of the property and revert to the lessor at the end of the lease, the

Decision Insight   *e*

Employee Intangible Assets   A study of entrepreneurs who make accommodations to employees finds that such employees are more productive and loyal and work to solve problems. One entrepreneur even lists employees' personal appointments on the company calendar so everyone can plan around those dates.

lessee amortizes these costs over the life of the lease or the life of the improvements, whichever is shorter. The amortization entry debits Rent Expense and credits Accumulated Amortization—Leasehold Improvements.

Franchises and Licenses

Franchises and **licenses** are rights that a company or government grants an entity to deliver a product or service under specified conditions. Many organizations grant franchise and license rights—McDonald's, Pizza Hut, Major League Baseball, and professional football and basketball leagues are just a few examples. The costs of franchises and licenses are debited to a *Franchises and Licenses* asset account and are amortized over the lives of the agreements.

Decision Track 8.4   *d*

Decision Point	Information Search	Analyze & Evaluate
What is the estimated useful life of (amortizable) intangible assets? Is the estimate reasonable?	Financial statement notes (useful life is estimated by dividing intangible asset cost by amortization expense) and competitor data.	Income can be overstated (and amortization understated) with a useful life that is too high; a useful life that is too low yields opposite results.

Goodwill

Point: IBM's balance sheet includes an item called *Investments and Sundry Assets*. A note to this item reports that it includes more than $1 billion of goodwill.

Goodwill has a specific meaning in accounting. **Goodwill** is the amount by which a company's value exceeds the value of its individual assets and liabilities. This usually implies that the company as a whole has certain valuable attributes not measured among its individual assets and liabilities. These can include superior management, skilled workforce, good supplier or customer relations, quality products or services, good location, or other competitive advantages.

Goodwill Illustration

Conceptually, a company has goodwill when its expected future income is greater than the normal income for its industry (competitors). To illustrate, consider the information in Exhibit 8.20 for two competing companies (Z2 and Burton) of roughly equal size in the snowboard industry.

Exhibit 8.20

Data for Goodwill Illustration

	Z2	Burton
Net assets* (excluding goodwill)	$190,000	$190,000
Normal return on net assets in the industry	10%	10%
Normal net income	$ 19,000	$ 19,000
Expected net income	24,000	19,000
Expected net income above normal	$ 5,000	$ 0

* Net assets (also called *equity*) equal total assets minus total liabilities.

The expected net income for Z2 is $24,000. This is $5,000 higher than the $19,000 industry norm based on the 10% return on net assets (equity) for its competitors. This implies that Z2 has goodwill that yields above normal net income. In contrast, Burton's expected income of $19,000 equals the norm for this industry. This implies zero goodwill for Burton. For Z2, it implies that buyers are willing to pay more than just the value of its net assets—specifically, to acquire its goodwill asset.

Point: Accounting for goodwill is different for financial accounting and tax accounting. The IRS requires the amortization of goodwill over a period not to exceed 15 years.

In accounting, goodwill is recorded when an entire company or business segment is purchased. The buyer and seller can estimate goodwill in more than one way. For instance, how do we value Z2's $5,000 per year above normal net income? One method is to value goodwill at some *multiple* of above normal net income. If we choose a multiple of 6, our goodwill estimate for Z2 is 6 × $5,000, or $30,000. Another method is to assume the $5,000 above normal net income continues indefinitely (often called *capitalizing*). This is like an *annuity*. For example, if we assume a 16% discount (interest) rate, the goodwill estimate is

$5,000/16%, or $31,250. Whatever method we choose, the value of goodwill is confirmed only by the price the seller is willing to accept and the buyer is willing to pay.

Accounting for Goodwill

To keep accounting information from being too subjective, goodwill is not recorded unless it is purchased. Purchased goodwill is measured by taking the purchase price of the company and subtracting the market value of its individual net assets (excluding goodwill). Goodwill is a major part of many company purchases. For instance, Yahoo! paid nearly $3.0 billion in stock and options to acquire GeoCities; about $2.8 of the $3.0 billion was for goodwill and other intangibles.

Goodwill is measured as the excess of the cost of an acquired entity over the value of the acquired net assets. Goodwill is recorded as an asset, and it is *not* amortized. Instead, the FASB (*SFAS 142*) requires that goodwill be annually tested for impairment. If the book value of goodwill does not exceed its fair value, goodwill is not impaired. However, if the book value of goodwill does exceed its fair value, an impairment loss is recorded equal to that excess. (Details of this test are in advanced courses.)

Global: International accounting standards call for charging goodwill against income. The amortization period suggested is 5 or fewer years unless a longer period (up to 20 years) is justified.

Trademarks and Trade Names

Companies often adopt unique symbols or select unique names and brands in marketing their products. A **trademark** or **trade (brand) name** is a symbol, name, phrase, or jingle identified with a company, product, or service. Examples are Nike swoosh, Marlboro Man, Big Mac, Coca-Cola, and Corvette. Ownership and exclusive right to use a trademark or trade name is often established by showing that one company used it before another. Ownership is best established by registering a trademark or trade name with the government's Patent Office. The cost of developing, maintaining, or enhancing the value of a trademark or trade name (such as advertising) is charged to expense when incurred. If a trademark or trade name is purchased, however, its cost is debited to an asset account and then amortized over its useful life.

Point: McDonald's "golden arches" symbol is one of the world's most valuable trademarks, yet this asset is not reported on McDonald's balance sheet.

Decision Insight

What's in a Name? The Nike swoosh is one of the world's best-known trademarks. It has helped Nike pump out sales and earnings growth exceeding its competitors. Equally impressive is the brand identity that Intel Corporation's "Intel Inside" campaign created for a product that most consumers never see and few understand.

Global: Some Australian and U.K. companies value brand names separately on their balance sheets.

Quick Check

13. Give an example of a natural resource and of an intangible asset.

14. A company pays $650,000 for an ore deposit. The deposit is estimated to have 325,000 tons of ore that will be mined over the next 10 years. During the first year, it mined, processed, and sold 91,000 tons. What is that year's depletion expense?

15. On January 6, 2002, a company pays $120,000 for a patent with a 17-year legal life to produce a toy expected to be marketable for three years. Prepare entries to record its acquisition and the December 31, 2002, adjustment.

Answers—p. 359

Most long-term asset acquisitions and disposals impact the statement of cash flows. Cash acquisitions of long-term assets are reported in the investing section of the statement of cash flows. Most acquisitions are an immediate *use* of cash, and the amount paid at acquisition is deducted in the statement. Nike, for instance, reports the following under investing activities in its statement of cash flows in Appendix A: "Additions to property, plant and equipment (*$ millions*) . . . $(419.9)."

Disposals of long-term assets usually create an immediate receipt of cash. When they do, they are reported as a *source* of cash (an addition) in the investing section of the statement of cash flows. Nike reports its disposals in Appendix A as follows: "Disposals of property, plant and equipment (*$ millions*) . . . $ 25.3." Note that a gain or loss from an asset disposal is the difference between an asset's book value and the value received—neither reflects any cash flows. Depreciation and amortization also do *not* yield cash flows.

Cash Flow Impacts of Long-Term Assets

C4 Identify cash flow impacts of long-term asset transactions.

Decision Analysis   Total Asset Turnover

A2   Compute total asset turnover and apply it to analyze a company's use of assets.

A company's assets are important in determining its ability to generate sales and earn income. Managers devote much attention to deciding what assets a company acquires, how much it invests in assets, and how to use assets most efficiently and effectively. One important measure of a company's ability to use its assets is **total asset turnover.** The formula for total asset turnover is in Exhibit 8.21.

Exhibit 8.21

Total Asset Turnover

$$\text{Total asset turnover} = \frac{\text{Net sales}}{\text{Average total assets}}$$

Total asset turnover can be computed for any type of company, including manufacturing, merchandising, and service companies. The numerator, net sales, reflects amounts earned from the sale of products and services. The denominator, average total assets, reflects the total resources devoted to operating the company and generating sales.

    To illustrate, let's look at total asset turnover for two competing companies: Coors and Anheuser-Busch. Exhibit 8.22 reports total asset turnover for these two companies.

Exhibit 8.22

Analysis Using Total Asset Turnover

Company	Figure ($ in millions)	2000	1999	1998
Coors	Net sales	$ 2,414	$ 2,236	$ 2,072
	Total assets	$ 1,629	$ 1,546	$ 1,461
	Total asset turnover	1.52	1.49	1.44
Anheuser-Busch	Net sales	$12,262	$11,704	$11,246
	Total assets	$13,085	$12,640	$12,484
	Total asset turnover	0.95	0.93	0.93

To show how we compute and use total asset turnover, let's look at the numbers for Coors. We compute Coors's 2000 total asset turnover as follows: $2,414/[($1,629 + $1,546)/2] = 1.52. We express Coors's use of assets in generating net sales by saying "it turned its assets over 1.52 times during the year." This means that each $1.00 of assets produced $1.52 of net sales for the year. Is a total asset turnover of 1.52 good or bad? It is safe to say that all companies desire a high total asset turnover. Like many ratio analyses, however, a company's total asset turnover must be interpreted in comparison with that of prior years and of its competitors. Interpreting the total asset turnover also requires an understanding of the company's operations. Some operations are capital intensive, meaning that a relatively large amount is invested in assets to generate sales. This suggests a relatively lower total asset turnover. Other companies' operations are labor intensive, meaning that they generate sales more by the efforts of people than the use of assets. In that case, we expect a higher total asset turnover.[2] Coors's turnover has been steady over the past three years and is superior to that for Anheuser-Busch. Total asset turnover for Coors's competitors, available in industry publications such as Dun & Bradstreet, is generally in the range of 1.0 to 1.1 over this same period. Overall, Coors appears to be competitive and doing slightly better than its competitors on total asset turnover.

Decision Maker

Environmentalist A paper manufacturer claims it cannot afford more environmental controls. It points to its low total asset turnover of 1.9 and argues that it cannot compete with companies whose total asset turnover is much higher. Examples cited are food stores (5.5) and auto dealers (3.8). How do you respond?

Answer—p. 358

---

[2] There is a relation between total asset turnover and profit margin. Companies with low total asset turnover require higher profit margins (examples are hotels and real estate); companies with high total asset turnover can succeed with lower profit margins (examples are food stores and toy merchandisers).

On July 14, 2002, Tulsa Company pays $600,000 to acquire a fully equipped factory. The purchase involves the following assets:

Demonstration Problem

Asset	Appraised Value	Salvage Value	Useful Life	Depreciation Method
Land	$160,000			Not depreciated
Land improvements	80,000	$ 0	10 years	Straight-line
Building	320,000	100,000	10 years	Double-declining-balance
Machinery	240,000	20,000	10,000 units	Units-of-production*
Total	$800,000			

* The machinery is used to produce 700 units in 2002 and 1,800 units in 2003.

Required

1. Allocate the total $600,000 purchase cost among the separate assets.

2. Compute the 2002 (six months) and 2003 depreciation expense for each asset and compute total depreciation expense for both years.

3. On the first day of 2004, Tulsa exchanged the machinery that was acquired on July 14, 2002, and $5,000 cash for similar machinery with a $210,000 market value. Journalize the exchange of these similar assets.

4. On the last day of calendar year 2004, Tulsa discarded machinery that had been on its books for five years. The machinery's original cost is $12,000 (estimated life of five years) and its salvage value is $2,000. No depreciation had been recorded for the fifth year when the disposal occurred. Journalize the fifth year of depreciation (straight-line method) and the asset's disposal.

5. At the beginning of year 2004, Tulsa purchased a patent for $100,000 cash. The company estimated the patent's useful life to be 10 years. Journalize the patent acquisition and its amortization for the year 2004.

6. Late in the year 2004, Tulsa acquired an ore deposit for $600,000 cash. It added roads and shafts for an additional cost of $80,000. Salvage value of the mine is estimated to be $20,000. The company estimated 330,000 tons of available ore. In year 2004, Tulsa mined and sold 10,000 tons of ore. Journalize the mine's acquisition and its first year's depletion.

Planning the Solution

- Complete a three-column table showing these amounts for each asset: appraised value, percent of total value, and apportioned cost.

- Using allocated costs, compute depreciation for 2002 (only one-half year) and 2003 (full year) for each asset. Summarize those computations in a table showing total depreciation for each year.

- Remember that gains on exchanges of similar assets are not recognized. Make a journal entry to add the acquired machinery to the books and to remove the old machinery, along with its accumulated depreciation, and the cash given in the exchange.

- Remember that depreciation must be recorded up to date before discarding an asset. Calculate and record depreciation expense for the fifth year using the straight-line method. Since salvage value is not received at the end of a discarded asset's life, the amount of any salvage value becomes a loss on disposal. Record the loss on the disposal as well as the removal of the discarded asset and its related accumulated depreciation.

- Record the patent (an intangible asset) at its purchase price. Use straight-line amortization over its useful life to calculate amortization expense.

- Record the ore deposit (a natural resource asset) at its cost, including any added costs to ready the mine for use. Calculate depletion per ton using the depletion formula. Multiply the depletion per ton by the amount of tons mined and sold to calculate depletion expense for the year.

Solution to Demonstration Problem

1. Allocation of the total cost of $600,000 among the separate assets:

Asset	Appraised Value	Percent of Total Value	Apportioned Cost
Land	$160,000	20%	$120,000 ($600,000 × 20%)
Land improvements	80,000	10	60,000 ($600,000 × 10%)
Building	320,000	40	240,000 ($600,000 × 40%)
Machinery	240,000	30	180,000 ($600,000 × 30%)
Total	$800,000	100%	$600,000

2. Depreciation for each asset. (*Note:* Land is not depreciated.)

Land Improvements

Cost	$ 60,000
Salvage value	0
Depreciable cost	$ 60,000
Useful life	10 years
Annual depreciation expense ($60,000/10 years)	$ 6,000
2002 depreciation ($6,000 × 6/12)	$ 3,000
2003 depreciation	$ 6,000

Building

Straight-line rate = 100%/10 years = 10%
Double-declining-balance rate = 10% × 2 = 20%

2002 depreciation ($240,000 × 20% × 6/12)	$ 24,000
2003 depreciation [($240,000 − $24,000) × 20%]	$ 43,200

Machinery

Cost	$180,000
Salvage value	20,000
Depreciable cost	$160,000
Total expected units of production	10,000 units
Depreciation per unit ($160,000/10,000 units)	$ 16
2002 depreciation ($16 × 700 units)	$ 11,200
2003 depreciation ($16 × 1,800 units)	$ 28,800

Total depreciation expense:

	2002	2003
Land improvements	$ 3,000	$ 6,000
Building.................	24,000	43,200
Machinery...............	11,200	28,800
Total	$38,200	$78,000

3. Record the exchange of similar assets (machinery) with a gain on the exchange: The book value on the exchange date is $180,000 (cost) − $40,000 (accumulated depreciation). The book value of the machinery given up in the exchange ($140,000) plus the $5,000 cash paid is less than the

$210,000 value of the machine acquired. The entry to record this exchange of similar assets does not recognize the $65,000 gain on exchange:

Machinery (new)	145,000*	
Accumulated Depreciation—Machinery (old)	40,000	
Machinery (old)		180,000
Cash		5,000
To record exchange of similar assets.		

* Market value of the acquired asset of $210,000 minus $65,000 gain.

4. Record the depreciation up to date on the discarded asset:

Depreciation Expense—Equipment	2,000	
Accumulated Depreciation—Equipment		2,000
To record depreciation on date of disposal: ($12,000 − $2,000)/5		

Record the removal of the discarded asset and its loss on disposal:

Accumulated Depreciation—Machinery	10,000	
Loss on Disposal of Machinery	2,000	
Machinery		12,000
To record the discarding of machinery with a $2,000 book value.		

5.

Patent	100,000	
Cash		100,000
To record patent acquisition.		

Amortization Expense—Patent	10,000	
Accumulated Amortization—Patent		10,000
To record amortization expense: $100,000/10 years = $10,000.		

6.

Ore Deposit	680,000	
Cash		680,000
To record ore deposit acquisition and its related costs.		

Depletion Expense—Ore Deposit	20,000	
Accumulated Depletion—Ore Deposit		20,000
To record depletion expense: ($680,000 − $20,000)/330,000 tons = $2 per ton. 10,000 tons mined and sold × $2 = $20,000 depletion.		

Summary

C1 **Describe plant assets and issues in accounting for them.**
Plant assets are tangible assets used in the operations of a company and have a useful life of more than one accounting period. Plant assets are set apart from other tangible assets by two important features: use in operations and useful lives longer than one period. The four main accounting issues with plant assets are (1) computing their costs, (2) allocating their costs to the periods they benefit, (3) accounting for subsequent expenditures, and (4) recording their disposal.

C2 **Explain depreciation and the factors affecting its computation.** Depreciation is the process of allocating to expense the cost of a plant asset over the accounting periods that benefit from its use. Depreciation does not measure the decline in a plant asset's market value or its physical deterioration. Three factors determine depreciation: cost, salvage value, and useful life. Salvage value is an estimate of the asset's value at the end of its benefit period. Useful (service) life is the length of time an asset is productively used.

C3 **Explain depreciation for partial years and changes in estimates.** Partial-year depreciation is often required because assets are bought and sold throughout the year. Depreciation is revised when changes in estimates such as salvage value and useful life occur. If the useful life of a plant asset changes, for instance, the remaining cost to be depreciated is spread over the remaining (revised) useful life of the asset.

C4 **Identify cash flow impacts of long-term asset transactions.** Acquisition and disposal of long-term assets for cash impact the investing section of the statement of cash flows. Acquisitions are a use of cash; disposals are a source of cash.

A1 **Compare and analyze alternative depreciation methods.** The amount of depreciation expense per period is usually different for different methods, yet total depreciation expense over an asset's life is the same for all methods. Each method starts with the same total cost and ends with the same salvage value. The difference is in the pattern of depreciation expense over the asset's life. Common methods are straight-line, double-declining-balance, and units-of-production.

A2 **Compute total asset turnover and apply it to analyze a company's use of assets.** Total asset turnover measures a company's ability to use its assets to generate sales. It is defined as net sales divided by average total assets. While all companies desire a high total asset turnover, it must be interpreted in comparison with that for prior years and its competitors.

P1 **Apply the cost principle to compute the cost of plant assets.** Plant assets are recorded at cost when purchased. Cost includes all normal and reasonable expenditures necessary to get the asset in place and ready for its intended use. The cost of a lump-sum purchase is allocated among its individual assets.

P2 **Compute and record depreciation using the straight-line, units-of-production, and declining-balance methods.** The straight-line method divides cost less salvage value by the asset's useful life to determine depreciation expense per period. The units-of-production method divides cost less salvage value by the estimated number of units the asset will produce over its life to determine depreciation per unit. The declining-balance method multiplies the asset's beginning-period book value by a factor that is often double the straight-line rate.

P3 **Distinguish between revenue and capital expenditures, and account for these expenditures.** Revenue expenditures expire in the current period and are debited to expense accounts and matched with current revenues. Ordinary repairs are an example of revenue expenditures. Capital expenditures benefit future periods and are debited to asset accounts. Examples of capital expenditures are extraordinary repairs and betterments.

P4 **Account for asset disposal through discarding, selling, or exchanging an asset.** When a plant asset is discarded, sold, or exchanged, its cost and accumulated depreciation are removed from the accounts. Any cash proceeds from discarding or selling an asset are recorded and compared to the asset's book value to determine gain or loss. When similar assets are exchanged, losses are recognized but gains are not. When gains are not recognized, the new asset account is debited for the book value of the old asset plus any cash (assets) paid.

P5 **Account for natural resource assets and their depletion.** The cost of a natural resource is recorded in an asset account. Depletion of a natural resource is recorded by allocating its cost to depletion expense using the units-of-production method. Depletion is credited to an Accumulated Depletion account.

P6 **Account for intangible assets.** An intangible asset is recorded at the cost incurred to purchase it. The cost of an intangible asset with a definite useful life is allocated to expense using the straight-line method and is called *amortization*. Goodwill and intangible assets with an indefinite useful life are not amortized—they are annually tested for impairment. Intangible assets include patents, copyrights, leaseholds, goodwill, and trademarks.

Guidance Answers to **Decision Maker** and **Decision Ethics**

Controller The president's instruction may reflect an honest and reasonable prediction of the future. Since the company is struggling financially, the president may have concluded that the normal pattern of replacing assets every three years cannot continue. Perhaps the strategy is to avoid costs of frequent replacements and stretch use of equipment a few years longer until financial conditions improve. However, if you believe the president's decision is unprincipled, you might confront the president with your opinion that it is unethical to change the estimate to increase income. Another possibility is to wait and see whether the auditor will prohibit this change in estimate. In either case, you should insist that the statements be based on reasonable estimates.

Entrepreneur Treating an expense as a capital expenditure means that reported expenses will be lower and income higher in the short run. This is so because a capital expenditure is not expensed immediately but is spread over the asset's useful life. Treating an expense as a capital expenditure also means that asset and equity totals are reported at larger amounts in the short run. This continues until the asset is fully depreciated. Your friend is probably trying to help, but the suggestion is misguided. Only an expenditure benefiting future periods is a capital expenditure.

Environmentalist The paper manufacturer's comparison of its total asset turnover with food stores and auto dealers is misdirected. These other industries' turnovers are higher because their profit margins are lower (about 2%). Profit margins for the paper industry are usually 3% to 3.5%. You need to collect data from competitors in the paper industry to show that a 1.9 total asset turnover is about right for this industry. You might also want to collect data on this company's revenues and expenses, along with compensation data for its high-ranking officers and employees.

Guidance Answers to **Quick Checks**

1. a. Supplies—current assets
   b. Office equipment—plant assets
   c. Inventory—current assets
   d. Land for future expansion—long-term investments
   e. Trucks used in operations—plant assets
2. a. Land   **b.** Land Improvements
3. $700,000 + $49,000 − $21,000 + $3,500 + $3,000 + $2,500 = $737,000
4. a. Straight-line with 7-year life: ($77,000/7) = $11,000
   b. Straight-line with 10-year life: ($77,000/10) = $7,700
5. Depreciation is a process of allocating the cost of plant assets to the accounting periods that benefit from the assets' use.
6. a. Book value using straight-line depreciation:
   $96,000 − [($96,000 − $8,000)/5] = $78,400
   b. Book value using units of production:
   $96,000 − [($96,000 − $8,000) × (10,000/100,000)]
   = $87,200
7. ($3,800 − $200)/3 = $1,200 (original depreciation per year)
   $1,200 × 2 = $2,400 (accumulated depreciation)
   ($3,800 − $2,400)/2 = $700 (revised depreciation)

8.

Machinery	12,000	
Cash		12,000

9. A revenue expenditure benefits only the current period and should be charged to expense in the current period. A capital expenditure yields benefits that extend beyond the end of the current period and should be charged to an asset.

10. A betterment involves modifying an existing plant asset to make it more efficient, usually by replacing part of the asset with an improved or superior part. The cost of a betterment should be debited to the asset's account.

11.

Depreciation Expense	3,500	
Accumulated Depreciation		3,500
Cash	32,000	
Accumulated Depreciation	10,500	
Gain on Sale of Equipment		500
Equipment		42,000

12.

(a)

Equipment	45,000	
Loss on Exchange of Assets	3,600	
Accumulated Depreciation—Equip.	23,400	
Equipment		30,000
Cash ($45,000 − $3,000)		42,000

(b)

Equipment (reflects $400 unrecognized gain)	44,600	
Accumulated Depreciation—Equip.	23,400	
Equipment		30,000
Cash ($45,000 − $7,000)		38,000

13. Examples of natural resources are timberlands, mineral deposits, and oil reserves. Examples of intangible assets are patents, copyrights, leaseholds, leasehold improvements, goodwill, trademarks, and licenses.

14. ($650,000/325,000 tons) × 91,000 tons = $182,000

15.

Jan. 6	Patents	120,000	
	Cash		120,000
Dec. 31	Amortization Expense	40,000*	
	Accumulated Amortization—Patents		40,000

* $120,000/3 years = $40,000.

Glossary

Accelerated depreciation method Method that produces larger depreciation charges in the early years of an asset's life and smaller charges in its later years. (p. 338)

Amortization Process of allocating the cost of an intangible asset to expense over its estimated useful life. (p. 349)

Betterments Expenditures to make a plant asset more efficient or productive; also called *improvements*. (p. 344)

Book value Total cost of an asset less its accumulated depreciation (or depletion, or amortization). (p. 337)

Capital expenditures Additional costs of plant assets that provide material benefits extending beyond the current period; also called *balance sheet expenditures*. (p. 343)

Change in an accounting estimate Change in an accounting estimate that results from new information, subsequent developments, or improved judgment. (p. 342)

Copyright Right giving the owner the exclusive privilege to publish and sell musical, literary, or artistic work during the creator's life plus 50 years. (p. 350)

Cost All normal and reasonable expenditures necessary to get a plant asset in place and ready for its intended use. (p. 333)

Declining-balance method Method that determines depreciation charge for the period by multiplying a depreciation rate (often twice the straight-line rate) by the asset's beginning-period book value. (p. 338)

Depletion Process of allocating the cost of natural resources to periods when they are consumed. (p. 348)

Depreciation Process of allocating the cost of a plant asset to expense in the periods benefiting from its use. (p. 335)

Extraordinary repairs Major repairs that extend the useful life of a plant asset beyond prior expectations; treated as a capital expenditure. (p. 344)

Franchises, Licenses Privileges granted by a company or government to sell a product or service under specified conditions. (p. 352)

Goodwill Amount by which a company's value exceeds the value of its individual assets and liabilities. (p. 352)

Inadequacy Condition in which the capacity of plant assets is too small to meet the company's production demands. (p. 336)

Intangible assets Nonphysical assets (used in operations) that confer on their owners long-term rights, privileges, or competitive advantages. (p. 349)

Land improvements Assets that increase the benefits of land, have a limited useful life, and are depreciated. (p. 334)

Lease Contract specifying the rental of property. (p. 351)

Leasehold Rights the lessor grants to the lessee under the terms of a lease. (p. 351)

Leasehold improvements Alterations or improvements to leased property such as partitions and storefronts. (p. 351)

Lessee Party to a lease who secures the right to possess and use the property from another party (the lessor). (p. 351)

Lessor Party to a lease who grants another party (the lessee) the right to possess and use its property. (p. 351)

Licenses (See *franchises*.)

Modified Accelerated Cost Recovery System (MACRS) Depreciation system required by federal income tax law. (p. 341)

Natural resources Assets physically consumed when used; examples are timber, mineral deposits, and oil and gas fields; also called *wasting assets*. (p. 348)

Obsolescence Condition in which, because of new inventions and improvements, a plant asset can no longer be used to produce goods or services with a competitive advantage. (p. 336)

Ordinary repairs Repairs to keep a plant asset in normal, good operating condition; treated as a revenue expenditure. (p. 343)

Patent Exclusive right granted to its owner to manufacture and sell an item or to use a process for 17 years. (p. 350)

Plant assets Tangible assets used in a company's operations that have a useful life of more than one period. (p. 332)

Revenue expenditures Expenditures reported on the current income statement as an expense because they do not provide benefits in future periods. (p. 343)

Salvage value Estimate of amount to be recovered at the end of an asset's useful life; also called *residual*, or *scrap, value*. (p. 335)

Straight-line depreciation Method that allocates an equal portion of the total depreciation for a plant asset (cost minus salvage) to each accounting period in its useful life. (p. 336)

Total asset turnover Measure of a company's ability to use its assets to generate sales; computed by dividing net sales by average total assets. (p. 354)

Trademark or **trade (brand) name** Symbol, name, phrase, or jingle identified with a company, product, or service. (p. 353)

Units-of-production depreciation Method that charges a varying amount to depreciation expense per period of an asset's useful life depending on usage. (p. 338)

Useful life Length of time an asset will be productively used in the operations of a business; also called *service life*. (p. 335)

Questions

1. What is the general rule for costs included in a plant asset?
2. 🛅 What characteristics of a plant asset make it different from other assets?
3. What is the balance sheet classification for land that is held for future expansion? Why is such land not classified as a plant asset?
4. What is different between land and land improvements?
5. Why is the Modified Accelerated Cost Recovery System not generally accepted for financial accounting purposes?
6. 🛅 Does the balance in the Accumulated Depreciation—Machinery account represent funds to replace the machinery when it wears out? If not, what does it represent?
7. 🛅 What accounting principle justifies charging low-cost plant asset purchases immediately to an expense account?
8. What is the difference between ordinary repairs and extraordinary repairs? How should each be recorded?
9. 🛅 Identify events that might lead to disposal of a plant asset.
10. What is the process of allocating the cost of natural resources to expense as they are used?
11. What are the characteristics of an intangible asset?
12. Is the declining-balance method an acceptable way to compute depletion of natural resources?
13. What general procedures are applied in accounting for the acquisition and potential cost allocation of intangible assets?
14. 🛅 When do we know that a company has goodwill? When can goodwill appear in a company's balance sheet?
15. 🛅 Assume that a company buys another business and pays for its goodwill. If the company plans to incur costs each year to maintain the value of the goodwill, must it also amortize this goodwill?
16. How does accounting for long-term assets impact the statement of cash flows?
17. 🛅 How is total asset turnover computed? Why would a financial statement user be interested in total asset turnover?
18. Refer to Nike's balance sheet in Appendix A. What title does Nike use for its plant assets? **NIKE** What is its book value of plant assets as of May 31, 2000, and May 31, 1999?
19. Refer to Reebok's balance sheet in Appendix **Reebok** A. How are Reebok's plant assets and intangibles reported (with amounts) on its 1999 balance sheet?
20. Refer to the January 29, 2000, balance sheet of Gap in Appendix A. What long-term assets discussed in this chapter are reported? **GAP**

U-Bowl installs automatic scorekeeping equipment with an invoice price of $190,000. The electrical work required for the installation costs $20,000. Additional costs are $4,000 for delivery and $13,700 for sales tax. During the installation, a component of the equipment is carelessly left on a lane and hit by the automatic lane-cleaning machine. The cost of repairing the component is $1,850. What is the recorded cost of the automatic scorekeeping equipment?

QUICK STUDY

QS 8-1 🖉
Cost of plant P1
assets

Identify the main difference between (1) plant assets and current assets, (2) plant assets and inventory, and (3) plant assets and long-term investments.

QS 8-2 🖉
Defining assets C1

On January 2, 2002, the Young Country Band acquires sound equipment for concert performances at a cost of $65,800. The band estimates it will use this equipment for four years, during which time it anticipates performing about 200 concerts. It estimates that after four years it can sell the equipment for $2,000. During year 2002, the band performs 45 concerts. Compute the year 2002 depreciation using the (1) straight-line method and (2) units-of-production method.

QS 8-3
Depreciation methods

P2

Refer to the facts in QS 8–3. Assume that Young Country Band chose straight-line depreciation but realizes early in the second year that due to concert bookings beyond expectations, this equipment will last only a total of three years. The salvage value remains unchanged. Compute the revised depreciation for both the second and third years.

QS 8-4
Computing revised C3
depreciation

A fleet of refrigerated delivery trucks is acquired on January 5, 2002, at a cost of $830,000 with an estimated useful life of eight years and an estimated salvage value of $75,000. Compute the depreciation expense for the first three years using the double-declining-balance method.

QS 8-5
Double-declining- P2
balance method

1. Classify the following as either a revenue or a capital expenditure:
   a. Completed an addition to an office building for $225,000 cash.
   b. $175 monthly cost of replacement filters on an air-conditioning system.
   c. Cost of annual tune-ups for delivery trucks, $200 cash per truck.
   d. Replaced a compressor on a refrigeration system for $40,000 cash that extends its useful life by four years.
2. Prepare the journal entries to record transactions *a* and *d* of part 1.

QS 8-6 🖉
Revenue and capital
expenditures

P3

Fife Co. owns a machine that costs $42,400 with accumulated depreciation of $18,400. Fife exchanges the machine for a similar but newer model that has a market value of $52,000. Record the exchange assuming Fife also paid cash of (1) $30,000 and (2) $22,000.

QS 8-7
Similar asset P4
exchange

Outback Company acquires an ore mine at a cost of $1,400,000. It incurs additional costs of $400,000 to access the mine, which is estimated to hold 1,000,000 tons of ore. The estimated value of the land after the ore is removed is $200,000.
1. Prepare the entry(ies) to record the cost of the ore mine.
2. Prepare the year-end adjusting entry if 180,000 tons of ore are mined and sold the first year.

QS 8-8
Natural resources
and depletion

P5

Which of the following assets are reported on the balance sheet as intangible assets? Which are reported as natural resources? (*a*) Oil well, (*b*) Trademark, (*c*) Leasehold, (*d*) Gold mine, (*e*) Building.

QS 8-9 🖉
Classify assets P5 P6

On January 4 of this year, Belair Boutique incurs a $105,000 cost to modernize its store. Improvements include new floors, ceilings, wiring, and wall coverings. These improvements are estimated to yield benefits for 10 years. Belair leases its store and has eight years remaining on the lease. Prepare the entry to record (1) the cost of modernization and (2) amortization at the end of this current year.

QS 8-10
Intangible assets P6
and amortization

For each of the following investing activities, identify whether it is a source (A) or use (B) of cash.
A. Cash provided by investing activities.
B. Cash used by investing activities.
1. _____ Purchase of timberland for cash   **3.** _____ Cash purchase of machinery
2. _____ Cash sale of factory warehouse   **4.** _____ Sale of patents for cash

QS 8-11 🖉
Cash impacts from
acquisitions and disposals

C4

QS 8-12 🖉
Computing total
asset turnover **A2**

Eastman Company reports the following: net sales of $14,880 million for 2003 and $13,990 million for 2002; end-of-year total assets of $15,869 million for 2003 and $17,819 million for 2002. Compute its total asset turnover for 2003.

EXERCISES

Exercise 8-1 🖉
Cost of plant assets
P1

Rip Curl Co. purchases a machine for $12,500, terms 2/10, n/60, FOB shipping point. The seller pre-paid the $360 freight charges, adding the amount to the invoice and bringing its total to $12,860. The machine requires special steel mounting and power connections costing $895. Another $475 is paid to assemble the machine and get it into operation. In moving the machine to its steel mounting, $180 in damages occurred. Also, $40 of materials is used in adjusting the machine to produce a satisfactory product. The adjustments are normal for this machine and are not the result of the damages. Compute the cost recorded for this machine. (Rip Curl pays for this machine within the cash discount period.)

Exercise 8-2
Recording costs
of assets
C1 P1

Ashgrove Manufacturing purchases a large lot on which an old building is located as part of its plans to build a new plant. The negotiated purchase price is $280,000 for the lot plus $110,000 for the old building. The company pays $33,500 to tear down the old building and $47,000 to landscape the lot. It also pays a total of $1,540,000 in construction costs—this amount consists of $1,452,200 for the new building and $87,800 for lighting and paving a parking area next to the building. Prepare a single journal entry to record these costs incurred by Ashgrove, all of which are paid in cash.

Exercise 8-3
Lump-sum purchase
of plant assets **C1**

Reese Company pays $375,280 for real estate plus $20,100 in closing costs. The real estate consists of land appraised at $156,820; land improvements appraised at $57,540; and a building appraised at $178,300. Allocate the total cost among the three purchased assets and prepare the journal entry to record the purchase.

Exercise 8-4
Depreciation methods
P2

In early January 2002, LabOne purchases computer equipment for $154,000 to use in operating activities for the next four years. It estimates the equipment's salvage value at $25,000. Prepare tables showing depreciation and book value for each of the four years assuming (1) straight-line and (2) double-declining-balance depreciation.

Exercise 8-5
Depreciation methods **P2**

Spoon Company installs a computerized manufacturing machine in its factory at a cost of $43,500. The machine's useful life is estimated at 10 years, or 385,000 units of product, with a $5,000 salvage value. During its second year, the machine produces 32,500 units of product. Determine the machine's second-year depreciation under the (1) straight-line, (2) units-of-production, and (3) double-declining-balance methods.

Check   (3) $6,960

Exercise 8-6
Depreciation methods;
partial year depreciation **C3**

On April 1, 2002, Admiral's Backhoe Co. purchases a trencher for $280,000. The machine is expected to last five years and have a salvage value of $40,000. Compute depreciation expense for year 2003 using the (1) straight-line and (2) double-declining-balance methods.

Exercise 8-7
Revising depreciation **C3**

Top Notch Fitness Club uses straight-line depreciation for a machine costing $23,860, with an estimated four-year life and a $2,400 salvage value. At the beginning of the third year, Top Notch determines that the machine has three more years of remaining useful life, after which it will have an estimated $2,000 salvage value. Compute (1) the machine's book value at the end of its second year and (2) the amount of depreciation for each of the final three years given the revised estimates.

Check   (2) $3,710

Exercise 8-8 🖉
Income effects of
depreciation methods **A1**

MES Enterprises pays $238,400 for equipment that will last five years and have a $43,600 salvage value. By using the machine in its operations for five years, the company expects to earn $88,500 annually, after deducting all expenses except depreciation. Prepare a table showing income before depreciation, depreciation expense, and net (pretax) income for each year and the total five-year period, assuming (1) straight-line depreciation and (2) double-declining-balance depreciation.

Check   (2) Year 4 NI, $80,606

Exercise 8-9 🖉
Extraordinary repairs;
plant asset age **P3**

Mustang Company owns a building that appears on its prior year-end balance sheet at its original $572,000 cost less $429,000 accumulated depreciation. The building is depreciated on a straight-line basis assuming a 20-year life and no salvage value. During the first week in January of the current calendar year, major structural repairs are completed on the building at a $68,350 cost. The repairs extend its useful life for 7 years beyond the 20 years originally estimated.

1. Determine the building's age (plant asset age) as of the end of the prior calendar year.
2. Prepare the entry to record the cost of the structural repairs that are paid in cash.
3. Determine the book value of the building immediately after the repairs are recorded.
4. Prepare the entry to record the current calendar year's depreciation.

Check   (3) $211,350

Archer Company pays $264,000 for equipment expected to last four years and have a $25,000 salvage value. Prepare journal entries to record the following costs related to the equipment:

1. During the second year of the equipment's life, $22,000 cash is paid for a new component expected to increase the equipment's productivity by 10% a year.
2. During the third year, $6,250 cash is paid for normal repairs necessary to keep the equipment in good working order.
3. During the fourth year, $14,870 is paid for repairs expected to increase the useful life of the equipment from four to five years.

Exercise 8-10
Ordinary repairs, extraordinary repairs, and betterments
P3

Blackbelt Construction trades in an old tractor for a new tractor, receiving a $29,000 trade-in allowance and paying the remaining $83,000 in cash. The old tractor had cost $96,000, and straight-line accumulated depreciation of $52,500 had been recorded to date under the assumption that it would last eight years and have a $12,000 salvage value. Answer the following questions:

1. What is the book value of the old tractor at the time of exchange?
2. What is the loss on this similar asset exchange?
3. What amount should be recorded (debited) in the asset account for the new tractor?

Exercise 8-11 *d*
Exchanging similar assets
P4

Check   (2) $14,500

On January 2, 2002, Ritchfield Co. disposes of a machine costing $44,000 with accumulated depreciation of $24,625. Prepare the entries to record the disposal under each of the following separate assumptions:

1. Machine is sold for $18,250 cash.
2. Machine is traded in on a similar but newer machine having a $60,200 cash price. A $25,000 trade-in allowance is received, and the balance is paid in cash.
3. Machine is traded in on a similar but newer machine having a $60,200 cash price. A $15,000 trade-in allowance is received, and the balance is paid in cash.

Exercise 8-12
Recording plant asset disposals
P4
Check   (2) Dr. Machinery, $54,575

Finesse Co. purchases and installs a machine on January 1, 2002, at a total cost of $105,000. Straight-line depreciation is taken each year for four years assuming a seven-year life and no salvage value. The machine is disposed of on July 1, 2006, during its fifth year of service. Prepare entries to record the partial year's depreciation on July 1, 2006, and to record the disposal under the following separate assumptions: (1) the machine is sold for $45,000 cash, and (2) Finesse receives an insurance settlement of $25,000 resulting from the total destruction of the machine in a fire.

Exercise 8-13
Partial year depreciation; disposal of plant asset
P4

On April 2, 2002, Cascade Mining Co. pays $3,736,250 for an ore deposit containing 1,525,000 tons. The company installs machinery in the mine costing $213,500, with an estimated seven-year life and no salvage value. The machinery will be abandoned when the ore is completely mined. Cascade began mining on May 1, 2002, and mined and sold 166,200 tons of ore during the remaining eight months of 2002. Prepare the December 31, 2002, entries to record both the ore deposit depletion and the mining machinery depreciation. Mining machinery depreciation should be in proportion to the mine's depletion.

Exercise 8-14
Depletion of natural resources
P5

Uptown Gallery purchases the copyright on an oil painting for $418,000 on January 1, 2002. The copyright legally protects its owner for 19 more years. However, the company plans to market and sell prints of the original for only 12 years. Prepare entries to record the purchase of the copyright on January 1, 2002, and its annual amortization on December 31, 2002.

Exercise 8-15
Amortization of   **P6**
intangible assets

Exercise 8-16
Goodwill estimation

P6

Check   (2) $453,750

Tracey Losh has devoted years to developing a profitable business that earns an attractive return. Losh is now considering selling the business and is attempting to estimate its goodwill. The value of the business's net assets (excluding goodwill) is $537,000, and in a typical year net income is about $90,000. Most businesses of this type are expected to earn a return of about 10% on their net assets. Estimate the value of this business's goodwill for the following separate cases assuming it is (1) equal to 10 times the amount that net income is above normal and (2) computed by capitalizing at a rate of 8% the amount that net income is above normal.

Exercise 8-17
Cash flows related to assets

C4   GAP

Refer to the statement of cash flows for **Gap** in Appendix A for the 52 week period ended January 29, 2000, to answer the following:

1. What amount of cash is used to purchase property and equipment?
2. How much depreciation and amortization are recorded?
3. What total amount of net cash is used in investing activities?
4. What amount of cash is used to acquire lease rights?

Exercise 8-18
Evaluating efficient **A2**
use of assets

Klink Co. reports net sales of $5,865,000 for 2002 and $8,689,000 for 2003. End-of-year balances for total assets are: 2001, $1,686,000; 2002, $1,800,000; and 2003, $1,982,000. Compute Klink's total asset turnover for 2002 and 2003 and comment on its efficiency in using assets.

PROBLEM SET A

Problem 8-1A
Plant asset costs;
depreciation methods

C1 C2 A1 P1 P2

Check   (2) $26,604
            (3) $9,624

Gunner Construction negotiates a lump-sum purchase of several assets from a company that is going out of business. The purchase is completed on January 1, 2002, at a total cash price of $802,000 for a building, land, land improvements, and six vehicles. The estimated market values of the assets are building, $506,000; land, $302,000; land improvements, $28,500; and six vehicles, $124,500. The company's fiscal year ends on December 31.

Required

1. Prepare a table to allocate the lump-sum purchase price to the separate assets purchased (round percents to the nearest 1%). Prepare the journal entry to record the purchase.
2. Compute the depreciation expense for year 2002 on the building using the straight-line method, assuming a 15-year life and a $26,000 salvage value.
3. Compute the depreciation expense for year 2002 on the land improvements assuming a five-year life and double-declining-balance depreciation.

Analysis Component

4. Defend or refute this statement: Accelerated depreciation results in payment of less taxes over the asset's life.

Problem 8-2A
Asset cost allocation;
straight-line depreciation

C1 C2 P1 P2

Check   (1) Land costs, $2,487,800;
Building 2 costs, $736,000

In January 2002, Moonscapes pays $3,200,000 for a tract of land with two buildings on it. It plans to demolish Building 1 and build a new store in its place. Building 2 will be a company office; it is appraised at $645,000, with a useful life of 20 years and a $60,000 salvage value. A lighted parking lot near Building 1 has improvements (Land Improvements 1) valued at $420,000 that are expected to last another 14 years with no salvage value. Without the buildings and improvements, the tract of land is valued at $1,735,000. Moonscapes also incurs the following additional costs:

Cost to demolish Building 1	$ 328,400
Cost of additional landscaping	175,400
Cost to construct new building (Building 3), having a useful life of 25 years and a $392,000 salvage value	2,202,000
Cost of new land improvements (Land Improvements 2) near Building 2 having a 20-year useful life and no salvage value	164,000

Required

1. Prepare a table with the following column headings: Land, Building 2, Building 3, Land Improvements 1, and Land Improvements 2. Allocate the costs incurred by Moonscapes to the appropriate columns and total each column (round percents to the nearest 1%).

2. Prepare a single journal entry to record all the incurred costs assuming they are paid in cash on January 1, 2002.

3. Using the straight-line method, prepare the December 31 adjusting entries to record depreciation for the 12 months of 2002 when these assets were in use.

Check   (3) Depr.—Land Improv. 1 and 2, $34,286 and $8,200

Clampett Contractors completed the following transactions and events involving the purchase and operation of equipment in its business:

2002

Jan.   1   Paid $287,600 cash plus $11,504 in sales tax and $1,500 in transportation (FOB shipping point) for a new loader. The loader is estimated to have a four-year life and a $20,604 salvage value. Loader costs are recorded in the Equipment account.

Jan.   3   Paid $4,800 to enclose the cab and install air conditioning in the loader to enable operations under harsher conditions. This increased the estimated salvage value of the loader by another $1,396.

Dec. 31   Recorded annual straight-line depreciation on the loader.

2003

Jan.   1   Paid $5,400 to overhaul the loader's engine, which increased the loader's estimated useful life by two years.

Feb. 17   Paid $820 to repair the loader after the operator backs it into a tree.

Dec. 31   Recorded annual straight-line depreciation on the loader.

Required

Prepare journal entries to record these transactions and events.

Problem 8-3A
Computing and revising depreciation; revenue and capital expenditures

C3 P1 P3

Check   Dec. 31, 2002, Dr. Depr. Expense—Equip., $70,851

Check   Dec. 31, 2003, Dr. Depr. Expense—Equip., $43,591

ACT Company completed the following transactions and events involving its delivery trucks:

2002

Jan.   1   Paid $20,515 cash plus $1,485 in sales tax for a new delivery truck estimated to have a five-year life and a $2,000 salvage value. Delivery truck costs are recorded in the Trucks account.

Dec. 31   Recorded annual straight-line depreciation on the truck.

2003

Dec. 31   Due to new information obtained earlier in the year, the truck's estimated useful life was changed from five to four years, and the estimated salvage value was increased to $2,500. Recorded annual straight-line depreciation on the truck.

2004

Dec. 31   Recorded annual straight-line depreciation on the truck.

Dec. 31   Sold the truck for $5,200 cash.

Required

Prepare journal entries to record these transactions and events.

Problem 8-4A
Computing and revising depreciation; selling plant assets

C3 P2 P4

Check   Dec. 31, 2003, Dr. Depr. Expense—Trucks, $5,167

Check   Dec. 31, 2004, Dr. Loss on Disposal of Trucks, $2,466

Part 1. A machine costing $257,500 with a four-year life and an estimated $20,000 salvage value is installed in Carlton Company's factory on January 1. The factory manager estimates the machine will produce 475,000 units of product during its life. It actually produces the following units: year 1, 220,000; year 2, 124,600; year 3, 121,800; and year 4, 15,200. The total number of units produced by the end of year 4 exceeds the original estimate—this difference was not predicted. (The machine must not be depreciated below its estimated salvage value.)

Required

Prepare a table with the following column headings and compute depreciation for each year (and total depreciation of all years combined) for the machine under each depreciation method.

Problem 8-5A
Depreciation methods; disposal of plant asset

C3 P1 P2 P4

Check   Year 4: Units-of-Production Depreciation, $4,300; DDB Depreciation, $12,187

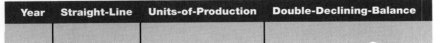

Year	Straight-Line	Units-of-Production	Double-Declining-Balance

Part 2. Casablanca purchases a used machine for $178,000 cash on January 2 and readies it for use the next day at a $2,840 cost. On January 3, it is installed on a new platform costing $1,160, and it began operating. The company predicts the machine will be used for six years and have a $15,000 salvage value. Depreciation is to be charged on a straight-line basis. On December 31, at the end of its fifth year in operations, it is disposed of.

Required

a. Prepare journal entries to record the machine's purchase and the costs to ready and install it. Cash is paid for all costs incurred.

Check (b) Depr. Exp., $27,833

b. Prepare journal entries to record depreciation of the machine at December 31 of its first year in operations and at December 31 in the year of its disposal.

Check (iii) Dr. Loss from Fire, $12,835

c. Prepare journal entries to record the machine's disposal under each of the following separate assumptions: (i) it is sold for $15,000 cash; (ii) it is sold for $50,000 cash; and (iii) it is destroyed in a fire and the insurance company pays $30,000 cash to settle the loss claim.

Problem 8-6A
Intangible assets and
natural resources

A1 P5 P6

G

Part 1. On July 1, 2000, Sweetman Company signs a contract to lease space in a building for 15 years. The lease contract calls for annual (prepaid) rental payments of $80,000 on each July 1 throughout the life of the lease, and that the lessee will pay for all additions and improvements to the leased property. On June 25, 2005, Sweetman decides to sublease the space to Kirk & Associates for the remaining 10 years of the lease—Kirk pays $200,000 to Sweetman for the right to sublease and it agrees to assume the obligation to pay the $80,000 annual rent to the building owner beginning July 1, 2005. After taking possession of the leased space, Kirk pays for improving the office portion of the leased space at a $130,000 cost. The improvements are paid for on July 5, 2005 and are estimated to have a useful life equal to the 16 years remaining in the life of the building.

Required

Check Dr. Rent Expense for:
(d) $10,000, (e) $6,500, (f) $40,000

Prepare entries for Kirk to record (a) its payment to Sweetman for the right to sublease the building space, (b) its payment of the 2005 annual rent to the building owner, and (c) its payment for the office improvements. Prepare Kirk's year-end adjusting entries required at December 31, 2005, to (d) amortize the $200,000 cost of the sublease, (e) amortize the office improvements, and (f) record rent expense.

Part 2. On July 23 of the current year, Denver Mining Co. pays $4,725,000 for land estimated to contain 5,125,000 tons of recoverable ore. It installs machinery costing $400,000 that has a 10-year life and no salvage value and is capable of mining the ore deposit in eight years. The machinery is paid for on July 25, seven days before mining operations begin. The company removes and sells 480,000 tons of ore during its first five months of operations. Depreciation of the machinery is in proportion to the mine's depletion as the machinery will be abandoned after the ore is mined.

Required

Preparation Component

Check (c) Depletion, $442,560;
(d) Depreciation, $37,440

Prepare entries to record (a) the purchase of the land, (b) the cost and installation of machinery, (c) the first five months' depletion assuming the land has a net salvage value of zero after the ore is mined, and (d) the first five months' depreciation on machinery.

Analysis Component

Describe both the similarities and differences in amortization, depletion, and depreciation.

Problem 8-7A
Goodwill estimation
and analysis

P6 E**x**

Rent-A-Way, an equipment rental business, has the following balance sheet on December 31, 2002:

Assets		
Cash		$ 87,800
Equipment	$725,300	
Accumulated depreciation—Equipment	303,500	421,800
Buildings	360,000	
Accumulated depreciation—Buildings	160,000	200,000
Land		102,000
Total assets		$811,600

[continued on next page]

[continued from previous page]

Liabilities and Equity	
Accounts payable	$100,400
Long-term note payable	285,400
Equity	425,800
Total liabilities and equity	$811,600

In this industry, normal annual net income averages 20% of equity. Rent-A-Way regularly expects to earn $100,000 annually. The balance sheet amounts are reasonable estimates of market values for both assets (except goodwill) and liabilities. In negotiations to sell the business, Rent-A-Way proposes to measure goodwill by capitalizing at a rate of 15% the amount of above-normal net income. The potential buyer thinks that goodwill should be valued at five times the amount of above-normal net income.

Required

1. Compute the amount of goodwill as proposed by Rent-A-Way.
2. Compute the amount of goodwill as proposed by the potential buyer.
3. The buyer purchases the business for the net asset amount (assets less liabilities) reported on the December 31, 2002, balance sheet plus the amount proposed by Rent-A-Way for goodwill. What is the buyer's purchase price?
4. If the buyer earns $100,225 of net income in its first year after acquiring the business under the terms in part 3, what rate of return does the buyer earn on this investment for the first year? Explain how goodwill impacts the buyer's net income computation.

Check   (1) $98,933
(2) $74,200

Check   (4) 19.1%

Asheville Company negotiates a lump-sum purchase of several assets from a contractor who is relocating. The purchase is completed on January 1, 2002, at a total cash price of $1,720,000 for a building, land, land improvements, and six trucks. The estimated market values of the assets are building, $895,400; land, $430,200; land improvements, $248,200; and six trucks, $205,200. The company's fiscal year ends on December 31.

Required

1. Prepare a table to allocate the lump-sum purchase price to the separate assets purchased (round percents to the nearest 1%). Prepare the journal entry to record the purchase.
2. Compute the depreciation expense for year 2002 on the building using the straight-line method, assuming a 12-year life and a $120,000 salvage value.
3. Compute the depreciation expense for year 2002 on the land improvements assuming a 10-year life and double-declining-balance depreciation.

Analysis Component

4. Defend or refute this statement: Accelerated depreciation results in payment of more taxes over the asset's life.

PROBLEM SET B

Problem 8-1B 🖫
Plant asset costs; depreciation methods

C1 C2 A1 P1 P2

Check   (2) $61,667
(3) $48,160

In January 2002, BuyTech pays $1,550,000 for a tract of land with two buildings. It plans to demolish Building A and build a new shop in its place. Building B will be a company office; it is appraised at a $489,900 value, with a useful life of 15 years and a $100,000 salvage value. A lighted parking lot near Building B has improvements (Land Improvements B) valued at $127,200 that are expected to last another six years with no salvage value. Without the buildings and improvements, the tract of land is valued at $800,900. BuyTech also incurs the following additional costs:

Problem 8-2B
Asset cost allocation; straight-line depreciation

C1 C2 P1 P2

Cost to demolish Building A	$ 122,000
Cost of additional landscaping	174,500
Cost to construct new building (Building C), having a useful life of 20 years and a $258,000 salvage value	1,458,000
Cost of new land improvements (Land Improvements C) near building C, having a 10-year useful life and no salvage value	103,500

Required

1. Prepare a table with the following column headings: Land, Building B, Building C, Land Improvements B, and Land Improvements C. Allocate the costs incurred by BuyTech to the appropriate columns and total each column (round percents to the nearest 1%).

2. Prepare a single journal entry to record all incurred costs assuming they are paid in cash on January 1, 2002.

3. Using the straight-line method, prepare the December 31 adjusting entries to record depreciation for the 12 months of 2002 when these assets were in use.

Problem 8-3B
Computing and revising
depreciation; revenue and
capital expenditures

C3 P1 P3

Pronto Delivery Service completed the following transactions and events involving the purchase and operation of its equipment for its business:

2002

Jan. 1   Paid $25,860 cash plus $1,810 in sales tax for a new delivery van that was estimated to have a five-year life and a $3,670 salvage value. Van costs are recorded in the Equipment account.

Jan. 3   Paid $1,850 to install sorting racks in the van for more accurate and quicker delivery of packages. This increases the estimated salvage value of the van by another $230.

Dec. 31   Recorded annual straight-line depreciation on the van.

2003

Jan. 1   Paid $2,080 to overhaul the van's engine, which increased the van's estimated useful life by two years.

May 10   Paid $800 to repair the van after the driver backed it into a loading dock.

Dec. 31   Record annual straight-line depreciation on the van.

Required

Prepare journal entries to record these transactions and events.

Problem 8-4B
Computing and revising
depreciation; selling plant
assets

C3 P2 P4

Precision Instruments completed the following transactions and events involving its machinery:

2002

Jan. 1   Paid $107,800 cash plus $6,470 in sales tax for a new machine. The machine is estimated to have a six-year life and a $10,270 salvage value.

Dec. 31   Recorded annual straight-line depreciation on the machinery.

2003

Dec. 31   Due to new information obtained earlier in the year, the machine's estimated useful life was changed from six to four years, and the estimated salvage value was increased to $14,100. Recorded annual straight-line depreciation on the machinery.

2004

Dec. 31   Recorded annual straight-line depreciation on the machinery.

Dec. 31   Sold the machine for $25,240 cash.

Required

Prepare journal entries to record these transactions and events.

Problem 8-5B
Depreciation methods;
disposal of plant assets

C3 P1 P2 P4

Part 1. On January 2, Brodie Co. purchases and installs a new machine costing $324,000 with a five-year life and an estimated $30,000 salvage value. Management estimates the machine will produce 1,470,000 units of product during its life. Actual production of units is as follows: year 1, 355,600; year 2, 320,400; year 3, 317,000; year 4, 342,600; and year 5, 138,500. The total number of units produced by the end of year 5 exceeds the original estimate—this difference was not predicted. (The machine must not be depreciated below its estimated salvage value.)

Required

Prepare a table with the following column headings and compute depreciation for each year (and to-tal depreciation of all years combined) for the machine under each depreciation method.

Year	Straight-Line	Units-of-Production	Double-Declining-Balance

Part 2. On January 1, Trek purchases a used machine for $150,000 and readies it for use the next day at a cost of $3,510. On January 4, it is mounted on a new platform costing $4,600, and it began operating. Management estimates the machine will be used for seven years and have an $18,110 sal-vage value. Depreciation is to be charged on a straight-line basis. On December 31, at the end of its sixth year of use, the machine is disposed of.

Required

a. Prepare journal entries to record the machine's purchase and the costs to ready and install it. Cash is paid for all costs incurred.

b. Prepare journal entries to record depreciation of the machine at December 31 of its first year in operations and at December 31 in the year of its disposal.

c. Prepare journal entries to record the machine's disposal under each of the following separate as-sumptions: (i) it is sold for $28,000 cash; (ii) it is sold for $52,000 cash; and (iii) it is destroyed in a fire and the insurance company pays $25,000 cash to settle the loss claim.

Part 1. On January 1, 2000, Grandview Co. enters into a 12-year lease on a building. The lease con-tract requires: (1) annual (prepaid) rental payments of $36,000 each January 1 throughout the life of the lease and (2) that the lessee will pay for all additions and improvements to the leased property. On January 1, 2007, Grandview decides to sublease the space to Moberly Co. for the remaining five years of the lease—Moberly pays $40,000 to Grandview for the right to sublease and agrees to as-sume the obligation to pay the $36,000 annual rent to the building owner beginning Jan. 1, 2007. After taking possession of the leased space, Moberly pays for improving the office portion of the leased space at a $20,000 cost. The improvements are paid for on Jan. 3, 2007, and are estimated to have a useful life equal to the 13 years remaining in the life of the building.

Problem 8-6B [icon]
Intangible assets and natural resources
A1 P5 P6

Required

Prepare entries for Moberly to record (a) its payment to Grandview for the right to sublease the build-ing space, (b) its payment of the 2007 annual rent to the building owner, and (c) its payment for the office improvements. Prepare Moberly's year-end adjusting entries required on December 31, 2007, to (d) amortize the $40,000 cost of the sublease, (e) amortize the office improvements, and (f) record rent expense.

Part 2. On February 19 of the current year, Rock Solid Co. pays $5,400,000 for land estimated to contain 4 million tons of recoverable ore. It installs machinery costing $400,000 that has a 16-year life and no salvage value and is capable of mining the ore deposit in 12 years. The machinery is paid for on March 21, 11 days before mining operations begin. The company removes and sells 254,000 tons of ore during its first nine months of operations. Depreciation of the machinery is in proportion to the mine's depletion as the machinery will be abandoned after the ore is mined.

Required

Preparation Component

Prepare entries to record (a) the purchase of the land, (b) the cost and installation of machinery, (c) the first nine months' depletion assuming the land has a net salvage value of zero after the ore is mined, and (d) the first nine months' depreciation on machinery.

Analysis Component

Describe both the similarities and differences in amortization, depletion, and depreciation.

Problem 8-7B 📖
Goodwill estimation
and analysis

P6

Tiki Casual Wear has the following balance sheet on December 31, 2003:

Assets		
Cash		$ 148,700
Merchandise inventory		608,950
Buildings	$ 452,800	
Accumulated depreciation—Buildings	212,800	240,000
Land		185,900
Total assets		$1,183,550
Liabilities and Equity		
Accounts payable		$ 108,520
Long-term note payable		415,975
Equity		659,055
Total liabilities and equity		$1,183,550

In this industry, normal annual net income averages 28% of equity. Tiki regularly expects to earn $200,000 annually. The balance sheet amounts are reasonable estimates of market values for both assets (except goodwill) and liabilities. In negotiations to sell the business, Tiki proposes to measure goodwill by capitalizing at a rate of 10% the amount of above-normal net income. The potential buyer believes that goodwill should be valued at eight times the amount of above-normal net income.

Required

Check (1) $154,650
(2) $123,720

1. Compute the amount of goodwill as proposed by Tiki.

2. Compute the amount of goodwill as proposed by the potential buyer.

3. The buyer purchases the business for the net asset amount (assets less liabilities) reported on the December 31, 2003, balance sheet plus the amount proposed by Tiki for goodwill. What is the buyer's purchase price?

Check (4) 24.6%

4. If the buyer earns $200,175 of net income in its first year after acquiring the business under the terms in part 3, what rate of return does the buyer earn on this investment for the first year? Is the goodwill asset amortized or not? Explain.

BEYOND THE NUMBERS

Reporting in Action

C4 A1 A2 📖

NIKE

BTN 8-1   Refer to the financial statements for **Nike** in Appendix A to answer the following:

1. What percent of the original cost of Nike's property, plant, and equipment remains to be depreciated as of May 31, 2000, and May 31, 1999? Assume these assets have no salvage value.

2. Over what length(s) of time is Nike amortizing its intangible assets?

3. What is the change in total property, plant, and equipment (before accumulated depreciation) for the year ended May 31, 2000? What is the amount of cash provided (used) by investing activities for property, plant, and equipment for the year ended May 31, 2000? What is one possible explanation for the difference between these two amounts?

4. Compute Nike's total asset turnover for the year ended May 31, 2000.

Swoosh Ahead

5. Access Nike's financial statements for fiscal years ending after May 31, 2000, at its Web site (www.nike.com) or the SEC's EDGAR database (www.sec.gov). Recompute Nike's total asset turnover for the additional years' data you collect. Comment on any differences relative to the turnover computed in part 4.

BTN 8-2   Key comparative figures ($ in millions) for Nike and Reebok follow:

Key Figures	Nike			Reebok		
	Current Year	One Year Prior	Two Years Prior	Current Year	One Year Prior	Two Years Prior
Total assets	$5,856.9	$5,247.7	$5,397.4	$1,564.1	$1,684.6	$1,756.1
Net sales	8,995.1	8,776.9	9,553.1	2,899.9	3,224.6	3,643.6

Required

1. Compute total asset turnover for the most recent two years for both Nike and Reebok using the data shown.
2. Which company is more efficient in generating net sales given the total assets it employs?

BTN 8-3   Janice Griffin owns a small business and manages its accounting. Her company just finished a year in which a large amount of borrowed funds were invested in a new building addition as well as in equipment and fixture additions. Janice's banker requires her to submit semiannual financial statements so he can monitor the financial health of her business. He has warned her that if profit margins erode, he might raise the interest rate on the borrowed funds to reflect the increased loan risk from the bank's point of view. Janice knows profit margin is likely to decline this year. As she prepares year-end adjusting entries, she decides to apply the following depreciation rule: all asset additions are considered to be in use on the first day of the following month. (The previous rule assumed assets are in use on the first day of the month nearest to the purchase date.)

Required

1. Identify decisions that managers like Janice must make in applying depreciation methods.
2. Is Janice's rule an ethical violation, or is it a legitimate decision in computing depreciation?
3. How will Janice's depreciation rule affect the profit margin of her business?

BTN 8-4   Teams are to select an industry, and each team member is to select a different company in that industry. Each team member is to acquire the financial statements (form 10-K) of the company selected—see the company's Web site or the SEC's EDGAR database (www.sec.gov). Use the financial statements to compute total asset turnover. Communicate with teammates via a meeting, e-mail, or telephone to discuss the meaning of this ratio, how different companies compare to each other, and the industry norm. The team must prepare a one-page report that describes the ratios for each company and identifies the conclusions reached during the team's discussion.

BTN 8-5   Access Adaptec's (ticker: ADPT) 10-K report for its fiscal year ended March 31, 2000, filed on June 27, 2000, at www.edgar-online.com to answer the following.

Required

1. Read the overview of Adaptec's business and briefly describe the types of products it produces.
2. On page 7 of its 10-K, what information is provided regarding the company's patents?
3. Does Adaptec show any patent-related revenue or expense on its consolidated statement of operations (income statement)?

BTN 8-6   Each team member is to become an expert on one depreciation method to facilitate teammates' understanding of that method. Follow these procedures:

a. Each team member is to select an area for expertise from one of the following depreciation methods: straight-line, units-of-production, or double-declining-balance.

Point: This activity can follow an overview of each method. Step 1 allows for three areas of expertise. Larger teams will have some duplication of areas, but the straight-line choice should not be duplicated. Expert teams can use the book and consult with the instructor.

b. Expert teams are to be formed from those who have selected the same area of expertise. The instructor will identify the location where each expert team meets.

c. Using the following data, expert teams are to collaborate and develop a presentation answering the requirements. Expert team members must write the presentation in a format they can show to their learning teams.

Data and Requirements On January 8, 2002, Whitewater Riders purchases a van to transport rafters back to the point of departure at the conclusion of the rafting adventures they operate. The cost of the van is $44,000. It has an estimated salvage value of $2,000 and is expected to be used for four years and driven 60,000 miles. The van is expected to be driven 12,000 miles in 2002, 18,000 miles in 2003, 21,000 in 2004, and 10,000 in 2005.

1. Compute annual depreciation expense for each year of the van's estimated useful life.

2. Explain when and how annual depreciation is recorded.

3. Explain the impact on income of this depreciation method versus others over the van's life.

4. Identify the van's book value for each year of its life and illustrate the reporting of this amount for any one year.

d. Re-form original learning teams. In rotation, experts are to present to their teams the results from part *c*. Experts are to encourage and respond to questions.

Business Week Activity
C1 P6

BTN 8-7 Read the commentary "Goodwill Accounting" in the August 30, 1999, issue of *Business Week*. (The book's Web site provides a free link.)

Required

1. Explain how goodwill is calculated in accounting terms.

2. Describe how goodwill was accounted for prior to 1970.

3. How was goodwill accounted for from 1970 through 2001?

4. What is the current (new) standard in accounting for goodwill?

Entrepreneurial Decision
A2
e *d*

BTN 8-8 Jason Gannon is an entrepreneur and owner of Game Haven, which is a game-room gallery providing high-tech action games aimed at teenagers and young adults. Game Haven consistently earns annual net sales of $350,000 on an average total asset investment of $100,000. To increase sales, Gannon proposes to expand the game room, which would increase average total assets by $50,000. This expansion is expected to increase net sales by $250,000.

Required

1. Compute this company's total asset turnover under (*a*) current conditions and (*b*) proposed conditions.

2. Evaluate and comment on the merits of Gannon's proposal given your analysis in part (1). Identify any concerns you would express about the proposal.

Hitting the Road
C1 P5 P6

BTN 8-9 Team up with one or more classmates for this activity. Identify companies in your community or area of the country that must account for at least one of the following assets: natural resource; patent; lease; leasehold improvement; copyright; trademark; and goodwill. You might need to identify seven different companies for the seven assets, or you might find a company having more than one type of asset. Once you identify a company with a specific asset, describe the accounting this company uses to allocate the cost of that asset to the periods benefited from its use.

9

Reporting and Analyzing Current Liabilities

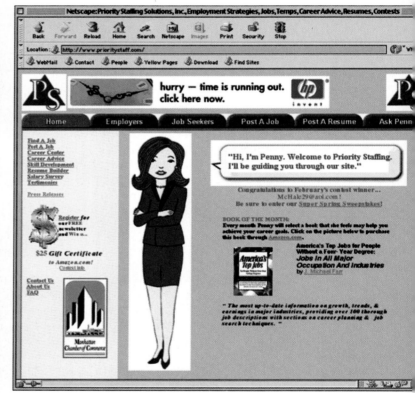

"We've created a friendly, comfortable, and professional atmosphere"—Deborah Wainstein

A Look Back

Chapter 8 focused on long-term assets including plant assets, natural resources, and intangibles. We showed how to record their costs, allocate their costs to periods benefiting from their use, record their disposal, and assess their turnover.

A Look at This Chapter

This chapter emphasizes current liabilities and introduces long-term liabilities. We explain how to identify, compute, record, and report current liabilities in financial statements. We also analyze and interpret these liabilities.

A Look Ahead

Chapter 10 focuses on long-term liabilities. We explain how these liabilities are valued, recorded, amortized, and reported in financial statements. We also describe the accounting for leases and pensions.

Learning Objectives

Conceptual

C1 Describe current and long-term liabilities and their characteristics.

C2 Identify and describe known current liabilities.

C3 Explain how to account for contingent liabilities.

Analytical

A1 Compute the times interest earned ratio and use it to analyze liabilities.

Procedural

P1 Prepare entries to account for short-term notes payable.

P2 Compute and record *employee* payroll deductions and liabilities.

P3 Compute and record *employer* payroll expenses and liabilities.

P4 Account for estimated liabilities, including warranties and income taxes.

Decision Feature

Se Habla Temp

e NEW YORK—Need a Spanish-speaking secretary, a Korean interpreter, or a salesperson fluent in Hindi? Deborah Wainstein's **Priority Staffing Solutions (www.PriorityStaff.com)** can deliver. A multicultural phenomenon herself, Wainstein is the daughter of a Russian-Jewish father and a Colombian mother. Wainstein was educated in Hebrew, and spoke Spanish with her mother at home. "I remember being picked on, we were so different," the Brooklyn native says. "Now I've been able to work it to my benefit."

The 27-year-old Wainstein stumbled into staffing, joining a friend's company. In 1999, she went solo. "I work probably 70 hours a week," she says. "I'm here at 8 o'clock in the morning and I don't leave until . . . well, let's just say 9 P.M. is an early night." But Wainstein is not complaining. Priority Staffing now has nine permanent employees, sends out 60 multilingual temps a day, and has 80 clients, including big outfits like **Revlon** and telecom provider **RCN Corporation.**

To succeed, Wainstein learned to handle many aspects of business, including the crucial task of managing liabilities for payroll, supplies, employee benefits, vacations, training, and taxes. Without her effective management of liabilities, Priority Staffing would not be where it is today. If you want your business to be a success, Wainstein says, "you need to realize [that liability management is] not something you walk away from." This chapter focuses on measuring and analyzing current liabilities, tasks that Wainstein emphasizes. Wainstein projects her annual sales at $4 million. And that's a success in any language. [Sources: Priority Staffing Solutions Web site, January 2002; *Entrepreneur*, April 2001; *Business Week*, April 2, 2001.]

Previous chapters introduced us to liabilities such as accounts payable, notes payable, wages payable, and unearned revenues. In this chapter, we learn more about these liabilities and additional ones such as warranties, taxes, payroll, vacation pay, and deferred taxes. We also describe contingent liabilities and introduce some long-term liabilities. Our focus is on how to define, classify, measure, and analyze liabilities in order to report useful information about them to business decision makers.

Characteristics of Liabilities

C1 Describe current and long-term liabilities and their characteristics.

This section discusses important characteristics of liabilities and how they are classified and reported.

Defining Liabilities

A *liability* is a probable future payment of assets or services that a company is presently obligated to make as a result of past transactions or events. This definition includes three crucial factors:

- ■ A past transaction or event.
- ■ A present obligation.
- ■ A future payment of assets or services.

Exhibit 9.1

Characteristics of a Liability

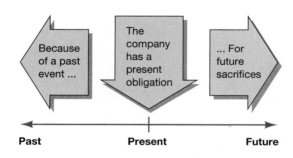

Because of a past event ... → The company has a present obligation → ... For future sacrifices

Past   Present   Future

These three important elements are portrayed visually in Exhibit 9.1. Liabilities do not include all expected future payments. For example, most companies expect to pay wages to their employees in upcoming months and years, but these future payments are not liabilities because no past event such as employee work resulted in a present obligation. Instead, the liabilities arise when employees perform their work and earn the wages.

Classifying Liabilities

Information about liabilities is more useful when the balance sheet identifies them as either current or long term. Decision makers need to know when obligations are due so they can plan for them and take appropriate action.

Current Liabilities

Current liabilities, also called *short-term liabilities,* are obligations due within one year or the company's operating cycle, whichever is longer. They are expected to be paid using current assets or by creating other current liabilities. Common examples of current liabilities are accounts payable, short-term notes payable, wages payable, warranty liabilities, lease liabilities, taxes payable, and unearned revenues.

Point: Improper classification of liabilities can distort key ratios used in financial statement analysis and decision making.

Current liabilities are different across companies because they depend on the type of company operations. **Harley-Davidson,** for instance, recently included the following current accrued liabilities related to its motorcycle operations ($000s):

Warranty/recalls	$14,655
Dealer incentive programs	40,322

Global: In some countries such as France, the balance sheet does not separate current liabilities into their own category.

Univision, the leading Spanish-language television broadcaster in the United States, reports a much different set of current liabilities. It discloses more than $140 million in current liabilities made up of items such as television programming and license fee liabilities.

Long-Term Liabilities

A company's obligations not expected to be paid within the longer of one year or the company's operating cycle are reported as **long-term liabilities.** They can include long-term notes payable, warranty liabilities, lease liabilities, and bonds payable. They are sometimes reported on the balance sheet in a single long-term liabilities total or in multiple categories. Domino's Pizza, for instance, reports the following long-term liabilities ($ millions): long-term debt, $696; insurance reserves, $15; other, $22. They are reported after current liabilities. A single liability also can be divided between the current and noncurrent sections if a company expects to make payments toward it in both the short and long term. Domino's reports ($ millions) long-term debt, $696; and current portion of long-term debt, $21. The second item is reported in current liabilities. We sometimes see liabilities that do not have a fixed due date but instead are payable on the creditor's demand. These are reported as current liabilities because of the possibility of payment in the near term. Exhibit 9.2 shows amounts of current and long-term liabilities for selected companies.

Point: The current ratio will be overstated if a company fails to classify any portion of long-term debt due next period as a current liability.

Decision Track 9.1		*d*
Decision Point	**Information Search**	**Analyze & Evaluate**
What is the company's current ability to obtain (immediate) short-term financing?	Financial statement notes; available lines of credit.	Identify available lines of credit; lines of credit should be higher when liquid assets are low when compared to current liabilities.

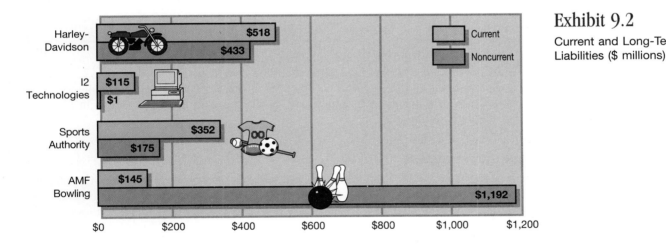

Exhibit 9.2

Current and Long-Term Liabilities ($ millions)

Uncertainty in Liabilities

Accounting for liabilities involves addressing three important questions: Whom to pay? When to pay? How much to pay? Answers to these questions are often decided when a liability is incurred. For example, if a company has a $100 account payable to a specific individual, payable on March 15, the answers are clear. The company knows whom to pay, when to pay, and how much to pay. However, the answers to one or more of these three questions are uncertain for some liabilities.

Uncertainty in Whom to Pay

Liabilities can involve uncertainty in whom to pay. For instance, a company can create a liability with a known amount when issuing a note that is payable to its holder. In this case, a specific amount is payable to the note's holder at a specified date, but the company does not know who the holder is until that date. Despite this uncertainty, the company reports this liability on its balance sheet.

Uncertainty in When to Pay

A company can have an obligation of a known amount to a known creditor but not know when it must be paid. For example, a legal services firm can accept fees in advance from a client who plans to use the firm's services in the future. This means that the firm has a liability that it settles by providing services at an unknown future date. Although this uncertainty exists, the firm's balance sheet must report this liability. These types of obligations are reported as current liabilities because they are likely to be settled in the short term.

Uncertainty in How Much to Pay

A company can be aware of an obligation but not know how much will be required to settle it. For example, a company using electrical power is billed only after the meter has been read. This cost is incurred and the liability created before a bill is received. A liability to the power company is reported as an estimated amount if the balance sheet is prepared before a bill arrives.

Quick Check

1. What is a liability?

2. Is every expected future payment a liability?

3. If a liability is payable in 15 months, is it classified as current or long term?

Answers—p. 402

Known (Determinable) Liabilities

Most liabilities arise from situations with little uncertainty. They are set by agreements, contracts, or laws and are measurable. These liabilities are **known liabilities,** also called *definitely determinable liabilities.* Known liabilities include accounts payable, notes payable, payroll, sales taxes, unearned revenues, and leases. We describe how to account for these known liabilities in this section.

C2 Identify and describe known current liabilities.

Accounts Payable

Accounts payable, or trade accounts payable, are amounts owed to suppliers for products or services purchased with credit. Accounting for accounts payable is explained and illustrated in several prior chapters. Much of our discussion of merchandising activities in Chapters 4 and 5, for instance, dealt with accounts payable.

Sales Taxes Payable

Nearly all states and many cities levy taxes on retail sales. Sales taxes are stated as a percent of selling prices. The retailer (seller) collects sales taxes from customers when sales occur and remits these collections (often monthly) to the proper government agency. Since retailers currently owe these collections to the government, this amount is a current liability for retailers. Home Depot, for instance, reports sales taxes payable of $269 million in its recent annual report. To illustrate, if Home Depot sells materials on August 31 for $6,000 cash that are subject to a 5% sales tax, the revenue portion of this transaction is recorded as follows:

Assets = Liabilities + Equity
+6,300   +300   +6,000

Aug. 31	Cash	6,300	
	Sales		6,000
	Sales Taxes Payable ($6,000 × 0.05)		300
	To record cash sales and 5% sales tax.		

Sales Taxes Payable is debited and Cash credited when it remits these collections to the government. Sales Taxes Payable is not an expense. It arises because laws require retailers to collect this cash from customers for the government.

Unearned Revenues

Unearned revenues (also called *deferred revenues, collections in advance,* and *prepayments*) are amounts received in advance from customers for future products or services. Advance ticket sales for sporting events or music concerts are examples. The **Boston Celtics**, for instance, reported "deferred game revenues" including advance ticket sales of $10.4 million in its recent balance sheet. When the Celtics sell $5 million of season tickets, its entry is

Point: To *defer* a revenue means to postpone recognition of a revenue collected in advance until it is earned. Sport teams must defer recognition of ticket sales until games are played.

June 30	Cash	5,000,000	
	Unearned Season Ticket Revenue		5,000,000
	To record sale of Celtic season tickets.		

Assets = Liabilities + Equity
+5,000,000   +5,000,000

When each game is played, the Celtics record revenue for the portion earned:

Oct. 31	Unearned Season Ticket Revenue	60,000	
	Season Ticket Revenue		60,000
	To record Celtic season ticket revenues earned.		

Assets = Liabilities + Equity
              −60,000   +60,000

Unearned Season Ticket Revenue is an unearned revenue account and is reported as a current liability. Unearned revenues also arise with airline ticket sales, magazine subscriptions, construction projects, hotel reservations, and custom orders.

Short-Term Notes Payable

A **short-term note payable** is a written promise to pay a specified amount on a definite future date within one year or the company's operating cycle, whichever is longer. These promissory notes are negotiable (as are checks), meaning they can be transferred from party to party by endorsement. The written documentation provided by notes is helpful in resolving disputes and for pursuing legal actions involving these liabilities. Most notes payable bear interest to compensate for use of the money amount until payment is made. Short-term notes payable can arise from many transactions. A company that purchases merchandise on credit can sometimes extend the credit period by signing a note to replace an account payable. Such notes also can arise when money is borrowed from a bank. We describe both of these cases in this section.

P1 Prepare entries to account for short-term notes payable.

Point: Required characteristics for negotiability of a note: (1) unconditional promise, (2) in writing, (3) specific amount, and (4) definite due date.

Note Given to Extend Credit Period

A company can replace an account payable with a note payable. A common example is a creditor that requires the substitution of an interest-bearing note for an overdue account payable that does not bear interest. A less common situation occurs when a debtor's weak financial condition motivates the creditor to obtain a note, sometimes for a lesser amount, and to close the account to ensure that this customer makes no additional credit purchases.

Illustration of note to extend credit period. To illustrate, let's assume that on August 23, Irwin asks to extend its past-due $600 account payable to McGraw. After some negotiations, McGraw agrees to accept $100 cash and a 60-day, 12%, $500 note payable to replace the account payable. Irwin records the transaction with this entry:

Assets = Liabilities + Equity
−100   −600
+500

Aug. 23	Accounts Payable—McGraw	600	
	Cash		100
	Notes Payable—McGraw		500
	Gave $100 cash and a 60-day, 12% note for payment on account.		

Point: Accounts payable are detailed in a subsidiary ledger, but notes payable are sometimes not. A file with copies of notes often serves as a subsidiary ledger.

Signing the note does not pay Irwin's debt. Instead, the form of debt is changed from an account payable to a note payable. McGraw prefers the note payable over the account payable because it earns interest and it is written documentation of the debt's existence, term, and amount. When the note comes due, Irwin pays the note and interest by giving McGraw a check for $510. This payment is recorded with this entry:

Assets = Liabilities + Equity
−510   −500   −10

Oct. 22	Notes Payable—McGraw	500	
	Interest Expense	10	
	Cash		510
	Paid note with interest ($500 × 12% × 60/360).		

Point: Companies commonly compute interest using a 360-day year. This is known as the *banker's rule.*

Interest expense is computed by multiplying the principal of the note ($500) by the annual interest rate (12%) for the fraction of the year the note is outstanding (60 days/360 days).

Note Given to Borrow from Bank

Point: Cash received from long-term borrowing is reported on the statement of cash flows as a source of financing (cash from short-term borrowing is part of operating activities). Interest incurred on a note is reported on the income statement as an expense.

Point: If a client borrows money from a bank, the loan is reported as an asset (receivable) on the bank's balance sheet.

A bank nearly always requires a borrower to sign a promissory note when making a loan. When the note matures, the borrower repays the note with an amount larger than the amount borrowed. The difference between the amount borrowed and the amount repaid is *interest.* This section considers two types of notes. The first type states that the note's signer promises to pay *principal* (the amount borrowed) plus interest. In this case, the *face value* of the note equals principal. Face value is the value shown on the face (front) of the note. The second type occurs when a bank has a borrower sign a note with a face value that includes both principal and interest. In this case, the note's signer receives *less* than the note's face value. The difference between the borrowed amount and the note's face value is interest. Since the borrowed amount is less than the note's face value, the difference is called **discount on note payable.** To illustrate these two types of notes, assume that a company needs $2,000 for a project and borrows this money from a bank at 12% annual interest. The loan is made on September 30, 2002, and is due in 60 days.

Face value equals amount borrowed. Assume that the borrowing company signs a note with a face value equal to the amount borrowed. The note includes a statement similar to this: *"I promise to pay $2,000 plus interest at 12% within 60 days after September 30."* This simple note is shown in Exhibit 9.3.

Exhibit 9.3

Note with Face Value Equal to Amount Borrowed

Promissory Note

$2,000
Face Value

Sept. 30, 2002
Date

Sixty days after date, *I* promise to pay to the order of

National Bank
Boston, MA

Two thousand and no/100 - **Dollars**

plus interest at the annual rate of 12% .

Janet Lee

The borrower records its receipt of cash and the new liability with this entry:

Sept. 30	Cash	2,000	
	Notes Payable		2,000
	Borrowed $2,000 cash with a 60-day, 12%, $2,000 note.		

Assets = Liabilities + Equity
+2,000   +2,000

When principal and interest are paid, the borrower records payment with this entry:

Nov. 29	Notes Payable	2,000	
	Interest Expense	40	
	Cash		2,040
	Paid note with interest ($2,000 × 12% × 60/360).		

Assets = Liabilities + Equity
−2,040   −2,000   −40

Face value equals amount borrowed plus interest. Assume that the borrower signs a note with the interest included in its face value. This type of note includes a promise similar to this: *"I promise to pay $2,040 within 60 days after September 30."* This note is shown in Exhibit 9.4. In this case assume that the borrower receives $2,000 cash; notice that the note does not refer to the rate used to compute the $40 of interest included in the $2,040 face value. In other respects, this note is similar to the one in Exhibit 9.3. Since this note lacks a stated interest rate, it is sometimes called a **noninterest-bearing note,** which can be misleading since the note does bear interest that is included in the face value.

Point: When interest is included in face value, the borrowing process is referred to as *discounting a note* since the borrower receives less than the face value, or a discounted amount.

Promissory Note

$2,040   Sept. 30, 2002
Face Value   **Date**

Sixty days   after date,   *I*   promise to pay to the order of

National Bank
Boston, MA

Two thousand forty and no/100 --------------------------- **Dollars.**

Janet Lee

Exhibit 9.4

Note with Face Value Equal to Amount Borrowed plus Interest

When the face value of a note includes principal and interest, the borrower usually records this note with an entry to credit Notes Payable for its face value and to record the interest in a Discount on Notes Payable account as follows:

Point: Use of a contra liability account allows us to always enter face value when recording notes payable.

Sept. 30	Cash	2,000	
	Discount on Notes Payable	40	
	Notes Payable		2,040
	Borrowed $2,000 cash with a 60-day, $2,040 note.		

Assets = Liabilities + Equity
+2,000   +2,040
          −40

Discount on Notes Payable is a contra liability account to the Notes Payable account. If a balance sheet is prepared after this transaction on September 30, the $40 discount is subtracted from the $2,040 note to reflect the $2,000 net amount borrowed:[1]

Point: A discount reflects deferred interest expense. The matching principle supports regular recognition of this expense over time.

| Notes payable .... | $2,040 | |
| Less discount on notes payable ...... | 40 | $2,000 |

---

[1] We can approximate the annual interest rate on a short-term loan as **(Interest paid ÷ Amount received) × (360 days ÷ Loan period in days).** For the note in Exhibit 9.4, this formula yields: ($40/$2,000) × (360/60) = 12%.

When this note matures 60 days later on November 29, the entry to record the company's $2,040 payment to the bank is

$$Assets = Liabilities + Equity$$
$$-2,040 \quad -2,040 \quad -40$$
$$+40$$

Nov. 29	Notes Payable	2,040	
	Interest Expense	40	
	Cash		2,040
	Discount on Notes Payable		40
	Paid note with interest.		

End-of-Period Adjustment to Notes

When the end of an accounting period occurs between the signing of a note payable and its maturity date, the *matching principle* requires us to record the accrued but unpaid interest on the note. To illustrate, let's return to the earlier short-term note and assume that the company borrows $2,000 cash on December 16, 2002, instead of September 30. This 60-day note matures on February 14, 2003, and the company's fiscal year ends on December 31. Thus, we need to record interest expense for the final 15 days in December. The adjusting entry depends on the type of note.

Face value equals amount borrowed. When the note's face value equals the amount borrowed, any accrued interest is charged to expense and credited to an Interest Payable account. Specifically, we know that 15 days of the 60-day loan period for the $2,000, 12% note have elapsed by December 31. This means that one-fourth (15 days/60 days) of the $40 total interest is an expense of year 2002. The borrower records this expense with the following adjusting entry:

2002			
Dec. 31	Interest Expense	10	
	Interest Payable		10
	To record accrued interest on note ($2,000 ×		
	12% × 15/360).		

When this note matures on February 14, the borrower must recognize 45 days of interest expense for year 2003 and remove the balances of the two liability accounts:

2003			
Feb. 14	Interest Expense*	30	
	Interest Payable	10	
	Notes Payable	2,000	
	Cash		2,040
	*Paid note with interest. *($2,000 × 12% × 45/360)*		

Face value equals amount borrowed plus interest. When the face value of the note *includes* interest, any accrued interest is charged to Interest expense with an adjustment to the Discount on Notes Payable account. Specifically, for the $2,040 noninterest-bearing note entered into on December 16, the adjusting entry on December 31 needs to record the accrual for 15 days of interest. Accrued interest is recorded by reducing the balance of the contra

---

Example: What is the annual interest rate for a (1) $2,000, 12%, 60-day note and (2) $2,000 noninterest-bearing, 60-day note with 12% interest included in its face? *Hint:* In the first case, the borrower receives $2,000; in the second, the borrower receives $1,960 ($2,000 less $40 interest). *Answer:*
Case 1 rate = $40/$2,000 = 2.0% for 60 days (or 12.0% annually).
Case 2 rate = $40/$1,960 = 2.041% for 60 days (or 12.245% annually).

$$Assets = Liabilities + Equity$$
$$+10 \quad -10$$

Example: If this note is dated December 1 instead of December 16, how much expense is recorded on December 31? *Answer:*
$2,000 × 12% × 30/360 = $20

$$Assets = Liabilities + Equity$$
$$-2,040 \quad -10 \quad -30$$
$$-2,000$$

liability account from $40 to $30. This adjustment increases the net liability to $2,010 ($2,040 note less $30 discount):

2002			
Dec. 31	Interest Expense	10	
	Discount on Notes Payable		10
	To record accrued interest on note ($40 × 15/60).		

Assets = Liabilities + Equity
+10   −10

When this note matures, we need an entry both to accrue interest expense for its last 45 days and to record payment of both principal and interest:

2003			
Feb. 14	Interest Expense*	30	
	Notes Payable	2,040	
	Discount on Notes Payable		30
	Cash		2,040
	*Paid note with interest. *($40 × 45/60)*		

Assets = Liabilities + Equity
−2,040   −2,040   −30
                    +30

Quick Check

4. Why does a creditor prefer a note payable to a past-due account payable?

5. A company borrows money by signing a $1,050, six-month note payable. In recording the transaction, the company correctly debits $50 to Discount on Notes Payable. How much cash is borrowed? What annual rate of interest is charged?

Answers—p. 402

Payroll Liabilities

An employer incurs several expenses and liabilities from having employees. These expenses and liabilities are often large and arise from salaries and wages earned, from employee benefits, and from payroll taxes levied on the employer. **Anheuser-Busch**, for instance, reports payroll-related current liabilities of more than $250 million from "accrued salaries, wages and benefits." We discuss payroll liabilities and related accounts in this section. The appendix to this chapter describes important details about payroll reports, records, and procedures.

P2 Compute and record *employee* payroll deductions and liabilities.

Employee Payroll Deductions

Gross pay is the total compensation an employee earns including wages, salaries, commissions, bonuses, and any compensation earned before deductions such as taxes. (*Wages* usually refer to payments to employees at an hourly rate. *Salaries* usually refer to payments to employees at a monthly or yearly rate.) **Net pay,** also called *take-home pay,* is gross pay less all deductions. **Payroll deductions,** commonly

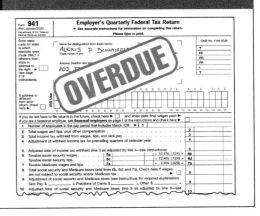

Decision Insight

Pay or Else Delay or failure to pay withholding taxes to the government has severe consequences. For example, a 100% penalty can be levied, with interest, on the unpaid balance. The government can even close a company, take its assets, and pursue legal actions against those involved.

called *withholdings,* are amounts withheld from an employee's gross pay, either required or voluntary. Required deductions result from laws and include income taxes and Social Security taxes. Voluntary deductions, at an employee's option, include pension and health contributions, union dues, and charitable giving. Exhibit 9.5 shows the typical payroll deductions of an employee. The employer withholds payroll deductions from employees' pay and is obligated to transmit this money to the designated organization. The employer records

Exhibit 9.5

Payroll Deductions

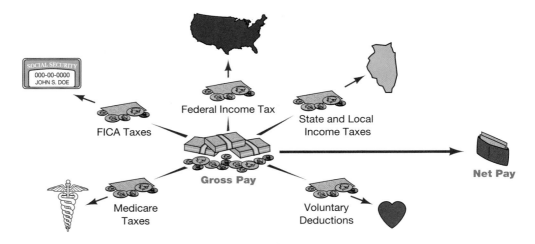

Topic Tackler 9-1

payroll deductions as current liabilities until these amounts are transmitted. This section discusses the major payroll deductions.

Employee FICA taxes. The federal Social Security system provides retirement, disability, survivorship, and medical benefits to qualified workers. Laws *require* employers to withhold **Federal Insurance Contributions Act (FICA) taxes** from employees' pay to cover costs of the system. Employers usually separate FICA taxes into two groups: (1) retirement, disability, and survivorship and (2) medical. For the first group, the Social Security system provides monthly cash payments to qualified retired workers for the rest of their lives. These payments are often called *Social Security benefits.* Taxes related to this group are often called *Social Security taxes.* For the second group, the system provides monthly payments to deceased workers' surviving families and to disabled workers who qualify for assistance. These payments are commonly called *Medicare benefits;* like those in the first group, they are paid with *Medicare taxes* (part of FICA taxes).

Law requires employers to withhold FICA taxes from each employee's salary or wages on each payday. The taxes for Social Security and Medicare are computed separately. For example, for the year 2000, the amount withheld from each employee's pay for Social Security tax was 6.2% of the first $76,200 the employee earns in the calendar year, or a maximum of $4,724.40. The Medicare tax was 1.45% of *all* wages the employee earns. Medicare tax has no maximum amount because the government wants to maintain the solvency of this program.

Employers must pay withheld taxes to the Internal Revenue Service (IRS) on specific filing dates during the year. Employers who fail to send the withheld taxes to the IRS on time can be assessed substantial penalties. Until all the taxes are sent to the IRS, they are included in employers' current liabilities. For any changes in rates or with the maximum earnings level, check the IRS Web site at www.IRS.USTreas.gov.

Employee income tax. Most employers are required to withhold federal income tax from each employee's paycheck. The amount withheld is computed using tables published by the IRS. The amount depends on the employee's annual earnings rate and the number of *withholding allowances* the employee claims. Allowances reduce the amount of taxes one owes the government. The more allowances one claims, the less tax the employer will withhold. Employees can claim allowances for themselves and their dependents. They also can claim additional allowances if they expect major declines in their taxable income for medical expenses. (An employee who claims more allowances than appropriate is subject to a fine.) Most states and many local governments require employers to withhold income taxes from employees' pay and to remit them promptly to the proper government agency. Until they are paid, withholdings are reported as a current liability on the employer's balance sheet.

Point: Part-time employees may claim "exempt from withholding" if they did not have any income tax liability in the prior year and do not expect any in the current year.

Point: IRS withholding tables are based on projecting weekly (or other period) pay into an annual figure.

Employee voluntary deductions. Beyond Social Security, Medicare, and income taxes, employers often withhold other amounts from employees' earnings. These withholdings arise from employee requests, contracts, unions, or other agreements. They can include amounts for charitable giving, medical insurance premiums, pension contributions, and union dues. Until they are paid, such withholdings are reported as part of employers' current liabilities.

Recording employee payroll deductions. Employers must accrue payroll expenses and liabilities at the end of each pay period. To illustrate, assume that an employee earns a salary of $2,000 per month. At the end of January, the employer's entry to accrue payroll expenses and liabilities for this employee is

				Assets = Liabilities + Equity
Jan. 31	Salaries Expense	2,000		
	FICA—Social Security Taxes Payable (6.2%)		124	+124 −2,000
	FICA—Medicare Taxes Payable (1.45%) . . .		29	+29
	Employee Federal Income Taxes Payable* . .		213	+213
	Employee Medical Insurance Payable*		85	+85
	Employee Union Dues Payable*		25	+25
	Accrued Payroll Payable		1,524	+1,524
	To record accrued payroll for January.			

* Amounts taken from employer's accounting records.

Salaries Expense (debit) shows that the employee earns a gross salary of $2,000. The first five payables (credits) show the liabilities the employer owes on behalf of this employee to cover FICA taxes, income taxes, medical insurance, and union dues. The Accrued Payroll Payable account (credit) records the $1,524 net pay the employee receives from the $2,000 gross pay earned. When the employee is paid, another entry (or a series of entries) is required to record the check written and distributed (or funds transferred). The entry to record cash payment to this employee is to debit Accrued Payroll Payable and credit Cash for $1,524.

Employer Payroll Taxes

Employers must pay payroll taxes in addition to those required of employees. Employer taxes include FICA and unemployment taxes.

Employer FICA tax. Employers must pay FICA taxes *equal in amount to* the FICA taxes withheld from their employees. An employer's tax is credited to the same FICA Taxes Payable accounts used to record the Social Security and Medicare taxes withheld from employees. (A self-employed person must pay both the employee and employer FICA taxes.)

Federal and state unemployment taxes. The federal government participates with states in a joint federal–state unemployment insurance program. Each state administers its own program. These programs provide unemployment benefits to qualified workers. The federal government approves state programs and pays a portion of their administrative expenses.

Federal Unemployment Taxes (FUTA). Employers are subject to a federal unemployment tax on wages and salaries paid to their employees. For the year 2000, employers were required to pay FUTA taxes of as much as 6.2% of the first $7,000 earned by each employee. This federal tax can be reduced by a credit of up to 5.4% for taxes paid to a state program. As a result, the net federal unemployment tax is often only 0.8%.

State Unemployment Taxes (SUTA). All states support their unemployment insurance

> **Decision Insight**
>
> **Payroll Control**   More than $600 million is lost annually to check schemes. Companies are fighting back with an internal control method called *positive pay*. Here's how it works: A company regularly (daily) sends the bank a "positive file" listing all checks written. When a check reaches the bank for payment, the bank compares the check against the positive file. This flags any forged checks, as well as authentic checks that have been altered.

P3   Compute and record *employer* payroll expenses and liabilities.

> **Decision Insight**
>
> **Tax Aid**   Technology helps reduce errors and increase speed in computing taxes as compared with manual use of tax tables. Tax tables can be downloaded off the Web (www.IRS.USTreas.gov) and then used to accurately and quickly compute payroll taxes.

programs by placing a payroll tax on employers. (A few states require employees to make a contribution. In our assignments, we assume that this tax is only on the employer.) In most states, the base rate for SUTA taxes is 5.4% of the first $7,000 paid each employee. This base rate is adjusted according to an employer's merit rating. The state assigns a **merit rating** that reflects a company's stability or instability in employing workers. A good rating reflects stability in employment and means an employer can pay less than the 5.4% base rate. A low rating reflects high turnover or seasonal hirings and layoffs. To illustrate, an employer with 50 employees who each earn $7,000 or more per year saves $15,400 annually if it has a merit rating of 1.0% versus 5.4%. This is computed by comparing taxes of $18,900 at the 5.4% rate to only $3,500 at the 1.0% rate.

Decision Ethics   *d*

Web Designer   You take a summer job working for a family friend who runs a small IT service. On your first payday, the owner slaps you on the back, gives you full payment in cash, winks, and adds: "No need to pay those high taxes, eh." What action do you take?

Answer—p. 402

Recording employer payroll taxes. Employer payroll taxes are an added expense beyond the wages and salaries earned by employees. These taxes are often recorded in an entry separate from the one recording payroll expenses and deductions. To illustrate, assume that the $2,000 recorded salaries expense from the previous example is earned by an employee whose earnings have not yet reached $5,000 for the year. Also assume that the federal unemployment tax rate is 0.8% and the state unemployment tax rate is 5.4%. Consequently, the FICA portion of the employer's tax is $153, computed by multiplying both the 6.2% and 1.45% by the $2,000 gross pay. Moreover, state unemployment (SUTA) taxes are $108 (5.4% of the $2,000 gross pay), and federal unemployment (FUTA) taxes are $16 (0.8% of $2,000). The entry to record the employer's payroll tax expense and related liabilities is

Example: If the employer's merit rating in this example reduces its SUTA rate to 2.9%, what is its SUTA liability? *Answer:* SUTA payable = $2,000 × 2.9% = $58

Assets = Liabilities + Equity
+124   −277
+29
+108
+16

Jan. 31	Payroll Taxes Expense	277	
	FICA—Social Security Taxes Payable (6.2%)		124
	FICA—Medicare Taxes Payable (1.45%) . .		29
	State Unemployment Taxes Payable		108
	Federal Unemployment Taxes Payable		16
	To record employer payroll taxes.		

Quick Check

6. A company pays its one employee $3,000 per month. This company's FUTA rate is 0.8% on the first $7,000 earned; its SUTA rate is 4.0% on the first $7,000; its Social Security tax rate is 6.2% of the first $76,200; and its Medicare tax rate is 1.45% of all amounts earned. The entry to record this company's March payroll includes what amount for total payroll taxes expense?

7. Identify whether the employer or employee or both pays each of the following: (*a*) FICA taxes, (*b*) FUTA taxes, (*c*) SUTA taxes, and (*d*) withheld income taxes.

Answers—p. 402

Estimated Liabilities

P4 Account for estimated liabilities, including warranties and income taxes.

An **estimated liability** is a known obligation that is of an uncertain amount but that can be reasonably estimated. Common examples are employee benefits such as pensions, health care and vacation pay, warranties offered by a seller, and income taxes. We discuss each of these in this section. Other examples of estimated liabilities include property taxes and certain contracts to provide future services.

Health and Pension Benefits

Many companies provide **employee benefits** beyond salaries and wages. An employer often pays all or part of medical, dental, life, and disability insurance. Many employers also contribute to *pension plans,* which are agreements by employers to provide benefits (payments) to employees after retirement. Many companies also provide medical care and insurance benefits to their retirees. When payroll taxes and charges for employee benefits are totaled, payroll cost often exceeds employees' gross earnings by 25% or more.

> ### Decision Insight
>
> **Postgame Benefits**   Several ex-players are suing **Major League Baseball** over a pension system they say unfairly excludes them and fails to reward their contributions. Gripes include failure to extend pensions to players whose careers ended before 1947, were interrupted by World War II, or were spent in the Negro League. A full pension exceeds $120,000 per year.
>
>

To illustrate, assume that an employer agrees to (1) pay an amount for medical insurance equal to $8,000 and (2) contribute an additional 10% of the employees' $120,000 gross salary to a retirement program. The entry to record these benefits is

Jan. 31	Employee Benefits Expense.	20,000	
	Employee Medical Insurance Payable		8,000
	Employee Retirement Program Payable . . .		12,000
	To record costs of employee benefits.		

Assets = Liabilities + Equity
+8,000   −20,000
+12,000

Vacation Pay

Many employers offer paid vacation benefits. For example, employees might earn 2 weeks' vacation per year. This benefit increases employers' payroll expenses because employees are paid for 52 weeks but work for only 50 weeks. Total annual salary is the same, but the cost per week worked is greater than the amount paid per week. To illustrate, if an employee is paid $20,800 for 52 weeks but works only 50 weeks, the weekly salary expense to the employer is $416 ($20,800/50 weeks) instead of the $400 paid weekly to the employee ($20,800/52 weeks). The $16 difference between these two amounts is recorded weekly to Salary Expense and Vacation Pay Liability. When the employee takes a vacation, the employer reduces the vacation pay liability but does not record any additional expense.

Global: Bonuses are considered part of salary expense in most countries. In Japan, bonuses to members of the board of directors and to external auditors are directly charged against equity rather than treated as an expense.

Bonus Plans

Many companies offer bonuses to employees, and many of the bonuses depend on net income. To illustrate, assume that an employer offers a bonus to its employees equal to 5% of the company's annual net income (to be equally shared by all). The company's expected annual net income is $210,000. The year-end adjusting entry to record this benefit is

Dec. 31	Employee Bonus Expense*	10,000	
	Bonus Payable		10,000
	To record expected bonus costs.		

Assets = Liabilities + Equity
+10,000   −10,000

* Bonus Expense is deducted in computing net income. This means it equals 5% of $210,000 *less the bonus*—computed as:

$$B = 0.05\,(\$210,000 - B)$$
$$B = \$10,500 - 0.05B$$
$$1.05B = \$10,500$$
$$B = \$10,500/1.05 = \$10,000$$

When the bonus is paid, Bonus Payable is debited and Cash is credited for $10,000.

Warranty Liabilities

A **warranty** is a seller's obligation to replace or correct a product (or service) that fails to perform as expected within a specified period. Most new cars, for instance, are sold with a warranty covering parts for a specified period of time. **Ford Motor Company** reported more than $10 billion in "dealer and customer allowances and claims" in its recent annual report. To

Point: Zenith recently reported $32.1 million on its balance sheet for warranties.

comply with the *full disclosure* and *matching principles,* the seller reports the expected warranty expense in the period when revenue from the sale of the product or service is reported. The seller reports this warranty obligation as a liability, although the existence, amount, payee, and date of future sacrifices are uncertain. However, such warranty costs are probable and the amount of this liability can be estimated using, for instance, past experience with warranties.

To illustrate, a dealer sells a used car for $16,000 on December 1, 2002, with a maximum one-year or 12,000-mile warranty covering parts. This dealer's experience shows that warranty expense averages about 4% of a car's selling price, or $640 in this case ($16,000 × 4%). The dealer records the estimated expense and liability related to this sale with this entry:

Assets = Liabilities + Equity
+640   −640

2002			
Dec. 1	Warranty Expense	640	
	Estimated Warranty Liability		640
	To record estimated warranty expense.		

Point: Recognition of expected warranty liabilities is necessary to comply with the matching and full disclosure principles.

This entry alternatively could be made as part of end-of-period adjustments. Either way, the estimated warranty expense is reported on the 2002 income statement. It also results in a warranty liability on the balance sheet. To further extend this example, suppose the customer returns the car for warranty repairs on January 9, 2003. The dealer performs this work by replacing parts costing $200. The entry to record partial settlement of the estimated warranty liability is

Assets = Liabilities + Equity
−200   −200

2003			
Jan. 9	Estimated Warranty Liability.	200	
	Auto Parts Inventory.		200
	To record costs of warranty repairs.		

This entry reduces the balance of the estimated warranty liability. Warranty expense was previously recorded in 2002, the year the car was sold with the warranty. What happens if total warranty expenses are more or less than the estimated 4%, or $640? The answer is that management should monitor actual warranty expenses to see whether the 4% rate is accurate. If experience reveals a large difference from the estimate, the rate for current and future sales should be changed. Differences are expected, but they should be small.

Income Tax Liabilities

Corporations are subject to income taxes and must estimate their income tax liability when preparing financial statements. Since income tax expense is created by earning income, a liability is incurred when income is earned. This tax must be paid quarterly under federal regulations. To illustrate, consider a corporation that prepares monthly financial statements. Based on its income in January 2002, this corporation estimates that it owes income taxes of $12,100. The following adjusting entry records this estimate:

Assets = Liabilities + Equity
        +12,100   −12,100

Jan. 31	Income Taxes Expense	12,100	
	Income Taxes Payable		12,100
	To accrue January income taxes.		

The tax liability is recorded each month until the first quarterly payment is made. If estimated taxes for this first quarter total $30,000, the entry to record its payment is

Assets = Liabilities + Equity
−30,000   −30,000

Apr. 10	Income Taxes Payable.	30,000	
	Cash		30,000
	Paid estimated quarterly income taxes based on first quarter income.		

This process of accruing and then paying estimated income taxes continues through the year. When annual financial statements are prepared at year-end, the corporation knows its actual total income and the actual amount of income taxes it must pay. This information allows it to properly record income taxes expense for the fourth quarter so that the total of the four quarters' expense amounts equals the taxes paid to the government.

Deferred Income Tax Liabilities

An income tax liability for corporations can arise when the amount of income before taxes that the corporation reports on its income statement is not the same as the amount of income reported on its income tax return. This difference occurs because income tax laws and GAAP measure income differently.[2]

Some differences between tax laws and GAAP are temporary. *Temporary differences* arise when the tax return and the income statement report a revenue or expense in different years. As an example, companies are often able to deduct higher amounts of depreciation in the early years of an asset's life and smaller amounts in later years for tax reporting in comparison to GAAP. This means that in the early years, depreciation for tax reporting is often more than depreciation on the income statement. In later years, depreciation for tax reporting is often less than depreciation on the income statement. When temporary differences exist between taxable income on the tax return and the income before taxes on the income statement, corporations compute income taxes expense based on the income reported on the income statement. The result is that income taxes expense reported in the income statement is often different from the amount of income taxes payable to the government. This difference is the **deferred income tax liability.**

To illustrate, assume that in recording its usual quarterly income tax payments, a corporation computes $25,000 of income taxes expense. It also determines that only $21,000 is currently due and $4,000 is deferred to future years (a timing difference). The entry to record this end-of-period adjustment is

Dec. 31	Income Taxes Expense	25,000	
	Income Taxes Payable		21,000
	Deferred Income Tax Liability.		4,000
	To record tax expense and deferred tax liability.		

Assets = Liabilities + Equity
+21,000   −25,000
+4,000

The credit to Income Taxes Payable reflects the amount currently due to be paid. The credit to Deferred Income Tax Liability reflects tax payments deferred until future years when the temporary difference reverses. Coca-Cola Bottling, for instance, reports deferred income taxes of $125 million among liabilities on its balance sheet.

Temporary differences also can cause a company to pay income taxes *before* they are reported on the income statement as expense. If so, the company reports a *Deferred Income Tax Asset* on its balance sheet. Dell Computer, for instance, reports deferred income taxes of $535 million as an asset in its balance sheet.

Quick Check

8. Estimated liabilities involve an obligation to pay which of these? (a) An uncertain but reasonably estimated amount owed on a known obligation, or (b) A known amount to a specific entity on an uncertain due date.

9. A car is sold for $15,000 on June 1, 2002, with a one-year warranty on parts. Warranty expense is estimated at 1.5% of selling price. On March 1, 2003, the car is returned for warranty repairs costing $135. The amount recorded as warranty expense on March 1 is (a) $0; (b) $60; (c) $75; (d) $135; (e) $225.

10. Why does a corporation accrue an income tax liability for quarterly reports?

Answers—p. 402

---

[2] Differences between tax laws and GAAP arise because Congress uses tax laws to generate receipts, stimulate the economy, and influence behavior, whereas GAAP are intended to provide financial information useful for decision making. Also, tax accounting often follows the cash basis, whereas GAAP follows the accrual basis.

Contingent Liabilities

C3 Explain how to account for contingent liabilities.

	Probable	Reasonably Possible	Remote
Amount estimable	Record contingent liability	Disclose liability in notes	No action
Amount not estimable	Disclose liability in notes	Disclose liability in notes	No action

Point: A contingency is an *if*. Namely, if a future event occurs, then financial consequences are likely for the entity.

Point: A discounted note receivable is a contingent liability. It becomes a liability only if the original signer of the note fails to pay it at maturity.

A **contingent liability** is a potential obligation that depends on a future event arising from a past transaction or event. An example is a lawsuit pending in court. Here, a past transaction or event leads to a lawsuit whose result depends on the court's decision. Generally, future payment of a contingent liability depends on whether an uncertain future event occurs.

Accounting for Contingent Liabilities

Accounting for contingent liabilities depends on the likelihood that a future event will occur and the ability to estimate the future amount owed if this event occurs. Three categories are identified. (1) The future event is *probable* (likely) and the amount owed can be *reasonably estimated*. We record this amount as a liability. Examples are the estimated liabilities described earlier such as warranties, vacation pay, and income taxes. (2) The future event is *remote* (unlikely). We do not record or disclose information on remote contingent liabilities. (3) Likelihood of the future event is between these two extremes. That is, if the future event is *reasonably possible* (could occur), we disclose information about the contingent liability in notes to the financial statements. This section identifies contingent liabilities that often fall in the third category—when the future event is reasonably possible. Disclosing information about contingencies in this third category is motivated by the *full-disclosure principle*, which requires information relevant to decision makers be reported.

Reasonably Possible Contingent Liabilities

This section discusses common examples of reasonably possible contingent liabilities.

Potential Legal Claims. Many companies are sued or at risk of being sued. The accounting question is: whether the defendant should recognize a liability on its balance sheet or disclose a contingent liability in its notes while a lawsuit is outstanding and not yet settled. The answer is that a potential claim is recorded in the accounts *only* if payment for damages is probable and the amount can be reasonably estimated. If the potential claim cannot be reasonably estimated or is less than probable but reasonably possible, it is disclosed. **Ford Motor Company**, for example, includes the following note in its recent annual report: "Various legal actions, governmental investigations and proceedings and claims are pending . . . against the company . . . arising out of alleged defects in the company's products."

Decision Insight

Boiling Mad Remember the infamous lawsuit against **McDonald's** that awarded an 81-year-old New Mexico woman $2.9 million—later reduced to $640,000—after she spilled hot coffee in her lap? Well, copycat litigation is booming. Fast-food chains are beset by suits over hot-drink and food spills. Companies from **Burger King** to **Starbucks** now print cautions on coffee cups, chili bowls, and so forth.

Debt Guarantees. Sometimes a company guarantees the payment of debt owed by a supplier, customer, or another company. The guarantor usually discloses the guarantee in its financial statement notes as a contingent liability. If it is probable that the debtor will default, the guarantor needs to record and report the guarantee in its financial statements as a liability. The **Boston Celtics** report a unique guarantee when it comes to coaches and players: "Certain of the contracts provide for guaranteed payments which must be paid even if the employee is injured or terminated."

Other Contingencies. Other examples of contingencies include environmental damages, possible tax assessments, insurance losses, and government investigations. **Sun**, for instance, reports that "federal, state, local and foreign laws

Decision Insight

Eco Cops What's it worth to see from one side of the Grand Canyon to the other? What's the cost when beaches are closed due to pollution? One method to measure these environmental liabilities is **contingent valuation,** by which people are surveyed and asked to answer such questions. Regulators use their answers to levy fines, assess punitive damages, and measure cleanup costs.

Point: Auditors and managers often have different views about whether a contingency is recorded, disclosed, or omitted.

. . . result in loss contingencies . . . at Sun's refineries, service stations, terminals, pipelines and truck transportation facilities." Many of these contingencies require disclosure in notes to financial statements since they are reasonably possible. These contingencies can sometimes carry characteristics that cause them to be recorded as liabilities or, alternatively, omitted altogether.

Uncertainties. All organizations face uncertainties from future events such as natural disasters and the development of new competing products or services. If these events occur, they can damage a company's assets or drive it out of business. These uncertainties are not contingent liabilities because they are future events *not* arising from past transactions. Undue speculation about the effects of possible future uncertainties such as these reduces the usefulness of financial statements; accordingly, they are not disclosed.

Topic Tackler 9-2

Quick Check

11. A future payment is reported as a liability on the balance sheet if payment is contingent on a future event that (*a*) is reasonably possible but the payment cannot be reasonably estimated; (*b*) is probable and the payment can be reasonably estimated; or (*c*) is not probable but the payment is known.

12. Under what circumstances is a future payment reported in the notes to the financial statements as a contingent liability?

Answers—p. 402

Long-term liabilities are a company's obligations not requiring a payment within one year or its operating cycle, whichever is longer. Long-term liabilities often are identical to current liabilities except for the longer time interval until the obligation comes due. Long-term liabilities can arise from many different transactions and events. Probably their most common source is money borrowed from a bank in return for a note. They also occur when a company enters into a multiyear lease agreement similar to buying an asset. We explain long-term liabilities in the context of discussing known, estimated, and contingent long-term liabilities. The main discussion of accounting for long-term liabilities is in Chapter 10.

Long-Term Liabilities

Known Long-Term Liabilities

Many known or determinable liabilities are long term. These include unearned revenues and notes payable. For example, if **Sports Illustrated** sells a five-year magazine subscription, it records amounts received for this subscription in an Unearned Subscription Revenues account. Amounts in this account are liabilities, but are they current or long term? They are *both.* The portion of the Unearned Subscription Revenues account that will be fulfilled in the next year is reported as a current liability. The remaining portion is reported as a long-term liability.

Decision Insight

e

Entrepreneurial Financing The Small Business Administration (www.sba.gov) publishes a yearly report of likely sources of small business loans by state. The report shows that small businesses number more than 25 million, employ 53% of the private workforce, make 47% of all sales, create most new jobs, and produce 55% of innovations. It also shows that about 70% of small businesses with loans obtain this money from commercial banks.

The same analysis applies to notes payable. For example, a borrower reports a three-year note payable as a long-term liability in the first two years it is outstanding. In the third year, the borrower reclassifies this note as a current liability since it is due within one year or the operating cycle, whichever is longer. The **current portion of long-term debt** refers to that part of long-term debt due within one year or the operating cycle, whichever is longer. Long-term debt is reported under long-term liabilities, but the *current portion due* is reported under current liabilities. To illustrate, assume that a $7,500 debt is paid in installments of $1,500 per year for five years. The $1,500 due within the year is reported as a current liability. No journal entry is necessary for this reclassification. Instead, we simply classify the amounts for debt as either current or long term when the balance sheet is prepared.

Some known liabilities are rarely reported in long-term liabilities. These include accounts payable, sales taxes, and wages and salaries.

Estimated Long-Term Liabilities

Estimated liabilities are both current and long term. Examples include employee benefits and deferred income taxes. Pension liabilities to employees are long term to workers who will not retire within the next period. For employees who are retired or will retire within the next period, a portion of pension liabilities is current. The same analysis applies to employee health benefits, deferred income taxes payable for corporations, and warranties. For example, many warranties are for 30 or 60 days in length. Estimated costs under these warranties are properly reported in current liabilities, yet many automobile warranties are for three years or 36,000 miles. A portion of these warranties is reported as long term.

Contingent Long-Term Liabilities

Contingent liabilities can be either, or both, current and long term. This extends to nearly every contingent liability, including litigation, debt guarantees, environmental cleanup, government investigations, and tax assessments.

Decision Track 9.2		*d*
Decision Point	**Information Search**	**Analyze & Evaluate**
Is a company exposed to contingent liabilities? What is its related risk?	Balance sheet liabilities; financial statement notes; knowledge of business activities.	Identify contingent losses; the greater their likelihood, amount, and financial impact, the greater the risk.

Decision Analysis   **Times Interest Earned Ratio**

A company incurs interest expense on many of its current and long-term liabilities. Examples extend from its short-term notes and the current portion of long-term liabilities to its long-term notes and bonds. The amount of these liabilities is likely to remain in one form or another for a substantial period of time. Accordingly, interest expense is often viewed as a *fixed expense*. This means that the amount of interest is unlikely to fluctuate due to changes in sales or other operating activities. While fixed costs can be advantageous when a company is growing, they create risk. This risk stems from the possibility that a company might be unable to pay fixed expenses if sales decline. To illustrate, consider X-Caliber's results for year 2002 and two possible outcomes for year 2003 shown in Exhibit 9.6.

A1   Compute the times interest earned ratio and use it to analyze liabilities.

Exhibit 9.6

X-Caliber's Actual and Projected Results

		Year 2003	
($ thousands)	**Year 2002**	**Sales Increase**	**Sales Decrease**
Sales	$600	$900	$300
Expenses (75% of sales)	450	675	225
Income before interest	150	225	75
Interest expense (fixed)	60	60	60
Net income	$ 90	$165	$ 15

Expenses excluding interest are at, and expected to remain at, 75% of sales. Expenses such as these that change with sales volume are called *variable expenses*. However, interest expense is at, and expected to remain at, $60,000 per year due to its fixed nature.

The middle numerical column of Exhibit 9.6 shows that X-Caliber's income nearly doubles if sales increase by 50% to $900,000. In contrast, the far right column shows that income falls sharply if sales decline by 50% to $300,000. These results reveal that the amount of fixed interest expense affects a company's risk. This risk is numerically reflected in the **times interest earned** ratio defined in Exhibit 9.7.

Decision Maker

Entrepreneur You wish to invest in a franchise for one of two national chains. Each franchise has an expected annual net income *after* interest and taxes of $100,000. Net income for the first franchise includes a regular fixed interest charge of $200,000. The fixed interest charge for the second franchise is $40,000. Which franchise is riskier to you if sales forecasts are not met? Does your decision change if the first franchise has more variability in its income stream?

Answer—p. 402

$$\text{Times interest earned} = \frac{\text{Income before interest expense and income taxes}}{\text{Interest expense}}$$

Exhibit 9.7

Times Interest Earned

For 2002, X-Caliber's times interest earned is computed as $150,000/$60,000, or 2.5 times. This ratio suggests that X-Caliber faces low to moderate risk because its sales must decline sharply before it would be unable to cover its interest expenses. (X-Caliber is an S-corporation and does not pay income taxes.)

Experience shows that when times interest earned falls below 1.5 to 2.0 and remains at that level or lower for several periods, the default rate on liabilities increases sharply. This reflects increased risk for companies and their creditors. We also must interpret the times interest earned ratio in light of information about the variability of a company's income before interest. If income is stable from year to year or if it is growing, the company can afford to take on added risk by borrowing. If its income greatly varies from year to year, fixed interest expense can increase the risk that it will not earn a positive return and be unable to pay interest expense.

Point: Circuit City's times interest earned ratio was 7.6, 3.2, and 14.0 for the years 1998, 1999, and 2000, respectively.

The following transactions and events took place at Kern Company during its recent calendar-year reporting period (Kern does not use reversing entries):

a. In September 2002, Kern sold $140,000 of merchandise covered by a 180-day warranty. Prior experience shows that costs of the warranty equal 5% of sales. Compute September's warranty expense and prepare the adjusting journal entry for the warranty liability as recorded at September 30. Also prepare the journal entry on October 8 to record a $300 cash expenditure to provide warranty service on an item sold in September.

b. On October 12, 2002, Kern arranged with a supplier to replace Kern's overdue $10,000 account payable by paying $2,500 cash and signing a note for the remainder. The note matures in 90 days and has a 12% interest rate. Prepare the entries recorded on October 12, December 31, and January 10, 2003, related to this transaction.

c. In late December, Kern learns it is facing a product liability suit filed by an unhappy customer. Kern's lawyer advises that although it will probably suffer a loss from the lawsuit, it is not possible to estimate the amount of damages at this time.

d. Sally Kline works for Kern. For the pay period ended November 30, her gross earnings are $3,000. Sally has $800 deducted for federal income taxes and $200 for state income taxes from each paycheck. Additionally, a $35 premium for her health care insurance and a $10 donation for the United Way are deducted. Sally pays FICA Social Security taxes at a rate of 6.2% and FICA Medicare taxes at a rate of 1.45%. She has not earned enough this year to be exempt from FICA taxes. Journalize the payment of Sally's wages by Kern.

e. On November 1, Kern borrows $5,000 cash from a bank in return for a 60-day, 12%, $5,000 note. Record the note's issuance on November 1 and its repayment with interest on December 31.

f. On December 16, Kern receives $2,000 cash by signing a noninterest-bearing note promising to pay $2,080 within 60 days. Record the issuance of the note, the interest accrual on December 31, and the repayment of the note on February 14 ($80 of interest is included in the note's face value of $2,080).

Demonstration Problem

g. Kern has estimated and recorded its quarterly income tax payments. In reviewing its year-end tax adjustments, it identifies an additional $5,000 of income tax expense that should be recorded. A portion of this additional expense, $1,000, is deferrable to future years. Record this year-end income taxes expense adjusting entry.

h. Kern's net income for the year is $1,000,000. Its interest expense for the year is $275,000. Income taxes expense for the year is $225,000. Calculate Kern's times interest earned ratio.

Planning the Solution

- For *a,* compute the warranty expense for September and record it with an estimated liability. Record the October expenditure as a decrease in the liability.
- For *b,* eliminate the liability for the account payable and create the liability for the note payable. Compute interest expense for the 80 days that the note is outstanding in 2002 and record it as an additional liability. Record the payment of the note, being sure to include the interest for the 10 days in 2003.
- For *c,* decide whether the company's contingent liability needs to be disclosed or accrued (recorded) according to the two necessary criteria: probable loss and reasonably estimable.
- For *d,* set up payable accounts for all items in Sally's paycheck that require deductions. After deducting all necessary items, credit the remaining amount to Accrued Payroll Payable.
- For *e,* record the issuance of the note. Calculate 60 days' interest due using the 360-day convention in the interest formula.
- For *f,* record the note as a noninteresting-bearing note. Use the contra account Discount on Notes Payable for the interest portion of the proceeds upon issuance. Make the year-end adjustment for 15 days' interest to Interest Expense and to Discount on Notes Payable. Record the repayment of the note, being sure to include the interest for the 45 days in 2003.
- For *g,* determine how much of the income taxes expense is payable in the current year and how much needs to be deferred.
- For *h,* apply and compute times interest earned.

Solution to Demonstration Problem

a. Warranty expense $= 5\% \times \$140,000 = \$7,000$

Sept. 30	Warranty Expense	7,000	
	Estimated Warranty Liability		7,000
	To record warranty expense for the month.		
Oct. 8	Estimated Warranty Liability	300	
	Cash		300
	To record the cost of the warranty service.		

b. Interest expense for 2002 $= 12\% \times \$7,500 \times 80/360 = \$200$
Interest expense for 2003 $= 12\% \times \$7,500 \times 10/360 = \$25$

Oct. 12	Accounts Payable	10,000	
	Notes Payable		7,500
	Cash		2,500
	Paid $2,500 cash and gave a 90-day, 12% note to extend the due date on the account.		
Dec. 31	Interest Expense	200	
	Interest Payable		200
	To accrue interest on note payable.		
Jan. 10	Interest Expense	25	
	Interest Payable	200	
	Notes Payable	7,500	
	Cash		7,725
	Paid note with interest, including the accrued interest payable.		

c. Disclose the pending lawsuit in the financial statement notes. Although the loss is probable, no liability can be accrued since the loss cannot be reasonably estimated.

d.

Nov. 30	Salaries Expense	3,000.00	
	FICA—Social Security Taxes Payable (6.2%)		186.00
	FICA—Medicare Taxes Payable (1.45%) . .		43.50
	Employee Federal Income Taxes Payable . .		800.00
	Employee State Income Taxes Payable . . .		200.00
	Employee Medical Insurance Payable		35.00
	Employee United Way Payable		10.00
	Accrued Payroll Payable		1,725.50
	To record Kline's accrued payroll.		

e.

Nov. 1	Cash	5,000	
	Notes Payable		5,000
	Borrowed cash with a 60-day, 12% note.		

When the note and interest are paid 60 days later, Kern Company records this entry:

Dec. 31	Notes Payable	5,000	
	Interest Expense	100	
	Cash		5,100
	Paid note with interest ($5,000 × 12% × 60/360).		

f.

Dec. 16	Cash	2,000	
	Discount on Notes Payable	80	
	Notes Payable		2,080
	Borrowed cash with a 60-day note.		
Dec. 31	Interest Expense	20	
	Discount on Notes Payable		20
	To record accrued interest (15/60 days × $80).		

When the note matures on February 14, 2003, Kern records this entry:

Feb. 14	Interest Expense (45/60 days × $80)	60	
	Notes Payable	2,080	
	Cash		2,080
	Discount on Notes Payable		60
	Paid note with interest.		

g.

Dec. 31	Income Taxes Expense	5,000	
	Income Taxes Payable		4,000
	Deferred Income Tax Liability		1,000
	To record added income taxes expense and the deferred tax liability.		

h. Times interest earned $= \dfrac{\$1,000,000 + \$275,000 + \$225,000}{\$275,000} = \underline{\underline{5.45 \text{ times}}}$

9A   Payroll Reports, Records, and Procedures

Understanding payroll procedures and keeping adequate payroll reports and records are essential to a company's success. Many companies now use accounting software to maintain their payroll records. This appendix focuses on payroll accounting and its reports, records, and procedures.

Payroll Reports

Most employees and employers are required to pay local, state, and federal payroll taxes. Payroll expenses involve liabilities to individual employees, to federal and state governments, and to other organizations such as insurance companies. Beyond paying these liabilities, employers are required to prepare and submit reports explaining how they computed these payments.

Reporting FICA Taxes and Income Taxes

C4   Identify and describe payroll reporting.

The Federal Insurance Contributions Act (FICA) requires each employer to file an Internal Revenue Service (IRS) **Form 941,** the *Employer's Quarterly Federal Tax Return,* within one month after the end of each calendar quarter. A sample Form 941 is shown in Exhibit 9A.1 for Phoenix Sales & Service, a landscape design company. Accounting information and software are helpful in tracking payroll transactions and reporting the accumulated information on Form 941. Specifically, the employer reports total wages subject to income tax withholding on line 2 of Form 941. (For simplicity, this appendix uses *wages* to refer to both wages and salaries.) The income tax withheld is reported on lines 3 and 5. The combined amount of employees' and employer's FICA (Social Security) taxes for Phoenix Sales & Service is reported on line 6a (taxable Social Security wages, $36,599 \times 12.4\% = \$4,538.28$). The 12.4% is the sum of the Social Security tax withheld, computed as 6.2% tax withheld from the employees' wages for the quarter plus the 6.2% tax levied on the employer. The combined amount of employees' Medicare wages is reported on line 7. The 2.9% is the sum of 1.45% withheld from employees' wages for the quarter plus 1.45% tax levied on the employer. Total FICA taxes are reported on lines 8 and 10 and are added to the total income taxes withheld of $3,056.47 to yield a total of $8,656.11. For this year, assume that income up to $76,200 is subject to Social Security tax. There is no income limit on amounts subject to Medicare tax. Congress sets annual limits on the amount owed for Social Security tax.

The total of amounts deposited in a **federal depository bank** is subtracted to determine whether a balance remains to be paid. Federal depository banks are authorized to accept deposits of amounts payable to the federal government. Deposit requirements depend on the amount of tax owed. For example, when the sum of FICA taxes plus the employees' income taxes is less than $500 for a quarter, the taxes can be paid when Form 941 is filed. Companies with large payrolls are often required to pay monthly or even semiweekly. If taxes owed are $100,000 or more at the end of any day, they must be paid by the end of the next banking day.

Reporting FUTA Taxes and SUTA Taxes

An employer's federal unemployment taxes (FUTA) are reported on an annual basis by filing an *Annual Federal Unemployment Tax Return,* IRS **Form 940.** It must be mailed on or before January 31 following the end of each tax year. Ten more days are allowed if all required tax deposits are filed on a timely basis and the full amount of tax is paid on or before January 31. FUTA payments are made quarterly to a federal depository bank if the total amount due exceeds $100. If $100 or less is due, the taxes are remitted annually. Requirements for paying and reporting state unemployment taxes (SUTA) vary depending on the laws of each state. Most states require quarterly payments and reports.

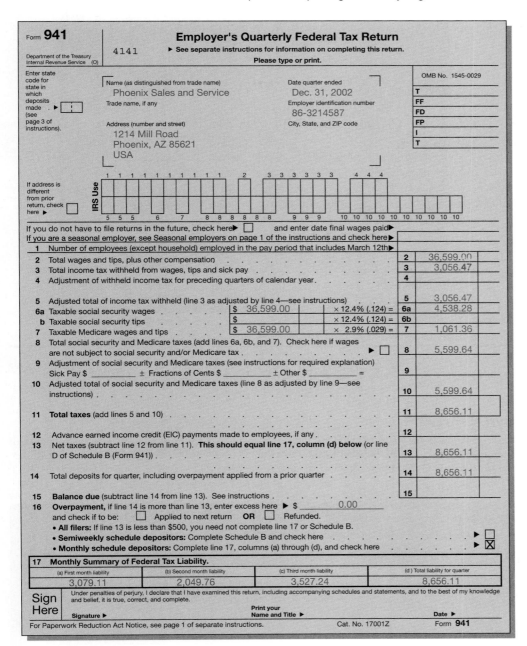

Exhibit 9A.1

Form 941

Reporting Wages and Salaries

Employers are required to give each employee an annual report of his or her wages subject to FICA and federal income taxes along with the amounts of these taxes withheld. This report is called a *Wage and Tax Statement*, or **Form W-2.** It must be given to employees before January 31 following the year covered by the report. Exhibit 9A.2 shows Form W-2 for one of the employees at Phoenix Sales & Service. Copies of the W-2 Form must be sent to the Social Security Administration, where the amount of the employee's wages subject to FICA taxes and FICA taxes withheld are posted to each employee's Social Security account. These posted amounts become the basis for determining an employee's retirement and survivors' benefits. The Social Security Administration also transmits to the IRS the amount of each employee's wages subject to federal income taxes and the amount of taxes withheld.

Exhibit 9A.2

Form W-2

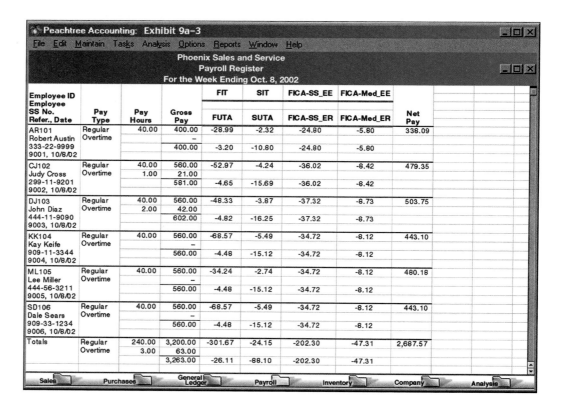

Payroll Records

Employers must keep certain payroll records in addition to reporting and paying taxes. These records usually include a payroll register and an individual earnings report for each employee.

Payroll Register

C5 Identify and describe payroll records.

A **payroll register** shows the pay period dates, hours worked, gross pay, deductions, and net pay of each employee for each pay period. Exhibit 9A.3 shows a payroll register for Phoenix Sales & Service. It is organized into nine columns:

Exhibit 9A.3

Payroll Register

Peachtree Accounting: Exhibit 9a-3

File Edit Maintain Tasks Analysis Options Reports Window Help

Phoenix Sales and Service
Payroll Register
For the Week Ending Oct. 8, 2002

Employee ID Employee SS No. Refer., Date	Pay Type	Pay Hours	Gross Pay	FIT	SIT	FICA-SS_EE	FICA-Med_EE	Net Pay
				FUTA	SUTA	FICA-SS_ER	FICA-Med_ER	
AR101 Robert Austin 333-22-9999 9001, 10/8/02	Regular Overtime	40.00	400.00 –	-28.99	-2.32	-24.80	-5.80	338.09
			400.00	-3.20	-10.80	-24.80	-5.80	
CJ102 Judy Cross 299-11-9201 9002, 10/8/02	Regular Overtime	40.00 1.00	560.00 21.00	-52.97	-4.24	-36.02	-8.42	479.35
			581.00	-4.65	-15.69	-36.02	-8.42	
DJ103 John Diaz 444-11-9090 9003, 10/8/02	Regular Overtime	40.00 2.00	560.00 42.00	-48.33	-3.87	-37.32	-8.73	503.75
			602.00	-4.82	-16.25	-37.32	-8.73	
KK104 Kay Keife 909-11-3344 9004, 10/8/02	Regular Overtime	40.00	560.00 –	-68.57	-5.49	-34.72	-8.12	443.10
			560.00	-4.48	-15.12	-34.72	-8.12	
ML105 Lee Miller 444-56-3211 9005, 10/8/02	Regular Overtime	40.00	560.00 –	-34.24	-2.74	-34.72	-8.12	480.18
			560.00	-4.48	-15.12	-34.72	-8.12	
SD106 Dale Sears 909-33-1234 9006, 10/8/02	Regular Overtime	40.00	560.00 –	-68.57	-5.49	-34.72	-8.12	443.10
			560.00	-4.48	-15.12	-34.72	-8.12	
Totals	Regular Overtime	240.00 3.00	3,200.00 63.00	-301.67	-24.15	-202.30	-47.31	2,687.57
			3,263.00	-26.11	-88.10	-202.30	-47.31	

Sales   Purchases   General Ledger   Payroll   Inventory   Company   Analysis

Col. 1 Employee identification (ID); Employee name; Social Security number (SS No.); Reference (check number) and Date (date check issued)

Col. 2 Pay Type (regular and overtime)

Col. 3 Pay Hours (number of hours worked as regular and overtime)

Col. 4 Gross Pay (amount of gross pay)[3]

Col. 5 FIT (federal income taxes withheld); FUTA (federal unemployment taxes)

Col. 6 SIT (state income taxes withheld); SUTA (state unemployment taxes)

Col. 7 FICA-SS_EE (social security taxes withheld, employee); FICA-SS_ER (social security taxes, employer)

Col. 8 FICA-Med_EE (medicare tax withheld, employee); FICA-Med_ER (medicare tax, employer)

Col. 9 Net pay (Gross pay less amounts withheld from employees)

Net pay for each employee is computed as gross pay minus the items on the first line of columns 5–8. The employer's payroll tax for each employee is computed as the sum of items on the third line of columns 5–8. A payroll register includes all data necessary to record payroll in the general journal. In some software programs the entries to record payroll are made in a *payroll journal.*

Payroll Check

Payment of payroll is usually done by check or electronic funds transfer. Exhibit 9A.4 shows a *payroll check* for a Phoenix employee. This check is accompanied with a detachable *statement of earnings* (at top) showing gross pay, deductions, and net pay.

Exhibit 9A.4

Check and Statement of Earnings

Employee Earnings Report

An **employee earnings report** is a cumulative record of an employee's hours worked, gross earnings, deductions, and net pay. Payroll information on this report is taken from the payroll register. The employee earnings report for R. Austin at Phoenix Sales & Service is shown in Exhibit 9A.5.

---

[3] The Gross Pay column shows regular hours worked on the first line multiplied by the regular pay rate—this equals regular pay. Overtime hours multiplied by the overtime premium rate equals overtime premium pay reported on the second line. If employers are engaged in interstate commerce, federal law sets a minimum overtime rate of pay to employees. For this company, it is 50% of the regular rate for hours worked in excess of 40 per week. This means workers earn at least 150% of their regular rate for hours in excess of 40 per week.

Exhibit 9A.5

Employee Earnings Report

Peachtree Accounting: Exhibit 12a–5

File Edit Maintain Tasks Analysis Options Reports Window Help

Phoenix Sales and Service
Employee Earnings Report
For the Month Ending Dec. 31, 2002

Employee ID Employee SS No.	Date Reference	Gross Pay	FIT / FUTA	SIT / SUTA	FICA-SS_EE / FICA-SS_ER	FICA-Med_EE / FICA-Med_ER	Net Pay
Beginning Balance for Robert Austin		2,910.00	-188.42	-15.08	-180.42	-42.20	2,483.88
			-23.28	-78.57	-180.42	-42.20	
AR101 Robert Austin 333-22-9999	12/3/02 9049	400.00	-28.99	-2.32	-24.80	-5.80	338.09
			-3.20	-10.80	-24.80	-5.80	
AR101 Robert Austin 333-22-9999	12/10/02 9055	400.00	-28.99	-2.32	-24.80	-5.80	338.09
			-3.20	-10.80	-24.80	-5.80	
AR101 Robert Austin 333-22-9999	12/17/02 9061	400.00	-28.99	-2.32	-24.80	-5.80	338.09
			-3.20	-10.80	-24.80	-5.80	
AR101 Robert Austin 333-22-9999	12/24/02 9067	400.00	-28.99	-2.32	-24.80	-5.80	338.09
			-3.20	-10.80	-24.80	-5.80	
AR101 Robert Austin 333-22-9999	12/31/02 9073	400.00	-28.99	-2.32	-24.80	-5.80	338.09
			-3.20	-10.80	-24.80	-5.80	
Total 12/1/02 thru 12/31/02		2,000.00	-144.95	-11.60	-124.00	-29.00	1,690.45
			-16.00	-54.00	-124.00	-29.00	
Year-to-date Total for Robert Austin		4,910.00	-333.37	-26.68	-304.42	-71.20	4,174.33
			-39.28	-132.57	-304.42	-71.20	

Sales   Purchases   General Ledger   Payroll   Inventory   Company   Analysis

---

Decision Insight

High-Tech Reports Off-the-shelf and Web-based programs can produce many payroll reports including the (1) payroll register, (2) payroll checks, and (3) employee earnings report.

An employee earnings report accumulates information that can show when an employee's earnings reach the tax-exempt points for FICA, FUTA, and SUTA taxes. It also gives data an employer needs to prepare Form W-2.

Payroll Procedures

Employers must be able to compute federal income tax for payroll purposes. This section explains how we compute this tax and how to use a payroll bank account.

Computing Federal Income Taxes

P5 Compute payroll taxes.

To compute the amount of taxes withheld from each employee's wages, we need to determine both the employee's wages earned and the employee's number of *withholding allowances.* Each employee records the number of withholding allowances claimed on a withholding allowance certificate, **Form W-4,** filed with the employer. When the number of withholding allowances increases, the amount of income taxes withheld decreases.

Employers often use a **wage bracket withholding table** similar to the one shown in Exhibit 9A.6 to compute the federal income taxes withheld from each employee's gross pay. The table in Exhibit

Exhibit 9A.6

Wage Bracket Withholding Table

SINGLE Persons—**WEEKLY** Payroll Period
(For Wages Paid)

If the wages are –		And the number of withholding allowances claimed is —										
At least	But less than	0	1	2	3	4	5	6	7	8	9	10
		The amount of income tax to be withheld is —										
$600	$610	95	80	68	60	52	44	36	29	21	13	5
610	620	97	83	69	61	53	46	38	30	22	15	7
620	630	100	86	71	63	55	47	39	32	24	16	8
630	640	103	88	74	64	56	49	41	33	25	18	10
640	650	106	91	77	66	58	50	42	35	27	19	11
650	660	109	94	79	67	59	52	44	36	28	21	13
660	670	111	97	82	69	61	53	45	38	30	22	14
670	680	114	100	85	70	62	55	47	39	31	24	16
680	690	117	102	88	73	64	56	48	41	33	25	17
690	700	120	105	91	76	65	58	50	42	34	27	19
700	710	123	108	93	79	67	59	51	44	36	28	20
710	720	125	111	96	82	68	61	53	45	37	30	22
720	730	128	114	99	84	70	62	54	47	39	31	23
730	740	130	116	102	87	73	64	56	48	40	33	25
740	750	134	119	105	90	76	65	57	50	42	34	26

9A.6 is for a single employee paid weekly. Tables are also provided for married employees and for biweekly, semimonthly, and monthly pay periods (most payroll software includes these tables). When using a wage bracket withholding table to compute federal income tax withheld from an employee's gross wages, we need to locate an employee's wage bracket within the first two columns of the table. We then find the amount withheld by looking in the withholding allowance column for that employee.

Payroll Bank Account

Companies with few employees often pay them with checks drawn on the company's regular bank account. Companies with many employees often use a special **payroll bank account** to pay employees. When this account is used, a company either (1) draws one check for total payroll on the regular bank account and deposits it in the payroll bank account or (2) executes an *electronic funds transfer* to the payroll bank account. Individual payroll checks are then drawn on this payroll bank account. Since only one check for the total payroll is drawn on the regular bank account each payday, use of a special payroll bank account helps with internal control. It also helps in reconciling the regular bank account. When companies use a payroll bank account, they usually include check numbers in the payroll register. The payroll register in Exhibit 9A.3 shows check numbers in column 1. For instance, Check No. 9001 is issued to Robert Austin. With this information, the payroll register serves as a supplementary record of wages earned by and paid to employees.

P6 Record payment of payroll.

Quick Check

13. What two items determine the amount deducted from an employee's wages for federal income taxes?

14. What amount of income tax is withheld from the salary of an employee who is single with three withholding allowances and earnings of $675 in a week? (*Hint:* Use the wage bracket withholding table in Exhibit 9A.6.)

15. Which of the following steps are executed when a company draws one check for total payroll and deposits it in a special payroll bank account? (*a*) Write a check to the payroll bank account for the total payroll and record it with a debit to Accrued Payroll Payable and a credit to Cash. (*b*) Deposit a check (or transfer funds) for the total payroll in the payroll bank account. (*c*) Issue individual payroll checks drawn on the payroll bank account. (*d*) All of the above.

Answers—p. 403

Summary

C1 Describe current and long-term liabilities and their characteristics. Liabilities are probable future payments of assets or services that past transactions or events obligate an entity to make. Current liabilities are due within one year or the operating cycle, whichever is longer. All other liabilities are long term.

C2 Identify and describe known current liabilities. Known (determinable) current liabilities are set by agreements or laws and are measurable with little uncertainty. They include accounts payable, sales taxes payable, unearned revenues, notes payable, payroll liabilities, and the current portion of long-term debt.

C3 Explain how to account for contingent liabilities. If an uncertain future payment depends on a probable future

event and the amount can be reasonably estimated, the payment is recorded as a liability. The uncertain future payment is reported as a contingent liability (in the notes) if (*a*) the future event is reasonably possible but not probable or (*b*) the event is probable but the payment amount cannot be reasonably estimated.

C4 Identify and describe payroll reporting. Employers report FICA taxes and federal income tax withholdings using Form 941. FUTA taxes are reported on Form 940. Earnings and deductions are reported to each employee and the federal government on Form W-2.

C5 Identify and describe payroll records. An employer's payroll records include a payroll register for each pay period, payroll checks and statements of earnings, and individual employee earnings reports.

A1 **Compute the times interest earned ratio and use it to analyze liabilities.** Times interest earned is computed by dividing a company's net income before interest expense and income taxes by the amount of interest expense. The times interest earned ratio reflects a company's ability to pay interest obligations.

P1 **Prepare entries to account for short-term notes payable.** Short-term notes payable are current liabilities; most bear interest. When a short-term note's face value equals the amount borrowed, it identifies a rate of interest to be paid at maturity. When a short-term note's face value equals the amount to be paid at maturity, its face value includes interest.

P2 **Compute and record *employee* payroll deductions and liabilities.** Employee payroll deductions include FICA taxes, income taxes, and voluntary deductions such as for pensions and charities. They make up the difference between gross and net pay.

P3 **Compute and record *employer* payroll expenses and liabilities.** An employer's payroll expenses include employees'

gross earnings, and benefits, and payroll taxes levied on the employer. Payroll liabilities include employees' net pay amounts withheld from their wages and benefits, and the employer's payroll taxes.

P4 **Account for estimated liabilities, including warranties and income taxes.** Liabilities for health and pension benefits, warranties, bonuses, and income taxes are recorded with estimated amounts. These items are recognized as expenses when incurred and to match with revenues generated.

P5 **Compute payroll taxes.** Federal income tax deductions depend on the employee's earnings and the number of withholding allowances claimed. Wage bracket withholding tables are available for different pay periods and employee classes.

P6 **Record payment of payroll.** Employers with a large number of employees often use a separate payroll bank account. When this is done, the payment of employees is recorded with a transfer of cash from the regular bank account to the payroll bank account.

Guidance Answers to **Decision Maker** and **Decision Ethics**

Rock Band Both banks agree to give the band $30,000 cash and require repayment in six months. Provided terms in these contracts are similar, the only potential difference is in the amount of interest the band must pay. The second bank's contract makes this clear—since $30,000 is borrowed and the band must pay $32,000, the interest [charged] is $2,000. For the first bank, we must compute interest on the contract. It is $2,100, computed as $30,000 × 14% × 6/12. The band prefers the contract requiring less interest, which is the one reading: "Band promises to pay $32,000 within 6 months."

Web Designer You need to be concerned about being an accomplice to unlawful payroll activities. Not paying federal and state taxes on wages earned is illegal and unethical. Such payments also will not provide the employee with Social Security and some

Medicare credits. The best course of action is to request payment by check. If this fails to change the owner's payment practices, you must consider quitting this job.

Entrepreneur Risk is partly reflected by the times interest earned ratio. This ratio for the first franchise is 1.5 [($100,000 + $200,000)/$200,000], whereas the ratio for the second franchise is 3.5 [($100,000 + $40,000)/$40,000]. This analysis shows that the first franchise is more at risk of incurring a loss if its sales decline. The second question asks about variability of income. If income greatly varies, this increases the risk an owner will not earn sufficient income to cover interest. Since the first franchise has the greater variability, it is a riskier investment.

Guidance Answers to **Quick Checks**

1. A liability involves a probable future payment of assets or services that an entity is presently obligated to make as a result of past transactions or events.

2. No, an expected future payment is not a liability unless an existing obligation was created by a past event or transaction.

3. In most cases, a liability due in 15 months is classified as long term. It is classified as a current liability if the company's operating cycle is 15 months or longer.

4. A creditor prefers a note payable instead of an account payable so as to (*a*) charge interest and/or (*b*) have evidence of the debt and its terms for potential litigation or disputes.

5. The amount borrowed is $1,000 cash ($1,050 − $50). The rate of interest is 5% ($50/$1,000) for six months, which approximates an annual rate of 10%.

6. $1,000(.008) + $1,000(.04) + $3,000(.062) + $3,000(.0145) = $277.50

7. (*a*) FICA taxes are paid by both the employee and employer.
   (*b*) FUTA taxes are paid by the employer.
   (*c*) SUTA taxes are paid by the employer.
   (*d*) Withheld income taxes are paid by the employee.

8. (*a*)

9. (*a*) Warranty expense was previously estimated and recorded.

10. A corporation accrues an income tax liability for its quarterly financial statements because income tax expense is incurred when income is earned, not just at year-end.

11. (*b*)

12. A future payment is reported in the notes as a contingent liability if (*a*) the uncertain future event is probable but the amount of payment cannot be reasonably estimated or (*b*) the uncertain future event is not probable but has a reasonable possibility of occurring.

13. An employee's gross earnings and number of withholding allowances determine the deduction for federal income taxes.

14. $70

15. (*d*)

Glossary

Contingent liability Potential liability that depends on a future event arising from a past transaction. (p. 390)

Current liabilities Obligations due within a year or the company's operating cycle, whichever is longer; paid using current assets or by creating other current liabilities. (p. 376)

Current portion of long-term debt Portion of long-term debt due within one year or the operating cycle, whichever is longer; reported under current liabilities. (p. 391)

Deferred income tax liability Corporation income taxes that are deferred until future years because of temporary differences between GAAP and tax rules. (p. 389)

Discount on note payable Difference between the face value of a note payable and the amount borrowed; the interest to be paid on the note over its life. (p. 380)

Employee benefits Additional compensation paid to or on behalf of employees, such as premiums for medical, dental, life, disability insurance, and contributions to pension plans. (p. 387)

Employee earnings report Record of an employee's net pay, gross pay, deductions, and year-to-date information. (p. 399)

Estimated liability Obligation of an uncertain amount that can be reasonably estimated. (p. 386)

Federal depository bank Bank authorized to accept deposits of amounts payable to the federal government. (p. 396)

Federal Insurance Contributions Act (FICA) Taxes Taxes assessed on both employers and employees; for Social Security and Medicare programs. (p. 384)

Federal Unemployment Taxes (FUTA) Payroll taxes on employers assessed by the federal government to support its unemployment insurance program. (p. 385)

Form 940 IRS form used to report an employer's federal unemployment taxes (FUTA) on an annual filing basis. (p. 396)

Form 941 IRS form filed to report FICA taxes owed and remitted. (p. 396)

Form W-2 Annual report by an employer to each employee showing the employee's wages subject to FICA and federal income taxes along with amounts withheld. (p. 397)

Form W-4 A withholding allowance certificate, filed with the employer, identifying the number of withholding allowances claimed. (p. 400)

Gross pay Total compensation earned by an employee. (p. 383)

Known liabilities Obligations of a company with little uncertainty; set by agreements, contracts, or laws; also called *definitely determinable liabilities.* (p. 378)

Long-term liabilities Obligations *not* requiring payment within one year or the operating cycle, whichever is longer. (p. 377)

Merit rating Rating assigned to an employer by a state based on the employer's record of employment. (p. 386)

Net pay Gross pay less all deductions; also called *take-home pay.* (p. 383)

Noninterest-bearing note Note with no stated rate of interest; interest is included in the face value of the note. (p. 381)

Payroll bank account Bank account used solely for paying employees; each pay period an amount equal to the total employees' net pay is deposited in it and the payroll checks are drawn on it. (p. 401)

Payroll deductions Amounts withheld from an employee's gross pay; also called *withholdings.* (p. 383)

Payroll register Record for a pay period that shows the pay period dates, regular and overtime hours worked, gross pay, net pay, and deductions. (p. 398)

Short-term note payable Current obligation in the form of a written promissory note. (p. 379)

State Unemployment Taxes (SUTA) State payroll taxes on employers to support its unemployment programs. (p. 385)

Times interest earned Ratio of income before interest expense (and any income taxes) divided by interest expense; reflects risk of interest commitments when income varies. (p. 393)

Wage bracket withholding table Table of the amounts of income tax withheld from employees' wages. (p. 400)

Warranty Agreement that obligates the seller to correct or replace a product or service when it fails to perform properly within a specified period. (p. 387)

Superscript letter ^A *denotes assignments based on Appendix 9A.*

Questions

1. What are the three important questions concerning the uncertainty of liabilities?

2. What is the difference between a current and a long-term liability?

3. What is an estimated liability?

4. What is the combined amount (in percent) of the employees' and employer's Social Security tax rate?

5. What is the current Medicare tax rate? This rate is applied to what maximum level of salary and wages?

6. What determines the amount deducted from an employee's wages for federal income taxes?

7. Which payroll taxes are the employee's responsibility and which are the employer's responsibility?

8. What is an employer's unemployment merit rating? How are these ratings assigned to employers?

9. 𝑑 Why are warranty liabilities usually recognized on the balance sheet as liabilities even when they are uncertain?

10. 𝑑 Suppose that a company has a facility located where disastrous weather conditions often occur. Should it report a probable loss from a future disaster as a liability on its balance sheet? Explain.

11.ᴬ What is a wage bracket withholding table?

12.ᴬ What amount of income tax is withheld from the salary of an employee who is single with two withholding allowances

and earning $725 per week? What if the employee earned $625 and has no withholding allowances? (Use Exhibit 9A.6.)

13. 𝑑 Refer to Nike's financial statements in Appendix A. Explain the change in current notes payable during fiscal year 2000 with reference to a statement other than the balance sheet.

14. 𝑑 Refer to Reebok's balance sheet in Appendix A. What accounts related to income taxes are on the balance sheet? Identify the meaning of each income tax account you identify.

15. Refer to Gap's balance sheet in Appendix A. Which current liability account reports the payroll-related liabilities (if any) of Gap as of January 29, 2000?

QUICK STUDY

QS 9-1
Classifying liabilities **C1**

Which of the following items are normally classified as a current liability for a company that has a 15-month operating cycle?

1. Note payable maturing in 2 years.
2. Note payable due in 11 months.
3. Portion of long-term note due in 15 months.
4. Salaries payable.
5. Note payable due in 18 months.
6. FICA taxes payable.

QS 9-2
Accounting for sales taxes **C2**

Cube Computing sells merchandise for $6,000 cash on September 30 (cost of merchandise is $3,900). The sales tax law requires Cube to collect 4% sales tax on every dollar of merchandise sold. Record the entry for the $6,000 sale and its applicable sales tax. Also record the entry that shows the remittance of the 4% tax on this sale to the state government on October 15.

QS 9-3 𝑑
Unearned revenue **C2**

Ticketmaster receives $5,000,000 in advance ticket sales for a four-date tour of the Rolling Stones. Record the advance ticket sales on October 31. Record the revenue earned for the first concert date of November 5 assuming it represents one-fourth of the advance ticket sales.

QS 9-4 𝑑
Interest-bearing note transactions **P1**

On November 7, 2002, Eager Company borrows $160,000 cash by signing a 90-day, 8% note payable with a face value of $160,000. (1) Compute the accrued interest payable on December 31, 2002, and (2) prepare the journal entry to record payment of the note at maturity.

QS 9-5
Noninterest-bearing note transactions **P1**

Hamm Company signs a noninterest-bearing note dated December 16 and promising to pay $5,120 within 60 days. Record the signing of the note, the interest accrual on December 31, and the repayment of the note on February 14. (The note's face value of $5,120 includes $120 of interest.)

QS 9-6
Record employer payroll taxes **P2 P3**

Regis Co. has five employees, each of whom earns $2,500 per month and has been employed since January 1. FICA Social Security taxes are 6.2% of gross pay and FICA Medicare taxes are 1.45% of gross pay. FUTA taxes are 0.8% and SUTA taxes are 2.8% of the first $7,000 paid to each employee. Prepare the March 31 journal entry to record March payroll taxes expense.

QS 9-7
Recording warranty repairs **P4**

On September 11, 2002, Maxims sells a mower for $500 with a one-year warranty that covers parts. Warranty expense is estimated at 5% of sales. On July 24, 2003, the mower is brought in for repairs covered under the warranty requiring $55 in materials taken from the Repair Parts Inventory. Prepare the July 24, 2003, entry to record the warranty repairs.

QS 9-8
Record deferred income tax liability **P4**

Ivanhoe Corporation has made and recorded its quarterly income tax payments. After a final review of taxes for the year, the company identifies an additional $40,000 of income tax expense that should be recorded. A portion of this additional expense, $6,000, is deferred for payment in future years. Record Ivanhoe's year-end adjusting entry for income tax expense.

Fabrique Company offers an annual bonus to employees if the company meets certain net income goals. Prepare the journal entry to record a $15,000 bonus owed to workers (to be shared equally) at calendar year-end.

QS 9-9
Accounting for bonuses P4

The following legal claims exist for Kalamazoo Co. Identify the accounting treatment for each claim as either (*a*) a liability that is recorded or (*b*) an item described in notes to its financial statements.

1. Kalamazoo (defendant) estimates that a pending lawsuit could result in damages of $1,250,000; it is reasonably possible that the plaintiff will win the case.
2. Kalamazoo faces a probable loss on a pending lawsuit; the amount is not reasonably estimable.
3. Kalamazoo estimates damages in a case at $3,500,000 with a high probability of losing the case.

QS 9-10
Accounting for contingent liabilities

C3

Compute the times interest earned for Sarafin Company, which reports income before interest expense and income taxes of $1,885,000 and interest expense of $145,000. Interpret its times interest earned—assume that its competitors average ratio is 4.0.

QS 9-11
Times interest earned A1

The following items appear on the balance sheet of a company with a two-month operating cycle. Identify the proper classification of each item as follows: *C* if it is a current liability, *L* if it is a long-term liability, or *N* if it is not a liability.

_____ **1.** Sales taxes payable.	_____ **6.** Notes payable (due in 6 to 12 months).
_____ **2.** Income taxes payable.	_____ **7.** Notes payable (mature in five years).
_____ **3.** Accrued payroll payable.	_____ **8.** Current portion of long-term debt.
_____ **4.** Accounts receivable.	_____ **9.** Notes payable (due in 120 days).
_____ **5.** Wages payable.	_____ **10.** Notes payable (due in 13 to 24 months).

EXERCISES

Exercise 9-1
Classifying liabilities

C1

Prepare any necessary adjusting entries at December 31, 2002, for Delta Company's year-end financial statements given the following information:

1. During December, Delta Company sold 4,000 units of a product that carries a 60-day warranty. December sales for this product total $150,000. The company expects 8% of the units to need warranty repairs, and it estimates the average repair cost per unit will be $17.
2. A disgruntled employee is suing Delta Company. Legal advisers believe that the company will probably have to pay damages, but the amount cannot be reasonably estimated.
3. Employees earn vacation pay at a rate of one day per month. During December, 20 employees qualify for one vacation day each. Their average daily wage is $105 per employee.
4. Delta Company guarantees the $7,500 debt of a supplier. The supplier will probably not default on the debt.
5. Delta Company records an adjusting entry for $750,000 of previously unrecorded cash sales along with the sales taxes of 5%. The costs of those merchandise sales total $500,000.
6. The company earned $75,000 of $100,000 previously received in advance for services.

Exercise 9-2
Adjusting entries for liabilities

C2 C3 P4

For the year ended December 31, 2002, Warner Company has implemented an employee bonus program equal to 3% of Warner's net income that employees will share equally. Warner's net income (pre-bonus) is expected to be $500,000, and bonus expense is deducted in computing net income.

1. Compute the amount of the bonus payable to the employees at year-end (use the method described in the chapter and round to the nearest dollar).
2. Prepare the journal entry at December 31, 2002, to record the bonus due the employees.
3. Prepare the journal entry at January 19, 2003, to record payment of the bonus to employees.

Exercise 9-3
Computing and recording bonuses C2

Check (1) $14,563

Peerless Systems borrows $104,000 cash on May 15, 2002, by signing a 60-day, 12% note.

1. On what date will this note mature?
2. Suppose the face value of the note equals $104,000, the principal of the loan. Prepare the journal entries to record issuance of the note and its payment at maturity.

Exercise 9-4
Interest-bearing and noninterest-bearing notes payable P1

Check (2) Interest expense, $2,080

3. Suppose the face value of the note is $106,080, which includes both the principal of the loan ($104,000) and the interest to be paid at maturity. Prepare the journal entries to record issuance of the note and its payment at maturity.

Exercise 9-5 🗹

Interest-bearing and noninterest-bearing notes payable with year-end adjustments

P1

Check (2) $3,000

(3) $1,500

Excel Co. borrows $200,000 cash on November 1, 2002, by signing a 90-day, 9% note with a face value of $200,000.

1. On what date will this note mature?

2. How much interest expense results from this note in 2002? (Assume a 360-day year.)

3. How much interest expense results from this note in 2003? (Assume a 360-day year.)

4. Prepare journal entries to record issuance of the note, accrual of interest at the end of 2002, and payment of the note at maturity.

5. Suppose the face value of the note is $204,500 (instead of $200,000), which includes both the principal of the loan ($200,000) and its interest ($4,500). Prepare journal entries to record issuance of the note, accrual of interest at the end of 2002, and payment of the note at maturity.

Exercise 9-6

Computing payroll taxes

P2 P3

TSI Co. has one employee, and the company is subject to the following taxes:

Tax	Rate	Applied To
FICA—Social Security	6.20%	First $76,200
FICA—Medicare	1.45	Gross pay
FUTA	0.80	First $7,000
SUTA	2.90	First $7,000

Compute TSI's amounts for each of these four taxes as applied to the employee's gross earnings for September under each of three separate situations (a), (b), and (c):

	Gross Pay through August	Gross Pay for September
a.	$ 6,800	$ 900
b.	19,200	2,200
c.	71,200	8,000

Check (a) FUTA, $1.60; SUTA, $5.80

Exercise 9-7

Payroll-related **P2 P3** journal entries

Using the data in situation a of Exercise 9-6, prepare the employer's September 30 journal entries to record (1) salary expense and its related payroll liabilities for this employee and (2) the employer's payroll taxes expense and its related liabilities. The employee's federal income taxes withheld by the employer are $100 for this pay period.

Exercise 9-8 🗹

Warranty expense and liability computations and entries

P4

Check (1) $240

Check (4) $31

Yoko Co. sold a copier costing $4,800 with a two-year parts warranty to a customer on August 16, 2002, for $6,000 cash (Yoko uses the perpetual inventory system). On November 22, 2003, the copier requires on-site repairs that are completed the same day. The repairs cost $209 for materials taken from the Repair Parts Inventory. These are the only repairs required in 2003 for this copier. Based on experience, Yoko expects to incur warranty costs equal to 4% of sales. It records warranty expense with an adjusting entry at the end of each year.

1. How much warranty expense does the company report in 2002 for this copier?

2. How much is the estimated warranty liability for this copier as of December 31, 2002?

3. How much warranty expense does the company report in 2003 for this copier?

4. How much is the estimated warranty liability for this copier as of December 31, 2003?

5. Prepare journal entries to record (a) the copier's sale; (b) the adjustment on December 31, 2002, to recognize the warranty expense; and (c) the repairs that occur in November 2003.

Caper Corporation prepares financial statements each month. As part of its accounting process, estimated income taxes are accrued each month for 30% of the current month's net income. The income taxes are paid in the first month of each quarter for the amount accrued for the prior quarter. The following information is available for the last quarter of year 2002. When tax computations are completed on January 20, 2003, Caper determines that the quarter's Income Taxes Payable account balance should be $28,300 on December 31, 2002 (its unadjusted balance is $24,690).

October net income	$28,600
November net income	19,100
December net income	34,600

1. Determine the amount of the accounting adjustment (dated as of December 31, 2002) to produce the proper ending balance in the Income Taxes Payable account.
2. Prepare journal entries to record (*a*) the December 31, 2002, adjustment to the Income Taxes Payable account and (*b*) the January 20, 2003, payment of the fourth-quarter taxes.

Exercise 9-9
Accounting for income taxes
P4

Check   (1) $3,610

Use the following information from separate companies *a* through *f* to compute times interest earned. Which company indicates the strongest ability to pay interest expense as it comes due?

	Net Income (Loss)	Interest Expense	Income Taxes
a.	$115,000	$44,000	$ 35,000
b.	110,000	10,000	50,000
c.	100,000	12,000	70,000
d.	235,000	14,000	130,000
e.	59,000	14,000	30,000
f.	(5,000)	10,000	0

Exercise 9-10
Computing and interpreting times interest earned
A1

The payroll records of Classic Software show the following information about Trish Nyhart, an employee, for the weekly pay period ending September 30, 2002. Trish is single and claims one allowance. Compute her Social Security tax (6.2%), Medicare tax (1.45%), federal income tax withholding, state income tax (0.5%), and net pay for the current pay period. The state income tax is 0.5 percent on $9,000 maximum. (Use the withholding table in Exhibit 9A.6.)

| Total (gross) earnings for current pay period   . . . | $ 725 |
| Cumulative earnings of previous pay periods . . . | 9,600 |

Exercise 9-11^A

Exercise 9-11[A]
Net pay and tax computations
P5

Check   Net pay, $555.54

Wendy Geiger, an unmarried employee, works 48 hours in the week ended January 12. Her pay rate is $14 per hour, and her wages are subject to no deductions other than FICA—Social Security, FICA—Medicare, and federal income taxes. She claims two withholding allowances. Compute her regular pay, overtime pay (overtime premium is 50% of the regular rate for hours in excess of 40 per week), and gross pay. Then compute her FICA tax deduction (use 6.2% for the Social Security portion and 1.45% for the Medicare portion), income tax deduction (use the wage bracket withholding table of Exhibit 9A.6), total deductions, and net pay.

Exercise 9-12[A]
Gross and net pay computation
P5 P6

Check   Net pay, $573.30

Langholz Co. entered into the following transactions involving short-term liabilities in 2002 and 2003.

2002

| Apr. 20 | Purchased $40,250 of merchandise on credit from Fitz, terms are 1/10, n/30. Langholz uses the perpetual inventory system. |
| May 19 | Replaced the April 20 account payable to Fitz with a 90-day, $35,000 note bearing 10% annual interest along with paying $5,250 in cash. |

PROBLEM SET A

Problem 9-1A
Short-term notes payable transactions and entries
P1

July 8	Borrowed $80,000 cash from Firstar Bank by signing a 120-day, 9% interest-bearing note with a face value of $80,000.
?	Paid the amount due on the note to Fitz at the maturity date.
?	Paid the amount due on the note to Firstar Bank at the maturity date.
Nov. 28	Borrowed $42,000 cash by signing a noninterest-bearing note with a face value of $42,560 to UMB Bank that matures in 60 days. The face value includes principal of $42,000 and interest of $560.
Dec. 31	Recorded an adjusting entry for accrued interest on the note to UMB Bank.

2003

| ? | Paid the amount due on the note to UMB Bank at the maturity date. |

Required

1. Determine the maturity date for each of the three notes described.
2. Determine the interest due at maturity for each of the three notes. (Assume a 360-day year.)
3. Determine the interest expense to be recorded in the adjusting entry at the end of 2002.
4. Determine the interest expense to be recorded in 2003.
5. Prepare journal entries for all the preceding transactions and events for years 2002–2003.

Check (2) Fitz, $875
(3) $308
(4) $252

Problem 9-2A
Warranty expense and
liability estimation

P4

On October 29, 2002, Shaver Co. began operations by purchasing electric razors for resale at $75 each. Shaver uses the perpetual inventory method. The razors have a 90-day warranty that requires the company to replace any nonworking razor. When a razor is returned, the company discards it and mails a new one from Merchandise Inventory to the customer. The company's cost per new razor is $20 in both 2002 and 2003. The manufacturer has advised the company to expect warranty costs to equal 8% of dollar sales. The following transactions and events occurred in 2002 and 2003:

2002

Nov. 11	Sold 105 razors for $7,875 cash.
30	Recognized warranty expense related to November sales with an adjusting entry.
Dec. 9	Replaced 15 razors that were returned under the warranty.
16	Sold 220 razors for $16,500 cash.
29	Replaced 30 razors that were returned under the warranty.
31	Recognized warranty expense related to December sales with an adjusting entry.

2003

Jan. 5	Sold 150 razors for $11,250 cash.
17	Replaced 50 razors that were returned under the warranty.
31	Recognized warranty expense related to January sales with an adjusting entry.

Required

1. Prepare journal entries to record these transactions and adjustments for 2002 and 2003.
2. How much warranty expense is reported for November 2002 and for December 2002?
3. How much warranty expense is reported for January 2003?
4. What is the balance of the Estimated Warranty Liability account as of December 31, 2002?
5. What is the balance of the Estimated Warranty Liability account as of January 31, 2003?

Check (3) $900
(4) $1,050 Cr.
(5) $950 Cr.

Problem 9-3A
Computing and analyzing
times interest earned

A1

Shown here are condensed income statements for two different companies (both are organized as S corporations and pay no income taxes):

Acme Co.	
Sales	$1,000,000
Variable expenses (80%)	800,000
Income before interest	$ 200,000
Interest expense (fixed)	60,000
Net income	$ 140,000

Nadir Co.	
Sales	$1,000,000
Variable expenses (60%)	600,000
Income before interest	$ 400,000
Interest expense (fixed)	260,000
Net income	$ 140,000

Required

1. Compute times interest earned for Acme Co.

2. Compute times interest earned for Nadir Co.

3. What happens to each company's net income if sales increase by 30%?

4. What happens to each company's net income if sales increase by 50%?

5. What happens to each company's net income if sales increase by 80%?

6. What happens to each company's net income if sales decrease by 10%?

7. What happens to each company's net income if sales decrease by 20%?

8. What happens to each company's net income if sales decrease by 40%?

Check (3) Acme net income, $200,000 (43% increase)

Check (6) Nadir net income, $100,000 (29% decrease)

Analysis Component

9. Comment on the results from parts 3 through 8 in relation to the fixed-cost strategies of the two companies and the ratio values you computed in parts 1 and 2.

Legal Eagles pays its employees each week. Its employees' gross pay is subject to these taxes:

Problem 9-4A
Payroll expenses, withholdings, and taxes

P2 P3

Tax	Rate	Applied To
FICA—Social Security	6.20%	First $76,200
FICA—Medicare	1.45	Gross pay
FUTA	0.80	First $7,000
SUTA	2.15	First $7,000

The company is preparing its payroll calculations for the week ended August 25. Payroll records show the following information for the company's four employees:

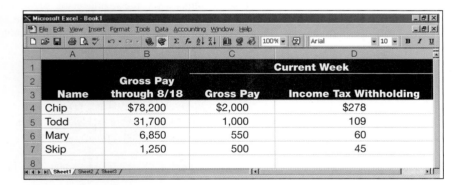

Name	Gross Pay through 8/18	Gross Pay	Income Tax Withholding
		Current Week	
Chip	$78,200	$2,000	$278
Todd	31,700	1,000	109
Mary	6,850	550	60
Skip	1,250	500	45

In addition to gross pay, the company must pay one-half of the $34 per employee weekly health insurance; each employee pays the remaining one-half. The company also contributes an extra 8% of each employee's gross pay (at no cost to employees) to a pension fund.

Required

Compute the following for the week ended August 25 (round amounts to the nearest cent):

1. Each employee's FICA withholdings for Social Security.

2. Each employee's FICA withholdings for Medicare.

3. Employer's FICA taxes for Social Security.

4. Employer's FICA taxes for Medicare.

5. Employer's FUTA taxes.

6. Employer's SUTA taxes.

Check (3) $127.10
(4) $58.73
(5) $5.20

7. Each employee's net (take-home) pay.

8. Employer's total payroll-related expense for each employee.

Problem 9-5A

Entries for payroll transactions

P2 P3

On January 8, the end of the first weekly pay period of the year, Kidwear Company's payroll register showed that its employees earned $22,760 of office salaries and $65,840 of sales salaries. Withholdings from the employees' salaries include FICA Social Security taxes at the rate of 6.2%, FICA Medicare taxes at the rate of 1.45%, $12,860 of federal income taxes, $1,340 of medical insurance deductions, and $840 of union dues. No employee earned more than $7,000 in this first period.

Required

1. Calculate FICA Social Security taxes payable and FICA Medicare taxes payable. Prepare the journal entry to record Kidwear Company's January 8 (employee) payroll expenses and liabilities.

2. Prepare the journal entry to record Kidwear's (employer) payroll taxes resulting from the January 8 payroll. Kidwear's merit rating reduces its state unemployment tax rate to 4.0% of the first $7,000 paid each employee. The federal unemployment tax rate is 0.8%.

Problem 9-6A[A]

Entries for payroll transactions

P2 P3 P5 P6

Friesen Company has 10 employees, each of whom earns $2,700 per month and is paid on the last day of each month. All 10 have been employed continuously at this amount since January 1. Friesen uses a payroll bank account and special payroll checks to pay its employees. On March 1, the following accounts and balances exist in its general ledger:

a. FICA—Social Security Taxes Payable, $3,348; FICA—Medicare Taxes Payable, $783. (The balances of these accounts represent total liabilities for *both* the employer's and employees' FICA taxes for the February payroll only.)

b. Employees' Federal Income Taxes Payable, $4,000 (liability for February only).

c. Federal Unemployment Taxes Payable, $432 (liability for January and February together).

d. State Unemployment Taxes Payable, $2,160 (liability for January and February together).

During March and April, the company had the following payroll transactions:

Mar. 15   Issued check payable to Fleet Bank, a federal depository bank authorized to accept employers' payments of FICA taxes and employee income tax withholdings. The $8,131 check is in payment of the February FICA and employee income taxes.

31   Recorded the March payroll and transferred funds from the regular bank account to the payroll bank account. Issued checks payable to each employee in payment of the March payroll. The payroll register shows the following summary totals for the March pay period:

Salaries and Wages				Federal	
Office Salaries	Shop Wages	Gross Pay	FICA Taxes*	Income Taxes	Net Pay
$10,800	$16,200	$27,000	$1,674.00	$4,000	$20,934.50
			$ 391.50		

* FICA taxes are Social Security and Medicare, respectively.

31   Recorded the employer's payroll taxes resulting from the March payroll. The company has a merit rating that reduces its state unemployment tax rate to 4.0% of the first $7,000 paid each employee. The federal rate is 0.8%.

Apr. 15   Issued check to Fleet Bank in payment of the March FICA and employee income taxes.

15   Issued check to the State Tax Commission for the January, February, and March state unemployment taxes. Mailed the check and the first quarter tax return to the Commission.

30   Issued check payable to Fleet Bank in payment of the employer's FUTA taxes for the first quarter of the year.

30   Mailed Form 941 to the IRS, reporting the FICA taxes and the employees' federal income tax withholdings for the first quarter.

Required

Prepare journal entries to record the transactions and events for both March and April.

Quinn Co. entered into the following transactions involving short-term liabilities in 2002 and 2003.

2002

Apr. 22   Purchased $5,000 of merchandise on credit from Cascade Products, terms are 1/10, n/30. Quinn uses the perpetual inventory system.

May 23   Replaced the April 22 account payable to Cascade Products with a 60-day, $4,600 note bearing 15% annual interest along with paying $400 in cash.

July 15   Borrowed $12,000 cash from Fall River Bank by signing a 120-day, 10% interest-bearing note with a face value of $12,000.

____?____   Paid the amount due on the note to Cascade Products at maturity.

____?____   Paid the amount due on the note to Fall River Bank at maturity.

Dec. 6   Borrowed $8,000 cash by signing a noninterest-bearing note with a face value of $8,090 to City Bank that matures in 45 days. The face value includes principal of $8,000 and interest of $90.

     31   Recorded an adjusting entry for accrued interest on the note to City Bank.

2003

____?____   Paid the amount due on the note to City Bank at maturity.

Problem 9-1B
Short-term notes payable
transactions and entries

P1

Required

1. Determine the maturity date for each of the three notes described.

2. Determine the interest due at maturity for each of the three notes. (Assume a 360-day year.)

3. Determine the interest expense to be recorded in the adjusting entry at the end of 2002.

4. Determine the interest expense to be recorded in 2003.

5. Prepare journal entries for all the preceding transactions and events for years 2002–2003.

On November 10, 2002, Maleta Co. began operations by purchasing coffee grinders for resale at $50 each. Maleta uses the perpetual inventory method. The grinders have a 60-day warranty that requires the company to replace any nonworking grinder. When a grinder is returned, the company discards it and mails a new one from Merchandise Inventory to the customer. The company's cost per new grinder is $24 in both 2002 and 2003. The manufacturer has advised the company to expect warranty costs to equal 10% of dollar sales. The following transactions and events occurred in 2002 and 2003.

Problem 9-2B
Warranty expense and
liability estimation

P4

2002

Nov. 16   Sold 50 grinders for $2,500 cash.
     30   Recognized warranty expense related to November sales with an adjusting entry.
Dec. 12   Replaced six grinders that were returned under the warranty.
     18   Sold 200 grinders for $10,000 cash.
     28   Replaced 17 grinders that were returned under the warranty.
     31   Recognized warranty expense related to December sales with an adjusting entry.

2003

Jan. 7   Sold 40 grinders for $2,000 cash.
     21   Replaced 38 grinders that were returned under the warranty.
     31   Recognized warranty expense related to January sales with an adjusting entry.

Required

1. Prepare journal entries to record these transactions and adjustments for 2002 and 2003.

2. How much warranty expense is reported for November 2002 and for December 2002?

3. How much warranty expense is reported for January 2003?

4. What is the balance of the Estimated Warranty Liability account as of December 31, 2002?

5. What is the balance of the Estimated Warranty Liability account as of January 31, 2003?

Problem 9-3B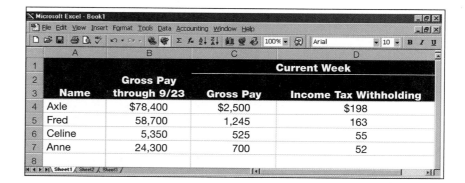
Computing and analyzing
times interest earned

A1

Shown here are condensed income statements for two different companies (both are organized as LLCs and pay no income taxes):

Scorpio Co.	
Sales	$240,000
Variable expenses (50%)	120,000
Income before interest	$120,000
Interest expense (fixed)	90,000
Net income	$ 30,000

Gemini Co.	
Sales	$240,000
Variable expenses (75%)	180,000
Income before interest	$ 60,000
Interest expense (fixed)	30,000
Net income	$ 30,000

Required

1. Compute times interest earned for Scorpio.
2. Compute times interest earned for Gemini.
3. What happens to each company's net income if sales increase by 10%?
4. What happens to each company's net income if sales increase by 40%?
5. What happens to each company's net income if sales increase by 90%?
6. What happens to each company's net income if sales decrease by 20%?
7. What happens to each company's net income if sales decrease by 50%?
8. What happens to each company's net income if sales decrease by 80%?

Analysis Component

9. Comment on the results from parts 3 through 8 in relation to the fixed cost strategies of the two companies and the ratio values you computed in parts 1 and 2.

Check   (4) Scorpio net income, $78,000 (160% increase)

Check   (6) Gemini net income, $18,000 (40% decrease)

Problem 9-4B
Payroll expenses,
withholdings, and taxes

P2 P3

Seahawk Company pays its employees each week. Employees' gross pay is subject to these taxes:

Tax	Rate	Applied To
FICA—Social Security	6.20%	First $76,200
FICA—Medicare	1.45	Gross pay
FUTA	0.80	First $7,000
SUTA	1.75	First $7,000

The company is preparing its payroll calculations for the week ended September 30. Payroll records show the following information for the company's four employees:

		Current Week	
Name	**Gross Pay through 9/23**	**Gross Pay**	**Income Tax Withholding**
Axle	$78,400	$2,500	$198
Fred	58,700	1,245	163
Celine	5,350	525	55
Anne	24,300	700	52

In addition to gross pay, the company must pay one-half of the $40 per employee weekly health insurance; each employee pays the remaining one-half. The company also contributes an extra 5% of each employee's gross pay (at no cost to employees) to a pension fund.

Required

Compute the following for the week ended September 30 (round amounts to the nearest cent):

1. Each employee's FICA withholdings for Social Security.
2. Each employee's FICA withholdings for Medicare.
3. Employer's FICA taxes for Social Security.
4. Employer's FICA taxes for Medicare.
5. Employer's FUTA taxes.
6. Employer's SUTA taxes.
7. Each employee's net (take-home) pay.
8. Employer's total payroll-related expense for each employee.

Check   (3) $153.14
(4) $72.06
(5) $4.20

(7) Total net pay, $4,196.80

Genie Company's first weekly pay period of the year ends on January 8. On that date, the column totals in Genie's payroll register indicate its sales employees earned $34,745, its office employees earned $21,225, and its delivery employees earned $1,030. The employees are to have withheld from their wages FICA Social Security taxes at the rate of 6.2%, FICA Medicare taxes at the rate of 1.45%, $8,625 of federal income taxes, $1,160 of medical insurance deductions, and $138 of union dues. No employee earned more than $7,000 in the first pay period.

Problem 9-5B
Entries for payroll transactions
P2 P3

Required

1. Calculate FICA Social Security taxes payable and FICA Medicare taxes payable. Prepare the journal entry to record Genie Company's January 8 (employee) payroll expenses and liabilities.
2. Prepare the journal entry to record Genie's (employer) payroll taxes resulting from the January 8 payroll. Genie's merit rating reduces its state unemployment tax rate to 3.4% of the first $7,000 paid each employee. The federal unemployment tax rate is 0.8%.

Check   (1) Cr. Accrued Payroll
Payable, $42,716.50
(2) Dr. Payroll Taxes
Expense, $6,754.50

CMI Company has five employees, each of whom earns $1,400 per month and is paid on the last day of each month. All five have been employed continuously at this amount since January 1. CMI uses a payroll bank account and special payroll checks to pay its employees. On June 1, the following accounts and balances exist in its general ledger:

a. FICA—Social Security Taxes Payable, $868; FICA—Medicare Taxes Payable, $203. (The balances of these accounts represent total liabilities for *both* the employer's and employees' FICA taxes for the May payroll only.)
b. Employees' Federal Income Taxes Payable, $1,050 (liability for May only).
c. Federal Unemployment Taxes Payable, $112 (liability for April and May together).
d. State Unemployment Taxes Payable, $560 (liability for April and May together).

During June and July, the company had the following payroll transactions:

June 15   Issued check payable to Security Bank, a federal depository bank authorized to accept employers' payments of FICA taxes and employee income tax withholdings. The $2,121 check is in payment of the May FICA and employee income taxes.

30   Recorded the June payroll and transferred funds from the regular bank account to the payroll bank account. Issued checks payable to each employee in payment of the June payroll. The payroll register shows the following summary totals for the June pay period:

Problem 9-6B[A]
Entries for payroll transactions
P2 P3 P5 P6

Check   Cr. Accrued Payroll
Payable, $5,414.50

| Salaries and Wages | | | | Federal | |
Office Salaries	Shop Wages	Gross Pay	FICA Taxes*	Income Taxes	Net Pay
$2,800	$4,200	$7,000	$434.00 $101.50	$1,050	$5,414.50

* FICA taxes are Social Security and Medicare, respectively.

30   Recorded the employer's payroll taxes resulting from the June payroll. The company has a merit rating that reduces its state unemployment tax rate to 4.0% of the first $7,000 paid each employee. The federal rate is 0.8%.

Check   Dr. Payroll Taxes
Expenses, $535.50

Check   July 15, Cr. Cash $2,121

July 15   Issued check payable to Security Bank in payment of the June FICA and employee income taxes.

15   Issued check to the State Tax Commission for the April, May, and June state unemployment taxes. Mailed the check and the second quarter tax return to the State Tax Commission.

31   Issued check payable to Security Bank in payment of the employer's FUTA taxes for the second quarter of the year.

31   Mailed Form 941 to the IRS, reporting the FICA taxes and the employees' federal income tax withholdings for the second quarter.

Required

Prepare journal entries to record the transactions and events for both June and July.

COMPREHENSIVE PROBLEM

BeGone Exterminators
(Review of Chapters 1–9)

Peachtree

BeGone Exterminators provides pest control services and also sells extermination products manufactured by other companies. The following six-column table contains the company's unadjusted trial balance as of December 31, 2002.

BEGONE EXTERMINATORS December 31, 2002					
	Unadjusted Trial Balance		Adjustments		Adjusted Trial Balance
Cash	$ 18,000				
Accounts receivable	5,000				
Allowance for doubtful accounts		$ 928			
Merchandise inventory	12,700				
Trucks	40,000				
Accum. depreciation—Trucks		0			
Equipment	55,000				
Accum. depreciation—Equip.		14,400			
Accounts payable		4,800			
Estimated warranty liability		1,400			
Unearned services revenue		0			
Long-term notes payable		15,000			
Discount on notes payable	3,974				
Common stock		20,000			
Retained earnings		32,600			
Extermination services revenue		70,000			
Interest revenue		872			
Sales (of merchandise)		80,000			
Cost of goods sold	54,017				
Depreciation expense—Trucks	0				
Depreciation expense—Equip.	0				
Wages expense	32,500				
Interest expense	0				
Rent expense	10,000				
Bad debts expense	0				
Miscellaneous expense	1,338				
Repairs expense	671				
Utilities expense	6,800				
Warranty expense	0				
Totals	$240,000	$240,000			

The following information applies to the company at the end of the current year:

a. The bank reconciliation as of December 31, 2002, includes these facts:

Balance per bank	$16,100
Balance per books	18,000
Outstanding checks	1,800
Deposit in transit	1,450
Interest earned	52
Service charges (miscellaneous expense)	15

Included with the bank statement is a canceled check that the company failed to record. (Information from the bank reconciliation allows you to determine the amount of this check, which is a payment on account.)

b. An examination of customers' accounts shows that accounts totaling $779 should be written off as uncollectible. Using an aging of receivables, the company determines that the ending balance of the Allowance for Doubtful Accounts should be $800.

c. A truck is purchased and placed in service on January 1, 2002. Its cost is being depreciated with the straight-line method using these facts and estimates:

Original cost	$40,000
Expected salvage value	5,000
Useful life (years)	5

d. Two items of equipment (a sprayer and an injector) were purchased and put into service early in January 2000. They are being depreciated with the straight-line method using these facts and estimates:

	Sprayer	Injector
Original cost	$35,000	$20,000
Expected salvage value	3,000	4,000
Useful life (years)	8	5

e. On August 1, 2002, the company is paid $7,680 in advance to provide monthly service for an apartment complex for one year. The company began providing the services in August. When the cash was received, the full amount was credited to the Extermination Services Revenue account.

f. The company offers a warranty for the services it sells. The expected cost of providing warranty service is 2.5% of sales. No warranty expense has been recorded for 2002. All costs of servicing warranties in 2002 were properly debited to the Estimated Warranty Liability account.

g. The $15,000 long-term note is a five-year, noninterest-bearing note that was issued to First National Bank on December 31, 2000. The market interest rate on the issuance of the loan was 8% and interest expense (not yet recorded) is $882 for year 2002.

h. The ending inventory of merchandise is counted and determined to have a cost of $12,700. Be-Gone uses a perpetual inventory system.

Required

1. Use the preceding information to determine amounts for the following items:
   a. Correct (reconciled) ending balance of Cash and the amount of the omitted check.
   b. Adjustment needed to obtain the correct ending balance of the Allowance for Doubtful Accounts.
   c. Depreciation expense for the truck acquired in January.
   d. Depreciation expense for the two items of equipment used during year 2002.
   e. Adjusted ending balances of the Extermination Services Revenue and Unearned Services Revenue accounts.
   f. Adjusted ending balances of the accounts for Warranty Expense and Estimated Warranty Liability.
   g. Adjusted ending balances of the accounts for Interest Expense and Discount on Notes Payable. (Round amounts to nearest whole dollar.)

2. Use the results of part 1 to complete the six-column table by first entering the appropriate adjustments for items *a* through *g* and then completing the adjusted trial balance columns. (*Hint:* Item *b* requires two adjustments.)

Check   (1a) Cash, $15,750
(1b) $651 credit

Check   Adjusted trial balance Totals, $253,837

3. Prepare journal entries to record the adjustments entered on the six-column table. Assume Be-Gone's adjusted balance for Merchandise Inventory matches the year-end physical count.

Check   Net income, $23,370; Total assets, $98,271

4. Prepare a single-step income statement, a statement of retained earnings (dividends during 2002 were $10,000), and a classified balance sheet.

BEYOND THE NUMBERS

Reporting in Action

A1 P4 🖾

NIKE

BTN 9-1   Refer to the financial statements for Nike in Appendix A to answer the following:
1. Compute times interest earned for the years ended May 31, 2000, 1999, and 1998. Comment on Nike's ability to cover its interest expense for this period.
2. What evidence can you identify for an indication that Nike has temporary differences between income reported on its income statement and income reported on its tax return?

Swoosh Ahead
3. Access Nike's financial statements for fiscal years ending after May 31, 2000, at its Web site (www.nike.com) or the SEC's EDGAR database (www.sec.gov). Compute Nike's times interest earned for years ending after May 31, 2000, and compare your results to those in part 1.

Comparative Analysis

A1 🖾

NIKE

Reebok

BTN 9-2   Key comparative figures ($ millions) for both Nike and Reebok follow:

	Nike			Reebok		
Key Figures	**Current Year**	**One Year Prior**	**Two Years Prior**	**Current Year**	**One Year Prior**	**Two Years Prior**
Net income	$579.1	$451.4	$399.6	$11.0	$23.9	$135.1
Income taxes . . .	340.1	294.7	253.4	10.1	11.9	12.5
Interest expense .	45.0	44.1	60.0	49.7	60.7	64.4

Required
1. Compute times interest earned for the three years' data shown for each company.
2. Comment on which company appears stronger in its ability to pay interest obligations if income should decline.

Ethics Challenge

P4 🖾

BTN 9-3   Mike Gates is a sales manager for an automobile dealership. He earns a bonus each year based on revenue from the number of autos sold in the year less related warranty expenses. Actual warranty expenses have varied over the prior 10 years from a low of 3% of an automobile's selling price to a high of 10%. In the past, Mike has tended to estimate warranty expenses on the high end to be conservative. He must work with the dealership's accountant at year-end to arrive at the warranty expense accrual for cars sold each year.
1. Does the warranty accrual decision create any ethical dilemma for Gates?
2. Since warranty expenses vary, what percent do you think Gates should choose for the current year? Justify your response.

Communicating in Practice

C3 🖾

BTN 9-4   Matthew Stafford is the accounting and finance manager for a manufacturer. At year-end, he must determine how to account for the company's contingencies. His manager, John Harris, objects to Matthew's proposal to recognize an expense and a liability for warranty service on units of a new product introduced in the fourth quarter. John comments, "There's no way we can estimate this warranty cost. We don't owe anyone anything until a product breaks and is returned. Let's report an expense if and when we do repairs."

Required

Prepare a one-page memorandum for Matthew to send to John defending his proposal.

BTN 9-5 Access the March 28, 2000, filing of the December 31, 1999, annual 10-K report of McDonald's Corporation (Ticker: MCD), which is available from www.edgar-online.com.

Required

1. Identify the current liabilities on McDonald's balance sheet as of December 31, 1999.
2. What portion (in percent) of McDonald's long-term debt matures within the next 12 months?
3. Use the consolidated statement of income for the year ended December 31, 1999, to compute McDonald's times interest earned ratio.

Taking It to the Net

C1 A1

BTN 9-6 Assume that your team is in business and you must borrow $6,000 cash for short-term needs. You have been shopping banks for a loan, and you have the following two options:

A. Sign a $6,000, 90-day, 11% interest-bearing note dated June 1.

B. Sign a $6,172.50, 90-day, noninterest-bearing note dated June 1.

Required

1. Discuss these two options and determine the best choice. Ensure that all teammates concur with the decision and understand the rationale.
2. Each member of the team is to prepare *one* of the following journal entries:
   a. Option A—at date of issuance.
   b. Option B—at date of issuance.
   c. Option A—at maturity date.
   d. Option B—at maturity date.
3. In rotation, each member is to explain the entry he/she prepared in part 2 to the team. Ensure that all team members concur with and understand the entries.
4. Assume that the funds are borrowed on December 1 (instead of June 1) and your business operates on a calendar-year reporting period. Each member of the team is to prepare *one* of the following entries:
   a. Option A—the year-end adjustment.
   b. Option B—the year-end adjustment.
   c. Option A—at maturity date.
   d. Option B—at maturity date.
5. In rotation, each member is to explain the entry he/she prepared in part 4 to the team. Ensure that all team members concur with and understand the entries.

Teamwork in Action

C2 P1 🖉

BTN 9-7 Read the article "The Second Income: Is It Worth It?" in the August 25, 1997, issue of *Business Week*. (This book's Web site provides a free link.)

Required

1. What assumptions does the article's analysis make regarding the couple's location, income, family members, mortgage, and 401(k) plans?
2. Based on the analysis in the table, what is the couple's take-home pay when the husband works and the wife stays home? What is the pretax value of the 401(k) savings in this first scenario?
3. Based on the analysis reported in the table, what is the couple's take-home pay when both the husband and the wife work? What is the pretax value of the 401(k) savings in this second scenario?
4. What conclusions can you draw from this one example of whether it pays for both members of this couple to work full-time?

***Business Week* Activity**

P4 🖉

BTN 9-8 Shania Swain is an entrepreneur and owner of The Edge, LLC, a manufacturer of skateboards and accessories. The Edge is considering a major technological investment in its manufacturing process. This investment would cut variable costs from 60% of sales to 45% of sales. However, fixed interest expense would increase from $90,000 per year to $190,000 per year to fund the $800,000

Entrepreneurial Decision

A1 🖻 🖉

plant asset investment (with zero salvage, 50-year life, and depreciated using straight-line). Its recent income statement follows (it pays zero income taxes as a LLC):

THE EDGE
Income Statement
For Year Ended January 31, 2002

Sales	$500,000
Depreciation	10,000
Variable expenses (60%)	300,000
Income before interest	$190,000
Interest expense (fixed)	90,000
Net income	$100,000

Required

1. Compute The Edge's times interest earned ratio at January 31, 2002.

2. If the Edge expects sales to remain at $500,000, what would net income and times interest earned equal if it makes the investment?

3. What would net income and times interest earned equal if sales increase to $600,000 and the investment is (*a*) not made and (*b*) made?

4. What would net income and times interest earned equal if sales increase to $773,333 and the investment is (*a*) not made and (*b*) made? (Round amounts to the nearest thousand dollars.)

5. What would net income and times interest earned equal if sales increase to $900,000 and the investment is (*a*) not made and (*b*) made?

6. Comment on the results from parts 1 through 5 and their relation to the times interest earned ratio.

Hitting the Road
P2

BTN 9-9   Check your phone book or the Social Security Administration Web site (www.ssa.gov) to locate the Social Security office near you. Visit the office to request a personal earnings and estimate form. Fill out the form and mail according to the instructions. You will receive a statement from the Social Security Administration regarding your earnings history and future Social Security benefits you can receive. (Note: Formerly the request could be made online. The online service has been discontinued and is now under review by the Social Security Administration due to security concerns.) It is good to request an earnings and benefit statement every 5 to 10 years to make sure you have received credit for all wages earned and for which you and your employer have paid taxes into the system.

10

Reporting and Analyzing Long-Term Liabilities

"I promise it won't be boring"—David Bowie

A Look Back

Chapter 9 primarily focused on current liabilities and secondarily on long-term liabilities. We explained how liabilities are identified, computed, recorded, and reported in financial statements. We also described analysis of these liabilities.

A Look at This Chapter

This chapter describes the accounting and analysis for bonds and notes. We explain their characteristics, payment patterns, interest computations, retirement, and reporting requirements. An appendix to this chapter explains accounting for leases and pensions.

A Look Ahead

Chapter 11 extends our discussion of the corporate form of organization. We describe stock issuances, dividends, and other equity transactions. We also explain how income, earnings per share, and retained earnings are reported and analyzed.

Bowie Bonds

e NEW YORK—David Bowie continues to jam. Well known for his unique style and innovations in the world of music, he's now rocking Wall Street with the introduction of "Bowie bonds." Bowie, the godfather of "glam rock," created and issued bonds backed by his greatest hits. The bond issue generated millions for Bowie and enabled him to pursue some of his other passions, including his online Internet services at **www.DavidBowie.com**.

The Bowie bonds are called *secured bonds,* meaning they are backed by other assets. Secured bonds are common in business and are backed by assets such as land, homes, and automobiles. Secured bonds are less risky than other bonds because bondholders can potentially demand that assets be sold to cover interest and principal. This lower risk has led to an asset-backed bond market that exceeds $200 billion, yet Bowie's secured bonds are unique—the assets backing them are his expected future royalties from 25 of his past albums. These include *Ziggy Stardust, Thin White Duke,* and *Let's Dance.*

Such securities—especially ones backed by future royalties of a rock star—are normally considered risky and thus shunned by Wall Street, but Moody's Investors Service gave the Bowie bonds the highest investment-grade rating (AAA). Moreover, Prudential Insurance Company dove in, snatching up all Bowie bonds for a cool $55 million. Prudential will earn a 7.9% return over the 10-year life of the bonds. The success of the bond issue has intrigued other musical artists wanting to raise cash to fund ambitious projects. These artists include Rod Stewart, Michael Jackson, and Crosby, Stills and Nash.

So what's next for Bowie? Derivatives? Options? Nobody knows for sure. The only thing certain is that he remains on the cutting edge. Says Bowie, "I don't know where I'm going from here, but I promise it won't be boring." Wall Street is certainly not underestimating him. He might just ch-ch-ch-change everything! [Sources: CNN's Web site, September 2001; DavidBowie Web site, March 2002; *Fortune,* June 8, 1998.]

Learning Objectives

Conceptual

C1 Describe the types of bonds and the procedures for issuing them.

C2 Explain the types and payment patterns of notes.

Analytical

A1 Compare bond financing with stock financing.

A2 Explain collateral agreements and their effects on loan risk.

A3 Compute the ratio of pledged assets to secured liabilities and explain its use.

Procedural

P1 Prepare entries to record bond issuance and bond interest expense.

P2 Compute and record amortization of bond discount.

P3 Compute and record amortization of bond premium.

P4 Record the retirement of bonds.

P5 Prepare entries to account for notes.

Chapter Preview

Individuals, companies, and governments issue bonds to finance their activities. In return for financing, bonds promise to repay the lender with interest. This chapter explains the basics of bonds and the accounting for their issuance and retirement. The chapter also describes long-term notes as another financing source, including interest-bearing, noninterest-bearing, and installment notes. We explain how present value concepts impact both the accounting for and reporting of bonds and notes. Appendixes to this chapter discuss present value concepts applicable to liabilities and the accounting for leases and pensions. Explaining how bonds, notes, and other liabilities are used to a company's advantage is an important goal of this chapter.

Basics of Bonds

Many companies finance operations and borrow money by issuing bonds. This section explains the basics of bonds and a company's motivation for issuing them.

Bond Financing

Companies can finance their business activities in several ways, including issuing notes, leasing assets, and using owner investments. Projects that demand large amounts of money often are funded from bond issuances. (Bonds are issued by both for-profit and nonprofit companies, as well as by governmental units, such as nations, states, cities, and school districts.) A **bond** is its issuer's written promise to pay an amount identified as the par value of the bond along with interest. The **par value of a bond,** also called the *face amount* or *face value,* is paid at a specified future date known as the bond's *maturity date.* Most bonds also require the issuer to make semiannual interest payments. The amount of interest paid each period is determined by multiplying the par value of the bond by the bond's contract rate of interest. This section explains both advantages and disadvantages of bond financing.

A1 Compare bond financing with stock financing.

Advantages of Bonds

There are three main advantages of bond financing:

1. *Bonds do not affect owner control.* Equity financing reflects ownership in a company, whereas bond financing does not. A person who contributes $1,000 of a company's $10,000 equity financing typically controls one-tenth of all owners' decisions. A person who owns a $1,000, 11%, 20-year bond has no ownership right. This person, or bondholder, is to receive from the bond issuer 11% interest, or $110, each year the bond is outstanding and $1,000 when it matures in 20 years.

2. *Interest on bonds is tax deductible.* Bond interest payments are tax deductible, but equity payments (distributions) to owners are not. This feature is important for corporations. For example, assume that a corporation with no bond financing earns $15,000 in income *before* paying taxes at a 40% tax rate. This corporation would owe $6,000 ($15,000 × 40%) in taxes. If a portion of its financing is in bonds, however, the resulting bond interest is deducted in computing taxable income. That is, if bond interest expense is $10,000, the taxes owed would be $2,000 ([$15,000 − $10,000] × 40%), which is much less than the $6,000 owed with no bond financing.

3. *Bonds can increase return on equity.* A company earning a higher return with the borrowed funds than it pays in interest, increases its return on equity. This process is called *financial leverage* or *trading on the equity.*

To illustrate the third point, consider Magnum Co., which has $1 million in equity and is planning a $500,000 expansion to meet increasing demand for its product. Magnum predicts the $500,000 expansion will yield $125,000 in additional income before paying any interest. Magnum currently earns $100,000 per year and has no interest expense. Magnum is considering three plans. Plan A is not to expand. Plan B is to expand and raise $500,000 from equity financing. Plan C is to expand and issue $500,000 of bonds that pay 10% annual interest ($50,000). Exhibit 10.1 shows how these three plans affect Magnum's net income, equity, and return on equity (net income/equity). Analysis shows that the owner(s) will earn a higher return on equity if expansion occurs. Moreover, the preferred expansion

Point: Financial leverage can be achieved by issuing either bonds, notes, or preferred stock.

	Plan A Do not Expand	Plan B Equity Financing	Plan C Bond Financing
Income before interest expense	$ 100,000	$ 225,000	$ 225,000
Interest expense	—	—	(50,000)
Net Income	**$ 100,000**	**$ 225,000**	**$ 175,000**
Equity	$1,000,000	$1,500,000	$1,000,000
Return on equity	**10.0%**	**15.0%**	**17.5%**

Exhibit 10.1

Financing with Bonds versus Equity

plan is to issue bonds. Projected net income under Plan C ($175,000) is smaller than under Plan B ($225,000), but the return on equity is larger because of less equity investment. Further, Plan C has another advantage if income is taxable. This illustration reflects a general rule: *Return on equity increases when the expected rate of return from the new assets is greater than the rate of interest expense on the bonds.*

Disadvantages of Bonds

The two main disadvantages of bond financing are:

1. *Bonds can decrease return on equity.* When a company earns a lower return with the borrowed funds than it pays in interest, it decreases its return on equity. This is the downside risk of financial leverage; it is more likely to arise when a company has periods of low income or net losses.
2. *Bonds require payment of both periodic interest and the par value at maturity.* Bond payments can be especially burdensome when income and cash flow are low. Equity financing, in contrast, does not require any payments because cash withdrawals (dividends) are paid at the discretion of the owner (or board).

A company must weigh the risks and returns of the disadvantages and advantages of bond financing when deciding whether to issue bonds to finance operations.

Example: Compute return on equity for all three plans if Magnum currently earns $150,000 instead of $100,000. *Answer ($ in 000s):*
Plan A = 15%   ($150/$1,000)
Plan B = 18.3%   ($275/$1,500)
Plan C = 22.5%   ($225/$1,000)

Decision Track 10.1   *d*

Decision Point	Information Search	Analyze & Evaluate
What mix of debt and equity financing should a company aim for?	Balance sheet; income statement; financial statement notes; forecasts of future performance.	More willingness to take on debt when interest is tax deductible, control is desirable, and return on equity is high relative to interest rates on the debt.

Types of Bonds

We describe the more common types of bonds and their characteristics in this section.

C1 Describe the types of bonds and the procedures for issuing them.

Secured and Unsecured Bonds

Secured bonds have specific assets of the issuer pledged (or *mortgaged*) as collateral. This arrangement gives bondholders added protection against the issuer's default. If the issuer fails to pay interest or par value, the secured bondholders can demand that the collateral be sold and the proceeds used to pay the bond obligation. **Unsecured bonds,** also called *debentures,* are backed by the issuer's general credit standing. Unsecured bonds are riskier than secured bonds. An issuer generally must be financially strong to successfully issue debentures at a favorable interest rate. *Subordinated debentures* refer to

Secured Bond   **Unsecured Bond**

creditors whose claims on the issuer's assets are second to those of other unsecured liabilities. In a liquidation, subordinated debentures are not repaid until the claims of the more senior, unsecured liabilities have been settled.

Term and Serial Bonds

Term Bond

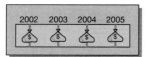

Serial Bond

Term bonds are scheduled for maturity at a single specified date. **Serial bonds** mature at more than one date (often in series) and thus are usually repaid over a number of periods. For instance, $1,000,000 of serial bonds might mature at the rate of $10,000 each year from 6 to 15 years after they are issued. This involves 10 groups (or series) of bonds of $10,000 each with one series maturing after six years, another after seven years, and another each successive year until the final series is repaid. Many bonds are also **sinking fund bonds.** To reduce the holder's risk, sinking fund bonds require the issuer to create a *sinking fund* of assets set aside at specified amounts and dates to repay the bonds at maturity.

Registered Bonds and Bearer Bonds

Registered Bond

Bearer Bond

Bonds issued in the names and addresses of their holders are **registered bonds.** The issuer makes bond payments by sending checks (or cash transfers) to these registered holders. When a registered holder sells a bond to another holder, the issuer must be notified of the change. Registered bonds offer the issuer the practical advantage of not having to actually issue bond certificates. This arrangement protects holders against loss or theft of bonds.

Bonds payable to whoever holds them (the *bearer*) are called **bearer bonds,** or *unregistered bonds.* Since sales or exchanges might not be recorded, the holder of a bearer bond is presumed to be its rightful owner. As a result, lost or stolen bearer bonds are difficult to replace. Many bearer bonds are also **coupon bonds.** This term reflects interest coupons that are attached to these bonds. Each coupon matures on a specific interest payment date. When each coupon matures, the holder presents it to a bank or broker for collection. At maturity, the holder follows the same process and presents the bond certificate for collection. Income tax law discourages companies from issuing coupon bonds because there is no readily available record of who actually receives the interest.

Convertible and Callable Bonds

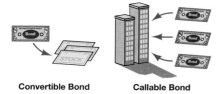

Convertible Bond   Callable Bond

Convertible bonds can be exchanged for a fixed number of shares of the issuing corporation's common stock. Convertible bonds offer bondholders the potential to participate in future increases in a stock's market value. Bondholders receive periodic interest while the bonds are held and will receive the par value if the bond is held to maturity. In most cases, it is the bondholders who decide whether and when to convert the bonds to stock. **Callable bonds** have an option exercisable by the issuer to retire them at a stated dollar amount prior to maturity.

Bond Trading

Bonds are securities that can be readily bought and sold. A large number of bonds trade on both the New York Exchange and the American Exchange. A bond issue consists of a number of bonds, usually in denominations of $1,000 or $5,000, and is sold to many different lenders. After bonds are issued, they often are bought and sold by investors, meaning that any particular bond probably has a number of owners before it matures. Since bonds are exchanged (bought and sold) in the market, they have a market value (price). For convenience, bond market values are expressed as a percent of their par (face) value. For example, a company's bonds might be trading at 103½, meaning they can be bought or sold for 103.5% of their par value. Bonds can also trade below par value. For instance, if a company's bonds are trading at 95, they can be bought or sold at 95% of their par value.

Bond-Issuing Procedures

State and federal laws govern bond issuances. Bond issuers also want to ensure that they do not violate any of their existing contractual agreements when issuing bonds. Authorization of bond issuances includes the number of bonds authorized, their par value, and the contract interest rate. The legal document identifying the rights and obligations of both the bond-holders and the issuer is called the **bond indenture,** which acts as the legal contract between the issuer and the bondholders. A bondholder may also receive a bond certificate as evidence of the company's debt. A **bond certificate,** such as that shown in Exhibit 10.2, includes specifics such as the issuer's name, the bond's par value, the contract interest rate, and the maturity date. Many companies reduce costs by not issuing certificates to bond-holders.

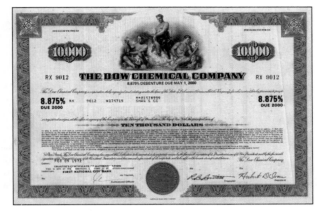

Exhibit 10.2

Bond Certificate

The issuing company normally sells its bonds to an investment firm called an *underwriter,* which then resells them to the public. An issuing company can also sell bonds directly to investors. When an underwriter sells bonds to a large number of investors, a *trustee* represents and protects the bondholders' interests. The trustee monitors the issuer to ensure that it complies with the obligations in the bond indenture. Most trustees are large banks or trust companies. The trustee writes and accepts the terms of a bond indenture before it is issued. When bonds are offered to the public, called *floating an issue,* they must be registered with the Securities and Exchange Commission (SEC). SEC registration requires the issuer to file certain financial information. Most company bonds are issued in par value units of $1,000 or $5,000. A *baby bond* is a bond with a par value of less than $1,000, such as $100.

Bond Issuances

This section explains accounting for bond issuances at par, below par (discount), and above par (premium). We also describe the amortization of a discount or premium and how to record bonds issued between interest payment dates.

P1 Prepare entries to record bond issuance and bond interest expense.

Issuing Bonds at Par

To illustrate an issuance of bonds at par value, suppose a company receives authorization to issue $800,000 of 9%, 20-year bonds dated January 1, 2002, that mature on December 31, 2021, and pay interest semiannually on each June 30 and December 31. After the trustee accepts the bond indenture on behalf of the bondholders, all or a portion of the bonds can be sold to an underwriter. If all bonds are sold at par value, the issuer records the sale as:

Assets = Liabilities + Equity
+800,000   +800,000

2002			
Jan. 1	Cash	800,000	
	Bonds Payable		800,000
	Sold bonds at par.		

This entry reflects increases in both the issuer's cash and its long-term liabilities.

The issuer records the first semiannual interest payment as follows:

Assets = Liabilities + Equity
−36,000   −36,000

2002			
June 30	Bond Interest Expense	36,000	
	Cash		36,000
	Paid semiannual interest (9% × $800,000 ×		
	½ year).		

Topic Tackler 10-1

Assets = Liabilities + Equity
−800,000 −800,000

The issuer pays and records its semiannual interest obligation every six months until the bonds mature. When they mature, the issuer records its payment of principal:

2021			
Dec. 31	Bonds Payable	800,000	
	Cash		800,000
	Paid bonds at maturity.		

Decision Insight

Ratings Game   Many bond buyers rely on rating services to assess bond risk. The best known are Standard & Poor's and Moody's. These services focus on the issuer's financial statements in setting ratings. Standard & Poor's ratings, from best quality to default, are AAA, AA, A, BBB, BB, B, CCC, CC, C, and D. Ratings can include a plus (+) or minus (−) to show relative standing within a category.

Point: Business acquisitions are sometimes financed by issuing "junk bonds" that carry high market rates of interest but offer little security. Bondholders can suffer huge losses if the acquired companies do not generate adequate cash flows to pay interest and principal.

Bond Discount or Premium

The bond issuer pays the interest rate specified in the indenture, which is called the **contract rate.** The contract rate is also referred to as the *coupon rate, stated rate,* or *nominal rate.* The annual interest paid is determined by multiplying the bond par value by the contract rate. The contract rate is usually stated on an annual basis, even if interest is paid semiannually. For example, if a company issues a $1,000, 8% bond paying interest semiannually, its annual interest of $80 (8% × $1,000) is paid in two semiannual payments of $40 each.

The contract rate sets the amount of interest the issuer pays in *cash,* which is not necessarily the *bond interest expense* actually incurred by the issuer. Bond interest expense depends on the bond's market value at issuance, which is determined by market expectations of the risk of lending to the issuer. The bond's market rate of interest reflects this expected risk, as does the supply of and demand for bonds. The **market rate** is the rate that borrowers are willing to pay and lenders are willing to accept for a particular bond and its risk level. As the risk level increases, the rate increases. The increased market rate compensates purchasers for the bonds' increased risk. Also, the market rate is generally higher when the time period until the bond matures is longer. This is so because many events can occur with a company over a longer period of time.

Many bond issuers try to set a contract rate of interest equal to the market rate they expect as of the bond issuance date. When the contract rate and market rate are equal, a bond sells at par value, but when they are not equal, a bond does not sell at par value. Instead, it is sold at a *premium* above par value or at a *discount* below par value. Exhibit 10.3 shows the relation between the contract rate, market rate, and a bond's issue price.

Exhibit 10.3

Relation between Bond Issue Price, Contract Rate, and Market Rate

Contract Rate Is		Bond Sells
Above market rate	➡	At a premium
Equal to market rate	➡	At par value
Below market rate	➡	At a discount

Quick Check

1. Unsecured bonds backed only by the issuer's general credit standing are called (a) serial bonds, (b) debentures, (c) registered bonds, or (d) convertible bonds.
2. How do you compute the amount of interest a bond issuer pays in cash each year?
3. When the contract rate is above the market rate, do bonds sell at a premium or a discount? Do purchasers pay more or less than the par value of the bonds?

Answers—p. 451

Issuing Bonds at a Discount

A **discount on bonds payable** occurs when a company issues bonds with a contract rate less than the market rate. This means that the issue price is less than par value. To illustrate, assume that Fila announces an offer to issue bonds with a $100,000 par value, an 8% annual contract rate (paid semiannually), and a five-year life. Also assume that the market rate for Fila bonds is 10%. The Fila bonds will sell at a discount since the contract rate is less than the market rate. The exact issue price for these bonds is 92.277 (or 92.277% of par value)—we show how to compute this issue price later in the chapter. These bonds obligate the issuer to pay two separate types of future cash flows:

P2 Compute and record amortization of bond discount.

1. Par value of $100,000 cash at the end of the bonds' five-year life.
2. Cash interest payments of $4,000 (4% × $100,000) at the end of each semiannual period during the bonds' five-year life.

The exact pattern of cash flows for the Fila bonds is shown in Exhibit 10.4.

Point: The difference between the contract rate and the market rate of interest on a new bond issue is usually a fraction of a percent. We use a difference of 2% to emphasize the effects.

Exhibit 10.4
Cash Flows for Fila Bonds

When Fila accepts $92,277 cash for its bonds on the issue date of December 31, 2002, it records the sale as follows:

Dec. 31	Cash	92,277	
	Discount on Bonds Payable	7,723	
	Bonds Payable		100,000
	Sold bonds at a discount on their issue date.		

Assets = Liabilities + Equity
+92,277   +100,000
                 −7,723

These bonds are reported in the long-term liability section of the issuer's December 31, 2002, balance sheet as shown in Exhibit 10.5.

Point: Book value at issuance always equals the cash amount borrowed.

Exhibit 10.5
Balance Sheet Presentation of Bond Discount

Long-term liabilities		
Bonds payable, 8%, due December 31, 2007	$100,000	
Less discount on bonds payable	7,723	$92,277

A discount is deducted from the par value of bonds to yield the **carrying (book) value** of the bonds payable. Discount on Bonds Payable is a contra liability account.

Amortizing a Bond Discount

Fila receives $92,277 for its bonds; in return it must pay bondholders $100,000 after five years (plus semiannual interest payments). The $7,723 discount is paid to bondholders at maturity and is part of the cost of using the $92,277 for five years. The upper portion of Exhibit 10.6 shows that total bond interest expense of $47,723 is the difference between the total amount repaid to bondholders ($140,000) and the amount borrowed from bondholders ($92,277). Alternatively, we can compute total bond interest expense as the sum of the 10 interest payments and the bond discount. This alternative computation is shown in the lower portion of Exhibit 10.6.

Decision Maker *d*

Bond Rater You must assign a rating to a bond that reflects its risk to bondholders. Identify factors you consider in assessing bond risk. For the factors you identify, indicate their likely levels (relative to the norm) for a bond that sells at a discount.

Answer—p. 451

Point: *Zero-coupon bonds* do not pay periodic interest (contract rate is zero). These bonds always sell at a discount because their 0% contract rate is always below the market rate.

Exhibit 10.6

Total Interest Expense for
Bonds Issued at a Discount

Amount repaid to bondholders	
Ten interest payments of $4,000	$ 40,000
Par value at maturity	100,000
Total repaid to bondholders	$140,000
Less amount borrowed from bondholders	(92,277)
Total bond interest expense	$ 47,723
Alternative Computation	
Ten payments of $4,000	$ 40,000
Plus discount	7,723
Total bond interest expense	$ 47,723

The total $47,723 bond interest expense
must be allocated across the 10 semiannual periods in the bonds' life, and the carrying value
of the bonds must be updated at each balance
sheet date. Two alternative methods accomplish
this: the straight-line and the effective interest
methods. Both methods systematically reduce
the discount on the bonds to zero over their
five-year life. This process is called *amortizing
a bond discount*.

Straight-Line Method

Global: Some countries such as
Italy report bonds and notes at their
par (face) value, and not at book
(carrying) value.

Point: The straight-line method
was more widely used before
development of inexpensive
computers.

The **straight-line method** is the simpler of the two methods to amortize a bond discount. It
allocates an equal portion of the total bond interest expense to each interest period. To apply
the straight-line method to Fila's bonds, we divide the total bond interest expense of $47,723
by 10 (the number of semiannual periods in the bonds' life). This gives us a bond interest
expense of $4,772 per period (all computations, including those for assignments, are rounded
to the nearest whole dollar). Alternatively, we can find this number by dividing the $7,723
original discount by 10. The resulting $772 is the amount of discount to be amortized in each
interest period. When the $772 of amortized discount is added to the $4,000 cash payment,
the bond interest expense for each semiannual period is $4,772. In either case, the issuer
records bond interest expense and updates the balance of the bond liability account for *each*
semiannual period (June 30, 2003, through Dec. 31, 2007):

2003–2007			
June 30 and	Bond Interest Expense	4,772	
Dec. 31	Discount on Bonds Payable		772
	Cash		4,000
	To record semiannual interest and discount amortization (straight-line method).		

Assets = Liabilities + Equity
−4,000   +772   −4,772

This entry is made at the end of each of the 10 semiannual interest periods. The $772 credit
to the Discount on Bonds Payable account *increases* the bonds' carrying value. This increase
occurs because a credit *decreases* the debit balance of the Discount on Bonds Payable (contra) account, which is subtracted from the Bonds Payable account. Exhibit 10.7 shows this
pattern of decreases in the Discount on Bonds Payable account, along with the increase in
the bonds' carrying value. The following points summarize straight-line amortization of the
Fila discount bonds:

Global: Accounting for a discount
and premium varies across
countries. In some countries such as
Belgium, Sweden, and Japan, a
discount and premium can be
immediately written off.

1. The $92,277 cash received from the bond issuance equals the $100,000 par value less
   the initial $7,723 discount from issuing the bonds at less than par.
2. Semiannual bond interest expense of $4,772 equals total bond interest expense of $47,723
   divided by the 10 semiannual periods (alternatively computed as the $4,000 cash paid

plus the periodic discount amortization of $772).

3. The $772 semiannual credit to the Discount on Bonds Payable account equals the total $7,723 discount divided by 10 semiannual periods.

4. The $4,000 semiannual interest payment equals the bonds' $100,000 par value multiplied by the 4% semiannual contract rate.

5. Carrying (or book) value of bonds continues to increase each period by the $772 discount amortization until it equals par value when the bonds mature.

Semiannual Period-End	Unamortized Discount*	Carrying Value†
12/31/2002	$7,723	$ 92,277
6/30/2003	6,951	93,049
12/31/2003	6,179	93,821
6/30/2004	5,407	94,593
12/31/2004	4,635	95,365
6/30/2005	3,863	96,137
12/31/2005	3,091	96,909
6/30/2006	2,319	97,681
12/31/2006	1,547	98,453
6/30/2007	775	99,225
12/31/2007	0‡	**100,000**

* Total bond discount ($7,723) less accumulated periodic amortization ($772 per semiannual period).

† Bond par value less unamortized discount.

‡ Adjusted for rounding.

Exhibit 10.7

Straight-Line Amortization of Bond Discount

Notice that Fila incurs a $4,772 bond interest expense each period but pays only $4,000 cash. The $772 unpaid portion of this expense is added to the carrying value of the bonds by decreasing the Discount on Bonds Payable account balance. (The $7,723 unamortized discount is "paid" when the bonds mature—namely, $100,000 is paid at maturity when only $92,277 was received at issuance.)

Effective Interest Method

The straight-line method yields changes in the bonds' carrying value (see Exhibit 10.7) while the amount for bond interest expense remains constant (always equal to $4,772 for Fila bonds). This gives the impression of a changing interest rate when users divide a constant bond interest expense over a changing carrying value. As a result, accounting standards allow use of the straight-line method only when its results do not differ materially from those obtained using the effective interest method. The **effective interest method,** or simply *interest method,* allocates total bond interest expense over the life of the bonds in a way that yields a constant rate of interest. This constant rate of interest is the market rate at the issue date. This means that bond interest expense for a period equals the carrying value of the bond at the beginning of that period multiplied by the market rate when issued.

An *amortization table* can help track interest allocation and the balances of bond-related accounts. Exhibit 10.8 shows an effective interest amortization table for the Fila bonds. The key difference between the effective interest and straight-line methods lies in computing bond interest expense. Instead of assigning an equal amount of bond interest expense to each period, the effective interest method assigns a bond interest expense amount that increases over the life of a discount bond. Both methods allocate the *same* $47,723 of total bond interest expense to the bonds' life, but in different patterns. Specifically, as with the straight-line method, the amortization table in Exhibit 10.8 shows that the balance of the discount (column D) is amortized until it reaches zero. Also, the bonds' carrying value (column E) changes each period until it equals par value at maturity. Compare columns D and E to the corresponding columns in Exhibit 10.7 to see the amortization patterns. Still, total bond interest expense is $47,723—composed of $40,000 of semiannual cash payments and $7,723 of the original bond discount—the same for both methods.

Except for differences in amounts, journal entries recording the expense and updating the liability balance are the same under the effective interest method and the straight-line method. For instance, we record the interest payment at the end of the first semiannual period as:

Topic Tackler 10-2

Global: The United States generally requires use of the effective interest method, but some countries prefer straight-line amortization, and Brazil requires it.

Point: The effective interest method consistently computes bond interest expense using the market rate at issuance. This rate is applied to a changing carrying value.

2003				
June 30	Bond Interest Expense	4,614		
	Discount on Bonds Payable		614	
	Cash			4,000
	To record semiannual interest and discount amortization (effective interest method).			

Assets = Liabilities + Equity
−4,000   +614   −4,614

Exhibit 10.8

Effective Interest
Amortization of
Bond Discount

	Bonds: $100,000 Par Value, Semiannual Interest Payments, Five-Year Life, 4% Semiannual Contract Rate, 5% Semiannual Market Rate					
	(A)	(B)	(C)	(D)	(E)	
Semiannual Interest Period-end	Cash Interest Paid	Bond Interest Expense	Discount Amortization	Unamortized Discount	Carrying Value	
12/31/2002				$7,723	$ 92,277	
6/30/2003	$ 4,000	$ 4,614	$ 614	7,109	92,891	
12/31/2003	4,000	4,645	645	6,464	93,536	
6/30/2004	4,000	4,677	677	5,787	94,213	
12/31/2004	4,000	4,711	711	5,076	94,924	
6/30/2005	4,000	4,746	746	4,330	95,670	
12/31/2005	4,000	4,784	784	3,546	96,454	
6/30/2006	4,000	4,823	823	2,723	97,277	
12/31/2006	4,000	4,864	864	1,859	98,141	
6/30/2007	4,000	4,907	907	952	99,048	
12/31/2007	4,000	4,952	952	0	100,000	
	$40,000	$47,723	$7,723			

Column **(A)** is par value ($100,000) multiplied by the semiannual contract rate (4%).

Column **(B)** is prior period's carrying value multiplied by the semiannual market rate (5%).

Column **(C)** is the difference between interest paid and bond interest expense, or $[(B) - (A)]$.

Column **(D)** is the prior period's unamortized discount less the current period's discount amortization.

Column **(E)** is par value less unamortized discount, or $[\$100,000 - (D)]$.

We can use the numbers in Exhibit 10.8 to record each semiannual entry throughout the five-year life of the bonds (June 30, 2003, through December 31, 2007).

Quick Check

Five-year, 6% bonds with a $100,000 par value are issued at a price of $91,893. Interest is paid semiannually, and the bonds' market rate is 8% on the issue date. Use this information to answer the following questions:

4. Are these bonds issued at a discount or a premium? Explain your answer.

5. What is the issuer's journal entry to record the issuance of these bonds?

6. What is the amount of bond interest expense recorded at the first semiannual period using the (a) straight-line method and (b) effective interest method?

Answers—p. 451

Issuing Bonds at a Premium

P3 Compute and record amortization of bond premium.

When bonds have a contract rate higher than the market rate, they sell at a price higher than par value. The amount by which the bond price exceeds par value is the **premium on bonds.** To illustrate, assume that Adidas issues bonds with a $100,000 par value, a 12% annual contract rate, semiannual interest payments, and a five-year life. Also assume that the market rate for Adidas bonds is 10% on the issue date. The Adidas bonds will sell at a premium because the contract rate is higher than the market rate. The exact issue price for these bonds is 107.72 (or 107.72% of par value)—we show how to compute this issue price later in the chapter. These bonds obligate the issuer to pay out two separate future cash flows:

1. Par value of $100,000 cash at the end of the bonds' five-year life.
2. Cash interest payments of $6,000 (6% × $100,000) at the end of each semiannual period during the bonds' five-year life.

The exact pattern of cash flows for the Adidas bonds is shown in Exhibit 10.9.

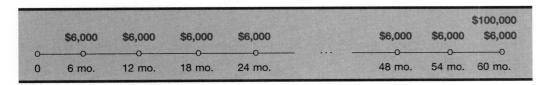

Exhibit 10.9

Cash Flows for Adidas Bonds

When Adidas accepts $107,720 cash for its bonds on the issue date of December 31, 2002, it records this transaction as follows:

Dec. 31	Cash	107,720	
	Premium on Bonds Payable		7,720
	Bonds Payable		100,000
	Sold bonds at a premium on their issue date.		

Assets = Liabilities + Equity
+107,720 +100,000
             +7,720

These bonds are reported in the long-term liability section of the issuer's December 31, 2002, balance sheet as shown in Exhibit 10.10.

Long-term liabilities		
Bonds payable, 12%, due December 31, 2007	$100,000	
Plus premium on bonds payable	**7,720**	**$107,720**

Exhibit 10.10

Balance Sheet Presentation of Bond Premium

A premium is added to par value to yield the carrying (book) value of bonds payable. Premium on Bonds Payable is an adjunct (also called *accretion*) liability account.

Amortizing a Bond Premium

Adidas receives $107,720 for its bonds; in return it will pay bondholders $100,000 after five years (plus semiannual interest payments). The $7,720 premium not repaid to bondholders at maturity goes to reduce the expense of using the $107,720 for five years. The upper portion of Exhibit 10.11 shows that total bond interest expense of $52,280 is the difference between the total amount repaid to bondholders ($160,000) and the amount borrowed from bondholders ($107,720). Alternatively, we can compute total bond interest expense as the sum of the 10 interest payments less the bond premium. The premium is subtracted because it will not be paid to bondholders when the bonds mature—see the lower portion of Exhibit 10.11. Total bond interest expense must be allocated over the 10 semiannual periods using either the straight-line or the effective interest method.

Amount repaid to bondholders	
Ten interest payments of $6,000	$ 60,000
Par value at maturity	100,000
Total repaid to bondholders	$160,000
Less amount borrowed from bondholders	(107,720)
Total bond interest expense	**$ 52,280**
Alternative Computation	
Ten payments of $6,000	$ 60,000
Less premium	(7,720)
Total bond interest expense	**$ 52,280**

Exhibit 10.11

Total Interest Expense for Bonds Issued at a Premium

Straight-Line Method

We explained earlier how the straight-line method allocates an equal portion of total bond interest expense to each of the bonds' semiannual interest periods. To apply the straight-line method to Adidas bonds, we divide the five years' total bond interest expense of $52,280 by 10 (the number of semiannual periods in the bonds' life). This gives a total bond interest expense of $5,228 per period. The issuer records bond interest expense and updates the balance of the bond liability account for *each* semiannual period (June 30, 2003, through Dec. 31, 2007) as follows:

Assets = Liabilities + Equity
−6,000 −772   −5,228

2003–2007			
June 30 and	Bond Interest Expense	5,228	
Dec. 31	Premium on Bonds Payable	772	
	Cash		6,000
	To record semiannual interest and premium amortization (straight-line method).		

The $772 debit to the Premium on Bonds Payable account *decreases* the bonds' carrying value. Exhibit 10.12 shows this decrease in the unamortized premium during the five-year bond life.

Exhibit 10.12

Straight-Line Amortization of Bond Premium

Semiannual Period-End	Unamortized Premium*	Carrying Value†
12/31/2002	$7,720	$107,720
6/30/2003	6,948	106,948
12/31/2003	6,176	106,176
6/30/2004	5,404	105,404
12/31/2004	4,632	104,632
6/30/2005	3,860	103,860
12/31/2005	3,088	103,088
6/30/2006	2,316	102,316
12/31/2006	1,544	101,544
6/30/2007	772	100,772
12/31/2007	0	100,000

* Total bond premium ($7,720) less accumulated periodic amortization ($772 per semiannual period).

† Bond par value plus unamortized premium.

Effective Interest Method

Exhibit 10.13 shows the amortization table using the effective interest method for Adidas bonds. Column A lists the semiannual cash payments. Column B shows the amount of bond interest expense, computed as the 5% semiannual market rate at issuance multiplied by the beginning-of-period carrying value. The amount of cash paid in column A is larger than the bond interest expense because the cash payment is based on the higher 6% semiannual contract rate. The excess cash payment over the interest expense reduces the principal. These amounts are shown in column C. Column E shows the carrying value after deducting the amortized premium in column C from the prior period's carrying value. Column D shows how the premium is reduced by periodic amortization. When the issuer makes the first semiannual interest payment, the effect of premium amortization on bond interest expense and bond liability is recorded as follows:

Assets = Liabilities + Equity
−6,000 −614   −5,386

2003			
June 30	Bond Interest Expense	5,386	
	Premium on Bonds Payable	614	
	Cash		6,000
	To record semiannual interest and premium amortization (effective interest method).		

Similar entries with different amounts are recorded at each payment date until the bond matures at the end of 2007. The effective interest method yields decreasing amounts of bond interest expense and increasing amounts of premium amortization over the bonds' life.

Decision Track 10.2

Decision Point	Information Search	Analyze & Evaluate
What bond amortization method should a company adopt?	Bond dollar amounts and interest rates.	The effective interest method is preferred when making business decisions from debt-related information; an exception is when the straight-line method yields similar results.

Exhibit 10.13
Effective Interest Amortization of Bond Premium

Bonds: $100,000 Par Value, Semiannual Interest Payments, Five-Year Life, 6% Semiannual Contract Rate, 5% Semiannual Market Rate

Semiannual Interest Period-end	(A) Cash Interest Paid	(B) Bond Interest Expense	(C) Premium Amortization	(D) Unamortized Premium	(E) Carrying Value
12/31/2002				$7,720	$107,720
6/30/2003	$ 6,000	$ 5,386	$ 614	7,106	107,106
12/31/2003	6,000	5,355	645	6,461	106,461
6/30/2004	6,000	5,323	677	5,784	105,784
12/31/2004	6,000	5,289	711	5,073	105,073
6/30/2005	6,000	5,254	746	4,327	104,327
12/31/2005	6,000	5,216	784	3,543	103,543
6/30/2006	6,000	5,177	823	2,720	102,720
12/31/2006	6,000	5,136	864	1,856	101,856
6/30/2007	6,000	5,093	907	949	100,949
12/31/2007	6,000	5,051*	949	0	100,000
	$60,000	$52,280	$7,720		

Column **(A)** is par value ($100,000) multiplied by the semiannual contract rate (6%).

Column **(B)** is prior period's carrying value multiplied by the semiannual market rate (5%).

Column **(C)** is the difference between interest paid and bond interest expense, or [(A) − (B)].

Column **(D)** is the prior period's unamortized premium less the current period's premium amortization.

Column **(E)** is par value plus unamortized premium, or [$100,000 + (D)].

* Adjusted for rounding.

Issuing Bonds between Interest Dates

An issuer can sell bonds at a date other than an interest payment date. When this occurs, the buyers normally pay the issuer the purchase price plus any interest accrued since the prior interest payment date. This accrued interest is then repaid to these buyers on the next interest payment date. To illustrate, suppose Avia sells $100,000 of its 9% bonds at par on March 1, 2002, two months after the stated issue date. The interest on Avia bonds is payable semiannually on each June 30 and December 31. Since two months have passed, the issuer collects two months' interest from the buyers at the time of issuance. This amount is $1,500 ($100,000 × 9% × 2/12 year). This case is reflected in Exhibit 10.14.

Decision Insight

Excel Amortization Spreadsheet and accounting software such as Excel and Peachtree make amortization tables easier. We need only enter the bonds' par value, selling price, contract rate, and life to get a complete amortization table.

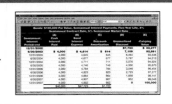

Exhibit 10.14

Accruing Interest between
Interest Payment Dates

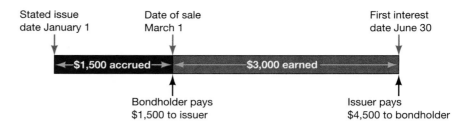

Avia records the issuance of these bonds on March 1, 2002, as follows:

Assets = Liabilities + Equity
+101,500 +100,000
          +1,500

Mar. 1	Cash	101,500	
	Interest Payable		1,500
	Bonds Payable		100,000
	Sold bonds at par with accrued interest.		

Example: How much interest is collected from a buyer of $50,000 of Avia bonds sold at par on June 1, 2002? *Answer:* $1,875 (computed as $50,000 × 9% × ⁵⁄₁₂ year)

Note that liabilities for interest payable and bonds payable are recorded in separate accounts. When the June 30, 2002, semiannual interest date arrives, Avia pays a full six months' interest of $4,500 ($100,000 × 9% × ½ year) to the bondholders. This payment includes the four months' interest of $3,000 earned by the bondholders from March 1 to June 30 *plus* the repayment of two months' accrued interest collected by Avia when the bonds were sold. Avia records this first semiannual interest payment as follows:

Assets = Liabilities + Equity
−4,500   −1,500   −3,000

June 30	Interest Payable	1,500	
	Bond Interest Expense	3,000	
	Cash		4,500
	Paid semiannual interest on the bonds.		

The practice of collecting and then repaying accrued interest with the next interest payment is to simplify the issuer's administrative efforts. To explain, suppose an issuer sells bonds on 15 or 20 different dates between the stated issue date and the first interest payment date. If the issuer did not collect accrued interest from buyers, it would need to pay different amounts of cash to each of them according to the time that had passed since they purchased the bonds. The issuer would need to keep detailed records of buyers and the dates they bought bonds. Issuers avoid this recordkeeping by having each buyer pay accrued interest at the time of purchase. Issuers then pay a full six months' interest to all buyers, regardless of when they bought bonds.

Global: In some countries such as Kuwait, Saudi Arabia, and Iran, charging explicit interest for use of money is rare due to Islamic law.

Accruing Bond Interest Expense

If a bond's interest period does not coincide with the issuer's accounting period, an adjusting entry is necessary to recognize bond interest expense accrued since the most recent interest payment. To illustrate, assume that the Adidas bonds described in Exhibit 10.13 are sold on the stated issue date of September 1, 2002, instead of December 31, 2002. As a result, four months' interest (and premium amortization) accrue before the end of the 2002 calendar year. Interest for these four months equals $3,591, which is ⁴⁄₆ of the first six months' interest of $5,386. Also, the premium amortization is $409, which is ⁴⁄₆ of the first six months' amortization of $614. The sum of the bond interest expense and the amortization is $4,000 ($3,591 + $409), which equals ⁴⁄₆ of the $6,000 cash payment due on February 28, 2003. Adidas records these effects with an adjusting entry at December 31, 2002:

Assets = Liabilities + Equity
        −409   −3,591
       +4,000

Dec. 31	Bond Interest Expense	3,591	
	Premium on Bonds Payable	409	
	Interest Payable		4,000
	To record four months' accrued interest and premium amortization.		

Similar entries with different amounts are made on each December 31 throughout the five-year life of the bonds. When the $6,000 cash payment occurs on each February 28 interest payment date, Adidas must recognize bond interest expense and amortization for January and February. It must also eliminate the interest payable liability created by the December 31 adjusting entry. For example, Adidas records payment on February 28, 2003, as:

Feb. 28	Interest Payable	4,000	
	Bond Interest Expense ($5,386 × ⅔)	1,795	
	Premium on Bonds Payable ($614 × ⅔)	205	
	Cash		6,000
	To record two months' interest and amortization, and to eliminate accrued interest liability.		

Assets = Liabilities + Equity
−6,000   −4,000   −1,795
         −205

The interest payments made each August 31 are recorded as usual because the entire six-month interest period is included within this company's calendar year reporting period.

Bond Pricing

Prices for bonds traded on an organized exchange are often published in newspapers and available through online services. This information normally includes the bond price (called *quote*), its contract rate, and its current market (called *yield*) rate. However, only a fraction of bonds are traded on organized exchanges. To compute the price of a bond, we apply present value concepts. This section explains how we use *present value concepts* to price the Fila discount bond and the Adidas premium bond described earlier.

Point: Access Bond-Online.com for information on investing in bonds.

Present Value of a Discount Bond

The issue price of bonds is found by computing the present value of the bonds' cash payments, discounted at the bonds' market rate. When computing the present value of the Fila bonds, we work with *semiannual* compounding periods because this is the time between interest payments; the annual market rate of 10% is considered as a semiannual rate of 5%. Also, the five-year bond life is viewed as 10 semiannual periods. The price computation is twofold: (1) find the present value of the $100,000 par value paid at maturity and (2) find the present value of the series of 10 semiannual payments of $4,000 each; see Exhibit 10.4. These present values can be found by using present value tables. Appendix B at the end of this book shows present value tables and describes their use. Table B.1 in Appendix B is used for the single $100,000 maturity payment, and Table B.3 in Appendix B is used for the $4,000 series of interest payments. Specifically, we go to Table B.1, row 10, and across to the 5% column to identify the present value factor of 0.6139 for the maturity payment. Next, we go to Table B.3, row 10, and across to the 5% column, where the present value factor is 7.7217 for the series of interest payments. We compute bond price by multiplying the cash flow payments by their corresponding present value factors and adding them together—see Exhibit 10.15.

Point: A bond's market value (issue price) at issuance equals the present value of all its future cash payments (where the interest rate equals the bond's market rate).

Point: Many calculators provide present value functions for computation of bond prices.

Point: The general approach to bond pricing is identical for discount bonds and premium bonds.

Cash Flow	Table	Present Value Factor	Amount		Present Value
$100,000 par (maturity) value	B.1	0.6139	× $100,000	=	$61,390
$4,000 interest payments	B.3	7.7217	× 4,000	=	30,887
Price of bond					$92,277

Exhibit 10.15

Computing Issue Price for Fila Bonds

Present Value of a Premium Bond

We get the issue price of the Adidas bonds by using the market rate to compute the present value of its future cash flows. When computing the present value of these bonds, we again work with *semiannual* compounding periods because this is the time between interest pay-

Point: InvestingInBonds.com is an excellent bond research and learning source.

ments. The annual 10% market rate is applied as a semiannual rate of 5%, and the five-year bond life is viewed as 10 semiannual periods. The computation is twofold: (1) find the present value of the $100,000 par value paid at maturity and (2) find the present value of the series of 10 payments of $6,000 each; see Exhibit 10.9. These present values can be found by using present value tables. First, go to Table B.1, row 10, and across to the 5% column where the present value factor is 0.6139 for the maturity payment. Second, go to Table B.3, row 10, and across to the 5% column, where the present value factor is 7.7217 for the series of interest payments. The bonds' price is computed by multiplying the cash flow payments by their corresponding present value factors and adding them together—see Exhibit 10.16.

Point: There are nearly 5 million individual U.S. bond issues—ranging from huge treasuries to tiny municipalities. This compares to about 12,000 individual U.S. stocks that are traded.

Exhibit 10.16

Computing Issue Price for Adidas Bonds

Cash Flow	Table	Present Value Factor		Amount		Present Value
$100,000 par (maturity) value	B.1	0.6139	×	$100,000	=	$61,390
$6,000 interest payments	B.3	7.7217	×	6,000	=	46,330
Price of bond						$107,720

Quick Check

On December 31, 2001, a company issues 16%, 10-year bonds with a par value of $100,000. Interest is paid on June 30 and December 31. The bonds are sold to yield a 14% annual market rate at an issue price of $110,592. Use this information to answer questions 7 through 9:

7. Are these bonds issued at a discount or a premium? Explain your answer.

8. Using the effective interest method to allocate bond interest expense, the issuer records the second interest payment (on December 31, 2002) with a debit to Premium on Bonds Payable in the amount of (a) $7,741, (b) $259, or (c) $277.

9. How are these bonds reported in the long-term liability section of the issuer's balance sheet as of December 31, 2002?

10. On May 1, a company sells 9% bonds with a $500,000 par value that pays semiannual interest on each January 1 and July 1. The bonds are sold at par plus interest accrued since January 1. The issuer records the first semiannual interest payment on July 1 with (a) a debit to Interest Payable for $15,000, (b) a debit to Bond Interest Expense for $22,500, or (c) a credit to Interest Payable for $7,500.

Answers—p. 451

Bond Retirement

This section describes the retirement of bonds (1) at maturity, (2) before maturity, and (3) by converting them to stock.

Bond Retirement at Maturity

P4 Record the retirement of bonds.

The carrying value of bonds at maturity always equals par value. For example, both Exhibits 10.8 (a discount) and 10.13 (a premium) show that the carrying value of bonds at the end of their five-year life equals par value ($100,000). To record retirement of these bonds at maturity, assuming interest is already paid and entered, is recorded as follows:

Assets = Liabilities + Equity
−100,000 −100,000

2007			
Dec. 31	Bonds Payable	100,000	
	Cash		100,000
	To record retirement of bonds at maturity.		

Bond Retirement before Maturity

Issuers sometimes wish to retire some or all of their bonds prior to maturity. For instance, if interest rates decline significantly, an issuer may wish to replace high-interest-paying bonds with new low-interest bonds. Two common ways to retire bonds before maturity are to (1) exercise a call option or (2) purchase them on the open market. In the first instance, an issuer can reserve the right to retire bonds early by issuing callable bonds. The bond indenture can give the issuer an option to *call* the bonds before they mature by paying the par value plus a *call premium* to bondholders. In the second case, the issuer retires bonds by repurchasing them on the open market at their current price. Whether bonds are called or repurchased, the issuer is unlikely to pay a price that exactly equals their carrying value. When a difference exists between the bonds' carrying value and the amount paid, the issuer records a gain or loss equal to the difference. (Gains and losses from retiring bonds and other debt must be reported on the issuer's income statement as an extraordinary item.)

To illustrate the accounting for retiring callable bonds, assume that a company issued callable bonds with a par value of $100,000. The call option requires the issuer to pay a call premium of $3,000 to bondholders in addition to the par value. Next, assume that after the June 30, 2002, interest payment, the bonds have a carrying value of $104,500. Then on July 1, 2002, the issuer calls these bonds and pays $103,000 to bondholders. The issuer recognizes a $1,500 gain from the difference between the bonds' carrying value of $104,500 and the retirement price of $103,000. The issuer records this bond retirement as:

Point: Bond retirement is also referred to as *bond redemption*.

Global: Some countries such as Spain, Germany, and Korea offer no specific accounting guidelines for retirement of bonds or debt.

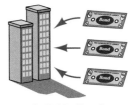

Callable Bond

July 1	Bonds Payable	100,000	
	Premium on Bonds Payable	4,500	
	Gain on Bond Retirement (extraordinary) ...		1,500
	Cash		103,000
	To record retirement of bonds before maturity.		

Assets = Liabilities + Equity
−103,000 −100,000 +1,500
−4,500

An issuer usually must call all bonds when it exercises a call option. However, to retire as many or as few bonds as it desires, an issuer can purchase them on the open market. If it retires less than the entire class of bonds, it recognizes a gain or loss for the difference between the carrying value of those bonds retired and the amount paid to acquire them.

Bond Retirement by Conversion

We described convertible bonds earlier in the chapter and explained how these bondholders have the right to convert their bonds to stock. When conversion occurs, the bonds' carrying value is transferred to equity accounts and no gain or loss is recorded (the market prices of the bonds and stock are not relevant to the entry for conversion). Knowledge of the material in Chapter 11 is helpful in understanding this transaction. To illustrate, assume that on January 1 the $100,000 par value bonds of Converse, with a carrying value of $100,000, are converted to 15,000 shares of $2 par value common stock. The entry to record this conversion is:

Convertible Bond

Decision Insight

Cruis'n Convertibles Over the past decade, convertible bonds have delivered about 80% of the returns of diversified stock funds but with only 66% of the price volatility. Convertibles protect holders against stock price declines, yet they give holders the chance to make more money if stock prices increase by converting bonds to stock.

Bonds	Return
Convertible Bonds	17.8%
L-T Gov. Bonds	12.1
L-T Corp. Bonds	11.3
L-T Munis	9.9
International Bonds	9.9
All Bond Funds	9.4

Jan. 1	Bonds Payable	100,000	
	Common Stock		30,000
	Contributed Capital in Excess of Par Value .		70,000
	To record retirement of bonds by conversion.		

Assets = Liabilities + Equity
−100,000 +30,000
+70,000

Answer—p. 451

> ### Quick Check
>
> **11.** Six years ago, a company issued $500,000 of 6%, eight-year bonds at a price of 95. The current carrying value is $493,750. The company decides to retire 50% of these bonds by buying them on the open market at a price of 102½. What is the amount of gain or loss on retirement of these bonds?

Long-Term Notes Payable

Like bonds, notes are issued to obtain assets such as cash. Unlike bonds, notes are typically transacted with a *single* lender such as a bank. An issuer initially records a note at its selling price—the note's face value minus any discount or plus any premium. Over the note's life, the amount of interest expense allocated to each period is computed by multiplying the market rate (at issuance of the note) by the beginning-of-period balance of the note. The note's carrying (book) value at any time equals its face value minus any unamortized discount or plus any unamortized premium—carrying value is computed as the present value of all remaining future payments, discounted using the market rate at the time of issuance.

Installment Notes

An **installment note** is an obligation requiring a series of periodic payments to the lender. Installment notes are common for franchises and other businesses when lenders and borrowers agree to spread costs over several periods. When an installment note is used to borrow money or pay for assets, the borrower records the note with an increase (debit) to cash or other assets and an increase (credit) to the Notes Payable liability account. To illustrate, assume that Foghog borrows $60,000 from a bank to purchase equipment. Foghog signs an 8% installment note requiring six annual payments of principal plus interest and records the note's issuance as follows:

Assets = Liabilities + Equity
+60,000   +60,000

Dec. 31	Cash	60,000	
	Notes Payable		60,000
	Borrowed $60,000 by signing an 8%, six-year installment note.		

Alternatively, Foghog could issue a note directly to the seller of the equipment. In this case, it records the equipment received instead of cash.

C2 Explain the types and payment patterns of notes.

Payments on an installment note normally include the interest expense accruing to the date of the payment plus a portion of the amount borrowed (the *principal*). Generally, we can identify two payment pattern types: (1) accrued interest plus equal principal payments and (2) equal payments. This section describes these two patterns and how we account for them.

Accrued Interest plus Equal Principal Payments

One common payment pattern for an installment note is accrued interest plus equal amounts of principal. This pattern creates cash flows that decrease in size over the note's life. This decrease occurs because each principal payment reduces the note's principal balance, yielding less accrued interest expense for the next period.

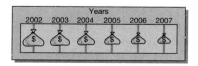

To illustrate, assume that Foghog's $60,000, 8% note requires it to make a payment at the end of each of six years equal to *accrued interest plus $10,000 of principal*. Exhibit 10.17 shows these payments and the changes in the balance of this note. Column A lists the note's annual beginning balance. Columns B, C, and D list each annual cash payment and its division between interest and principal. Specifically, column B shows interest expense for each year at 8% of the beginning balance. Column C shows that each principal payment reduces the Notes Payable account balance by $10,000. Column D is the total annual payment. Column E shows the note's ending balance, which equals the beginning balance in column A minus the principal payment in column C. We include *debit* or *credit* in column headings to show the accounting effects. Note that the sum of debits to both interest expense and notes payable equals the credit to Cash. Also notice that total interest expense is

P5 Prepare entries to account for notes.

Period Ending Date	(A) Beginning Balance	(B) *Debit* Interest Expense 8% × (A)	+	(C) *Debit* Notes Payable $60,000/6	=	(D) *Credit* Cash (B) + (C)	(E) Ending Balance (A) − (C)
			Payments				
12/31/2002	$60,000	$ 4,800		$10,000		$14,800	$50,000
12/31/2003	50,000	4,000		10,000		14,000	40,000
12/31/2004	40,000	3,200		10,000		13,200	30,000
12/31/2005	30,000	2,400		10,000		12,400	20,000
12/31/2006	20,000	1,600		10,000		11,600	10,000
12/31/2007	10,000	800		10,000		10,800	0
		$16,800		$60,000		$76,800	

Exhibit 10.17

Installment Note: Accrued Interest plus Equal Principal Payments

$16,800 and total principal is $60,000, which means cash payments for the five years total $76,800. The graph in the lower portion of Exhibit 10.17 shows the decreasing pattern in total payments—made up of decreasing accrued interest and constant principal payments. Foghog records its first two payments (for years 2002 and 2003) as follows:

2002			
Dec. 31	Interest Expense	4,800	
	Notes Payable	10,000	
	Cash		14,800
	To record first installment payment.		

Assets = Liabilities + Equity
−14,800   −10,000   −4,800

2003			
Dec. 31	Interest Expense	4,000	
	Notes Payable	10,000	
	Cash		14,000
	To record second installment payment.		

Assets = Liabilities + Equity
−14,000   −10,000   −4,000

After all six payments are recorded, the balance of the Notes Payable account is zero.

Equal Total Payments

Another type of installment note requires the borrower to make a series of equal payments that consist of changing amounts of both interest and principal. To illustrate, assume that Foghog borrows $60,000 by signing a $60,000 note that requires six *equal payments* of $12,979 at the end of each year. (The present value of an annuity of six annual payments of $12,979, discounted at 8%, equals $60,000—we show this computation later in the section.) The $12,979 includes both interest and principal, the amounts of which change with each payment. Exhibit 10.18 shows the pattern of equal total payments and its two parts, interest and principal. Column A shows the note's beginning balance. Column B shows accrued interest for each year at 8% of the beginning note balance. Column C shows the impact on the note's principal, which equals the difference between the total payment in column D and the interest expense in column B. Column E shows the note's year-end balance.

Although the six cash payments are equal, accrued interest decreases each year because the principal balance of the note declines. As the amount of interest decreases each year, the portion of each payment applied to principal increases. This pattern is graphed in the lower part of Exhibit 10.18. Foghog uses the amounts in Exhibit 10.18 to record its first two payments (for years 2002 and 2003) as follows:

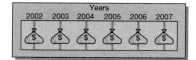

Point: Most consumer notes are installment notes that require equal total payments.

		2002		
Dec. 31	Interest Expense	4,800	
	Notes Payable	8,179	
	Cash		12,979
	To record first installment payment.		

Assets = Liabilities + Equity
−12,979   −8,179   −4,800

		2003		
Dec. 31	Interest Expense	4,146	
	Notes Payable	8,833	
	Cash		12,979
	To record second installment payment.		

Assets = Liabilities + Equity
−12,979   −8,833   −4,146

Decision Insight *e*

Entrepreneur Aid The Small Business Administration (SBA) provides loan programs, workshops, software, and other useful services for start-ups. It also operates an online library with facts and advice for entrepreneurs (www.sba.gov). It reports that reliable accounting is crucial in securing financing at favorable terms.

Foghog records similar entries but with different amounts for each of the remaining four payments. After six years, the Notes Payable account balance is zero.

It is useful to compare the two payment patterns in Exhibits 10.17 and 10.18. The series of equal total payments yields more interest expense over the life of the note because the first three payments in Exhibit 10.18 are smaller and do not reduce the principal as quickly as the first three payments in Exhibit 10.17.[1]

Example: Suppose the $60,000 installment loan has an 8% interest rate with eight equal annual payments. What is the annual payment? *Answer* (using Table B.3): $60,000/5.7466 = $10,441

Mortgage Notes

A **mortgage** is a legal agreement that helps protect a lender if a borrower fails to make required payments on bonds or notes. A mortgage gives the lender a right to be paid from the cash proceeds of the sale of a borrower's assets identified in the mortgage. A legal document, called a *mortgage contract,* describes the mortgage terms.

---

[1] Table B.3 in Appendix B is used to compute the dollar amount of the six payments equivalent to the initial note balance of $60,000 at 8% interest. We go to Table B.3, row 6, and across to the 8% column, where the value is 4.6229. The payment amount is then computed by solving this relation:

Table	Present Value Factor		Amount		Present Value
B.3 . . .	4.6229	×	?	=	60,000

We solve for the payment amount by dividing $60,000 by 4.6229, yielding $12,979.

| Period Ending Date | (A) Beginning Balance | Payments | | (E) Ending Balance (A) − (C) |
		(B) Debit Interest Expense 8% × (A) +	(C) Debit Notes Payable (D) − (B) =	(D) Credit Cash (computed)	
12/31/2002	$60,000	$ 4,800	$ 8,179	$12,979	$51,821
12/31/2003	51,821	4,146	8,833	12,979	42,988
12/31/2004	42,988	3,439	9,540	12,979	33,448
12/31/2005	33,448	2,676	10,303	12,979	23,145
12/31/2006	23,145	1,852	11,127	12,979	12,018
12/31/2007	12,018	961	12,018	12,979	0
		$17,874	$60,000	$77,874	

Exhibit 10.18

Installment Note: Equal Total Payments

☐ Principal

☐ Interest

Increasing Principal Component

Decreasing Accrued Interest

Equal Total Payments

End of Year	
2007	$12,018 · $961
2006	$11,127 · $1,852
2005	$10,303 · $2,676
2004	$9,540 · $3,439
2003	$8,833 · $4,146
2002	$8,179 · $4,800

0   $2,500 $5,000 $7,500 $10,000 $12,500 $15,000

Cash Payment Pattern

Mortgage notes carry a mortgage contract pledging title to specific assets as security for the note. While less common, *mortgage bonds* backed by the issuer's assets also exist. A mortgage contract is given to the lender who accepts a mortgage note or to the trustee of mortgage bonds. This contract usually requires the issuer (borrower) to pay all property taxes on the mortgaged assets, to maintain them properly, and to carry adequate insurance against fire and other types of losses. These requirements are designed to keep the property from losing value and avoid diminishing the lender's security. Mortgage notes are especially popular in the purchase of homes and the acquisition of plant assets.

Accounting for mortgage notes and bonds is essentially the same as accounting for unsecured notes and bonds. The primary difference is that the mortgage agreement needs to be disclosed. For instance, more than 10% of **Musicland**'s long-term liabilities are in mortgage notes. Musicland reports that its "mortgage note pay-

Point: The Truth-in-Lending Act requires lenders to provide consumers information about the cost of their loans. This includes finance charges and the annual interest rate.

Decision Maker

Entrepreneur You are an electronics retailer planning a holiday sale on a custom stereo system that requires no payments for two years. At the end of two years, buyers must pay the full amount. The system's suggested retail price is $4,100, but you are willing to sell it today for $3,000 cash. What is your holiday sale price if payment will not occur for two years and the market interest rate is 10%?

Answer—p. 451

able is collateralized by land, buildings and certain fixtures of three of the Company's Media Play stores." Musicland's note carries a variable interest rate, also called a *floating rate*.

Most mortgage contracts grant the lender the right to *foreclose* on the property if the borrower fails to pay in accordance with the terms of the agreement. If foreclosure occurs, a court either orders the property to be sold or simply grants legal title for the mortgaged property to the lender. If the property is sold, the proceeds are first applied to court costs and then to the mortgage holder's claims. The borrower receives any additional proceeds subject to claims from its other creditors.

Global: Countries vary in the preference given to debtholders vs. stockholders when a company is in financial distress. Some countries such as Germany, France, and Japan give preference to stockholders over the interests of debtholders.

Quick Check

12. Which of the following is true for an installment note requiring a series of equal total cash payments? (*a*) Payments consist of increasing interest and decreasing principal; (*b*) Payments consist of changing amounts of principal but constant interest; or (*c*) Payments consist of decreasing interest and increasing principal.

13. How is the interest portion of an installment note payment computed?

14. When a borrower records an interest payment on an installment note, how are the balance sheet and income statement affected?

Answers—p. 451

Decision Analysis   Pledged Assets to Secured Liabilities

This section explains how lenders can reduce their risk of loss and how borrowers can achieve more favorable terms by entering into collateral agreements. Also, this section describes an important measure of this risk.

Collateral Agreements

A2 Explain collateral agreements and their effects on loan risk.

Collateral agreements can reduce the risk of loss for both bonds and notes. Unsecured bonds and notes are riskier because the issuer's obligation to pay interest and principal has the same priority as all other unsecured liabilities in the event of bankruptcy. If a company is unable to pay its debts in full, the unsecured creditors (including the holders of debentures) lose all or a portion of their balances.

A company's ability to borrow money with or without collateral agreements depends on its credit rating. In some cases, debt financing is unavailable unless the borrower can provide security to creditors with a collateral agreement. Even if unsecured loans are available, the creditors are likely to charge a higher rate of interest to compensate for the added risk. To borrow funds at a more favorable rate, many bonds and notes are secured by collateral agreements in the form of mortgages. Information about a company's security agreements with its lenders is important to users. Notes to financial statements sometimes describe the amounts of assets pledged as security against liabilities. The next section describes a ratio used to assess a borrower's situation with respect to its security agreements.

Ratio of Pledged Assets to Secured Liabilities

A3 Compute the ratio of pledged assets to secured liabilities and explain its use.

Buyers (investors) of a company's secured debt obligations need to determine whether the debtor's pledged assets provide adequate security. One method to evaluate this is to compute the ratio of **pledged assets to secured liabilities.** This is computed by dividing the book value of the company's assets pledged as collateral by the book value of liabilities secured by these collateral agreements as shown in Exhibit 10.19.

Exhibit 10.19

Pledged Assets to Secured Liabilities

$$\text{Pledged assets to secured liabilities} = \frac{\text{Book value of pledged assets}}{\text{Book value of secured liabilities}}$$

To illustrate, assume that a company owns assets with a book value of $230,000 pledged against loans with a balance of $100,000. The pledged assets to secured liabilities ratio is 2.3 (often expressed as 2.3 to 1) and is computed as $230,000/$100,000. There are no exact guidelines for interpreting the value for this ratio, but a 2.3 value is sufficiently high to provide secured creditors with some comfort that their loans are covered by the borrower's assets. As another example, a recent annual report of Chock Full O'Nuts reveals that "borrowings under the Loan Agreements . . . are collateralized by . . . accounts receivable and inventories, and substantially all of the machinery and equipment and real estate." We can use this information to compute its pledged assets to secured liabilities ratio of 20.6 ($206 million/$10 million). This ratio implies that more than $20 of collateral exists for each $1 of secured liabilities. This huge collateral commitment likely accounts for the low 8.5% interest that Chock Full O'Nuts pays on these secured liabilities.

Pledging assets for the benefit of secured creditors also affects unsecured creditors. When a larger portion of assets is pledged, the unsecured creditors are at greater risk. Namely, secured creditors often demand a high ratio when they perceive that (1) the values of the assets in liquidation are low and (2) the likelihood that the company will meet its obligations from operating cash flows is not high. Consequently, unsecured creditors also gain information from the ratio of pledged assets to secured liabilities.

When using this ratio, we must be aware that reported book values of a company's assets are unlikely to exactly reflect market values. This ratio is improved if we can determine the assets' market values and then use them in the ratio instead of book values. A company's lenders can sometimes obtain this information directly by asking the borrower to provide recent appraisals. Using the ratio also requires knowledge about secured liabilities and pledged assets— how they are both measured and reported. This requires analysis of information in both the financial statements and their notes.

Decision Maker

Bond Investor   You plan to purchase debenture bonds from one of two companies in the same industry that are similar in size and performance. The first company has $350,000 of unsecured liabilities, $575,000 of secured liabilities, and $1,265,000 in book value of pledged assets. The second company has $1,200,000 of unsecured liabilities, $800,000 of secured liabilities, and $2,000,000 in book value of pledged assets. Which company's debenture bonds are less risky based on the ratio of pledged assets to secured liabilities?

Answer—p. 451

Demonstration Problem

Water Sports Company (WSC) patented and successfully test-marketed a new product. To expand its ability to produce and market the new product, WSC needs to raise $800,000 of financing. On January 1, 2002, the company obtains the money in two ways:

a. WSC signs a $400,000, 10% installment note to be repaid with five equal annual installments. The payments will be made on December 31 of 2002 through 2006.

b. WSC issues five-year bonds with a par value of $400,000. The bonds have a 12% annual contract rate and pay interest on June 30 and December 31. The annual market rate for the bonds is 10% as of January 1, 2002.

Required

1. For the installment note, (a) compute the size of each annual payment, (b) prepare an amortization table such as Exhibit 10.18, and (c) prepare the journal entry for the first payment.

2. For the bonds, (a) compute their issue price; (b) prepare the January 1, 2002, journal entry to record their issuance; (c) prepare an amortization table using the effective interest method; (d) prepare the June 30, 2002, journal entry to record the first interest payment; and (e) prepare a journal entry to record retiring the bonds at a $416,000 call price on January 1, 2004.

Planning the Solution

• For the installment note, divide the borrowed amount by the annuity factor (from Table B.3) using the 10% rate and five payments. Prepare a table similar to Exhibit 10.18 and use the numbers in the table's first line for the journal entry.

- For the bonds, compute the issue price by using the market rate to find the present value of the bonds' cash flows (use tables found in Appendix B). Then use this result to record the bonds' issuance. Next, prepare an amortization table like Exhibit 10.13 and use it to get the numbers needed for the journal entry. Also use the table to find the carrying value as of the date of the bonds' retirement that you need for the journal entry.

Solution to Demonstration Problem

Part 1: Installment Note

a. Annual payment = Note balance/Annuity factor = $400,000/3.7908 = $105,519 (Note: Annuity factor is for five payments and a rate of 10%.)

b. Amortization table:

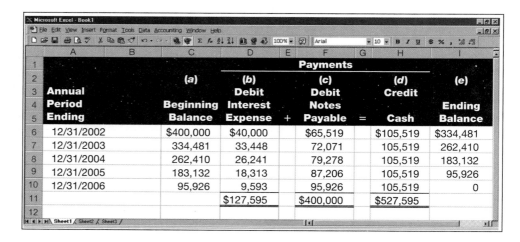

Annual Period Ending	(a) Beginning Balance	(b) Debit Interest Expense +	(c) Debit Notes Payable =	(d) Credit Cash	(e) Ending Balance
12/31/2002	$400,000	$40,000	$65,519	$105,519	$334,481
12/31/2003	334,481	33,448	72,071	105,519	262,410
12/31/2004	262,410	26,241	79,278	105,519	183,132
12/31/2005	183,132	18,313	87,206	105,519	95,926
12/31/2006	95,926	9,593	95,926	105,519	0
		$127,595	$400,000	$527,595	

c. Journal entry for December 31, 2002, payment:

Dec. 31	Interest Expense	40,000	
	Notes Payable	65,519	
	Cash		105,519
	To record first installment payment.		

Part 2: Bonds

a. Compute the bonds' issue price:

Cash Flow	Table	Present Value Factor*		Amount		Present Value
Par (maturity) value	B.1 in App. B (PV of 1)	0.6139	×	400,000	=	$245,560
Interest payments	B.3 in App. B (PV of annuity)	7.7217	×	24,000	=	185,321
Price of bond						$430,881

* Present value factors are for 10 payments using an interest rate of 5%.

b. Journal entry for January 1, 2002, issuance:

Jan. 1	Cash	430,881	
	Premium on Bonds Payable		30,881
	Bonds Payable		400,000
	Sold bonds at a premium.		

c. Amortization table:

Semiannual Interest Period	(A) Cash Interest Paid 6% × $400,000	(B) Interest Expense 5% × Prior (E)	(C) Premium Amortization (A) – (B)	(D) Unamortized Premium Prior (D) – (C)	(E) Carrying Value $400,000 + (D)
1/1/2002				$30,881	$430,881
6/30/2002	$ 24,000	$ 21,544	$ 2,456	28,425	428,425
12/31/2002	24,000	21,421	2,579	25,846	425,846
6/30/2003	24,000	21,292	2,708	23,138	423,138
12/31/2003	24,000	21,157	2,843	20,295	420,295
6/30/2004	24,000	21,015	2,985	17,310	417,310
12/31/2004	24,000	20,866	3,134	14,176	414,176
6/30/2005	24,000	20,709	3,291	10,885	410,885
12/31/2005	24,000	20,544	3,456	7,429	407,429
6/30/2006	24,000	20,371	3,629	3,800	403,800
12/31/2006	24,000	20,200*	3,800	0	400,000
	$240,000	$209,119	$30,881		

* Adjusted for rounding.

d. Journal entry for June 30, 2002, payment:

June 30	Bond Interest Expense	21,544	
	Premium on Bonds Payable	2,456	
	Cash		24,000
	Paid semiannual interest on bonds.		

e. Journal entry for January 1, 2004, bond retirement:

Jan. 1	Bonds Payable	400,000	
	Premium on Bonds Payable	20,295	
	Cash		416,000
	Gain on Retirement of Bonds		4,295
	To record retirement of bonds (carrying value determined as of December 31, 2003).		

Present Values of Bonds and Notes

10A

Accounting for long-term liabilities such as bonds and notes presents challenges because of the extended time period until these obligations are settled. This appendix explains how to apply present value techniques both to measure a long-term liability when it is created and to assign interest expense to the periods until it is settled. Appendix B at the end of the book provides additional discussion of present value concepts.

C3 Explain and compute the present value of an amount to be paid at a future date.

Present Value Concepts

Accounting for long-term liabilities requires some understanding of present value concepts. The basic present value concept is the idea that cash paid (or received) in the future has less value now than the same amount of cash paid (or received) today. To illustrate, if we must pay $1 one year from now, its present value is less than $1. To see this, assume that we borrow $0.9259 today that must be paid back in one year with 8% interest. Our interest expense for this loan is computed as $0.9259 × 8%, or $0.0741. When the $0.0741 interest is added to the $0.9259 borrowed, we get the $1 payment necessary to repay our loan with interest. This is formally computed in Exhibit 10A.1. The $0.9259 borrowed is the present value of the $1 future payment. More generally, an amount borrowed equals the present value of the future payment. (This same interpretation applies to an investment. If $0.9259 is invested at 8%, it yields $0.0741 in revenue after one year. This amounts to $1, made up of principal and interest.)

Exhibit 10A.1

Components of a
One-Year Loan

Amount borrowed	$0.9259
Interest for one year at 8%	0.0741
Amount owed after 1 year	$1.0000

To extend this example, assume that we owe $1 two years from now instead of one year, and the 8% interest is compounded annually. *Compounded* means that interest during the second period is based on the total of the amount borrowed plus the interest accrued from the first period. The second period's interest is then computed as 8% multiplied by the sum of the amount borrowed plus interest earned in the first period. Exhibit 10A.2 shows how we compute the present value of $1 to be paid in two years. This amount is $0.8573. The first year's interest of $0.0686 is added to the principal so that the second year's interest is based on $0.9259. Total interest for this two-year period is $0.1427, computed as $0.0686 plus $0.0741.

Point: Benjamin Franklin is said to have described compounding as "the money, money makes, makes more money."

Exhibit 10A.2

Components of a
Two-Year Loan

Amount borrowed	**$0.8573**
Interest for first year ($0.8573 × 8%)	0.0686
Amount owed after 1 year	$0.9259
Interest for second year ($0.9259 × 8%)	0.0741
Amount owed after 2 years	$1.0000

Present Value Tables

The present value of $1 that we must repay at some future date can be computed by using this formula: $1/(1 + i)^n$. The symbol i in the formula is the interest rate per period and n is the number of periods until the future payment must be made. Applying this formula to our two-year loan, we get $1/(1.08)^2$, or $0.8573. This is the same value shown in Exhibit 10A.2. We can use this formula to find any present value. However, a simpler method is to use a *present value table,* which lists present values computed with this formula for various interest rates and time periods. Many people find it helpful in learning present value concepts to first work with the table and then move to using a calculator.

Example: If interest in this example is 6% instead of 8%, what amount does the borrower receive for a promise to pay $1 in 1 year? How much is interest?
Answer: Amount borrowed: $1/1.06 = $0.9434. Interest for 1 year: 6% × $0.9434 = $0.0566

Exhibit 10A.3

Present Value of 1

Periods	Rate		
	6%	8%	10%
1	0.9434	**0.9259**	0.9091
2	0.8900	**0.8573**	0.8264
3	0.8396	0.7938	0.7513
4	0.7921	0.7350	0.6830
5	0.7473	0.6806	0.6209
6	0.7050	0.6302	0.5645
7	0.6651	0.5835	0.5132
8	0.6274	0.5403	0.4665
9	0.5919	0.5002	0.4241
10	0.5584	0.4632	0.3855

Exhibit 10A.3 shows a present value table for a future payment of 1 for up to 10 periods at three different interest rates. Present values in this table are rounded to four decimal places. This table is drawn from the larger and more complete Table B.1 in Appendix B at the end of the book. Notice that the first value in the 8% column is 0.9259, the value we computed earlier for the present value of a $1 loan for one year at 8% (see Exhibit 10A.1). Go to the second row in the same 8% column and find the present value of 1 discounted at 8% for two years, or 0.8573. This $0.8573 is the present value of our obligation to repay $1 after two periods at 8% interest (see Exhibit 10A.2).

Example: Use Exhibit 10A.3 to find the present value of $1 discounted for 2 years at 6%.
Answer: Present value = $0.8900

Applying a Present Value Table

To illustrate how to measure a liability using a present value table, assume that a company plans to borrow cash and repay it as follows:

Payment after 1 year	$ 2,000
Payment after 2 years	3,000
Payment after 3 years	5,000
Total payments	$10,000

How much does this company receive today if the interest rate is 10% on this loan? For the answer, we need to compute the present value of the three future payments, discounted at 10%. This computation is shown in Exhibit 10A.4 using present values from Exhibit 10A.3. The company can borrow $8,054 today at 10% interest in exchange for its promise to make these three payments at the scheduled dates.

Exhibit 10A.4

Present Value of a Series of Unequal Payments

Periods	Payments	Present Value of 1 at 10%	Present Value of Payments
1	$2,000	0.9091	$1,818
2	3,000	0.8264	2,479
3	5,000	0.7513	3,757
Present value of all payments			**$8,054**

Present Value of an Annuity

The $8,054 present value for the loan in Exhibit 10A.4 equals the sum of the present values of the three payments. When payments are not equal, their combined present value is best computed by adding the individual present values as shown in Exhibit 10A.4. Sometimes payments follow an **annuity,** which is a series of *equal* payments at equal time intervals. The present value of an annuity is readily computed.

C4 Explain and compute the present value of a series of equal amounts to be paid at future dates.

To illustrate, assume that a company must repay a 6% loan with a $5,000 payment at each year-end for the next four years. This loan amount equals the present value of the four payments discounted at 6%. Exhibit 10A.5 shows how to compute this loan's present value of $17,326 by multiplying each payment by its matching present value factor taken from Exhibit 10A.3. Since the series of $5,000 payments is an annuity, we can compute its present value with either of two shortcuts. First, the third column of Exhibit 10A.5 shows that the sum of the present values of 1 at 6% for periods 1 through 4 equals 3.4651. One shortcut is to multiply this total of 3.4651 by the $5,000 annual payment to get the combined present value of $17,326. It requires one multiplication instead of four.

The second shortcut uses an *annuity table* such as the one shown in Exhibit 10A.6, which is drawn from the more complete Table B.3 in Appendix B. We go directly to the annuity table to get the present value factor for a specific number of payments and interest rate. We then multiply this factor by the amount of the payment to find the present value of the annuity. Specifically, find the row for four periods and go across to the 6% column, where the factor is 3.4651. This factor equals the present value of an annuity with four payments of 1, discounted at 6%. We then multiply 3.4651 by $5,000 to get the $17,326 present value of the annuity.

Exhibit 10A.5

Present Value of a Series of Equal Payments (Annuity) by Discounting Each Payment

Periods	Payments	Present Value of 1 at 6%	Present Value of Payments
1	$5,000	0.9434	$ 4,717
2	5,000	0.8900	4,450
3	5,000	0.8396	4,198
4	5,000	0.7921	3,961
Present value of all payments		**3.4651**	**$17,326**

Exhibit 10A.6

Present Value of an Annuity of 1

Periods	Rate		
	6%	8%	10%
1	0.9434	0.9259	0.9091
2	1.8334	1.7833	1.7355
3	2.6730	2.5771	2.4869
4	**3.4651**	3.3121	3.1699
5	4.2124	3.9927	3.7908
6	4.9173	4.6229	4.3553
7	5.5824	5.2064	4.8684
8	6.2098	5.7466	5.3349
9	6.8017	6.2469	5.7590
10	7.3601	6.7101	6.1446

Example: Use Exhibit 10A.6 to find the present value of an annuity of eight $15,000 payments with an 8% interest rate. *Answer:* Present value = $15,000 × 5.7466 = $86,199

Compounding Periods Shorter than a Year

Our present value examples all involved periods of a year. In many situations, however, interest is compounded over shorter periods. For example, the interest rate on bonds is usually stated as an annual rate but interest is often paid every six months (semiannually). This means that the present value of interest payments from such bonds must be computed using interest periods of six months.

Assume that a borrower wants to know the present value of a series of 10 *semiannual payments* of $4,000 made over five years at an *annual interest rate* of 12%. The interest rate is stated as an annual rate of 12%, but it is actually a rate of 6% per semiannual interest period. To compute the present value of this series of $4,000 payments, go to row 10 of Exhibit 10A.6 and across to the 6% column to find the factor 7.3601. The present value of this annuity is $29,440 (7.3601 × $4,000).

We recommend reading Appendix B to learn more about present value concepts. It also includes more complete present value tables and additional assignments.

Example: If this borrower makes five semiannual payments of $8,000, what is the present value of this annuity at a 12% annual rate?
Answer: 4.2124 × $8,000 = $33,699

Quick Check

15. A company enters into an agreement to make four annual year-end payments of $1,000 each, starting one year from now. The annual interest rate is 8%. The present value of these four payments is (*a*) $2,923, (*b*) $2,940, or (*c*) $3,312.

16. Suppose a company has an option to pay either (*a*) $10,000 after one year or (*b*) $5,000 after six months and another $5,000 after one year. Which choice has the lower present value?

Answers—p. 452

APPENDIX

10B   Leases and Pensions

This appendix explains the accounting and analysis for both leases and pensions.

Lease Liabilities

C5 Describe the accounting for leases and pensions.

A **lease** is a contractual agreement between a *lessor* (asset owner) and a *lessee* (asset renter or tenant) that grants the lessee the right to use the asset for a period of time in return for cash (rent) payments. Nearly one-fourth of all equipment purchases is financed with leases. The advantages of lease financing include the lack of an immediate large cash payment and the potential to deduct rental payments in computing taxable income. From an accounting perspective, leases can be classified as either operating or capital leases.

Operating Leases

Point: Home Depot's recent annual report indicates that its rental expenses from operating leases total more than $250 million.

Operating leases are short-term (or cancelable) leases in which the lessor retains the risks and rewards of ownership. Examples include most car and apartment rental agreements. The lessee records such lease payments as expenses; the lessor records them as revenue. To illustrate, if an employee of Amazon leases a car for $300 at an airport while on company business, Amazon (lessee) records this cost as:

Assets = Liabilities + Equity
−300   −300

July 4	Rental Expense	300	
	Cash		300
	To record lease rental payment.		

The lessee does not report the leased item as an asset or a liability (it is the lessor's asset).

Capital Leases

Capital leases are long-term (or noncancelable) leases in which the lessor transfers substantially all risks and rewards of ownership to the lessee.[2] Examples include most leases of airplanes and department store buildings. The lessee records the leased item as its own asset along with a lease liability at the start of the lease term; the amount recorded equals the present value of all lease payments. To illustrate, assume that K2 Co. enters into a six-year lease of a building in which it will sell sporting equipment. The lease transfers all the risks and rewards of building ownership to K2 (the present value of its $12,979 annual lease payments is $60,000). K2 records this transaction as follows:

2002			
Jan. 1	Leased Asset—Building	60,000	
	Lease Liability		60,000
	To record leased asset and lease liability.		

Assets = Liabilities + Equity
+60,000 +60,000

K2 reports the leased asset as a plant asset. The lease liability is reported as a long-term liability. The portion of the lease liability expected to be paid in the next year is reported as a current liability.[3] At each year-end, K2 records depreciation on the leased asset (assume straight-line depreciation, six-year lease term, and no salvage value) as follows:

Point: Home Depot reports *"certain retail locations are leased under capital leases."* The net present value of its Lease Liability is about $150 million.

Dec. 31	Depreciation Expense—Building	10,000	
	Accumulated Depreciation—Building		10,000
	To record depreciation on leased asset.		

Assets = Liabilities + Equity
−10,000   −10,000

K2 also accrues interest on the lease liability at each year-end. Interest expense is computed by multiplying the remaining lease liability by the interest rate on the lease. Specifically, K2 records its annual interest expense as part of its annual lease payment ($12,979) as follows (for its first year):

2002			
Dec. 31	Interest Expense	4,800	
	Lease Liability	8,179	
	Cash		12,979
	*To record first annual lease payment.**		

Assets = Liabilities + Equity
−12,979 −8,179   −4,800

* These numbers are computed from a *lease payment schedule.* For simplicity, we use the same numbers from Exhibit 10.18 for this lease payment schedule—with different headings as follows:

			Payments		
	(A)	(B) *Debit*	(C) *Debit*	(D) *Credit*	(E)
Period Ending Date	Beginning Balance of Lease Liability	Interest on Lease Liability 8% × (A)	+ Lease Liability (D) − (B)	= Cash Lease Payment	Ending Balance of Lease Liability (A) − (C)
12/31/2002	$60,000	$ 4,800	$ 8,179	$12,979	$51,821
12/31/2003	51,821	4,146	8,833	12,979	42,988
12/31/2004	42,988	3,439	9,540	12,979	33,448
12/31/2005	33,448	2,676	10,303	12,979	23,145
12/31/2006	23,145	1,852	11,127	12,979	12,018
12/31/2007	12,018	961	12,018	12,979	0
		$17,874	$60,000	$77,874	

---

[2] A capital lease is one that meets any one or more of four criteria: (1) transfers title of leased asset to lessee, (2) contains a bargain purchase option, (3) has a lease term that is 75% or more of the leased asset's useful life, or (4) has a present value of lease payments that is 90% or more of the leased asset's market value.

[3] Most lessees try to keep leased assets and lease liabilities off their balance sheets by failing to meet one of the four criteria of a capital lease because a lease liability increases a company's total liabilities, making it more difficult to obtain additional financing. The acquisition of assets with liabilities not reported on the balance sheet is called **off-balance-sheet financing.**

Pension Liabilities

A **pension plan** is a contractual agreement between an employer and its employees for the employer to provide benefits (payments) to employees after they retire. Most employers pay the full cost of the pension, but sometimes employees pay part of the cost. An employer records its payment into a pension plan with a debit to Pension Expense and a credit to Cash. A *plan administrator* receives payments from the employer, invests them in pension assets, and makes benefit payments to *pension recipients* (retired employees). Insurance and trust companies often serve as pension plan administrators.

Many pensions are known as *defined benefit plans* that define future benefits, where the employer's contributions vary, depending on assumptions about future pension assets and liabilities. Several disclosures are necessary in this case. Specifically, a pension liability is reported when the accumulated benefit obligation is *more than* the plan assets, a so-called *underfunded plan*. The accumulated benefit obligation is the present value of promised future pension payments to retirees. *Plan assets* refer to the market value of assets the plan administrator holds. A pension asset is reported when the accumulated benefit obligation is *less than* the plan assets, a so-called *overfunded plan*. An employer reports pension expense when it receives the benefits from the employees' services, which is sometimes decades before it pays pension benefits to employees. (*Other Postretirement Benefits* refer to nonpension benefits such as health care and life insurance benefits. Similar to a pension, costs of these benefits are estimated and liabilities accrued when the employees earn them.)

Summary

C1 **Describe the types of bonds and the procedures for issuing them.** Certain bonds are secured by the issuer's assets; other bonds, called *debentures,* are unsecured. Serial bonds mature at different points in time; term bonds mature at one time. Registered bonds have each bondholder's name recorded by the issuer; bearer bonds are payable to the holder. Convertible bonds are exchangeable for shares of the issuer's stock. Callable bonds can be retired by the issuer at a set price. Bonds are often issued by an underwriter and monitored by a trustee.

C2 **Explain the types and payment patterns of notes.** Notes repaid over a period of time are called *installment notes* and usually follow one of two payment patterns: (1) decreasing payments of interest plus equal amounts of principal or (2) equal total payments. Mortgage notes also are common.

C3 **Explain and compute the present value of an amount to be paid at a future date.** The basic concept of present value is that an amount of cash to be paid or received in the future is worth less than the same amount of cash to be paid or received today. Another important present value concept is that interest is compounded, meaning interest is added to the balance and used to determine interest for succeeding periods.

C4 **Explain and compute the present value of a series of equal amounts to be paid at future dates.** An annuity is a series of equal payments occurring at equal time intervals. An annuity's present value can be computed as the sum of individual present values for each payment. An alternative and preferred approach is to compute the present value of the series using the present value table for an annuity (or a calculator).

C5 **Describe the accounting for leases and pensions.** A lease is a rental agreement between the lessor and the lessee. When the lessor retains the risks and rewards of asset ownership (called an *operating lease*), the lessee debits Rent Expense and credits Cash for its lease payments. When the lessor substantially transfers the risks and rewards of asset ownership to the lessee (called a *capital lease*), the lessee capitalizes the leased asset and

records a lease liability. Pension agreements can result in either pension assets or pension liabilities.

A1 **Compare bond financing with stock financing.** Bond financing is used to fund business activities. Advantages of bond financing versus stock include (1) no effect on owner control, (2) tax savings, and (3) increased earnings due to financial leverage. Disadvantages include (1) interest and principal payments and (2) amplification of poor performance.

A2 **Explain collateral agreements and their effects on loan risk.** Collateral agreements alter the risk of loss for creditors. Unsecured bonds and notes are riskier because the issuer's obligation to pay interest and principal has the same priority as all other unsecured liabilities in the event of bankruptcy. To borrow funds at a more favorable rate, many bonds and notes are secured by collateral agreements called *mortgages.*

A3 **Compute the ratio of pledged assets to secured liabilities and explain its use.** Both secured and unsecured creditors are concerned about the relation between the amount of assets the debtor owns and the amount of secured liabilities. Secured creditors are at less risk when the ratio of pledged assets to secured liabilities is larger, but the risks of unsecured creditors are often increased when this ratio is high because their claims to assets are secondary to secured creditors.

P1 **Prepare entries to record bond issuance and bond interest expense.** When bonds are issued at par, Cash is debited and Bonds Payable is credited for the bonds' par value. At bond interest payment dates (usually semiannual), Bond Interest Expense is debited and Cash credited for an amount equal to the bond par value multiplied by the bond contract rate.

P2 **Compute and record amortization of bond discount.** Bonds are issued at a discount when the contract rate is less than the market rate, making the issue (selling) price less than par. When this occurs, the issuer records a credit to Bonds Payable (at par) and debits both Discount on Bonds Payable and Cash. The amount of bond interest expense assigned to each period is computed using either the straight-line or effective interest method. The straight-line method can be used only if the results are not materially different from the effective interest method.

P3 **Compute and record amortization of bond premium.** Bonds are issued at a premium when the contract rate is higher than the market rate, making the issue (selling) price greater than par. When this occurs, the issuer records a debit to Cash and credits both Premium on Bonds Payable and Bonds Payable (at par). The amount of bond interest expense assigned to each period is computed using either the straight-line or effective interest method. The Premium on Bonds Payable is allocated to reduce bond interest expense over the life of the bonds.

P4 **Record the retirement of bonds.** Bonds are retired at maturity with a debit to Bonds Payable and a credit to Cash at

par value. The issuer can retire the bonds early by exercising a call option or by purchasing them in the market. Bondholders can also retire bonds early by exercising a conversion feature on convertible bonds. The issuer recognizes a gain or loss for the difference between the amount paid and the bond carrying value.

P5 **Prepare entries to account for notes.** Interest is allocated to each period in a note's life by multiplying its beginning-period carrying value by its market rate at issuance. If a note is repaid with equal payments, the payment amount is computed by dividing the borrowed amount by the present value of an annuity factor (taken from a present value table) using the market rate and the number of payments.

Guidance Answers to **Decision Maker**

Bond Rater Bonds that have longer repayment periods (life) have higher risk. Also, bonds issued by companies in financial difficulties or facing higher than normal uncertainties have higher risk. Moreover, companies with higher than normal debt and with large fluctuations in earnings are considered of higher risk.

Entrepreneur This is a "present value" question. The market interest rate (10%) and present value ($3,000) are known, but the payment required two years later is unknown. This amount ($3,630) can be computed as $3,000 × 1.10 × 1.10. This means that the sale price is $3,630 when no payments are received for two years. Note that the $3,630 received two years from today is equivalent to $3,000 cash today.

Bond Investor The ratio of pledged assets to secured liabilities for the first company is 2.2 ($1,265,000/$575,000) and for the second company is 2.5 ($2,000,000/$800,000), suggesting that the second company's secured creditors are at less risk than secured creditors of the first company. But *debenture bonds are unsecured.* Therefore, since the first company has fewer secured liabilities, it is of lower risk for unsecured debenture bonds. The first company also has fewer liabilities and, since the companies are of equal size, the first company's liabilities make up a smaller portion of total assets. Consequently, as a buyer of unsecured debenture bonds, you prefer the first company.

Guidance Answers to **Quick Checks**

1. (b)

2. Multiply the bond's par value by its contract rate of interest.

3. Bonds sell at a premium when the contract rate exceeds the market rate and the purchasers pay more than their par value.

4. The bonds are issued at a discount, meaning that issue price is less than par value. A discount occurs because the bond contract rate (6%) is less than the market rate (8%).

5.

Cash	91,893	
Discount on Bonds Payable	8,107	
Bonds Payable		100,000

6. (a) $3,811 (Total bond interest expense of $38,107 divided by 10 periods, or the $3,000 semiannual cash payment plus the $8,107 discount divided by 10 periods.)

    (b) $3,676 (Beginning carrying value of $91,893 multiplied by the 4% semiannual market rate at issuance.)

7. The bonds are issued at a premium, meaning issue price is higher than par value. A premium occurs because the bonds' contract rate (16%) is higher than the market rate (14%).

8. (c) On 6/30/2002: $110,592 × 7% = $7,741 bond interest expense; $8,000 − $7,741 = $259 premium amortization; $110,592 − $259 = $110,333 bond payable carrying value. On 12/31/2002: $110,333 × 7% = $7,723 bond interest expense; $8,000 − $7,723 = $277 premium amortization.

9.

Bonds payable, 16%, due 12/31/2011 .	$100,000
Plus premium on bonds payable	10,056* $110,056

* Original premium balance of $10,592 less $259 and $277 amortized on 6/30/2002 and 12/31/2002, respectively.

10. (a) Reflects payment of accrued interest recorded back on May 1.

11. $9,375 loss. Computed as the difference between the repurchase price of $256,250 [50% of ($500,000 × 102.5%)] and the carrying value of $246,875 (50% of $493,750).

12. (c)

13. The interest portion of an installment payment equals the period's beginning loan balance multiplied by the market interest rate at the time of issuance.

14. On the balance sheet, the account balances of the related liability (note payable) and asset (cash) accounts are decreased.
On the income statement, interest expense is recorded.

15. (*c*) Computed as 3.3121 × $1,000 = $3,312.

16. The option of paying $10,000 after one year has a lower pres-
ent value. It postpones paying the first $5,000 by six months.
More generally, the present value of a further delayed payment
is always lower than a less delayed payment.

Glossary

Annuity Series of equal payments at equal
intervals. (p. 447)

Bearer bonds Bonds made payable to
whoever holds them (the *bearer*); also
called *unregistered bonds.* (p. 424)

Bond Written promise to pay the bond's
par (or face) value and interest at a stated
contract rate; often issued in denominations
of $1,000. (p. 422)

Bond certificate Document containing
bond specifics such as issuer's name, bond
par value, contract interest rate, and maturity date. (p. 425)

Bond indenture Contract between the
bond issuer and the bondholders; identifies
the parties' rights and obligations. (p. 425)

Callable bonds Bonds that give the issuer
an option to retire them at a stated amount
prior to maturity. (p. 424)

Capital leases Long-term leases in which
the lessor transfers substantially all risk
and rewards of ownership to the lessee.
(p. 449)

Carrying value of bonds Net amount at
which bonds are reported on the balance
sheet; equals the par value of the bonds less
any unamortized discount or plus any unamortized premium; also called *carrying
amount* or *book value.* (p. 427)

Contract rate Interest rate specified in a
bond indenture; multiplied by the bonds'
par value to determine the interest paid
each period; also called *coupon rate, stated
rate,* or *nominal rate.* (p. 426)

Convertible bonds Bonds that bondholders can exchange for a set number of the
issuer's shares. (p. 424)

Coupon bonds Bonds with interest
coupons attached to their certificates;

bondholders present coupons to a bank or
broker for interest collection. (p. 424)

Discount on bonds payable Difference
between a bond's par value and its lower
carrying value; occurs when the contract
rate is less than the market rate. (p. 427)

Effective interest method Allocates interest expense over the bond life to yield a
constant rate of interest; interest expense
for a period is found by multiplying the balance of the liability at the beginning of the
period by the bond market rate at issuance;
also called *interest method.* (p. 429)

Installment note Liability requiring a series of periodic payments to the lender.
(p. 438)

Lease Contractual agreement between
lessor and *lessee* that grants a lessee the
right to use an asset for a period of time in
return for cash payments. (p. 448)

Market rate Interest rate borrowers are
willing to pay and lenders are willing to accept for a specific debt agreement given its
risk level. (p. 426)

Mortgage Legal agreement that protects a
lender by giving the lender the right to be
paid from the cash proceeds from the sale
of a borrower's assets identified in the
mortgage. (p. 440)

Off-balance-sheet financing Acquisition
of assets by agreeing to liabilities not reported on the balance sheet. (p. 449)

Operating leases Short-term (or cancelable) leases in which the lessor retains risks
and rewards of ownership. (p. 448)

Par value of a bond Amount the bond issuer agrees to pay at maturity and the
amount on which cash interest payments

are based; also called *face amount* or *face
value.* (p. 422)

Pension plan Contractual agreement between an employer and its employees for
the employer to provide benefits to employees after they retire. (p. 450)

Pledged assets to secured liabilities
Ratio of the book value of a company's
pledged assets to the book value of its secured liabilities. (p. 442)

Premium on bonds Difference between a
bond's par value and its higher carrying
value; occurs when the contract rate is
higher than the market rate. (p. 430)

Registered bonds Bonds owned by investors whose names and addresses are
recorded by the issuer; interest payments
are made to the registered owners. (p. 424)

Secured bonds Bonds that have specific
assets of the issuer pledged as collateral.
(p. 423)

Serial bonds Bonds consisting of separate
amounts that mature at different dates.
(p. 424)

Sinking fund bonds Bonds that require
the issuer to make deposits to a separate
account; bondholders are repaid at maturity from that account. (p. 424)

Straight-line method Method allocating
an equal amount of interest expense to each
period in the life of bonds. (p. 428)

Term bonds Bonds scheduled for payment (maturity) at a single specified date.
(p. 424)

Unsecured bonds Bonds backed only by
the issuer's credit standing; almost always
riskier than secured bonds; also called
debentures. (p. 423)

The superscript ^B *denotes assignments based on Appendix 10B.*

Questions

1. What is the main difference between a bond and a share of
stock?

2. What is the main difference between notes payable and
bonds payable?

3. What are the duties of a trustee for bondholders?

4. What is the advantage of issuing bonds instead of obtaining financing from the company's owners?

5. What is a bond indenture? What provisions are usually included in an indenture?

6. What is the *contract* rate and the *market* rate for bonds?

7. What factors affect the market rates for bonds?

8. Does the straight-line or effective interest method produce an allocation of interest expense that yields a constant rate of interest over a bond's life? Explain.

9. Why does a company that issues bonds between interest dates collect accrued interest from the bonds' purchasers?

10. If you know the par value of bonds, the contract rate, and the market rate, how do you compute the bonds' price?

11. What is the issue price of a $2,000 bond sold at 98¼? What is the issue price of a $6,000 bond sold at 101½?

12. Describe two common alternative payment patterns for installment notes.

13. Explain why unsecured creditors are concerned when the pledged assets to secured liabilities ratio for a borrower increases.

14. Refer to Nike's annual report in Appendix A. Is there any indication that Nike has issued bonds? **NIKE**

15. Refer to the statement of cash flows for Reebok in Appendix A. For the year ended December 31, 1999, what is Reebok's "Net borrowings (payments) of notes payable to banks"?

16. Refer to the annual report for Gap in Appendix A. For the 52 weeks ended January 29, 2000, did Gap raise more cash by issuing stock or debt? **GAP**

17. What obligation does an entrepreneur have to investors that purchase bonds to finance the business?

18.[B] When can a lease create both an asset and a liability for the lessee?

19.[B] Compare and contrast an operating lease with a capital lease.

20.[B] Describe the two basic types of pension plans.

Enter the letter of the description *A* through *H* that best fits each term 1 through 8.

A. Records and tracks the bondholders' names.

B. Is unsecured; backed only by the issuer's credit standing.

C. Has varying maturity dates for amounts owed.

D. Identifies rights and responsibilities of the issuer and the bondholders.

E. Can be exchanged for shares of the issuer's stock.

F. Is unregistered; interest is paid to whoever possesses them.

G. Maintains a separate asset account from which bondholders are paid at maturity.

H. Pledges specific assets of the issuer as collateral.

1. _____ Bond indenture

2. _____ Debentures

3. _____ Bearer bonds

4. _____ Registered bonds

5. _____ Convertible bonds

6. _____ Sinking fund bonds

7. _____ Serial bonds

8. _____ Secured bonds

QUICK STUDY

QS 10-1
Bond terminology

C1

Gore Company issues 8%, 10-year bonds with a par value of $250,000 and semiannual interest payments. On the issue date, the annual market rate for these bonds is 10%, which implies a selling price of 87½. The straight-line method is used to allocate interest expense.

1. What are the issuer's cash proceeds from issuance of these bonds?

2. What total amount of bond interest expense will be recognized over the life of these bonds?

3. What is the amount of bond interest expense recorded on the first interest payment date?

QS 10-2
Bond computations—
straight-line

P1 P2

Top Tier issues 10%, 15-year bonds with a par value of $240,000 and semiannual interest payments. On the issue date, the annual market rate for these bonds is 8%, which implies a selling price of 117¼. The effective interest method is used to allocate interest expense.

1. What are the issuer's cash proceeds from issuance of these bonds?

2. What total amount of bond interest expense will be recognized over the life of these bonds?

3. What is the amount of bond interest expense recorded on the first interest payment date?

QS 10-3
Bond computations—
effective interest

P1 P3

QS 10-4
Journalize bond **P1**
issuance

Prepare the journal entry for the issuance of the bonds in both QS 10-2 and QS 10-3. Assume that both bonds are issued for cash on January 1, 2002.

QS 10-5
Computing **P2 P3**
bond price

Using the bond details in both QS 10-2 and QS 10-3, confirm that the bonds' selling prices given in each problem are approximately correct. Use the present value tables B.1 and B.3 in Appendix B.

QS 10-6
Issuing bonds between **P1**
interest dates

Lafrentz Company plans to issue 8% bonds on January 1, 2002, with a par value of $4,000,000. The company sells $3,600,000 of the bonds on January 1, 2002. The remaining $400,000 sell at par on March 1, 2002. The bonds pay interest semiannually as of June 30 and December 31. Record the entry for the March 1 sale of bonds.

QS 10-7
Bond retirement by **P4**
call option

On July 1, 2002, Hamm Company exercises an $8,000 call option (plus par value) on its outstanding bonds that have a carrying value of $416,000 and par value of $400,000. The company exercises the call option after the semiannual interest is paid on June 30, 2002. Record the entry to retire the bonds.

QS 10-8
Bond retirement by **P4**
stock conversion

On January 1, 2002, the $2,000,000 par value bonds of Lott Company with a carrying value of $2,000,000 are converted to 1,000,000 shares of $1.00 par value common stock. Record the entry for the conversion of the bonds.

QS 10-9
Computing equal **C2**
payments for an
installment note

Sydney Company borrows $340,000 cash from a bank and in return it signs an installment note that calls for five annual payments of equal amount, with the first payment due one year after the note is signed. Use Table B.3 in Appendix B to compute the amount of the annual payment for each of the following annual market rates: (a) 4%, (b) 8%, and (c) 12%.

QS 10-10
Interpretation of collateral
agreement

A2

Note 2 of **Collins Industries**' annual report states: "The credit facility [line] is collateralized by receivables, inventories, equipment and certain real property. Under the terms of the Agreement, the Company is required to maintain certain financial ratios and other financial conditions. The Agreement also prohibits the Company from incurring certain additional indebtedness, limits certain investments, advances or loans and restricts substantial asset sales, capital expenditures and cash dividends." What restrictions are placed on Collins Industries by the bank that has granted the credit?

QS 10-11
Ratio of pledged assets to
secured liabilities

A3

Compute the ratio of pledged assets to secured liabilities for the following two companies. Which company appears to have the riskier secured liabilities?

	Xiang Co.	Xu Co.
Pledged assets	$402,000	$175,000
Total assets	587,000	510,000
Secured liabilities	165,000	172,000
Unsecured liabilities . . .	272,000	293,000

QS 10-12[B]
Recording operating **C5**
leases

Sarah Morris, an employee of ETrain.com, leases a car when she arrives at O'Hare airport for a three-day business trip. The cost of the rental is $250. Prepare the entry by ETrain.com to record Sarah's short-term car lease cost.

QS 10-13[B]
Recording capital **C5**
leases

Bazooka, Inc., signs a five-year lease for office equipment with Office Interiors. The present value of the lease payments is $15,499. Prepare the journal entry that Bazooka will record at the inception of this capital lease.

Round dollar amounts to the nearest whole dollar. Assume no reversing entries are used.

EXERCISES

On January 1, 2002, Cruise Enterprises issues bonds that have a $3,400,000 par value, mature in 20 years, and pay 9% interest semiannually on June 30 and December 31. The bonds are sold at par.

1. How much interest will Cruise pay (in cash) to the bondholders every six months?

2. Prepare journal entries to record (*a*) the issuance of bonds on January 1, 2002; (*b*) the first interest payment on June 30, 2002; and (*c*) the second interest payment on December 31, 2002.

3. Prepare the journal entry for issuance assuming the bonds are issued at (*a*) 98 and (*b*) 102.

Exercise 10-1
Recording bond issuance and interest
P1

TMP issues bonds with a par value of $180,000 on January 1, 2002. The annual contract rate on the bonds is 8%, and interest is paid semiannually on June 30 and December 31. The bonds mature in three years. The annual market rate at the date of issuance is 10%, and the bonds are sold for $170,862.

1. What is the amount of the discount on these bonds at issuance?

2. How much total bond interest expense will be recognized over the life of these bonds?

3. Prepare an amortization table like Exhibit 10.7 for these bonds; use the straight-line method to amortize the discount.

Exercise 10-2
Straight-line amortization of bond discount
P2

Shapiro Company issues bonds dated January 1, 2002, with a par value of $500,000. The annual contract rate on the bonds is 9%, and interest is paid semiannually on June 30 and December 31. The bonds mature in three years. The annual market rate at the date of issuance is 12%, and the bonds are sold for $463,140.

1. What is the amount of the discount on these bonds at issuance?

2. How much total bond interest expense will be recognized over the life of these bonds?

3. Prepare an amortization table like Exhibit 10.8 for these bonds; use the effective interest method to amortize the discount.

Exercise 10-3
Effective interest amortization of bond discount
P2

Mountain View Company issues bonds dated January 1, 2002, with a par value of $400,000. The annual contract rate is 13%, and interest is paid semiannually on June 30 and December 31. The bonds mature in three years. The annual market rate at the date of issuance is 12%, and the bonds are sold for $409,850.

1. What is the amount of the premium on these bonds at issuance?

2. How much total bond interest expense will be recognized over the life of these bonds?

3. Prepare an amortization table like Exhibit 10.13 for these bonds; use the effective interest method to amortize the premium.

Exercise 10-4
Effective interest amortization of bond premium
P3

Couric Company issues bonds with a par value of $800,000 on their stated issue date. The bonds mature in 10 years and pay 6% annual interest in semiannual payments. On the issue date, the annual market rate for the bonds is 8%.

1. What is the amount of each semiannual interest payment for these bonds?

2. How many semiannual interest payments will be made on these bonds over their life?

3. Use the interest rates given to determine whether the bonds are issued at par, at a discount, or at a premium.

4. Compute the price of the bonds as of their issue date.

5. Prepare the journal entry to record the bonds' issuance.

Exercise 10-5
Computing bond interest and price, and recording bond issuance
P2

Check (4) $691,287

Tyler, Inc., issues bonds with a par value of $150,000 on their stated issue date. The bonds mature in five years and pay 10% annual interest in semiannual payments. On the issue date, the annual market rate for the bonds is 8%.

1. What is the amount of each semiannual interest payment for these bonds?

2. How many semiannual interest payments will be made on these bonds over their life?

3. Use the interest rates given to determine whether the bonds are issued at par, at a discount, or at a premium.

4. Compute the price of the bonds as of their issue date.

5. Prepare the journal entry to record the bonds' issuance.

Exercise 10-6
Computing bond interest and price, and recording bond issuance
P3

Check (4) $162,172

Exercise 10-7
Bond computations, straight-line amortization, and bond retirement

P2 P4

Check (6) $8,190 loss

On January 1, 2002, Stryker issues $700,000 of 10%, 15-year bonds at a price of 97¾. Six years later, on January 1, 2008, Stryker retires 20% of these bonds by buying them on the open market at 104½. All interest is accounted for and paid through December 31, 2007, the day before the purchase. The straight-line method is used to amortize any bond discount.

1. How much does the company receive when it issues the bonds on January 1, 2002?
2. What is the amount of the discount on the bonds at January 1, 2002?
3. How much amortization of the discount is recorded on the bonds for the entire period from January 1, 2002, through December 31, 2007?
4. What is the carrying (book) value of the bonds as of the close of business on December 31, 2007? What is the carrying value of the 20% soon-to-be-retired bonds on this same date?
5. How much did the company pay on January 1, 2008, to purchase the bonds that it retired?
6. What is the amount of the recorded gain or loss from retiring the bonds?
7. Prepare the journal entry to record the bond retirement at January 1, 2008.

Exercise 10-8
Recording bond issuance with accrued interest

P1

Check (1) $102,000

On May 1, 2002, Cruise Enterprises issues bonds dated January 1, 2002, that have a $3,400,000 par value, mature in 20 years, and pay 9% interest semiannually on June 30 and December 31. The bonds are sold at par plus four months' accrued interest.

1. How much accrued interest is paid to Cruise by the purchasers of its bonds on May 1, 2002?
2. Prepare journal entries to record (a) the issuance of bonds on May 1, 2002; (b) the first interest payment on June 30, 2002; and (c) the second interest payment on December 31, 2002.

Exercise 10-9
Straight-line amortization and accrued bond interest expense

P1 P2

Simon issues 4-year bonds with a par value of $100,000 on June 1, 2002. The annual contract rate is 7%, and interest is paid semiannually on November 30 and May 31. The bonds are issued at a price of $95,948.

1. Prepare an amortization table like Exhibit 10.7 for these bonds. Use the straight-line method of interest amortization.
2. Prepare journal entries to record the first two interest payments and to accrue interest as of December 31, 2002.

Exercise 10-10
Installment note with equal principal payments

C2 P5

Check (1) $12,500

On January 1, 2003, JET borrows $50,000 cash by signing a four-year, 7% installment note that requires annual payments of accrued interest and equal amounts of principal on December 31 of each year from 2003 through 2006.

1. How much principal is included in each of the four annual payments?
2. Prepare an amortization table for this installment note like the one in Exhibit 10.17.

Exercise 10-11
Installment note entries **P5**

Use the information in Exercise 10-10 to prepare the journal entries for JET to record the loan on January 1, 2003, and the four payments from December 31, 2003, through December 31, 2006.

Exercise 10-12
Installment note with equal total payments **C2 P5**

Check (1) $29,523

On January 1, 2003, Tucker borrows $100,000 cash by signing a four-year, 7% installment note. The note requires four equal total payments of accrued interest and principal on December 31 of each year from 2003 through 2006.

1. Compute the amount of each of the four equal total payments.
2. Prepare an amortization table for this installment note like the one in Exhibit 10.18.

Exercise 10-13
Installment note entries **P5**

Use the information in Exercise 10-12 to prepare the journal entries for Tucker to record the loan on January 1, 2003, and the four payments from December 31, 2003, through December 31, 2006.

Exercise 10-14
Pledged assets to secured liabilities **A3**

An unsecured creditor of Telnet Co. has been monitoring Telnet's financing activities. Two years ago, Telnet's ratio of pledged assets to secured liabilities was 1.9. One year ago, the ratio climbed to 2.5, and the most recent financial report shows the ratio is now 3.3. Describe what this trend likely indicates about the company's activities, specifically from the point of view of this unsecured creditor.

For each separate case 1 through 3, indicate whether the company has entered into an operating lease or a capital lease.

1. The lessor retains title to the asset and the lease term is three years on an asset that has a five-year useful life.

2. The title is transferred to the lessee, the lessee can purchase the asset for $1 at the end of the lease, and the lease term is five years. The leased asset has an expected useful life of six years.

3. The present value of the lease payments is 95% of the leased asset's market value, and the lease term is 70% of the leased asset's useful life.

Exercise 10-15ᴮ
Identifying capital and operating leases

C5

Dextech (lessee) signs a 5-year capital lease for office equipment requiring a $10,000 annual lease payment. The present value of the five annual lease payments is $41,000, based on a 7% interest rate with the lease.

1. Prepare the journal entry Dextech will record at inception of the lease?

2. If the leased asset has a 5-year useful life with no salvage value, prepare the journal entry Dextech will record each year to recognize depreciation expense related to the leased asset?

Exercise 10-16ᴮ
Accounting for capital lease

C5

General Motors ran an advertisement offering three alternatives for a 25-month lease on a new Blazer. The three alternatives are (1) zero dollars down and a lease payment of $590 per month for 25 months, (2) $2,000 down and $498 per month for 25 months, or (3) $12,975 down and no payments for 25 months. Use the present value Table B.3 in Appendix B (page B-13) to determine which is the best alternative (assume you have enough cash to accept any of the three alternatives and the annual interest rate is 12% compounded monthly).

Exercise 10-17ᴮ
Analyzing lease options

C3 C4 C5

Round dollar amounts to the nearest whole dollar. Assume no reversing entries are used.

KC Research issues bonds dated January 1, 2003, that pay interest semiannually on June 30 and December 31. The bonds have a $40,000 par value, the annual contract rate is 10%, and the bonds mature in 10 years.

Required

For each of the following three separate situations, (*a*) determine the bonds' issue price on January 1, 2003, and (*b*) prepare the journal entry to record their issuance.

1. Market rate at the date of issuance is 8%.

2. Market rate at the date of issuance is 10%.

3. Market rate at the date of issuance is 12%.

PROBLEM SET A

Problem 10-1A
Computing bond price and recording issuance

P1 P2 P3

Check (1) Premium, $5,437
(3) Discount, $4,588

Harrigan issues $4,000,000 of 6%, 15-year bonds dated January 1, 2002, that pay interest semiannually on June 30 and December 31. The bonds are issued at a price of $3,456,448.

Required

1. Prepare the January 1, 2002, journal entry to record the bonds' issuance.

2. For each semiannual period, compute (*a*) the cash payment, (*b*) the straight-line discount amortization, and (*c*) the bond interest expense.

3. Determine the total bond interest expense that will be recognized over the life of these bonds.

4. Prepare the first two years of an amortization table like Exhibit 10.7 using the straight-line method.

5. Prepare the journal entries in which Harrigan would record the first two interest payments.

6. Assume that the bonds are issued at a price of $4,895,980. Repeat parts 1 through 5.

Problem 10-2A
Straight-line amortization of both bond discount and bond premium

P1 P2 P3

Eₓ

Check (3) $4,143,552;
(4) 12/31/2003 carrying
value, $3,528,920

GM issues 6.5%, five-year bonds dated January 1, 2002, with a par value of $250,000. The bonds pay interest on June 30 and December 31 and are issued at a price of $255,333. The annual market rate on these bonds is 6% on the issue date.

Required

1. Calculate the total bond interest expense over the life of these bonds.

2. Prepare an effective interest amortization table like Exhibit 10.13 for the life of these bonds.

Problem 10-3A
Effective interest amortization of bond premium; computing bond price

P1 P3

Check (2) 6/30/2004 carrying
value, $252,865; (4) $252,326

3. Prepare the journal entries in which GM would record the first two interest payments.

4. Use the market rate at issuance to compute the present value of the remaining cash flows for these bonds as of December 31, 2004. Compare your answer with the amount shown on the amortization table as the balance for that date (from part 2) and explain your findings.

Problem 10-4A

Effective interest amortization of bond discount

P1 P2

E **X**

Check   (2) $97,819;
          (3) 12/31/2003 carrying
          value, $307,308

Sweetman issues $325,000 of 5%, four-year bonds dated January 1, 2002, that pay interest semiannually on June 30 and December 31. The bonds are issued at a price of $292,181. The market rate on these bonds is 8% at the issue date.

Required

1. Prepare the January 1, 2002, journal entry to record the bonds' issuance.

2. Determine the total bond interest expense that will be recognized over the life of these bonds.

3. Prepare an effective interest amortization table like Exhibit 10.8 for the bonds' first two years.

4. Prepare the journal entries in which Sweetman would record the first two interest payments.

Analysis Component

5. Assume the market rate on January 1, 2002, is 4% instead of 8%. Without providing numbers, describe how this change would affect the amounts reported on Sweetman's financial statements.

Problem 10-5A

Effective interest amortization of bond premium; retiring bonds

P1 P3 P4

E **X**

Check   (3) 6/30/2003 carrying
          value, $182,448
          (5) $5,270 gain

McNeil issues $180,000 of 11%, three-year bonds dated January 1, 2002, that pay interest semiannually on June 30 and December 31. The bonds are issued at a price of $184,566. The market rate on these bonds is 10% at the issue date.

Required

1. Prepare the January 1, 2002, journal entry to record the bonds' issuance.

2. Determine the total bond interest expense that will be recognized over the life of these bonds.

3. Prepare an effective interest amortization table like Exhibit 10.13 for the bonds' first two years.

4. Prepare the journal entries in which McNeil would record the first two interest payments.

5. Prepare the journal entry to record the retirement of these bonds on January 1, 2004, at a price of 98.

Analysis Component

6. Assume that the market rate on January 1, 2002, is 12% instead of 10%. Without presenting numbers, describe how this change would affect the amounts reported on McNeil's financial statements.

Problem 10-6A

Installment notes

C2 P5

Check   (2) 10/31/2006 ending
          balance, $46,382

          (4) 10/31/2005 ending
          balance, $80,000

On November 1, 2002, Cook Ltd. borrows $200,000 cash from a bank by signing a five-year installment note bearing 8% interest. The note requires equal total payments each year on October 31.

Required

1. Compute the total amount of each installment payment.

2. Complete an amortization table for this installment note similar to Exhibit 10.18.

3. Prepare the journal entries in which Cook would record accrued interest as of December 31, 2002 (the end of its annual reporting period), and the first annual payment on the note.

4. Assume that the note does not require equal total payments but requires five payments of accrued interest and equal amounts of principal. Complete an amortization table for this note similar to Exhibit 10.17. Prepare the journal entries to record accrued interest as of December 31, 2002 (the end of its annual reporting period), and the first annual payment on the note.

Problem 10-7A

Ratio of pledged assets to secured liabilities

A2 A3

On January 1, 2002, Badger Company issues at par its 11%, four-year bonds with a $270,000 par value. They are secured by a mortgage that specifies assets totaling $360,000 as collateral. Also on January 1, 2002, Spartan Company issues at par its 11%, four-year bonds with a par value of $120,000. Spartan secures its bonds with a mortgage that includes $250,000 of pledged assets. The December 31, 2001, balance sheet information for both companies follows:

	Badger Co.	**Spartan Co.**
Total assets	$1,000,000*	$550,000[†]
Liabilities		
Secured	$ 260,000	$100,000
Unsecured	200,000	240,000
Equity	540,000	210,000
Total liabilities and equity	$1,000,000	$550,000

* 43% are pledged. [†] 54% are pledged.

Required

1. Compute the ratio of pledged assets to secured liabilities for each company at January 1, 2002.   **Check**   Badger, 1.49 to 1

Analysis Component

2. Which company's bonds appear less risky? What other information might help to evaluate the risks of these companies' bonds?

Gould Company signs a five-year capital lease to lease office equipment from Frazier Company. The annual lease payment is $10,000, and the interest rate is 8%.

Required

1. Compute the present value of the 5-year lease payments for Gould Company.

2. Prepare the journal entry to record the capital lease for Gould at the inception of the lease.

3. Complete a lease payment schedule for the five years of the lease with the following headings. Assume that the beginning balance of the lease liability (present value of lease payments) is $39,927. (*Hint:* To find the amount allocated to interest in year one, multiply the interest rate by the beginning-of-year lease liability. The amount of the annual lease payment not allocated to interest will be allocated to principal. Reduce the lease liability by the amount allocated to principal to update the lease liability at each year-end.)

Problem 10-8A[B]
Capital lease accounting

C5

Check   (1) $39,927

(3) Year 3 ending balance, $17,833

Period Ending Date	Beginning Balance of Lease Liability	Interest on Lease Liability	Reduction of Lease Liability	Cash Lease Payment	Ending Balance of Lease Liability

4. Use straight-line depreciation and prepare the journal entry to depreciate the leased asset at the end of year 1. Assume zero salvage value and a 5-year life for the office equipment.

Synergy Systems issues bonds dated January 1, 2003, that pay interest semiannually on June 30 and December 31. The bonds have a $90,000 par value, the annual contract rate is 12%, and the bonds mature in five years.

Required

For each of the following three separate situations, (*a*) determine the bonds' issue price on January 1, 2003, and (*b*) prepare the journal entry to record their issuance.

1. Market rate at the date of issuance is 10%.

2. Market rate at the date of issuance is 12%.

3. Market rate at the date of issuance is 14%.

PROBLEM SET B

Problem 10-1B
Computing bond price and recording issuance

P1 P2 P3

Check   (1) Premium, $6,948
(3) Discount, $6,326

Problem 10-2B
Straight-line amortization of both bond discount and bond premium

P1 P2 P3

ParView issues $3,400,000 of 10%, 10-year bonds dated January 1, 2002, that pay interest semiannually on June 30 and December 31. The bonds are issued at a price of $3,010,000.

Required

1. Prepare the January 1, 2002, journal entry to record the bonds' issuance.
2. For each semiannual period, compute (*a*) the cash payment, (*b*) the straight-line discount amortization, and (*c*) the bond interest expense.
3. Determine the total bond interest expense that will be recognized over the life of these bonds.
4. Prepare the first two years of an amortization table like Exhibit 10.7 using the straight-line method.
5. Prepare the journal entries in which ParView would record the first two interest payments.
6. Assume that the bonds are issued at a price of $4,192,932. Repeat parts 1 through 5.

Problem 10-3B
Effective interest amortization of bond premium; computing bond price

P1 P3

Tiger Company issues 9%, five-year bonds dated January 1, 2002, with a par value of $320,000. The bonds pay interest on June 30 and December 31 and are issued at a price of $332,988. The annual market rate on these bonds is 8% on the issue date.

Required

1. Calculate the total bond interest expense over the life of these bonds.
2. Prepare an effective interest amortization table like Exhibit 10.13 for the life of these bonds.
3. Prepare the journal entries in which Tiger would record the first two interest payments.
4. Use the market rate at issuance to compute the present value of the remaining cash flows for these bonds as of December 31, 2004. Compare your answer with the amount shown on the amortization table as the balance for that date (from part 2) and explain your findings.

Problem 10-4B
Effective interest amortization of bond discount

P1 P2

Morris issues $240,000 of 6%, 15-year bonds dated January 1, 2002, that pay interest semiannually on June 30 and December 31. The bonds are issued at a price of $198,494. The market rate on these bonds is 8% at the issue date.

Required

1. Prepare the January 1, 2002, journal entry to record the bonds' issuance.
2. Determine the total bond interest expense that will be recognized over the life of these bonds.
3. Prepare an effective interest amortization table like Exhibit 10.8 for the bonds' first two years.
4. Prepare the journal entries in which Morris would record the first two interest payments.

Problem 10-5B
Effective interest amortization of bond premium; retiring bonds

P1 P3 P4

Hamm issues $450,000 of 13%, four-year bonds dated January 1, 2002, that pay interest semiannually on June 30 and December 31. The bonds are issued at a price of $493,608. The market rate on these bonds is 10% at the issue date.

Required

1. Prepare the January 1, 2002, journal entry to record the bonds' issuance.
2. Determine the total bond interest expense that will be recognized over the life of these bonds.
3. Prepare an effective interest amortization table like Exhibit 10.13 for the bonds' first two years.
4. Prepare the journal entries in which Hamm would record the first two interest payments.
5. Prepare the journal entry to record the retirement of these bonds on January 1, 2004, at a price of 106.

Analysis Component

6. Assume that the market rate on January 1, 2002, is 14% instead of 10%. Without presenting numbers, describe how this change would affect the amounts reported on Hamm's financial statements.

Problem 10-6B
Installment notes **C2 P5**

On October 1, 2002, Venice Enterprises borrows $150,000 cash from a bank by signing a three-year installment note bearing 10% interest. Terms of the note require equal total payments each year on September 30.

Required

1. Compute the total amount of each installment payment.

2. Complete an amortization table for this installment note similar to Exhibit 10.18.

3. Prepare the journal entries in which Venice would record accrued interest as of December 31, 2002 (the end of its annual reporting period) and the first annual payment on the note.

4. Assume that the note does not require equal total payments but requires three payments of accrued interest and equal amounts of principal. Complete an amortization table for this note similar to Exhibit 10.17. Prepare the journal entries to record accrued interest as of December 31, 2002 (the end of its annual reporting period) and the first annual payment on the note.

Check   (2) 9/30/2004 ending balance, $54,836

(4) 9/30/2004 ending balance, $50,000

On January 1, 2003, Pine Company issues $50,000 of its 12%, 10-year bonds at par that are secured by a mortgage that specifies assets totaling $125,000 as collateral. Also on January 1, 2003, Maple Company issues its 12%, 10-year bonds at their par value of $160,000. Maple secures its bonds by a mortgage that includes $235,000 of pledged assets. The December 31, 2002, balance sheet information for both companies follows:

Problem 10-7B
Ratio of pledged assets to secured liabilities

A2 A3

	Pine Co.	Maple Co.
Total assets	$185,000*	$755,000†
Liabilities		
Secured	$ 41,000	$ 59,000
Unsecured	43,000	507,500
Equity	101,000	188,500
Total liabilities and equity	$185,000	$755,000

* 32% are pledged. † 10% are pledged.

Required

1. Compute the ratio of pledged assets to secured liabilities for each company at January 1, 2003.

Check   Pine, 2.02 to 1

Analysis Component

2. Which company's bonds appear less risky? What other information might help to evaluate the risks of these companies' bonds?

Parker Company signs a five-year capital lease to lease office equipment from Starbuck Company. The annual lease payment is $20,000, and the interest rate is 10%.

Problem 10-8B[B]
Capital lease accounting

C5

Required

1. Compute the present value of the lease payments for Parker Company.

2. Prepare the journal entry to record the capital lease for Parker at the inception of the lease.

3. Complete a lease payment schedule for the five years of the lease with the following headings. Assume that the beginning balance of the lease liability (present value of lease payments) is $75,816. (*Hint:* To find the amount allocated to interest in year one, multiply the interest rate by the beginning-of-year lease liability. The amount of the annual lease payment not allocated to interest will be allocated to principal. Reduce the lease liability by the amount allocated to principal to update the lease liability at each year-end.)

Check   (1) $75,816

(3) Year 3 ending balance, $34,712

Period Ending Date	Beginning Balance of Lease Liability	Interest on Lease Liability	Reduction of Lease Liability	Cash Lease Payment	Ending Balance of Lease Liability

4. Use straight-line depreciation and prepare the journal entry to depreciate the leased asset at the end of year 1. Assume zero salvage value and a 5-year life for the office equipment.

BEYOND THE NUMBERS

Reporting in Action
C1 A1 *a*

BTN 10-1　Refer to Nike's financial statements in Appendix A to answer the following questions:

1. Does Nike have any bonds or long-term notes payable that are issued and outstanding?
2. How much cash is paid to reduce long-term debt for the year ended May 31, 2000?
3. Did it have any additions to long-term debt that provided cash for the year ended May 31, 2000?

Swoosh Ahead

4. Access Nike's financial statements for a year ending after May 31, 2000, from its Web site (www.nike.com) or the SEC's EDGAR database (www.sec.gov). Has Nike issued additional long-term debt since the year ended May 31, 2000?

Comparative Analysis
A3 *a*

NIKE　Reebok

BTN 10-2　Key comparative figures ($ millions) for both Nike and Reebok follow:

	Nike		Reebok	
Key Figures	**Current Year**	**Prior Year**	**Current Year**	**Prior Year**
Accounts receivable, net	$1,567.2	$1,540.1	$417.4	$517.8
Inventory	1,446.0	1,170.6	414.6	535.2
Property and equipment, net	1,583.4	1,265.8	178.1	172.6
Long-term debt (includes current portion)	520.4	387.1	555.5	641.1

Required

1. Assume that both Nike and Reebok have pledged substantially all of their accounts receivable, inventory, and property and equipment to collateralize their long-term debt. Compute the ratio of pledged assets to secured liabilities for both companies.
2. Use the ratio you computed in part 1 to determine which company's long-term debt is less risky.

Ethics Challenge
C5 A1 *a*

BTN 10-3　Brevard County needs a new building for its county government that would cost $24 million. The politicians feel that voters are unlikely to approve a municipal bond issue to fund the building since it would increase taxes. They opt for a different approach. They have a state bank issue $24 million of tax-exempt securities to pay for the building construction. The county then will make yearly lease payments (of principal and interest) to repay the obligation. Unlike conventional municipal bonds, the lease payments are not binding obligations on the county and therefore, no voter approval is required.

Required

1. Do you think the actions of the politicians and the bankers are ethical in this situation?
2. How do the tax-exempt securities used to pay for the building compare in risk to a conventional municipal bond issued by Brevard County?

Communicating in Practice P3

BTN 10-4　Your business associate mentions that she is considering investing in corporate bonds currently selling at a premium. She says that since the bonds are selling at a premium, they are highly valued and her investment will yield more than the going rate of return for the risk involved. Reply with a memorandum to confirm or correct your associate's interpretation of premium bonds.

Taking It to the Net
C1 *a*

BTN 10-5　Access the March 9, 2000, filing of the 1999 calendar-year 10-K report of Coca-Cola Co. (Ticker KO) from www.edgar-online.com. Refer to Coca-Cola's statement of cash flows for the year ended December 31, 1999, to answer the following questions.

Required

1. Did the company issue any new debt in 1999?
2. Did the company repay any of its debt in 1999?
3. Did the company raise more new capital in 1999 from issuing debt or from issuing stock?
4. The company's 10-K report shows three years of cash flow data. Is the company showing a trend of issuing more or less debt over this three-year period?

BTN 10-6   Break into teams and complete the following requirements.

1. Each team member is to independently prepare a blank table with proper headings for amortization of a bond premium. When all have finished, compare tables and ensure all are in agreement.

Parts 2 and 3 require use of these facts: On January 1, 2002, BC issues $100,000, 9%, five-year bonds at 104.1. The market rate at issuance is 8%. BC pays interest semiannually on June 30 and December 31.

2. In rotation, *each* team member must explain how to complete *one* line of the bond amortization table, including all computations for his or her line. (Round amounts to the nearest dollar.) All members are to fill in their tables during this process. You need not finish the table; stop after all members have explained a line.

3. In rotation, *each* team member is to identify a separate column of the table and indicate what the final number in that column will be and explain the reasoning.

4. Reach a team consensus as to what the total bond interest expense on this bond issue will be if the bond is not retired before maturity.

5. As a team, prepare a list of similarities and differences between the amortization table just prepared and the amortization table if the bond had been issued at a discount.

Teamwork in Action

P2 P3 🖉

Hint: Rotate teams to report on parts 4 and 5. Consider requiring entries for issuance and interest payments.

BTN 10-7   Read the article "The Debt That's Dragging Nissan Downhill" from the April 5, 1999, issue of *Business Week*. (The book's Web site provides a free link.)

Required

1. In the fourth paragraph of the article, the sentence begins, "Nissan's big losses make it tougher for the company to service its own debt." What does the phrase *to service its debt* mean?
2. How much does Nissan Motor Company pay in interest each year on its debt?
3. What accounting rule that took effect in April 2000 impacts how Nissan reports its debt on its balance sheet?
4. What steps has Nissan taken to repay its debt?

Business Week Activity

C1 🖉

BTN 10-8   Andrew Hamill is the young entrepreneur and owner of WebWorks, a provider of Internet services and Web site development. WebWorks has $250,000 in equity and is considering a $100,000 expansion to meet increased demand. The $100,000 expansion will yield $16,000 in additional annual income before interest expense. WebWorks currently earns $40,000 annual income before interest expense of $10,000, yielding a return on equity of 12% ($30,000/$250,000). To fund the expansion, WebWorks is considering the issuance of a 10-year, $100,000 note with annual interest payments and with the principal amount due at the end of 10 years.

Required

1. Using return on equity as the decision criterion, show computations to support or reject WebWorks' expansion if interest on the $100,000 note is (*a*) 10%, (*b*) 15%, (*c*) 16%, (*d*) 17%, and (*e*) 20%.
2. What general rule do the results in part 1 illustrate?

Entrepreneurial Decision

A1

🅔 🖉

BTN 10-9   Visit your city or county library. Ask the librarian to help you locate the recent financial records of your city or county government. Examine the records.

Required

1. Determine the amount of long-term bonds and notes currently outstanding.
2. Read the supporting information to your municipality's financial statements and record:
   a. Market interest rate(s) when the bonds and/or notes were issued.
   b. Date(s) when the bonds and/or notes will mature.
   c. Any rating(s) on the bonds and/or notes received from Moody's, Standard & Poor's, or another rating agency.

Hitting the Road

A1 🖉

11

Reporting and Analyzing Equity

"Somebody has to have the final word, and that's me"—Vince McMahon (pinned on mat).

A Look Back

Chapter 10 focused on long-term liabilities. We explained how these liabilities are valued, recorded, amortized, and reported in financial statements. We also described the accounting for leases and pensions.

A Look at This Chapter

This chapter further describes the corporate form of organization. The accounting concepts and procedures for equity transactions are explained. We also describe how income, earnings per share, and retained earnings are reported and analyzed.

A Look Ahead

Chapter 12 focuses on reporting and analyzing a company's cash flows. Special emphasis is directed to the statement of cash flows and its interpretation.

Decision Feature

Blood, Sweat, and Corporations

e STAMFORD, CT—What's not unusual is that a company issued its stock to the public. What is unusual is that the company is the **World Wrestling Federation (www.WWF.com),** the brainchild of wrestling entrepreneur Vince McMahon. McMahon, who started as a wrestling commentator and script writer, has fought to turn a schlocky sport into mass entertainment with soap-opera scripts and enough cheeseball villains and heroes to make fans scream—and reach for their wallets. WWF's initial public offering (IPO) of its stock raised $179.3 million for more rock-'em, sock-'em action.

McMahon, a self-described juvenile delinquent who went to military school as a teenager to avoid a reformatory stint, is creating an entertainment empire that claims 35 million fans. Many are fervent in their devotion to pumped-up stars such as Stone Cold Steve Austin, The Rock, The Undertaker, Triple H, Chyna, and Kane and Kurt Angle. Such interest has helped annual sales exceed $400 million. This performance has catapulted WWF to No. 3 on *Business Week's* Hot Growth companies list—and has broadcasters salivating. Viacom and USA Networks are battling in court for the rights to WWF shows.

Although recent controversies have dragged WWF stock down, fans do not share whatever worry stockholders may have. Advertising and sponsorship sales are up over $30 million; a CD featuring the theme songs of WWF stars rose to No. 2 on the music charts; and a biography by wrestler Mankind topped *The New York Times* best-seller list. McMahon says he's just beginning. Next up: an action-adventure series, a late-night talk show featuring WWF talent, and international franchises in Australia, Britain, France, and Japan. Vince, who calls the WWF his mistress, boldly proclaims: "I don't mind people doubting us. We'll just have to prove them wrong." [Sources: *Business Week*, January 24, 2000, and October 30, 2000; WWF Web site, March 2002.]

Chapter Preview

This chapter focuses on corporations and accounting for them. Understanding the advantages and disadvantages of a corporation is important to each of us, including Vince McMahon of the **World Wrestling Federation**. The first part of this chapter describes the basics of the corporate form of organization, and explains the accounting for common and preferred stock. We then focus on several special financing transactions, including cash and stock dividends, stock splits, and treasury stock. Next, we discuss the form and content of a complete income statement as well as earnings per share. The final section considers accounting for retained earnings, including prior period adjustments, retained earnings restrictions, and reporting guidelines.

Corporate Form of Organization

A **corporation** is an entity created by law and separate from its owners. It has most of the rights and privileges granted to individuals. Owners of corporations are called *stockholders* or *shareholders*. Corporations can be separated into privately held and publicly held corporations. A *privately held* (or *closely held*) corporation does not offer its stock for public sale and usually has few stockholders. A *publicly held* corporation offers its stock for public sale and can have thousands of stockholders. *Public sale* usually refers to issuance and trading on an organized stock market.

Characteristics of Corporations

C1 Identify characteristics of corporations and their organization.

Corporations represent an important type of organization because of the advantages offered by their unique characteristics. This section describes these characteristics.

Separate Legal Entity

As a separate legal entity, a corporation conducts its affairs with the same rights, duties, and responsibilities of a person. It takes actions through its agents, who are its officers and managers.

Limited Liability of Stockholders

A corporation is responsible for its own acts and its own debt because it is a separate legal entity. However, its stockholders are not liable for either. From the stockholders' viewpoint, this limited liability is an important advantage of the corporate form.

Ownership Rights Are Transferable

Point: The *business entity principle* requires a corporation to be accounted for separately from its owners (shareholders).

Ownership of a corporation is by shares of stock that usually are easily bought and sold. The transfer of shares from one stockholder to another usually has no effect on the corporation or its operations. (A transfer of ownership can create significant effects if it causes a change in the directors who control or manage the corporation.) Millions of shares of many corporations are bought and sold daily in stock exchanges across the world.

Continuous Life

A corporation's life can continue indefinitely because it is not tied to the physical lives of its owners. Its life is sometimes initially limited by the laws of the state of its incorporation, but its charter can be renewed and its life extended when the stated time expires. Therefore, a corporation can have an indefinite life as long as it continues to be successful.

Stockholders Are Not Corporate Agents

A corporation acts through its agents, who are its officers and managers. Stockholders, who are not its officers or managers, do not have the power to bind the corporation to contracts. This is referred to as *lack of mutual agency*. Instead, stockholders impact the corporation's affairs by voting in stockholder meetings and by electing the board of directors.

Ease of Capital Accumulation

Global: U.S., U.K., and Canadian corporations finance much of their operations with stock issuances, but companies in countries such as France, Germany, and Japan finance primarily with note and bond issuances.

Buying stock in a corporation often is attractive to investors because (1) stockholders are not liable for the corporation's actions and debts, (2) stock usually is transferred easily, (3) the life of the corporation is unlimited, and (4) stockholders are not agents of the corporation. These advantages enable corporations to accumulate large amounts of capital from the combined investments of many stockholders. A corporation's capacity for raising capital is limited only by its ability to convince investors that it can use their funds profitably relative to other investment opportunities.

Decision Insight

Young Stock   Marc Andreessen cofounded **Netscape** at the age of 22, only four months after earning his degree. One year later, Andreessen and friends issued Netscape shares to the public. The stock, offered at $28 a share, soared to nearly $75 before ending its first trading day at $58. This made Andreessen a multimillionaire at 23.

Governmental Regulation

A corporation must meet requirements of a state's incorporation laws, which subject the corporation to state regulation and control. Proprietorships and partnerships escape many of the regulations and governmental reports required of corporations.

Corporate Taxation

Corporations are subject to the same property and payroll taxes as proprietorships and partnerships, but corporations are subject to *additional* taxes. The most burdensome of these are federal and state income taxes that together can take 40% or more of a corporation's pretax income. This results in the income of a corporation being taxed twice, first as income of the corporation and second as personal income to stockholders when cash is distributed to them as dividends. This is called *double taxation*. Proprietorships and partnerships are not subject to income taxes. Their income is taxed as the personal income of their owners. An *S corporation* also has the same tax status as a proprietorship and partnership. Consequently, the corporation's tax situation is usually a disadvantage. Yet, until the corporation pays dividends, its income is taxed only once at the lower corporate rate—at least temporarily until the stock is sold or dividends are paid.

Point: Double taxation is less severe when an owner-manager of a corporation collects a salary that is taxed only once as part of his or her personal income.

Decision Track 11.1

Decision Point	Information Search	Analyze & Evaluate
When, if ever, should a company incorporate?	Business characteristics; capital and growth expectations; tax status.	Depends on situation: corporations have limited liability and ease of capital accumulation; but they suffer from double taxation and added regulations.

Organizing and Managing a Corporation

This section describes the incorporation, costs, and management of corporate organizations.

Incorporation

A corporation is created by obtaining a charter from a state government. Charter requirements vary across states. A charter application usually must be signed by the prospective stockholders called *incorporators* or *promoters* and then filed with the proper state official. When the application process is complete and all fees have been paid, the charter is issued and the corporation is formed. Investors then purchase the corporation's stock, meet as stockholders, and elect a board of directors. Directors are responsible for overseeing a corporation's affairs.

Decision Insight

Start-up Money   Sources for start-up money: (1) Seek "angel" investors such as parents, siblings, friends, or anyone else who believes in your company, (2) run a bare-bones operation and pay employees, investors, and even suppliers with stock, (3) seek venture capitalists (investors) who have a record of success with entrepreneurs, and (4) check out the National Venture Capital Association (www.nvca.org).

Organization Expenses

Organization expenses (also called *organization costs*) are the costs to organize a corporation; they include legal fees, promoters' fees, and amounts paid to obtain a charter. The corporation records (debits) these costs to an expense account called *Organization Expenses.* Although these costs are expected to benefit the corporation throughout its life, it is difficult to determine the amount and timing of the future benefits. Accordingly, organization costs are expensed as incurred.

Management of a Corporation

The ultimate control of a corporation rests with stockholders. Stockholders control a corporation by electing its *board of directors,* or simply, *directors.* Each stockholder usually has one vote for each share of stock owned. This control relation is shown in Exhibit 11.1. A corporation's board of directors is responsible for and has final authority for managing the corporation's activities. It can act only as a collective body. An individual director has no power to transact corporate business. Although the board has broad authority, it usually limits its actions to establishing general policy.

Exhibit 11.1

Corporation Authority Structure

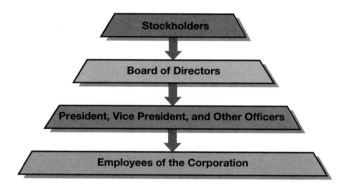

A corporation usually holds a stockholder meeting at least once a year to elect directors and transact business as required by its bylaws. A group of stockholders owning or controlling votes of more than a 50% share of a corporation's stock can elect the board and control the corporation. In many corporations, only a small percent of stockholders attend the annual meeting or participate in the voting process. Therefore, a smaller percent of stockholders is often able to dominate the election of board members. Still, stockholders who do not attend stockholders' meetings must have an opportunity to delegate their voting rights to an agent. A stockholder does this by signing a **proxy,** a document that gives a designated agent the right to vote the stock. Prior to a stockholders' meeting, a corporation's board of directors usually mails each stockholder an announcement of the meeting and a proxy listing the existing board chairperson as the voting agent of the stockholder. The announcement asks the stockholder to sign and return the proxy.

Day-to-day direction of corporate business is delegated to executive officers appointed by the board. A corporation's chief executive officer (CEO) is often its president. Several vice presidents, who report to the president, are commonly assigned specific areas of management responsibility such as finance, production, and marketing. The corporation secretary keeps minutes of stockholders' and directors' meetings and ensures that all legal responsibilities are met. In a small corporation, the secretary often is responsible for keeping a record of current stockholders and amounts of their stock interest. Another common corporate structure is the dual role of both the chairperson of the board of directors and the CEO. In this case, the president is usually designated the chief operating officer (COO).

Stock of a Corporation

This section explains stockholder rights, stock purchases and sales, and the role of registrar and transfer agents.

Rights of Stockholders

When investors buy stock, they acquire all *specific* rights the corporation's charter grants to stockholders. They also acquire *general* rights granted stockholders by the laws of the state in which the company is incorporated. When a corporation has only one class of stock, it is identified as **common stock,** which represents *residual equity,* meaning that creditors rank ahead of common stockholders if a corporation is liquidated. State laws vary, but common stockholders usually have the general right to

1. Vote at stockholders' meetings.
2. Sell or otherwise dispose of their stock.
3. Purchase their proportional share of any common stock later issued by the corporation. This right, called the **preemptive right,** protects stockholders' proportionate interest in the corporation. For example, a stockholder who owns 25% of a corporation's common stock has the first opportunity to buy 25% of any new common stock issued. This enables the stockholder to maintain a 25% interest if desired.
4. Share equally with other common stockholders in any dividends. This means that each common share receives the same dividend.
5. Share equally in any assets remaining after creditors are paid when, and if, the corporation is liquidated. Therefore, each common share receives the same amount of remaining liquidated assets.

Stockholders also have the right to receive timely financial reports.

Global: Stockholders' access to financial information varies across countries both in scope and by level of ownership. For instance, stockholders of Mexican companies holding small percent ownership often have difficulty obtaining quality financial information.

Stock Certificates and Transfer

When investors buy a corporation's stock, they sometimes receive a *stock certificate* as proof of share ownership. Many corporations issue only one certificate for each block of stock purchased. A certificate can be for any number of shares. Exhibit 11.2 shows an actual stock certificate of the Green Bay Packers. A certificate shows the company name, stockholder name, number of shares, and other crucial information. (Issuance of certificates is becoming less common. Instead, many stockholders maintain accounts with the corporation or their stockbrokers and never receive actual certificates.)

When selling stock, a stockholder completes and signs a transfer endorsement on the back of the certificate and sends it to the corporation's secretary or transfer agent. The secretary or agent cancels and files the old certificate and issues a new certificate to the new stockholder if the company issues certificates. If the old certificate represents more shares than were sold, the corporation issues two new certificates, one to the new stockholder for the shares purchased and the other to the selling stockholder for the remaining unsold shares. When stockholders have their shares held in the name of their stock brokerage, the corporation's secretary or registrar records who owns the shares but does not send certificates to stockholders.

Exhibit 11.2

Stock Certificate

Registrar and Transfer Agents

If a corporation's stock is traded on a major stock exchange, the corporation must have a *registrar* and a *transfer agent*. A registrar keeps stockholder records and prepares official lists of stockholders for stockholder meetings and dividend payments. A transfer agent assists with purchases and sales of shares by receiving and issuing certificates as necessary. Registrars and transfer agents are usually large banks or trust companies having computer facilities and staff to do this work.

Decision Insight

Online Trading   Online brokerage service fees are as low as $5 to $10 per trade. These fees are a fraction of those charged by full-service firms. Online brokerage firms say technology has slashed their costs and eliminated most order-entry errors.

Basics of Capital Stock

Capital stock is a general term that refers to a corporation's stock used in obtaining its capital (owner financing). This section introduces capital stock terminology and some of the basics in accounting for capital stock.

C2   Describe the components of stockholders' equity.

Authorized Stock

Authorized stock is the total amount of stock that a corporation's charter authorizes it to sell. Most corporations authorize more stock than they anticipate selling either initially or in the near future. Therefore, the number of authorized shares usually exceeds the number of shares issued (and outstanding), often by a large amount. (*Outstanding stock* refers to issued stock held by stockholders. This distinction is important since corporations can buy back their issued stock, called *treasury stock*.) No formal journal entry is required for stock authorization. A corporation must apply to the state for a change in its charter if it wishes to issue more shares than previously authorized. A corporation discloses the number of shares authorized in the equity section of its balance sheet or notes. **Reebok**'s balance sheet in Appendix A reports 250 million shares authorized.

Global: Some countries, such as Switzerland, have no particular reporting standards for stockholders' equity.

Decision Insight

Sizing Up an IPO   A prospectus accompanies an initial public offering (IPO) of stock, giving financial information about the company issuing the stock. A prospectus should help answer these questions to price an IPO: (1) Is the underwriter reliable? (2) Is there growth in revenues, profits, and cash flows? (3) What is management's view of operations? (4) Are current owners selling? (5) What are the risks?

Selling Stock

A corporation can sell stock either directly or indirectly. To *sell directly,* it advertises its stock issuance to potential buyers. This type of issuance is most common with privately held corporations. To *sell indirectly,* a corporation pays a brokerage house (investment banker) to issue its stock. Some brokerage houses *underwrite* an indirect issuance of stock; that is, they buy the stock from the corporation and take all gains or losses from its resale to stockholders.

Market Value of Stock

Market value per share is the price at which a stock is bought and sold. Expected future earnings, dividends, growth, and other company and economic factors influence market value. Traded stocks' market values are reported daily in newspapers such as *The Wall Street Journal* and are available online from the Web. The current market value of previously issued shares (for example, the price of stock in trades between investors) does not impact the issuing corporation's stockholders' equity.

Classes of Stock

Point: Managers are motivated to set a low par value when minimum legal capital and state issuance taxes are based on par value.

A corporation's charter authorizes it to issue a specified number of shares. If all authorized shares have the same rights and characteristics, the stock is called *common stock*. A corporation is sometimes authorized to issue more than one class of stock, including preferred stock and different classes of common stock. **American Greetings**, for instance, has two types of common stock outstanding: Class A stock has 1 vote per share and Class B stock has 10 votes per share.

Decision Insight

Stock Quotes   The **Nike** stock quote shown is interpreted as (left to

52 Weeks				Yld	Vol				Net
Hi	Lo	Stock Sym	Div	% PE	100s	Hi	Lo	Close	Chg
58^{50}	25^{81}	Nike B NKE	.48	1.3 18	6047	37^{75}	36^{44}	37^{06}	-1^{31}

right): **Hi,** highest price in past 52 weeks; **Lo,** lowest price in past 52 weeks; **Stock,** company; **Sym,** exchange symbol; **Div,** dividends paid per share in past year; **Yld %,** dividend divided by closing price; **PE,** stock price per share divided by earnings per share; **Vol 100s,** number of shares traded (in 100s); **Hi,** highest price for the day; **Lo,** lowest price for the day; **Close,** closing price for the day; **Net Chg,** change in closing price from the prior day.

Par Value Stock

Many stocks carry a **par value** established when they are authorized. **Par value stock** is a class of stock assigned a par value per share by the corporation in its charter. For example, **Novell**'s common stock has a par value of $0.10. Other commonly assigned par values are $25, $10, $5, $1 and $0.01. There is no restriction on the assigned par value. In many states, the par value of a stock etablishes **minimum legal capital,** which refers to the least amount that the buyers of stock must contribute to the corporation or be subject to making up anything less at a future date. For example, if a corporation issues 1,000 shares of $10 par value stock, the minimum legal

Point: Minimum legal capital requirements often prohibit dividends if dividends would reduce equity below the minimum amount.

capital of the corporation in these states would be $10,000. Minimum legal capital is intended to protect a corporation's creditors. Since creditors cannot demand payment from the personal assets of stockholders, their claims are limited to the corporation's assets. Minimum legal capital limits a corporation's ability to distribute assets to stockholders. A corporation must maintain minimum legal capital until it is liquidated. At liquidation, all creditor claims are paid before any amounts are distributed to stockholders.

Point: Minimum legal capital was intended to protect creditors by requiring a minimum amount of net assets be kept in the corporation. However, such net assets can be lost by unprofitable operations.

No-Par Value Stock

No-par value stock, or simply *no-par stock,* is stock *not* assigned a value per share by the corporate charter. Nearly all states permit issuance of stock without par value. Its advantage is that it can be issued at any price without the possibility of a minimum legal capital deficiency. The entire proceeds from sale of no-par stock becomes minimum legal capital in some states.

Stated Value Stock

Stated value stock is no-par stock to which the directors assign a "stated" value per share. Many states permit stated value stock. Stated value per share becomes the minimum legal capital per share in these cases.

Frequency of Par, No-Par, and Stated Value Common Stock

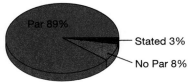

Point: Par, no-par, and stated value do *not* set the stock's market value.

Stockholder's Equity

A corporation's equity is known as **stockholders' equity,** also called *shareholders' equity* or *corporate capital*. Stockholders' equity consists of (1) contributed (or paid-in) capital and (2) retained earnings—see Exhibit 11.3. **Contributed capital** reflects the total amount of cash and other assets the corporation receives from its stockholders in exchange for common stock. **Retained earnings** represent the cumulative net income (and loss) retained by a corporation. Details of shareholders' equity are described in the remainder of this chapter.

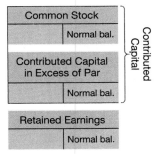

Corporation

Exhibit 11.3

Equity Composition

Point: Contributed capital comes from stock-related transactions, whereas retained earnings comes from operations.

Accounting for the issuance of common stock affects only contributed capital accounts; no retained earnings accounts are affected.

Common Stock

Issuing Par Value Stock

Par value stock can be issued at par, at a premium, or at a discount. In each case, stock can be exchanged for either cash or noncash assets.

P1 Record the issuance of corporate stock.

Topic Tackler 11-1

Assets = Liabilities + Equity
+300,000   +300,000

Issuing Par Value Stock at Par

When common stock is issued at par value, we record amounts for both the asset(s) received and the par value stock issued. Stock is usually issued in exchange for cash. To illustrate, the entry to record Dillon Snowboards' issuance of 30,000 shares of $10 par value stock for $300,000 cash on June 5, 2002, is as follows

June 5	Cash	300,000	
	Common Stock, $10 Par Value		300,000
	Issued 30,000 shares of $10 par value		
	common stock at par.		

Exhibit 11.4 shows the stockholders' equity of Dillon Snowboards at year-end 2002 (its first year of operations), after income of $65,000 and no dividend payments.

Exhibit 11.4

Stockholders' Equity for Stock Issued at Par

Stockholders' Equity	
Contributed capital	
Common Stock—$10 par value; 50,000 shares authorized;	
30,000 shares issued and outstanding	$300,000
Retained earnings	65,000
Total stockholders' equity	$365,000

Issuing Par Value Stock at a Premium

A **premium on stock** occurs when a corporation sells its stock for more than par (or stated) value. To illustrate, if Dillon Snowboards issues its $10 par value common stock at $12 per share, this implies that its stock is sold at a $2 per share premium. The premium, known as **contributed capital in excess of par value,** is accounted for separately from par value. This premium is reported as part of equity; it is not a revenue and is not listed on the income statement. The entry to record Dillon Snowboards' issuance of 30,000 shares of $10 par value stock for $12 per share on June 5, 2002, follows

Point: The Contributed Capital in Excess of Par Value, Common Stock account is also called Premium on Common Stock.

Assets = Liabilities + Equity
+360,000   +300,000
                  +60,000

June 5	Cash	360,000	
	Common Stock, $10 Par Value		300,000
	Contributed Capital in Excess of		
	Par Value, Common Stock		60,000
	Sold and issued 30,000 shares of $10 par		
	value common stock at $12 per share.		

Point: The *Contributed Capital* terminology is interchangeable with *Paid-In Capital.*

The Contributed Capital in Excess of Par Value account is added to the par value of the stock in the equity section of the balance sheet as shown in Exhibit 11.5.

Issuing Par Value Stock at a Discount

A **discount on stock** occurs when a corporation sells its stock for less than par (or stated) value. Most states prohibit the issuance of stock at a discount because stockholders would be investing less than minimum legal capital. In states that allow stock issued at a discount, its purchasers usually become contingently liable to the corporation's creditors for the discount. If stock is issued at a discount, the amount by which issue price is less than par is debited to a *Discount on Common Stock* account, a contra to the common stock account,

Stockholders' Equity		
Contributed capital		
Common Stock—$10 par value; 50,000 shares authorized; 30,000 shares issued and outstanding	$300,000	
Contributed capital in excess of par value, common stock	60,000	
Total contributed capital		$360,000
Retained earnings		65,000
Total stockholders' equity		$425,000

Exhibit 11.5

Stockholders' Equity for Stock Issued at a Premium

and its balance is subtracted from the par value of stock in the equity section of the balance sheet. This discount is not an expense and does not appear on the income statement.

Issuing No-Par Value Stock

When no-par stock is issued and is not assigned a stated value, the amount the corporation receives becomes legal capital and is recorded as Common Stock. Thus, the entire proceeds are credited to a no-par stock account. To illustrate, if a corporation issues 1,000 shares of no-par stock for $40 per share, it is recorded as follows:

Point: Retained earnings can be negative, reflecting accumulated losses. For example, Amazon.com had an accumulated deficit of $2.3 billion at the start of 2001.

Oct. 20	Cash	40,000	
	Common Stock, No-Par Value		40,000
	Issued 1,000 shares of no-par value common stock at $40 per share.		

Assets = Liabilities + Equity
+40,000   +40,000

Issuing Stated Value Stock

When no-par stock is issued and assigned a stated value, its stated value becomes legal capital and is credited to a stated value stock account. Assuming that stated value stock is issued at an amount in excess of stated value, the excess is credited to Contributed Capital in Excess of Stated Value, Common Stock. To illustrate, if a corporation issues 1,000 shares of no-par common stock with a stated value of $40 per share for cash of $50 per share, it is recorded as follows: $1 $20

Oct. 20	Cash	50,000	
	Common Stock, $40 Stated Value		40,000
	Contributed Capital in Excess of Stated Value, Common Stock		10,000
	Issued 1,000 shares of $40 per share stated value stock at $50 per share.		

Assets = Liabilities + Equity
+50,000   +40,000
                           +10,000

The Contributed Capital in Excess of Stated Value, Common Stock account is reported in the contributed capital part of the stockholders' equity section.

Issuing Stock for Noncash Assets

A corporation can receive assets other than cash in exchange for its stock. (It can also assume liabilities on the assets received such as a mortgage on property received.) The corporation records the assets received at their market values as of the date of the transaction. The stock given in exchange is recorded at its par (or stated) value with any excess recorded in the Contributed Capital in Excess of Par (or Stated) Value account. (If no-par stock is issued, the stock is recorded at the assets' market value.) To illustrate, the entry to record receipt of land valued at $105,000 in return for issuance of 4,000 shares of $20 par value common stock is

Point: Par value (or stated value) of issued shares is recorded in the common stock account. A premium is the amount by which the issue price exceeds par (or stated) value and it is recorded in a separate equity account.

June 10	Land	105,000	
	Common Stock, $20 Par Value		80,000
	Contributed Capital in Excess of Par Value,		
	Common Stock		25,000
	Exchanged 4,000 shares of $20 par value		
	common stock for land.		

Assets   = Liabilities +   Equity
+ 105,000   + 80,000
                             + 25,000

Point: Any type of stock can be issued for noncash assets.

Specifically, stock issued for noncash assets should be recorded at the market value of either the stock or the noncash asset, whichever is more clearly determinable.

A corporation sometimes gives shares of its stock to promoters in exchange for their services in organizing the corporation. In this case the corporation records the costs of Organization Expenses in exchange for stock. The entry to record receipt of services valued at $12,000 in organizing the corporation in return for issuance of 600 shares of $15 par value common stock is

June 5	Organization Expenses	12,000	
	Common Stock, $15 Par Value		9,000
	Contributed Capital in Excess of Par Value,		
	Common Stock		3,000
	Gave promoters 600 shares of $15 par value		
	common stock in exchange for their services.		

Assets = Liabilities +   Equity
                      − 12,000
                      + 9,000
                      + 3,000

Corporations sometimes issue stock through a **stock subscription,** which involves sale of stock when the investor agrees to buy a certain number of shares at specified future dates and prices. The usual case occurs when a new corporation is formed and the organizers recognize both an immediate and a future need for financing.

Quick Check

4. A company issues 7,000 shares of its $10 par value common stock in exchange for equipment valued at $105,000. The entry to record this transaction includes a credit to (a) Contributed Capital in Excess of Par Value, Common Stock, for $35,000. (b) Retained Earnings for $35,000. (c) Common Stock, $10 Par Value, for $105,000.

5. What is a premium on stock?

6. Who is intended to be protected by minimum legal capital?

Answers—p. 501

Preferred Stock

A corporation can issue two kinds of stock, common and preferred. **Preferred stock** has special rights that give it priority (or senior status) over common stock in one or more areas. Special rights typically include a preference for receiving dividends and for the distribution of assets if the corporation is liquidated. Preferred stock carries all rights of common stock unless the corporate charter nullified them. Most preferred stock, for instance, does not confer the right to vote. **Nike** has preferred stock outstanding without general voting rights (see Appendix A, Note 7). Exhibit 11.6 shows that preferred stock is issued by about one-fourth of large corporations. All corporations issue common stock.

Exhibit 11.6

Corporations and Preferred Stock

No Preferred Stock 73%

Issued Preferred Stock 27%

C3 Explain characteristics of common and preferred stock.

Issuing Preferred Stock

Preferred stock usually has a par value. Like common stock, it can be sold at a price different from par. Preferred stock is recorded in its own separate contributed capital accounts.

To illustrate, if Dillon Snowboards issues 50 shares of $100 par value preferred stock for $6,000 cash on July 1, 2002, the entry is

July 1	Cash	6,000	
	Preferred Stock, $100 Par Value		5,000
	Contributed Capital in Excess of Par Value, Preferred Stock		1,000
	Issued preferred stock for cash.		

Assets = Liabilities + Equity
+6,000   +5,000
                               +1,000

The preferred stock accounts are included as part of contributed capital. The equity section of the year-end balance sheet for Dillon Snowboards, including preferred stock, is shown in Exhibit 11.7. (This exhibit assumes that common stock was issued at par.) Note that issuing no-par preferred stock is similar to issuing no-par common stock. Also, the entries for issuing preferred stock for noncash assets are similar to those for common stock.

Stockholders' Equity

Contributed capital

Common stock—$10 par value; 50,000 shares authorized; 30,000 shares issued and outstanding	$300,000	
Preferred stock—$100 par value; 1,000 shares authorized; 50 shares issued and outstanding	5,000	
Contributed capital in excess of par value, preferred stock	1,000	
Total contributed capital		$306,000
Retained earnings		65,000
Total stockholders' equity		$371,000

Exhibit 11.7

Stockholders' Equity with Common and Preferred Stock

Dividend Preference

Preferred stock usually carries a preference for dividends, meaning that preferred stockholders are allocated their dividends before any dividends are allocated to common stockholders. The dividends allocated to preferred stockholders are usually expressed as a dollar amount per share or a percent applied to par value. A preference for dividends does *not* ensure dividends. If the directors do not declare a dividend, neither the preferred nor the common stockholders receive one.

P2 Distribute dividends between common stock and preferred stock.

Cumulative or Noncumulative Dividend

Most preferred stocks carry a cumulative dividend right. **Cumulative preferred stock** has a right to be paid both the current and all prior periods' unpaid dividends before any dividend is paid to common stockholders. When preferred stock is cumulative and the directors either do not declare a dividend to preferred stockholders or declare one that does not cover the total amount of cumulative dividend, the unpaid dividend amount is called **dividend in arrears.** Accumulation of dividends in arrears on cumulative preferred stock does not guarantee they will be paid. **Noncumulative preferred stock** confers no right to prior periods' unpaid dividends if they were not declared in those prior periods.

To illustrate the difference between cumulative and noncumulative preferred stock, assume that a corporation's outstanding stock includes (1) 1,000 shares of $100 par, 9% preferred stock and (2) 4,000 shares of $50 par common stock. During 2002, the first year of operations, the directors declare cash dividends of $5,000. In year 2003, they declare cash dividends of $42,000. Allocation of total dividends for these two years is shown in Exhibit 11.8. Note that allocation of year 2003 dividends depends on whether the preferred stock is noncumulative or cumulative. With noncumulative preferred, the preferred stockholders

Point: Dividend preference does not imply that preferred stockholders receive more dividends than common stockholders, nor does it guarantee a dividend.

Exhibit 11.8

Allocation of Dividends
(noncumulative vs. cumulative
preferred stock)

	Preferred	Common
Preferred Stock Is Noncumulative		
Year 2002	$ 5,000	$ 0
Year 2003		
Step 1: Current year's preferred dividend	$ 9,000	
Step 2: Remainder to common		$33,000
Preferred Stock Is Cumulative		
Year 2002	$ 5,000	$ 0
Year 2003		
Step 1: Dividend in arrears	$ 4,000	
Step 2: Current year's preferred dividend	9,000	
Step 3: Remainder to common		$29,000
Totals for year 2003	$13,000	$29,000

Example: What dividends do cumulative preferred stockholders receive in 2003 if the corporation paid only $2,000 of dividends in 2002? How does this affect dividends to common stockholders in 2003? *Answers:* $16,000 ($7,000 dividends in arrears, plus $9,000 current preferred dividends). Dividends to common stockholders decrease to $26,000.

never receive the $4,000 skipped in 2002. If the preferred stock is cumulative, the $4,000 in arrears is paid in 2003 before any other dividends are paid.

A liability for a dividend does not exist until the directors declare a dividend. If a preferred dividend date passes and the corporation's board fails to declare the dividend on its cumulative preferred stock, the dividend in arrears is not a liability. The *full-disclosure principle* requires a corporation to report (usually in a note) the amount of preferred dividends in arrears as of the balance sheet date.

Participating or Nonparticipating Dividend

Nonparticipating preferred stock has a feature that limits dividends to a maximum amount each year. This maximum is often stated as a percent of the stock's par value or as a specific dollar amount per share. Once preferred stockholders receive this amount, the common stockholders receive any and all additional dividends. **Participating preferred stock** has a feature allowing preferred stockholders to share with common stockholders in any dividends paid in excess of the percent or dollar amount stated on the preferred stock. This participation feature does not apply until common stockholders receive dividends equal to the preferred stock's dividend percent. Many corporations are authorized to issue participating preferred stock but rarely do, and most managers never expect to issue it.[1]

Convertible Preferred Stock

Preferred stock is more attractive to investors if it carries a right to exchange preferred shares for a fixed number of common shares. **Convertible preferred stock** gives holders the option to exchange their preferred shares for common shares at a specified rate, a feature offering a higher potential return. When a company prospers and its common stock increases in value, convertible preferred stockholders can share in this success by converting their

---

[1] Participating preferred stock is usually authorized as a defense against a possible corporate *takeover* by an "unfriendly" investor (or a group of investors) who intends to buy enough voting common stock to gain control. Taking a term from spy novels, the financial world refers to this type of plan as a *poison pill* that a company swallows if enemy investors threaten its capture. A poison pill usually works as follows: A corporation's common stockholders on a given date are granted the right to purchase a large amount of participating preferred stock at a very low price. This right to purchase preferred shares is *not* transferable. If an unfriendly investor buys a large block of common shares (whose right to purchase participating preferred shares does *not* transfer to this buyer), the board can issue preferred shares at a low price to the remaining common shareholders who retained the right to purchase. Future dividends are then divided between the newly issued participating preferred shares and the common shares. This usually transfers value from common shares to preferred shares, causing the unfriendly investor's common stock to lose much of its value and reduces the potential benefit of a hostile takeover.

preferred stock into more valuable common stock. These holders also benefit from increases in the value of common stock without converting their preferred stock because the convertible preferred stock's market value is impacted by changes in common stock value.

Callable Preferred Stock

Callable preferred stock gives the issuing corporation the right to purchase (retire) this stock from its holders at specified future prices and dates. Many issues of preferred stock are callable. The amount paid to call and retire a preferred share is its **call price,** or *redemption value,* and is set when the stock is issued. The call price normally includes the stock's par value plus a premium giving holders additional return on their investment. When the issuing corporation calls and retires a preferred stock, it usually must pay the call price *and* any dividends in arrears.

Point: The issuing corporation has the right, or option, to retire its callable preferred stock.

Motivation for Preferred Stock

Corporations issue preferred stock for several reasons. One is to raise capital without sacrificing control. For example, suppose a company's organizers have $100,000 cash to invest and wish to organize a corporation needing $200,000 of capital to start. If they sold $200,000 worth of common stock (with $100,000 to the organizers), they would have only 50% control and would need to negotiate extensively with other stockholders in making policy. However, if they issue $100,000 worth of common stock to themselves and sell outsiders $100,000 of 8%, cumulative preferred stock with no voting rights, they retain control.

A second reason to issue preferred stock is to boost the return earned by common stockholders. To illustrate, suppose a corporation's organizers expect their new company to earn an annual after-tax income of $24,000 on an investment of $200,000. If they sell and issue $200,000 worth of common stock, the $24,000 income produces a 12% return on the $200,000 of common stockholders' equity. However, if they issue $100,000 of 8% preferred stock to outsiders and $100,000 of common stock to themselves, their own return increases to 16% per year, as shown in Exhibit 11.9.

Net (after-tax) income	$24,000
Less preferred dividends at 8%	(8,000)
Balance to common stockholders	$16,000
Return to common stockholders ($16,000/$100,000)	16%

Exhibit 11.9

Return to Common Stockholders When Preferred Stock Is Issued

Common stockholders earn 16% instead of 12% because assets contributed by preferred stockholders are invested to earn $12,000 while the preferred dividend is only $8,000. Use of preferred stock to increase return to common stockholders is an example of **financial leverage** (also called *trading on the equity*). As a general rule, when the dividend rate on preferred stock is less than the rate the corporation earns on its assets, the effect of issuing preferred stock is to increase (or *lever*) the rate earned by common stockholders. Financial leverage also occurs when debt is issued and the interest rate paid on it is less than the rate earned from using the assets the creditors lend the corporation.

Other reasons for issuing preferred stock include its appeal to some investors who believe that the corporation's common stock is too risky or that the expected return on common stock is too low. Also, if a corporation's management wants to issue common stock but believes the current market price for common stock is too low, the corporation may issue preferred stock that is convertible into common stock. If and when the price of common stock increases, the preferred stockholders can convert their shares into common shares.

Decision Maker *d*

Concert Organizer Assume that you alter your business strategy from organizing concerts targeted at under 1,000 people to those targeted at between 5,000 to 20,000 people. You also incorporate because of increased risk of lawsuits and a desire to issue stock for financing. It is important that you control the company for decisions on whom to schedule. What types of stock issuances do you offer?

Answer—p. 501

Point: Financial leverage is a main reason for borrowing. The borrower hopes to earn a return on borrowed funds in excess of the borrowing rate.

Answers—p. 501

Dividends

P3   Record transactions involving cash dividends.

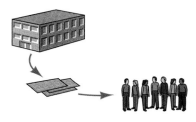

A corporation's retained earnings ordinarily equal the total cumulative amount of reported net income less any net losses and dividends declared since the company started operating. This section describes dividend transactions involving both cash and stock.

Cash Dividends

Many state laws allow a corporation to pay cash dividends only if it has a sufficient amount of retained earnings. A corporation also must have cash in addition to retained earnings to pay a cash dividend. The decision to pay cash dividends rests with the board of directors and involves more than evaluating retained earnings and cash. The directors, for instance, may decide to keep the cash to invest in the corporation's growth, to meet emergencies, to take advantage of unexpected opportunities, or to pay off debt. Many corporations pay regular cash dividends to their stockholders at regular dates. These cash flows provide a return to investors and almost always affect the stock's market value.

Dividend Types and Their Frequency

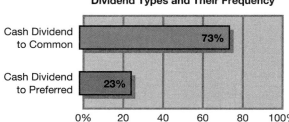

Cash Dividend to Common — 73%

Cash Dividend to Preferred — 23%

0%   20   40   60   80   100%

Global: International accounting standards allow companies to reduce equity by an amount equal to any proposed dividends and prior to their date of declaration.

Point: A cash dividend reduces a company's assets (and its working capital).

Accounting for Cash Dividends

We sometimes assume for simplicity that dividends are declared and paid at the same time, but in practice their payment involves three important dates: declaration, record, and payment. **Date of declaration** is the date the directors vote to declare and pay a dividend. Stockholders receive a dividend only if the directors vote to declare one. Declaring a dividend creates a legal liability of the corporation to its stockholders. **Date of record** is the future date specified by the directors for identifying those stockholders listed in the corporation's records to receive dividends. The date of record usually follows the date of declaration by at least two weeks. Persons who own stock on the date of record receive dividends. **Date of payment** is the date when the corporation makes payment; it follows the date of record by enough time to allow the corporation to arrange checks, money transfers, or other means to pay its stockholders dividends.

To illustrate, the entry to record a January 9 declaration of a $1 per share cash dividend by the directors of Z-Tech, Inc., with 5,000 outstanding shares is

Date of Declaration

Jan. 9	Retained Earnings	5,000	
	Common Dividend Payable		5,000
	Declared $1 per common share cash dividend.[2]		

Assets = Liabilities + Equity
        +5,000   −5,000

---

[2] An alternative entry is to debit Dividends Declared instead of Retained Earnings. The balance in Dividends Declared is then closed to Retained Earnings at the end of the reporting period. Thus, the effect is the same: Retained Earnings is decreased and a Dividend Payable is increased. For simplicity, all assignments use the Retained Earnings account to record dividend declarations.

Common Dividend Payable reflects a corporation's current liability to its stockholders. The date of record for the Z-Tech dividend is January 22. Those who own stock on this date will receive the dividend. *No journal entry is needed on the date of record.* The February 1 date of payment requires an entry to record distribution of the cash dividend. This entry records both the settlement of the liability and the reduction of the cash balance, as follows:

Topic Tackler 11-2

Date of Payment

Feb. 1	Common Dividend Payable	5,000	
	Cash		5,000
	Paid $1 per common share cash dividend.		

Assets = Liabilities + Equity
−5,000   −5,000

Deficits and Cash Dividends

A corporation with a debit (abnormal) balance for retained earnings is said to have a **retained earnings deficit,** which arises when a company incurs cumulative losses and/or pays more dividends than total earnings from current and prior years. A deficit is reported as a deduction on the balance sheet, as shown in Exhibit 11.10. Most states prohibit a corporation with a deficit from paying a cash dividend to its stockholders. This legal restriction is designed to protect creditors by preventing distribution of assets to stockholders when the company may be in financial difficulty.

Point: The Retained Earnings Deficit account is also called Accumulated Deficit.

Common stock—$10 par value, 5,000 shares authorized, issued, and outstanding	$50,000
Retained earnings deficit	**(6,000)**
Total stockholders' equity	$44,000

Exhibit 11.10

Stockholders' Equity with a Deficit

Some state laws allow cash dividends to be paid by returning a portion of the capital contributed by stockholders. This type of dividend is called a **liquidating cash dividend,** or simply *liquidating dividend,* because it returns a part of the original investment back to the stockholders. This requires a debit entry to one of the contributed capital accounts instead of Retained Earnings at the declaration date.

Decision Insight

Dividend Decline   Cash dividends have declined as a percent of stock prices in U.S. markets. Cash dividends are increasingly viewed as an inefficient way to reward shareholders. Rates for dividend taxes, which are inescapable, can be nearly 40%. Companies are instead buying back shares, paying down debt, or expanding business.

Point: It is often said a dividend is a distribution of retained earnings, but it is more precise to describe a dividend as a distribution of assets to satisfy stockholder claims.

Quick Check

10. The Common Dividend Payable account is what type of an account?

11. What three crucial dates are involved in the process of paying a cash dividend?

12. When does a dividend become a company's legal obligation?

Answers—p. 501

Stock Dividends

A **stock dividend** is a distribution of additional shares of the corporation's own stock to its stockholders without the receipt of any payment in return. Stock dividends and cash dividends are different. A stock dividend does not reduce a corporation's assets and equity, but simply transfers a portion of equity from retained earnings to contributed capital. A stock dividend is declared by a corporation's directors.

P4 Account for stock dividends and stock splits.

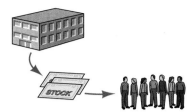

Reasons for Stock Dividends

Stock dividends are declared and distributed for at least two reasons. First, directors are said to use stock dividends to keep the market price of the stock affordable. For example, if a corporation continues to earn income but does not distribute it to shareholders through cash dividends, the price of its common stock likely increases. The price of such a stock may become so high that it discourages some investors from buying the stock (especially in lots of 100 and 1,000). When a corporation declares a stock dividend, it increases the number of outstanding shares and lowers the per share price of its stock. Another reason for declaring a stock dividend is to provide evidence of management's confidence that the company is doing well and will continue to do well.

Accounting for Stock Dividends

A stock dividend does not affect assets or total equity, but it does affect the components of equity. It does this by transferring part of retained earnings to contributed capital accounts, sometimes described as *capitalizing* retained earnings. Accounting for a stock dividend depends on whether it is a small or large stock dividend. A **small stock dividend** is a distribution of 25% or less of previously outstanding shares. It is recorded by capitalizing retained earnings for an amount equal to the market value of the shares to be distributed. A **large stock dividend** is a distribution of more than 25% of previously outstanding shares. It is likely to have a noticeable effect on the stock's market price. A large stock dividend is recorded by capitalizing retained earnings for the minimum amount required by state law governing the corporation. Most states require capitalizing retained earnings equal to the par or stated value of the stock.

To illustrate both small and large stock dividends, we use the equity section of X-Quest's balance sheet shown in Exhibit 11.11 just *before* its declaration of a stock dividend on December 31.

Exhibit 11.11

Stockholders' Equity <u>before</u> Declaring a Stock Dividend

Stockholders' Equity (before dividend)	
Common stock—$10 par value, 15,000 shares authorized, 10,000 shares issued and outstanding	$100,000
Contributed capital in excess of par value, common stock	8,000
Total contributed capital	$108,000
Retained earnings	35,000
Total stockholders' equity	$143,000

Recording a small stock dividend. Assume that X-Quest's directors declare a 10% stock dividend on December 31. This stock dividend of 1,000 shares, computed as 10% of its 10,000 issued and outstanding shares, is to be distributed on January 20 to the stockholders of record on January 15. Since the market price of X-Quest's stock on December 31 is $15 per share, this small stock dividend declaration is recorded as follows:

Date of Declaration

Dec. 31	Retained Earnings	15,000	
	Common Stock Dividend Distributable		10,000
	Contributed Capital in Excess of Par Value, Common Stock		5,000
	Declared a 1,000-share (10%) stock dividend.		

The $10,000 credit in the declaration entry equals the par value of the dividend shares and is recorded in a contributed capital account called *Common Stock Dividend Distributable*.

Its balance exists only until the shares are actually issued. The $5,000 credit equals the amount by which market value exceeds par value for the dividend shares. This amount increases the Contributed Capital in Excess of Par Value account in anticipation of the issue of shares. A stock dividend is never a liability on a balance sheet because it never reduces assets. Instead, any declared but undistributed stock dividend appears on the balance sheet as a part of contributed capital. In particular, a balance sheet changes in three ways when a company declares a stock dividend. First, the amount of equity attributed to common stock increases—for X-Quest, from $100,000 to $110,000 for 1,000 additional declared shares. Second, contributed capital in excess of par increases by the excess of market value over par value for the declared shares. Third, retained earnings decreases, reflecting the transfer of amounts to both common stock and contributed capital in excess of par. The stockholders' equity of X-Quest is shown in Exhibit 11.12 *after* its 10% stock dividend is declared on December 31.

Point: The credit to Contributed Capital in Excess of Par Value is recorded when the stock dividend is declared. This account is not affected when stock is later distributed.

Stockholders' Equity (after dividend)	
Common stock—$10 par value, 15,000 shares authorized, 10,000 shares issued and outstanding	$100,000
Common stock dividend distributable—1,000 shares	**10,000**
Contributed capital in excess of par value, common stock	**13,000**
Total contributed capital	$123,000
Retained earnings	**20,000**
Total stockholders' equity	$143,000

Exhibit 11.12

Stockholders' Equity <u>after</u> Declaring a Stock Dividend

No entry is made on the date of record for a stock dividend. On January 20, the date of payment, X-Quest distributes the new shares to stockholders and records this entry:

Date of Payment

Jan. 20	Common Stock Dividend Distributable	10,000	
	Common Stock, $10 Par Value		10,000
	To record issuance of common stock dividend.		

Assets = Liabilities + Equity
−10,000
+10,000

The combined effect of these three stock dividend entries is to transfer (or capitalize) $15,000 of retained earnings to contributed capital accounts. The amount of capitalized retained earnings equals the market value of the 1,000 issued shares ($15 × 1,000 shares).

A stock dividend has no effect on the ownership percent of individual stockholders. To show this, assume that we own 200 shares of X-Quest's stock prior to the 10% stock dividend. When X-Quest sends each stockholder one new share for each 10 shares held, we receive 20 new shares (10% × 200 shares). Exhibit 11.13 shows no change in the book value of X-Quest and our shares from this dividend. Before the stock dividend, we owned 2% of X-Quest's stock, computed as 200 divided by 10,000 outstanding shares. After the dividend, we hold 220 shares, but our holding still equals 2% (220 divided by 11,000 shares now outstanding). Also, total book value of our holding remains at $2,860. Before the stock dividend, we owned 200 shares with a book value of $14.30 per share. After the dividend, we hold 220 shares with a book value of $13.00 per share. The only change in our 2% investment is that it is now divided among 220 shares instead of 200 shares. The only effect on equity is a transfer of $15,000 from retained earnings to contributed capital—total equity remains the same.

Decision Maker *e*

Entrepreneur A company you cofounded and own stock in announces a 50% stock dividend. Has the value of your stock investment increased, decreased, or remained the same?

Answer—p. 501

Point: A small stock dividend does not affect a company's assets (or its working capital).

Exhibit 11.13

Financial Effects of
Small Stock Dividend

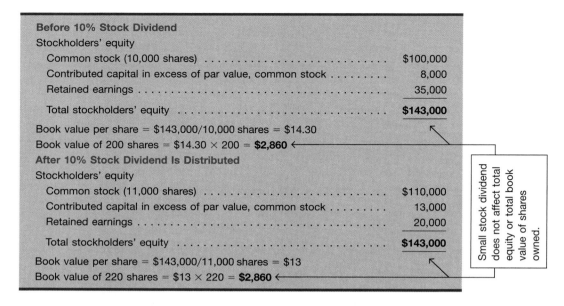

Before 10% Stock Dividend
Stockholders' equity
    Common stock (10,000 shares) $100,000
    Contributed capital in excess of par value, common stock 8,000
    Retained earnings 35,000
    Total stockholders' equity **$143,000**
Book value per share = $143,000/10,000 shares = $14.30
Book value of 200 shares = $14.30 × 200 = **$2,860** ←
After 10% Stock Dividend Is Distributed
Stockholders' equity
    Common stock (11,000 shares) $110,000
    Contributed capital in excess of par value, common stock 13,000
    Retained earnings 20,000
    Total stockholders' equity **$143,000**
Book value per share = $143,000/11,000 shares = $13
Book value of 220 shares = $13 × 220 = **$2,860** ←

Small stock dividend does not affect total equity or total book value of shares owned.

Recording a large stock dividend. A corporation capitalizes retained earnings equal to the minimum amount required by state law for a large stock dividend. For most states, this amount is the par or stated value of the newly issued shares. To illustrate, suppose X-Quest's board declares a stock dividend of 30% instead of 10% on December 31. Since this dividend is more than 25%, it is treated as a large stock dividend. Thus, the par value of the 3,000 dividend shares is capitalized instead of the market value at the date of declaration with this entry:

Point: Large stock dividends are recorded at par or stated value.

Date of Declaration

Dec. 31	Retained Earnings	30,000	
	Common Stock Dividend Distributable		30,000
	Declared a 3,000-share (30%) stock dividend.		

Assets = Liabilities + Equity
    −30,000
    +30,000

This transaction decreases retained earnings and increases contributed capital by $30,000. Subsequent entries related to a large stock dividend use the same accounts a small stock dividend uses. Also, the effects from a large stock dividend on balance sheet accounts are similar to those for a small stock dividend except for the absence of any effect on contributed capital in excess of par.

Stock Splits

A **stock split** is the distribution of additional shares to stockholders according to their percent ownership. When a stock split occurs, the corporation "calls in" its outstanding shares and issues more than one new share in exchange for each old share. Splits can be done in any ratio, including 2-for-1, 3-for-1, or higher. Stock splits reduce the par or stated value per share.

    To illustrate, CompTec has 100,000 outstanding shares of $20 par value common stock with a current market value of $88 per share. A 2-for-1 stock split cuts par value in half, from $20 to $10 per share and replaces 100,000 shares of $20 par value stock with 200,000 shares of $10 par value stock. Also, market value is reduced from $88 per share to about $44 per share. The split does not affect any equity amounts reported on the balance sheet or any individual stockholder's percent ownership. Both the Contributed Capital and Retained Earnings accounts are unchanged by a split, and *no journal entry is made.* The only effect on the accounts is a change in the stock account description. CompTec's 2-for-1 split on its $20 par value stock means that after the split, it changes its stock account title to

Point: A reverse stock split is the opposite of a stock split. It increases both the market value per share and the par or stated value per share by specifying the split ratio to be less than 1-for-1, such as 1-for-2. A reverse stock split results in fewer shares.

Common Stock, $10 Par Value. This stock's description on the balance sheet also changes to reflect the additional authorized, issued, and outstanding shares and the new par value.

The difference between stock splits and large stock dividends is often blurred. Many companies report stock splits in their financial statements without calling in the original shares and simply changing their par value. This type of "split" is really a large stock dividend and results in additional shares issued to stockholders by capitalizing retained earnings or transferring other contributed capital to Common Stock. This approach avoids administrative costs of splitting the stock. Harley-Davidson recently declared a 2-for-1 stock split executed in the form of a 100% stock dividend.

Quick Check

13. How does a stock dividend impact assets and retained earnings?

14. What distinguishes a large stock dividend from a small stock dividend?

15. What amount of retained earnings is capitalized for a small stock dividend?

Answers—p. 501

Treasury Stock

Corporations acquire shares of their own stock for several reasons. First, they can use their shares to acquire another corporation. Second, they can repurchase shares to avoid a hostile takeover by an investor seeking to take control of the company. Third, they can buy shares and reissue them to employees as compensation. Hewlett-Packard, for example, has a stock repurchase program to compensate employees. Fourth, they can buy shares to maintain a strong or stable market for their stock. This is often done when a stock quickly and markedly declines in price. By buying shares, management shows its confidence in the price of its shares.

A corporation's reacquired shares are called **treasury stock,** which is similar to unissued stock in several ways. That is, neither treasury stock nor unissued stock is an asset. Neither receives cash dividends or stock dividends. Neither allows the exercise of voting rights. Still, treasury stock does differ from unissued stock in one major way. Specifically, the corporation can resell the stock at less than par without having the buyers incur a liability, provided the treasury stock was originally issued at par value or higher. As shown in the margin, most large corporations have acquired some of their own stock.

Treasury stock purchases require management to exercise ethical sensitivity because corporate funds are being paid to specific stockholders instead of all stockholders. Managers must be sure the purchase is in the best interest of all stockholders. These concerns cause most companies to fully disclose treasury stock transactions.

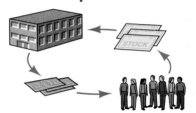

Corporations and Treasury Stock

With Treasury Stock 62%

No Treasury Stock 38%

Purchasing Treasury Stock

Purchasing treasury stock reduces the corporation's assets and equity by equal amounts. (We describe the *cost method* of accounting for treasury stock, which is the most widely used method. The *par value* method is another method explained in advanced courses.) To illustrate, Exhibit 11.14 shows Cyber Corporation's account balances *before* any treasury stock purchase.

P5 Record purchases and sales of treasury stock and the retirement of stock.

Assets		Stockholders' Equity	
Cash	$ 30,000	Common stock—$10 par; 10,000 shares authorized, issued, and outstanding	$100,000
Other assets	95,000	Retained earnings	25,000
Total assets	$125,000	Total stockholders' equity	$125,000

Exhibit 11.14

Account Balances before Purchasing Treasury Stock

Cyber then purchases 1,000 of its own shares for $11,500, which is recorded as follows:

Assets = Liabilities + Equity
−11,500   −11,500

May 1	Treasury Stock, Common	11,500	
	Cash		11,500
	Purchased 1,000 treasury shares at $11.50 per share.		

This entry reduces equity through the debit to the Treasury Stock account, which is a contra equity account. Exhibit 11.15 shows account balances *after* this transaction.

Exhibit 11.15

Account Balances <u>after</u> Purchasing Treasury Stock

Assets		Stockholders' Equity	
Cash	$ 18,500	Common stock—$10 par; 10,000 shares authorized and issued; 1,000 shares in treasury	$100,000
Other assets	95,000	Retained earnings, $11,500 restricted by treasury stock purchase	25,000
		Less cost of treasury stock	(11,500)
Total assets	$113,500	Total stockholders' equity	$113,500

The treasury stock purchase reduces Cyber's cash, total assets, and total equity by $11,500 but does not reduce the balance of either the Common Stock or the Retained Earnings account. The equity reduction is reported by deducting the cost of treasury stock in the equity section. Two disclosures in this section describe the effects of the transaction. First, the stock description tells us 1,000 issued shares are in treasury, leaving only 9,000 shares outstanding. Second, the description for retained earnings tells us it is partly restricted.

Decision Insight

Buybacks Explode Buybacks, which refer to a company's purchase of its own stock, have exploded. Some believe buybacks explain the market's reduced dividend yield because shareholders' capital gains are taxed at more favorable rates than the more highly taxed cash dividends.

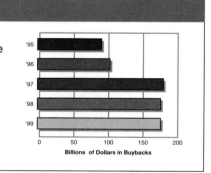

Billions of Dollars in Buybacks

Reissuing Treasury Stock

Treasury stock can be reissued by selling it at cost, above cost, or below cost. This section explains the accounting for reissuing treasury stock.

Selling Treasury Stock at Cost

If treasury stock is reissued at cost, the entry is the opposite of the entry made to record the purchase. For instance, if on May 21 Cyber reissues 100 of the treasury shares purchased on May 1 at the same $11.50 per share cost, the entry to record this sale is

Assets = Liabilities + Equity
+1,150   +1,150

May 21	Cash	1,150	
	Treasury Stock, Common		1,150
	Received $11.50 per share for 100 treasury shares costing $11.50 per share.		

Selling Treasury Stock *above* Cost

If treasury stock is sold for more than cost, the amount received in excess of cost is credited to the Contributed Capital, Treasury Stock account. This account is reported as a separate item in the contributed capital section of stockholders' equity. No gain is ever reported from the sale of treasury stock. To illustrate, if Cyber receives $12 cash per share for 400 treasury shares costing $11.50 per share, the entry is

June 3	Cash	4,800	
	Treasury Stock, Common		4,600
	Contributed Capital, Treasury Stock		**200**
	Received $12 per share for 400 treasury		
	shares costing $11.50 per share.		

Assets = Liabilities + Equity
+4,800   +4,600
                            +200

Selling Treasury Stock *below* Cost

When treasury stock is sold below cost, the entry to record the sale depends on whether the Contributed Capital, Treasury Stock account has a credit balance. If it has a zero balance, the excess of cost over the sales price is debited to Retained Earnings. If the Contributed Capital, Treasury Stock account has a credit balance, it is debited for the excess of the cost over the selling price, but not to exceed the balance in this account. When the credit balance in this contributed capital account is eliminated, any remaining difference between the cost and selling price is debited to Retained Earnings. To illustrate, if Cyber sells its remaining 500 shares of treasury stock at $10 per share, the company's equity is reduced by $750 (500 shares × $1.50 per share excess of cost over selling price), as shown in this entry:

Point: The term treasury stock is believed to arise from the fact that reacquired stock is held in a corporation's treasury.

Point: The Contributed Capital, Treasury Stock account can have a zero or credit balance but never a debit balance.

July 10	Cash	5,000	
	Contributed Capital, Treasury Stock	**200**	
	Retained Earnings	**550**	
	Treasury Stock, Common		5,750
	Received $10 per share for 500 treasury		
	shares costing $11.50 per share.		

Assets = Liabilities + Equity
+5,000   −200
                            −550
                            +5,750

This entry eliminates the $200 credit balance in the contributed capital account created on June 3 and then reduces the Retained Earnings balance by the remaining $550 excess of cost over selling price. A company never reports a loss (or gain) from the sale of treasury stock.

Decision Insight

Online Trading   The volume of online stock trading has skyrocketed. Charles Schwab, for instance, reports $100 billion in online customer assets. It also reports more than a million active online accounts and over a million daily visits to its Web site.

Retiring Stock

A corporation can purchase its own stock and retire it. Retiring stock reduces the number of issued shares. Retired stock is the same as authorized and unissued shares. Purchases and retirements of stock are permissible under state law only if they do not jeopardize the interests of creditors and stockholders. When stock is purchased for retirement, we remove all contributed capital amounts related to the retired shares. If the purchase price exceeds the net amount removed from contributed capital, this excess is debited to Retained Earnings. If the net amount removed from contributed capital exceeds the purchase price, this excess is credited to the Contributed Capital from Retirement of Stock account. A company's assets and equity are always reduced by the amount paid for the retiring stock.

Point: Wrigley Company recently reported that its "Board of Directors adopted a resolution retiring the entire balance of shares of Common Stock held in the corporate treasury."

Point: Recording stock retirement results in canceling the equity from the original issuance of the shares.

Point: An increase in equity from retiring stock is never credited to a gain account.

Quick Check

16. Purchase of treasury stock (*a*) has no effect on assets; (*b*) reduces total assets and total equity by equal amounts; or (*c*) is recorded with a debit to Retained Earnings.

17. Southern Co. purchases shares of Northern Corp. Should either company classify these shares as treasury stock?

18. How does treasury stock affect the authorized, issued, and outstanding shares?

19. When a company purchases treasury stock, (*a*) retained earnings are restricted by the amount paid; (*b*) Retained Earnings are credited; or (*c*) it is retired.

Answers—p. 501

Reporting Income Information

When a company's revenue and expense transactions are from normal, continuing operations, a simple income statement is usually adequate for describing its performance. This format shows revenues followed by a list of operating expenses and then net income. However, a company's activities can include income-related events not part of its normal, continuing operations. A company needs to provide useful information on these items in a format that helps users understand both current and past events and predict future performance. To meet these objectives, companies often separate the income statement into different sections. The major sections are continuing operations, discontinued segments, extraordinary items, changes in accounting principles, and earnings per share. Exhibit 11.16 shows such an income statement for CompUS.

Continuing Operations

C4   Explain the form and content of a complete income statement.

The first major section (①) of an income statement shows the revenues, expenses, and income generated by the company's continuing operations. Users especially rely on information in this section to predict the results of future operations. Many users view this section as the most important. Earlier chapters explained both the nature of the items and the measures comprising income from continuing operations.

Discontinued Segments

Many companies have different lines of business and deal with different groups of customers. A **segment of a business** is a part of a company's operations that serves a particular line of business or class of customers. A segment has assets, liabilities, and financial results of operations that can be distinguished from those of other parts of the company.

The gain or loss a company incurs from selling or closing down a segment is reported in a separate section of the income statement. Section ② of Exhibit 11.16 reports both (1) income from operating the discontinued segment for the current period prior to its disposal and (2) the loss from disposing of the segment's net assets. The income tax effects of each are also reported and are separate from the income taxes expense in section ①. The purpose of separately reporting gains and losses from discontinued segments is to isolate these results from continuing operations.

Extraordinary Items

Section ③ of the income statement in Exhibit 11.16 reports **extraordinary gains and losses,** which are those that are *both unusual* and *infrequent.* An **unusual gain or loss** is abnormal or otherwise unrelated to the company's regular activities and environment. An **infrequent gain or loss** is not expected to recur given the company's operating environment. Reporting extraordinary items in a separate category helps users predict future performance, absent the effects of extraordinary items. Few items qualify as extraordinary because they must be both *unusual* and *infrequent.* The following items are *not* considered extraordinary:

- Write-downs of inventories and write-offs of receivables.
- Gains and losses from disposing of segments.
- Financial effects of labor strikes.

Items that are usually considered extraordinary include these:

- Expropriation (taking away) of property by a foreign government.
- Condemning of property by a domestic government body.
- Prohibition against using an asset by a newly enacted law.
- Losses and gains from an unusual and infrequent calamity ("act of God").

Point: Chiquita recently reported an extraordinary loss of $22.84 million from retirement of debt.

Gains and losses that are neither unusual nor infrequent are reported as part of continuing operations. Gains and losses that are *either* unusual *or* infrequent, but *not* both, are reported

Exhibit 11.16

Income Statement (all-inclusive) for a Corporation

CompUS
Income Statement
For Year Ended December 31, 2002

Net sales		$8,478,000
Operating expenses		
Cost of goods sold	$5,950,000	
Depreciation expense	35,000	
Other selling, general, and administrative expenses	515,000	
Interest expense	20,000	
① Total operating expenses		(6,520,000)
Other gains (losses)		
Loss on plant relocation		(45,000)
Gain on sale of surplus land		72,000
Income from continuing operations before taxes		1,985,000
Income taxes expense		(595,500)
Income from continuing operations		1,389,500
Discontinued segment		
② Income from operating Division A (net of $180,000 taxes)	420,000	
Loss on disposal of Division A (net of $66,000 tax benefit)	(154,000)	266,000
Income before extraordinary items and cumulative effect of change in accounting principle		1,655,500
Extraordinary items		
③ Gain on land expropriated by state (net of $61,200 taxes)	142,800	
Loss from earthquake damage (net of $270,000 tax benefit)	(630,000)	(487,200)
Cumulative effect of a change in accounting principle		
④ Effect on prior years' income (through Dec. 31, 2001) of changing depreciation methods (net of $24,000 taxes)		56,000
Net income		$1,224,300
Earnings per common share (200,000 outstanding shares)		
Income from continuing operations		$ 6.95
Discontinued operations		1.33
⑤ Income before extraordinary items and cumulative effect of change in accounting principle		8.28
Extraordinary items		(2.44)
Cumulative effect of a change in accounting principle		0.28
Net income (basic earnings per share)		$ 6.12

as part of continuing operations *but* below the normal revenues and expenses. Accounting standards require that certain items be reported as extraordinary to highlight their occurrence even when they do not meet the two criteria. One such item frequently encountered is a gain or loss from retiring debt.

Decision Maker

Small Business Owner   You own an orange grove near Jacksonville, Florida. A bad frost destroys about one-half of your oranges. You are currently preparing an income statement for a bank loan. Can you claim the loss of oranges as extraordinary?

Answer—p. 501

Changes in Accounting Principles

The *consistency principle* requires that a company apply the same accounting principles across periods. However, a company can change from one acceptable accounting principle (such as FIFO, LIFO, or straight-line) to another as long as the change improves the usefulness of information in its financial statements. (Changes in principles are sometimes required when new accounting standards are issued.) Changes in accounting principles usually affect income in more than one way. To illustrate, CompUS purchased its only depreciable asset early in 1999 for $320,000. This asset has an eight-year life, a $40,000 salvage value, and was depreciated using double-declining-balance for the past three years. During 2002, CompUS decides its income statement would be more useful if depreciation is computed using straight-line instead of double-declining-balance. Exhibit 11.17 compares the results of applying the two depreciation methods to the initial three years of this asset's life. Double-declining-balance yields $185,000 of depreciation from 1999 through 2001. If the straight-line method had been used, only $105,000 of depreciation would have been reported. To adjust accounts to the balances they would be under straight-line, CompUS needs to decrease (debit) accumulated depreciation on this asset by $80,000. Also, since CompUS is subject to a 30% income tax, we offset this debit with credits of $24,000 (30% × $80,000) to deferred income taxes and $56,000 (remainder) to equity. Equity is increased because straight-line depreciation is less than that for double-declining-balance for these years.

Exhibit 11.17

Computing Cumulative
Effect of a Change in
Accounting Principle

	Double-Declining Depreciation	Straight-Line Depreciation	Pretax Difference	After-Tax Difference
Prior to Change				
1999	$ 80,000	$ 35,000		
2000	60,000	35,000		
2001	45,000	35,000		
Totals	$185,000	$105,000	$80,000	$56,000*
Year of Change				
2002	33,750	35,000†		
After Change				
2003–2006		35,000		

* Reported on the year 2002 income statement as the cumulative adjustment for the differences in the three years prior to the change in 2002, net of $24,000 additional taxes to be paid (30% × $80,000).
† Reported on the year 2002 income statement as depreciation expense.

The income statement in Exhibit 11.16 shows how to report a change in an accounting principle. First, section ① reports $35,000 of depreciation using the newly adopted straight-line method. Straight-line depreciation also will be used in 2003 through 2006. Second, the income statement reports the $56,000 catch-up adjustment in section ④. This item is the cumulative effect of the change in accounting principle. Finally, a note should describe the accounting change and why it is an improvement. The note should also describe what income would have been under the prior method. For CompUS, its note reports that 2002 depreciation of $33,750 would have been reported using double-declining-balance instead of $35,000 under straight-line.

Quick Check

20. Which of the following is an extraordinary item? (a) A settlement paid to a customer injured while using the company's product. (b) A loss to a plant from damages caused by a meteorite. (c) A loss from selling old equipment.

21. Identify the five major sections of an income statement that are potentially reported.

22. A company using FIFO for the past 15 years decides to switch to LIFO. The effect of this event on past years' net income is (a) reported as a prior period adjustment to retained earnings; (b) ignored, because it is a change in an accounting estimate; or (c) reported on the current year's income statement.

Answers—p. 501

Earnings per Share

The final section of the income statement in Exhibit 11.16 reports earnings per share results. Corporations must report earnings per share figures and usually report the amount of earnings per share for each of the four subcategories of income (continuing operations, discontinued segments, extraordinary items, and the effect of accounting principle changes) when they exist. **Earnings per share,** also called *net income per share,* is the amount of income earned per each share of a company's outstanding common stock. Investors find this ratio useful in the valuation of common shares, especially when compared with the market price per share discussed later in this chapter. The **basic earnings per share** formula is in Exhibit 11.18.

A1 Compute earnings per share and describe this ratio's use.

Exhibit 11.18
Basic Earnings per Share

$$\text{Basic earnings per share} = \frac{\text{Net income} - \text{Preferred dividends}}{\text{Weighted-average common shares outstanding}}$$

This formula shows that the basic earnings per share (EPS) computation depends not only on net income but also on (1) any preferred dividends and (2) the weighted-average common shares outstanding. Our explanation of earnings per share begins by considering the simple case that has no changes in shares outstanding during the period. We then look at what happens when the number of common shares outstanding changes.

No Changes in Common Shares Outstanding. To illustrate, assume that Quantum Co. earns $40,000 net income in 2002 and declares dividends of $7,500 on its noncumulative preferred stock.[3] Quantum has 5,000 common shares outstanding during all of 2002. Its basic EPS is

Point: Earnings per share is often referred to as *EPS.*

Global: Some countries, such as Mexico, Spain, Switzerland, and Sweden, have no requirements to report earnings per share.

$$\text{Basic earnings per share} = \frac{\$40,000 - \$7,500}{5,000 \text{ shares}} = \$6.50$$

Changes in Common Shares Outstanding (Stock Sales and Purchases). When a company sells additional shares or purchases treasury shares during the period, the denominator of the basic EPS formula is adjusted to equal the weighted-average number of outstanding shares. The idea behind this computation is to compare earnings to the average number of shares outstanding during the period. To illustrate, assume that Quantum earns $40,000 in 2002 and declares preferred dividends of $7,500. Also assume that Quantum begins the year with 5,000 common shares outstanding, sells 4,000 additional shares on July 1, and purchases 3,000 treasury shares on November 1. Thus, 5,000 shares were outstanding for the first six months, 9,000 were outstanding for July through October (four months), and 6,000 were outstanding for the final two months. Exhibit 11.19 shows how to compute Quantum's weighted-average number of shares outstanding for 2002.

Global: Some countries, such as France, Japan, and Australia, use the number of shares outstanding at the end of the period when computing EPS.

Exhibit 11.19
Computing Weighted-Average Shares Outstanding

Time Period	Outstanding Shares		Fraction of Year		Weighted Average
January–June	5,000	×	6/12	=	2,500
July–October	9,000	×	4/12	=	3,000
November–December	6,000	×	2/12	=	1,000
Weighted-average shares outstanding					6,500

Quantum's basic EPS is

$$\text{Basic earnings per share} = \frac{\$40,000 - \$7,500}{6,500 \text{ shares}} = \$5$$

[3] If preferred stock is *non*cumulative, the income available (numerator) is the current period's net income less any preferred dividends *declared* in that same period. If preferred stock is cumulative, the income available (numerator) is the current period's net income less the preferred dividends whether declared or not.

Changes in Common Shares Outstanding (Stock Splits and Dividends). Both a stock split and a stock dividend affect the computation of the weighted-average number of shares outstanding. We must restate the number of shares outstanding during the period to reflect a stock split or dividend *as if it occurred at the beginning of the period.* To illustrate, in addition to the facts above assume that Quantum executed a 2-for-1 stock split on December 1, 2002, that doubles the number of shares outstanding on December 1. In computing weighted-average shares outstanding we include an additional column reflecting the effect of the split as shown in Exhibit 11.20. The December shares already reflect the split and do not require adjustment.

Exhibit 11.20

Computing Weighted-Average Shares Outstanding when Stock Splits (and Dividends) Occur

Time Period	Outstanding Shares		Effect of Split		Fraction of Year		Weighted Average
January–June	5,000	×	2	×	6/12	=	5,000
July–October	9,000	×	2	×	4/12	=	6,000
November	6,000	×	2	×	1/12	=	1,000
December	12,000	×	1	×	1/12	=	1,000
Weighted-average shares outstanding							13,000

Quantum's basic EPS under the 2-for-1 stock split is

$$\text{Basic earnings per share} = \frac{\$40,000 - \$7,500}{13,000 \text{ shares}} = \$2.50$$

We use the same computations when stock dividends occur. For instance, if the 2-for-1 stock split had been a 10% stock dividend, the outstanding shares prior to the dividend are multiplied by 1.1 instead of 2.0 because 110% (or 1.1) of the original number of shares are now outstanding, computed as 100% + 10%.[4]

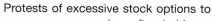

Stock Options

The majority of corporations whose shares are publicly traded issue **stock options,** which are rights to purchase common stock at a fixed price over a specified period. As the stock's price rises above the fixed price, the option's value increases. Use of stock options is growing in popularity as a way to pay both managers and employees for performance. **Starbucks** and **Home Depot**, for instance, are leaders in offering stock options to both full- and part-time employees. Stock options are said to motivate managers and employees to (1) fo-

---

[4] A corporation can be classified as having either a simple or complex capital structure. The term **simple capital structure** refers to a company with only common stock and nonconvertible preferred stock outstanding. The term **complex capital structure** refers to companies with dilutive securities. **Dilutive securities** include options, rights to purchase common stock, and any bonds or preferred stock that are convertible into common stock. A company with a complex capital structure must often report two EPS figures: basic and diluted. **Diluted earnings per share** is computed by adding all dilutive securities to the denominator of the basic EPS computation. It reflects the decrease in basic EPS *assuming* that all dilutive securities are converted into common shares. Since CompUS has a simple capital structure, it need report only basic EPS.

cus on company performance, (2) take a long-run perspective, and (3) remain with the company. A stock option is like having an investment with no risk (or "a carrot with no stick").

To illustrate, Quantum grants each of its employees the option to purchase 100 shares of its $1 par value common stock at its current market price of $50 per share anytime within the next 10 years. If Quantum's stock price exceeds $50 per share, employees can exercise the option at a profit. For instance, if the stock price rises to $70 per share, an employee can exercise the option at a gain of $20 per share (acquire a $70 stock at the $50 option price). With 100 shares, a single employee would have a total gain of $2,000, computed as $20 × 100 shares.

When options are granted, the difference between their estimated value and their exercise price is considered compensation expense and it is either recorded as compensation expense or, more commonly, reported in notes to the financial statements.

> **Decision Ethics** *d*
>
> **Director** The board of Intex is planning its stockholders' meeting agenda. The first item is whether to disclose a contract just signed that will increase future income. One officer argues, "The meeting should focus on actual results." After agreeing not to disclose the contract, the next item is a motion for stockholders to approve a two-year option to managers to buy shares at a price equal to the average stock price over the next 30 days. What action (if any) do you take?
>
> Answer—p. 501

Point: MCI recently reported stock option compensation expense of nearly $100 million; PepsiCo reported nearly $70 million.

Quick Check

23. FDI reports 2002 net income of $250,000 and pays preferred dividends of $70,000. On January 1, 2002, FDI had 25,000 outstanding common shares, and it purchased 5,000 treasury shares on July 1. Its 2002 basic EPS is (a) $8; (b) $9; or (c) $10.

24. How are stock splits and stock dividends treated in computing the weighted-average number of outstanding common shares?

25. What EPS figures are reported for a complex capital structure company?

Answers—p. 501

Retained Earnings

C5 Explain the items reported in retained earnings.

Retained earnings generally consist of a company's cumulative net income less any net losses and dividends declared since its inception. Retained earnings are part of stockholders' claims on the company's net assets, but it does *not* imply that a certain amount of cash or other assets is available to pay stockholders. For example, **Harley-Davidson** has $1.1 billion in retained earnings, but only $0.2 billion in cash. This section describes important events and transactions affecting retained earnings and how retained earnings are reported. However, we first define both restricted and appropriated retained earnings.

The term **restricted retained earnings** refers to both statutory and contractual restrictions placed on corporate activities that depend on the amount of retained earnings. For instance, most states restrict the amount of treasury stock purchases to the amount of retained earnings. This is called a *statutory* (or legal) *restriction*. The balance sheet in Exhibit 11.15 identifies *restricted retained* earnings created by treasury stock purchases. Certain *contractual restrictions* such as loan agreements can also restrict retained earnings. They often include restrictions on paying dividends beyond a specified amount or percent of retained earnings. When important restrictions exist, they are usually described in the notes. The term **appropriated retained earnings** refers to a voluntary transfer of amounts from Retained Earnings to Appropriated Retained Earnings to inform users of special activities that require funds. For example, a corporation's directors can voluntarily limit dividends to fund purchases of new facilities. Alternatively, management need not set up an Appropriated Retained Earnings account but can simply disclose in the letter to shareholders or other means of where funds are being directed.

Global: Some countries, such as France, Germany, and Japan, require companies to set up reserves at specified rates for the protection of creditors.

Point: Retained earnings restrictions are different from retained earnings appropriations.

Prior Period Adjustments

Prior period adjustments are corrections of material errors in prior periods' financial statements. These errors include making arithmetic mistakes, using unacceptable accounting principles, and ignoring relevant facts. Prior period adjustments are reported in the *statement of*

Exhibit 11.21

Statement of Retained Earnings with a Prior Period Adjustment

CompUS Statement of Retained Earnings For Year Ended December 31, 2002	
Retained earnings, Dec. 31, 2001, as previously reported	$4,745,000
Prior period adjustment:	
Cost of land incorrectly expensed (net of $63,000 income taxes)	**147,000**
Retained earnings, Dec. 31, 2001, as adjusted	$4,892,000
Plus net income	1,224,300
Less cash dividends declared	(301,800)
Retained earnings, Dec. 31, 2002	$5,814,500

Point: If a year 2000 error is discovered in 2001, the company records the adjustment in 2001. But if the retained earnings statement includes 2000 and 2001 figures, the adjustment is not reported as a correction of 2001's beginning balance. Instead, the statement reports the correct amount of income for 2000, and a note describes the correction.

Point: Accounting for changes in accounting estimates is sometimes criticized as two wrongs to make a right. Consider a change in an asset's useful life. Neither the depreciation before the change nor the depreciation after the change is the amount computed if the revised estimate had been originally selected. Regulators chose this approach to avoid restating prior periods' numbers.

retained earnings (or the statement of changes in stockholders' equity), net of any income tax effects. Prior period adjustments result in changing the beginning balance of retained earnings for events occurring prior to the earliest period reported in the current set of financial statements. To illustrate, assume that CompUS makes an error in a 2000 journal entry for the purchase of land by incorrectly debiting an expense account. When this is discovered in 2002, the statement of retained earnings includes a prior period adjustment, as shown in Exhibit 11.21. This exhibit also shows the usual format of the statement of retained earnings.

Changes in Accounting Estimates

Many items reported in financial statements are based on estimates. Future events are certain to reveal that some of these estimates were inaccurate even when based on the best data available at the time. These inaccuracies are *not* considered errors and are *not* reported as prior period adjustments. Instead, they are identified as **changes in accounting estimates** and are accounted for in current and future periods. To illustrate, we know that depreciation is based on estimated useful lives and salvage values. As time passes and new information becomes available, managers may need to change these estimates and the resulting depreciation expense. These types of changes in accounting estimates are applied in the current and future periods, and do not change prior period reports.

Statement of Changes in Stockholders' Equity

Few companies report a separate statement of retained earnings. Instead, they usually report a statement of changes in stockholders' equity that includes changes in retained earnings. A **statement of changes in stockholders' equity** lists the beginning and ending balances of each equity account and describes the changes that occur during the period. For instance, Nike, Reebok, and Gap report such a statement as shown in Appendix A. The usual format is to provide a column for each component of equity and use the rows to describe events occurring in the period. Exhibit 11.22 shows a condensed statement for WWF.

Exhibit 11.22

Statement of Changes in Stockholders' Equity

WORLD WRESTLING FEDERATION Statement of Changes in Stockholders' Equity					
($ thousands)	Common Stock	Contributed Capital in Excess of Par	Accumulated Other Comprehensive Income (Loss)	Retained Earnings	Total
Balance, April 30, 1999	$567	$ 1	$ (87)	$71,779	$ 72,260
Net (comprehensive) income	—	—	192	58,908	59,100
Initial public offering (net)	115	179,208	—	—	179,323
Stock option charges	—	15,330	—	—	15,330
Other	—	27,996	—	(95,472)	(67,476)
Balance, April 30, 2000	$682	$222,535	$105	$35,215	$258,537

This section explains the computation of, and analysis using, book value per share, dividend yield, and the price-earnings ratio.

Book Value per Share

Case 1: Common Stock (Only) Outstanding. **Book value per common share,** defined in Exhibit 11.23, is the recorded amount of stockholders' equity applicable to *common* shares on a per share basis.

A2 Compute book value and explain its use in analysis.

$$\text{Book value per common share} = \frac{\text{Stockholders' equity applicable to common shares}}{\text{Number of common shares outstanding}}$$

Exhibit 11.23

Book Value per Common Share

To illustrate, we compute the book value per common share for Dillon Snowboards at the end of year 2002 using data in Exhibit 11.4. Dillon has 30,000 outstanding common shares, and the stockholders' equity applicable to common shares is $365,000. Dillon's book value per common share is $12.17, computed as $365,000 divided by 30,000 shares.

Case 2: Common and Preferred Stock Outstanding. To compute book value when both common and preferred shares are outstanding, we must allocate total stockholders' equity between the two types of shares. The **book value per preferred share** is computed first; its computation is shown in Exhibit 11.24.

Point: Book value per share is also referred to as *stockholders' claim to assets on a per share basis.*

Point: Investors often use book value per share when estimating market value per share.

$$\text{Book value per preferred share} = \frac{\text{Stockholders' equity applicable to preferred shares}}{\text{Number of preferred shares outstanding}}$$

Exhibit 11.24

Book Value per Preferred Share

The stockholders' equity applicable to preferred shares equals the preferred share's call price (or par value if the preferred is not callable) plus any cumulative dividends in arrears. The remaining stockholders' equity is the portion applicable to common shares. To illustrate, consider MusicLive's stockholders' equity section in Exhibit 11.25. Its preferred stock is callable at $108 per share, and two years of cumulative preferred dividends are in arrears.

Exhibit 11.25

Stockholders' Equity with Preferred and Common Stock

Stockholders' Equity	
Preferred stock—$100 par value, 7% cumulative, 2,000 shares authorized, 1,000 shares issued and outstanding	$100,000
Common stock—$25 par value, 12,000 shares authorized, 10,000 shares issued and outstanding	250,000
Contributed capital in excess of par value, common stock	15,000
Retained earnings	82,000
Total stockholders' equity	$447,000

The book value of both preferred and common shares for MusicLive is computed in Exhibit 11.26. Notice that we must first allocate equity to preferred shares before we compute the book value of common shares.

Exhibit 11.26

Computing Book Value per Preferred and Common Share

Total stockholders' equity		$447,000
Less equity applicable to preferred shares		
Call price (1,000 shares × $108)	$108,000	
Dividends in arrears ($100,000 × 7% × 2 years)	14,000	(122,000)
Equity applicable to common shares		$325,000
Book value per preferred share ($122,000/1,000 shares)		**$ 122.00**
Book value per common share ($325,000/10,000 shares)		**$ 32.50**

Point: If preferred shares have no call price, the book value of preferred shares is lower and of common shares is higher (because par value is less than call price).

Book value per share reflects the value of
each share if a company is liquidated at
amounts reported on the balance sheet. Book
value is also the starting point in many stock
valuation models. Other uses include merger
negotiations, price setting for public utilities,
and loan contracts. The main limitation in using book value is the potential difference be-
tween recorded value and market value for both assets and liabilities. Investors often adjust
their analysis for estimates of these differences.

Dividend Yield

A3 Compute dividend yield
and explain its use in
analysis.

Investors buy shares of a company's stock in anticipation of receiving a return from either
or both cash dividends and stock price increases. Stocks that pay large dividends on a regular basis, called *income stocks,* are attractive to investors who want recurring cash flows
from their investments. In contrast, some stocks pay little or no dividends but are still attractive to investors because of their expected stock price increases. The stocks of companies that distribute little or no cash but use their cash to finance expansion are called *growth
stocks.* One way to help identify whether a stock is an income stock or a growth stock is to
analyze its dividend yield. **Dividend yield,** defined in Exhibit 11.27, shows the annual
amount of cash dividends distributed to common shares relative to their market value.

Exhibit 11.27

Dividend Yield

$$\text{Dividend yield} = \frac{\textbf{Annual cash dividends per share}}{\textbf{Market value per share}}$$

Dividend yield can be computed for both current and prior periods using data on actual div-
idends and stock prices. It can also be computed for future periods using expected values.
Exhibit 11.28 shows recent dividend and stock price data for Microsoft and Philip Morris.
Dividend yields are also reported.

Exhibit 11.28

Dividend and Stock
Price Information

Company	Cash Dividends per Share	Market Value per Share	Dividend Yield
Microsoft	$0.00	$70	0.0%
Philip Morris	1.92	30	6.4

Point: The *payout ratio* equals
cash dividends declared on common
stock divided by net income. A low
ratio suggests that a company is
retaining earnings for future growth.

We can compare dividend yields to assess the importance of dividends relative to earnings reinvestment for companies' stock values. Dividend yield is zero for Microsoft. Its stock
is classified in the growth stock category. An investor who purchases Microsoft would look
for increases in stock prices (and eventual cash from the sale of stock). Philip Morris has a
dividend yield of 6.4%. Its stock is classed as an income stock, implying that dividends are
an important factor in assessing its value.

Price-Earnings Ratio

A4 Compute price-earnings
ratio and describe its
use in analysis.

Point: The average PE ratio for the
1950–2000 period is about 14.
However, the PE ratio exceeds 16
when inflation is below 3.5%.

A stock's market value is determined by its *expected* future cash flows. A comparison of a
company's EPS and its market value per share reveals information about market expectations. This comparison is traditionally made using a **price-earnings (or PE) ratio,** expressed
as *price earnings, price to earnings,* or *PE.* Some analysts interpret this ratio as what price
the market is willing to pay for a company's current earnings stream. Price-earnings ratios
can differ across companies that have the same earnings because of either higher or lower
expectations of future earnings. The price-earnings ratio is defined in Exhibit 11.29.

Exhibit 11.29

Price-Earnings Ratio

$$\text{Price-earnings ratio} = \frac{\textbf{Market value (price) per share}}{\textbf{Earnings per share}}$$

This ratio is often computed using EPS from the most recent period. However, many users compute this ratio using *expected* EPS for the next period.

Some analysts apply the price-earnings ratio to search for over- or underpriced stocks. Such analysts view stocks with high PE ratios (say, higher than 20 to 25) as more likely to be overpriced and stocks with low PE ratios (say, less than 5 to 8) as more likely to be underpriced. These investors prefer to sell or avoid buying stocks with high PE ratios, and to buy or hold stocks with low PE ratios. However, investment decision making is rarely so simple as to rely on a single ratio. For instance, a stock with a high PE ratio may prove to be a good investment if its earnings continue to increase beyond current expectations. Similarly, a stock with a low PE ratio may prove to be a poor investment if its earnings decline below expectations. As with dividend yield, the price-earnings ratio is important in users' decisions but is only one piece of information.

Point: Average PE ratios for U.S. stocks have increased over the past two decades. Some analysts interpret this as a signal the market is overpriced. But higher ratios may at least partly reflect accounting changes that have reduced reported earnings.

Decision Maker

Manager You plan to invest in one of two companies that you have identified as having identical future prospects. One has a PE of 19 and the other a PE of 25. Which do you invest in? Does it matter if your *personal estimate* of PE for these two companies is 29 as opposed to 22?

Answer—p. 501

Demonstration Problem 1

Barton Corporation began operations on January 1, 2002. The following transactions relating to stockholders' equity occurred in the first two years of the company's operations.

2002

Jan. 1 Authorized the issuance of 2 million shares of $5 par value common stock and 100,000 shares of $100 par value, 10% cumulative, preferred stock.

Jan. 2 Issued 200,000 shares of common stock for $12 cash per share.

Jan. 3 Issued 100,000 shares of common stock in exchange for a building valued at $820,000 and merchandise inventory valued at $380,000.

Jan. 4 Paid $10,000 cash to the company's founders for organization activities.

Jan. 5 Issued 12,000 shares of preferred stock for $110 cash per share.

2003

June 4 Issued 100,000 shares of common stock for $15 cash per share.

Required

1. Prepare journal entries to record these transactions.

2. Prepare the stockholders' equity section of the balance sheet as of December 31, 2002, and December 31, 2003, based on these transactions.

3. Prepare a table showing dividend allocations and dividends per share for 2002 and 2003 assuming Barton declares the following cash dividends: 2002, $50,000; and 2003, $300,000.

4. Prepare the January 2, 2002, journal entry for Barton's issuance of 200,000 shares of common stock for $12 cash per share assuming

   a. Common stock is no-par stock without a stated value.

   b. Common stock is no-par stock with a stated value of $10 per share.

Planning the Solution

- Record journal entries for the transactions for 2002 and 2003.
- Determine the balances for the 2002 and 2003 equity accounts for the balance sheet.
- Prepare the contributed capital portion of the 2002 and 2003 balance sheets.
- Prepare a table similar to Exhibit 11.8 showing dividend allocations for 2002 and 2003.
- Record the issuance of common stock under both specifications of no-par stock.

Solution to Demonstration Problem 1

1. Journal entries:

2002				
Jan. 2	Cash		2,400,000	
		Common Stock, $5 Par Value		1,000,000
		Contributed Capital in Excess of Par Value, Common Stock		1,400,000
	Issued 200,000 shares of common stock.			
Jan. 3	Building		820,000	
	Merchandise Inventory		380,000	
		Common Stock, $5 Par Value		500,000
		Contributed Capital in Excess of Par Value, Common Stock		700,000
	Issued 100,000 shares of common stock.			
Jan. 4	Organization Expenses		10,000	
		Cash		10,000
	Paid founders for organization costs.			
Jan. 5	Cash		1,320,000	
		Preferred Stock, $100 Par Value		1,200,000
		Contributed Capital in Excess of Par Value, Preferred Stock		120,000
	Issued 12,000 shares of preferred stock.			
2003				
June 4	Cash		1,500,000	
		Common Stock, $5 Par Value		500,000
		Contributed Capital in Excess of Par Value, Common Stock		1,000,000
	Issued 100,000 shares of common stock.			

2. Balance sheet presentations:

	As of December 31	
	2002	**2003**
Stockholders' Equity		
Contributed capital:		
Preferred stock—$100 par value, 10% cumulative, 100,000 shares authorized, 12,000 shares issued and outstanding	$1,200,000	$1,200,000
Contributed capital in excess of par value, preferred stock	120,000	120,000
Total capital contributed by preferred stockholders	1,320,000	1,320,000
Common stock—$5 par value, 2,000,000 shares authorized, 300,000 shares issued and outstanding in 2002, and 400,000 shares issued and outstanding in 2003	1,500,000	2,000,000
Contributed capital in excess of par value, common stock	2,100,000	3,100,000
Total capital contributed by common stockholders	3,600,000	5,100,000
Total contributed capital	$4,920,000	$6,420,000

3. Dividend allocation table:

	Common	Preferred
2002 ($50,000)		
Preferred—current year (12,000 shares × $10 = $120,000)	$ 0	$ 50,000
Common—remainder (300,000 shares outstanding)	0	0
Total for the year	$ 0	$ 50,000
2003 ($300,000)		
Preferred—dividend in arrears from 2002 ($120,000 − $50,000)	$ 0	$ 70,000
Preferred—current year	0	120,000
Common—remainder (400,000 shares outstanding)	110,000	0
Total for the year	$110,000	$190,000
Dividends per share		
2002	$ 0.00	$ 4.17
2003	$ 0.28	$ 15.83

4. Journal entries:

a. For 2002:

Jan. 2	Cash	2,400,000	
	Common Stock, No-Par Value		2,400,000
	Issued 200,000 shares of no-par common stock at $12 per share.		

b. For 2002:

Jan. 2	Cash	2,400,000	
	Common Stock, $10 Stated Value		2,000,000
	Contributed Capital in Excess of Stated Value, Common Stock		400,000
	Issued 200,000 shares of $10 stated value common stock at $12 per share.		

Demonstration Problem 2

Precision Company began year 2002 with the following balances in its stockholders' equity accounts:

Common stock—$10 par, 500,000 shares authorized, 200,000 shares issued and outstanding	$2,000,000
Contributed capital in excess of par, common stock	1,000,000
Retained earnings	5,000,000
Total	$8,000,000

All outstanding common stock was issued for $15 per share when the company was created.

Part 1

Prepare journal entries to account for the following transactions during year 2002:

Jan. 10   The board declared a $0.10 cash dividend per share to shareholders of record Jan. 28.
Feb. 15   Paid the cash dividend declared on January 10.
Mar. 31   Declared a 20% stock dividend. The market value of the stock is $18 per share.
May 1   Distributed the stock dividend declared on March 31.
July 1   Purchased 30,000 shares of treasury stock at $20 per share.
Sept. 1   Sold 20,000 treasury shares at $26 cash per share.
Dec. 1   Sold the remaining 10,000 shares of treasury stock at $7 cash per share.

Part 2

Use the following information to prepare a complete income statement for year 2002, including EPS results for each category of income for Precision (a technology consulting company).

Cumulative effect of a change in depreciation method (net of tax benefit)	$ (136,500)
Operating expenses related to continuing operations	(2,072,500)
Extraordinary gain on debt retirement (net of tax)	182,000
Gain on disposal of discontinued segment's assets (net of tax)	29,000
Gain on sale of long-term investments	400,000
Loss from operating discontinued segment (net of tax benefit)	(120,000)
Income taxes on income from continuing operations	(225,000)
Prior period adjustment for error (net of tax benefit)	(75,000)
Net sales	4,140,000
Loss on sale of equipment	(650,000)

Planning the Solution

* Calculate the total cash dividend to record by multiplying the cash dividend declared by the number of shares as of the date of record.
* Decide whether the stock dividend is a small or large dividend. Then analyze each event to determine the accounts affected and the appropriate amounts to be recorded.
* Based on shares of outstanding stock at the beginning of the year and the transactions during the year, compute the weighted-average number of outstanding shares for the year.
* Assign each listed item to an appropriate income statement category.
* Prepare an income statement similar to Exhibit 11.16, including EPS results.

Solution to Demonstration Problem 2

Part 1

Jan. 10	Retained Earnings	20,000	
	Common Dividend Payable		20,000
	Declared a $0.10 per share cash dividend.		
Feb. 15	Common Dividend Payable	20,000	
	Cash		20,000
	Paid $0.10 per share cash dividend.		
Mar. 31	Retained Earnings	720,000	
	Common Stock Dividend Distributable		400,000
	Contributed Capital in Excess of Par Value, Common Stock		320,000
	Declared a small stock dividend of 20% or 40,000 shares; market value is $18 per share.		
May 1	Common Stock Dividend Distributable	400,000	
	Common Stock		400,000
	Distributed 40,000 shares of common stock.		
July 1	Treasury Stock, Common	600,000	
	Cash		600,000
	Purchased 30,000 common shares at $20 per share.		
Sept. 1	Cash	520,000	
	Treasury Stock, Common		400,000
	Contributed Capital, Treasury Stock		120,000
	Sold 20,000 treasury shares at $26 per share.		

Dec. 1	Cash	70,000	
	Contributed Capital, Treasury Stock	120,000	
	Retained Earnings	10,000	
	Treasury Stock, Common		200,000
	Sold 10,000 treasury shares at $7 per share.		

Part 2

Compute the weighted-average number of outstanding common shares:

Time Period	Outstanding Shares		Effect of Dividend		Fraction of Year		Weighted Average
January–April	200,000	×	1.2	×	4/12	=	80,000
May–June	240,000*	×	1	×	2/12	=	40,000
July–August	210,000	×	1	×	2/12	=	35,000
September–November	230,000	×	1	×	3/12	=	57,500
December	240,000	×	1	×	1/12	=	20,000
Weighted-average shares outstanding ...							**232,500**

* 200,000 shares × 1.2 = 240,000 shares.

PRECISION COMPANY Income Statement For Year Ended December 31, 2002		
Net sales		$4,140,000
Operating expenses		(2,072,500)
Other gains (losses)		
Gain on sale of long-term investments		400,000
Loss on sale of equipment		(650,000)
Income from continuing operations before taxes		1,817,500
Income taxes expense		225,000
Income from continuing operations		1,592,500
Discontinued segment		
Loss from operating discontinued segment (net of tax benefit)	$(120,000)	
Gain on disposal of discontinued segment (net of tax)	29,000	(91,000)
Income before extraordinary item and cumulative effect of a change in accounting principle		1,501,500
Extraordinary item		
Extraordinary gain on debt retirement (net of tax)		182,000
Cumulative effect of a change in accounting principle		
Cumulative effect of change in deprec. method (net of tax benefit)		(136,500)
Net income		$1,547,000
Earnings per share (232,500 weighted-average shares):		
Income from continuing operations		$ 6.85
Discontinued operations		(0.39)
Income before extraordinary item and cumulative effect of change in accounting principle		6.46
Extraordinary item		0.78
Cumulative effect of change in accounting principle		(0.59)
Net income (basic earnings per share)		$ 6.65

Summary

C1 Identify characteristics of corporations and their organization. Corporations are legal entities whose stockholders are not liable for its debts. Stock is easily transferred, and the life of a corporation does not end with the incapacity of a stockholder. A corporation acts through its agents, who are its officers and managers. Corporations are regulated and subject to income taxes.

C2 Describe the components of stockholders' equity. Authorized stock is the stock that a corporation's charter authorizes it to sell. Issued stock is the portion of authorized shares sold. Par value stock is a value per share assigned by the charter. No-par value stock is stock *not* assigned a value per share by the charter. Stated value stock is no-par stock assigned a value per share by the directors. Stockholders' equity is made up of (1) contributed capital and (2) retained earnings. Contributed capital consists of funds raised by stock issuances. Retained earnings consists of cumulative net income (losses) not distributed.

C3 Explain characteristics of common and preferred stock. Preferred stock has a priority (or senior status) relative to common stock in one or more areas. The usual areas include (1) dividends and (2) assets in case of liquidation. Preferred stock usually does not carry voting rights and can be convertible or callable. Convertibility permits the holder to convert preferred to common. Callability permits the issuer to buy back preferred stock under specified conditions.

C4 Explain the form and content of a complete income statement. An income statement has five *potential* sections: (1) continuing operations, (2) discontinued segments, (3) extraordinary items, (4) changes in accounting, and (5) earnings per share.

C5 Explain the items reported in retained earnings. Many companies face statutory and contractual restrictions on retained earnings. Corporations can voluntarily appropriate retained earnings to inform others about their disposition. Prior period adjustments are corrections of errors in prior financial statements.

A1 Compute earnings per share and describe this ratio's use. A company with a simple capital structure computes basic EPS by dividing net income less any preferred dividends by the weighted-average number of outstanding common shares. A company with a complex capital structure must usually report both basic and diluted EPS.

A2 Compute book value and explain its use in analysis. Book value per common share is equity applicable to common shares divided by the number of outstanding common shares. Book value per preferred share is equity applicable to preferred shares divided by the number of outstanding preferred shares.

A3 Compute dividend yield and explain its use in analysis. Dividend yield is the ratio of a stock's annual cash dividends per share to its market value (price) per share. Dividend yield can be compared with the yield of other companies to determine whether the stock is expected to be an income or growth stock.

A4 Compute price-earnings ratio and describe its use in analysis. A common stock's price-earnings (PE) ratio is computed by dividing the stock's market value (price) per share by its EPS. A stock's PE is based on expectations that may prove to be better or worse than eventual performance.

P1 Record the issuance of corporate stock. When stock is issued, its par or stated value is credited to the stock account and any excess is credited to a separate contributed capital account. If a stock has neither par nor stated value, the entire proceeds are credited to the stock account. Stockholders must contribute assets equal to minimum legal capital or be potentially liable for the deficiency.

P2 Distribute dividends between common stock and preferred stock. Preferred stockholders usually hold the right to dividend distributions before common stockholders. When preferred stock is cumulative and in arrears, the amount in arrears must be distributed to preferred before any dividends are distributed to common.

P3 Record transactions involving cash dividends. Cash dividends involve three events. On the date of declaration, the directors bind the company to pay the dividend. A dividend declaration reduces retained earnings and creates a current liability. On the date of record, recipients of the dividend are identified. On the date of payment, cash is paid to stockholders and the current liability is removed.

P4 Account for stock dividends and stock splits. Neither a stock dividend nor a stock split alters the value of the company. However, the value of each share is less due to the distribution of additional shares. The distribution of additional shares is according to individual stockholders' ownership percent. Small stock dividends ($\leq 25\%$) are recorded by capitalizing retained earnings equal to the market value of distributed shares. Large stock dividends ($> 25\%$) are recorded by capitalizing retained earnings equal to the par or stated value of distributed shares. Stock splits do not yield journal entries but do yield changes in the description of stock.

P5 Record purchases and sales of treasury stock and the retirement of stock. When a corporation purchases its own previously issued stock, it debits the cost of these shares to Treasury Stock. Treasury Stock is subtracted from equity in the balance sheet. If treasury stock is reissued, any proceeds in excess of cost are credited to Contributed Capital, Treasury Stock. If the proceeds are less than cost, they are debited to Contributed Capital, Treasury Stock to the extent a credit balance exists. Any remaining amount is debited to Retained Earnings. When stock is retired, all accounts related to the stock are removed.

Guidance Answers to **Decision Maker** and **Decision Ethics**

Concert Organizer   You have two basic options: (1) different classes of common stock or (2) common and preferred stock. Your objective is to issue stock to yourself that has all or a majority of the voting power. The other class of stock you issue would carry limited or no voting rights. In this way, you maintain control and are able to raise the necessary funds.

Entrepreneur   The 50% stock dividend provides you no direct income. A stock dividend often reveals management's optimistic expectations about the future and can improve a stock's marketability by making it affordable to more investors. Accordingly, a stock dividend usually reflects "good news" and because of this it likely increases (slightly) the market value for your stock.

Small Business Owner   The frost loss is probably not extraordinary. Jacksonville experiences enough recurring frost damage to make it difficult to argue this event is both unusual and infrequent. Still, you want to highlight the frost loss and hope the bank views this uncommon event separately from continuing operations.

Director   This case deals with insider trading in a company's stock. The ethical conflict is between your director responsibilities to stockholders (and the public) and your interest in increasing personal wealth from the options. If information about the new con-

tract is kept private until after the option plan is approved and the options are priced, you are likely to make more money. (*Note:* Insider trading laws may make nondisclosure in this case a crime.) You should raise ethical and legal concerns to the board. You might also consider whether staying on the board of this company is proper since it appears there was some intent to deceive outsiders.

Investor   Book value reflects recorded values. Ride's book value is $4 per common share. Stock price reflects the market's expectation of net asset value (both tangible and intangible items). Ride's market value is about $7 per common share. Comparing these figures suggests Ride's market value of net assets is higher than its recorded values (by an amount of $7 versus $4 per share).

Manager   Since one company requires a payment of $19 for each $1 of earnings, and the other requires $25, you should purchase the stock with the PE of 19—it is a better deal given identical prospects. You should make sure these companies' earnings computations are roughly the same—for example, no extraordinary items, unusual events, and so forth. Also, your PE estimates for these companies do matter. If you are willing to pay $29 for each $1 of earnings for these companies, both are solid investments because you obviously expect both to exceed current market expectations.

Guidance Answers to **Quick Checks**

1. (*b*)

2. A corporation pays taxes on its income, and its stockholders pay personal income taxes on any cash dividends received from the corporation.

3. A proxy is a legal document used to transfer a stockholder's right to vote to another person.

4. (*a*)

5. A stock premium is an amount in excess of par (or stated) value paid by purchasers of newly issued stock.

6. Minimum legal capital intends to protect creditors of a corporation by constraining a corporation from excessive payments to stockholders.

7. Typically, preferred stock has a preference in receipt of dividends and distribution of assets.

8. (*a*)

9. (*b*)

Total cash dividend	$288,000
To preferred shareholders	135,000*
Remainder to common shareholders . . .	$153,000

* 9,000 × $50 × 10% × 3 years = $135,000.

10. Common Dividend Payable is a current liability account.

11. The date of declaration, date of record, and date of payment.

12. A dividend is a legal liability at the date of declaration and it is also recorded as a liability on the date of declaration.

13. A stock dividend does not transfer assets to stockholders, but it does require retained earnings to be capitalized (reduced).

14. A small stock dividend is 25% or less of the previous outstanding shares. A large stock dividend is more than 25%.

15. Retained earnings equal to the distributable shares' market value should be capitalized for a small stock dividend.

16. (*b*)

17. No. The shares are an investment for Southern Co. and are issued and outstanding shares for Northern Corp.

18. Treasury stock does not affect the number of authorized or issued shares, but it reduces the outstanding shares.

19. (*a*)

20. (*b*)

21. The five major sections are income from continuing operations, discontinued segments, extraordinary items, cumulative effects of changes in accounting principles, and earnings per share.

22. (*c*)

23. (*a*) Weighted-average shares: $(25,000 \times 6/12) + (20,000 \times 6/12) = 22,500$. Earnings per share: $(\$250,000 - \$70,000)/22,500 = \$8$.

24. The number of shares previously outstanding is retroactively restated to reflect the stock split or stock dividend as if it occurred at the beginning of the period.

25. Basic EPS and diluted EPS.

Glossary

Appropriated retained earnings Retained earnings reported separately to inform stockholders of funding needs. (p. 491)

Authorized stock Total amount of stock that a corporation's charter authorizes it to sell. (p. 470)

Basic earnings per share Net income less preferred dividends divided by weighted-average common shares outstanding. (p. 489)

Book value per common share Recorded amount of equity applicable to common shares divided by the number of common shares outstanding. (p. 493)

Book value per preferred share Equity applicable to preferred shares (equals its call price [or par value if it is not callable] plus any cumulative dividends in arrears) divided by the number of preferred shares outstanding. (p. 493)

Callable preferred stock Preferred stock that the issuing corporation, at its option, may retire by paying the call price plus any dividends in arrears. (p. 477)

Call price Amount that must be paid to call and retire a preferred share. (p. 477)

Capital stock General term referring to a corporation's stock used in obtaining capital (owner financing). (p. 469)

Changes in accounting estimates Revisions to previous estimates of future events and outcomes; accounted for in current and future periods. (p. 492)

Common stock A corporation's basic stock; usually carries voting rights for controlling the corporation. (p. 468)

Complex capital structure Capital structure that includes outstanding rights or options to purchase common stock, or securities that are convertible into common stock. (p. 490)

Contributed capital Total amount of cash and other assets received from stockholders in exchange for stock. (p. 471)

Convertible preferred stock Preferred stock with an option to exchange it for common stock at a specified rate. (p. 476)

Contributed capital in excess of par value Difference between the par value of stock and its issue price when issued at a price above par. (p. 472)

Corporation Entity created by law and separate from its owners. (p. 466)

Cumulative preferred stock Preferred stock on which undeclared dividends accumulate until paid; common stockholders cannot receive dividends until cumulative dividends are paid. (p. 475)

Date of declaration Date the directors vote to pay a dividend. (p. 478)

Date of payment Date the corporation makes the dividend payment. (p. 478)

Date of record Date specified by directors for identifying stockholders to receive dividends. (p. 478)

Diluted earnings per share Earnings per share calculation that requires dilutive securities be added to the denominator of the basic EPS calculation. (p. 490)

Dilutive securities Securities having the potential to increase common shares outstanding; examples are options, rights, and convertible bonds and preferred stock. (p. 490)

Discount on stock Difference between the par value of stock and its issue price when issued at a price below par value. (p. 472)

Dividend in arrears Unpaid dividend on cumulative preferred stock; must be paid before any regular dividends on preferred stock and before any dividends on common stock. (p. 475)

Dividend yield Ratio of the annual amount of cash dividends distributed to common shareholders relative to the common stock's market value (price). (p. 494)

Earnings per share (EPS) Amount of income earned by each share of a company's outstanding common stock; also called *net income per share*. (p. 489)

Extraordinary gains or losses Gains or losses reported separately from continuing operations because they are both unusual and infrequent. (p. 486)

Financial leverage Earning a higher return on equity by paying dividends on preferred stock or interest on debt at a rate lower than the return earned with the assets from issuing preferred stock or debt. (p. 477)

Infrequent gain or loss Gain or loss not expected to recur, given the operating environment of the business. (p. 486)

Large stock dividend Stock dividend that is more than 25% of the previously outstanding shares. (p. 480)

Liquidating cash dividend Distribution of assets that returns part of the original investment to stockholders; charged to contributed capital accounts. (p. 479)

Market value per share Price at which stock is bought or sold. (p. 470)

Minimum legal capital Amount of assets defined by law that stockholders must (potentially) invest in a corporation; usually defined as par value of the stock; intended to protect creditors. (p. 470)

Noncumulative preferred stock Preferred stock on which the right to receive dividends is lost for any period when dividends are not declared. (p. 475)

Nonparticipating preferred stock Preferred stock on which dividends are limited to a maximum amount each year. (p. 476)

No-par value stock Stock class that has not been assigned a par value by the corporate charter. (p. 471)

Organization expenses (costs) Costs such as legal fees and promoter fees to bring an entity into existence. (p. 467)

Participating preferred stock Preferred stock that shares with common stockholders any dividends paid in excess of the percent stated on preferred stock. (p. 476)

Par value Value assigned a share of stock by the corporate charter when the stock is authorized. (p. 470)

Par value stock Class of stock assigned a par value by the corporate charter. (p. 470)

Preemptive right Stockholders' right to maintain their proportionate interest in a corporation with any additional shares issued. (p. 469)

Preferred stock Stock with a priority status over common stockholders in one or more ways, such as paying dividends or distributing assets. (p. 474)

Premium on stock See *contributed capital in excess of par*. (p. 472)

Price-earnings (PE) ratio Ratio of a company's current market value per share to its earnings per share. (p. 494)

Prior period adjustment Correction of an error in a prior year that is reported in the statement of retained earnings (or statement of changes in stockholders' equity) net of any income tax effects. (p. 491)

Proxy Legal document giving a stockholder's agent the power to exercise the stockholder's voting rights. (p. 468)

Restricted retained earnings Retained earnings not available for dividends because of legal or contractual limitations. (p. 491)

Retained earnings Cumulative income less cumulative losses and dividends. (p. 471)

Retained earnings deficit Debit (abnormal) balance in Retained Earnings: occurs when cumulative losses and dividends exceed cumulative income. (p. 479).

Reverse stock split Occurs when a corporation calls in its stock and replaces each share with less than one new share; increases both market value per share and any par or stated value per share. (p. 482)

Segment of a business Part of operations that serves a line of business or class of customers and that has assets, liabilities, and operating results distinguishable from other parts. (p. 486)

Simple capital structure Capital structure that consists of only common stock and nonconvertible preferred stock; consists of no dilutive securities. (p. 490)

Small stock dividend Stock dividend that is 25% or less of a corporation's previously outstanding shares. (p. 480)

Stated value stock No-par stock assigned a stated value per share; this amount is recorded in the stock account when the stock is issued. (p. 471)

Statement of changes in stockholders' equity Financial statement that lists the beginning and ending balances of each major equity account and describes all changes in those accounts. (p. 492)

Stock dividend Corporation's distribution

of its own stock to its stockholders without the receipt of any payment. (p. 479)

Stockholders' equity A corporation's equity; also called *shareholders' equity* or *corporate capital.* (p. 471)

Stock options Rights to purchase common stock at a fixed price over a specified period of time. (p. 490)

Stock split Occurs when a corporation calls in its stock and replaces each share with more than one new share; decreases both the market value per share and any par or stated value per share. (p. 482)

Stock subscription Investor's contractual commitment to purchase unissued shares at future dates and prices. (p. 474)

Treasury stock Corporation's own stock that it reacquired and still holds. (p. 483)

Unusual gain or loss Gain or loss that is abnormal or unrelated to the company's ordinary activities and environment. (p. 486)

Questions

1. What are organization expenses? List examples.
2. How are organization expenses reported?
3. Who is responsible for directing a corporation's affairs?
4. What is the preemptive right of common stockholders?
5. List the general rights of common stockholders.
6. Why would an investor find convertible preferred stock attractive?
7. What is the difference between the par value and the call price of a share of preferred stock?
8. Identify and explain the importance of the three dates relevant to corporate dividends.
9. Why is the term *liquidating dividend* used to describe cash dividends debited against contributed capital accounts?
10. How does declaring a stock dividend affect the corporation's assets, liabilities, and total equity? What effects does the eventual distribution of the stock have?
11. What is the difference between a stock dividend and a stock split?
12. Courts have ruled that a stock dividend is not taxable income to stockholders. What justifies this decision?
13. How does the purchase of treasury stock affect the purchaser's assets and total equity?
14. Why do laws place limits on treasury stock purchases?
15. Where on the income statement does a company report an unusual gain not expected to occur more often than once every two years?

16. After taking five years of straight-line depreciation expense for an asset that was expected to have an eight-year useful life, a company decides that the asset will last six more years. Is this decision a change in accounting principles? How do the financial statements describe this change?
17. How are EPS results computed for a corporation with a simple capital structure?
18. Review the balance sheet for Nike in Appendix A and determine the classes of stock that it has issued.
19. Refer to the financial statements for Nike in Appendix A. What cash amount is paid to purchase treasury stock for the year ended May 31, 2000? May 31, 1999?
20. Refer to the balance sheet for Reebok in Appendix A. What is the par value of its common stock? Suggest a rationale for the amount of par value it assigned.
21. Refer to the financial statements for Reebok in Appendix A. How many treasury stock shares does Reebok report as of December 31, 1999? Compute the average cost per treasury share.
22. Refer to the financial statements for Gap in Appendix A. Was Gap a net seller or net purchaser of treasury stock for the fiscal year ended May 31, 2000? Explain.
23. What steps did Vince McMahon need to take to receive a corporate charter for WWF?

QUICK STUDY

QS 11-1

Characteristics of corporations

C1

Of the following statements, which are true for the corporate form of organization?
1. It is a separate legal entity.
2. Ownership rights cannot be easily transferred.
3. Owners are not agents of the corporation.
4. Capital is more easily accumulated than with most other forms of organization.
5. It has a limited life.
6. Owners have unlimited liability for corporate debts.
7. Distributed income is usually taxed twice.

QS 11-2

Issuance of common stock   P1

Prepare the journal entry to record each separate transaction. (*a*) On March 1, DVD Co. issues 42,500 shares of $4 par value common stock for $297,500 cash. (*b*) On April 1, GT Co. issues no-par value common stock for $70,000 cash. (*c*) On April 6, MTV issues 2,000 shares of $25 par value common stock for $45,000 of inventory, $145,000 of machinery, and acceptance of a $94,000 note payable.

QS 11-3

Dividend allocation between classes of shareholders   P2

Harmon Company's stockholders' equity includes 80,000 shares of $5 par value, 8% cumulative preferred stock and 250,000 shares of $1 par value common stock. Harmon did not declare any dividends in the prior year and now declares and pays a $110,000 cash dividend in the current year. Determine the amount distributed to each class of stockholders for this two-year-old company.

QS 11-4

Accounting for cash dividends   P3

Prepare journal entries to record the following transactions for Delta Corporation:

May 15   Declared a $54,000 cash dividend payable to common stockholders.
July 31   Paid the dividend declared on May 15.

QS 11-5

Accounting for small stock dividend

C2 P4

The stockholders' equity section of Roanoke Company's balance sheet as of April 1 follows. On April 2, Roanoke declares and distributes a 10% stock dividend. The stock's per share market value on April 2 is $20. Prepare the stockholders' equity section immediately after the stock dividend.

Common stock—$5 par value, 375,000 shares authorized, 200,000 shares issued and outstanding	$1,000,000
Contributed capital in excess of par value, common stock	600,000
Total contributed capital	$1,600,000
Retained earnings	833,000
Total stockholders' equity	$2,433,000

QS 11-6

Purchase and sale of treasury stock   P5

On May 3, Cypher Corporation purchased 4,000 shares of its own stock for $36,000 cash. On November 4, Cypher reissued 850 shares of this treasury stock for $8,500. Prepare the May 3 and November 4 journal entries to record Cypher's purchase and reissuance of treasury stock.

QS 11-7

Accounting for changes in estimates; error adjustments

C4 C5

Answer the following questions related to a company's activities for the current year:
1. A review of the notes payable files discovers that three years ago the company reported the entire amount of a payment (principal and interest) on an installment note payable as interest expense. This mistake had a material effect on the amount of income in that year. How should the correction be reported in the current year financial statements?
2. After using an expected useful life of seven years and no salvage value to depreciate its office equipment over the preceding three years, the company decided early this year that the equipment will last only two more years. How should the effects of this decision be reported in the current-year financial statements?

QS 11-8

Basic earnings per share   A1

Chastain Company earned a net income of $900,000 this year. The number of common shares outstanding during the entire year was 400,000, and preferred shareholders received a cash dividend totaling $20,000. Compute Chastain Company's basic earnings per share.

On January 1, Ventura Company had 200,000 shares of common stock outstanding. On February 1, it issued 40,000 additional shares of common stock. On June 1, it issued another 80,000 shares of common stock. Compute Ventura's weighted-average shares outstanding for the calendar-year.

QS 11-9
Weighted-average A1
shares outstanding

On January 1, Benton Company had 300,000 shares of common stock outstanding. On April 1, it purchased 24,000 treasury shares and on June 2, it declared a 10% stock dividend. Compute Benton's weighted-average shares outstanding for the calendar-year.

QS 11-10
Weighted-average A1 **P4**
shares outstanding

The stockholders' equity section of Aurora Company's balance sheet follows. The preferred stock's call price is $40. Determine the book value per share of the common stock.

QS 11-11
Book value per common share

A2

Preferred stock—5% cumulative, $10 par value, 20,000 shares authorized, issued and outstanding	$ 200,000
Common stock—$5 par value, 200,000 shares authorized, 150,000 shares issued and outstanding	750,000
Retained earnings	890,000
Total stockholders' equity	$1,840,000

Fiva Company expects to pay a $2.30 per share cash dividend this year on its common stock. The current market value of Fiva stock is $32.50 per share. Compute the expected dividend yield on the Fiva stock. Would you classify the Fiva stock as a growth or an income stock?

QS 11-12
Dividend yield   A3

Compute Pax Company's price-earnings ratio if its common stock has a market value of $32.60 per share and its EPS is $3.95. Would an analyst likely consider this stock as potentially over- or underpriced?

QS 11-13
Price-earnings ratio A4

Describe how each of the following characteristics of organizations applies to corporations.

EXERCISES

1. Owners' authority and control	5. Duration of life
2. Ease of formation	6. Owners' liability
3. Transferability of ownership	7. Legal status
4. Ability to raise large capital amounts	8. Tax status of income

Exercise 11-1
Characteristics of C1
corporations

HiLife Corporation issues 19,000 shares of its common stock for $152,000 cash on February 20. Prepare journal entries to record this event under each of the following separate situations:

Exercise 11-2
Accounting for par and no-par stock issuances

P1

1. The stock has neither par nor stated value.
2. The stock has a $2 par value.
3. The stock has a $5 stated value.

Prepare journal entries to record the following four separate issuances of stock:

Exercise 11-3
Recording stock issuances

P1

1. Two thousand shares of no-par common stock are issued to the corporation's promoters in exchange for their efforts, estimated to be worth $40,000. The stock has no stated value.
2. Two thousand shares of no-par common stock are issued to the corporation's promoters in exchange for their efforts, estimated to be worth $40,000. The stock has a $1 per share stated value.
3. Four thousand shares of $5 par value common stock are issued for $35,000 cash.
4. One thousand shares of $50 par value preferred stock are issued for $60,000 cash.

Exercise 11-4

Identifying characteristics of preferred stock

C2 C3

Match each description 1 through 6 with the characteristic of preferred stock that it best describes by writing the letter of the characteristic in the blank next to each description.

A. Callable   **B.** Convertible   **C.** Cumulative
D. Noncumulative   **E.** Nonparticipating   **F.** Participating

____ **1.** Holders of the stock are not entitled to receive dividends in excess of the stated rate.

____ **2.** Holders of the stock lose any dividends that are not declared in the current year.

____ **3.** Holders of the stock are entitled to receive current and all past dividends before common stockholders receive any dividends.

____ **4.** Holders of this stock can exchange it for shares of common stock.

____ **5.** The issuing corporation can retire the stock by paying a prespecified price.

____ **6.** Holders of the stock can receive dividends exceeding the stated rate under certain conditions.

Exercise 11-5

Dividends on common and noncumulative preferred stock

P2

Citishop's outstanding stock consists of (a) 80,000 shares of noncumulative 7.5% preferred stock with a $5 par value and (b) 200,000 shares of common stock with a $1 par value. During its first four years of operation, the corporation declared and paid the following cash dividends:

2002	$ 20,000
2003	28,000
2004	200,000
2005	350,000

Check Total paid to preferred, $108,000

Determine the amount of dividends paid each year to each of the two classes of stockholders. Also compute the total dividends paid to each class for the four years combined.

Exercise 11-6

Dividends on common and cumulative preferred stock

P2

Use the data in Exercise 11-5 to determine the amount of dividends paid each year to each of the two classes of stockholders assuming that the preferred stock is cumulative. Also determine the total dividends paid to each class for the four years combined.

Exercise 11-7

Stock dividends and splits

P4

On June 30, 2002, American Corporation's common stock is priced at $62 per share before any stock dividend or split, and the stockholders' equity section of its balance sheet appears as follows:

Common stock—$10 par value, 120,000 shares authorized, 50,000 shares issued and outstanding	$ 500,000
Contributed capital in excess of par value, common stock	200,000
Total contributed capital	$ 700,000
Retained earnings	660,000
Total stockholders' equity	$1,360,000

1. Assume that the company declares and immediately distributes a 50% stock dividend. This event is recorded by capitalizing retained earnings equal to the stock's par value. Answer these questions about stockholders' equity as it exists *after* issuing the new shares:

   a. What is the retained earnings balance?

Check (1b) $1,360,000

   b. What is the amount of total stockholders' equity?

   c. How many shares are outstanding?

2. Assume that the company implements a 3-for-2 stock split instead of the stock dividend in part *a*. Answer these questions about stockholders' equity as it exists *after* issuing the new shares:

Check (2a) $660,000

   a. What is the retained earnings balance?

   b. What is the amount of total stockholders' equity?

   c. How many shares are outstanding?

3. Explain the difference, if any, to a stockholder from receiving new shares distributed under a large stock dividend versus a stock split.

The stockholders' equity of Biz.Com at the beginning of the day on February 5 follows:

Common stock—$10 par value, 150,000 shares authorized, 60,000 shares issued and outstanding	$ 600,000
Contributed capital in excess of par value, common stock	425,000
Total contributed capital	$1,025,000
Retained earnings	550,000
Total stockholders' equity	$1,575,000

Exercise 11-8
Stock dividends and per share book values
P4

On February 5, the directors declare a 20% stock dividend distributable on February 28 to the February 15 stockholders of record. The stock's market value is $40 per share on February 5 before the stock dividend. The stock's market value is $33.40 per share on February 28.

1. Prepare entries to record both the dividend declaration and its distribution.
2. One stockholder owned 800 shares on February 5 before the dividend. Compute the book value per share and total book value of this stockholder's shares immediately before and after the stock dividend of February 5.
3. Compute the total market value of the investor's shares in part 2 as of February 5 and February 28.

Check (2) Book value per share: before, $26.25; after, $21.875

On October 10, the stockholders' equity of Perry Systems consists of the following:

Common stock—$10 par value, 72,000 shares authorized, issued, and outstanding	$ 720,000
Contributed capital in excess of par value, common stock	216,000
Total contributed capital	$ 936,000
Retained earnings	864,000
Total stockholders' equity	$1,800,000

Exercise 11-9
Recording and reporting treasury stock transactions
P5

814000

1. Prepare journal entries to record the following transactions for Perry Systems:
   a. Purchased 5,000 shares of its own common stock at $25 per share on October 11.
   b. Sold 1,000 treasury shares on November 1 for $31 cash per share.
   c. Sold all remaining treasury shares on November 25 for $20 cash per share.
2. Explain how Perry's equity section changes after the October 11 treasury stock purchase.

Check (1c) Dr. Retained Earnings, $14,000

In 2002, Piazza Merchandise, Inc., sold its interest in a chain of wholesale outlets, taking the company completely out of the wholesaling business. The company still operates its retail outlets. A listing of the major sections of an income statement follows:

Exercise 11-10
Income statement categories
C4

A. Income (loss) from continuing operations
B. Income (loss) from operating a discontinued segment
C. Gain (loss) on disposal of a discontinued segment
D. Extraordinary gain (loss)
E. Cumulative effect of a change in accounting principle

Indicate where each of the following income-related items for this company appears on its 2002 income statement by writing the letter of the appropriate section in the blank beside each item.

Section	Item	Debit	Credit
_____	1. Net sales		$2,900,000
_____	2. Gain on state's condemnation of company property (net of tax)		230,000
_____	3. Cost of goods sold	$1,480,000	
_____	4. Effect of change from FIFO to LIFO (net of tax)		125,000
_____	5. Income taxes expense	217,000	
_____	6. Depreciation expense	232,500	
_____	7. Gain on sale of wholesale business segment (net of tax)		775,000
_____	8. Loss from operating wholesale business segment (net of tax)	444,000	
_____	9. Salaries expense	640,000	

Exercise 11-11
Income statement C4
presentation

Use the financial data for Piazza Merchandise, Inc., in Exercise 11-10 to prepare its income statement for calendar-year 2002. (Ignore the earnings per share section.)

Exercise 11-12 *d*
Reporting a change in
accounting principle

C4 C5

Fast Tek put an asset costing $450,000 into service on January 1, 2002. Its predicted useful life is six years with an expected salvage value of $45,000. The company uses double-declining-balance depreciation and records $150,000 of depreciation in 2002 and $100,000 of depreciation in 2003. The scheduled depreciation expense for 2004 is $66,667. After consulting with the company's auditors, management decides to change to straight-line depreciation in 2004 without changing either the predicted useful life or salvage value. Under this new method, the annual depreciation expense for this asset is $67,500. This company has a 35% income tax rate.

Check (1) After-tax cumulative
effect, $74,750

1. Prepare a table like Exhibit 11.17 to analyze this change in accounting principle.

2. How much depreciation expense is reported on the company's income statement for this asset in 2004 and in each of the remaining years of its life?

3. What amount is reported on the company's 2004 income statement as the after-tax cumulative effect of the change in accounting principle?

Exercise 11-13
Weighted-average shares and
earnings per share

A1

TSR Company reports $2,700,000 of net income for 2002 and declares $390,000 of cash dividends on its preferred stock for 2002. At the beginning of 2002, the company had 540,000 outstanding shares of common stock. Two events change the number of outstanding common shares during 2002:

May 1   Issued 360,000 common shares for cash.
Nov. 1   Purchased 216,000 shares of its own common stock.

1. What amount of net income is available to common stockholders for 2002?

Check (2) 744,000 shares

2. What is the weighted-average number of common shares outstanding for 2002?

3. What is the company's basic EPS for 2002?

Exercise 11-14
Weighted-average shares and
earnings per share

A1

CT Company reports $960,000 of net income for 2002 and declares $130,000 of dividends on its preferred stock for 2002. At the beginning of 2002, the company had 100,000 outstanding shares of common stock. Three events change the number of outstanding common shares during year 2002.

June 1   Issued 60,000 common shares for cash.
Sept. 1   Purchased 26,000 shares of its own common stock.
Oct. 1   Completed a 3-for-1 stock split.

1. What amount of net income is available to common stockholders for 2002?

Check (2) 379,000 shares

2. What is the weighted-average number of common shares outstanding for 2002?

3. What is the company's basic EPS for 2002?

Exercise 11-15 *d*
Book value per share

A2

The equity section of Tabak Corporation's balance sheet shows the following:

Preferred stock—6% cumulative, $25 par value, $30 call price, 10,000 shares issued and outstanding	$ 250,000
Common stock—$10 par value, 80,000 shares issued and outstanding	800,000
Retained earnings	535,000
Total stockholders' equity	$1,585,000

Determine the book value per share of the preferred and common stock under two separate situations:

Check (1) Book value of common,
$16.06

1. No preferred dividends are in arrears.

2. Three years of preferred dividends are in arrears.

Compute the dividend yield for each of these four separate companies. Which company's stock would probably *not* be classified as an income stock?

Exercise 11-16
Dividend yield computation and interpretation

A3

	Annual Cash	Market Value
Company	Dividend per Share	per Share
1	$16.00	$220.00
2	14.00	136.00
3	4.00	72.00
4	1.00	80.00

Compute the price-earnings ratio for each of these four separate companies. Which stock might an analyst likely investigate as being potentially undervalued by the market?

Exercise 11-17
Price-earnings ratio computation and interpretation

A4

	Earnings	Market Value
Company	per Share	per Share
1	$12.00	$176.00
2	10.00	96.00
3	7.50	94.00
4	50.00	250.00

Context Co. is incorporated at the beginning of this year and engages in a number of transactions. The following journal entries impacted its stockholders' equity during its first year of operations:

PROBLEM SET A

Problem 11-1A
Stockholders' equity transactions and analysis

C2 C3 P1

a.	Cash	300,000	
	Common Stock, $25 Par Value		250,000
	Contributed Capital in Excess of		
	Par Value, Common Stock		50,000
b.	Organization Expenses	150,000	
	Common Stock, $25 Par Value		125,000
	Contributed Capital in Excess of		
	Par Value, Common Stock		25,000
c.	Cash	43,000	
	Accounts Receivable	15,000	
	Building	81,500	
	Notes Payable		59,500
	Common Stock, $25 Par Value		50,000
	Contributed Capital in Excess of		
	Par Value, Common Stock		30,000
d.	Cash	120,000	
	Common Stock, $25 Par Value		75,000
	Contributed Capital in Excess of		
	Par Value, Common Stock		45,000

Required

1. Explain each journal entry *a* through *d*.

2. How many shares of common stock are outstanding at year-end?

Check   (2) 20,000 shares

3. What is the amount of minimum legal capital (based on par value) at year-end?

4. What is the total contributed capital at year-end?

5. What is the book value per share of the common stock at year-end if contributed capital plus retained earnings equals $695,000?

Problem 11-2A

Cash dividends, treasury stock, and statement of retained earnings

C2 C5 P3 P5

Ⓖ

Tetrix Corporation reports the following components of stockholders' equity on December 31, 2001:

Common stock—$10 par value, 100,000 shares authorized, 40,000 shares issued and outstanding	$400,000
Contributed capital in excess of par value, common stock	60,000
Retained earnings	270,000
Total stockholders' equity	$730,000

In year 2002, the following transactions affected its stockholders' equity accounts:

Jan.	1	Purchased 4,000 shares of its own stock at $20 cash per share.
Jan.	5	Directors declared a $2 per share cash dividend payable on Feb. 28 to the Feb. 5 stockholders of record.
Feb.	28	Paid the dividend declared on January 5.
July	6	Sold 1,500 of the treasury shares at $24 cash per share.
Aug.	22	Sold 2,500 of the treasury shares at $17 cash per share.
Sept.	5	Directors declared a $2 per share cash dividend payable on October 28 to the September 25 stockholders of record.
Oct.	28	Paid the dividend declared on September 5.
Dec.	31	Closed the $388,000 credit balance (from net income) in the Income Summary account to Retained Earnings.

Required

1. Prepare journal entries to record these transactions for 2002.

2. Prepare a statement of retained earnings for the year ended December 31, 2002.

3. Prepare the stockholders' equity section of the company's balance sheet as of December 31, 2002.

Problem 11-3A

Equity changes—journal entries and account balances

P3 P4

At September 30, the end of Navstar Company's third quarter, the following stockholders' equity accounts are reported:

Common stock, $12 par value	$360,000
Contributed capital in excess of par value, common stock	90,000
Retained earnings	320,000

In the fourth quarter, the following entries related to its equity accounts are recorded:

Date	Account	Debit	Credit
Oct. 2	Retained Earnings	60,000	
	Common Dividend Payable		60,000
Oct. 25	Common Dividend Payable	60,000	
	Cash		60,000
Oct. 31	Retained Earnings	75,000	
	Common Stock Dividend Distributable		36,000
	Contributed Capital in Excess of Par Value, Common Stock		39,000
Nov. 5	Common Stock Dividend Distributable	36,000	
	Common Stock, $12 Par Value		36,000
Dec. 1	Memo—Change the title of the common stock account to reflect the new par value of $4.		
Dec. 31	Income Summary	210,000	
	Retained Earnings		210,000

Required

1. Explain each journal entry.

2. Complete the following table showing the equity account balances at each indicated date:

	Oct. 2	Oct. 25	Oct. 31	Nov. 5	Dec. 1	Dec. 31
Common stock	$____	$____	$____	$____	$____	$____
Common stock dividend distributable	____	____	____	____	____	____
Contributed capital in excess of par, common stock .	____	____	____	____	____	____
Retained earnings	____	____	____	____	____	____
Total equity	$____	$____	$____	$____	$____	$____

Check Total equity: Oct. 2, $710,000; Dec. 31, $920,000

The equity sections from EOG Group's 2002 and 2003 year-end balance sheets follow:

Problem 11-4A
Analysis of changes in stockholders' equity accounts

C5 P3 P4 P5

Stockholders' Equity (December 31, 2002)

Common stock—$4 par value, 100,000 shares authorized, 40,000 shares issued and outstanding	$160,000
Contributed capital in excess of par value, common stock	120,000
Total contributed capital	$280,000
Retained earnings	320,000
Total stockholders' equity	$600,000

Stockholders' Equity (December 31, 2003)

Common stock—$4 par value, 100,000 shares authorized, 47,400 shares issued, 3,000 shares in treasury	$189,600
Contributed capital in excess of par value, common stock	179,200
Total contributed capital	$368,800
Retained earnings ($30,000 restricted by treasury stock)	400,000
	$768,800
Less cost of treasury stock	(30,000)
Total stockholders' equity	$738,800

The following transactions and events affected its equity accounts during year 2003:

Jan. 5	Declared a $0.50 per share cash dividend, date of record January 10.
Mar. 20	Purchased treasury stock for cash.
Apr. 5	Declared a $0.50 per share cash dividend, date of record April 10.
July 5	Declared a $0.50 per share cash dividend, date of record July 10.
July 31	Declared a 20% stock dividend when the stock's market value is $12 per share.
Aug. 14	Issued stock dividend that was declared on July 31.
Oct. 5	Declared a $0.50 per share cash dividend, date of record October 10.

Required

1. How many common shares are outstanding on each cash dividend date?

2. What is the total dollar amount for each of the four cash dividends?

3. What is the amount of the capitalization of retained earnings for the stock dividend?

4. What is the per share cost of the treasury stock purchased?

5. How much net income did the company earn during year 2003?

Check (3) $88,800;

(4) $10;

(5) $248,000

Problem 11-5A
Income statement
computations and format

C4

Selected account balances from the adjusted trial balance for Emulox Corporation as of its calendar year-end December 31, 2002, follow:

	Debit	Credit
a. Interest revenue		$ 14,000
b. Depreciation expense—Equipment	$ 34,000	
c. Loss on sale of equipment	25,850	
d. Accounts payable		44,000
e. Other operating expenses	106,400	
f. Accumulated depreciation—Equipment		71,600
g. Gain from settlement of lawsuit		40,000
h. Cumulative effect of change in accounting principle (pretax)	61,000	
i. Accumulated depreciation—Buildings		174,500
j. Loss from operating a discontinued segment (pretax)	18,250	
k. Gain on retirement of debt (pretax)		29,125
l. Net sales		998,500
m. Depreciation expense—Buildings	52,000	
n. Correction of overstatement of prior year's sales (pretax)	16,000	
o. Gain on sale of discontinued segment's assets (pretax)		34,000
p. Loss from settlement of lawsuit	23,750	
q. Income taxes expense	?	
r. Cost of goods sold	482,500	

Required

Answer each of the following questions by providing supporting computations:

1. Assuming that the company's income tax rate is 30% for all items, identify the tax effects and after-tax amounts of the five items labeled pretax.

2. What is the amount of income from continuing operations before income taxes? What is the amount of the income taxes expense? What is the amount of income from continuing operations?

Check (3) $11,025;

(4) $240,625;

(5) $218,312

3. What is the total amount of after-tax income (loss) associated with the discontinued segment?

4. What is the amount of income (loss) before the extraordinary items and the cumulative effect of changes in accounting principle?

5. What is the amount of net income for the year?

Problem 11-6A
Change in accounting
principle (depreciation)
and its disclosure

C4

On January 1, 2002, Alliance, Inc., purchases equipment costing $300,000 with an expected salvage value of $15,000 at the end of its five-year useful life. Depreciation is allocated to 2002, 2003, and 2004 with the double-declining-balance method. Early in 2005, the company decides to change to the straight-line method to produce more useful financial statements and to be consistent with other firms in the industry.

Required

1. Do generally accepted accounting principles allow Alliance to change depreciation methods in 2005?

Check (2) 2003, $72,000;

(3) 2003, $57,000;

(4) After-tax cumulative
effect, $44,940

2. Prepare a table to show the annual amount of depreciation expense allocated to 2002 through 2004 using the double-declining-balance method.

3. Prepare a table to show the annual amount of depreciation expense that would have been allocated to 2002 through 2004 using the straight-line method.

4. Organize your answers from parts 2 and 3 into a table like Exhibit 11.17 and compute the pretax and after-tax cumulative effects of the accounting change. The company's income tax rate is 30%. (Round to the nearest dollar.)

5. How should the cumulative effect of the change in accounting principle be reported? Does the cumulative effect increase or decrease net income?

6. How much depreciation expense is reported on the company's income statement for 2005?

Analysis Component

7. Assume that Alliance mistakenly treats the change in depreciation methods as a change in accounting estimate. Using your answers from parts 2, 3, and 4, describe the effect of this error on the 2005 financial statements.

The annual income statements for Crestline, Inc., as reported when they were initially published in 2002, 2003, and 2004 follow:

Problem 11-7A
Earnings per share calculation and presentation

C4 A1

Ex

	2002	2003	2004
Net sales	$740,000	$850,000	$825,000
Operating expenses	465,000	520,000	491,000
Income from continuing operations	$275,000	$330,000	$334,000
Loss on discontinued segment	(105,000)	—	—
Income before extraordinary items	$170,000	$330,000	$334,000
Extraordinary gain (loss)	—	66,000	(140,000)
Net income	$170,000	$396,000	$194,000

The company also experienced changes in the number of outstanding shares from the following events:

Outstanding shares on December 31, 2001	80,000
2002	
Treasury stock purchase on April 1	− 8,000
Issuance of new shares on June 30	+ 24,000
10% stock dividend on October 1	+ 9,600
Outstanding shares on December 31, 2002	105,600
2003	
Issuance of new shares on July 1	+ 32,000
Treasury stock purchase on November 1	− 9,600
Outstanding shares on December 31, 2003	128,000
2004	
Issuance of new shares on August 1	+ 40,000
Treasury stock purchase on September 1	− 8,000
3-for-1 stock split on October 1	+320,000
Outstanding shares on December 31, 2004	480,000

Required

1. Compute the weighted average of the common shares outstanding for year 2002.

2. Compute the EPS component amounts to report with the year 2002 income statement for: income from continuing operations, the loss on discontinued segment, and net income.

3. Compute the weighted average of the common shares outstanding for year 2003.

4. Compute the EPS component amounts to report with the year 2003 income statement for: income from continuing operations, the extraordinary gain, and net income.

5. Compute the weighted average of the common shares outstanding for year 2004.

6. Compute the EPS component amounts to report with the year 2004 income statement for: income from continuing operations, the extraordinary loss, and net income.

Analysis Component

7. Explain how you would use the EPS data from part 6 to predict EPS for 2005.

Check (1) 94,600 shares;
(2) EPS, $1.80;

(3) 120,000 shares;
(4) EPS, $3.30

Problem 11-8A
Computation of book values
and dividend allocations

C3 A2 P2

Reliant Corporation's common stock is currently selling on a stock exchange at $85 per share, and its current balance sheet shows the following stockholders' equity section:

Preferred stock—5% cumulative, $___ par value, 1,000 shares authorized, issued, and outstanding	$ 50,000
Common stock—$___ par value, 4,000 shares authorized, issued, and outstanding	80,000
Retained earnings	150,000
Total stockholders' equity	$280,000

Required

1. What is the current market value (price) of this corporation's common stock?
2. What are the par values of the corporation's preferred stock and its common stock?
3. If no dividends are in arrears, what are the book values per share of the preferred stock and the common stock?

Check (4) Book value of common, $56.25;

(5) Book value of common, $55;

(6) Dividends per common share, $1

4. If two years' preferred dividends are in arrears, what are the book values per share of the preferred stock and the common stock?
5. If two years' preferred dividends are in arrears and the preferred stock is callable at $55 per share, what are the book values per share of the preferred stock and the common stock?
6. If two years' preferred dividends are in arrears and the board of directors declares cash dividends of $11,500, what total amount will be paid to the preferred and to the common shareholders? What is the amount of dividends per share for the common stock?

Analysis Component

7. What are some factors that can contribute to a difference between the book value of common stock and its market value (price)?

PROBLEM SET B

Problem 11-1B
Stockholders' equity
transactions and analysis

C2 C3 P1

Knight Company is incorporated at the beginning of this year and engages in a number of transactions. The following journal entries impacted its stockholders' equity during its first year of operations:

a.	Cash	120,000	
	Common Stock, $1 Par Value		3,000
	Contributed Capital in Excess of Par Value, Common Stock		117,000
b.	Organization Expenses	40,000	
	Common Stock, $1 Par Value		1,000
	Contributed Capital in Excess of Par Value, Common Stock		39,000
c.	Cash	13,300	
	Accounts Receivable	8,000	
	Building	37,000	
	Notes Payable		18,300
	Common Stock, $1 Par Value		800
	Contributed Capital in Excess of Par Value, Common Stock		39,200
d.	Cash	60,000	
	Common Stock, $1 Par Value		1,200
	Contributed Capital in Excess of Par Value, Common Stock		58,800

Required

1. Explain each journal entry *a* through *d*.

Check (2) 6,000 shares

2. How many shares of common stock are outstanding at year-end?

3. What is the amount of minimum legal capital (based on par value) at year-end?

4. What is the total contributed capital at year-end?

5. What is the book value per share of the common stock at year-end if contributed capital plus retained earnings equals $283,000?

Check (3) $6,000;
(4) $260,000

Unocol Corp. reports the following components of stockholders' equity on December 31, 2001:

Common stock—$1 par value, 320,000 shares authorized, 200,000 shares issued and outstanding	$ 200,000
Contributed capital in excess of par value, common stock	1,400,000
Retained earnings	2,160,000
Total stockholders' equity	$3,760,000

Problem 11-2B
Cash dividends, treasury stock, and statement of retained earnings

C2 C5 P3 P5

It completed the following transactions related to stockholders' equity in year 2002:

Jan. 10	Purchased 40,000 shares of its own stock at $12 cash per share.
Mar. 2	Directors declared a $1.50 per share cash dividend payable on March 31 to the March 15 stockholders of record.
Mar. 31	Paid the dividend declared on March 2.
Nov. 11	Sold 24,000 of the treasury shares at $13 cash per share.
Nov. 25	Sold 16,000 of the treasury shares at $9.50 cash per share.
Dec. 1	Directors declared a $2.50 per share cash dividend payable on January 2, 2003, to the December 10 stockholders of record.
Dec. 31	Closed the $1,072,000 credit balance (from net income) in the Income Summary account to Retained Earnings.

Required

1. Prepare journal entries to record these transactions for 2002.

2. Prepare a statement of retained earnings for the year ended December 31, 2002.

3. Prepare the stockholders' equity section of the company's balance sheet as of December 31, 2002.

Check (2) Retained earnings, Dec. 31, 2002, $2,476,000

At December 31, the end of Open Channel Communication's third quarter, the following stockholders' equity accounts are reported:

Common stock, $10 par value	$ 960,000
Contributed capital in excess of par value, common stock	384,000
Retained earnings	1,600,000

Problem 11-3B
Equity changes —journal entries and account balances

P3 P4

In the fourth quarter, the following entries related to its equity accounts are recorded:

Jan. 17	Retained Earnings	96,000	
	Common Dividend Payable		96,000
Feb. 5	Common Dividend Payable	96,000	
	Cash		96,000
Feb. 28	Retained Earnings	252,000	
	Common Stock Dividend Distributable		120,000
	Contributed Capital in Excess of Par Value, Common Stock		132,000
Mar. 14	Common Stock Dividend Distributable	120,000	
	Common Stock, $10 Par Value		120,000
Mar. 25	Memo—Change the title of the common stock account to reflect the new par value of $5.		
Mar. 31	Income Summary	720,000	
	Retained Earnings		720,000

Required

1. Explain each journal entry.

2. Complete the following table showing the equity account balances at each indicated date:

	Jan. 17	Feb. 5	Feb. 28	Mar. 14	Mar. 25	Mar. 31
Common stock	$_____	$_____	$_____	$_____	$_____	$_____
Common stock dividend distributable	_____	_____	_____	_____	_____	_____
Contributed capital in excess of par, common stock	_____	_____	_____	_____	_____	_____
Retained earnings	_____	_____	_____	_____	_____	_____
Total equity	$_____	$_____	$_____	$_____	$_____	$_____

Check Total equity: Jan. 17, $2,848,000; Mar. 31, $3,568,000

Problem 11-4B [i]

Analysis of changes in stockholders' equity accounts

C5 P3 P4 P5

The equity sections from Scanat Corporation's 2002 and 2003 balance sheets follow:

Stockholders' Equity (December 31, 2002)

Common stock—$20 par value, 30,000 shares authorized, 17,000 shares issued and outstanding	$340,000
Contributed capital in excess of par value, common stock	60,000
Total contributed capital	$400,000
Retained earnings	270,000
Total stockholders' equity	$670,000

Stockholders' Equity (December 31, 2003)

Common stock—$20 par value, 30,000 shares authorized, 19,000 shares issued, 1,000 shares in treasury	$380,000
Contributed capital in excess of par value, common stock	104,000
Total contributed capital	$484,000
Retained earnings ($40,000 restricted by treasury stock)	295,200
	$779,200
Less cost of treasury stock	(40,000)
Total stockholders' equity	$739,200

The following transactions and events affected its equity accounts during year 2003:

Feb. 15	Declared a $0.40 per share cash dividend, date of record five days later.
Mar. 2	Purchased treasury stock for cash.
May 15	Declared a $0.40 per share cash dividend, date of record five days later.
Aug. 15	Declared a $0.40 per share cash dividend, date of record five days later.
Oct. 4	Declared a 12.5% stock dividend when the stock's market value is $42 per share.
Oct. 20	Issued stock dividend that was declared on October 4.
Nov. 15	Declared a $0.40 per share cash dividend, date of record five days later.

Required

1. How many common shares are outstanding on each cash dividend date?

2. What is the total dollar amount for each of the four cash dividends?

Check (3) $84,000;

(4) $40;

(5) $136,000

3. What is the amount of the capitalization of retained earnings for the stock dividend?

4. What is the per share cost of the treasury stock purchased?

5. How much net income did the company earn during year 2003?

Selected account balances from the adjusted trial balance for PXG Corp. as of its calendar year-end December 31, 2002, follow:

	Debit	Credit
a. Accumulated depreciation—Buildings		$ 400,000
b. Interest revenue		20,000
c. Cumulative effect of change in accounting principle (pretax)		92,000
d. Net sales		2,640,000
e. Income taxes expense	$?	
f. Loss on retirement of debt (pretax)	64,000	
g. Accumulated depreciation—Equipment		220,000
h. Other operating expenses	328,000	
i. Depreciation expense—Equipment	100,000	
j. Loss from settlement of lawsuit	36,000	
k. Gain from settlement of lawsuit		68,000
l. Loss on sale of equipment	24,000	
m. Loss from operating a discontinued segment (pretax)	120,000	
n. Depreciation expense—Buildings	156,000	
o. Correction of overstatement of prior year's expense (pretax)		48,000
p. Cost of goods sold	1,040,000	
q. Loss on sale of discontinued segment's assets (pretax)	180,000	
r. Accounts payable		132,000

Problem 11-5B
Income statement computations and format

C4

Required

Answer each of the following questions by providing supporting computations:

1. Assuming that the company's income tax rate is 25% for all items, identify the tax effects and after-tax amounts of the five items labeled pretax.
2. What is the amount of income from continuing operations before income taxes? What is the amount of income taxes expense? What is the amount of income from continuing operations?
3. What is the total amount of after-tax income (loss) associated with the discontinued segment?
4. What is the amount of income (loss) before the extraordinary items and the cumulative effect of changes in accounting principle?
5. What is the amount of net income for the year?

Check   (3) $(225,000);

(4) $558,000;

(5) $579,000

On January 1, 2002, Couric Corp. purchases equipment costing $400,000 with an expected salvage value of zero at the end of its five-year useful life. Depreciation is allocated to 2002, 2003, and 2004 with the double-declining-balance method. Early in 2005, the company decides to change to the straight-line method to produce more useful financial statements and to be consistent with other firms in the industry.

Problem 11-6B
Change in accounting principle (depreciation) and its disclosure

C4

Required

1. Do generally accepted accounting principles allow Couric to change depreciation methods in 2005?
2. Prepare a table to show the annual amount of depreciation expense allocated to 2002 through 2004 using the double-declining-balance method.
3. Prepare a table to show the annual amount of depreciation expense that would have been allocated to 2002 through 2004 using the straight-line method.
4. Organize your answers from parts 2 and 3 into a table like Exhibit 11.17 and compute the pretax and after-tax cumulative effect of the change. The company's income tax rate is 25%.
5. How should the cumulative effect of the change in accounting principle be reported? Does the cumulative effect increase or decrease net income?
6. How much depreciation expense is reported on the company's income statement for 2005?

Check   (2) 2003, $96,000;

(3) 2003, $80,000;

(4) After-tax cumulative effect, $55,200

Analysis Component

7. Assume that Couric mistakenly treats the change in depreciation methods as a change in accounting estimate. Using your answers from parts 2, 3, and 4, describe the effect of this error on the 2005 financial statements.

Problem 11-7B
Earnings per share calculation and presentation

C4 A1

The annual income statements for Bix, Inc., as reported when they were initially published in 2002, 2003, and 2004 follow:

	2002	2003	2004
Net sales	$500,000	$600,000	$800,000
Operating expenses	320,000	430,000	540,000
Income from continuing operations	$180,000	$170,000	$260,000
Loss on discontinued segment	(52,290)	—	—
Income before extraordinary items	$127,710	$170,000	$260,000
Extraordinary gain (loss)	—	28,200	(74,250)
Net income	$127,710	$198,200	$185,750

The company also experienced changes in the number of outstanding shares from the following events:

Outstanding shares on December 31, 2001	20,000
2002	
Treasury stock purchase on July 1	− 2,000
Issuance of new shares on September 30	+ 7,000
20% stock dividend on December 1	+ 5,000
Outstanding shares on December 31, 2002	30,000
2003	
Issuance of new shares on March 31	+ 8,000
Treasury stock purchase on October 1	− 3,000
Outstanding shares on December 31, 2003	35,000
2004	
Issuance of new shares on July 1	+ 6,000
Treasury stock purchase on October 1	− 3,500
2-for-1 stock split on November 1	+37,500
Outstanding shares on December 31, 2004	75,000

Required

Check (1) 24,900 shares;
(2) EPS, $5.13;

(3) 35,250 shares;
(4) EPS, $5.62

1. Compute the weighted-average of the common shares outstanding for year 2002.
2. Compute the EPS component amounts to report with the year 2002 income statement for: income from continuing operations, the loss on discontinued segment, and net income.
3. Compute the weighted-average of the common shares outstanding for year 2003.
4. Compute the EPS component amounts to report with the year 2003 income statement for: income from continuing operations, the extraordinary gain, and net income.
5. Compute the weighted-average of the common shares outstanding for year 2004.
6. Compute the EPS component amounts to report with the year 2004 income statement for: income from continuing operations, the extraordinary loss, and net income.

Analysis Component

7. Explain how you would use the EPS data from part 6 to predict EPS for 2005.

Big Hat, Inc.'s common stock is currently selling on a stock exchange at $90 per share, and its current balance sheet shows the following stockholders' equity section:

Problem 11-8B 🅐
Computation of book values
and dividend allocations
C3 A2 P2

Preferred stock—8% cumulative, $___ par value, 1,500 shares authorized, issued, and outstanding	$ 375,000
Common stock—$___ par value, 18,000 shares authorized, issued, and outstanding	900,000
Retained earnings	1,125,000
Total stockholders' equity	$2,400,000

Required

1. What is the current market value (price) of this corporation's common stock?
2. What are the par values of the corporation's preferred stock and its common stock?
3. If no dividends are in arrears, what are the book values per share of the preferred stock and the common stock?
4. If two years' preferred dividends are in arrears, what are the book values per share of the preferred stock and the common stock?
5. It two years' preferred dividends are in arrears and the preferred stock is callable at $280 per share, what are the book values per share of the preferred stock and the common stock?
6. If two years' preferred dividends are in arrears and the board of directors declares cash dividends of $100,000, what total amount will be paid to the preferred and to the common shareholders? What is the amount of dividends per share for the common stock?

Check (4) Book value of common, $109.17;

(5) Book value of common, $106.67;

(6) Dividends per common share, $0.56

Analysis Component

7. Discuss why the book value of common stock may not always be a good estimate of its market value.

BEYOND THE NUMBERS

BTN 11-1   Refer to Nike's financial statements in Appendix A to answer the following:

1. Has Nike issued any preferred stock? If so, what are its features?
2. How many shares of both class A and class B common stock are outstanding at the end of fiscal years 2000 and 1999? How do these numbers compare with the weighted-average common shares outstanding at the end of fiscal years 2000 and 1999?
3. What is the book value of its entire common stock at May 31, 2000?
4. What is its cash dividend declared per common share for fiscal years 2000 and 1999? What is the total amount of cash dividends paid to common and preferred stockholders for fiscal years 2000 and 1998?
5. Identify and compare basic EPS amounts across years 2000, 1999, and 1998. Identify and comment on any significant changes.
6. Does Nike hold any treasury stock as of May 31, 2000? As of May 31, 1999?
7. Does Nike report any changes in accounting principles or the occurrence of extraordinary items for fiscal years ended May 31, 2000 or 1999? Are there gains or losses on disposal of a business segment for fiscal years 2000 or 1999?

Reporting in Action
C2 C3 C4 A1 A2 🅐
NIKE

Swoosh Ahead

8. Access Nike's financial statements for fiscal years ending after May 31, 2000, from its Web site (www.nike.com) or the SEC's EDGAR database (www.sec.gov). Is the redeemable preferred stock still outstanding? Has the number of common shares outstanding increased since May 31, 2000? Has Nike increased the total amount of cash dividends paid compared to fiscal year 2000?

Comparative Analysis

A1 A2 A3 A4

NIKE   Reebok

BTN 11-2   Key comparative figures for both Nike and Reebok follow:

Key Figures	Nike	Reebok
Net income (in millions)	$ 579.1	$ 11.0
Cash dividends declared per common share	$ 0.48	$ 0.00
Common shares outstanding (in millions)	269.6	56.3
Market value (price) per share	$ 42.88	$ 8.19
Equity applicable to common shares (in mil.)	$3,136.0	$528.8

Required

1. Compute the book value per common share for each company using these data.
2. Compute the basic EPS for each company using these data.
3. Compute the dividend yield for each company using these data. Does the dividend yield of either company characterize it as an income or growth stock? Explain.
4. Compute, compare, and interpret the price-earnings ratio for each company using these data.

Ethics Challenge

C4

BTN 11-3   This chapter describes CompUS's change in accounting principle from the double-declining-balance method of depreciation to the straight-line method. CompUS argues that its income statement now is more useful when depreciation is computed using the straight-line method. This change in accounting principle adds $56,000 to net income for year 2002. As this company's auditor, you must review the decision to change the accounting principle. You review the equipment in question and learn that it is a piece of high-tech equipment, whose risk of obsolescence in the near future is high. You also are aware that management receives year-end bonuses based on net income.

Required   As the auditor, would you support the change in depreciation method or ask management to continue using the double-declining-balance method? Justify your response.

Communicating in Practice

A1 A4

Hint: Make a transparency of each team's memo for a class discussion.

BTN 11-4   Teams are to select an industry, and each team member is to select a different company in that industry. Next, each team member is to acquire the selected company's financial statements (or Form 10-K) from the SEC EDGAR site (www.sec.gov). Use these data to determine basic EPS. Use the financial press (or www.quote.yahoo.com) to determine the market price of this stock, and then compute the price-earnings ratio. Communicate with teammates via a meeting, e-mail, or telephone to discuss the meaning of this ratio, how companies compare, and the industry norm. The team must prepare a single memorandum reporting the ratio for each company and identifying the team conclusions or consensus of opinion. The memorandum is to be duplicated and distributed to the instructor and teammates.

Taking It to the Net

A1 A3 A4

BTN 11-5   Access the March 21, 2000, filing of the 1999 calendar-year 10-K report of Quaker Oats Company (ticker OAT) from www.edgar-online.com.

Required

1. How many classes of stock has the Quaker Oats Company issued?
2. What are the par values of the classes of stock you identified in part 1?
3. How much cash did Quaker Oats raise in 1999 from issuing stock?
4. What total amount of cash did Quaker Oats pay in 1999 to repurchase stock?
5. What amount did Quaker Oats pay out in cash dividends for 1999?

BTN 11-6 This activity requires teamwork to reinforce understanding of accounting for treasury stock.

1. Write a brief team statement (a) generalizing what happens to a corporation's financial position when it engages in a stock "buyback" and (b) identifying reasons that a corporation would engage in this activity.

2. Assume that an entity acquires 100 shares of its $100 par value common stock at a cost of $134 cash per share. Discuss the entry to record this acquisition. Next, assign *each* team member to prepare *one* of the following entries (assume each entry applies to all shares):

   a. Reissue treasury shares at cost.

   b. Reissue treasury shares at $150 per share.

   c. Reissue treasury shares at $120 per share—assume the contributed capital account from treasury shares has a $1,500 balance.

   d. Reissue treasury shares at $120 per share—assume the contributed capital account from treasury shares has a $1,000 balance.

   e. Reissue treasury shares at $120 per share—assume the contributed capital account from treasury shares has a zero balance.

3. In sequence, each member is to present his/her entry to the team and explain the *similarities* and *differences* between that entry and the previous entry.

Teamwork in Action

P5

Hint: Instructor should be sure each team accurately completes part 1 before proceeding.

BTN 11-7 Read the article "Paul Harris Aims to Get Spruced Up" from the October 26, 1998, issue of *Business Week*. (The book's Web site provides a free link.)

Required

1. What type of stores are the Paul Harris stores?

2. Describe the price behavior of the Paul Harris stock, including its 1997 high and its price as of October 8, 1998.

3. In September 1998, what action did Paul Harris management take in response to its stock price?

4. Access Paul Harris's stock prices (ticker PAUHQ) for 1998, 1999, and 2000 at www.datek.com. Obtain a print-out of its stock price history for these years. Comment on any trends.

5. In retrospect, does it seem management took the correct action in September 1998? Explain.

Business Week **Activity**

P5 🅐

BTN 11-8 An entrepreneur planning to start a new business needs $312,500 of start-up capital. This entrepreneur contributes $250,000 of personal assets in return for 5,000 shares of common stock but needs to raise another $62,500 in cash. There are two alternative plans for raising the additional cash. Plan A is to sell 1,250 shares of common stock to one or more investors for $62,500 cash. Plan B is to sell 625 shares of cumulative preferred stock to one or more investors for $62,500 cash (this preferred stock would have a $100 par value, an annual 8% dividend rate, and be issued at par).

1. If the business is expected to earn $45,000 of after-tax net income in the first year, what rate of return on beginning equity will this entrepreneur personally earn under each alternative? Which plan will provide the higher expected return to the entrepreneur?

2. If the business is expected to earn $10,500 of after-tax net income in the first year, what rate of return on beginning equity will the entrepreneur personally earn under each alternative? Which plan will provide the higher expected return to the entrepreneur?

3. Analyze and interpret the differences between the results for parts 1 and 2.

Entrepreneurial Decision

C2 C3 P3

🅔 🅐

BTN 11-9 Watch 30 to 60 minutes of financial news on the CNBC television channel. Take notes on company happenings that are catching the attention of analysts. You might hear reference to over- and undervaluation of firms. You might also hear reports about PE ratios, dividend yields, and earnings per share. Be prepared to give a brief description to the class of your observations of CNBC.

Hitting the Road

A1 A3 A4

12

Reporting and Analyzing Cash Flows

A Look Back

Chapter 11 focused on the corporate form of organization. We described its characteristics and its important transactions. We also explained corporate accounting and the reporting of income, earnings per share, and retained earnings.

A Look at This Chapter

This chapter focuses on reporting and analyzing cash inflows and cash outflows. We emphasize how to prepare and interpret the statement of cash flows.

A Look Ahead

Chapter 13 focuses on tools to help us analyze financial statements. We describe comparative analysis and the application of ratios for financial analysis.

"We're making very significant progress"—
Ken Seiff

Singing the Blues

e NEW YORK—While cash may not be king, it can be an executioner. Just ask Ken Seiff, the young owner of **Bluefly (www.Bluefly.com)**, an Internet retailer of designer fashions at discount prices. Seiff opened Bluefly's doors in 1998. Since that time, its revenues have gone from under $1 million to nearly $20 million a year. But instead of singing its praises, Bluefly investors are singing the blues. Bluefly's stock price is down from nearly $20 per share to $2 per share. What's the scoop? Seiff argues that Bluefly "has been overlooked by the private market's irrational lack of interest." A less passionate viewpoint suggests that cash flow is the culprit. That is, while revenues reached record highs, cash outflows were piling up. Bluefly went from a net cash inflow of $2.8 million in its first year to a net cash *outflow* of $2.6 million this past year, which included an operating cash outflow of $21.7 million. Such is the recipe of financial distress.

Seiff insists that Bluefly's revenue performance is solid and that its business plan is gaining momentum. "We are extremely pleased with . . . results, especially considering that we achieved triple-digit revenue growth while operations became more efficient," says Seiff. But cash flows tell another story. This chapter focuses on cash flows—their measurement, presentation, analysis, and interpretation. It describes the importance of analyzing cash flows separately by operating, investing, and financing activities. It also explains the computation of the statement of cash flows. Bluefly's Seiff would have benefited from increased attention to cash flows. Admits Seiff, "We're not there yet, but we're making very significant progress." Only time and cash flow will reveal how much progress. [Sources: Bluefly Web site, March 2002; *Entrepreneur*, November 2000; atNewYork.com, August 10, 2000; Bluefly 10-K, December 31, 2000.]

Learning Objectives

Conceptual

C1 Explain the purpose and importance of cash flow information.

C2 Distinguish among operating, investing, and financing activities.

C3 Identify and disclose noncash investing and financing activities.

C4 Describe the format of the statement of cash flows.

Analytical

A1 Analyze the statement of cash flows.

A2 Compute and apply the cash flow on total assets ratio.

Procedural

P1 Prepare a statement of cash flows.

P2 Compute cash flows from operating activities using the direct method.

P3 Compute cash flows from operating activities using the indirect method.

P4 Determine cash flows from both investing and financing activities.

Chapter Preview

Profitability is a primary goal of most managers, but not the only goal. A company cannot achieve or maintain profits without carefully managing cash. Managers and other users of information pay close attention to a company's cash position and the events and transactions affecting cash. Information about these events and transactions is reported in the statement of cash flows. This chapter explains how we prepare, analyze, and interpret a statement of cash flows. It also discusses the importance of cash flow information for predicting future performance and making managerial decisions. More generally, effectively using the statement of cash flows is crucial for managing and analyzing the operating, investing, and financing activities of businesses.

Basics of Cash Flow Reporting

This section describes the basics of cash flow reporting, including its purpose, measurement, classification, format, and preparation.

Purpose of the Statement of Cash Flows

C1 Explain the purpose and importance of cash flow information.

The purpose of the **statement of cash flows** is to report all major cash receipts (inflows) and cash payments (outflows) during a period. This includes separately identifying the cash flows related to operating, investing, and financing activities. The statement of cash flows does more than simply report changes in cash. It is the detailed disclosure of individual cash flows that makes this statement useful to users. Information in this statement helps users answer questions such as these:

- How does a company obtain its cash?
- Where does a company spend its cash?
- What explains the change in the cash balance?

The statement of cash flows addresses important questions such as these by summarizing, classifying, and reporting a company's cash inflows and cash outflows for each period.

Importance of Cash Flows

Point: An income statement reports revenues, gains, expenses, and losses on an accrual basis. The statement of cash flows reports cash received and cash paid for operating, financing, and investing activities.

Information about cash flows can influence decision makers in important ways. For instance, we look more favorably at a company that is financing its expenditures with cash from operations than one that does it by selling its assets. Information about cash flows also helps users decide whether a company has enough cash to pay its existing debts as they mature. It is also relied upon to evaluate a company's ability to meet unexpected obligations and pursue unexpected opportunities. External information users especially want to assess a company's ability to take advantage of new business opportunities. Internal users such as managers use cash flow information to plan day-to-day operating activities and make long-term investment decisions.

Macy's striking turnaround is an example of how analysis and management of cash flows can lead to improved financial stability. A few years ago, Macy's obtained temporary protection from bankruptcy, at which time it desperately needed to improve its cash flows. It did so by engaging in aggressive cost-cutting measures. As a result of this effort, Macy's annual cash flow rose to $210 million—up from a negative cash flow of $38.9 million in the prior year. Macy's eventually met its financial obligations and then successfully merged with **Federated Department Stores**.

The case of **W. T. Grant Co.** is a classic example of the importance of cash flow information in predicting a company's future performance and financial strength. Grant reported net income of more than $40 million per year for three consecutive years. At that same time, it was experiencing an alarming decrease in cash provided by operations. For instance, net cash outflow was more than $90 million by the end of that three-year period. Grant soon went bankrupt. Users who relied solely on Grant's income numbers were unpleasantly surprised.

Decision Insight

Cash Valuation Some experts who value private companies do so on the basis of a multiple of operating cash flow. For example, medium-sized private companies usually sell for five to seven times their operating cash flows. Larger companies can command somewhat higher multiples.

This reminds us that cash flows as well as income statement and balance sheet information are crucial in making business decisions.

Measuring Cash Flows

Cash and Cash Equivalents

Cash flows are defined to include both *cash* and *cash equivalents* in the statement of cash flows. The statement of cash flows explains the difference between the beginning and ending balances of cash and cash equivalents. We continue to use the phrases *cash flows* and the *statement of cash flows,* but we must remember that both phrases refer to cash and cash equivalents. As we discussed in Chapter 6, a cash equivalent must satisfy two criteria: (1) be readily convertible to a known amount of cash and (2) be sufficiently close to its maturity so its market value is unaffected by interest rate changes. In most cases, a security must be within three months of its maturity to satisfy these criteria. Classifying short-term, highly liquid investments as cash equivalents is based on the idea that companies make these investments to earn a return on idle cash balances. Companies must follow a clear policy for determining cash and cash equivalents.

Global: International accounting standards define cash flows as *net monetary assets*—meaning cash, demand deposits, and highly liquid investments minus short-term loans.

> ### Decision Insight
>
> **Cash Analysis** "A lender must have a complete understanding of a borrower's cash flows to assess both the borrowing needs and repayment sources. This requires information about the major types of cash inflows and outflows. I have seen many companies, whose financial statements indicate good profitability, experience severe financial problems because the owners or managers lacked a good understanding of cash flows."—Mary E. Garza, **NationsBank**.

These policies are disclosed in notes to their financial statements and must be followed consistently from period to period. **American Express**, for example, defines its cash equivalents as "time deposits with original maturities of 90 days or less, excluding those that are restricted by law or regulation."

Point: Internal users rely on the statement of cash flows to make investing and financing decisions. External users rely on this statement to assess the amount and timing of a company's cash flows.

Classifying Cash Flows

Since we treat cash and cash equivalents as a single item on the statement of cash flows, the statement does not report transactions between cash and cash equivalents such as cash paid to purchase cash equivalents and cash received from selling cash equivalents. However, all other cash receipts and cash payments are classified and reported on the statement as operating, investing, or financing activities. Individual cash receipts and payments for each of these three categories are labeled to identify their source transactions or events. Cash receipts and payments are then summarized for each category by netting them against each other. A net cash inflow (source) occurs when the receipts in a category exceed the payments. A net cash outflow (use) occurs when the payments in a category exceed the receipts.

C2 Distinguish among operating, investing, and financing activities.

Operating Activities

Operating activities include those transactions and events that determine net income. Examples are the production and purchase of merchandise, the sale of goods and services to customers, and the expenditures toward administering the business. Not all items in income, such as unusual gains and losses, are operating activities (we discuss these exceptions later in the chapter). Exhibit 12.1 lists the more common cash inflows and outflows from operating activities.

Global: Several countries such as Saudi Arabia and Italy do not require the statement of cash flows.

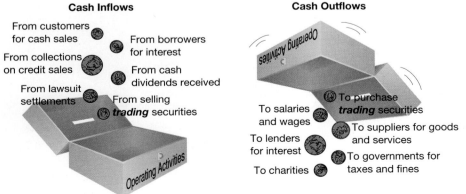

Exhibit 12.1

Cash Flows from Operating Activities

Topic Tackler 12-1

Investing Activities

Investing activities generally include those transactions and events that affect long-term assets—namely, the purchase and sale of long-term assets. However, they also include the (1) purchase and sale of short-term investments other than cash equivalents and trading securities, and (2) lending and collecting money for notes receivable. Exhibit 12.2 lists examples of cash flows from investing activities. Proceeds from collecting the principal amounts of notes deserve special mention. If the note results from sales to customers, its cash receipts are classed as operating activities whether short term or long term. If the note results from a loan to another party apart from sales, however, the cash receipts from collecting the principal of the note are classed as an investing activity. The FASB requires the collection of interest on loans be reported as an operating activity.

Exhibit 12.2

Cash Flows from Investing Activities

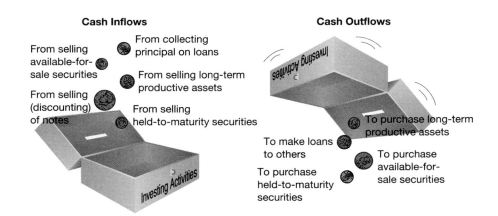

Financing Activities

Financing activities include those transactions and events that affect long-term liabilities and equity. Examples are (1) obtaining cash from issuing debt and repaying the amounts borrowed and (2) cash received from or distributed to owners. These activities all involve transactions with a company's owners and creditors. They also often involve borrowing and repaying principal amounts relating to both short- and long-term debt. Notice that payments of interest expense are classified as operating activities. Also, cash payments to settle credit purchases of merchandise, whether on account or by note, are operating activities. Exhibit 12.3 lists examples of cash flows from financing activities.

Exhibit 12.3

Cash Flows from Financing Activities

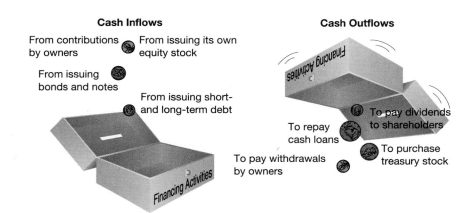

Decision Track 12.1   *d*

Decision Point	Information Search	Analyze & Evaluate
Does the difference between operating cash flow and operating income warrant scrutiny?	Compute: Cash flow from operations divided by net sales; Income from operations divided by net sales.	Compare these ratios across periods and competitors; large differences often foretell *aggressive* (improper) *accounting.*

Noncash Investing and Financing

Some important investing and financing activities do not affect cash receipts or payments. Important noncash investing and financing activities are disclosed at the bottom of the statement of cash flows or in a note to the statement because of their importance and the *full-disclosure principle*. One example of such a transaction is the purchase of long-term assets by giving a long-term note payable. This transaction involves both investing and financing activities, but it does not affect any cash inflow or outflow and is not reported in any of the three sections of the statement of cash flows. Other examples are investing and financing activities involving cash receipts or payments for only part of the transaction.

To illustrate, assume that Goorin purchases land for $12,000 by paying $5,000 cash and trading in used equipment with a $7,000 market value. The investing section of the statement of cash flows reports only the $5,000 cash outflow for the land purchase. The $12,000 investing transaction is only partially described in the body of the statement of cash flows, yet this information is potentially important to users because it changes the makeup of assets. Goorin could either describe the transaction in a note or include a small schedule at the bottom of its statement that lists the $12,000 land purchase along with the cash financing of $5,000 and a $7,000 trade-in of used equipment. Seagate Technology discloses its noncash investing and financing activity in a note as follows: "receipt of note receivable for sale of building, $5,000,000." Union Camp discloses its noncash investing and financing activity in a separate schedule ($ thousands) as follows:

C3 Identify and disclose noncash investing and financing activities.

Decision Maker   *e*

Entrepreneur You are considering purchasing a start-up business that recently reported a $110,000 annual net loss and a $225,000 annual net cash inflow. How are these results possible?

Answer—p. 556

Fair value of assets acquired	$8,345
Less: Cash paid	7,115
Liabilities incurred or assumed	$1,230

The Union Camp schedule describes an exchange of assets involving both cash and non-cash elements. It reports the $7,115 cash payment in the statement of cash flows as an investing activity. More generally, exhibit 12.4 lists some transactions commonly disclosed as noncash investing and financing activities.

Point: A stock dividend transaction involving a transfer from retained earnings to common stock, or a credit to contributed capital, is *not* considered a noncash investing and financing activity because the company receives no consideration (asset) for shares issued.

- ■ Retirement of debt by issuing equity stock.
- ■ Conversion of preferred stock to common stock.
- ■ Lease of assets in a capital lease transaction.
- ■ Purchase of long-term asset by issuing a note or bond.
- ■ Exchange of noncash assets for other noncash assets.
- ■ Purchase of noncash assets by issuing equity or debt.

Exhibit 12.4

Examples of Noncash Investing and Financing Activities

Format of the Statement of Cash Flows

C4 Describe the format of the statement of cash flows.

Accounting standards require companies to include a statement of cash flows in a complete set of financial statements. This statement must report information about a company's cash receipts and cash payments during the period. Exhibit 12.5 shows the usual format of the statement of cash flows. A company must report cash flows from three activities: operating, investing, and financing. Detailed cash inflows and cash outflows are reported for each category. The statement explains how transactions and events impact the beginning-of-period cash (and cash equivalents) balance to produce its end-of-period balance.

Exhibit 12.5

Format of the Statement of Cash Flows

Global: International accounting standards require a statement of cash flows separated into operating, investing, and financing activities.

COMPANY NAME Statement of Cash Flows For *period* Ended *date*		
Cash flows from operating activities		
[List of individual inflows and outflows]		
Net cash provided (used) by operating activities	$	#
Cash flows from investing activities		
[List of individual inflows and outflows]		
Net cash provided (used) by investing activities		#
Cash flows from financing activities		
[List of individual inflows and outflows]		
Net cash provided (used) by financing activities		#
Net increase (decrease) in cash	$	#
Cash (and equivalents) balance at beginning of period		#
Cash (and equivalents) balance at end of period	$	#

Note: Separate schedule or note disclosure of any "noncash investing and financing transactions" is required.

Quick Check

1. Does a statement of cash flows disclose cash payments to purchase cash equivalents? Does it disclose cash receipts from selling cash equivalents?

2. Identify the categories of cash flows reported separately on the statement of cash flows.

3. Identify the cash activity category for each transaction: (*a*) purchase equipment for cash, (*b*) payment of wages, (*c*) sale of common stock for cash, (*d*) receipt of cash dividends from stock investment, (*e*) cash collection from customers, (*f*) bonds issuance for cash.

Answers—pp. 556–557

Preparing the Statement of Cash Flows

P1 Prepare a statement of cash flows.

Preparation of a statement of cash flows involves five steps: (1) compute the net increase or decrease in cash; (2) compute and report net cash provided (used) by operating activities (using either the direct or indirect method—both are explained in this chapter); (3) compute and report net cash provided (used) by investing activities; (4) compute and report net cash provided (used) by financing activities; and (5) compute net cash flow by combining net cash provided (used) by operating, investing, and financing activities and then *prove it* by adding it to the beginning cash balance to show that it equals the ending cash balance. Moreover, all important noncash investing and financing activities are disclosed in either a note or a separate schedule to the statement.

Point: View the change in cash as a *target* number that you will fully explain and prove in the statement of cash flows.

    Computing the net increase or net decrease in cash is a simple but crucial computation. It equals the current period's cash balance minus the prior period's cash balance. This is the *bottom-line* figure for the statement of cash flows and is a helpful check on the accuracy of one's work. The information we need to prepare a statement of cash flows comes from a variety of sources including comparative balance sheets at the beginning and end of the period, and an income statement for the period—essentially an analysis of noncash accounts. Alternatively, because cash inflows and cash outflows are captured in the accounting system, we can examine the transactions that affect the Cash account. This section briefly describes these two alternative approaches to preparing the statement: (1) analyzing the Cash account and (2) analyzing noncash accounts.

Analyzing the Cash Account

A company's cash receipts and cash payments are recorded in the Cash account in its general ledger. The Cash account is therefore a natural place to look for information about cash flows from operating, investing, and financing activities. To illustrate, review the summarized Cash T-account of Genesis, Inc., in Exhibit 12.6. Individual cash transactions are summarized in this Cash account according to the major types of cash receipts and cash payments. For instance, only the total of cash receipts from all customers is listed. Individual cash transactions underlying these totals can number in the thousands. Accounting software programs are available to provide summarized cash accounts similar to the one illustrated.

Preparing a statement of cash flows from Exhibit 12.6 requires us to determine whether an individual cash inflow or outflow is an operating, investing, or financing activity, and then to list each by activity. This yields the statement shown in Exhibit 12.7. However, preparing the statement of cash flows from an analysis of the summarized Cash account has two limitations. First, most companies have many individual cash receipts and payments, making it difficult to review them all. Accounting software greatly minimizes this burden, but it is still a task requiring professional judgment for many transactions. Second, the Cash account does not usually carry an adequate description of each cash transaction, making assignment of all cash transactions according to activity difficult.

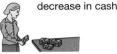
Step 1: Compute net increase or decrease in cash

Step 2: Compute net cash from operating activities

Step 3: Compute net cash from investing activities

Step 4: Compute net cash from financing activities

Step 5: Prove and report beginning and ending cash balances

Peachtree Accounting: 12–06			
Cash			
Balance, Dec. 31, 2001	12,000		
Receipts from customers	570,000	Payments for merchandise	319,000
Receipts from asset sales	12,000	Payments for wages and operating expenses	218,000
Receipts from stock issuance	15,000	Payments for interest	8,000
		Payments for taxes	5,000
		Payments for assets	10,000
		Payments to retire bonds	18,000
		Payments for dividends	14,000
Balance, Dec. 31, 2002	17,000		

Exhibit 12.6

Summarized Cash Account

Analyzing Noncash Accounts

A second approach to preparing the statement of cash flows is based on analyzing noncash accounts. This approach uses the fact that when a company records cash inflows and outflows with debits and credits to the Cash account (as reflected in the prior section), it also records credits and debits in other noncash accounts (reflecting double-entry accounting). Many of these noncash accounts are balance sheet accounts, for instance, from the sale of land for cash. Others are revenue and expense accounts that are closed to equity. For instance, the sale of services for cash yields a credit to Services Revenue that is closed to Retained Earnings for a corporation. In sum, *all cash transactions eventually affect noncash balance sheet accounts.* Thus, we can determine cash inflows and outflows by analyzing changes in noncash balance sheet accounts. We are not limited to analyzing the Cash account.

Exhibit 12.8 uses the accounting equation to show the important relation between the Cash account and the noncash balance sheet accounts. This exhibit starts with the familiar accounting equation at the top. We then expand it in line (2) to separate cash from noncash asset accounts. Next, we move noncash asset accounts to the right-hand side of the equality in line (3) where they are subtracted. This shows that cash equals the sum of the liability and equity accounts *minus* the noncash asset accounts. Line (4) points out that *changes* on one side of the accounting equation equal *changes* on the other side. It shows that we can explain changes in cash by analyzing changes in the noncash accounts consisting of liability accounts, equity accounts, and noncash assets accounts. By analyzing all noncash balance sheet accounts and any related income statement accounts, we have the information for preparing a statement of cash flows.

Global: Some countries require a statement of funds flow instead of a statement of cash flows—*funds* are often defined as *working capital* (current assets minus current liabilities).

Exhibit 12.7

Statement of Cash Flows—
Direct Method

GENESIS Statement of Cash Flows For Year Ended December 31, 2002		
Cash flows from operating activities		
Cash received from customers	$570,000	
Cash paid for merchandise	(319,000)	
Cash paid for wages and other operating expenses	(218,000)	
Cash paid for interest	(8,000)	
Cash paid for taxes	(5,000)	
Net cash provided by operating activities		$20,000
Cash flows from investing activities		
Cash received from sale of plant assets	12,000	
Cash paid for purchase of plant assets	(10,000)	
Net cash provided by investing activities		2,000
Cash flows from financing activities		
Cash received from issuing stock	15,000	
Cash paid to retire bonds	(18,000)	
Cash paid for dividends	(14,000)	
Net cash used in financing activities		(17,000)
Net increase in cash		$ 5,000
Cash balance at beginning of year		12,000
Cash balance at end of year		$17,000

Information to Prepare the Statement

Information to prepare the statement of cash flows usually comes from three sources: (1) comparative balance sheets, (2) current income statement, and (3) additional information. Comparative balance sheets are used to compute changes in noncash accounts from the beginning to the end of the period. The current income statement is used to help compute cash flows from operating activities. Additional information often includes details on transactions and events that help explain both the cash flows and noncash investing and financing activities.

Decision Insight

E-Cash Every credit transaction on the Net leaves a trail that a hacker, a marketer, or the government can pick up. Enter e-cash—digital money that can be used as freely and anonymously as cash. With e-cash, the encryption protects your money from snoops and thieves, and it cannot be traced back to you —not even by the issuing bank.

Exhibit 12.8

Relation between Cash and Noncash Accounts

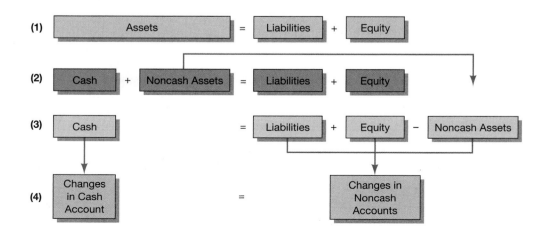

This section describes the reporting of cash flows from operating activities using the direct method and the indirect method. *These two different methods apply only to the operating activities section.*

Cash Flows from Operating

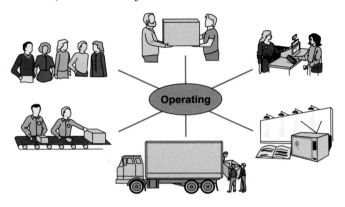

Reporting Operating Cash Flows

The net cash flows provided (used) by operating activities can be reported in one of two ways: the *direct method* or the *indirect method*. The **direct method** separately lists each major item of operating cash receipts (such as cash received from customers) and each major item of operating cash payments (such as cash paid for merchandise). The cash payments are subtracted from cash receipts to determine the net cash provided (used) by operating activities. The operating activities section of Exhibit 12.7 is an example of the direct method of reporting operating cash flows.

The **indirect method** reports net income and then adjusts it for items necessary to obtain net cash provided (used) by operating activities. It does *not* report individual items of cash inflows and cash outflows from operating activities. Instead, the indirect method reports the necessary adjustments to reconcile net income to net cash provided (used) by operating activities. The operating activities section prepared under the indirect method is shown in Exhibit 12.9 for Genesis.

Cash flows from operating activities		
Net income		$38,000
Adjustments to reconcile net income to net cash provided by operating activities		
Increase in accounts receivable	(20,000)	
Increase in merchandise inventory	(14,000)	
Increase in prepaid expenses	(2,000)	
Decrease in accounts payable	(5,000)	
Decrease in interest payable	(1,000)	
Increase in income taxes payable	10,000	
Depreciation expense	24,000	
Loss on sale of plant assets	6,000	
Gain on retirement of bonds	(16,000)	
Net cash provided by operating activities		**$20,000**

Exhibit 12.9

Operating Activities Section—Indirect Method

Note that the amount of net cash provided by operating activities is *identical* under both the direct and indirect methods. This equality always exists. The difference in these methods is with the computation and presentation of this amount.

The indirect method of reporting operating cash flows does not provide as much detail about the sources and uses of cash as does the direct method. The FASB recommends the direct method, but since it is not required and the indirect method is arguably easier to compute, most companies report operating cash flows using the indirect method. The direct method is presented like the income statement, and therefore many people find the direct method easier to understand when first learning about cash flow reporting. Many internal users such as managers and budget officers use the direct method to predict future cash requirements and availability.

To illustrate both methods, we prepare the operating activities section of the statement of cash flows for Genesis, Inc. Exhibit 12.10 shows the December 31, 2001, and 2002, balance sheets of Genesis along with its year 2002 income statement. We use this information to prepare a statement of cash flows to explain the $5,000 increase in cash for year 2002 as reported in its balance sheets. This $5,000 is computed as Cash of $17,000 at the end of

Point: To better understand the direct and indirect methods of reporting operating cash flows, identify the similarities and differences between Exhibits 12.7 and 12.17.

Point: The direct method is usually viewed as *user friendly* because less accounting knowledge is required to understand and use it.

Point: Operating activities are generally related to activities that determine income, which are often reflected in changes in current assets and current liabilities.

Point: Refer to Exhibit 12.10 and identify the $5,000 change in cash for Genesis. This is what we wish to explain in the statement of cash flows. The $5,000 change in cash also serves as a check figure.

2002 minus Cash of $12,000 at the end of 2001. Genesis discloses additional information about year 2002 transactions as follows:

a. Accounts payable balances result from merchandise inventory purchases.

b. Plant assets costing $70,000 are purchased by paying $10,000 cash and issuing $60,000 of bonds payable.

c. Plant assets with an original cost of $30,000 and accumulated depreciation of $12,000 are sold for $12,000 cash—yielding a $6,000 loss.

d. Cash of $15,000 is received from issuing 3,000 shares of common stock.

e. Paid $18,000 to retire bonds with a book value of $34,000—yielding a $16,000 gain.

f. Cash dividends of $14,000 are declared and paid.

Exhibit 12.10

Financial Statements

GENESIS Balance Sheet December 31, 2002 and 2001		
	2002	**2001**
Assets		
Current assets		
Cash..........................	$ 17,000	$ 12,000
Accounts receivable............	60,000	40,000
Merchandise inventory..........	84,000	70,000
Prepaid expenses	6,000	4,000
Total current assets	$167,000	$126,000
Long-term assets		
Plant assets	250,000	210,000
Accumulated depreciation	(60,000)	(48,000)
Total assets	$357,000	$288,000
Liabilities		
Current liabilities		
Accounts payable	$ 35,000	$ 40,000
Interest payable	3,000	4,000
Income taxes payable	22,000	12,000
Total current liabilities	$ 60,000	$ 56,000
Long-term liabilities		
Bonds payable	90,000	64,000
Total liabilities	$150,000	$120,000
Equity		
Common stock, $5 par	$ 95,000	$ 80,000
Retained earnings	112,000	88,000
Total equity	$207,000	$168,000
Total liabilities and equity	$357,000	$288,000

GENESIS Income Statement For Year Ended December 31, 2002		
Sales		$590,000
Cost of goods sold	$300,000	
Wages & other operating expenses ..	216,000	
Interest expense	7,000	
Depreciation expense.............	24,000	(547,000)
Other gains (losses)		
Loss on sale of plant assets		(6,000)
Income before taxes.............		$ 37,000
Income taxes expense*		(15,000)
Income from continuing operations ...		$ 22,000
Extraordinary item		
Gain on retirement of debt*		16,000
Net income		$ 38,000

* Income Taxes Expense is restated to include the taxes related to the extraordinary gain. This means the $16,000 extraordinary gain is at its gross amount, not net of tax. This restatement is made prior to preparing the statement of cash flows because the FASB requires *all income taxes paid be classified as operating cash outflows.*

Topic Tackler 12-2

The next section describes the direct method. The section following that one describes the indirect method (see p. 538). An instructor may choose to cover either one or both methods for preparing a statement of cash flows. Neither section depends on the other.

Direct Method of Reporting

P2 Compute cash flows from operating activities using the direct method.

We compute cash flows from operating activities under the direct method by adjusting accrual-based income statement items to the cash basis. The usual approach is to adjust income statement accounts related to operating activities for changes in their related balance sheet accounts as follows:

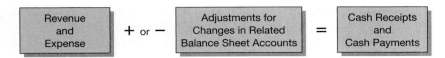

The framework for reporting these cash receipts and payments is shown in Exhibit 12.11. This framework is for the operating section of the cash flow statement under the direct method. We consider cash receipts first and then cash payments.

Global: Some countries such as Australia require the direct method of reporting.

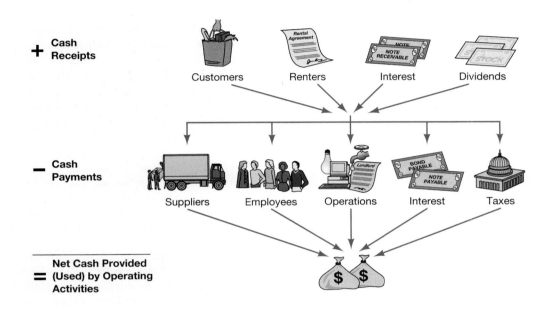

Exhibit 12.11

Major Classes of Operating Cash Flows

Operating Cash Receipts

A review of Exhibit 12.10 and the additional information reported by Genesis suggests only one potential cash receipt—sales to customers. This section, therefore, starts with sales to customers as reported on the income statement and then adjusts it as necessary to obtain cash received from customers to report on the statement of cash flows.

Cash received from customers. If all sales are for cash, the amount of cash received from customers equals the sales reported on the income statement. When some or all sales are on account, however, we must adjust the amount of sales revenue for the change in Accounts Receivable. It is often helpful to use *account analysis* for this purpose. This usually involves setting up a T-account and reconstructing its major entries, with emphasis on cash receipts and payments. To illustrate, we set up a T-account that includes accounts receivable balances for Genesis on December 31, 2001 and 2002. The beginning balance is $40,000 and the ending balance is $60,000. Next, the income statement shows sales of $590,000, which we enter on the debit side of this account. We now can reconstruct the Accounts Receivable account to determine the amount of cash received from customers as follows:

Point: An accounts receivable increase implies cash received from customers is less than sales (the converse is also true).

Accounts Receivable			
Bal., Dec. 31, 2001	40,000		
Sales	590,000	Cash receipts =	570,000
Bal., Dec. 31, 2002	60,000		

This T-account shows that the Accounts Receivable balance begins at $40,000 and increases to $630,000 from sales of $590,000, yet its ending balance is only $60,000. This implies that cash receipts from customers are $570,000, computed as $40,000 + $590,000 − [?] = $60,000. This computation can be rearranged to express cash received as equal to sales of

Example: If the ending balance of accounts receivable is $20,000, what is cash received from customers? *Answer:* $610,000

$590,000 minus a $20,000 increase in accounts receivable. This computation is summarized as a general rule in Exhibit 12.12. The statement of cash flows in Exhibit 12.7 reports the $570,000 cash received from customers as a cash inflow from operating activities.

Exhibit 12.12

Formula to Compute Cash Received from Customers— Direct Method

$$\text{Cash received from customers} = \text{Sales} \begin{cases} + \text{ Decrease in accounts receivable} \\ \quad\quad\quad\quad\quad \text{or} \\ - \text{ Increase in accounts receivable} \end{cases}$$

Point: Net income and cash flows from operations are different. Net income is measured using accrual accounting. Cash flows from operations are measured using cash basis accounting.

Other cash receipts. While Genesis's cash receipts are limited to collections from customers, we often see other types of cash receipts. The most common are cash receipts involving rent, interest, and dividends. We compute cash received from these items by subtracting an increase in their respective receivable or adding a decrease. For instance, if rent receivable increases in the period, cash received from renters is less than rent revenue reported on the income statement. If rent receivable decreases, cash received is more than reported rent revenue. The same logic applies to interest and dividends. The formulas for these computations are summarized in Exhibit 12.16 later in this section.

Operating Cash Payments

A review of Exhibit 12.10 and the additional information from Genesis shows four operating expenses: cost of goods sold, wages and other operating expenses, interest expense, and taxes expense. We analyze each of these expenses to compute their cash amounts for the statement of cash flows. (We then examine depreciation and the other losses and gains.)

Cash paid for merchandise. We compute cash paid for merchandise by analyzing both cost of goods sold and merchandise inventory. If all merchandise purchases are for cash and the ending balance of Merchandise Inventory is unchanged from the beginning balance, the amount of cash paid for merchandise equals cost of goods sold—an uncommon situation. We usually see some change in the Merchandise Inventory balance in a period. Also, some or all merchandise purchases are often made on credit, and this yields changes in the Accounts Payable balance. When the balances of Merchandise Inventory and Accounts Payable change, we must adjust the cost of goods sold for changes in both accounts to compute cash paid for merchandise. This is a two-step adjustment.

First, we use the change in the account balance of Merchandise Inventory and the cost of goods sold amount to compute cost of purchases for the period. An increase in merchandise inventory implies that we bought more than we sold, and we add this inventory increase to cost of goods sold to compute cost of purchases. A decrease in merchandise inventory implies that we bought less than we sold, and we subtract the inventory decrease from cost of goods sold to compute purchases.

Point: Many farms face cash flow problems. When market prices fall, some farms are forced to sell assets to meet debt payments. This reduces farm assets, which in turn, lowers future cash inflows and income and can lead to bankruptcy.

The second step uses the change in the balance of Accounts Payable along with the amount of cost of purchases to compute cash paid for merchandise. A decrease in accounts payable implies that we paid for more goods than we acquired this period, and we then add the accounts payable decrease to cost of purchases to compute cash paid for merchandise. An increase in accounts payable implies that we paid for less than the amount of goods acquired, and we subtract the accounts payable increase from purchases to compute cash paid for merchandise.

We illustrate this two-step process for Genesis. The *first step* is to use account analysis of Merchandise Inventory to compute cost of purchases. We do this by reconstructing the Merchandise Inventory account:

Merchandise Inventory			
Bal., Dec. 31, 2001	70,000		
Purchases =	**314,000**	Cost of goods sold	300,000
Bal., Dec. 31, 2002	84,000		

The beginning balance is $70,000, and the ending balance is $84,000. The income statement shows that cost of goods sold is $300,000, which we enter on the credit side of this account. With this information, we determine the amount for cost of purchases to be $314,000. This computation can be rearranged to express cost of purchases as equal to cost of goods sold of $300,000 plus the $14,000 increase in inventory. The *second step* is to compute cash paid for merchandise by adjusting purchases for the change in accounts payable. This is done by reconstructing the Accounts Payable account:

Accounts Payable			
		Bal., Dec. 31, 2001	40,000
Cash payments =	319,000	Purchases	314,000
		Bal., Dec. 31, 2002	35,000

This account shows that its beginning balance of $40,000 plus purchases of $314,000 minus an ending balance of $35,000 yields cash paid of $319,000 (or $40,000 + $314,000 − [?]= $35,000). Alternatively, we can express cash paid for merchandise as equal to purchases of $314,000 plus the $5,000 decrease in accounts payable. Exhibit 12.7 shows that the $319,000 cash paid for merchandise is reported on the statement of cash flows as a cash outflow under operating activities. We summarize this two-step adjustment to cost of goods sold to compute cash paid for merchandise inventory in Exhibit 12.13.

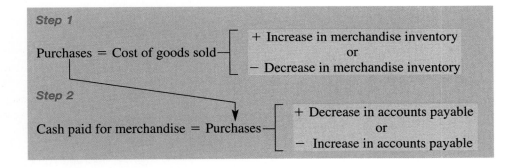

Exhibit 12.13

Two Steps to Compute Cash Paid for Merchandise—Direct Method

Cash paid for wages and operating expenses (excluding depreciation). The income statement of Genesis shows wages and other operating expenses of $216,000 (see Exhibit 12.10). To compute cash paid for wages and other operating expenses, we adjust this amount for any changes in their related balance sheet accounts. We begin by looking for any prepaid expenses and accrued liabilities related to wages and other operating expenses in the balance sheets of Genesis in Exhibit 12.10. The balance sheets show prepaid expenses but no accrued liabilities, meaning that adjustment is limited to the change in prepaid expenses. The amount of adjustment is computed by assuming that all cash paid for wages and other operating expenses is initially debited to Prepaid Expenses. This assumption allows us to reconstruct the Prepaid Expenses account:

Prepaid Expenses			
Bal., Dec. 31, 2001	4,000		
Cash payments =	218,000	Wages and other operating exp.	216,000
Bal., Dec. 31, 2002	6,000		

Prepaid Expenses increases by $2,000 in the period, meaning that cash paid for wages and other operating expenses exceeds the reported expense by $2,000. Alternatively, we can

Point: A decrease in prepaid expenses implies that reported expenses include an amount(s) that did not require a cash outflow in the period.

express cash paid for wages and other operating expenses as equal to its reported expenses of $216,000 plus the $2,000 increase in prepaid expenses.[1]

Exhibit 12.14 summarizes the adjustments to wages (including salaries) and other operating expenses. While the Genesis balance sheet did not report accrued liabilities, we would add them to explain the adjustment to cash when they do exist. A decrease in accrued liabilities implies that we paid cash for more goods or services than received this period, and we would add the decrease in accrued liabilities to the expense amount to obtain cash paid for these goods or services. An increase in accrued liabilities implies that we paid cash for less than what was acquired, and we would subtract this increase in accrued liabilities from the expense amount to get cash paid.

Exhibit 12.14

Formula to Compute Cash Paid for Wages and Operating Expenses—Direct Method

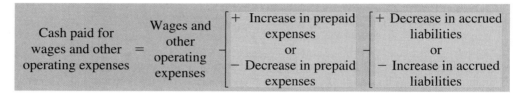

Cash paid for interest and income taxes. Computing operating cash flows for interest and taxes is similar to that for operating expenses. Both require adjustments to their amounts reported on the income statement for changes in their related balance sheet accounts. We begin with the Genesis income statement showing interest expense of $7,000 and income taxes expense of $15,000. To compute the cash paid, we adjust interest expense for the change in interest payable and then the income taxes expense for the change in income taxes payable. These computations involve reconstructing both liability accounts:

Interest Payable			
		Bal., Dec. 31, 2001	4,000
Cash paid for interest =	8,000	Interest expense	7,000
		Bal., Dec. 31, 2002	3,000

Income Taxes Payable			
		Bal., Dec. 31, 2001	12,000
Cash paid for taxes =	5,000	Income taxes expense	15,000
		Bal., Dec. 31, 2002	22,000

These accounts reveal cash paid for interest of $8,000 and cash paid for income taxes of $5,000. The formulas to compute these amounts are shown in Exhibit 12.15. Both of these cash payments are reported as operating cash outflows on the statement of cash flows in Exhibit 12.7.

Exhibit 12.15

Formulas to Compute Cash Paid for Both Interest and Taxes—Direct Method

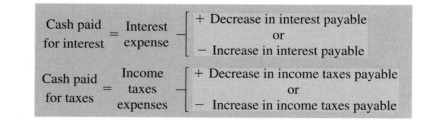

Analysis of additional expenses, gains, and losses. Genesis has three additional items reported on its income statement: depreciation, loss on sale of assets, and gain on retirement of debt. We must consider each of these for their potential cash effects.

---

[1] The assumption that all cash payments for wages and operating expenses are initially debited to Prepaid Expenses is not necessary for our analysis to hold. If cash payments are debited directly to the expense account, the total amount of cash paid for wages and other operating expenses still equals the $216,000 expense plus the $2,000 increase in Prepaid Expenses (which arise from end-of-period adjusting entries).

Depreciation expense Depreciation expense is $24,000. It is often called a *noncash expense* because there are no cash flows from depreciation. Depreciation expense is an allocation of the depreciable cost of an asset. The cash outflow with a plant asset is reported as part of investing activities when it is paid for. This means that depreciation expense is *never* reported on a statement of cash flows using the direct method. Depletion and amortization expenses are treated similarly.

Loss on sale of assets Sales of assets frequently result in gains and losses reported as part of net income, but the amount of recorded gain or loss does *not* reflect any cash flows in these transactions. Asset sales result in cash inflow equal to the cash amount received, regardless of whether the asset was sold at a gain or a loss. This cash inflow is reported under investing activities, meaning that the loss or gain on a sale of assets is *never* reported on a statement of cash flows using the direct method.

Gain on retirement of debt A retirement of debt usually yields a gain or loss reported as part of net income, but that gain or loss does *not* reflect cash flow in this transaction. Debt retirement results in cash outflow equal to the cash paid to settle the debt, regardless of whether the debt is retired at a gain or loss. This cash outflow is reported under financing activities, meaning that the loss or gain from retirement of debt is *never* reported on a statement of cash flows using the direct method.

Summary of Adjustments for Direct Method

Exhibit 12.16 summarizes common adjustments for items making up net income to yield net cash provided (used) by operating activities under the direct method.

Item	From Income Statement	Adjustments to Obtain Cash Flow Numbers	
Receipts			
From sales	Sales Revenue	⌠ +Decrease in Accounts Receivable ⌡ −Increase in Accounts Receivable	
From rent	Rent Revenue	⌠ +Decrease in Rent Receivable ⌡ −Increase in Rent Receivable	
From interest	Interest Revenue	⌠ +Decrease in Interest Receivable ⌡ −Increase in Interest Receivable	
From dividends	Dividend Revenue	⌠ +Decrease in Dividends Receivable ⌡ −Increase in Dividends Receivable	
Payments			
To suppliers	Cost of Goods Sold	⌠ +Increase in Inventory ⌡ −Decrease in Inventory	⌠ +Decrease in Accounts Payable ⌡ −Increase in Accounts Payable
For operations	Operating Expense	⌠ +Increase in Prepaids ⌡ −Decrease in Prepaids	⌠ +Decrease in Accrued Liabilities ⌡ −Increase in Accrued Liabilities
To employees	Wages (Salaries) Expense	⌠ +Decrease in Wages (Salaries) Payable ⌡ −Increase in Wages (Salaries) Payable	
For interest	Interest Expense	⌠ +Decrease in Interest Payable ⌡ −Increase in Interest Payable	
For taxes	Income Tax Expense	⌠ +Decrease in Income Tax Payable ⌡ −Increase in Income Tax Payable	

Exhibit 12.16

Summary of Selected Adjustments for Direct Method

Direct Method Format of Operating Activities Section

Exhibit 12.7 shows the Genesis statement of cash flows using the direct method. Major items of cash inflows and cash outflows are listed separately in the operating activities section. The format requires that operating cash outflows be subtracted from operating cash inflows to get net cash provided (used) by operating activities. The FASB recommends that the operating activities section of the statement of cash flows be reported using the direct method, which is considered more useful to financial statement users. *However, the FASB requires a reconciliation of net income to net cash provided (used) by operating activities when the direct method is used* (which can be reported in the notes). This reconciliation is similar to preparing the operating activities section of the statement of cash flows using the indirect method. The next section describes this indirect method.

Point: Some preparers argue that it is easier to prepare a statement of cash flows using the indirect method. This likely explains its greater frequency in financial statements.

Decision Insight

B-Cash The NBA's **Boston Celtics** report operating cash flows using the direct method. The team's operating activities section from its recent statement of cash flows is shown here ($ in 000s). For this same period, its operating income is $9,011 (in 000s).

Basketball regular season receipts:	
Ticket sales	$37,851
Television and radio broadcast fees	28,074
Other, principally advertising	8,308
Costs and expenses:	
Basketball regular season expenditures .	(49,559)
General and administrative expenses . . .	(5,048)
Selling and promotional expenses	(4,059)
Other expenses and income	(4,065)
Net cash flows from operations	$11,502

Quick Check

4. Is the direct or indirect method of reporting operating cash flows more informative? Explain. Which method is more common in practice?

5. Net sales in a period are $590,000, beginning accounts receivable are $120,000, and ending accounts receivable are $90,000. What cash amount is collected from customers in the period?

6. The Merchandise Inventory account balance decreases in the period from a beginning balance of $32,000 to an ending balance of $28,000. Cost of goods sold for the period is $168,000. If the Accounts Payable balance increases $2,400 in the period, what is the cash amount paid for merchandise inventory?

7. Wages and other operating expenses total $112,000. Beginning-of-period prepaid expenses totaled $1,200, and its ending balance is $4,200. The end-of period wages payable equal $5,600, whereas there were no accrued liabilities at period-end. How much cash is paid for wages and other operating expenses?

Answers—p. 557

Indirect Method of Reporting

P3 Compute cash flows from operating activities using the indirect method.

Net income is computed using accrual accounting, which recognizes revenues when earned and expenses when incurred. Revenues and expenses do not necessarily reflect the receipt and payment of cash. The indirect method of computing and reporting net cash flows from operating activities involves adjusting the net income figure to obtain the net cash provided (used) by operating activities. This includes subtracting noncash increases (credits) from net income and adding noncash charges (debits) back to net income.

Point: Noncash *credits* refer to *revenue amounts* reported on the income statement that are *not collected in cash* this period. Noncash *charges* refer to *expense amounts* reported on the income statement that are *not paid* this period.

We use the Genesis statements in Exhibit 12.10 to illustrate the indirect method. The indirect method begins with Genesis net income of $38,000 and adjusts it to obtain net cash provided (used) by operating activities. Exhibit 12.17 shows the results of the indirect method of reporting operating cash flows for Genesis. The net cash provided by operating activities is $20,000. This amount is the same as that for the direct method of reporting operating cash flows (see Exhibit 12.7). *The two methods always yield the same net cash flow provided (used) by operating activities.* Only the computations and presentation are different.

The indirect method does not report individual operating cash inflows or outflows. Instead, it adjusts net income for three types of adjustments as identified in Exhibit 12.17. There are adjustments ① to reflect changes in noncash current assets and current liabilities relating to operating activities, ② to income statement items involving operating activities that do not affect cash inflows or outflows in the period, and ③ to eliminate gains and losses resulting from investing and financing activities (not part of operating activities). This section describes each of these three types of adjustments.

Global: Some countries such as Spain require the indirect method of reporting.

Exhibit 12.17

Statement of Cash Flows— Indirect Method

GENESIS Statement of Cash Flows For Year Ended December 31, 2002		
Cash flows from operating activities		
Net income	$38,000	
Adjustments to reconcile net income to net cash provided by operating activities:		
① Increase in accounts receivable	(20,000)	
Increase in merchandise inventory	(14,000)	
Increase in prepaid expenses	(2,000)	
Decrease in accounts payable	(5,000)	
Decrease in interest payable	(1,000)	
Increase in income taxes payable	10,000	
② Depreciation expense	24,000	
③ Loss on sale of plant assets	6,000	
Gain on retirement of bonds	(16,000)	
Net cash provided by operating activities		$20,000
Cash flows from investing activities		
Cash received from sale of plant assets	12,000	
Cash paid for purchase of plant assets	(10,000)	
Net cash provided by investing activities		2,000
Cash flows from financing activities		
Cash received from issuing stock	15,000	
Cash paid to retire bonds	(18,000)	
Cash paid for dividends	(14,000)	
Net cash used in financing activities		(17,000)
Net increase in cash		$ 5,000
Cash balance at beginning of year		12,000
Cash balance at end of year		$17,000

① Adjustments for Changes in Current Assets and Current Liabilities

This section describes adjustments for changes in noncash current assets and current liabilities for determining operating cash flows using the indirect method.

Adjustments for changes in noncash current assets. Changes in noncash current assets are normally the result of operating activities. Examples are sales affecting accounts receivable and rented asset usage affecting prepaid rent expense. Specifically, one adjustment to net income in computing operating cash flows under the indirect method is to reflect decreases in noncash current assets as follows:

Decreases in noncash current assets are added to net income.

To see the logic for this adjustment, consider that a decrease in a noncash current asset such as accounts receivable suggests more available cash at the end of the period compared to the beginning. This is so because a decrease in accounts receivable implies higher cash receipts than reflected in sales. We add these higher cash receipts (from decreases in noncash current assets) to net income when computing net cash flow from operations.

In contrast, an increase in noncash current assets such as accounts receivable implies less cash receipts than reflected in sales. As another example, an increase in prepaid rent expense indicates that more cash is paid for rent than is deducted as rent expense. We therefore subtract this increase in prepaid rent from net income in computing the amount of cash flow from operations. These examples dictate the following adjustment to reflect increases in noncash current assets under the indirect method of reporting operating cash flows:

Increases in noncash current assets are subtracted from net income.

We apply both of these adjustments to the Genesis noncash current assets in Exhibit 12.10.

Accounts receivable   Accounts Receivable *increase* $20,000 in the period, from a beginning balance of $40,000 to an ending balance of $60,000. This increase implies that Genesis collects less cash than its reported sales for the period. It also means that some of these sales are in the form of accounts receivable, leaving accounts receivable with an increase. The lower amount of cash receipts compared to sales is reflected in the Accounts Receivable T-account:

Accounts Receivable			
Bal., Dec. 31, 2001	40,000		
Sales	590,000	Cash receipts =	570,000
Bal., Dec. 31, 2002	60,000		

Accordingly, the $20,000 increase in Accounts Receivable is subtracted from net income as part of the adjustments to obtain net cash provided by operating activities (see Exhibit 12.17). Notice that subtracting it adjusts sales to the cash receipts amount.

Merchandise inventory   Merchandise inventory *increases* by $14,000 in the period, from a $70,000 beginning balance to an $84,000 ending balance. This increase implies that Genesis had a larger amount of cash purchases than cost of goods sold this period. This larger amount of cash purchases is in the form of inventory, resulting in an increase in the Merchandise Inventory account:

Merchandise Inventory			
Bal., Dec. 31, 2001	70,000		
Purchases =	314,000	Cost of goods sold	300,000
Bal., Dec. 31, 2002	84,000		

The $14,000 increase in Merchandise Inventory is subtracted from net income as part of the adjustments to determine net cash provided by operating activities (see Exhibit 12.17).

Prepaid expenses   Prepaid expenses *increase* $2,000 in the period, from a $4,000 beginning balance to a $6,000 ending balance. This increase implies that Genesis's cash payments exceed its expenses (related to its prepaids) incurred this period. These higher cash payments increase the amount of Prepaid Expenses, as reflected in its T-account:

Prepaid Expenses			
Bal., Dec. 31, 2001	4,000		
Cash payments =	218,000	Wages and other operating exp.	216,000
Bal., Dec. 31, 2002	6,000		

The $2,000 increase in Prepaid Expenses is subtracted from net income as part of the adjustments to determine net cash provided by operating activities (see Exhibit 12.17). Subtracting it adjusts operating expenses to a cash payments amount.

Adjustments for changes in current liabilities. Changes in current liabilities are normally the result of operating activities. An example is a purchase that affects accounts payable. One adjustment to net income in computing operating cash flows under the indirect method is to reflect increases in current liabilities as follows:

Increases in current liabilities are added to net income.

To see the logic for this adjustment, consider that an increase in the Accounts Payable account suggests that cash payments are less than the related (cost of goods sold) expense. As another example, an increase in wages payable implies that wages expense exceeds cash paid for wages during the period. Since more is deducted as an expense than is paid in cash, we would add the increase in wages payable to net income when computing net cash flow from operations.

Conversely, when current liabilities decrease in the period, the indirect method for reporting operating cash flows requires the following adjustment:

Decreases in current liabilities are subtracted from net income.

We apply both of these adjustments to the current liabilities shown in Exhibit 12.10.

Accounts payable   Accounts Payable *decrease* $5,000 in the period, from a beginning balance of $40,000 to an ending balance of $35,000. This decrease implies that its cash payments to suppliers exceed its merchandise purchases by $5,000 for the period, which is reflected in the Accounts Payable T-account:

Accounts Payable			
		Bal., Dec. 31, 2001	40,000
Cash payments =	319,000	Purchases	314,000
		Bal., Dec. 31, 2002	35,000

The $5,000 decrease in Accounts Payable is subtracted from net income as part of the adjustments to determine net cash provided by operating activities (see Exhibit 12.17).

Interest payable   Interest Payable *decreases* $1,000 in the period, from a $4,000 beginning balance to a $3,000 ending balance. This decrease indicates that cash paid for interest exceeds interest expense for the period by $1,000. This larger cash payment compared to reported interest expense is reflected in the Interest Payable T-account:

Interest Payable			
		Bal., Dec. 31, 2001	4,000
Cash paid for interest =	8,000	Interest expense	7,000
		Bal., Dec. 31, 2002	3,000

The $1,000 decrease in Interest Payable is subtracted from net income as part of the adjustments to get net cash provided by operating activities (see Exhibit 12.17).

Income taxes payable   Income Taxes Payable *increases* $10,000 in the period, from a $12,000 beginning balance to a $22,000 ending balance. This increase implies that income taxes incurred exceed the cash paid for taxes by $10,000. This smaller cash payment for taxes compared to taxes expense is reflected in the Income Taxes Payable T-account:

Income Taxes Payable			
		Bal., Dec. 31, 2001	12,000
Cash paid for taxes =	5,000	Income taxes expense	15,000
		Bal., Dec. 31, 2002	22,000

The $10,000 increase in Income Taxes Payable is added to net income as part of the adjustments to determine net cash provided by operating activities (see Exhibit 12.17).

② Adjustments for Operating Items Not Providing or Using Cash

The income statement usually includes some expenses that do not reflect cash outflows in the period. Examples are depreciation, amortization, depletion, and bad debts expense. The indirect method for reporting operating cash flows requires that

Expenses with no cash outflows are added back to net income.

To see the logic of this adjustment, recall that items such as depreciation, amortization, depletion, and bad debts originate from debits to expense accounts and credits to noncash accounts. These entries have *no* cash effect, and we need to add them back to net income when computing net cash flows from operations. Adding them back cancels their deductions.

Similarly, when net income includes revenues that do not reflect cash inflows in the period, the indirect method for reporting operating cash flows requires that

Revenues with no cash inflows are subtracted from net income.

We apply these adjustments to the Genesis operating items that do not provide or use cash.

Depreciation. Depreciation expense is the only Genesis operating item that does not affect cash flows in the period. We must add back the $24,000 depreciation expense to net income to obtain net cash provided by operating activities. (Later in the chapter, we explain that the cash outflow to acquire a plant asset is reported as an investing activity.)

③ Adjustments for Nonoperating Items

Net income often includes losses that are not part of operating activities but instead are part of either investing or financing activities. Examples are a loss from the sale of a plant asset and a loss from retirement of a bond payable. Thus, the indirect method for reporting operating cash flows requires that

Nonoperating losses are added back to net income.

To see the logic, consider that items such as a plant asset sale and a bond retirement are normally recorded by recognizing the cash, removing all plant asset or bond accounts, and recognizing any loss or gain. The cash received or paid is not part of operating activities but instead is part of either investing or financing activities. *No* operating cash flow effect occurs. However, since the nonoperating loss is a deduction in computing net income, we need to add it back to net income when computing the net cash flow from operations. Adding it back cancels the deduction.

Similarly, when net income includes gains not part of operating activities, the indirect method for reporting operating cash flows requires that

Nonoperating gains are subtracted from net income.

These net income adjustments are part of computations to determine net cash provided by operating activities. We now look at the nonoperating items of Genesis.

Loss on sale of plant assets. Genesis reports a $6,000 loss on sale of plant assets as part of net income. This loss is a proper deduction in computing income, but it is *not part of operating activities*. Instead, a sale of plant assets is part of investing activities. The $6,000 nonoperating loss is added back to net income as part of our adjustments to determine cash provided by operating activities (see Exhibit 12.17). Adding it back cancels the loss. Later we explain how to report the cash inflow from the asset sale in investing activities.

Gain on retirement of debt. A $16,000 gain on retirement of debt is reported in net income. This gain is properly included in net income, but it is *not part of operating activities*. The $16,000 nonoperating gain is subtracted from net income as part of our adjustments to obtain net cash provided by operating activities (see Exhibit 12.17). Subtracting it cancels the recorded gain. Later we describe how to report the cash outflow to retire debt.

Summary of Adjustments for Indirect Method

Exhibit 12.18 summarizes common adjustments to net income when computing net cash provided (used) by operating activities under the indirect method.

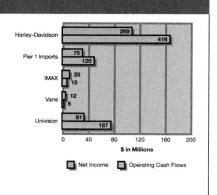

Decision Insight

Cash or Income   The difference between net income and operating cash flows can be large. The bar chart to the side shows net income and operating cash flows for five companies. Note that operating cash flows can be either higher or lower than net income. The difference between net income and operating cash flows is a focus of many analysts.

Net Income

   + Decrease in noncash current asset

   − Increase in noncash current asset

   + Increase in current liability*

   − Decrease in current liability*

   + Depreciation, depletion, and amortization

   + Accrued expenses

   − Accrued revenues

   + Loss on disposal of long-term asset

   + Loss on retirement of debt

   − Gain on disposal of long-term asset

   − Gain on retirement of debt

Net cash provided (used) by operating activities

① Adjustments for changes in current assets and current liabilities

② Adjustments for operating items not providing or using cash

③ Adjustments for nonoperating items

Exhibit 12.18

Summary of Selected Adjustments for Indirect Method

* Excludes current portion of long-term debt and any short-term notes payable if unrelated to sales—both are financing activities.

The computations in determining net cash provided (used) by operating activities are different for the direct and indirect methods, but the result is identical. Both methods yield the same $20,000 figure for net cash provided (used) by operating activities for Genesis—see Exhibits 12.7 and 12.17.

Quick Check

8. Determine net cash provided (used) by operating activities using the following data: net income, $74,900; decrease in accounts receivable, $4,600; increase in inventory, $11,700; decrease in accounts payable, $1,000; loss on sale of equipment, $3,400; payment of cash dividends, $21,500.

9. Why are expenses such as depreciation and amortization added to net income when cash flow from operating activities is computed by the indirect method?

10. A company reports net income of $15,000 that includes a $3,000 gain on the sale of plant assets. Why is this gain subtracted from net income in computing cash flow from operating activities using the indirect method?

Answers—p. 557

The third major step in preparing the statement of cash flows is to compute and report net cash flows from investing activities. We normally do this by identifying changes in (1) all noncurrent asset accounts and (2) the current accounts for both notes receivable and investments in securities (excluding trading securities). We then analyze changes in these accounts using available information to determine their effect, if any, on cash. Results of this analysis are reported in the investing activities section of the statement of cash flows. *Reporting of investing activities is identical under the direct method and the indirect method.*

   Information to compute cash flows from investing activities is usually taken from beginning and ending balance sheets and the income statement. We use a three-step process to determine net cash provided (used) by investing activities: (1) identify changes in investing-related accounts, (2) explain these changes using reconstruction analysis, and (3) report their cash flow effects.

Analysis of Noncurrent Assets

Information provided earlier in the chapter about the Genesis transactions reveals that the company both purchased and sold plant assets during the period. Both transactions are investing activities and are analyzed for their cash flow effects in this section.

Cash Flows from Investing

P4 Determine cash flows from both investing and financing activities.

Point: Investing activities include (1) purchasing and selling long-term assets, (2) lending and collecting on notes receivable, and (3) purchasing and selling short-term investments other than cash equivalents and trading securities.

Point: Financing and investing info is available in ledger accounts to help explain changes in comparative balance sheets. Post references lead to relevant entries and explanations.

Assets = Liabilities + Equity
+70,000   +60,000
−10,000

Assets = Liabilities + Equity
+12,000   −6,000
−30,000
+12,000

Assets = Liabilities + Equity
−24,000   −24,000

Example: If a plant asset costing $40,000 with $37,000 of accumulated depreciation is sold at a $1,000 loss, what is the cash flow? What is the cash flow if this asset is sold at a gain of $3,000? *Answers:* +$2,000; +$6,000.

Plant asset transactions. The first step in analyzing the Plant Assets account and its related Accumulated Depreciation is to identify any changes in these accounts from comparative balance sheet information in Exhibit 12.10. This analysis reveals a $40,000 increase in plant assets from $210,000 to $250,000 and a $12,000 increase in accumulated depreciation from $48,000 to $60,000. The second step is to explain these changes. Items *b* and *c* of the additional information reported for Genesis (page 532) are relevant in this case. Recall that the Plant Assets account is affected by both its purchases and sales, while its Accumulated Depreciation account is normally increased from depreciation and decreased from the removal of accumulated depreciation from asset sales. To explain changes in these accounts and to identify their cash flow effects, we prepare *reconstructed entries,* which are recreations of entries from prior transactions; *they are not the actual entries by the preparer.* Item *b* reports that Genesis purchases plant assets of $70,000 by issuing $60,000 in bonds payable to the seller and paying $10,000 in cash. The reconstructed entry for analysis of item *b* follows:

Reconstruction	Plant Assets	70,000	
	Bonds Payable		60,000
	Cash		**10,000**

This entry reveals a $10,000 cash outflow for plant assets, and a $60,000 noncash investing and financing transaction involving bonds exchanged for plant assets.

Item *c* reports that Genesis sells plant assets costing $30,000 (with $12,000 of accumulated depreciation) for cash of $12,000, resulting in a loss of $6,000. The reconstructed entry for analysis of item *c* follows:

Reconstruction	**Cash**	**12,000**	
	Accumulated Depreciation	12,000	
	Loss on Sale of Plant Assets	6,000	
	Plant Assets		30,000

This entry reveals a $12,000 cash inflow from assets sold. The $6,000 loss is computed by comparing the asset book value to the cash received and does not reflect any cash inflow or outflow. In addition, we also reconstruct the entry for Depreciation Expense using information from the income statement:

Reconstruction	Depreciation Expense	24,000	
	Accumulated Depreciation		24,000

This entry shows that Depreciation Expense results in no cash flow effect. These three reconstructed entries are reflected in the following accounts.

Plant Assets			
Bal., Dec. 31, 2001	210,000		
Purchase	**70,000**	**Sale**	**30,000**
Bal., Dec. 31, 2002	250,000		

Accumulated Depreciation—Plant Assets			
		Bal., Dec. 31, 2001	48,000
Sale	**12,000**	**Depr. expense**	**24,000**
		Bal., Dec. 31, 2002	60,000

We have now reconstructed plant asset and related accounts by explaining how the beginning balances of these accounts are affected by purchases, sales, and depreciation in yielding their ending balances. Specifically, the change in plant assets from $210,000 to $250,000 is fully explained by the $70,000 purchase and the $30,000 sale. Also, the change in accumulated depreciation from $48,000 to $60,000 is fully explained by the sale of assets (removal of $12,000 in accumulated depreciation) and depreciation expense of $24,000. (Note:

Preparers of the statement of cash flows have the entire ledger and additional information at their disposal. For brevity reasons, we are given only the additional information needed for reconstructing accounts and verifying that our analysis of the investing-related accounts is complete.)

The final step in analyzing investing activities is to make the necessary disclosures on the statement of cash flows. Disclosure of the two cash flow effects in the investing section of the statement appears as follows (also see Exhibit 12.7 or 12.17):

Cash flows from investing activities	
Cash received from sale of plant assets	$12,000
Cash paid for purchase of plant assets	(10,000)

The $60,000 portion of the purchase described in item *b* and financed by issuing the bonds is a noncash investing and financing activity. It can be reported in a note or in a separate schedule to the statement as follows:

Noncash investing and financing activity	
Purchased plant assets with issuance of bonds	$60,000

Analysis of Other Assets

Many other asset transactions (including those involving current notes receivable and investments in certain securities) are considered investing activities and can affect a company's cash flows. Since Genesis did not enter into other investing activities impacting assets, we do not need to extend our analysis to these other assets. If such transactions did exist, we would analyze them using the same three-step process illustrated for plant assets.

Point: Equity and debt investments usually refer to investments in stocks and bonds, respectively.

Decision Track 12.2

Decision Point	Information Search	Analyze & Evaluate
Is a company's operating cash flow adequate to meet asset growth?	**Cash coverage of growth** = Cash flow from operations divided by cash outflow for long-term assets.	A low ratio (less than 1) suggests a financing need; conversely, a very high ratio can reflect limited growth opportunities.

Quick Check

11. Equipment costing $80,000 with accumulated depreciation of $30,000 is sold at a loss of $10,000. What is the cash receipt from this sale? In what section of the statement of cash flows is this transaction reported?

Answer—p. 557

The fourth major step in preparing the statement of cash flows is to compute and report net cash flows from financing activities. We normally do this by identifying changes in all non-current liability accounts (including the current portion of any notes and bonds) and the equity accounts. These accounts include long-term debt, notes payable, bonds payable, common stock, and retained earnings. Changes in these accounts are then analyzed using available information to determine their effect, if any, on cash. Results of this analysis are reported in the financing activities section of the statement. *Reporting of financing activities is identical under the direct method and indirect method.*

We again use a three-step process to determine net cash provided (used) by financing activities: (1) identify changes in financing-related accounts, (2) explain these changes using reconstruction analysis, and (3) report their cash flow effects.

Cash Flows from Financing

Point: Financing activities generally refer to changes in the noncurrent liability and the equity accounts. Examples are (1) receiving cash from issuing debt or repaying amounts borrowed and (2) receiving cash from or distributing cash to owners.

Analysis of Noncurrent Liabilities

Information provided earlier about Genesis reveals two transactions involving noncurrent liabilities. We have analyzed one of those—the $60,000 issuance of bonds payable to purchase plant assets. This transaction is reported as a significant noncash investing and financing activity in a note or a separate schedule to the statement of cash flows. The other remaining transaction involving noncurrent liabilities is the cash retirement of bonds payable, which we analyze in this section.

Bonds payable transactions. The first step in analysis of bonds is to review comparative balance sheet information from Exhibit 12.10 for bonds payable, which reveals an increase in bonds payable from $64,000 to $90,000. The second step is to explain this change. Item *e* of the additional information for Genesis (page 532) reports that bonds with a carrying value of $34,000 are retired for $18,000 cash, resulting in a $16,000 gain. The reconstructed entry for analysis of item *e* follows:

Assets = Liabilities + Equity
−18,000 −34,000   +16,000

Reconstruction	Bonds Payable	34,000	
	Gain on retirement of debt		16,000
	Cash		**18,000**

This entry reveals an $18,000 cash outflow for retirement of bonds and a $16,000 gain from comparing the bonds payable carrying value to the cash received. This gain does not reflect any cash inflow or outflow. In addition, item *b* of the additional information reports that Genesis purchased plant assets costing $70,000 by issuing $60,000 in bonds payable to the seller and paying $10,000 in cash. We reconstructed this entry for analysis of investing activities—it increased bonds payable by $60,000 and is reported as a noncash investing and financing transaction. The Bonds Payable account reflects (and is fully explained by) these reconstructed entries as follows:

Bonds Payable			
		Bal., Dec. 31, 2001	64,000
Retired bonds	34,000	**Issued bonds**	**60,000**
		Bal., Dec. 31, 2002	90,000

The third step is to disclose the cash flow effect of the bond retirement in the financing section of the statement as follows (also see Exhibit 12.7 or 12.17):

Cash flows from financing activities	
Cash paid to retire bonds	$(18,000)

We have now reconstructed the Bonds Payable account by showing how the change in bonds payable from $64,000 to $90,000 is explained by the $34,000 retirement and the $60,000 issuance.

Analysis of Equity

The Genesis information reveals two transactions involving equity accounts. The first is the issuance of common stock for cash. The second is the declaration and payment of cash dividends. We analyze both transactions in this section.

Common stock transactions. The first step in analyzing common stock is to review comparative balance sheet information from Exhibit 12.10, which reveals an increase in common stock from $80,000 to $95,000. The second step

Decision Insight

Free Cash Flow *Free cash flow* refers to operating cash flows available after allowing for investing and financing requirements. Free cash flow is often estimated as operating cash flows minus capital expenditures and cash dividends. Growth and financial flexibility depend on adequate free cash flow.

is to explain this change. Item *d* of the Genesis additional information reports that it issued 3,000 shares of common stock at par for $5 per share. The reconstructed entry for analysis of item *d* follows:

Reconstruction	**Cash**	**15,000**		Assets	= Liabilities + Equity
	Common Stock		15,000	+15,000	+15,000

This entry reveals a $15,000 cash inflow from stock issuance and is reflected in (and explains) the Common Stock account as follows:

Common Stock		
	Bal., Dec. 31, 2001	80,000
	Issued stock	**15,000**
	Bal., Dec. 31, 2002	95,000

The third step is to disclose the cash flow effect from stock issuance in the financing section of the statement as follows (also see Exhibit 12.7 or 12.17):

Cash flows from financing activities	
Cash received from issuing stock	$15,000

The $15,000 stock issuance fully explains the change in the Common Stock account.

Retained earnings transactions. The first step in analyzing the Retained Earnings account is to review comparative balance sheet information from Exhibit 12.10. This reveals an increase in retained earnings from $88,000 to $112,000. The second step is to explain this change. Item *f* of the additional information for Genesis reports that it paid cash dividends of $14,000. The reconstructed entry for analysis of item *f* follows:

Reconstruction	Retained Earnings	14,000		Assets	= Liabilities + Equity
	Cash		**14,000**	−14,000	−14,000

This entry reveals a $14,000 cash outflow for cash dividends. Retained earnings is also impacted by net income of $38,000. (Net income was analyzed under the operating section of the statement of cash flows.) Our reconstruction analysis is reflected in (and explains) the Retained Earnings account as follows:

Retained Earnings			
		Bal., Dec. 31, 2001	88,000
Cash dividend	**14,000**	**Net income**	**38,000**
		Bal., Dec. 31, 2002	112,000

The third step is to disclose the cash flow effect from the cash dividend in the financing section of the statement as follows (also see Exhibit 12.7 or 12.17):

Cash flows from financing activities	
Cash paid for dividends	$(14,000)

The $14,000 dividend payment and the $38,000 of net income explain the change in Retained Earnings.

We now have identified and explained all of the Genesis cash inflows and cash outflows along with one noncash investing and financing transaction. Specifically, our analysis has reconciled changes in all noncash balance sheet accounts.

Point: Financing activities not affecting cash flow include *declaration* of a cash dividend, *declaration* of a stock dividend, payment of a stock dividend, and a stock split.

Global: There are no requirements to separate domestic and international cash flows, leading some users to ask "Where in the world is cash flow?"

Decision Track 12.3   *d*

Decision Point	Information Search	Analyze & Evaluate
Is a company's operating cash flow adequate to meet long-term obligations?	**Cash coverage of debt** = Cash flow from operations divided by noncurrent liabilities	A low ratio suggests a risk of insolvency; conversely, a high ratio suggests a greater ability to meet long-term obligations

Proving Cash Balances

The fifth and final step in preparing the statement is to report the beginning and ending cash balances and prove that the *net change in cash* is explained by operating, investing, and financing net cash flows. This step is shown here for Genesis.

Net cash provided by operating activities	$20,000
Net cash provided by investing activities	2,000
Net cash used in financing activities	(17,000)
Net increase in cash	**$ 5,000**
Cash balance at beginning of 2002	12,000
Cash balance at end of 2002	$17,000

Decision Maker   *d*

Reporter   Management grants you an interview and highlights a recent $600,000 net loss that involves a $930,000 extraordinary loss and a total net cash outflow of $550,000 (which includes net cash outflows of $850,000 for investing activities and $350,000 for financing activities). What is your assessment of this company?

Answer—p. 556

The table above shows that the $5,000 net increase in cash, from $12,000 at the beginning of the period to $17,000 at the end, is reconciled by net cash flows from operating ($20,000 inflow), investing ($2,000 inflow), and financing ($17,000 outflow) activities. This is formally reported at the bottom of the statement of cash flows as shown in both Exhibits 12.7 and 12.17.

Decision Analysis   *d*   Cash Flow Analysis

This section explains analysis of the statement of cash flows and describes the usefulness of the cash flow on total assets ratio.

Analyzing Cash Sources and Uses

 A1   Analyze the statement of cash flows.

Most managers stress the importance of understanding and predicting cash flows for many business decisions. In addition, creditors evaluate a company's ability to generate cash before deciding whether to lend money. Investors also assess cash inflows and outflows before buying and selling stock. Information in the statement of cash flows helps address these and other questions such as (1) How much cash is generated from or used in operations? (2) What expenditures are made with cash from operations? (3) What is the source of cash for debt payments? (4) What is the source of cash for distributions to owners? (5) How is the increase in investing activities financed? (6) What is the source of cash for new plant assets? (7) Why is cash flow from operations different from income? (8) How is cash from financing used? Cash flows from investing and financing activities are important in these decisions, but we pay special attention to operating cash flows. A statement of cash flows helps by separating investing, financing, and operating activities.

To illustrate the importance of separately analyzing cash flows by activities, consider data from three different companies in Exhibit 12.19. These companies operate in the same industry and have been in business for several years.

($ in thousands)	Fisher	Sprint	Tektron
Cash provided (used) by operating activities	$90,000	$40,000	$(24,000)
Cash provided (used) by investing activities			
Proceeds from sale of plant assets			26,000
Purchase of plant assets	(48,000)	(25,000)	
Cash provided (used) by financing activities			
Proceeds from issuance of debt			13,000
Repayment of debt	(27,000)		
Net increase (decrease) in cash	$15,000	$15,000	$ 15,000

Exhibit 12.19

Cash Flows of Competing Companies

Each company generates an identical $15,000 net increase in cash flows, but their sources and uses of cash flows are very different. Fisher's operating activities provide net cash flows of $90,000, allowing it to purchase additional plant assets for $48,000 and repay $27,000 of its debt. Sprint's operating activities provide $40,000 of cash flows, limiting its purchase of plant assets to $25,000. Tektron's $15,000 net cash increase is due to selling plant assets and incurring additional debt. Its operating activities yield a net cash outflow of $24,000. Overall, analysis of these cash flows reveals that Fisher is more capable of generating cash to meet its future obligations than is Sprint or Tektron. Also, Fisher's strong operating cash flows bode well for future performance, while Tektron's operating outlook is poor. This evaluation is, of course, tentative and must be supported by other information, including data from the balance sheet and income statement.

Cash Flow on Total Assets

Cash flow accounting recognizes cash inflows when received (not necessarily earned) and cash outflows when paid (not necessarily incurred). Cash flow information has limitations, but it can help us measure a company's ability to meet its obligations, pay dividends, expand operations, and obtain financing. Users often compute and analyze a cash-based ratio called *cash flow on total assets*. It is similar to return on total assets except that its numerator is net cash flows from operating activities (not net income). The **cash flow on total assets** ratio is defined in Exhibit 12.20.

A2   Compute and apply the cash flow on total assets ratio.

$$\text{Cash flow on total assets} = \frac{\text{Cash flow from operations}}{\text{Average total assets}}$$

Exhibit 12.20

Cash Flow on Total Assets

The cash flow on total assets ratio reflects actual cash flows and is not affected by the accounting constraints of income recognition and measurement. It can also help business decision makers estimate the amount and timing of cash flows when planning and analyzing operating activities.

To illustrate, consider the cash flow on total assets ratio for Nike at May 31, 2000. It is computed as follows ($ millions): $759.9/[($5,856.9 + $5,247.7)/2] = 13.7\%$. Is a 13.7% cash flow on total assets ratio good or bad for Nike? To help answer this question, we can compare this ratio with the ratios of prior years, its competitors, and the market. For example, we show Nike's cash flow on total assets ratio for its most recent five years in the second column of Exhibit 12.21. Its return on total assets is provided in the third column.

Nike's cash flow on total assets has increased in the past two years relative to the prior three years. Moreover, the ratio exceeds its return on total assets for the period 1998–2000, leading some analysts to infer that Nike's *earnings quality* is high for

Year	Cash Flow on Total Assets	Return on Total Assets
2000	13.7%	10.4%
1999	18.1	8.5
1998	9.6	7.4
1997	6.9	17.1
1996	9.6	15.6

Exhibit 12.21

Nike's Cash Flow on Total Assets

this period. These analysts presume higher earnings quality when more earnings are realized in the form of cash.

In sum, the statement of cash flows is an important bridge between the income statement and balance sheet and is valuable in financial analysis. The cash flow on total assets ratio is a useful part of this analysis and can be an indicator of earnings quality.

Demonstration Problem

Umlauf's comparative balance sheets, income statement, and additional information follow.

UMLAUF COMPANY
Income Statement
For Year Ended December 31, 2002

Sales		$446,100
Cost of goods sold	$222,300	
Other operating expenses	120,300	
Depreciation expense	25,500	(368,100)
Other gains (losses)		
Loss on sale of equipment		(3,300)
Income before taxes		$ 74,700
Income taxes expense*		(13,725)
Income from continuing oper.		$ 60,975
Extraordinary item		
Loss on retirement of bonds*		(825)
Net income		$ 60,150

UMLAUF COMPANY
Balance Sheet
December 31, 2002 and 2001

	2002	2001
Assets		
Cash	$ 43,050	$ 23,925
Accounts receivable	34,125	39,825
Merchandise inventory	156,000	146,475
Prepaid expenses	3,600	1,650
Equipment	135,825	146,700
Accum. depreciation—Equip.	(61,950)	(47,550)
Total assets	$310,650	$311,025
Liabilities and Equity		
Accounts payable	$ 28,800	$ 33,750
Income taxes payable	5,100	4,425
Dividends payable	0	4,500
Bonds payable	0	37,500
Common stock, $10 par	168,750	168,750
Retained earnings	108,000	62,100
Total liabilities and equity	$310,650	$311,025

* Income Taxes Expense is restated to include the tax effects from the extraordinary loss. This means that the $825 extraordinary loss is at its gross amount, not net of tax.

Additional Information

a. All sales are made on credit.

b. All merchandise inventory purchases are on credit.

c. Accounts Payable balances result from merchandise inventory purchases.

d. Prepaid expenses relate to "other operating expenses."

e. Equipment costing $21,375 with accumulated depreciation of $11,100 is sold for cash.

f. Equipment purchases are for cash.

g. Accumulated Depreciation is affected by depreciation expense and the sale of equipment.

h. The balance of Retained Earnings is affected by dividend declarations and net income.

Required

1. Prepare a statement of cash flows using the direct method for year 2002.

2. Prepare a statement of cash flows using the indirect method for year 2002.

Planning the Solution

- Prepare two blank statements of cash flows with sections for operating, investing, and financing activities using the (1) direct method format and (2) indirect method format.

- Compute cash received from customers, cash paid for merchandise, cash paid for other operating expenses, and cash paid for taxes as illustrated in the chapter.
- Compute the cash paid for equipment and the cash received from the sale of equipment using the additional information provided along with the amount for depreciation expense and the change in the balances of equipment and accumulated depreciation. Use T-accounts to help chart the effects of the sale and purchase of equipment on the balances of the Equipment account and the Accumulated Depreciation account.
- Calculate the effect of net income on the change in the Retained Earnings account balance. Assign the difference between the change in retained earnings and the amount of net income to dividends declared. Adjust the dividends declared amount for the change in the Dividends Payable balance.
- Enter the cash effects of reconstruction entries to the appropriate section(s) of the statement.
- Total each section of the statement, determine the total net change in cash, and add it to the beginning balance to get the ending balance of cash.

Solution to Demonstration Problem

Supporting computations for cash receipts and cash payments:

(1) Sales	$446,100
Add decrease in accounts receivable	5,700
Cash received from customers	**$451,800**
(2) Cost of goods sold	$222,300
Plus increase in merchandise inventory	9,525
Purchases	$231,825
Plus decrease in accounts payable	4,950
Cash paid for merchandise	**$236,775**
(3) Other operating expenses	$120,300
Plus increase in prepaid expenses	1,950
Cash paid for other operating expenses	**$122,250**
(4) Income taxes expense	$ 13,725
Less increase in income taxes payable	(675)
Cash paid for income taxes	**$ 13,050**
(5) *Cost of equipment sold	$ 21,375
Accumulated depreciation of equipment sold	(11,100)
Book value of equipment sold	$ 10,275
Loss on sale of equipment	(3,300)
Cash received from sale of equipment	**$ 6,975**
Cost of equipment sold	$ 21,375
Less decrease in the equipment account balance . . .	(10,875)
Cash paid for new equipment	**$ 10,500**

*Supporting T-account analysis for part 5 above:

Equipment			
Bal., Dec. 31, 2001	146,700		
Cash purchase	10,500	Sale	21,375
Bal., Dec. 31, 2002	135,825		

Accumulated Depreciation—Equipment			
		Bal., Dec. 31, 2001	47,550
Sale	11,100	Depr. expense	25,500
		Bal., Dec. 31, 2002	61,950

(6) Loss on retirement of bonds	$ 825
Carrying value of bonds retired	37,500
Cash paid to retire bonds	**$ 38,325**
(7) Net income	$ 60,150
Less increase in retained earnings	45,900
Dividends declared	$ 14,250
Plus decrease in dividends payable	4,500
Cash paid for dividends	**$ 18,750**

UMLAUF COMPANY
Statement of Cash Flows (Direct Method)
For Year Ended December 31, 2002

Cash flows from operating activities		
Cash received from customers	$451,800	
Cash paid for merchandise	(236,775)	
Cash paid for other operating expenses	(122,250)	
Cash paid for income taxes	(13,050)	
Net cash provided by operating activities		$79,725
Cash flows from investing activities		
Cash received from sale of equipment	6,975	
Cash paid for equipment	(10,500)	
Net cash used in investing activities		(3,525)
Cash flows from financing activities		
Cash paid to retire bonds payable	(38,325)	
Cash paid for dividends	(18,750)	
Net cash used in financing activities		(57,075)
Net increase in cash		$19,125
Cash balance at beginning of year		23,925
Cash balance at end of year		$43,050

UMLAUF COMPANY
Statement of Cash Flows (Indirect Method)
For Year Ended December 31, 2002

Cash flows from operating activities		
Cash flows from operating activities:		
Net income	$60,150	
Adjustments to reconcile net income to net cash provided by operating activities		
Decrease in accounts receivable	5,700	
Increase in merchandise inventory	(9,525)	
Increase in prepaid expenses	(1,950)	
Decrease in accounts payable	(4,950)	
Increase in income taxes payable	675	
Depreciation expense	25,500	
Loss on sale of plant assets	3,300	
Loss on retirement of bonds	825	
Net cash provided by operating activities		$79,725

[continued on next page]

[continued from previous page]

Cash flows from investing activities		
Cash received from sale of equipment	$ 6,975	
Cash paid for equipment	(10,500)	
Net cash used in investing activities		(3,525)
Cash flows from financing activities		
Cash paid to retire bonds payable	(38,325)	
Cash paid for dividends	(18,750)	
Net cash used in financing activities		(57,075)
Net increase in cash		$19,125
Cash balance at beginning of year		23,925
Cash balance at end of year		$43,050

APPENDIX

Spreadsheet Preparation of the Statement of Cash Flows

12A

This appendix explains how to use a spreadsheet to prepare the statement of cash flows under the indirect method.

Preparing the Indirect Method Spreadsheet

Analyzing noncash accounts can be challenging when a company has a large number of accounts and many operating, investing, and financing transactions. A *spreadsheet*, also called *work sheet* or *working paper*, can help us organize the information needed to prepare a statement of cash flows. A spreadsheet also makes it easier to check the accuracy of our work. To illustrate, we return to the comparative balance sheets and income statement shown in Exhibit 12.10. Information needed for the spreadsheet in preparing the statement of cash flows along with identifying letters *a* through *m* follow:

P5 Illustrate spreadsheet use in preparing a statement of cash flows.

a. Net income is $38,000.

b. Accounts receivable increase by $20,000.

c. Merchandise inventory increases by $14,000.

d. Prepaid expenses increase by $2,000.

e. Accounts payable decrease by $5,000.

f. Interest payable decreases by $1,000.

g. Income taxes payable increase by $10,000.

h. Depreciation expense is $24,000.

i. Plant assets costing $30,000 with accumulated depreciation of $12,000 are sold for $12,000 cash. This yields a loss on sale of assets of $6,000.

j. Bonds with a book value of $34,000 are retired with a cash payment of $18,000—yielding a $16,000 gain on retirement of bonds.

k. Plant assets costing $70,000 are purchased with a cash payment of $10,000 and an issuance of bonds payable for $60,000.

l. Issued 3,000 shares of common stock for $15,000 cash.

m. Paid cash dividends of $14,000.

Exhibit 12A.1 shows the indirect method spreadsheet for Genesis. We enter both beginning and ending balance sheet amounts on the spreadsheet. We also enter information in the Analysis of Changes columns (keyed to the additional information items *a* through *m*) to explain changes in the accounts and determine the cash flows for operating, investing, and financing activities. Information about non-cash investing and financing activities is reported near the bottom.

Exhibit 12.A1

Spreadsheet for
Preparing Statement
of Cash Flows—
Indirect Method

GENESIS
Spreadsheet for Statement of Cash Flow–Indirect Method
For Year Ended December 31, 2002

	Dec. 31, 2001		Analysis of Changes Debit		Credit	Dec. 31, 2002
Balance Sheet—Debits						
Cash	$ 12,000					$ 17,000
Accounts receivable	40,000	*(b)*	$ 20,000			60,000
Merchandise inventory	70,000	*(c)*	14,000			84,000
Prepaid expenses	4,000	*(d)*	2,000			6,000
Plant assets	210,000	*(k1)*	70,000	*(i)*	$ 30,000	250,000
	$336,000					$417,000
Balance Sheet—Credits						
Accumulated depreciation	$ 48,000	*(i)*	$ 12,000	*(h)*	$ 24,000	$ 60,000
Accounts payable	40,000	*(e)*	5,000			35,000
Interest payable	4,000	*(f)*	1,000			3,000
Income taxes payable	12,000			*(g)*	10,000	22,000
Bonds payable	64,000	*(j)*	34,000	*(k2)*	60,000	90,000
Common stock, $5 par value	80,000			*(l)*	15,000	95,000
Retained earnings	88,000	*(m)*	14,000	*(a)*	38,000	112,000
	$336,000					$417,000
Statement of Cash Flows						
Operating activities						
Net income		*(a)*	$ 38,000			
Increase in accounts receivable				*(b)*	$ 20,000	
Increase in merchandise inventory				*(c)*	14,000	
Increase in prepaid expenses				*(d)*	2,000	
Decrease in accounts payable				*(e)*	5,000	
Decrease in interest payable				*(f)*	1,000	
Increase in income taxes payable		*(g)*	10,000			
Depreciation expense		*(h)*	24,000			
Loss on sale of plant assets		*(i)*	6,000			
Gain on retirement of bonds				*(j)*	16,000	
Investing activities						
Receipts from sale of plant assets		*(i)*	12,000			
Payment for purchase of plant assets				*(k1)*	10,000	
Financing activities						
Payment to retire bonds				*(j)*	18,000	
Receipts from issuing stock		*(l)*	15,000			
Payments of cash dividends				*(m)*	14,000	
Noncash Investing and Financing Activities						
Purchase of plant assets with bonds		*(k2)*	60,000	*(k1)*	60,000	
			$337,000		$337,000	

Entering the Analysis of Changes on the Spreadsheet

The following sequence of procedures is used to complete the spreadsheet after the beginning and ending balances of the balance sheet accounts are entered:

① Enter net income as the first item in the Statement of Cash Flows section for computing operating cash inflow (debit) and as a credit to Retained Earnings.

② In the Statement of Cash Flows section, adjustments to net income are entered as debits if they increase cash flows and as credits if they decrease cash flows. Applying this same rule, adjust net income for the change in each noncash current asset and current liability account related to operating activities. For each adjustment to net income, the offsetting debit or credit must help reconcile the beginning and ending balances of a current asset or current liability account.

③ Enter adjustments to net income for income statement items not providing or using cash in the period. For each adjustment, the offsetting debit or credit must help reconcile a noncash balance sheet account.

④ Adjust net income to eliminate any gains or losses from investing and financing activities. Since the cash from a gain must be excluded from operating activities, the gain is entered as a credit in the operating activities section. Losses are entered as debits. For each adjustment, the related debit and/or credit must help reconcile balance sheet accounts and involve reconstructed entries to show the cash flow from investing or financing activities.

⑤ After reviewing any unreconciled balance sheet accounts and related information, enter the remaining reconciling entries for investing and financing activities. Examples are purchases of plant assets, issuances of long-term debt, stock issuances, and dividend payments. Some of these may require entries in the noncash investing and financing section of the spreadsheet (reconciled).

⑥ Check accuracy by totaling the Analysis of Changes columns and by determining that the change in each balance sheet account has been explained (reconciled).

We illustrate these steps in Exhibit 12A.1 for Genesis:

Point: Analysis of the changes on the spreadsheet can be summarized as follows:

1. Cash flows from operating activities generally affect net income, current assets, and current liabilities.

2. Cash flows from investing activities generally affect noncurrent asset accounts.

3. Cash flows from financing activities generally affect noncurrent liability and the equity accounts.

Step	Entries
①.....	(a)
②.....	(b) through (g)
③.....	(h)
④.....	(i) through (j)
⑤.....	(k) through (m)

Since adjustments *i*, *j*, and *k* are more challenging, we show them in the following debit and credit format. These entries are for purposes of our understanding—they are *not* the entries actually made in the journals. Changes in the Cash account are identified as sources or uses of cash.

		Debit	Credit
i.	Loss from sale of plant assets	6,000	
	Accumulated depreciation	12,000	
	Receipt from sale of plant assets **(source of cash)**	12,000	
	Plant assets		30,000
	To describe sale of plant assets.		
j.	Bonds payable	34,000	
	Payments to retire bonds **(use of cash)**		18,000
	Gain on retirement of bonds		16,000
	To describe retirement of bonds.		
k1.	Plant assets	70,000	
	Payment to purchase plant assets **(use of cash)**		10,000
	Purchase of plant assets financed by bonds		60,000
	To describe purchase of plant assets.		
k2.	Purchase of plant assets financed by bonds	60,000	
	Bonds payable		60,000
	To issue bonds for purchase of assets.		

Summary

C1 **Explain the purpose and importance of cash flow information.** The main purpose of the statement of cash flows is to report the major cash receipts and cash payments for a period. This includes identifying cash flows as relating to either operating, investing, or financing activities. Most business decisions involve evaluating activities that provide or use cash.

C2 **Distinguish among operating, investing, and financing activities.** Operating activities include transactions and events that determine net income. Investing activities include transactions and events that mainly affect long-term assets. Financing activities include transactions and events that mainly affect long-term liabilities and equity.

C3 **Identify and disclose noncash investing and financing activities.** Noncash investing and financing activities must be disclosed in either a note or in a separate schedule to the statement of cash flows. Examples are the retirement of debt by issuing equity and the exchange of a note payable for plant assets.

C4 **Describe the format of the statement of cash flows.** The statement of cash flows separates cash receipts and payments into operating, investing, or financing activities.

A1 **Analyze the statement of cash flows.** To understand and predict cash flows, users stress identification of the sources and uses of cash flows by operating, investing, and financing activities. Emphasis is on operating cash flows since they derive from continuing operations.

A2 **Compute and apply the cash flow on total assets ratio.** The cash flow on total assets ratio is defined as operating cash flows divided by average total assets. Analysis of current and past values for this ratio can reflect on a company's ability to yield regular and positive cash flows. It is also viewed as a measure of earnings quality.

P1 **Prepare a statement of cash flows.** Preparation of a statement of cash flows involves five steps: (1) Compute the net increase or decrease in cash; (2) compute net cash provided (used) by operating activities (*using either the direct or indirect method*); (3) compute net cash provided (used) by investing activities; (4) compute net cash provided (used) by financing activities; and (5) report the beginning and ending cash balance and prove that it is explained by net cash flows. Noncash investing and financing activities are also disclosed.

P2 **Compute cash flows from operating activities using the direct method.** The direct method for reporting net cash provided (used) by operating activities lists major operating cash inflows less cash outflows to yield net cash inflow or outflow from operations. The FASB recommends the direct method.

P3 **Compute cash flows from operating activities using the indirect method.** The indirect method for reporting net cash provided (used) by operating activities starts with net income and then adjusts it for three items: (1) changes in noncash current assets and current liabilities related to operating activities, (2) revenues and expenses not providing (using) cash, and (3) gains and losses from investing and financing activities.

P4 **Determine cash flows from both investing and financing activities.** Cash flows from both investing and financing activities are determined by identifying the cash flow effects of transactions and events affecting each balance sheet account related to these activities. All cash flows from these activities are identified when we can explain changes in these accounts from the beginning to the end of the period.

P5 **Illustrate spreadsheet use in preparing a statement of cash flows.** A spreadsheet is a useful tool in preparing a statement of cash flows. Six key steps (see appendix) are applied when using the spreadsheet to prepare the statement.

Guidance Answers to **Decision Maker**

Entrepreneur Several factors might explain an increase in net cash flows when a net loss is reported, including (1) early recognition of expenses relative to revenues generated (such as research and development), (2) advances on long-term sales contracts not yet recognized in income, (3) issuances of debt or equity to finance expansion, (4) selling of assets, (5) delay of cash payments, and (6) prepayment on sales. Analysis needs to focus on the components of both the net loss and the net cash flows and their implications for future performance.

Reporter Your initial reaction is not positive—based on the company's $600,000 loss with a $550,000 decrease in net cash flows. However, closer scrutiny reveals a different picture. Cash flow from operating activities is $650,000, computed as [?] − $850,000 − $350,000 = $(550,000). You also note net income *before* the extraordinary loss is $330,000, computed as [?] − $930,000 = $(600,000). This information reveals a more positive picture of this company's performance.

Guidance Answers to **Quick Checks**

1. No to both. The statement of cash flows reports changes in the sum of cash plus cash equivalents. It does not report transfers between cash and cash equivalents.

2. The three categories of cash inflows and outflows are operating activities, investing activities, and financing activities.

3. a. Investing   c. Financing   e. Operating
   b. Operating   d. Operating   f. Financing

4. The direct method is probably most informative because it separately lists each major item of operating cash receipts and each major item of operating cash payments. However, the indirect method is most often reported.

5. $590,000 + ($120,000 − $90,000) = $620,000

6. $168,000 − ($32,000 − $28,000) − $2,400 = $161,600

7. $112,000 + ($4,200 − $1,200) − $5,600 = $109,400

8. $74,900 + $4,600 − $11,700 − $1,000 + $3,400 = $70,200

9. Expenses such as depreciation and amortization do not require current cash outflows. Therefore, adding these expenses back to net income eliminates these noncash items from the net income number, converting it to a cash basis.

10. A gain on the sale of plant assets is subtracted from net income because a sale of plant assets is not an operating activity; it is an investing activity for the amount of cash received from its sale. Also, such a gain yields no cash effects.

11. $80,000 − $30,000 − $10,000 = $40,000 cash receipt. The $40,000 cash receipt is reported as an investing activity.

Glossary

Cash flow on total assets Ratio of operating cash flows to average total assets; not affected by income recognition and measurement; reflects earnings quality. (p. 549)

Direct method Presentation of net cash from operating activities that lists major operating cash receipts less major operating cash payments. (p. 531)

Financing activities Transactions with owners and creditors that include obtaining cash from issuing debt, repaying amounts borrowed, and obtaining cash from or distributing cash to owners. (p. 526)

Indirect method Presentation that reports net income and then adjusts it by adding and subtracting items to yield net cash from operating activities. (p. 531)

Investing activities Transactions that involve purchasing and selling of long-term assets, including making and collecting notes receivable and investments in other than cash equivalents. (p. 526)

Operating activities Activities that involve the production or purchase of merchandise and the sale of goods or services to customers, including expenditures related to administering the business. (p. 525)

Statement of cash flows Financial statement that reports cash inflows and cash outflows for an accounting period and classifies them as operating, investing, or financing activities. (p. 524)

The superscript ^{A} denotes assignments based on Appendix 12A.

Questions

1. When a statement of cash flows is prepared by the direct method, what are some operating cash flows?

2. What is the direct method of reporting cash flows from operating activities?

3. What is the indirect method of reporting cash flows from operating activities?

4. What are some investing activities reported on the statement of cash flows?

5. What are some financing activities reported on the statement of cash flows?

6. Where on the statement of cash flows is the payment of cash dividends reported?

7. ⚿ Assume that a company purchases land for $100,000, paying $20,000 cash and borrowing the remainder with a long-term note payable. How should this transaction be reported on a statement of cash flows?

8. ⚿ On June 3, a company borrows $50,000 cash by giving its bank a 160-day, interest-bearing note. On the statement of cash flows, where should this be reported?

9. ⚿ If a company reports positive net income for the year, is it possible for the company to show a net cash outflow from operating activities? Explain.

10. ⚿ Is depreciation a source of cash flow?

11. ⚿ Refer to Nike's statement of cash flows in Appendix A. (*a*) Which method is used to compute its net cash provided by operating activities? (*b*) While its balance sheet shows an increase in receivables from fiscal years 1999 to 2000, why is this increase in receivables subtracted when computing net cash provided by operating activities for fiscal year 2000?

NIKE

12. ⚿ Refer to Reebok's statement of cash flows in Appendix A. What are its cash flows from financing activities for 1999?

Reebok

13. ⚿ Refer to Gap's statement of cash flows in Appendix A. What investing activities result in cash outflows for the year ended January 29, 2000?

QUICK STUDY

QS 12-1 *⫶*
Statement
of cash
flows

C1 C2 C3

The statement of cash flows is one of the four primary financial statements.

1. Describe the contents and presentation of a statement of cash flows, including its three separate sections.
2. List at least three transactions classified as investing activities in a statement of cash flows.
3. List at least three transactions classified as financing activities in a statement of cash flows.
4. List at least three transactions classified as significant noncash financing and investing activities in the statement of cash flows.

QS 12-2 *⫶*
Transaction classification
by activity

C2

Classify the following cash flows as operating, investing, or financing activities:

1. Cash from sale of long-term investments.
2. Received cash payments from customers.
3. Paid wages and salaries.
4. Purchased inventories for cash.
5. Paid cash dividends.

6. Issued common stock for cash.
7. Received interest on a note.
8. Paid interest on outstanding bonds.
9. Cash from sale of land at a loss.
10. Paid property taxes on building.

QS 12-3 *⫶*
Computing cash received
from customers

P2

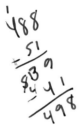

Use the following balance sheet and income statement to answer QS 12-3 through QS 12-8. (1) How much cash is received from sales to customers for year 2002? (2) What is the net increase or decrease in cash for year 2002?

ORWELL, INC. Income Statement For Year Ended December 31, 2002		
Sales		$488,000
Cost of goods sold		(314,000)
Gross profit		$174,000
Operating expenses		
Depreciation expense	$37,600	
Other expenses	89,100	(126,700)
Income before taxes		$ 47,300
Income taxes		(17,300)
Net income		$ 30,000

ORWELL, INC. Comparative Balance Sheet December 31, 2002		
	2002	**2001**
Assets		
Cash	$ 94,800	$ 24,000
Accounts receivable (net)	41,000	51,000
Inventory	85,800	95,800
Prepaid expenses	5,400	4,200
Furniture	109,000	119,000
Accum. depreciation—Furniture	(17,000)	(9,000)
Total assets	$319,000	$285,000
Liabilities and Equity		
Accounts payable	$ 15,000	$ 21,000
Wages payable	9,000	5,000
Income taxes payable	1,400	2,600
Notes payable (long-term)	29,000	69,000
Common stock, $5 par value	229,000	179,000
Retained earnings	35,600	8,400
Total liabilities and equity	$319,000	$285,000

QS 12-4 *⫶*
Computing operating **P2**
cash outflows

Refer to the data in QS 12-3. (1) How much cash is paid to acquire merchandise inventory during year 2002? (2) How much cash is paid for operating expenses during year 2002?

QS 12-5 *⫶*
Computing cash from **P2**
operations (direct)

Refer to the data in QS 12-3. Using the direct method, prepare the cash provided (used) from operating activities section only of the statement of cash flows.

Refer to the data in QS 12-3. Using the indirect method, prepare the cash provided (used) from operating activities section only of the statement of cash flows.

QS 12-6 🖉
Computing cash from **P3**
operations (indirect)

Refer to the data in QS 12-3. Furniture costing $55,000 is sold at its book value in 2002. Acquisitions of furniture total $45,000 cash, on which no depreciation is necessary since it is acquired at year-end. What is the cash inflow related to the sale of furniture?

QS 12-7 🖉
Computing cash **P4**
from asset sales

Refer to the data in QS 12-3. (1) Assume that all common stock is issued for cash. What amount of cash dividends is paid during 2002? (2) Assume that no additional notes payable are issued in 2002. What cash amount is paid to reduce the notes payable balance in 2002?

QS 12-8 🖉
Computing financing **P4**
cash outflows

Financial data from three competitors in the same industry are shown below.
1. Which of the three competitors is in the strongest position as shown by their cash flow statements?
2. Compare the strength of Fox's cash flow on total assets ratio to that of Wolf.

QS 12-9 🖉
Analyses of sources
and uses of cash

A1 A2

($ in thousands)	Fox	Wolf	Zetrix
Cash provided (used) by operating activities	$ 70,000	$ 60,000	$ (24,000)
Cash provided (used) by investing activities			
Proceeds from sale of operating assets			26,000
Purchase of operating assets	(28,000)	(34,000)	
Cash provided (used) by financing activities			
Proceeds from issuance of debt			23,000
Repayment of debt	(6,000)		
Net increase (decrease) in cash	$ 36,000	$ 26,000	$ 25,000
Average total assets	$ 790,000	$ 625,000	$ 300,000

When a spreadsheet for a statement of cash flows is prepared, all changes in noncash balance sheet accounts are fully explained on the spreadsheet. Explain how we use noncash balance sheet accounts to fully account for cash flows on a spreadsheet.

QS 12-10ᴬ
Noncash accounts **P5**
on a spreadsheet

For each of the following three separate cases, use the information provided about the calendar-year 2002 operations of Riley Company to compute the required cash flow information:

EXERCISES

Exercise 12-1
Computation of cash flows
(direct)

P2

Case A: Compute cash received from customers:

Sales	$515,000
Accounts receivable, December 31, 2001	27,200
Accounts receivable, December 31, 2002	33,600

Case B: Compute cash paid for rent:

Rent expense	$139,800
Rent payable, December 31, 2001	7,800
Rent payable, December 31, 2002	6,200

Case C: Compute cash paid for merchandise:

Cost of goods sold	$525,000
Merchandise inventory, December 31, 2001	158,600
Accounts payable, December 31, 2001	66,700
Merchandise inventory, December 31, 2002	130,400
Accounts payable, December 31, 2002	82,000

Exercise 12-2 🗍

Cash flow classification (direct)

C2

C3

P2

The following transactions and events occurred during the year. Assuming that this company uses the direct method to report cash provided by operating activities, indicate the accounting classification for each item on the statement of cash flows by placing an *x* in the appropriate column.

	Statement of Cash Flows			Noncash Investing and Financing Activities	Not Reported on Statement or in Note
	Operating Activities	Investing Activities	Financing Activities		
a. Long-term bonds payable are retired by issuing common stock.	____	____	____	____	____
b. Depreciation expense recorded.	____	____	____	____	____
c. Cash dividend declared in a prior period is paid this period.	____	____	____	____	____
d. Inventory is sold for cash.	____	____	____	____	____
e. Borrowed cash from bank by signing a 9-month note payable.	____	____	____	____	____
f. Paid cash to purchase a patent.	____	____	____	____	____
g. Six-month note receivable accepted in exchange for plant assets.	____	____	____	____	____

Exercise 12-3 🗍

Cash flow classification (indirect)

C2

C3

P3

The following transactions and events occurred during the year. Assuming that this company uses the indirect method to report cash provided by operating activities, indicate the accounting classification for each item on its statement of cash flows by placing an *x* in the appropriate column.

	Statement of Cash Flows			Noncash Investing and Financing Activities	Not Reported on Statement or in Note
	Operating Activities	Investing Activities	Financing Activities		
a. Paid cash to purchase inventory.	____	____	____	____	____
b. Purchased land by issuing common stock.	____	____	____	____	____
c. Accounts receivable decreased in the year. . . .	____	____	____	____	____
d. Sold equipment at a loss.	____	____	____	____	____
e. Recorded depreciation expense.	____	____	____	____	____
f. Income taxes payable increased in the year. . .	____	____	____	____	____
g. Declared and paid a cash dividend.	____	____	____	____	____

Exercise 12-4

Preparation of statement of cash flows (direct) and supporting note

C2 C3 C4 P1

Use the following information about the cash flows of Sanuk Company to prepare a complete statement of cash flows (direct method) for the year ended December 31, 2002. Use a note disclosure for any noncash investing and financing activities.

Cash and cash equivalents balance, December 31, 2001	$ 40,000
Cash and cash equivalents balance, December 31, 2002	148,000
Cash received as interest	3,500
Cash paid for salaries	76,500
Bonds payable retired by issuing common stock (no gain or loss on retirement)	185,500

[continued on next page]

[continued from previous page]

Cash paid to retire long-term notes payable	100,000
Cash received from sale of equipment	60,250
Cash received in exchange for six-month note payable	35,000
Land purchased by issuing long-term note payable	105,250
Cash paid for store equipment	24,750
Cash dividends paid	10,000
Cash paid for other expenses	20,000
Cash received from customers	495,000
Cash paid for merchandise	254,500

Use the following income statement and information about changes in noncash current assets and current liabilities to prepare the cash flows from operating activities section only of the statement of cash flows using the direct method:

Exercise 12-5
Cash flows from operating activities (direct)

P2

BRADHAM COMPANY
Income Statement
For Year Ended December 31, 2002

Sales		$1,828,000
Cost of goods sold		(991,000)
Gross profit		$ 837,000
Operating expenses		
Salaries expense	$245,535	
Depreciation expense	44,200	
Rent expense	49,600	
Amortization expenses—Patents	4,200	
Utilities expense	18,125	(361,660)
Gain on sale of equipment		6,200
Net income		$ 481,540

Changes in current asset and current liability accounts for the year that relate to operations follow:

Accounts receivable	$30,500 increase	Accounts payable	$12,500 decrease
Merchandise inventory	25,000 increase	Salaries payable	3,500 decrease

Refer to the information about Bradham Company in Exercise 12-5. Use the indirect method to prepare the cash provided (used) by operating activities section only of the statement of cash flows.

Exercise 12-6
Cash flows from operating activities (indirect) **P3**

Mandela Company's calendar-year 2002 income statement shows the following: Net Income, $374,000; Depreciation Expense, $44,000; Amortization Expense, $7,200; Gain on Sale of Plant Assets, $6,000. An examination of the company's current assets and current liabilities reveals the following changes (all from operating activities): Accounts Receivable decrease, $17,100; Merchandise Inventory decrease, $42,000; Prepaid Expenses increase, $4,700; Accounts Payable decrease, $8,200; Other Payables increase, $1,200. Use the indirect method to compute cash flow from operating activities.

Exercise 12-7
Cash flows from operating activities (indirect)

P3

Exercise 12-8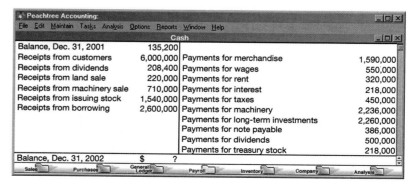

Preparation of statement of cash flows (direct)

C2 A2 P1 P2 P4

Use the financial statements and additional information shown to (1) prepare a statement of cash flows for the year ended June 30, 2002, using the direct method, and (2) compute the cash flow on total assets ratio for Passat, Inc., for its fiscal year 2002.

PASSAT INC.
Income Statement
For Year Ended June 30, 2002

Sales		$678,000
Cost of goods sold		(411,000)
Gross profit		$267,000
Operating expenses		
Depreciation expense	$58,600	
Other expenses	67,000	
Total operating expenses		(125,600)
Other gains (losses)		
Gain on sale of equipment		2,000
Income before taxes		$143,400
Income taxes		(43,890)
Net income		$ 99,510

PASSAT INC.
Comparative Balance Sheet
June 30, 2002

	2002	2001
Assets		
Cash	$ 86,500	$ 44,000
Accounts receivable (net)	65,000	51,000
Inventory	63,800	86,500
Prepaid expenses	4,400	5,400
Equipment	125,000	115,000
Accum. depreciation—Equip.	(27,000)	(9,000)
Total assets	$317,700	$292,900
Liabilities and Equity		
Accounts payable	$ 25,000	$ 30,000
Wages payable	6,000	15,000
Income taxes payable	3,400	3,800
Notes payable (long term)	30,000	60,000
Common stock, $5 par value	220,000	160,000
Retained earnings	33,300	24,100
Total liabilities and equity	$317,700	$292,900

Additional Information

a. A $30,000 note payable is retired at its carrying (book) value in exchange for cash.

b. The only changes affecting retained earnings are net income and cash dividends paid.

c. New equipment is acquired for $58,600 cash.

d. Received cash for the sale of equipment that had cost $48,600, yielding a $2,000 gain.

e. Prepaid Expenses and Wages Payable relate to Other Expenses on the income statement.

f. All purchases and sales of merchandise inventory are on credit.

Exercise 12-9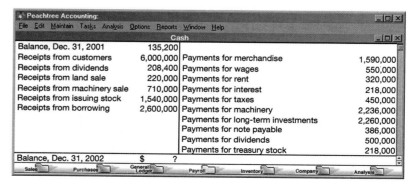

Preparation of statement of cash flows (direct) from Cash T-account

C2 A1 P1 P2 P4

The following summarized Cash T-account reflects the total debits and total credits to the Cash account of Triangle Corporation for calendar year 2002. (1) Use this information to prepare a complete statement of cash flows for year 2002. The cash provided (used) by operating activities should be reported using the direct method. (2) Refer to the statement of cash flows you prepared for part 1 to answer the following questions: (*a*) Which section—operating, investing, or financing—shows the largest cash (i) inflow and (ii) outflow? (*b*) What is the largest individual item among the investing cash outflows? (*c*) Are the cash proceeds larger from issuing notes or issuing stock? (*d*) Does the company have a net cash inflow or outflow from borrowing activities?

```
Peachtree Accounting:                                              _ □ ×
File Edit Maintain Tasks Analysis Options Reports Window Help
                              Cash                                  _ □ ×
Balance, Dec. 31, 2001      135,200
Receipts from customers   6,000,000  Payments for merchandise       1,590,000
Receipts from dividends     208,400  Payments for wages               550,000
Receipts from land sale     220,000  Payments for rent                320,000
Receipts from machinery sale 710,000 Payments for interest            218,000
Receipts from issuing stock 1,540,000 Payments for taxes              450,000
Receipts from borrowing   2,600,000  Payments for machinery         2,236,000
                                     Payments for long-term investments 2,260,000
                                     Payments for note payable        386,000
                                     Payments for dividends           500,000
                                     Payments for treasury stock      218,000
Balance, Dec. 31, 2002     $    ?
Sales   Purchases   General Ledger   Payroll   Inventory   Company   Analysis
```

Bushtex Company, a merchandiser, recently completed its calendar-year 2002 operations. For the year, (1) all sales are credit sales, (2) all credits to Accounts Receivable reflect cash receipts from customers, (3) all purchases of inventory are on credit, (4) all debits to Accounts Payable reflect cash payments for inventory, and (5) Other Expenses are paid in advance and are initially debited to Prepaid Expenses. Bushtex's balance sheet and income statement follow:

PROBLEM SET A

Problem 12-1A
Statement of cash flows
(direct method)

C2 C3 A1
P1 P2 P4

BUSHTEX COMPANY
Comparative Balance Sheet
December 31, 2002

	2002	2001
Assets		
Cash	$ 49,800	$ 73,500
Accounts receivable	65,810	50,625
Merchandise inventory	275,656	251,800
Prepaid expenses	1,250	1,875
Equipment	157,500	108,000
Accum. depreciation—Equip.	(36,625)	(46,000)
Total assets	$513,391	$439,800
Liabilities and Equity		
Accounts payable	$ 53,141	$114,675
Short-term notes payable	10,000	6,000
Long-term notes payable	65,000	48,750
Common stock, $5 par value	162,750	150,250
Contributed capital in excess of par, common stock	37,500	0
Retained earnings	185,000	120,125
Total liabilities and equity	$513,391	$439,800

BUSHTEX COMPANY
Income Statement
For Year Ended December 31, 2002

Sales		$582,500
Cost of goods sold		(285,000)
Gross profit		297,500
Operating expenses		
Depreciation expense	$ 20,750	
Other expenses	132,400	(153,150)
Other gains (losses)		
Loss on sale of equipment		(5,125)
Income before taxes		$139,225
Income taxes expense		(24,250)
Net income		$114,975

Additional Information on Year 2002 Transactions

a. The loss on the cash sale of equipment is $5,125 (details in *b*).

b. Sold equipment costing $46,875, with accumulated depreciation of $30,125, for $11,625 cash.

c. Purchased equipment costing $96,375 by paying $30,000 cash and signing a long-term note payable for the balance.

d. Borrowed $4,000 cash by signing a short-term note payable.

e. Paid $50,125 cash to reduce the long-term notes payable.

f. Issued 2,500 shares of common stock for $20 cash per share.

g. Declared and paid cash dividends of $50,100.

Required

1. Prepare a complete statement of cash flows; report its operating activities using the direct method. Disclose any noncash investing and financing activities in a note.

Check Cash from operating activities, $40,900

Analysis Component

2. Analyze and discuss the statement of cash flows prepared in part 1, giving special attention to the wisdom of the cash dividend payment.

Refer to Bushtex Company's financial statements and related information in Problem 12-1A.

Required

Prepare a complete statement of cash flows; report its operating activities according to the indirect method. Disclose any noncash investing and financing activities in a note.

Problem 12-2A
Statement of cash flows (indirect method)

C3 P1
P3 P4

Check Cash used in financing activities, $(46,225)

Problem 12-3A^A

Cash flows spreadsheet
(indirect method)

P1 P3 P4 P5

Refer to the information reported about Bushtex Company in Problem 12-1A.

Required

Prepare a complete statement of cash flows using a spreadsheet as in Exhibit 12A.1; report its operating activities using the indirect method. Identify the debits and credits in the Analysis of Changes columns with letters that correspond to the following list of transactions and events:

 a. Net income is $114,975.

 b. Accounts receivable increased.

 c. Merchandise inventory increased.

 d. Prepaid expenses decreased.

 e. Accounts payable decreased.

 f. Depreciation expense is $20,750.

 g. Sold equipment costing $46,875, with accumulated depreciation of $30,125, for $11,625 cash. This yielded a loss of $5,125.

 h. Purchased equipment costing $96,375 by paying $30,000 cash and **(i.)** by signing a long-term note payable for the balance.

 j. Borrowed $4,000 cash by signing a short-term note payable.

 k. Paid $50,125 cash to reduce the long-term notes payable.

 l. Issued 2,500 shares of common stock for $20 cash per share.

Check Analysis of Changes column totals, $600,775

 m. Declared and paid cash dividends of $50,100.

Problem 12-4A

Statement of cash flows
(direct method)

C3 P1 P2 P4

Pierpont Corp., a merchandiser, recently completed its 2002 operations. For the year, (1) all sales are credit sales, (2) all credits to Accounts Receivable reflect cash receipts from customers, (3) all purchases of inventory are on credit, (4) all debits to Accounts Payable reflect cash payments for inventory, (5) Other Expenses are all cash expenses, and (6) any change in Income Taxes Payable reflects the accrual and cash payment of taxes. Pierpont's balance sheet and income statement follow:

PIERPONT CORPORATION
Comparative Balance Sheet
December 31, 2002

	2002	2001
Assets		
Cash	$ 164,000	$107,000
Accounts receivable	83,000	71,000
Merchandise inventory	601,000	526,000
Equipment	335,000	299,000
Accum. depreciation—Equip.	(158,000)	(104,000)
Total assets	$1,025,000	$899,000
Liabilities and Equity		
Accounts payable	$ 87,000	$ 71,000
Income taxes payable	28,000	25,000
Common stock, $2 par value	592,000	568,000
Contributed capital in excess of par value, common stock	196,000	160,000
Retained earnings	122,000	75,000
Total liabilities and equity	$1,025,000	$899,000

PIERPONT CORPORATION
Income Statement
For Year Ended December 31, 2002

Sales		$1,792,000
Cost of goods sold		(1,086,000)
Gross profit		$ 706,000
Operating expenses		
Depreciation expense	$ 54,000	
Other expenses	494,000	(548,000)
Income before taxes		$ 158,000
Income taxes expense		(22,000)
Net income		$ 136,000

Additional Information on Year 2002 Transactions

 a. Purchased equipment for $36,000 cash.

 b. Issued 12,000 shares of common stock for $5 cash per share.

 c. Declared and paid $89,000 in cash dividends.

Required

Prepare a complete statement of cash flows; report its cash inflows and cash outflows from operating activities according to the direct method.

Check Cash from operating activities, $122,000

Refer to Pierpont Corporation's financial statements and related information in Problem 12-4A.

Required

Prepare a complete statement of cash flows; report its cash flows from operating activities according to the indirect method.

Problem 12-5A

Statement of cash flows (indirect method)

P1 P3 P4 **E**x

Check Cash used in financing activities, $(29,000)

Refer to the information reported about Pierpont Corporation in Problem 12-4A.

Required

Prepare a complete statement of cash flows using a spreadsheet as in Exhibit 12A.1; report operating activities under the indirect method. Identify the debits and credits in the Analysis of Changes columns with letters that correspond to the following list of transactions and events:

a. Net income is $136,000.

b. Accounts receivable increased.

c. Merchandise inventory increased.

d. Accounts payable increased.

e. Income taxes payable increased.

f. Depreciation expense is $54,000.

g. Purchased equipment for $36,000 cash.

h. Issued 12,000 shares at $5 cash per share.

i. Declared and paid $89,000 of cash dividends.

Problem 12-6A[A]

Cash flows spreadsheet (indirect method)

P1 P3 P4 P5 **E**x

Check Analysis of Changes column totals, $481,000

Keller Corporation, a merchandiser, recently completed its calendar-year 2002 operations. For the year, (1) all sales are credit sales, (2) all credits to Accounts Receivable reflect cash receipts from customers, (3) all purchases of inventory are on credit, (4) all debits to Accounts Payable reflect cash payments for inventory, and (5) Other Expenses are paid in advance and are initially debited to Prepaid Expenses. Keller's balance sheet and income statement follow:

PROBLEM SET B

Problem 12-1B 🎧

Statement of cash flows (direct method)

C2 C3 A1
P1 P2 P4

KELLER CORPORATION
Comparative Balance Sheet
December 31, 2002

	2002	2001
Assets		
Cash	$123,450	$ 61,550
Accounts receivable	77,100	80,750
Merchandise inventory	240,600	250,700
Prepaid expenses	15,100	17,000
Equipment	262,250	200,000
Accum. depreciation—Equip.	(110,750)	(95,000)
Total assets	$607,750	$515,000
Liabilities and Equity		
Accounts payable	$ 17,750	$ 102,000
Short-term notes payable	15,000	10,000
Long-term notes payable	100,000	77,500
Common stock, $5 par	215,000	200,000
Contributed capital in excess of par, common stock	30,000	0
Retained earnings	230,000	125,500
Total liabilities and equity	$607,750	$515,000

KELLER CORPORATION
Income Statement
For Year Ended December 31, 2002

Sales		$1,185,000
Cost of goods sold		(595,000)
Gross profit		$ 590,000
Operating expenses		
Depreciation expense	$ 38,600	
Other expenses	362,850	
Total operating expenses		(401,450)
Other gains (losses)		
Loss on sale of equipment		(2,100)
Income before taxes		$ 186,450
Income taxes expense		(28,350)
Net income		$ 158,100

Additional Information on Year 2002 Transactions

a. The loss on the cash sale of equipment is $2,100 (details in *b*).

b. Sold equipment costing $51,000, with accumulated depreciation of $22,850, for $26,050 cash.

c. Purchased equipment costing $113,250 by paying $43,250 cash and signing a long-term note payable for the balance.

d. Borrowed $5,000 cash by signing a short-term note payable.

e. Paid $47,500 cash to reduce the long-term notes payable.

f. Issued 3,000 shares of common stock for $15 cash per share.

g. Declared and paid cash dividends of $53,600.

Required

Check Cash from operating activities, $130,200

1. Prepare a complete statement of cash flows; report its operating activities using the direct method. Disclose any noncash investing and financing activities in a note.

Analysis Component

2. Analyze and discuss the statement of cash flows prepared in part 1, giving special attention to the wisdom of the cash dividend payment.

Problem 12-2B
Statement of cash flows
(indirect method)

C3 P1 P3 P4

Check Cash used in financing activities, $(51,100)

Refer to Keller Corporation's financial statements and related information in Problem 12-1B.

Required

Prepare a complete statement of cash flows; report its operating activities according to the indirect method. Disclose any noncash investing and financing activities in a note.

Problem 12-3B^A
Cash flows spreadsheet
(indirect method)

P1 P3 P4 P5

Refer to the information reported about Keller Corporation in Problem 12-1B.

Required

Prepare a complete statement of cash flows using a spreadsheet as in Exhibit 12A.1; report its operating activities using the indirect method. Identify the debits and credits in the Analysis of Changes columns with letters that correspond to the following list of transactions and events:

a. Net income is $158,100.

b. Accounts receivable decreased.

c. Merchandise inventory decreased.

d. Prepaid expenses decreased.

e. Accounts payable decreased.

f. Depreciation expense is $38,600.

g. Sold equipment costing $51,000, with accumulated depreciation of $22,850, for $26,050 cash. This yielded a loss of $2,100.

h. Purchased equipment costing $113,250 by paying $43,250 cash and **(i.)** by signing a long-term note payable for the balance.

j. Borrowed $5,000 cash by signing a short-term note payable.

k. Paid $47,500 cash to reduce the long-term notes payable.

Check Analysis of Changes column totals, $681,950

l. Issued 3,000 shares of common stock for $15 cash per share.

m. Declared and paid cash dividends of $53,600.

Problem 12-4B
Statement of cash flows
(direct method)

C3 P1 P2 P4

Takisha Co., a merchandiser, recently completed its 2002 operations. For the year, (1) all sales are credit sales, (2) all credits to Accounts Receivable reflect cash receipts from customers, (3) all purchases of inventory are on credit, (4) all debits to Accounts Payable reflect cash payments for inventory, (5) Other Expenses are cash expenses, and (6) any change in Income Taxes Payable reflects the accrual and cash payment of taxes. Takisha's balance sheet and income statement follow:

TAKISHA COMPANY
Comparative Balance Sheet
December 31, 2002

	2002	2001
Assets		
Cash	$ 58,750	$ 28,400
Accounts receivable	20,222	25,860
Merchandise inventory	165,667	140,320
Equipment	107,750	77,500
Accum. depreciation—Equip.	(46,700)	(31,000)
Total assets	$305,689	$241,080
Liabilities and Equity		
Accounts payable	$ 20,372	$157,530
Income taxes payable	2,100	6,100
Common stock, $5 par	40,000	25,000
Contributed capital in excess of par, common stock	68,000	20,000
Retained earnings	175,217	32,450
Total liabilities and equity	$305,689	$241,080

TAKISHA COMPANY
Income Statement
For Year Ended December 31, 2002

Sales		$750,800
Cost of goods sold		(269,200)
Gross profit		$481,600
Operating expenses		
Depreciation expense	$ 15,700	
Other expenses	173,933	(189,633)
Income before taxes		$291,967
Income taxes expense		(89,200)
Net income		$202,767

Additional Information on Year 2002 Transactions

a. Purchased equipment for $30,250 cash.

b. Issued 3,000 shares of common stock for $21 cash per share.

c. Declared and paid $60,000 of cash dividends.

Required

Prepare a complete statement of cash flows; report its cash inflows and cash outflows from operating activities according to the direct method.

Check Cash from operating activities, $57,600

Refer to Takisha Company's financial statements and related information in Problem 12-4B.

Required

Prepare a complete statement of cash flows; report its cash flows from operating activities according to the indirect method.

Problem 12-5B
Statement of cash flows (indirect method)

P1 P3 P4

Check Cash from financing activities, $3,000

Refer to the information reported about Takisha Company in Problem 12-4B.

Required

Prepare a complete statement of cash flows using a spreadsheet as in Exhibit 12A.1; report operating activities under the indirect method. Identify the debits and credits in the Analysis of Changes columns with letters that correspond to the following list of transactions and events:

a. Net income is $202,767.

b. Accounts receivable decreased.

c. Merchandise inventory increased.

d. Accounts payable decreased.

e. Income taxes payable decreased.

f. Depreciation expense is $15,700.

g. Purchased equipment for $30,250 cash.

h. Issued 3,000 shares at $21 cash per share.

i. Declared and paid $60,000 of cash dividends.

Problem 12-6B[A]
Cash flows spreadsheet (indirect method)

P1 P3 P4 P5

Check Analysis of Changes column totals, $543,860

BEYOND THE NUMBERS

Reporting in Action

C4 A1 🖉

NIKE

BTN 12-1   Refer to Nike's financial statements in Appendix A to answer the following:

1. Is Nike's statement of cash flows prepared under the direct method or the indirect method?
2. For each of the fiscal years 2000, 1999, and 1998, is the amount of cash provided by operating activities more or less than the cash paid for dividends?
3. What is the largest amount in reconciling the difference between net income and cash flow from operating activities in 2000? In 1999? In 1998?
4. Identify the major cash flows for investing and for financing activities in 2000 and in 1999.

Swoosh Ahead

5. Obtain Nike's financial statements for a fiscal year ending after May 31, 2000, from either its Web site (www.nike.com) or the SEC's EDGAR database (www.sec.gov). Since May 31, 2000, what are Nike's largest cash outflows and inflows in the investing and in the financing sections of its cash flow statement?

Comparative Analysis

A1 A2 🖉

NIKE

Reebok

BTN 12-2   Key comparative figures ($ millions) for both Nike and Reebok follow:

	Nike			Reebok		
Key Figures	Current Year	1 year Prior	2 years Prior	Current Year	1 year Prior	2 years Prior
Operating cash flows	$ 759.9	$ 961.0	$ 517.5	$ 281.6	$ 151.8	$ 127.0
Total assets	5,856.9	5,247.7	5,397.4	1,564.1	1,684.6	1,756.1

Required

1. Compute the recent two years' cash flow on total assets ratios for both Nike and Reebok.
2. What does the cash flow on total assets ratio measure?
3. Which company has the higher cash flow on total assets ratio?
4. Does the cash flow on total assets ratio reflect on the quality of earnings? Explain.

Ethics Challenge

C1 C2 A1 🄴 🖉

BTN 12-3   Julie Vignery is preparing for a meeting with her banker. Her business is finishing its fourth year of operations. In the first year, it had negative cash flows from operations. In the second and third years, cash flows from operations turned positive. However, inventory costs rose significantly in year 4, and cash flows from operations will probably be down 25%. Julie wants to secure a line of credit from her banker as a financing buffer. From experience, she knows a focus of the meeting will be cash flows from operations. The banker will scrutinize cash flows for years 1 through 4 and will want a projected number for year 5. Julie knows that a steady progression upward in cash flows for years 1 through 4 will help her case. She decides to use her discretion as owner and considers several business actions that will turn her cash flow in year 4 from a decrease to an increase over year 3.

Required

1. Identify two business actions Julie might take to improve cash flows from operations.
2. Comment on the ethics and possible consequences of Julie's decision to pursue these actions.

Communicating in Practice

C1 C4 🄴 🖉

BTN 12-4   Your friend, Jenny Hunter, recently completed the second year of her business and just received annual financial statements from her accountant. Jenny finds the income statement and balance sheet informative, but she does not understand the statement of cash flows. She says the first section is especially confusing because it contains a lot of additions and subtractions that do not make sense to her. Jenny adds, "The income statement tells me the business is more profitable than last year and that's most important. If I want to know how cash changes, I can look at comparative balance sheets."

Required

Write a half-page memorandum to your friend explaining the purpose of the statement of cash flows. Speculate as to why the first section is so confusing and how it might be rectified.

BTN 12-5   Access the April 25, 2000, filing date of the 10-K report (for year ending January 29, 2000) of J. Crew Group, Inc., at www.edgar-online.com.

Taking It to the Net

A1 🖉

Required

1. Does J. Crew use the direct or indirect method to construct its consolidated statement of cash flows?

2. For the fiscal year ended January 29, 2000, what is the largest item recorded in reconciling the net loss to cash flow provided by operations?

3. Over the past three years, J. Crew has recorded a net loss. Has the company been more successful in generating operating cash flows over this time period than in generating net income?

4. In the year ended January 29, 2000, what was the largest cash outflow for investing activities and for financing activities?

5. What items does J. Crew present as supplementary cash flow information?

6. Does J. Crew report any noncash financing activities?

BTN 12-6   Team members are to coordinate and independently answer one question within each of the following three sections. Team members should then report to the team and confirm or correct teammates' answers.

Teamwork in Action

C1 C4 A1
P2 P3 🖉

1. Answer *one* of the following questions about the statement of cash flows:

   a. What is this statement's reporting objectives?

   b. What two methods are used to prepare it? Identify similarities and differences between them.

   c. What steps are followed to prepare the statement?

   d. What types of analyses are often made from this statement's information?

2. Identify and explain the formula for computing cash flows from operating activities using the direct method for *one* of the following items:

   a. Cash receipts from sales to customers.

   b. Cash paid for merchandise inventory.

   c. Cash paid for wages and operating expenses.

   d. Cash paid for interest and taxes.

3. Identify and explain the adjustment from net income to obtain cash flows from operating activities using the indirect method for *one* of the following items:

   a. Noncash operating revenues and expenses.

   b. Nonoperating gains and losses.

   c. Increases and decreases in noncash current assets.

   d. Increases and decreases in current liabilities.

Note: For teams of more than four, some pairing within teams is necessary. Use as an in-class activity or as an assignment. If used in class, specify a time limit on each part. Conclude with reports to the entire class, using team rotation. Each team can prepare responses on a transparency.

BTN 12-7   Read the article "Making Sure the Price Is Right" in the March 29, 1999, issue of *Business Week*. (The book's Web site provides a free link.)

Business Week Activity

A1 🄴 🖉

Required

1. Why is it important for a business owner to know the value of his/her business?

2. In the article, how did the professional business appraiser calculate the value of VTE?

3. How is *free cash flow* defined?

4. How much would it likely cost for an appraisal of a business with about $1 million in sales?

5. In today's business environment, which businesses might be easiest to sell?

Entrepreneurial Decision

C2 A1 A2

e *d*

BTN 12-8   Jenna and Matt Wilder are completing their second year of operating Mountain High, a downhill ski area and resort. Mountain High reports a net loss of $(10,000) this year, which includes an $85,000 extraordinary loss from fire. This past year also involved major purchases of plant assets for renovation and expansion, yielding a year-end total asset amount of $800,000. Mountain High's net cash outflow for this year is $(5,000); a summarized version of its statement of cash flows follows:

Net cash flow provided by operating activities	$295,000
Net cash flow used by investing activities	(310,000)
Net cash flow provided by financing activities	10,000

Required

Write a one-page memorandum to the Wilders evaluating Mountain High's current performance and assessing its future. Give special emphasis to cash flow data and their interpretation.

Hitting the Road

C1

BTN 12-9   Visit The Motley Fool's Web site (www.fool.com). Click on the sidebar link titled *School*. Identify and select the link *Valuation: Principles and Practice*. (*a*) How does the Fool's school define cash flow? (*b*) Per the school's instruction, why do analysts focus on earnings before interest and taxes (EBIT)? (*c*) Visit other links at this Web site that interest you such as "A Journey through the Balance Sheet," or find out what the "Fool's Ratio" is. Write a half-page report on what you find.

13

Financial Statement Analysis and Interpretation

A Look Back

Chapter 12 focused on reporting and analyzing cash inflows and cash outflows. We explained how to prepare and interpret the statement of cash flows.

A Look at This Chapter

This chapter emphasizes the analysis and interpretation of financial statement information. We learn to apply horizontal, vertical, and ratio analyses to better understand company performance and financial condition.

"What goes on at The Motley Fool every day is similar to what goes on in a library"—Tom Gardner

Decision Feature

Fool's Gold?

e ALEXANDRIA, VA—Seven years ago, with less than $10,000 in start-up money, then 26-year-old David Gardner and his 28-year-old brother, Tom, launched **The Motley Fool (www.TheMotleyFool.com)**. The name derives from Elizabethan drama (Shakespeare's *As You Like It*), in which only the fool could tell the king the truth without getting his head lopped off. The Gardners view themselves as modern-day fools "dedicated to educating, amusing, and enriching individuals in the search of the truth," according to their Web site. The truth to which they refer involves the financial world. Their site argues that "the financial world preys on ignorance and fear." According to Tom Gardner, "There is such a great need in the general populace for financial information." Given their huge success—Web site, radio shows, newspaper columns, online store, stock research reports, and international expansion—few can argue.

Still, there is a concern that individuals fail to fully exploit the available information in financial statements. The Motley Fool's bulletin board often finds "discussions" that could be readily resolved with reference to reliable accounting data. This suggests that more "education and enriching" of individuals is required. This chapter takes on that challenge. It introduces horizontal and vertical analyses—key tools to reveal crucial trends and insights from financial information. It also summarizes and expands on ratio analysis—applying basic tools to reveal insights into a company's financial condition and performance. With knowledge from this chapter, along with The Motley Fool's guidance on investing, individuals will be in a much stronger position to succeed in the financial markets. [Sources: The Motley Fool Web site, March 2002, *Entrepreneur*, July 1997.]

Chapter Preview

This chapter shows how to use information in financial statements to further evaluate a company's financial performance and condition. We describe the purpose of financial statement analysis, its basic building blocks, the information available, standards for comparisons, and tools of analysis. Three major analysis tools are emphasized: horizontal analysis, vertical analysis, and ratio analysis. We illustrate the application of each of these tools using Nike's financial statements. We also introduce comparative analysis using Reebok's financial statements. Moreover, this chapter expands and organizes the ratio analyses introduced at the end of each chapter. Understanding financial statement analysis is crucial to effective business decision making.

Basics of Analysis

Financial statement analysis applies analytical tools to general-purpose financial statements and related data for making business decisions. It involves transforming accounting data into useful information. Financial statement analysis reduces our reliance on hunches, guesses, and intuition. It also reduces our uncertainty in decision making. It does not lessen the need for expert judgment; instead, it provides us an effective and systematic basis for making business decisions. This section describes the purpose of financial statement analysis, its information sources, the use of comparisons, and some issues in computations.

Purpose of Analysis

C1 Explain the purpose of analysis.

The purpose of financial statement analysis is to help users make better business decisions. These users include decision makers both internal and external to the company.

Internal users of accounting information are the individuals involved in managing and operating the company. They include managers, officers, internal auditors, consultants, budget officers, and market researchers. Internal users make a company's strategic and operating decisions. The purpose of financial statement analysis for these users is to provide information helpful in improving the company's efficiency and effectiveness in providing products and services.

External users of accounting information are *not* directly involved in running the company. They include shareholders, lenders, directors, customers, suppliers, regulators, lawyers, brokers, and the press. These users are affected by, and sometimes affect, the company's activities. External users rely on financial statement analysis to make better and more informed decisions in pursuing their own goals.

Point: Financial statement analysis tools are also used for personal financial investment decisions.

We can identify many examples of the use of financial statement analysis. Shareholders and creditors assess company prospects for investing and lending decisions. A board of directors analyzes financial statements in monitoring management's decisions. Employees and unions use information in financial statements in labor negotiations. Suppliers use financial statement information in establishing credit terms. Customers analyze financial statements in deciding whether to establish supply relationships. Public utilities set customer rates by analyzing financial statements. Auditors use financial statements in assessing the "fair presentation" of their clients' financial reports. Analyst services such as Dun & Bradstreet, Moody's, and Standard & Poor's use financial statements in making buy-sell recommendations and setting credit ratings. The common goal of these users is to evaluate company performance and financial condition. This includes evaluating (1) past and current performance, (2) current financial position, and (3) future performance and risk.

Point: Financial statement analysis is an important topic on the CPA, CMA, CIA, and CFA exams.

Building Blocks of Analysis

C2 Identify the building blocks of analysis.

Financial statement analysis focuses on one or more elements of a company's financial condition or performance. Our analysis emphasizes four areas of inquiry—with varying degrees of importance. These four areas are described and illustrated in this chapter and are considered the *building blocks* of financial statement analysis:

■ **Liquidity** and **efficiency**—ability to meet short-term obligations and to efficiently generate revenues.
■ **Solvency**—ability to generate future revenues and meet long-term obligations.

- **Profitability**—ability to provide financial rewards sufficient to attract and retain financing.
- **Market prospects**—ability to generate positive market expectations.

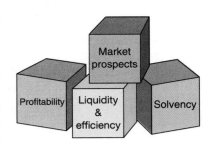

Applying the building blocks of financial statement analysis involves determining (1) the objectives of analysis and (2) the relative emphasis among the building blocks. We distinguish among these four building blocks to emphasize the different aspects of a company's financial condition or performance, yet we must remember that these areas of analysis are interrelated. For instance, a company's operating performance is affected by the availability of financing and short-term liquidity conditions. Similarly, a company's credit standing is not limited to satisfactory short-term liquidity but depends also on its profitability and efficiency in using assets. Early in our analysis, we need to determine the relative emphasis of each building block and the order of their analysis given our objectives. Emphasis and analysis can later change as a result of evidence collected.

Decision Insight

Chips and Brokers The term *blue chips* is used to refer to stock of big, profitable companies. The term comes from poker—where the most valuable chips are the blue ones. *Brokers* execute orders to buy or sell stock. The term comes from wine retailers—individuals who broach (break) wine casks.

Information for Analysis

We explained how decision makers such as managers, employees, directors, customers, suppliers, current and potential owners, current and potential lenders, brokers, regulatory authorities, lawyers, economists, labor union leaders, analysts, and consultants need to analyze financial statements. Some of these people, such as managers and a few regulatory authorities, are able to receive special financial reports prepared to meet their needs. However, most users must rely on general-purpose financial statements that companies periodically release. **General-purpose financial statements** include the (1) income statement, (2) balance sheet, (3) statement of changes in equity (or statement of retained earnings), (4) statement of cash flows, and (5) notes to these statements.

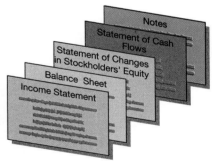

General-purpose financial statements are part of financial reporting. **Financial reporting** refers to the communication of relevant financial information to decision makers. It includes not only financial statements but also information from 10-K or other filings with the Securities and Exchange Commission, news releases, shareholders' meetings, forecasts, management letters, auditors' reports, and analyses published in annual reports. Financial reporting broadly refers to information useful for making investment, credit, and other business decisions. It helps users assess the amounts, timing, and uncertainty of future cash inflows and outflows.

One example of useful information outside the traditional financial statements is the Management Discussion and Analysis (MD&A). Nike's MD&A (available at www.nikebiz.com), for example, begins with a list of four highlights: net income, revenues, gross margins, and expenses. It then proceeds to compare operating activities for 2000 with 1999, and 1999 with 1998. This analysis includes a breakdown of Nike's revenues between footwear and apparel and between domestic and international activities. The third part of its analysis examines liquidity and capital resources—roughly equivalent to investing and financing activities. The fourth and final part explains Nike's market risk—including its exposure to currency changes, interest rates, and derivatives. The MD&A is an excellent starting point in understanding the business activities of a company.

Point: Decision makers rely on financial statement analysis to help them better understand the financial position and profitability of a business. Auditors use financial statement analysis to assess the reasonableness of amounts presented in those statements.

Decision Insight

Analysis Online Many Web sites offer free access and screening of companies by key financial numbers such as earnings, sales, and book value. For instance, Standard & Poor's has information for more than 10,000 stocks (www.standardpoor.com).

Standards for Comparisons

When computing and interpreting analysis measures as part of a financial statement analysis, we need to decide whether these measures suggest good, bad, or average performance. To make these judgments, we need standards (benchmarks) for comparisons. Standards for comparisons can include these:

- *Intracompany*—The company under analysis can provide its own standards for comparisons based on prior performance and relations between its financial items. **Nike**'s current net income, for instance, can be compared with its prior years' net income and in relation to its revenues or total assets.
- *Competitor*—One or more direct competitors of the company being analyzed can provide standards for comparisons. **Coca-Cola**'s profit margin, for instance, can be compared with **PepsiCo**'s profit margin.
- *Industry*—Industry statistics can provide standards of comparisons. Published industry statistics are available from several services such as Dun & Bradstreet, Standard & Poor's, and Moody's.
- *Guidelines (rules of thumb)*—General standards of comparisons can develop from past experiences. Examples are the 2:1 level for the current ratio or 1:1 level for the acid-test ratio. These guidelines, or rules of thumb, must be carefully applied since their context is often crucial.

Point: Each chapter's *Reporting in Action* problems engage students in *intracompany* analysis, whereas *Comparative Analysis* problems require analyzing information relative to a competitor (Nike vs. Reebok).

All of these standards of comparisons are useful when properly applied, yet analysis measures taken from a selected competitor or group of competitors are often the best. Intracompany and industry measures are also important parts of all analyses. Guidelines or rules of thumb should be applied with care, and then only if they seem reasonable in light of past experience and industry norms.

Quick Check

1. Who are the intended users of general-purpose financial statements?
2. General-purpose financial statements consist of what information?
3. Which of the following is *least* useful as a basis for comparison when analyzing ratios? (*a*) Company results from a different economic setting. (*b*) Subjective standards from past experience. (*c*) Rule-of-thumb standards. (*d*) Industry averages.
4. What is the preferred basis of comparison for ratio analysis?

Answers—p. 600

Decision Insight

Ticker Prices *Ticker prices* refer to a band of moving data on a monitor carrying up-to-the-minute stock prices. The term comes from *ticker tape*—a 1-inch-wide strip of paper spewing stock prices from a printer that ticked as it ran. Most of today's investors have never seen actual ticker tape, but the term survives.

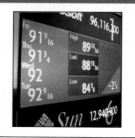

Tools of Analysis

Three of the most common tools of financial statement analysis are

1. **Horizontal analysis**—Comparison of a company's financial condition and performance across time.
2. **Vertical analysis**—Comparison of a company's financial condition and performance to a base amount.
3. **Ratio analysis**—Measurement of key relations between financial statement items.

The remainder of this chapter describes these tools of analysis and how to apply them.

Analysis of any single financial number is of limited value. Instead, financial analysis must use the important relations that exist between items and across time. Much of financial statement analysis involves identifying and describing relations between numbers, groups of numbers, and changes in those numbers. Horizontal analysis is a tool to evaluate changes in financial statement data *across time*. [The term *horizontal analysis* arises from the left-to-right (or right-to-left) movement of our eyes as we review comparative financial statements across time.]

Horizontal Analysis

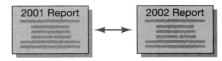

Comparative Statements

Comparing amounts for two or more successive periods often helps in analyzing financial statement data. **Comparative financial statements** facilitate this comparison by showing financial amounts in side-by-side columns on a single statement. Each financial statement is presented in a *comparative format*. For instance, **Nike**'s *Financial History* report in Appendix A is a comparative statement based on six years of financial performance. Using figures from Nike's financial statements, this section explains how to compute dollar changes and percent changes for comparative statements.

P1 Explain and apply methods of horizontal analysis.

Topic Tackler 13-1

Computation of Dollar Changes and Percent Changes

Comparing financial statements over relatively short time periods—two to three years—is often done by analyzing changes in line items. A change analysis usually includes analysis of absolute dollar amount changes as well as percent changes. Both analyses are relevant since dollar changes can yield large percent changes inconsistent with their importance. For instance, a 50% change from a base figure of $100 is less important than the same percent change from a base amount of $100,000 in the same statement. Reference to dollar amounts is necessary to retain a proper perspective and to assess the importance of changes. We compute the *dollar change* for a financial statement item as follows:

$$\text{Dollar change} = \text{Analysis period amount} - \text{Base period amount}$$

Analysis period is the point or period of time for the financial statements under analysis, and *base period* is the point or period of time for the financial statements used for comparison purposes. The prior year is commonly used as a base period. We compute the *percent change* by dividing the dollar change by the base period amount and then multiplying this quantity by 100 as follows:

$$\text{Percent change } (\%) = \frac{\text{Analysis period amount} - \text{Base period amount}}{\text{Base period amount}} \times 100$$

We can always compute a dollar change, but we must be aware of a few rules in working with percent changes. To illustrate, look at four separate cases in this chart:

Case	Analysis Period	Base Period	Change Analysis Dollar	Change Analysis Percent
A	$ 1,500	$(4,500)	$6,000	—
B	(1,000)	2,000	(3,000)	—
C	8,000	—	8,000	—
D	0	10,000	(10,000)	(100%)

When a negative amount appears in the base period and a positive amount in the analysis period (or vice versa), we cannot compute a meaningful percent change—see cases A and B. Also, when no value is in the base period, no percent change is computable—see case C. Finally, when an item has a value in the base period and zero in the analysis period, the decrease is 100 percent—see case D.

It is common when using horizontal analysis to compare amounts to either average or median values from prior periods.[1] Comparing changes to average or median values computed from more than one prior period highlights unusual happenings because average and median values smooth out erratic or unusual fluctuations. We also commonly round percents and ratios to one or two decimal places, but practice on this matter is not uniform. Computations are as detailed as necessary, which is judged by whether or not rounding potentially affects users' decisions. Computations should not be so excessively detailed that important relations are lost among a mountain of decimal points and digits.

Comparative Balance Sheet

One of the most useful comparative statements is the comparative balance sheet. It consists of amounts from two or more balance sheet dates arranged side by side. The usefulness of comparative financial statements is often improved by showing each item's dollar change and percent change. This type of presentation highlights large dollar and percent changes for decision makers. Exhibit 13.1 shows a comparative balance sheet for Nike.

Analysis of comparative financial statements begins by focusing on items that show large dollar or percent changes. We then try to identify the reasons for these changes and, if possible, determine whether they are favorable or unfavorable. We also follow up on items with small changes when we expected the changes to be large.

Example: If cash and equivalents increased in 2000 by an additional $100 million, what is the percent change in cash and equivalents? *Answer:* ($254.3 + $100.0 − $198.1)/$198.1 = 78.8%

With Nike's comparative balance sheet in Exhibit 13.1, a few items stand out. Among current assets, Cash and Equivalents, with a $56.2 million increase (28.4%), and Inventories, with a $275.4 million increase (23.5%), are notable. The statement of cash flows in Appendix A reveals that a substantial portion of the increase in cash is due to cash flows from financing activities, mainly cash from issuance of notes payable. Moreover, the footnotes reveal that much of the increase in inventories is due to finished goods inventory. The comparative analysis also shows that Nike's total current liabilities increased by $693.1 million with most of this attributed to notes payable. Further analysis reveals a large increase ($317.6 million) in property, plant and equipment. This increase is larger in magnitude than that in any other asset account. We need to monitor this increase in productive assets to be certain that such expansion is the best use of available resources. Finally, we see an overall increase in debt (liability) financing and a decrease in equity financing.

Point: Business consultants use comparative statement analysis to provide management advice.

Comparative Income Statement

A comparative income statement is prepared similarly to the comparative balance sheet. Amounts for two or more periods are placed side by side, with additional columns for dollar and percent changes. Exhibit 13.2 shows Nike's comparative income statement.

Point: We can also compute percent changes by dividing the current period by the prior period and subtracting 1.0. For example, the 2.5% revenue increase of Exhibit 13.2 is computed as: ($8,995.1/$8,776.9) − 1.

Nike's growth in revenues in 2000 was small, as shown by its 2.5% revenues increase in Exhibit 13.2. Since Nike is a consumer products company, its revenues depend heavily on consumer tastes. Changes in consumer tastes were not especially favorable for Nike in 2000. This might partly explain the increase in finished goods inventory evidenced in Exhibit 13.1. To counter the slow revenue growth, Nike spent $179.8 million more on selling and administrative activities. Nike is not currently reaping adequate benefits from the increase in these expenses. Exhibit 13.2 also shows an increase in gross margin (revenues − cost of sales). This is evident from the 2.5% revenue increase coupled with the 1.6% decrease in cost of sales. Specifically, its gross margin ratio rises to 39.9% of revenues in 2000, compared to 37.4% in 1999.

Decision Insight

Analysis Tech   Spreadsheet programs can help with horizontal, vertical, and ratio analyses, including graphical depictions of financial relations. The key is using this information properly and effectively for business decision making.

---

[1] *Median* is the middle value in a group of numbers. For instance, if five prior years' incomes are (in 000s) $15, $19, $18, $20, and $22, the median value is $19. When there are two middle numbers, we can take their average. For instance, if four prior years' sales are (in 000s) $84, $91, $96, and $93, the median is $92 (computed as the average of $91 and $93).

Exhibit 13.1

Comparative Balance Sheet

NIKE
Comparative Balance Sheet
May 31, 2000 and 1999

(in millions)	2000	1999	Dollar Change	Percent* Change
Assets				
Current assets				
Cash and equivalents	$ 254.3	$ 198.1	$ 56.2	28.4%
Accounts receivable, less allowance for				
doubtful accounts of $65.4 and $73.2	1,567.2	1,540.1	27.1	1.8
Inventories	1,446.0	1,170.6	275.4	23.5
Deferred income taxes	111.5	120.6	(9.1)	(7.5)
Income taxes receivable	2.2	15.9	(13.7)	(86.2)
Prepaid expenses	215.2	219.6	(4.4)	(2.0)
Total current assets	$3,596.4	$3,264.9	$ 331.5	10.2
Property, plant and equipment, net	1,583.4	1,265.8	317.6	25.1
Identifiable intangible assets and goodwill	410.9	426.6	(15.7)	(3.7)
Deferred income taxes and other assets	266.2	290.4	(24.2)	(8.3)
Total assets	$5,856.9	$5,247.7	$ 609.2	11.6
Liabilities and Equity				
Current liabilities				
Current portion of long-term debt	$ 50.1	$ 1.0	$ 49.1	4,910.0%
Notes payable	924.2	419.1	505.1	120.5
Accounts payable	543.8	473.6	70.2	14.8
Accrued liabilities	621.9	553.2	68.7	12.4
Total current liabilities	$2,140.0	$1,446.9	$ 693.1	47.9
Long-term debt	470.3	386.1	84.2	21.8
Deferred income taxes and other liabilities	110.3	79.8	30.5	38.2
Commitments and contingencies	—	—		
Redeemable preferred stock	0.3	0.3	0.0	0.0
Shareholders' equity				
Common stock at stated value				
Class A convertible—99.2 and 100.7				
shares outstanding	0.2	0.2	0.0	0.0
Class B—170.4 and 181.6				
shares outstanding	2.6	2.7	(0.1)	(3.7)
Capital in excess of stated value	369.0	334.1	34.9	10.4
Unearned stock compensation	(11.7)	—	(11.7)	—
Accumulated other comprehensive income ...	(111.1)	(68.9)	(42.2)	(61.2)
Retained earnings	2,887.0	3,066.5	(179.5)	(5.9)
Total shareholders' equity	$3,136.0	$3,334.6	$(198.6)	(6.0)
Total liabilities and equity	$5,856.9	$5,247.7	$ 609.2	11.6

* Percents are rounded to tenths.

Trend Analysis

Trend analysis, also called *trend percent analysis* or *index number trend analysis,* is a form of horizontal analysis that can reveal patterns in data across successive periods. It involves computing trend percents for a series of financial numbers and is a variation on the use of percent changes. The difference is that trend analysis does not subtract the base period amount in the numerator. To compute trend percents, we do the following:

1. Select a *base period* and assign each item in the base period a weight of 100%.
2. Express financial numbers as a percent of their base period number.

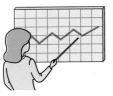

Exhibit 13.2

Comparative Income
Statement

(in millions, except per share data)	2000	1999	Dollar Change	Percent* Change
NIKE Comparative Income Statement For Years Ended May 31, 2000 and 1999				
Revenues	$8,995.1	$8,776.9	$218.2	2.5%
Costs and expenses				
Costs of sales	5,403.8	5,493.5	(89.7)	(1.6)
Selling and administrative	2,606.4	2,426.6	179.8	7.4
Interest expense	45.0	44.1	0.9	2.0
Other income and expense, net	23.2	21.5	1.7	7.9
Restructuring charge, net	(2.5)	45.1	(47.6)	—
Total costs and expenses	$8,075.9	$8,030.8	$ 45.1	0.6
Income before income taxes	919.2	746.1	173.1	23.2
Income taxes	340.1	294.7	45.4	15.4
Net income	$ 579.1	$ 451.4	$127.7	28.3
Basic earnings per common share	$ 2.10	$ 1.59	$ 0.51	32.1
Average common shares outstanding	275.7	283.3		

* Percents are rounded to tenths.

Specifically, a *trend percent,* also called an *index number,* is computed as follows:

Point: *Index* refers to the comparison of the analysis period to the base period. Percents determined for each period are called *index numbers.*

$$\text{Trend percent } (\%) = \frac{\text{Analysis period amount}}{\text{Base period amount}} \times 100$$

To illustrate trend analysis, we use selected Nike data as reported in Exhibit 13.3.

Exhibit 13.3

Revenues and Expenses

($ in millions)	2000	1999	1998	1997	1996	1995
Revenues	$8,995.1	$8,776.9	$9,553.1	$9,186.5	$6,470.6	$4,760.8
Costs of sales	5,403.8	5,493.5	6,065.5	5,503.0	3,906.7	2,865.3
Selling and administrative . .	2,606.4	2,426.6	2,623.8	2,303.7	1,588.6	1,209.8

Point: In trend analysis, the first period in a series of periods is usually chosen as the base period.

These data are from Nike's financial history in Appendix A and its prior statements. We select 1995 as the base period and compute the trend percent in each subsequent year by dividing each year's amount by its 1995 amount. For instance, the revenue trend percent for 2000 is 188.9%, computed as $8,995.1/$4,760.8. The trend percents using the data from Exhibit 13.3 are shown in Exhibit 13.4.

Exhibit 13.4

Trend Percents of Revenues
and Expenses

(in percents)	2000	1999	1998	1997	1996	1995
Revenues	188.9%	184.4%	200.7%	193.0%	135.9%	100%
Costs of sales	188.6	191.7	211.7	192.1	136.3	100
Selling and administrative	215.4	200.6	216.9	190.4	131.3	100

Point: Trend analysis expresses a percent of base, not a percent of change.

Graphical depictions often aid analysis of trend percents. Exhibit 13.5 shows the trend percents from Exhibit 13.4 in a *line graph,* which can help us identify trends and detect changes in direction or magnitude. It reveals that, through 1997, costs of sales increased at a rate almost identical to the increase in revenues. In particular, at no time did the revenues and costs of sales lines deviate by more than 1%. However, in 1998, cost of sales jumped 11.0% above revenues (211.7% vs. 200.7%). By 2000, Nike has cost of sales back in line with earlier relations (revenues [green line] at 188.9% vs. cost of sales [red line] at 188.6%). The graph also reveals that both revenues and costs of sales markedly increased from 1995 to 1998, but flatten out in 1999–2000. The line graph in Exhibit 13.5 also shows that the increase in selling and administrative expenses exceeded the increase in both revenues and costs of sales in 1998–2000. Its trend line rises to 215.4% in 2000 compared to 100% in 1995. As suggested from Exhibit 13.2, we should continue to monitor these expenses.

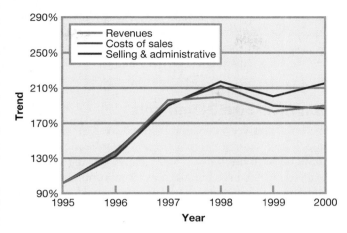

Exhibit 13.5

Trend Percent Lines for Revenues and Expenses

Exhibit 13.6 compares **Nike**'s revenue trend line to that of **Reebok** for this recent six-year period. Nike's revenues sharply increased in 1996–1997, while those of Reebok did not. Both companies' revenues declined in 1999, but Nike's revenues for 2000 slightly increased while Reebok's did not.

Trend analysis of financial statement items also can include comparisons of relations between items on different financial state-

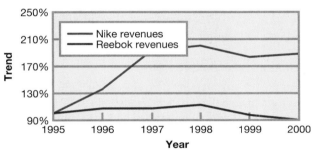

Exhibit 13.6

Trend Percent Lines—
Nike vs. Reebok

ments. For instance, Exhibit 13.7 is a comparison of Nike's revenues and total assets. The rate of increase in total assets (186.4%) is slightly less than the increase in revenues (188.9%). Is this result favorable or not? It suggests that Nike was slightly more efficient in using its assets in 2000 than in earlier years.

Overall we must remember that an important role of financial statement analysis is identifying questions and areas of interest, which often direct us to important factors bearing on a company's future. Accordingly, financial statement analysis should be seen as a continuous process of refining our understanding and expectations of company performance and financial condition.

Decision Maker *d*

Auditor   Your tests reveal a 3% increase in sales from $200,000 to $206,000 and a 4% decrease in expenses from $190,000 to $182,400. Both changes are within your "reasonableness" criterion of ± 5%, and thus you don't pursue additional tests. The audit partner in charge questions your lack of follow-up and mentions the *joint relation* between sales and expenses. To what is the partner referring?

Answer—p. 600

Decision Track 13.1 *d*

Decision Point	Information Search	Analyze & Evaluate
Has a company's financial condition and performance changed across time?	Financial statements—the company, key competitors, and industry statistics.	Investigate changes in comparative financial statements (*horizontal analysis*) with dollar and percent changes—compared to a base year; also review trend percents.

Exhibit 13.7

Revenues and Total Assets Data for Nike

	2000	1995	Trend Percent (2000 vs. 1995)
Revenues	$8,995.1	$4,760.8	188.9%
Total assets	5,856.9	3,142.7	186.4

Vertical Analysis

P2 Describe and apply methods of vertical analysis.

Vertical analysis is a tool to evaluate individual financial statement items or a group of items in terms of a specific base amount. We usually define a key aggregate figure as the base, which for an income statement is usually revenue and a balance sheet is usually total assets. This section explains vertical analysis and applies it to **Nike**. [The term *vertical analysis* arises from the up-down (or down-up) movement of our eyes as we review common-size financial statements. Vertical analysis is also called *common-size analysis*.]

Common-Size Statements

The comparative statements in Exhibits 13.1 and 13.2 show the change in each item over time, but they do not emphasize the relative importance of each item. We use **common-size financial statements** to reveal changes in the relative importance of each financial statement item. All individual amounts in common-size statements are redefined in terms of common-size percents. A *common-size percent* is measured by dividing each individual financial statement amount under analysis by its base amount:

$$\text{Common-size percent (\%)} = \frac{\text{Analysis amount}}{\text{Base amount}} \times 100$$

Common-Size Balance Sheet

Point: The *base* amount in common-size analysis is an *aggregate* amount from the same period's financial statement.

Common-size statements express each item as a percent of a *base amount,* which for a common-size balance sheet is usually total assets. It is assigned a value of 100%. This implies that the total amount of liabilities plus equity equals 100% since this amount equals total assets. We then compute a common-size percent for each asset, liability, and equity item using total assets as the base amount. When we present a company's successive balance sheets in this way, changes in the mixture of assets, liabilities, and equity are apparent.

Point: Common-size statements often are used to compare two or more companies in the same industry.

Exhibit 13.8 shows a common-size comparative balance sheet for Nike. Some relations that stand out on both a magnitude and percent basis include (1) an increase in inventory (22.3% to 24.7%); (2) an increase in property, plant, and equipment (24.1% to 27.0%); and (3) an increase in notes payable (8.0% to 15.8%). None of these happenings is necessarily favorable to Nike. In particular, the increasing inventory warrants attention due to risk of excess and slow-moving products. Also, an increase in property, plant, and equipment must be offset with increased net income in current and/or future periods to support such asset acquisitions.

Decision Track 13.2		d
Decision Point	**Information Search**	**Analyze & Evaluate**
Has the makeup of a company's financial condition and performance changed?	Financial statements—the company, key competitors, and industry statistics.	Investigate major changes in common-size financial statements as a percent of a base amount (*vertical analysis*) across time and/or companies.

Common-Size Income Statement

Point: Common-size statements are useful in comparing firms that report in different currencies.

Our analysis also benefits from examining a common-size income statement. Revenues is usually the base amount, which is assigned a value of 100%. Each common-size income statement item appears as a percent of revenues. If we think of the 100% revenues amount as representing one sales dollar, the remaining items show how each revenue dollar is distributed among costs, expenses, and income.

Exhibit 13.8

Common-Size Comparative
Balance Sheet

NIKE
Common-Size Comparative Balance Sheet
May 31, 2000 and 1999

(in millions)	2000	1999	Common-Size Percents* 2000	1999
Assets				
Current assets				
Cash and equivalents	$ 254.3	$198.1	4.3%	3.8%
Accounts receivable, less allowance for doubtful accounts of $65.4 and $73.2	1,567.2	1,540.1	26.8	29.3
Inventories	1,446.0	1,170.6	24.7	22.3
Deferred income taxes	111.5	120.6	1.9	2.3
Income taxes receivable	2.2	15.9	0.0	0.3
Prepaid expenses	215.2	219.6	3.7	4.2
Total current assets	$3,596.4	$3,264.9	61.4%	62.2%
Property, plant, and equipment, net	1,583.4	1,265.8	27.0	24.1
Intangible assets and goodwill	410.9	426.6	7.0	8.1
Deferred taxes and other assets	266.2	290.4	4.6	5.6
Total assets	$5,856.9	$5,247.7	100.0%	100.0%
Liabilities and Shareholders' Equity				
Current liabilities				
Current portion of long-term debt	$ 50.1	$ 1.0	0.8%	0.0%
Notes payable	924.2	419.1	15.8	8.0
Accounts payable	543.8	473.6	9.3	9.0
Accrued liabilities	621.9	553.2	10.6	10.5
Total current liabilities	$2,140.0	$1,446.9	36.5%	27.5%
Long-term debt	470.3	386.1	8.0	7.4
Deferred taxes and other liabilities	110.3	79.8	1.9	1.5
Commitments and contingencies	—	—		
Redeemable preferred stock	0.3	0.3	0.0	0.0
Shareholders' equity:				
Common stock at stated value				
Class A convertible—99.2 and 100.7 shares outstanding	0.2	0.2	0.0	0.0
Class B—170.4 and 181.6 shares outstanding	2.6	2.7	0.1	0.1
Capital in excess of stated value	369.0	334.1	6.3	6.4
Unearned stock compensation	(11.7)	—	(0.2)	—
Accumulated other comprehensive income	(111.1)	(68.9)	(1.9)	(1.3)
Retained earnings	2,887.0	3,066.5	49.3	58.4
Total shareholders' equity	$3,136.0	$3,334.6	53.5%	63.5%
Total liabilities and equity	$5,856.9	$5,247.7	100.0%	100.0%

* Percents are rounded to tenths.

Exhibit 13.9 shows the common-size income statement for each dollar of Nike's revenues. The exhibit shows that Nike's costs and expenses, as a percent of revenues, decreased from 1999 (91.5%) to 2000 (89.8%). The largest change is a decrease in costs of sales, from 62.6 cents on the dollar to 60.1 cents. This favorable change overcomes the unfavorable increase in selling and administrative expenses from 27.7% to 29.0%. One advantage of computing common-size percents for successive income statements is that it helps uncover potentially important changes in a company's expenses. Evidence of no changes, especially when changes are expected, is also informative for analysis purposes.

Global: International companies sometimes disclose "convenience" financial statements, which are statements translated in other languages and currencies. However, these statements rarely adjust for differences in accounting principles across countries.

Exhibit 13.9
Common-Size Comparative
Income Statement

NIKE Common-Size Comparative Income Statement For Years Ended May 31, 2000 and 1999			Common-Size Percents*	
(in millions, except per share data)	2000	1999	2000	1999
Revenues	$8,995.1	$8,776.9	100.0%	100.0%
Costs and expenses				
Costs of sales	5,403.8	5,493.5	60.1	62.6
Selling and administrative	2,606.4	2,426.6	29.0	27.7
Interest expense	45.0	44.1	0.5	0.5
Other income and expense, net	23.2	21.5	0.2	0.2
Restructuring charge, net	(2.5)	45.1	(0.0)	0.5
Total costs and expenses	$8,075.9	$8,030.8	89.8%	91.5%
Income before income taxes	919.2	746.1	10.2	8.5
Income taxes	340.1	294.7	3.8	3.4
Net income	$ 579.1	$ 451.4	6.4%	5.1%
Basic earnings per common share	$ 2.10	$ 1.59		
Average common shares outstanding	275.7	283.3		

* Percents are rounded to tenths.

Common-Size Graphics

Two of the most common tools of common-size analysis are trend analysis of common-size statements and graphical analysis. The trend analysis of common-size statements is similar to that of comparative statements discussed under vertical analysis. It is not illustrated here because the only difference is the substitution of common-size percents for trend percents. Instead, this section discusses graphical analysis of common-size statements.

An income statement readily lends itself to common-size graphical analysis. This is so because revenues affect nearly every item in an income statement. Exhibit 13.10 shows Nike's 2000 common-size income statement in graphical form. This pie chart highlights the contribution of each component of revenues.

Exhibit 13.10
Common-Size Graphic of
Nike Income Statement

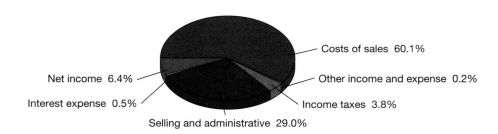

Exhibits 13.11 and 13.12 give a preview of more complex graphical analyses available and the insights they provide. The data for these graphs are taken from Nike's MD&A. The bar chart in Exhibit 13.11 shows a graphical breakdown of 2000 versus 1998 by apparel and footwear for both U.S. and non-U.S. revenues. It is immediately apparent from this chart that each segment's revenues remained about the same or decreased from 1998 to 2000. Exhibit 13.12 shows a bar chart measuring each segment's revenues as a percent of its annual revenues. This presentation highlights the decline in magnitude of U.S. apparel revenues for Nike's total operations. In particular, its U.S. apparel revenues made up

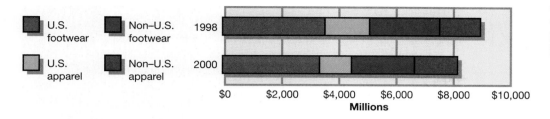

Exhibit 13.11

Nike Revenue Breakdown
in Dollars

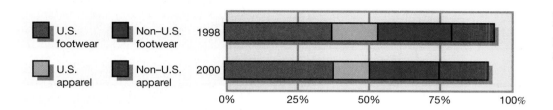

Exhibit 13.12

Nike Revenue Breakdown
as Percent of Total

15.2% of its total revenues in 1998, but by 2000 it declined to 12.8% of total revenues. In contrast, non-U.S. revenues increased (as a percent of the total) for both footwear and apparel. This raises Nike's risk exposure to changes in the global economy.

Graphical analysis is also useful in evaluating a balance sheet. It is especially helpful in identifying (1) sources of financing including the distribution among current liabilities, noncurrent liabilities, and equity capital and (2) types of investing activities, including the distribution among current and noncurrent assets. Common-size balance sheet analysis is often extended to examine the composition of subgroups. For instance, in assessing liquidity of current assets, knowing what proportion of current assets consists of inventories is often important, and not simply what proportion inventories are of total assets. Exhibit 13.13 shows a common-size graphical display of Nike's assets.

Common-size financial statements are also useful in comparing different companies. Exhibit 13.14 shows common-size graphics of both Nike and Reebok on financing sources. This graphic highlights the much larger percent of debt financing for Reebok compared to that for Nike. However, common-size statements fail to reflect the relative sizes of companies. Comparison of a company's common-size statements with competitors' or industry common-size statistics alerts our attention to differences in the structure or distribution of its financial statements, but not to their dollar magnitude.

Cash and equivalents 4.3%

Accounts receivable 26.8%

Inventories 24.7%

S-T deferred taxes 1.9%
Prepaid expenses 3.7%

Property, plant
and equipment 27.0%

Intangible assets 7.0%
L-T deferred taxes 4.6%

Exhibit 13.13

Common-Size Graphic of Nike
Asset Components

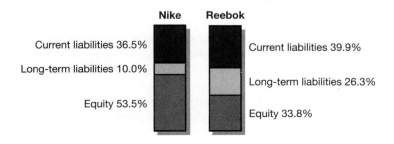

Exhibit 13.14

Common-Size Graphic of
Financing Sources—
Competitor Analysis

Answers—p. 600

Ratio Analysis

P3 Define and apply ratio analysis.

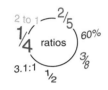

Topic Tackler 13-2

Point: Some sources for industry norms are *Annual Statement Studies* by Robert Morris Associates, *Industry Norms & Key Business Ratios* by Dun & Bradstreet, *Standard & Poor's Industry Surveys,* and www.MarketGuide.com.

Ratios are among the more popular and widely used tools of financial analysis. They provide clues to and symptoms of underlying conditions. Ratios, properly interpreted, identify areas requiring further investigation. A ratio can help us uncover conditions and trends difficult to detect by inspecting individual components making up the ratio. Ratios, like other analysis tools, are usually future oriented—that is, they are often adjusted for their probable future trend and magnitude, and their usefulness depends on skillful interpretation of them.

A ratio expresses a mathematical relation between two quantities. It can be expressed as a percent, rate, or proportion. For instance, a change in an account balance from $100 to $250 can be expressed as (1) 150%, (2) 2.5 times, or (3) 2.5 to 1 (or 2.5:1). Computation of a ratio is a simple arithmetic operation, but its interpretation is not. To be meaningful, a ratio must refer to an economically important relation. For example, a direct and crucial relation exists between an item's sales price and its cost. Accordingly, the ratio of cost of goods sold to sales is significant. In contrast, no obvious relation exists between freight costs and the balance of long-term investments.

This section describes an important set of financial ratios and shows how to apply them. The selected ratios are organized into the four building blocks of financial statement analysis: (1) liquidity and efficiency, (2) solvency, (3) profitability, and (4) market prospects. All of these ratios have been previously explained at relevant points in prior chapters. The purpose here is to organize and apply them under a summary framework. As we discussed earlier, we use four common standards for comparisons: intracompany, competitor, industry, and guidelines. Our analysis of **Nike** uses three of the four standards in varying degrees: intracompany, competitor (**Reebok**), and guideline comparisons. Since no obvious industry comparison is available for Nike, we do not use industry standards as we normally would. For instance, constructing industry standards using Reebok, Adidas, and Fila might be useful, but since Adidas and Fila are non-U.S. companies and do not publish statements readily comparable to those of Nike, this is not done.

Liquidity and Efficiency

Liquidity refers to the availability of resources to meet short-term cash requirements. A company's short-term liquidity is affected by the timing of cash inflows and outflows along with its prospects for future performance. Our analysis of liquidity is aimed at a company's funding requirements. *Efficiency* refers to how productive a company is in using its assets. Efficiency is usually measured relative to how much revenue is generated from a certain level of assets. Both liquidity and efficiency are important and complementary in our analysis. If a company fails to meet its current obligations, its continued existence is doubtful. Viewed in this light, all other measures of analysis are of secondary importance. Although accounting measurements assume the company's continued existence, our analysis must always assess the validity of this assumption using liquidity measures. Moreover, inefficient use of assets can cause liquidity problems. A lack of liquidity often precedes lower profitability and fewer opportunities. It can foretell a loss of owner control or loss of investment. To a company's creditors, lack of liquidity can yield delays in collecting interest and principal payments or the loss of amounts due them. A company's customers and suppliers of goods and services are affected by short-term liquidity problems. Implications include a company's inability to execute contracts and potential damage to important customer and supplier relationships. This section describes and illustrates key ratios relevant to accessing liquidity and efficiency.

Working Capital and Current Ratio

The amount of current assets less current liabilities is called **working capital,** or *net working capital.* A company needs an adequate amount of working capital to meet current debts, carry sufficient inventories, and take advantage of cash discounts. A company that runs low on working capital is less likely to meet current obligations or continue operating. When evaluating a company's working capital, we must look beyond the dollar amount of current assets less current liabilities. We also must consider the relation between the amounts of current assets and current liabilities. Recall from Chapter 3 that the *current ratio* reflects a company's ability to pay its short-term obligations and is defined as follows:

$$\text{Current ratio} = \frac{\text{Current assets}}{\text{Current liabilities}}$$

Drawing on information in Exhibit 13.1, Nike's working capital and current ratio for both 2000 and 1999 are shown in Exhibit 13.15. Reebok's current ratio of 1.99 is shown in the margin. It is higher than Nike's current ratio (1.68), but neither company appears in danger of defaulting on loan payments. A high current ratio suggests a strong liquidity position and an ability to meet current obligations. A company can have a current ratio that is too high. An excessively high current ratio means that the company has invested too much in current assets compared to its current obligations. Since current assets normally generate a low return on investment (compared with long-term assets), an excessive investment in current assets is not an efficient use of funds.

($ in millions)	2000	1999
Current assets	$3,596.4	$3,264.9
Current liabilities	2,140.0	1,446.9
Working capital	$1,456.4	$1,818.0
Current ratio		
$3,596.4/$2,140.0	1.68 to 1	
$3,264.9/$1,446.9		2.26 to 1

Point: Amazon.com's stock price decline corresponded with its decline in working capital (WC):

Date	Price	WC (mil.)
Mar. 31, 2000	$67.00	$704
June 30, 2000	36.31	559
Sept. 29, 2000	38.44	504
Dec. 29, 2000	15.56	386

Example: Refer to Reebok's financial statements in Appendix A. What is its working capital on Dec. 31, 1999? *Answer (in mil.):*

Current assets	$1,243.118
Current liabilities	(623.903)
Working capital	$ 619.215

Exhibit 13.15

Nike's Working Capital and Current Ratio

Reebok
Current ratio = 1.99

Many users apply a guideline of 2:1 for the current ratio in helping evaluate a company's debt-paying ability. A company with a 2:1 or higher current ratio is generally thought to be a good credit risk in the short run. Such a guideline or any analysis of the current ratio must recognize at least three additional factors: (1) type of business, (2) composition of current assets, and (3) turnover rate of current asset components.

Type of Business. The type of business a company operates affects an assessment of its current ratio. A service company that grants little or no credit and carries no inventories can probably operate on a current ratio of less than 1:1 if its revenues generate enough cash to pay its current liabilities. On the other hand, a company selling high-priced clothing or furniture requires a higher ratio because of difficulties in judging customer demand and cash receipts. For instance, if demand falls, this company's inventory may not generate as much cash as expected. Accordingly, analysis of the current ratio should include a comparison with ratios from successful companies in the same industry and from prior periods. We must also recognize that a company's accounting methods, especially choice of inventory method, affect the current ratio. For instance, a company using LIFO tends to report a smaller amount of current assets than if it uses FIFO when costs are rising. These factors should be considered before we decide whether a given current ratio is adequate.

Composition of Current Assets. The composition of a company's current assets is important to an evaluation of short-term liquidity. For instance, cash, cash equivalents, and short-term investments are more liquid than accounts and notes receivable. Also, short-term receivables normally are more liquid than merchandise inventory. Cash, of course, can be

Point: When a firm uses LIFO in a period of rising costs, the standard for an adequate current ratio usually is lower than if it used FIFO.

Global: Ratio analysis helps overcome most currency translation problems, but it does *not* overcome differences in accounting principles.

used to immediately pay current debts. Items such as accounts receivable and inventory, however, normally must be converted into cash before payment is made. An excessive amount of receivables and inventory weakens a company's ability to pay current liabilities. The acid-test ratio (see below) can help with this assessment.

Turnover Rate of Assets. Asset turnover measures a company's efficiency in using its assets. One relevant measure of asset efficiency is the revenue generated. A measure of total asset turnover is revenues divided by total assets, but evaluation of turnover for individual assets is also useful. We discuss total asset turnover with both receivables turnover and inventory turnover in the next section.

Acid-Test Ratio

Chapter 4 introduced us to the *acid-test ratio,* also called *quick ratio,* which focuses on current asset composition. Quick assets are cash, short-term investments, accounts receivable, and current notes receivable. These are the most liquid types of current assets. We compute the acid-test ratio as follows:

$$\text{Acid-test ratio} = \frac{\text{Cash + Short-term investments + Current receivables}}{\text{Current liabilities}}$$

Using information in Exhibit 13.1, we compute Nike's acid-test ratio in Exhibit 13.16.

Exhibit 13.16

Nike Acid-Test Ratio

($ in millions)	2000	1999
Cash and equivalents	$ 254.3	$ 198.1
Accounts receivable, less allowance	1,567.2	1,540.1
Total quick assets	$1,821.5	$1,738.2
Current liabilities	$2,140.0	$1,446.9
Acid-test ratio		
$1,821.5/$2,140.0	0.85 to 1	
$1,738.2/$1,446.9		1.20 to 1

Reebok
Acid-test ratio = 1.12

Nike's 2000 acid-test ratio (0.85) is less than both Reebok's (1.12) and the common guideline for an acceptable acid-test ratio of 1:1, but it appears adequate. Similar to our analysis of the current ratio, we need to consider other factors. For instance, the frequency with which a company converts its current assets into cash affects its working capital requirements. This implies that our analysis of short-term liquidity should also include an analysis of receivables and inventories. We next consider these analyses.

Accounts Receivable Turnover

We can measure how frequently a company converts its receivables into cash by computing *accounts receivable turnover*. As explained in Chapter 7, it is computed as follows:

$$\text{Accounts receivable turnover} = \frac{\text{Net sales}}{\text{Average accounts receivable}}$$

Short-term receivables from customers are also often included in the denominator along with accounts receivable. Also, accounts receivable turnover is more precise if credit sales are used for the numerator, but external users generally use net sales (or net revenues) because information about credit sales is typically not reported. Nike's 2000 accounts receivable turnover is computed as follows ($ millions):

$$\frac{\$8,995.1}{(\$1,567.2 + \$1,540.1)/2} = 5.8 \text{ times}$$

Reebok
Accounts receivable turnover = 6.2

Nike's value of 5.8 is slightly lower than Reebok's 6.2. Note that if accounts receivable are collected quickly, the accounts receivable turnover is high. A high turnover is favorable because it means the company need not commit large amounts of capital to accounts receivable. However, an accounts receivable turnover can be too high; this can occur when credit terms are so restrictive that they negatively affect sales volume. Also, some users prefer using gross accounts receivable (before subtracting the allowance for doubtful accounts) to avoid the influence of a manager's bad debts estimates.

Point: Ending accounts receivable is sometimes substituted for the average balance in computing accounts receivable turnover. This is acceptable if the difference between ending and average receivables is insignificant.

Point: *Average collection period* is estimated by dividing 365 by the accounts receivable turnover ratio. For example, 365 divided by an accounts receivable turnover of 6.1 indicates a 60-day average collection period.

Inventory Turnover

How long a company holds inventory before selling it affects working capital requirements. One measure of this effect is the *inventory turnover,* also called *merchandise turnover* or *merchandise inventory turnover.* Inventory turnover is defined in Chapter 5:

$$\text{Inventory turnover} = \frac{\text{Cost of goods sold}}{\text{Average inventory}}$$

Using costs of sales (Nike's term for cost of goods sold) and inventories information from Exhibits 13.1 and 13.2, we compute Nike's inventory turnover for 2000:

$$\frac{\$5,403.8}{(\$1,446.0 + \$1,170.6)/2} = 4.1 \text{ times}$$

Reebok
Inventory turnover = 3.8

Average inventory is estimated by averaging the beginning and the ending inventories for 2000. If the beginning and ending inventories do not represent the amount normally available, an average of quarterly or monthly inventories can be used. Nike's inventory turnover of 4.1 is slightly higher than Reebok's 3.8. A company with a high turnover requires a smaller investment in inventory than one producing the same sales with a lower turnover. Inventory turnover can be too high, however, if the inventory a company keeps is so small that it restricts sales volume.

Days' Sales Uncollected

We already described the use of accounts receivable turnover to evaluate how frequently a company collects its accounts. Another measure of this activity is *days' sales uncollected,* defined in Chapter 6:

$$\text{Days' sales uncollected} = \frac{\text{Accounts receivable}}{\text{Net sales}} \times 365$$

Any short-term notes receivable from customers are normally included in the numerator.
We illustrate this ratio's application by using Nike's information from Exhibits 13.1 and 13.2. The days' sales uncollected on May 31, 2000, is as follows:

$$\frac{\$1,567.2}{\$8,995.1} \times 365 = 63.6 \text{ days}$$

Reebok
Day's sales uncollected = 52.5

Nike's days' sales uncollected of 63.6 days is longer than the 52.5 days for Reebok. Days' sales uncollected is more meaningful if we know Nike's and Reebok's credit terms. A rough guideline states that days' sales uncollected should not exceed $1\frac{1}{3}$ times the days in its (1) credit period, if discounts are not offered or (2) discount period, if favorable discounts are offered.

Days' Sales in Inventory

Chapter 5 explained how *days' sales in inventory* is a useful measure in evaluating inventory liquidity. Days' sales in inventory is linked to inventory in a way that days' sales uncollected is linked to receivables. We compute days' sales in inventory as follows:

$$\text{Days' sales in inventory} = \frac{\text{Ending inventory}}{\text{Cost of goods sold}} \times 365$$

We compute Nike's days' sales in inventory for 2000 as follows:

Reebok
Days' sales in inventory = 84.8

$$\frac{\$1,446.0}{\$5,403.8} \times 365 = 97.7 \text{ days}$$

If the products in Nike's inventory are in demand by customers, this formula estimates that its inventory will be converted into receivables (or cash) in 97.7 days. If all of Nike's sales are credit sales, the conversion of inventory to receivables in 97.7 days *plus* the conversion of receivables to cash in 63.6 days implies that inventory will be converted to cash in about 161.3 days (97.7 + 63.6).

Total Asset Turnover

Total asset turnover describes a company's ability to use its assets to generate sales. We explained in Chapter 8 the computation of this ratio:

$$\text{Total asset turnover} = \frac{\text{Net sales}}{\text{Average total assets}}$$

In computing Nike's total asset turnover for 2000, we follow the usual practice of averaging total assets at the beginning and the end of the year. Taking the information from Exhibits 13.1 and 13.2, this computation is

Reebok
Total asset turnover = 1.79

$$\frac{\$8,995.1}{(\$5,856.9 + \$5,247.7)/2} = 1.62 \text{ times}$$

Total asset turnover is an important part of operating efficiency. Nike's performance on this factor is not as strong as Reebok's.

Quick Check

8. Information from Paff Co. at Dec. 31, 2002, follows: cash, $820,000; accounts receivable, $240,000; inventories, $470,000; plant assets, $910,000; accounts payable, $350,000; and income taxes payable, $180,000. Compute its (a) current ratio and (b) acid-test ratio.

9. On Dec. 31, 2001, Paff Company (question 8) had accounts receivable of $290,000 and inventories of $530,000. During 2002, net sales amounted to $2,500,000 and cost of goods sold was $750,000. Compute (a) accounts receivable turnover, (b) days' sales uncollected, (c) inventory turnover, and (d) days' sales in inventory.

Answers—p. 600

Solvency

Solvency refers to a company's long-run financial viability and its ability to cover long-term obligations. All business activities of a company—financing, investing, and operating—affect its solvency. Analysis of solvency is long term and uses less precise but more encompassing measures as compared to liquidity. One of the most important components of solvency analysis is the composition of a company's capital structure. *Capital structure*

refers to a company's sources of financing. It ranges from relatively permanent equity financing to riskier or more temporary short-term financing. Assets represent security for financiers ranging from loans secured by specific assets to the assets available as general security to unsecured creditors. This section describes the tools of solvency analysis. Our analysis focuses on a company's ability to both meet its obligations and provide security to its creditors *over the long run*. Indicators of this ability include *debt* and *equity* ratios, the relation between *pledged assets and secured liabilities,* and the company's capacity to earn sufficient income to *pay fixed interest charges*.

Debt and Equity Ratios

One element of solvency analysis is to assess the portion of a company's assets contributed by its owners and the portion contributed by creditors. This relation is reflected in the debt ratio described in Chapter 2. Recall that the *debt ratio* expresses total liabilities as a percent of total assets. The **equity ratio** provides complementary information by expressing total equity as a percent of total assets. Nike's debt and equity ratios are computed here:

Point: Bank examiners from the FDIC and other regulatory agencies use debt and equity ratios to monitor compliance with regulatory capital requirements imposed on banks and S&Ls.

($ in millions)	2000	Ratios	
Total liabilities	$2,720.9	46.5%	[Debt ratio]
Total equity	3,136.0	53.5	[Equity ratio]
Total liabilities and equity	$5,856.9	100.0%	

Reebok
Debt ratio = 66.2%
Equity ratio = 33.8%

Nike's financial statements reflect less debt than equity. Also, its debt mainly consists of current liabilities—comprising nearly 80% of its total liabilities, computed as $2,140/$2,720.9. A company is considered less risky if its capital structure (equity and long-term debt) contains more equity. One risk factor is the required payment for interest and principal when debt is outstanding. Another factor is the amount of financing provided by stockholders (owners). The greater is stockholder financing, the more losses a company can absorb through equity before the assets become inadequate to satisfy creditors' claims. From the stockholders' point of view, including debt in a company's capital structure is desirable so long as risk is not too great. If a company earns a return on borrowed capital that is higher than the cost of borrowing, the difference represents increased income to stockholders. Since debt can have the effect of increasing the return to stockholders, the inclusion of debt is described as *financial leverage*. Companies are said to be highly leveraged if a large portion of their assets is financed by debt.

Pledged Assets to Secured Liabilities

We explained in Chapter 10 how we use the ratio of pledged assets to secured liabilities to evaluate the risk of nonpayment faced by secured creditors. This ratio also is relevant to unsecured creditors because of what it implies about the remaining assets available. We compute the ratio as follows:

$$\text{Pledged assets to secured liabilities} = \frac{\text{Book value of pledged assets}}{\text{Book value of secured liabilities}}$$

The information needed to compute this ratio is not often reported in financial statements. This means that the ratio is used primarily by persons who have the ability to obtain information directly from the company, such as bankers and lenders. A generally agreed minimum value for this ratio is about 2:1 (from a secured creditor perspective), but the ratio needs careful interpretation because it is based on the *book value* of pledged assets. Book values are not necessarily intended to reflect amounts to be received from assets in event of liquidation. Also, a company's long-run earning ability can be more important than the value of its pledged assets. Creditors prefer that a debtor be able to pay with cash generated by operating activities rather than with cash obtained by liquidating assets.

Times Interest Earned

Chapter 9 explained the *times interest earned* ratio. Its purpose is to reflect the creditors' risk of loan repayments with interest. The amount of income before deductions for interest expense and income taxes is the amount available to pay interest expense. We compute this ratio as follows:

$$\text{Times interest earned} = \frac{\text{Income before interest expense and income taxes}}{\text{Interest expense}}$$

Decision Insight

Bears and Bulls A *bear market* is a declining market. The phrase comes from bear-skin jobbers who often sold the skins before the bears were caught. The term *bear* was then used to describe investors who sold shares they did not own in anticipation of a price decline. A *bull market* is a rising market. This phrase comes from the once popular sport of bear and bull baiting. The term *bull* came to mean the opposite of *bear.*

The larger this ratio, the less risky is the company for lenders. A guideline for this ratio says that creditors are reasonably safe if the company earns its fixed interest expense by two or more times each year. Exhibit 13.2 shows Nike's interest expense of $45.0 million. Its times interest earned ratio is computed as follows and its value suggests that Nike's creditors have little risk of non-repayment.

Reebok
Times interest earned = 1.4

$$\frac{\$579.1 + \$340.1 + \$45.0}{\$45.0} = 21.4$$

Profitability

We are especially interested in a company's ability to use its assets efficiently to produce profits (and positive cash flows). *Profitability* refers to a company's ability to generate an adequate return on invested capital. Return is judged by assessing earnings relative to the level and sources of financing. Profitability is also relevant to solvency. This section describes key profitability measures and their importance to financial statement analysis. We also explain variations in return measures and their interpretation. We analyze the components of return on assets for additional insights.

Profit Margin

A company's operating efficiency and profitability can be expressed by two components. The first is its *profit margin.* We explained in Chapter 3 that profit margin reflects a company's ability to earn a net income from sales. It is measured by expressing net income as a percent of sales (*sales* and *revenues* are similar terms). We use the information in Exhibit 13.2 to compute **Nike**'s 2000 profit margin:

Reebok
Profit margin = 0.4%

$$\text{Profit margin} = \frac{\text{Net income}}{\text{Net sales}} = \frac{\$579.1}{\$8,995.1} = 6.4\%$$

To evaluate profit margin, we must consider the industry. For instance, a publishing company might require a profit margin between 10% and 15%; a retail supermarket might require a profit margin of 1% or 2%. The second component of operating efficiency is *total asset turnover.* We described this ratio earlier in this section. Both profit margin and total asset turnover make up the two basic components of operating efficiency. These ratios also reflect management performance since managers are ultimately responsible for operating efficiency. The next section explains how we use both measures to analyze return on total assets.

Return on Total Assets

The two components of operating efficiency, profit margin and total asset turnover, are used to compute a summary measure. This summary measure is the *return on total assets* we described in Chapter 1. It is computed as follows:

$$\text{Return on total assets} = \frac{\text{Net income}}{\text{Average total assets}}$$

Nike's return on total assets for 2000 is:

$$\frac{\$579.1}{(\$5,856.9 + \$5,247.7)/2} = 10.4\%$$

Reebok
Return on total assets = 0.7%

Nike's 10.4% return on total assets is lower than that for many businesses but is higher than Reebok's return of 0.7%. We need comparisons with other competitors and alternative investment opportunities, however, before drawing reliable conclusions. We also should evaluate any trend in the rate of return. The following computation shows the important relation between profit margin, total asset turnover, and return on total assets:

Point: Many analysts add back *Interest expense x (1 − Tax rate)* to net income in computing return on total assets.

$$\text{Profit margin} \times \text{Total asset turnover} = \text{Return on total assets}$$

or

$$\frac{\text{Net income}}{\text{Net sales}} \times \frac{\text{Net sales}}{\text{Average total assets}} = \frac{\text{Net income}}{\text{Average total assets}}$$

Notice that both profit margin and total asset turnover contribute to overall operating efficiency, as measured by return on total assets. If we apply this formula to Nike, we get

$$6.4\% \times 1.62 = 10.4\%$$

Reebok: 0.4% × 1.79 = 0.7%

This analysis shows that, while Nike has a less favorable total asset turnover compared to that for Reebok, it has both a higher profit margin and a higher return on assets.

Return on Common Stockholders' Equity

Perhaps the most important goal in operating a company is to earn net income for its owner(s). The *return on common stockholders' equity* measures a company's success in reaching this goal. We explained in Chapter 2 how we compute return on equity. This return measure is slightly modified for a corporation with preferred stock as follows:

$$\text{Return on common stockholders' equity} = \frac{\text{Net income} - \text{Preferred dividends}}{\text{Average common stockholders' equity}}$$

Nike's *Note 7* reports that it has $0.03 million in dividends on redeemable preferred stock in 2000. From this information and data in its statements, we compute Nike's 2000 return on common stockholders' equity as follows:

$$\frac{\$579.1 - \$0.03}{(\$3,136.0 + \$3,334.6)/2} = 17.9\%$$

Reebok
Return on common stockholders'
equity = 2.1%

The denominator in this computation is the book value of common equity. In the numerator, the dividends on Nike's cumulative preferred stock are subtracted whether they are declared or are in arrears. If preferred stock is noncumulative, its dividends are subtracted only if declared.

Market Prospects

Market measures are useful for analyzing corporations with publicly traded stock. These market measures use stock price, which reflects

Decision Insight

Wall Street *Wall Street* is synonymous with financial markets and capitalism. Its name comes from the street location of the original New York Stock Exchange. The street's name derives from stockades built by early settlers to protect New York from pirate attacks.

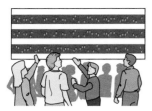

the market's (public's) expectations for the company. This includes expectations of both company return and risk—as the market perceives it.

Price-Earnings Ratio

We explained in Chapter 11 the computation of the *price-earnings ratio* as follows:

$$\text{Price-earnings ratio} = \frac{\text{Market price per common share}}{\text{Earnings per share}}$$

Point: The PE ratio can be viewed as an indicator of the market's expected growth and risk for a stock. A high level of expected risk suggests a low PE ratio. A high growth rate suggests a high PE ratio.

We also noted that the predicted earnings per share for the next period is often used in the denominator of this computation. Reported earnings per share for the most recent period is also commonly used. In both cases, the ratio is used as an indicator of the future growth and risk of a company's earnings as perceived by the stock's buyers and sellers.

The market price of Nike's common stock during fiscal 2000 ranged from a low of $26.563 to a high of $64.125, with a year-end price of $42.875 at May 31, 2000. Using Nike's $2.10 basic earnings per share reported in Exhibit 13.2, we compute its price-earnings ratio as follows (some analysts compute this ratio at both the low and high stock price):

Reebok
PE (year-end) = 40.9

$$\frac{\$42.875}{\$2.10} = 20.4$$

Point: Some investors avoid stocks with high PE ratios under the belief they are "overpriced." Alternatively, some investors *sell these stocks short*—hoping for price declines.

Nike's price-earnings ratio is higher than many companies' ratios. (Reebok's ratio is high due to abnormally low earnings.) Nike's high ratio reflects investors' expectation that the company will continue to grow at a rate faster than the typical company. Alternatively, some might suggest that its stock is priced quite high given its recent earnings per share level.

Dividend Yield

We explained in Chapter 11 how to use *dividend yield* to compare the dividend-paying performance of different investment alternatives. We compute dividend yield as follows:

$$\text{Dividend yield} = \frac{\text{Annual cash dividends per share}}{\text{Market price per share}}$$

Nike's dividend yield, based on its fiscal year-end market price per share of $42.875 and its $0.48 cash dividends per share from its financial history section, is computed as follows:

Reebok
Dividend yield = 0.0%

$$\frac{\$0.48}{\$42.875} = 1.1\%$$

Point: Corporate PE ratios and dividend yields are found in daily stock market quotations listed in *The Wall Street Journal, Investor's Business Daily,* or other business publications and Web services.

Some companies decide not to declare and pay dividends because they prefer to reinvest their cash. **Microsoft,** for instance, does not pay cash dividends on its common stock.

Summary of Ratios

Exhibit 13.17 summarizes several of the major financial statement analysis ratios illustrated in this chapter and throughout the book. This summary includes each ratio's title, its formula, and the purpose for which it is commonly used.

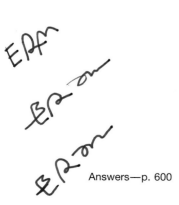

Quick Check

10. Which ratio best reflects a company's ability to meet immediate interest payments? (*a*) Debt ratio. (*b*) Equity ratio. (*c*) Times interest earned.

11. Which ratio best measures a company's success in earning net income for its owner(s)? (*a*) Profit margin. (*b*) Return on common stockholders' equity. (*c*) Price-earnings ratio. (*d*) Dividend yield.

12. If a company has net sales of $8,500,000, net income of $945,000, and total asset turnover of 1.8 times, what is its return on total assets?

Answers—p. 600

Exhibit 13.17

Financial Statement Analysis Ratios*

Ratio	Formula	Measure of
Liquidity and Efficiency		
Current ratio	$= \dfrac{\text{Current assets}}{\text{Current liabilities}}$	Short-term debt-paying ability
Acid-test ratio	$= \dfrac{\text{Cash} + \text{Short-term investments} + \text{Current receivables}}{\text{Current liabilities}}$	Immediate short-term debt-paying ability
Accounts receivable turnover	$= \dfrac{\text{Net sales}}{\text{Average accounts receivable}}$	Efficiency of collection
Inventory turnover	$= \dfrac{\text{Cost of goods sold}}{\text{Average inventory}}$	Efficiency of inventory management
Days' sales uncollected	$= \dfrac{\text{Accounts receivable}}{\text{Net sales}} \times 365$	Liquidity of receivables
Days' sales in inventory	$= \dfrac{\text{Ending inventory}}{\text{Cost of goods sold}} \times 365$	Liquidity of inventory
Total asset turnover	$= \dfrac{\text{Net sales}}{\text{Average total assets}}$	Efficiency of assets in producing sales
Solvency		
Debt ratio	$= \dfrac{\text{Total liabilities}}{\text{Total assets}}$	Creditor financing and leverage
Equity ratio	$= \dfrac{\text{Total equity}}{\text{Total assets}}$	Owner financing
Pledged assets to secured liabilities	$= \dfrac{\text{Book value of pledged assets}}{\text{Book value of secured liabilities}}$	Protection to secured creditors
Times interest earned	$= \dfrac{\text{Income before interest expense and income taxes}}{\text{Interest expense}}$	Protection in meeting interest payments
Profitability		
Profit margin ratio	$= \dfrac{\text{Net income}}{\text{Net sales}}$	Net income in each sales dollar
Gross margin ratio	$= \dfrac{\text{Net sales} - \text{Cost of goods sold}}{\text{Net sales}}$	Gross margin in each sales dollar
Return on total assets	$= \dfrac{\text{Net income}}{\text{Average total assets}}$	Overall profitability of assets
Return on common stockholders' equity	$= \dfrac{\text{Net income} - \text{Preferred dividends}}{\text{Average common stockholders' equity}}$	Profitability of owner's investment
Book value per common share	$= \dfrac{\text{Shareholders' equity applicable to common shares}}{\text{Number of common shares outstanding}}$	Liquidation at reported amounts
Basic earnings per share	$= \dfrac{\text{Net income} - \text{Preferred dividends}}{\text{Weighted-average common shares outstanding}}$	Net income per common share
Market Prospects		
Price-earnings ratio	$= \dfrac{\text{Market price per common share}}{\text{Earnings per share}}$	Market value relative to earnings
Dividend yield	$= \dfrac{\text{Annual cash dividends per share}}{\text{Market price per share}}$	Cash return per common share

*Several additional ratios were also examined in previous chapters including: credit risk ratio; plant asset useful life; plant asset age; days' cash expense coverage; cash coverage of growth; cash coverage of debt; free cash flow; cash flow on total assets; and payout ratio. Many of these are defined on the back inside cover of the book.

A1   Summarize and report results of analysis.

Understanding the purpose of financial statement analysis is crucial to the usefulness of any analysis. This understanding leads to efficiency of effort, effectiveness in application, and relevance in focus. The purpose of most financial statement analyses is to reduce uncertainty in business decisions through a rigorous and sound evaluation. A *financial statement analysis report* helps by directly addressing the building blocks of analysis and by identifying weaknesses in inference by requiring explanation—it forces us to organize our reasoning and to verify the flow and logic of analysis. A report also serves as a communication link with readers, and the writing process reinforces our judgments and vice versa. Finally, the report helps us (re)evaluate evidence and refine conclusions on key building blocks. A good analysis report usually consists of six sections:

1. **Executive summary**—brief focus on important analysis results and conclusions.
2. **Analysis overview**—background on the company, its industry, and its economic setting.
3. **Evidential matter**—financial statements and information used in the analysis, including ratios, trends, comparisons, statistics, and all analytical measures assembled; often organized under the building blocks of analysis.
4. **Assumptions**—identification of important assumptions regarding a company's industry and economic environment, and other important assumptions for estimates.
5. **Key factors**—list of important favorable and unfavorable factors, both quantitative and qualitative, for company performance; usually organized by areas of analysis.
6. **Inferences**—forecasts, estimates, interpretations, and conclusions drawing on all sections of the report.

We must remember that the user dictates relevance, meaning that the analysis report should include a brief table of contents to help readers focus on those areas most relevant to their decisions. All irrelevant matter must be eliminated. For example, decades-old details of obscure transactions and detailed miscues of the analysis are irrelevant. Ambiguities and qualifications to avoid responsibility or hedging inferences should be eliminated. Finally, writing is important. Mistakes in grammar and errors of fact compromise the credibility of the analysis.

Decision Insight

Short Selling   *Short selling* refers to selling stock before you buy it. Here's an example: You borrow 100 shares of Nike stock, sell them in the market at $40 each, and receive money from their sale. You then wait. Your hope is that Nike's stock price falls to, say, $35 each and you can replace the borrowed stock for less money than you sold it for—reaping a profit of $5 each less any transaction costs.

Demonstration Problem

Use the following financial statements of Precision Co. to complete these requirements:

1. Prepare a comparative income statement showing the percent increase or decrease for year 2002 in comparison to year 2001.
2. Prepare a common-size comparative balance sheet for years 2002 and 2001.
3. Compute the following ratios as of December 31, 2002, or for the year ended December 31, 2002, and identify its building block category for financial statement analysis:

   a. Current ratio
   b. Acid-test ratio
   c. Accounts receivable turnover
   d. Days' sales uncollected
   e. Inventory turnover
   f. Debt ratio

   g. Pledged assets to secured liabilities
   h. Times interest earned
   i. Profit margin ratio
   j. Total asset turnover
   k. Return on total assets
   l. Return on common stockholders' equity

PRECISION COMPANY
Comparative Income Statement
For Years Ended December 31, 2002 and 2001

	2002	2001
Sales	$2,486,000	$2,075,000
Cost of goods sold	1,523,000	1,222,000
Gross profit	$ 963,000	$ 853,000
Operating expenses		
Advertising expense	145,000	100,000
Sales salaries expense	240,000	280,000
Office salaries expense	165,000	200,000
Insurance expense	100,000	45,000
Supplies expense	26,000	35,000
Depreciation expense	85,000	75,000
Miscellaneous expenses	17,000	15,000
Total operating expenses	$ 778,000	$ 750,000
Operating income	$ 185,000	$ 103,000
Interest expense	44,000	46,000
Income before taxes	$ 141,000	$ 57,000
Income taxes	47,000	19,000
Net income	$ 94,000	$ 38,000
Earnings per share	$ 0.99	$ 0.40

PRECISION COMPANY
Comparative Balance Sheet
December 31, 2002 and 2001

	2002	2001
Assets		
Current assets		
Cash	$ 79,000	$ 42,000
Short-term investments	65,000	96,000
Accounts receivable (net)	120,000	100,000
Merchandise inventory	250,000	265,000
Total current assets	$ 514,000	$ 503,000
Plant assets		
Store equipment (net)	400,000	350,000
Office equipment (net)	45,000	50,000
Buildings (net)	625,000	675,000
Land	100,000	100,000
Total plant assets	$1,170,000	$1,175,000
Total assets	$1,684,000	$1,678,000
Liabilities		
Current liabilities		
Accounts payable	$ 164,000	$ 190,000
Short-term notes payable	75,000	90,000
Taxes payable	26,000	12,000
Total current liabilities	$ 265,000	$ 292,000
Long-term liabilities		
Notes payable (secured by mortgage on buildings)	400,000	420,000
Total liabilities	$ 665,000	$ 712,000
Stockholders' Equity		
Common stock, $5 par value	$ 475,000	$ 475,000
Retained earnings	544,000	491,000
Total stockholders' equity	$1,019,000	$ 966,000
Total liabilities and equity	$1,684,000	$1,678,000

Planning the Solution

- Set up a four-column income statement; enter the 2002 and 2001 amounts in the first two columns and then enter the dollar change in the third column and the percent change from 2001 in the fourth column.
- Set up a four-column balance sheet; enter the 2002 and 2001 year-end amounts in the first two columns and then compute and enter the amount of each item as a percent of total assets.
- Compute the required ratios using the data provided. Use the average of beginning and ending amounts when appropriate (see Exhibit 13.17 for definitions).

Solution to Demonstration Problem

1.

PRECISION COMPANY
Comparative Income Statement
For Years Ended December 31, 2002 and 2001

	2002	2001	Increase (Decrease) in 2002 Amount	Increase (Decrease) in 2002 Percent
Sales	$2,486,000	$2,075,000	$411,000	19.8%
Cost of goods sold	1,523,000	1,222,000	301,000	24.6
Gross profit	$ 963,000	$ 853,000	$110,000	12.9
Operating expenses				
Advertising expense	145,000	100,000	45,000	45.0
Sales salaries expense	240,000	280,000	(40,000)	(14.3)
Office salaries expense	165,000	200,000	(35,000)	(17.5)
Insurance expense	100,000	45,000	55,000	122.2
Supplies expense	26,000	35,000	(9,000)	(25.7)
Depreciation expense	85,000	75,000	10,000	13.3
Miscellaneous expenses	17,000	15,000	2,000	13.3
Total operating expenses	$ 778,000	$ 750,000	$ 28,000	3.7
Operating income	$ 185,000	$ 103,000	$ 82,000	79.6
Interest expense	44,000	46,000	(2,000)	(4.3)
Income before taxes	$ 141,000	$ 57,000	$ 84,000	147.4
Income taxes	47,000	19,000	28,000	147.4
Net income	$ 94,000	$ 38,000	$ 56,000	147.4
Earnings per share	$ 0.99	$ 0.40	$ 0.59	147.5

2.

PRECISION COMPANY
Common-Size Comparative Balance Sheet
December 31, 2002 and 2001

	December 31 2002	December 31 2001*	Common-Size Percents 2002	Common-Size Percents 2001*
Assets				
Current assets				
Cash	$ 79,000	$ 42,000	4.7%	2.5%
Short-term investments	65,000	96,000	3.9	5.7
Accounts receivable (net)	120,000	100,000	7.1	6.0
Merchandise inventory	250,000	265,000	14.8	15.8
Total current assets	$ 514,000	$ 503,000	30.5	30.0
Plant Assets				
Store equipment (net)	400,000	350,000	23.8	20.9
Office equipment (net)	45,000	50,000	2.7	3.0
Buildings (net)	625,000	675,000	37.1	40.2
Land	100,000	100,000	5.9	6.0
Total plant assets	$1,170,000	$1,175,000	69.5	70.0
Total assets	$1,684,000	$1,678,000	100.0	100.0

[continued on next page]

[continued from previous page]

PRECISION COMPANY Common-Size Comparative Balance Sheet December 31, 2002 and 2001	December 31		Common-Size Percents	
	2002	2001*	2002	2001*
Liabilities				
Current liabilities				
Accounts payable	$ 164,000	$ 190,000	9.7%	11.3%
Short-term notes payable	75,000	90,000	4.5	5.4
Taxes payable	26,000	12,000	1.5	0.7
Total current liabilities	$ 265,000	$ 292,000	15.7	17.4
Long-term liabilities				
Notes payable (secured by mortgage on buildings & land)	400,000	420,000	23.8	25.0
Total liabilities	$ 665,000	$ 712,000	39.5	42.4
Stockholders' Equity				
Common stock, $5 par value	$ 475,000	$ 475,000	28.2	28.3
Retained earnings	544,000	491,000	32.3	29.3
Total stockholders' equity	$1,019,000	$ 966,000	60.5	57.6
Total liabilities and equity	$1,684,000	$1,678,000	100.0	100.0

* Columns do not always exactly add to 100 due to rounding.

3. **Ratios for 2002:**
   a. Current ratio: $514,000/$265,000 = 1.9 : 1 (liquidity and efficiency)
   b. Acid-test ratio: ($79,000 + $65,000 + $120,000)/$265,000 = 1.0:1 (liquidity and efficiency)
   c. Average receivables: ($120,000 + $100,000)/2 = $110,000
      Accounts receivable turnover: $2,486,000/$110,000 = 22.6 times (liquidity and efficiency)
   d. Days' sales uncollected: ($120,000/$2,486,000) $\times$ 365 = 17.6 days (liquidity and efficiency)
   e. Average inventory: ($250,000 + $265,000)/2 = $257,500
      Inventory turnover: $1,523,000/$257,500 = 5.9 times (liquidity and efficiency)
   f. Debt ratio: $665,000/$1,684,000 = 39.5% (solvency)
   g. Pledged assets to secured liabilities: ($625,000)/$400,000 = 1.56 : 1 (solvency)
   h. Times interest earned: $185,000/$44,000 = 4.2 times (solvency)
   i. Profit margin ratio: $94,000/$2,486,000 = 3.8% (profitability)
   j. Average total assets: ($1,684,000 + $1,678,000)/2 = $1,681,000
      Total asset turnover: $2,486,000/$1,681,000 = 1.48 times (liquidity and efficiency)
   k. Return on total assets: $94,000/$1,681,000 = 5.6% or 3.8% $\times$ 1.48 = 5.6% (profitability)
   l. Average total common equity: ($1,019,000 + $966,000)/2 = $992,500
      Return on common stockholders' equity: $94,000/$992,500 = 9.5% (profitability)

Summary

C1 Explain the purpose of analysis. The purpose of financial statement analysis is to help users make better business decisions. Internal users want information to improve company efficiency and effectiveness in providing products and services. External users want information to make better and more informed decisions in pursuing their goals. The common goals of all users are to evaluate a company's (1) past and current performance, (2) current financial position, and (3) future performance and risk.

C2 Identify the building blocks of analysis. Financial statement analysis focuses on four "building blocks" of analysis: (1) liquidity and efficiency—ability to meet short-term obligations and to efficiently generate revenues; (2) solvency—ability to generate future revenues and meet long-term obligations, (3) profitability—ability to provide financial rewards sufficient to attract and retain financing; and (4) market prospects—ability to generate positive market expectations.

C3 **Describe standards for comparisons in analysis.** Standards for comparisons include (1) intracompany—prior performance and relations between financial items for the company under analysis; (2) competitor—one or more direct competitors of the company; (3) industry—industry statistics; and (4) guidelines (rules of thumb)—general standards developed from past experiences and personal judgments.

C4 **Identify the tools of analysis.** The three most common tools of financial statement analysis are (1) horizontal analysis—comparing a company's financial condition and performance across time; (2) vertical analysis—comparing a company's financial condition and performance to a base amount such as revenues or total assets; and (3) ratio analysis—using and quantifying key relations among financial statement items.

A1 **Summarize and report results of analysis.** A financial statement analysis report is often organized around the building blocks of analysis. A good report separates interpretations and conclusions of analysis from the information underlying them. An analysis report often consists of six sections: (1) executive summary, (2) analysis overview, (3) evidential matter, (4) assumptions, (5) key factors, and (6) inferences.

P1 **Explain and apply methods of horizontal analysis.** Horizontal analysis is a tool to evaluate changes in data across time. Two important tools of horizontal analysis are comparative statements and trend analysis. Comparative statements show amounts for two or more successive periods, often with changes disclosed in both absolute and percent terms. Trend analysis is used to reveal important changes occurring from one period to the next.

P2 **Describe and apply methods of vertical analysis.** Vertical analysis is a tool to evaluate each financial statement item or group of items in terms of a base amount. Two tools of vertical analysis are common-size statements and graphical analyses. Each item in common-size statements is expressed as a percent of a base amount. For the balance sheet, the base amount is usually total assets, and for the income statement, it is usually sales.

P3 **Define and apply ratio analysis.** Ratio analysis provides clues and symptoms of underlying conditions. Ratios, properly interpreted, identify areas requiring further investigation. A ratio expresses a mathematical relation between two quantities such as a percent, rate, or proportion. Ratios can be organized into the building blocks of analysis: (1) liquidity and efficiency, (2) solvency, (3) profitability, and (4) market prospects.

Guidance Answers to **Decision Maker**

Auditor The *joint relation* referred to is the combined increase in sales and the decrease in expenses yielding more than a 5% increase in income. Both *individual* accounts (sales and expenses) yield percent changes within the ±5% acceptable range. However, a joint analysis suggests a different picture. For example, consider a joint analysis using the profit margin ratio. The client's profit margin is 11.46% ($206,000 − $182,400/$206,000) for the current year compared with 5.0% ($200,000 − $190,000/$200,000) for the prior year—yielding a 129% increase in profit margin! This is what concerns the partner, and it suggests expanding audit tests to verify or refute the client's figures.

Banker Your decision on the loan application is positive for at least two reasons. First, the current ratio suggests a strong ability to meet short-term obligations. Second, current assets of $160,000 and a current ratio of 4:1 imply current liabilities of $40,000 (one-fourth of current assets) and a working capital excess of $120,000. This working capital excess is 60% of the loan amount. However, if the application is for a 10-year loan, our decision is less optimistic. The current ratio and working capital suggest a good safety margin, but there are indications of inefficiency in operations. In particular, a 4:1 current ratio is more than double its key competitors' ratio. This is characteristic of inefficient asset use.

Guidance Answers to **Quick Checks**

1. General-purpose financial statements are intended for a variety of users interested in a company's financial condition and performance—users without the power to require it to prepare specialized financial reports to meet their specific needs.

2. General-purpose financial statements include the income statement, balance sheet, statement of changes in stockholders' (owner's) equity, and statement of cash flows, plus the notes related to these statements.

3. (*a*)

4. Data from one or more direct competitors are usually preferred for comparative purposes.

5. (*d*)

6. Percents on a comparative income statement show the increase or decrease in each item from one period to the next. On a common-size comparative income statement, each item is shown as a percent of net sales for that period.

7. (*c*)

8. (*a*); ($820,000 + $240,000 + $470,000)/ ($350,000 + $180,000) = 2.9 to 1.
   (*b*); ($820,000 + $240,000)/($350,000 + $180,000) = 2:1.

9. (*a*); $2,500,000/[($290,000 + $240,000)/2] = 9.43 times.
   (*b*); ($240,000/$2,500,000) × 365 = 35 days.
   (*c*); $750,000/[($530,000 + $470,000)/2] = 1.5 times.
   (*d*); ($470,000/$750,000) × 365 = 228.7 days.

10. (*c*)

11. (*b*)

12. Profit margin × $\dfrac{\text{Total asset}}{\text{turnover}}$ = $\dfrac{\text{Return on}}{\text{total assets}}$

$$\frac{\$945,000}{\$8,500,000} \times 1.8 = 20\%$$

Glossary

Common-size financial statement Statement that expresses each amount as a percent of a base amount. In the balance sheet, total assets is usually the base. In the income statement, net sales is usually the base. (p. 582)

Comparative financial statement Statement with data for two or more successive periods placed in side-by-side columns, often with changes shown in dollar amounts and percents. (p. 577)

Efficiency Company's productivity in using its assets; usually measured relative to how much revenue a certain level of assets generates. (p. 574)

Equity ratio Portion of total assets provided by equity, computed as total equity divided by total assets. (p. 591)

Financial reporting Process of communicating information relevant to investors, creditors, and others in making investment, credit, and business decisions. (p. 575)

Financial statement analysis Application of analytical tools to general-purpose financial statements and related data for making business decisions. (p. 574)

General-purpose financial statements Statements published periodically for use by a variety of interested parties; includes the income statement, balance sheet, statement of changes in equity (or statement of retained earnings), statement of cash flows, and notes to these statements. (p. 575)

Horizontal analysis Comparison of a company's financial condition and performance across time. (p. 576)

Liquidity Availability of resources to meet short-term cash requirements. (p. 574)

Market prospects Expectations (both good and bad) about a company's future performance as assessed by users and other interested parties. (p. 575)

Profitability Company's ability to generate an adequate return on invested capital. (p. 575)

Ratio analysis Determination of key relations between financial statement items. (p. 576)

Solvency Company's long-run financial viability and its ability to cover long-term obligations. (p. 574)

Vertical analysis Evaluation of each financial statement item or group of items in terms of a specific base amount. (p. 576)

Working capital Current assets minus current liabilities. (p. 587)

Questions

1. What is the difference between comparative financial statements and common-size comparative statements?

2. Which items are usually assigned a 100% value on (*a*) a common-size balance sheet and (*b*) a common-size income statement?

3. Explain the difference between financial reporting and financial statements.

4. What three factors would influence your evaluation as to whether a company's current ratio is good or bad?

5. Suggest several reasons that a 2:1 current ratio may not be adequate for a particular company.

6. Why is working capital given special attention in the process of analyzing balance sheets?

7. What does the number of days' sales uncollected indicate?

8. What does a relatively high accounts receivable turnover indicate about a company's short-term liquidity?

9. Why is a company's capital structure, as measured by debt and equity ratios, important to financial statement users?

10. How does inventory turnover provide information about a company's short-term liquidity?

11. What ratios would you compute to evaluate management performance?

12. Why must the ratio of pledged assets to secured liabilities be interpreted with caution?

13. Why would a company's return on total assets be different from its return on common stockholders' equity?

14. Using Nike's financial statements in Appendix A, compute its return on total assets for the years ended May 31, 2000 and 1999. Total assets at May 31, 1998, are $5,397.4 million. **NIKE**

15. Refer to Reebok's financial statements in Appendix A. Compute its equity ratio as of December 31, 1999 and 1998. **Reebok**

16. Refer to Gap's financial statements in Appendix A. Compute its profit margin for the fiscal year ended January 29, 2000. **GAP**

Which of the following items (1) through (9) are part of financial reporting but are not included as part of general-purpose financial statements? (1) stock price information and analysis, (2) statement of cash flows, (3) management discussion and analysis of financial performance, (4) income statement, (5) company news releases, (6) balance sheet, (7) financial statement notes, (8) statement of changes in equity, (9) prospectus.

QUICK STUDY

QS 13-1
Financial reporting C1

QS 13-2 📓

Standard of comparison **C3**

What are four possible standards of comparison used to analyze financial statement ratios? Which of these is generally considered to be the most useful? Which one is least likely to provide a good basis for comparison?

QS 13-3

Horizontal analysis

P1

Compute the dollar changes and the percent changes for each of the following financial accounts:

	2002	2001
Short-term investments	$220,000	$160,000
Accounts receivable	38,000	44,000
Notes payable	60,000	0

QS 13-4

Common-size and trend percents

P1 P2

Use the following information for Neef Corporation to determine (1) the 2001 and 2002 common-size percents for cost of goods sold using net sales as the base and (2) the 2001 and 2002 trend percents for net sales using 2001 as the base year.

	2002	2001
Net sales	$202,800	$116,200
Cost of goods sold	110,600	61,400

QS 13-5

Building blocks of analysis

C2 C4 P3

Match the ratio to the building block of financial statement analysis to which it best relates.

A. Liquidity and efficiency   **C.** Profitability

B. Solvency   **D.** Market prospects

1. _____ Gross margin ratio	**6.** _____ Book value per common share
2. _____ Acid-test ratio	**7.** _____ Days' sales in inventory
3. _____ Equity ratio	**8.** _____ Accounts receivable turnover
4. _____ Return on total assets	**9.** _____ Pledged assets to secured liabilities
5. _____ Dividend yield	**10.** _____ Times interest earned

QS 13-6 📓

Identifying financial ratios

C4 P3

1. Which two ratios are key components in measuring a company's operating efficiency? Which ratio summarizes these two components?

2. Which two short-term liquidity ratios measure how frequently a company collects its accounts?

3. What measure reflects the difference between current assets and current liabilities?

QS 13-7 📓

Ratio interpretation

P3

For each ratio listed, identify whether the change in ratio value from 2001 to 2002 is usually regarded as favorable or unfavorable.

Ratio	2002	2001	Ratio	2002	2001
1. Profit margin	9%	8%	5. Accounts receivable turnover	5.5	6.7
2. Debt ratio	47%	42%	6. Basic earnings per share	$1.25	$1.10
3. Gross margin	34%	46%	7. Inventory turnover	3.6	3.4
4. Acid-test ratio	1.00	1.15	8. Dividend yield	2%	1.2%

EXERCISES

Exercise 13-1 📓

Computation and analysis of trend percents

P1

Compute trend percents for the following financial items, using 2000 as the base year. State whether the situation as revealed by the trends appears to be favorable or unfavorable for each item.

	2004	2003	2002	2001	2000
Sales	$282,880	$270,800	$252,600	$234,560	$150,000
Cost of goods sold	128,200	122,080	115,280	106,440	67,000
Accounts receivable	18,100	17,300	16,400	15,200	9,000

Common-size and trend percents for TLC Company's sales, cost of goods sold, and expenses follow. Determine whether net income increased, decreased, or remained unchanged in this three-year period.

	Common-Size Percents			Trend Percents		
	2003	**2002**	**2001**	**2003**	**2002**	**2001**
Sales	100.0%	100.0%	100.0%	105.4%	104.2%	100.0%
Cost of goods sold	63.4	61.9	59.1	103.0	101.1	100.0
Expenses	15.3	14.8	15.1	95.0	91.0	100.0

Exercise 13-2 🅐

Determination of income effects from common-size and trend percents

P1 P2

Express the following comparative income statement in common-size percents and assess whether or not this company's situation has improved in the most recent year.

GERALDO CORPORATION		
Comparative Income Statement		
For Years Ended December 31, 2002 and 2001		
	2002	**2001**
Sales	$740,000	$625,000
Cost of goods sold	560,300	290,800
Gross profit	$179,700	$334,200
Operating expenses	128,200	218,500
Net income	$ 51,500	$115,700

Exercise 13-3 🅐

Common-size percent computation and interpretation

P2

The following information is available for Tuff Company and Tesa Company, similar firms operating in the same industry. Write a half-page report comparing Tuff and Tesa using the available information. Your discussion should include their ability to meet current obligations and to use current assets efficiently.

Exercise 13-4 🅐

Analysis of short-term financial condition

A1 P3

```
X Microsoft Excel - Book1                                                    _ 0 X
File Edit View Insert Format Tools Data Accounting Window Help               _ 8 X
D ☞ 🖫 🖨 🖺 ✖ ᵃᵇ⁄  ∽ ▾ ∽ ▾  🖴 🏶  Σ fₓ  A↓ Z↓  🛍 🏶 🌠  100% ▾  🔊   Arial        ▾ 10 ▾  B I U  $ % ,  ⁎.₀₈ ₊.₀₈
```

	A	B	C	D	E	F	G	H
1			**Tuff**				**Tesa**	
2		**2003**	**2002**	**2001**		**2003**	**2002**	**2001**
3	Current ratio	1.7	1.8	2.1		3.2	2.7	1.9
4	Acid-test ratio	1.0	1.1	1.2		2.8	2.5	1.6
5	Accounts receivable turnover	30.5	25.2	29.2		16.4	15.2	16.0
6	Merchandise inventory turnover	24.2	21.9	17.1		14.5	13.0	12.6
7	Working capital	$70,000	$58,000	$52,000		$131,000	$103,000	$78,000
8								

```
I◄ ◄ ► ►I  Sheet1  Sheet2  Sheet3 /                      I◄I                          ►I
```

Team Project: Assume that the two companies apply for a one-year loan from the team. Identify additional information the companies must provide before the team can make a loan decision.

Rison Company and Kearse Company are similar firms that operate in the same industry. Kearse began operations in 2002 and Rison in 1999. In 2004, both companies pay 7% interest on their debt to creditors. The following additional information is available:

Exercise 13-5 🅐

Analysis of efficiency and financial leverage

A1 P3

	Rison Company			Kearse Company		
	2004	**2003**	**2002**	**2004**	**2003**	**2002**
Total asset turnover	3.1	2.8	3.0	1.7	1.5	1.2
Return on total assets	9.0%	9.6%	8.8%	5.9%	5.6%	5.3%
Profit margin ratio	2.4%	2.5%	2.3%	2.8%	3.0%	2.9%
Sales	$410,000	$380,000	$396,000	$210,000	$170,000	$110,000

Write a half-page report comparing Rison and Kearse using the available information. Your analysis should include their ability to use assets efficiently to produce profits. Also comment on their success in employing financial leverage in 2004.

Exercise 13-6
Common-size percents

P2

Dixon Company's year-end balance sheets follow. Express the balance sheets in common-size percents. Round amounts to the nearest one-tenth of a percent. Analyze and comment on the results.

	2003	2002	2001
Cash	$ 31,800	$ 35,625	$ 37,800
Accounts receivable, net	89,500	62,500	50,200
Merchandise inventory	112,500	82,500	54,000
Prepaid expenses	10,700	9,375	5,000
Plant assets, net	278,500	255,000	230,500
Total assets	$523,000	$445,000	$377,500
Accounts payable	$129,900	$ 75,250	$ 51,250
Long-term notes payable secured by mortgages on plant assets	98,500	101,500	83,500
Common stock, $10 par value	163,500	163,500	163,500
Retained earnings	131,100	104,750	79,250
Total liabilities and equity	$523,000	$445,000	$377,500

Exercise 13-7
Liquidity analysis **P3**

Refer to Dixon Company's balance sheet accounts in Exercise 13-6. Analyze the year-end short-term liquidity position of this company at the end of 2003, 2002, and 2001 by computing (1) the current ratio and (2) the acid-test ratio. Comment on the ratio results.

Exercise 13-8
Liquidity analysis and interpretation

P3

Refer to the information in Exercise 13-6 about Dixon Company. The company's income statements for the years ended December 31, 2003 and 2002, follow. For the years ended December 31, 2003 and 2002, assume that all sales are on credit and then compute the following: (1) days' sales uncollected, (2) accounts receivable turnover, (3) inventory turnover, and (4) days' sales in inventory. Comment on the changes in the ratios from 2002 to 2003.

	2003		2002	
Sales		$673,500		$532,000
Cost of goods sold	$411,225		$345,500	
Other operating expenses	209,550		134,980	
Interest expense	12,100		13,300	
Income taxes	9,525		8,845	
Total costs and expenses		(642,400)		(502,625)
Net income		$ 31,100		$ 29,375
Earnings per share		$ 1.90		$ 1.80

Exercise 13-9
Risk and capital **P3** structure analysis

Refer to the information in Exercises 13-6 and 13-8 about Dixon Company. Compare the company's long-term risk and capital structure positions at the end of 2003 and 2002 by computing these ratios: (1) debt and equity ratios, (2) pledged assets to secured liabilities, and (3) times interest earned. Comment on these ratio results.

Exercise 13-10
Efficiency and **P3** profitability analysis

Refer to Dixon Company's financial information in Exercises 13-6 and 13-8. Evaluate the company's efficiency and profitability by computing the following: (1) profit margin ratio, (2) total asset turnover, and (3) return on total assets. Comment on these ratio results.

Refer to Dixon Company's financial information in Exercises 13-6 and 13-8. Additional information about the company follows. To help evaluate the company's profitability, compute the following ratios for 2003 and 2002: (1) return on common stockholders' equity, (2) price-earnings ratio on December 31, and (3) dividend yield.

Exercise 13-11
Profitability analysis

P3

Common stock market price, December 31, 2003 . . .	$30.00
Common stock market price, December 31, 2002 . . .	28.00
Annual cash dividends per share in 2003	0.29
Annual cash dividends per share in 2002	0.24

Selected comparative financial statements of Bartiromo Company follow:

PROBLEM SET A

Problem 13-1A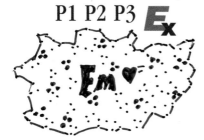
Ratios, common-size statements, and trend percents

P1 P2 P3

BARTIROMO COMPANY Comparative Income Statement For Years Ended December 31, 2003, 2002, and 2001			
	2003	**2002**	**2001**
Sales	$555,000	$340,000	$278,000
Cost of goods sold	283,500	212,500	153,900
Gross profit	$271,500	$127,500	$124,100
Selling expenses	102,900	46,920	50,800
Administrative expenses	50,668	29,920	22,800
Total expenses	$153,568	$ 76,840	$ 73,600
Income before taxes	$117,932	$ 50,660	$ 50,500
Income taxes	40,800	10,370	15,670
Net income	$ 77,132	$ 40,290	$ 34,830

BARTIROMO COMPANY Comparative Balance Sheet December 31, 2003, 2002, and 2001			
	2003	**2002**	**2001**
Assets			
Current assets	$ 52,390	$ 37,924	$ 51,748
Long-term investments	0	500	3,950
Plant assets, net	100,000	96,000	60,000
Total assets	$152,390	$134,424	$115,698
Liabilities and Equity			
Current liabilities	$ 22,800	$ 19,960	$ 20,300
Common stock	72,000	72,000	60,000
Other contributed capital	9,000	9,000	6,000
Retained earnings	48,590	33,464	29,398
Total liabilities and equity	$152,390	$134,424	$115,698

Required

1. Compute each year's current ratio.

2. Express the income statement data in common-size percents.

3. Express the balance sheet data in trend percents with 2001 as the base year.

Analysis Component

4. Comment on any significant relations revealed by the ratios and percents computed.

Check (3) 2003, Total assets trend, 131.71%

Problem 13-2A 🖉

Calculation and analysis of trend percents

A1 P1

Selected comparative financial statements of Lazar Company follow:

LAZAR COMPANY Comparative Income Statement ($000) For Years Ended December 31, 2007–2001							
	2007	2006	2005	2004	2003	2002	2001
Sales	$1,694	$1,496	$1,370	$1,264	$1,186	$1,110	$928
Cost of goods sold	1,246	1,032	902	802	752	710	586
Gross profit	$ 448	$ 464	$ 468	$ 462	$ 434	$ 400	$342
Operating expenses	330	256	234	170	146	144	118
Net income	$ 118	$ 208	$ 234	$ 292	$ 288	$ 256	$224

LAZAR COMPANY Comparative Balance Sheet ($000) December 31, 2007–2001							
	2007	2006	2005	2004	2003	2002	2001
Assets							
Cash	$ 58	$ 78	$ 82	$ 84	$ 88	$ 86	$ 89
Accounts receivable, net	490	514	466	360	318	302	216
Merchandise inventory	1,838	1,364	1,204	1,032	936	810	615
Other current assets	36	32	14	34	28	28	9
Long-term investments	0	0	0	146	146	146	146
Plant assets, net	2,020	2,014	1,752	944	978	860	725
Total assets	$4,442	$4,002	$3,518	$2,600	$2,494	$2,232	$1,800
Liabilities and Equity							
Current liabilities	$1,220	$1,042	$ 718	$ 614	$ 546	$ 522	$ 282
Long-term liabilities	1,294	1,140	1,112	570	580	620	400
Common stock	1,000	1,000	1,000	850	850	650	650
Other contributed capital	250	250	250	170	170	150	150
Retained earnings	678	570	438	396	348	290	318
Total liabilities and equity	$4,442	$4,002	$3,518	$2,600	$2,494	$2,232	$1,800

Required

1. Compute trend percents for all components of both statements using 2001 as the base year.

Check   (1) 2007, Total assets trend, 246.8%

Analysis Component

2. Analyze and comment on the financial statements and trend percents from part 1.

Problem 13-3A

Transactions, working capital, and liquidity ratios

P3

Check   May 2: Current ratio, 2.27; Acid-test, 0.93

Peak Corporation began the month of May with $700,000 of current assets, a current ratio of 2.50:1, and an acid-test ratio of 1.10:1. During the month, it completed the following transactions (the company uses a perpetual inventory system):

May 2   Purchased $50,000 of merchandise inventory on credit.
  8   Sold merchandise inventory that cost $55,000 for $110,000 cash.
  10   Collected $20,000 cash on an account receivable.
  15   Paid $22,000 cash to settle an account payable.

17 Wrote off a $5,000 bad debt against the Allowance for Doubtful Accounts account.
22 Declared a $1 per share cash dividend on the 50,000 shares of outstanding common stock.
26 Paid the dividend declared on May 22.
27 Borrowed $100,000 cash by giving the bank a 30-day, 10% note.
28 Borrowed $80,000 cash by signing a long-term secured note.
29 Used the $180,000 cash proceeds from the notes to buy new machinery.

Check May 29: Current ratio, 1.80; Working capital, $325,000

Required

Prepare a table showing Peak's (1) current ratio, (2) acid-test ratio, and (3) working capital after each transaction. Round ratios to hundredths.

Selected year-end financial statements of McCune Corporation follow. (Note that all sales are on credit; and selected balance sheet amounts at December 31, 2001, were inventory, $48,900; total assets, $189,400; common stock, $90,000; and retained earnings, $22,748.)

Problem 13-4A
Calculation of financial statement ratios

P3 Ex

McCUNE CORPORATION Income Statement For Year Ended December 31, 2002	
Sales	$ 448,600
Cost of goods sold	297,250
Gross profit	$151,350
Operating expenses	98,600
Interest expense	4,100
Income before taxes	$ 48,650
Income taxes	19,598
Net income	$ 29,052

McCUNE CORPORATION
Balance Sheet
December 31, 2002

Assets		Liabilities and Equity	
Cash	$ 10,000	Accounts payable	$ 17,500
Short-term investments	8,400	Accrued wages payable	3,200
Accounts receivable, net	29,200	Income taxes payable	3,300
Notes receivable (trade)*	4,500	Long-term note payable, secured	
Merchandise inventory	32,150	by mortgage on plant assets	63,400
Prepaid expenses	2,650	Common stock, $1 par value	90,000
Plant assets, net	153,300	Retained earnings	62,800
Total assets	$240,200	Total liabilities and equity	$240,200

* These are short-term notes receivable arising from customer (trade) sales.

Required

Compute the following: (1) current ratio, (2) acid-test ratio, (3) days' sales uncollected, (4) inventory turnover, (5) days' sales in inventory, (6) ratio of pledged assets to secured liabilities, (7) times interest earned, (8) profit margin ratio, (9) total asset turnover, (10) return on total assets, and (11) return on common stockholders' equity.

Check Acid-test ratio, 2.2 to 1; Inventory turnover, 7.3

Problem 13-5A ⓐ
Comparative ratio **A1 P3**
analysis
Ⓖ

Summary information from the financial statements of two companies competing in the same industry follows:

	Rowland Company	Pierce Company		Rowland Company	Pierce Company
Data from the current year-end balance sheets:			**Data from the current year's income statement:**		
Assets			Sales	$770,000	$880,200
Cash	$ 19,500	$ 34,000	Cost of goods sold	585,100	632,500
Accounts receivable, net	37,400	57,400	Interest expense	7,900	13,000
Current notes receivable (trade)	9,100	7,200	Income tax expense	14,800	24,300
Merchandise inventory	84,440	132,500	Net income	162,200	210,400
Prepaid expenses	5,000	6,950	Basic earnings per share	4.51	5.11
Plant assets, net	290,000	304,400			
Total assets	$445,440	$542,450			
			Beginning-of-year balance sheet data:		
Liabilities and Equity			Accounts receivable, net	$ 29,800	$ 54,200
Current liabilities	$ 61,340	$ 93,300	Current notes receivable (trade)	0	0
Long-term notes payable	80,800	101,000	Merchandise inventory	55,600	107,400
Common stock, $5 par value	180,000	206,000	Total assets	398,000	382,500
Retained earnings	123,300	142,150	Common stock, $5 par value	180,000	206,000
Total liabilities and equity	$445,440	$542,450	Retained earnings	98,300	93,600

Required

Check (1) Pierce: Accounts
receivable turnover, 14.8; inventory
turnover, 5.3

1. For both companies compute the following: (*a*) current ratio, (*b*) acid-test ratio, (*c*) accounts (including notes) receivable turnover, (*d*) inventory turnover, (*e*) days' sales in inventory, and (*f*)
days' sales uncollected. Identify the company you consider to be the better short-term credit risk
and explain why.

Check (2) Rowland: Profit margin,
21.1%; PE, 16.6

2. For both companies compute the following: (*a*) profit margin ratio, (*b*) total asset turnover, (*c*) return on total assets, and (*d*) return on common stockholders' equity. Assuming that each company
paid cash dividends of $3.80 per share and each company's stock can be purchased at $75 per
share, compute their (*e*) price-earnings ratios and (*f*) dividend yields. Identify which company's
stock you would recommend as the better investment and explain why.

PROBLEM SET B

Problem 13-1B ⓐ
Ratios, common-size
statements, and trend percents

P1 P2 P3

Selected comparative financial statements of Terradyne Corporation follow:

TERRADYNE CORPORATION Comparative Income Statement For Years Ended December 31, 2003, 2002, and 2001			
	2003	**2002**	**2001**
Sales	$198,800	$166,000	$143,800
Cost of goods sold	108,890	86,175	66,200
Gross profit	$ 89,910	$ 79,825	$ 77,600
Selling expenses	22,680	19,790	18,000
Administrative expenses	16,760	14,610	15,700
Total expenses	$ 39,440	$ 34,400	$ 33,700
Income before taxes	$ 50,470	$ 45,425	$ 43,900
Income taxes	6,050	5,910	5,300
Net income	$ 44,420	$ 39,515	$ 38,600

TERRADYNE CORPORATION
Comparative Balance Sheet
December 31, 2003, 2002, and 2001

	2003	2002	2001
Assets			
Current assets	$ 54,860	$ 32,660	$ 36,300
Long-term investments	0	1,700	10,600
Plant assets, net	112,810	113,660	79,000
Total assets	$167,670	$148,020	$125,900
Liabilities and Equity			
Current liabilities	$ 22,370	$ 19,180	$ 16,500
Common stock	46,500	46,500	37,000
Other contributed capital	13,850	13,850	11,300
Retained earnings	84,950	68,490	61,100
Total liabilities and equity	$167,670	$148,020	$125,900

Required

1. Compute each year's current ratio.

2. Express the income statement data in common-size percents.

3. Express the balance sheet data in trend percents with 2001 as the base year.

Analysis Component

4. Comment on any significant relations revealed by the ratios and percents computed.

Check (3) 2003, Total assets trend, 133.18%

Selected comparative financial statements of Chow Company follow:

Problem 13-2B 𝑎
Calculation and analysis of trend percents

A1 **P1**

CHOW COMPANY
Comparative Income Statement ($000)
For Years Ended December 31, 2007–2001

	2007	2006	2005	2004	2003	2002	2001
Sales	$560	$610	$630	$680	$740	$770	$860
Cost of goods sold	276	290	294	314	340	350	380
Gross profit	$284	$320	$336	$366	$400	$420	$480
Operating expenses	84	104	112	126	140	144	150
Net income	$200	$216	$224	$240	$260	$276	$330

CHOW COMPANY
Comparative Balance Sheet ($000)
December 31, 2007–2001

	2007	2006	2005	2004	2003	2002	2001
Assets							
Cash	$ 44	$ 46	$ 52	$ 54	$ 60	$ 62	$ 68
Accounts receivable, net	130	136	140	144	150	154	160
Merchandise inventory	166	172	178	180	186	190	208
Other current assets	34	34	36	38	38	40	40
Long-term investments	36	30	26	110	110	110	110
Plant assets, net	510	514	520	412	420	428	454
Total assets	$920	$932	$952	$938	$964	$984	$1,040

[continued on next page]

[continued from previous page]

CHOW COMPANY Comparative Balance Sheet ($000) December 31, 2007–2001							
	2007	2006	2005	2004	2003	2002	2001
Liabilities and Equity							
Current liabilities	$148	$156	$186	$190	$210	$260	$ 280
Long-term liabilities	92	120	142	148	194	214	260
Common stock	160	160	160	160	160	160	160
Other contributed capital	70	70	70	70	70	70	70
Retained earnings	450	426	394	370	330	280	270
Total liabilities and equity	$920	$932	$952	$938	$964	$984	$1,040

Required

1. Compute trend percents for all components of both statements using 2001 as the base year.

Check (1) 2007, Total assets trend, 88.5%

Analysis Component

2. Analyze and comment on the financial statements and trend percents from part 1.

Problem 13-3B
Transactions, working capital, and liquidity ratios

P3

Check June 1: Current ratio, 2.88; Acid-test, 2.40

Check June 30: Working capital, $(10,000); Current ratio, 0.97

Ready Corporation began the month of June with $300,000 of current assets, a current ratio of 2.50:1, and an acid-test ratio of 1.40:1. During the month, it completed the following transactions (the company uses a perpetual inventory system):

June 1	Sold merchandise inventory that cost $75,000 for $120,000 cash.
3	Collected $88,000 cash on an account receivable.
5	Purchased $150,000 of merchandise inventory on credit.
7	Borrowed $100,000 cash by giving the bank a 60-day, 10% note.
10	Borrowed $120,000 cash by signing a long-term secured note.
12	Purchased machinery for $275,000 cash.
15	Declared a $1 per share cash dividend on the 80,000 shares of outstanding common stock.
19	Wrote off a $5,000 bad debt against the Allowance for Doubtful Accounts account.
22	Paid $12,000 cash to settle an account payable.
30	Paid the dividend declared on June 15.

Required

Prepare a table showing the company's (1) current ratio, (2) acid-test ratio, and (3) working capital after each transaction. Round ratios to hundredths.

Problem 13-4B
Calculation of financial statement ratios

P3

Selected year-end financial statements of Upland Corporation follow. (Note that all sales are on credit; and selected balance sheet amounts at December 31, 2001, were inventory, $17,400; total assets, $94,900; common stock, $35,500; and retained earnings, $18,800.)

UPLAND CORPORATION Income Statement For Year Ended December 31, 2002	
Sales	$315,500
Cost of goods sold	236,100
Gross profit	$ 79,400
Operating expenses	49,200
Interest expense	2,200
Income before taxes	$ 28,000
Income taxes	4,200
Net income	$ 23,800

UPLAND CORPORATION Balance Sheet December 31, 2002			
Assets		**Liabilities and Equity**	
Cash	$ 6,100	Accounts payable	$ 11,500
Short-term investments	6,900	Accrued wages payable	3,300
Accounts receivable, net	12,100	Income taxes payable	2,600
Notes receivable (trade)*	3,000	Long-term note payable, secured	
Merchandise inventory	13,500	by mortgage on plant assets	30,000
Prepaid expenses	2,000	Common stock, $5 par value	35,000
Plant assets, net	73,900	Retained earnings	35,100
Total assets	$117,500	Total liabilities and equity	$117,500

* These are short-term notes receivable arising from customer (trade) sales.

Required

Compute the following: (1) current ratio, (2) acid-test ratio, (3) days' sales uncollected, (4) inventory turnover, (5) days' sales in inventory, (6) ratio of pledged assets to secured liabilities, (7) times interest earned, (8) profit margin ratio, (9) total asset turnover, (10) return on total assets, and (11) return on common stockholders' equity.

Check Acid-test ratio, 1.6 to 1; Inventory turnover, 15.3

Summary information from the financial statements of two companies competing in the same industry follows:

Problem 13-5B
Comparative ratio analysis **A1 P3**

	Lincoln Company	Mertz Company			Lincoln Company	Mertz Company
Data from the current year-end balance sheet:				**Data from the current year's income statement:**		
Assets				Sales	$393,600	$667,500
Cash	$ 20,000	$ 36,500		Cost of goods sold	290,600	480,000
Accounts receivable, net	77,100	70,500		Interest expense	5,900	10,400
Current notes receivable (trade)	11,600	9,000		Income tax expense	5,700	12,300
Merchandise inventory	86,800	82,000		Net income	33,850	61,700
Prepaid expenses	9,700	10,100		Basic earnings per share	1.27	2.19
Plant assets, net	176,900	252,300				
Total assets	$382,100	$460,400				
Data from the current year-end balance sheet:				**Beginning-of-year balance sheet data:**		
Liabilities and Equity				Accounts receivable, net	$ 72,200	$ 73,300
Current liabilities	$ 90,500	$ 97,000		Current notes receivable (trade)	0	0
Long-term notes payable	93,000	93,300		Merchandise inventory	105,100	80,500
Common stock, $5 par value	133,000	141,000		Total assets	383,400	443,000
Retained earnings	65,600	129,100		Common stock, $5 par value	133,000	141,000
Total liabilities and equity	$382,100	$460,400		Retained earnings	49,100	109,700

Required

1. For both companies compute the following: (a) current ratio, (b) acid-test ratio, (c) accounts (including notes) receivable turnover, (d) inventory turnover, (e) days' sales in inventory, and (f) days' sales uncollected. Identify the company you consider to be the better short-term credit risk and explain why.

Check (1) Lincoln: Accounts receivable turnover, 4.9; inventory turnover, 3.0

2. For both companies compute the (a) profit margin ratio, (b) total asset turnover, (c) return on total assets, and (d) return on common stockholders' equity. Assuming that each company paid cash dividends of $1.50 per share and each company's stock can be purchased at $25 per share, compute their (e) price-earnings ratios and (f) dividend yields. Identify which company's stock you would recommend as the better investment and explain why.

Check (2) Mertz: Profit margin, 9.2%; PE, 11.4

BEYOND THE NUMBERS

Reporting in Action
A1 P1 P2 📖
NIKE

BTN 13-1   Refer to Nike's financial statements in Appendix A to answer the following:

1. Using 1998 as the base year, compute trend percents for 1998, 1999, and 2000 for revenues, cost of sales, selling and administrative expenses, income taxes, and net income. (Round to the nearest whole percent.)

2. Compute common-size percents for 2000 and 1999 for the following categories of assets: (*a*) total current assets, (*b*) property, plant and equipment—net, (*c*) identifiable intangible assets and goodwill, and (*d*) deferred income taxes and other assets. (Round to the nearest tenth percent.)

3. Comment on any significant changes across the years for the income statement trends computed in part 1 and the balance sheet percents computed in part 2.

Swoosh Ahead

4. Access Nike's financial statements for fiscal years ending after May 31, 2000, from Nike's Web site (www.nike.com) or the SEC database (www.sec.gov). Update your work for parts 1, 2, and 3 using the new information accessed.

Comparative Analysis
C3 P2 📖
NIKE Reebok

BTN 13-2   Key comparative figures ($ millions) for both Nike and Reebok follow:

Key Figures	Nike	Reebok	Key Figures	Nike	Reebok
Cash and equivalents ...	$ 254.3	$ 281.7	Income taxes	$ 340.1	$ 10.1
Accounts receivable	1,567.2	417.4	Revenues (Nike)	8,995.1	—
Inventories	1,446.0	414.6	Net sales (Reebok) ...	—	2,899.9
Retained earnings	2,887.0	1,170.9	Total assets	5,856.9	1,564.1
Costs of sales	5,403.8	1,783.9			

Required

1. Compute common-size percents for both companies using the data provided.
2. Which company incurs a higher percent of its revenues (net sales) in income taxes?
3. Which company retains a higher portion of cumulative net income in the company?
4. Which company has a higher gross margin ratio on sales?
5. Which company holds a higher percent of its total assets as inventory?

Ethics Challenge
A1 📖

BTN 13-3   As controller of Boxer Company, you are responsible for keeping the board of directors informed about its financial activities. At the board meeting, you present the following:

	2003	2002	2001
Sales trend percent	147.0%	135.0%	100.0%
Selling expenses to net sales	10.1%	14.0%	15.6%
Sales to plant assets ratio	3.8 to 1	3.6 to 1	3.3 to 1
Current ratio	2.9 to 1	2.7 to 1	2.4 to 1
Acid-test ratio	1.1 to 1	1.4 to 1	1.5 to 1
Inventory turnover	7.8 times	9.0 times	10.2 times
Accounts receivable turnover	7.0 times	7.7 times	8.5 times
Total asset turnover	2.9 times	2.9 times	3.3 times
Return on total assets	9.1%	9.7%	10.4%
Return on stockholders' equity	9.75%	11.50%	12.25%
Profit margin ratio	3.6%	3.8%	4.0%

After the meeting, the company's CEO holds a press conference with analysts in which she mentions the following ratios:

	2003	**2002**	**2001**
Sales trend percent	147.0%	135.0%	100.0%
Selling expenses to net sales	10.1%	14.0%	15.6%
Sales to plant assets ratio	3.8 to 1	3.6 to 1	3.3 to 1
Current ratio	2.9 to 1	2.7 to 1	2.4 to 1

Required

1. Why do you think the CEO decided to report 4 ratios instead of the 11 prepared?

2. Comment on the possible consequences of the CEO's reporting decision.

BTN 13-4 Each team is to select a different industry, and each team member is to select a different company in that industry and acquire its financial statements. Use those statements to analyze the company, using at least one ratio from each of the four building blocks of analysis. When necessary, use the financial press to determine the market price of its stock. Communicate with teammates via a meeting, e-mail, or telephone to discuss how different companies compare to each other and to industry norms. The team is to prepare a single one-page memorandum reporting on its analysis and the conclusions reached.

Communicating in Practice

C2 A1 P3 🖉

BTN 13-5 Access the March 30, 2000, filing of the 10-K report of Yahoo! Inc. (ticker YHOO) at www.edgaronline.com. The profitability of Yahoo! and other Internet companies is becoming an increasingly important issue in the stock market.

Taking It to the Net

C4 P3 🖉

Required

Compute or locate the following profitability ratios for Yahoo! for its fiscal years ending December 31, 1999 *and* 1998. Interpret its profitability using these ratio results.

1. Profit margin ratio

2. Gross profit ratio

3. Return on total assets (Note: 1997 total assets were $143,512,000.)

4. Return on common stockholders' equity (Note: 1997 total shareholders' equity was $118,358,000.)

5. Basic earnings per share

BTN 13-6 A team approach to learning financial statement analysis is often useful.

Teamwork in Action

C2 P1 P2 P3 🖉

Required

1. Each team should write a description of horizontal and vertical analysis that all team members agree with and understand. Illustrate each description with an example.

2. *Each* member of the team is to select *one* of the following categories of ratio analysis. Explain what the ratios in that category measure. Choose one ratio from the category selected, present its formula, and explain what it measures.

a. Liquidity and efficiency **c.** Profitability

b. Solvency **d.** Market prospects

3. Each team member is to present his or her notes from part 2 to teammates. Team members are to confirm or correct other teammates' presentation.

Hint: Pairing within teams may be necessary for part 2. Use as an in-class activity or as an assignment. Consider presentations to the entire class using team rotation with transparencies.

BTN 13-7 Read the article "Research Firm Off the Record Is on the Mark" in the December 6, 1999, issue of *Business Week*. (The book's Web site provides a free link.)

Business Week Activity

C1 C4

Required

1. What is the name of the research firm highlighted in the article?

2. How does it conduct research?

3. How does its research interface with traditional financial statement analysis?

4. What incentive does it offer its survey respondents?

5. As an individual, you cannot access the firm's research. What can you learn, however, from the firm's methods?

Entrepreneurial Decision

A1 P1 P2 P3

ℓ d

BTN 13-8   Jose Sanchez owns and operates Western Gear, a small merchandiser in outdoor recreational equipment. You have been hired to review the three most recent years of operations for Western Gear. Your financial statement analysis reveals the following results:

	2002	2001	2000
Sales trend percents	137.0%	125.0%	100.0%
Selling expenses to net sales	9.8%	13.7%	15.3%
Sales to plant assets ratio	3.5 to 1	3.3 to 1	3.0 to 1
Current ratio	2.6 to 1	2.4 to 1	2.1 to 1
Acid-test ratio	0.8 to 1	1.1 to 1	1.2 to 1
Merchandise inventory turnover	7.5 times	8.7 times	9.9 times
Accounts receivable turnover	6.7 times	7.4 times	8.2 times
Total asset turnover	2.6 times	2.6 times	3.0 times
Return on total assets	8.8%	9.4%	10.1%
Return on equity	9.75%	11.50%	12.25%
Profit margin ratio	3.3%	3.5%	3.7%

Required

Use these data to answer each of the following questions with explanations:

1. Is it becoming easier for the company to meet its current liabilities on time and to take advantage of any available cash discounts?
2. Is the company collecting its accounts receivable more rapidly?
3. Is the company's investment in accounts receivable decreasing?
4. Is the company's investment in plant assets increasing?
5. Is the owner's investment becoming more profitable?
6. Did the dollar amount of selling expenses decrease during the three-year period?

Hitting the Road

C1 P3 d

BTN 13-9   You are to devise a savings/investment strategy whereby you are able to accumulate $1,000,000 by age 65. Start by making some assumptions about your salary. Next compute the percent of your salary that you will be able to save each year. If you will receive any lump-sum monies, you can include those amounts in your calculations. Historically, stocks have delivered average annual returns of 10–11%. Given this history, you should probably not assume that you will earn above 10% on the money you invest. It is not necessary to specify exactly what types of assets you will buy for your investments; just make an assumption about a rate you expect to earn. Use the future value tables in Appendix B to calculate how your savings will grow. Experiment a bit with your figures to see how much less you have to save if you start at, for example, age 25 versus age 35 or 40. (For this assignment, do not include inflation in your calculations.)

Financial Statement Information

This appendix includes financial information for (1) Nike, (2) Reebok, and (3) Gap. This information is taken from their annual reports. An **annual report** is a summary of a company's financial results for the year, along with its current financial condition and future plans. This report is directed to external users of financial information, but it also affects the actions and decisions of internal users.

A company uses an annual report to showcase itself and its products. Many annual reports include attractive photos, diagrams, and illustrations related to the company. The primary objective of annual reports, however, is the *financial section*, which communicates much information about a company, with most data drawn from the accounting information system. The layout of an annual report's financial section is fairly established and typically includes the following:

- Letter to Shareholders
- Financial History and Highlights
- Management Discussion and Analysis
- Management's Report
- Report of Independent Accountants (Auditor's Report)
- Financial Statements
- Notes to Financial Statements
- List of Directors and Officers

This appendix provides the financial statements for Nike (plus selected notes), Reebok, and Gap. The appendix is organized as follows:

- Nike   **A-2** through **A-10**
- Reebok   **A-11** through **A-14**
- Gap   **A-15** through **A-18**

Many assignments at the end of each chapter refer to information in this appendix. We encourage readers to spend time with these assignments; they are especially useful in showing the relevance and diversity of financial accounting and reporting.

Special note: The SEC maintains the EDGAR (**E**lectronic **D**ata **G**athering, **A**nalysis, and **R**etrieval) database at **www.sec.gov**. The **Form 10-K** is the annual report form for most companies. It provides electronically accessible information. The **Form 10-KSB** is the annual report form filed by "small businesses." It requires slightly less information than the Form 10-K. One of these forms must be filed within 90 days after the company's fiscal year-end. (Forms 10-K405, 10-KT, 10-KT405, and 10-KSB405 are slight variations of these usual forms due to certain regulations or rules.)

NIKE

Financial History

(in millions, except per share data, financial ratios and number of shareholders)

YEAR ENDED MAY 31,	2000	1999	1998	1997	1996	1995
Revenues	$8,995.1	$8,776.9	$9,553.1	$9,186.5	$6,470.6	$4,760.8
Gross margin	3,591.3	3,283.4	3,487.6	3,683.5	2,563.9	1,895.6
Gross margin %	39.9%	37.4%	36.5%	40.1%	39.6%	39.8%
Restructuring charge	(2.5)	45.1	129.9	—	—	—
Net income	579.1	451.4	399.6	795.8	553.2	399.7
Basic earnings per common share	2.10	1.59	1.38	2.76	1.93	1.38
Diluted earnings per common share	2.07	1.57	1.35	2.68	1.88	1.36
Average common shares outstanding	275.7	283.3	288.7	288.4	286.6	289.6
Diluted average common shares outstanding	279.4	288.3	295.0	297.0	293.6	294.0
Cash dividends declared						
per common share	0.48	0.48	0.46	0.38	0.29	0.24
Cash flow from operations	759.9	961.0	517.5	323.1	339.7	254.9
Price range of common stock						
High	64.125	65.500	64.125	76.375	52.063	20.156
Low	26.563	31.750	37.750	47.875	19.531	14.063

MAY 31,						
Cash and equivalents	$ 254.3	$ 198.1	$ 108.6	$ 445.4	$ 262.1	$ 216.1
Inventories	1,446.0	1,170.6	1,396.6	1,338.6	931.2	629.7
Working capital	1,456.4	1,818.0	1,828.8	1,964.0	1,259.9	938.4
Total assets	5,856.9	5,247.7	5,397.4	5,361.2	3,951.6	3,142.7
Long-term debt	470.3	386.1	379.4	296.0	9.6	10.6
Redeemable Preferred Stock	0.3	0.3	0.3	0.3	0.3	0.3
Shareholders' equity	3,136.0	3,334.6	3,261.6	3,155.9	2,431.4	1,964.7
Year-end stock price	42.875	60.938	46.000	57.500	50.188	19.719
Market capitalization	11,559.1	17,202.2	13,201.1	16,633.0	14,416.8	5,635.2

FINANCIAL RATIOS						
Return on equity	17.9%	13.7%	12.5%	28.5%	25.2%	21.6%
Return on assets	10.4%	8.5%	7.4%	17.1%	15.6%	14.5%
Inventory turns	4.1	4.3	4.4	4.8	5.0	5.2
Current ratio at May 31	1.7	2.3	2.1	2.1	1.9	1.8
Price/Earnings ratio at May 31 (diluted)	20.7	38.8	34.1	21.5	26.6	14.5

GEOGRAPHIC REVENUES						
United States	$5,017.4	$5,042.6	$5,460.0	$5,538.2	$3,964.7	$2,997.9
Europe	2,350.9	2,255.8	2,096.1	1,789.8	1,334.3	980.4
Asia Pacific	955.1	844.5	1,253.9	1,241.9	735.1	515.6
Americas (exclusive of United States)	671.7	634.0	743.1	616.6	436.5	266.9
Total Revenues	$8,995.1	$8,776.9	$9,553.1	$9,186.5	$6,470.6	$4,760.8

All per common share data has been adjusted to reflect the 2-for-1 stock splits paid October 23, 1996, October 30, 1995 and October 5, 1990. The Company's Class B Common Stock is listed on the New York and Pacific Exchanges and trades under the symbol NKE. At May 31, 2000, there were approximately 153,000 shareholders of Class A and Class B common stock.

Nike, Inc. Consolidated Statement of Income

(in millions, except per share data)

YEAR ENDED MAY 31,	2000	1999	1998
Revenues	$8,995.1	$8,776.9	$9,553.1
Costs and expenses:			
Cost of sales	5,403.8	5,493.5	6,065.5
Selling and administrative	2,606.4	2,426.6	2,623.8
Interest expense (Notes 4 and 5)	45.0	44.1	60.0
Other income/expense, net (Notes 1, 10 and 11)	23.2	21.5	20.9
Restructuring charge, net (Note 13)	(2.5)	45.1	129.9
Total costs and expenses	8,075.9	8,030.8	8,900.1
Income before income taxes	919.2	746.1	653.0
Income taxes (Note 6)	340.1	294.7	253.4
Net income	$ 579.1	$ 451.4	$ 399.6
Basic earnings per common share (Notes 1 and 9)	$ 2.10	$ 1.59	$ 1.38
Diluted earnings per common share (Notes 1 and 9)	$ 2.07	$ 1.57	$ 1.35

NIKE

Nike, Inc. Consolidated Balance Sheet

(in millions)

MAY 31,	2000	1999
ASSETS		
Current Assets:		
Cash and equivalents	$ 254.3	$ 198.1
Accounts receivable, less allowance for doubtful accounts of $65.4 and $73.2	1,567.2	1,540.1
Inventories (Note 2)	1,446.0	1,170.6
Deferred income taxes (Notes 1 and 6)	111.5	120.6
Income taxes receivable	2.2	15.9
Prepaid expenses (Note 1)	215.2	219.6
Total current assets	3,596.4	3,264.9
Property, plant and equipment, net (Note 3)	1,583.4	1,265.8
Identifiable intangible assets and goodwill (Note 1)	410.9	426.6
Deferred income taxes and other assets (Notes 1 and 6)	266.2	290.4
Total assets	$5,856.9	$5,247.7
LIABILITIES AND SHAREHOLDERS' EQUITY		
Current Liabilities:		
Current portion of long-term debt (Note 5)	$ 50.1	$ 1.0
Notes payable (Note 4)	924.2	419.1
Accounts payable (Note 4)	543.8	473.6
Accrued liabilities	621.9	553.2
Total current liabilities	2,140.0	1,446.9
Long-term debt (Notes 5 and 14)	470.3	386.1
Deferred income taxes and other liabilities (Notes 1 and 6)	110.3	79.8
Commitments and contingencies (Notes 12 and 15)	—	—
Redeemable Preferred Stock (Note 7)	0.3	0.3
Shareholders' Equity :		
Common stock at stated value (Note 8):		
Class A convertible – 99.2 and 100.7 shares outstanding	0.2	0.2
Class B – 170.4 and 181.6 shares outstanding	2.6	2.7
Capital in excess of stated value	369.0	334.1
Unearned stock compensation	(11.7)	—
Accumulated other comprehensive income	(111.1)	(68.9)
Retained earnings	2,887.0	3,066.5
Total shareholders' equity	3,136.0	3,334.6
Total liabilities and shareholders' equity	$5,856.9	$5,247.7

Nike, Inc. Consolidated Statement of Cash Flows
(in millions)

YEAR ENDED MAY 31,	2000	1999	1998
Cash provided (used) by operations:			
Net income	$579.1	$451.4	$399.6
Income charges (credits) not affecting cash:			
Depreciation	188.0	198.2	184.5
Non-cash portion of restructuring charge	—	28.0	59.3
Deferred income taxes	36.8	37.9	(113.9)
Amortization and other	35.6	30.6	49.0
Changes in certain working capital components:			
(Increase) decrease in inventories	(275.4)	226.0	(58.0)
(Increase) decrease in accounts receivable	(27.1)	134.3	79.7
Decrease (increase) in other current assets and income taxes receivable	65.6	25.0	(12.6)
Increase (decrease) in accounts payable, accrued liabilities and income taxes payable	157.3	(170.4)	(70.1)
Cash provided by operations	759.9	961.0	517.5
Cash provided (used) by investing activities:			
Additions to property, plant and equipment	(419.9)	(384.1)	(505.9)
Disposals of property, plant and equipment	25.3	27.2	16.8
Increase in other assets	(51.3)	(60.8)	(87.4)
Increase (decrease) in other liabilities	5.9	1.2	(18.5)
Cash used by investing activities	(440.0)	(416.5)	(595.0)
Cash provided (used) by financing activities:			
Additions to long-term debt	0.1	—	101.5
Reductions in long-term debt including current portion	(1.8)	(1.5)	(2.5)
Increase (decrease) in notes payable	505.1	(61.0)	(73.0)
Proceeds from exercise of options	23.9	54.4	32.2
Repurchase of stock	(646.3)	(299.8)	(202.3)
Dividends – common and preferred	(133.1)	(136.2)	(127.3)
Cash used by financing activities	(252.1)	(444.1)	(271.4)
Effect of exchange rate changes on cash	(11.6)	(10.9)	12.1
Net increase (decrease) in cash and equivalents	56.2	89.5	(336.8)
Cash and equivalents, beginning of year	198.1	108.6	445.4
Cash and equivalents, end of year	$254.3	$198.1	$108.6
Supplemental disclosure of cash flow information:			
Cash paid during the year for:			
Interest	$ 45.0	$ 47.1	$ 52.2
Income taxes	221.1	231.9	360.5
Non-cash investing and financing activity:			
Assumption of long-term debt to acquire property, plant, and equipment	$108.9	—	—

NIKE

Nike, Inc. Consolidated Statement of Shareholders' Equity

(in millions)

	Common Stock Class A Shares	Class A Amount	Class B Shares	Class B Amount	Capital in Excess of Stated Value	Unearned Stock Compensation	Accumulated Other Comprehensive Income	Retained Earnings	Total
BALANCE AT MAY 31, 1997	101.7	$0.2	187.6	$2.7	$210.6	$ —	$ (31.3)	$2,973.7	$3,155.9
Stock options exercised			2.1		57.2				57.2
Conversion to Class B Common Stock	(0.2)		0.2						
Repurchase of Class B Common Stock			(4.4)		(5.3)			(197.0)	(202.3)
Dividends on common stock								(132.9)	(132.9)
Comprehensive income:									
Net income								399.6	399.6
Foreign currency translation (net of tax benefit of $3.7)							(15.9)		(15.9)
Comprehensive income							(15.9)	399.6	383.7
BALANCE AT MAY 31, 1998	101.5	0.2	185.5	2.7	262.5	—	(47.2)	3,043.4	3,261.6
Stock options exercised			2.7		80.5				80.5
Conversion to Class B Common Stock	(0.8)		0.8						
Repurchase of Class B Common Stock			(7.4)		(8.9)			(292.7)	(301.6)
Dividends on common stock								(135.6)	(135.6)
Comprehensive income:									
Net income								451.4	451.4
Foreign currency translation (net of tax benefit of $12.5)							(21.7)		(21.7)
Comprehensive income							(21.7)	451.4	429.7
BALANCE AT MAY 31, 1999	100.7	0.2	181.6	2.7	334.1	—	(68.9)	3,066.5	3,334.6
Stock options exercised			1.3		38.7				38.7
Conversion to Class B Common Stock	(1.5)		1.5						
Repurchase of Class B Common Stock			(14.5)	(0.1)	(17.3)			(627.1)	(644.5)
Dividends on common stock								(131.5)	(131.5)
Issuance of shares to employees			0.5		13.5	(13.5)			—
Amortization of unearned compensation						1.8			1.8
Comprehensive income:									
Net income								579.1	579.1
Foreign currency translation (net of tax benefit of $9.3)							(42.2)		(42.2)
Comprehensive income							(42.2)	579.1	536.9
BALANCE AT MAY 31, 2000	99.2	$0.2	170.4	$2.6	$369.0	$ (11.7)	$(111.1)	$2,887.0	$3,136.0

Nike, Inc. Notes to Consolidated Financial Statements

NOTE 1—SUMMARY OF SIGNIFICANT ACCOUNTING POLICIES:

Basis of consolidation: The consolidated financial statements include the accounts of NIKE, Inc. and its subsidiaries (the Company). All significant intercompany transactions and balances have been eliminated.

Recognition of revenues: Revenues recognized include sales and fees earned on sales by licensees. Revenues are recognized when title passes based on the terms of the sale, which are generally upon shipment.

Advertising and promotion: Advertising production costs are expensed the first time the advertisement is run. Media (TV and print) placement costs are expensed in the month the advertising appears. Accounting for endorsement contracts, the majority of the Company's promotional expenses, is based upon specific contract provisions. Generally, endorsement payments are expensed uniformly over the term of the contract after giving recognition to periodic performance compliance provisions of the contracts. Contracts requiring prepayments are included in prepaid expenses or other assets depending on the length of the contract. Total advertising and promotion expenses were $978.2 million, $978.6 million and $1,129.1 million for the years ended May 31, 2000, 1999 and 1998, respectively. Included in prepaid expenses and other assets was $158.7 million and $180.9 million at May 31, 2000 and 1999, respectively, relating to prepaid advertising and promotion expenses.

Cash and equivalents: Cash and equivalents represent cash and short-term, highly liquid investments with original maturities of three months or less.

Inventory valuation: Inventories are stated at the lower of cost or market. Inventories are valued on a first-in, first-out (FIFO) basis. In the fourth quarter of fiscal year 1999, the Company changed its method of determining cost for substantially all of its U.S. inventories from last-in, first-out (LIFO) to FIFO. See Note 11.

Property, plant and equipment and depreciation: Property, plant and equipment are recorded at cost. Depreciation for financial reporting purposes is determined on a straight-line basis for buildings and leasehold improvements over 2 to 30 years and principally on a declining balance basis for machinery and equipment over 2 to 8 years. Computer software is depreciated on a straight-line basis over 3 to 7 years.

Identifiable intangible assets and goodwill: At May 31, 2000 and 1999, the Company had patents, trademarks and other identifiable intangible assets with a value of $215.2 million and $213.0 million, respectively. The Company's excess of purchase cost over the fair value of net assets of businesses acquired (goodwill) was $323.5 million and $324.8 million at May 31, 2000 and 1999, respectively.

Identifiable intangible assets and goodwill are being amortized over their estimated useful lives on a straight-line basis over five to forty years. Accumulated amortization was $127.8 million and $111.2 million at May 31, 2000 and 1999, respectively. Amortization expense, which is included in other income/expense, was $18.5 million, $19.4 million and $19.8 million for the years ended May 31, 2000, 1999 and 1998, respectively. Intangible assets are periodically reviewed by the Company for impairments to assess if the fair value is less than the carrying value.

Foreign currency translation: Adjustments resulting from translating foreign functional currency financial statements into U.S. dollars are included in the currency translation adjustment, a component of accumulated other comprehensive income in shareholders' equity.

Derivatives: The Company enters into foreign currency contracts in order to reduce the impact of certain foreign currency fluctuations. Firmly committed transactions and the related receivables and payables may be hedged with forward exchange contracts or purchased options. Anticipated, but not yet firmly committed, transactions may be hedged through the use of purchased options. Premiums paid on purchased options and any realized gains are included in prepaid expenses or accrued liabilities and are recognized in earnings when the transaction being hedged is recognized. Gains and losses arising from foreign currency forward and option contracts, and cross-currency swap transactions are recognized in income or expense as offsets of gains and losses resulting from the underlying hedged transactions. Hedge effectiveness is determined by evaluating whether gains and losses on hedges will offset gains and losses on the underlying exposures. This evaluation is performed at inception of the hedge and periodically over the life of the hedge. Occasionally, hedges may cease to be effective and are thus terminated prior to recognition of the underlying transaction. Gains and losses on these hedges are deferred until the point in time ineffectiveness is determined and will be included in the basis of the underlying transaction. Hedges will also be terminated if the underlying transaction is no longer expected to occur. When this occurs all related deferral gains and losses are recognized in earnings immediately. Cash flows from risk management activities are classified in the same category as the cash flows from the related investment, borrowing or foreign exchange activity. See Note 15 for further discussion.

Income taxes: Income taxes are provided currently on financial statement earnings of non-U.S. subsidiaries expected to be repatriated. The Company intends to determine annually the amount of undistributed non-U.S. earnings to invest indefinitely in its non-U.S. operations. The Company accounts for income taxes using the asset and liability method. This approach requires the recognition of deferred tax assets and liabilities for the expected future tax consequences of temporary differences between the carrying amounts and the tax bases of other assets and liabilities. See Note 6 for further discussion.

Earnings per share: Basic earnings per common share is calculated by dividing net income by the average number of common shares outstanding during the year. Diluted earnings per common share is calculated by adjusting outstanding shares, assuming conversion of all potentially dilutive stock options and awards. See Note 9 for further discussion.

Management estimates: The preparation of financial statements in conformity with generally accepted accounting principles requires management to make estimates, including estimates relating to assumptions that affect the reported amounts of assets and liabilities and disclosure of contingent assets and liabilities at the date of financial statements and the reported amounts of revenues and expenses during the reporting period. Actual results could differ from these estimates.

Reclassifications: Certain prior year amounts have been reclassified to conform to fiscal year 2000 presentation. These changes had no impact on previously reported results of operations or shareholders' equity.

NOTE 2 – INVENTORIES:

Inventories by major classification are as follows:

(in millions)

MAY 31,	2000	1999
Finished goods	$1,416.6	$1,127.6
Work-in-progress	17.3	21.2
Raw materials	12.1	21.8
	$1,446.0	$1,170.6

As stated in Note 1, the Company changed its inventory valuation method for substantially all U.S. inventories in fiscal year 1999.

NOTE 3 – PROPERTY, PLANT AND EQUIPMENT:

Property, plant and equipment includes the following:

(in millions)

MAY 31,	2000	1999
Land	$ 180.6	$ 99.6
Buildings	503.4	374.2
Machinery and equipment	981.9	923.3
Leasehold improvements	279.6	273.4
Construction in process	448.3	330.8
	2,393.8	2,001.3
Less accumulated depreciation	810.4	735.5
	$1,583.4	$1,265.8

Capitalized interest expense incurred was $4.8 million, $6.9 million and $6.5 million for the fiscal years ended May 31, 2000, 1999 and 1998, respectively.

NOTE 7 – REDEEMABLE PREFERRED STOCK:

NIAC is the sole owner of the Company's authorized Redeemable Preferred Stock, $1 par value, which is redeemable at the option of NIAC at par value aggregating $0.3 million. A cumulative dividend of $0.10 per share is payable annually on May 31 and no dividends may be declared or paid on the common stock of the Company unless dividends on the Redeemable Preferred Stock have been declared and paid in full. There have been no changes in the Redeemable Preferred Stock in the three years ended May 31, 2000. As the holder of the Redeemable Preferred Stock, NIAC does not have general voting rights but does have the right to vote as a separate class on the sale of all or substantially all of the assets of the Company and its subsidiaries, on merger, consolidation, liquidation or dissolution of the Company or on the sale or assignment of the NIKE trademark for athletic footwear sold in the United States.

NOTE 9 – EARNINGS PER SHARE:

The following represents a reconciliation from basic earnings per share to diluted earnings per share. Options to purchase 9.7 million and 3.3 million shares of common stock were outstanding at May 31, 2000 and May 31, 1998, respectively, but were not included in the computation of diluted earnings per share because the options' exercise prices were greater than the average market price of the common shares and, therefore, the effect would be antidilutive. No such antidilutive options were outstanding at May 31, 1999.

(in millions, except per share data)

YEAR ENDED MAY 31,	2000	1999	1998
Determination of shares:			
Average common shares outstanding	275.7	283.3	288.7
Assumed conversion of dilutive stock options and awards	3.7	5.0	6.3
Diluted average common shares outstanding	279.4	288.3	295.0
Basic earnings per common share	$ 2.10	$ 1.59	$ 1.38
Diluted earnings per common share	$ 2.07	$ 1.57	$ 1.35

NOTE 10 – BENEFIT PLANS:

The Company has a profit sharing plan available to substantially all employees. The terms of the plan call for annual contributions by the Company as determined by the Board of Directors. Contributions of $15.7 million, $12.8 million and $11.2 million to the plan are included in other expense in the consolidated financial statements for the years ended May 31, 2000, 1999 and 1998, respectively. The Company has a voluntary 401(k) employee savings plan. The Company matches a portion of employee contributions with common stock, vesting that portion over 5 years. Company contributions to the savings plan were $6.7 million, $7.4 million and $8.1 million for the years ended May 31, 2000, 1999 and 1998, respectively, and are included in selling and administrative expenses.

NOTE 11 – OTHER INCOME/EXPENSE, NET:

Included in other income/expense for the years ended May 31, 2000, 1999, and 1998, was interest income of $13.6 million, $13.0 million and $16.5 million, respectively. In addition, included in other income/expense in fiscal 1999 was income of $15.0 million related to the change in accounting for inventories in the U.S. from the LIFO to the FIFO method. The change was effected in the fourth quarter of fiscal 1999 and was not considered significant to show the cumulative effect or to restate comparable income statements as dictated by Accounting Principles Board Opinion No. 20.

NIKE

NOTE 12 – COMMITMENTS AND CONTINGENCIES:

The Company leases space for its offices, warehouses and retail stores under leases expiring from one to seventeen years after May 31, 2000. Rent expense aggregated $145.5 million, $129.5 million and $129.6 million for the years ended May 31, 2000, 1999 and 1998, respectively. Amounts of minimum future annual rental commitments under non-cancelable operating leases in each of the five fiscal years 2001 through 2005 are $121.1 million, $107.3 million, $89.0 million, $69.9 million, $59.3 million, respectively, and $299.5 million in later years.

At May 31, 2000, the Company had letters of credit outstanding totaling $678.2 million. These letters of credit were issued for the purchase of inventory.

Lawsuits arise during the normal course of business. In the opinion of management, none of the pending lawsuits will result in a significant impact on the consolidated results of operations or financial position.

NOTE 16 – OPERATING SEGMENTS AND RELATED INFORMATION:

Revenues by Major Product Lines: Revenues to external customers for NIKE Brand products are attributable to sales of Footwear, Apparel, and Equipment & Other NIKE Brand. Revenues to external customers for Other Brands include external sales by the non-NIKE brand subsidiaries.

(in millions)

YEAR ENDED MAY 31,	2000	1999	1998
Footwear	$5,561.5	$5,218.4	$5,959.0
Apparel	2,698.6	2,822.9	2,885.7
Equipment	328.2	316.8	277.4
Other brands	406.8	418.8	431.0
	$8,995.1	$8,776.9	$9,553.1

Report of Independent Accountants

Portland, Oregon
June 29, 2000
To the Board of Directors and
Shareholders of NIKE, Inc.

In our opinion, the accompanying consolidated balance sheet and the related consolidated statements of income, of cash flows and of shareholders' equity present fairly, in all material respects, the financial position of NIKE, Inc. and its subsidiaries at May 31, 2000 and 1999, and the results of their operations and their cash flows for each of the three years in the period ended May 31, 2000 in conformity with accounting principles generally accepted in the United States. These financial statements are the responsibility of the Company's management; our responsibility is to express an opinion on these financial statements based on our audits. We conducted our audits of these statements in accordance with auditing standards generally accepted in the United States, which require that we plan and perform the audit to obtain reasonable assurance about whether the financial statements are free of material misstatement. An audit includes examining, on a test basis, evidence supporting the amounts and disclosures in the financial statements, assessing the accounting principles used and significant estimates made by management, and evaluating the overall financial statement presentation. We believe that our audits provide a reasonable basis for the opinion expressed above.

PricewaterhouseCoopers LLP

REEBOK INTERNATIONAL LTD.

CONSOLIDATED STATEMENTS OF INCOME

	Year Ended December 31		
	1999	1998	1997
	(Amounts in thousands, except per share data)		
Net sales	$2,899,872	$3,224,592	$3,643,599
Other income (expense)	(8,635)	(19,167)	(6,158)
	2,891,237	3,205,425	3,637,441
Costs and expenses:			
Cost of sales	1,783,914	2,037,465	2,294,049
Selling, general and administrative expenses	971,945	1,043,199	1,069,433
Special charges	61,625	35,000	58,161
Amortization of intangibles	5,183	3,432	4,157
Interest expense	49,691	60,671	64,366
Interest income	(9,159)	(11,372)	(10,810)
	2,863,199	3,168,395	3,479,356
Income before income taxes and minority interest	28,038	37,030	158,085
Income taxes	10,093	11,925	12,490
Income before minority interest	17,945	25,105	145,595
Minority interest	6,900	1,178	10,476
Net income	$ 11,045	$ 23,927	$ 135,119
Basic earnings per share	$ .20	$ .42	$ 2.41
Diluted earnings per share	$ .20	$ .42	$ 2.32

Reebok

REEBOK INTERNATIONAL LTD.

CONSOLIDATED BALANCE SHEETS

	December 31	
	1999	**1998**
	(Amounts in thousands, except share data)	

Assets

Current assets:

Cash and cash equivalents	$ 281,744	$ 180,070
Accounts receivable, net of allowance for doubtful accounts (1999, $46,217; 1998, $47,383)	417,404	517,830
Inventory	414,616	535,168
Deferred income taxes	88,127	79,484
Prepaid expenses and other current assets	41,227	50,309
Total current assets	1,243,118	1,362,861
Property and equipment, net	178,111	172,585

Other non-current assets:

Intangibles, net of amortization	68,892	68,648
Deferred income taxes	43,868	43,147
Other	30,139	37,383
	142,899	149,178
Total Assets	$1,564,128	$1,684,624

Liabilities and Stockholders' Equity

Current liabilities:

Notes payable to banks	$ 27,614	$ 48,070
Current portion of long-term debt	185,167	86,640
Accounts payable	153,998	203,144
Accrued expenses	248,822	177,133
Income taxes payable	8,302	27,597
Total current liabilities	623,903	542,584
Long-term debt, net of current portion	370,302	554,432
Minority interest and other long-term liabilities	41,107	46,672
Commitments and contingencies		
Outstanding redemption value of equity put options		16,559

Stockholders' equity:

Common stock, par value $.01; authorized 250,000,000 shares; issued shares 92,985,737 in 1999; 93,306,642 shares in 1998	930	933
Retained earnings	1,170,885	1,156,739
Less 36,716,227 shares in treasury at cost	(617,620)	(617,620)
Unearned compensation		(26)
Accumulated other comprehensive income (expense)	(25,379)	(15,649)
	528,816	524,377
Total Liabilities and Stockholders' Equity	$1,564,128	$1,684,624

REEBOK INTERNATIONAL LTD.
CONSOLIDATED STATEMENTS OF STOCKHOLDERS' EQUITY

	Shares	Total	Common Stock (Par Value $.01)	Retained Earnings	Treasury Stock	Unearned Compensation	Accumulated Other Comprehensive Income (Expense)
			(Dollar amounts in thousands)				
Balance, December 31, 1996	92,556,295	$381,234	$926	$ 992,563	$(617,620)	$(283)	$ 5,648
Comprehensive income:							
Net income		135,119		135,119			
Adjustment for foreign currency translation		(26,933)					(26,933)
Comprehensive income		108,186					
Issuance of shares to certain employees	9,532			431		(431)	
Amortization of unearned compensation		566				566	
Shares repurchased and retired	(313)	8				8	
Shares issued under employee stock purchase plans	151,210	4,363	1	4,362			
Shares issued upon exercise of stock options	399,111	10,044	4	10,040			
Income tax reductions relating to exercise of stock options		2,756		2,756			
Balance, December 31, 1997	93,115,835	507,157	931	1,145,271	(617,620)	(140)	(21,285)
Comprehensive income:							
Net income		23,927		23,927			
Adjustment for foreign currency translation		5,636					5,636
Comprehensive income		29,563					
Issuance of shares to certain employees	14,704			458		(458)	
Amortization of unearned compensation		387				387	
Shares repurchased and retired	(114,920)	(3,181)	(1)	(3,365)		185	
Shares issued under employee stock purchase plans	223,583	3,821	2	3,819			
Shares issued upon exercise of stock options	67,440	1,187	1	1,186			
Put option contracts outstanding		(16,559)		(16,559)			
Premium received from unexercised equity put options		2,002		2,002			
Balance, December 31, 1998	93,306,642	524,377	933	1,156,739	(617,620)	(26)	(15,649)
Comprehensive income:							
Net income		11,045		11,045			
Adjustment for foreign currency translation		(9,730)					(9,730)
Comprehensive income		1,315					
Issuance of shares to certain employees	4,449			116		(116)	
Amortization of unearned compensation		142				142	
Shares repurchased pursuant to equity put options	(625,000)	0	(6)	6			
Shares issued under employee stock purchase plans	292,432	2,885	3	2,882			
Shares issued upon exercise of stock options	7,214	97		97			
Balance, December 31, 1999	92,985,737	$528,816	$930	$1,170,885	$(617,620)	$ (0)	$(25,379)

Reebok

REEBOK INTERNATIONAL LTD.

CONSOLIDATED STATEMENTS OF CASH FLOWS

	Year Ended December 31		
	1999	1998	1997
	(Amounts in thousands)		
Cash flows from operating activities:			
Net income	$ 11,045	$ 23,927	$ 135,119
Adjustments to reconcile net income to net cash provided by operating activities:			
Depreciation and amortization	48,643	48,017	47,423
Minority interest	6,900	1,178	10,476
Deferred income taxes	(9,364)	(28,074)	(17,285)
Special charges	61,625	35,000	58,161
Changes in operating assets and liabilities:			
Accounts receivable	85,698	63,951	(13,915)
Inventory	109,381	39,134	(47,937)
Prepaid expenses and other	5,986	8,626	(4,155)
Accounts payable and accrued expenses	(18,338)	(65,616)	18,295
Income taxes payable	(19,951)	25,634	(59,257)
Total adjustments	270,580	127,850	(8,194)
Net cash provided by operating activities:	281,625	151,777	126,925
Cash flows from investing activity:			
Payments to acquire property and equipment	(51,197)	(53,616)	(23,910)
Net cash used for investing activity	(51,197)	(53,616)	(23,910)
Cash flows from financing activities:			
Net borrowings (repayments) of notes payable to banks	(22,269)	2,048	27,296
Repayments of long-term debt	(85,020)	(121,016)	(156,966)
Proceeds from issuance of common stock to employees	2,982	5,008	17,163
Proceeds from premium on equity put options		2,002	
Dividends to minority shareholders	(17,966)	(6,649)	(3,900)
Repurchases of common stock	(16,559)	(3,366)	
Net cash used for financing activities	(138,832)	(121,973)	(116,407)
Effect of exchange rate changes on cash	10,078	(5,884)	(9,207)
Net increase (decrease) in cash and cash equivalents	101,674	(29,696)	(22,599)
Cash and cash equivalents at beginning of year	180,070	209,766	232,365
Cash and cash equivalents at end of year	$ 281,744	$ 180,070	$ 209,766
Supplemental disclosures of cash flow information:			
Interest paid	$ 43,620	$ 58,224	$ 59,683
Income taxes paid	35,147	26,068	115,985

GAP, Inc.

CONSOLIDATED STATEMENTS OF EARNINGS

($000 except per share amounts)	52 Weeks Ended Jan. 29, 2000	Percentage to Sales	52 Weeks Ended Jan. 30, 1999	Percentage to Sales	52 Weeks Ended Jan. 31, 1998	Percentage to Sales
Net sales	$11,635,398	100.0%	$ 9,054,462	100.0%	$ 6,507,825	100.0%
Costs and expenses						
Cost of goods sold and occupancy expenses	6,775,262	58.2	5,318,218	58.7	4,021,541	61.8
Operating expenses	3,043,432	26.2	2,403,365	26.5	1,635,017	25.1
Net interest expense (income)	31,755	0.3	13,617	0.2	(2,975)	0.0
Earnings before income taxes	1,784,949	15.3	1,319,262	14.6	854,242	13.1
Income taxes	657,884	5.6	494,723	5.5	320,341	4.9
Net earnings	$ 1,127,065	9.7%	$ 824,539	9.1%	$ 533,901	8.2%
Weighted-average number of shares–basic	853,804,924		864,062,060		891,404,945	
Weighted-average number of shares–diluted	895,029,176		904,374,383		922,951,706	
Earnings per share–basic	$ 1.32		$ 0.95		$ 0.60	
Earnings per share–diluted	1.26		0.91		0.58	

See Notes to Consolidated Financial Statements.

GAP

GAP, Inc.

CONSOLIDATED BALANCE SHEETS

($000 except par value)	Jan. 29, 2000	Jan. 30, 1999
Assets		
Current Assets		
Cash and equivalents	$ 450,352	$ 565,253
Merchandise inventory	1,462,045	1,056,444
Other current assets	285,393	250,127
Total current assets	2,197,790	1,871,824
Property and Equipment		
Leasehold improvements	1,426,537	1,040,959
Furniture and equipment	2,083,604	1,601,572
Land and buildings	278,422	160,776
Construction-in-progress	414,725	245,020
	4,203,288	3,048,327
Accumulated depreciation and amortization	(1,487,973)	(1,171,957)
Property and equipment, net	2,715,315	1,876,370
Lease rights and other assets	275,651	215,725
Total assets	$5,188,756	$3,963,919
Liabilities and Shareholders' Equity		
Current Liabilities		
Notes payable	$ 168,961	$ 90,690
Accounts payable	805,945	684,130
Accrued expenses and other current liabilities	751,710	655,770
Income taxes payable	26,263	122,513
Total current liabilities	1,752,879	1,553,103
Long-Term Liabilities		
Long-term debt	784,925	496,455
Deferred lease credits and other liabilities	417,907	340,682
Total long-term liabilities	1,202,832	837,137
Shareholders' Equity		
Common stock $.05 par value		
Authorized 2,300,000,000 shares; issued 1,007,356,790 and 997,496,214 shares; outstanding 850,498,941 and 857,960,032 shares	50,368	49,875
Additional paid-in capital	669,490	349,037
Retained earnings	4,172,796	3,121,360
Accumulated other comprehensive loss	(6,759)	(12,518)
Deferred compensation	(23,150)	(31,675)
Treasury stock, at cost	(2,629,700)	(1,902,400)
Total shareholders' equity	2,233,045	1,573,679
Total liabilities and shareholders' equity	$5,188,756	$3,963,919

See Notes to Consolidated Financial Statements.

GAP, Inc.

CONSOLIDATED STATEMENTS OF CASH FLOWS

($000)	52 Weeks Ended Jan. 29, 2000	52 Weeks Ended Jan. 30, 1999	52 Weeks Ended Jan. 31, 1998
Cash Flows from Operating Activities			
Net earnings	$1,127,065	$ 824,539	$ 533,901
Adjustments to reconcile net earnings to net cash provided by operating activities:			
Depreciation and amortization	436,184	326,447	269,706
Tax benefit from exercise of stock options and vesting of restricted stock	211,891	79,808	23,682
Deferred income taxes	2,444	(34,766)	(13,706)
Change in operating assets and liabilities:			
Merchandise inventory	(404,211)	(322,287)	(156,091)
Prepaid expenses and other	(55,519)	(77,292)	(44,736)
Accounts payable	118,121	265,296	63,532
Accrued expenses	89,071	231,178	107,365
Income taxes payable	(94,893)	38,805	(8,214)
Deferred lease credits and other long-term liabilities	47,775	62,433	69,212
Net cash provided by operating activities	1,477,928	1,394,161	844,651
Cash Flows from Investing Activities			
Net purchase of property and equipment	(1,238,722)	(797,592)	(465,843)
Acquisition of lease rights and other assets	(39,839)	(28,815)	(19,779)
Net maturity of short-term investments	—	—	174,709
Net purchase of long-term investments	—	—	(2,939)
Net cash used for investing activities	(1,278,561)	(826,407)	(313,852)
Cash Flows from Financing Activities			
Net increase in notes payable	84,778	1,357	44,462
Net issuance of long-term debt	311,839	—	495,890
Issuance of common stock	76,211	36,655	23,309
Net purchase of treasury stock	(707,125)	(879,383)	(585,798)
Cash dividends paid	(75,795)	(76,888)	(79,503)
Net cash used for financing activities	(310,092)	(918,259)	(101,640)
Effect of exchange rate fluctuations on cash	(4,176)	2,589	(1,634)
Net (decrease) increase in cash and equivalents	(114,901)	(347,916)	427,525
Cash and equivalents at beginning of year	565,253	913,169	485,644
Cash and equivalents at end of year	$ 450,352	$ 565,253	$ 913,169

See Notes to Consolidated Financial Statements.

GAP, Inc.

CONSOLIDATED STATEMENTS OF SHAREHOLDERS' EQUITY

($000 except share and per share amounts)	Common Stock Shares	Common Stock Amount	Additional Paid-in Capital	Retained Earnings	Accumulated Other Comprehensive Loss	Deferred Compensation	Treasury Stock Shares	Treasury Stock Amount	Total	Comprehensive Earnings
Balance at January 31, 1998	989,826,394	$ 49,491	$ 205,393	$2,392,750	$ (15,230)	$ (38,167)	(105,277,081)	$(1,010,251)	$1,583,986	$ 523,858
Issuance of common stock pursuant to stock option plans	7,575,195	380	46,709			(10,351)			36,738	
Net issuance of common stock pursuant to management incentive restricted stock plans	94,625	4	4,361			(3,873)			492	
Tax benefit from exercise of stock options by employees and from vesting of restricted stock			79,808						79,808	
Adjustments for foreign currency translation ($1,893) and fluctuations in fair market value of financial instruments ($819)					2,712				2,712	2,712
Amortization of restricted stock and discounted stock options						20,716			20,716	
Purchase of treasury stock							(35,714,475)	(910,387)	(910,387)	
Reissuance of treasury stock			12,766				1,455,374	18,238	31,004	
Net earnings				824,539					824,539	824,539
Cash dividends ($.11 per share)				(95,929)					(95,929)	
Balance at January 30, 1999	997,496,214	$ 49,875	$ 349,037	$3,121,360	$ (12,518)	$ (31,675)	(139,536,182)	$(1,902,400)	$1,573,679	$ 827,251
Issuance of common stock pursuant to stock option plans	9,933,713	497	81,456			(9,186)			72,767	
Net cancellations of common stock pursuant to management incentive restricted stock plans	(73,137)	(4)	2,583			(3,411)			(832)	
Tax benefit from exercise of stock options by employees and from vesting of restricted stock			211,891						211,891	
Adjustments for foreign currency translation ($3,305) and fluctuations in fair market value of financial instruments ($2,454)					5,759				5,759	5,759
Amortization of restricted stock and discounted stock options			72			21,122			21,194	
Purchase of treasury stock			4,276				(18,500,000)	(745,056)	(740,780)	
Reissuance of treasury stock			20,175				1,178,333	17,756	37,931	
Net earnings				1,127,065					1,127,065	1,127,065
Cash dividends ($.09 per share)				(75,629)					(75,629)	
Balance at January 29, 2000	1,007,356,790	$ 50,368	$ 669,490	$4,172,796	$ (6,759)	$ (23,150)	(156,857,849)	$(2,629,700)	$2,233,045	$1,132,824

See Notes to Consolidated Financial Statements.

B

Present and Future Values in Accounting

Learning Objectives

Conceptual

C1 Describe the earning of interest and the concepts of present and future values.

Procedural

P1 Apply present value concepts to a single amount by using interest tables.

P2 Apply future value concepts to a single amount by using interest tables.

P3 Apply present value concepts to an annuity by using interest tables.

P4 Apply future value concepts to an annuity by using interest tables.

Appendix Preview

The concepts of present and future values are important to modern business activity. The purpose of this appendix is to explain, illustrate, and compute present and future values. We apply these concepts with reference to both business and everyday activities.

Present and Future Value Concepts

C1 Describe the earning of interest and the concepts of present and future values.

The old saying "Time is money" reflects the notion that as time passes, the value of our assets and liabilities changes. This change is due to *interest,* which is the payment to the owner of an asset for its use by a borrower. The most common example of interest is a savings account asset. As we keep a balance of cash in the account, it earns interest that the financial institution pays us. An example of a liability is a car loan. As we carry the balance of the loan, we accumulate interest costs on it. We must ultimately repay this loan with interest.

Present and future value computations enable us to measure or estimate the interest component of holding assets or liabilities over time. The present value computation is important when we want to know the value of future-day assets *today.* The future value computation is important when we want to know the value of present-day assets *at a future date.* The first section focuses on the present value of a single amount. The second section focuses on the future value of a single amount. Then both the present and future values of a series of amounts (called an *annuity*) are defined and explained.

Present Value of a Single Amount

Exhibit B.1

Present Value of a Single Amount Diagram

We graphically express the present value, called *p,* of a single future amount, called *f,* that is received or paid at a future date in Exhibit B.1.

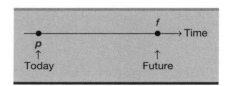

The formula to compute the present value of a single amount is shown in Exhibit B.2, where *p* = present value; *f* = future value; *i* = rate of interest per period; and *n* = number of periods. (Interest is also called the *discount,* and an interest rate is also called the *discount rate.*)

Exhibit B.2

Present Value of a Single Amount Formula

$$p = \frac{f}{(1 + i)^n}$$

To illustrate present value concepts, assume that we need $220 one period from today. We want to know how much we must invest now, for one period, at an interest rate of 10% to provide for this $220. For this illustration, the *p,* or present value, is the unknown amount—the specifics are shown graphically as follows:

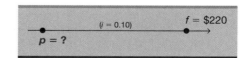

Conceptually, we know *p* must be less than $220. This is obvious from the answer to this question: Would we rather have $220 today or $220 at some future date? If we had $220 today, we could invest it and see it grow to something more than $220 in the future. Therefore, we would prefer the $220 today. This means that if we were promised $220 in the future, we would take less than $220 today. But how much less? To answer that question, we compute an estimate of the present value of the $220 to be received one period from now using the formula in Exhibit B.2 as follows:

$$p = \frac{f}{(1 + i)^n} = \frac{\$220}{(1 + 0.10)^1} = \$200$$

We interpret this result to say that given an interest rate of 10%, we are indifferent between $200 today or $220 at the end of one period.

We can also use this formula to compute the present value for *any number of periods.* To illustrate, consider a payment of $242 at the end of two periods at 10% interest. The present value of this $242 to be received two periods from now is computed as follows:

$$p = \frac{f}{(1 + i)^n} = \frac{\$242}{(1 + 0.10)^2} = \$200$$

Together, these results tell us we are indifferent between $200 today, or $220 one period from today, or $242 two periods from today given a 10% interest rate per period.

The number of periods (n) in the present value formula does not have to be expressed in years. Any period of time such as a day, a month, a quarter, or a year can be used. Whatever period is used, the interest rate (i) must be compounded for the same period. This means that if a situation expresses n in months and i equals 12% per year, then i is transformed into interest earned per month (or 1%). In this case, interest is said to be *compounded monthly.*

I will pay your allowance at the end of the month. Do you want to wait or receive its present value today?

A present value table helps us with present value computations. It gives us present values (factors) for a variety of both interest rates (i) and periods (n). Each present value in a present value table assumes that the future value (f) equals 1. When the future value (f) is different from 1, we simply multiply the present value (p) from the table by that future value to give us the estimate. The formula used to construct a table of present values for a single future amount of 1 is shown in Exhibit B.3.

P1 Apply present value concepts to a single amount by using interest tables.

$$p = \frac{1}{(1 + i)^n}$$

Exhibit B.3

Present Value of 1 Formula

This formula is identical to that in Exhibit B.2 except that f equals 1. Table B.1 at the end of this appendix is such a present value table. It is often called a **present value of 1 table.** A present value table involves three factors: p, i, and n. Knowing two of these three factors allows us to compute the third. (A fourth is f, but as already explained, we need only multiply the 1 used in the formula by f.) To illustrate the use of a present value table, consider three cases.

Case 1 (solve for p when knowing i and n). To show how we use a present value table, let's again look at how we estimate the present value of $220 (the f value) at the end of one period ($n = 1$) where the interest rate (i) is 10%. To solve this case, we go to the present value table (Table B.1) and look in the row for 1 period and in the column for 10% interest. Here we find a present value (p) of 0.9091 based on a future value of 1. This means, for instance, that $1 to be received one period from today at 10% interest is worth $0.9091 today. Since the future value in this case is not $1 but $220, we multiply the 0.9091 by $220 to get an answer of $200.

Case 2 (solve for n when knowing p and i). To illustrate, assume a $100,000 future value ($f$) that is worth $13,000 today ($p$) using an interest rate of 12% (i) but where n is unknown. In particular, we want to know how many periods (n) there are between the present value and the future value. To put this in context, it would fit a situation in which we want to re-tire with $100,000 but currently have only $13,000 that is earning a 12% return. How long will it be before we can retire? To answer this, we go to Table B.1 and look in the 12% in-terest column. Here we find a column of present values (p) based on a future value of 1. To use the present value table for this solution, we must divide $13,000 ($p$) by $100,000 ($f$), which equals 0.1300. This is necessary because *a present value table defines f equal to 1, and p as a fraction of 1.* We look for a value nearest to 0.1300 (p), which we find in the row for 18 periods (n). This means that the present value of $100,000 at the end of 18 periods at 12% interest is $13,000 or, alternatively stated, we must work 18 more years.

Case 3 (solve for i when knowing p and n). In this case, we have, say, a $120,000 fu-ture value ($f$) that is worth $60,000 today ($p$) when there are nine periods (n) between the present and future values but the interest rate is unknown. As an example, suppose we want to retire with $120,000, but we have only $60,000 and hope to retire in nine years. What interest rate must we earn to retire with $120,000 in nine years? To answer this, we go to the present value table (Table B.1) and look in the row for nine periods. To use the present value table, we must divide $60,000 ($p$) by $120,000 ($f$), which equals 0.5000. Recall that this step is necessary because a present value table defines f equal to 1, and p as a fraction of 1. We look for a value in the row for nine periods that is nearest to 0.5000 (p), which we find in the column for 8% interest (i). This means that the present value of $120,000 at the end of nine periods at 8% interest is $60,000 or, in our example, we must earn 8% annual interest to retire in nine years.

Quick Check

1. A company is considering an investment expected to yield $70,000 after six years. If this company demands an 8% return, how much is it willing to pay for this investment?

Answer—p. B-8

Future Value of a Single Amount

Exhibit B.4
Future Value of a Single Amount Formula

We must modify the formula for the present value of a single amount to obtain the formula for the future value of a single amount. In particular, we multiply both sides of the equa-tion in Exhibit B.2 by $(1 + i)^n$ to get the result shown in Exhibit B.4.

$$f = p \times (1 + i)^n$$

The future value (f) is defined in terms of p, i, and n. We can use this formula to deter-mine that $200 ($p$) invested for 1 ($n$) period at an interest rate of 10% (i) yields a future value of $220 as follows:

$$f = p \times (1 + i)^n$$
$$= \$200 \times (1 + 0.10)^1$$
$$= \$220$$

This formula can also be used to compute the future value of an amount for *any number of periods* into the future. To illustrate, assume that $200 is invested for three periods at 10%. The future value of this $200 is $266.20, computed as follows:

$$f = p \times (1 + i)^n$$
$$= \$200 \times (1 + 0.10)^3$$
$$= \$266.20$$

A future value table makes it easier for us to compute future values (f) for many different combinations of interest rates (i) and time periods (n). Each future value in a future value table assumes the present value (p) is 1. As with a present value table, if the future amount is something other than 1, we simply multiply our answer by that amount. The formula used to construct a table of future values (factors) for a single amount of 1 is in Exhibit B.5.

P2 Apply future value concepts to a single amount by using interest tables.

$$f = (1 + i)^n$$

Exhibit B.5

Future Value of 1 Formula

Table B.2 at the end of this appendix shows a table of future values for a current amount of 1. This type of table is called a **future value of 1 table**.

There are some important relations between Tables B.1 and B.2. In Table B.2, for the row where $n = 0$, the future value is 1 for each interest rate. This is so because no interest is earned when time does not pass. Also notice that Tables B.1 and B.2 report the same information but in a different manner. In particular, one table is simply the *inverse* of the other. To illustrate this inverse relation, let's say we invest $100 annually for a period of five years at 12% per year. How much do we expect to have after five years? We can answer this question using Table B.2 by finding the future value (f) of 1, for five periods from now, compounded at 12%. From that table we find $f = 1.7623$. If we start with $100, the amount it accumulates to after five years is $176.23 ($100 × 1.7623). We can alternatively use Table B.1. Here we find that the present value (p) of 1, discounted five periods at 12%, is 0.5674. Recall the inverse relation between present value and future value. This means that $p = 1/f$ (or equivalently, $f = 1/p$). We can compute the future value of $100 invested for five periods at 12% as follows: $f = \$100 \times (1/0.5674) = \$176.24$.

A future value table involves three factors: f, i, and n. Knowing two of these three factors allows us to compute the third. To illustrate, consider these three possible cases.

Case 1 (solve for f when knowing i and n). Our preceding example fits this case. We found that $100 invested for five periods at 12% interest accumulates to $176.24.

Case 2 (solve for n when knowing f and i). In this case, we have, say, $2,000 ($p$) and we want to know how many periods (n) it will take to accumulate to $3,000 ($f$) at 7% ($i$) interest. To answer this, we go to the future value table (Table B.2) and look in the 7% interest column. Here we find a column of future values (f) based on a present value of 1. To use a future value table, we must divide $3,000 ($f$) by $2,000 ($p$), which equals 1.500. This is necessary because *a future value table defines p equal to 1, and f as a multiple of 1*. We look for a value nearest to 1.50 (f), which we find in the row for six periods (n). This means that $2,000 invested for six periods at 7% interest accumulates to $3,000.

Case 3 (solve for i when knowing f and n). In this case, we have, say, $2,001 ($p$) and in nine years ($n$), we want to have $4,000 ($f$). What rate of interest must we earn to accomplish this? To answer that, we go to Table B.2 and search in the row for nine periods. To use a future value table, we must divide $4,000 ($f$) by $2,001 ($p$), which equals 1.9990. Recall that this is necessary because a future value table defines p equal to 1 and f as a multiple of 1. We look for a value nearest to 1.9990 (f), which we find in the column for 8% interest (i). This means that $2,001 invested for nine periods at 8% interest accumulates to $4,000.

Quick Check

2. Assume that you win a $150,000 cash sweepstakes. You decide to deposit this cash in an account earning 8% annual interest, and you plan to quit your job when the account equals $555,000. How many years will it be before you can quit working?

Answer—p. B-8

Present Value of an Annuity

An annuity is a series of equal payments occurring at equal intervals. One example is a series of three annual payments of $100 each. An *ordinary annuity* is defined as equal end-of-period payments at equal intervals. An ordinary annuity of $100 for 3 periods and its present value (*p*) are illustrated in Exhibit B.6.

Exhibit B.6

Present Value of an Ordinary Annuity Diagram

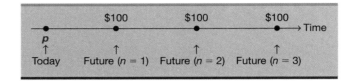

P3 Apply present value concepts to an annuity by using interest tables.

One way for us to compute the present value of an ordinary annuity is to find the present value of each payment using our present value formula from Exhibit B.3. We then add each of the three present values. To illustrate, let's look at three $100 payments at the end of each of the next three periods with an interest rate of 15%. Our present value computations are

$$p = \frac{\$100}{(1 + 0.15)^1} + \frac{\$100}{(1 + 0.15)^2} + \frac{\$100}{(1 + 0.15)^3} = \$228.32$$

This computation is identical to computing the present value of each payment (from Table B.1) and taking their sum or, alternatively, adding the values from Table B.1 for each of the three payments and multiplying their sum by the $100 annuity payment.

A more direct way is to use a present value of annuity table. Table B.3 at the end of this appendix is one such table. This table is called a **present value of an annuity of 1 table**. If we look at Table B.3 where $n = 3$ and $i = 15\%$, we see the present value is 2.2832. This means that the present value of an annuity of 1 for three periods, with a 15% interest rate, equals 2.2832.

A present value of an annuity formula is used to construct Table B.3. It can also be constructed by adding the amounts in a present value of 1 table. To illustrate, we use Table B.1 and B.3 to confirm this relation for the prior example:

Decision Insight

Goin' Fish'n   Frank and Shirley Capaci went fishing in Pell Lake, WI—fishing for money, that is. They purchased a ticket in the powerball lottery and hit the jackpot. The Capacis had to choose between a $196 million annuity over 25 years or a single amount of $104 million. They chose the latter, making it one of the largest one-time payments in lottery history.

From Table B.1		From Table B.3	
$i = 15\%, n = 1$	0.8696		
$i = 15\%, n = 2$	0.7561		
$i = 15\%, n = 3$	0.6575		
Total.	2.2832	$i = 15\%, n = 3$	2.2832

We can also use business calculators or spreadsheet programs to find the present value of an annuity.

Quick Check

3. A company is considering an investment paying $10,000 every six months for three years. The first payment would be received in six months. If this company requires an annual return of 8%, what is the maximum amount it is willing to pay for this investment?

Answer—p. B-8

Future Value of an Annuity

The future value of an *ordinary annuity* is the accumulated value of each annuity payment with interest as of the date of the final payment. To illustrate, let's consider the earlier annuity of three annual payments of $100. Exhibit B.7 shows the point in time for the future value (f). The first payment is made two periods prior to the point when future value is determined, and the final payment occurs on the future value date.

Exhibit B.7

Future Value of an Ordinary Annuity Diagram

One way to compute the future value of an annuity is to use the formula to find the future value of *each* payment and add them. If we assume an interest rate of 15%, our calculation is

$$f = \$100 \times (1 + 0.15)^2 + \$100 \times (1 + 0.15)^1 + \$100 \times (1 + 0.15)^0 = \$347.25$$

This is identical to using Table B.2 and summing the future values of each payment, or by adding the future values of the three payments of 1 and multiplying the sum by $100.

A more direct way is to use a table showing future values of annuities. Such a table is called a **future value of an annuity of 1 table**. Table B.4 at the end of this appendix is one such table. Note that in Table B.4 when $n = 1$, the future values equal 1 ($f = 1$) for all rates of interest. This is so because such an annuity consists of only one payment and the future value is determined on the date of that payment—no time passes between the payment and its future value. The future value of an annuity formula is used to construct Table B.4. We can also construct it by adding the amounts from a future value of 1 table. To illustrate, we use Tables B.2 and B.4 to confirm this relation for the prior example:

P4 Apply future value concepts to an annuity by using interest tables.

From Table B.2		From Table B.4	
$i = 15\%, n = 0$	1.0000		
$i = 15\%, n = 1$	1.1500		
$i = 15\%, n = 2$	1.3225		
Total.	3.4725	$i = 15\%, n = 3$	3.4725

Note that the future value in Table B.2 is 1.0000 when $n = 0$, but the future value in Table B.4 is 1.0000 when $n = 1$. Is this a contradiction? No. When $n = 0$ in Table B.2, the future value is determined on the date when a single payment occurs. This means that no interest is earned, since no time has passed, and the future value equals the payment. Table B.4 describes annuities with equal payments occurring at the end of each period. When $n = 1$, the annuity has one payment, and its future value equals 1 on the date of its final and only payment. Again, no time passes from the payment and its future value date.

Quick Check

4. A company invests $45,000 per year for five years at 12% annual interest. Compute the value of this annuity investment at the end of five years.

Answer—p. B-8

Summary

C1 **Describe the earning of interest and the concepts of present and future values.** Interest is payment by a borrower to the owner of an asset for its use. Present and future value computations are a way for us to estimate the interest component of holding assets or liabilities over a period of time.

P1 **Apply present value concepts to a single amount by using interest tables.** The present value of a single amount received at a future date is the amount that can be invested now at the specified interest rate to yield that future value.

P2 **Apply future value concepts to a single amount by using interest tables.** The future value of a single amount

invested at a specified rate of interest is the amount that would accumulate by the future date.

P3 **Apply present value concepts to an annuity by using interest tables.** The present value of an annuity is the amount that can be invested now at the specified interest rate to yield that series of equal periodic payments.

P4 **Apply future value concepts to an annuity by using interest tables.** The future value of an annuity invested at a specific rate of interest is the amount that would accumulate by the date of the final payment.

Guidance Answers to Quick Checks

1. $70,000 × 0.6302 = $44,114 (use Table B.1, $i = 8\%$, $n = 6$).

2. $555,000/$150,000 = 3.7000; Table B.2 shows this value is not achieved until after 17 years at 8% interest.

3. $10,000 × 5.2421 = $52,421 (use Table B.3, $i = 4\%$, $n = 6$).

4. $45,000 × 6.3528 = $285,876 (use Table B.4, $i = 12\%$, $n = 5$).

QUICK STUDY

QS B-1

Identifying interest rates in tables **C1**

Assume that you must make future value estimates using the *future value of 1 table* (Table B.2). Which interest rate column do you use when working with the following rates?

1. 8% compounded quarterly

2. 12% compounded annually

3. 6% compounded semiannually

4. 12% compounded monthly

QS B-2

Interest rate on **P1** an investment

Ken Francis is offered the possibility of investing $2,745 today and then in return would receive $10,000 after 15 years. What is the annual rate of interest for this investment? (Use Table B.1.)

QS B-3

Number of periods **P1** of an investment

Megan Brink is offered the possibility of investing $6,651 today at 6% interest per year in a desire to accumulate $10,000. How many years must Brink wait to accumulate $10,000? (Use Table B.1.)

QS B-4

Present value **P1** of an amount

Flaherty is considering an investment that, if paid for immediately, is expected to return $140,000 five years from now. If Flaherty demands a 9% return, how much is she willing to pay for this investment?

CII, Inc., invests $630,000 in a project expected to earn a 12% annual rate of return. The earnings will be reinvested in the project each year until the entire investment is liquidated 10 years later. What will the cash proceeds be when the project is liquidated?

QS B-5
Future value P2
of an amount

Beene Distributing is considering a project that will return $150,000 annually at the end of each year for six years. If Beene demands an annual return of 7% and pays for the project immediately, how much is it willing to pay for the project?

QS B-6
Present value P3
of an annuity

Claire Fitch is planning to begin an individual retirement program in which she will invest $1,500 at the end of each year. Fitch plans to retire after making 30 annual investments in the program earning a return of 10%. What is the value of the program on the date of the last payment?

QS B-7
Future value P4
of an annuity

Bill Thompson expects to invest $10,000 at 12% and, at the end of a certain period, receive $96,463. How many years will it be before Thompson receives the payment? (Use Table B.2.)

EXERCISES

Exercise B-1
Number of periods P2
of an investment

Ed Summers expects to invest $10,000 for 25 years, after which he wants to receive $108,347. What rate of interest must Summers earn? (Use Table B.2.)

Exercise B-2
Interest rate on P2
an investment

Jones expects an immediate investment of $57,466 to return $10,000 annually for eight years, with the first payment to be received one year from now. What rate of interest must Jones earn? (Use Table B.3.)

Exercise B-3
Interest rate on P3
an investment

Keith Riggins expects an investment of $82,014 to return $10,000 annually for several years. If Keith earns a return of 10%, how many annual payments will he receive? (Use Table B.3.)

Exercise B-4
Number of periods P3
of an investment

Algoe expects to invest $1,000 annually for 40 years to yield an accumulated value of $154,762 on the date of the last investment. For this to occur, what rate of interest must Algoe earn? (Use Table B.4.)

Exercise B-5
Interest rate on P4
an investment

Kate Beckwith expects to invest $10,000 annually that will earn 8%. How many annual investments must Kate make to accumulate $303,243 on the date of the last investment? (Use Table B.4.)

Exercise B-6
Number of periods P4
of an investment

Sam Weber finances a new automobile by paying $6,500 cash and agreeing to make 40 monthly payments of $500 each, the first payment to be made one month after the purchase. The loan bears interest at an annual rate of 12%. What is the cost of the automobile?

Exercise B-7
Present value P3
of an annuity

Spiller Corp. plans to issue 10%, 15-year, $500,000 par value bonds payable that pay interest semiannually on June 30 and December 31. The bonds are dated December 31, 2002, and are issued on that date. If the market rate of interest for the bonds is 8% on the date of issue, what will be the total cash proceeds from the bond issue?

Exercise B-8
Present value P1 P3
of bonds

McAdams Company expects to earn 10% per year on an investment that will pay $606,773 six years from now. Use Table B.1 to compute the present value of this investment.

Exercise B-9
Present value P1
of an amount

Exercise B-10

Present value of **P1 P3**
an amount and
of an annuity

Compute the amount that can be borrowed under each of the following circumstances:

1. A promise to repay $90,000 seven years from now at an interest rate of 6%.

2. An agreement made on February 1, 2002, to make three separate payments of $20,000 on February 1 of 2003, 2004, and 2005. The annual interest rate is 10%.

Exercise B-11

Present value **P1**
of an amount

On January 1, 2002, a company agrees to pay $20,000 in three years. If the annual interest rate is 10%, determine how much cash the company can borrow with this agreement.

Exercise B-12

Present value **P1**
of an amount

Find the amount of money that can be borrowed today with each of the following separate debt agreements *a* through *f*:

Case	Single Future Payment	Number of Periods	Interest Rate
a.	$40,000	3	4%
b.	75,000	7	8
c.	52,000	9	10
d.	18,000	2	4
e.	63,000	8	6
f.	89,000	5	2

Exercise B-13

Present values of annuities

P3

C&H Ski Club recently borrowed money and agrees to pay it back with a series of six annual payments of $5,000 each. C&H subsequently borrows more money and agrees to pay it back with a series of four annual payments of $7,500 each. The annual interest rate for both loans is 6%.

1. Use Table B.1 to find the present value of these two separate annuities. (Round amounts to the nearest dollar.)

2. Use Table B.3 to find the present value of these two separate annuities.

Exercise B-14

Present value with semiannual
compounding

C1 P3

Otto Co. borrows money on April 30, 2002, by promising to make four payments of $13,000 each on November 1, 2002; May 1, 2003; November 1, 2003; and May 1, 2004.

1. How much money is Otto able to borrow if the interest rate is 8%, compounded semiannually?

2. How much money is Otto able to borrow if the interest rate is 12%, compounded semiannually?

3. How much money is Otto able to borrow if the interest rate is 16%, compounded semiannually?

Exercise B-15

Future value **P2**
of an amount

Mark Welsch deposits $7,200 in an account that earns interest at an annual rate of 8%, compounded quarterly. The $7,200 plus earned interest must remain in the account 10 years before it can be withdrawn. How much money will be in the account at the end of 10 years?

Exercise B-16

Future value **P4**
of an annuity

Kelly Malone plans to have $50 withheld from her monthly paycheck and deposited in a savings account that earns 12% annually, compounded monthly. If Kelly continues with her plan for two and a half years, how much will be accumulated in the account on the date of the last deposit?

Exercise B-17

Future value of **P2 P4**
an amount plus
an annuity

Starr Company decides to establish a fund that it will use 10 years from now to replace an aging production facility. The company will make an initial contribution of $100,000 to the fund and plans to make quarterly contributions of $50,000 beginning in three months. The fund earns 12%, compounded quarterly. What will be the value of the fund 10 years from now?

Exercise B-18

Future value of **P2**
an amount

Catten, Inc., invests $163,170 today earning 7% per year for nine years. Use Table B.2 to compute the future value of the investment nine years from now.

For each of the following situations, identify (1) the case as either (*a*) a present or a future value and (*b*) a single amount or an annuity, (2) the table you would use in your computations (but do not solve the problem), and (3) the interest rate and time periods you would use.

a. You need to accumulate $10,000 for a trip you wish to take in four years. You are able to earn 8% compounded semiannually on your savings. You plan to make only one deposit and let the money accumulate for four years. How would you determine the amount of the one-time deposit?

b. Assume the same facts as in part *a* except that you will make semiannual deposits to your savings account.

c. You want to retire after working 40 years with savings in excess of $1,000,000. You expect to save $4,000 a year for 40 years and earn an annual rate of interest of 8%. Will you be able to retire with more than $1,000,000 in 40 years?

d. A sweepstakes agency names you a grand prize winner. You can take $225,000 immediately or elect to receive annual installments of $30,000 for 20 years. You can earn 10% annually on any investments you make. Which prize do you choose to receive?

Exercise B-19
Using present and future value tables

C1 P1 P2
P3 P4

Table B.1

Present Value of 1

$$p = 1/(1 + i)^n$$

Periods	1%	2%	3%	4%	5%	6%	7%	8%	9%	10%	12%	15%
1	0.9901	0.9804	0.9709	0.9615	0.9524	0.9434	0.9346	0.9259	0.9174	0.9091	0.8929	0.8696
2	0.9803	0.9612	0.9426	0.9246	0.9070	0.8900	0.8734	0.8573	0.8417	0.8264	0.7972	0.7561
3	0.9706	0.9423	0.9151	0.8890	0.8638	0.8396	0.8163	0.7938	0.7722	0.7513	0.7118	0.6575
4	0.9610	0.9238	0.8885	0.8548	0.8227	0.7921	0.7629	0.7350	0.7084	0.6830	0.6355	0.5718
5	0.9515	0.9057	0.8626	0.8219	0.7835	0.7473	0.7130	0.6806	0.6499	0.6209	0.5674	0.4972
6	0.9420	0.8880	0.8375	0.7903	0.7462	0.7050	0.6663	0.6302	0.5963	0.5645	0.5066	0.4323
7	0.9327	0.8706	0.8131	0.7599	0.7107	0.6651	0.6227	0.5835	0.5470	0.5132	0.4523	0.3759
8	0.9235	0.8535	0.7894	0.7307	0.6768	0.6274	0.5820	0.5403	0.5019	0.4665	0.4039	0.3269
9	0.9143	0.8368	0.7664	0.7026	0.6446	0.5919	0.5439	0.5002	0.4604	0.4241	0.3606	0.2843
10	0.9053	0.8203	0.7441	0.6756	0.6139	0.5584	0.5083	0.4632	0.4224	0.3855	0.3220	0.2472
11	0.8963	0.8043	0.7224	0.6496	0.5847	0.5268	0.4751	0.4289	0.3875	0.3505	0.2875	0.2149
12	0.8874	0.7885	0.7014	0.6246	0.5568	0.4970	0.4440	0.3971	0.3555	0.3186	0.2567	0.1869
13	0.8787	0.7730	0.6810	0.6006	0.5303	0.4688	0.4150	0.3677	0.3262	0.2897	0.2292	0.1625
14	0.8700	0.7579	0.6611	0.5775	0.5051	0.4423	0.3878	0.3405	0.2992	0.2633	0.2046	0.1413
15	0.8613	0.7430	0.6419	0.5553	0.4810	0.4173	0.3624	0.3152	0.2745	0.2394	0.1827	0.1229
16	0.8528	0.7284	0.6232	0.5339	0.4581	0.3936	0.3387	0.2919	0.2519	0.2176	0.1631	0.1069
17	0.8444	0.7142	0.6050	0.5134	0.4363	0.3714	0.3166	0.2703	0.2311	0.1978	0.1456	0.0929
18	0.8360	0.7002	0.5874	0.4936	0.4155	0.3503	0.2959	0.2502	0.2120	0.1799	0.1300	0.0808
19	0.8277	0.6864	0.5703	0.4746	0.3957	0.3305	0.2765	0.2317	0.1945	0.1635	0.1161	0.0703
20	0.8195	0.6730	0.5537	0.4564	0.3769	0.3118	0.2584	0.2145	0.1784	0.1486	0.1037	0.0611
25	0.7798	0.6095	0.4776	0.3751	0.2953	0.2330	0.1842	0.1460	0.1160	0.0923	0.0588	0.0304
30	0.7419	0.5521	0.4120	0.3083	0.2314	0.1741	0.1314	0.0994	0.0754	0.0573	0.0334	0.0151
35	0.7059	0.5000	0.3554	0.2534	0.1813	0.1301	0.0937	0.0676	0.0490	0.0356	0.0189	0.0075
40	0.6717	0.4529	0.3066	0.2083	0.1420	0.0972	0.0668	0.0460	0.0318	0.0221	0.0107	0.0037

Table B.2

Future Value of 1

$$f = (1 + i)^n$$

Periods	1%	2%	3%	4%	5%	6%	7%	8%	9%	10%	12%	15%
0	1.0000	1.0000	1.0000	1.0000	1.0000	1.0000	1.0000	1.0000	1.0000	1.0000	1.0000	1.0000
1	1.0100	1.0200	1.0300	1.0400	1.0500	1.0600	1.0700	1.0800	1.0900	1.1000	1.1200	1.1500
2	1.0201	1.0404	1.0609	1.0816	1.1025	1.1236	1.1449	1.1664	1.1881	1.2100	1.2544	1.3225
3	1.0303	1.0612	1.0927	1.1249	1.1576	1.1910	1.2250	1.2597	1.2950	1.3310	1.4049	1.5209
4	1.0406	1.0824	1.1255	1.1699	1.2155	1.2625	1.3108	1.3605	1.4116	1.4641	1.5735	1.7490
5	1.0510	1.1041	1.1593	1.2167	1.2763	1.3382	1.4026	1.4693	1.5386	1.6105	1.7623	2.0114
6	1.0615	1.1262	1.1941	1.2653	1.3401	1.4185	1.5007	1.5869	1.6771	1.7716	1.9738	2.3131
7	1.0721	1.1487	1.2299	1.3159	1.4071	1.5036	1.6058	1.7138	1.8280	1.9487	2.2107	2.6600
8	1.0829	1.1717	1.2668	1.3686	1.4775	1.5938	1.7182	1.8509	1.9926	2.1436	2.4760	3.0590
9	1.0937	1.1951	1.3048	1.4233	1.5513	1.6895	1.8385	1.9990	2.1719	2.3579	2.7731	3.5179
10	1.1046	1.2190	1.3439	1.4802	1.6289	1.7908	1.9672	2.1589	2.3674	2.5937	3.1058	4.0456
11	1.1157	1.2434	1.3842	1.5395	1.7103	1.8983	2.1049	2.3316	2.5804	2.8531	3.4785	4.6524
12	1.1268	1.2682	1.4258	1.6010	1.7959	2.0122	2.2522	2.5182	2.8127	3.1384	3.8960	5.3503
13	1.1381	1.2936	1.4685	1.6651	1.8856	2.1329	2.4098	2.7196	3.0658	3.4523	4.3635	6.1528
14	1.1495	1.3195	1.5126	1.7317	1.9799	2.2609	2.5785	2.9372	3.3417	3.7975	4.8871	7.0757
15	1.1610	1.3459	1.5580	1.8009	2.0789	2.3966	2.7590	3.1722	3.6425	4.1772	5.4736	8.1371
16	1.1726	1.3728	1.6047	1.8730	2.1829	2.5404	2.9522	3.4259	3.9703	4.5950	6.1304	9.3576
17	1.1843	1.4002	1.6528	1.9479	2.2920	2.6928	3.1588	3.7000	4.3276	5.0545	6.8660	10.7613
18	1.1961	1.4282	1.7024	2.0258	2.4066	2.8543	3.3799	3.9960	4.7171	5.5599	7.6900	12.3755
19	1.2081	1.4568	1.7535	2.1068	2.5270	3.0256	3.6165	4.3157	5.1417	6.1159	8.6128	14.2318
20	1.2202	1.4859	1.8061	2.1911	2.6533	3.2071	3.8697	4.6610	5.6044	6.7275	9.6463	16.3665
25	1.2824	1.6406	2.0938	2.6658	3.3864	4.2919	5.4274	6.8485	8.6231	10.8347	17.0001	32.9190
30	1.3478	1.8114	2.4273	3.2434	4.3219	5.7435	7.6123	10.0627	13.2677	17.4494	29.9599	66.2118
35	1.4166	1.9999	2.8139	3.9461	5.5160	7.6861	10.6766	14.7853	20.4140	28.1024	52.7996	133.176
40	1.4889	2.2080	3.2620	4.8010	7.0400	10.2857	14.9745	21.7245	31.4094	45.2593	93.0510	267.864

$$p = \left[1 - \frac{1}{(1 + i)^n}\right]/i$$

Table B.3

Present Value of an Annuity of 1

Periods	1%	2%	3%	4%	5%	6%	7%	8%	9%	10%	12%	15%
1	0.9901	0.9804	0.9709	0.9615	0.9524	0.9434	0.9346	0.9259	0.9174	0.9091	0.8929	0.8696
2	1.9704	1.9416	1.9135	1.8861	1.8594	1.8334	1.8080	1.7833	1.7591	1.7355	1.6901	1.6257
3	2.9410	2.8839	2.8286	2.7751	2.7232	2.6730	2.6243	2.5771	2.5313	2.4869	2.4018	2.2832
4	3.9020	3.8077	3.7171	3.6299	3.5460	3.4651	3.3872	3.3121	3.2397	3.1699	3.0373	2.8550
5	4.8534	4.7135	4.5797	4.4518	4.3295	4.2124	4.1002	3.9927	3.8897	3.7908	3.6048	3.3522
6	5.7955	5.6014	5.4172	5.2421	5.0757	4.9173	4.7665	4.6229	4.4859	4.3553	4.1114	3.7845
7	6.7282	6.4720	6.2303	6.0021	5.7864	5.5824	5.3893	5.2064	5.0330	4.8684	4.5638	4.1604
8	7.6517	7.3255	7.0197	6.7327	6.4632	6.2098	5.9713	5.7466	5.5348	5.3349	4.9676	4.4873
9	8.5660	8.1622	7.7861	7.4353	7.1078	6.8017	6.5152	6.2469	5.9952	5.7590	5.3282	4.7716
10	9.4713	8.9826	8.5302	8.1109	7.7217	7.3601	7.0236	6.7101	6.4177	6.1446	5.6502	5.0188
11	10.3676	9.7868	9.2526	8.7605	8.3064	7.8869	7.4987	7.1390	6.8052	6.4951	5.9377	5.2337
12	11.2551	10.5753	9.9540	9.3851	8.8633	8.3838	7.9427	7.5361	7.1607	6.8137	6.1944	5.4206
13	12.1337	11.3484	10.6350	9.9856	9.3936	8.8527	8.3577	7.9038	7.4869	7.1034	6.4235	5.5831
14	13.0037	12.1062	11.2961	10.5631	9.8986	9.2950	8.7455	8.2442	7.7862	7.3667	6.6282	5.7245
15	13.8651	12.8493	11.9379	11.1184	10.3797	9.7122	9.1079	8.5595	8.0607	7.6061	6.8109	5.8474
16	14.7179	13.5777	12.5611	11.6523	10.8378	10.1059	9.4466	8.8514	8.3126	7.8237	6.9740	5.9542
17	15.5623	14.2919	13.1661	12.1657	11.2741	10.4773	9.7632	9.1216	8.5436	8.0216	7.1196	6.0472
18	16.3983	14.9920	13.7535	12.6593	11.6896	10.8276	10.0591	9.3719	8.7556	8.2014	7.2497	6.1280
19	17.2260	15.6785	14.3238	13.1339	12.0853	11.1581	10.3356	9.6036	8.9501	8.3649	7.3658	6.1982
20	18.0456	16.3514	14.8775	13.5903	12.4622	11.4699	10.5940	9.8181	9.1285	8.5136	7.4694	6.2593
25	22.0232	19.5235	17.4131	15.6221	14.0939	12.7834	11.6536	10.6748	9.8226	9.0770	7.8431	6.4641
30	25.8077	22.3965	19.6004	17.2920	15.3725	13.7648	12.4090	11.2578	10.2737	9.4269	8.0552	6.5660
35	29.4086	24.9986	21.4872	18.6646	16.3742	14.4982	12.9477	11.6546	10.5668	9.6442	8.1755	6.6166
40	32.8347	27.3555	23.1148	19.7928	17.1591	15.0463	13.3317	11.9246	10.7574	9.7791	8.2438	6.6418

Table B.4

Future Value of an Annuity of 1

$$f = [(1 + i)^n - 1]/i$$

Periods	1%	2%	3%	4%	5%	6%	7%	8%	9%	10%	12%	15%
1	1.0000	1.0000	1.0000	1.0000	1.0000	1.0000	1.0000	1.0000	1.0000	1.0000	1.0000	1.0000
2	2.0100	2.0200	2.0300	2.0400	2.0500	2.0600	2.0700	2.0800	2.0900	2.1000	2.1200	2.1500
3	3.0301	3.0604	3.0909	3.1216	3.1525	3.1836	3.2149	3.2464	3.2781	3.3100	3.3744	3.4725
4	4.0604	4.1216	4.1836	4.2465	4.3101	4.3746	4.4399	4.5061	4.5731	4.6410	4.7793	4.9934
5	5.1010	5.2040	5.3091	5.4163	5.5256	5.6371	5.7507	5.8666	5.9847	6.1051	6.3528	6.7424
6	6.1520	6.3081	6.4684	6.6330	6.8019	6.9753	7.1533	7.3359	7.5233	7.7156	8.1152	8.7537
7	7.2135	7.4343	7.6625	7.8983	8.1420	8.3938	8.6540	8.9228	9.2004	9.4872	10.0890	11.0668
8	8.2857	8.5830	8.8923	9.2142	9.5491	9.8975	10.2598	10.6366	11.0285	11.4359	12.2997	13.7268
9	9.3685	9.7546	10.1591	10.5828	11.0266	11.4913	11.9780	12.4876	13.0210	13.5795	14.7757	16.7858
10	10.4622	10.9497	11.4639	12.0061	12.5779	13.1808	13.8164	14.4866	15.1929	15.9374	17.5487	20.3037
11	11.5668	12.1687	12.8078	13.4864	14.2068	14.9716	15.7835	16.6455	17.5603	18.5312	20.6546	24.3493
12	12.6825	13.4121	14.1920	15.0258	15.9171	16.8699	17.8885	18.9771	20.1407	21.3843	24.1331	29.0017
13	13.8093	14.6803	15.6178	16.6268	17.7130	18.8821	20.1406	21.4953	22.9534	24.5227	28.0291	34.3519
14	14.9474	15.9739	17.0863	18.2919	19.5986	21.0151	22.5505	24.2149	26.0192	27.9750	32.3926	40.5047
15	16.0969	17.2934	18.5989	20.0236	21.5786	23.2760	25.1290	27.1521	29.3609	31.7725	37.2797	47.5804
16	17.2579	18.6393	20.1569	21.8245	23.6575	25.6725	27.8881	30.3243	33.0034	35.9497	42.7533	55.7175
17	18.4304	20.0121	21.7616	23.6975	25.8404	28.2129	30.8402	33.7502	36.9737	40.5447	48.8837	65.0751
18	19.6147	21.4123	23.4144	25.6454	28.1324	30.9057	33.9990	37.4502	41.3013	45.5992	55.7497	75.8364
19	20.8109	22.8406	25.1169	27.6712	30.5390	33.7600	37.3790	41.4463	46.0185	51.1591	63.4397	88.2118
20	22.0190	24.2974	26.8704	29.7781	33.0660	36.7856	40.9955	45.7620	51.1601	57.2750	72.0524	102.444
25	28.2432	32.0303	36.4593	41.6459	47.7271	54.8645	63.2490	73.1059	84.7009	98.3471	133.334	212.793
30	34.7849	40.5681	47.5754	56.0849	66.4388	79.0582	94.4608	113.283	136.308	164.494	241.333	434.745
35	41.6603	49.9945	60.4621	73.6522	90.3203	111.435	138.237	172.317	215.711	271.024	431.663	881.170
40	48.8864	60.4020	75.4013	95.0255	120.800	154.762	199.635	259.057	337.882	442.593	767.091	1,779.09

Reporting and Analyzing Long-Term Investments

Learning Objectives

Conceptual

C1 Distinguish long-term investments from short-term investments.

C2 Identify classes of securities in long-term investments.

C3 Describe how to report equity securities with controlling influence.

Procedural

P1 Account for held-to-maturity securities.

P2 Account for available-for-sale securities.

P3 Account for equity securities with significant influence.

Appendix Preview

This appendix's focus is long-term investments. Many companies have long-term investments, and many of these are in the form of debt and equity securities issued by other companies. We describe long-term investments in these securities and how they are accounted for.

Classifying Investments

In this section, we first describe the distinction between short- and long-term investments and then describe the different classifications of long-term investments.

Short-Term versus Long-Term Investments

We explained in Chapter 7 how to account for short-term investments in debt and equity securities. *Short-term investments* are current assets that must meet two requirements. First, they are expected to be converted into cash within one year or the current operating cycle, whichever is longer. Second, they are readily convertible to cash. Short-term investments are usually held as an investment of cash for use in current operations. (It is helpful to review short-term investments in Chapter 7 and the basics of bonds and stocks in Chapters 10 and 11.)

C1 Distinguish long-term investments from short-term investments.

Long-term investments are investments in debt and equity securities that are not readily convertible to cash or are not intended to be converted into cash in the short term. Long-term investments also include funds earmarked for a special purpose, such as bond sinking funds and investments in land or other assets not used in the company's operations. Long-term investments are reported in the noncurrent section of the balance sheet, often in its own separate section titled *Long-Term Investments*.

Classes of Long-Term Investments

Accounting for long-term investments depends on two factors. The first factor is whether the securities can be classified as (1) debt securities *held-to-maturity* or (2) debt and equity securities *available-for-sale*. These two classes of investments are either long term or short term depending on what the company intends to do with them. (Note that investments in trading securities always are short-term investments.) The second factor applies to equity securities and depends on the company's (investor's) percent ownership in the other company's (investee's) shares. Exhibit C.1 classifies long-term securities on the basis of these two factors and describes the accounting required. The four classifications shown are (1) debt securities *held-to-maturity,* (2) debt and equity securities *available-for-sale,* (3) equity securities with a significant influence over an investee, and (4) equity securities with control over an investee. We describe each of these four classes of securities and how to account for them.

C2 Identify classes of securities in long-term investments.

Exhibit C.1

Accounting for Long-Term Investments in Securities

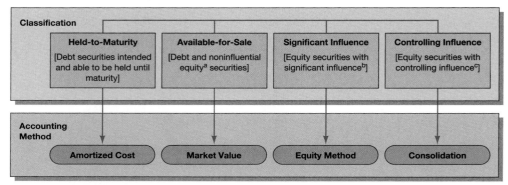

^a Holding less than 20% of voting stock (equity securities only). ^b Holding 20% or more, but not more than 50%, of voting stock.
^c Holding more than 50% of voting stock.

Long-Term Investments in Securities

Similar to the accounting for short-term investments, a long-term investment in securities is recorded at cost when purchased. *Cost* is defined as all necessary expenditures to acquire the investment, including any commissions or brokerage fees paid. After the purchase, the accounting treatment for long-term investments depends on its classification.

Held-to-Maturity Securities

Held-to-maturity securities are *debt* securities a company intends and is able to hold until maturity. Debt securities held to maturity are classified as long-term investments when their maturity dates extend beyond one year or the operating cycle, whichever is longer. They are recorded at cost when purchased. Interest revenue for long-term investments in held-to-maturity debt securities must be recorded as it accrues.

P1   Account for held-to-maturity securities.

   The cost of an investment in a held-to-maturity debt security can be either higher or lower than the maturity value of the debt security. When the investment is long term, the difference between cost and maturity value is amortized over the remaining life of the security. Chapter 10 explains how we amortize such a premium or discount. Here we assume for ease of computations that the cost of a debt security equals its maturity value.

Illustration: Held-to-Maturity debt security. Music City paid $29,500 plus a $500 brokerage fee on September 1, 2002, to buy Improv's 7%, two-year bonds payable with a $30,000 par value. The bonds pay interest semiannually on August 31 and February 28. The amount of each interest payment is $1,050, computed as $30,000 par value × 7% interest × 6/12 year. Music City intends to hold the bonds until they mature on August 31, 2004. The entry to record this purchase is

2002			
Sept. 1	Long-Term Investments	30,000	
	Cash		30,000
	Purchased bonds to be held to maturity.		

Assets = Liabilities + Equity
+30,000
−30,000

On December 31, 2002, at the end of its accounting period, Music City accrues interest receivable as follows:

Dec. 31	Interest Receivable	700	
	Interest Revenue		700
	Accrue interest earned ($30,000 × 7% × ¹/₁₂).		

Assets = Liabilities + Equity
+700   +700

The $700 reflects 4/6 of the semiannual cash receipt of interest. This is the portion Music City earned as of December 31. Relevant sections of Music City's financial statements at December 31, 2002, are shown in Exhibit C.2.

On the income statement for year 2002:	
Interest revenue	**$ 700**
On the December 31, 2002, balance sheet:	
Long-term investments—Held-to-maturity securities (at amortized cost)	**$30,000**

Exhibit C.2

Financial Statement Effects of Held-to-Maturity Securities

On February 28, 2003, Music City records receipt of semiannual interest:

Feb. 28	Cash	1,050	
	Interest Receivable		700
	Interest Revenue		350
	Received 6 months' interest on Improv bonds.		

Assets = Liabilities + Equity
+1,050   +350
 −700

When the bonds mature, their proceeds are recorded as follows:

2004			
Aug. 31	Cash	30,000	
	Long-Term Investments.		30,000
	Received cash from matured bonds.		

Assets = Liabilities + Equity
+30,000
−30,000

This illustration reflects what is called the *cost method* of accounting for long-term investments in held-to-maturity debt securities. This method is required.

Available-for-Sale Securities

Available-for-sale securities are held with the intent to sell them in the future. If the intent is to hold them at least through the next year or operating cycle, they are classified as long-term investments. Exhibit C.1 shows that long-term investments in available-for-sale securities can include both debt securities and noninfluential equity securities. This section describes the accounting for both of these available-for-sale securities.

Available-for-Sale <u>Debt</u> Securities

Accounting for **available-for-sale debt securities** is similar to accounting for held-to-maturity debt securities. First, debt securities are recorded at cost when purchased. Second, while debt securities are held, interest is recorded as it accrues. The difference in accounting for held-to-maturity debt securities versus available-for-sale debt securities is the amount reported on the balance sheet. Held-to-maturity debt securities are reported at cost, adjusted for the amortized amount of any difference between cost and maturity value. Available-for-sale debt securities are reported at (fair) market value.

To illustrate the accounting for an available-for-sale debt security, assume that Music City does not intend to hold the Improv bonds to maturity (see the prior case). The Improv bonds are then classified as available-for-sale securities. The entries in the prior section to record the purchase of the Improv bonds on September 1, the accrual of interest on December 31, 2002, and the receipt of interest on February 28, 2003, remain the same provided the bonds are not yet sold. If Music City were to sell the bonds as planned (before they mature), any gain or loss on this sale is reported in the income statement. Also, (1) there is no amortization of any discount or premium and (2) any unrealized gain or loss from adjusting these securities to market value is reported in the equity section of the balance sheet.

Available-for-Sale <u>Equity</u> Securities

The accounting is similar for short-term and long-term investments in **available-for-sale equity securities.** First, these investments are recorded at cost. Second, cash dividends received are credited to Dividend Revenue and reported in the income statement. Third, when the shares are sold, proceeds from the sale are compared with the cost of the investment, and any gain or loss on the sale is reported in the income statement. (If a long-term investment in an equity security gives the investor significant influence over the investee, it cannot be classified as available-for-sale. Significant influence usually exists if the investor owns 20% or more of the investee company's voting stock.)

Point: Some users of financial statements are concerned that certain managers hold available-for-sale securities that have incurred losses, while selling those that incur gains (which increases income).

To illustrate, Music City purchases 1,000 shares of Intex common stock at par value for $86,000 on October 10, 2002, and it records this purchase as follows:

Assets = Liabilities + Equity
+86,000
−86,000

Oct. 10	Long-Term Investments	86,000	
	Cash		86,000
	Purchased 1,000 shares of Intex.		

On November 2, Music City receives a $1,720 quarterly cash dividend on the Intex shares, which it records as follows:

Assets = Liabilities + Equity
+1,720   +1,720

Nov. 2	Cash	1,720	
	Dividend Revenue		1,720
	Received dividend of $1.72 per share.		

On December 20, Music City sells 500 of the Intex shares for $45,000 and records this sale:

Assets = Liabilities + Equity
+45,000   +2,000
−43,000

Dec. 20	Cash	45,000	
	Long-Term Investments		43,000
	Gain on Sale of Long-Term Investments ...		2,000
	Sold 500 Intex shares ($86,000 × 500/1,000).		

Reporting market value of available-for-sale securities. Long-term investments in available-for-sale (both debt and equity) securities are reported at (fair) market value on the balance sheet. Any unrealized holding gain or loss on these securities is not reported on the standard income statement. Instead, it bypasses the income statement and is directly reported in equity (as part of *comprehensive income*). All changes in equity for a period, except those from investments by and distributions to owners, make up *comprehensive income*. The items making up comprehensive income (beyond the standard income statement items) are typically reported in the equity section of the balance sheet and as part of the statement of changes in equity. (Two other options are to report these items in a separate comprehensive income statement or in a combined statement of comprehensive income. These options are left for advanced courses.)

To illustrate the reporting on available-for-sale securities, assume that Music City had no prior investments in available-for-sale securities other than the bonds purchased on September 1 and the stock purchased on October 10. Exhibit C.3 shows both the book value and market value of these investments on December 31, 2002.

	Book Value	Market Value
Improv bonds	$30,000	$29,050
Intex common stock, 500 shares	43,000	45,500
Total	$73,000	$74,550

Exhibit C.3

Book and Market Value of Available-for-Sale Securities

The entry to record the market value of these investments follows:

Dec. 31	Market Adjustment—Available-for-Sale	1,550	
	Unrealized Gain—Equity		1,550
	To record adjustment to market value of available-for-sale securities.		

It is common to combine the cost of investments with the balance in the Market Adjustment account and report the net as a single amount. Exhibit C.4 shows this reporting approach for Music City's December 31, 2002, balance sheet.

Long-Term Investments—Available-for-sale at market (cost is $73,000)	$74,550
Equity:	
. . . *usual equity accounts* . . .	
Add: Unrealized gain on available-for-sale securities*	$ 1,550

* Often included under the caption Accumulated Other Comprehensive Income.

Exhibit C.4

Balance Sheet Presentation of Available-for-Sale Securities

Next, let's extend this illustration and assume that at the end of its next calendar year (December 31, 2003), Music City's available-for-sale securities have an $81,000 book (cost) value and an $82,000 market value. It would record the adjustment to market value as follows:

Dec. 31	Unrealized Gain—Equity	550	
	Market Adjustment—Available-for-Sale		550
	To record adjustment to market value of available-for-sale securities.		

Example: What is the entry if Music City sells 500 Intex shares for $41,000? *Answer:*

Cash 41,000
Loss on Sale of
  L-T Invest. . . . 2,000
    L-T Investments 43,000

Example: If market value in Exhibit C.3 is $70,000 (instead of $74,550), what entry is made? *Answer:*
Unreal. Loss—Equity . . . 3,000
  Market Adj.—AFS . . . 3,000

Assets = Liabilities + Equity
+1,550   +1,550

Point: Unrealized Loss—Equity and Unrealized Gain—Equity are *permanent* (balance sheet) *accounts.*

Assets = Liabilities + Equity
−550   −550

The effects of year 2002 and 2003 securities transactions are reflected in the following T-accounts:

Market Adjustment — Available-for-Sale (LT)					Unrealized Gain — Equity			
Bal. 12/31/02	1,550	Adj. 12/31/03	550		Adj. 12/31/03	550	Bal. 12/31/02	1,550
Bal. 12/31/03	1,000						Bal. 12/31/03	1,000

Amounts reconcile.

Investment in Equity Securities with Significant Influence

P3 Account for equity securities with significant influence.

A long-term investment classified in **equity securities with significant influence** implies that the investor can exert significant influence over the investee. An investor that owns 20% or more (but not more than 50%) of a company's voting stock is usually presumed to have a significant influence over the investee. In some cases, however, the 20% test of significant influence is overruled by other, more persuasive, evidence. This evidence can either lower the 20% requirement or increase it. The **equity method** of accounting and reporting is used for long-term investments in equity securities with significant influence.

Long-term investments in equity securities with significant influence are recorded at cost when acquired. To illustrate, Micron Co. records the purchase of 3,000 shares (30%) of JVT common stock at a total cost of $70,650 on January 1, 2002, as follows:

Assets = Liabilities + Equity
+70,650
−70,650

Jan. 1	Long-Term Investments	70,650	
	Cash		70,650
	To record purchase of 3,000 JVT shares.		

Under the equity method, earnings of the investee (JVT) increase both the investee's net assets and the investor's (Micron) claim on the investee's net assets. Thus, when the investee reports its earnings, the investor records its share of those earnings in its investment account. To illustrate, assume that JVT reports net income of $20,000 for 2002. Micron then records its 30% share of those earnings as follows:

Assets = Liabilities + Equity
+6,000   +6,000

Dec. 31	Long-Term Investments	6,000	
	Earnings from Long-Term Investment		6,000
	To record 30% equity in investee earnings.		

The debit reflects the increase in Micron's equity in JVT. The credit reflects 30% of JVT's net income that appears on Micron's income statement. If the investee incurs a net loss instead of a net income, the investor records its share of the loss and reduces (credits) its investment account. The investor closes this earnings or loss account to Income Summary.

The receipt of cash dividends is not revenue under the equity method because the investor has already recorded its share of the earnings reported by the investee. Instead, cash dividends received by an investor from an investee are viewed as a conversion of one asset to another. Dividends thus reduce the balance of the investor's investment account. To illustrate, JVT declares and pays $10,000 in cash dividends on its common stock. Micron records its 30% share of these dividends received on January 9, 2003:

Assets = Liabilities + Equity
+3,000
−3,000

Jan. 9	Cash	3,000	
	Long-Term Investments		3,000
	To record share of dividend paid by JVT.		

The book value of an investment under the equity method equals the cost of the investment plus (minus) the investor's equity in the *undistributed* (*distributed*) earnings of the investee. Once we record these transactions for Micron, its investment account appears as shown in Exhibit C.5.

Date	Explanation	Debit	Credit	Balance
2002				
Jan. 1	Investment acquisition	70,650		70,650
Dec. 31	Share of earnings	6,000		76,650
2003				
Jan. 9	Share of dividend		3,000	73,650

Exhibit C.5

Investment in JVT Common
Stock (Ledger Account)

Micron's account balance on January 9, 2003, for its investment in JVT is $73,650. This is the investment's cost *plus* Micron's equity in JVT's earnings since its purchase *less* Micron's equity in JVT's cash dividends since its purchase. When an investment in equity securities is sold, the gain or loss is computed by comparing proceeds from the sale with the book value of the investment on the date of sale. If Micron sells its JVT stock for $80,000 on January 10, 2003, it records the sale as:

Jan. 10	Cash	80,000	
	Long-Term Investments		73,650
	Gain on Sale of Investment		6,350
	Sold 3,000 shares of stock for $80,000.		

Assets = Liabilities + Equity
+80,000   +6,350
−73,650

Investment in Equity Securities with Controlling Influence

A long-term investment classified as **equity securities with controlling influence** implies that the investor can exert a controlling influence over the investee. An investor who owns more than 50% of a company's voting stock has control over the investee. This investor can dominate all other shareholders in electing the corporation's board of directors and has control over the investee's management. In some cases, controlling influence can extend to situations of

C3 Describe how to report equity securities with controlling influence.

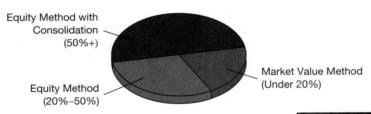

Equity Method with
Consolidation
(50%+)

Equity Method
(20%–50%)

Market Value Method
(Under 20%)

Exhibit C.6

Accounting for Equity
Investments by Percent
of Ownership

less than 50% ownership. Exhibit C.6 summarizes the accounting for investments in equity securities based on an investor's ownership in the stock.

The equity method is used to account for long-term investments in equity securities with controlling influence. The investor reports *consolidated financial statements* when owning such securities. The controlling investor is called the **parent** and the investee is called the **subsidiary.** Many companies are parents with subsidiaries. Examples are (1) McGraw-Hill, the parent of *Business Week,* Standard & Poor's, and Compustat; (2) Gap, Inc., the parent of Gap, Old Navy, and Banana Republic; and (3) Brunswick, the parent of Mercury Marine, Sea Ray, and U.S. Marine. A company owning all the outstanding stock of a subsidiary can, if it desires, take over the subsidiary's assets, retire the subsidiary's stock, and merge the subsidiary into the parent. However, there often are financial, legal, and tax advantages if a business operates as a parent controlling one or more subsidiaries. When a company operates as a parent with subsidiaries, each entity maintains separate accounting records. From a legal viewpoint, the parent and each subsidiary are separate entities with all rights, duties, and responsibilities of individual companies.

Consolidated financial statements show the financial position, results of operations, and cash flows of all entities under the parent's control, including all subsidiaries. These statements are prepared as if the business were organized as one entity. The parent uses the equity method in its accounts, but the investment account is *not* reported on the parent's financial statements. Instead, the individual assets and liabilities of the parent and its subsidiaries are

combined on one balance sheet. Their revenues and expenses also are combined on one income statement and their cash flows are combined on one statement of cash flows. The detailed procedures for preparing consolidated financial statements are included in advanced courses.

Accounting Summary for Investments in Securities

Exhibit C.7 summarizes the accounting for investments in securities. Recall that many investment securities can be classified as either short term or long term depending on management's intent and ability to convert them in the future. Understanding the accounting for these investments enables us to draw better conclusions from financial statements in making business decisions.

Exhibit C.7

Accounting for Investments in Securities

Class of Investment Securities	Accounting Method
Short-Term Investment in Securities	
Held-to-maturity (debt) securities	Cost (without any discount or premium amortization)
Trading (debt and equity) securities	Market value (with market adjustment to income)
Available-for-sale (debt and equity) securities	Market value (with market adjustment to equity)
Long-Term Investment in Securities	
Held-to-maturity (debt) securities	Cost (with discount or premium amortization)
Available-for-sale (debt and equity) securities	Market value (with market adjustment to equity)
Equity securities with significant influence	Equity method
Equity securities with controlling influence	Equity method (with consolidation)

Comprehensive Income

The term **comprehensive income** refers to all changes in equity for a period except those due to investments and distributions to owners. This means that it includes (1) the revenues, gains, expenses, and losses reported in net income, *and* (2) the gains and losses that bypass net income but affect equity. An example of an item that bypasses net income is unrealized gains and losses on available-for-sale securities. These items make up *other comprehensive income* and are usually reported as a part of the statement of changes in stockholders' equity. (Two other options are as a second separate income statement or as a combined income statement of comprehensive income—these less common options are described in advanced courses.) Most often this simply requires one additional column for Other Comprehensive Income in the usual columnar form of the statement of changes in equity (the details of this are left for advanced courses). The FASB encourages, but does *not* require, other comprehensive income items to be grouped under the caption *Accumulated Other Comprehensive Income* in the equity section of the balance sheet, which would include unrealized gains and losses on available-for-sale securities. For instructional benefits, we use actual account titles for these items in the equity section instead of this general, less precise caption.

Demonstration Problem

The following transactions relate to Brown Company's long-term investment activities during 2002 and 2003. Brown did not own any long-term investments prior to 2002. Show (1) the appropriate journal entries and (2) the portions of each year's balance sheet and income statement that reflect these transactions for both 2002 and 2003.

2002

Sept. 9   Purchased 1,000 shares of Packard, Inc., common stock for $80,000 cash. These shares represent 30% of Packard's outstanding shares.

Oct. 2   Purchased 2,000 shares of AT&T common stock for $60,000 cash. These shares represent less than a 1% ownership in AT&T.

    17   Purchased as a long-term investment 1,000 shares of Apple Computer common stock for $40,000 cash. These shares are less than 1% of Apple's outstanding shares.

Nov. 1   Received $5,000 cash dividend from Packard.

    30   Received $3,000 cash dividend from AT&T.

Dec. 15   Received $1,400 cash dividend from Apple.
    31   Packard's 2002 net income is $70,000.
    31   Market values for the investments in equity securities are Packard, $84,000; AT&T, $48,000; and Apple Computer, $45,000.
    31   After closing the accounts, select account balances on Brown Company's books are Common Stock, $500,000, and Retained Earnings, $350,000.

2003

Jan.   1   Sold Packard, Inc., shares for $108,000 cash.
May 30   Received $3,100 cash dividend from AT&T.
June 15   Received $1,600 cash dividend from Apple.
Aug. 17   Sold the AT&T stock for $52,000 cash.
    19   Purchased 2,000 shares of Coca-Cola common stock for $50,000 cash as a long-term investment. The stock represents less than a 5% ownership in Coca-Cola.
Dec. 15   Received $1,800 cash dividend from Apple.
    31   Market values of the investments in equity securities are Apple, $39,000, and Coca-Cola, $48,000.
    31   After closing the accounts, select account balances on Brown Company's books are Common Stock, $500,000, and Retained Earnings, $410,000.

Solution to Demonstration Problem

1. Journal entries for 2002:

Sept. 9	Long-Term Investments (Packard)	80,000	
	Cash		80,000
	Acquired 1,000 shares, representing a 30% equity in Packard.		
Oct. 2	Long-Term Investments (AT&T)	60,000	
	Cash		60,000
	Acquired 2,000 shares as a long-term investment in available-for-sale securities.		
Oct. 17	Long-Term Investments (Apple)	40,000	
	Cash		40,000
	Acquired 1,000 shares as a long-term investment in available-for-sale securities.		
Nov. 1	Cash	5,000	
	Long-Term Investments (Packard)		5,000
	Received dividend from Packard.		
Nov. 30	Cash	3,000	
	Dividend Revenue		3,000
	Received dividend from AT&T.		
Dec. 15	Cash	1,400	
	Dividend Revenue		1,400
	Received dividend from Apple.		
Dec. 31	Long-Term Investments (Packard)	21,000	
	Earnings from Investment (Packard)		21,000
	To record 30% share of Packard's annual earnings of $70,000.		
Dec. 31	Unrealized Loss—Equity	7,000	
	Market Adjustment—Available-for-Sale* . . .		7,000
	To record change in market value of long-term available-for-sale securities.		

* Market adjustment computations:

	Cost	Market Value
AT&T	$ 60,000	$48,000
Apple	40,000	45,000
Total	$100,000	$93,000

Required credit balance of Market Adjustment
    —Available-for-Sale (LT) account:
    ($100,000 − $93,000) $7,000
Existing balance   0
Necessary credit adjustment $7,000

2. The December 31, 2002, balance sheet items appear as follows:

Assets	
Long-term investments:	
Available-for-Sale securities (at market value)	$93,000
Investment in (significant) equity securities	96,000
Total long-term investments	$189,000
Stockholders' Equity	
Common stock	500,000
Retained earnings.........................	350,000
Unrealized loss—Equity.....................	(7,000)

The income statement items for the year ended December 31, 2002, appear as follows:

Dividend revenue	$ 4,400
Earnings from investment	21,000

1. Journal entries for 2003:

Jan. 1	Cash	108,000	
	Long-Term Investments (Packard)		96,000
	Gain on Sale of Investments		12,000
	Sold 1,000 shares for cash.		
May 30	Cash	3,100	
	Dividend Revenue		3,100
	Received dividend from AT&T.		
June 15	Cash	1,600	
	Dividend Revenue		1,600
	Received dividend from Apple.		
Aug. 17	Cash	52,000	
	Loss on Sale of Investments	8,000	
	Long-Term Investments (AT&T)		60,000
	Sold 2,000 shares for cash.		
Aug. 19	Long-Term Investments (Coca-Cola)	50,000	
	Cash		50,000
	Acquired 2,000 shares as a long-term investment in available-for-sale securities.		
Dec. 15	Cash	1,800	
	Dividend Revenue		1,800
	Received dividend from Apple.		
Dec. 31	Market Adjustment—Available-for-Sale*.	4,000	
	Unrealized Loss—Equity		4,000
	To record change in market value of long-term available-for-sale securities.		

* Market adjustment computations:

	Cost	Market Value
Apple	$40,000	$39,000
Coca Cola ...	50,000	48,000
Total	$90,000	$87,000

Required credit balance of Market Adjustment —Available-for-Sale (LT) account:	
($90,000 − $87,000)	$3,000
Existing credit balance	7,000
Necessary debit adjustment	$4,000

2. The December 31, 2003, balance sheet items appear as follows:

Assets	
Long-term investments:	
Available-for-Sale securities (at market value)	$ 87,000
Stockholders' Equity	
Common stock	500,000
Retained earnings	410,000
Unrealized loss—Equity	(3,000)

The income statement items for the year ended December 31, 2003, appear as follows:

Dividend revenue	$ 6,500
Gain on sale of investments	12,000
Loss on sale of investments	(8,000)

Summary

C1 Distinguish long-term investments from short-term investments. Short-term investments in securities are current assets that meet two criteria. First, they are expected to be converted into cash within one year or the current operating cycle of the business, whichever is longer. Second, they are readily convertible to cash, or *marketable*. All other investments in securities are long-term investments. Long-term investments also include assets not used in operations and those held for special purposes, such as land for expansion.

C2 Identify classes of securities in long-term investments. Long-term investments in securities are classified into one of four groups: (1) debt securities held-to-maturity, (2) debt and equity securities available-for-sale, (3) equity securities in which an investor has a significant influence over the investee, and (4) equity securities in which an investor has a controlling influence over the investee.

C3 Describe how to report equity securities with controlling influence. If an investor owns more than 50% of another company's voting stock and controls the investee, the investor's financial reports are prepared on a consolidated basis. These reports are prepared as if the company were organized as one entity.

P1 Account for held-to-maturity securities. Debt securities held-to-maturity are reported at cost when purchased. Interest revenue is recorded as it accrues. The cost of held-to-maturity securities is adjusted for the amortization of any difference between cost and maturity value.

P2 Account for available-for-sale securities. Debt and equity securities available-for-sale are recorded at cost when purchased. Available-for-sale securities are reported at their market values with unrealized gains or losses shown in the equity section of the balance sheet. Gains and losses realized on the sale of these investments are reported in the income statement.

P3 Account for equity securities with significant influence. The equity method is used when an investor has a significant influence over an investee. This usually exists when an investor owns 20% or more of the investee's voting stock but not more than 50%. The equity method means an investor records its share of investee earnings with a debit to the investment account and a credit to a revenue account. Dividends received satisfy the investor's equity claims and reduce the investment account balance.

Glossary

Available-for-sale debt securities Investments in debt securities held with the intent to sell them in the future. (p. C-4)

Available-for-sale equity securities Investments in noninfluential equity securities held with the intent to sell them in the future. (p. C-4)

Comprehensive income Net change in equity for a period, excluding owner investments and distributions. (p. C-8)

Consolidated financial statements Financial statements that show all (combined) activities under the parent's control, including those of any subsidiaries. (p. C-7)

Equity method Accounting method used for long-term investments when the in-

vestor has "significant influence" over the investee. (p. C-6)

Equity securities with controlling influence Long-term investment when the investor is able to exert controlling influence over the investee; investors owning 50% or more of voting stock are presumed to exert control. (p. C-7)

Equity securities with significant influence Long-term investment when the investor is able to exert significant influence over the investee; investors owning 20% or more (but less than 50%) of voting stock are presumed to exert significant influence. (p. C-6)

Held-to-maturity securities Debt securities that the company has the intent and ability to hold until they mature. (p. C-4)

Long-term investments Investments in equity and debt securities that are not marketable or, if marketable, are not intended to be converted into cash in the short term; also special-purpose funds and assets not used in operations. (p. C-2)

Parent Company that owns a controlling interest in a corporation (requires more than 50% of voting stock). (p. C-7)

Subsidiary Entity controlled by another entity (parent) in which the parent owns more than 50% of the subsidiary's voting stock. (p. C-7)

QUICK STUDY

QS C-1

Debt securities **P1**
transactions

On February 1, 2002, Bob Dejonge purchased 6% bonds issued by Cross Utilities at a cost of $40,000, which equals their par value. The bonds pay interest semiannually on July 31 and January 31. Prepare the entries to record the July 31 receipt of interest and the December 31 year-end interest accrual.

QS C-2

Recording equity securities

P2

On May 20, 2002, Cornwell Co. paid $1,000,000 to acquire 25,000 shares (10%) of JVM Corp.'s outstanding common shares as a long-term investment. On August 5, 2004, Cornwell sold half of these shares for $625,000. What method should be used to account for this stock investment? Prepare entries to record both the acquisition of these shares and their sale.

QS C-3

Equity method transactions

P3

Assume the same facts as in QS C-2 except that the stock acquired represents 40% of JVM Corp.'s outstanding stock. Also assume that JVM Corp. paid a $100,000 dividend on November 1, 2002, and reported a net income of $700,000 for 2002. Prepare the entries to record the receipt of the dividend and the December 31, 2002, year-end adjustment required for the investment account.

QS C-4

Recording market adjustment for securities

P2

During the current year, Ross Consulting Group acquires long-term investment securities at a $70,000 cost. These securities are classified as available-for-sale. At its December 31 year-end, these securities had a market value of $58,000. The consulting group owns no other long-term investments.

1. Prepare the necessary year-end adjustment related to these securities.

2. Explain how each account used in part 1 is reported in the financial statements.

EXERCISES

Exercise C-1

Transactions in short- and long-term investments

C1 P1 P2

Prepare journal entries to record the following transactions involving both the short- and long-term investments of Cascade Corp., all of which occurred during calendar year 2002. Use the account Short-Term Investments for any transactions that you determine are short term.

a. On February 15, paid $160,000 cash to purchase American General's 120-day short-term notes at par, which are dated February 15 and pay 10% interest.

b. On March 22, bought 700 shares of Franklin Industries common stock at $51 cash per share plus a $150 brokerage fee.

c. On June 15, received a check from American General in payment of the principal and 120 days' interest on the notes purchased in transaction *a*.

d. On July 30, paid $100,000 cash to purchase MP3 Electronics' 8% notes at par, dated July 30, 2002, and maturing on January 30, 2003.

e. On September 1, received a $1 per share cash dividend on the Franklin Industries common stock purchased in transaction *b*.

f. On October 8, sold 350 shares of Franklin Industries common stock for $64 cash per share, less a $125 brokerage fee.

g. On October 30, received a check from MP3 Electronics for three months' interest on the notes purchased in transaction *d*.

Exercise C-2

Recording adjustment to market value for long-term securities

P2

On December 31, 2002, Stillwater Co. held the following long-term available-for-sale securities:

	Cost	Market Value
Nintendo Co. common stock	$44,450	$48,900
Atlantic Richfield Co. bonds payable ...	49,000	47,000
Kellogg Co. notes payable	25,000	23,200
McDonald's Corp. common stock	46,300	44,800

Stillwater had no long-term securities investments prior to the current period. Prepare the December 31, 2002, year-end adjusting entry to record the market adjustment for these securities.

Big Board Services began operations in 2002 and regularly makes long-term investments in available-for-sale securities. Annual total cost and market value for these investments follow:

	Cost	Market Value
On December 31, 2002	$372,000	$360,860
On December 31, 2003	428,500	455,800
On December 31, 2004	600,200	700,500
On December 31, 2005	876,900	780,200

Prepare journal entries to record the market adjustment of these securities at each year-end.

Exercise C-3
Market value adjustments for available-for-sale securities

P2

Prepare journal entries to record the following transactions and events of Kinney Company:

2002

Jan. 2   Purchased 30,000 shares of Montex Co. common stock for $408,000 cash plus a broker's fee of $3,000 cash. Montex has 90,000 shares of common stock outstanding and admits its policies will be significantly influenced by Kinney.
Sept. 1   Montex declared and paid a cash dividend of $1.50 per share.
Dec. 31   Montex announced that net income for the year is $486,900.

2003

June 1   Montex declared and paid a cash dividend of $2.10 per share.
Dec. 31   Montex announced that net income for the year is $702,750.
Dec. 31   Kinney sold 10,000 shares of Montex for $320,000 cash.

Exercise C-4
Securities transactions; equity method

P3

Kobe Security, which began operations in 2002, invests in long-term available-for-sale securities. Following is a series of transactions and events determining its long-term investment activity:

2002

Jan. 20   Purchased 1,000 shares of Johnson & Johnson at $20.50 per share plus a $240 commission.
Feb. 9   Purchased 1,200 shares of Sony at $46.20 per share plus a $225 commission.
June 12   Purchased 1,500 shares of Mattel at $27.80 per share plus a $195 commission.
Dec. 31   Per share market values for stocks in the portfolio are Johnson & Johnson, $21.50; Mattel, $30.90; Sony, $38.00.

2003

Apr. 15   Sold 1,000 shares of Johnson & Johnson at $23.50 per share less a $525 commission.
July 5   Sold 1,500 shares of Mattel at $23.90 per share less a $235 commission.
July 22   Purchased 600 shares of Sara Lee at $22.50 per share plus a $480 commission.
Aug. 19   Purchased 900 shares of Eastman Kodak at $17.00 per share plus a $198 commission.
Dec. 31   Per share market values for stocks in the portfolio are Kodak, $19.25; Sara Lee, $20.00; Sony, $35.00

2004

Feb. 27   Purchased 2,400 shares of Microsoft at $67.00 per share plus a $525 commission.
June 21   Sold 1,200 shares of Sony at $48.00 per share less an $880 commission.
June 30   Purchased 1,400 shares of Black & Decker at $36.00 per share plus a $725 commission.
Aug. 3   Sold 600 shares of Sara Lee at $16.25 per share less a $435 commission.
Nov. 1   Sold 900 shares of Eastman Kodak at $22.75 per share less a $625 commission.
Dec. 31   Per share market values for stocks in the portfolio are Black & Decker, $39.00; Microsoft, $69.00.

Exercise C-5
Transactions and market adjustments for long-term investments in securities

P2

Required

1. Prepare journal entries to record these transactions and events and any year-end adjustments needed to record the market values of these long-term investments.

2. Prepare a table that shows the total cost, total market adjustment, and total market value of the long-term investments at each year-end.

3. For each year, prepare a table that shows the realized gains and losses included in earnings and the total unrealized gains or losses at each year-end.

Exercise C-6
Accounting for long-term investments in securities; with and without significant influence

P3

Case Steel Co. began operations on January 4, 2002. The following transactions and events subsequently occurred in its long-term investments:

2002

Jan.   5   Case purchased 60,000 shares (20%) of Kildaire's common stock for $1,560,000.
Oct. 23   Kildaire declared and paid a cash dividend of $3.20 per share.
Dec. 31   Kildaire's net income for 2002 is $1,164,000, and the market value of its stock at December 31 is $30.00 per share.

2003

Oct. 15   Kildaire declared and paid a cash dividend of $2.60 per share.
Dec. 31   Kildaire's net income for 2003 is $1,476,000, and the market value of its stock at December 31 is $32.00 per share.

2004

Jan.   2   Case sold all of its investment in Kildaire for $1,894,000 cash.

Part 1

Assume that Case has a significant influence over Kildaire with its 20% share of stock.

Required

1. Prepare journal entries to record the preceding transactions and events for Case.

2. Compute the carrying (book) value per share of Case's investment in Kildaire common stock as reflected in the investment account on January 1, 2004.

3. Compute the change in Case's equity from January 5, 2002, through January 2, 2004, resulting from its investment in Kildaire.

Part 2

Assume that although Case owns 20% of Kildaire's outstanding stock, circumstances indicate that it does not have a significant influence over the investee.

Required

1. Prepare journal entries to record the preceding transactions and events for Case. Also prepare an entry dated January 2, 2004, to remove any balance related to the market adjustment.

2. Compute the cost per share of Case's investment in Kildaire common stock as reflected in the investment account on January 1, 2004.

3. Compute the change in Case's equity from January 5, 2002, through January 2, 2004, resulting from its investment in Kildaire.

Credits

Index

Chart of Accounts

Assets

Current Assets

101 Cash
102 Petty cash
103 Cash equivalents
104 Short-term investments
105 Market adjustment, _____ securities (S-T)
106 Accounts receivable
107 Allowance for doubtful accounts
108 Legal fees receivable
109 Interest receivable
110 Rent receivable
111 Notes receivable
115 Subscriptions receivable, Common stock
116 Subscriptions receivable, Preferred stock
119 Merchandise inventory
120 _____ inventory
121 _____ inventory
124 Office supplies
125 Store supplies
126 _____ supplies
128 Prepaid insurance
129 Prepaid interest
131 Prepaid rent
132 Raw materials inventory
133 Goods in process inventory, _____
134 Goods in process inventory, _____
135 Finished goods inventory

Long-Term Investments

141 Long-term investments
142 Market adjustment, _____ securities (L-T)
144 Investment in _____
145 Bond sinking fund

Plant Assets

151 Automobiles
152 Accumulated depreciation, Automobiles
153 Trucks
154 Accumulated depreciation, Trucks
155 Boats
156 Accumulated depreciation, Boats
157 Professional library
158 Accumulated depreciation, Professional library
159 Law library
160 Accumulated depreciation, Law library
161 Furniture
162 Accumulated depreciation, Furniture
163 Office equipment
164 Accumulated depreciation, Office equipment
165 Store equipment
166 Accumulated depreciation, Store equipment
167 _____ equipment
168 Accumulated depreciation, _____ equipment
169 Machinery
170 Accumulated depreciation, Machinery
173 Building _____
174 Accumulated depreciation, Building _____
175 Building _____
176 Accumulated depreciation, Building _____
179 Land improvements _____
180 Accumulated depreciation, Land improvements _____
181 Land improvements _____
182 Accumulated depreciation, Land improvements _____
183 Land

Natural Resources

185 Mineral deposit
186 Accumulated depletion, Mineral deposit

Intangible Assets

191 Patents
192 Leasehold
193 Franchise
194 Copyrights
195 Leasehold improvements
196 Licenses

Liabilities

Current Liabilities

201 Accounts payable
202 Insurance payable
203 Interest payable
204 Legal fees payable
207 Office salaries payable
208 Rent payable
209 Salaries payable
210 Wages payable
211 Accrued payroll payable
214 Estimated warranty liability
215 Income taxes payable
216 Common dividend payable
217 Preferred dividend payable
218 State unemployment taxes payable
219 Employee federal income taxes payable
221 Employee medical insurance payable
222 Employee retirement program payable
223 Employee union dues payable
224 Federal unemployment taxes payable
225 FICA taxes payable
226 Estimated vacation pay liability

Unearned Revenues

230 Unearned consulting fees
231 Unearned legal fees
232 Unearned property management fees
233 Unearned _____ fees
234 Unearned _____ fees
235 Unearned janitorial revenue
236 Unearned _____ revenue
238 Unearned rent

Notes Payable

240 Short-term notes payable
241 Discount on short-term notes payable
245 Notes payable
251 Long-term notes payable
252 Discount on long-term notes payable

Long-Term Liabilities

253 Long-term lease liability
255 Bonds payable
256 Discount on bonds payable
257 Premium on bonds payable
258 Deferred income tax liability

Equity

Owner's Equity

301 _____, Capital
302 _____, Withdrawals
303 _____, Capital
304 _____, Withdrawals
305 _____, Capital
306 _____, Withdrawals

Contributed Capital

307 Common stock, $ _____ par value
308 Common stock, no-par value
309 Common stock, $ _____ stated value
310 Common stock dividend distributable
311 Contributed capital in excess of par value, Common stock
312 Contributed capital in excess of stated value, No-par common stock
313 Contributed capital from retirement of common stock
314 Contributed capital, Treasury stock
315 Preferred stock
316 Contributed capital in excess of par value, Preferred stock

Retained Earnings

318 Retained earnings
319 Cash dividends declared
320 Stock dividends declared

Other Equity Accounts

321 Treasury stock, Common
322 Unrealized gain—Equity
323 Unrealized loss—Equity

Revenues

401 _____ fees earned
402 _____ fees earned
403 _____ services revenue
404 _____ services revenue
405 Commissions earned
406 Rent revenue (or Rent earned)
407 Dividend revenue (or Dividend earned)
408 Earnings from investment in _____
409 Interest revenue (or Interest earned)
410 Sinking fund earnings
413 Sales
414 Sales returns and allowances
415 Sales discounts

Cost of Sales

Cost of Goods Sold

502 Cost of goods sold
505 Purchases
506 Purchases returns and allowances
507 Purchases discounts
508 Transportation-in

Manufacturing

520 Raw materials purchases
521 Freight-in on raw materials
530 Factory payroll
531 Direct labor
540 Factory overhead
541 Indirect materials
542 Indirect labor
543 Factory insurance expired
544 Factory supervision
545 Factory supplies used
546 Factory utilities
547 Miscellaneous production costs
548 Property taxes on factory building
549 Property taxes on factory equipment
550 Rent on factory building
551 Repairs, factory equipment
552 Small tools written off
560 Depreciation of factory equipment
561 Depreciation of factory building

Standard Cost Variance

580 Direct material quantity variance
581 Direct material price variance
582 Direct labor quantity variance
583 Direct labor price variance
584 Factory overhead volume variance
585 Factory overhead controllable variance

Expenses

Amortization, Depletion, and Depreciation

601 Amortization expense—_____
602 Amortization expense—_____
603 Depletion expense—_____
604 Depreciation expense—Boats
605 Depreciation expense—Automobiles
606 Depreciation expense—Building _____
607 Depreciation expense—Building _____
608 Depreciation expense—Land improvements _____
609 Depreciation expense—Land improvements _____
610 Depreciation expense—Law library
611 Depreciation expense—Trucks
612 Depreciation expense—_____ equipment
613 Depreciation expense—_____ equipment
614 Depreciation expense—_____
615 Depreciation expense—_____

Employee-Related Expenses

620 Office salaries expense
621 Sales salaries expense
622 Salaries expense
623 _____ wages expense
624 Employees' benefits expense
625 Payroll taxes expense

Financial Expenses

630 Cash over and short
631 Discounts lost
632 Factoring fee expense
633 Interest expense

Insurance Expenses

635 Insurance expense—Delivery equipment
636 Insurance expense—Office equipment
637 Insurance expense—_____

Rental Expenses

640 Rent expense
641 Rent expense—Office space
642 Rent expense—Selling space
643 Press rental expense
644 Truck rental expense
645 _____ rental expense

Supplies Expenses

650 Office supplies expense
651 Store supplies expense
652 _____ supplies expense
653 _____ supplies expense

Miscellaneous Expenses

655 Advertising expense
656 Bad debts expense
657 Blueprinting expense
658 Boat expense
659 Collection expense
661 Concessions expense
662 Credit card expense
663 Delivery expense
664 Dumping expense
667 Equipment expense
668 Food and drinks expense
669 Gas, oil, and repairs expense
671 Gas and oil expense
672 General and administrative expense
673 Janitorial expense
674 Legal fees expense
676 Mileage expense
677 Miscellaneous expenses
678 Mower and tools expense
679 Operating expense
680 Organization expense
681 Permits expense
682 Postage expense
683 Property taxes expense
684 Repairs expense—_____
685 Repairs expense—_____
687 Selling expense
688 Telephone expense
689 Travel and entertainment expense
690 Utilities expense
691 Warranty expense
695 Income taxes expense

Gains and Losses

701 Gain on retirement of bonds
702 Gain on sale of machinery
703 Gain on sale of investments
704 Gain on sale of trucks
705 Gain on _____
706 Foreign exchange gain or loss
801 Loss on disposal of machinery
802 Loss on exchange of equipment
803 Loss on exchange of _____
804 Loss on sale of notes
805 Loss on retirement of bonds
806 Loss on sale of investments
807 Loss on sale of machinery
808 Loss on _____
809 Unrealized gain—Income
810 Unrealized loss—Income

Clearing Accounts

901 Income summary
902 Manufacturing summary

FUNDAMENTALS

① Accounting Equation

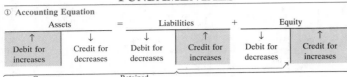

Assets	=	Liabilities	+	Equity
↑ Debit for increases	↓ Credit for decreases	↓ Debit for decreases	↑ Credit for increases	↓ Debit for decreases	↑ Credit for increases

Common Stock	+	Retained Earnings	+	Revenues	−	Expenses
↓ Dr. for decreases	↑ Cr. for increases	↓ Dr. for decreases	↑ Cr. for increases	↓ Dr. for decreases	↑ Cr. for increases	↑ Dr. for increases	↓ Cr. for decreases

▨ Indicates normal balance.

② Accounting Cycle

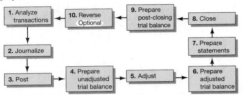

1. Analyze transactions
2. Journalize
3. Post
4. Prepare unadjusted trial balance
5. Adjust
6. Prepare adjusted trial balance
7. Prepare statements
8. Close
9. Prepare post-closing trial balance
10. Reverse Optional

③ Adjustments and Entries

Type	Adjusting Entry	
Prepaid Expense	Dr. Expense	Cr. Asset*
Unearned Revenues	Dr. Liability	Cr. Revenue
Accrued Expenses	Dr. Expense	Cr. Liability
Accrued Revenues	Dr. Asset	Cr. Revenue

*For depreciation, credit Accumulated Depreciation (contra asset).

④ 3-Step Closing Process

<1> Transfer revenue and gain account balances to Income Summary.
<2> Transfer expense and loss account balances to Income Summary.
<3> Transfer Income Summary balance to Retained Earnings.

⑤ Accounting Concepts

Characteristics	Assumptions	Principles	Constraints
Relevance	Business entity	Historical cost	Cost-benefit
Reliability	Going concern	Revenue recognition	Materiality
Comparability	Monetary unit	Matching	Industry practice
Consistency	Periodicity	Full disclosure	Conservatism

⑥ Ownership of Inventory

	Ownership transfers when goods passed to	Transportation costs paid by
FOB Shipping Point	Carrier	Buyer
FOB Destination	Buyer	Seller

⑦ Inventory Costing Methods

Specific Identification
First-In, First-Out (FIFO)*
Last-In, First-Out (LIFO)
Weighted Average

*FIFO Inventory = LIFO Inventory + LIFO Reserve
FIFO COGS = LIFO COGS − Increase (or + Decrease) in LIFO Reserve

⑧ Depreciation and Depletion

Straight-Line: $\dfrac{\text{Cost} - \text{Salvage value}}{\text{Useful life in periods}} \times \text{Periods expired}$

Units-of-Production: $\dfrac{\text{Cost} - \text{Salvage value}}{\text{Useful life in units}} \times \text{Units produced}$

Declining-Balance: $\text{Rate}^* \times \text{Beginning-of-period book value}$
*Rate is often double the straight-line rate, or $2 \times (1/\text{useful life})$

Depletion: $\dfrac{\text{Cost} - \text{Salvage value}}{\text{Total capacity in units}} \times \text{Units extracted}$

⑨ Interest Computation

Interest = Principal (face) × Rate × Time

⑩ Accounting for Investment Securities

Short-term investment in securities	
Held-to-maturity (debt) securities	Cost (without any discount or premium amortization)
Trading (debt and equity) securities	Market value (with market adjustment to income)
Available-for-sale (debt and equity) securities	Market value (with market adjustment to equity)
Long-term investment in securities	
Held-to-maturity (debt) securities	Cost (with any discount or premium amortization)
Available-for-sale (debt and equity) securities	Market value (with market adjustment to equity)
Equity securities with significant influence	Equity method

ANALYSES

① Liquidity and Efficiency

Current ratio $= \dfrac{\text{Current assets}}{\text{Current liabilities}}$ — p. 127

Working capital = Current assets − Current liabilities — p. 587

Acid-test ratio $= \dfrac{\text{Cash} + \text{Short-term investments} + \text{Current receivables}}{\text{Current liabilities}}$ — p. 180

Accounts receivable turnover $= \dfrac{\text{Net sales}}{\text{Average accounts receivable}}$ — p. 311

Credit risk ratio $= \dfrac{\text{Allowance for doubtful accounts}}{\text{Accounts receivable}}$ — p. 297

Inventory turnover $= \dfrac{\text{Cost of goods sold}}{\text{Average inventory}}$ — p. 224

Days' sales uncollected $= \dfrac{\text{Accounts receivable}}{\text{Net sales}} \times 365^*$ — p. 269

Days' sales in inventory $= \dfrac{\text{Ending inventory}}{\text{Cost of goods sold}} \times 365^*$ — p. 224

Total asset turnover $= \dfrac{\text{Net sales}}{\text{Average total assets}}$ — p. 354

Plant asset useful life $= \dfrac{\text{Plant asset cost}}{\text{Depreciation expense}}$ — p. 336

Plant asset age $= \dfrac{\text{Accumulated depreciation}}{\text{Depreciation expense}}$ — p. 344

Days' cash expense coverage $= \dfrac{\text{Cash and cash equivalents}}{\text{Average daily cash expenses}}$ — p. 267

*360 days is also commonly used.

② Solvency

Debt ratio $= \dfrac{\text{Total liabilities}}{\text{Total assets}}$ — p. 71

Equity ratio $= \dfrac{\text{Total equity}}{\text{Total assets}}$ — p. 591

Pledged assets to secured liabilities $= \dfrac{\text{Book value of pledged assets}}{\text{Book value of secured liabilities}}$ — p. 442

Times interest earned $= \dfrac{\text{Income before interest expense and income taxes}}{\text{Interest expense}}$ — p. 393

Cash coverage of growth $= \dfrac{\text{Cash flow from operations}}{\text{Cash outflow for long-term assets}}$ — p. 545

Cash coverage of debt $= \dfrac{\text{Cash flow from operations}}{\text{Total noncurrent liabilities}}$ — p. 548

Free cash flow $= \dfrac{\text{Cash flow from}}{\text{operations}} - \dfrac{\text{Capital}}{\text{expenditures}} - \dfrac{\text{Cash}}{\text{dividends}}$ — p. 546

③ Profitability

Profit margin ratio $= \dfrac{\text{Net income}}{\text{Net sales}}$ — p. 126

Gross margin ratio $= \dfrac{\text{Net sales} - \text{Cost of goods sold}}{\text{Net sales}}$ — p. 181

Return on total assets $= \dfrac{\text{Net income}}{\text{Average total assets}}$ — p. 21 & 593
$= \text{Profit margin ratio} \times \text{Total asset turnover}$

Return on common stockholders' equity $= \dfrac{\text{Net income} - \text{Preferred dividends}}{\text{Average common stockholders' equity}}$ — p. 70 & 593

Book value per common share $= \dfrac{\text{Stockholders' equity applicable to common shares}}{\text{Number of common shares outstanding}}$ — p. 493

Basic earnings per share $= \dfrac{\text{Net income} - \text{Preferred dividends}}{\text{Weighted-average common shares outstanding}}$ — p. 489

Cash flow on total assets $= \dfrac{\text{Cash flow from operations}}{\text{Average total assets}}$ — p. 549

Payout ratio $= \dfrac{\text{Cash dividends declared on common stock}}{\text{Net income}}$ — p. 494

④ Market

Price-earnings ratio $= \dfrac{\text{Market price per common share}}{\text{Earnings per share}}$ — p. 494

Dividend yield $= \dfrac{\text{Annual cash dividends per share}}{\text{Market price per share}}$ — p. 494